Joseph Foster

Oxford Men

1880-1892

Joseph Foster

Oxford Men
1880-1892

ISBN/EAN: 9783744693608

Printed in Europe, USA, Canada, Australia, Japan

Cover: Foto ©ninafisch / pixelio.de

More available books at **www.hansebooks.com**

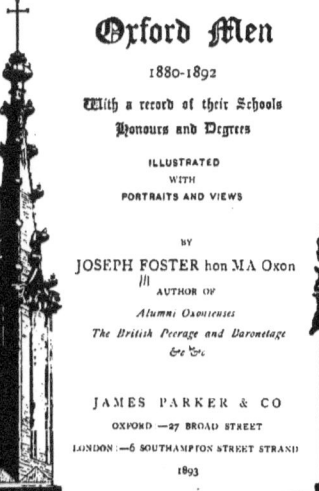

Oxford Men

1880-1892

With a record of their Schools Honours and Degrees

ILLUSTRATED
WITH
PORTRAITS AND VIEWS

BY

JOSEPH FOSTER hon M.A Oxon

AUTHOR OF

Alumni Oxonienses
The British Peerage and Baronetage
&c &c

JAMES PARKER & CO
OXFORD :—27 BROAD STREET
LONDON :—6 SOUTHAMPTON STREET STRAND
1893

PINNACLES AND BATTLEMENT OF MERTON CHAPEL TOWER
[*From Mackenzie and Pugin*]

COMPANION VOLUME.

Oxford Men and their Colleges.

ILLUSTRATED WITH PORTRAITS AND VIEWS.

A work of reference the copiousness of which cannot be too highly praised.—*The Times.*

I have received the magnificent book.—*The Bishop of Oxford.*

A very attractive book to the Oxford men.—*The Provost of Queen's.*

. . . the truly splendid volume on the Oxford men of the present day.—*The President of Corpus.*

Your magnificent work on the Colleges of Oxford and its Alumni.—*The Master of Pembroke.*

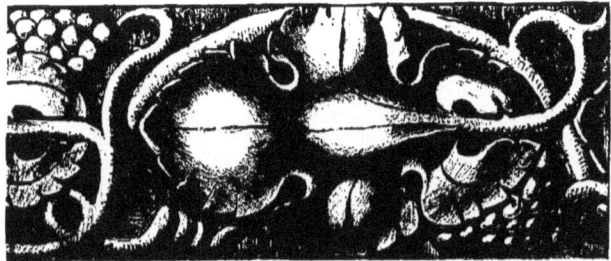

PREFACE.

T had originally been my intention to append the contents of this volume to my "Oxford Men and Their Colleges," but owing to the elaboration of my plan, the book would have attained unwieldy proportions; and I was thus compelled to divide it into two parts.

The present work continues and completes "*Alumni Oxonienses*," containing the MATRICULATION REGISTER from 1880 to 1892 alphabetically arranged as a distinct division, to which has been added where practicable birthdays, schools, honours, and degrees. It also includes cross-references to all the biographical notices under the respective colleges or elsewhere in the other portion of the work, in addition to the index in that volume.

While the MATRICULATION REGISTER has been placed at my service as before by the University Authorities, the Heads of Houses have allowed me full access to their COLLEGE RECORDS, from which, in the majority of instances, I have been enabled to glean the birthdays and schools of their members since 1880, thus accentuating and perpetuating the link between the Schools and the Universities. Moreover, from the official University publications, viz.: the Honours register, Calendar, and Gazette, I have incorporated the particulars of the Honours, the degrees, and the appointments relating to each individual. This elaborate array of facts, together with the miscellaneous annotations from Crockford and my own collections, especially parliamentary and legal, should prove a trustworthy and unique guide, such as can be found nowhere else, to the rising generation of Oxford Men, destined to play so large a part in the government and intellectual life of this country.

The novel feature that I have ventured on this occasion to introduce will, I trust, add considerably to the present interest and future value of these pages. It is my hope that as types of Oxford men and as investing the Register with actuality, my illustrations may prove acceptable.

In the other portion of this work I have illustrated the Colleges as homes, but no picture of Oxford Life could lay claim to completeness which did not show their members at play as well as at work. Indeed, the College Coat, with its distinctive arms, or perhaps its badge, introduces even into the sports of to-day the historic life of Oxford, and reminds us that heraldry, here, at least, has never lost its significance or its pride. The "eight," the "eleven," and the football teams are an integral part of College and University life, and I have included among my illustrations several typical crews and teams by the aid of the collotype process and the agency of Waterlow and Sons, from photographs by Messrs. Hills & Saunders and Messrs. Gillman and Co., Oxford. If the proposition meets with sufficient encouragement I should also some day hope to illustrate the *personnel* of the University, by groups of its Fellows, Professors, and other distinguished Alumni. It would, I believe, be possible thus to form an illustrated record which should possess a permanent and ever increasing value.

JOSEPH FOSTER.

21, BOUNDARY ROAD, LONDON, N.W.

VIEW BY BEREBLOCK, 1566. [*Facsimile from Hearne.*]

LIST OF ILLUSTRATIONS.

PORTRAIT OF MR. JUSTICE CHITTY, facing title page.	
ST. GEORGE'S HALL, now demolished, from Skelton, xv.	
UNIVERSITY CREW, 1893, from a photograph by *Hills and Saunders* . . . facing	1 and 2
UNIVERSITY FOOTBALL TEAMS, 1892-3, Rugby and Association, from photographs by *Hills and Saunders* . . . facing	1 and 2
THE ANCIENT NORTH ENTRANCE INTO OXFORD, taken down 1771, from an engraving by Skelton . . . . facing	15-16
PEG TANKARD, in the Ashmolean, from Shaw	21-22
REMAINS OF REWLEY ABBEY, from Skelton .	23-24
UNIVERSITY College Football Team, Association 1892-3, facing 39-40, and Torpid 1893 (facing 41-2), from photographs by *Hills and Saunders*.	
BALLIOL, Torpid 1893, from a photo by *Gillman and Co.*, facing 71-72, followed by	
BALLIOL Football Teams 1892-3, Rugby and Association, from photos by *Hills and Saunders*.	
VIEW OF OXFORD FROM HEADINGTON HILL, after J. M. W. Turner, from Skelton facing	79-80
HENRY VIII's CHAIR, in the Ashmolean, from Storer	91-92
ANCIENT LANTERN OF BRONZE, in the Ashmolean, from Shaw	93-94
GREAT LION HALL, now demolished, from Skelton	95-96
MERTON Football Teams, Rugby and Association, 1892-3, and 1st Torpid 1893, from photos by *Hills and Saunders* . . facing	103-4
EXETER Torpid 1893, from photo by *Hills and Saunders* . . . . facing	119-120
EXETER Football Tenm, Association, 1892-3, from photo by *Gillman and Co.* . facing	121-122
ORIEL Torpid, 1893, from photograph by *Gillman and Co.* . . . . facing	127-8
BODLEIAN LIBRARY, by A. Pugin, from Ackerman . . . . . . facing	143-144
WOODEN STALL ELBOWS, Beauchamp Chapel, Warwick, by Pugin . . . facing	147-150
EAST GATE, now demolished, from Skelton .	159-160
PART OF LITTLE GATE, now demolished, from Skelton	161-162
QUEEN'S Torpid, 1893, and Football Teams, 1892-3, Rugby and Association, from photos by *Gillman and Co.* . . facing	167-8
VIGNETTE USED IN THE UNIVERSITY PRESS, 1517, from Ingram	179-180
VIGNETTE USED IN THE UNIVERSITY PRESS, 1585, from Ingram	181-182
NEW COLL. 1st Torpid, 1893, from a photograph by *Hills and Saunders* . facing	191-2
DIVINITY SCHOOL, by F. Mackenzie, from Ackerman . . . . . facing	207-208
ST. GEORGE'S HALL, now demolished, from Skelton	223-224
LINCOLN Football Team, Association, 1892-3, facing 247-8; and Torpid 1893, facing 249-250, from photos by *Hills and Saunders*.	
STONE ANIMALS, Rouen Cathedral, Pugin 253-258, 435-43⁶, 447-448	
INTERIOR OF ST. MARY'S CHURCH, by F. Mackenzie . . . . facing	271-272

MAGDALEN Torpid, 1893, from photo by *Gillman and Co.* . . . facing	295-6
MAGDALEN Football Teams, 1892-3, Rugby and Association, from photos by *Hills and Saunders* . . . . facing	295-6
BRASENOSE 1st Torpid, 1893, and Rugby XV., 1892-3, from photos by *Hills & Saunders*, facing	311-312
BRASENOSE Association XI., 1892-3, from photo by *Gillman and Co.* . facing	311-312
THE SHELDONIAN, from Oxford Almanac, 1820 . . . . . facing	319-320
CORPUS CHRISTI Torpid 1893, and Football Teams 1892-3, Rugby and Association, from photographs by *Gillman and Co.* facing	343-4
STONE BOSSES, Chapter House, St. George de Boucherville, near Rouen, Pugin .	351-354
THE STATUE GALLERY, after W. Westall, from Ackerman . . . facing	367-368
CANDELABRA, Radcliffe Library, from Lascelles	385-386
CHRIST CHURCH 1st Torpid 1893, from a photo by *Gillman and Co.* . .	391-2
CHRIST CHURCH Football Teams 1892-3, Rugby and Association, from photos by *Hills and Saunders* . . . facing	391-2
RADCLIFFE OBSERVATORY, Interior, after F. Mackenzie, from Ackerman . facing	399-400
RADCLIFFE OBSERVATORY, Exterior, after F. Mackenzie, from Ingram . facing	415-416
TRINITY Torpid 1893, from a photo by *Hills and Saunders* . . . facing	431-2
ST. JOHN'S Torpid 1893, from a photo by *Hills and Saunders* . . facing	479-80
JESUS COLL. Torpid 1893, from a photo by *Hills and Saunders*. . . facing	495-6
RADCLIFFE LIBRARY, or CAMERA, Interior, after F. Mackenzie, from Ingram facing	511-512
ORNAMENT, from New College	529-530
WADHAM Torpid 1893, from a photo by *Hills and Saunders* . . . facing	535-6
WADHAM Football Teams, 1892-3, Rugby and Association, from photos by *Gillman and Co.* . . . facing	535-6
PENBROKE Football Team, Association, 1892-3, facing 567-8; and Torpid 1893, facing 569-70, from photos by *Gillman and Co.*	
COINS, Bodleian	587-588
RADCLIFFE INFIRMARY, Exterior, after F. Mackenzie, from Ingram . . facing	591-592
WORCESTER Torpid 1893, from photo by *Gillman and Co.* . . .	615-616
WORCESTER Football Team, Rugby, 1892-3, from photo by *Hills and Saunders* facing	617-618
HERTFORD Football Team, Association, 1892-3, facing 647-8, and Torpid 1893, facing 649-650, from photos by *Gillman and Co.*	
THE UNIVERSITY PRINTING HOUSE, from the Infirmary, after F. Mackenzie, from Ingram's Memorials . . . facing	655-656
STONE BRACKET, York Minster, Pugin .	677-678
KEBLE Torpids 1893, 1st and 2nd, from photos by *Gillman and Co.* . facing	679-682
COINS, Bodleian	681-682
STONE BRACKET, York Minster, Pugin .	685-686
PATERAS, Beauchamp Chapel, Warwick .	687-688

PORTRAITS OF BLUES.

Facing page 1.

Baker, Cecil Douglas, of Merton. Captain University F. C. Rugby 1892-3.
Bliss, Edward Church, of Oriel. University F. C. Association 1892-3.
Buzzard, Edward Farquhar, of Magdalen. University F. C. Association 1892-3.
Carey, Godfrey Mohun, of Exeter. University F. C. Rugby 1892-3.
Colvile, Algernon Holland, of Merton. University F. C. Rugby 1892-3.
Cookson, George Heinrich Frederic, of Lincoln. University F. C. Rugby 1892-3.
Cotton, Hugh Benjamin, of Magdalen. VIII. 1893.
Donaldson, William Patrick, of Brasenose. University F. C. Rugby 1892-3.
Elwes, Albert Cary, of St. John's. University F. C. Rugby 1892-3.
Fletcher, William Alfred Littledale, of Christ Church. VIII. 1893.
Ford, James Arthur, of Brasenose. VIII. 1893.
Fry, Charles Burgess, of Wadham. University F. C. Association 1892-3.
Grant, Alfred Hamilton, of Balliol. University F. C. Association 1892-3.
Hewitt, Copley Delisle, of Magdalen. University F. C. Association 1892-3.
Humfrey, Lebbeus Charles, of Keble. University F. C. Rugby 1892-3.
Latter, Algernon, of Trinity. University F. C. Rugby 1892-3.
Legge, Hugh, of Trinity. VIII. 1893.
[Maclean, Douglas Hamilton, Coach of the VIII. 1893.]
Morrison, James Archibald, of New Coll. VIII. 1893.
Mortimer, Leonard, of Exeter. University F. C. Rugby 1892-3.
Nickalls, Vivian, of Magdalen. VIII. 1893.
Oakley, William John, of Christ Church. University F. C. Association 1892-3.
Pilkington, Malcolm Carlisle, of Magdalen. VIII. 1893.
Pitman, Charles Murray, of New Coll. VIII. 1893.
Poole, Francis Oswald, of Keble. University F. C. Rugby 1892-3.
Portman, Lionel, of University Coll. VIII. 1893.
Raikes, George Barkley, of Magdalen. University F. C. Association 1892-3.
Rees, John Conway, of Jesus Coll. University F. C. Rugby 1892-3.
Robinson, Thomas Chambers, of Oriel. University F. C. Association 1892-3.
Salt, Reginald John, of New Coll. University F. C. Association 1892-3.
Smith, Gilbert Oswald, of Keble. University F. C. Association 1892-3.
Smith, James Arthur, of Trinity. University F. C. Rugby 1892-3.
Stewart, William Burton, of Brasenose. University F. C. Rugby 1892-3.
Street, Frank, of Christ Church. Captain University F. C. Association 1892-3.
Taberer, Henry Melville, of Keble. University F. C. Association 1892-3.
Wakefield, William Henry, of New Coll. University F. C. Rugby 1892-3.
Walker, John Allsop, of Magdalen. University F. C. Association 1892-3.

ORNAMENT FROM STRING COURSE, MAGDALEN COLL.—*A. Pugin.*

PORTRAITS
IN FOOTBALL AND TORPID GROUPS.

THOSE MARKED THUS (†) ARE ALSO "BLUES," SEE PRECEDING PAGE.

		PAGE
Abbott, Evelyn Robbins. Balliol F.C. Rugby	1892-3 facing	71
Allen, Arthur Henry B. Corpus F.C. Rugby	,, ,,	343
Allen, Basil Copleston. Corpus F.C. Rugby	,, ,,	343
Allen, William Heriah. Hertford F.C. Association	,, ,,	647
Anderson, Frank. Exeter Torpid	1893 ,,	121
Anderson, James Finlay. Brasenose F.C. Association	1892-3 ,,	311
Andrews, Reginald Arthur W. Keble 1st Torpid	1893 ,,	679
Anstie, William Henry. Wadham F.C. Rugby	1892-3 ,,	535
Arkwright, Harold Arthur. Magdalen F.C. Association	,, ,,	295
Arkwright, John Stanhope. Christ Church F.C. Rugby	,, ,,	391
Arnold, George Frederick. Queen's F.C. Rugby	,, ,,	167
Arnold, George Frederick. Queen's F.C. Association	,, ,,	167
Ashwin, Collins. Merton F.C. Rugby	,, ,,	103
Ashwin, Collins. Merton F.C. Association	,, ,,	103
Aspinall, Algernon Edward. Magdalen 1st Torpid	1893 ,,	295
Atkinson, Ernest Cuthbert. St. John's Torpid	,, ,,	479
Ayre, Algernon Early. Wadham F.C. Rugby	1892-3 ,,	535
Badcock, Henry. Cox Lincoln Torpid	1893 ,,	249
Badcock, Henry. Lincoln F.C. Association	1892-3 ,,	247
Baker, Percy Charles. Christ Church F.C. Rugby	,, ,,	391
Balcarres, Lord. Magdalen F.C. Rugby	,, ,,	295
Balfour, Charles Frederick. Corpus F.C. Rugby	,, ,,	343
Balfour, Charles Frederick. Corpus F.C. Association	,, ,,	343
Balfour, Patrick. Bow Balliol 1st Torpid	1893 ,,	71
Barkley, MacDonald. Lincoln F.C. Association	1892-3 ,,	247
Barlow, Hugh Christopher H. Stroke Lincoln Torpid	1893 facing	249
Barlow, Micah Yates. University coll. F.C. Association	1892-3 ,,	41
Barnes, Lewis Carrington. Wadham F.C. Association	,, ,,	535
Barnes, Herbert Charles. Christ Church F.C. Association	,, ,,	391
Barrows, Wilfred Murdoch. Merton F.C. Rugby	,, ,,	103
Barry, Arthur Joseph. Cox University coll. Torpid	1893 ,,	41
Barth, Jacob William. Wadham Torpid	,, ,,	535
Bawden, Henry Bartram. Jesus coll. 1st Torpid	,, ,,	495
Beavis, Charles Edward H. Keble 1st Torpid	,, ,,	679
Bell, James Arthur W. Corpus F.C. Rugby	1892-3 ,,	343
Bell, James Arthur W. Corpus F.C. Association	,, ,,	343
Bennett, George Edward M. Lincoln Torpid	1893 ,,	249
Bennett, Henry Pearson. Hertford Torpid	,, ,,	649
Bentley, Alfred Leonard. Wadham F.C. Rugby	1892-3 ,,	535
Berens, Edward. Christ Church F.C. Association	,, ,,	391
Birnbaum, Albert Bernard. Merton 1st Torpid	1893 ,,	103
Bischoff, Charles Edward. Trinity Torpid	,, ,,	431
Booker, Arthur John N. Christ Church F.C. Association	1892-3 ,,	391
Bosworth-Smith, Bertrand Nigel. Magdalen F.C. Association	,, ,,	295
Bouch, Joseph. Bow Queen's Torpid	1893 ,,	167
Bourne, Walter Kemp. Worcester F.C. Rugby	1892-3 ,,	617
Bousfield, Hugh Delabere. Queen's F.C. Rugby	,, ,,	167
Bovill, Francis Henry. Christ Church 1st Torpid	1893 ,,	391
Bowker, Benjamin Turner. Brasenose F.C. Association	1892-3 ,,	311
Bowman, Paget Mervyn. Magdalen 1st Torpid	1893 ,,	295

b

PORTRAITS IN FOOTBALL AND TORPID GROUPS, 1893.

Name	Year	Page
Boyd-Carpenter, Archibald. Cox Balliol Torpid	1893 facing	71
Brinton, Percival Robert. Balliol F.C. Association	1892-3 ,,	71
Brittain, William. Stroke Exeter Torpid	1893 ,,	121
Broadbent, Percy Goolden A. Keble 2nd Torpid	,, ,,	679
Brock, Hugh Hulkeley P. Brasenose F.C. Association	1892-3 ,,	311
Bros, Henry Alwyn. Magdalen F.C. Association	,, ,,	295
Brown, Lionel George. Merton F.C. Rugby	,, ,,	103
Bruce, Francis Rosslyn C. Worcester F.C. Rugby	,, ,,	617
Brunskill, Hubert Fawcett. Exeter F.C. Association	,, ,,	119
Bryden, Charles Lumsdaine. Christ Church 1st Torpid	1893 ,,	391
Bull, Allen Wilfred. Wadham F.C. Rugby	1892-3 ,,	535
Burrell, Percy Saville. Queen's Torpid	1893 ,,	167
Bury, Arthur Maxwell. Hertford F.C. Association	1892-3 ,,	647
Butler, Thomas Harrison. Corpus Torpid	1893 ,,	343
Butler, William Albert. Worcester Torpid	,, ,,	615
†Buzzard, Edward Farquhar. Magdalen F.C. Association	1892-3 ,,	295
Cain, Charles Smith. Queen's F.C. Rugby	,, ,,	167
Callaway, Robert Furley. Corpus Torpid	1893 ,,	343
Carr, Douglas Ward. Brasenose F.C. Rugby	1892-3 ,,	311
Causton, Charles Guy. University coll. F.C. Association	,, ,,	39
Champernowne, Amyas Walter. Christ Church 1st Torpid	1893 ,,	391
Champernowne, Amyas Walter. Christ Church F.C. Rugby	1892-3 ,,	391
Chaplin, Wyndham Allen. Cox Keble 2nd Torpid	1893 ,,	679
Cholmeley, Roger James. Cox Corpus Torpid	,, ,,	343
Chorlton, John Henwood. Wadham F.C. Association	1892-3 ,,	535
Cinnamond, Arthur. Christ Church F.C. Rugby	,, ,,	391
Clark, Robert Moorhouse. Lincoln F.C. Association	,, ,,	247
Clarke, Charles Philip S. Christ Church F.C. Rugby	,, ,,	391
Clarke, John Grey. St. John's Torpid	1893 ,,	479
Clarke, Leycester Annand G. Jesus coll. Torpid	,, ,,	495
Clarke, Loftus Otway. Christ Church 1st Torpid	,, ,,	391
Clayton, Frederick George H. University coll. F.C. Association	1892-3 ,,	39
Cleave, Ernest. Exeter F.C. Association	,, ,,	119
Clegg, Ernest Bernulf. New coll. 1st Torpid	,, ,,	191
Cockcroft, Edward Francis. Brasenose F.C. Association	,, ,,	311
Collinge, William. Cox Christ Church 1st Torpid	1893 ,,	391
Collis, Harold. Worcester Torpid	,, ,,	615
†Colvile, Algernon Holland. Merton F.C. Rugby	1892-3 ,,	103
Combe, Ralph Molyneux. Exeter F.C. Association	,, ,,	119
Conder, Edward Baines. Cox Wadham Torpid	1893 facing	535
Cook, Arther Wilstead. Pembroke F.C. Association	1892-3 ,,	567
Cooke, Arthur George. Bow Corpus Torpid	1893 ,,	343
Cornes, Julian. Corpus F.C. Rugby	1892-3 ,,	343
Cornes, Julian. Corpus F.C. Association	,, ,,	343
Coupland, Herbert. Corpus F.C. Rugby	1892-3 ,,	343
Coupland, Herbert. Corpus F.C. Association	,, ,,	343
Coverston, Alfred Laurence. St. John's Torpid	1893 ,,	479
Cowan, Charles Howard. Brasenose F.C. Rugby	1892-3 ,,	311
Cox, William Spiller. Stroke Queen's Torpid	1893 ,,	167
Crump, Eldon Annesley. Cox Exeter Torpid	,, ,,	121
Crump, Frederick Cuthbert. Merton F.C. Rugby	1892-3 ,,	103
Cunliffe, Arthur Tabor. Balliol 1st Torpid	1893 ,,	71
Currie, Donald. University coll. F.C. Association	,, ,,	41
Currie, John Ronald. Lincoln F.C. Association	1892-3 ,,	247
Dallin, Francis Thomas. Queen's Torpid	1893 ,,	167
Dallin, Francis Thomas. Queen's F.C. Rugby	1892-3 ,,	167
Danks, Eric. Queen's F.C. Rugby	,, ,,	167
Davidson, Frederick Lewis M. St. John's Torpid	1893 ,,	479
Davies, Robert Bennet W. University coll. F.C. Association	1892-3 ,,	39
Davis, Charles Thomas. Balliol F.C. Rugby	,, ,,	71
Deakin, Carrick Ransome. Corpus F.C. Rugby	,, ,,	343
Dickson, James William. Captain Exeter F.C. Association	,, ,,	119
Dinwoody, Frank Kenelm. Cox Hertford Torpid	1893 ,,	649
Dixon, Arthur Lee. Merton F.C. Rugby	1892-3 ,,	103
Dixon, Frederick Percival. Exeter F.C. Rugby	1893 ,,	121
Dobell, Walter Duffield. Magdalen F.C. Rugby	1892-3 ,,	295
Dobson, Louis Lempriere. Stroke Magdalen 1st Torpid	1893 ,,	295
Doherty, William Vernon. Christ Church F.C. Rugby	1892-3 ,,	391
Donaldson, James Gordon. Christ Church F.C. Rugby	,, ,,	391
†Donaldson, William Patrick. Brasenose F.C. Rugby	,, ,,	311
†Donaldson, William Patrick. Brasenose F.C. Association	,, ,,	311
Drage, William Henry. Merton 1st Torpid	1893 ,,	103
Dredge, Joseph Alan. Balliol F.C. Association	1892-3 ,,	71
Dun, Robert Hay. Brasenose F.C. Rugby	,, ,,	311
Dutton, Frederick Hugh. Stroke Hertford Torpid	1893 ,,	649
Ebden, Frederick Rogers. Magdalen F.C. Association	1892-3 ,,	295
Eliot, Montague Charles. Exeter F.C. Association	,, ,,	119
Ellis, Thomas Peter. Lincoln F.C. Association	,, ,,	247
Ellwood, Henry Whalley. Brasenose 1st Torpid	1893 ,,	311

		PAGE
Elwell, James Dudley. St. John's Torpid	1893 facing	479
Encombe, Lord, Captain Magdalen F.C. Association	1892-3 ,,	295
English, Edward James. Merton F.C. Rugby	,, ,,	103
Erskine, Alan David. Magdalen F.C. Association	,, ,,	295
Evans, Francis Duntze. Brasenose F.C. Rugby	,, ,,	311
Evans, Lewis Herbert. Pembroke F.C. Association	,, ,,	567
Everitt, Walter Lewis R. G. Stroke Merton 1st Torpid	,, ,,	103
Fairclough, William Robert. Hertford Torpid	1893 ,,	649
Farquharson, Arthur Spencer L. University coll. Torpid	1893 ,,	41
Farquharson, Arthur Spencer L. University coll. F.C. Association	1892-3 ,,	39
Farrer, Roland John. Balliol F.C. Association	1892-3 ,,	71
Faunthorpe, Bertram Platt. Keble and Torpid	1893 ,,	679
Ferguson, William Harold. Keble 1st Torpid	,, ,,	679
Finch, Hugh Earnshaw. Keble 1st Torpid	,, ,,	679
Fisher, John Cecil. Brasenose F.C. Association	1892-3 ,,	311
Fitzgerald, Reginald Patrick. Balliol F.C. Association	,, ,,	71
Fleming, Charles James N. Queen's F.C. Rugby	,, ,,	167
Flemmick, Arthur Helmuth. Balliol 1st Torpid	1893 ,,	71
Fletcher, Hamilton. Pembroke Torpid	,, ,,	569
Foley, Blanchard. Merton F.C. Association	1892-3 ,,	103
Forster, John Gibson. Queen's F.C. Rugby	,, ,,	167
Foster, Gerald Harman. Magdalen F.C. Rugby	,, ,,	295
Frend, Edwin George C. Wadham Torpid	1893 ,,	535
†Fry, Charles Burgess. Wadham F.C. Rugby	1892-3 ,,	535
†Fry, Charles Burgess. Wadham F.C. Association	,, ,,	535
Furniss, Thomas Sanderson. Cox Merton 1st Torpid	1893 ,,	103
Gairdner, Harry Hamilton. Cox Brasenose 1st Torpid	,, ,	311
Galloway, Thomas Percival. Wadham F.C. Rugby	1892-3 ,,	535
Galloway, Thomas Percival. Wadham F.C. Association	,, ,,	535
Garrett, Abraham. Brasenose F.C. Rugby	,, ,,	311
Gibson, Alan Graeme. University coll. Torpid	1893 ,,	41
Gilbert, Harry Upfield. Merton 1st Torpid	,, ,,	103
Gillison, Maurice Paget. University coll. Torpid	,, ,,	41
Goldschmidt, Charles Alfred. Balliol F.C. Rugby	1892-3 ,,	71
Goode, John. Brasenose F.C. Association	,, ,,	311
Goodwin, Harry Smyth. Queen's F.C. Rugby	,, ,,	167
Goodwin, Harry Smyth. Queen's F.C. Association	,, ,,	167
Gordon, Edward. Queen's F.C. Rugby	,, ,,	167
Gordon, Percival Wilmot. Christ Church F.C. Rugby	,, ,,	391

		PAGE
Gosling, Walter Charles. Merton F.C. Association	1892-3 facing	103
Gough, Arthur Valentine. Brasenose F.C. Rugby	,, ,,	311
Graham, Cecil William N. Stroke Trinity Torpid	1893 ,,	431
†Grant, Alfred Hamilton. Balliol F.C. Rugby	1892-3 ,,	71
Greaves, Arthur Ivan. Keble 1st Torpid	1893 ,,	679
Greig, Ronald Alister. University coll. F.C. Association	1892-3 ,,	39
Griffiths, Trevor. Worcester F.C. Rugby	,, ,,	617
Grotrian, Harold Hunter. Brasenose F.C. Association	,, ,,	311
Groves, Charles Nixon. Stroke Keble and Torpid	1893 ,,	679
Gwyther, Edward Newill. Bow Exeter Torpid	,, ,,	121
Hailey, William Malcolm. Corpus Torpid	,, ,,	343
Haldane, Henry Chicheley. Brasenose 1st Torpid	,, ,,	311
Haldane, Henry Chicheley. Brasenose F.C. Association	1892-3 ,,	311
Hale, James Rashleigh. Hertford F.C. Association	,, ,,	647
Hall, Bertram Alexander. Captain Christ Church F.C. Rugby	,, ,,	391
Hallifax, Henry Francis. Balliol F.C. Rugby	,, ,,	71
Hampson, Henry Christian. Brasenose F.C. Rugby	,, ,,	311
Hannay, Robert Kerr. University coll. F.C. Association	,, ,,	39
Hanreitté, Charles James. Queen's Torpid	1893 ,,	167
Harrison, Oliver Ormerod. Oriel Torpid	,, ,,	127
Harrison, Spencer Henry. Pembroke F.C. Association	1892-3 ,,	567
Hartley, Edward. Captain University coll. F.C. Association	,, ,,	39
Hawkin, Robert Crawford. Pembroke F.C. Rugby	1893 ,,	569
Hayden, Oswald Ernest. Christ Church F.C. Rugby	1892-3 ,,	391
Hayes-Robinson, Roger. Merton F.C. Association	,, ,,	103
Healey, Gerald Edward C. Trinity Torpid	1893 ,,	431
Hemmerde, Edward George. University coll. F.C. Association	1892-3 ,,	39
Hemsley, George Herbert. Bow Merton 1st Torpid	1893 ,,	103
Hemsley, George Herbert. Merton F.C. Association	1892-3 ,,	103
Henderson, Bernard William. Bow Lincoln Torpid	1893 ,,	249
Henderson, Edward Lowry. Stroke Oriel Torpid	,, ,,	127
Henlé, Frederick Thomas B. Balliol F.C. Rugby	1892-3 ,,	71
Henley, Hon. Anthony Morton. Balliol 1st Torpid	1893 ,,	71
Henley, Edward Cornish. Lincoln F.C. Association	1892-3 ,,	247
Henning, Edward Nares. Corpus F.C. Rugby	,, ,,	343
Henriques, Quentin Quixano. Corpus Torpid	,, ,,	343
Henson, John. Worcester F.C. Rugby	,, ,,	617
†Hewitt, Copley Delisle. Magdalen F.C. Association	,, ,,	295
Hichens, Richard Arthur J. Exeter Torpid	1893 ,,	121

xii   PORTRAITS IN FOOTBALL AND TORPID GROUPS, 1893.

Name	Year		PAGE
Hickey, Godfrey Michael V. Queen's F.C. Association	1892-3	facing	167
Hill, Ernest George. Magdalen F.C. Rugby	"	"	295
Hill, Gerard Robert. Balliol F.C. Association	"	"	71
Hilliard, Francis Porteus T. Magdalen 1st Torpid	1893	"	295
Hirst, Francis Wrigley. Wadham F.C. Rugby	1892-3	"	535
Hirst, William Alfred. Worcester F.C. Rugby	"	"	617
Hives, Charles Vesey. Corpus F.C. Rugby	"	"	343
Hives, Charles Vesey. Corpus F.C. Association	"	"	343
Hodges, Frederick George. Wadham F.C. Rugby	1892-3	"	535
Hodges, William Richardson. Wadham F.C. Association	"	"	535
Hodgson, Archibald Sanford. New Coll. 1st Torpid	1893	"	191
Holland, Robert Erskine. Bow Oriel Torpid	"	"	127
Home, Robert. Queen's F.C. Association	1892-3	"	167
Home, Robert. Queen's Torpid	1893	"	167
Home, Edward Richard. Wadham F.C. Rugby	"	"	535
Hooke, George. New Coll. 1st Torpid	"	"	191
Hope, Robert Philip. Merton 1st Torpid	"	"	103
Houghton, Arthur Villiers. Hertford F.C. Association	1892-3	"	647
How, John Hall. Wadham Torpid	1893	"	535
Hughes-Games, Harold G. W. Worcester F.C. Rugby	1892-3	"	617
Humble, William Eustace E. Queen's F.C. Rugby	"	"	167
Humble, William Eustace E. Queen s F.C. Association	"	"	167
Hutchinson, Frederick William. Keble 1st Torpid	1893	"	679
Irish, Harold John H. Brasenose F.C. Rugby	1892-3	"	311
Jackson, George Erskine. Corpus Torpid	1893	"	343
Jackson, George Erskine. Corpus F.C. Rugby	1892-3	"	343
James, Benjamin. Merton F.C. Rugby	"	"	103
James, Charles Wilford. Lincoln Torpid	1893	"	249
James, Charles Wilford. Lincoln F.C. Association	1892-3	"	247
James, George Fitzhugh B. Merton F.C. Rugby	"	"	103
Jeffcock, Charles Augustus C. Bow Keble 1st Torpid	1893	"	679
Jenkins, Griffith Wight. Wadham F.C. Rugby	1892-3	"	535
Jennison, George. Balliol F.C. Association	"	"	71
Jephson, William Vincent. Stroke Keble 1st Torpid	1893	"	679
Jex-Blake, Arthur J. Magdalen 1st Torpid	"	"	295
Jex-Blake, Thomas B. Balliol 1st Torpid	"	"	71
Johnson, Walter Lyulph. Stroke New coll. 1st Torpid	"	"	191
Jones, Arthur John. Capt. Lincoln F.C. Association	1892-3	"	247
Jones, Arthur Mervyn. University coll. Torpid	1893	"	41
Jones, Charles Lerigo. Bow Worcester Torpid	"	"	615

Name	Year		PAGE
Jones, Charles Sydney. Cox Magdalen 1st Torpid	1893	facing	295
Jones, Frederick William. Magdalen F.C. Rugby	1892-3	"	295
Jones, Walter Hugh. Merton F.C. Association	"	"	103
Kennard, Charles Heywood. Brasenose F.C. Association	"	"	311
Kenrick, Cyril Cranmer C. Merton F.C. Association	"	"	103
Kent, Sidney Joseph F. Wadham F.C. Association	"	"	535
Kershaw, John Felix. Stroke Balliol 1st Torpid	1893	"	71
Kidston, George Jardine. New coll. 1st Torpid	"	"	191
Kilby, Reginald George. Pembroke F.C. Association	1892-3	"	567
King, Hugh Charles. Oriel Torpid	1893	"	127
Kirby, Walter Reginald. Exeter F.C. Association	1892-3	"	119
Kirby, William Henry. Balliol F.C. Association	"	"	71
Kitson, James Butler. Pembroke F.C. Association	"	"	567
Kitson, John Archibald. Keble and Torpid	1893	"	679
Lake, Kenneth Alexander. Captain Magdalen F.C. Rugby	1892-3	"	295
Lambert, George Bancroft. Magdalen F.C. Rugby	"	"	295
Langley, Alexander. Pembroke F.C. Association	"	"	567
Lawrence, Henry. Queen's F.C. Rugby	"	"	167
Lawrence, Henry. Queen's F.C. Association	"	"	167
Lawrence, James Frederic N. Balliol 1st Torpid	1893	"	71
Lee, Henry Kenneth. Bow New coll. 1st Torpid	"	"	191
Lee, William Stevens. Wadham F.C. Rugby	1892-3	"	535
Legh, Edmund Willoughby. Stroke University coll. Torpid	1893	"	41
Lempriere, Charles Cyril. Worcester F.C. Rugby	1892-3	"	617
Lempriere, Lancelot Raoul. Worcester F.C. Rugby	"	"	617
Leslie-Jones, Leycester H. Brasenose 1st Torpid	1893	"	311
Leslie-Jones, Leycester H. Brasenose F.C. Rugby	1892-3	"	311
L'Estrange, Perceval Hastings. Queen's F.C. Rugby	"	"	167
Lewis, John Wilfred. Jesus coll. Torpid	1893	"	495
Lewis, William Henry. Bow Jesus coll. Torpid	"	"	495
Lindsay, Patrick Charles N. Pembroke Torpid	"	"	567
Lister, Alfred James. Pembroke F.C. Association	1892-3	"	567
Lister, Edward. Wadham F.C. Association	"	"	535
Littlehales, Charles Gough. Exeter F.C. Association	"	"	119
Littlewood, Reginald Basil. Wadham F.C. Association	"	"	535
Lloyd, Thomas Owen. Brasenose 1st Torpid	1893	"	311
Longmore, Philip Raynsford. Magdalen F.C. Rugby	1892-3	"	295
Lovat, Lord. Magdalen F.C. Rugby	"	"	295
Lubbock, Geoffrey. Trinity Torpid	1893	"	431
Luxmoore, William Cyril. Bow Keble and Torpid	"	"	679

OXFORD MEN 1880-1892.

Name	Year	Page
Lyall, Francis Frederick. Balliol F.C. Rugby	1892-3 facing	71
Lydall, Cecil Wykeham. Worcester Torpid	1893 ,,	615
Lynam, Alfred Edward. Exeter Torpid	,, ,,	121
Lyon, George Herbert. Brasenose F.C. Rugby	1892-3 ,,	311
Lyon, Leopold Playfair. Bow Hertford Torpid	1893 ,,	649
McArthur, Malcolm Stewart H. Cox Queen's Torpid	,, ,,	167
McArthur, William Lyon. Worcester F.C. Rugby	1892-3 ,,	617
Mackenzie, William K. S. Cox St. John's Torpid	1893 ,,	479
Macvey, Thomas. Wadham F.C. Rugby	1892-3 ,,	535
Mair, Robert Bird R. Queen's F.C. Rugby	,, ,,	167
Maitland, David Baxter. Magdalen F.C. Rugby	,, ,,	295
Majendie, Lionel Robert. Bow Christ Church 1st Torpid	1893 ,,	391
Maling, Arthur Freville. Exeter F.C. Association	1892-3 ,,	113
Mallam, Herbert Edward. Hertford F.C. Association	,, ,,	647
Marshall, Reginald. Stroke Wadham Torpid	1893 ,,	535
Marshall, Reginald. Wadham F.C. Association	1892-3 ,,	535
Marten, Clarence Henry K. Balliol F.C. Association	,, ,,	71
Mawson, William Willmott. Merton 1st Torpid	1893 ,,	103
Mayo, John Pym. Balliol F.C. Rugby	1892-3 ,,	71
Meggy, Douglas Henry. Christ Church F.C. Association	,, ,,	391
Menzies, John Herbert. Exeter Torpid	1893 ,,	121
Millett, Harold Wake. Pembroke F.C. Association	1892-3 ,,	567
Millington, William Algernon. Worcester F.C. Rugby	,, ,,	617
Mirrlees, Charles Alexander R. Merton F.C. Rugby	,, ,,	103
Mitchell, Alexander. Balliol F.C. Rugby	,, ,,	71
Moffat, Henry Elias. Pembroke Torpid	1893 ,,	569
Montagnon, Louis Langlois. Hertford Torpid	,, ,,	649
Montgomery, Charles James. Lincoln F.C. Association	1892-3 ,,	247
Moore, Pierce Langrishe. Christ Church F.C. Rugby	,, ,,	391
Mordaunt, Gerald John. University coll. F.C. Association	,, ,,	39
Morison, Lennox James. Pembroke Torpid	1893 ,,	569
Moseley, Herbert Harvey. Worcester, Torpid	,, ,,	615
Mullins, Reginald Cuthbert. Keble 2nd Torpid	,, ,,	679
Murray, Wilfred George R. Balliol F.C. Association	1892-3 ,,	71
Mytton, George Herbert. New coll. 1st Torpid	1893 ,,	191
Nathan, Geoffrey. Worcester F.C. Rugby	1892-3 ,,	617
Nelson, Alfred Leonard. Captain Merton F.C. Association	,, ,,	103
Newman, Richard. Brasenose F.C. Rugby	,, ,,	311
Newsom, George Ernest. Merton F.C. Rugby	,, ,,	103
Nicholson, Harold. Exeter Torpid	1893 ,,	121
Nutter, Alfred Barrett. Brasenose 1st Torpid	1893 facing	311
†Oakley, William John. Christ Church F.C. Association	1892-3 ,,	391
O'Flaherty, Alfred Ernest. Oriel Torpid	1893 ,,	127
Otto, John Ellison. Magdalen F.C. Rugby	1892-3 ,,	295
Oxmantown, Lord. Stroke Christ Church 1st Torpid	1893 ,,	391
Paddison, George Frederick. Queen's F.C. Rugby	1892-3 ,,	167
Paddison, George Frederick. Queen's F.C. Association	,, ,,	167
Pantin, Robert Gerald. Wadham Torpid	1893 ,,	535
Parker, Frederic Moore S. Merton F.C. Association	1892-3 ,,	103
Partridge, Walter Ernest C. Keble 2nd Torpid	1893 ,,	679
Pattinson, Reginald. Oriel Torpid	,, ,,	127
Pearson, Robert Barclay. Brasenose 1st Torpid	,, ,,	311
Pearson, Robert Barclay. Brasenose F.C. Rugby	1892-3 ,,	311
Pechey, Richard Francis. Hertford F.C. Association	,, ,,	647
Peel, John Douglas. Magdalen F.C. Association	,, ,,	295
Petitit, Oliver Stanley. Lincoln F.C. Association	,, ,,	247
Phillips, Francis Ashley. Exeter F.C. Association	,, ,,	119
Pocock, Richard Lawrence. Stroke Pembroke Torpid	1893 ,,	569
Pocock, Theodore Innes. Corpus F.C. Rugby	1892-3 ,,	343
Porter, John Scott. Stroke Brasenose 1st Torpid	1893 ,,	311
Pountney, Arthur Meek. University coll. Torpid	,, ,,	41
Pyatt, Henry Robert. Hertford F.C. Association	1892-3 ,,	647
Radley, Harold Yelf. Brasenose F.C. Rugby	,, ,,	311
†Raikes, George Barkley. Magdalen F.C. Association	,, ,,	295
Rankin, James Reginald Len. Corpus Torpid	1893 ,,	343
Ransome, Chas. Arthur H. Wadham F.C. Association	1892-3 ,,	535
Ravenshaw, John. Merton F.C. Association	,, ,,	103
Rawstorne, Edward Buckley. Balliol F.C. Rugby	,, ,,	71
Renwick, Arthur. Cox Worcester Torpid	1893 ,,	615
Reynolds, George Reynolds. Stroke St. John's Torpid	,, ,,	479
Reynolds, Leonard William. Exeter F.C. Association	1892-3 ,,	119
Richards, Cyril James R. Exeter F.C. Association	,, ,,	119
Richards, Morley John B. Lincoln Torpid	1893 ,,	249
Rivington, Henry Gibson. Worcester Torpid	,, ,,	615
Rivington, Henry Gibson. Worcester F.C. Rugby	1892-3 ,,	617
Robbs, Charles Haldane H. Merton F.C. Rugby	,, ,,	103
Roberts, Paul Ernest. Worcester F.C. Rugby	,, ,,	617
Robertson-Glasgow, Charles P. Magdalen F.C. Rugby	,, ,,	295
Roche, Alexander Adair. Wadham F.C. Rugby	,, ,,	535

PORTRAITS IN FOOTBALL AND TORPID GROUPS, 1893.

Name	Year	Page
Roche, Alexander Adair. Wadham F.C. Association	1892-3 facing	535
Rogers, Herbert Lionel. Christ Church F.C. Association	,, ,,	391
Russell, Charles. Hertford Torpid	1893 ,,	649
Russell, Thomas Brownloe. Pembroke F.C. Association	1892-3 ,,	567
Ryley, Cyril List. Jesus coll. Torpid	1893 ,,	495
St. Hill, Ralph Woodward. Bow Trinity Torpid	,, ,,	431
Salmon, Thomas. Magdalen F.C. Association	1892-3 ,,	295
Salt, Frederick John. Christ Church F.C. Rugby	,, ,,	391
Sanderson, F. University coll. Torpid	1893 ,,	41
Sanger, William. Corpus Torpid	,, ,,	343
Sanger, William. Corpus F.C. Rugby	1892-3 ,,	343
Sant, Ivor. Jesus coll. Torpid	1893 ,,	495
Scanlan, Arthur Dennison. Cox Oriel Torpid	,, ,,	127
Scott, Russell. Balliol F.C. Rugby	1892-3 ,,	71
Scott, Thomas Gilbert. Hertford F.C. Association	,, ,,	647
Sells, Arthur Clement. Queen's Torpid	1893 ,,	167
Sharpley, Hugo. Corpus F.C. Association	1892-3 ,,	343
Shaw, Harold Lancaster. Cox Pembroke Torpid	1893 ,,	569
Shepheard, Harold Beaumont. Trinity Torpid	,, ,,	431
Sherwood, Edward Charles. Magdalen 1st Torpid	,, ,,	295
Sich, Alexander Ernest. Lincoln Torpid	,, ,,	249
Simon, John Allsebrook. Wadham Torpid	,, ,,	535
Simon, Maurice. Wadham F.C. Rugby	1892-3 ,,	535
Simpson, Edgar Hope. Balliol F.C. Rugby	,, ,,	71
Simpson, Frederick Charles. Queen's Torpid	1893 ,,	167
Sing, Mark. Christ Church 1st Torpid	,, ,,	391
Slater, Thomas. Bow Pembroke Torpid	,, ,,	569
Slocock, Charles Edward. Merton F.C. Association	1892-3 ,,	103
Smallwood, Arthur William. Corpus F.C. Association	,, ,,	343
Smith, Botcler Chernocke. Keble 1st Torpid	1893 ,,	679
Smith, Frederick Edwin. Wadham F.C. Rugby	1892-3 ,,	535
Smith, Thomas Oliphant. Trinity Torpid	1893 ,,	431
Smyth, George Muckleston T. Queen's F.C. Association	1892-3 ,,	167
Sparrow, Isaac. Corpus F.C. Association	,, ,,	343
Sperling, Rowland Arthur C. Cox New coll. 1st Torpid	1893 ,,	191
Stangar-Leathes, Thomas D. Brasenose F.C. Rugby	1892-3 ,,	311
Steedman, James William. Christ Church F.C. Association	,, ,,	391
Stephenson, Hugh Lansdown. Christ Church F.C. Association	1892-3 ,,	391
Stevinson, John Sandilands. Pembroke F.C. Association	,, ,,	567
†Stewart, William Burton. Brasenose F.C. Rugby	,, ,,	311
Stewart, Walter James L. St. John's Torpid	1893 ,,	479
Stocks, Edward Varlelle. Wadham Torpid	1893 facing	535
†Street, Frank. Christ Church F.C. Association	1892-3 ,,	391
Stutfield, Vincent Corbett. Jesus coll. Torpid	1893 ,,	495
Sully, Arthur Blount. Lincoln Torpid	,, ,,	249
Symonds, Francis Henry. University coll. F.C. Association	1892-3 ,,	39
Tassell, Douglas Spencer M. Christ Church F.C. Rugby	,, ,,	391
Taylor, Arthur Ernest. Bow St. John's Torpid	1893 ,,	479
Tetley, James George Wynn. Pembroke Torpid	,, ,,	569
Tew, Edward Grosvenor. Magdalen 1st Torpid	,, ,,	327
Tew, Ernest William. Stroke Worcester Torpid	,, ,,	615
Thomas, Edward Aubrey. Bow Magdalen 1st Torpid	,, ,,	295
Thomas, Edward Swayne. Queen's F.C. Rugby	1892-3 ,,	167
Tollinton, Henry Phillips. Balliol F.C. Association	,, ,,	71
Tombleson, James Bennett. Corpus F.C. Association	,, ,,	343
Tomkins, Percy Smith. Cox Keble 1st Torpid	1893 ,,	679
Trendall, Edwin Percivall. Worcester F.C. Rugby	1892-3 ,,	617
Tudor-Owen, Edward. Christ Church F.C. Association	,, ,,	391
Twidell, John Cook. Trinity Torpid	1893 ,,	431
Underdown, William Goodwin. Wadham F.C. Association	1892-3 ,,	535
Underhill, Charles Bernard. Balliol F.C. Rugby	,, ,,	71
Van Cooten, Harold. Jesus coll. Torpid	1893 ,,	495
Varley, Frederick John. Oriel Torpid	,, ,,	127
Veale, Rawdon Augustus. Queen's F.C. Association	1892-3 ,,	167
Vesey, Sidney Philip Chas. Christ Church F.C. Rugby	,, ,,	391
Veysey, John Waldegrave. Pembroke F.C. Association	,, ,,	567
Wade-Smith, Molineux. Hertford F.C. Association	,, ,,	647
Walcot, John Owen H. Hertford F.C. Association	,, ,,	647
†Walker, John Allsop. Magdalen F.C. Association	,, ,,	295
Wall, Reginald Cecil B. Queen's F.C. Association	,, ,,	167
Waller, David Grierson. Cox Trinity Torpid	1893 ,,	431
Walters, David. Merton F.C. Rugby	1892-3 ,,	103
Ward, Francis. Bow Wadham Torpid	1893 ,,	535
Warman, Arthur Seager. Corpus F.C. Rugby	1892-3 ,,	343
Warman, Arthur Seager. Corpus F.C. Association	,, ,,	343
Warre, Ernald Roger. Balliol 1st Torpid	1893 ,,	71
Warre, Ernald Roger. Balliol F.C. Association	1892-3 ,,	71
Warrington, Thomas Cotterill. Stroke Jesus coll. Torpid	1893 ,,	495
Watling, Henry John W. Lincoln Torpid	,, ,,	249
Watson, William Donald Paul. Brasenose 1st Torpid	,, ,,	311

PORTRAITS IN FOOTBALL AND TORPID GROUPS, 1893. xv

Watson, William Donald Paul. Brasenose F.C. Association		PAGE 1892-3 facing 311
Wedd, Henry George. Brasenose F.C. Association	,,	,, 311
Weigall, Cecil Edward. Stroke Corpus Torpid	1893	,, 343
Welch-Thornton, Henry. Merton 1st Torpid	,,	,, 103
West, Tom. Queen's F.C. Association	1892-3	,, 167
White, Wallis Harry B. Lincoln F.C. Association	,,	,, 247
Wickham, Reginald William. Magdalen F.C. Rugby	,,	,, 295
Wigram, Robert. Merton F.C. Association	,,	,, 103
Wilkinson, Charles Robert. Hertford Torpid	1893	,, 649
Willett, John Abernethy. University coll. F.C. Association	1892-3	,, 39
Williams, David James. Worcester F.C. Rugby	,,	,, 617
Williams, John Larden. Corpus F.C. Rugby	,,	,, 343

Willimott, Andrew Beauchamp. Wadham F.C. Association		PAGE 1892-3 facing 535
Wingate-Saul, Ernest. Christ Church F.C. Rugby	,,	,, 391
Wingfield Digby, Stephen H. Christ Church 1st Torpid	1893	,, 391
Witt, Robert Clermont. New coll. 1st Torpid	,,	,, 191
Wolfe, Benjamin Spencer. Magdalen F.C. Rugby	1892-3	,, 295
Wood, George Ronald. Merton F.C. Association	,,	,, 103
Wood, Robert Boardman. Hertford Torpid	1893	,, 649
Woolcombe, Charles Kenneth. Worcester Torpid	,,	,, 615
Wright, Charles Ernest. Oriel Torpid	,,	,, 127
Wybergh, Cecil Hilton. Hertford F.C. Association	1892-3	,, 647
Wynn-Williams, Ernest. Corpus F.C. Association	,,	,, 343
Zwezdakoff, Victor. Lincoln F.C. Association	,,	,, 247

ST. GEORGE'S HALL, NOW DEMOLISHED.—*From Skelton.*

Alumni Oxonienses (1500—1886).

Vols. in 4, large 8vo.; handsomely bound in Half-Roan, gilt top. 1500—1714, 4 Vols. in 2, eight guineas; 1715—1886, 4 Vols. in 2, eight guineas.

OPINIONS OF THE PRESS, &c.

'Since Anthony Wood, the famous Oxford antiquary, completed and published his "Athenæ Oxonienses," just 200 years ago, no such important contribution has been made to what may be called the biographical history of the University of Oxford as Mr. Joseph Foster has now made, by the publication of his monumental work, entitled "Alumni Oxonienses." . . . Mr. Foster is an expert in scientific genealogy, an enthusiast for rigid biographical accuracy, and his well-known labours in other quarters of this field of research have enabled him to bring to the work of annotation a fund of collateral information which is accessible to no other man. . . . The earlier instalments of his work have been recognized by all competent authorities. . . . We cannot but congratulate Mr. Foster on the completion of his gigantic undertaking, and bespeak for it a cordial and, we trust, not un-remunerative recognition. Such labours as his are almost necessarily a work of love rather than of profit; but, at least, they are entitled to a fuller measure of credit and distinction than have so far fallen to his share.'—*The Times*.

'By far the most important publication relating to Oxford University. . . . We have also to praise, in every respect, the mechanical execution of the book.'—*The Oxford Magazine*.

'We are glad to be able to congratulate Mr. Foster on the result of this great undertaking. That a single individual should have the energy and the patience to carry through a book of so laborious a character, is a striking testimony to his knowledge and his powers. Three thousand two hundred and sixty-four closely-printed pages, each of them teeming with scores of facts, and positively bristling with dates, represent an achievement of which any man might be proud, and the more so when the general accuracy of this vast mass of information has been so widely and authoritatively acknowledged.'—*Athenæum*.

'This most laborious, extensive, and, considering the space over which it travels, surprisingly full and accurate collection of names, will, henceforth, be absolutely indispensable for the student of academic history.'—*Preface to the History of Corpus Christi College, by its President*.

'Of the many standard books of reference to which we have been indebted, one at least calls for special recognition. Mr. Joseph Foster's "Alumni Oxonienses" has been of the greatest service to us in identifying many of the names in this Register. We can only hope that the Cambridge Matriculations, when they come to be published, will be edited with as much care and thoroughness as Mr. Foster's valuable work.'—*Preface to Westminster School Register*.

'Oxford has reason to be thankful to Mr. Foster's zeal and patience.'—*English Historical Review*.

'A most valuable addition to our sources of genealogical and biographical information. . . . Clearly printed and well got up, its accuracy will be taken for granted by all who know the character of Mr. Foster's earlier publications.'—*Saturday Review*.

'To every member of either University, to every genealogist, and to all engaged in historical or biographical pursuits, the mere title of the work involves its full recommendation, and tells how formidable a labour Mr. Foster has undertaken. . . . Mr. Foster's spirited efforts will win him grateful recognition, and we are anxious to give a task such as he now undertakes all the publicity in our power. . . . No public library can indeed afford to be without a work to which the historian and the genealogist must perpetually turn. That a work of this class should be accomplished by private energy and enterprise is nothing short of a marvel.'—*Notes and Queries*.

'A boon to the nonplussed genealogist . . . and handy book of reference of perpetual use. . . . Everything is ready at hand, complete, concise, authentic. . . . The wonder is how, with the immense mass of matter, with unexceptional paper and print, the volume can be issued at the price.'—*The Tablet*.

'Upon the extraordinary value of this great undertaking for biographical and genealogical purposes it is unnecessary to dwell. We must content ourselves with calling attention to the rapidity with which it has been passed through the press, and to the low price at which it is issued.'—*Academy*.

'Here is preserved indubitable proof of those needful facts which are daily sought for with infinite labour by the historian and genealogist.'—*Genealogist*.

'Mr. Joseph Foster's book, "Alumni Oxonienses," issued this week, is one of those works which inspire with unbounded respect the most casual examiner of their pages. . . . Of its extreme value there can be no possible doubt, and genealogists will not be the only class to regard Mr. Foster as one of their greatest benefactors. . . . The information supplied is for the most part absolutely correct.'—*The Record*.

'The book arrived safely. Beautiful and interesting.'—THE BISHOP OF OXFORD.

'I wish to express my admiration of the manner in which the book has been prepared and edited, and my appreciation of its great value and utility.'—J. BELLAMY, D.D., VICE CHANCELLOR.

'A magnificent book. . . . The "Alumni" will be of priceless service to all future workers at the History of Oxford. . . . I have worked through A and B of the new volume, and marvel at its accuracy. . . . By the publication of these transcripts Mr. Foster has conferred a great boon on students of recent academic history. . . . Of inestimable value, and very unlikely to be ever superseded. In helping him, I felt I was helping all future students of the history of Oxford.'—THE PROVOST OF QUEEN'S COLLEGE.

'We have obtained to-day the first volume of your early series of "Alumni Oxonienses," and the admirable way in which you have produced the work certainly fills one with feelings of gratitude. Of the labour involved I understand something, and I find it difficult to comprehend how you accomplish so much with such thoroughness and perfect arrangement. I trust that you will meet with some reward in the recognition of the magnitude of your services on the part of those who, like contributors to our Dictionary, benefit by your labours immediately.'—SIDNEY LEE.

'It is a splendid piece of work, and I am daily grateful for it.'—F. MADAN, BODLEIAN LIBRARY.

'The accuracy is greater than I am used to find in books of reference.'—M. H. GREEN, TRINITY COLL.

'We are much indebted to you for the trouble you have taken in compiling so useful a book of reference.'—LI. J. M. BEBB, LIBRARIAN, BRASENOSE COLLEGE.

'How you have contrived to complete so gigantic a task in so short a time is a mystery, and I heartily congratulate you. In looking through the books, I have found errors; but how could it be otherwise? No man but yourself would have dared to attempt to annotate such a list.'—H. SYDNEY GRAZEBROOK.

'I find the "Alumni Oxonienses" a most useful book, in fact, better so every time I open it; it is quite a boon.'—EDW. H. OWEN.

'I am fairly astonished at the vast amount of labour it must have cost you to compile these volumes. I am greatly pleased with them, and consider them the most valuable books of reference in my library. Posterity will owe you a deep debt of gratitude for your labours in this direction.'—F. A. BLAYDES.

'I consider it the most valuable book of reference I have.'—VERE L. OLIVER.

'It is a valuable book of reference, and should be in every public library, in addition to private ones.'—R. S. ARNOLD.

'"Alumni Oxonienses" is a work of which you may well be proud. The labour involved in producing it cannot be estimated, and no words can adequately express its value as a book of reference.'—W. H. RICHARDSON.

'All antiquaries and all Oxford men are under deep debt of a obligation to you for your arduous labours. I only hope the book may have a very largely increased sale. It is splendidly done, and of the highest value and use. The fund of information you give is beyond all conception.'—W. G. DIMOCK-FLETCHER.

'Allow me to have the pleasure of adding my testimony to the invaluable benefit you have conferred upon every student and lover of biography and genealogical research, by the compilation and publication of such a vast treasury of information full of interest and assistance.'—E. M. S. PARKER.

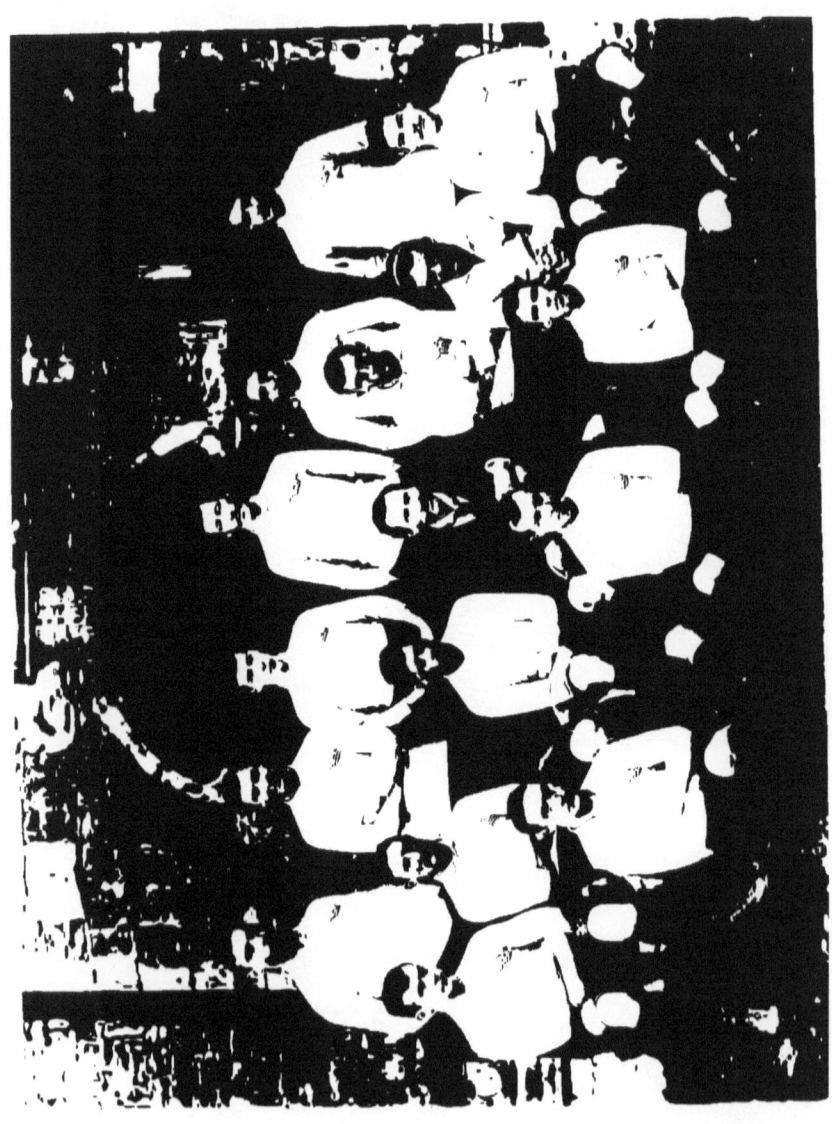

[WOODEN ORNAMENT FROM ROUEN CATHEDRAL.—*Pugin.*]

A

Abbay, Richard, M.A., fellow WADHAM 69-79, where see.

Abbey, Charles John, M.A., fellow UNIVERSITY COLL. 62-66, where see.

Abbey, John, born at Wheldrake, Yorks, 1841; 1s. Matthew, pleb. NON-COLLEGIATE, matric. 29 April, 81, aged 40.

Abbey, Roland Walter, born at Checkendon, Oxon, 1866; 1s. Charles John, cler. NON-COLLEGIATE, matric. 15 Jan., 87, aged 20; migrated to ST. EDMUND HALL, B.A. 89.

Abbot, Reginald Charles Edward, baron Colchester, M.A., fellow ALL SOULS' 64-9, where see.

Abbot, rev. Wilfred Henry, born at Dublin 7 June, 1867; 2s. Frederick James, cler. KEBLE, matric. 19 Oct., 86, aged 19 (from Bradfield coll.), B.A. 89.

Abbott, Albert, born at Adlington, Lancashire, 7 March, 1872; 2s. George Thomas, gen. NON-COLLEGIATE, matric. 17 Oct., 91, aged 19, from Blackrod and Rivington school.

Abbott, Evelyn Robins, born at Derby 9 May, 1873; 1s. Samuel, C.E., deceased. BALLIOL, matric. 20 Oct., 91, aged 18 (from Bath coll.); a selected candidate (10th) Indian civil service 91.

Abbott, Evelyn, M.A., fellow BALLIOL 74, where see.

Abbott, John Herbert Roxby, born at Rathmines, co. Dublin, 24 Aug., 1873; 1s. Matthew William, late lieut. R.N. HERTFORD, matric. 22 Oct., 92, aged 19, from Bedford gr. school.

Abbott, John Ralph, born at Hampstead, Middlesex, 1868; 2s. Thomas, arm. HERTFORD, matric. 29 Oct., 87, aged 19.

Abbott, Norman Josiah, born at The Elms, Essex, 3 Jan., 1870; 2s. John, gen. MERTON, matric. 19 Oct., 89, aged 19, from Uppingham school.

Abbott, Robert Lamb, M.A., tutor NON-COLLEGIATE students, where see.

Abbott, rev. Thomas Kingsmill, born at Coogah, New South Wales, 18 Feb., 1866; s. Kingsmill, MERTON, matric. 19 Oct., 89, aged 23 (from Sydney gr. school, and university), B.A. 91; HONOURS :—3 classics 91.

Abbott, Walter John, born in London 1873; 1s. Walter, M.A., cler. CHRIST CHURCH, matric. 14 Oct., 92, aged 19, from Haileybury.

Abbott, Wilfred Horace, born in Bermondsey, Surrey, 25 Dec., 1867; 2s. George Isaac Worley, gen. NON-COLLEGIATE, matric. 16 May, 91, aged 23 (from St. Mark's coll., Chelsea); migrated to TRINITY 92.

Abbott, rev. William Martin, born in Bermuda 1861; o.s. Charles Thompson, D.Med. NON-COLLEGIATE, matric. 24 Feb., 81, aged 19 (from Royse's school, Abingdon); curate of Salisbury St. Thomas 91.

Abel, sir Frederick Augustus, K.C.B. Created D.C.L. 13 June, 1883 (s. John Leopold); professor of chemistry war department, C.B. 27 Oct., 77, knighted 20 April 83, K.C.H. 91, LL.D. Cambridge 88; a member of the royal commission on mines 83, organizing secretary of the Imperial Institute since 87, president of the Institute of chemistry, of the society of telegraph engineers and electricians, and of the British association 90. See *Alumni Oxonienses*, page 3.

Abel, Horace Marshall, born at Harrogate, Yorks, 24 June, 1863; y.s. Alfred, gent. MERTON, matric. 17 Oct., 82, aged 19 (from St. Edward's school, Summertown), B.A. 86.

Abell, Francis Martin George, born at Worcester 1869; 1s. Martin, arm. HERTFORD, matric. 29 Jan., 89, aged 19, from Clifton coll.

Abell, William Henry, born at Norton, co. Worcester, 20 Sept., 1873; 2s. Martin, banker. BRASENOSE, matric. 21 Oct., 92, aged 19, from Rugby.

Abernethy, Frank Nicholson, born at Lambeth 1864; y.s. George, gen. NEW COLL., matric. 14 Jan., 90, aged 25, B.Mus. 90.

Abernethy, John Scott, born in London 31 May, 1866; 4s. James, arm. WORCESTER, matric. 27 Oct., 80, aged 20 (from Westminster school), B.A. 86, M.A. 88; bar.-at-law, Middle Temple, 87.

Abrahall, John Leigh Hoskyns, born at Combe, Oxon, 6 June, 1865; 1s. John Hoskyns, vicar. MAGDALEN, matric. 19 Oct., 83, aged 18 (from Eton), demy 83, B.A. 87 (HONOURS :—2 mathematical mods. 85, 1 chemistry 87); died 1 Oct., 91.

Abrahams, Barnett Lionel, born in London 9 Dec., 1869; 1s. Mordecai, gen. BALLIOL, matric. 18 Oct., 88, aged 18 (from city of London school), scholar 87, Jenkyns exhibitioner 92; HONOURS :—proxime accessit Hertford scholarship 88 and 89, 1 classical mods. 90, 2 classics 92.

Abrahamson, Albert, born at Kovno, in Russia, 1859; s. Alexander. NON-COLLEGIATE, matric. 16 May, 91, aged 32.

Acheson, Guy Francis Hamilton, born at Gosport, Hants, 1864; y.s. John Inglefield, arm. UNIVERSITY COLL., matric. 14 Oct., 82, aged 18 (from Birkenhead school), exhibitioner 82-6, B.A. 86; HONOURS :—a mathematical mods. 84, 2 mathematics 86.

Ackerley, Frederic George, born at Mytton, Yorks, 12 Nov., 1871; o.s. George Biglands, cler, ST. MARY HALL, matric. 27 Oct., 91, aged 19.

Ackerley, Richard, born at Birkenhead, Cheshire, 21 Feb., 1861; 1s. Richard. gent. CORPUS CHRISTI, matric. 21 Oct., 80, aged 19 (from Liverpool coll.), B.A. 83, M.A. and B.Med. 88; HONOURS :—3 classical mods. 82.

Acland, right hon. Arthur Herbert Dyke, M.A., hon. fellow BALLIOL, where see.

Acland, sir Henry Wentworth, bart., K.C.B., D.Med., hon. student CHRIST CHURCH 58, where see.

Acland, Henry Dyke, born at Wellington, New Zealand, 21 Sept., 1867; 2s. John Barton Arundell, M.L.C., N.Z., arm. CHRIST CHURCH, matric. 12 June, 86, aged 18, B.A. 89 (HONOURS :—3 history 89); bar.-at-law, Inner Temple, 91.

Acland, John Dyke, born at Christ Church, New Zealand, 17 Feb., 1863; 1s. John Barton Arundell, M.L.C., N.Z., arm. CHRIST CHURCH, matric. 25 May, 83, aged 20.

Acland, right hon. sir Thomas Dyke, bart., M.A., D.C.L., fellow ALL SOULS' 13-9, where see.

Acton, Edward, born at Stretford, co. Lancaster, 6 Nov., 1865; o.s. Henry Thorell, one of the editors of "The Manchester Guardian." WADHAM, matric. 11 Oct., 84, aged 18 (from Uppingham school), scholar 83, B.A. 89 (HONOURS :—1 classical mods. 86, 2 classics 88); bar.-at-law, Inner Temple, 91.

Acton, John Emerich Edward, lord, created D.C.L. 22 June, 1887; hon. fellow ALL SOULS' 90, where see.

Acton, hon. Richard Maximilian Dalberg, born at Tegernsee, near Munich, Bavaria, 7 Aug., 1870; o.s. John Emerich Edward, baron Acton. MAGDALEN, matric. 16 Oct., 88, aged 18.

Acworth, George Pelham Aufrère, born at Rochester, 3 July, 1864; 1s. George Brindley, gent. WORCESTER, matric. 18 Oct., 83, aged 19 (from Bradfield coll.) (HONOURS :—2 classical mods. 85); lieut. R.E. 86.

Acworth, Robert William Harrison, born at Rochester 1870; 2s. George Brindley, gent. WORCESTER, matric. 14 Oct., 89, aged 19, from Lancing coll.

Adair, Alexander Cecil, born at Taunton, Somerset, 10 Oct., 1872; 2s. Henry Atkinson, major. CHRIST CHURCH, matric. 10 Oct., 90, aged 18, from St. Edward's school, Summertown.

Adair, Robert Shafto, born at Bradford, Somerset, 18 Aug., 1862; 2s. Hugh Edward, of Flixton Hall, Suffolk, arm. CHRIST CHURCH, matric. 15 Oct., 80, aged 18, B.A. 84; bar.-at-law, Inner Temple, 90.

Adam, Clement George Montague, born in London, 13 April, 1871; o.s. George Robert, vicar of Shoulden, Kent. NEW COLL., matric. 11 Oct., 89, aged 18, from Radley coll.

Adam, Edward Percy, born at Hulme, Manchester, 28 July, 1873; 1s. Joseph, evangelist. MERTON, matric. 18 Oct., 92, aged 19 (from Nottingham high school), exhibitioner 92.

Adam, James, born in Edinburgh, 6 May, 1870; o.s. James, lord Adam. MERTON, matric. 22 Jan., 89, aged 19.

Adams, Alfred, born at Bromley, Kent, 21 Aug., 1863; 3s. Henry Cadwallader, vicar of Dry Sandford, Berks. MAGDALEN, matric. 15 Oct., 81, aged 18 (from Radley coll.), demy 80-5 (HONOURS :—1 classical mods. 83, 2 history 85); bar.-at-law, Lincoln's Inn 88, as Alfred Arthur.

Adams, Alfred, born at Stockcross, Berks 1865; o.s. John, cler. EXETER, matric. 18 Oct., 83, aged 18, B.A. 87 (from Marlborough), M.A. and B.Med. 92.

Adams, Arthur Conrade Cuffe, born at Bath, 1861; o.s. Thomas, arm. ST. JOHN'S, matric. 16 Oct., 80, aged 19.

Adams, Charles George, born at Bath 1861; o.s. George, gent. NON-COLLEGIATE, matric. 14 Oct., 82, aged 21.

Adams, rev. Edward Charles, M.A., fellow WORCESTER 50-83, where see.

Adams, Henry Cadwallader, M.A., fellow MAGDALEN 43-52, where see.

Adams, rev. Harold Thomas, born in London 1865; 2s. Francis Bryant, gent. UNIVERSITY COLL., matric. 13 Oct., 83, aged 18 (from Bradfield coll.), B.A. 87, M.A. 90 (HONOURS :—3 classical mods. 85, 4 law 87); student Lincoln's Inn 83; curate of St. Barnabas, Oxford, 88.

Adams, Henry Augustus, born at Wing, near Leighton Buzzard, 15 Dec., 1862; 3s. Henry Charles, gent. NON-COLLEGIATE, matric. 18 Oct., 80, aged 17 (from Stony Stratford school); migrated to QUEEN'S, B.A. 83. M.A. 88.

Adams, Herbert, born at Stockcross, Berks, 1862; 1s. John, cler. HERTFORD, matric. 18 Oct., 80, aged 18 (from Marlborough coll.); died 7 April, 83.

Adams, John William Bateman, born at Finchley, Middlesex, 1868; o.s. William Bateman, gen. PEMBROKE, matric. 29 Jan., 91, aged 22.

Adams, Walter Marsham, M.A., fellow NEW COLL. 56-62, where see.

Adams, Walter Frederick, born at Clifton, co. Gloucester, Jan. 1871; 2s. Frederick Morice, cler. KEBLE, matric. 11 Oct., 90, aged 19, from Bristol gr. school.

Adams, William Dacres, born at Wokingham, Berks, 19 Aug., 1864; 1s. William Fulford, of Bowden, Devon, cler. EXETER, matric. 18 Jan., 83, aged 18, from Radley coll.

Adamson, Charles Stennott, born at Ealing, Middlesex, 1867; 2s. Frank, gen. ST. JOHN'S, matric. 16 Oct., 86, aged 19 (from Merchant Taylors' school), scholar 86, B.A. 90, senior scholar 91; HONOURS : —1 classical mods. 88, and 1 mathematical mods. 88, 1 mathematics 89, 1 classics 91.

Addenbroke, rev. Albert Edward, born at Wombourne, co. Stafford, 1866; 2s. George. gent. ST. EDMUND HALL, matric. 22 Oct. 84, aged 18, B.A. 87; curate of Berkeley, co. Gloucester, 88, dock chaplain at Sharpness 90.

Adderley, Ralph Bowyer, born at Arley, co. Warwick, 9 Oct., 1872; 1s. hon. Charles Leigh. CHRIST CHURCH, matric. 29 May, 91, aged 19, from Eton.

Addison, John Joseph, born at Wigton, Cumberland, 1863; 2s. Joseph, arm. NEW INN HALL, matric. 20 Oct., 86, aged 23; migrated to BALLIOL, 87.

Addleshaw, Stanley, born at Whalley Range, co. Lancaster, 1872; 4s. John William, solicitor. PEMBROKE, matric. 25 Oct., 90, aged 18.

Addleshaw, William Percy, born at Bowdon, Cheshire, Sept. 1866; 1s. John William, solicitor. CHRIST CHURCH, matric. 12 June, 86, aged 19 (from Shrewsbury school), B.A. 90; HONOURS : — Ægrotat law 90.

Adeane, Charles Robert Whorwood, born in London, 2 Nov., 1863; o.s. Henry, arm. CHRIST CHURCH, matric. 22 April, 84, aged 20.

A'Deane, Walter Whetham Wratislaw, born at Napier in New Zealand 1869; 2s. John, arm. UNIVERSITY COLL., matric. 15 Oct., 87, aged 18, B.A. 90; HONOURS :—3 law 90.

Adkins, William Ryland Dent, born at Northampton 1862; o.s. William, arm. BALLIOL, matric. 1 Feb., 82, aged 19 (from Mill Hill school), exhibitioner 81-6; bar.-at-law, Inner Temple, 90.

Adler, Berthold, born in London 12 May, 1871; 1s. Louis, merchant. BALLIOL, matric. 17 Oct., 89, aged 18 (from University coll. school, London); HONOURS:—2 classical mods. 91.

Agate, William, born at Emsworth, Hants, 1857; 1s. Joseph, gent. QUEEN'S, matric. 25 Jan., 88, aged 30, B.Mus. 90.

Agius, Edward Charles Tancred, born in London 1875; 1s. Edward Tancred, esq. UNIVERSITY COLL., matric. 15 Oct., 92, aged 17, from St. Augustine's coll., Canterbury.

Agnew, Harold, born at Eccles, co. Lanc., 27 May, 1862; 2s. John Henry, arm. ORIEL, matric. 24 Nov., 80, aged 18 (from Rugby), B.A. 84, M.A. 87; HONOURS:—4 history 84.

Agnew, Patrick Dalreagle, born in Victoria; 1s. William Henry, arm. BALLIOL, matric. 19 Oct., 87, aged — (from Bedford school); selected candidate (5th) Indian civil service 87, 8th in final 89.

Agnew, Philip Leslie, born at Pendleton, co. Lancaster, 30 June, 1863; 4s. William, publisher. NEW COLL., matric. 14 Oct., 82, aged 19 (from Rugby), B.A. 87, M.A. 90 (HONOURS:—2 classical mods. 84, 2 history 86); bar.-at-law, Lincoln's Inn, 90.

Aiken, John Chetwode Chetwood-, born at Stoke Bishop, Bristol, 25 April, 1873; 3s. John Chetwood C.-A., banker. UNIVERSITY COLL., matric. 15 Oct., 92, aged 19, from Marlborough.

Ainger, Alfred, M.A., select preacher 92-3, see part i. col. 4.

Ainger, Edward Barnard, M.A., fellow PEMBROKE 56-78, where see.

Ainslie, Douglas, born in Paris 16 Dec., 1865; 1s. Ainslie Douglas, arm. (see Ainslie Grant-Duff, *Al. Ox.* 391). NON-COLLEGIATE, matric. 13 Oct., 84, aged 18; migrated to EXETER 21 Oct., 85.

Ainslie, Ralph St. John, born at Corfe, Somerset, 26 Jan., 1861; 2s. Alexander Colvin, cler. ORIEL, matric. 19 Oct., 80, aged 19 (from Sherborne school), scholar 80-5, B.A. 85 (HONOURS:—3 classical mods. 82, 2 classics 84); master Sedbergh school, Yorks.

Aitchison, Archibald John Thomas Francis, born in London 11 Nov., 1861; o.s. gen. sir John. G.C.B. QUEEN'S, matric. 22 Oct., 84, aged 22, B.A. 88, M.A. 91.

Aitken, Arthur William Grant, born in London 6 June, 1868; 1s. William Hay Macdowall Hunter, cler. MERTON, matric. 22 Oct., 87, aged 19 (from Bedford school); postmaster 87, B.A. 91; HONOURS: —2 classical mods. 89, 2 classics 91.

Aitken, Charles, born in York 12 Sept., 1869; 2s. Henry Martin, gen., deceased. NEW COLL., matric. 18 Oct., 87, aged 18 (from Clifton coll.), exhibitioner 87, B.A. 91; HONOURS:—3 classical mods. 89, 2 history 91.

Aitken, George Herbert, born at Whittle-le-Woods, co. Lancaster, 17 May 1863; 1s. Robert, gent. ORIEL, matric. 1 June, 82, aged 19 (from Fettes coll. and Rugby), B.A. 85; student Inner Temple 85; curate of St. Jude, Whitechapel, 86.

Aitken, Robert Aubrey, born in London 15 Aug., 1870; 2s. William Hay Macdowall Hunter, cler. MERTON, matric. 19 Oct., 89, aged 19, from Bedford school.

Albery, Frederick John, born at Sydney, N.S.W., 1863; 1s. Mark, gen. CHRIST CHURCH, matric. 12 Oct., 88, aged 25 (from Sydney school), B.A. 91; curate of Longton St. John 91.

Alcock, Arthur Ernest, born at Warminster, Wilts, 12 April, 1871; 3s. Charles, gen. WADHAM, matric. 13 Oct., 90, aged 19 (from Warminster school).

Alcock, rev. John Mark, born at Bickley, Kent, 25 April, 1866; 1s. John Price, cler. ORIEL, matric. 9 Dec., 84, aged 18 (from Canterbury school), B.A. 88, M.A. 91 (HONOURS:—3 theology 88); curate of Evershot, Dorset, 91.

Alcock, rev. Percy Christopher, born at Lee, Kent, 1868; 3s. John, gen. NON-COLLEGIATE, matric. 21 April, 88, aged 20, B.A. 92.

Alcock, Wilfrid Owen, born at Lee, Kent, 19 June, 1874; 4s. John, captain R.N. BALLIOL, matric. 11 Feb., 92, aged 17 (from Tiverton school), exhibitioner 91.

Alden, Lewis, born at Oxford, 11 June, 1869; 5s. Isaac, gen. WADHAM, matric. 15 Oct., 88, aged 19 (from Oxford high school), exhibitioner 88, B.A. 92; HONOURS:—2 classical mods. 90, 2 classics 92.

Alden, Percy, born at Oxford, 6 June, 1865; 3s. Isaac, gen. BALLIOL, matric. 15 Oct., 84, aged 19, B.A. 88, M.A. 91; HONOURS:—3 classical mods. 86, and 3 classics 88.

Alderson, Charles Henry, M.A., fellow ALL SOULS' 57-67, where see.

Alderson, Edward Hall, born at Dunedin, New Zealand, 1864; 1s. Francis John, gent. CHARSLEY'S HALL, matric. 25 Jan., 84, aged 19; migrated to BRASENOSE 84, B.A. 88; bar.-at-law, Inner Temple, 91.

Alderson, rev. Ellerton Garside, born at Worksop, Notts, 23 Feb., 1868; 1s. Daniel Fossick, gen. NEW COLL., matric. 14 Oct., 87, aged 19 (from Leamington coll.), B.A. 91; HONOURS:—2 classical mods. 89, 2 theology 91); curate of Burghclere, Hants, 92.

Alderson, Montague Frederick, born at Holdenby, Northants, 20 July. 1869; 2s. Frederick Cecil, cler. MERTON, matric. 22 Oct., 87, aged 18 (from Winchester), B.A. 90; HONOURS:—2 history 90.

Aldous, Arthur George, born at Islington, 3 Jan., 1867; 5s. James Robert, arm. HERTFORD, matric. 22 Oct., 85, aged 19 (from Sherborne school), scholar 85, B.A. 90; HONOURS:—2 classical mods. 88, 3 classics 90.

Aldred, Philip Foster, M.A., D.C.L., HERTFORD, where see.

Aldridge, Herbert Henry, born in London 25 Feb., 1869; 3s. John, of St. Leonard's Forest, Sussex, lieut.-col. 21st regt. NEW COLL., matric. 12 Oct., 88, aged 19, from Winchester.

Aldridge, James Eyre, born at Parkstone, Dorset, 24 Nov., 1866; 2s. William Wheeler, cler. WORCESTER, matric. 22 Oct., 85, aged 18 (from Malvern coll.), B.A. 92.

Aldridge, John Wheeler, born at Parkstone, Dorset, 26 May, 1865; 1s. William Wheeler, vicar of Emmanuel, Weston-super-Mare. NON-COLLEGIATE, matric. 26 Jan., 85, aged 19 (from Malvern coll.); migrated to WADHAM 15 Feb., 86, to CHARSLEY HALL, B.A. 90.

Aldridge, Robert Beauclerk, born in Chelsea 11 June, 1865; 1s. John, of St. Leonard's Forest, Sussex, arm. UNIVERSITY COLL., matric. 11 Oct., 84, aged 19 (from Eton); of St. Leonard's Forest, capt. 3rd batt. Royal Sussex regiment.

Aldworth, rev. Arthur Ernest, born at Haig, co. Lancaster, 24 May, 1864; 1s. John, cler. WORCESTER, matric. 18 Oct., 83, aged 19 (from Marlborough coll.), B.A. 88.

Alexander, Charles Henry, born in East Indies 1870; 1s. William, arm. TURRELL'S HALL, matric. 15 May, 86, aged 16.

ALEXANDER. — MATRICULATIONS, 1880 TO 1892. — ALLEN.

Alexander, Claude, born in London 24 Feb., 1867; o.s. Claude, arm. (now baronet). NEW COLL., matric. 16 Oct., 85, aged 18 (from Eton), B.A. 89; lieut. 3rd batt. Royal Scots Fusiliers.

Alexander, Edward Bruce, born at Mainpoori, N.W.P., 3 March, 1872; 1s. Richard Dundas, E.I.C.S. TRINITY, matric. 17 Oct., 91, aged 19, from Forest school.

Alexander, Philip Frederick, born in London 1864; elder son Frederick. arm. HERTFORD, matric. 14 Oct., 84, aged 20, B.A. 87, M.A. 91.

Alexander, Samuel, M.A., fellow LINCOLN 82, where see.

Alexander, rev. Sidney Arthur, born at Hampstead, Middlesex, 2 April, 1866; 2s. Frederick, gent. TRINITY, matric. 17 Oct., 85, aged 19 (from St. Paul's school), scholar 84, B.A. 89, tutor KEBLE 92, M.A. 92 (HONOURS:—1 classical mods. 87, 1 classics 89; Septuagint prize 86 and 91, English verse 87, Greek testament prize 88 and 91, Denyer and Johnson theological scholarship 90); curate St. Michael, Oxford, 89-93; reader at the Temple 93.

Alexander, William Frederick, born at Calcutta 6 Feb., 1864; o.s. William Stuart, arm. LINCOLN, matric. 17 Jan., 83, aged 18 (from Ewell school), B.A. 87, M.A. 89; HONOURS:—3 history 86.

Alington, Cyril Argentine, born at Ipswich, Suffolk, 22 Aug., 1872; 2s. Henry Giles, cler. and inspector of schools. TRINITY, matric. 17 Oct., 91, aged 19 (from Marlborough coll.), scholar 90.

Alington, Hildebrand Thomas Giles, born at Marlborough, Wilts, 27 April, 1866; 1s. Henry Giles, cler. MAGDALEN, matric. 23 Oct., 85, aged 19 (from Marlborough coll.), exhibitioner 85, B.A. 90; HONOURS:—2 classical mods. 87, 3 classics 89.

Alison, Arthur James, born at Glasgow 26 March, 1870; 1s. Arthur, gen. CORPUS CHRISTI, matric. 25 Oct., 89, aged 19 (from Rugby), scholar 88; HONOURS:—1 classical mods. 91.

Alker, George Howard Vandeleur, born at Preston, co. Lanc., 25 July, 1872; 1s. George, cler. KEBLE, matric. 20 Oct., 91, aged 19, from Rossall school.

Allan, Edwin Francis, born at Clapton, Surrey, 10 Nov., 1867; 1s. Francis, arm. CHRIST CHURCH, matric. 16 Oct., 85, aged 17 (from Westminster school), scholar 85; HONOURS:—3 mathematical mods. 87.

Allan, Henry, born at Witnoon, co. Argyll, 1866; 6s. Alexander, arm. BALLIOL, matric. 21 Oct., 85, aged 19 (from Glasgow university), B.A. 90; HONOURS:—2 law 89.

Allan, James Bryce, born at Montreal 13 June, 1862; 5s. Andrew, arm. ORIEL, matric. 1 Nov., 81, aged 19 (from Rugby), B.A. 85 (HONOURS:—2 law 84, 3 civil law 85); student of Lincoln's Inn 83, barrister and solicitor at Montreal.

Allan, William Lewis Campbell, born at Dalhousie, in East Indies, 6 July, 1873; 1s. William, major general. BRASENOSE, matric. 14 Oct., 90, aged 19, from Wellington coll.

Allcroft, Arthur Hadrian, born at Ashby, co. Lanc., 1865; 2s. Walter, cler. CHRIST CHURCH, matric. 12 Oct., 83, aged 18 (from Exeter school), scholar 89, B.A. 89, M.A. 91; HONOURS:—1 classical mods. 84, 1 classics 87.

Allen, Alfred, born at Torquay, Devon, 1853; 3s. William, gent. NON-COLLEGIATE, matric. 18 Oct., 80, aged 27, from Torquay school.

Allen, Arthur Acland, born at Prestwich, co. Lanc., 11 Aug., 1868; y.s. Peter, arm. UNIVERSITY COLL., matric. 15 Oct., 87, aged 19 (from Rugby), scholar 87, B.A. 91; HONOURS:—1 classical mods. 89, 2 history 91.

Allen, Arthur Clement, born at Lilleshall, Salop, 29 May, 1868; 3s. William, vicar of Eccleshall, co. Staff. NEW COLL., matric. 14 Oct., 87, aged 19 (from Repton school), B.A. 91 (HONOURS:—2 classical mods. 89, 4 classics 91).

Allen, Arthur Henry Burliton, born at Blackheath, Kent, 20 March, 1872; 2s. James Henry, arm. CORPUS CHRISTI, matric. 16 Oct., 90, aged 18 (from Marlborough coll.), scholar 90; HONOURS:—1 classical mods. 92.

Allen, Arthur John, born at Shepton Mallet, Somerset, 6 Nov., 1869; 3s. Joseph, gen. LINCOLN, matric. 18 Oct., 88, aged 18 (from Bristol gr. school), B.A. 92; HONOURS:—4 classics 92.

Allen, Basil Copleston, born at Stoke Newington, Middlesex, 12 July, 1870; 5s. Arthur John, gen. CORPUS CHRISTI, matric. 25 Oct., 89, aged 19 (from Haileybury), scholar 89 (HONOURS:—1 classical mods. 91); selected candidate (21st) Indian civil service 92.

Allen, Bernard, born in Norwich, 16 Dec., 1872; o.s. Joseph, M.R.C.S., and L.S.A. TRINITY, matric. 17 Oct., 91, aged 18, from Lancing coll.

Allen, Bernard Meredith, born in London 1864; 3s. Charles, gent. BALLIOL, matric. 17 Oct., 82, aged 18 (from Highgate school), scholar 81-6, B.A. 86, M.A. 89; HONOURS:—1 classical mods. 83, accessit Ireland scholarship 83, 1 classics 86.

Allen, Cecil John Mead, born at Southampton 30 July, 1872; 1s. Leonard Frederick, gen. NON-COLLEGIATE, matric. 17 Oct., 91, aged 19, from Merchant Taylors' school.

Allen, Charles George Hillersden, born at Leicester 1864; 2s. Robert James, cler. BALLIOL, matric. 16 Oct., 83, aged 19 (from Haileybury), assistant magistrate and collector, Chittagong, Bengal civil service.

Allen, Charles Peter, born at Prestwich, co. Lanc., 2 Dec., 1861; 2s. Peter, gent. UNIVERSITY COLL., matric. 26 Jan., 82, aged 19 (from Rugby), B.A. 85, M.A. 88 (HONOURS:—3 history 84); bar.-at-law, Inner Temple, 86, journalist at Manchester.

Allen, Edward Cuthbert, born at Shepton Mallet, Somerset, 1872; 4s. Joseph, gen. LINCOLN, matric. 20 Oct., 90, aged 18 (from the Charterhouse), exhibitioner LINCOLN 90; HONOURS:—2 classical mods. 92.

Allen, Francis, born at Barraclough, co. Cork, 6 Nov., 1865; 1s. Francis Sealy, arm. MERTON, matric. 21 Oct., 86, aged 20 (from Harrow), B.A., 90.

Allen, Frederick Charles, born at Brighton 23 April, 1851; 3s. John, cler. NON-COLLEGIATE, matric. 5 Dec., 84, aged 33; migrated to EXETER 21 Oct., 85, B.A. 88.

Allen, Frederick John, born at Burnham, Somerset, April, 1867; o.s. Joseph, arm. KEBLE, matric. 19 Oct., 86, aged 19 (from Clifton coll.), B.A. 91; HONOURS:—3 history 90.

Allen, George Henry, born in London 30 Nov., 1873; o.s. George, gent. TRINITY, matric. 15 Oct., 92, aged 18 (from St. Paul's school), exhibitioner 92.

Allen, Herbert, born at Leicester 1867; 3s. Charles, gen. NON-COLLEGIATE, matric. 25 Jan., 88, aged 21, from Wyggeston school, Leicester.

Allen, rev. Herbert Reginald, born at Bushby, co. Worc., 1862; 4s. Charles, cler. BRASENOSE, matric. 10 June, 81, aged 19 (from Clifton coll.), B.A. 84; curate of Taunton St. Andrew 85-7, and St. John Evangelist 87.

Allen, Hugh Percy, born at Reading 1870; 4s. John Herbert, cler. QUEEN'S, matric. 16 March, 92, aged 22.

Allen, James Edward Rothwell, born at Padiham, co. Lanc., 1866; 2s. Edward, cler. PEMBROKE, matric. 27 Oct., 83, aged 17 (from Manchester gr. school), scholar 83-5, B.A. 87, M.A. 90; HONOURS:—1 classical mods. 84, 2 classics 87.

Allen, John Edward Taylor, born at Prestwich, co. Lanc., 11 Sept., 1864; 3s. Peter, gent. UNIVERSITY COLL., matric. 17 Oct., 85, aged 21 (from Rugby), B.A. 88; HONOURS :—3 law 88.

Allen, John George, born at Brighton 1868; 1s. John, cler. UNIVERSITY COLL., matric. 18 Oct., 86, aged 18 (from Brighton coll.), B.A. 90 (HONOURS :—3 history 89); bar.-at-law, Inner Temple, 93.

Allen, John Hugh Honeywood, born in Liverpool 1867; 1s. John, cler. CORPUS CHRISTI, matric. 20 Oct., 86, aged 19 (from Leamington coll.), B.A. 90; HONOURS :—2 classical mods. 88, 4 classics 90.

Allen, John William, born in London 29 March, 1865; 1s. John William, gent. BALLIOL, matric. 15 Oct., 84, aged 19 (from Marlborough coll.), exhibitioner 83, B.A. 88, M.A. 91; HONOURS :—1 history 87.

Allen, rev. Kenneth Buchanan, born at Worcester 2 April, 1864; o.s. Thomas, gent. WORCESTER, matric. 22 Oct., 85, aged 21 (from blind coll., Worcester), B.A. 88, M.A. 92; curate of Bp. Ryder's church, Birmingham, 89.

Allen, Leonard Arthur Cecil, born at Whitchurch, Dorset, 1873; 2s. Francis Edwin, cler. ALL SOULS', matric. 24 Oct., 91, aged 18 (from King's coll. school, London), bible clerk 91.

Allen, Percival Burt, born at Shepton Mallet, Somerset, 7 Feb., 1868; 4s. James, gent. WORCESTER, matric. 17 Oct., 87, aged 19 (from Independent coll., Taunton), exhibitioner 86, B.A. 91; HONOURS :—2 mathematical mods. 89, 3 mathematics 91, 2 history 92.

Allen, Percy Stafford, born at Twickenham, Middlesex, 7 July, 1869; 2s. Joseph, gen. CORPUS CHRISTI, matric. 20 Oct., 88, aged 19 (from Clifton coll.), scholar 88, B.A. 92; HONOURS :—1 classical mods. 90, 2 classics 92.

Allen, Percy Underhill, born at Shepton Mallet, Somerset, 22 March, 1867; 2s. Joseph, gent. MAGDALEN, matric. 23 Oct, 85, aged 19 (from Cheltenham coll. and university coll. school, London), B.A. 88 (HONOURS :—2 Indian languages 88); assistant magistrate Allahabad.

Allen, rev. Roland, born at Derby 1869; 3s. Charles Fletcher, cler. ST. JOHN'S, matric. 15 Oct., 87, aged 18 (from Bristol school), scholar 87, B.A. 91; HONOURS :—2 classical mods. 89, 2 history 91, Lothian essay 91.

Allen, Robert William, born at Brampton Abbots rectory, co. Hereford, 1873; o.s. Evans Mynor, of Upton Bishop, capt. 21st Scots Fusiliers. ORIEL, matric. 27 Oct., 92, aged 19, from Harrow.

Allen, Stephen Henry, born at Easlover, Hants, 1867; 2s. Stephen Henry, gent. ST. JOHN'S, matric. 16 Oct., 86, aged 19 (from Rossall school), B.A. 90.

Allen, Thomas William, born in London 9 May, 1862; 1s. Thomas Bull, gent. QUEEN'S, matric. 28 Oct., 81, aged 19 (from University coll., London), scholar 81-6, B.A. 85, M.A. 89, fellow 90 (HONOURS :—1 classical mods. 82, 1 classics 85, Craven travelling fellowship 87), fellow University coll., Lond., 86.

Allen, William Beriah, born near Broseley, Salop, 21 Dec., 1873; o.s. William, esq. HERTFORD, matric. 22 Oct., 92, aged 18, from S. Oswald's coll., Ellesmere, Salop.

Allen, William Dennis, M.A., fellow MAGDALEN 71-82, where see.

Allen, William Edward, born in London 18 March, 1869; o.s. Algernon, gent. LINCOLN, matric. 2 May, 89, aged 20 (from united Westminster schools), scholar 90, B.A. 92; HONOURS :—2 classical mods. 90, 2 classics 92.

Allen, William John, born in Sheffield 1 April, 1866; 3s. William Daniel, gent. EXETER, matric. 61 Oct., 84, aged 18 (from Cheltenham coll.), B.A. 89, M.A. 91.

Allen, Willoughby Charles, born at Derby 7 Oct., 1867; 3s. Charles Fletcher, cler. EXETER, matric. 19 Oct., 87, aged 20 (from Clergy orphan school, Canterbury, and Cambridge, NON-COLLEGIATE, matric. 21 Oct., 86); scholar 87, B.A. 90; HONOURS: —1 theology 90, Hebrew scholarship 90 and 92, Syriac prize 92, 1 Semitic languages 92.

Allfrey, Edward Wilfrid, born at Blackheath, Kent, 5 Sept., 1869; 1s. Edward Richmond, arm. TRINITY, matric. 13 Oct., 88, aged 19 (from the Charterhouse); HONOURS :—3 classical mods. 90, 3 history 92.

Allies, Thomas William, M.A., fellow WADHAM 33-40, where see.

Alliott, Richard, born at Bishop Stortford, Herts, 1870; 1s. Richard, cler. BALLIOL, matric. 17 Oct., 89, aged 19, from Bishop Stortford gr. school.

Allison, Charles Vernon, born at Sheffield, 1868; o.s. John, gen. NON-COLLEGIATE, matric. 12 Oct., 89, aged 21, from Sheffield collegiate school.

Allison, Francis Henry, born at Louth, co. Lincoln, 23 Sept., 1869; 3s. William, gen. LINCOLN, matric. 18 Oct., 88, aged 19 (from K. Edward gr. school, Louth), B.A. 92; HONOURS :—4 history 92.

Allison, Malcolm, born at Clayton, Yorks, 1862; 2s. William Horn, gen. QUEEN'S, matric. 29 Jan., 89, aged 27.

Allison, Thomas, born at Lisbon 19 July, 1869; 2s. Thomas Dunlop, D.Med., surgeon R.N. LINCOLN, matric. 17 Oct., 89, aged 20 (from Nairne academy, Edinburgh, and university of Edinburgh), scholar 89; HONOURS :—2 classical mods. 91.

Allnutt, Henry Sheppard, born at Windsor 21 Oct., 1863; 1s. Henry, gent. MAGDALEN, matric. 16 Oct., 82, aged 18 (from Magdalen coll. school), B.A. 87; HONOURS :—3 classical mods. 84.

Allport, Joseph Steevens, born at Reading 1862; 1s. William, gent. BALLIOL, matric. 21 Oct., 80, aged 18 (from Reading school), exhibitioner 79-84, B.A. 84; HONOURS :—2 mathematical mods. 82, 3 classics 84.

Allsebrook, William Carmont, born at Liverpool 10 March, 1868; 1s. William, gen. NON-COLLEGIATE, matric. 13 Oct., 88, aged 20 (from Sheffield gr. school and Liverpool coll.); migrated to JESUS COLL. 20 Jan., 90, B.A. 91.

Alsop, James Carteret, born at Newton Abbot, Devon, 26 April, 1871; 2s. Henry, gen. MERTON, matric. 15 Oct., 90, aged 19 (from Newton Abbot coll.), postmaster 90; HONOURS :—1 mathematical mods.

Alston, Alfred, born at Sydenham, Kent, 6 April, 1871; 7s. Thomas Rowland, gen. WADHAM, matric. 13 Oct., 90, aged 19, from Lancing coll.

Alston, Conyers William, born in London, 12 Feb., 1873; 4s. sir Francis Beilby, kt. QUEEN'S, matric. 27 Oct., 91, aged 18, from Rugby.

Alston, rev. Frank Simpson, born at Dennington, Suffolk, 6 Dec., 1863; 8s. Edward Constable, cler. EXETER, matric. 27 May, 82, aged 18 (from Marlborough coll.), B.A. 85, M.A. 89; vicar of Wispington, co. Lincoln, 90.

Alvarez, Thomas Edgar, born at Chorlton on Medlock, co. Lanc., 2 Oct., 1870; 3s. William Thomas, professor of Spanish, Victoria university. JESUS COLL., matric. 14 Oct., 89, aged 19 (from Manchester gr. school), scholar 89; HONOURS :—2 classical mods. 91.

Ambrose, William Gerald, born in London 1869; 1s. William, arm. UNIVERSITY COLL., matric. 18 Oct., 86, aged 17, B.A. 90; HONOURS :—3 law 90.

Amery, Leopold Charles Maurice Stennett, born at Gorrekpore, N.W.P., India, 22 Nov. 1873; 1s. Charles Stennett, late Inspector of H.M's. Indian forestry. BALLIOL, matric. 18 Oct. 92, aged 18, (from Harrow), exhibitioner 91.

Ames, Felix Lyde, born at Long Horsley, Northumberland, 17 Aug., 1862; 2s. Henry Metcalf, of Linden, arm. MERTON, matric. 3 June, 81, aged 18, from Harrow.

Ames, Hugh Laurenson, born in London 23 April, 1866; 7s. Lionel, of the Hyde, Beds, arm. ORIEL, matric. 23 Oct., 84, aged 18 (from the Charterhouse), B.A. 87.

Ames, William Herbert, born in Remenham juxta Hurley, Berks, 8 July, 1868; o.s. Charles Herbert, late of Remenham, arm., deceased. NEW COLL., matric. 14 Oct., 87, aged 19 (from Eton), B.A. 91; HONOURS:—2 classical mods. 89, 3 classics 91.

Amory, Ian Murray Heathcot, born at Bolham, near Tiverton, 16 April, 1865; 1s. sir John Heathcot, bart. CHRIST CHURCH, matric. 31 May, 84, aged 19, from Eton.

Amphlett, George L'Estrange, born at Bridgnorth, Salop, 3 Sept., 1868; 3s. Charles, late of Four Ashes Hall, co. Staff., cler., deceased. MAG-DALEN, matric. 22 Oct., 87, aged 19 (from Wellington coll.), B.A. 90; HONOURS:—3 history 90.

Anderson, Edgar James Varden, born at Blairgowrie, co. Perth, 1872; 1s. James Chapman, arm. CHARSLEY'S HALL, matric. 14 Oct., 89, aged 17, from Bedford school.

Anderson, rev. Edward Paterson, born at Glasgow 1864; 5s. John, gent. EXETER, matric. 16 Oct., 84, aged 20, B.A. 88, M.A. 91; curate of Nottingham St. Thomas 90.

Anderson, Francis Geoffrey Hartwell, born at Paddington 1870; 1s. Francis Edward, of London, arm. BALLIOL, matric. 18 Oct., 88, aged 18 (from Bath coll.), scholar 86 (HONOURS:—accessit Hertford scholarship 89, 1 classical mods. 90, 1 classics 92); selected candidate (5th) Indian civil service 92.

Anderson, Francis Molison, born at Dundee, co. Forfar, 7 Oct., 1868; 2s. Patrick, merchant, deceased. BALLIOL, matric. 17 Oct., 89, aged 21, from St. Andrew's university; HONOURS:—2 classics 92.

Anderson, Frank, born at Erith, Kent, 22 Nov., 1871; 3s. William, D.C.L., director-general ordnance factories. EXETER, matric. 13 Oct. 90, aged 18 (from Marlborough coll.), scholar 90; HONOURS:—2 classical mods. 92.

Anderson, Frederick Hubert Wright-, born at Reading 13 June, 1869; 1s. Frederick, cler. WORCESTER, matric. 16 Oct., 88, aged 19, from Cheltenham coll.

Anderson, James Finlay, born at East Melbourn 19 June, 1870; 2s. James, late captain 14th Light Infantry. BRASENOSE, matric. 14 Oct., 89, aged 19, from Harrow.

Anderson, John George Clarke, born at Edenkillie, co. Moray, 1871; 4s. Alexander, clergyman free church, Scotland. CHRIST CHURCH, matric. 16 Oct., 91, aged 20 (from Aberdeen university), exhibitioner 92.

Anderson, John Pratt, born at Edinburgh 1870; 1s. William, arm. UNIVERSITY, matric. 12 Oct., 89, aged 19.

Anderson, Kenneth Skelton, born in London 21 Dec., 1866; 3s. James, arm. NEW COLL., matric. 16 Oct., 85, aged 18, from Harrow.

Anderson, Lawrence, born at Tokyo, Japan, 25 July, 1874; 1s. W., F.R.C.S. CHRIST CHURCH, matric. 14 Oct., 92, aged 18, from Westminster school.

Anderson, Maurice Robert, born in isle of Mauritius 1863; 1s. William Mather, gent. PEMBROKE, matric. 2 May, 82, aged 19.

Anderson, William Cliffe Foley, born at Upper Falls, co. Antrim, 1865; 1s. Samuel, cler. NON-COLLEGIATE, matric. 28 Jan., 84, aged 19 (from royal academical institution Belfast, and Durham university), exhibitioner ORIEL 84 (HONOURS:—2 classical mods. 85, 2 classics 87), 1st classics Durham 81, professor of classics, Firth coll., Sheffield, 90.

Andrew, James, M.A., D.Med., hon. fellow WADHAM 87, where see.

Andrew, John Chapman, born at Whitby, Yorks, 13 Dec., 1865; 2s. John Chapman, cler. CORPUS CHRISTI, matric. 26 Oct., 85, aged 19, B.A. 89, (HONOURS:—2 law 89); bar.-at-law, Lincoln's Inn, 90.

Andrew, Richard Hambley, born in London 1869; o.s. Richard, arm. PEMBROKE, matric. 28 Jan., 87, aged 18.

Andrew, Samuel Ogden, born at Ashton, co. Lanc., 1868; 1s. Samuel, gent. ORIEL, matric. 19 Oct., 86, aged 18 (from Manchester gr. school), scholar 86, B.A. 91; HONOURS:—1 classical mods. 88, 1 classics 90.

Andrews, Arthur Edward, born at Salisbury 1860; 3s. John, gent. ST. EDMUND HALL, matric. 22 Jan., 80, aged 20.

Andrewes, Frederick William, M.A., B.Med., fellow PEMBROKE 86, where see.

Andrewes, George Gerrard, born at Morden, Surrey, July, 1862; 2s. William Gerrard, cler. CHRIST CHURCH, matric. 4 June, 81, aged 18 (from Eton), student Inner Temple 84.

Andrewes, Percy Lancelot, born at Reading 10 Nov., 1866; 6s. Charles James, gent. QUEEN'S, matric. 30 Oct., 85; aged 18 (from Reading gr. school), scholar 85, B.A. 89, M.A. 92; HONOURS:—1 mathematical mods. 87, 3 mathematics 89.

Andrews, Arthur Westlake, born at Hastings 12 Dec., 1868; 2s. William Ryton, rector of Teffont. MAGDALEN, matric. 22 Oct., 87, aged 18 (from the Charterhouse), exhibitioner 87, B.A. 91; HONOURS:—2 classical mods. 89, 2 classics 91.

Andrews, Cecil Rollo Peyton, born in London 2 Feb., 1870; 1s. John Marshall, vicar of St. Michael's, Highgate. ST. JOHN'S, matric. 13 Oct., 88, aged 18 (from Merchant Taylors' school), scholar 88, B.A. 92; HONOURS:—1 classical mods. 90, 2 classics 92.

Andrews, Herbert Tom, born at Oxford 22 Dec., 1864; 1s. Thomas, gent. MAGDALEN, matric. 19 Oct., 83, aged 18 (from Oxford central school), demy 83, B.A. 87; HONOURS:—1 classical mods. 85, 2 classics 87, Septuagint prize 89, Ellerton theological essay 89, Denyer and Johnson theological scholarship 90.

Andrews, Lawford, born at Blackheath, Kent, June, 1861; 3s. Henry William, arm. CHRIST CHURCH, matric. 21 May, 80, aged 18 (from Radley coll.), B.A. 84 (HONOURS:—4 law 84); bar.-at-law, Inner Temple, 88.

Andrews, Maynard Percy, born at Whitchurch, Salop, 1870; o.s. Percy, cler. ORIEL, matric. 25 Jan., 89, aged 19, from Sedbergh school.

Andrews, Reginald Arthur Ward, born at Monkstown, Dublin, Jan., 1872; 1s. Arthur, gen. KEBLE, matric. 20 Oct., 91, aged 19, from Shrewsbury gr. school.

Andrews, Septimus, M.A., student CHRIST CHURCH 51-69, where see.

Anger, Joseph Humphrey, born at Ashbury, Berks, 1863; 4s. Moses, gent. NEW COLL., matric. 30 Jan., 82, aged 19, B.Mus. 89.

Annesley, Arthur Dighton, born at Horsmath, co. Cambridge, 20 Oct., 1866; 1s. Francis Hanbury, cler. TRINITY, matric. 17 Oct., 85, aged 18 (from Marlborough coll.), B.A. 88; HONOURS—3 classical mods. 87.

Ansell, John Percy, born at Tottenham, Middlesex, 1849; 4s. Charles, gent. NON-COLLEGIATE, matric. 17 March, 88, aged 46.

Anson, Ernest, born at Sudbury, co. Derby, 26 Sept., 1864; 8s. Frederick, cler. ORIEL, matric. 27 Oct., 83, aged 19, B.A. and M.A. 90.

Anson, rev. Harold, born at Sudbury, co. Derby, 4 Dec., 1867; 8s. Frederick, cler. CHRIST CHURCH, matric. 12 June, 86, aged 18, B.A. 89 (HONOURS:—2 history 89); curate of St. Pancras, London, 90, domestic chaplain to bishop of St. Albans 91.

Anson, rev. Hugh Richard, born at Sudbury, co. Derby, 5 April, 1869; 9s. Frederick, cler. KEBLE, matric. 17 Oct., 87, aged 18 (from Clifton coll.), B.A. 90.

Anson, sir William Reynell, bart., D.C.L., warden of ALL SOULS' 81, where see.

Anstey, Arthur Henry, born at Bristol April, 1872; 1s. Arthur Campbell Clements, cler. KEBLE, matric. 11 Oct., 90, aged 18. from the Charterhouse.

Anstey, rev. Harry Christopher Scott, born at Ryde, isle of Wight, Jan., 1864; o.s. Charles Christopher, cler. KEBLE, matric. 18 Oct., 81, aged 17 (from Hammersmith school), B.A. 84, M.A. 86 (HONOURS:—3 theology 84); curate of Bilton, co. Warwick, 90.

Anstice, John Christian Appold, born at Madeley, Salop, Aug., 1861; 1s. John, gent. CHRIST CHURCH, matric. 21 May, 80, aged 18 (from Eton), captain and dragoon guards 88.

Anstie, William Henry, born in London 4 May, 1872; o.s. William Henry, gent., deceased. WADHAM, matric. 20 Oct., 91, aged 19 (from Dulwich coll.), scholar 90.

Anthony, Henry Montesquieu, born at Westbury-on-Trym, co. Gloucester, 1 April, 1873; 1s. Joseph Montesquieu, merchant. LINCOLN, matric. 25 Oct., 92, aged 19, from Clifton coll.

Antrobus, George Lancelot Neville, born in London 2 March, 1864; 3s. George, vicar of Beighton, co. Derby, deceased. NEW COLL., matric. 12 Oct., 83, aged 19 (from St Paul's school), B.A. 87, M.A. 90; HONOURS:—2 classical mods. 84, 2 classics 87.

Anwyl, Edward, born at Chester 5 Aug., 1866; 1s. John, gent. ORIEL, matric. 23 Oct., 83, aged 19 (from Chester gr. school), scholar 84, B.A. 90 (HONOURS:—2 classical mods. 87, 1 classics 89); professor of Welsh at Aberystwyth coll. 92.

Apcar, John Alexander, born at Calcutta 7 Feb., 1863; 5s. Alexander, arm. MAGDALEN, matric. 16 Oct., 80, aged 17, from Harrow.

Appach, Arthur Richard, born in London 1864; 2s. Francis Hobson, arm. BRASENOSE, matric. 22 April, 84, aged 20 (from Eton), B.A. 88, M.A. 91; bar.-at-law, Lincoln's Inn, 92.

Appleford, Frank Langley, born at High Lee, 8 March, 1865; 3s. John William, cler. NON-COLLEGIATE, matric. 20 Oct., 84, aged 19 (from St. Columba coll., Dublin); migrated to WORCESTER, B.A. 90; curate of St. John, Johnstone, N.B. 91.

Appleton, Henry William, born at Bradford, Yorks, 1865; 2s. Thomas William, gent. UNIVERSITY COLL., matric. 13 Oct., 83, aged 18 (from Bradford school), scholar 83, B.A. 88, M.A. 92 (HONOURS:—1 classical mods. 85, 1 classics 87, 1 history 88); professor of history at Firth coll., Sheffield, 92.

Applewhaite, rev. Frederick Arthur, born at Great Yarmouth 1866; 3s. Edward Archer Thornhill, arm. EXETER, matric. 16 Oct., 84, aged 18, B.A. 88; curate of Moordown, Winton, 89.

Appleyard, William Arthur, born at Brixton, Surrey, 7 May, 1869; 1s. Joseph, gen. QUEEN'S, matric. 20 Oct., 88, aged 19 (from K. Edward's school, Birmingham), scholar 87; HONOURS:—2 classical mods. 90.

Arbuthnot, Robert Edward Vaughan, born at Sempringham, co. Lincoln, 15 Jan., 1871; 1s. Robert Keith, vicar of St. James, Ratcliffe. ST. JOHN'S, matric. 12 Oct., 89, aged 18 (from Merchant Taylors' school), scholar 89 (HONOURS:—2 Indian languages 92); selected candidate (44th) Indian civil service 90, 16th in final 92.

Archdale, Nicholas Francis, born at Magheracross, Ireland, 18 Feb., 1862; 3s. Nicholas, of co. Fermanagh, arm. PEMBROKE, matric. 4 Feb., 81, aged 18, B.A. 84.

Archer, John Rubidge, born at Peterborough in Canada, 1 March, 1871; o.s. Francis Edward, gen. WADHAM, matric. 14 Oct., 89, aged 18, from Merchant Taylors' school.

Archibald, Richard George, Fereday fellow ST. JOHN'S 64-5, where see.

Archibald, William Frederick Alphonse, M.A., Fereday fellow ST. JOHN'S 69-72, where see.

Arden, rev. Lawrence Eric, born at Beverley, Yorks, 10 Nov., 1862; 3s. Charles, gent. NEW COLL., matric. 9 Oct., 81, aged 19 (from St. Edward's school, Summertown), B.A. 85, M.A. 90 (HONOURS:—3 theology 85); curate of Banbury, Oxford, 88.

Argenti, Ambrose, born in London 15 Aug., 1866; 2s. Nicholas, arm. TRINITY, matric. 17 Oct., 85, aged 19 (from the Charterhouse), B.A. 88.

Aris, John Whitton, born at Long Weedon, Northants, 11 April, 1867; 1s. John, gent. HERTFORD, matric. 22 Oct., 86, aged 19 (from Westminster school), scholar 87, B.A. 90; HONOURS:—3 classical mods. 88, 2 history 90.

Arkell, Charles Ernest, born at Boxted, Essex, 6 May, 1865; 2s. John, cler. CHARLSLEY'S HALL, matric. 21 Oct., 86, aged 21.

Arkell, rev. Henry Herbert, born at Portishead, Somerset, 23 Jan., 1869; 4s. John, cler. NON-COLLEGIATE, matric. 15 Oct., 87, aged 18 (from Magdalen coll. school); migrated to JESUS COLL. 20 Jan., 90, B.A. 91; HONOURS:—4 theology 91.

Arkell, John, M.A. PEMBROKE, where see.

Arkell, rev. John Norris, born at Boxted, Essex, 9 Dec., 1866; 3s. John, cler. NON-COLLEGIATE, matric. 16 Oct., 86, aged 19 (from Magdalen coll. school), B.A. 90 (HONOURS:—3 theology 90); curate of Grey Friars, Reading, 91.

Arkell, Thomas Norman, born 1864; 1s. John, cler. CORPUS CHRISTI, matric. 19 Oct., 82, aged 18 (from Magdalen coll. school), B.A. 86, M.A. 89; HONOURS:—3 classical mods. 84, 2 law 86.

Arkwright, Ernest Henry, born at Pencombe, co. Hereford, 23 March, 1868; 4s. George, cler. UNIVERSITY COLL., matric. 18 Oct., 86, aged 18, B.A. 91; HONOURS:—2 chemistry 91.

Arkwright, Godfrey Edward Pellew, born in London 10 April, 1864; 3s. Godfrey Harry, vicar of Heath. BALLIOL, matric. 16 Oct., 83, aged 18 (from Eton); HONOURS:—2 classical mods. 85, 4 classics 87.

Arkwright, Harold Arthur, born at Oswestry, Salop, 10 Nov., 1872; 2s. Arthur Chandos, of Tholy Priory, Essex, colonel in the army. MAGDALEN, matric. 18 Oct., 92, aged 20, from Eton.

Arkwright, Hubert Seymour, born at Pencombe, co. Hereford, 24 April, 1865; 3s. George, cler. CORPUS CHRISTI, matric. 23 Oct., 84, aged 19 (from Haileybury), B.A. 88 (HONOURS:—3 classical mods. 86); curate of Cossall, Notts, 89.

Arkwright, John Stanhope, born in London 20 July, 1872; 1s. John Hungerford, esq., of Hampton Court, co. Hereford. CHRIST CHURCH, matric. 16 Oct., 91, aged 19, from Eton.

Arkwright, Richard Eden St. Aubyn, born at Pencombe, co. Hereford, 6 May, 1870; 5s. George, cler. CORPUS CHRISTI, matric. 25 Oct., 89, aged 19, from Haileybury.

Arkwright, Sidney John, born in London 23 Dec., 1863; 2s. George, cler. ORIEL, matric. 31 Oct., 82, aged 18 (from Halleybury), B.A. 85; HONOURS: —2 classical mods. 83, 2 law 85.

Arkwright, Walter George, born at Sutton Scarsdale, co. Derby, 22 July, 1865; 4s. Godfrey Henry, cler. BALLIOL, matric. 28 Jan., 84, aged 18 (from Limpsfield school), exhibitioner 83; HONOURS:—2 classical mods. 85, 2 history 87.

Arkwright, Wilfrid Lionel Tyrell, born at Hatfield Peverell, Essex, 7 Feb., 1871; 1s. Arthur Chandos, arm. NEW COLL., matric. 10 Oct., 90, aged 19, from Eton.

Arlosh, Godfrey William Liddell, born at Southsea, Hants, 9 March, 1870; o.s. James, cler. BRASENOSE, matric. 11 Dec., 89, aged 19 (from Eton); died 1 July, 90.

Armitstead, John Hornby, born at Sandbach, Cheshire, 31 Aug., 1868; 1s. John Richard, cler. CHRIST CHURCH, matric. 3 June, 87, aged 18 (from Westminster school), B.A. 91.

Armitage, Edward, M.A., fellow MAGDALEN 48-56, where see.

Armitage, Frederick Lionel, born at Paramatta, Australia, 7 April, 1862; 2s. Frederick, arm. TRINITY, matric. 15 Oct., 83, aged 21 (from Gotha gymnasium), B.A. 87, M.A. 91; HONOURS:—3 classical mods. 85, Taylorian (Italian) exhibition 86.

Armitage, rev. George Edwin, born at Pudsey, Yorks, 1868; 3s. Samuel, gent. HERTFORD, matric. 5 Feb., 86, aged 18, B.A. 89, M.A. 92 (HONOURS: —3 classical mods. 87, 3 classics 89); curate of Seacombe, Cheshire, 90.

Armitage, George Herbert, born at Silverdale, co. Stafford, 30 Aug., 1863; 1s. George, cler. QUEEN'S, matric. 30 Oct., 85, aged 22 (from Repton school), sometime of Manchester.

Armitstead, Edward, born at Sandbach, Cheshire, 10 Sept., 1872; 3s. John Richard, vicar. MAGDALEN, matric. 22 Oct., 91, aged 19, from Oswestry school.

Armitstead, John Richard, M.A., student CHRIST CHURCH 48-63, where see.

Armitstead, Lawrence, born at Sandbach, Cheshire, 26 Feb., 1871; 2s. John Richard, vicar. MAGDALEN, matric. 28 Jan., 89, aged 18 (from Oswestry gr. school), B.A. 92; HONOURS:—2 classical mods. 90, 3 classics 92.

Armitstead, William George, M.A., student CHRIST CHURCH 59-6, where see.

Armour, Henry Crawford, born at Sefton, co. Lanc., 6 April, 1868; o.s. Samuel Crawford, cler. TRINITY, matric. 15 Oct., 87, aged 19 (from Rossall school), B.A. 92.

Armstrong, rev. Alexander Nenon, born at Reading 17 Dec., 1861; 4s. John, arm. ST. MARY HALL, matric. 19 Oct., 81, aged 19, exhibitioner 81-5, B.A. 84; curate of St. Sidwell, Exeter, 89.

Armstrong, Alfred Archibald, born at Ripley, Yorks, 1864; 3s. Rowley, cler. WORCESTER, matric. 19 Oct., 82, aged 18 (from Denstone coll.), B.A. 86, M.A. 89.

Armstrong, Charles Frederick, born at Richmond, Surrey, Sept., 1868; 1s. Charles, cler. CHRIST CHURCH, matric. 12 June, 86, aged 18, from Uppingham school.

Armstrong, Edward, M.A., fellow QUEEN'S 69.

Armstrong, Frank Philip, born at Kensington 16 Oct., 1871; 2s. Carlyon Hughes, capt. in the army. MAGDALEN, matric. 14 Oct., 90, aged 19, from the Charterhouse.

Armstrong, James, born at Seal, Kent, Nov., 1862; o.s. James, gent. PEMBROKE, matric. 6 Feb., 82, aged 19, from Lancing coll.

Armstrong, Lawrence McKnight, born at Manchester 11 Nov., 1868; 4s. John Alexander, Wesleyan minister. QUEEN'S, matric. 25 Oct., 86, aged 17 (from Kingswood school), scholar 86, B.A. 90; HONOURS:—3 mathematical mods. 88, 3 mathematics 90.

Armstrong, Percy, born at Cheetham, co. Lanc., 15 Oct., 1866; 4s. John Alexander, Wesleyan minister. JESUS COLL., matric. 23 Oct., 85, aged 19 (from Kingswood school), scholar 85, B.A. 89, M.A. 92; HONOURS:—2 mathematical mods. 87, 1 mathematics 89.

Armstrong, Thomas Percy, born at Manchester 1861; 1s. Thomas, arm. BRASENOSE, matric. 22 Oct., 80, aged 19 (from King's school, Canterbury), B.A. 83; HONOURS:—a history 83.

Arnall-Thompson, Harry Thompson, of BRASENOSE, 1883. See Thompson.

Arnold, Arthur Claude, born in Paris 29 June, 1864; 2s. Frederick, cler. NON-COLLEGIATE, matric. 19 Jan., 85, aged 20 (from Queen's school, Bath, and Brighton gr. school), B.A. 92.

Arnold, George Frederick, born at Winchester 11 Jan., 1870; 2s. George Benjamin, gen. QUEEN'S, matric. 20 Oct., 88, aged 18 (from Merchant Taylors' school), scholar 88 (HONOURS:—2 classical mods 90, 1 classics 92); selected candidate (8th) Indian civil service 92.

Arnold, Robert Antony, born at Rochester 11 July, 1869; 1s. Augustus Alfred, arm. TRINITY, matric. 13 Oct., 88, aged 20 (from Tonbridge school), B.A. 91; HONOURS:—3 law 91.

Arnold, Thomas Kerchever, born at Wimbledon, Surrey, 4 March, 1865; 1s. Charles Thomas, solicitor. MAGDALEN, matric. 19 Oct., 83, aged 18 (from Clifton coll.), demy 83, B.A. 87; HONOURS: —accessit Hertford scholarship 84, 2 classical mods. 85, 3 classics 87.

Arnold, William Channing, born at Sidcup, Kent, 1869; 2s. Edwin (K.C.S.I.) UNIVERSITY COLL., matric. 15 Oct., 87, aged 18, B.A. 91 (HONOURS:— 3 classical mods. 89, 3 history 90); bar.-at-law, Inner Temple, 92.

Arnott, Arthur Philip, M.A., TRINITY, where see.

Arnott, Scott, born at Nairn Sept., 1871; 2s. Henry, D.D., KEBLE, matric. 11 Oct., 90, aged 19, from Lancing coll.

Arnould, Henry Lloyd, born at Whitecross, Cholsey, Berks, 12 April, 1872; 3s. Alfred Henry, of London, solicitor, D.C.L. CORPUS CHRISTI, matric. 19 Oct., 91, aged 19, from St. Paul's school.

Arrowsmith, Richard Staines, born at Darlington, co. Durham, 22 Sept., 1873; 1s. William Nixon, F.R.C.S. Eng. CORPUS CHRISTI, matric. 19 Oct., 91, aged 18, from Darlington gr. school.

Arrowsmith, Robert Henry, born at Walsgrave, co. Warwick, Oct., 1868; o.s. Robert, cler. ORIEL, matric. 18 Oct., 87, aged 19 (from Harrow), B.A. 90.

Arthur, Oswald George, born at Satara, East Indies, 16 July, 1869; 2s. John Raynor, of Bombay c.s., arm. CHRIST CHURCH, matric. 12 Oct., 88, aged 19 (from Winchester), scholar 88; assist. magistrate Iludaun, N.W.P. India, 90.

Arthur, Richard Wells, born at Petersfield, Devon, 8 June, 1867; o.s. Edward, of Wonton, Devon, judge high court India. EXETER, matric. 18 Jan., 1887, aged 19, from Bradfield coll.

Arthur, Sigismund Raynor, born at Satara, East Indies, 9 Feb., 1867; 1s. John Raynor, of Bombay c.s. NEW COLL., matric. 15 Oct., 86, aged 19 (from the Charterhouse), supy. assist. collector and magistrate Rohri (sub-division), Sind, Bombay c.s.

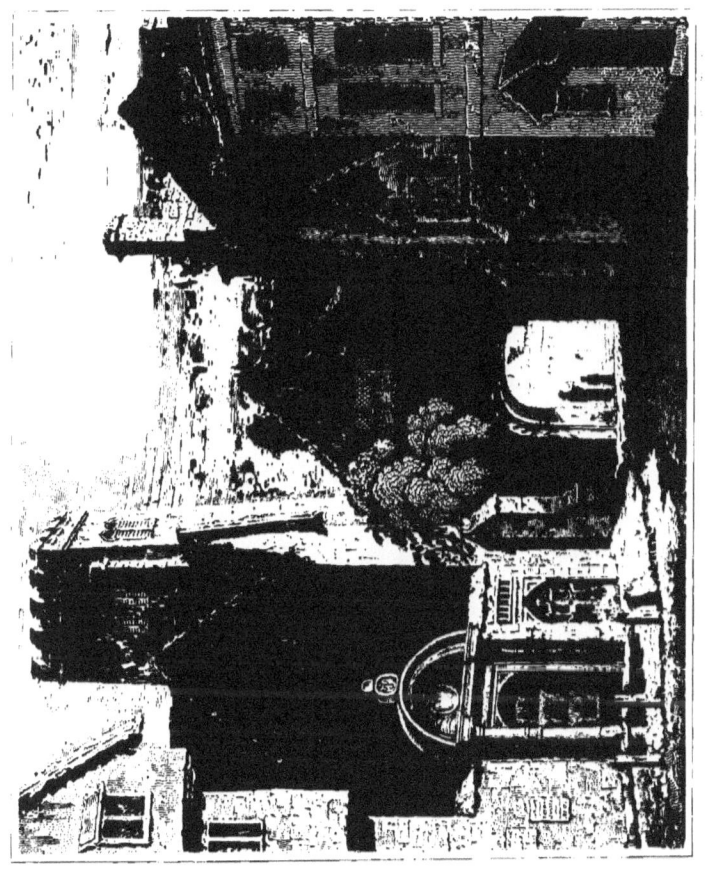

THE ANCIENT NORTH ENTRANCE INTO OXFORD, TAKEN DOWN 1771
From an Engraving by Shelton

Arton, William Denby, born at Shipley, Yorks, 17 June, 1864; o.s. Thomas, gent. HERTFORD, matric. 18 Oct., 83, aged 19 (from Rugby), B.A. 86; bar.-at-law, Inner Temple, 89.

Arthure, rev. Harry Edgar Erskine, born at Worcester 1865; 3s. Bennet, cler. HERTFORD, matric. 14 Oct., 84, aged 19 (from Worcester cathedral school), scholar 83, B.A. 88, M.A. 91 (HONOURS :—2 classical mods. 86, 3 classics 88); curate of Rugby 90.

Arundel, Walter Charles, born at St. Neots, Hunts, 1857; 2s. Alfred, gent. NEW COLL., matric. 24 Jan., 81, aged 24 (from Hipperholme gr. school, Yorks, and Wesleyan coll., Taunton); migrated to EXETER, B.A. 86.

Arundell, Gilbert Harris, born at Lifton, Devon, 18 Oct., 1869; 8s. William Reinfred Arundell Harris, gen. BALLIOL, matric. 22 Jan., 89, aged 19 (from Tiverton school), exhibitioner 87.

Ash, Percy Clayton, born at Birmingham 13 March, 1868; 1s. Alfred, major Warwickshire rifles and J.P. WORCESTER, matric. 17 Oct., 87, aged 19 (from Shrewsbury gr. school.

Ashburner, Walter, born at West Roxbury, America, 1864; 2s. Samuel, gent. BALLIOL, matric. 16 Oct., 83, aged 19 (from University coll. school, London), exhibitioner 82, Jenkyns exhibitioner 86; fellow MERTON 87, B.A. 87, M.A. 90 [HONOURS :—1 classical mods. 84, 1 classics 87, proxime accessit Ireland scholarship 84, and accessit 85 (*b/s*), proxime accessit Hertford scholarship 85, Greek prose 85, Craven scholarship 86]; fellow University coll., London, 88; bar.-at-law, Lincoln's Inn, 92.

Ashby, Harold Francis, born at Staines, Middlesex, 11 May, 1874; 1s. Francis Tillyer, gent. MAGDALEN, matric. 18 Oct., 92, aged 18, from Harrow.

Ashby, rev. Paul Ogilvie, born at Cobham, Surrey, 1867; 4s. Richard Wallace, gent. BRASENOSE, matric. 23 Oct., 85, aged 18 (from Aldenham school), B.A. 88; curate of St. Jude's, Gray's Inn Road, London, 91.

Ashe, Herbert, born at Eccles, co. Lancaster, 19 Jan., 1868; 6s. Edward, stockbroker. WADHAM, matric. 16 Oct., 86, aged 18 (from Manchester gr. school), B.A. 89; HONOURS :—3 theology 89.

Asher, Augustus Gordon Grant, born at Poonah, East Indies, 1862; 1s. John Gordon, D.Med. BRASENOSE, matric. 10 June, 81, aged 19 (from Loretto school), B.A. 85, in the University eleven 83.

Ashley, Wilfred William, born in London 13 Sept., 1867; 1s. hon. Anthony Evelyn. MAGDALEN, matric. 23 Oct., 85, aged 18, from Harrow.

Ashley, William James, M.A., fellow LINCOLN 85-8, where see.

Ashmore, Thomas Digby, born in London Nov. 1861; 4s. Charles, arm. KEBLE, matric. 19 Oct., 80; aged 18 (from St. Paul's school), B.A. 85, M.A. 87; HONOURS :—2 classical mods. 82.

Ashpitel, Ernest Hurst, born at Great Hampden, Bucks, 13 May, 1867; 3s. Francis, vicar of Flitwick, Beds. UNIVERSITY COLL., matric. 18 Oct., 86, aged 19 (from Haileybury); HONOURS :—3 classical mods. 88.

Ashton, rev. John William, born at Wakefield, Yorks, 1867; 1s. George, gent. UNIVERSITY COLL., matric. 17 Oct., 85, aged 18 (from Wakefield school), scholar 85, B.A. 89, M.A. 92 (HONOURS :—2 mathematical mods. 86, 1 mathematics 89); licentiate in theology, university of Durham, 90, curate of Terrington St. Clement 91.

Ashton, Joseph William, born at Lwynegryn, Flints, 22 Oct., 1865; 2s. Charles Ellis, stockbroker, deceased. MAGDALEN, matric. 29 Jan., 85, aged 19, from Eton.

Ashton, Thomas Knight, born at Balham, Surrey, 29 July, 1869; 4s. Thomas Knight, arm. TRINITY, matric. 15 Oct., 87, aged 18 (from Canterbury school), B.A. 91; HONOURS :—4 history 91.

Ashwin, Collins, born at Bretforton, co. Worcester, 17 March, 1870; 5s. William Henry, arm. MERTON, matric. 19 Oct., 89, aged 19.

Ashworth, Edward Thomas, born at Exeter 31 May, 1865; 1s. Edward, gent. BALLIOL, matric. 17 Oct., 82, aged 17 (from Newton Abbott coll.), a selected candidate (7th) Indian civil service 82, 11th in final 84.

Ashworth, Ernest Horatio, born at Highgate, Middlesex, 27 July, 1870; 3s. Howard Haughton, chartered accountant. ST. JOHN's, matric. 12 Oct., 89, aged 19 (from Merchant Taylors' school), scholar 89; HONOURS :—1 classical mods. 91.

Ashworth, George Harry, born at Bolton, co. Lanc., 14 May, 1865; 1s. George Binns, of Turton, gent. NEW COLL., matric. 16 Jan., 85, aged 19 (from Eton), B.A. 88; HONOURS :—accessit Hertford scholarship 85, 1 classical mods. 86, 2 classics 88, Latin essay 90.

Ashworth, rev. John Thomas, born at Rawtenstall, co. Lanc., 4 Feb., 1864; 1s. John, gent. NON-COLLEGIATE, matric. 30 Jan., 90, aged 26 (from Peterborough school); migrated to BRASENOSE, B.A. 92; HONOURS :—3 theology 92.

Askew, David Hugh Watson, born at Edinburgh 21 Oct., 1863; 1s. Watson, of Pallinsburn, Northumberland, arm. CHRIST CHURCH, matric. 2 May, 82, aged 18 (from Eton), B.A. 85; bar.-at-law, Inner Temple, 88.

Askew, John Bertram, born at Edinburgh 11 Oct., 1869; 3s. Watson, of Pallinsburn, Northumberland, arm. CHRIST CHURCH, matric. 1 June, 88, aged 18, from Eton.

Askew, William Haggerstone, born at Edinburgh 4 Oct., 1868; 2s. Watson, of Pallinsburn, Northumberland, arm. CHRIST CHURCH, matric. 18 Jan., 89, aged 20, B.A. 92.

Askwith, George Ranken, born at Waltham Abbey, Essex, 17 Feb., 1861; 2s. William Harrison, arm. BRASENOSE, matric. 22 Oct., 80, aged 19 (from Marlborough coll.), scholar 80-3, exhibitioner 83-6, B.A. 84, M.A. 87 (HONOURS :—3 classical mods. 81, 1 history 84); bar.-at-law, Inner Temple, 86.

Aspinall, Algernon Edward, born in London, 12 May, 1871; 2s. Robert Augustus, J.P., deceased. MAGDALEN, matric. 14 Oct., 90, aged 18, from Eton.

Aspinall, rev. Noel Lake, born at Bebington, Cheshire, 1861; 1s. Clarke, arm. ST. JOHN's, matric. 16 Oct., 80, aged 19, B.A. 84, M.A. 90; curate of Eccleshall, Yorks, 88.

Asprey, Lionel Charles, born at Putney, Surrey, 1874; 1s. Charles, esq. HERTFORD, matric. 20 Oct., 92, aged 18, from the Charterhouse.

Asquith, right hon. Herbert Henry, M.A., Q.C., M.P., home secretary, fellow BALLIOL 74-82, where see.

Assinder, George Frederick, born at Birmingham 1857; 3s. George. ST. JOHN's, matric. 10 Dec., 92, aged 35.

19 ASTBURY. —— MATRICULATIONS, 1880 TO 1892. —— AVAASKER. 20

Astbury, Charles John, born at Prestwich, co. Lanc., 7 Aug., 1873; 3s. Frederick James, chartered accountant. BRASENOSE, matric. 21 Oct., 92, aged 19 (from Hereford cathedral school), scholar 92.

Atherton, Richard Percy, born at Speke, co. Lanc., 17 Sept., 1860; 1s. Richard, gent. TRINITY, matric. 13 Oct., 88, aged 19 (from Canterbury school); HONOURS:—3 classical mods. 90, 4 classics 92.

Atkin, James Richard, born at Brisbane, Australia, 28 Nov., 1867; 1s. Robert Travers, arm. MAGDALEN, matric. 23 Oct., 85, aged 17 (from Brecon coll.), demy 84, B.A. 91 (HONOURS:—2 classical mods. 87, 2 classics 89); bar.-at-law, Gray's Inn, 91.

Atkins, Charles Herbert, born at Coventry 31 Dec., 1870; 1s. John, gent. BALLIOL, matric. 17 Oct., 89, aged 18 (from Coventry school), assistant commissioner Punjab 91.

Atkins, Ivor Algernon, born at Llandaff, co. Glamorgan, 1870; 5s. Frederick Pyke, B.Mus. QUEEN'S, matric. 16 March, 90, aged 22, B.Mus. 27 Oct., 92.

Atkins, John Burnaby-, born at Halstend, Kent, 15 Sept., 1873; 1s. Thomas Frederick, M.A., J.P., and D.L. MAGDALEN, matric. 18 Oct., 92, aged 19, from Eton.

Atkins, rev. Lancelot White, born at Bedhampton, Hants, 1862; 1s. Richard White, cler. ST. JOHN'S, matric. 9 May, 81, aged 19, B.A. 84, curate of Wyke, Hants, 87.

Atkinson, rev. Arthur George Breeks, born at Madras Aug., 1866; 1s. Arthur Johnston, arm. ORIEL, matric. 23 Oct., 85, aged 19 (from Canterbury school), B.A. 88, M.A. 92 (HONOURS:—4 history 88); curate of St. Thomas, Portman Square, London, 91.

Atkinson, Arthur Richmond, born at Taranaki, New Zealand, 8 Aug., 1863; o.s. Arthur Samuel, arm. CORPUS CHRISTI, matric. 19 Oct., 82, aged 19 (from Clifton coll.), scholar 82-6, B.A. 87 (HONOURS:—1 classical mods. 83, 2 classics 86); bar.-at-law, Lincoln's Inn, 87.

Atkinson, Cecil Daly, born at Hull, Dec., 1872; 1s. Henry Sadgrove, cler. KEBLE, matric. 11 Oct., 90, aged 17, from the Charterhouse.

Atkinson, Ernest Cuthbert, born at Beckenham, Kent, 22 June, 1873; 5s. William, c.E. ST. JOHN'S, matric. 17 Oct., 91, aged 18 (from Merchant Taylors' school), scholar 91; HONOURS:—1 mathematical mods. 92.

Atkinson, rev. Francis, born at Scofton, Notts, 1870; 5s. William, gen. NON-COLLEGIATE, matric. 13 Oct., 88, aged 18 (from Durham gr. school), B.A. 92; HONOURS:—3 history 91.

Atkinson, Henry Ernest, born at Exmouth, Devon, 21 April, 1871; 1s. Francis Horne, cler. EXETER, matric. 13 Oct., 90, aged 19 (from Victoria coll., Jersey), scholar 90.

Atkinson, Henry William Almeric Bradford, born at Broughton, Oxon, 20 Aug., 1869; 3s. Ralph, of Angerton, Northumberland, arm. MERTON, matric. 17 Oct., 88, aged 19, from Eton.

Atkinson, James, born at West Hartlepool, co. Durham, 9 Jan., 1869; 2s. James, D.Med. LINCOLN, matric. 21 Oct., 87, aged 18 (from Bilton grange school, Harrowgate), B.A. 92.

Atkinson, rev. Robert Leighton, born at Leeds 1862; 3s. Edward, gent. NON-COLLEGIATE, matric. 14 Oct., 82, aged 20, B.A. 86, M.A. 89 (HONOURS:—2 theology 86); curate of Hunslet, Yorks, 90.

Attlee, Bernard Henry Bravery, born at Putney, Surrey, 6 May, 1873; 2s. Henry, solicitor. MERTON, matric. 18 Oct., 92, aged 19, from Haileybury.

Attlee, Robert Bravery, born at Putney, Surrey, July, 1871; 1s. Henry, arm. ORIEL, matric. 25 Oct., 89, aged 18 (from Haileybury), B.A. 92; HONOURS:—3 classical mods. 91.

Attwood, Thomas Arthur Careless, born at Edington, co. Warwick, May, 1863; o.s. Thomas Aurelius, arm. PEMBROKE, matric. 25 Jan., 83, aged 19 (from Uppingham), B.A. 86, M.A. 89; student Inner Temple 84.

Aubin, Alfred Lerrier, born at Kingswinford, co. Stafford, 1 Aug., 1866; 1s. Thomas John, D.Med. JESUS COLL., matric. 23 Oct., 85, aged 19 (from Victoria college, Jersey), B.A. 90; HONOURS:—2 classical mods. 87, 3 classics 89.

Auden, Eustace George, born at Shrewsbury 1872; 4s. Thomas, cler. CHRIST CHURCH, matric. 71 Oct., 90, aged 18 (from Shrewsbury school), exhibitioner 90.

Auden, John Ernest, born at Silverdale, co. Stafford, 13 Dec., 1860; 1s. John, of Shrewsbury, cler. LINCOLN, matric. 23 Oct. 80, aged 19 (from Shrewsbury school), B.A. 83, M.A. 87 (HONOURS:—3 classical mods. 82); curate of Montford with Shrawardine, Salop, 89.

Augeraud, William, born in London March, 1863; 1s. William, arm. CHRIST CHURCH, matric. 4 June, 81, aged 18 (from Eton), B.A. and M.A. 88.

Austen, Edward Thomas, M.A., fellow ST. JOHN'S 42-55, where see.

Austin, Alfred, born at Brixton, Surrey, 30 July, 1863; o.s. Alfred, arm. MERTON, matric. 17 Jan., 83, aged 19 (from Malvern coll.), B.A. 86; HONOURS:—3 classical mods. 84, 2 law 86.

Austin, Charles Alleyne Summers, M.A., D.C.L., fellow ST. JOHN'S 55, where see.

Austin, Frank Ernest, born at Hackney 28 March, 1870; 2s. Cornelius Howard, gent. NON-COLLEGIATE, matric. 11 Oct., 90, aged 20, from a Northampton school.

Austin, John Worsley, born at Cirencester, co. Glouc., 9 Nov., 1872; 2s. Henry, Unitarian minister. NON-COLLEGIATE, matric. 15 Oct., 92, aged 19, from Cirencester school, Mason coll., Birmingham, and Manchester new coll., Oxford.

Austin, Robert Frederick, born in London 1871; 1s. Ebenezer, gent. UNIVERSITY COLL., matric. 12 Oct., 89, aged 18 (from King's coll. school, London), exhibitioner 89; HONOURS:—2 classical mods. 91.

Austin, Robert Gordon Lefroy, born at Cheltenham, co. Glouc., 28 Dec., 1871; 2s. Christopher Edward Lefroy, cler. ORIEL, matric. 27 Oct., 91, aged 19, from Cheltenham coll.

Austin, Stanley, born at Glastonbury, Somerset, 1 Dec., 1861; 3s. James, gent. LINCOLN, matric. 23 Oct., 80, aged 18 (from Clifton coll.), B.A. 83; HONOURS:—3 law 83.

Austin, William Edward Plercy, born at Georgetown, British Guiana, 5 Nov., 1869; 1s. William George Gardiner, cler., inspector of schools. MAGDALEN, matric. 19 Jan., 80, aged 19 (from Reading school), B.A. 83, M.A. 89; HONOURS:—3 classical mods. 81, 4 history 83.

Avaasker, Moses Abraham, born at Bombay 1861; 3s. Abraham David, arm. NON-COLLEGIATE, matric. 27 May, 82, aged 21 (from Robert Money institution, Bombay), B.A. 85; HONOURS:—4 law 85, 3 civil law 86.

Aveling, Claude Lindsay Clifford, born at Erith, Kent, 26 Oct., 1869; 2s. Stephen Thomas, arm. CHRIST CHURCH, matric. 12 Oct., 88, aged 18 (from Westminster school), scholar 88; HONOURS: —3 classical mods. 90, 4 classics 92.

Averill, rev. Alfred Walter, born at Stafford, 1865; 1s. Henry Alcock, gent. ST. JOHN'S, matric. 11 Oct., 84, aged 19, B.A. 87, M.A. 91 (HONOURS:— 2 theology 87); curate of St. George's, Hanover square, 88-91, and of Holy Trinity, Dalston, 91.

Awdry, William, M.A., fellow QUEEN'S 66-9, where see.

Aynsley, Frederick, born at Stoke-on-Trent 1860; 4s. John, gent. CHRIST CHURCH, matric. 14 Oct., 81, aged 21, B.A. 85; bar.-at-law, Inner Temple, 86.

Ayre, Algernon Early, born at Hull 3 July, 1872; o.s. Algernon Sidney, arm. WADHAM, matric. 13 Oct., 90, aged 18 (from Merchant Taylors' school), exhibitioner 90.

Ayres, Herbert Ernest, born at Barnes, Surrey, 21 June, 1865; 2s. William, gent. QUEEN'S, matric. 8 Feb., 86, aged 20, from Q. Eliz. coll., Guernsey.

PEG TANKARD IN THE ASHMOLEAN MUSEUM, OXFORD.—*From Shaw's Ancient Furniture.*

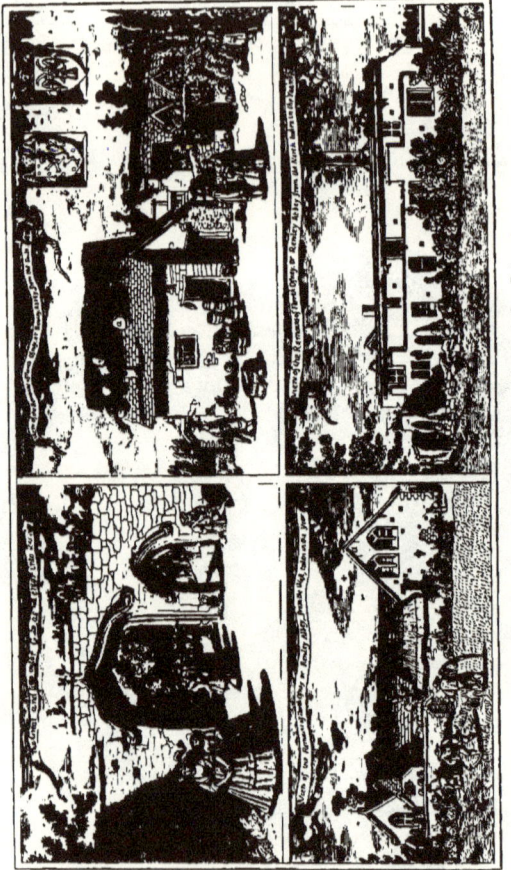

REMAINS OF REWLEY ABBEY.—*From Skelton's Oxonia Antiqua Restaurata.*

[STRING COURSE FROM WESTMINSTER ABBEY.—*Pugin*.]

B

Baber, Francis Villiers, born in London 1865; 3s. John, D.Med. BALLIOL, matric. 15 Oct., 84, aged 19 (from Brighton coll.), B.A. 90 (HONOURS :— 2 classical mods. 86, 2 classics 88); died in New Zealand 4 Dec., 91.

Bacchus, George Reginald, born at St. Leonard's, Sussex, 1 June, 1873; 1s. George Henry, late captain Austrian army. EXETER, matric. 18 Oct., 92, aged 19, from Clifton coll.

Back, Walter, born at Stretton S. Mary, Norfolk, Feb., 1863; 2s. Leonard, arm. KEBLE, matric. 19 Oct., 80, aged 17 (from Norwich gr. school), B.A. 85.

Backhouse, Edmund Trelawny, born at Middleton Tyas, Yorks, 20 Oct., 1873; 1s. Jonathan Edmund, banker. MERTON, matric. 18 Oct., 92, aged 18 (from Winchester coll.), postmaster 92.

Bacon, James Salisbury Frederick, born at Baxterley, co. Warwick, 25 Feb., 1865; 1s. Hugh, cler. WORCESTER, matric. 18 Oct., 83, aged 18 (from Marlborough coll.), scholar 83, B.A. 89, M.A. 90 (HONOURS :—2 classical mods. 85, 2 classics 87); bar.-at-law, Inner Temple, 90.

Bacon, John Cæsar, born at Shillington, Beds, 26 Feb., 1870; o.s. John Joseph, formerly capt. 92nd regt. HERTFORD, matric. 19 Oct., 88, aged 18, from Rugby.

Bacon, Thomas Walter, born at Gainsborough, co. Linc., 16 Sept., 1863; 2s. sir Henry, of Thorrock Hall, co. Lincoln, bart. CHRIST CHURCH, matric. 13 Oct., 82, aged 19, from Eton.

Badcock, Charles, born at Cuxham, Oxon, 14 Jan., 1867; 1s. Charles, gent. LINCOLN, matric. 22 Oct., 86, aged 19 (from Magdalen coll. school), exhibitioner 86, B.A. 90 (HONOURS :—2 classics 90); brother of Henry.

Badcock, Francis John, born in London 27 Feb., 1869; 1s. Philip, gent. NEW COLL., matric. 12 Oct., 88, aged 19 (from Marlborough coll.), B.A. 92; HONOURS :—2 classical mods. 90, 2 classics 92.

Badcock, Henry, born at Oxford 13 Feb., 1873; 2s. Charles, gent. LINCOLN, matric. 25 Oct., 92, aged 19 (from Magdalen coll. school); brother of Charles.

Badcock, rev. Henry Edward Otley, born at Taunton, Somerset, 1868; 1s. Henry Jeffries, cler. CHRIST CHURCH, matric. 1 Feb., 86, aged 18 (from Winchester), B.A. 90, M.A. 93.

Badcock, Hugh Daniel, born at Taunton, Somerset, 9 Jan., 1871; 1s. Daniel, of Kilve Court, Bridgewater, J.P. BALLIOL, matric. 14 Oct., 90, aged 19 (from Eton); HONOURS :—2 mathematical mods. 92.

[25]

Badcock, Laurence Henry, born in London 30 July, 1873; 1s. Isaac, bar.-at-law. TRINITY, matric. 15 Oct., 92, aged 19, from Winchester coll.

Badger, Alfred Bernard, born at King's Norton, co. Stafford, 6 May, 1864; 2s. Edward William, gent. NEW COLL., matric. 10 Oct., 84, aged 20 (from K. Edward's school, and Mason coll., Birmingham), exhibitioner 84, B.A. 88, M.A. 92; HONOURS :—Morphology 88, Burdett-Coutts scholarship (geology) 89, 1 geology 89.

Badger, George Edwin, born at Birmingham 23 Dec., 1868; 3s. Samuel Thomas, M.R.C.S.Eng. NON-COLLEGIATE, matric. 11 Oct., 90, aged 21, from K. Edward's high school, Birmingham.

Badham, Francis Pritchett, born at Charlton, Kent, 16 March, 1864; o.s. Francis, cler. EXETER, matric. 18 Oct., 83, aged 19 (from Merchant Taylors' school), exhibitioner 83, B.A. 87, M.A. 92; HONOURS :—2 history 87.

Bagguley, Alfred, born at Newcastle, co. Stafford, 1865; 5s. Henry, gen. NON COLLEGIATE, matric. 17 Oct., 91, aged 26, from Newcastle middle school.

Bagnall, William Herbert, born at Handsworth, co. Stafford, 24 Aug., 1867; 1s. William Henry, of Charlton Kings, co. Glouc., arm. ORIEL, matric. 18 Oct., 87, aged 20 (from Cheltenham coll.), B.A. 90.

Bagnell, Henry William James, born at Kurrachee, E. Indies, 1861; 1s. Henry William, cler. KEBLE, matric. 19 Oct., 80, aged 19 (from Eastbourne coll.); and assistant coll. and magistrate, Bombay, 82.

Bagot, Cecil Villiers, born in London 5 Sept., 1865; 1s. Frederick, rector of Harpsden, Oxon. PEMBROKE, matric. 30 Jan., 84, aged 18 (from Radley coll.), scholar 83, B.A. 87, M.A. 90; HONOURS :—2 classical mods. 85, 3 classics 87.

Bagot, Sidney Charles, born at Harpsden rectory, Oxon, 10 April, 1873; 3s. Frederic, rector. KEBLE matric. 15 Oct., 92, aged 19, from Radley coll.

Bagott, rev. Charles Hodgetts, born at Dudley, co. Worcester, 9 Sept., 1867; 1s. Henry, gent. WORCESTER, matric. 19 Oct., 86, aged 19 (from Dudley gr. school), B.A. 89; curate of Pelsall, co. Staff., 90.

Bagram, John George, born at Calcutta 1866; o.s. John Simon, gent. ST. EDMUND HALL, matric. 22 Oct., 83, aged 17, B.A. 86; bar.-at-law, Middle Temple, 88.

Bailey, Alfred, M.A., student CHRIST CHURCH 1845-58, where see.

[26]

Bailey, Cyril, born in London 1871; 1s. Alfred, arm. BALLIOL, matric. 14 Oct., 90, aged 19 (from St. Paul's school), scholar 89; | HONOURS :—proxime accessit Hertford scholarship90, Hertford scholarship 91, and Craven scholarship 91, 1 classical mods. 92.

Bailey, rev. Gerard Chilton, born at Panton, co. Lincoln, 1863; 2s. Anthony Winter. EXETER, matric. 20 Oct., 81, aged 18 (from Newark school), B.A. 87, M.A. 88; curate of St. Cyprian, Durban, 88-91, and of Newcastle, Natal, 91.

Bailey, Herbert Crawshay, born at Llangattock, co. Brecon, 23 June, 1871; 4s. Joseph Russell, bart. MAGDALEN COLL., matric. 20 Jan., 90, aged 18, from Eton.

Bailey, James Blake, born at Oxford 9 July, 1848; 3s. Samuel. NON-COLLEGIATE, matric. 18 April, 91, aged 42 (from Choir school, Oxford); librarian of Royal college of Surgeons, England.

Bailey, John Cann, born at Norwich 10 Jan., 1864; 3s. Elijah Crosier, solicitor. NEW COLL., matric. 14 Oct., 82, aged 18 (from York school and Haileybury), B.A. 86, M.A. 89 (HONOURS :—2 classical mods. 84, 2 classics 86); bar.-at-law, Inner Temple, 92.

Bailey, rev. Maurice Roach, born at Southampton 9 July, 1867; 3s. James, gent. EXETER, matric. 23 Oct., 85, aged 18 (from Tiverton school), B.A. 90; curate of Exeter St. James 91.

Bailey, Wilfred Ormrod, born at Bolton, co. Lanc., 13 Aug., 1870; 2s. Arthur, gent. TRINITY, matric. 12 Oct., 89, aged 19 (from Repton school); scholar 88; HONOURS :—1 classical mods. 91, Greek verse 92.

Baily, John Macdonald, born 1865; 1s. Johnson, rector of Ryton-on-Tyne 91. ORIEL, matric. 23 Oct., 84, aged 19 (from Magdalen coll. school), B.A. 89, M.A. 92 (HONOURS :—3 law 88); bar.-at-law, Inner Temple, 90.

Baily, Robert Neale, born at Frome, Somerset, 20 July, 1869; 1s. Thomas, arm. BRASENOSE, matric. 22 Oct., 91, aged 22, from Clifton coll.

Bain, Francis William, born at Bothwell, co. Renfrew, 2 April, 1863; 3s. Joseph, gent. CHRIST CHURCH, matric. 13 Oct., 82, aged 19 (from Westminster school), scholar 82, B.A. 86; fellow ALL SOULS' 89, M.A. 89 (HONOURS :—2 classical mods. 84, 1 classics 86); capt. Oxford University assoc. football club; professor of history and political economy Deccan coll., Bombay.

Baines, Alfred George Pisani, born at High Wycombe, Bucks, Nov., 1871; 6s. William Vincent, colliery owner. KEBLE, matric. 15 Oct., 92, aged 20, from Bedford gr. school.

Baines, rev. Charles Frederick, born at Birmingham 26 March, 1862; 3s. James, gent. WADHAM, matric. 26 Jan., 82, aged 19, B.A. 85, M.A. 89; acting chaplain Aldershot 91.

Baines, Philip Henry, born at Oxford 26 Oct., 1873; 1s. Henry, solicitor. NON-COLLEGIATE, matric. 18 April, 91, aged 17, from Warwick school.

Bainton, Arthur William, born at Beverley, Yorks, 14 May, 1862; 3s. William, arm. MAGDALEN, matric. 27 April, 81, aged 18 (from Shrewsbury school), B.A. 85; bar.-at-law, Inner Temple, 88.

Baird, John Lawrence, born in London April, 1874; 1s. Alexander, lord-lieut. Kincardineshire. CHRIST CHURCH, matric. 14 Oct., 92, aged 18, from Eton.

Baiss, Reginald Sydney Habershon, born at Belvedere, Kent, 6 March, 1873; 1s. Sydney Standring, merchant. NON-COLLEGIATE, matric. 15 Oct., 92, aged 19, from Tonbridge school.

Baker, Arthur, born at Byculla, E. Indies, 1863; 3s. William Adolphus, arm. BALLIOL, matric. 21 Oct., 80, aged 17 (from Clifton coll.), B.A. 84, M.A. 87 (HONOURS :—2 classics 84); student Inner Temple 80, selected candidate (3rd) for Indian c.s. 80.

Baker, Cecil Douglas, born at Lewisham, Surrey, 5 Dec., 1870; 3s. Arthur Henry, arm. MERTON, matric. 15 Oct., 90, aged 19, from Sherborne school.

Baker, Charles Maurice, born at Cobham, Kent, 3 March, 1872; 7s. Thomas Henry, gent. TRINITY, matric. 11 Oct., 90, aged 18 (from Tonbridge school), exhibitioner 89, 1 classical mods. 92.

Baker, Daniel, born at Filleigh, Devon, 17 Nov., 1844; 4s. William, gen. EXETER, matric. 17 Oct., 88, aged 42 or 44.

Baker, D'Arcy, born at Thruxton, Hants, 12 July, 1862; 1s. Henry de Foe, cler. WORCESTER, matric. 26 Jan., 82, aged 19; died 26 April, 85; brother of Henry C.

Baker, rev. Edward Turner, born at Wilton, Wilts, 12 Dec., 1862; o.s. Edward Turner, cler. ST. JOHN'S, matric. 21 Jan., 82, aged 19 (from Merchant Taylors' school), B.A. 86, M.A. 89; curate of St. Andrew, Hillingdon, Middlesex, 91.

Baker, Frederick Ekins, born in London 1860; 1s. Charles, cler. ST. EDMUND HALL, matric. 25 Oct., 81, aged 21, from Trinity coll., Stratford-on-Avon.

Baker, rev. George, born in London 19 Nov., 1863; 1s. George, gent. TRINITY, matric. 14 Oct., 82, aged 18 (from Clifton coll.), B.A. 86, M.A. 90 (HONOURS :—2 theology 86); curate of St. Mary, Bathwick, 90.

Baker, George Edward, M.A., fellow MAGDALEN 70-81; where see.

Baker, George Henry, born at Beaulieu, Hants, 1851; 3s. Frederick Walter, cler. CORPUS CHRISTI, matric. 18 May, 83, aged 19 (from Radley coll.), exhibitioner 84-6, B.A. 87, M.A. 91; HONOURS :—3 classical mods. 84, 4 history 86.

Baker, Harold Vining, born at Clifton, co. Glouc., 16 July, 1874; 2s. Arthur, of Henbury, near Bristol, gent. MAGDALEN, matric. 18 Oct., 92, aged 18, from Radley coll.

Baker, Harry Drury, born at Montreal 1868; o.s. James Bowyer, arm. NON-COLLEGIATE, matric. 25 Jan., 88, aged 20, from Magdalen coll. school.

Baker, rev. Henry Charleton, born at Thruxton, Hants, 17 Nov., 1863; 2s. Henry de Foe, rector. BRASENOSE, matric. 22 Oct., 83, aged 19 (from Cheltenham coll.), B.A. 88 (HONOURS :—3 history 87); curate of Penistone, Yorks, 88-91, and of Hornsey St. Paul, Middlesex, 91; brother of D'Arcy.

Baker, rev. Henry Grant, born in London 21 April, 1861; o.s. Henry Grant, gent. WORCESTER, matric. 24 Jan., 80, aged 18 (from Merchant Taylors' school), B.A. 83, M.A. 87; curate of Aylesford 85-90, and of St. Luke, New Brompton, Chatham, 90.

Baker, Henry Mills, born at Stapleton, co. Gloucester, 24 Oct., 1866; 3s. Thomas, gent. ORIEL, matric. 23 Oct., 85, aged 18 (from Rugby), B.A. 89, M.A. 92; HONOURS :—3 law 89.

Baker, Henry Prideaux, born at Henkl, Cape of Good Hope, 12 Sept., 1873; 5s. George, South African missionary. NON-COLLEGIATE, matric. 11 Oct., 90, aged 17 (from Watson's coll., Edinburgh); brother of John Chubb same date.

Baker, Henry William Clinton, born at Haydfordbury, Herts, 16 March, 1868; 1s. William, arm. CHRIST CHURCH, matric. 16 Jan., 85, aged 19, from Eton.

Baker, Herbert Brereton, born at Livesey, co. Lancaster, 1862; 2s. John, cler. BALLIOL, matric. 21 Oct., 80, aged 18 (from Manchester gr. school), scholar 79-84, B.A. 84, M.A. 88; HONOURS :—1 natural science 83.

Baker, James Bernard, born at Winchester 5 Oct., 1862; 1s. James, cler. NON-COLLEGIATE, matric. 13 Oct., 83, aged 21 (from Radley coll.), B.A. 87, M.A. 90; HONOURS :—1 classical mods. 85, 2 history 87.

Baker, John Chubb, born at Heald, Cape of Good Hope, 29 July, 1875; 6s. George, South African missionary. NON-COLLEGIATE, matric. 11 Oct., 90, aged 15 (from Watson's coll., Edinburgh); brother of Henry Prideaux same date.

Baker, John Ffolliot, born at Clifton-on-Teme, co. Worcester, 10 Feb., 1870; 4s. Slade, cler. KEBLE, matric. 13 Oct., 88, aged 18, from Cheltenham coll.

Baker, Joseph, M.A., fellow WORCESTER 42-56, where see.

Baker, Maurice Mills, born at Stoke Bishop, co. Gloucester, 8 March, 1867; 2s. William Mills, arm. ORIEL, matric. 18 Oct., 87, aged 20 (from Rugby), B.A. 91.

Baker, Michael Granville Lloyd, born at Hardwicke, co. Gloucester, 16 Jan., 1873; 1s. Granville Edwin, arm. CHRIST CHURCH, matric. 29 May, 91, aged 18, from Eton.

Baker, Percy Charles, born at Bromley, Kent, 2 May, 1874; 2s. Alfred John, solicitor. CHRIST CHURCH, matric. 14 Oct., 92, aged 18.

Baker, Percy Thomas, born at Cobham 13 Nov., 1867; 5s. Thomas Henry, arm. TRINITY, matric. 16 Oct., 86, aged 18 (from Tonbridge school), B.A. 90; HONOURS :—3 classical mods. 88, 3 history 90.

Baker, Reginald John Edward, born at Portsmouth, Feb., 1874; 1s. John, M.P., and J.P. CHRIST CHURCH, matric. 14 Oct., 92, aged 18, from Portsmouth gr. school.

Baker, Richard Philip, born at Condover, Salop, 1866; 1s. William, gent. BALLIOL, matric. 15 Oct., 84, aged 18 (from Clifton coll.), scholar 83; HONOURS :—2 mathematical mods. 86.

Baker, rev. Richard Whittington, born at Tellisford, Somerset, 10 Sept., 1865; 5s. Charles Francis, rector. MAGDALEN, matric. 16 Oct., 84, aged 19 (from Honiton gr. school), B.A. 88, M.A. 92 (HONOURS :—2 classical mods. 86, 2 theology 88, septuagint prize 89); rector of Tellisford, 90.

Baker, rev. Slade Raymond, born at Clifton-on-Teme, co. Worc., 15 Oct., 1861; 1s. Slade, cler. LINCOLN, matric. 29 Jan., 81, aged 19 (from Marlborough coll.), scholar 80-4, B.A. 84, M.A. 89 (HONOURS :—2 classical mods. 82, 4 classics 84); curate of Kidderminster 90.

Baker, rev. Stanley, born at Blackburn, co. Lancaster, 14 Oct., 1868; 3s. John, cler. QUEEN'S, matric. 21 Oct., 87, aged 19 (from Manchester gr. school), exhibitioner 87, B.A. 92; HONOURS :—3 classics 91.

Baker, Walter George, born at Beaulieu, near New Forest, 1862; 2s. Frederick Walter, arm. UNIVERSITY COLL., matric. 16 Oct., 80, aged 18 (from Radley coll.); sometime in the army.

Baker William, D.D., fellow ST. JOHN'S 60-70, where see.

Baker, William Henry, born at North Shields 1862; 1s. Joseph, gent. ST. EDMUND HALL, matric. 16 Jan., 83, aged 20 (from Durham gr. school), B.A. 86; assistant master Hull and East Riding coll. 86-8, curate of St. Mary, Kingston-upon-Hull, 87-9; London diocesan home missionary 89.

Baker, William Henry, born at Handborough, Oxon, 1872; 1s. William, gent. ST. JOHN'S, matric. 15 Oct., 92, aged 20, from Magdalen coll. school.

Baker, William Thomas Webb, born at Abergavenny, co. Mon., 6 Dec., 1873; 1s. Henry Laurence, solicitor. EXETER, matric. 18 Oct., 92 (from Rugby), scholar 92.

Bakewell, John Scales, born at Lendenham, co. Lincoln, 1865; o.s. John, gent. EXETER, matric. 12 May, 83, aged 18.

Balderston, William, born at Bainbridge, near Bedale, 18 Jan., 1864; 1s. William, cler. QUEEN'S, matric. 22 Oct., 83, aged 19 (from Sedbergh school), exhibitioner 83, B.A. 87; HONOURS :—2 classical mods. 85.

Baldwin, Leonard, born at Kemerton, co. Gloue. 1857; 1s. Bernard, arm. EXETER, matric. 27 April, 81, aged 24; migrated to NEW INN HALL (BALLIOL 87), B.A. 88; M.A. from Exeter 89, as Baldwyn.

Balfour, right hon. Arthur James; 1s. James Maitland, of Whittinghame, N.B.; 1st lord of the treasury and leader of the house of commons 91-2, created D.C.L. 17 June, 91, and St. Andrew's 85. TRINITY COLL., Camb. 67 (from Eton), B.A. 70, M.A. 73, LL.D. 88 (HONOURS :—2nd class moral science 69), hon. LL.D. Edinburgh 81; president of local government board June 85 to Jan. 86, secretary for Scotland July 86 to March 87, chief secretary for Ireland March 87-91, M.P. Hertford 74-85, East Manchester 85, F.R.S. 88, rector of St. Andrew's university 86-9, and lord rector of Glasgow university 90, etc.; born 25 July, 48. See Men and Women of the Time.

Balfour, Charles Frederick, born at Valparaiso, Chili, 18 Nov., 1872; 1s. James Robert, merchant. CORPUS CHRISTI, matric. 19 Oct., 91, aged 18 (from Clifton coll.), scholar 91.

Balfour, Frederick Stephen, born at Mount Alyn, co. Denbigh, 11 March, 1873; 1s. Alexander, M.A. TRINITY, matric. 15 Oct., 92, aged 19, from Loretto school.

Balfour, Henry, born at Croydon, Surrey, 11 April, 1863; o.s. Lewis, gent. TRINITY, matric. 3 June, 81, aged 18 (from the Charterhouse), B.A. 85, M.A. 88 (HONOURS :—2 natural science 85), curator of the Pitt-Rivers Collection.

Balfour, Isaac Bayley, M.A., D.Med., fellow MAGDALEN 84-88, where see.

Balfour, Maxwell, born at Valparaiso, Chili, 8 Feb., 1874; 2s. James Robert. esq., deceased. NEW COLL., matric. 14 Oct., 92, aged 18, from Clifton coll.

Balfour, Patrick, born in Edinburgh 1870; 1s. John Blair. BALLIOL, matric. 17 Oct., 89, aged 19, from Harrow.

Ball, Cecil Herbert Shirley Shirley, born at Ballyhaise House, Cavan, 18 March, 1872; 2s. Arthur William Shirley, captain 8th Hussars. ORIEL, matric. 27 Oct., 91, aged 19, from Cheltenham coll.

Ball, rev. Frederick, born at Torquay, Devon, 1862; 2s. William, gent. EXETER, matric. 20 Oct., 81, aged 19 (from Newton Abbot coll. and Basingstoke school), scholar 81-5, B.A. 85, M.A. 88 (HONOURS :—2 mathematical mods. 83, 2 mathematics 85); chaplain royal navy 90, H.M.S. Boadicea 91.

Ball, rev. Herbert, born at Bristol 2 Aug., 1863; 2s. Alfred William, cler. TRINITY, matric. 15 Oct., 83, aged 20 (from Coventry school), B.A. 87 (HONOURS :—2 classical mods. 85, 3 history 87); curate of Fisherton Anger, Wilts, 91.

Ball, Sidney, M.A., fellow ST. JOHN's 82-92, where see.

31   BALLANTYNE. —— MATRICULATIONS, 1880 TO 1892. —— BARKER.   32

Ballantyne, George Monck Mason, born at Edinburgh Nov. 1859; 2s. James Robert, arm. UNIVERSITY COLL., matric. 22 Jan., 80, aged 20 (from Bradfield coll.), exhibitioner 80-4, B.A. 83, M.A. 86 (HONOURS:—1 mathematical mods. 81, 2 mathematics 83); died 23 March, 80, in Barbados.

Ballantyne, Walter Reeve, born at Dalkeith, N.B., 1874; 1s. John, gent. PEMBROKE, matric. 28 Oct., 92, aged 18.

Balleine, George Orange, M.A., fellow QUEEN'S 65-9, where see.

Balleine, George Reginald, born at Bletchingdon, Oxon, 1 April, 1873; 1s. George Orange, dean of Jersey. QUEEN'S, matric. 27 Oct., 91, aged 18, from Marlborough and Victoria college, Jersey.

Balloch, Robert Hugh, born at Kilcreggan, co. Dumbarton, 14 July, 1863; 3s. Robert, gent. NEW COLL., matric. 19 Oct., 82, aged 19 (from Uppingham school), B.A. 86, M.A. 89 (HONOURS:—2 classical mods. 84, 2 law 86); bar.-at-law, Inner Temple, 89.

Balmer, rev. Edward Liddell, M.A., fellow HERTFORD 75-88, where see.

Balston, Stanworth, born at Poole, Dorset, 10 Jan., 1869; 4s. Alfred, gent. LINCOLN, matric. 18 Oct., 88, aged 19 (from Bath coll.), scholar 88, B.A. 93; HONOURS:—2 classical mods. 90, 3 classics 92.

Bancroft, George Pleydell, born in London 1 Nov., 1868; 2s. Squire, arm. BRASENOSE, matric. 16 Oct., 88, aged 19 (from Eton), B.A. 92 (HONOURS: —3 law 92); bar.-at-law, Inner Temple, 93.

Banister, Herbert, born at Denmark Hill, Surrey, 1864; o.s. Frederick Dale, gent. PEMBROKE, matric. 27 Oct., 83, aged 19, B.A. 89.

Bankes, Ralph Vincent, born at Northop, Flints, 1867; 3s. John Scott, arm. UNIVERSITY COLL., matric. 18 Oct., 86, aged 19 (from Winchester), B.A. 89 (HONOURS:—2 law 89); bar.-at-law, Inner Temple, 90.

Banks, rev. Ernest William, born at Aylesbury, Bucks, 1864; 2s. William Henry, gen. NON-COLLEGIATE, matric. 15 Oct., 87, aged 23 (from King's coll., London), B.A. 91; HONOURS:—4 theology 91.

Banks, Morris Lawden, born at Edgbaston, co. Warwick, 14 Dec., 1862; o.s. Morris, gent. LINCOLN, matric. 21 Jan., 83, aged 20 (from K. Edward's school, Birmingham), B.A. 86, M.A. 90; HONOURS:—3 history 86.

Bannister, rev. Arthur Thomas, born at Chester 21 March, 1861; o.s. Joseph, gent. LINCOLN, matric. 23 Oct., 80, aged 19 (from King's school, Chester), B.A. 84, M.A. 88 (HONOURS:—1 classical mods. 82, 3 classics 84); curate of Birchington, Kent, 91.

Barber, Alfred Stephen, born at Orpington, Kent, 20 Oct., 1872; 1s. Alfred Graeff, stockbroker, deceased. KEBLE, matric. 15 Oct., 92, aged 19, from Haileybury.

Barber, George Edward, born at Radley, Berks, 19 Aug., 1870; 1s. Edward, archdeacon of Chester. WORCESTER, matric. 16 Oct., 88, aged 18 (from Radley coll.), scholar 88, B.A. 92; HONOURS:—2 classical mods. 90, 4 classics 92.

Barber, Howard Cambridge, born in London 9 Dec., 1871; 1s. William Cambridge, gent. QUEEN'S, matric. 24 Oct., 90, aged 18 (from Bradford school), exhibitioner 90; HONOURS:—2 classical mods. 92.

Barber, William Priestley, born in London 17 Aug., 1869; 1s. William, Q.C., county court judge. WORCESTER, matric. 17 Jan., 88, aged 18 (from Marlborough), B.A. 90.

Barbour, John Milne, born in co. Antrim, Ireland, 1868; 2s. John Doherty, arm. BRASENOSE, matric. 23 Oct., 85, aged 17 (from Leamington coll.), B.A. 88, M.A. 92.

Barchard, Francis, born at Hove, Sussex, March, 1863; 1s. Elphinstone, arm. CHRIST CHURCH, matric. 4 June, 81, aged 18 (from Winchester), B.A. 84 (HONOURS:—4 history 84); bar.-at-law, Inner Temple, 88.

Barchard, Herbert Pulman, born at Eccles, co. Lanc., 1864; 3s. William Burnett, gent. BRASENOSE, matric. 21 Jan., 84, aged 19 (from Shrewsbury school), B.A. 87.

Barclay, George Alexander Noel, born at Ipswich 11 Nov., 1866; 1s. Henry Alexander, of Brighton, cler. MAGDALEN, matric. 23 Oct., 85, aged 18, (from Haileybury), on the Stock Exchange 86.

Bardsley, Cyril Charles Bowman, born at Greenwich 13 Feb., 1870; 3s. James Wareing, cler. NEW COLL., matric. 11 Oct., 89, aged 19 (from Marlborough coll.), B.A. 92; HONOURS:—ægrotat in law 92.

Bardsley, rev. Ernest John, born at Greenwich, Kent, 15 Oct., 1868; 2s. James Wareing, cler. WORCESTER, matric. 17 Oct., 87, aged 19 (from Marlborough coll.), B.A. 90 (HONOURS:—3 theology 90); curate of Sandal Magna, Yorks, 91.

Bardsley, rev. Herbert James, born at Islington 9 Jan., 1865; 1s. James Wareing, cler. WORCESTER, matric. 18 Oct., 83, aged 18 (from Merchant Taylors' school), exhibitioner 83, B.A. 87, M.A. 90 (HONOURS:—2 classical mods. 85, 2 classics 87, 2 theology 88); curate of Sandal Magna.

Bardsley, Samuel Martyn, born at Wandsworth, Surrey, 1863; 2s. Samuel, cler. CHRIST CHURCH, matric. 13 Oct., 82, aged 19 (from St. Paul's school), scholar 82-6, B.A. 86, M.A. 90; HONOURS:—2 mathematical mods. 84, 3 history 86.

Bardswell, Charles Hamilton, born at Surbiton, Surrey, 8 Sept., 1867; 1s. Charles William, bar.-at-law. NEW COLL., matric. 15 Oct., 86, aged 19 (from Sherborne school), B.A. 90; HONOURS:—3 classical mods. 88, 2 classics 90.

Barff, rev. Herbert Henry, born at Hawkley, Hants, July, 1863; 1s. Henry Tootal, cler. KEBLE, matric. 17 Jan., 83, aged 19 (from Clifton coll.), B.A. 86; curate St. Nicholas cathedral, Newcastle-on-Tyne, 90.

Barford, Bernard Weight, born at Wokingham, Berks, 1862; 1s. James Gale, gent. EXETER, matric. 14 June, 80, aged 18 (from Wellington coll.), migrated to New Inn Hall (BALLIOL), B.A. 88.

Baring, hon. Alexander Henry, born 4 Sept., 1869; 3s. Alexander Hugh, baron Ashburton. NEW COLL., matric. 12 Oct., 88, aged 19, from Eton.

Baring, hon. Cecil, born at Kingston-on-Thames 12 Sept., 1864; 2s. Edward Charles, lord Revelstoke (85). BALLIOL, matric. 28 Jan., 84, aged 19 (from Eton), exhibitioner 84, B.A. 87; HONOURS:—1 classical mods. 85, 3 classics 87.

Baring, Godfrey Nigel Everard, born at High Beech, Essex, 1 Oct., 1870; 2s. Thomas Charles, arm. HERTFORD, matric. 14 Oct., 89, aged 19, from Harrow.

Baring, Harold Hermann John, born in London 4 March, 1869; 1s. Thomas Charles, arm. HERTFORD, matric. 26 Oct., 88, aged 19, from Harrow.

Barker, rev. Aislabie Denham, born at Camberwell, Surrey, 1862; 1s. Ephraim David Edmund, gent. ST. EDMUND HALL, matric. 25 Oct., 81, aged 19, B.A. 86, M.A. 88; curate of St. Barnabas, Hove, Sussex, 89.

Barker, Alfred Herbert, born at Bourgn, near Smyrna, 1864; 1s. Alfred James Frederick, banker. EXETER, matric. 27 May, 82, aged 18, B.A. 86.

Barker, Algernon Prest Bird, born at Hexham, Northumberland, 28 July, 1868; 1s. Henry Christopher, cler. EXETER, matric. 16 Oct., 89, aged 21 (from Clifton coll., and Trinity coll., Cambridge, 87), B.A. 91; HONOURS:—3 history 91.

Barker, Edmund John Perrott Ross-, born at Enfield, Middlesex, Oct., 1869; 1s. John Ross, cler. BRASENOSE, matric. 16 Oct., 88, aged 19 (from Aldenham school), exhibitioner 88, B.A. 92; HONOURS:—1 classical mods. 90, 2 classics 92.

Barker, Frederick George, born at Sherfield, Hants, 27 Oct., 1866; 1s. Alfred Gresley, cler. BRASENOSE, matric. 24 March, 86, aged 19 (from Eton), B.A. 91.

Barker, Geoffrey Claude, born at Hendingley, Yorks, 27 July, 1870; 3s. Frederick, arm. MAGDALEN, matric. 14 Oct., 89, aged 19 (from the Charterhouse); HONOURS:—3 classical mods. 91.

Barker, George Crossley, born at Crosby, co. Lanc., 6 Nov., 1868; 1s. George, gen. MERTON, matric. 22 Oct., 87, aged 18 (from University coll., Liverpool), B.A. 90; HONOURS:—3 classical mods. 89.

Barker, Gerald Edgar, born in London 1868; o.s. Edgar, D. Med. BRASENOSE, matric. 24 April, 88, aged 20, from Eton.

Barker, Harry, born at Great Grimsby, co. Lincoln, 1863; 1s. Henry, gent. CHRIST CHURCH, matric. 15 Oct., 86, aged 23.

Barker, Henry Raine, M.A., student CHRIST CHURCH 48-64, where see.

Barker, Herbert Arthur, born at East Bridgeford, Notts, 28 Jan., 1866; o.s. Arthur Alcock, rector. MAGDALEN, matric. 16 Oct., 84, aged 18 (from Clifton coll.), B.A. 88.

Barker, Hildebrand Samuel, born at Smyrna 18 June, 1869; 3s. Alfred Frederick, of Constantinople, banker. PEMBROKE, matric. 26 Oct., 89, aged 20, from Cheltenham coll.

Barker, John Raymond, born at Albrighton, Salop, Nov., 1869; 1s. George James, arm. CHRIST CHURCH, matric. 12 Oct., 88, aged 18 (from Shrewsbury school), B.A. 91.

Barker, Joseph, born at Doncaster 27 Jan., 1867; ¾s. Samuel, gen. NON-COLLEGIATE, matric. 6 Dec., 90, aged 23, from Trinity coll., near Harrogate.

Barker, Thomas Child, M.A., student CHRIST CHURCH 46-57, where see.

Barkley, MacDonald, born at Tacklestone, Norfolk, 26 April, 1871; o.s. Henry Charles, c.e. LINCOLN, matric. 23 Oct., 91, aged 20, from Haileybury.

Barlow, Herbert William Leyland, born at Manchester Aug., 1856; 1s. Robert, gent. TRINITY, matric. 16 Oct., 86, aged 20 (from Manchester gr. school), scholar 86, B.A. 91; HONOURS:—1 chemistry 89, 2 physiology 91.

Barlow, Hugh Christopher Heneage, born at Bristol 25 Feb., 1872; 3s. William Hagger, cler. LINCOLN, matric. 23 Oct., 91, aged 19 (from Marlborough coll.), scholar 91.

Barlow, Micah Yates, born at Bury, co. Lanc., 6 Feb., 1873; 1s. Micah, manufacturer. UNIVERSITY COLL., matric. 15 Oct., 92, aged 19, from Harrow.

Barlow, Walter Charles, born at St. Leonard's, Sussex, 1867; 2s. Henry Walter, gen. PEMBROKE, matric. 26 Oct., 89, aged 22 (from Hnth coll.), B.A. 92.

Barmby, Francis James, born at Durham 21 Dec., 1863; 2s. James, B.D., vicar of Pittington, co. Durham. MAGDALEN, matric. 16 Oct., 82, aged 18 (from the Charterhouse), B.A. 86, M.A. 91; HONOURS:—2 classical mods. 84, 3 classics 86.

Barmby, Henry Temple, born at Durham 1868; 4s. James, B.D., vicar of Pittington, co. Durham. KEBLE, matric. 19 Oct., 86, aged 18, from Durham gr. school.

Barmby, James, B.D., fellow MAGDALEN 1846-59, where see.

Barmby, Sydney Charles, born at Durham 15 June, 1862; 1s. James, B.D., vicar of Pittington, co. Durham. MAGDALEN, matric. 21 Jan., 82, aged 19, from Uppingham school.

Barnard, Thomas, born at Weston-super-Mare, Somerset, 1871; 1s. Thomas, gen. NON-COLLEGIATE, matric. 17 Oct., 91, aged 20, from college for the Blind, Powyke.

Barnes, rev. Arthur Stapylton, born in Kussowli, E. Indies, 31 May, 1861; o.s. George, arm. UNIVERSITY COLL., matric. 16 Oct., 80, aged 19 (from Eton), B.A. 83, M.A. 87 (HONOURS:—3 history 83); vicar of St. Ives, Hunts, 91.

Barnes, Herbert Charles, born in London 1870; 1s. Herbert, arm. CHRIST CHURCH, matric. 11 Oct., 89, aged 19 (from Westminster school), exhibitioner 89; HONOURS:—2 classical mods. 91.

Barnes, Herbert Grafton, born at Tideford, Cornwall, Feb., 1869; 1s. Frederick, cler. KEBLE, matric. 17 Oct., 87, aged 18 (from Stratford-on-Avon school), B.A. 90; HONOURS:—3 theology 90.

Barnes, Horace William, born at Farnley, Yorks, 25 Nov., 1861; 1s. William, vicar of Little Holbeck. QUEEN'S, matric. 4 June, 81, aged 19 (from Leeds gr. school), commoner 81-5, B.A. 85, M.A. 89; HONOURS:—2 classical mods. 83, 2 classics 85.

Barnes, Reginald Garrould, born at Morningthorpe, Norfolk, 1869; 2s. John Matthew, arm. BRASENOSE, matric. 16 Oct., 88, aged 19 (from Ipswich school), scholar 87, B.A. 92; HONOURS:—1 mathematical mods. 90, 2 mathematics 92.

Barnes, rev. Thomas, born at Mowbray, Cumberland, 1 July, 1862; 2s. Robert, pleb. NEW COLL., matric. 15 Oct., 81, aged 19 (from Penrith school), B.A. 85, M.A. 89 (HONOURS:—3 classical mods. 83, and 3 classics 85); curate of St. Anne, Limehouse, London, 87.

Barnett, Richard Whieldon, born at Forest Hill, Surrey, 6 Dec., 1863; 1s. Richard, D.Med. WADHAM, matric. 19 Jan., 84, aged 20 (from Methodist coll., Belfast), B.A. 87, M.A. and B.C.L. 90 (HONOURS:—3 classical mods. 85, a law 87, a civil law 89); bar.-at-law, Middle Temple, 89.

Barnston, Harry, born at Edinburgh 12 Dec., 1870; 1s. Harry, gen. ST. JOHN'S, matric. 18 Oct., 90, aged 19 (from Bournemouth school).

Barnwell, Charles Thomas, born at Norwich 1869; 1s. Charles, gen. NON-COLLEGIATE, matric. 12 Oct., 89, aged 20, from Wiesbaden gymnasium and St. Edward's coll., London.

Baron, rev. Charles William, born at Hungerford, Berks, 1862; 2s. William Joseph, cler. CHRIST CHURCH, matric. 14 Oct., 81, aged 19 (from Christ's hospital), exhibitioner 81-5, B.A. 86, M.A. 91; HONOURS:—2 classical mods. 83, 3 classics 85.

Barrett, John Bernhard Steinlen, born at Waiblingen, Germany, 4 Feb., 1868; 3s. John Cook, gen. CORPUS CHRISTI, matric. 22 Oct., 87, aged 19 (from Kingswood school), scholar 87; HONOURS:—2 classical mods. 89, 4 classics 91.

Barrett, Alexander Gould, born at North Curry, Somerset, 17 Nov., 1866; 3s. William, major in militia. LINCOLN, matric. 13 May, 86, aged 19 (from Eton), B.A. 90.

Barrett, rev. Frank Moulton, born at Bampton, Devon, 30 April, 1865; 2s. Henry, of Dunsland, arm. MAGDALEN, matric. 19 Oct., 83, aged 18 (from Marlborough), B.A. 87, M.A. 90, curate of Harpenden, Herts, 88.

Barrett, Nugent James, born at Cambridge 30 April, 1868; 7s. Arthur Charles, arm. NON-COLLEGIATE, matric. 12 June, 86, aged 28, migrated to EXETER, B.A. 89; HONOURS :—4 history 89.

Barrett, Wilfred Tufnell, born at Barrow-in-Furness Nov., 1865; 4s. Tuffnell Samuel, cler. CHRIST CHURCH, matric. 12 Oct., 1888, aged 22, from Shrewsbury school.

Barrett, rev. William Carter, born at Wimborne, Dorset, 24 Nov., 1863; 2s. Charles Carter, late captain 33rd reg. JESUS COLL., matric. 18 Oct., 82, aged 18 (from Stratford-on-Avon school), scholar 82-4, B.A. 86; curate of St. John the Divine, Richmond, Surrey, 89.

Barrington, Arthur, born in London July, 1878; 2s. Arthur, gen., deceased. KEBLE, matric. 15 Oct., 92, aged 19, from Harpenden school.

Barron, Albert Harold, born at Hollymount, co. Mayo, 5 Jan., 1871; 3. Gerald Edward, physician. ST. JOHN'S, matric. 16 Oct., 88, aged 17 (from Merchant Taylors' school), scholar 88; HONOURS : —2 classical mods. 90, 3 classics 92.

Barron, rev. Henry Marshall, born at Barking, Essex, 5 June, 1866; 1s. Henry Stracey, C.E. NON-COLLEGIATE, matric. 17 Oct., 85, aged 19 (from Merchant Taylors' school); migrated to WADHAM 19 Oct., 87, B.A. 89 (HONOURS :—3 law 89); curate of Lynesack, co. Durham, 90.

Barron, John Hall, born at Inverarie, Aberdeen, 1 April, 1873; 1s. James, merchant. EXETER, matric. 18 Oct., 92, aged 19 (from Aberdeen university), scholar 92.

Barron, Robert Harrison, born in London 10 Dec., 1862; 2s. Francis John, gent. WORCESTER, matric. 26 Jan., 82, aged 19, from Merchant Taylors' school.

Barrow, John Graham, born at Clareborough, Notts, 1857; 2s. Richard James, cler. NON-COLLEGIATE, matric. 21 Jan., 82, aged 25 (from Brewood gr. school), B.A. from ST. EDMUND HALL 87, and M.A. 90, as John G. B.

Barrow, Percy James, born at Cowes, isle of Wight, 10 Oct., 1872; 3s. Richard, gen. KEBLE, matric. 20 Oct., 91, aged 19, from Portsmouth gr. school.

Barrow, Reginald Pocock, born at Worcester 9 March, 1864; 1s. Francis Wynford, arm. TRINITY, matric. 15 Oct., 83, aged 19; assistant collector and magistrate, Hyderabad and Tando, sub-division, Sind Bo. c.s. 85.

Barrows, Wilfred Murdock, born at Banbury, Oxon, 19 Sept., 1871; 4s. Thomas Welch, gen. MERTON, matric. 22 Oct., 91, aged 20, from Cheltenham coll.

Barry, Arthur Joseph, born at Grahamstown, S. Africa, 6 June, 1873; 2s. sir Jacob Dirk, B.A., judge in S. Africa. UNIVERSITY COLL., matric. 15 Oct., 92, aged 19, from St. Andrew's coll., Grahamstown, and Sherborne school.

Barry, Douglas Heron, born at Beckenham, Kent, 1862; 3s. Francis Ypress, arm. M.P. BRASENOSE, matric. 21 May, 80, aged 18 (from Harrow); brother of William James.

Barry, Francis Henry, born at Sydenham, Kent, 8 Oct., 1866; 2s. Francis Charles, arm. MERTON, matric. 24 Oct., 85, aged 19 (from Cranbrook and King's coll. school, London), B.A. 89; HONOURS :—3 classical mods. 87, 3 law 89.

Barry, rev. Henry Boothby, M.A., fellow QUEEN'S 44-56, where see.

Barry, rev. John Shafto, born at Allahabad, E. Indies, 1862; o.s. Thomas Posgrove, gent. ST. EDMUND HALL, matric. 29 Jan., 81, aged 19, B.A. 83, M.A. 89, curate of Lightcliffe, Yorks, 90.

Barry, Lionel Edward, born in London 1863; 1s. Edward Middleton, arm. BRASENOSE, matric. 10 June, 81, aged 18, from Eton.

Barry, William James, born at Beckenham, Kent, 1864; 4s. Francis Ypress, arm. (M.P.) BRASENOSE, matric. 19 Oct., 82, aged 18 (from Harrow), B.A. 86; brother of Douglas Heron.

Barsdorf, Ralph Bismarck, born at Port Elizabeth, Cape of Good Hope, 1870; 2s. Augustus, arm. BRASENOSE, matric. 16 Oct., 88, aged 18 (from Clifton coll.), B.A. 91.

Barter, Charles, B.C.L., fellow NEW COLL. 39-53, where see.

Barth, Jacob William, born in London 23 July, 1871; 1s. William Wright, arm. WADHAM, matric. 13 Oct., 90, aged 19, from Battersea school.

Bartholomew, Arthur John, born at Maidstone, Kent, 1862; 1s. Edward John, gent. BRASENOSE, matric. 21 Jan., 82, aged 20, from Maidstone school.

Bartleet, rev. Edward John, born at Knowle, co. Worcester, 1865; 1s. John Robert, gent. HERTFORD, matric. 20 Jan., 83, aged 18, B.A. and M.A. 89; curate of Weston-super-Mare 91.

Bartleet, Edwin Berry, born at Edgbaston, co. Warwick, 12 April, 1872; 1s. Thomas Heron, surgeon. WADHAM, matric. 16 Oct., 91, aged 19, from Marlborough and Clifton colls.

Bartlet, James Vernon, born at Scarborough, Yorks, 1863; o.s. George Donald, baptist minister. EXETER, matric. 18 Oct., 82, aged 19 (from Highgate school), scholar 82, B.A. 86, M.A. 89 (fellow Mansfield coll. 89); HONOURS :—1 classical mods. 83, 2 classics 86, 1 theology 87, Greek testament prize 89.

Bartlet, Philip Perring, born at Dorking, Surrey, March, 1868; 2s. John Moysey, cler. ST. JOHN'S, matric. 15 Oct., 87, aged 19, B.A. 92.

Bartlet, rev. Alfred James, born at Stone, Herts, Aug., 1866; 2s. John Barnes, of Weston-super-Mare, cler. ORIEL, matric. 23 Oct., 85, aged 19 (from Haileybury), B.A. 90.

Bartlett, Arthur Henry, born in London 1864; 1s. Thomas Henry, arm. ORIEL, matric. 27 Oct., 83, aged 19 (from Eton), bible clerk 83, B.A. 87, M.A. and B.C.L. 90; HONOURS :—2 classical mods. 84, 2 law 87, 1 civil law 88.

Bartlett, rev. Charles Oldfield, born at Blandford, Dorset, 1859; 2s. Robert Leach, cler. NON-COLLEGIATE, matric. 6 Feb., 80, aged 21 (from Christ's hospital), migrated to EXETER, B.A. 83, M.A. 86 (HONOURS :—4 theology 82); rector of Willersey, co. Worc., 91.

Bartlett, Frank, born at Pershore, co. Worcester, 27 Jan., 1872; 3s. Robert Edward, cler. TRINITY, matric. 17 Oct., 91, aged 19, from Rugby.

Bartlett, John Adams, born at Liverpool 14 March, 1868; 1s. William, arm. CHRIST CHURCH, matric. 25 April, 87, aged 19 (from Uppingham), B.A. 90.

Bartlett, rev. Richard Grosvenor, born at Thurlaxton, Somerset, 5 Dec., 1858; 6s. Robert Leach, vicar. NON-COLLEGIATE, matric. 16 Oct., 86, aged 17 (from Crewkerne gr. school), migrated to WADHAM 17 Oct., 87, B.A. 90 (HONOURS :—3 history 89); curate of Whitchurch-Canonicorum, Dorset, 91.

Bartlett, Robert Edward, M.A., fellow TRINITY 53-60, where see.

Barton, Alfred Thomas, M.A., fellow PEMBROKE 65, where see.

Barton, Arnold Binney, born in London 1867; 2s. Henry, gen. ST. JOHN'S, matric. 13 Oct., 88, aged 21, from Haileybury.

Barton, rev. George, born at Woburn, Beds, Oct., 1863; 1s. Samuel Henry, gent. ST. JOHN'S, matric. 14 Oct., 82, aged 18 (from Lincoln gr. school), B.A. 86; curate of South Banbury, OXON, 91.

Barton, Harry Scott, born at Kingston-on-Thames 1862; 2s. Bertram Francis, arm. BRASENOSE, matric. 21 May, 80, aged 18 (from Eton), B.A. 85, M.A. 88.

Barton, Henry Alexander, born at Kidderminster, co. Worcester, 24 Sept., 1862; 4s. John Edward, gent. TRINITY, matric. 29 Jan., 81, aged 18 (from Rugby), B.A. 84, M.A. 88, solicitor and acting deputy atty.-general British Columbia 91.

Barton, Henry John Hope, born in London Feb., 1873; o.s. John Hope, arm. CHRIST CHURCH, matric. 2 Dec., 90, aged 17, from Eton.

Barton, Henry Newell, M.A., fellow PEMBROKE 44-9, where see.

Barton, William Henry, born at Ampthill, Beds, 24 Sept., 1867; 2s. Samuel Henry, solicitor. WADHAM, matric. 26 Oct., 86, aged 19 (from Lincoln school), B.A. 90.

Bartram, Algernon Howard, born at Cirencester 10 Dec., 1860; 4s. William, cler. LINCOLN, matric. 29 April, 81, aged 20, migrated to ST. MARY HALL.

Bartram, rev. Reginald Swayne, born at Chichester 1864; 3s. William, cler. NON-COLLEGIATE, matric. 14 April, 83, aged 19, B.A. 87; curate of Haydock, co. Lanc., 89.

Bartrum, Edward Stothert, born at Berkhampstead, Herts, 9 Feb., 1868; 1s. Edward, D.D. MERTON, matric. 22 Oct., 87, aged 19 (from Berkhamsted school), B.A. 92.

Bartrum, rev. Henry Hooke, born at Charlcombe, Somerset, 11 Nov., 1861; y.s. Benjamin, arm. MERTON, matric. 16 Oct., 84, aged 21 (from Felsted school), B.A. 87, M.A. 91 (HONOURS:—1 theology 87); curate of Beckenham, Kent, 89-91.

Barwell, Charles Sedley William, born at Norwich 4 May, 1869; 2s. John, gent. HERTFORD, matric. 19 Oct., 88, aged 19, from Westminster school.

Bashall, John, born at Richmond, Surrey, 1867; 4s. William, cler. ST. JOHN'S, matric. 15 Oct., 87, aged 20, from King's coll., London.

Basilon, Edmund Anthony, born at Trinidad 1853; 1s. Charles Sylvester, gen. NON-COLLEGIATE, matric. 11 Oct., 90, aged 37, from St. Mary's coll., Port-of-Spain.

Baskett, Bertram George Mortimer, born at Manchester 9 May, 1862; o.s. George Crooks, gent. QUEEN'S, matric. 28 Oct., 81, aged 19 (from York school), exhibitioner 81-5, B.A. 85; HONOURS:—2 classical mods. 83, 3 law 85.

Bassano, Alfred Hill, born at Old Hill, co. Worcester, 1863; 1s. Walter, gent. BALLIOL, matric. 16 Jan., 83, aged 20 (from Leamington coll.), B.A. 86; HONOURS:—3 classical mods. 84.

Bassano, rev. Charles Walter, born at Old Hill, co. Worcester, 1864; 2s. Walter, gen. BALLIOL, matric. 16 Jan., 83, aged 19 (from Leamington coll.), B.A. 86 (HONOURS:—2 classical mods. 84); curate of Holy Trinity, Cheltenham, 88-91.

Bassett, Alexander Willis, born at Southampton 1866; 3s. Robert Goodenough, arm. BRASENOSE, matric. 25 May, 83, aged 17, B.A. 87, M.A. 90; bar.-at-law, Inner Temple, 90.

Bassett, Hubert, born at Stanton St. John, OXON, 5 Oct., 1867; 5s. Edward, gen. NON-COLLEGIATE, matric. 15 Oct., 87, aged 20 (from an Oxford school), in the Oxford eleven 89, 90, 91.

Bassett, Stuart Tilney, born at Bath 1862; 2s. Frederick Tilney, cler. ST. EDMUND HALL, matric. 19 Oct., 82, aged 20, migrated to CHARSLEY HALL, B.A. 88; M.A. from ST. EDMUND HALL 90; vicar of Goodersione, Norfolk, 91.

Bastard, Edward William, born at Wilton, Somerset, 28 Feb., 1862; 2s. Henry Horlock, cler. WADHAM, matric. 15 Oct., 81, aged 19 (from Sherborne school), scholar 81-5, B.A. 85, M.A. 88 (HONOURS:—3 classical mods. 83, 3 classics 85), in the Oxford eleven 83, 4, 5.

Bastard, James Mayo, born at Taunton, Somerset, 1867; 4s. Henry Horlock, cler. ST. JOHN'S, matric. 17 Oct., 85, aged 18 (from Sherborne school), scholar 89, B.A. 90, M.A. 92; HONOURS:—2 classical mods. 87, 3 history 89.

Bastard, John Muston, born at Taunton 1863; 3s. Henry Horlock, cler. ST. JOHN'S, matric. 14 Oct., 82, aged 19 (from Sherborne school), B.A. 85, M.A. 89.

Bastard, William Edmund Pollexfen, born at Yealmpton, Devon, 1864; o.s. William, cler. ST. JOHN'S, matric. 21 April, 84, aged 19, B.A. 88.

Batcholor, Beetham Arthur Leeman, born at Worcester Park, Surrey, 5 Dec., 1871; 1s. George Beetham, arm. TRINITY, matric. 11 Oct., 90, aged 18, from Wellington coll.

Bate, Herbert Newell, born at Brixton, Surrey, 31 May, 1871; 5s. George Osborn, cler. TRINITY, matric. 12 Oct., 89, aged 18 (from St. Paul's school), scholar 88; HONOURS:—1 classical mods. 91.

Bate, Launcelot Brabant, born at Wembdon, Somerset, 1873; o.s. Charles Robert, gen. EXETER, matric. 25 Jan., 90, aged 17, from Tiverton school.

Bate, Robert Shelton, born at Bridgwater, Somerset, 30 Sept., 1862; 4s. Robert, conveyancer. EXETER, matric. 4 June, 81, aged 18 (from Bristol gr. school), scholar 81-4; HONOURS:—2 classical mods. 83.

Bateman, Edward Sacheverell, born at Kew, Surrey, 1 Dec., 1870; 1s. Alfred Edmund, of the board of trade, C.M.G. UNIVERSITY COLL., matric. 12 Oct., 89, aged 18 (from St. Peter's coll., Radley); HONOURS:—3 classical mods. 91.

Bateman, John, born in London 1831; 2s. John, of Islington, gent. NON-COLLEGIATE, matric. 23 Oct., 80, aged 49.

Bateman, Robert Bowness, born at Penrith, Cumberland, 1846; elder son of Thomas, pleb. NEW COLL., matric. 30 Jan., 82, aged 36, B.Mus. 87.

Bateman, Rowland Lloyd Jones, M.A., fellow NEW COLL. 1846-59, where see.

Bates, Ernest, born at Blaxhall, Suffolk, 18 Nov., 1858; 1s. Alfred, cler. WORCESTER, matric. 17 Oct., 87, aged 18 (from Ipswich gr. school), B.A. 91.

Bates, Guy Lockington, born at Iden, Sussex, 26 Aug., 1856; 2s. John Lockington, cler. EXETER, matric. 17 Oct., 88, aged 22.

Bates, rev. Henry James, born at Bredwardine, co. Hereford, 1862; 3s. George. BRASENOSE, matric. 22 Oct., 80, aged 18 (from Hereford school), scholar 80-4; migrated to MAGDALEN, B.A. 85; curate of St. Paul, Burton-on-Trent, 89.

Bates, John Higgs, born at Leicester, 25 April, 1871; 1s. John Oscar, arm. deceased. NEW COLL., matric. 10 Oct., 90, aged 19 (from Finchleycoll.); HONOURS:—2 classical mods. 92.

Bates, rev. Raymond Cooper, born at Birmingham, Oct., 1863; 4s. John, gent. KEBLE, matric. 16 Oct., 83, aged 20 (from Magdalen coll. school, and chorister 74-7), scholar 83, B.A. 87, M.A. 90 (HONOURS:—2 classical mods. 85, 3 classics 87); curate of St. Paul, Worcester, 91.

Bateson, Alexander Dingwall, born at Allerton, near Liverpool, 30 April, 1866; 6s. William Gandy, arm. TRINITY, matric. 17 Oct., 85, aged 19 (from Rugby), B.A. 88 (HONOURS:—3 classical mods. 87); bar.-at-law, Inner Temple, 91.

Bateson, rev. James Swinburne, born at Somersal, co. Lancaster, 20 July, 1860; o.s. Richard, arm. QUEEN'S, matric. 24 Jan., 80, aged 19 (from Manchester gr. school), B.A. 83, M.A. 86 (HONOURS:—3 classical mods. 81, 4 classics 83); rector of St. Mark, Cheetham Hill, Manchester, 91, co-editor " Manchester Diocesan Directory," etc.

Bath, Samuel, born in London 1863; 1s. Samuel, gent. NEW COLL., matric. 25 Jan., 88, aged 25.

Bathe, Arthur Allan, born at Coventry, co. Warwick, 1868; 1s. Stephen Brown, cler. CHRIST CHURCH, matric. 14 Oct., 87, aged 17 (from Shrewsbury school), B.A. 91; HONOURS:—2 chemistry 91.

Bather, Francis Arthur, born at Richmond, Surrey, 17 Feb., 1864; 1s. Arthur Henry, of the admiralty. NEW COLL., matric. 14 Oct., 82, aged 19 (from Winchester), scholar 81, B.A. 86, M.A. 90; HONOURS:—1 morphology 86, Rolleston memorial prize 92.

Bathurst, Algernon, M.A., B.C.L., fellow NEW COLL. 39-61, where see.

Bathurst, Arthur Henry, born in London 29 Aug., 1872; 2s. Charles, bar.-at-law. NEW COLL., matric. 22 Oct., 90, aged 18 (from Sherborne school), passed into Sandhurst 93.

Bathurst, Charles, born in London 25 Sept., 1867; 1s. Charles, bar.-at-law. UNIVERSITY COLL., matric. 18 Oct., 86, aged 19 (from Sherborne school), B.A. 90 (HONOURS:—3 classical mods. 88, 3 law 90); bar.-at-law, Inner Temple, 92.

Bathurst, hon. Lancelot Julian, born 24 Jan., 1868; 2s. Allen Alexander, earl Bathurst. NEW COLL., matric. 15 Oct., 86, aged 18 (from Eton) (HONOURS: 3 classical mods. 88, 4 law 90); master of Exmoor foxhounds.

Bathurst, Lawrence Charles Villebois, born at Gressenhall, Norfolk, 4 June, 1871; 4s. Henry, arm. TRINITY, matric. 17 Dec., 90, aged 19, from Radley coll.

Bathurst, Robert Andrew, M.A., fellow NEW COLL. 35-52, where see.

Bathurst, Seymour Henry, lord Apsley, born 21 July, 1864; 1s. Allen Alexander, earl Bathurst. CHRIST CHURCH, matric. 25 May, 83, aged 18 (from Eton); 7th earl Bathurst.

Bathurst, Stuart Eyre, M.A., fellow MERTON 39-45, where see.

Bathurst, Stuart Leslie, born in London Feb. 1862; 1s. Algernon, bar.-at-law. QUEEN'S, matric. 15 May, 80, aged 18 (from Bradfield coll.), B.A. 85 (HONOURS:—2 classical mods. 82, 2 classics 84); bar.-at-law, Lincoln's Inn, 88.

Batson, Vincent Lascelles, born at Ramsbury, Wilts, 1861; 7s. Alfred, gent. NON-COLLEGIATE, matric. 15 Oct., 81, aged 20, B.A. 86, M.A. 89.

Batten, Henry George Summers, born at Ilminster, Somerset, 1871; 1s. Henry, gen. NON-COLLEGIATE, matric. 14 Jan., 88, aged 17, B.A. 91.

Batton, John Kaye, born at Almora, E. Indies, 26 Aug., 1865; 5s. John Hallet, arm. ORIEL, matric. 23 Oct., 84, aged 19 (from Haileybury); Indian c.s. 84; special assistant and magistrate at Malupuram, Madras, 90.

Battersby, Herbert Dillon, born in London 14 Jan., 1872; 2s. John Prevost, major-general, retired. ST. JOHN'S, matric. 17 Oct., 91, aged 19, from an Ealing school.

Battersby, rev. William John, born at Lancaster 1867; 1s. William, gent. ST. JOHN'S, matric. 17 Oct., 85, aged 18 (from Manchester gr. school), B.A. 88, M.A. 93 (HONOURS:—3 theology 88); curate of St. Clement, Salford, 90.

Batty, rev. Arthur Montague, born at Fulham 1868-1 3s. William Edmund, cler. ORIEL, matric. 14 Dec., 87, aged 19, B.A. 90; HONOURS :—3 history 90.

Batty, Edward Joseph, born at Paddington 1867; 2s. Caleb, gen. NON-COLLEGIATE, matric. 3 Nov., 88, aged 21, from Christ's hospital.

Battye, Aubyn Bernard Rochfort, born at Havers, Kent, 1866; 2s. William Wilberforce, cler. NON-COLLEGIATE, matric. 28 Jan., 82, aged 16; migrated to CHRIST CHURCH, B.A. 89.

Baty, Thomas, born at Carlisle 8 Feb., 1869; o.s. William Thomas, gen. QUEEN'S, matric. 20 Oct., 88, aged 19 (from Carlisle gr. school), exhibitioner 88, B.A. 92; HONOURS :—3 mathematical mods. 90, 2 law 92.

Baughan, John Edward, born at Putney, Surrey, 6 May, 1866; o.s. John, gent. WADHAM, matric. 17 Oct., 85, aged 19 (from Brighton coll.), B.A. 89.

Baumgarten, rev. Charles Ord, born at Calcutta 21 July, 1862; 1s. Edward Picton, captain. MERTON, matric. 18 Oct., 80, aged 18 (from Merchant Taylors' school), B.A. 84, M.A. 87 (HONOURS :—3 history 84); migrated to TRINITY 88; Trinity coll. missioner at Stratford 88-91, and of S. Mary, Johannesburg, Transvaal, 91.

Baverstock, Albany Henry, born at Stratford, Essex, 1871; 1s. Edwin Henry, gen. KEBLE, matric. 11 Oct., 90, aged 19 (from Merchant Taylors' school), scholar 89; HONOURS :—2 classical mods. 92.

Bawden, Henry Bertram, born at Truro 6 Aug., 1872; 2s. John Henry, gen. JESUS COLL., matric. 20 Oct., 91, aged 19, from Newton Abbott coll.

Bax, Arthur Nesham, born at Hamble, Hants, 21 March, 1871; 1s. Bonham Ward, late captain R.N. deceased. BALLIOL, matric. 17 Oct., 89, aged 18 (from Kelly coll., Tavistock), exhibitioner 88, B.A. 92; HONOURS :—2 history 92.

Baxter, Arthur William, born at Manchester 1 Jan., 1865; 1s. David, gent. LINCOLN, matric. 19 Oct., 83, aged 18 (from Owens coll., Manchester), scholar 83, B.A. 87, M.A. 91; HONOURS :—2 classical mods. 85, 1 classics 87,

Baxter, Dudley, born at Atherstone, co. Warwick, 1872; 2s. Dudley, lawyer. UNIVERSITY COLL., matric. 17 Oct., 91, aged 19.

Baxter, Henry, born at Sutton, co. Lanc., 1864; 2s. Henry, arm. UNIVERSITY COLL., matric. 18 Jan., 82, aged 18 (from Eton), B.A. 85, M.A. 88 ; HONOURS :—2 history 85.

Baxter, rev. John Thomas Chatterton, born at Cupar Angus 23 Nov., 1859; o.s. James Howard, gent. ST. MARY HALL, matric. 13 April, 80, aged 20 (from Dundee high school and Aberdeen university); migrated to NEW INN HALL, B.A. 83, M.A. 87; HONOURS:— 4 theology 87.

Baxter, rev. William, born at Wigonby, Cumberland, 14 Aug., 1867; o.s. William, gen. QUEEN'S, matric. 25 Oct., 86, aged 20 (from Carlisle gr. school), exhibitioner 86, B.A. 90; HONOURS :—2 classical mods. 88, 2 classics 90, 2 history 91.

Bayley, Arthur, born at Brixton, Surrey, 27 April, 1868; o.s. William Rutter, cler. PEMBROKE, matric. 28 Oct., 86, aged 18 (from Harrow), B.A. 90; HONOURS :—3 history 90.

Bayley, Frank, born at Lambeth, Surrey, 6 Feb., 1871; 2s. Edward Hodson, manufacturer. EXETER, matric. 13 Feb., 92, aged 21, from Uppingham and King's coll. school, Lond.

Bayley, Thomas Henry, born at Wrexham, co. Denbigh, 1862; 1s. Thomas, gent. UNIVERSITY COLL., matric. 15 Oct., 81, aged 19, exhibitioner 83-5, B.A. 85, M.A. 88; HONOURS :—3 classical mods. 83, 4 classics 85.

Baylis, Moseley Serjeant, born at Worcester 16 Sept., 1869; 1s. Charles William, gen. LINCOLN, matric. 4 Nov., 90, aged 21, from Worcester cathedral school.

Bayliss, William Maddock, born at Wednesbury, co. Stafford, 2 May, 1860; o.s. Moses, gent. WADHAM, matric. 19 Oct., 85, aged 25 (from University coll., London), B.A. 88; Oxford HONOURS :—1 physiology 88; London HONOURS :—1 zoology 81.

Bayly, John, born at Plymouth 28 May, 1869; 1s. Robert, arm. BRASENOSE, matric. 16 Oct., 88, aged 19 (from Haileybury), B.A. 91.

Bayne, rev. Percy Matheson, born at South Weald, Essex, 1865; 4s. George Smith, cler. HERTFORD, matric. 14 Oct., 84, aged 19 (from Highgate school), scholar 83, B.A. 88, M.A. 91 (HONOURS :—1 classical mods. 86, 3 classics 88); curate of Holy Trinity, Barking Road, 90.

Bayne, rev. Thomas Vere, M.A., student CHRIST CHURCH 49, where see.

Baynes, Robert Edward, M.A., senior student CHRIST CHURCH 73, where see.

Bazely, Thomas Tyssen, M.A., fellow BRASENOSE 31-40, where see.

Bazley, Gardner Sebastian, born at Rostherne, Cheshire, 14 Oct., 1863; 1s. Thomas Sebastian, arm. (after bart.) MAGDALEN, matric. 16 Oct., 82, aged 19 (from Eton), B.A. 86, M.A. 89 (HONOURS :—3 classical mods. 84, 2 law 86); bar.-at-law, Inner Temple, 88.

Beach, John Newton, born at Liverpool 1864; 1s. John Newton, gent. CORPUS CHRISTI, matric. 19 Oct., 82, aged 18 (from University coll. school, London), B.A. 86, M.A. 89; HONOURS :—2 classical mods. 83.

Beak, George Bailey, born at Stanmore, Berks, 14 Sept., 1872; 1s. Worthy, gent., deceased. QUEEN'S, matric. 28 April, 92, aged 19, from Salisbury school.

Beale, Stanley Leonard, born at Waltham St. Lawrence, Berks, 19 Jan., 1872; 3s. William Lansdowne, gent. MERTON, matric. 22 Jan., 91, aged 19, from Rugby.

Beale, Walter Herbert, born at Tenterden, Kent, 13 Oct., 1872; 3s. Seaman Curtis Fross, M.A., Oxon, vicar of S. Michael, Tenterden. WADHAM, matric. 26 Oct., 92, aged 20, from

Besley, Frank Alfred John, born at Middlesborough 1867; 1s. John Kay, cler. EXETER, matric. 14 Dec., 92, aged 25, from

Beall, rev. William Alfred Baker, born at Brockley, Kent, 1866; 2s. John, gent. ST. EDMUND HALL, matric. 26 April, 88, aged 22, B.A. 91 (HONOURS :—3 history 91); curate of St. Mark, Kennington, 91.

Beatty, Octavius Holmes, born at Marantiam, Brazil, 1863; y.s. Pakenham, gent. EXETER, matric. 25 Jan., 82, aged 16, B.A. 84, M.A. 88; bar.-at-law, Middle Temple, 86; LL.B. Trinity coll., Dublin.

Beaufort, Claude St. Lawrence Paul, born at Kilroan, co. Cork, 3 Aug., 1863; 1s. William Augustus, cler. MERTON, matric. 25 Jan., 84, aged 20 (from Malvern coll.), B.A. 87, M.A. 90.

Beaufort, Louis Walter William, born at Kilroan, co. Cork, 23 April, 1867; 2s. William Augustus, cler. WORCESTER, matric. 19 Oct., 86, aged 19, from Rossall school.

Beaumont, Arthur Merton, born in London 1861; 1s. Joseph, arm. ST. JOHN'S, matric. 16 Oct., 80, aged 19, B.A. 84.

Beaumont, Francis Henry, born at Hove, near Brighton, May, 1868; 3s. Henry, D.D. CHRIST CHURCH, matric. 3 June, 87, aged 19.

Beaumont, Francis Morton, M.A., fellow ST. JOHN'S 56-69, where see.

Beaumont, Harry, born at Thurnacoe, Yorks, 26 May, 1865; 1s. Alfred, gent. QUEEN'S, matric. 25 Oct., 86, aged 21, from K. Ravensworth and Richmond gr. schools.

Beaumont, Henry Hamond Dawson, born at Chelmondiston, Suffolk, 1867; 3s. Thomas George, cler. BALLIOL, matric. 19 Oct., 86, aged 19 (from Winchester), B.A. 90; HONOURS :—3 history 89.

Beaumont, Hubert George, born in London 2 March, 1864; 2s. Wentworth Blackett, arm. BALLIOL, matric. 16 Jan., 83, aged 18 (from Eton and Cheltenham coll.), B.A. 85; HONOURS :—4 history 86.

Beaumont, William Beresford, M.A., student CHRIST CHURCH, where see.

Beavan, Samuel Sydney, born at Dartmouth, Devon, 5 Jan., 1864; 1s. John Griffiths, arm. ST. MARY HALL, matric. 1 Feb., 82, aged 18.

Beavis, Charles Edward Hartnell, born at Crosby, co. Lanc., 1873; 1s. Samuel Tanner, captain Cunard Line. KEBLE, matric. 15 Oct., 92, aged 19 (from Christ's hospital), exhibitioner 92.

Beazley, Michael Wornum, born at Portland, Dorset, 7 Feb., 1866; o.s. Alexander, architect, C.E. LINCOLN, matric. 14 Oct., 85, aged 18 (from Malvern coll.), B.A. 89, M.A. 91.

Beazley, Charles Raymond, born at Lewisham, Kent, 1868; o.s. Joseph, gent. BALLIOL, matric. 19 Oct., 86, aged 18 (from St. Paul's school and King's coll., London), scholar 85; fellow Merton 89, B.A. 90; HONOURS :—1 history 89, Lothian essay prize 89.

Beazor, John Augustus Thomas Lovell, born at Minster Lovell, Oxon, 22 Dec., 1869; 1s. John Augustus, cler. WORCESTER, matric. 14 Oct., 90, aged 20, from Weymouth coll.

Bebb, Thomas William, born at Kington, co. Hereford, 16 June, 1870; 4s. William, vicar of Kennington, Berks. MAGDALEN, matric. 14 Oct., 89, aged 19 (from Christ's hospital), demy 88 (HONOURS :—1 classical mods. 91); died 13 Oct., 92.

Bebb, rev. Llewellyn John Montford, born at St. John's, Cape Town, 16 Feb., 1862; 1s. William, vicar of St. John's, Cape Town. NEW COLL., matric. 15 Oct., 81, aged 19 (from Winchester), scholar 81-5, B.A. 85; fellow BRASENOSE 85, M.A. 88, tutor 89, librarian 92, and pro-proctor 92 (HONOURS :—3 mathematical mods. 82, 1 classical mods. 83, 1 classics 85, Greek testament prize 84 and 88, Denyer and Johnson theological scholarship 87, Ellerton theological essay 88), lecturer at Kirtlington, Oxon, 87.

Beckford, Edward Hastings, born in Toronto, Canada, 1870; 1s. Edward Oscar, gen. LINCOLN, matric. 26 April, 88, aged 18.

Beckton, Arthur Curtis, born at Eccles, co. Lanc., 30 July, 1864; 1s. Joseph, gent., deceased. NEW COLL., matric. 4 Oct., 83, aged 18 (from St. Paul's coll., Stony Stratford), B.A. 86, M.A. 90; HONOURS :—3 classical mods. 84, 3 classics 86.

Beckwith, Edward George Ambrose, born at Winchester 29 May, 1869; 1s. George, cler., deceased. MAGDALEN, matric. 16 Oct., 88, aged 19 (from Winchester coll.), exhibitioner 88; HONOURS :—2 classical mods. 90, 3 classics 92.

Beckwith, Ernest George, born at Blymhill, co. Staff., 12 Jan., 1861 or 63; 3s. George Langton, vicar of Collingham, Yorks. NEW COLL., matric. 9 Dec., 81, aged 18 (from Bradfield coll.), B.A. 86, M.A. 89.

Beckwith, rev. Herbert Birley, born at Shifnal, co. Stafford, 12 Oct., 1864; 4s. George Langton, vicar of Collingham, Yorks. NEW COLL., matric. 12 Oct., 83, aged 19 (from Bradfield coll.), scholar 83, B.A. 87, M.A. 90 (HONOURS :—1 mathematical mods. 85, 2 mathematics 87); curate of Collingham, Yorks, nl.

Beckwith, John, born at Surbiton, Surrey, 29 May, 1861 ; y.s. Edward Lonsdale, C.E. NEW COLL., matric. 16 Oct., 80, aged 19 (from Wellington coll.), B.A. 84; HONOURS :—4 law 83.

Beckwith, Sidney, born at Chelsea, Middlesex, 1867; 1s. Thomas Percival, arm. CORPUS CHRISTI, matric. 26 Oct., 85, aged 18 (from Eton), B.A. 91.

Bedale, rev. Frederick, born at Clapham, Surrey, 4 June, 1852 ; 3s. Edward, gen. WORCESTER, matric. 16 Oct., 88, aged 36, B.A. 91 (HONOURS :—3 theology); curate of Christ Church, Luton, 91.

Beddington, Charles Lindsay, born in London 1867; 2s. Samuel Henry, gent PEMBROKE, matric. 27 Oct., 84, aged 17; bar.-at-law, Inner Temple, 89.

Beddington, George Stuart, born in London 1865 ; 1s. Samuel Henry, gent. PEMBROKE, matric. 27 Oct., 84, aged 19.

Bedford, rev. Albert Edward Riland, born at Portobello, Scotland, 27 Dec., 1864 ; 4s. William Kirkpatrick, cler. BRASENOSE, matric. 22 Oct., 84, aged 19 (from Westminster school), B.A. 86, M.A. 90 ; curate of St. Nicholas, Warwick, 90.

Bedford, rev. Arthur William, born at Cheltenham 28 Sept., 1863; 1s. William Fanshawe, general in the army. ORIEL, matric. 2 June, 82, aged 18 (from Haileybury), B.A. 85, M.A. 89 ; curate of Holy Trinity, Clapham, 88.

Bedford, Bernard Francis Riland, born in London 16 Jan., 1868 ; 6s. William Kirkpatrick, cler. BRASENOSE, matric. 20 Oct., 86, aged 18, from Leamington coll.

Bedford, Edward Gordon Guthrie, born at Armidale, N.S.W., 3 July, 1870 ; 1s. William James Guthrie, M.R.C.S. (BRASENOSE, matric. 22 Oct., 91, aged 21.

Bedford, James Perch, born at Langharne, co. Carmarthen, 1868 ; o.s. James, arm. BALLIOL, matric. 19 Oct., 87, aged 19 (from Clifton coll.) ; assistant to collector and magistrate, Tinnevelly, Madras civil service, 89.

Beebe, Arthur Henry Thompson, born at Stockwell, Surrey, 1864 ; 2s. Henry Thomas, cler. NON-COLLEGIATE, matric. 13 Oct., 84, aged 20 (from Magdalen coll. school), B.A. 90.

Beechey, William John, born at Devizes 2 March, 1862 ; o.s. William Henry Jones, gent. NON-COLLEGIATE, matric. 29 April, 81, aged 19; migrated to MERTON, M.A. 88.

Beeching, Frank Staverton, born at Brighton 16 May, 1871 ; o.s. Francis, arm. NEW COLL., matric. 10 Oct., 90, aged 19 (from Harrow) ; HONOURS :—3 classical mods. 92.

Beeching, Harold Antony, born at Tunbridge Wells 12 Oct., 1865 ; 1s. Thomas, banker, deceased. MAGDALEN, matric. 19 Oct., 83, aged 18 (from Ramsgate school), B.A. 86, M.A. 90 ; HONOURS : —4 history 86.

Beeching, Horace Arthur, born at Tonbridge, Kent, 10 Dec., 1864 ; 1s. Arthur Thomas, of Ferox Hall, arm. ORIEL, matric. 27 Oct., 83, aged 18 (from Haileybury), B.A. 86, M.A. 90.

Beeching, Walter Charles, born at Tonbridge, Kent, 12 April, 1866 ; 2s. Arthur Thomas, arm. TRINITY, matric. 11 Oct., 84, aged 18 (from Tonbridge school), B.A. 88.

Beedle, rev. Alfred John, born at Weston-super-Mare 11 Aug., 1867 ; 3s. Thomas, gen. ST. MARY HALL, matric. 24 Oct., 87, aged 20, B.A. 90 ; curate of Frenchay, co. Gloucester, 91.

Beerbohm, Henry Maximilian, born in London 24 Aug., 1872 ; 4s. Julius Ewald, arm. MERTON, matric. 15 Oct., 90, aged 18 (from the Charterhouse), HONOURS :—3 classical mods. 92.

Beeton, Mayson Moss, born at Greenhithe, Kent, 29 Jan., 1865 ; 4s. Samuel Orchard, publisher, deceased. MAGDALEN, matric. 19 Oct., 83, aged 18 (from Marlborough coll.), demy 83, B.A. 87 ; HONOURS : —2 classical mods. 85, 2 history 87.

Beggs, rev. John, born in Dublin 15 Aug., 1856 ; 1s. David, gen. WORCESTER, matriculated 12 May, 87, aged 30 (matric. NON-COLLEGIATE, Cambridge, 21 Oct., 84, and migrated to ST. JOHN'S, Cambridge, Easter, 85) ; curate of Ardwick, St. Thomas, co. Lanc., 86.

Behrens, George Benjamin, born at Manchester 1865; 3s. Edward, gent. CORPUS CHRISTI, matric. 19 Oct., 84, aged 18 (from Wellington coll.) ; HONOURS : —2 classical mods. 85.

Behrens, Oliver Philip, born at Manchester 21 Aug., 1863 ; 2s. Edward, arm. ORIEL, matric. 30 Jan., 82, aged 18 (from Rugby and Owens coll.), B.A. 85 ; HONOURS :—2 history 85.

Beibitz, rev. Joseph Hugh, born at Worcester 1868 ; o.s. Joseph, gen. HERTFORD, matric. 22 Oct., 86, aged 18 (from Worcester cathedral school), scholar 85, B.A. 91 ; HONOURS :—2 classical mods. 88, 1 theology 91, Denyer and Johnson theological scholarship 92.

Belcher, Herbert George, born at Farringdon or Little Amwell, Berks, 10 Aug., 1866 ; 5s. Charles, gent., deceased. EXETER, matric. 23 Oct., 85, aged 19 (from Bedford gr. school), scholar 84, B.A. 89, M.A. 92 ; HONOURS :—2 classical mods. 87, 2 classics 89.

Belcher, William Edward, born at Handsworth-juxta-Birmingham 1865 ; 2s. William Thomas, gen. QUEEN'S, matric. 29 Jan., 89, aged 24.

Beldam, James Ward, born at Royston, co. Cambridge, 1861 ; 3s. Edward, arm. BALLIOL, matric. 21 Oct., 80, aged 19 (from Eton), B.A. 86, M.A. 88 ; HONOURS :—3 classical mods. 82.

Beldam, Percival Edward, born at Royston, co. Cambridge, 27 Nov., 1862 ; 4s. Edward, bar.-at-law, deceased. MAGDALEN, matric. 13 Jan., 83, aged 20 (from Harrow), B.A. 86.

Belfield, Frederick, born at Paignton, Devon, 3 June, 1863; 4s. John, arm. NEW COLL., matric. 19 Oct., 82, aged 19 (from Clifton coll.), scholar 82-6, B.A. 87, M.A. 89 ; HONOURS :—1 classical mods. 84, 2 classics 86.

Belk, Oswald, born at Hartlepool, co. Durham, 1863 ; 10s. Thomas, gent. QUEEN'S, matric. 23 Oct., 82, aged 19, B.A. 85, M.A. 89.

Bell, Alexander Dunlop, born at "Friockheim," co. Forfar, 14 Nov., 1873 ; 1s. Benjamin, presbyterian minister. TRINITY, matric. 15 Oct., 92, aged 18, from Manchester gr. school.

Bell, Alexander James Montgomerie, M.A. BALLIOL, where see.

Bell, Archibald William, born at Leeds 24 June, 1870 ; 1s. William Pool, gen. WORCESTER, matric. 14 Oct., 90, aged 20, from Leeds gr. school.

Bell, Bertie Edward, born at Fonthill-Gifford, Wilts, 1867; 2s. Edward William, gent. ST. JOHN'S, matric. 17 Oct., 85, aged 18 (from Sherborne school), B.A. 88; HONOURS:—4 law 88.

Bell, Charles Alfred, born at Colchester 31 Oct., 1870; 3s. Henry, bar.-at-law. NEW COLL., matric. 11 Oct., 89, aged 18 (from Winchester); assistant magistrate and collector (24-Pergunnahs), Bengal C.S. 91.

Bell, Charles Cameron, born at Pudsey, Yorks, 2 June, 1871; o.s. Peter Macdonald, gen. QUEEN'S, matric. 24 Oct., 90, aged 19 (from Leeds gr. school), exhibitioner 90; HONOURS:—2 classical mods. 92.

Bell, rev. Charles Carlyle, born at Tichfield, Hants, Sept., 1868; 1s. William Warden, arm. KEBLE, matric. 17 Oct., 87, aged 19 (from Tonbridge school), B.A. 90 (HONOURS:—3 theology 90); curate of St. Pancras, London, 91.

Bell, Charles William, born at South Moor, co. Durham, 16 Sept., 1867; 3s. Thomas, arm. TRINITY, matric. 16 Oct., 86, aged 19 (from Durham gr. school), exhibitioner 86, B.A. 90; HONOURS:—2 classical mods. 88, 3 classics 90.

Bell, Edward, born at Reigate, Surrey, July, 1863; o.s. Edward, arm. HERTFORD, matric. 22 April, 84, aged 20.

Bell, Francis de Beauvoir, born at Guernsey 1867; 1s. William, colonel in the army. EXETER, matric. 21 Jan., 85, aged 18 (from Elizb. coll., Guernsey), B.A. 87.

Bell, rev. Frank Lendon, born at Randwick in Australia, 9 April, 1864; 3s. Henry, arm. MERTON, matric. 25 Jan., 82, aged 17 (from King's school, Parramatta, N.S.W.), B.A. 85, M.A. 89 (HONOURS: —1 law 85); bar.-at-law, Inner Temple, 89, curate of Wing, Oxon, 91.

Bell, Frederick, born at Preston, co. Lancaster, 27 Feb., 1862; 2s. William, D.Med. NEW COLL., matric. 24 Jan., 81, aged 18 (from Preston gr. school), B.A. 85; HONOURS:—3 mathematical mods. 82, 3 natural science 84.

Bell, George Arthur Campbell, born at Penrith, Cumberland, 15 July, 1868; 3s. William, principal of Penrith high school. ST. EDMUND HALL, matric. 22 Oct., 91, aged 23.

Bell, rev. George Charles, M.A., fellow WORCESTER 75-71, where see.

Bell, George Milner, born in London 23 May, 1872; o.s. George Charles, cler., head master of Marlborough coll. NEW COLL., matric. 16 Oct., 91, aged 19 (from Marlborough), scholar 91.

Bell, James Arthur William, born at Rochester 18 Nov., 1871; o.s. James Vincent, D.Med. CORPUS CHRISTI, matric. 16 Oct., 90, aged 18 (from Winchester), exhibitioner 90; HONOURS:—2 classical mods. 92.

Bell, James Frederick Spencer Spencer, born at Borovere, Hants, 3 May, 1863; 1s. James, of Fawe Park, Keswick, deceased. MAGDALEN, matric. 16 Oct., 82, aged 19, a student Lincoln's Inn 83; drowned in Derwentwater lake 9 Sept., 86.

Bell, James Robertson, born at Glasgow 25 May, 1861, o.s. James, arm. TRINITY, matric. 16 Oct., 80, aged 19 (from Westminster school), B.A. 84; student Inner Temple 81.

Bell, rev. Maurice Frederick, born in London 1862; 2s. George William, arm. HERTFORD, matric. 18 Oct., 80, aged 18 (from Eastbourne coll.); migrated to HERTFORD, B.A. 84, M.A. 87 (HONOURS:—3 theology 84); vicar of Appleton-le-Street, Yorks, 89.

Bell, Nicholas Dodd Beatson, born at Aberdeen 1867; 2s. Andrew Beatson, gent. BALLIOL, matric. 19 Oct., 86, aged 19 (from Edinburgh academy), B.A. 89 (HONOURS:—1 Indian languages 89, Boden Sanskrit scholarship 89); assistant magistrate and collector, Putna, Bengal C.S. 88.

Bell, Richard Graham, born at Everton, co. Lanc., 1865; 2s. Richard, gen. NON-COLLEGIATE, matric. 17 Jan., 91, aged 26.

Bell, Thomas Alfred, born at Thornley, co. Durham, 30 Dec., 1864; 2s. Thomas, arm. TRINITY, matric. 13 Oct., 88, aged 23 (from Durham gr. school), B.A. 92; HONOURS:—2 classical mods. 90, 2 history 92.

Bell, William Lawrence Leonard, born at Peterborough 1865; o.s. William Lawrence, gent. ST. JOHN'S, matric.' 16 Oct., 86, aged 21 (from Southampton school), Abbott scholar 86, B.A. 90; bar.-at-law, Inner Temple, (see 90); bar.-at-law, Inner Temple, (see 90).

Bellairs, Cecil Sebastian, born at Bombay, India, 25 May, 1871; 3s. Henry Spencer Kenrick, cler. NON-COLLEGIATE, matric. 15 Oct., 92, aged 21, from Hunstanton school.

Bellairs, Ralph Hamon, born at Belgraum, East Indies, 5 Sept., 1867; 2s. Henry Spencer Kenrick, cler. BALLIOL, matric. 16 Oct., 86, aged 19 (from Westminster school), Abbott scholar 86, B.A. 90; HONOURS:—2 classical mods. 88, 3 classics 90.

Bellamy, Arthur Theodore, born at Clenchwarton, Norfolk, 22 April, 1870; 1s. Arthur, cler. ST. MARY HALL, matric. 21 Jan., 89, aged 18 (from Marlborough), B.A. 92.

Bellamy, James, D.D., president ST. JOHN'S 71, where see.

Bellamy, William Montagu, born at Hereford, June, 1871; 2s. Arthur, cler. KEBLE, matric. 17 Dec., 88, aged 17 (from Marlborough), B.A. 92.

Bellewes, George Oliver, born at Blackheath, Kent, 22 April, 1862; 1s. George, cler. BRASENOSE, matric. 22 Oct., 80, aged 18 (from King's coll., London), scholar 80-5, B.A. 84, M.A. 87 (HONOURS: —2 classical mods. 82, 3 classics 84); librarian of the Oxford union society 84, president 85; bar.-at-law, Middle Temple, 86.

Bellhouse, Walter, born at Altrincham, Cheshire, 11 Jan., 1867; 1s. Ernest, gent. MAGDALEN, matric. 23 Oct., 85, aged 18 (from Uppingham school), B.A. 89.

Bellot, Hugh Hale Leigh, born at Leamington, co. Warwick, 19 Oct., 1861; o.s. William Henry, D.Med. TRINITY, matric. 21 Oct., 80, aged 18 (from Leamington coll.), B.A., B.A., M.A. and B.C.L. 91 (HONOURS:—2 history 84); bar.-at-law, Inner Temple, 90.

Benbow, rev. Mountford, born at Anerley, Surrey, 21 Aug., 1868; 1 son. George. LINCOLN, matric. 18 Oct., 88, aged 20 (from Appuldurcombe school, I.W.), B.A. 92 (HONOURS:—4 theology 91); curate of Bexley, Kent, 91.

Benbow, William Leonard, born at Uxbridge, Middx., 11 July, 1863; 4s. John, merchant. CHRIST CHURCH, matric. 15 Oct., 82, aged 19 (from Westminster school), scholar 82, B.A. 86; HONOURS:— 1 classical mods. 84, 2 classics 86.

Benecke, Edward Felix Mendelssohn, born at Roehampton, Surrey, 26 March, 1870; 2s. Charles Victor, arm. BALLIOL, matric. 16 Oct., 88, aged 18 (from Haileybury), exhibitioner 87, B.A. 92; HONOURS: —1 classical mods. 89, 2 Semitic languages 92.

Benecke, Paul Victor Mendelssohn, born at Roehampton, Surrey, 7 June, 1868; 1s. Charles Victor, arm. MAGDALEN, matric. 16 Oct., 86, aged 18 (from Haileybury), demy 86, B.A. 90, fellow 91; HONOURS:—1 classical mods. 88, 1 classics 90, 1 theology 91, Greek testament prize 90, 92, Denyer and Johnson theological scholarship 91.

Bengough, Ernest Henry, born at Wotton-under-Edge, co. Glouc., 29 Nov., 1866; 4s. John Charles, arm. ORIEL, matric. 5 Feb., 86, aged 19 from Rugby, died.

Benham, Charles Daniel, born in London 7 Sept., 1870; 3s. Henry, gen. NEW COLL., matric. 11 Oct., 89, aged 19 (from Rugby), B.A. 92 (HONOURS: —2 history 92); bar.-at-law, Inner Temple, 93.

Von Benkendorff-Hindenburg, Herbert Alexander, born in Berlin 1 April, 1872; 1s. general Conrad von B.-H. BALLIOL, matric. 9 June, 92, aged 20, from collège Royal Français, Berlin.

Bennett, Ambrose, born at Margate 8 July, 1864; 3s. Henry, cler., deceased. NON-COLLEGIATE, matric. 17 Oct., 91, aged 27, from city of London school.

Bennett, rev. Charles William, born at Pershore, co. Worcester, 14 May, 1865; 2s. Hugh, cler. WORCESTER, matric. 17 Oct., 84, aged 19 (from Stratford-on-Avon school), B.A. 87 (HONOURS:—4 history 87); curate of Harpenden, Herts, 90.

Bennett, Edward Pitt, born at Solihull, co. Warwick, 16 Dec., 1869; 3s. James Hatchard, cler. EXETER, matric. 17 Oct., 88, aged 20 (from Honiton school and Heidelberg), B.A. 92.

Bennett, Ernest Nathaniel, born at Colombo, Ceylon, 12 Dec., 1865; o.s. George, rector of Redo, Suffolk. WADHAM, matric. 19 Oct., 85, aged 19 (from Durham cathedral school); scholar HERTFORD 85, B.A. 90, fellow 91, M.A. 92; HONOURS:—1 classical mods. 87, 1 classics 89, 1 theology 90, Greek testament prize 91.

Bennett, Ernest William, born at South Cadbury, Somerset, 29 March, 1866; 1s. James Arthur, rector. NEW COLL., matric. 10 Oct., 84, aged 18 (from Winchester), B.A. 88; HONOURS:—3 law 88.

Bennett, Francis F., of St. David's coll., Lampeter; HONOURS:—3 mathematical mods. 92.

Bennett, rev. Frank Selwyn Macaulay, born at Torquay, Devon, 28 Oct., 1866; 2s. Henry Edward, arm. KEBLE, matric. 22 Oct., 85, aged 18 (from Sherborne school), scholar 85, B.A. 89; HONOURS:—2 classics 89.

Bennett, Geoffrey Thomas, born at Solihull, co. Warwick, 1864; 2s. James Hatchard, cler. UNIVERSITY COLL., matric. 11 Oct., 84, aged 20 (from Sherborne school), B.A. 87; HONOURS:—4 history 87.

Bennett, George, M.A., fellow NEW COLL. 51-88, where see.

Bennett, George Edward Macaulay, born at Sparkford, Bath, Somerset, 3 July, 1873; 3s. Henry Edward, B.A. LINCOLN, matric. 26 Oct., 92, aged 19, from Clifton coll.

Bennett, Hugh Frederick, born at Elmley Castle, co. Worc., Nov., 1862; 1s. Hugh, cler. NON-COLLEGIATE, matric. 11 Feb., 82, aged 19 (from Bradfield coll.); migrated to WORCESTER, B.A. 84; HONOURS:—3 classical mods. 83.

Bennett, Lawrence Henry, born at Bedminster 27 Nov., 1861; 3s. Henry, gent. TRINITY, matric. 16 Oct., 80, aged 18 (from Clifton coll.), B.A. 84, M.A. and B.Med. 90 (HONOURS:—4 natural science 84); I.R.C.P. and M.R.C.S. 89.

Bennett, Reginald Arthur Renaud, born at Kemerton, co. Glouc., 1866; 2s. Frederick Hamilton, cler., deceased. MAGDALEN, matric. 26 Jan., 86, aged 19, B.A. 88, M.A. 92.

Bennett, Richard Alexander, born at Bournemouth, Hants, Dec., 1872; 1s. Alexander Sykes, cler. CHRIST CHURCH, matric. 29 May, 91, aged 18, from Eton.

Bennetts, Henry Johnson Treloar, born at Helston, Cornwall, 23 April, 1868; o.s. Henry Jenkin, gen.

Non-Collegiate, matric. 15 Oct., 87, aged 19 (from Truro gr. school); migrated to EXETER, B.A. 91; HONOURS:—3 classical mods. 89.

Benoy, rev. John, born at Kidwelly, co. Carmarthen, 6 June, 1865; 2s. James, gent. JESUS COLL., matric. 16 Oct., 84, aged 19 (from Birmingham school), B.A. 88 (HONOURS:—2 mathematical mods. 86, 3 mathematics 88); Incumbent of St. John, Harrisville, Queensland, 91.

Benskin, Frederick George, born at Princes Risborough, Bucks, 1872; 1s. Frederick John, baptist minister. CHRIST CHURCH, matric. 16 Oct., 91, aged 19 (from Huddersfield school), scholar 90.

Benson, Edward White, archbishop of Canterbury 1883, created D.C.L. 24 April, 1884 (s. Edward White Benson, of York and Birmingham Heath), born 14 July, 1829; scholar TRINITY COLL., Camb., 50 (from K. Ed. gr. school, Birmingham), B.A. 52, fellow 53-9, M.A. 55, B.D. 62, D.D. 67 (HONOURS: —Latin essay 51, 14th senior optime and 8th classics 52, 1st chancellor's medal 52); admitted *ad eundem* 4 June, 56, and select preacher Oxford 75; 1st bishop of Truro 77-83. See *Al. Ox.* 96.

Benson, Florance John, born in London 1865; 5s. Henry Roxby, arm. CHRIST CHURCH, matric. 25 May, 83, aged 18.

Benson, George Frederick, born at Montreal 1865; 1s. William Thomas, arm. UNIVERSITY COLL., matric. 13 Oct., 83, aged 18.

Benson, Godfrey Rathbone, born at Alresford, Hants, 6 Nov., 1864; 4s. William, arm. BALLIOL, matric. 16 Oct., 83, aged 18 (from Winchester), exhibitioner 83, B.A. 88, M.A. 90 (HONOURS:—2 classical mods. 84, 1 classics 87); M.P. Mid. Oxon, 92.

Benson, Ralph Beaumont, born in London 10 March, 1862; 1s. Ralph Augustus, arm. BALLIOL, matric. 21 Oct., 80, aged 18 (from Harrow), scholar 80 (HONOURS:—2 classical mods. 81); student Inner Temple, 82.

Benson, Ralph Herbert, born at Gonuckpore, E. Indies, 11 Sept., 1870; 3s. William Ralph, of London, late B.C.S. UNIVERSITY COLL., matric. 14 Oct., 89, aged 19.

Benson, Richard Cuming, born at Clifton, co. Glouc., 1860; 1s. Richard Matthew, arm. MERTON, matric. 26 May, 80, aged 20, B.A. 83, M.A. and B.C.L. 86 (HONOURS:—1 law 83); bar.-at-law, Lincoln's Inn, 85; died 22 April, 89.

Benson, Richard Meux, M.A., student CHRIST CHURCH 46, where see.

Benson, rev. Sawrey Brownlow, born at Pulverbatch, Salop, 1861; 3s. Richard Brownlow, arm. CHRIST CHURCH, matric. 4 June, 81, aged 20 (from Shrewsbury school), exhibitioner 82, scholar 85-6, B.A. 85, M.A. 88 (HONOURS:—2 classical mods. 83, 2 classics 85); curate of Holy Trinity, Oxford, 87-91, and of Aston, by Birmingham, 91.

Benson, Wilfrid, born at Ripon, Yorks, 15 July, 1870; o.s. George, gen. PEMBROKE, matric. 26 Oct., 89, aged 19 (from Ripon school); HONOURS:—2 classical mods. 91.

Bent, Godfrey Thomas, born at Thetford, Norfolk, 1869; 7s. Frederick Charles, cler. ORIEL, matric. 20 Oct., 88, aged 19 (from Lancing coll.), B.A. 92.

Bentinck, lord Henry Cavendish, born at Everaleigh, Hants, 28 May, 1863; 2s. Arthur Charles, general in the army. CHRIST CHURCH, matric. 14 Oct., 81, aged 18 (from Eton); M.P. Norfolk (North-West) July 86—July 92; heir-presumptive to the dukedom of Portland.

Bentinck, lord William Augustus Cavendish, born in London 31 Jan., 1865; 2s. Arthur Charles, general in the army. CHRIST CHURCH, matric. 25 May, 83, aged 18.

Bentley, Alfred Leonard, born in London 15 March, 1874; 1s. Alfred Wilson, major 3rd Middlesex rifle volunteers. WADHAM, matric. 26 Oct., 92, aged 18.

Bentley, Bertram Henry, born at Withington, co. Lanc., 1873; 1s. John Eugene, gent. KEBLE, matric. 15 Oct., 92, aged 19 (from Shrewsbury school), exhibitioner 92.

Bentley, rev. Frederick William, born at Swansea, co. Glamorgan, 30 Dec., 1861; 2s. Frederick, gent. WADHAM, matric. 17 Oct., 82, aged 20 (from King's college London), B.A. 85, M.A. 89 (HONOURS :—2 theology 85); curate of St. Stephen, Hammersmith, 85.

Berdmore, Samuel Charles James, M.A., student CHRIST CHURCH, 25-38, where see.

Bere, rev. Montague Acland, born at Tiverton, Devon, 19 Oct., 1866; 1s. Charles Sandford, cler. NON-COLLEGIATE, matric. 23 May, 85, aged 18 (from Marlborough coll.); migrated to LINCOLN, B.A. 88 (HONOURS :—4 history 88); curate Holy Trinity, Harrow Green, 90.

Berens, Edward, born at Kevington, St. Mary Cray, Kent, 24 Oct., 1873; 5s. Richard Benyon, M.A. CHRIST CHURCH, matric. 14 Oct., 92, aged 18, from Winchester coll.

Berens, rev. George, born at St. Mary Cray, Kent, 11 Jan., 1866; 2s. Richard Benyon, arm. CHRIST CHURCH, matric. 10 Oct., 84, aged 18 (from Westminster school), B.A. 88, M.A. 91; curate of St. Andrew, Bethnal Green, 89.

Berens, Richard, born at St. Mary Cray, Kent, 28 Jan., 1864; 1s. Richard Benyon, arm. CHRIST CHURCH, matric. 13 Oct., 82, aged 18 (from Westminster school), B.A. 87, M.A. 90; bar.-at-law, Inner Temple, 92.

Beresford, rev. Charles John, born at Birmingham 1868; 1s. John William Wellington, gen. NON-COLLEGIATE, matric. 15 Oct., 87, aged 19 (from Sutton Coldfield gr. school); migrated to ST. EDMUND HALL, B.A. 91 (HONOURS :—2 classical mods. 89, 2 theology 91); curate of St. Peter, Coventry, 91.

Beresford, Denis Robert Pack, born at Dublin 23 March, 1864; 1s. Denis, of Fenagh, co. Carlow, arm. CHRIST CHURCH, matric. 12 Oct., 83, aged 21 (from Rugby), B.A. 88; student Inner Temple 84.

Beresford, Robert Oswald de la Poer, born at Dalkey, co. Dublin, 15 Jan., 1866; 1s. Robert de la Poer, D.Med. WADHAM, matric. 11 Oct., 84, aged 18 (from Oswestry gr. school); HONOURS :—2 classical mods. 86, 3 history 88.

Beresford, rev. Walter Vevers de la Poer, born at Bedale, Yorks, 22 June, 1864; 5s. John George, cler. KEBLE, matric. 11 Dec., 83, aged 19 (from Canterbury gr. school), B.A. 87; curate of Staningley, Yorks, 91.

Beresford, hon. William Marcus de la Poer Horsley, born 12 Jan., 1865; 1s. William, baron de Decies. CHRIST CHURCH, matric. 16 Jan., 85, aged 20, from Eton.

Berkeley, George Fitz-Hardinge, born at Dublin 1870; o.s. George Sackville, arm. KEBLE, matric. 12 Oct., 89, aged 19 (from Wellington coll.), scholar 89; in Oxford eleven 90, 1, 2.

Berkley, Maurice, born at Navestock, Essex, 6 Sept., 1872; 1s. William, cler. HERTFORD, matric. 20 Oct., 91 (from Fettes coll.), scholar 90.

Berkley, William, M.A., fellow TRINITY 62-8, where see.

Bernard, Edward Russell, M.A., fellow MAGDALEN 66-78, where see.

Bernard, James Henry, born at Nagpur, E. Indies, 1863; 1s. Charles Edward, gent. BALLIOL, matric. 17 Oct., 82, aged 19 (from Clifton coll.), student Middle Temple 82; joint manager and deputy collector Shahabad, Bengal c.s. 84.

Bernard, John Henry, B.D., select preacher 93-4, where see page 5.

Bernays, rev. Steward Frederick Lewis, born at Stanmore, Middx., 3 Oct., 1866; 4s. Leopold John, gent. TRINITY, matric. 23 Oct., 85, aged 19 (from Durham school), B.A. 89 (HONOURS :—2 history 89); lecturer of Boston, co. Linc., 92.

Berridge, Douglas Jesse Penford, born at Leicester 13 Sept., 1869; 1s. Thomas, solicitor, deceased. WADHAM, matric. 14 Oct., 89, aged 20 (from Magdalen school), B.A. 92; HONOURS :—2 chemistry 92.

Berridge, rev. Frederick Henry, born in London 24 Feb., 1859; 1s. Frederick, gent. TRINITY, matric. 14 Oct., 82, aged 23 (from Marylebone school), B.A. 85 (HONOURS :—2 theology 85); curate of Broughton St. John, Manchester 87.

Berridge, Richard, born at Norwood, Surrey, 21 April, 1870; o.s. Richard, arm. QUEEN'S, matric. 20 Oct., 88, aged 18.

Berry, Albert James, born at Brasted, Kent, 11 Feb., 1868; 1s. James, schoolmaster. NON-COLLEGIATE, matric. 21 Oct., 91, aged 23 (from St. John's coll., Battersea); migrated to WADHAM 25 June, 92.

Berry, Arthur, born at Skeffling, Yorks, 1861; 3s. John, gent. ST. MARY HALL, matric. 23 Oct., 82, aged 21.

Berry, Charles Walter, born at Edinburgh 1865; 3s. Walter, gent. NON-COLLEGIATE, matric. 13 Oct., 83, aged 20 (from Loretto school); migrated to BRASENOSE 84.

Berry, George Godfrey, born at Huddersfield 1866; 1s. Edward, gent. BALLIOL, matric. 15 Oct., 84, aged 18 (from Clifton coll.), scholar 84, B.A. 90; HONOURS :—1 classical mods. 85, 1 mathematical mods. 86, 2 classics 88.

Berry, Henry Walter Birkhead, born at Pinner, Middx., 2 Oct., 1870; o.s. Henry Samuel, B.A., vicar of Norton Cuckney, Notts. NON-COLLEGIATE, matric. 27 April, 89, aged 18 (from Trent coll., Notts); HONOURS :—3 theology 92.

Berthod, Charles Henry, born at Hall End, Essex, 31 May, 1872; 2s. Alphonse Henry, foreign banker. NEW COLL., matric. 12 Dec., 91, aged 19, from Uppingham school.

Bertie, rev. the hon. Henry William, D.C.L., fellow ALL SOULS' 36, where see.

Bertram, Julius, born in London 8 Nov., 1866; 1s. Julius Alfred, solicitor. NEW COLL., matric. 16 Oct., 85, aged 18 (from Repton school), B.A. 89; HONOURS :—3 classical mods. 87, 2 history 89.

Besant, Herbert Albert, born at Chipperfield, Herts, 6 Jan., 1862; o.s. Charles, gent. NON-COLLEGIATE, matric. 21 Jan., 82, aged 20.

Best, rev. Edward Shiffner, born at Chute, Hants, 11 April, 1862; 2s. Thomas, arm. MAGDALEN, matric. 16 Oct., 82, aged 20 (from Bradfield coll.), B.A. 88, M.A. 90; curate of Lower Brixham, Devon, 90.

Best, Thomas Alexander Vans, born at Aberdeen 8 Oct., 1870; 2s. Alphonse Henry, D.Med. MAGDALEN, matric. 19 Jan., 91, aged 20, from Cheltenham coll.

Bethell, Wilfrid Philip, born at Kensington 25 Nov., 1870; o.s. Charles Ithell, gen. MERTON, matric. 19 Oct., 89, aged 18; passed into Sandhurst 91.

Bettany, Frederick George, born at Colchester 1868; 14. Jesse, gent. CHRIST CHURCH, matric. 15 Oct., 86, aged 18 (from Leeds gr. school), scholar 86, B.A. 90; senior demy MAGDALEN 90; HONOURS :—1 classical mods. 88, 1 classics 90, 1 history 91.

Bettany, William Arthur Lewis, born at Brighton 10 Sept., 1869; 2s. Jesse. QUEEN'S, matric. 20 Oct., 88, aged 19 (from Leeds gr. school), exhibitioner 88; HONOURS :—3 classical mods. 90.

Betterton, Henry Bucknall, born at Blackfordby, co. Leicester, 15 Aug., 1872; 1s. Henry Inman, gen. CHRIST CHURCH, matric. 6 June, 90, aged 17, from Rugby.

Bevan, Benjamin, born at Nevin, co. Carnarvon, 12 Jan., 1863; s. Evan, cler. ST. MARY HALL, matric. 23 Jan., 88, aged 25.

Bevan, rev. Edward Latham, born at Weymouth, Dorset, 1862; 3s. William Latham, cler. HERTFORD, matric. 1 Feb., 81, aged 19, B.A. 84, M.A. 89; chaplain Gordon boys' home, Chatham, 91.

Bevan, Edwyn Robert, born in London 15 Feb., 1870; 7s. Robert Cooper Lee, banker, deceased. NEW COLL., matric. 12 Oct., 88, aged 18 (from Monkton Combe school), scholar 88, B.A. 92; HONOURS:—1 classical mods. 90, 1 classics 92.

Bevan, Greville, born at Esher, Surrey, 29 June, 1867; 1s. Frederick Lincoln, gen. EXETER, matric. 21 Oct., 86, aged 19, from Wellington coll.

Bevan, Richard Hunter, born at Brighton 1862; 1s. Richard Alexander, arm. BRASENOSE, matric. 10 June, 81, aged 19, B.A. 85.

Beven, rev. Osmond James Clement, born at Colombo, isle of Ceylon, 1861; 8s. John, arm. NON-COLLEGIATE, matric. 18 Oct., 80, aged 19, B.A. 84, M.A. 88 (HONOURS:—3 classical mods. 82, 2 theology 84); curate of St. Paul, Pettah, Colombo, 85-89, and incumbent 89, also incumbent of St. Matthew 89.

Bevenot, Clovis Maurice Camille, born at Hainault, Belgium, 1862; 1s. Hippolyte, gen. BALLIOL, matric. 21 Oct., 80, aged 38 (from Cambrai school), Taylorian exhibitioner (Italian) 82; HONOURS:—3 classical mods. 82.

Beverley, Ernest Orme, born at Brighton July, 1870; 1s. Henry Weber, cler. KEBLE, matric. 12 Oct., 89, aged 19 (from Radley coll.); HONOURS:—3 classical mods. 91.

Bewley, Edward Dawson, born at Dublin 9 July, 1868; 1s. Edmund Thomas, bar.-at-law. NEW COLL., matric. 14 Oct., 87, aged 19 (from Winchester); scholar 87, B.A. 91; HONOURS:—1 mathematical mods. 88, proxime accessit junior mathematical exhibition 89, 2 mathematics 91.

Bickersteth, Montagu Cyril, M.A., NEW COLL., where see.

Bickham, George William, born at Bowdon, Cheshire, 7 July, 1870; 1s. Spencer Henry, gen. NEW COLL., matric. 11 Oct., 89, aged 19 (from Clifton coll.), B.A. 92; HONOURS:—3 classical mods. 91, 3 law 92.

Bickmore, Arthur Laurence, born at Kenilworth, co. Warwick, 1859; 2s. William Frederick, cler. WORCESTER, matric. 29 April, 81, aged 22 (from Leamington coll.), B.A. 85; HONOURS:—3 classical mods. 82.

Bickmore, Charles Edward, M.A., fellow NEW COLL. 72-86, where see.

Bickmore, Claude Egerton, born at Kenilworth, co. Warwick, 1868; 6s. William Frederick, cler. NON-COLLEGIATE, matric. 12 Oct., 89, aged 21, from Sherborne school.

Bickmore, Harry Christopher, born at Kenilworth, co. Warwick, 1863; 4s. William Frederick, cler. NON-COLLEGIATE, matric. 17 Oct., 85, aged 22 (from Rossall school), B.A. 90; HONOURS:—2 history 89.

Bicknell, Ethrayne Adsimar, born in London 3 Dec., 1873; 2s. Algernon Sidney, gent. TRINITY, matric. 17 Dec., 92, aged 19, from Eton.

Bicknell, Worman Leslie, born at Brighton Dec., 1868; 1s. Percy, gen. CHRIST CHURCH, matric. 1 June, 88 aged 19 (from Harrow), B.A. 91.

Bidder, Henry Jardine, B.D.; fellow ST. JOHN'S 71, where see.

Biddle, rev. Alexander Ross, born at Wimborne, Dorset, 1864; 2s. Waring Alexander, arm. UNIVERSITY COLL., matric. 13 Oct., 83, aged 19 (from Sherborne school), B.A. 87 (HONOURS:—4 history 86); curate of St. Luke, Maidenhead, 90.

Biddle, Waring Alfred Rolles, born at Lougham, Dorset, 1862; 1s. Waring Alexander, arm. UNIVERSITY COLL., matric. 14 Oct., 82, aged 20 (from Sherborne school), B.A. 87; HONOURS:—3 classical mods. 84, 3 history 86.

Biddulph, John Michael Gordon, born in London 9 Nov., 1869; 1s. Michael, arm. CHRIST CHURCH, matric. 12 Oct., 88, aged 18 (from Eton), B.A. 92.

Bidlake, rev. Walter, born at Wellington, Salop, 1866; 2s. John, solicitor. EXETER, matric. 31 May, 84, aged 18 (from the Leys sch., Cambridge), B.A. 87, M.A. 91 (HONOURS:—4 theology 87); curate of Coppenhall St. Paul, Cheshire, 90.

Bidwell, rev. Edward John, born at Stanton, Suffolk, 26 Nov., 1866; 4s. George Shelford, rector of Sympson, Bucks. WADHAM, matric. 19 Oct., 85, aged 18 (from Bradfield coll.); scholar 84, B.A. 89 (HONOURS:—2 classical mods. 87, 2 classics 89), assist. master Leamington coll. 90.

Bigg, Charles, D.D., senior student CHRIST CHURCH, 62-7, where see.

Bigg, Charles Sale, born at Cheltenham 30 Dec., 1867; 1s. Charles, D.D. WORCESTER, matric. 19 Oct., 86, aged 18 (from Cheltenham coll.), exhibitioner 86, B.A. 90; HONOURS:—2 classical mods. 88, 4 classics 90; brother of Lionel and William.

Bigg, Lionel Thursfield, born at Cheltenham 19 June, 1870; 3s. Charles, D.D. ORIEL, matric. 25 Oct., 89, aged 19 (from Cheltenham coll.), B.A. 92.

Bigg, William Edward, born at Cheltenham 15 May, 1869; 2s. Charles, D.D. ORIEL, matric. 18 Oct., 87, aged 18 (from Haileybury), B.A. 91.

Bigge, Denys Leighton Selby, born at Bourton, Salop, 11 Sept., 1864; 3s. Charles, arm. CHRIST CHURCH, matric. 27 May, 82, aged 17.

Bigge, Lewis Amherst Selby, M.A., fellow UNIVERSITY COLL. 83, where see.

Bigge, Philip Matthew, born at Wolverhampton 7 Feb., 1862; o.s. Matthew Robert, arm. NEW COLL., matric. 15 Oct., 81, aged 19 (from Winchester); HONOURS:—2 classical mods. 82.

Biggin, Thomas, born at Stamford, co. Lincoln, 26 July, 1871; o.s. Samuel, gen. CORPUS CHRISTI, matric. 16 Oct., 90, aged 19 (from Manchester gr. school); scholar 89; HONOURS:—1 mathematical mods. 91, proxime accessit junior mathematical exhibition 92.

Biggs, rev. Charles Richard Davey, born at Lichfield 1865; 4s. Sylvanus, gent. ST. JOHN'S, matric. 14 Oct., 82, aged 17 (from Derby school), scholar 82, B.A. 86, M.A. 89. Fereday fellow 91 (HONOURS:—2 classical mods. 84, 2 classics 86); vice-principal theological coll., Edinburgh, and chaplain of St. Mary cathedral, Edinburgh, 90.

Bilbrough, rev. Harold Ernest, born at Twickenham, Middx., 22 Feb., 1867; 2s. Arthur, gent. NEW COLL., matric. 15 Oct., 86, aged 19 (from Winchester), B.A. 89 (HONOURS:—3 theology 89); curate of St. Mary, S. Shields 90.

Biles, Robert MacBrair, born at Portsmouth 1865; 4s. John, gent. BALLIOL, matric. 16 Oct., 83, aged 18 (from Portsmouth gr. school), scholar 82, B.A. 86 (HONOURS:—1 mathematical mods. 84, 1 mathematics 86); died 24 Feb., 89, at Melbourne.

Bill, Arnold Francis, born at Coventry 8 Oct., 1865; 3s. John, arm. BRASENOSE, matric. 14 Oct., 84, aged 19 (from Rugby), scholar 84, B.A. 88; HONOURS:—2 classical mods. 86, 3 physiology 88.

Bill, Charles Fitz-Herbert, born at Alton, co. Stafford, July, 1872; 1s. Charles, M.P., M.A. NEW COLL., matric. 16 Oct., 91, aged 19, from Eton.

Billiat, Joseph, born at Barkston, co. Lincoln, Sept., 1863; o.s. Joseph, gent. CHARSLEY HALL, matric. 15 Oct., 84, aged 21, from Uppingham school.

Billing, Robert Claudius, born at Maidstone, Kent, 1834; 1s. Robert, cler. WORCESTER, matric. 25 Oct., 53, aged 19, B.A. 57, M.A. 86, created D.D. 21 June, 88; rector of Spitalfields 78, bishop suffragan of Bedford 88. See *Al. Ox.* 129.

Billings, John S., D.Med., created D.C.L. 26 June, 1889, of surgeon-general's office, war department, Washington, U.S. America.

Billson, Edgar Leicester, born at Birkenhead, 15 Sept., 1869; o.s. Alfred, solicitor. MAGDALEN, matric. 22 Oct., 87, aged 18 (from Eton), B.A. 89.

Billups, Howard Barclay, born at Chatteris, co. Cambridge, 9 Aug., 1872; 4s. Christopher Smith, gen. WORCESTER, matric. 22 Oct., 91, aged 18 (from Magdalen coll. school), scholar 90.

Billups, Lindsay Barclay, born at Chatteris, co. Cambridge, 23 Jan., 1867; 6s. Christopher Smith, gent. NON-COLLEGIATE, matric. 16 Oct., 86, aged 19 (from Hanley Castle school), B.A. 89.

Billups, Stanley Barclay, born at Chatteris, co. Cambridge, 14 April, 1870; 3s. Christopher Smith, gen. NON-COLLEGIATE, matric. 13 Oct., 88, aged 18 (from Hanley Castle school), B.A. 92; HONOURS: —3 physiology 92.

Bindley, rev. Thomas Herbert, born at Smethwick, co. Stafford, 21 Oct., 1861; 2s. Thomas Robert Bourn, gent. MERTON, matric. 18 Oct., 80, aged 18 (from Bromsgrove school), B.A. 84, M.A. 87 (HONOURS: —2 theology 84); *ad eundem* Durham 90; examining chaplain to bishop of Barbados; principal and prof. of theology Codrington coll., Barbados, 90. For list of his writings see *Crockford*.

Bindon, Ernest Rawle Rignud, born at Antigua 1866; o.s. Robert Holberton, cler. NON-COLLEGIATE, matric. 17 Oct., 85, aged 19, B.A. 88; HONOURS: —4 history 88.

Bingham, George Thomas, born at Kilkenny, Ireland, 28 June, 1873; o.s. Lucan, county inspector R. Irish constabulary. JESUS COLL., matric. 18 Oct., 92, aged 19 (from Bangor school), scholar 92.

Bingley, Arthur George Elton, born at Colchester 22 Dec., 1867; 1s. John George, cler. MERTON, matric. 21 Oct., 86, aged 18, from Canterbury school.

Bingley, Frederick Sparkes Norman, born in London 17 Sept., 1863; o.s. Alfred Williams, gent. MAG-DALEN, matric. 29 Jan., 85, aged 21 (from Brighton coll. and university coll. Lond.), B.A. 88, M.A. 91 (HONOURS: —4 chemistry 88); bar.-at-law, Inner Temple, 93.

Bingley, Robert Cecil, born at Colchester Sept., 1869; 2s. John George, cler. KEBLE, matric. 13 Oct., 86, aged 19, from King's school, Canterbury.

Bingley, Robert Noel Glanville, born at Braysworth, Suffolk, 25 Dec., 1864; 2s. Robert Mildred, cler. EXETER, matric. 23 Oct., 85, aged 20 (from the Charterhouse), B.A. 89.

Binney, Edward Hibbert, born at Clifton Hampden, Oxon, 26 Oct., 1872; 8s. Douglas Belcher, cler. EXETER, matric. 22 Oct., 91, aged 18 (from the Charterhouse), exhibitioner 91.

Binney, John Edward Hibbert, born at Halifax, N.S., 20 Dec., 1862; 2s. Hibbert, bishop of Nova Scotia. NEW COLL., matric. 15 Oct., 81, aged 18 (from Winchester), B.A. 86, M.A. 88.

Binns, Francis Aston, born at Warwick 1859; o.s. Thomas Aston, gent. BALLIOL, matric. 18 Oct., 81, aged 22 (from Bradford school), B.A. 86, M.A. 88 (HONOURS: —2 classical mods. 83, 3 classics 85, Taylorian exhibition (French) 85. and scholarship (Italian) 86]; a master at King's school, Sherborne, 91.

Binstead, Charles Herbert, born at Wakefield, Yorks, 1862; 1s. Charles Henry, gent. PEMBROKE, matric. 26 Oct., 81, aged 19, B.A. 84, M.A. 88.

Binyon, Robert Laurence, born at Lancaster 10 Aug., 1869; 2s. Frederick, cler. TRINITY, matric. 13 Oct., 88, aged 19 (from St. Paul's school), scholar 87; HONOURS: —English verse 90, 1 classical mods. 90, 2 classics 92.

Binyon, rev. Walter, born at Dowden, Cheshire, 24 Nov., 1862; 2s. Alfred, gent. UNIVERSITY COLL., matric. 4 June, 81, aged 18 (from Owens coll., Manchester), scholar 81, B.A. 85, M.A. 88 (HONOURS: —1 mathematical mods. 83, 1 mathematics 85), tutor St. Columba's coll., Dublin, 86-8.

Birch, Arthur Pershouse, born at Nottingham June, 1870; 2s. George Turner, cler. CHRIST CHURCH, matric. 10 Oct., 90, aged 20, from Wrexham gr. school.

Birch, Charles William, born at Whitchurch, co. Mon., 1863; 1s. Edward, gent. HERTFORD, matric. 14 Oct., 89, aged 26 (from Brampton school, Cumberland), B.A. 92.

Birch, Ernest Edward Holcombe, born in London 5 March, 1864; 2s. Edward, gent. NEW COLL., matric. 12 Oct., 83, aged 19 (from King's coll. school, London), B.A. 87 (HONOURS: —3 chemistry 87); bar.-at-law, Lincoln's Inn, 90.

Birch, rev. George Thomas, born at Liverpool 25 Dec., 1865; 1s. George Turner, cler. LINCOLN, matric. 27 Oct., 85, aged 19 (from Wrexham school), scholar 85, B.A. 89, M.A. 92 (HONOURS: —1 classical mods. 87, 3 classics 89); curate of St. John Evangelist, Altrincham, 92.

Birchall, Reginald, born at Accrington, co. Lancaster, 25 May, 1866; 2s. James, cler. LINCOLN, matric. 3 Feb., 86, aged 19 (from Rossall school); died 14 Nov., 90.

Bird, Arthur Horace, born at Highgate, Middlesex, 31 July, 1870; 1s. Arthur, arm. TRINITY, matric. 13 Oct., 89, aged 18 (from Harrow), B.A. 91; HONOURS: —3 law 91.

Bird, Benwell Harold, born at Birmingham 28 June, 1872; 1s. Benwell, cler. EXETER, matric. 13 Oct., 90, aged 18 (from Plymouth coll.), HONOURS: —2 classical mods. 92.

Bird, Cyril Henry Golding, born in London 18 Sept., 1874; 3s. Robert James G.-B., vicar of St. Bartholomew, Gray's Inn Road. LINCOLN, matric. 25 Oct., 92, aged 18, from Merchant Taylors' school and S. Andrew's theol. coll., N.B.

Bird, Douglas Smith, born at West Pennard, Dorset, 21 Nov., 1866; 5s. Charles James, cler., of Clifton, co. Glouc. MAGDALEN, matric. 16 Oct., 84, aged 18 (from Bristol gr. school), demy 84, B.A. 88; HONOURS: —1 mathematical mods. 85, 2 mathematics 88.

Bird, George Bertie, born at Peterborough 7 April, 1872; 3s. John, rector of Welton, co. Linc. QUEEN's, matric. 27 Oct., 92, aged 20.

Bird, Golding Golding, born in London 1870; 1s. Robert James G.-B., vicar of St. Bartholomew's, London. ST. EDMUND HALL, matric. 18 Oct., 88, aged 18 (from Merchant Taylors' school); migrated to HERTFORD, B.A. 91 (HONOURS: —3 theology 91); assumed the additional name of Golding.

Bird, rev. Harold Braginton, born in Cheshire 1864; o.s. Valentine, D.Med. CHRIST CHURCH, matric. 13 Oct., 82, aged 18, B.A. 86, M.A. 89 (HONOURS: —3 theology 86); curate of St. Mary Magdalen, Paddington, 91.

Bird, John Payne Edmund, born at Peterborough 26 Nov., 1865; 1s. John, cler. QUEEN's, matric. 30 Oct., 85, aged 19 (from Salisbury school), B.A. 89.

Bird, rev. Montague Bertie, born at Peterborough 8 Feb., 1869; 2s. John, cler. QUEEN'S, matric. 21 Oct., 87, aged 18, B.A. 91; HONOURS :—4 theology 90.

Bird, Reginald Edward Oliver, born at York 1870; 2s. William, D.Med. ALL SOULS' COLL., matric. 15 Oct., 88, aged 18 (from Leamington coll.), bible clerk 88; HONOURS :—3 classical mods. 90, 3 classics 92.

Birdwood, Francis Travers, born at Bombay 6 Dec., 1865; 3s. sir George Christopher Molesworth, knt. WORCESTER, matric. 17 Oct., 84, aged 18 (from Harrow), B.A. 87; HONOURS :—4 history 87.

Birkbeck, William Alexander, born at Newbold, co. Derby, Oct., 1866; o.s. John Addison, of Middlesborough, gent. KEBLE, matric. 19 Oct., 86, aged 20, from Middlesborough school.

Birkmyre, Henry Napier, born at Windsor 17 March, 1862; 3s. Adam, gent. NON-COLLEGIATE, matric. 17 Oct., 81, aged 19 (from Bristol gr. school, and Lancing coll.); migrated to WORCESTER, B.A. 85, M.A. 92; HONOURS :—3 classical mods. 83, 3 classics 85.

Birks, rev. Arthur Hatfield, born at Sheffield, Yorks, 1868; 2s. Joseph Twindon, gen. BRASENOSE, matric. 20 Oct., 87, aged 19 (from Sheffield collegiate school), B.A. 90 (HONOURS :—4 theology 90); curate of Southport St. Philip 91.

Birley, Maurice, born at Pendlebury, co. Lanc., 6 Oct., 1870; 3s. Arthur, gen. NEW COLL., matric. 11 Oct., 89, aged 19 (from Uppingham school); HONOURS :—3 classical mods. 91.

Birley, Percival Alfred Hugh, born at Esh, co. Durham, 22 July, 1870; o.s. Alfred, cler. LINCOLN, matric. 17 Oct., 89, aged 19 (from University coll., Liverpool), B.A. 93.

Birley, rev. Thomas Howard, born at Wrea Green, co. Lanc., 11 Dec., 1865; 1s. Hutton, arm. CHRIST CHURCH, matric. 12 Oct., 83, aged 17 (from Radley coll.), B.A. 88, M.A. 91; curate of St. German, Roath, co. Glam., 88.

Birnbaum, Albert Bernard, born in London 28 Oct., 1871; 5s. Bernard, arm. MERTON, matric. 15 Oct., 90, aged 18 (from city of London school); HONOURS :—2 classical mods. 92.

Bischoff, Charles Edward, born at Surbiton, Surrey, 24 Feb., 1873; 1.s. Thomas William, solicitor. TRINITY, matric. 17 Oct., 91, aged 18, from Rugby.

Biscoe, Vincent Hilton, B.A., student CHRIST CHURCH 56-70, where see.

Bishop, Frederick Sillery, M.A., Foreday fellow ST. JOHN'S 73-6, where see.

Bisset, Alexander, born at Aberdeen 7 May, 1866; 1s. Alexander, of Arbroath, postmaster. JESUS COLL., matric. 16 Oct., 84, aged 18 (from St. Andrew's university), scholar 84, B.A. and M.A. 92; HONOURS :—2 classical mods. 86, 3 classics 88.

Black, Arthur Strong, born at Hollywood, co. Down, 2 July, 1865; 2s. Christopher Strong, D.Med. WORCESTER, matric. 22 Oct., 85, aged 20.

Blackall, John Ofspring, born at Seal, Kent, 1864; 1s. Thomas Ofspring, cler. MERTON, matric. 17 Jan., 83, aged 18 (from Malvern coll.), B.A. 87; HONOURS :—3 history 86.

Blackburn, Ernest Woodhead, born at Barnsley, Yorks, 31 Dec., 1867; 2s. John, gent. ST. JOHN'S, matric. 16 Oct., 86, aged 18 (from Rugby), scholar 86, B.A. 90; HONOURS :—2 mathematical mods. 87, 1 chemistry 90.

Blackburn, Reginald Herbert, born in London 2 Jan., 1863; 1s. Herbert Cautley, arm., deceased. MAGDALEN, matric. 15 Oct., 81, aged 18 (from Winchester), B.A. 85.

Blackburn, Robert, M.A., fellow BRASENOSE 34-45, where see.

Blacker, Cecil Julius, born in London 31 May, 1863; 2s. Maxwell Julius, cler. NON-COLLEGIATE, matric. 13 Oct., 83, aged 20 (from Merchant Taylors' school and King's coll., London); migrated to MERTON, B.A. 89 (HONOURS :—3 classical mods. 85, 2 classics 87, 3 civil law 89), treasurer of Oxford union society 86, president 87; died 11 Oct., 89, in Virginia, U.S.A.

Blackett, Hugh Douglas, born in London March, 1873; 1s. general sir Edward Wentworth, bart. CHRIST CHURCH, matric. 14 Oct., 92, aged 19, from Eton.

Blackley, Travers Robert, born at Dublin 6 Jan., 1867; 1s. Travers Robert, major in the army. EXETER, matric. 23 Oct., 85, aged 18, from the Charterhouse.

Blackmore, Hubert Bertram, born at Lowestoft, Suffolk, 1868; o.s. James Baker, cler. TURRELL'S HALL, matric. 24 May, 86, aged 18.

Blackmore, William Downes, born at Lancing, Sussex, 29 Nov., 1871; 1s. Edmund, cler. PEMBROKE, matric. 25 Oct., 90, aged 18 (from Lancing coll.); HONOURS :—3 classical mods. 92.

Blackshaw, William, born at Walworth, Surrey, 7 May, 1866; 2s. Charles, gen. NON-COLLEGIATE, matric. 25 Oct., 90, aged 24, from city of London school.

Blackstone, Alan Cornwall, M.A., fellow NEW COLL. 51-73, where see.

Blackwood, Ion Basil Gawen Temple, baron Blackwood, born at Clandeboy, co. Down, 4 Nov., 1870; 3s. Frederick Temple, marquis (of) Dufferin). BALLIOL, matric. 17 Jan., 91, aged 20, from Harrow.

Bladon, Henry John Hunt, born at Nottingham 1865; 1s. George Thomas, gent. CHRIST CHURCH, matric. 12 Oct., 83, aged 18 (from Ashby de la Zouch school), B.A. 87.

Blagden, Charles Otto, born in London 30 Sept., 1864; 1s. William George, gent. CORPUS CHRISTI, matric. 19 Oct., 83, aged 19 (from Dulwich coll.), scholar 83, B.A. 87; HONOURS :—2 classical mods. 84, 1 classics 87.

Blagden, Claude Martin, born at Milcombe, Oxon, 18 April, 1874; 3s. Henry Charles, M.A., cler. CORPUS CHRISTI, matric. 18 Oct., 92, aged 18 (from Bradfield coll.), scholar 92.

Blagden, rev. James Nevill, born at Newbury, Berks, Feb., 1867; 1s. Henry, cler. CHRIST CHURCH, matric. 12 June, 86, aged 19 (from Lancing coll.), B.A. 89 (HONOURS :—4 history 89); curate of Mansfield, Notts, 90.

Blair, Alexander Stevenson, born in Edinburgh 1866; 1s. Patrick, arm. BRASENOSE, matric. 25 May, 83, aged 17 (from Loretto school), B.A. 86.

Blair, rev. Arthur Austin, born at Newcastle on Tyne 1863; 4s. James Samuel, cler. ST. EDMUND HALL, matric. 19 Oct., 82, aged 19, B.A. 85, M.A. 89 (HONOURS :—3 theology 85); curate of Gateshead St. James 88.

Blair, George Alexander, born at Glasgow 16 May, 1865; 1s. Alexander John, gen. NEW COLL., matric. 12 Oct., 88, aged 23 (from Bradford gr. school), six years assistant master.

Blake, Arthur Middleton, born 28 Nov., 1870; 1s. Arthur, arm., deceased. WADHAM, matric. 17 Oct., 89, aged 18, from a Ramsgate school.

Blake, Arthur Roddam Frederick, born at Cornhill-on-Tweed, Northumberland, 21 Dec., 1860; 2s. Francis, arm. BRASENOSE, matric. 10 June, 81, aged 20 (from Cheltenham coll.), B.A. 85.

Blake, Charles Frederick Sapte, born at Carisbrooke, Isle of Wight, 31 Dec., 1869; 1s. Edward Frederick, solicitor. EXETER, matric. 17 Oct., 88, aged 20, from Rugby.

Blake, rev. Godfrey Bernard, born at Wetherall, Cumberland, Dec., 1861; 2s. William, cler. ST. JOHN'S, matric. 21 Jan., 82, aged 20, B.A. 88; curate of Wetherall, Cumberland, 89.

Blake, James Martindale, born at Sunderland, co. Durham, 1863; o.s. George, cler. ST. EDMUND HALL, matric. 19 April, 82, aged 19, B.A. 89, M.A. 90.

Blake, Thomas, born at Sharrow, Yorks, 17 March, 1872; 1s. William Greaves, major 9th Lancers. MERTON, matric. 18 Oct., 92, aged 20, from Rugby.

Blakelock, Albert, born at Eccleshall, Yorks, 1 Sept., 1867; o.s. Ralph Blakelock-Smith, solicitor, deceased. MAGDALEN, matric. 21 Oct., 86, aged 19 (from Harrow), B.A. 89.

Blakelock, Ralph Blakelock Salts,- born at Leeds 12 July, 1867; 1s. Alfred Salts, vicar of Littleborough, co. Lanc. QUEEN'S, matric. 25 Oct., 86, aged 19 (from Leeds gr. school), scholar 86, B.A. 90; HONOURS:—2 classical mods. 88, 2 classics 90, 2 theology 91.

Blakemore, Arthur Villiers, born at Edgbaston, co. Warwick, 1866; o.s. Villiers, gent. PEMBROKE, matric. 27 Oct., 84, aged 18, B.A. 89.

Blakesley, Arthur Holmes, born at Ware, Herts, 26 July, 1863; 7s. Joseph Williams, dean of Lincoln. CHRIST CHURCH, matric. 13 Oct., 82, aged 19 (from the Charterhouse), scholar 82-6, B.A. 86 (HONOURS:—2 classical mods. 84, 2 classics 86, 1 theology 87); died in Calcutta 20 Aug., 89.

Blakesley, Edmund Holmes, born at Ware, Herts, 7 Oct., 1868; 7s. Joseph Williams, dean of Lincoln. CHRIST CHURCH, matric. 14 Oct., 87, aged 19 (from the Charterhouse), scholar 87; assistant commissioner Damoh, central provinces, Bengal C.S. 89.

Blakeway, Charles Edward, born at Much Wenlock, Salop, Oct., 1868; 2s. Roger Charles, arm. CHRIST CHURCH, matric. 12 Oct., 88, aged 20 (from Shrewsbury school), B.A. 92; HONOURS:—2 history 92.

Blakeway, rev. Philip John Thomas, born in London 11 March, 1864; 1s. Philip Edward, gent., deceased. MAGDALEN, matric. 13 Jan., 83, aged 18, B.A. 91; curate of St. Luke, Camberwell, 91.

Blakey, Eustace Henry, born at Stockholm 1866; 2s. Robert Healey, cler. ST. JOHN'S, matric. 11 Oct., 84, aged 18 (from Canterbury school), B.A. 87.

Blakiston, Archibald Charles Hugh, born at Monks Risborough, Bucks, 30 May, 1874; 1s. Charles Denly, cler. TRINITY, matric. 15 Oct., 92, aged 18 (from Malvern coll.), scholar 91.

Blakiston, rev. Herbert Edward Douglas, born at Hastings 5 Sept., 1862; 1s. Douglas Yeoman, vicar of East Grinstead, Sussex. TRINITY, matric. 15 Oct., 81, aged 19 (from Tonbridge school), scholar 81-5, B.A. 86, (fellow 87, M.A. 88, tutor 90 (HONOURS:—1 classical mods. 82, 1 classics 85); assistant master Clifton coll. 86-7.

Blakiston, Rochfort Folliot, born at Stoke, co. Stafford, 25 Nov., 1860; 1s. Matthew Folliott, arm. ORIEL, matric. 20 Jan., 80, aged 19 (from Clifton coll.), B.A. 83 (HONOURS:—3 classical mods. 81, 4 history 83); student Middle Temple 82.

Blanch, George Ernest, born at Malvern, co. Worcester, 30 July, 1864; 1s. , gent. CHRIST CHURCH, matric. 18 Oct., 83, aged 19 (from Kingswood school), scholar 82, B.A. 86, M.A. 90; HONOURS:—1 chemistry 86.

Bland, Isaac Hudson, born at Orton, Westmorland, 2 Sept., 1860; 3s. William, cler. QUEEN'S, matric. 25 Oct., 80, aged 20 (from Appleby gr. school), exhibitioner 80-5, B.A. 84, M.A. 87; HONOURS:—2 mathematical mods. 82, 3 mathematics 84.

Blandford, rev. Henry Weare, born at Fryerning, Essex, 12 Sept., 1863; 1s. Henry Weare, cler. ST. JOHN'S, matric. 11 Oct., 84, aged 21, B.A. 87 (HONOURS:—4 history 87); curate of Sydling St. Nicholas, Dorset, 90.

Blandy, John Cecil, born at Reading Feb., 1862; 2s. William Frank, arm. NON-COLLEGIATE, matric. 18 Oct., 80, aged 18, from Sherborne school.

Blathwayt, Theodore Ballantyne, born 1862; 4s. Raymond, cler. NON-COLLEGIATE, matric. 14 Oct., 82, aged 20, B.A. 85; HONOURS:—4 theology 85.

Bleackley, Horace William, born at Prestwich, co. Lancaster, 19 Jan., 1868; 1s. William, gen. UNIVERSITY COLL., matric. 15 Oct., 87, aged 19 (from Cheltenham coll. and Repton school), B.A. 91; HONOURS:—2 history 90.

Bleackley, John Arthur, born at Prestwich, co. Lancaster, 11 Oct., 1869; 1s. William, gen. ST. JOHN'S, matric. 25 April, 90, aged 20, from Repton school.

Bleiben, rev. William, born at Aston, co. Warwick, 5 June, 1863; o.s. Thomas, gent. NON-COLLEGIATE, matric. 13 Oct., 84, aged 21 (from K. Edward's school, Birmingham); migrated to WADHAM 17 Oct., 85, B.A. 87, M.A. 90; curate of St. Martin, Birmingham, 91.

Blencowe, William Poole, born at Chailey, Sussex, Feb. 1870; 3s. John George, arm. CHRIST CHURCH, matric. 17 Oct., 87; aged 17 (from Eton), B.A. 90.

Blennerhassett, Arthur Charles Francis Bernard, born at Munich, 14 April, 1871; 1s. Rowland, of co. Kerry, bart. BALLIOL, matric. 14 Oct., 90, aged 19, from Munich gymnasium.

Bligh, hon. Arthur Frederick Pelham, born 25 April, 1865; 3s. John Stuart, earl Darnley. CHRIST CHURCH, matric. 25 May, 83, aged 18.

Bligh, Stanley Price Morgan, born at Llanfaestree, co. Brecon, 15 Feb., 1870; 1s. Oliver Morgan, arm. TRINITY, matric. 13 Oct., 88, aged 18 (from Eton), B.A. 92 (HONOURS:—3 history 92); Welsh county councillor.

Bliss, Edward Church, born at Walsall, co. Stafford, 10 Oct., 1872; 1s. Edward, merchant. ORIEL, matric. 27 Oct., 91, aged 19, from the Charterhouse.

Bliss, rev. George Charles, M.A., NON-COLLEGIATE, where see.

Bliss, Howard Sweetser, born at Suk-el-Jhurb, in Syria, 1860; 2s. Daniel, D.D. NON-COLLEGIATE, matric. 22 Oct., 87, aged 27, from Amherst coll., Mass. and Union theol. seminary, U.S.A.

Block, William Edmonston, born in London 22 May, 1861; 4s. Samuel Wilson, arm. ORIEL, matric. 19 Oct., 80, aged 19 (from Haileybury), B.A. 85, M.A. 87 (HONOURS:—3 classical mods. 82); assistant master Bengeo 88-9; 2nd 14 July, 90.

Blockley, rev. Thomas Trotter, born at Pinner, Middx., 1864; 1s. Thomas, of Watford, arm. MAGDALEN, matric. 24 Jan., 84, aged 19 (from Harrow), B.A. 87, M.A. 90; curate of St. Alban cathedral 88.

Blomfield, right rev. Alfred, D.D., bishop suffragan of Colchester, fellow ALL SOULS' 55-69, where see.

Blomfield, Frederick Charles, born in London, 3 July, 1865; o.s. Frederick George, arm. NEW COLL., matric. 12 Oct., 83, aged 18, from Eton.

Blood, John Neptune, born in Cheltenham, 9 Nov., 1869; 1s. Francis Gamble, major 69th Regt. Light Infantry, deceased. MAGDALEN, matric. 16 Oct., 88, aged 18 (from Rugby), B.A. 91 (HONOURS:— 3 law 91); bar.-at-law, Inner Temple, 93.

Blood, Maurice, born at Westbury-on-Trym, co. Glouc., 15 Feb., 1870; o.s. George Edmund, gen. MERTON, matric. 19 Oct., 89, aged 19 (from Bristol gr. school), postmaster 89; HONOURS:— 2 mathematical mods. 91.

Bloor, (rev.) Robert Edward Underwood, born at Widford, Herts, 1867; 3s. John Usielli, gent. ST. JOHN'S, matric. 17 Oct., 85, aged 18 (from Highbury school), B.A. 88 (HONOURS:—4 history 88); curate of St. Sepulchre, London, 89.

Blore, George Henry, born at Bromsgrove, co. Worcester, 3 March, 1870; 1s. George John, D.D., hon. canon Canterbury. NEW COLL., matric. 11 Oct., 89, aged 19 (from Winchester), scholar 88; HONOURS:—1 classical mods. 91.

Blore, George John, D.D., hon. canon of Canterbury, student CHRIST CHURCH 56-61, senior student 61-7, where see.

Blount, George Hugh, born at Barnes, Surrey, 31 May, 1870; 1s. George Bouverie, of the admiralty. NEW COLL., matric. 12 Oct., 88, aged 18 (from Derby school), B.A. 91; HONOURS:—3 classical mods. 90, 3 law 91.

Bloxam, John Francis, born at Wimbledon, Surrey, 17 Dec., 1873; 3s. Edward, late a solicitor. EXETER, matric. 18 Oct., 92, aged 18, from Winchester coll.

Blucher von Wahlstatt, count, Gustav Gebhard Francis; born 1867; 2s. Prince Gebhard, of Radun, Austria. CHRIST CHURCH, matric. 5 Feb., 86, aged 19.

Blundell, Cecil Rickards, born at Newport, co. Mon., 28 April, 1870; 3s. Augustus Rickards, arm. EXETER, matric. 13 Oct., 90, aged 20, from Marlborough coll.

Blunt, Edward Henry, born at Windsor 12 March, 1865; 1s. James St. John, cler. CHRIST CHURCH, matric. 12 Oct., 83, aged 18 (from Winchester), lieut. princess Charlotte of Wales' (royal Berkshire Regt.) 91.

Blunt, Herbert William, born at Whittlesea, co. Cambr., 1864; 3s. James, arm. ORIEL, matric. 31 Oct., 82, aged 18 (from King's coll. sch., Lond.), scholar 82-6, B.A. 86; student CHRIST CHURCH 88, tutor and M.A. 87; HONOURS:—2 classical mods. 83, 1 classics 86, Arnold essay 87.

Blunt, Osmund Donald, born at Adrianople in Turkey, 1871; o.s. John Elijah, arm. UNIVERSITY COLL., matric. 13 Oct., 88, aged 17, from Wellington coll.

Blunt, Thomas Gaire Rockstro, born at Shrewsbury 1867; 1s. Thomas Porter, gent. CHRIST CHURCH, matric. 16 Oct., 85, aged 18 (from Shrewsbury school), exhibitioner 85, B.A. 89, M.A. 92; HONOURS:—2 classical mods. 87, 2 history 89.

Bluntschli, Jean Gaspard, created D.C.L. 8 Sept., 1880, privy councillor and professor of international law in the University of Heidelberg, ex-president of the "Institut de Droit International."

Blyth, George Francis Popham, bishop of Jerusalem, created D.D. 15 March, 87. See Al. Ox. 127.

Blyth, Percy Harold, born at Edinburgh 1866; 4s. Edward Lawrence Ireland, arm. BRASENOSE, matric. 7 June, 84, aged 18, from Loretto school.

Board, John William, born at Westerham, Kent, May or Aug., 1866; 1s. John, arm. MERTON, matric. 28 Jan., 86, aged 19, from Eton.

Boas, Frederick Samuel, born at Belfast 1862; 1s. Hermann, gent. BALLIOL, matric. 18 Oct., 81,

aged 19 (from Clifton coll.), exhibitioner 80, Jenkyns exhibitioner 85, B.A. 86, M.A. 89; HONOURS:—1 classical mods. 82, 1 classics 85, 1 history 86.

Boas, Henry Julius, born at Belfast 15 May, 1870; 3s. Hermann, gent. TRINITY, matric. 12 Oct., 89, aged 19 (from Clifton coll.); assistant magistrate Meerut, N.W.P. India 91.

Boase, rev. Charles William, M.A., fellow EXETER 50, where see.

Bode, (rev.) George Herbert, born at Dinton, Bucks, Jan., 1865; 3s. Henry, gent. ST. EDMUND HALL, matric. 30 Oct., 83, aged 18 (from St. Paul's coll., Stony Stratford), B.A. 87, M.A. 91 (HONOURS:—3 theology 86); curate of St. Mary with St. Peter, Hayling island, 90.

Bode, Reginald Heber, born at Newcastle, Australia, 12 Oct., 1865; 2s. George Charles, cler., deceased. NEW COLL., matric. 10 Oct., 84, aged 18 (from King's school, Parramatta, N.S.W.), B.A. 88; HONOURS:—3 classical mods. 86, 2 law 88.

Bodey, Ralph Thomas, born at Bristol 1 Jan., 1863; 3s. John Joseph, gent. TRINITY, matric. 14 Oct., 82, aged 19 (from Bristol mining school and Royal school of mines), scholar 80-6, B.A. 86, M.A. 89; HONOURS:—3 classical mods. 84, 1 chemistry 86.

Bodington, rev. Eric James, born at Harborne, co. Stafford, 1863; 2s. Thomas, arm. BRASENOSE, matric. 18 Oct., 81, aged 18 (from Hereford school), scholar 81-5, B.A. 85, M.A. 89 (HONOURS:—2 classics 85); domestic chaplain bishop of Salisbury 90, vicar of Christ church, Burghersdorp, Cape Colony, 90.

Bodington, Nathan, M.A., fellow LINCOLN 75-86, where see.

Boevey, Francis Hyde Crawley-, born at Newnham, co. Glouc., 25 April, 1868; 1s. Thomas Hyde, bart. CHRIST CHURCH, matric. 3 June, 87, aged 19, B.A. 91.

Boger, Alnod John, born at Plymouth 31 Aug., 1871; 1s. Heat, arm. MAGDALEN, matric. 14 Oct., 90, aged 19 (from Winchester), in Oxford eleven 91.

Boger, Edward M.A., fellow EXETER 43-9, where see.

Boileau, Maurice Colborne, born at Tacolnstone, Norfolk, 3 Dec., 1865; 2s. sir Francis George Manningham, bart. WORCESTER, matric. 8 May, 86, aged 20, B.A. 89, M.A. 92.

Boissier, George John, born at Turville, Berks, 11 Oct., 1857; 4s. Peter Henry, cler. NON-COLLEGIATE, matric. 13 Oct., 83, aged 26 (from Bristol gr. school); migrated to EXETER 23 June, 84, B.A. 87, M.A. 90.

Boles, Dennis Fortescue, born at Exeter Sept., 1861; 5s. James Thomas, cler. EXETER, matric. 4 June, 81, aged 19, from Bradfield coll.

Bolitho, William Edward Thomas, born at Penzance, Cornwall, 2 July, 1862; o.s. William, arm. TRINITY, matric. 15 Oct., 81, aged 19 (from Harrow), B.A. 85, in university eleven 83 and 85; a banker.

Bolton, Charles Ernest, born at Paddington 17 Aug., 1871; 2s. Thomas, arm. MERTON, matric. 9 Dec., 89, aged 18, from Marlborough coll.

Bolton, Charles Hicks, born at Oxford 2 June, 1869; 2s. Charles, gent. NON-COLLEGIATE, matric. 15 Oct., 92, aged 23, from S. Mark's coll., Chelsea.

Bolton, Frederick, born at Radcliffe, co. Lanc., 1866; 2s. Samuel, gen. NON-COLLEGIATE, matric. 11 Oct., 90, aged 24, from Farnworth gr. school.

Bolton, Henry Lushington, born in London 1863; 1s. Thomas, solicitor. MERTON, matric. 20 Oct., 81, aged 18 (from Winchester), B.A. 85, M.A. 88.

Bolton, Hubert Ernest Langtree, born at Newchurch-in-Rossendale, co. Lanc., Nov., 1872; 3s. Henry Hargreaves, engineer. CHRIST CHURCH, matric. 4 June, 92, aged 19.

Bolton, Maurice Egerton Augustus, born at Shrimpling, Suffolk, March, 1872; m. Augustus Charles Hope, cler. KEBLE, matric. 20 Oct., 91, aged 19; died 22 Dec., 91.

Bompas, Harold Buckland, born in London Aug., 1863; 1s. George Cox, arm. CHRIST CHURCH, matric. 27 May, 82, aged 18, B.A. 85, M.A. 91 HONOURS :—3 history 85; bar.-at-law, Inner Temple, 88.

Bond, Alexander Godolphin, born at Marlborough May 1870; 5s. Frederick Hookey, cler. KEBLE, matric. 12 Oct., 89, aged 19, from Weston-super-Mare school.

Bond, Edmund Delafosse, born at Marlborough, Wilts, Jan., 1874; 6s. Frederick Hookey, cler. KEBLE, matric. 15 Oct., 92, aged 18, from Clifton coll.

Bond, Edward, M.A., fellow QUEEN'S 69-91, where see.

Bond, Ernest Walter, born at Ipswich 6 April, 1866; 4s. Henry Cooper, arm. WORCESTER, matric. 29 Jan., 86, aged 19, from Shrewsbury school.

Bond, Frederick Hookey, M.A., fellow EXETER 43-52, where see.

Bond, John Wentworth Garneys, born in London 12 Sept., 1865; 1s. Nathaniel, arm. ORIEL, matric. 23 Oct., 84, aged 19 (from Eton), B.A. 87; HONOURS :—2 history 87.

Bond, Reginald Copleston, born at Marlborough, Wilts, 28 April, 1866; 4s. Frederick Hookey, cler. TRINITY, matric. 11 Oct., 84, aged 18, from Bath coll.), lieutenant Yorks L.I.

Bond, William Purnell, born at Kingdon, Somerset, 30 Sept., 1868; 2s. John James, gen. QUEEN'S, matric. 21 Oct., 87, aged 19 (from Merchant Taylors' school), scholar 87, B.A. 91; HONOURS :—2 classical mods. 89, 2 classics 91.

Bone, Charles Belfield, born at Stoke Damerell, Devon, 1862; 7s. Allan Belfield, solicitor. EXETER, matric. 15 May, 80, aged 18, B.A. 83; migrated to KEBLE, M.A. 92.

Bone, George Henry Kavanagh, born at Surbiton, Surrey, 26 Feb., 1871; 1s. Henry Kavanagh, arm. CHRIST CHURCH, matric. 6 June, 90, aged 19.

Bonghi, Ruggiero, created D.C.L. 20 June, 1888, member of the Italian parliament, late minister of public instruction Italy 74, professor of philosophy Milan 59, of Greek literature Turin university 64, and of ancient history at Rome and Naples. See *Men and Women of the Time.*

Bonner, George Albert, born at Spalding, co. Lincoln, 9 March, 1862; 2s. Charles Foster, solicitor. NEW COLL., matric. 17 Jan., 80, aged 17 (from Magdalen coll. school), B.A. 83 (HONOURS :—4 law 83); bar.-at-law, Inner Temple, 85.

Bonnin, Alfred, born at Adelaide, Australia, 16 June, 1867; 1s. Alfred, arm. TRINITY, matric. 11 Oct., 90, aged 23, from Cheltenham coll. and Adelaide university.

Bonus, Arthur Rivers, born at Karachi, E. Indies, 29 Dec., 1866; 2s. Joseph, arm. BALLIOL, matric. 15 Oct., 84, aged 17 (from Clifton coll.); assistant collector and magistrate Dharwar, Bombay C.S. 86.

Bonus, Ernest Melville, born at Hastings 22 Sept., 1867; 3s. Joseph, arm. NEW COLL., matric. 12 Oct., 88, aged 19 (from Clifton coll.), scholar 88; HONOURS :—1 classical mods. 90, 2 classics 92.

Boodle, Benjamin James, born at Chilcompton, Somerset, 9 March, 1868; s. Robert Hockin, gen. ST. JOHN'S, matric. 15 Oct., 87, aged 19 (from St. John's Wood school), scholar 90, B.A. 91; HONOURS :—2 classical mods. 89, 2 classics 91.

Boodle, Charles Edward, born at Chilcompton, 1862; 5s. Robert Hockin, arm. ST. JOHN'S, matric. 27 April, 82, aged 19, B.A. 84.

Booker, Arthur John Nussey, born at Kensington Nov., 1871; 3s. George, incumbent of St. John Baptist, Kensington. CHRIST CHURCH, matric. 17 Dec., 89, aged 18 (from Westminster school); brother of George and Josias.

Booker, Edward born at Redditch, co. Worcester, 1857; 1s. Edward, gen. NON-COLLEGIATE, matric. 28 May, 87, aged 30, from Redditch gr. school.

Booker, George Edward Nussey, born in London 14 March, 1867; 3s. George, cler. NON-COLLEGIATE, matric. 28 Jan., 84, aged 16, from Westminster school.

Booker, Josias Antony Nussey, born in London 15 July, 1865; 1s. George, cler. CHRIST CHURCH, matric. 12 Oct., 83, aged 18, from Westminster school.

Booker, Robert Penrice Lee, born at Sutton, Surrey, 25 Nov., 1864; 2s. John, vicar. NEW COLL., matric. 12 Oct., 83, aged 18 (from Winchester), scholar 82, B.A. 87, M.A. 90; HONOURS :—1 classical mods. 85, 2 classics 87.

Boone, Charles Frederick de Bohun, born at Nagod, E. Indies, 16 May, 1870; 1s. Frederick Brown, late col. 6th Regt. Madras, N.I. ORIEL, matric. 25 Oct., 89, aged 19 (from Haileybury); passed into R.M. coll., Sandhurst, Dec. 90.

Booth, Charles, born at Liverpool 1869; 1s. Alfred, arm. UNIVERSITY COLL., matric. 15 Oct., 87, aged 18, B.A. 92; HONOURS :—3 classical mods. 89, 2 history 91.

Booth, John, born at Warlaby, Yorks, 23 June, 1872; 3s. Thomas Christopher, gen. EXETER, matric. 22 Oct., 91, aged 19 (from Durham gr. school); twin brother of Wilfrid.

Booth, rev. John Bryan, born at Durham 1862; CHRIST CHURCH, matric. 16 Oct., 85, aged 23, scholar 86, B.A. 89 (*ad eundem* Durham 89), M.A. 92 (HONOURS :—3 history 88); 2 theology 90), vice-principal Culham training college 90-1, curate of St. John Baptist, Peterborough, 91.

Booth, Wilfrid, born at Warlaby, Yorks, 23 June, 1872; 4s. Thomas Christopher, gen. EXETER, matric. 22 Oct., 91, aged 19 (from Durham gr. school); twin brother of John.

Boothby, rev. Herbert Cecil, born at Welwyn, Herts, 2 Dec., 1863; 4s. sir Brooke, bart. NON-COLLEGIATE, matric. 18 March 85, aged 21 (from Clifton coll.); migrated to CHRIST CHURCH, B.A. 88 (HONOURS :—3 history 88); curate of St. Augustine, Stepney, 90-1.

Borel, Maurice Arnaud Hippolyte, born in Paris 1863; 2s. Paul, gent. BALLIOL, matric. 1 Feb., 82, aged 19, from Lycée Fontanes school.

Borough, Reginald John Maxwell, born at Derby Nov., 1869; 1s. John, gen. PEMBROKE, matric. 25 Oct., 87, aged 17 (from Repton school), B.A. 90; (HONOURS :—4 law 90); bar.-at-law, Lincoln's Inn, 93.

Borthwick, hon. Archibald Patrick Thomas, master of ; born 3 Sept., 1867; 1s. Connyngham, lord Borthwick. CHRIST CHURCH, matric. 30 May, 85, aged 17.

Borthwick, Oliver Andrew, born in London, 2 March, 1873; 1s. sir Algernon, bart., M.P. BALLIOL, matric. 18 Oct., 92, aged 19 (from Eton), exhibitioner 91.

Borthwick, William George Maxwell, born in London Aug., 1869; o.s. William David, arm. ORIEL, matric. 14 Dec., 87, aged 18, from Clifton coll.

Borwick, Frank, born at Walthamstow 16 Dec., 1866; 3s. Alfred, gen. TRINITY, matric. 16 Oct., 86, aged 19 (from Clifton coll.), B.A. 92; HONOURS :—3 classical mods. 88, 4 classics 90.

Bosanquet, Bernard, M.A., fellow UNIVERSITY COLL. 70-84, where see.

Bosanquet, rev. Claude Charles Courthorpe, born at St. Osyth, Essex, 19 Dec., 1862; 1s. Charles, cler. ORIEL, matric. 18 Oct., 81, aged 18 (from Rugby), B.A. 85, M.A. 88 (HONOURS:—2 theology 85); vicar of Lowdham, Notts, 91.

Bosanquet, George Richard Bosanquet Smith-, born at Broxbourne, Herts, 5 Feb., 1866; 1s. Horace James, arm. TRINITY, matric. 16 Oct., 86, aged 20, from Eton.

Bosanquet, Oswald Vyvian, born at Mahablishwar, E. Indies, 5 April, 1856; 3s. Arthur, arm. NEW COLL., matric. 16 Oct., 85, aged 19 (from Clifton coll.), assistant to the resident and assistant secretary for Berar, etc. Hyderabad, and at Nilgiris, Madras c.s. 87.

Bosanquet, rev. Reginald Albert, born at Rochester 12 June, 1867; 3s. Claude, cler. CHRIST CHURCH, matric. 12 June, 86, aged 18 (from Bath coll.), B.A. 89 (HONOURS:—4 theology 89); curate of Christ Church, Catton, Norfolk, 90.

Bosanquet, Robert Holford Macdowall, M.A., fellow ST. JOHN'S 70, where see.

Bosanquet, Samuel Courthope, M.A., student CHRIST CHURCH 51-62, where see.

Bosanquet, William Cecil, born at Whiligh, Sussex, 12 Oct., 1866; 1s. George Stanley, capt. R.N. NEW COLL., matric. 16 Oct., 85, aged 19 (from Eton), scholar 84, B.A. 89, fellow 90, M.A. 92; HONOURS:—1 classical mods. 87, 1 classics 89.

Bosoawen, Arthur Sackville Griffith-, born at Rossett, co. Denbigh, 18 Oct., 1865; y.s. Bosanwen Trevor, arm. QUEEN'S, matric. 22 Oct., 84, aged 19 (from Rugby), exhibitioner 84, B.A. 88 (HONOURS:— 2 classical mods. 86, 1 classics 88, 2 history 89), treasurer Oxford union society 87, president 88; M.P. south-west Kent 92.

Bosoawen, Hugh John, born at Hanmer, Flints, 22 July, 1862; 2s. William Henry, cler. NON-COLLEGIATE, matric. 15 Oct., 81, aged 19 (from St. John's school, Cowley); migrated to QUEEN'S, B.A. 86.

von Böselager, baron Dietrich, born at Schloss Hollinghoven, in Westphalia, 1858; 2s. baron Max. CHRIST CHURCH, matric. 21 Jan., 90, aged 22.

Bosville, Alexander Wentworth Macdonald, born at Settrington House, Yorks, 26 Sept., 1865; o.s. Godfrey Wentworth Bayard, capt. 7th Hussars, deceased. MAGDALEN, matric. 23 April, 84, aged 18, from Eton.

Boswell, Henry, created M.A. 23 Nov., 1886, "Cryptogamic botanist."

Boswell, John Douglas, born at Garrallan, co. Ayr, 16 Feb., 1867; 2s. Patrick Charles Douglas, arm. BRASE-NOSE, matric. 23 Oct., 85, aged 18 (from Loretto school), B.A. 88.

Bott, Arthur Thomas, born in London 1857; 1s. George James, gent. NON-COLLEGIATE, matric. 15 Oct., 81, aged 24 (from St. Mark's coll., Chelsea), B.A. 84, M.A. 88.

Bott, John Wilson Eagle, born at Sydenham, Kent, June, 1866; 2s. William, arm. ORIEL, matric. 23 Oct., 84, aged 18, from St. Edmund's school, Salisbury.

Botwood, George Benson Hall, born at Quebec 9 Sept., 1865; o.s. Edward, rector of St. Mary, St. John's, Newfoundland. LINCOLN, matric. 25 April, 84, aged 18.

Bonch, Joseph, born at Workington, Cumberland, 15 Oct., 1872; 1s. John, gent. QUEEN'S, matric. 27 Oct., 91, aged 19 (from Workington school), exhibitioner 91.

Boucher, William Armstrong, born at Ludlow, Salop, 1860; 1s. William Armstrong, gent. CHRIST CHURCH, matric. 15 Oct., 80, aged 20.

Boudler, rev. John Hervey, born at Warwick 20 March, 1859; 1s. Albert, cler. MAGDALEN, matric. 19 Jan., 80, aged 20; curate of Clutton, Bristol, 85.

Boulay, see **Du Boulay**.

Boulton, Charles Percy, born at Long Stratford, Bucks, 1 Sept., 1867; 1s. Charles George, of Stanmore, arm. deceased. MAGDALEN, matric. 23 Oct., 85, aged 18 (from Haileybury), B.A. 90; lieut. 4th batt. Beds. Militia.

Boulton, Frederick, born at Kingston-on-Thames 1865; o.s. Frederick, gent. CHARSLEY HALL, matric. 19 Jan., 85, aged 20.

Boulton, Matthew Ernest, born in London Oct., 1870; 1s. Matthew Piers Watt, arm. CHRIST CHURCH, matric. 8 June, 89, aged 18 (from Eton), B.A. 92.

Boulton, Oscar Evan, born at Charlton, Kent, 1866; 2s. Samuel Bagster, gent. BALLIOL, matric. 15 Oct., 84, aged 18 (from Harrow), B.A. 89; HONOURS:—3 classical mods. 86, 2 history 88.

Bou(r)ohier, Arthur, born at Newbury, Berks, June, 1863; o.s. Charles John, of Speen Lodge, Berks. CHRIST CHURCH, matric. 27 May, 82, aged 18 (from Eton); migrated to NEW INN HALL (Balliol); returned to CHRIST CHURCH, B.A. 88, M.A. 89. See Foster's *Our Noble and Gentle Families*.

Bourohier, Walter, M.A., fellow NEW COLL. 57-76, where see.

Bourne, Alfred Allinson, born at Atherstone, co. Warwick, 16 April, 1848; 3s. William, arm. Scholar ST. JOHN'S COLL., Cambridge, 69 (from Rugby), B.A. 71, M.A. 74 (HONOURS:—17th wrangler and 2nd class classics 71); incorporated from CORPUS CHRISTI 23 Nov., 82, aged 34, in the Cambridge eleven 70, head master Oxford military coll., Cowley, 81-4.

Bourne, Gilbert Charles, born at Bromsgrove 5 July, 1861; 1s. Robert, capt. in the army. NEW COLL., matric. 15 Oct., 81, aged 20 (from Eton), B.A. 85, fellow 87, M.A. 88 (HONOURS:—1 natural science 85),in the Oxford eight 82, 3.

Bourne, Herbert John, born at Dudley, co. Worcester, 1863; 3s. James Samuel, solicitor. EXETER, matric. 19 Oct., 82, aged 19 (from the Charterhouse); migrated to CHARSLEY HALL, B.A. 88.

Bourne, Malcolm Stuart, born at Trichinopoli, E. Indies, 1866; 1s. Malcolm Kemp, arm. UNIVERSITY COLL., matric. 11 Oct., 84, aged 18, B.A. 88, M.A. 91; HONOURS:—3 classical mods. 86, 2 history 88.

Bourne, Thomas William, born at Birkenhead 15 June, 1862; 1s. William, gent. NEW COLL., matric. 14 Oct., 82, aged 20 (from Shrewsbury school), B.A. 87, M.A. 91; HONOURS:—3 classical mods. 84.

Bourne, Walter Kemp, born at Atherstone, co. Warwick, 29 June, 1872; 2s. John Kemp, merchant. WORCESTER, matric. 22 Oct., 91, aged 19, from Rossall school.

Bousfield, rev. Edward Henry, born at Brixton, Surrey, 26 May, 1860; 1s. Edward Holroyd, gent. NEW COLL., matric. 21 Jan., 80, aged 19 (from King's coll. school, London) ; migrated to BALLIOL, B.A. and M.A. 87; vicar of Milton Abbas, Dorset, 91.

Bousfield, Hugh Delabere, born at Leeds 3 Aug., 1872; 4s. Charles Edward, gent. QUEEN'S, matric. 27 Oct., 91, aged 19 (from Leeds gr. school), exhibitioner 91.

Bousfield, John, born at Liverpool 4 Sept., 1866; o.s. John, gent. EXETER, matric. 28 Jan., 86, aged 19.

Boutflower, rev. Cecil Henry, born at Braithay, Westmorland, 15 Aug., 1863; 4s. Samuel Pench, cler. CHRIST CHURCH, matric. 13 Oct., 82, aged 19 (from Uppingham school), scholar 82, B.A. 86, M.A. 89 (HONOURS:—English verse 84, 2 classical mods. 84, 2 classics 86, 2 theology 87); domestic chaplain to bishop of Durham 90.

Bouth, Osmonde Norman Delamere, born at Rochdale, co. Lanc., 20 Dec., 1867; 3s. Frederick William, cotton spinner. LINCOLN, matric. 22 Oct., 86, aged 18, from Rugby.

Bouth, rev. Reginald Myddleton Delamere, born at Rochdale, co. Lanc., 21 Jan, 1867; 2s. Frederick William, cotton spinner. LINCOLN, matric. 27 Oct., 85, aged 18 (from Rugby), B.A. 89, M.A. 92.

Bovill, Francis Henry, born at Dorking, Surrey, 1870; 9s. John Edward, gen. CHRIST CHURCH, matric. 16 Oct., 91, aged 21, from Harrow.

Bovill, Frederick Walter, born at Dorking, Surrey, Feb., 1864; 3s. John Edward, gent., deceased. NEW COLL., matric. 12 Oct., 83, aged 19 (from Harrow), B.A. 87; HONOURS:—2 classical mods. 84, 3 classics 87.

Bovill, George Baxendale, born at Dorking, Surrey, 12 Oct., 1866; 7s. John Edward, arm., deceased. NEW COLL., matric. 16 Oct., 85, aged 19, from Harrow.

Bowden, Charles Stuart, born at Portsea, Hants, 1861; 2s. Herbert George, arm. HERTFORD, matric. 18 Oct., 80, aged 19 (from Fettes coll.), scholar 80-5, B.A. 84; HONOURS:—2 classical mods. 82, 3 classics 84.

Bowden, rev. James Richard, born at Staunton, co. Worcester, 1865; 1s. James, cler. EXETER, matric. 16 Oct., 84, aged 19 (from Bradfield coll.), B.A. 89, M.A. 91; curate of Southampton St. Paul 90.

Bowden, William Edmund, born at Oatlands, Surrey, 1 Nov., 1870; 3s. James, rector of Ardingly, Sussex. UNIVERSITY COLL., matric. 12 Oct., 89, aged 18, from isle of Wight coll., Ryde.

Bowden, William Hugh, born at Walsall, co. Stafford, 1854; 1s. William, gent. NON-COLLEGIATE, matric. 28 Jan., 84, aged 30 (from Walsall gr. school); rector of Nymet Tracy (or Bow), Devon, 86.

Bowdin, Ralph Horatio, born at Wakefield, Yorks, 1862; 2s. William, gent. BALLIOL, matric. 18 Oct., 81, aged 19 (from Wakefield gr. school), scholar 80-5, B.A. 85 (HONOURS:—1 mathematical mods. 82, junior mathematical scholarship 83, 1 mathematics 81, 1 physics 86); died (March?) 89.

Bowell, Ernest William, born at Hereford 8 Aug., 1872; 4s. William, cler. WADHAM, matric. 13 Oct., 90, aged 18 (from Hereford school), scholar 89; HONOURS:—2 classical mods. 92.

Bowen, right hon. sir Charles Synge Christopher, created D.C.L. 13 June, 83; visitor of BALLIOL, where see.

Bowen, right hon. sir George Ferguson, G.C.M.G., M.A., D.C.L., fellow BRASENOSE 44-54, where see.

Bowen, Hubert Cecil, born at Birkenhead, Cheshire, 1864; 2s. Essex, D.Med. BALLIOL, matric. 16 Oct., 83, aged 19 (from Birkenhead school), B.A. 88, M.A. 90; HONOURS:—2 classical mods. 84, 3 classics 87.

Bowen, (rev.) William Edward, born in London 28 Nov., 1862; 1s. Charles Synge Christopher, arm. (after a knight). BALLIOL, matric. 31 Jan., 82, aged 19 (from Harrow), B.A. and M.A. 86 (HONOURS:—3 classical mods. 83, 3 history 85); curate of St. Stephen, Westbourne Park, 91.

Bower, Alexander George, born at Vedlarpuram, 1854; 4s. Henry, cler. NON-COLLEGIATE, matric. 10 April, 80, aged 26 (from Doveton prot. coll. and s.P.G. theol. coll., Madras), B.A. 85, M.A. 86.

Bower, Charles Hawkins Syndercombe, born at Shaston, Dorset, Aug., 1871; 2s. Henry Syndercombe, arm. CHRIST CHURCH, matric. 6 June, 90, aged 18, from Radley coll.

Bower, George, born at Caistor, co. Lincoln, 1864; 4s. Anthony, cler. BALLIOL, matric. 17 Oct., 82, aged 18 (from Eton), deputy supt. of family domains of the Maharaja of Benares 84.

Bowers, Frank Gresty, born in Chester 1864; 3s. Thomas, gent. NON-COLLEGIATE, matric. 14 April, 83, aged 19 (from Chester school); migrated to WORCESTER, B.A. 86, M.A. 90; HONOURS:—3 classical mods. 84, 4 history 86.

Bowers, Herbert Edmund, born at Southampton, 1864; 3s. John, gent. HERTFORD, matric. 20 Jan., 83, aged 19, B.A. 87, M.A. 89.

Bowes, Charles Kessick, born at Herne Bay, Kent, 1863; 2s. John, arm. CHRIST CHURCH, matric. 4 June, 81, aged 18 (from Epsom coll.), scholar 81-5, B.A. 85, M.A. and B.Med. 89; HONOURS:—2 mathematical mods. 83, 2 mathematics 85.

Bowes, Frederick, born in Paris 10 Dec., 1867; Hely, journalist. WADHAM, matric. 18 Jan., 87, aged 19 (from Dover coll.), B.A. 90 (HONOURS:—2 classical mods. 88, 2 classics 90); passed for Eastern cadetship 91.

Bowett, John Henry, born at Worksop, Notts, 1859; 2s. Thomas, pleb. NON-COLLEGIATE, matric. 21 Jan., 82, aged 23; migrated to CHARSLEY H LL, B.A. 88.

Bowker, Benjamin Turner, born at Farnworth, co. Lanc., 26 Dec., 1871; 2s. James, deceased. BRASENOSE, matric. 21 Oct., 92, aged 20, from Farnworth gr. school.

Bowlby, right rev. Henry Bond, D.D., bishop suffragan of Coventry, fellow WADHAM 48-53, where see.

Bowlby, Henry Thomas, born at Chudleigh, co. Worcester, 15 June, 1864; o.s. Henry Bond (now bishop). BALLIOL, matric. 18 Oct., 83, aged 19 (from the Charterhouse), exhibitioner 82, B.A. 87, M.A. 91; HONOURS:—2 classical mods. 84, 3 classics 87.

Bowles, George Downing, M.A., student CHRIST CHURCH 45-67, where see.

Bowles, Thomas, M.A. QUEEN'S, where see.

Bowley, rev. James Lyon, M.A., chaplain CHRIST CHURCH, where see.

Bowman, rev. Alfred, born at Salford, co. Lanc., 26 April, 1863; 8s. William, gent. QUEEN'S, matric. 1 Feb., 81, aged 17 (from Manchester gr. school), clerk 81-2, scholar 82-5, B.A. 84 (HONOURS:—3 classical mods. 82, 3 classics 84); curate of Devonport St. James 88.

Bowman, Herbert Lister, born in London 16 March, 1874; o.s. John Herbert, assistant secretary board of England. NEW COLL., matric. 14 Oct., 92, aged 18, from Eton.

Bowman, Hubert, born at Adelaide, Australia, 1863; 3s. Edmund, arm. EXETER, matric. 22 Oct., 80, aged 17.

Bowman, Paget Mervyn, born in London 1 Sept., 1873; 1s. sir William Paget, bart., bar.-at-law, etc. MAGDALEN, matric. 18 Oct., 92, aged 19, from Eton.

Bowman, Philip Edward, born in Bristol 8 April, 1861; 4s. Thomas, cler. HERTFORD, matric. 18 May, 80, aged 19 (from Bristol school), scholar 79-84, B.A. 84; HONOURS:—1 mathematical mods. 81, 1 mathematics 84.

Bowman, Thomas, M.A., fellow MERTON 77, where see.

Bown, Frederick William, born at Handsworth, co. Staff., 1870; 1s. George, gen. UNIVERSITY COLL., matric. 13 Oct., 88, aged 18 (from Bromsgrove school), scholar 88, B.A. 92; HONOURS:—2 mathematical mods. 90, 4 physics 92.

Bown, George Herbert, born at Handsworth, co. Stafford, 11 Nov., 1871; 2s. George, gen. TRINITY, matric. 11 Oct., 90, aged 18 (from Bromsgrove school), scholar 89; HONOURS:—1 classical mods. 92.

Bowring, (rev.) Edgar George, born at St. Heliers, Jersey, 1866; 4s. Hubert, gent. HERTFORD, matric. 27 Oct., 85, aged 19 (from Victoria coll., Jersey), scholar 84, B.A. 89, M.A. 92 (HONOURS:—1 classical mods. 87, 2 classics 89); curate of All Saints, Hatcham Park, Surrey 90.

Bowring, Henry Illingworth, born at Liverpool 4 Jan., 1870; 1s. Henry Price, arm. TRINITY, matric. 13 Oct., 88, aged 18 (from Marlborough coll.), B.A. 91; HONOURS:—3 law 91, 3 civil law 92.

Box, George Herbert, born at Gravesend, Kent, 24 Sept., 1869; 1s. George, gen. ST. JOHN'S, matric. 12 Oct., 89, aged 20 (from Merchant Taylors' school), exhibitioner 89, scholar 93; HONOURS: —Hebrew scholarship 89, 1 theology 92.

Boxall, William, born at Albourne, Sussex, 23 Jan., 1861; ST. MARY HALL, matric. 27 April, 91, aged 30.

Boyd, Alexander Brooke, born May, 1863. CHRIST CHURCH, matric. 14 Oct., 81, aged 18 (from Clifton coll.), scholar 84-6, B.A. 85, M.A. and B.Med. 92; HONOURS:—2 natural science 85, 3 physiology 86.

Boyd, Andrew, born at Townland, co. Derry, 1863; 1s. George, gen. BALLIOL, matric. 18 Oct., 87, aged 24, from Queen's coll., Belfast.

Boyd, Charles Clifford, born in Edinburgh 24 April, 1869; 2s. James, arm. MAGDALEN, matric. 16 Oct., 88, aged 19 (from Haileybury); assist. collector and magistrate Belgaum, Bombay C.S. 90.

Boyd, Henry, D.D., principal of HERTFORD 77, where see.

Boyd, Hugh Arthur, born in Bombay 1870; 2s. Dugald Cameron, cler. BALLIOL, matric. 18 Oct., 88, aged 18 (from Aberdeen gymnasium); assist. magistrate and collector Cuttack, Bengal C.S. 90.

Boyd, James Craufurd, born in Edinburgh 5 March, 1868; 1s. James, arm. MERTON, matric. 15 Oct., 90, aged 22, from Clifton coll.

Boyd, William, M.A., archdeacon of Craven, fellow UNIVERSITY COLL. 33-6, where see.

Boyd, rev. William Grenville, born in London, 1867; 1s. Thomas, arm. HERTFORD, matric. 22 Oct., 85, aged 19 (from Sherborne school), exhibitioner 86, B.A. 90 (HONOURS:—3 classical mods. 88, 2 classics 90); curate of Portsea 91.

Boyle, Albert Sydney, born in London Feb., 1873; 3s. Charles, barrister-at-law. KEBLE, matric. 15 Oct., 92, aged 19, from Elizabeth coll., Guernsey.

Boyle, Charles Schofield, born in Sydenham, Kent, 1869; 1s. Charles, arm. PEMBROKE, matric. 25 Oct., 87, aged 18 (from Elizabeth coll., Guernsey), scholar 87, B.A. 91; HONOURS:—2 classical mods. 89, 2 classics 91.

Boyle, hon. Fitzadelm Alfred Wentworth, born 20 Aug., 1866; 3s. Richard, earl of Cork. NEW COLL., matric. 16 Jan., 85, aged 18 (from Eton), B.A. 88 (HONOURS:—3 classical mods. 86, 4 law 88); died 6 Jan. 90, at Cannes.

Boyle, Sydney Herbert, born at Woolwich 8 April, 1865; 2s. Robert, arm. KEBLE, matric. 17 Oct., 82, aged 19, from Fettes coll.

Brabant, Frederick Gaspard, M.A. CORPUS CHRISTI, where see.

Brabazon, Richard Carmichael, born at Bath 11 Jan., 1864; 4s. Antony Beaufort, D.Med. NON-COLLEGIATE, matric. 3 Jan., 83, aged 19; migrated to ST. MARY HALL, B.A. 86.

Brackenbury, Edmund Algernon, born at Bristol 12 Oct., 1868; 1s. Edmund Bennet, cler. KEBLE, matric. 13 Oct., 88, aged 20.

Brackenbury, Henry Langton, born at Colchester 26 April, 1868; o.s. Henry, major, etc. CORPUS CHRISTI, matric. 22 Oct., 87, aged 19 (from Lemington coll.), scholar 87; HONOURS:—2 classical mods. 89, 4 classics 91.

Brackenbury, rev. Robert Allen, born at Wimbledon, Surrey, April, 1860; 7s. John Matthew, cler. NON-COLLEGIATE, matric. 23 Oct., 80, aged 20 (from Sherborne school), B.A. 83, M.A. 90 (HONOURS:—3 theology 83); curate of Northover, Somerset, 83.

Bradburne, Charles Randal, born at Torquay, Devon, 26 Feb., 1866; 1s. Charles Randal, cler. TRINITY, matric. 11 Oct., 84, aged 18 (from Marlborough coll.), B.A. 87; HONOURS:—4 law 87.

Bradbury, John Swanwick, born at Winsford, Cheshire, 23 Sept., 1872; 1s. John, merchant, deceased. BRASENOSE, matric. 22 Oct., 91, aged 19 (from Manchester gr. school), scholar 91.

Brady, Edward Hugh Falquen, born at Harrow, Middx., 8 Nov. 1866; 2s. Edward Henry, D.D. ORIEL, matric., 23 Oct., 85, aged 18 (from Rugby), B.A. 88.

Brady, Godfrey Fox, born at Harrow, Middx., 21 May, 1863; 1s. Edward Henry, D.D. BALLIOL, matric. 17 Oct., 82, aged 19 (from Rugby), B.A. 87, M.A. 89 (HONOURS:—1 classical mods. 84, 2 classics 86); a master at Rugby 87.

Brady, Henry Christopher, born at Haileybury, Herts, 28 Dec., 1868; 3s. Edward Henry, cler., and head master of Haileybury. NEW COLL., matric. 14 Oct. 87, aged 18 (from Rugby), B.A. 92 (HONOURS:—1 classical mods. 89, 2 classics 91), in the University eleven 90.

Braddon, Edward, born at Upton-on-Severn, co. Gloucester, 1858; 3s. Charles, gent. WADHAM, matric. 26 Jan., 81, aged 22; migrated to BALLIOL, B.A. and M.A. 87.

Bradfield, Daniel, born in London 1859; 1s. Francis, gen. NEW COLL., matric. 18 Jan., 87, aged 28, B.Mus. 91.

Bradford, Basil Wyatt, born at Clyffe Pypard, Wilts, 1870; 2s. Charles William, cler. BRASENOSE, matric. 16 Oct., 88, aged 18 (from Clifton coll.), B.A. 92.

Bradford, Charles Cyril, born at Clyffe Pypard, Wilts, 1865; 1s. Charles William, cler. BRASENOSE, matric. 14 Oct., 84, aged 19 (from Clifton coll.), B.A. 88; HONOURS:—3 classical mods. 86, 2 history 88.

Bradford, rev. Edwin Emmanuel, born at Torquay, Devon, 1860; 4s. Edward Greendale, gent. EXETER, matric. 20 Oct., 81, aged 21 (from Castle coll., Torquay), B.A. 84 (HONOURS:—3 theology 84), assist. chaplain St. Petersburg 87-9, curate of English church Paris (Rue des Russins), 90.

Bradford, Montagu Edward, born at Poonah, E. Indies, 1867; 1s. Edward, arm. CHRIST CHURCH, matric. 15 Oct., 86, aged 19 (from Eton), selected candidate Indian C.S. 86; died 22 Aug., 90, at Calcutta.

Brackhurst, Augustus Maunsell, born in New York, 1866; o.s. Henry Maunsell, arm. CHRIST CHURCH, matric. 12 June, 86, aged 20.

Bradish, Henry Bell. NON-COLLEGIATE, matric. 27 Jan., 91, from K. Edward's school, Bromsgrove.

Bradley, Andrew Cecil, M.A., fellow BALLIOL 74-84, where see.

Bradley, Everard Gilbert, born at Nether Whitaker, co. Warwick, May, 1861; 1s. Gilbert, cler. KEBLE, matric. 19 Oct., 80, aged 19 (from Rossall school), B.A. 83, M.A. 91.

Bradley, Francis Herbert, M.A., fellow MERTON 70, where see.

Bradley, Frederick Lewis, born at Sale, Cheshire, 21 Sept., 1862; 3s. William Henry, gent. ST. JOHN'S, matric. 14 Oct., 82, aged 20, from Rugby.

Bradley, George Granville, D.D., dean of Westminster, master of UNIVERSITY COLL. 70-81, where see.

Bradley, Henry, president of the philological society of London, created M.A. 3 March, 91.

Bradshaw, Francis Thomas, born at Bucklebury, Berks, 18 April, 1862 ; 1s. Sandys Vnyr Burges, cler. WADHAM, matric. 15 Oct., 81, aged 19 (from Manchester gr. school), B.A. 85 (HONOURS :—3 classical mods. 83, 4 classics 85) ; bar.-at-law, Middle Temple, 87.

Braidwood, Harold Lithgow, born at Twickenham, Middx., 12 Aug., 1872; 2s. Lithgow, cler. CORPUS CHRISTI, matric. 19 Oct., 91, aged 19 (from St. Paul's school), scholar 91.

Brain, rev. Alfred, born at Oxford 26 June, 1862 ; 2s. William, gen. NON-COLLEGIATE, matric. 13 Oct., 88, aged 26 ; migrated to WORCESTER, B.A. 91 ; of diocesan registry Melbourne.

Brain, Joseph Hugh, born at Bristol 1863 ; 1s. Joseph Benjamin, gent. ORIEL, matric. 27 Oct., 83, aged 20 (from Clifton coll.), B.A. 88 (HONOURS :—3 classical mods. 85), in the University eleven 84, 5, 6, 7.

Brain, William Henry, born at Clifton, co. Glouc., July, 1870; 2s. Joseph Benjamin, gen. ORIEL, matric. 25 Oct., 89, aged 19 (from Clifton coll.), in the University eleven 91-2.

Braithwaite, rev. Herbert Morris, born at Kendal, Westmorland, 15 April, 1864 ; 4s. George Foster, arm. UNIVERSITY COLL., matric. 13 Oct., 83, aged 19, B.A. 86, M.A. 90 (HONOURS :—4 history 86) ; curate of St. Saviour, Liverpool, 86.

Bramley, Cyril Richard, born at Worsthorne, co. Lanc., 1865 ; 1s. Richard, cler. NON-COLLEGIATE, matric. 28 Jan., 84, aged 19, B.A. 86.

Bramley, Henry Ramsden, M.A., fellow MAGDALEN 57, where see.

Bramston, John, C.B., D.C.L., fellow ALL SOULS' 55-73, where see.

Bramston, John Trant, M.A., select preacher 91-2, where see page .

Bramwell, Ernest, born at Barrow Hill, Surrey, 1873 ; 3s. Addison, cler. ORIEL, matric. 27 Oct., 91, aged 18, from the Charterhouse.

Bramwell, Frederick Charles, born at Wiganthorpe, Yorks, 22 Jan., 1872 ; 2s. Henry, of Crown East Court, co. Worc., arm. MAGDALEN, matric. 14 Oct., 90, aged 18, from Eton.

Bramwell, sir Frederick Joseph, bart., created D.C.L. 20 June, 1886 ; (s. George, of London, banker), LL.D., Cambridge 92 ; F.R.S. 73, associate 56, member 62, and president of the Institution of civil engineers 85-6, hon. sec. Royal Institution 85, knighted 18 Aug., 81, created a baronet 89.

Branch, Charles Churchill, born in London May, 1866 ; o.s. Charles, arm. NEW COLL., matric. 10 Oct., 84, aged 18 (from Eton), B.A. 89 ; (HONOURS :—3 law 88) ; bar.-at-law, Inner Temple, 91.

Brand, John Arthur, born in London 20 May, 1867 ; 1s. John Alexander, arm. ST. MARY HALL, matric. 30 April, 85, aged 18.

Brandreth, (rev.) Frank Williams, born in London Aug., 1866 ; 1s. William Fredrick, gent. NON-COLLEGIATE, matric. 20 Jan., 86, aged 19 ; migrated to CHRIST CHURCH 87, B.A. 89, M.A. 92 ; curate of Buckland Newton, Dorset, 90.

Branthwaite, Thomas Albert, born at Dalston, Middx., 1871 ; 4s. William, arm. HERTFORD, matric. 14 Oct., 90, aged 19 (from Worcester cathedral school), scholar 89 ; HONOURS :—3 classical mods. 92.

Brashaw, rev. Thomas Littlewood, born at Darnall, Yorks, 8 April, 1868 ; o.s. Joseph, gen. ST. JOHN'S, matric. 15 Oct., 87, aged 19 (from Hemsworth school), B.A. 91 ; HONOURS :—3 theology 91.

Brassey, Henry Leonard Campbell, born at Leamington 7 March, 1870 ; 1s. Henry Arthur, arm. CHRIST CHURCH, matric. 1 June 88, aged 18, from Eton.

Brassey, Thomas, lord, born at Stafford, 11 Feb., 1836 ; 1s. Thomas, of Stafford, arm. UNIVERSITY COLL., matric. 30 May, 55, aged 19 (from Rugby), B.A. 59, M.A. 64, created D.C.L. 20 June, 86 ; bar.-at-law, Lincoln's Inn, 66, civil lord of the admiralty 80-4, secretary to admiralty Nov., 84-5, M.P. Devonport June—July, 65, Hastings 66-86, K.C.B. 81, created baron Brassey of Bulkley, Cheshire, 16 Aug., 85.

Brassey, hon. Thomas Allnutt, born at Beaufort Park, Sussex, 7 March 1863 ; 1s. sir Thomas, K.C.B. (baron 86). BALLIOL, matric. 17 Oct., 82, aged 19 (from Eton), B.A. 86 ; HONOURS :—2 history 86.

Bray, Joseph, born in London 1868 ; 4s. Joseph, arm. PEMBROKE, matric. 22 Jan., 88, aged 20, B.A. 91 ; HONOURS :—4 history 91.

Braybrooke, Arthur Philip, born at Leamington, co. Warwick, 19 Nov., 1870 ; 3s. Philip Watson, arm. TRINITY, matric. 12 Oct., 89, aged 18, from Wellington coll.

Brearley, Samuel, born at Rocky Hill, America, 1859 ; 7s. Samuel, gent. BALLIOL, matric. 17 Oct., 80, aged 21 (from Harvard coll., U.S.A.); died 87.

Broay, rev. Christopher Francis, born at Birmingham, 27 April, 1866 ; y.s. Henry Thomas, cler. MERTON, matric. 16 Oct., 84, aged 18, B.A. 89, M.A. 91 ; curate of St. Andrew, Peckham, Surrey, 89.

Breeds, James, born at Hastings 1862 ; 3s. James, arm. BRASENOSE, matric. 22 Oct., 80, aged 18, from Dulwich coll.

Brooks, Charles Wilkinson, born at Ootacamund, E. Indies, 11 Aug., 1870 ; 2s. James Wilkinson, arm. CHRIST CHURCH, matric. 18 Jan., 89, aged 18, from Rugby.

Brooks, William Denison, born at Ootacamund, E. Indies, 4 Nov., 1871 ; 3s. James Wilkinson, arm. NEW COLL., matric. 10 Oct., 90, aged 18, from Rugby.

Broese, Lewis Jorwerth, born at Portmadoc, co. Carnarvon, 1866 ; 2s. Edward, solicitor. EXETER, matric. 16 Oct., 84, aged 18 (from Shrewsbury school), drowned at Portmadoc 8 July, 86.

Bremridge, Richard Harding, born at Pimlico 30 Oct., 1870 ; 1s. Richard, sec. Pharmaceutical soc., London. MAGDALEN, matric. 30 Oct., 88, aged 17 (from Merchant Taylors' school), demy 89, B.A. 93 ; HONOURS :—1 classical mods. 91.

Brendon, Benjamin Adams, born at Plymouth 1871 ; 2s. William Turner, gent. BALLIOL, matric. 14 Oct., 90, aged 19 (from Plymouth coll.), selected candidate Indian c.s. 92.

Brendon, Ernest, born at Gosport, Hants, July, 1863 ; Algernon, arm. WORCESTER, matric. 27 Oct., 81, aged 18, from Bradfield coll. and Oxford military coll.

Brereton, Charles B.C.L., fellow NEW COLL. 32-40, where see.

Brereton, Charles Abdy, born at Worcester Park, Surrey, 1873 ; 2s. Charles William, colonel R.A. ST. JOHN'S, matric. 9 Feb., 92, aged 19, from Lancing coll.

Brereton, Reginald Hugh, born at Cheltenham 12 Nov., 1861 ; 3s. Ebenezer William, cler. BALLIOL, matric. 21 Oct., 80, aged 18 (from Cheltenham coll.), assist. commissioner Hamirpur, Oude, N.W.P., 82.

Bretherton, Walter Kington, born at Gloucester 27 Aug., 1871; 7s. Edward, gen. NON-COLLEGIATE, matric. 29 Oct., 90, aged 19 (from Bristol gr. school); HONOURS:—3 classical mods. 92.

Brett, Edward Adolphus de, born at Meeamecca, E. Indies, 21 June, 1867; 1s. Alfred, col. 18th Native Inf. NEW COLL., matric. 15 Oct., 86, aged 19 (from Winchester), assist. commissioner Narsinghpur, central provinces, 88.

Brett, Michael, born at Roehampton, Surrey, 23 July, 1871; 1s. John, A.R.A. NEW COLL., matric. 10 Oct., 90, aged 19, from Winchester.

Brettell, Samuel Sidaway, born at Quarry Bank, co. Stafford, 26 Dec., 1859; 2s. Thomas, gen. NON-COLLEGIATE, matric. 21 Oct., 89, aged 29, from Owens coll., Manchester, and Manchester new coll. London and Oxford.

Brewer, Alfred Herbert, born at Gloucester, 21 June, 1865; 1s. Alfred, of the probate office. EXETER, matric. 24 Jan., 84, aged 18 (from Gloucester collegiate school), organist 83-6.

Brewer, Edmund Williams Tom Llewellyn, born at Dan-y-Craig, co. Monmouth, Sept., 1865; o.s. Tom Llewellyn, arm. ST. JOHN'S, matric. 23 Jan., 86, aged 20 (from St. Edward's school, Summertown), B.A. 90.

Brewin, rev. Clement, born at Settle, Yorks, 22 Feb., 1863; 1s. Arthur, assistant master Giggleswick school. NEW COLL., matric. 14 Oct., 82, aged 19 (from Winchester), B.A. 85 (HONOURS:—3 classical mods. 83, 3 history 85); chaplain at Lausanne 90-1, curate St. Botolph, Lincoln, 91.

Brewin, Francis Henry, born at Isleworth, Middx., 26 Nov., 1873; 3. Arthur, stockbroker. NEW COLL., matric. 14 Oct., 92, aged 18 (from Winchester coll.); clerk of MAGDALEN 92.

Brewin, Lancelot, born at Giggleswick, Yorks, 1869; 4s. Arthur, assistant master. BALLIOL, matric. 18 Oct., 88, aged 19 (from Giggleswick school), exhibitioner 87, B.A. 92; HONOURS:—1 mathematical mods. 89, 1 mathematics 92.

Brewster, Arthur James, born at Daventry, Northants, 26 Aug., 1873; 1s. James George, M.A., rector of Stratford St. Mary, Suffolk. UNIVERSITY COLL., matric. 15 Oct., 92, aged 19, from Marlborough coll.

Brice, rev. Edward Henry, born at Bishops Lydeard, Somerset, 4 Nov., 1858; 1s. Henry, cler. MERTON, matric. 20 Oct., 87, aged 18 (from Newton Abbot coll.), B.A. 90 (HONOURS:—3 theology 90); curate of Charlton Kings, co. Gloucester, 90.

Brickdale, John Matthew Fortescue-, born at Upper Norwood Sept., 1869; 2s. Matthew Inglett, arm. CHRIST CHURCH, matric. 12 Oct., 88, aged 19 (from Dulwich coll.), B.A. 92.

Bricknell, (rev.) William Nash, born at Kendall, Westmorland, 8 March, 1863; o.s. Richard Nash, cler. ST. ALBAN HALL, matric. 19 Oct., 81, aged 18 (from Magdalen coll. school); migrated to MERTON, B.A. 86, M.A. 90; curate of Mirfield, Yorks, 87-91.

Bridge, George Fletcher, born at Opawa, New Zealand, 4 Feb., 1862; 2s. Charles Joseph, arm., deceased. NEW COLL., matric. 19 Oct., 80, aged 18 (from Malvern coll.), B.A. 84; HONOURS:—3 classical mods. 82, 3 history 84.

Bridge, John Ethelred Mangles, born at Piddle-Trenthide, Dorset, 1864; 3s. John Edward, arm. EXETER, matric. 18 Oct., 83, aged 19 (from Chardstock coll.), B.A. 87.

Bridges, George Theodore, born at Wallsintch, Salop, Oct., 1862; 1s. John Affleck, arm. CHRIST CHURCH, matric. 20 Jan., 82, aged 19, from Birmingham gr. school.

Bridges, James Albert, born at Stepney, Middx., 15 Oct., 1862; 4s. William Thomas, gen. ST. MARY HALL, matric. 21 May, 87, aged 25.

Bridges, John Henry, B.Med., fellow ORIEL 55-61, where see.

Bridgman, John Moore, born at Walreddon, Devon, 3 Dec., 1872; 4s. Christopher Vicary, solicitor. EXETER COLL., matric. 22 Oct., 91, aged 18, from Magdalen coll. school.

Bridson, Edward Ridgway, born at Bolton-le-Moors, co. Lanc., 11 April, 1864; 3s. Thomas, of Torquay, gent. MAGDALEN, matric. 19 Oct., 83, aged 19, B.A. 87, M.A. 90.

Bridson, Francis Charles, born at Bolton-le-Moors, co. Lanc., 1868; 4s. Thomas Ridgway, arm. BRASENOSE, matric. 20 Oct., 87, aged 19, from St. Edward's school, Summertown.

Brierley, William Booth, born at Chester 1870; 1s. John Colley, gen. NON-COLLEGIATE, matric. 15 March, 92, aged 22.

Briggs, Arthur Charlesworth, born at Ripley, Yorks, 15 Jan., 1867; 4s. Rawdon, arm. EXETER, matric. 21 Oct., 86, aged 19 (from Bedford gr. school), B.A. 90.

Briggs, (rev.) Arthur Nathaniel, born at Rawdon, Yorks, 1869; o.s. Arthur, arm. ORIEL, matric. 18 Oct., 87, aged 18 (from Loretto school), B.A. 90.

Briggs, (rev.) Douglas Hilton, born at Sunderland 1864; 1s. Charles James, arm. ST. JOHN'S, matric. 17 Oct., 85, aged 21, B.A. 88, M.A. 92; curate of Longton St. John, Stafford, 90.

Briggs, Francis, born at Wyke, near Bradford, Yorks, 5 Aug., 1872; o.s. Samuel, gen. QUEEN'S, matric. 27 Oct., 91, aged 19 (from Bradford gr. school), scholar 91.

Bright, James Frank, D.D., master of UNIVERSITY COLL., 81, where see.

Bright, right hon. John, created D.C.L. 30 June, 1886. See *Alumni Oxonienses*, and series, 160.

Bright, John Edward, M.A., student CHRIST CHURCH 39-47, where see.

Bright, William, D.D., canon of CHRIST CHURCH 68, where see.

Brightman, rev. Frank Edward, M.A. UNIVERSITY COLL., where see.

Brigstocke, Arthur Montague, born at Hamburg in Germany 1871; 1s. Claude Buchanan, cler. CHRIST CHURCH, matric. 21 Oct., 90, aged 19 (from Heidelberg), scholar 90; selected candidate Indian C.S. 90.

Brind, Charles Brownlow, born at Lee, Kent, 1865; 1s. Charles, gent. BALLIOL, matric. 17 Oct., 82, aged 17 (from a Blackheath school), selected candidate Indian C.S. 82.

Brindle, Joseph Fleury, born at Bacup, co. Lanc., 23 Jan., 1866; 1s. Joseph Furnival, cler. JESUS COLL., matric. 16 Oct., 84, aged 18 (from King William's coll., isle of Man), scholar 84, B.A. 88; HONOURS:—Abbott scholarship 84, 2 classical mods. 86, 3 classics 88.

Brindley, Charles Harry, born at Longton, co. Stafford, 16 Dec., 1869; 4s. William, gen. WORCESTER, matric. 17 Oct., 87, aged 17, from Stafford school.

Brine, rev. Algernon Lindesay, born at Wiesbaden, Germany, 1864; 4s. James Grant, cler. ST. JOHN'S, matric. 14 Oct., 82, aged 18, B.A. 85, M.A. 90 (HONOURS:—4 theology 85); curate of West Malling, Kent, 87.

Brine, James Gram, B.D., fellow ST. JOHN'S 37-54, where see.

Brinkworth, James Bardulph, born at Swindon, Wilts, 18 Feb., 1868; o.s. James Arthur, dissenting minister. NON-COLLEGIATE, matric. 11 Oct., 90, aged 22 (from K. Edward gr. school, Saffron Walden), B.A. Queen's coll., Cambridge, 89; HONOURS: 3 theology 89 and 3 Semitic languages 90.

Brinton, Hubert, born in London 13 Feb., 1863; 3s. William, D.Med., deceased. NEW COLL., matric. 14 Oct., 82, aged 19 (from Marlborough coll.), B.A. 86, M.A. 90; HONOURS :—1 classical mods. 83, 1 classics 86.

Brinton, John Chaytor, born at Stourport, co. Worcester, 5 April, 1867; 2s. John, of Moor Hall, arm. TRINITY, matric. 17 Oct., 85, aged 18 (from Bath coll.),lieut. and Life guards 92.

Brinton, Percival Robert, born at Lower Milton, co. Worc., 5 Feb., 1873; s. John, of Moor Hall, Stourport, arm. BALLIOL, matric. 20 Oct., 91, aged 18, from Winchester.

Brinton, Reginald Seymour, born at Lower Milton, co. Worc., 15 Dec., 1869; 3s. John, of Moor Hall, Stourport, arm. NEW COLL., matric. 12 Oct., 88, aged 18 (from Winchester), scholar 87; HONOURS : —2 classical mods. 90.

Brisay, rev. Henry Delacour de, M.A. UNIVERSITY COLL., where see.

Briscoe, Alfred Leigh, born at Hooton, Cheshire, 1870; 1s. John James, arm. CORPUS CHRISTI, matric. 20 Oct., 88, aged 18 (from Harrow), B.A. 91; HONOURS :—3 law 91.

Briscoe, Francis Percival, born at Drogheda, co. Meath, 25 Dec., 1862; 4s. James Reginald, cler. TRINITY, matric. 21 Jan., 82, aged 19 (from Malvern coll.), B.A. 85; died 86.

Briscoe, George, born at Rainhill, co. Lanc., 23 Sept., 1862; 1s. Walter, arm. TRINITY, matric. 16 Oct., 80, aged 18 (from Repton school), B.A. 83, M.A. 87; HONOURS :—3 classical mods. 81, 3 history 83.

Briscoe, Henry Meyrick Eliott Drake, born at Nutfield, Surrey, 12 Sept., 1870; 2s. Richard, D.D. JESUS COLL., matric. 14 Oct., 89, aged 19, from Hammersmith school.

Briscoe, Theodore Francis Heathfield, born at Nutfield, Surrey, 15 Oct., 1867; 1s. Richard, D.D. JESUS COLL., matric. 18 Jan., 87, aged 19 (from Hammersmith school), B.A. 92.

Briscoe, Francis, D.D., chancellor of Bangor, fellow JESUS COLL. 34-59, where see.

Brise, Harry Goodeve Ruggles-, born at Finchingfield, Essex, 1864; 5s. Samuel Brise, C.B., M.P. BALLIOL, matric. 17 Oct., 82, aged 18 (from Winchester), (HONOURS :—2 classical mods. 83); in university eleven 83, lieut. Grenadier guards 85.

Bristowe, Arthur Lynn, born at Herne Hill, Surrey, 9 Oct., 1862; 3s. Thomas Lynn, arm. MAGDALEN, matric. 16 Oct., 80, aged 18 (from Radley coll.), B.A. 83, M.A. 91 (HONOURS —4 history 83); bar.-at-law, Inner Temple, 85.

Brittain Henry Ernest, born at Ranmoor, near Sheffield, 24 Dec., 1873; 1s. William Henry, merchant. WORCESTER, matric. 18 Oct., 92, aged 18, from Rossall school.

Brittain, William, born at Tittensor, co. Stafford, 18 Dec., 1872; 4s. Thomas, paper manufacturer. EXETER, matric. 22 Oct., 91, aged 18, from Tunbridge school.

Britten, Frank Curzon, born at Blackburn, co. Lanc., 16 Jan., 1870; 3s. George, gen. CHRIST CHURCH, matric. 10 Oct., 90, aged 20 (from St. Paul's school), exhibitioner 89.

Britten, rev. George Edmund, born at Silverton, Northants, 21 May, 1868; 1s. Thomas Candy, late vicar of Somerby, Rutland. LINCOLN, matric. 21 Oct., 87, aged 19 (from Derby school), B.A. 90; curate of Wednesbury, co. Staff., 90.

Britton, Alfred Edward, born in London 21 Sept., 1872; 1s. George, of Putney, Surrey, gen. BALLIOL, matric. 20 Oct., 91, aged 19, from St. Paul's school.

Britton, rev. Robert William, born at Manchester 1854; 1s. Robert, gent. NON-COLLEGIATE, matric. 26 April, 80 (from Owens coll., Manchester, and St. Aidan's coll., Birkenhead); migrated to NEW INN HALL. 80 (BALLIOL 87); has held various curacies since 77.

Broad, Albert Sheppard Leigh, born at Plymouth 15 Feb., 1870; 1s. Alfred, gen. WORCESTER, matric. 14 Oct., 90, aged 20.

Broad, Charles Luther, born in London 1853; 2s. Peter, gent. NON-COLLEGIATE, matric. 17 Jan., 80, aged 27, from Clifton coll.

Broadbent, Arthur Carr, born at Collingham, Notts, 23 April, 1867; 7s. John, D.Med. MAGDALEN, matric. 21 Oct., 86, aged 19, from Newark and Sherborne school.

Broadbent, Henry, M.A., fellow EXETER 74, where see.

Broadbent, Herbert, born at Bradshaw, Yorks, 1870; 1s. Benjamin, arm. HERTFORD, matric. 19 Oct., 88, aged 18 (from the Charterhouse), exhibitioner 90, B.A. 92; HONOURS :—3 classical mods. 90, 3 history 92.

Broadbent, John Francis Harpin, born in London 16 Oct., 1865; 1s. William Henry, D.Med. HERTFORD, matric. 14 Oct., 84, aged 19 (from Rugby), scholar 83, B.A. 88, M.A. and B.Med. 92; HONOURS :—2 classical mods. 86, 3 physiology 88.

Broadbent, Percy Goolden Argentine, born at Reigate, Surrey, Jan. 1870; 3s. John, gen. KEBLE, matric. 14 Oct., 90, aged 20, from Croydon school.

Broadbent, Theodore Parker, born at Lewes, Sussex, 1868; 1s. James, gent. ORIEL, matric. 23 Oct., 85, aged 17 (from Lewes school), scholar 84, B.A. 90; HONOURS :—2 classical mods. 87.

Broadwater, rev. Richard, M.A., NON-COLLEGIATE, where see.

Brook, Arthur Clutton, born at Stourport, co. Worcester, 23 March, 1868; 1s. John Allan Clutton, banker. NEW COLL., matric. 14 Oct., 87, aged 19 (from Eton); HONOURS :—3 classical mods. 89, 3 classics 91.

Brook, Harry, born in Glasgow 1864; 1s. Henry, arm. CORPUS CHRISTI, matric. 19 Oct., 83, aged 19.

Brook, Hugh Bulkeley Price, born at Glasgow 20 Jan., 1871; 2s. Henry arm. BRASENOSE, matric. 14 Oct., 90, aged 19, from Loretto school.

Brook, Robert Coleman Hall, born at Philadelphia Jan., 1861; 5s. John Penn, arm. CHARSLEY'S HALL, matric. 19 Oct., 80, aged 19, from St. Paul's school, U.S.A.

Brocklebank, John Wilfrid Royds, born at Liverpool Aug. 1869; 1s. Thomas, arm. CHRIST CHURCH, matric. 11 Oct., 89, aged 20, from Eton.

Brockman, Elliot George Drake, born at Cawnpore, E. Indies, 2 Feb., 1867; 3s. William Drake, arm. TRINITY, matric. 16 Oct., 86, aged 19 (from Elizabeth coll., Guernsey); assist. magistrate and collector (24-Pergunnahs), Bengal c.s. 88.

Brookman, rev. Ralph Thomas, born in London 15 June, 1861; 2s. Ralph St. Leger, vicar of Kesgrave, Suffolk, deceased. NON-COLLEGIATE, matric. 14 Oct., 82, aged 19 from Huntingdon gr. school), B.A. 86, M.A. 91 (HONOURS :—2 theology 86); curate of Cowley St. John, Oxford, 90.

Brodhurst, Bernard Edward Spencer, born in London 1866; 1s. Bernard Edward, arm. MAGDALEN, matric. 23 Oct., 85, aged 19 (from Harrow), B.A. 88, M.A. and B.C.L. 92 (HONOURS :—3 law 88, 3 civil law 89); bar.-at-law, Inner Temple, 91.

Brodhurst, rev. Edward Henry Herbert, born at Barnsley, Yorks, 3 Aug., 1862; 1s. Frederick, cler. KEBLE, matric. 17 Oct., 82, aged 20 (from Marlborough coll.), B.A. 86, M.A. 90 (HONOURS :—2 history 85); incumbent of St. Peter, West End, Brisbane, Queensland, 91.

Brodie, sir Benjamin Vincent Sellon (3rd bart.), born at Oxford 19 June, 1862; 1s. Sir Benjamin Collins, bart. MAGDALEN, matric. 1 Nov., 81, aged 19 (from Owens coll.), B.A. 86, M.A. 89; bar.-at-law, Lincoln's Inn, 89.

Brodie, Norman Somerville, born in Colombo, Ceylon, 1865; 7s. William Church, gent. CHRIST CHURCH, matric. 15 Oct., 84, aged 19 (from University coll. school, London), scholar 84, B.A. 87, M.A. 92 (HONOURS:—2 Indian languages 87); assist. collector and magistrate, Malabar, Madras C.S. 86.
Brodie, Robert, M.A., senior student CHRIST CHURCH 64-9, where see.
Brodrick, Francis Hammond, born at Peasmarsh, Sussex, 7 Aug., 1867; 2s. William Richard, vicar of Peasmarsh. KEBLE, matric. 22 Oct., 85, aged 18 (from Winchester), B.A. 88.
Brodrick, hon. George Charles, D.C.L., warden of MERTON 81, where see.
Brodrick, hon. Laurence Alan, born 24 Jan., 1864; 2s. William, viscount Midleton. MERTON, matric. 17 Oct., 82, aged 18, B.A. 86; HONOURS:—3 history 86.
Brodrick, Reginald Snaith, born at Salisbury, 6 Oct., 1869; 3s. Thomas, gen. LINCOLN, matric. 18 Oct., 88, aged 19 (from Lancing coll.), B.A. 92.
Brodrick, Thomas Herbert, born in Salisbury 1863; 1s. Thomas, gent. WORCESTER, matric. 20 Oct., 81, aged 18.
Brodrick, William Edward Beninck, born at Peasmarsh, Sussex, 10 Dec., 1865; 1s. William Richard, vicar. PEMBROKE, matric. 27 Oct., 84, aged 18 (from Winchester), scholar 84, B.A. 88; HONOURS: —2 mathematical mods. 86, 3 mathematics 88.
Brodrick, William John Henry, born at Stagsden, Beds, 25 Jan., 1874; 2s. Alan, M.A., cler. CORPUS CHRISTI, matric. 18 Oct., 92, aged 18 (from the Charterhouse), exhibitioner 91.
Broke, rev. Horatio George, born in London 27 Nov., 1861; 1s. Horace, arm. UNIVERSITY COLL., matric. 16 Oct., 80, aged 18 (from Eton), B.A. 83, M.A. 88 (HONOURS:—3 classical mods. 82, 4 history 83); curate of East Dereham 90.
Broke, Philip Vere, born in London 9 Jan., 1867; 3s. Horace, arm. MERTON, matric. 24 Oct., 85, aged 18, as Philip (from Eton), postmaster 85, B.A. 89, as Philip Vere; HONOURS:—2 classical mods. 87, 2 history 89.
Bromet, Alfred, born at Tadcaster, Yorks, 30 Dec., 1865; 4s. John Addinell, solicitor. MAGDALEN, matric. 16 Oct., 84, aged 18 (from Harrow), B.A. 87, M.A. and B.C.L. 91 (HONOURS:—4 law 87, 3 civil law 90); bar.-at-law, Inner Temple, 90.
Bromet, William Ernest, born at Tadcaster, Yorks, 17 May, 1868; 7s. John Addinell, solicitor. WADHAM, matric. 16 Oct., 86, aged 18 (from Richmond gr. school), B.A. 90.
Bromfield, Harry Hickman, born at Warwick Jan., 1869; 1s. Henry, arm. HERTFORD, matric. 14 Oct., 90, aged 21, from Malvern coll.
Bromfield, rev. John Briscoe, born at Whitchurch, Salop, 1863; o.s. John. BRASENOSE, matric. 10 June, 81, aged 18 (from Shrewsbury school), B.A. 84, M.A. 91; curate of Eccleston, co. Lane., 91.
Bromley, Robert, born at Stoke Hall, Notts, 4 Jan., 1874; 1s. Henry, formerly in the army, who was son of Henry, bart. EXETER, matric. 18 Oct., 92, aged 18, from Eton.
Bromwich, rev. Frank Henry, born at Rugby, co. Warwick, 1864; 2s. Henry, gent. ST. JOHN'S, matric. 22 Jan., 84, aged 20, B.A. 89; curate of Burneston, Yorks, 90.
Brook, David, born at Elland, Yorks, 1855; o.s. Joseph, gent. NON-COLLEGIATE, matric. 10 April, 80, aged 25, B.A. 84, M.A. 87, B.C.L. 90.
Brook, rev. William, born at Mansfield Woodhouse, Yorks, March, 1868; 4s. Alfred, cler. KEBLE, matric. 17 Oct., 87, aged 19 (from Uppingham school), B.A. 90.

Brooke, Arthur Richard de Capell, born at Market Harborough, co. Leicester, 12 Oct., 1869; 1s. Richard de Capell, bart. CHRIST CHURCH, matric. 12 Oct., 88, aged 19, from Eton.
Brooke, Charles William Alfred, born at Montreal, Canada, 1861; 1s. Alfred, gent. NEW COLL., matric. 4 Feb., 84, aged 23.
Brooke, Ernest Brooke Cozens, born at Walsall, co. Stafford, 9 May, 1868; 1s. Harry, arm. WADHAM, matric. 15 Oct., 87, aged 19 (from Repton school), B.A. 92.
Brooke, Frederick William, born at Sibton, Suffolk, 31 Dec., 1860; 3s. John William, arm. BRASENOSE, matric. 21 May, 80, aged 19.
Brooke, Henry, born at Folkestone 9 July, 1870; 2s. John, arm. TRINITY, matric. 13 Oct., 88, aged 18 (from Dulwich coll.), B.A. 91; HONOURS:—2 law 91.
Brooke, Henry Richard Patton, born at Jaffna, Ceylon, 1861; o.s. Richard Henry, arm. KEBLE, matric. 19 Oct., 80, aged 19, B.A. 84.
Brooke, Herbert Otto Wildman Goodwyn, born at Tunbridge Wells, Kent, 30 April, 1871; 1s. William John, colonel late 30th Regt. MAGDALEN, matric. 14 Oct., 90, aged 19 (from Cheltenham coll.), demy 90; selected candidate Indian C.S. 90.
Brooke, Percy Cozens, born at Walsall, co. Stafford, 25 May, 1869; 2s. Harry, gen. HERTFORD, matric. 2 May, 90, aged 20, from Malvern coll.
Brooke, rev. William Holford, born at Hyde, Cheshire, 28 Jan., 1868; o.s. William, gent. WADHAM, matric. 16 Oct., 86, aged 18 (from Manchester gr. school), B.A. 89 (HONOURS:—3 theology 89); curate of East Ardsley, Yorks, 89.
Brooke, rev. William Ingham, born at Retford, Notts, 1862; 1s. Joshua Ingham, cler. NON-COLLEGIATE, matric. 23 Oct., 80, aged 18 (from Clifton coll.); migrated to EXETER 22 April, 81, B.A. and M.A. 87; student, Inner Temple, 83.
Brookes, rev. Charles Cunliffe, born at Steeple Aston, Oxon, 14 Dec., 1866; 2s. John Henry, rector. NEW COLL., matric. 16 Oct., 85, aged 18 (from Radley coll.), B.A. 88, M.A. 92 (HONOURS:—3 history 88); curate of St. Pancras, London, 90.
Brookes, Henry Langham, born at Preston Deanery, Northants, 4 Nov., 1864; 1s. John Henry, rector of Steeple Aston, Oxon. NEW COLL., matric. 12 Oct., 83, aged 19 (from the Charterhouse), B.A. 87, M.A. 90; HONOURS:—4 law 87.
Brookes, John Henry, M.A., fellow BRASENOSE 45-64, where see.
Brookes, rev. Joshua Alfred Rowland, born at Felpham, Middx., 30 March, 1865; 1s. Joshua Rowland, arm. PEMBROKE, matric. 27 Oct., 84, aged 19 (from Westminster school), B.A. 88, M.A. 91 (HONOURS:—3 classical mods. 86, 2 history 88); curate of Hednesford, co. Stafford, 89.
Brooks, Cecil Robert Lucas, born in London 10 Sept., 1872; 4s. Henry, gent. CHRIST CHURCH, matric. 14 Oct., 92, aged 20, from Elstree school.
Brooks, Francis, born at Heath, co. Worcester, 1861; 1s. John, gent. BALLIOL, matric. 21 Oct., 80, aged 19 (from Birmingham gr. school), scholar 79-84, B.A. 84, M.A. 87; HONOURS:—1 classical mods. 81, 3 classics 84.
Brooks, George William Desborough Cornwall, born at Streatham, Surrey, Nov., 1872; 1s. George Henry, solicitor. KEBLE, matric. 20 Oct., 91, aged 18, from Harpenden school.
Brooks, Phillips, rector of Trinity Church, Boston, U.S.A., born 13 Dec., 1835; created D.D. 16 June, 85, bishop of Massachusetts 91; died 23 Jan., 93.

Brooks, Walter Tyrrell, born at Stoke Newington, London, 1860; 3s. John, gent. CHRIST CHURCH, matric. 10 June, 84, aged 24 (from King's coll., London), B.A. 87, M.A. 91; clinical lecturer in medicine Radcliffe infirmary 87.

Brooksbank, George, born at Middleton, Yorks, 19 Oct., 1863; 3s. Arthur, arm. MERTON, matric. 25 Jan., 82, aged 18 (from Winchester), B.A. 85, M.A. 88; HONOURS :—4 history 85.

Brooksbank, rev. John Hoult, born at Tinsley, Yorks, 1862; o.s. Martin, gent. NON-COLLEGIATE, matric. 30 April, 85, aged 23, B.A. 88 (HONOURS :—3 history 88); curate of Heanor, co. Derby.

Brooksbank, John Lonsdale, born at Middleton Hall, near Beverley, Yorks, 7 April, 1862; 2s. Arthur, lieut.-col. MAGDALEN, matric. 16 Oct., 80, aged 18 (from Harrow), B.A. 85.

Broomfield, Reginald Cobden, born at Pyrmont, Australia, 15 June, 1864; 3s. John, arm. TRINITY, matric. 15 Oct., 83, aged 19 (from Sydney gr. school), B.A. 87; HONOURS :—2 classical mods. 85, 2 law 87.

Bros, Henry Alwyn, born in London 1 Aug., 1872; 1s. James Reade White, bar.-at-law. MAGDALEN, matric. 22 Oct., 91, aged 19, from Rugby.

Broughton, James Arthur, born at Bradford, Yorks, 10 Sept., 1861; 7s. Benjamin, gent. QUEEN'S, matric. 15 May, 80, aged 18 (from Thorp Arch grange school), clerk MAGDALEN 81-3.

Broughton, Reginald, M.A., fellow HERTFORD 74-7, where see.

Broughton, rev. Reginald Edmund, born at Norbury, co. Derby, 1851; 3s. Clement Francis, cler. KEBLE, matric. 22 Jan., 80, aged 19 (from Bromsgrove school), B.A. 84, M.A. 86 (HONOURS :—3 classical mods. 81); vicar of Prestbury, Cheshire, 89.

Broughton, Thomas Herbert, born at Cheltenham 20 May, 1865; o.s. Reginald, cler. NON-COLLEGIATE, matric. 17 Oct., 85, aged 20, from Cheltenham coll.

Broughton, rev. Walter Basil, born at Norbury, co. Derby, 1863; 4s. Clement Francis, cler. WORCESTER, matric. 26 Jan., 82, aged 19, B.A. 85, M.A. 88; curate of Tewkesbury 91.

Brown, Alfred, born at Tyldesley, co. Lanc., 1865; 3s. John, gent. BRASENOSE, matric. 28 Jan., 86, aged 21 (from Heversham school), B.A. 90, M.A. 92.

Brown, Alfred Vanhouse, born in London 29 Oct., 1873; 1s. Frederick, gen. QUEEN'S, matric. 27 Oct., 91, aged 17 (from Merchant Taylors' school), scholar 91.

Brown, Allen Bathurst, born at Ealing 11 May, 1874; 2s. John Allen, gent. EXETER, matric. 18 Oct., 92, aged 18, from Haileybury.

Brown, rev. Arthur Campion, born at Scarborough, Yorks, Jan., 1862; 1s. Arthur, arm. KEBLE, matric. 18 Oct., 81, aged 19 (from Lincoln and Tonbridge schools), B.A. 84, M.A. 89 (HONOURS : —3 theology 84); curate of Wigan, co. Lanc., 85.

Brown, rev. Arthur Ernest, born in London 1863; 3s. Augustus, D.Med. PEMBROKE, matric. 27 Oct., 83, aged 20 (from Lancing coll.), B.A. 88, M.A. 90; curate of Long Crichel, Dorset, 89.

Brown, Arthur Heber, born at Ross, co. Hereford, 26 March, 1864; 1s. William, gent. MAGDALEN, matric. 19 Oct., 83, aged 19 (from Ross, Taunton, and Stonehouse schools); migrated to ST. EDMUND HALL, B.A. 87, M.A. 90.

Brown, Arthur Neville, born at Nayland, Suffolk, 18 June, 1864; 1s. James Taylor, cler. QUEEN'S, matric. 16 Oct., 82, aged 18 (from ? Leatherhead and Huddersfield schools), exhibitioner 83, B.A. 87, M.A. 91; HONOURS :—2 classical mods. 85, 2 classics 87.

Brown, Cecil Hew, born at Ayr, Scotland, 1867; 2s. John, gent. EXETER, matric. 16 Oct., 84, aged 17 (from Harrow), B.A. 87, M.A. 91; HONOURS :—4 history 87.

Brown, Charles, born at Bow, Middx. 8 June, 1870; 1s. John Whitley, of the Hudson's bay company, gent. NON-COLLEGIATE, matric. 12 Oct., 89, aged 19 (from St. John's school, Iffley road, Oxford); migrated to JESUS COLL. 8 Feb., 92, B.A. 92.

Brown, Charles Dallas, born at Lahore, E. Indies, 1866; 3s. Thomas Edwin Burton, gent. BALLIOL, matric. 24 Oct., 85, aged 19 (from the Charterhouse), B.A. 88 (HONOURS :—4 Indian languages 88); assist. magistrate and collector Belgnaum, Bombay C.S. 87.

Brown, Charles Wreford, born at Clifton, co. Glouc., 1867; 2s. William, arm. ORIEL, matric. 5 Feb., 86, aged 19 (from the Charterhouse), B.A. 90.

Brown, Colin Campbell, born at Glasgow 1859; 1s. Colin, gent. NON-COLLEGIATE, matric. 14 Oct., 82, aged 23 (from Glasgow university), Chinese scholar 84.

Brown, rev. David Hepburn, born at Linlithgow, Scotland, 1860; 1s. David Hepburn, w.s., deceased. EXETER, matric. 15 May, 80, aged 20 (from Edinburgh academy), B.A. 83, M.A. 87; vicar of Elmton with Creswell, co. Derby, 91.

Brown, Edward Cotgrave, born at Kinwarton, co. Warwick, 1866; 5s. John, arm. ST. JOHN'S, matric. 17 Oct., 85, aged 19 (from Coventry school), scholar 85, B.A. 89; HONOURS :—3 mathematical mods. 87.

Brown, Francis Ernest, born at Bristol 1869; 4s. James, gen. HERTFORD, matric. 19 Oct., 88, aged 19 (from Bristol gr. school), scholar 87, B.A. 92; HONOURS :—1 mathematical mods. 89, 2 mathematics 92.

Brown, Frederick D., created M.A. 13 Feb., 1883, then demonstrator in chemistry at the Oxford museum, professor in New Zealand coll.

Brown, Frederick Hewlett (Burton), born at Lahore, E. Indies, 28 Sept., 1863; 1s. Thomas Edwin Burton, D.Med. MAGDALEN, matric. 16 Oct., 82, aged 19 (from the Charterhouse), demy 82, B.A. 86, M.A. and B.Med. 91; HONOURS :—1 physiology 86.

Brown, rev. Frederick John, M.A., BRASENOSE, where see.

Brown, George, born at Wigton, Cumberland, 25 April, 1868; 2s. Thomas, gen. QUEEN'S, matric. 20 Oct., 88, aged 20, from Wigton gr. school.

Brown, George Douglas, born at Ochiltree, Ayrshire, 1868; 1s. George Douglas, gen. BALLIOL, matric. 20 Oct., 91, aged 22 (from Glasgow university), exhibitioner 91.

Brown, rev. George Gibson, born at Edinburgh 1863; 2s. John Crombie, arm. NON-COLLEGIATE, matric. 13 Oct., 84, aged 21 (Pitt scholar Edinburgh university, and M.A. 84); migrated to BALLIOL 85, B.A. 86, M.A. 91 (HONOURS :—1 classical mods. 86, 2 classics 88); curate of Tudhoe Grange, co. Durham, 89.

Brown, rev. George Gilbert, born in London 1866; 1s. Alfred, gent. ST. JOHN'S, matric. 20 April, 85, aged 19, B.A. 88; curate of Welford, Berks, 89.

Brown, Gerard Baldwin, M.A., fellow BRASENOSE 74-7, where see.

Brown, Harold Alexander, born at Calcutta 1866; 1s. John, gent. EXETER, matric. 16 Oct., 84, aged 18, from Harrow.

Brown, Harold Holgate, born at Nayland, Suffolk, 1866; 2s. James Taylor, cler. HERTFORD, matric. 2 June, 84, aged 18 (from Clergy Orphan school, Canterbury), scholar 83, B.A. 88; HONOURS :— 2 classical mods. 86, 2 classics 88.

Brown, Harold Pearce, born at Shutlanger, Northants, 25 March, 1871; o.s. John, cler. BRASENOSE, matric. 14 Oct., 89, aged 18 (from Marlborough coll.), B.A. 92.

Brown, Henry Forbes Darell, born at Welland, co. Worc., 7 June, 1867; 1s. Lionel Edward, vicar. NEW COLL., matric. 23 Jan., 86, aged 18, from Marlborough coll.; brother of Otway.

Brown, Henry Rowland, born at Pinner, Middx., 19 May, 1865; o.s. Henry, arm. UNIVERSITY COLL., matric. 24 Jan., 84, aged 18 (from Rugby), B.A. 87; bar.-at-law, Lincoln's Inn, 89.

Brown, Herbert Hamilton, born in London 1867; 1s. Hamilton Lowther, arm. NON-COLLEGIATE, matric. 20 Oct., 90, aged 23, from Greenock academy.

Brown, Herbert Rochfort Johnson, born at Cheltenham 8 Oct., 1864; 3s. John, arm. KEBLE, matric. 16 Oct., 83, aged 19 (from Cheltenham coll.), B.A. 87, M.A. and B.Med. 92.

Brown, Herbert William, born at Tewkesbury, co. Glouc., July, 1873; 1s. Frederick James, solicitor. KEBLE, matric. 20 Oct., 91, aged 18, from Malvern coll.

Brown, Hercules Langford, born at Froxfield, Wilts, 10 July, 1865; 1s. Hercules Edwin, arm. EXETER, matric. 23 Oct., 85, aged 20 (from Winchester), B.A. 88.

Brown, John, born at St. Andrew's, Scotland, 1861; 1s. Thomas, gent. WORCESTER, matric. 20 Oct., 81, aged 20 (from St. Andrews university), scholar 81-5, B.A. 85; HONOURS:—1 classical mods. 83, 2 classics 85.

Brown, John Hope, born at St. Bees, Cumberland, 18 Feb., 1872; 1s. Thomas, arm. TRINITY, matric. 11 Oct., 90, aged 18, from St. Bees school.

Brown, John Kennett, born at Ealing 3 April, 1873; 1s. John Allen, gen. EXETER, matric. 22 Oct., 91, aged 18, from Haileybury; brother of Allen B.

Brown, Leslie John, born at Ayr, Scotland, 1869; 3s. John, gent. ST. JOHN's, matric. 20 April, 85, aged 16, B.A. 88, M.A. 92; HONOURS:—3 history 88.

Brown, Lionel George, born at Ancaster, co. Lincoln, 23 April, 1872; 4s. Francis, mayor. MERTON, matric. 22 Oct., 91, aged 19, from Bedford modern school.

Brown, Otway Darell Darell, born at Welland, co. Worcester, 7 Nov., 1872; 3s. Edward Lionel D.-B., M.A., cler., deceased. ST. JOHN's, matric. 22 Oct., 92, aged 19, from St. Edward's school, Summertown; brother of Henry F. D.

Brown, Richard Cecil, born at Preston, co. Lanc., Nov., 1868; 4s. James Taylor, cler. KEBLE, matric. 17 Oct., 87, aged 18 (from Clergy orphan school, Canterbury); assistant collector and magistrate Sholapur, Bombay c.s. 89.

Brown, Richard Cuthbert, born at Luton, Beds, 28 April, 1871; 1s. Richard, gen., deceased. BALLIOL, matric. 14 Oct., 90, aged 19, from Clifton coll.

Brown, Thomas Birkett, born at Clifton, co. Glouc., 1863; 1s. Thomas Edward, cler. CORPUS CHRISTI, matric. 19 Oct., 82, aged 19 (from Clifton coll.), B.A. 88; HONOURS:—3 classical mods. 83, 4 classics 86.

Brown, Thomas Edward, M.A., fellow ORIEL 54-8, where see.

Brown, rev. Thomas Temple, born at Feltham, Middx., 2 June, 1862; 1s. Thomas Davy, arm. NON-COLLEGIATE, matric. 17 Oct., 81, aged 19 (from Tonbridge school); migrated to TRINITY, B.A. 85 (HONOURS:—2 theology 85); curate of Trinity Higham 86-7.

Brown, rev. Waller, born at Dawsmar, co. Lincoln, 1869; 5s. William, gen. PEMBROKE, matric. 25 Oct., 87, aged 18 (from Snettisham school), B.A. 90; HONOURS:—4 history 90.

Brown, William Barclay, born at Dalry, co. Ayr, 1865; 3s. David, gen. BALLIOL, matric. 16 Oct., 83, aged 19 (from Ayr academy), B.A. 86 (HONOURS: —2 law 86); assist. commissioner North Lakhimpur, Assam, 85.

Brown, William Frederick, born at Bristol 1871; 4s. James, arm. HERTFORD, matric. 14 Oct., 90, aged 19 (from Bristol school), scholar 89; HONOURS:— 1 mathematical mods. 91, proxime accessit junior mathematical exhibition 91.

Brown, William Geraldton, born at Minton Stanley, S. Australia, 1868; 3s. James, gent. NON-COLLEGIATE, matric. 4 Nov., 86, aged 18, from Stanley gr. school, S. Australia.

Browne, Arthur Harold, born at Kilkenny, Ireland, 13 Feb., 1871; 2s. John James, vicar of Sutton Cheney, co. Leic. BALLIOL, matric. 17 Oct., 89, aged 18 (from Tiverton school), scholar 89; HONOURS:—1 classical mods. 91.

Browne, rev. Austin Leland, born at York, 1864; 1s. Thomas Leland, gen. ST. EDMUND HALL, matric. 19 Oct., 82, aged 18, B.A. 88 (HONOURS:—3 history 86); curate of Somerton, Somerset, 91.

Browne, Beauchamp Denis, born at Pallanza, in Italy, 1 Oct., 1871; o.s. Peter Denis, arm. BALLIOL, matric. 14 Oct., 90, aged 19, from Northcourt house school. See Foster's *Peerage*, M. SLIGO.

Browne, Bernard Emanuel, born at Norwich 6 Aug., 1872; 3s. Thomas Henry, of Lowestoft, gen. NON-COLLEGIATE, matric. 17 Oct., 91, aged 19.

Browne, rev. Charles Hotham, born at East Acklam, Yorks, 1867; 6s. Thomas Brierley, cler. BRASENOSE, matric. 20 Oct., 85, aged 19, B.A. 89; curate of St. Saviour, Eastbourne, 91; brother of L. R.

Browne, Dominick Sydney, born at Dublin 31 March, 1866; 1s. Dominick Andrew, arm. ST. JOHN'S, matric. 16 Jan., 85, aged 18; of Breaghwy, co. Mayo.

Browne, Edward Thomas, born in London 10 April, 1866; o.s. Edward Payne, gent. QUEEN'S, matric. 22 Oct., 84, aged 18 (from Faversham and Maidstone schools), B.A. 91.

Browne, Francis Drysdale, born at Lewisham, Kent, 20 March, 1872; 3s. Marcus Alexis Septimus, of London, gen. ST. JOHN'S, matric. 17 Oct., 91, aged 19, from Merchant Taylors' school.

Browne, Franklin Doughty, born in London 4 March, 1873; 1s. George Franklin, B.A., LL.B., solicitor. TRINITY, matric. 15 Oct., 92, aged 19, from Dulwich coll.

Browne, James William, M.A., B.Med., fellow WORCESTER 70-88, where see.

Browne, John Gordon, born at Carlow, Ireland, 20 Sept., 1867; 7s. John James, of Penkhull, co. Staff., cler. WORCESTER, matric. 19 Oct., 86, aged 19 (from Bath coll.), scholar 86, B.A. 91; HONOURS: —1 classical mods. 88, 2 classics 90.

Browne, Leonard, born at Brisbane, Queensland, 1873; 1s. Leonard, gen. KEBLE, matric. 20 Oct., 91, aged 18, from Brisbane gr. school.

Browne, Lionel Ravald, born at East Acklam, Yorks, 1869; 7s. Thomas Brierly, cler. BRASENOSE, matric. 16 Oct., 88, aged 19 (from Hereford cathedral school), scholar 88, B.A. 92 (HONOURS:—3 classical mods. 90, Greek testament, prize 91, 2 theology 92); brother of Charles H.

Browne, Montague Doughty, born in London 1871; 3s. Henry Doughty, gen. PEMBROKE, matric. 17 Oct., 88, aged 17 (from Eastbourne coll.); HONOURS: —4 history 91.

Browne, ven. Robert William, M.A., fellow ST. JOHN'S 27-39, where see.

Browne, Walter Woodgates, born at South Wootton, Norfolk, 30 Dec., 1871 ; 2s. Walter, rector of West Walton, co. Camb. ST. EDMUND HALL, matric. 14 Dec., 89, aged 17, from the King's school, Ely.

Browning, rev. Berthold Alexander, born at Walmer, Kent, April 1868 ; 3s. Montagu Charles, col. in the army. CHRIST CHURCH, matric. 14 Jan., 87, aged 18 (from Winchester), B.A. 90; HONOURS :— 3 theology 90.

Browning, Bertie Percy, born at Redditch, co. Worcester, 9 Dec., 1868 ; 2s. Harold Constantine, gen. BRASENOSE, matric. 20 Oct., 87, aged 18 (from Tonbridge school) ; HONOURS :—a classical mods. 89, 3 classics 91.

Browning, Colin Harington, born at Nagpore, E. Indies, 7 July, 1870 ; 4s. Colin Arrot Robinson, C.I.E. ST. JOHN'S, matric. 12 Oct., 89, aged 19 (from Merchant Taylors' school), scholar 92, B.A. 92 ; HONOURS :—1 history 92.

Browning, Frederick Henry, born at Barton Mere, Suffolk, 1 Aug., 1870 ; 4s. Montagu Charles, col. in the army. MAGDALEN, matric. 14 Oct., 89, aged 19, from Wellington coll.

Browning, Robert, created D.C.L. 14 June, 1882, born 7 May, 1812 ; died 12 Dec., 89. See Al. Ox. 78.

Brownrigg, Charles Edward, born at Maryborough, Ireland, 3 Feb., 1865 ; 2s. Thomas Mark, of Guildford, arm. MAGDALEN, matric. 19 Oct., 83, aged 18 (from Haileybury), exhibitioner 83, B.A. 87, M.A. 90 ; (HONOURS :—1 classical mods. 85, 2 classics 87), assistant master, Eton, Jan.—July, 88, and master Magdalen coll. school 89.

Bruce, Francis Rosslyn Courtenay, born at Barton, co. Lincoln, 14 Aug., 1871 ; 3s. Lloyd Stewart, cler. WORCESTER, matric. 14 Oct., 90, aged 19, from St. Edward's school, Summertown.

Bruce, George Lewis, born in London 17 Dec., 1862 ; 1s. Alan Cameron Bruce-Pryce, arm. BALLIOL, matric. 18 Oct., 81, aged 18, B.A. 86, M.A. 88 ; HONOURS :—2 classical mods. 82, 2 classics 85. See Foster's *Peerage,* B. ABERDARE.

Bruce, George Wyndham Hamilton Knight, created D.D. 23 Nov., 86, bishop of Bloemfontein. See Al. Ox. and series 179.

Bruce, Henry Austin, lord Aberdare, created D.C.L. 9 June, 1880 (i.e. John Bruce Bruce-Pryce, of Duffryn, co. Glam.), G.C.B. 7 Jan., 85 ; created a peer 23 Aug., 73, bar.-at-law, Lincoln's Inn, 37. M.P. Merthyr Tydvil 52-68, Renfrewshire 69-73, home secretary 69-73, etc. ; born 16 April, 1815. See Al. Ox. 179.

Bruce, rev. Robert Douglas, born at Barton-in-Fabis, Notts, 30 March, 1867 ; 1s. Lloyd Stewart, cler. WORCESTER, matric. 17 Oct., 84, aged 17 (from St. Edward's school, Summertown), B.A. 87, M.A. 92 (HONOURS :—4 history 87) ; curate of Lancaster 91.

Bruce, William Alexander, born at Aberdeen 21 March, 1873 ; o.s. William, gent. UNIVERSITY COLL., matric. 15 Oct., 92, aged 19 (from city of London school), exhibitioner 92.

Brumwell, George Murray, born at Mossley, co. Lanc., 19 May, 1872 ; 1s. George Murray, D.Med. TRINITY, matric. 15 Oct., 92, aged 20, from Manchester gr. school.

Brunskill, Hubert Fawcett, born at Torquay, Devon, 28 Feb., 1873 ; 1s. William Fawcett. EXETER, matric. 28 April, 92, aged 19, from Clifton coll.

Brunskill, rev. John Ritson, born at Hackthorpe, Westmorland, 11 May, 1865 ; o.s. Joseph, vicar of Threlkeld. QUEEN'S, matric. 22 Oct., 85, aged 18 (from Lowther and Appleby schools, Westmorland), exhibitioner 83, B.A. 87, M.A. 90 ; curate of Portwood, Cheshire, 88.

Brunyate, Thomas Tombieson, born at Crewe, Cheshire, 1866 ; 1s. Wesley, gent. CHRIST CHURCH, matric. 10 Oct., 84, aged 18 (from Kingswood school), scholar 83, B.A. 87, M.A. and B.Med. 92 ; HONOURS :—2 mathematical mods. 85, 2 mathematics 87.

Brutton, Cyril Octavius, born at North Shields May, 1873 ; 8s. Thomas, cler. KEBLE, matric. 20 Oct., 91, aged 18, from St. Edward's school, Summertown.

Bryan, rev. Edward Venn Eustace, born at Lavenheath, Suffolk, 1863 ; 4s. Wilmot, cler. NON-COLLEGIATE, matric. 13 Oct., 84, aged 21 (from Bath coll.) ; migrated to CHARSLEY HALL, B.A. 88, M.A. 91 (HONOURS :—4 theology 88) ; curate of Folkestone, Kent, 91.

Bryan, John Francis, born at Oxford 10 Aug., 1867 ; 1s. John, gent., deceased. NON-COLLEGIATE, matric. 26 Oct., 85, aged 18, B.A. 88.

Bryan, Walter Joseph, born at Oxford 1871 ; 2s. Job, gen. NON-COLLEGIATE, matric. 25 Jan., 88, aged 17, from Gloucester Green school, Oxford.

Bryans, Arthur Hugh, born at Elstree, Herts, 15 June, 1865 ; 2s. Richard, cler. MERTON, matric. 25 Jan., 84, aged 18 (from Marlborough), B.A. 89.

Bryans, rev. Reginald de Faur, born at Birkenhead, Cheshire, 18 Aug., 1864 ; 2s. Richard, arm. MAGDALEN, matric. 16 Oct., 84, aged 20 (from Shrewsbury school), B.A. 88, M.A. 92, curate of Cheshunt, Herts, 93.

Bryant, Archibald Festing, born at Brent Tor, Devon, 30 Sept., 1873 ; 6s. Francis John, rector of Tavy St. Peter. BRASENOSE, matric. 21 Oct., 92, aged 19, from Honiton gr. school.

Bryant, Francis John, born at Brent Tor, Devon, 11 Oct., 1862 ; 3s. Francis John, rector of Tavy St. Peter. WADHAM, matric. 23 Jan., 82, aged 19 (from Marlborough coll.), B.A. 88 ; bar.-at-law, Lincoln's Inn, 91.

Bryant, George Edward, born at St. Leonard's, Sussex, 22 May, 1868 ; 1s. George William, schoolmaster. WADHAM, matric. 16 Oct., 86, aged 18, from Lancing coll.

Bryant, Henry Chandos, born at Brent Tor, Devon, 4 May, 1869 ; 5s. Francis John, D.D. HERTFORD, matric. 19 Oct., 88, aged 19 (from Sherborne school) ; HONOURS :—3 classical mods. 90, 2 law school.

Bryant, Raymond Mackenzie Beadon, born at Horfield, Somerset, July, 1862 ; 2s. William Frederic, cler. KEBLE, matric. 18 Oct., 81, aged 19 (from Warrington school), B.A. 86.

Bryce, James, D.C.L., fellow ORIEL 62, where see.

Bryce, Paul John, born in Paris Nov., 1872 ; 1s. John Paul, esq. CHRIST CHURCH, matric. 16 Oct., 91, aged 18 (from Harrow) ; clerk in college 5 Oct., 92.

Bryden, Charles Lumsdaine, born at Simla, Bengal, Nov., 1872 ; o.s. James Lumsden, surgeon major and D.Med. CHRIST CHURCH, matric. 16 Oct., 91, aged 18, from Rugby.

Brydone, Reginald Marr, born at Petworth, Sussex, 21 July, 1873 ; 1s. Henry Gray, solicitor. NEW COLL., matric. 14 Oct., 92 (from Winchester coll.), scholar 91.

Bubb, Edward Wallis, born at Richmond, Surrey, 23 Aug., 1864 ; 1s. Charles, gent. NEW COLL., matric. 14 Oct., 84, aged 18 (from Winchester), B.A. 85 ; HONOURS :—3 law 85.

Bubb, George, born at Cheltenham, 31 Dec., 1872 ; 3s. William Henry, M.A., solicitor. WORCESTER, matric. 18 Oct., 92, aged 19 (from Eastbourne coll.), scholar 91.

Buchanan, rev. John, born at Tralee, co. Kerry, 1852 ; 1s. James, arm. NON-COLLEGIATE, matric. 13 Jan., 83, aged 21, B.A. 90 ; curate of Sedbergh, Yorks, 90.

Buchanan, Nigel Francis William, born in London 5 March, 1870; 2s. David William Ramsay, arm. EXETER, matric. 17 Oct., 88, aged 18 (from Honiton school), B.A. 91.

Buchanan, rev. Sidney James, born at Gt. Wishford, Wilts, 25 July, 1864; 1s. Thomas Broughton, archdeacon of Wilts. NEW COLL., matric. 12 Oct., 83, aged 19 (from Winchester), scholar 82, B.A. 87 (HONOURS :—1 classical mods. 85, 2 classics 87); curate of Salisbury St. Edmund 90.

Buchanan, Thomas Ryburn, M.A., fellow ALL SOULS' 71, where see.

Buchanan, Walter, born at Gt. Wishford, Wilts, 4 Aug., 1869; 3s. Thomas Boughton, archdeacon of Wilts. QUEEN'S, matric. 20 Oct., 88, aged 19 (from Westminster school), scholar 88, B.A. 91; HONOURS :—4 law 92.

Buck, Percy Carter, born at West Ham, Essex, 25 March, 1871; 3s. William Richard, gen. KEBLE, matric. 15 Jan., 91, aged 19 (from Merchant Taylors' school); migrated to WORCESTER, B.Mus. 92.

Buckell, Augustine Charles, born at Lewisham, Kent, 1875; 1s. William, cler. KEBLE, matric. 15 Oct., 92, from Brighton coll.

Buckhurst, Alfred Ernest, born at Rochester 10 April, 1865; 2s. Benjamin John, gent. UNIVERSITY COLL., matric. 13 Oct., 83, aged 18 (from Rochester school), scholar 84, B.A. 87; HONOURS :—2 classical mods. 84, 1 chemistry 87.

Buckland, Edward Hastings, born at Laleham, Middx., 20 June, 1864; 4s. Matthew Harvey, cler. NEW COLL., matric. 12 Oct., 83, aged 19 (from Marlborough), B.A. 86 (HONOURS :—3 law 86); in the University eleven 84, 5, 6.

Buckland, Philip Lindsay, born in London 12 Sept., 1874; 1s. Charles Edward, B.C.S. NEW COLL., matric. 14 Oct., 92, aged 18, from King's coll. London, and Eton.

Buckle, rev. David Purdy, born at Durham 1862; 1s. Mathew, gent. EXETER, matric. 20 Oct., 81, aged 19 (from Durham gr. school), exhibitioner 81, B.A. 85, M.A. 88 (HONOURS :—2 classical mods. 83, 3 classics 85); curate of Earls Henton, Yorks, 91.

Buckle, George, M.A., fellow ORIEL 43-53, where see.

Buckle, George Earle, M.A., fellow ALL SOULS' 77-85, where see.

Buckley, Edmund, born at Llandovery, co. Carmarthen, 7 May, 1861; 1s. Edmund, bart. ST. JOHN'S, matric. 3 Nov., 80, aged 19; migrated to New Inn Hall (BALLIOL); student Inner Temple, 84.

Buckley, rev. Eric Rede, born in London 31 Aug., 1868; 5s. Robert Alford, gent. ST. JOHN, matric. 16 Oct., 86, aged 19 (from Merchant Taylors' school), B.A. 89 (HONOURS :—2 history 89, 2 theology 91); curate of Bodmin 92.

Buckley, James Francis Hughes, born at Llanelly, co. Carmarthen, 20 Feb., 1869; 1s. James, gen. ORIEL, matric. 20 Oct., 88, aged 19 (from Rugby), B.A. 92; HONOURS :—3 law 92.

Buckley, Llewellyn Edison, born at Hampton Wick, Middx., 19 June, 1866; 3s. John Arthur, a taxing master in chancery. NEW COLL., matric. 16 Oct., 85, aged 19 (from Clifton coll.); assist. collector and magistrate North Arcot, Madras C.S. 87.

Buckley, Percy Falcon, born at Catcot, Somerset, 1868; 1s. Cecil William, arm. UNIVERSITY COLL., matric. 15 Jan., 87, aged 19, B.A. 90; HONOURS: —3 classical mods. 88, 3 law 90.

Buckley, St. John Maclean, born at Waitaki in New Zealand 1869; 3s. George, arm. MAGDALEN, matric. 22 Oct., 87, aged 18.

Buckley, William Frederick McLean, born at Lyttleton, New Zealand, 1861; 1s. George, gent. NON-COLLEGIATE, matric. 4 June, 81, aged 20 (from Christ Church school, N.Z.); migrated to CHRIST CHURCH, B.A. 86; bar.-at-law, Inner Temple, 89.

Buckmaster, William North, born at Ramsgate 9 April, 1873; 1s. John North, B.A., cler. UNIVERSITY COLL., matric. 15 Oct., 92, aged 19, from Sherborne school.

Bucknall, Edgar Allan, born at Sydenham, Kent, 1 Dec., 1869; 5s. HENRY, arm. MERTON, matric. 17 Oct., 88, aged 18 (from Eton), B.A. 91.

Bucknall, Ernest Corfield, born at Peckham, Kent, 22 Jan., 1867; 4s. Henry Corfield, gent. MERTON, matric. 24 Oct., 85, aged 17 (from Uppingham school), B.A. 88.

Bucknall, Henry Lechend, born at Sydenham 1862; 1s. Henry Corfield, arm. HERTFORD, matric. 18 Oct., 80, aged 18, from Uppingham school.

Bucknall, Herbert Merrick, born at Lisbon 1870; 3s. Richard Corfield, arm. HERTFORD, matric. 14 Oct., 89, aged 19, from Marlborough coll.

Bucknall, John Lloyd, born at Peckham, Kent, 1866; 3s. Henry Corfield, gent. PEMBROKE, matric. 30 Jan., 84, aged 18.

Bucknall, Norman Rixon, born at Sydenham, Surrey, 25 Jan., 1873; 8s. Henry Corfield, gen. MERTON, matric. 19 March, 91, aged 18, from Eton.

Bucknall, Roger Estcourt, born at Garratts Hall, Banstead, Surrey, 27 Oct., 1874; 7s. Henry Corfield, shipowner. MERTON, matric. 18 Oct., 92, aged 17, from Eton.

Bucknall, William St. Vincent, born at Dulwich, Surrey, 1863; 2s. Henry Corfield, gent. EXETER, matric. 18 Oct., 82, aged 19 (from Uppingham school), B.A. 86, M.A. 89.

Bucknill, John Alexander, born at Clifton, Bristol, 14 Sept., 1873; 1s. Thomas Townsend, Q.C. KEBLE, matric. 20 Oct., 91, aged 18, from the Charterhouse.

Budworth, David Philip Dutton, born at Greenstead, Essex, Sept., 1871; 3s. Philip John, captain, deceased. KEBLE, matric. 20 Oct., 91, aged 20.

Budworth, Richard Thomas Dutton, born at Greenstead, Essex, 17 Oct., 1867; 1s. Philip John, late in the army. MAGDALEN, matric. 20 Oct., 86, aged 18 (from Brecon coll.), B.A. 90; HONOURS :—2 classical mods. 88, 2 classics 90.

Bue, Jules T. T., M.A., Taylorian teacher in French 47, where see.

Bull, Allen Wilfred, born at Southampton 4 Dec., 1869; 2s. Edward Charles, architect. WADHAM, matric. 20 Oct., 91, aged 21, from King's coll., London.

Bull, (rev.) Bertie Paul, born at Richmond, Surrey, Dec. 1864; 4s. James Burrington, gent. WORCESTER, matric. 18 Oct., 83, aged 18 (from Hurstpierpoint coll.), B.A. 86, M.A. 90 (HONOURS :—3 history 86); assist. master Hurstpierpoint 87-91; diocesan missioner, Chichester, 91.

Bull, Charles Musgrave, M.A., fellow UNIVERSITY COLL. 53-66, where see.

Bull, Henry Foyster, born at Gestingthorpe, Essex, 1863; 1s. Henry Dawson Ellis, cler. EXETER, matric. 28 Jan., 81, aged 18 (from Malvern coll.), B.A. 85, M.A. 89.

Bull, Herbert, born at Hackney, Middx., 26 April, 1866; 5s. William, gent. UNIVERSITY COLL., matric. 17 Oct., 85, aged 19 (from Christ's hospital), scholar 84; HONOURS :—1 classical mods. 87, 2 classics 89.

Bull, rev. Herbert Edward Usher, born at Southampton 24 Aug., 1866; 1s. Edward Charles, gent. MAGDALEN, matric. 16 Oct., 84, aged 18 (from Spring Hill school, Southampton), B.A. 87, M.A. 91 (HONOURS :—2 classical mods. 86, 3 law 87); curate of Milford, Hants, 89.

Bull, Percival George, born at Madras, E. Indies, 20 Oct., 1862; o.s. James Vivian, cler. MERTON, matric. 18 Oct., 81, aged 18 (from Clifton coll.), B.A. 84, M.A. 88.

Bull, William Brooks, born at Bedhampton, Hants, 18 April, 1868; 1s. William, gen. WADHAM, matric. 15 Oct., 87, aged 19 (from Framlingham coll.), B.A. 91 (HONOURS :—4 history 91); died 17 Dec., 92.

Bullard, John Vincent, born at Rochester 9 June, 1869; 1s. Charles, arm. UNIVERSITY COLL., matric. 13 Oct., 88, aged 19 (from Rochester cathedral school), exhibitioner 88, B.A. 92; HONOURS :—3 classical mods. 90, 3 classics 92.

Bullen, rev. Hugh Alexander, born at Everton, co. Lanc., 1864; 2s. William, gent. PEMBROKE, matric. 26 Oct., 81, aged 17 (from Liverpool coll.), B.A. 84; curate of Smisby 91.

Buller, Charles William, B.A., fellow ALL SOULS' 71-91, where see.

Buller, rev. the hon. Reginald John Yarde, born in co. Gloucester 12 July, 1864; 5s. hon. John Buller Y.-B. CHRIST CHURCH, matric. 25 May, 83, aged 18 (from Radley coll.), B.A. 87, M.A. 90; curate of St. Mark, New Swindon, 89. See Foster's *Peerage*, B. CHURSTON.

Buller, rev. Richard Witherston, born at West Parley, Dorset, 24 March, 1847; 2s. Henry John, rector, deceased. NON-COLLEGIATE, matric. 15 Oct., 81, aged 34; migrated to NEW COLL. Dec., 82, B.A. 85, M.A. 88 (HONOURS :—4 natural science 85); sometime E.I.C.S. and late government inspector of telegraphs; perpetual curate Marsden, Yorks, 91. See Foster's *Peerage*, B. CHURSTON.

Bulley, Frederick Pocock, M.A., home bursar MAGDALEN, where see.

Bullivant, Thomas Pelham, born at Hackney, Middx., 30 May, 1864; 3s. William Munton, gent. BALLIOL, matric. 16 Oct., 83, aged 19 (from Cheltenham coll.); HONOURS :—2 classical mods. 85.

Bullock, rev. Edward, born in London July, 1866; 1s. Edward, arm. CHRIST CHURCH, matric. 31 May, 84, aged 17 (from the Charterhouse), B.A. 87, M.A. 91 (HONOURS :—3 law 87); curate of Holy Trinity, Leeds, 89.

Bullock, Edward Clifford, born at Barton-on-Humber, co. Lincoln, 24 Feb., 1866; 1s. Richard, cler. ORIEL, matric. 23 Oct., 85, aged 19 (from Malvern coll.), B.A. 90, M.A. 92; HONOURS :—3 history 89.

Bulman, John Frederick, born at Newcastle-on-Tyne 30 Sept., 1861; 3s. John, gent. ORIEL, matric. 16 Oct., 80, aged 19, from Bradfield coll.

Bulmer, Thornton Bulmer, born at Rotherhithe, Surrey, at Dec., 1868; eld 1 son of George Edward, arm. HERTFORD, matric. 27 Oct., 87, aged 18, (from Rugby), B.A. 91; bar.-at-law, Lincoln's Inn, 92.

Bulpit, Frederick William, born at Birmingham 1864; o.s. William, cler. BRASENOSE, matric. 22 Oct., 83, aged 19, from Manchester gr. school.

Bunbury, Cecil Edward Francis, born at Morar, E. Indies, 1 Dec., 1864; 1s. Henry Fox, capt. 35th Native Inf., India. KEBLE, matric. 16 Oct., 83, aged 18 (from Wellington coll.), assist. commissioner Punjab 85. See Foster's *Baronetage*.

Bunbury, George Alexander, born at Southampton June, 1870; 1s. William Reeves, arm. ORIEL, matric. 25 Oct., 89, aged 19 (from Bath coll.); HONOURS :—2 classical mods. 91.

Bunting, Sidney Percival, born in London 29 June, 1873; 1s. Percy William, bar.-at-law, and editor of "Contemporary Review." MAGDALEN, matric. 18 Oct., 92, aged 19 (from University coll., and St. Paul's schools), demy 92.

Burbey, John Leonard, born at Edmonton, Middx., 20 Feb., 1869; 1s. Robert, gen. EXETER, matric. 19 Oct., 87, aged 18 (from Clifton coll.), scholar 87; HONOURS :—2 classical mods. 89, 3 classics 91.

Burch, George James, born at Sewardstone, Essex, 1853; 2s. George, gent. NON-COLLEGIATE, matric. 23 Jan., 86, aged 33 (from Cheshunt school), B.A. 89; HONOURS :—2 chemistry 89.

Burch, Louis, born at Exeter July, 1863; 3s. Arthur, solicitor, EXETER, matric. 24 Jan., 84, aged 20 (from Exeter gr. school); migrated to TURRELL'S HALL, B.A. 7; returned to EXETER, M.A. 92.

Burchett, Jasper Comerford, born in London 1859; 1s. Henry, gent. NEW INN HALL, matric. 28 May, 81; aged 22.

Burchett, Lionel Godfrey, born at sea, off S. America, 1863; 2s. Henry, arm. WADHAM, matric. 16 Jan., 80, aged 17, from Berkhamstead school.

Burd, rev. Charles Ernest, born at Worthen, Salop, 17 April, 1867; 1s. Charles, vicar of Shirley, near Birmingham. NON-COLLEGIATE, matric. 17 Oct., 85, aged 18 (from K. Edward's high school, Birmingham); migrated to WADHAM 19 Oct., 86, B.A. 88.

Burd, Frederick Neville, born at Cound, Salop, 1866; 1s. Frederick, cler. KEBLE, matric. 22 Oct., 85, aged 19, from Eton.

Burd, Lawrence Arthur, born at Shrewsbury 1 June, 1863; 2s. Lawrence, gent. BALLIOL, matric. 1 Feb., 82, aged 18 (from Clifton coll.), exhibitioner 80-5, B.A. 85, M.A. 89; HONOURS :—1 classical mods. 83, 1 classics 85.

Burdekin, rev. Arthur Edward, born at Sheffield 1860; 2s. Benjamin, gent. ST. JOHN's, matric. 16 Oct., 86, aged 26 (from Sheffield school), scholar 88, B.A. 90 (HONOURS :—regrated law 90); curate of Stanhope, co. Durham, 91.

Burdon, John, M.A., fellow QUEEN's 35-45, where see.

Burdon-Sanderson, John Scott, M.A., fellow MAGDALEN 82, where see.

Burge, Hubert Murray, born at Meerut, E. Indies, 9 Aug., 1862; y. s. Milward, cler. UNIVERSITY COLL., matric. 14 Oct., 82, aged 20 (from Bedford gr. school), scholar 82-6, B.A. 86, fellow 90, M.A. 91; HONOURS :—1 classical mods. 83, 2 classics 86.

Burges, Frank, born at Winterbourne, co. Glouc., 1868; 1s. Frank, B.D., rector, deceased. MAGDALEN, matric. 21 Oct., 86, aged 18 (from Winchester); HONOURS :—2 classical mods. 88; in the army.

Burges, George Herbert, born in London 19 Sept., 1863; o.s. George, gent. MERTON, matric. 18 Oct., 81; aged 18 (from Winchester), B.A. 87.

Burges, Ynyr Richard Patrick, born in Dublin 15 March, 1865; 1s. Ynyr Henry, lieut.-col. CHRIST CHURCH, matric. 10 Oct., 84, aged 17, from Winchester.

Burke, John, born at Nahaut (?), Dublin, 3 June, 1865; 1s. John, of Orange, New Jersey, U.S., arm. TRINITY, matric. 15 Oct., 83, aged 18 (from Harrow), B.A. 88, M.A. 90; HONOURS :—2 classical mods. 85, 3 classics 87.

Burkitt, William John Dwyer, born at Banda, N.W.P., 28 Oct., 1872; 1s. William Robert, judge High Court, N.W.P. BALLIOL, matric. 20 Oct., 91, aged 18 (from Marlborough coll.); selected candidate Indian C.S. 91.

Burland, John Burland Harris, born at Aldershot 1 Nov., 1870; 1s. William Burland H.-B., major-general, deceased. EXETER, matric. 18 Oct., 92, aged 21, from Sherborne school.

Burn, John Henry, born at Newcastle-upon-Tyne 24 March, 1864; 1s. John Henry, gent. UNIVERSITY COLL., matric. 13 Oct., 83, aged 19 (from Rugby), B.A. 87, M.A. 90 (HONOURS :—1 classical mods. 84, 1 classics 87); bar.-at-law, Inner Temple, 90.

Burn, Richard, born at Liverpool 1 Feb., 1871; 1s. Richard, arm. CHRIST CHURCH, matric. 11 Oct., 89, aged 18 (from Liverpool Institute), scholar 89 (HONOURS :—2 mathematical mods. 90), assistant magistrate N.W.P., India, 91.

Burnaby, Robert Beaumont, born at Leicester 16 Feb., 1870; o.s. Robert William, vicar of East Cowes, Isle of Wight. CORPUS CHRISTI, matric. 20 Oct., 88, aged 18 (from Marlborough coll.), scholar 88, B.A. 92; HONOURS :—1 classical mods. 90, 2 classics 92.

Burne, Richard Higgins, born in London 5 April, 1868; 2s. Richard Higgins, solicitor, deceased. ORIEL, matric. 19 Oct., 86, aged 18 (from Winchester), B.A. 90; HONOURS :—3 chemistry 89.

Burne, Thomas Higgins, born in London 7 Oct., 1866; 1s. Richard Higgins, solicitor, deceased. MAGDALEN, matric. 21 Oct., 86, aged 20 (from Winchester); died 87.

Burnet, John, born at Edinburgh 1864; 1s. John, arm. BALLIOL, matric. 16 Oct., 83, aged 19 (from Edinburgh high school and university), scholar and Warner exhibitioner 82, Jenkyns exhibitioner 87, B.A. 87; fellow Merton 89, M.A. 90 (HONOURS :—1 classical mods. 84, Taylorian (French) scholar 85, 1 classics 87); professor of Greek at St. Andrew's 92.

Burnett, Harry Cleather, born in London 21 Nov., 1866; 1s. George Henry arm. BRASENOSE, matric. 23 Oct., 85, aged 18 (from Highgate school), scholar 85, B.A. 89; HONOURS :—1 classical mods. 87, 2 classics 89.

Burnett, rev. Thomas Mountford, born at Halton, Hants, 1863; 3s. Charles, D.Med. CORPUS CHRISTI, matric. 19 Oct., 82, aged 19 (from Epsom coll.), B.A. 87, M.A. 89; curate of Gt. Berkhamsted, Herts, 91.

Burnett, William Freshfield, born at Brighton 6 Nov., 1865; 2s. Frederick Wildman, bar.-at-law. NEW COLL., matric. 10 Oct., 84, aged 18 (from Winchester), B.A. 88, M.A. 91 (HONOURS :—2 classical mods. 86, 2 history 88); bar.-at-law, Lincoln's Inn, 91.

Burnett, William Ridley, born at Scotby, Cumberland, 1869; 3s. George, cler. ST. JOHN'S, matric. 13 Oct., 88, aged 19 (from Carlisle gr. school), B.A. 92; HONOURS :—3 classical mods. 89, 4 theology 92.

Burney, Charles Fox, born at Old Charlton, Kent, 1869; o.s. Charles George, gen. ST. JOHN'S, matric. 15 Oct., 87, aged 18 (from Merchant Taylors' school), exhibitioner 87, B.A. 90; HONOURS :—1 theology 90, Hebrew scholarship 87 and 90, Syriac prize 91, septuagint prize 92, 1 Semitic languages 92.

Burnham, Alfred Lee, born at Kingsthorpe, Northants, 18 May, 1872; 1s. Broughton. MAGDALEN, matric. 22 Oct., 91, aged 19 (from Magdalen coll. school Brackley 87-7, and Oxford 87-91), demy 91; HONOURS :—1 mathematical mods. 92.

Burnham, George Baird, M.A., B.C.L., UNIVERSITY COLL., where see.

Burns, rev. James Albert, born at Carlisle 11 Sept., 1865; 6s. John, gent. QUEEN'S, matric. 30 Oct., 85, aged 20 (from Carlisle gr. school), B.A. 88; HONOURS :—3 mathematical mods. 87.

Burns, rev. William Rothwell, born at Manchester 1866; 1s. William Henry, cler. NON-COLLEGIATE, matric. 16 Oct., 86, aged 20 (from Manchester gr. school), B.A. 90; curate of Elton St. Stephen, co. Lanc., 91.

Burr, rev. Edmund Godfrey, born at Burgh, Norfolk, 1865; 2s. Edmund, arm. ST. JOHN'S, matric. 11 Oct., 84, aged 19 (from Clifton coll.), B.A. 88, M.A. 91; HONOURS :—3 classical mods. 86, 4 classics 88.

Burr, Frederick John, born at Shrewsbury 1863; 3s. George, gent. UNIVERSITY COLL., matric. 14 Oct., 82, aged 19, B.A. 86; HONOURS :—4 law 86.

Burra, Henry Curteis, born at Rye, Sussex, 7 March, 1870; 1s. Henry, banker, deceased. MAGDALEN, matric. 30 Oct., 88, aged 18 (from the Charterhouse), B.A. 91; HONOURS :—3 history 91.

Burra, Richard Pomfret, born at Plagden, Sussex, 9 Jan. (or June), 1871; 2s. Henry, gen. BRASENOSE, matric. 27 Jan., 91, aged 19, from the Charterhouse.

Burrage, John Henry, born at Stratford-on-Avon 12 July, 1870; 1s. John William Westgate, arm. NEW COLL., matric. 11 Oct., 89, aged 19 (from St. Paul's school), exhibitioner 89.

Burrell, rev. Stephen Eliot Porter, born in New York 1868; 2s. Stephen Eliot, gen. MAGDALEN, matric. 20 Jan., 87, aged 19 (from Eton), B.A. 91 (HONOURS :—3 history 90); curate of Stokenham, Devon, 91.

Burrell, rev. Herbert John Edwin, born at Kirtling, co. Cambr., 15 Nov., 1866; 1s. John, of Frome Littlebury, Saffron Walden, gent. MAGDALEN, matric. 23 Oct., 85, aged 18 (from the Charterhouse), B.A. 89, M.A. 92; curate of Hillingdon, Middlesex, 90.

Burrell, Percy Saville, born at Leeds 11 Dec., 1871; 4s. Benjamin, gen. QUEEN'S, matric. 14 Oct., 90, aged 18 (from Leeds gr. school), scholar 90; HONOURS :—1 classical mods. 92.

Burrow, Francis Russell, born at Great Malvern, co. Worcester, 30 Jan., 1866; o.s. John Severn, gent. NEW COLL., matric. 10 Oct., 84 (from Harrow); migrated to TURRELL'S HALL, B.A. 89; bar.-at-law, Inner Temple, 90.

Burrowes, Henry Adrian, born at Exeter 8 Sept., 1873; 1s. Henry Adrian, decreased. EXETER, matric. 18 Oct., 92, aged 19, from Marlborough.

Burrows, Eustace Herbert, born at Lee, Kent, Oct., 1867; 5s. Arthur George, major-general, deceased. KEBLE, matric. 19 Oct., 86, aged 18 (from Clifton coll.), scholar 86, B.A. 91; HONOURS :—2 classical mods. 88, 2 history 90.

Burrows, James Cronyn, born at Kingston, Canada, 1863; 3s. Arthur George, major-general, deceased. HERTFORD, matric. 18 Oct., 83, aged 20.

Burrows, Leonard Francis, M.A., fellow WADHAM 46-56, where see.

Burrows, Montagu, M.A., fellow ALL SOULS' 62, where see.

Burrows, Ronald Montagu, born at Rugby 16 Aug., 1867; 3s. Leonard Francis, cler. CHRIST CHURCH, matric. 15 Oct., 86, aged 19 (from the Charterhouse), scholar 86, B.A. 90; HONOURS :—1 classical mods. 88, 1 classics 90.

Burrows, Winfrid Oldfield, M.A., student CHRIST CHURCH 83-92, where see.

Burt, Ernest Whitby, born at Yeovil, Somerset, 1867; 1s. William, gen. NON-COLLEGIATE, matric. 1 June, 89, aged 22 (from Baptist and University colls., Bristol); migrated to BALLIOL, B.A. 92 (HONOURS :—Chinese scholarship 90, 3 Oriental studies 92), B.A. London.

89   BURTON. —— MATRICULATIONS, 1880 TO 1892. —— BUZZARD.   90

Burton, rev. Albert Edward, born at Hertford 27 Sept., 1862; 1s. Edward Spedding, gent. WORCESTER, matric. 21 Oct., 80, aged 18 (from Berkhamstead school), scholar 80-5, B.A. 84, M.A. 89 (HONOURS :—2 mathematical mods. 82, 1 mathematics 84), assistant master Birkenhead gr. school 85-90, and of St. Peter's school, York, 90.

Burton, Charles Henry, born at Bickerstaff, co. Lanc. 13 Sept., 1867; 2s. William, gent. TRINITY, matric. 16 Oct., 86, aged 19 (from Liverpool coll.), B.A. 89; HONOURS :—4 law 89.

Burton, Edmund Charles, M.A., student CHRIST CHURCH 45-60, where see.

Burton, Edmund Gerald, born at Daventry Oct., 1872; 1s. Edmund Charles, solicitor. CHRIST CHURCH, matric. 16 Oct., 91, aged 19, from Westminster school.

Burton, John Robertson, born at Andover 5 March, 1872; 1s. Richard John, cler. TRINITY, matric. 17 Oct., 91, aged 19, from Monkton Combe school.

Burton, Thomas Musgrave, born at Soulbury, Bucks, 1865; 3s. William Schoolcroft, gent. ST. JOHN, matric. 11 Oct., 84, aged 19 (from Bedford school), B.A. 87 (HONOURS :—3 history 87); curate of Hagbourne, Berks, 88.

Burton, William Latham, born at Soberton, Hants, 1864; 2s. Roger Taylor, cler. PEMBROKE, matric. 23 Oct., 82, aged 18 (from Christ's hospital), scholar 82, B.A. 86; HONOURS :—2 mathematical mods. 84, 2 mathematics 86.

Bury, Herbert, born in Gwevne (? Geneva), 28 Jan., 1871; 5s. John, arm. CHRIST CHURCH, matric. 11 Oct., 89, aged 18 (from Cheltenham coll.), B.A. 92.

Bury, (rev.) William, born at Tickhill, Yorks, May, 1867; 1s. James Marshall, cler. HERTFORD, matric. 22 Oct., 86, aged 19 (from Hereford cath. school), B.A. 90; curate of Belgrave, co. Leic., 91.

Busbridge, Vernon Ashby, born at West Malling, Kent, 1862; 2s. George Frederick, gent. PEMBROKE, matric. 26 Oct., 81, aged 19.

Busby, Alexander Hamilton, born at Cassilis, New England, N.S.W., 18 Sept., 1869; 7s. William, gen. HERTFORD, matric. 25 Oct. 89, aged 20, from Sydney gr. school and King's coll., London.

Busby, rev. William, born at Richmond, Surrey, 21 Oct., 1866; 3s. Alexander, gent. NEW COLL., matric. 16 Oct., 85, aged 18 (from Winchester), scholar 84, B.A. 89, M.A. 92 (HONOURS :—1 classical mods. 87, 2 classics 89, 2 theology 90); curate of St. Mary the Virgin, London, 91.

Busby, rev. William Blundell, born at Hartington 22 Feb., 1860; 1s. James, gent. NON-COLLEGIATE, matric. 13 Oct., 83, aged 23; migrated to WORCESTER, B.A. 87, M.A. 90 (HONOURS :—3 mathematical mods. 85, 3 mathematics 87), chaplain Carmarthen training coll., 89-91, vice-principal York diocesan training coll. 91.

Bush, Harry Edgell, born at Trowbridge, Wilts, Sept., 1861; 3s. John James, arm. CHRIST CHURCH, matric. 13 Oct., 82, aged 21 (from Trowbridge school), B.A. 86; HONOURS :—4 history 86.

Bush, Herbert Cromwell, born at Duloe, Cornwall, 1862; 5s. Paul, cler. HERTFORD, matric. 18 Oct., 80, aged 18, B.A. 85, M.A. 89.

Bush, Herbert Wheler, born at Westbury-on-Trym, co. Gloucester, 1862; 2s. William Harrington, solicitor. EXETER, matric. 15 May, 80, aged 18 (from Clifton coll.), B.A. 86, M.A. 89.

Bush, Robert, born at Belfast 1867; 1s. John, arm. ST. JOHN'S, matric. 16 Oct., 86, aged 19 (from Harrow), B.A. 89.

Bushby, Dudley Jeffreys Charles, born in London 31 July, 1864; 2s. Henry Jeffreys, late Metropolitan magistrate. TRINITY, matric. 16 Oct., 86, aged 22 (from Eton); HONOURS :—3 theology 89.

Bushnell, Gilbert Duffus Sutherland, born at Grouville, in Jersey, March 1870; 2s. James Henry, arm. KEBLE, matric. 12 Oct., 89, aged 19 (from Dulwich coll.), B.A. 92.

Bussell, rev. Frederick William, born at Cadmore End, High Wycombe, Bucks, 23 April, 1862; 1s. Frederick, vicar of Great Marlow, deceased. MAGDALEN, matric. 15 Oct., 81, aged 19 (from the Charterhouse), demy 80-5, B.A. 85; fellow BRASENOSE 86, lecturer 86, M.A. 88, chaplain 91, B.Mus. and B.D. 92; HONOURS :—1 classical mods. 82, 1 classics 85, accessit Ireland scholarship 84 and 85, Craven scholarship 85, 1 theology 86.

Butcher, Samuel Henry, M.A., fellow UNIVERSITY COLL. 76-82, where see.

Butcher, William Harold, born at Harrogate, Yorks, 9 May, 1873; 1s. Charles Fosbery, gent. CHRIST CHURCH, matric. 4 June, 92, aged 19.

Butler, Alfred Joshua, M.A., fellow BRASENOSE 77, where see.

Butler, Arthur Gray, M.A., fellow ORIEL, where see.

Butler, Frederick George Augustus, born at Riddings, co. Derby, 5 April, 1873; 2s. Augustus Matthew, congregational minister. TRINITY, matric. 15 Oct., 92, aged 19 (from Bradford gr. school), exhibitioner 91.

Butler, Harold Bracher, born in Reading 26 Jan., 1871; 1s. George Russell, bar.-at-law. WADHAM, matric. 19 Jan., 89, aged 17.

Butler, Spencer Harcourt, born in London 1869; 2s. Spencer Perceval, arm. BALLIOL, matric 18 Oct., 88, aged 19 (from Harrow); assist. magistrate N.W.P., India, 90.

Butler, Thomas Harrison, born at Stanhope, co. Durham, 19 March, 1871; 1s. George William, cler. CORPUS CHRISTI, matric. 25 Oct., 89, aged 18 (from St. Paul's school), scholar 88.

Butler, William, born at Ilfracombe, Devon, 1863; o.s. William Henry, gent. NON-COLLEGIATE, matric. 5 Nov., 85, aged 22, B.A. 88, M.A. 92.

Butler, William Albert, born in London 22 Feb., 1873; 2s. James William, merchant. WORCESTER, matric. 25 Oct., 92, aged 19, from the Charterhouse.

Butler, William John Chesshyre, born at Folkestone, Kent, April 1864; 3s. Philip, arm. CHRIST CHURCH, matric. 13 Oct., 82, aged 18 (from the Charterhouse), B.A. 86 (HONOURS :—3 history 85); in the army.

Buttanshaw, John, M.A., fellow CORPUS CHRISTI 54-64, where see.

Butterfield, William John Atkinson, born at Camberwell 1867; 3s. William, gent. NON-COLLEGIATE, matric. 15 Oct., 87, aged 20 (from University coll., London); migrated to CHRIST CHURCH, B.A. 91; HONOURS :—3 chemistry 91.

Butters, William Middleton, born in Adelaide, South Australia, 1858; 3s. William, gent. NON-COLLEGIATE, matric. 16 Oct., 86, aged 28, from Tulse Hill school.

Butterworth, Alan, born at Southport, co. Lanc., 1864; 2s. Henry, arm. BALLIOL, matric. 16 Oct., 83, aged 19 (from Elizabeth coll., Guernsey); head assistant to collector and magistrate, Godavari, Madras C.S., 85.

Butterworth, John Abel, born at Rochdale 1849; 2s. John, gen. QUEEN'S, matric. 25 Jan., 88, aged 39.

Buxton, Travers, born at Camberwell, Surrey, 10 Dec., 1864; o.s. Travers, gent., deceased. NEW COLL., matric. 12 Oct., 83, aged 18 (from University coll. school, London), B.A. 87, M.A. 91; HONOURS :—2 classical mods. 85, 3 classics 87.

Buzzard, Edward Farquhar, born in London 20 Dec., 1871; 1s. Thomas, D.Med. MAGDALEN, matric. 14 Oct., 90, aged 18, from the Charterhouse.

Byass, Sydney Hutchinson, born at Reigate, Surrey, 1862; 2s. Robert Nichol, gen. UNIVERSITY COLL., matric. 15 Oct., 81, aged 19 (from Radley coll.); migrated to NEW INN HALL, B.A. 85.

Bygott, rev. John Parkinson, born at Lincoln 4 March, 1862; 1s. John Parkinson, gent. NON-COLLEGIATE, matric. 22 Jan., 81, aged 18 (from Lincoln gr. school); migrated to HERTFORD, B.A. 85, M.A. 87 (HONOURS:—3 classical mods. 82, 3 history 84, 3 law 85); vicar of Newchapel, Stoke-upon-Trent, 92.

Byham, Cyril Moncreiff, born at Ealing, Middx., 1870; 3s. George, gent. CHARSLEY'S HALL, matric. 20 May, 86, aged 16.

Byles, Roussell Davids, born at Leeds 26 Feb., 1870; 1s. Alfred Holden, nonconformist minister. BALLIOL, matric. 17 Oct., 89, aged 19 (from Rossall school), scholar 88; HONOURS:—3 mathematical mods. 91.

Byles, Walter John Barnard, born at Harefield, Middx., 1868; 2s. Walter Barnard, arm. UNIVERSITY COLL., matric. 15 Oct., 87, aged 19, B.A. 90; HONOURS:—2 history 90.

Byne, rev. Mordaunt Henry Martin, born at Bombay 1863; 1s. Henry, arm. PEMBROKE, matric. 25 Jan., 83, aged 20, B.A. and M.A. 89; curate of Tavistock 89.

Byrchmore, Joseph, born at Dunstable, Beds, 1846; o.s. Richard, gent. NON-COLLEGIATE, matric. 29 April, 81, aged 35, from Dunstable gr. school.

Byrne, Henry Barnes, M.A., fellow QUEEN'S 51-63, where see.

Byrne, Lionel Stanley Rice, born in London 3 July, 1863; o.s. John Rice, cler. TRINITY, matric. 14 Oct., 82, aged 19 (from Eton), B.A. 86, M.A. 89 (HONOURS:—3 classical mods. 84, 3 history 84), in the Oxford eight 86; a master at Eton.

Byron, rev. the hon. Frederick Ernest Charles, born 26 March, 1861; 2s. hon. Frederick. CHARSLEY'S HALL, matric. 28 Jan., 82, aged 20; migrated to EXETER, B.A. 87, M.A. 90; rector of Langford, Essex, 91.

Byron, Thomas, born at Caterham, Surrey, April, 1869; 1s. Edmund, arm. CHRIST CHURCH, matric. 3 June, 87, aged 18, from Eton.

Byron, rev. the hon. William, M.A., fellow ALL SOULS' 52-7, where see.

Bywater, Ingram, M.A., fellow EXETER 63 and 90, where see.

HENRY VIII.'S CHAIR, IN THE ASHMOLEAN.—*Storer.*

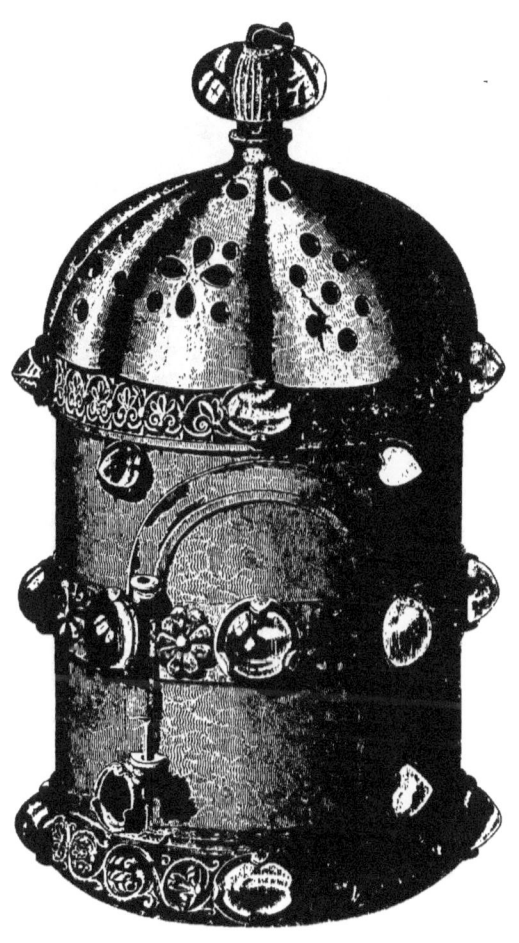

ANCIENT LANTERN OF BRONZE, STUDDED WITH CHRYSTALS, IN THE ASHMOLEAN.
[*From an Engraving by Henry Shaw, F.S.A.*]

GREAT LION HALL, NOW DEMOLISHED.—*Shehim.*

[STONE ORNAMENT FROM ROUEN CATHEDRAL.—*Pugin*.]

C

Cadell, Arthur William Rees, born at Chelsea, Middx., 1863; o.s. William Monteith, gent. BALLIOL, matric. 18 Oct., 81, aged 18 (from St. Paul's school); selected candidate Indian C.S. 81; died 15 March, 86.

Cadell, Patrick Robert, born at Ulwar, in E. Indies, 1871; 2s. Thomas, arm. BALLIOL, matric. 17 Oct., 89, aged 18 (from Haileybury); assist. collector and magistrate Admednugar, Bombay C.S. 91.

Cadogan, John Herbert, born at Walton, co. Warwick, Nov., 1866; 2s. Edward, cler. CHRIST CHURCH, matric. 1 June, 88, aged 21 (HONOURS :—3 history 92); sometime in the navy and blinded.

Caffin, Benjamin Charles, M.A., fellow WORCESTER 52-64, where see.

Cain, Charles Smith, born at Gosforth, Cumberland, 24 May, 1872; 2s. James Jackson, gen. QUEEN'S, matric. 27 Oct., 91, aged 19 (from St. Bees gr. school), exhibitioner 91.

Caine, William, born in Liverpool, 28 Aug., 1873; 1s. William Sproston, M.P., merchant. NON-COLLEGIATE, matric. 15 Oct., 92, aged 19, from Westminster school and St. Andrews university.

Caird, Edward, D.C.L., fellow MERTON 64-8, where see.

Cairns, hon. Douglas Halyburton, born at Glenquaich, N.B., 5 Sept., 1867; 4s. Hugh, earl Cairns. NEW COLL., matric. 15 Oct., 86, aged 19 (from Eton), B.A. 92.

Calcott, Roland Berkeley, born at Oundle, Northants, Feb., 1865; 5s. George Wallis Berkeley, gent. WORCESTER, matric. 18 Oct., 83, aged 18 (from Oundle school), B.A. 86.

Caldecott, Leslie, born at Pishobury, Herts, 10 May, 1870; 2s. Andrew, gen. NEW COLL., matric. 23 Nov., 89, aged 19, from Eton.

Calder, David Mann, born at Arbroath, co. Forfar, 16 Oct., 1867; 1s. David, gent. MERTON, matric. 26 Jan., 86, aged 18, as David (from Pieter-Maritzhurg school, Natal), B.A. 89, as David Mann; HONOURS :—4 law 89.

Calderon, George Leslie, born in London 2 Dec., 1868; 5s. Philip Hermogenes, R.A. TRINITY, matric. 15 Oct., 87, aged 18 (from Rugby), exhibitioner 86, B.A. 91 (HONOURS :—2 classical mods. 89, 2 classics 91.

Caldicott, rev. Arthur Henry, born at Bristol, 15 July, 1867; 2s. John William, D.D. CORPUS CHRISTI, matric. 20 Oct., 86, aged 19 (from Bristol gr. school), B.A. 90 (HONOURS :—3 classical mods. 88, 3 classics 90); assist. master Liverpool institute, and curate of St. Thomas, Toxteth Park, 91.

Caldicott, Cecil Bolton, born at Edgbaston 30 Oct., 1872; 1s. John Underhill, gen. CORPUS CHRISTI, matric. 19 Oct., 91, aged 18, from Repton school.

Caldicott, Herbert Vigors, born at Lambeth 19 Sept., 1873; 1s. Thomas Parker, of Upper Norwood, gent. UNIVERSITY COLL., matric. 15 Oct., 92, aged 19, from Haileybury.

Caldicott, John Croydon, born at Bristol 1866; 1s. John William, cler. CORPUS CHRISTI, matric. 26 Oct., 85, aged 19 (from Bristol school), B.A. 89, M.A. 92 (HONOURS :—4 law 89); bar.-at-law, Inner Temple, 92.

Caldwell, rev. William Henry McKennal, born at Melbourne 1 Jan., 1866; 2s. Gavin Ralston, arm., deceased, MAGDALEN, matric. 26 Jan., 86, aged 20 (from Eton), B.A. 89; curate of Sneinton St. Mathias, Notts, 91.

Callaway, Robert Furley, born at Harbledown, Kent, 9 Oct., 1872; 4s. John, of Guildford, Surrey, gent. CORPUS CHRISTI, matric. 19 Oct., 91, aged 19, from Bury St. Edmund's school.

Calthorpe, Walter Gough, born in London 2 May, 1873; 1s. hon. Augustus Cholmondely Gough. CHRIST CHURCH, matric. 29 May, 91, aged 18, from Eton.

Calver, Sydney Charles, born at Walthamstow, Essex, 1869; 3s. James William, gen. ST. EDMUND HALL, matric. 20 Oct., 92, aged 23, from Leyton school.

Calverley, Henry Calverley, M.A., fellow CORPUS CHRISTI 51-75, where see.

Cambridge, Arthur Wallace Pickard, born at Bloxworth, Dorset, 20 Jan., 1873; 3s. Octavius, rector, and F.R.S. BALLIOL, matric. 20 Oct., 91, aged 18 (from Weymouth coll.), scholar 91; HONOURS :—accessit Craven scholarship 92.

Cambridge, Charles Owen Pickard, born at Bloxworth, Dorset, 9 Nov., 1874; 4s. Octavius, M.A., rector, and F.R.S. BALLIOL, matric. 18 Oct., 92, aged 17 (from Weymouth coll.), scholar 91.

Cambridge, rev. Frederick Octavius Pickard, born at Warmwell, Dorset, 17 Dec., 1860; 4s. Edward, cler. ST. MARY HALL, matric. 20 Oct., 80, aged 19 (from Sherborne school); migrated to EXETER 28 Jan., 81, B.A. 84; curate of St. Cuthbert, Carlisle, 89.

Cambridge, Robert Jocelyn Pickard, born at Bloxworth, Dorset, 10 May, 1867; 1s. Octavius, M.A., rector and F.R.S. KEBLE, matric. 19 Oct., 86, aged 19 (from Forest school), B.A. 89.

Cameron, rev. Archibald Evan, born in London 1865; 1s. Archibald Henry Foley, D.Med. HERTFORD, matric. 14 Oct., 84, aged 19, B.A. 88 (HONOURS :— 4 theology 88) ; curate of Moturam-in-Longdendale, co. Lanc., 89 ; died 29 April, 90.

Cameron, Archibald Stuart, born at Daventry, Northants, 1867 ; o.s. Donald, cler. ST. JOHN'S, matric. 16 Oct., 86, aged 19 (from Hereford school), B.A. 89 ; HONOURS :—3 history 89.

Cameron, Donald John, born at Tallisher, co. Inverness, May, 1870; 3s. Donald Colin, gen. ORIEL, matric. 25 Oct., 89, aged 19, from Fettes coll.

Cameron, William, born at Kilmorack, Invernesshire, 9 March, 1862 ; 1s. Duncan, pleb. MAGDALEN, matric. 25 April, 83, aged 21 (from Aberdeen university, 1 classics 83), demy 81-3 ; drowned in the Rhine 83.

Camidge, Charles Edward, bishop of Bathurst, created D.D. 30 June, 87. See *Al. Ox.* 212.

Camm, Alfred Robert MacLean, born at Monkton Wyld, Dorset, 2 Oct., 1869; 2s. John Benedict Mary Aloysius, gen. WORCESTER, matric. 22 Oct., 91, aged 22, from Tiverton school.

Camm, (rev.) Reginald Percy John, born at Sunbury-on-Thames 26 Dec., 1864 ; 1s. John Brooke Maher, cler. KEBLE, matric. 16 Oct., 83, aged 18 (from Westminster school), B.A. 87 (HONOURS :—2 theology 87) ; seceded to Rome 90.

Campagnac, Ernest Trafford, born at Monghyr, India, 13 Nov., 1872 ; o.s. James Alden, cler. UNIVERSITY COLL., matric. 17 Oct., 91, aged 18 (from Bristol school), scholar 91.

Campbell, Archibald John, born at Cawnpore, E. Indies, 1 Feb., 1867 ; 2s. Henry Montgomery, captain in the army, deceased. MAGDALEN, matric. 23 Oct., 85, aged 18, from Bath coll.

Campbell, Arthur Minton, born at Ombersley, co. Worc., 1864 ; 3s. Arthur Minton, gent. HERTFORD, matric. 18 Oct., 83, aged 19 (from Worcester cathedral school), scholar 82-6, B.A. 87, M.A. and B.Med. 92 ; HONOURS :—2 classical mods. 85.

Campbell, Claud Herbert, born at Cannes in France 21 Jan., 1868 ; 1s. Douglas, arm. TRINITY, matric. 16 Oct., 86, aged 18 (from the Charterhouse), exhibitioner 87 (HONOURS :—2 classical mods. 88) ; and lieut. R, Scots.

Campbell, Harrison, born at Whitby, Yorks, 1864 ; 2s. Hugh Stillie, cler. CHARSLEY'S HALL, matric. 18 Oct., 87, aged 23.

Campbell, hon. Hugh Frederick Vaughan, born at Cantray, co. Nairn, 21 June, 1870; 1s. Frederick Archibald, viscount Emlyn. CHRIST CHURCH, matric. 8 June, 89, aged 18, from Eton.

Campbell, John Edward, born at Lisburn, Ireland, 1862 ; 3s. John, D.Med. HERTFORD, matric. 14 Oct., 84, aged 22 (from Queen's coll., Belfast), scholar 83 and fellow 87, B.A. 88, M.A. 91 (HONOURS :—1 mathematical mods. 85, 1 mathematics 87; junior 85 and senior mathematical scholarship 88, Herschel astronomical prize 88.

Campbell, John Fitzherbert, born at Stoke-on-Trent, co. Stafford, 6 July, 1867 ; 1s. Colin Minton, M.P., arm. NEW COLL., matric. 16 Oct., 80, aged 19 (from Eton) ; of Woodseat, co. Stafford, J.P., student Inner Temple 81.

Campbell, John Gordon Drummond, born at Dumdrum, E. Indies, 15 Feb., 1864 ; 2s. Archibald Neil, arm. CORPUS CHRISTI, matric. 19 Oct., 83, aged 19 (from the Charterhouse), scholar 83, B.A. 87 (HONOURS :—1 classical mods. 84, 1 classics 87) ; bar.-at-law, Lincoln's Inn, 90, H.M. inspector of schools 92.

Campbell, John Seymour, born at Sherwood, Notts, 1863 ; 1s. William, cler. HERTFORD, matric. 22 Oct., 81, aged 18 (from Uppingham school), B.A. 84, M.A. 88 ; HONOURS :—3 classical mods. 83.

Campbell, John Stratheden, born at Saugur, E. Indies, 21 Jan., 1863 ; 1s. John Scarlett, gent. BALLIOL, matric. 18 Oct., 81, aged 18 (from Rugby), student Inner Temple 82 ; joint magistrate N.W.P. India 83. See Foster's *Peerage*, B. STRATHEDEN.

Campbell, Lewis, M.A., fellow QUEEN'S 55-8, where see.

Campbell, Matthew John, born at Aberdovery Towyn, co. Merion., 7 Feb., 1867 ; 3s. Charles. JESUS COLL., matric. 20 Oct., 91, aged 26, from Ystrad-Meurig gr. school ; died 4 Nov., 92.

Campbell, Reginald John, born in London 1867 ; 2s. John, methodist minister of Gunthorpe, Notts. CHRIST CHURCH, matric. 14 Oct., 92, aged 25, from University coll., Nottingham.

Campbell, Richard Arthur Pleydell-Bouverie-, born at Salisbury 6 July, 1862 ; 1s. Richard Arthur, arm. MERTON, matric. 25 Jan., 82, aged 19, from Harrow. See Foster's *Peerage*, E. RADNOR.

Campion, rev. Charles Thomas, born at Manchester 1862 ; 1s. Henry, arm. CORPUS CHRISTI, matric. 21 Oct., 80, aged 18 (from the Charterhouse) ; scholar ORIEL 81-5, B.A. 84, M.A. 87 (HONOURS :—1 classical mods. 82, 2 classics 84) ; curate of Heaton Mersey, co. Lanc., 90.

Campion, Frederick Henry, born at Danny Park, Sussex, 8 Sept., 1872 ; 2s. William Henry, esquire. NEW COLL., matric. 16 Oct., 91, aged 19, from Eton.

Campion, rev. Herbert Roper, born at Manchester May, 1868 ; 4s. Henry, gent. KEBLE, matric. 19 Oct., 86, aged 18 (from the Charterhouse), B.A. 89; curate of Chendle, Cheshire, 91.

Campion, William Robert, born in London July, 1870 ; 1s. William Henry, arm. NEW COLL., matric. 11 Oct., 89, aged 19 (from Eton), B.A. 92 ; HONOURS :—4 history 92.

Cancellor, Henry Lannoy, born at Hamble, Hants, 16 Jan., 1862 ; 1s. John Henry, cler. UNIVERSITY COLL., matric. 15 May, 80, aged 18 (from Eton), B.A. 84, M.A. 87 (HONOURS :—3 classical mods. 82, 3 history 84) ; bar.-at-law, Inner Temple, 88.

Candland, Herbert William, born at Stoke-upon-Trent, co. Stafford, 5 Jan., 1863; 1s. William, gen. QUEEN'S, matric. 27 Oct., 91, aged 28, from Bedford county school.

Candler, rev. Eugene Ebenezer Temple, born in London 23 July, 1861; 1s. Eugene, arm. ST. MARY HALL, matric. 24 April, 80, aged 18 (from King's coll. school, London, B.A.), B.A. (NON-COLLEGIATE) 85, M.A. 88 ; curate 86-9, and vicar of Stockport St. Peter since 89.

Cane, *see* DuCane.

Cannan, Charles, M.A., fellow TRINITY 84, where see.

Cannan, Edwin, born at Funchal, Madeira, 3 Feb., 1861 ; 2s. David Alexander, arm. BALLIOL, matric. 29 Jan., 81, aged 19 (from Clifton coll.), B.A. 84, M.A. 87 ; HONOURS :—2 classical mods. 82, Lothian essay 85.

Canney, Maurice Arthur, born in London 1872 ; 1s. Edward, cler. ST. JOHN'S, matric. 17 Oct., 91, aged 19 (from Merchant Taylors' school), exhibitioner 91 ; HONOURS :—Hebrew scholarship 92.

Canney, Thomas Stanley Alfred, born at Willesden, Middx., 10 May ; 5s. Henry Edward, late of the admiralty, deceased. MAGDALEN, matric. 4 Nov., 91, aged 20, from Christ's hospital and University coll. school.

Canning, Charles Felix Algernon Stratford, born at Tahiti 30 Jan., 1870; 3s. Francis Alfred, arm. WADHAM, matric. 1 Nov., 87, aged 17 (from Perth high school, West Australia), B.A. 91 ; bar.-at-law, Inner Temple, 92.

Canning, George Cunningham, born at Tahiti 28 Nov., 1871; 4s. Francis Alfred, arm. CHRIST CHURCH, matric. 21 Jan., 90, aged 18; brother of the last named.

Canning, Hubert, born in London 7 Nov., 1868; o.s. Charles Bowyer, arm. BRASENOSE, matric. 18 Jan., 87, aged 19.

Capel, Arthur Carnegie, born in London 26 Sept., 1862; 1s. Arthur Risdon, gent. NEW COLL., matric. 15 Oct., 81, aged 19 (from Winchester), B.A. 84; HONOURS :—2 law 84.

Capell, hon. Arthur Algernon, born 27 July, 1864; 3s. Arthur Algernon, (6th) earl of Essex. MERTON, matric. 19 Oct., 83, aged 19 (from Marlborough); migrated to New Inn Hall (BALLIOL); bar.-at-law, Inner Temple, 92.

Capes, William Wolfe, M.A., fellow QUEEN'S 56-70, where see.

Carden, Frederick Henry Walter, born in London 17 Oct., 1873; 1s. lieut.-col. sir Frederick Walter, bart. PEMBROKE, matric. 26 Oct., 91, aged 18, from Marlborough.

Cardew, Reginald Kirby, born at Helmingham, Suffolk, 25 Nov., 1862; 2s. George, cler. KEBLE, matric. 17 Jan., 83, aged 20 (from Marlborough coll.), B.A. 87; HONOURS :—2 classical mods. 84, 3 classics 86.

Cardus, Thomas Arthur Barrow, born at Phyhembury, Devon, 14 May, 1872; 1s. Thomas Michael, gent. EXETER, matric. 22 Oct., 91, aged 19.

Carew, Walter Gawen, born at Bickleigh, Devon, 1 Sept., 1870; 2s. Robert Baker, cler. PEMBROKE, matric. 26 Oct., 89, aged 19, from Tiverton school.

Carey, (rev.) Albert Darell Tupper-, born at Weybridge, Surrey, 16 Feb., 1866; 1s. Tupper, cler. CHRIST CHURCH, matric. 31 May, 84, aged 18 (from Eton), B.A. 87, M.A. 91 (HONOURS :—2 history 88, 2 theology 89); curate of Leeds 90.

Carey, Gaspard William, born in London, 9 Aug., 1862; o.s. James Gaspard le Marchant, archdeacon of Essex. NEW COLL., matric. 12 Oct. 81, aged 19 (from Uppingham school), B.A. 87; HONOURS :—3 classical mods. 83, 2 history 87.

Carey, George Sausmarez, born in London 13 Oct., 1865; 1s. Ernest Adolphus, lieut.-col. Cheshire Regt. JESUS COLL., matric. 16 Oct., 84, aged 19 (from Rossall school), scholar 84; B.A. 91; HONOURS :—3 classical mods. 86.

Carey, Godfrey Mohun, born at St. Peter's Port, isle of Guernsey, 17 Aug., 1872; 3s. Thomas Godfrey, solicitor. EXETER, matric. 22 Oct., 91, aged 19 (from Sherborne school), scholar 91.

Carey, Harold Stafford, born at Alicante in Spain, 28 Sept., 1861; 1s. Julius Alphonsus. PEMBROKE, matric. 30 Oct., 80, aged 19 (from Victoria coll., Jersey), B.A. 84.

Carey, Lionel Slade, born at St. Peter Port, Guernsey, 19 Aug., 1861; 1s. Thomas Godfrey, arm. BALLIOL, matric. 21 Oct., 80, aged 19 (from Elizabeth coll., Guernsey), dep.-com. central provinces India 82.

Carey, Spencer Wooddill Seymour, born in London 18 Nov., 1861; 2s. William James, gent. QUEEN'S, matric. 1 Feb., 81, aged 19 (from Bradfield coll. 74-80), B.A. 84; HONOURS :—3 classical mods. 82, 4 history 84.

Carey, William Henry, born at Roston, co. Leicester, Aug., 1868; 5s. Alfred Henry, cler. KEBLE, matric. 17 Oct., 87, aged 19 (from Bedford gr. school), B.A. 90.

Carkeet, John Toone, born at Plymouth, Devon, 11 June, 1872; o.s. John, gen. EXETER, matric. 22 Oct., 91, aged 19, from Plymouth coll.

Carlton, Frederick William, born at Knutsford, Cheshire, 19 Aug., 1871; 4s. James, gen. TRINITY, matric. 17 Oct., 91, aged 20, from St. Mark's, Windsor.

Carlton, Harry Weston, born at Knutsford, Cheshire, 31 May, 1865; 2s. James, gent. LINCOLN, matric. 27 Oct., 85, aged 20 (from King's coll. school, London), exhibitioner 85, B.A. 92; HONOURS :— 2 classical mods. 87, 3 law 89.

Carlyle, rev. Alexander James, M.A., chaplain fellow UNIVERSITY COLL. 93, where see page 30.

Carlyle, Edward Irving, born in London 1871; 1s. Gavin, cler. ST. JOHN'S, matric. 16 Dec., 90, aged 19, exhibitioner 90; HONOURS :—3 mathematical mods. 92.

Carlyon, Hugh Tredenham, born at Torquay 1868; 1s. Horace, arm. ST. JOHN, matric. 15 Oct., 87, aged 19, from Eton.

Carmichael, Archibald John Thomas Hill Paterson, born at Edinburgh 1870; o.s. John, gen. ST. EDMUND HALL, matric. 16 March, 89, aged 19.

Carmichael, Evelyn George Massey, born at Worcester, 9 April, 1871; 1s. George Lynedock, arm. ORIEL, matric. 22 Oct., 90, aged 19, from Harrow.

Carmichael, George, born at Aberdeen 1866; 3s. George, gent. BALLIOL, matric. 15 Oct., 84, aged 18 (from Aberdeen gr. school), assist. commissioner at Yamethin, Burma, Bombay c.s. 86.

Carnduff, Herbert William Cameron, born in Calcutta 1862; 1s. David, gent. BALLIOL, matric. 18 Oct., 81, aged 19 (from Edinburgh university); registrar appellate side high court Calcutta 83.

Carne, Mansel Sydney Derkrolles, born at Demblands, co. Glamorgan, 1862; 2s. John Whitlock Stradling, D.C.L. NEW INN HALL, matric. 14 Oct., 82, aged 18; of Nash Manor, co. Glam.

Carnegie, hon. Lancelot Douglas, born in Edinburgh 26 Dec., 1867; 2s. James, earl of Southesk. CHRIST CHURCH, matric. 4 June, 81, aged 19, from Eton.

Carnsew, Walter Henry, born at Bude. Cornwall, 27 Oct., 1862; 1s. Thomas Stone, cler. KEBLE, matric. 18 Oct., 81, aged 18, from Cheltenham coll.

Carpenter, Archibald Boyd, born in London 26 March, 1873; 4s. William Boyd, D.D., bishop of Ripon. BALLIOL, matric. 18 Oct., 92, aged 19, from Harrow school.

Carpenter, William Boyd, scholar ST. CATHERINE COLL., Cambridge; 29th senior optime, and B.A. 1864, M.A. 67, D.D. 84, hon. fellow 87, created D.C.L. (Oxford), 26 June, 89; vicar of St. James, Holloway, 70-9, and of Christ Church, Lancaster Gate, 79-84, canon of Windsor 82-4, bishop of Ripon 84; select preacher at Cambridge 75 and 77 (and at Oxford 82), Hulsean lecturer 78, hon. chaplain to the Queen 79-83, and chaplain 83-4, Hampton lecturer Oxford 87.

Carr, Arthur, M.A., fellow ORIEL 68-72, where see.

Carr, Benjamin Lund, born at Conisbrough, Yorks, 1867; 1s. Thomas, gent. NON-COLLEGIATE, matric. 19 Jan., 89, aged 21, B.A. 89, M.A. 92.

Carr, Douglas Ward, born at Cranbrook, Kent, 17 March, 1872; 1s. Thomas Arnold, cler. NON-COLLEGIATE, matric. 11 Oct., 90, aged 18, from Sutton Valence gr. school.

Carr, Frank Collett, born at Ramsgate, Kent, 16 July, 1870 or 72; 3s. Thomas William, cler. WADHAM, matric. 14 Oct., 89, aged 19, from the Charterhouse.

Carr, George, M.A., schoolmaster QUEEN'S 75, where see.

Carr, Horace Fulton, born at Putney, Middx., 1874; 1s. Jonathan Thomas, gent. CHRIST CHURCH, matric. 14 Oct., 92, aged 18, from Westminster school.

Carr, Reginald Childers Culling, born at Cuddalore, E. Indies, 3 Aug., 1864; 3s. Francis, arm. TRINITY, matric. 15 Oct., 83, aged 19 (from the Charterhouse); assist. sec. to government of Madras, judicial and legislative departments 85.

Carr, Thomas William, born at Loddington, Northants, 1861; 1s. Thomas William, cler. CORPUS CHRISTI, matric. 24 Jan., 80, aged 19 (from Winchester), B.A. 83; HONOURS:—2 classical mods. 81, 2 law 83.

Carr, Walter Charles, born at Whitworth, co. Durham, Nov., 1863; 2s. Charles, cler. KEBLE, matric. 17 Oct., 82, aged 18 (from Richmond gr. school), B.A. 85, M.A. 89; HONOURS:—3 theology 85.

Carr, William, born at Gomersal, Yorks, 14 June, 1862; 1s. William, of Gomersal, arm. UNIVERSITY COLL., matric. 14 Oct., 82, aged 20 (from Marlborough coll.), B.A. 86; (HONOURS:—3 classical mods. 84, Stanhope essay 84, 2 history 86, Lothian essay 88, Arnold essay 90); bar.-at-law, Middle Temple, 89.

Carrack, James Masters, born at Liverpool 13 Sept., 1857; o.s. Aaron Thomas, gent. QUEEN'S, matric. 25 Oct., 80, aged 22 (from archbishop Holgate's school, York), B.A. 84; HONOURS:—3 theology 84.

Carreg, Robert Thomas, born at Pwllheli, co. Carnarvon, 28 July, 1868; 1s. Robert, gen. WORCESTER, matric. 21 Jan., 87, aged 18 (from Beaumaris gr. school), R.A. 90; passed into Sandhurst 91.

Carrington, John, born at Cottingham, Yorks, 15 May, 1867; 2s. Thomas, cler. MAGDALEN, matric. 22 Oct., 87, aged 20 (from King's coll. school, London), academical clerk 87; migrated to KING'S COLL., Cambridge, 9 May, 89.

Carroll, rev. William Alexander, born at Putney, Surrey, 1863; 1s. Herbert Alexander, arm. CHRIST CHURCH, matric. 13 Oct., 82, aged 19, B.A. 85; HONOURS:—3 theology 85.

Carruthers, George, born at Little Corby, Cumberland, 26 Sept., 1865; 1s. Richard, gent. QUEEN'S, matric. 20 Oct., 84, aged 19 (from Heversham school), exhibitioner 84; HONOURS:—3 mathematical mods. 86, 4 mathematics 88.

Cart, Alfred, born in London 1865; 2s. Henry Philip, gent. NEW INN HALL, matric. 19 Oct., 85, aged 20; of BALLIOL 87.

Cart, rev. Henry Thomas, born at Hampstead, Middx., 1860; 1s. Henry Philip, gent. ST. JOHN'S, matric. 17 Jan., 80, aged 20 (from King's coll., London), theological associate 80; migrated to CHARSLEY HALL, B.A. 83, M.A. 88; vicar of St. Luke's, New Kentish town, 89.

Carte, Lucas D'Oyly, born at Norwood, Surrey, 27 Dec., 1871; 1s. Richard, arm. MAGDALEN, matric. 14 Oct., 90, aged 18, from Winchester.

Cartre, Arthur Arnold, born at Oxford 7 Oct., 1869; 2s. George, M.A., master of New coll. choristers school. NEW COLL., matric. 12 Oct., 88, aged 19 (from Oxford high school) (HONOURS:—3 classical mods. 90); brother of Ernest George.

Carter, Arthur Cecil, born at Liverpool 26 July, 1866; 4s. Robert William, gen. NON-COLLEGIATE, matric. 15 Oct., 87, aged 21 (from Mercers' school, London); migrated to TRINITY 89, R.A. 91; HONOURS:—3 chemistry 91.

Carter, Charles Emerson, born in Calcutta 1861; o.s. Thomas Emerson, gent. WORCESTER, matric. 18 Oct., 83, aged 22, B.A. 87; HONOURS:—4 history 87.

Carter, rev. Cyril Robert, born at Eton 6 Jan., 1863; 8s. William Adolphus, vicar of Burnham, Berks. CORPUS CHRISTI, matric. 19 Oct., 82, aged 19 (from Eton and Cheltenham colleges); scholar 82-6, B.A. 86, M.A. 91 (HONOURS:—2 mathematical mods. 83, 2 classical mods. 84, 3 classics 86), in the Oxford eight 84, 5, 6; assistant master Wellington coll. 87.

Carter, Edgar Bonham, born in London 2 April, 1870; 5s. Henry Bonham, bar.-at-law. NEW COLL., matric. 11 Oct., 89, aged 19 (from Clifton coll.), B.A. 92; HONOURS:—2 law 92.

Carter, rev. Ernest Courtnay, born at Compton, Berks, 17 Feb., 1858; 3s. George, cler. NON-COLLEGIATE, matric. 18 Oct., 80, aged 22 (from the Charterhouse and Leamington coll.); migrated to ST. JOHN'S, B.A. 84; curate of Chieveley, Berks, 89.

Carter, Ernest George, born at Cowley, Oxon, 25 July, 1867; 1s. George, gent. WADHAM, matric. 16 Oct., 86, aged 19 (from Oxford high school); brother of Arthur Arnold.

Carter, Evan Eyare, born in Barbados 11 Aug., 1866; o.s. Eyre Poppin, gent. TRINITY, matric. 17 Oct., 85, aged 19 (from Canterbury school); lieut. Leicestershire Regt. 91, and of Army Service corps, Dublin, 91.

Carter, Fitzwilliam, born at Shelton, co. Stafford, 17 Feb., 1873; 1s. Conway Richard Dobbs, M.A., vicar of St. Erth. NON-COLLEGIATE, matric. 17 Oct., 91, aged 18, from Magdalen coll. school.

Carter, Frank, born at Great Crosby, co. Lincoln, 1862; 1s. Robert Oliver, cler. BALLIOL, matric. 21 Jan., 80, aged 18 (from Uppingham school), exhibitioner 80-3, B.A. 83; HONOURS:—1 classical mods. 81, 1 classics 83.

Carter, Henry St. John, born at Sutton on Hull, Yorks, March, 1872; 1s. John, cler. KEBLE, matric. 20 Oct., 91, aged 19, from Rossall school.

Carter, (rev.) James Holderness, born at Salisbury 1864; 2s. William, gen. NON-COLLEGIATE, matric. 2 June, 84, aged 20 (from Salisbury gr. school and Woolfardisworthy coll.); migrated to EXETER, B.A. 87, M.A. 92 (HONOURS:—3 theology 87); precentor Grahamstown cathedral church 90.

Carter, (rev.) James Octavius Holderness, born at Formby, Cheshire, 26 April, 1861; 2s. Thomas Fortescue, arm., deceased. MAGDALEN, matric. 2 March, 83, aged 21 (from St. Edmund's coll., Salisbury), clerk 83-6, B.A. and M.A. 90.

Carter, (rev.) John, born at Toronto 1862; 1s. John, prof. of music. EXETER, matric. 18 Oct., 83, aged 21 (from Trinity coll., Ontario, B.A. 82, M.A. 89), exhibitioner 83, B.A. 85, M.A. 90 (HONOURS:—3 classical mods. 85, 2 classics 87); curate of St. Anne Limehouse 87-9.

Carter, Langham, born at North Walsham, Norfolk, Oct., 1861; 1s. Robert, gent. CORPUS CHRISTI, matric. 21 Oct., 80, aged 18 (from Bradfield coll.), B.A. 84; HONOURS:—3 classical mods. 82, 3 law 84.

Carter, Norman Bonham, born in London 29 Dec., 1867; 4s. Henry, arm. BALLIOL, matric. 16 Oct., 86, aged 18 (from Rugby), assist. magistrate and collector, Bengal c.s. 88.

Carter, Reginald, born at Truro, Cornwall, 12 Jan., 1868; 1s. Richard Henry, gent. BALLIOL, matric. Oct., 86, aged 18 (from Clifton coll.), exhibitioner 86, R.A. 91; HONOURS:—1 classical mods. 88, proxime accessit Hertford scholarship 87, Greek prose 89, 2 classics 90.

Carter, Reginald, B.A., assistant classical tutor LINCOLN, matric 90.

Carter, Reginald Carlyle, born at Leamington, 25 Oct., 1869; 3s. Thomas Albert, arm. MAGDALEN, matric. 16 Oct., 88, aged 18 (from Leamington coll.), demy 88; HONOURS:—1 classical mods. 90, 2 classics 92.

Carter, William Charles, born at St. Bees, Cumberland, 8 April, 1868; 4s. John, gen. QUEEN'S, matric. 21 Oct., 87, aged 19 (from St. Bees gr. school), B.A. 92.

Carter, William Edward Dickson, M.A., fellow NEW COLL. 40-50, where see.

Carter, William Morris, born at Petworth, Sussex, 9 Dec., 1874; 1s. Sidney James, banker, deceased. BRASENOSE, matric. 21 Oct., 92, aged 18 (from King's school, Canterbury), exhibitioner 92.

Cartwright, Ernest Henry, born in London 1865; o.s. Henry Edmund, bar.-at-law. EXETER, matric. 18 Oct., 83, aged 18 (from the Charterhouse), scholar 83, B.A. 87, M.A. and B.Med. 92 (HONOURS :—2 physiology 87); M.R.C.S. 92.

Cartwright, rev. Harry Beauchamp, born in London 13 July, 1863; 3s. Thomas Broadbent, gent. CHRIST CHURCH, matric. 13 Oct., 82, aged 19 (from Merchant Taylors' school), scholar 83-6, B.A. 86 (HONOURS :—3 classical mods. 84, 2 theology 86); has served curacies in N.W. Canada.

Cartwright, Henry Everard, born at Braintree, Essex, 12 Aug., 1873; 1s. Thomas Everard, M.A., rector of Chatham St. John's. UNIVERSITY COLL., matric. 15 Oct., 92, aged 19, from Vicars school Ely and Rochester.

Cartwright, Philip Charles, born at Brighton 6 Oct., 1864; 4s. Richard Aubrey, of Edgecott, Northants, arm. NEW COLL., matric. 10 Oct., 84, aged 20, from Eton.

Cartwright, rev. Stephen Frederic, born at Brighton 25 Dec., 1862; 3s. Richard Aubrey, arm. MERTON, matric. 17 Oct., 82, aged 19 (from Limpsfield school and Eton), B.A. 86, M.A. 89, curate of Maidstone 88; brother of the last-named.

Cartwright, Theodore John, born at Preston Bagot, co. Warwick, 28 March, 1868; o.s. Theodore John, rector, deceased. NEW COLL., matric. 14 Oct., 87, aged 19 (from Rugby), B.A. 91; HONOURS :— 3 classical mods. 89, 4 classics 91.

Cartwright, Thomas George, born at Newport, co. Mon., 10 March, 1867; 1s. William George, arm. CHRIST CHURCH, matric. 3 June, 87, aged 20, from Rugby.

Cartwright, rev. William Digby, born in London 11 Feb., 1865; 3s. Henry, arm. CHRIST CHURCH, matric. 12 Oct., 83, aged 19 (from Eton), B.A. 87, M.A. 90 (HONOURS :—4 history 87); curate of New Ferry, Cheshire, 89.

Carver, Alfred Wright, born at North Brixton, Surrey, 30 Nov., 1866; 1s. Alfred Enoch, gent. NON-COLLEGIATE, matric. 17 Oct., 85, aged 18 (from Southwark gr. school), B.A. 89, M.A. 92; HONOURS: —3 classical mods. 87, 2 history 89.

Carver, Frank, born at Altrincham, Cheshire, 24 Feb., 1865; 1s. John, of Ealing, arm. MAGDALEN, matric. 16 Oct., 84, aged 19 (from Wellington coll.), B.A. 87; HONOURS :—3 law 87.

Carwithen, Reginald Master, born at Bareilly, E. Indies, 13 Dec., 1870; 2s. George Terry, arm. ST. MARY HALL, matric. 18 Jan., 90, aged 19 (from Wimbledon school), B.A. 92.

Cary, (rev.) Henry Lucius Moultrie, born at Warrington 31 Oct., 1866; o.s. Offley Henry, cler. ORIEL, matric. 23 Oct., 85, aged 18 (from Clifton coll.), scholar 84, B.A. 89 (HONOURS :—2 classical mods. 87), vice-principal Dorchester missionary coll. 91.

Case, Henry Ben, born at Trowbridge, Wilts, 14 Aug., 1864; 8s. Henry Hervey, gen., deceased. NON-COLLEGIATE, matric. 6 Feb., 92, aged 27, from Independent coll., Taunton.

Case, Montague James, born at Ufton, Berks, 1873; 1s. James, gent. NON-COLLEGIATE, matric. 1 Nov., 92, aged 19, from Eastbourne coll.

Case, Thomas, M.A., fellow MAGDALEN 90, where see.

Case, Thomas Bennett, born at Upton, Berks, 19 Feb., 1871; 1s. Thomas, M.A., professor of moral and natural philosophy. MAGDALEN, matric. 14 Oct., 89, aged 18 (from Winchester), in University eleven 91-2.

Case, William Sterndale, born at Oxford 24 Aug., 1873; 2s. Thomas, M.A., professor of moral and natural philosophy. MAGDALEN, matric. 30 April, 92, aged 18, from Winchester.

Cash, Christopher, born at Coventry 15 Sept., 1861; 4s. John, gent. TRINITY, matric. 29 Jan., 81, aged 19 (from Uppingham school), B.A. 87; HONOURS :—2 classical mods. 82, 3 classics 84.

Casher, rev. Charles James, born at North Brixton, Surrey, 1861; o.s. Charles Edward, cler. NON-COLLEGIATE, matric. 15 Oct., 81, aged 20 (from Brighton coll.), scholar ST. JOHN'S 84, B.A. 85, M.A. 88 (HONOURS :—2 theology 85, Denyer and Johnson theological scholarship 86); curate of St. Aldate's, Oxford, 88.

Cass, rev. Bingley, born at Amwell, Herts, 16 March, 1871; 5s. Charles, cler. WADHAM, matric. 13 Oct., 88, aged 21 (from Brighton coll.), B.A. 91; HONOURS :—3 theology 91.

Cass, rev. Frederick Charles Guise, born in London 1860; 1s. Frederick, cler. EXETER, matric. 28 Jan., 81, aged 21, B.A. 85, M.A. 89; curate of Monken-Hadley, Middlesex, 88-91, rector 91.

Cassel, Felix Maximilian Schoenbrunn, born at Cologne, 16 Sept., 1869; o.s. Louis Schoenbrunn, gen. CORPUS CHRISTI, matric. 20 Oct., 88, aged 19 (from Harrow), scholar 88; HONOURS :—1 classical mods. 90, 1 law 92.

Cassels, Walter Seytoun, born in London Aug., 1873; 4s. Andrew, a member of council of India. ORIEL, matric. 27 Oct., 91, aged 18, from Marlborough coll.

Cassidy, rev. Mark Mortimer, born at Sydenham, Ireland, 27 Dec., 1863; 4s. Robert, solicitor, deceased. WADHAM, matric. 23 Oct., 82, aged 18 (from Merchant Taylors' school), exhibitioner 82, B.A. 85, M.A. 92 (HONOURS :—2 history 85); curate of Bexley, Kent, 90.

Casson, Arthur Carroll Bazely, born at Old, Northants 1861; 1s. George, cler. BRASENOSE, matric. 10 June, 80, aged 19 (from Wellington), B.A. 85, M.A. 92; HONOURS :—3 classical mods. 83, 3 classics 85.

Casson, Ferdinand George, born at Old, Northants 5 March, 1864; 2s. George, cler. ORIEL, matric. 25 Jan., 83, aged 18 (from Marlborough coll.); lieut. the Northumberland Fusiliers 85.

Casson, George, M.A., fellow BRASENOSE 31-43, where see.

Casson, Herbert Alexander, born at Old Northants, 1867; 4s. George, cler. HERTFORD, matric. 22 Oct., 86, aged 19 (from Marlborough coll.), scholar 85, B.A. 89 (HONOURS :—3 Indian languages 89); assistant commissioner Punjab 88.

Casson, John Walker George, born at Dlaen-y-ddol, co. Merioneth, 1873; 1s. John, gent. BALLIOL, matric. 18 Oct., 92, aged 19, from Marlborough coll.

Casson, Thomas, born at Leeds 1868; o.s. Thomas, gent. ST. JOHN'S, matric. 16 Oct., 86, aged 18 (from Bury St. Edmund's school), B.A. 90; HONOURS :—3 history 90.

Casswell, rev. George Frank, born at Harpswell, co. Lincoln, 1862; 1s. George, gent. HERTFORD, matric. 4 May, 81, aged 19. B.A. 84; curate of Saxilby, co. Lincoln, 91.

Castens, Herbert Hayton, born at Port Elizabeth, Cape of Good Hope, 23 Nov., 1864; 1s. Emilius, gen. BRASENOSE, matric. 21 Jan., 84, aged 19 (from Rugby), B.A. 89; bar.-at-law, Inner Temple, 89.

Castle, Arthur Herbert, born at Putney, Surrey, 1864; 2s. Richard Henry Barton, gent. NON-COLLEGIATE, matric. 14 Oct., 82, aged 18; migrated to ST. JOHN'S, B.A. 86, M.A. 92; HONOURS:—3 theology 86.

Castle, George, born at Oxford 15 June, 1870; o.s. George, gen. ST. MARY HALL, matric. 26 Jan., 91, aged 20.

Castle, Harold Cyril Palmer, born in London 13 Nov., 1866; 1s. Edward James, bar.-at-law. MAGDALEN, matric. 22 Oct., 87, aged 18 (from the Charterhouse), exhibitioner 87, B.A. 91 (HONOURS:—3 classical mods. 89, 4 history 92); bar.-at-law, Inner Temple, 92.

Castle, rev. Joseph, born at Oxford 1859; 3s. Frederick, gent. HERTFORD, matric. 1 Feb., 81, aged 22, B.A. 85; curate of Faversham, Kent, 91.

Castlehow, William, born at Watermillock 1863; 2s. Thomas, arm. CORPUS CHRISTI, matric. 19 Oct., 82, aged 19 (from Sedbergh school), B.A. 88, M.A. 89; HONOURS:—3 classical mods. 84.

Cater, Herbert Elliott, born at Southgate, Middx., 23 Sept., 1870; 1s. John James, gen. LINCOLN, matric. 27 Jan., 90, aged 19, from Bath coll.

Cato, Thomas Butler, born at Ashford, Kent, 1867; 1s. Thomas Ensor, cler. ORIEL, matric. 13 May, 86, aged 19, B.A. 89.

Cator, Bertie John Lumley, born in London 6 Aug., 1861; 1s. John Thomas, gent. ST. ALBAN HALL, matric. 26 Jan., 81, aged 19 (from St. Edward's school, Summertown); migrated to EXETER 22 April following.

Cator, Ralph Bertie Peter, born in London Nov., 1861; 1s. Bertie Peter, arm. KEBLE, matric. 19 Oct., 80, aged 18 (from Radley coll.), B.A. 83; HONOURS:—2 history 83.

Cattell, Richard Henry Burdon, born at Erdington, co. Warwick, 23 March, 1871; 2s. Thomas, gen. EXETER, matric. 13 Oct., 90, aged 19, from Trinity coll., Stratford-on-Avon.

Caudwell, rev. Edmund Schuyler Sutton, born at Carnmenillis, Cornwall, 18 March, 1866; 2s. Francis, cler. ST. MARY HALL, matric. 20 Oct., 84, aged 18, B.A. 87; curate of All Hallows, East India docks, 88.

Causten, Charles Guy, born at Stutton, co. Glouc., 17 May, 1871; 2s. Charles Purefoy, rector of Stretton-on-the-Fosse, co. Gloucester. UNIVERSITY COLL., matric. 11 Oct., 90, aged 19, from Haileybury.

Cave, Arthur Wilson, M.A., MAGDALEN, where see.

Cave, Cecil Beckwith Cave-Brown-, born at Ellel, co. Lanc., 22 Nov., 1871; 2s. Fitzherbert Astley, vicar of Longridge, co. Lanc. BRASENOSE, matric. 14 Oct., 90, aged 18, from Eton.

Cave, Edward Wilkins, born at Surbiton, Yorks, 1 Aug., 1871; y.s. sir Lewis William, judge of high court. ORIEL, matric. 22 Oct., 90, aged 19 (from Rugby and King's coll. (London) schools), scholar 90; HONOURS:—2 classical mods. 92.

Cave, Harold Watkins, born at Kingston, Surrey, 18 Aug., 1862; 1s. sir Lewis William, judge of high court. BALLIOL, matric. 18 Oct., 81, aged 19 (from Rugby), B.A. and M.A. 88 (HONOURS:—2 classical mods. 82, 2 law 85); bar.-at-law, Lincoln's Inn, 88.

Cave, Henry William, born at Brackley, Northants, 23 Feb., 1854; 1s. William, pleb. NON-COLLEGIATE, matric. 14 Oct., 82, aged 28 (from Magdalen coll. school, Brackley); migrated to BALLIOL, B.A. 88; served in educational dept., Ceylon.

Cave, Herbert, born at Hartley Wintney, Hants, 1859; CHRIST CHURCH, matric. 14 Oct., 81, aged 22, scholar 85-6, B.A. 85, M.A. 89; HONOURS:—2 natural science 85.

Cave, Robert Moore, born at Weston-super-Mare, 1873; 2s. John O'Connell, gent. NON-COLLEGIATE, matric. 15 Oct., 92, aged 19, from Bristol school.

Cavenagh, James Lawrence, born at Torpoint, Cornwall, 11 Jan., 1870; 2s. James Lawrence, gen. NON-COLLEGIATE, matric. 13 Oct., 88, aged 18, (from Southwark gr. school); died 20 April, 92.

Cavendish, hon. Edwin William, born at Latimer, Bucks, 29 Oct., 1865; 3s. Charles Compton William, baron Chesham. CHRIST CHURCH, matric. 1 Feb., 86, aged 20.

Cawker, Louis Garnant, born at Sydney, Australia, 31 July, 1866; 1s. Lewis, gent. JESUS COLL., matric. 26 Oct., 85, aged 19 (from Brecon coll.), B.A. 90; HONOURS:—3 classical mods. 87.

Cawood, Edward Hay Crane, born at Penrose, co. Worcester, Sept., 1871; 6s. John, cler. KEBLE, matric. 11 Oct., 89, aged 19, from Rossall school.

Cawood, William Benjamin Crane, born at Pensax, co. Worc., Aug., 1869; 5s. John, cler. KEBLE, matric. 13 Oct., 88, aged 19 (from St. Edward's school, Summertown), B.A. 92; HONOURS:—2 history 91.

Cayzer, Charles William, born at Bombay July, 1869; 1s. Charles William, gen. CHRIST CHURCH, matric. 16 Oct., 91, aged 22, from Rugby.

Cazalet, William Marshall, born at St. Petersburgh, 8 July, 1865; 1s. Edward, arm. CHRIST CHURCH, matric. 30 May, 85, aged 19, B.A. 89.

Cecil, lord Edgar Algernon Robert, born 14 Sept., 1864; 3s. Robert Arthur, marquis of Salisbury. UNIVERSITY COLL., matric. 13 Jan., 83, aged 18 (from Eton), B.A. 85 (HONOURS:—2 law 86), treasurer and president of the Oxford union society 85; bar.-at-law, Inner Temple, 87.

Cecil, Evelyn, born in London 30 May, 1865; 1s. lord Eustace. NEW COLL., matric. 12 Oct., 83, aged 18 (from Eton), B.A. 87. M.A. 90 (HONOURS:—2 law 87); bar.-at-law, Inner Temple, 89.

Cecil, lord Hugh Richard Heathcote, born 14 Oct., 1869; 5s. Robert Arthur, marquis of Salisbury. UNIVERSITY COLL., matric. 15 Oct., 87, aged 18 (from Eton); fellow HERTFORD 91, B.A. 91; HONOURS:—1 history 91.

Cecil, James Edward Herbert Gascoyne ; viscount Cranborne, born 23 Oct., 1861; 1s. Robert Arthur, marquis of Salisbury. UNIVERSITY COLL., matric. 15 May, 80, aged 18 (from Eton), B.A. 85 (HONOURS:—3 mathematical mods. 82, 2 history 84); M.P. North East Lancashire (Darwen division) Dec., 85—July, 92, and Rochester 93, hon. col. 1 vol. batt. Essex Regt. 88, major 4 batt. (militia) Beds. Regt. 87.

Cecil, rev. lord William Rupert Ernest Gascoyne, born 9 March, 1863; 2s. Robert Arthur, marquis of Salisbury. UNIVERSITY COLL., matric. 21 Jan., 82, aged 18 (from Eton), B.A. 86, M.A. 88 (HONOURS:—3 law 85); rector of Bishops Hatfield 88.

Chadwick, Herbert Francis, born at Hopton, Yorks, 10 Oct., 1870; o.s. Samuel Joseph, solicitor. WADHAM, matric. 14 Oct., 89, aged 19 from York school), B.A. 92.

Chadwick, Samuel Thomas, born at Bathysford, Yorks, 15 May, 1869; 2s. Joseph, arm. TRINITY, matric. 11 Oct., 90, aged 21, from Sherborne school.

Chaffer, rev. William, born at Hull, Yorks, 18,42; 1s. Thomas, gen. NON-COLLEGIATE, matric. 4 Oct., 87, aged 45, B.A. 90; HONOURS:—4 theology 90.

Chaffey, Reginald Edward, born at Clapham, Surrey, 4 Jan., 1862; 6s. John Banyard, gent. QUEEN'S, matric. 4 May, 81, aged 19 (from Dulwich coll.), B.A. 90.

Chafy, John Westwood William, born at Camberwell, Surrey, 6 Oct., 1864; 2s. William Westwood, arm. CHRIST CHURCH, matric. 25 May, 83, aged 18, from Harrow.

Chaine, James, born in co. Antrim, Ireland, 25 Dec., 1866; 2s. James, arm., deceased. MAGDALEN, matric. 23 Oct., 85, aged 18 (from Marlborough coll.), B.A. 89.

Chalken, Frederick, M.A., fellow CORPUS CHRISTI 50-69, where see.

Challacombe, rev. William Allen Nicholas, born at High Wycombe, Bucks, 18 Nov., 1863; o.s. William Nicholas, gent. NON-COLLEGIATE, matric. 17 Oct., 85, aged 22 (from Billericay school); migrated to CHRIST CHURCH 86, and from thence to WORCESTER 87, B.A. 88, M.A. 92 (HONOURS:— a theology 88); curate of Christ Church, Dover, 88.

Chalmers, Alexander Gustavus Adolphus, born in London 2 March, 1869; o.s. Alexander, gent., deceased. HERTFORD, matric. 19 Feb., 92, aged 22, from a Bromley school.

Chalmers, Kenneth Ellmann, born in London 1873; 2s. Frederick William Marsh, banker. BALLIOL, matric. 18 Oct., 92, aged 19, from Eton.

Chamberlain, George Arthur, born at Madras 29 May, 1870; 1s. George Kenaway, late Madras c.s., retired. BRASENOSE, matric. 14 Oct., 89, aged 19 (from Clifton coll.), B.A. 92.

Chambers, (rev.) Arthur John, born at Ely, co. Cambridge, 25 Feb., 1867; 2s. John, vicar of Woodhead, co. Lane. MERTON, matric. 21 Oct., 86, aged 19 (from Manchester gr. school), exhibitioner MAGDALEN 87, B.A. 90 (HONOURS:—3 mathematical mods. 88, 3 mathematics 90); curate of Trinity, Kingston-on-Hull, 91.

Chambers, Charles Douglas, born at Douglas, isle of Man, 1867; 2s. Richard, arm. HERTFORD, matric. 27 Oct., 87, aged 20 (from Harrow), scholar B.A., B.A. 91; HONOURS:—1 classical mods. 89, 1 classics 91.

Chambers, Charles Grahame, born at West Ilsley, Berks, 12 July, 1870; 2s. William, cler. LINCOLN, matric. 17 Oct., 89, aged 19 (from Marlborough coll.), exhibitioner 89, B.A. 92; HONOURS:—3 law 92.

Chambers, Edmund Kerchever, born at West Ilsley, Berks, 16 March, 1866; 1s. William, cler. CORPUS CHRISTI, matric. 26 Oct., 85, aged 19 (from Marlborough coll.), scholar 85, B.A. 89 (HONOURS:— 1 classical mods. 87, 1 classics, 89, English essay 91), junior examiner education department 93.

Chambers, Frank Harding, born at Wolverhampton, Dec., 1867; 1s. Joseph James, gent. BALLIOL, matric. 24 Oct., 85, aged 18 (from Wolverhampton gr. school), exhibitioner 84, B.A. 88; HONOURS:— a mathematical mods. 86, 1 mathematics 88.

Chambers, (rev.) Henry, born at Sutton in Ashfield, Notts, 1859; 6s. William, gent. NON-COLLEGIATE, matric. 13 Oct., 84, aged 25, B.A. 87; curate of Emmanuel church, Loughborough, 91.

Chambers, John Miles, born at Wolverhampton 11 May, 1869; 2s. Joseph James, arm. UNIVERSITY COLL., matric. 15 Oct., 87, aged 18 (from Wolverhampton school), scholar 87; HONOURS:—2 mathematical mods. 88.

Chambers, William, M.A., fellow WORCESTER 56-65, where see.

Chambers, rev. Gordon Crewe, born at Wallasey, Cheshire, 1861; 1s. Charles Crewe, gent. BALLIOL, matric. 21 Oct., 80, aged 19 (from Dulwich coll.), exhibitioner 80-1; scholar CHRIST CHURCH 81-5, B.A.

84, M.A. 87 (HONOURS:—1 natural science 83); curate of Uttoxeter 88-91, and master Uttoxeter gr. school 88-91; headmaster Wigan school 91.

Chamot, Paul George François, born in Paris 11 April, 1862; 1s. Alexander Louis, arm. MAGDALEN, matric. 27 April, 81, aged 19, from Westminster school.

Champernowne, Amyas Walter, born at Dartington, Devon, Sept., 1873; 3s. Arthur, M.A. CHRIST CHURCH, matric. 14 Oct., 92, aged 19, from Newton Abbot school.

Champernowne, Arthur Melville, born at Totnes, Devon, 16 Aug., 1871; 1s. Arthur, of Dartington, arm. CHRIST CHURCH, matric. 10 Oct., 90, aged 19, from Eton.

Champernowne, Francis Gawayne, born at Dartington, Devon, 22 April, 1866; 3s. Richard, cler. KEBLE, matric. 5 Nov., 84, aged 18 (from Newton Abbott coll.); exhibitioner 84, B.A. 87; HONOURS:— 2 history 87.

Champernowne, John Edward, born at Bisley, co. Glouc., 5 March, 1870; y.s. Richard, cler. KEBLE, matric. 17 Jan., 91, aged 20, from St. Edward's school, Summertown.

Chance, Charles Richard, born in London, 13 July, 1861; 3s. George, metropolitan magistrate. TRINITY, matric. 16 Oct., 80, aged 19 (from Shrewsbury school; HONOURS:—3 classical mods. 82.

Chance, Joseph Selby, born at Malvern, co. Worcester, 13 Oct., 1862; 3s. Edward, arm. TRINITY, matric. 16 Oct., 80, aged 18 (from Harrow), B.A. 84; HONOURS:—3 history 84.

Chancellor, Edwin Beresford, born at Richmond, Surrey, Jan., 1868; 1s. Albert arm. CHRIST CHURCH, matric. 12 Oct., 88, aged 20, B.A. 92.

Chancellor, Frederick Wykeham, born at Chelmsford, Essex, 1865; 1s. Frederick, gent. PEMBROKE, matric. 27 Oct., 85, aged 20 (from Woking school), B.A. 89, M.A. 92.

Chandler, Arthur, M.A., fellow BRASENOSE 83-90, where see.

Chandler, rev. Frederick John, born at Newport, co. Mon., 1862; 1s. Frederick Robinson, gent. JESUS COLL., matric. 23 Oct., 80, aged 18 (from city of London school), scholar 80, B.A. 84, M.A. 87 (HONOURS:—2 classical mods. 82, 4 classics 84), organising sec. National society for northern province 91.

Channing, Francis Allston, M.A., fellow UNIVERSITY COLL. 66-70, where see.

Chaplin, Charles Slingsby, born at Ashfordby, co. Leic., 1864; 2s. Clifford Waterman, gent. PEMBROKE, matric. 2 May, 82, aged 18.

Chaplin, Edward James Morgan, born in London 1869; 1s. Edward, gent. CORPUS CHRISTI, matric. 19 Oct., 89, aged 21 (from Winchester), B.A. 87, M.A. 90 (HONOURS:—3 classical mods. 85, 3 history 87); bar.-at-law, Lincoln's Inn, 92.

Chaplin, Francis Drummond Percy, born at Twickenham 1866; o.s. Percy, arm. UNIVERSITY COLL., matric. 17 Oct., 85, aged 19 (from Harrow), scholar 84, B.A. 91 (HONOURS:—1 classical mods. 87, 2 classics 89); bar.-at-law, Lincoln's Inn, 91.

Chaplin, Robert John Morgan, born at Hamburg 5 July, 1864; 2s. Edward, gent. NEW COLL., matric. 10 Oct., 84, aged 20 (from Harsfield gym., Hesse Cassel, and Winchester), B.A. 89, M.A. 92; HONOURS:—3 classical mods. 86, Taylorian exhibition (German) 87.

Chaplin, Wyndham Allen, born at Trichinopoly Nov., 1872; 1s. Allen, colonel and deputy judge advocate. KEBLE, matric. 20 Oct., 91, aged 18.

Chapman, Arthur, born at Bromley by Bow, near London, 1865; 2s. Richard, gent. ST. JOHN'S, matric. 15 Oct., 81, aged 18 (from Merchant Taylors' school), scholar 81, B.A. 85, M.A. 88; HONOURS: —1 classical mods. 83, 2 classics 85.

Chapman, David Leonard, born at Wells-juxta-Mare, Norfolk, 1870; 1s. David, gen. CHRIST CHURCH, matric. 11 Oct., 89, aged 19 (from Manchester gr. school), exhibitioner 88.

Chapman, Edward, M.A., fellow MAGDALEN 82, where see.

Chapman, (rev.) Henry Palmer, born at Ashfield, Suffolk, April, 1865; 1s. Francis Robert, archdeacon of Sudbury. CHRIST CHURCH, matric. 12 Oct., 83, aged 18, exhibitioner 85, B.A. 87; HONOURS:—2 classical mods. 85, 1 classics 87, 3 theology 88.

Chapman, Horace Arthur Bruce, born at Roehampton, Surrey, 22 Sept., 1866; o.s. Horace Edward, cler. EXETER, matric. 21 Oct., 86, aged 20 (from Eton), B.A. 91.

Chapman, Macnaghten Hay, born at Lowestoft, Suffolk, 5 June, 1872; 5s. William Hay, cler. BRASENOSE, matric. 15 Oct., 90, aged 18, from Windermere old coll.

Chapman, (rev.) Thomas Alfred, born at Hanley, co. Stafford, 30 Nov., 1867; 1s. Thomas, cler. NON-COLLEGIATE, matric. 16 Oct., 86, aged 18 (from Middleton gr. school, co. Lanc.); migrated to EXETER 87, B.A. 89; curate of Charles, Plymouth, 89.

Chapman, Walter Charles Stephenson, born at Echelbruck 9 April, 1865; 1s. Harry Stephenson, of London, gent. QUEEN'S, matric. 30 April, 84, aged 19 (from Bruton and R. N. schools), B.A. 87; HONOURS:—3 mathematical mods. 85, 4 law 87.

Chapman, William Palmer, born in London 9 Nov., 1860; 1s. Thomas Palmer, arm. EXETER, matric. 15 May, 80, aged 19 (from Cheltenham and Bradfield colls.), B.A. 83, M.A. 87 (HONOURS:—3 law 83); student Inner Temple 82.

Chappel, (rev.) Henry Rivington, born at Camborne, Cornwall, 13 April, 1864; 3s. William Pestes, cler. EXETER, matric. 21 Oct., 86, aged 19 (from Marlborough coll.), scholar 85, B.A. 90 (HONOURS:—2 classical mods. 88, 3 classics 90, 2 theology 91); curate of St. Antholin, Nunhead, 91.

Chappel, William Henry, born at Tavistock, Devon, 31 Dec., 1869; o.s. Joseph George Winter, cler., deceased. ST. EDMUND HALL, matric. 22 Oct., 91, aged 21, from King's coll. school, London.

Chard, Henry George Augustine, born in India 1874; 1s. Charles Henry, cler. KEBLE, matric. 21 Oct., 92, aged 18, from Marlborough coll.

Chariates, Antonius, archbishop of Corfu, created D.D. 21 Feb., 1889.

Charles, Edward Eber, born in London 25 June, 1869; 1s. Arthur, a judge of the high court and a knight. NEW COLL., matric. 12 Oct., 88, aged 19 (from Clifton coll.), B.A. 92; HONOURS:—3 classical mods. 90, 3 classics 92.

Charles, Ernest Bruce, born in London 15 June, 1871; 2s. Arthur, a judge of the high court and a knight. NEW COLL., matric. 10 Oct., 90, aged 19, from Clifton coll.

Charles, Robert Henry, born at Cookstown, co. Tyrone, 6 Aug., 1855; 3s. David Hughes, D.Med., EXETER, incorporated 27 Jan., 91, aged 35; scholar Trinity coll., Dublin, 80, B.A. 81, M.A. 87 (HONOURS: —1 classics and gold medals 77 and 80, 2 ethics and logic 81, M.A. 77 and M.A. 80, QUEEN'S UNIVERSITY, BELFAST. A senior moderator in 1st classics 77, biblical Greek prize and Elrington theological prize 82, Ryan prize and theological exhibition 83. TRINITY COLL., DUBLIN), held various London curacies 83-9.

Charleston, Joseph, born at Newton Moor, Cheshire, 20 June, 1850; 1s. James, gen. WORCESTER, matric. 16 Oct., 88, aged 38 (from Culham coll.), B.A. 91 (HONOURS:—2 law 91); solicitor at Oxford.

Charlesworth, Basil Arthur, born in London 4 March, 1866; 2s. Frederick, gent. MAGDALEN, matric. 16 Oct., 84, aged 18 (from Winchester), B.A. 87, M.A. 91.

Charlesworth, Cyril, born in London June, 1864; 1s. Frederick, gen. CHRIST CHURCH, matric. 25 May, 83, aged 18, from Winchester.

Charlesworth, George Lindsay, born at Thornhill, Yorks, 5 April, 1865; 2s. George, gent. MAGDALEN, matric. 16 Oct., 84, aged 19 (from Bradford gr. school), exhibitioner 84, B.A. 88; HONOURS:—2 classical mods. 86, 3 classics 88.

Charlesworth, Guy Tudor, born at Leyton, Essex, 1867; 2s. Jesse Thomas, arm. CORPUS CHRISTI, matric. 20 Oct., 86, aged 19 (from Forest school), B.A. 90; HONOURS:—2 classical mods. 88, 3 classics 90.

Charlton, Francis Hartley, born at Manchester 1872; o.s. Francis, gent. CHRIST CHURCH, matric. 14 Oct., 92, aged 20, from Rugby.

Charrington, Francis, born at Herne Hill, Kent, 18 June, 1863; 2s. Nicholas George, cler. MERTON, matric. 3 June, 81, aged 18, B.A. 85.

Charsley, rev. Robert Harvey, M.A., ST. MARY HALL, where see.

Charteris, hon. Evan Edward, born in London 29 Jan., 1864; 3s. Francis Wemys, earl (Wemys). BALLIOL, matric. 19 Oct., 87, aged 23 (from Eton); bar.-at-law, Inner Temple, 91.

Charteris, Richard Butler, born in London 12 Oct., 1866; 1s. hon. Richard. CHRIST CHURCH, matric. 30 Oct., 85, aged 19.

Chase, rev. Drummond Percy, principal of ST. MARY HALL 1857, where see.

Chase, rev. Temple Hamilton, M.A., fellow QUEEN'S 43-55, where see.

Chataway, rev. Thomas Ernest Eagle, born at Malvern Link, co. Worc., 1857; 1s. Thomas Eagle, cler. NON-COLLEGIATE, matric. 10 April, 80, aged 23 (from Repton school); migrated to HERTFORD, B.A. 83, M.A. 87 (HONOURS:—3 theology '83); curate of Illadon, Oxon, 83.

Chattaway, Frederick Daniel, born at Foleshill, co. Warwick, 1870; 1s. Daniel Charles, gen. CHRIST CHURCH, matric. 13 Dec., 88, aged 18 (from University coll., Aberystwith, and Owens coll., Manchester); scholar 87; HONOURS:—1 chemistry 91.

Chatwin, Leslie Boughton, born at Harborne, co. Staff., 13 Aug., 1871; 1s. Julius Alfred, arm. MERTON, matric. 15 Oct., 90, aged 19, from Birmingham gr. school.

Chaundy, Edred Martin, born at Oxford 14 April, 1871; 6s. John, gen. NEW COLL., matric. 25 Jan., 88, aged 16 (from Oxford high school); NON-COLLEGIATE 89, B.Mus. 90, B.A. 92; HONOURS:— 2 theology 91, 3 history 92.

Chavasse, Albert Sidney, M.A., B.C.L., fellow UNIVERSITY COLL. 64, where see.

Chavasse, Francis James, M.A., CORPUS CHRISTI, where see.

Chaytor, Henry John, born at Starpool, co. Worc., 1871; 1s. Henry John, arm. ALL SOUL'S, matric. 14 Oct., 89, aged 18 (from Durham gr. school), bible clerk 91; HONOURS:—2 classical mods. 91.

Cheales, John Alan Carnegie, born at Brockham, Surrey, 29 Sept., 1861; 3s. Alan Benjamin, cler. NON-COLLEGIATE, matric. 23 Jan., 86, aged 23 (from Eton); migrated to EXETER, B.A. 89; HONOURS:—4 history 88.

Cheales, rev. John Pacey, born at Skendleby, co. Lincoln, Nov., 1865; 2s. Henry John, cler. KEBLE, matric. 14 Oct., 84, aged 18 (from Marlborough coll.), B.A. 87 (HONOURS:—3 history 87); curate of Friskney, co. Lincoln, 89.

Cheeke, George Alfred (Mosley), born at Sydney in Australia, 1872; 1s. George Ashwin, arm. ST. JOHN'S, matric. 11 Oct., 90, aged 18, from Cheltenham coll.

Cheesman, rev. Alfred Hunter, born at Bosham, Sussex, 10 Nov., 1864; 2s. Alfred, gent. WORCESTER, matric. 22 Oct., 85, aged 20 (from a Chichester school), B.A. 88, M.A. 92; curate of All Saints', Gloucester, 88.

Cheetham, Joshua Milne Compton, born at Preston, co. Lanc., 9 July, 1869; 2s. Joshua Milne, gen. CHRIST CHURCH, matric. 12 Oct., 88, aged 19 (from Rossall school), scholar 88, B.A. 92; HONOURS:—2 classical mods. 90, 2 classics 92, archæological studentship, Athens, 92.

Chelake, Edwin, born at Hereford 29 Jan., 1864; o.s. William, architect. WADHAM, matric. 19 Oct., 85, aged 21, from Reading school.

Cheshire, Cecil James, born at Hampton Lucy, co. Warwick, May, 1873; 3s. John Stanley, cler. KEBLE, matric. 20 Oct., 91, aged 18, from Marlborough coll.

Cheshire, rev. Reginald Stanley Pargiter, born at Hampton Lucy, co. Warwick, May, 1869; 1s. John Stanley, cler. KEBLE, matric. 13 Oct., 88, aged 19 (from Marlborough coll.), B.A. 92 (HONOURS:—3 classical mods. 90, 3 theology 92); curate of Kidderminster 93.

Chester, Joseph Lemuel, created D.C.L. 22 June, 1881. *See Al. Ox. 245.*

Chetwynd, Charles Richard Blaauw, born at Dover 17 Feb., 1863; 1s. hon. Charles Cornwallis, arm. CHRIST CHURCH, matric. 13 Oct., 82, aged 19. B.A. 86, M.A. 89; student Inner Temple 84; died 28 March, 91.

Chevallier, Clement Woodward Dumaresque, born at Aspall, Suffolk, 20 March, 1871; 3s. Charles Henry, cler. TRINITY, matric. 11 Oct., 90, aged 19, from Lancing coll.

Chevallier, rev. John, born at Ipswich, 24 Feb., 1862; 3s. Barrington, D.Med. Scholar TRINITY. COLL., Cambridge, 80 (from Winchester), B.A. 83 (HONOURS:—4th wrangler 83, 1st class mathematics 84); fellow NEW COLL., Oxford, 83-91, incorporated 18 Jan., 84, aged 21, M.A. 87 (HONOURS:—senior mathematical scholarship 84, Herschel astronomical prize 84), tutor MAGDALEN 84; 1 mathematics, London, 82 and 84; rector of Gt. Horwood, Bucks, 89.

Chevis, William, born at Andover, Hants, 1864; 2s. James, gen. BALLIOL. matric. 16 Oct. 83, aged 19 (from Lancing coll.); assist. commissioner Punjab, India, 85.

Cheyne, Thomas Kelly, M.A., fellow ORIEL 86, where see.

Chichester, (rev.) Charles, born at Voulston, Devon, 19 Aug., 1868; 7s. sir Arthur, bart. BRASENOSE, matric. 20 Oct., 86, aged 18 (from Gosport academy), B.A. 89; curate of Weymouth Holy Trinity 91.

Chichester, Charles Hamlyn, born at Bishops Tawton, Devon, 30 Oct., 1871; 1s. Charles, arm. PEMBROKE, matric. 29 Jan., 91, aged 19, from Eton.

Chichester, John, born at Tavistock, Devon, 18 Jan., 1870; 2s. William Henry, arm. EXETER, matric. 16 Oct., 89, aged 19.

Child, rev. Arthur Gascoigne, born at North Nibley, co. Glouc., 1865; 1s. Thomas Harrington, cler. KEBLE, matric. 20 Oct., 85, aged 18 (from Newton Abbot coll.), B.A. 88 (HONOURS:—4 theology 88); curate of St. John Baptist, Chester, 89.

Child, Coles, born in London 1862; 1s. Coles, arm. BRASENOSE, matric. 19 Oct., 82, aged 20 (from Eton); of Bromley Place, Kent, J.P.

Child, Gerald Alfred, born at Barnsley, co. Glouc., 1871; 1s. Alfred, cler. CHARSLEY'S HALL, matric. 24 May, 90, aged 19.

Child, Gilbert William, M.A., D.Med. of EXETER, where see.

Child, Harold Hannyngton, born at Gloucester 20 July, 1869; 2s. Thomas Hannyngton, cler. BRASENOSE, matric. 16 Oct., 88, aged 19 (from Winchester), scholar 88, B.A. 92; (HONOURS:—3 classical mods. 90, 2 classics 92.

Child, Nicholas Gilbert Louis, born at Oxford 23 June, 1866; 2s. Gilbert William, D.Med. EXETER, matric. 23 Oct., 85, aged 19 (from Malvern coll.), B.A. 89 (HONOURS:—3 law 89); bar.-at-law, Inner Temple, 91.

Child, Stephen Ambrose, born at Oxford 4 April, 1865; 1s. Gilbert William, D.Med. UNIVERSITY COLL., matric. 11 Oct., 84, aged 19 (from Clifton coll.), B.A. 87, M.A. and B.C.L. 91; HONOURS:—4 history 87, 3 civil law 90.

Childs, James Francis, born at Southsea, Hants, 13 July, 1868; 1s. James Linnington, gen. MAGDALEN, matric. 22 Oct., 87, aged 19 (from Portsmouth gr. school), demy 87, B.A. 92; HONOURS:—3 chemistry 91.

Childs, William Cuthbert, born at Portsea, Hants, 2 Sept., 1872; 2s. James Linnington, gen. CORPUS CHRISTI, matric. 19 Oct., 91, aged 18 (from Portsmouth gr. school), scholar 90; HONOURS:—1 mathematical mods. 92, proxime accessit, junior mathematical exhibition 93.

Childs, William Macbride, born at Carrington, co. Lincoln, 3 Jan., 1869; 2s. William Linnington, cler. KEBLE, matric. 19 Oct., 87, aged 18 (from Portsmouth gr. school), scholar 87, B.A. 91; HONOURS:—2 history 91.

Chilton, rev. Arthur, born at Manchester 1869; o.s. William, gent. CHRIST CHURCH, matric. 12 Oct., 83, aged 20 (from Christ's hospital), exhibitioner 83, B.A. 87, M.A. 91 (HONOURS:—1 classical mods. 85, 3 classics 87); curate of Holy Trinity, Upper Chelsea, 91.

Chinner, Charlton, born at Swindon, co. Staff., 1871; 2s. William, gent. EXETER, matric. 17 Jan., 89, aged 17 (from Wolverhampton gr. school), B.A. 92.

Chippindale, Arthur William, born in London 2 Jan., 1869; 1s. William, arm. NEW COLL., matric. 18 Oct., 80, aged 18 (from Margate school); migrated to QUEEN'S 81.

Chisholm, Hugh, born in London 22 Feb., 1866; o.s. Henry Williams, arm. CORPUS CHRISTI, matric. 23 Oct., 84, aged 18 (from Felsted school), scholar 84, B.A. 88 (HONOURS:—1 classical mods. 86, 1 classics 88); bar.-at-law, Middle Temple, 92.

Chittenden, George Scobell, born at Kirtlington, Oxon, 17 March, 1864; o.s. Thomas Knapp, D.D. ST. JOHN'S, matric. 14 Oct., 84, aged 18, B.A. 85, M.A. 89.

Chitty, Herbert, born in London 13 Jan., 1863; 3s. sir Joseph William (judge). BALLIOL, matric. 17 Oct., 82, aged 19 (from Winchester), B.A. 86, M.A. 89 (HONOURS:—1 classical mods. 84, 3 classics 86); bar.-at-law, Inner Temple, 89.

Chitty, James Charles Martin, born in London 1865; 2s. Thomas Edward, arm. PEMBROKE, matric. 25 Oct., 87, aged 22 (from Bath coll.), B.A. 92.

Chitty, Joseph Henry Pollock, born in London 11 Jan., 1861; 2s. sir Joseph William (judge) TRINITY, matric. 17 Oct., 79, aged 19 (from Winchester), B.A. 83, M.A. 86 (HONOURS:—3 classical mods. 81, 2 law 83); solicitor.

Chitty, sir Joseph William, M.A., fellow EXETER 52-8, where see.
Cholmeley, Charles Humphrey, M.A., fellow MAGDALEN 55-60, where see.
Cholmeley, Hugh Charles, born at Naples 24 Feb., 1864; 1s. Thomas Charles, arm. CHRIST CHURCH, matric. 10 Oct., 84, aged 20, from Oscott R. C. coll.
Cholmeley, James, M.A., fellow MAGDALEN 57-64, where see.
Cholmeley, Norman Goodford, born at Muddanpilly, E. Indies, 5 May, 1863; 2s. Montagu, arm. BALLIOL, matric. 18 Oct., 81, aged 18 (from the Charterhouse), B.A. 84; deputy commissioner Burma 83.
Cholmeley, Robert Arthur, born at Swabey, co. Lincoln, 3 May, 1867; 1s. James, cler. KEBLE, matric. 19 Oct., 86, aged 19 (from Highgate school), exhibitioner 87; B.A. 90; HONOURS :—2 classical mods. 88, 3 classics 90.
Cholmeley, Robert Francis, born at Charlton Rode, Norfolk, 22 Feb., 1862; 1s. John, cler. CORPUS CHRISTI, matric. 26 Oct., 81, aged 19 (from Marlborough coll.), scholar 81-5, B.A. 85, M.A. 88; HONOURS :—1 classical mods. 82, 2 classics 85.
Cholmeley, Roger James, born at Swabey, co. Lincoln, 4 Jan., 1872; 2s. James, cler. CORPUS CHRISTI, matric. 16 Oct., 90, aged 18 (from St. Edward's school, Summertown), scholar 90; HONOURS :—1 classical mods. 92.
Cholmondeley, rev. Charles Fiennes, born at Addlestrop, co. Glouc., 26 Nov., 1863; 5s. hon. Henry Pitt, cler. NEW COLL., matric. 12 Oct., 83, aged 19 (from Clifton coll.), B.A. 87, M.A. 90 (HONOURS :—4 classics 87); curate of Christ Church, Albany Street, London, 91.
Cholmondeley, Francis Grenville, M.A. fellow ALL SOULS' 74, where see.
Cholmondeley, hon. and rev. Henry Pitt, M.A., fellow ALL SOULS' 41-8, where see.
Chope, Basil Stafford, born at South Kensington 30 Aug., 1868; 3s. Richard Robert, cler. ST. JOHN'S, matric. 13 Oct., 88, aged 20, from Westminster school.
Chorley, rev. Charles Faulkner, born at Congleton, Cheshire, 24 May, 1867; 1s. Charles Robert, gent. LINCOLN, matric. 22 Jan., 87, aged 19 (from Leeds gr. school); migrated to CHARSLEY HALL, but returned to LINCOLN 12 Jan., 88, B.A. 91.
Chorley, Henry Sutton, born at Congleton, Cheshire, 14 April, 1869; 2s. Charles Robert, arm. TRINITY, matric. 13 Oct., 88, aged 19 (from Leeds gr. school), B.A. 91; HONOURS :—a history 91.
Chorlton, John Henwood, born at Sheffield 29 June, 1869; 2s. Samuel, vicar of Pitsmoor, Sheffield, NON-COLLEGIATE, matric. 12 Oct., 89, aged 20 (from Firth coll., Sheffield); migrated to WADHAM 19 Jan., 91.
Chorlton, rev. Samuel Woodward, born at Sheffield 17 Nov., 1867; 1s. Samuel, vicar of Pitsmoor, NON-COLLEGIATE, matric. 14 Jan., 88, aged 20 (from Sheffield gr. school); migrated to WADHAM 27 April, 89, B.A. 90; curate of Nottingham St. Mark 91.
Chown, Thomas Lionel Collingwood, born in London 1875; 1s. Thomas Collingwood, gent. PEMBROKE, matric. 26 Oct., 91, aged 16, from Eton.
Chretien, Charles Peter, M.A., fellow ORIEL 43-64, where see.
Christian, Frederick William, born at Putney, Surrey, June, 1867; o.s. Elias Hiscutt, arm. BALLIOL, matric. 19 Oct., 86, aged 19 (from Eton), B.A. 90; HONOURS :—2 classical mods. 88.

Christian, Robert Bertram Keough, born at Enniskillen, co. Fermanagh, 17 May, 1870; 1s. Robert Cuthbertson, cler. LINCOLN, matric. 17 Oct., 89, aged 19 (from Christ's hospital and B.A., Trinity coll., Dublin), scholar 89; HONOURS :—2 classical mods. 91.
Christie, Henry James, born in London May, 1864; o.s. James Traill, arm. CHRIST CHURCH, matric. 18 Jan., 84, aged 19 (from Eton), B.A. 87; HONOURS :—4 law 87.
Christie, James Archibald, born in London 5 April, 1873; o.s. James Henry Brooke, esq. MAGDALEN, matric. 22 Oct., 91, aged 18, from the Charterhouse.
Christie, Octavius Francis, born at Hoddesdon, Herts, 30 April, 1867; 4s. Charles Peter, gent. TRINITY, matric. 16 Oct., 86, aged 19 (from Clifton coll.), scholar 85, B.A. 90 (HONOURS :—2 classical mods. 88, 3 classics 90); bar.-at-law, Inner Temple, 92.
Christie, William Pensi, born at York 7 Feb., 1868; o.s. Tobias, gen. QUEEN'S, matric. 20 Oct., 88, aged 20 (from Bradford gr. school), exhibitioner 88; HONOURS :—2 classical mods. 90.
Christopher, Alfred Millard William, M.A. (Cantab.), see TRINITY.
Christopherson, Percy, born at Blackheath, Kent, 31 March, 1866; 5s. Derman, gent. UNIVERSITY COLL., matric. 17 Oct., 85, aged 19 (from Marlborough and Bedford gr. school), B.A. 89, M.A. 93; HONOURS :—3 classics 89.
Christy, William Miller, born at Fairfield, co. Lanc., Jan., 1863; 1s. Richard, arm. CHRIST CHURCH, matric. 27 May, 82, aged 19 (from Eton), B.A. 86, M.A. 90; bar.-at-law, Inner Temple, 90.
Church, Alfred Francis Bentley, born in London 22 Aug., 1864; 1s. Alfred John, cler. WORCESTER, matric. 17 Oct., 84, aged 20 (from Aldenham school), exhibitioner 84, B.A. 89; HONOURS :—2 classical mods. 86, 3 classics 88.
Church, Arthur Henry, born at Plymouth, Devon, 28 March, 1865; 1s. Henry, gen. JESUS COLL., matric. 20 Oct., 91, aged 26 (from University coll., Aberystwith), scholar 91.
Church, Charles Cunningham, born at Liverpool 1864; 1s. Charles, arm. ST. JOHN'S, matric. 14 Oct., 82, aged 18.
Church, Francis William King-, born at Albury, Surrey, 27 Aug., 1870; 1s. William Thomas, arm. TRINITY, matric. 13 Oct., 88, aged 18, from the Charterhouse.
Church, Maurice Richard, born at Wells, Somerset, 19 Jan., 1872; 2s. Charles Maire, cler. KEBLE, matric. 11 Oct., 91, aged 18, from Lancing coll.
Church, Norman Laurie King-, born at Albury, Surrey, 17 April, 1873; 2s. William Thomas, arm. TRINITY, matric. 15 Oct., 92, aged 19, from the Charterhouse.
Church, Percy William Palmer, born at Liverpool 2 March, 1867; 2s. Charles, arm., deceased. MAGDALEN, matric. 23 Oct., 85, aged 18, from Eton.
Church, William Selby, M.A., D.Med., student CHRIST CHURCH 60-9, where see.
Churchill, lord Edward Spencer, born 28 March, 1853; 5s. George, duke of Marlborough. NON-COLLEGIATE, matric. 11 Nov., 86, aged 33, from Eton.
Churchill, William Fleetwood Smith, born at Atherstone, co. Warwick, 22 June, 1870; 1s. Smith Wild, cler. CHRIST CHURCH, matric. 11 Oct., 89, aged 19 (from Manchester gr. school), scholar 88; HONOURS :—1 mathematical mods. 91.
Churton, Edward Temple, born at Erith, Kent, 1869; 2s. Thomas, D.Med. NON-COLLEGIATE, matric. 14 Jan., 88, aged 19; HONOURS :—4 history 91.
Churton, Edward Townson, bishop of Nassau, created D.D. 28 Nov., 1886. See *Al. Ox.* 2nd series 252.

Chutter, Frederick George, born at Chard, Somerset, 1857; 1s. George, gen. NON-COLLEGIATE, matric. 22 Oct., 91, aged 34, from Andover theological sem. U.S.A.

Cinnamond, Arthur, born at Belfast, Dec., 1872; 1s. Arthur, merchant. CHRIST CHURCH, matric. 14 Oct., 92, aged 19, from Queen's coll., Belfast.

Clack, George Reginald Sadler, born at Middleham, Yorks, 16 Nov., 1873; 1s. George Robert, vicar of Downholme, Yorks, deceased. NON-COLLEGIATE, matric. 15 Oct., 92, aged 18, from Kent county school, Birchington, etc.

Clapton, rev. Edward Louis Churchill, born at Lee, Kent, 25 April, 1865; o.s. Edward, D.Med. NEW COLL., matric. 10 Dec., 81, aged 18 (from Harrow), B.A. 85, M.A. 88 (HONOURS :—3 theology 85); vicar of St. Michael, Battersea, 91.

Clark, Albert Curtis, M.A., fellow QUEEN'S 82, where see.

Clark, Andrew, M.A., fellow LINCOLN 80, where see.

Clark, Andrew Gladstone, born in London 18 Dec., 1870; 2s. Andrew, bart. CHRIST CHURCH, matric. 8 June, 89, aged 18 (from Westminster school), B.A. 92.

Clark, Charles Reginald, born at Christ Church, New Zealand, 26 July, 1866; 1s. Charles, gen. EXETER, matric. 21 Oct., 86, aged 20, B.A. 90; bar.-at-law, Middle Temple, 90.

Clark, rev. Edward, born at East Hothley, Sussex, 4 Oct., 1862; 1s. Edward, gent. NEW COLL., matric. 14 Oct., 81, aged 19 (from Winchester), B.A. 85, M.A. 88 (HONOURS :—2 classical mods. 83, 3 classics 85); curate of St. Werburgh, Derby, 90.

Clark, Edwin William, born at Hordle, Hants, 1860; 1s. Edwin John, gent. CHRIST CHURCH, matric. 12 Oct., 83, aged 23 (from Dorset county school), exhibitioner 83, B.A. 91; HONOURS :—1 classical mods. 85, 3 mathematical mods. 85, 4 history 87.

Clark, Erland Aubrey, born at Leamington 1863; 2s. James Fenn, arm. TRINITY, matric. 15 Oct., 81, aged 18 (from Leamington coll.), migrated to NEW INN HALL (Balliol), B.A. and M.A. 88.

Clark, Ernest Holman, born at East Hothley, Sussex, 22 April, 1864; 2s. Edward, arm. NEW COLL., matric. 14 Oct., 82, aged 18, B.A. 86, M.A. 89 (HONOURS :—2 classical mods. 84, 3 law 86); bar.-at-law, Inner Temple, 88.

Clark, Henry Alfred Ready, born at Ipswich 5 Oct., 1868; 3s. Francis Storer, cler. WORCESTER, matric. 17 Oct., 87, aged 19 (from Merchant Taylors' school), scholar 87, B.A. 92; HONOURS :—1 classical mods. 89, 2 classics 91.

Clark, Henry Douglas Gee, born at Worcester 10 Aug., 1871; 1s. Henry William, gen. NON-COLLEGIATE, matric. 22 Oct., 91, aged 20, from Cheltenham coll.

Clark, Henry Herbert Gordon, born in London 1862; 1s. Gordon Wyatt, arm. EXETER, matric. 22 Jan., 80, aged 18 (from Winchester), B.A. 82, M.A. 86; HONOURS :—4 law 82.

Clark, Herbert Kelsey, born at Botley, Hants, 3 Feb., 1868; o.s. Edward Henry, arm. WORCESTER, matric. 13 Dec., 86, aged 18, from Portsmouth gr. school.

Clark, James, born at Peterhead, co. Aberdeen, 1867; 1s. James, gen. CHRIST CHURCH matric. 14 Oct., 87, aged 20 (from King's coll., Aberdeen), exhibitioner 87, B.A. 91; HONOURS :—2 classical mods. 89, 2 classics 91.

Clark, rev. James Curtis, born at Haileybury 22 July, 1865; o.s. Albert Charles, a master at Haileybury coll. QUEEN'S, matric. 22 Oct., 83, aged 18 (from Hertford gr. school), B.A. 87;

Clark, John, born at Foveran, co. Aberdeen, 1865; 2s. John Sim, cler. BALLIOL, matric. 15 Oct., 84, aged 19 (from Old Aberdeen gr. school); assist. commissioner Assam 85.

Clark, John Norman D'Arcy, born at Derby 29 March, 1874; 1s. George D'Arcy, gent. ORIEL, matric. 27 Oct., 92, aged 18, from Rugby.

Clark, Phillips, born at St. Louis, Missouri, U.S.A., April 1873; o.s. Charles Sumner, gent. PEMBROKE, matric. 26 Oct., 91, aged 18.

Clark, rev. Robert Benjamin, born at Ipswich 1866; 1s. Francis Storer, cler. ST. JOHN'S, matric. 17 Oct., 85, aged 19 (from Merchant Taylors' school), scholar 85, B.A. 89; HONOURS :—2 classical mods. 87, 2 classics 89, 2 theology 90.

Clark, Robert Ernest, born at Chelsea, Middx., 1870 ; 3s. John Arthur, gen. QUEEN'S, matric. 11 June, 91, aged 21.

Clark, Robert Moorhouse, born at Helmsley, Yorks, 23 May, 1872; 1s. Moorhouse. LINCOLN, matric. 23 Oct., 91, aged 19 (from Denstone coll.), scholar 91.

Clark, rev. Thomas Charles, born at Trowbridge, Wilts, 31 Aug., 1863; 2s. William Perkins, gent. NEW COLL., matric. 14 Oct., 82, aged 19 (from Sherborne school), B.A. 86, M.A. 89 (HONOURS :—3 classical mods. 84, 3 theology 86); curate of Holy Trinity, Clifton, Bristol, 88.

Clark, Walter John, born at Dulwich, Surrey, 10 Aug., 1871; 2s. John Meek, cler. NEW COLL., matric. 10 Oct., 90, aged 19 (from Marlborough coll.); HONOURS :—1 classical mods. 92.

Clarke, rev. Alfred Edward, born at Calcutta 1863; 2s. Samuel Edward James, gent. ST. EDMUND HALL, matric 19 Oct., 82, aged 19, B.A. 87; HONOURS :—3 classical mods. 84.

Clarke, Alfred Walter George, born at Ormside, Westmorland, 27 Oct., 1861; 2s. Thomas, cler. QUEEN'S, matric. 31 Jan., 82, aged 20 (from Appleby school, Westmorland), exhibitioner 82, B.A. 85.

Clarke, Arthur David, born at Poonamalee, E. Indies, 16 Jan., 1868; 2s. David George, cler. KEBLE, matric. 17 Oct. 87, aged 19 (from St. Edward's school, Summertown), B.A. 91; HONOURS :—3 classical mods. 89.

Clarke, Arthur Henry Penkivil, born at Kennington 13 Dec., 1869; 1s. William Henry Chatfeild, of Niton, isle of Wight, arm. MAGDALEN, matric. 14 Oct., 89, aged 19, from Harrow.

Clarke, Charles Agacy, born at Calcutta 14 May, 1872 ; 5s. Samuel Edward James, sec. to Bengal chamber of commerce, NEW COLL., matric. 17 Oct., 91, aged 19, from St. Paul's school; brother of Robert L. H.

Clarke, rev. Charles Granville, M.A., fellow WORCESTER 59-64, where see.

Clarke, Charles Leopold Stanley, B.C.L., fellow NEW COLL. 37-49, where see.

Clarke, Charles Noel, born at Great Barr, co. Stafford, 7 Feb., 1858; 6s. Frederick, arm. TRINITY, matric. 16 Oct., 86, aged 18 (from Westminster school), B.A. 90; HONOURS :—3 law 90.

Clarke, Charles Philip Stewart, born at Whitechill, co. Glouc., 1872; 2s. Charles, cler. CHRIST CHURCH, matric. 10 Oct., 90, aged 18 (from Clifton coll.), scholar 89.

Clarke, Frederick Arthur, M.A., fellow CORPUS CHRISTI 76, where see.

Clarke, Henry Butler, born at Somersall, co. Stafford, 9 Nov., 1863; 1s. Henry, cler. WADHAM, matric. 19 Oct., 85, aged 21, B.A. 89, M.A. 92 (HONOURS :—2 classical mods. 87, Taylorian scholarship (Spanish) 88); University teacher of Spanish 90.

Clarke, James Walter, born at Moreton-in-the-Marsh, co. Gloucester, Oct. 1868; 1s. James William, NON-COLLEGIATE, matric. 25 Jan., 88, aged 19, from Rossall school.

Clarke, John Grey, born at Wingham, Kent, 21 Oct., 1871; 2s. William, vicar of Rumburgh, Suffolk. ST. JOHN'S, matric. 11 Oct., 90, aged 18 (from Merchant Taylors' school), scholar 90; HONOURS: —2 classical mods. 92.

Clarke, Leslie, born in London 16 March, 1873; o.s. Arthur Leslie, merchant. UNIVERSITY COLL., matric. 15 Oct., 92, aged 19, from Highgate school.

Clarke, Leycester Annand Grey, born at Wingham, Kent, 15 July, 1870; 1s. William, vicar of Rumburgh, Suff. JESUS COLL., matric. 14 Oct., 89, aged 19 (from Merchant Taylors' school), exhibitioner 89 (HONOURS :—2 classical mods. 92); Indian C.S. 92.

Clarke, Lionel James, born at Armathwaite, Cumberland, 1865; 6s. Anthony William, D.Med. EXETER, matric. 16 Oct., 84, aged 19 (from Marlborough coll.), B.A. 87; cox. of the Oxford eight 87.

Clarke, Loftus Otway, born at Dublin 1872; 2s. Marshal Neville, arm. CHRIST CHURCH, matric. 10 Oct., 90, aged 18 (from the Charterhouse), scholar 90; HONOURS :—2 classical mods. 92.

Clarke, Reginald Warlow, born at Llanfair, co. Monmouth, 31 Oct., 1871; 5s. John Thomas, vicar of Whitchurch. JESUS COLL., matric. 15 Oct., 90, aged 18 (from Brecon coll.), exhibitioner 90; HONOURS :—2 classical mods. 92.

Clarke, Richard Augustine, born at Taunton 1864; 4s. Frederick Ricketts, gent. NON-COLLEGIATE, matric. 14 Oct., 82, aged 18 (from Taunton collegiate school); migrated to BALLIOL 83, B.A. 86, M.A. 90 (HONOURS :—2 classical mods. 84, 2 classics 86); brother of Rupert Charles and Frederick Arthur.

Clarke, Richard Frederick, M.A., fellow ST. JOHN'S 56-69, where see.

Clarke, Robert Sutton, born in London 1867; 5s. Thomas Chatfield, gent. PEMBROKE, matric. 27 Oct., 85, aged 18 (from Harrow), B.A. 88.

Clarke, Robert Lucas Hyrapiet, born at Calcutta 1 Jan., 1871; 4s. Samuel Edward James, sec. to Bengal chamber of commerce. NEW COLL., matric. 14 Oct., 92, aged 22 (from St. Paul's school); selected candidate (3rd) for Indian civil service 92; brother of Charles A.

Clarke, rev. Rupert Charles, born at Taunton, Somerset, 4 July, 1866; 3s. Frederick Ricketts, gent. BALLIOL, matric. 15 Oct., 84, aged 18 (from Taunton collegiate school); scholar EXETER 84, B.A. 88, M.A. 92 (HONOURS :—2 classical mods. 86, 2 classics 88); curate of St. Mary the Virgin, Reading, 89; brother of Richard A.

Clarke, Rupert Turner Havelock, born 16 March, 1865; 1s. sir William John, of Rupertstown, Bourke co., Victoria, bart. NEW INN HALL, matric. 22 Oct., 84, aged 19; BALLIOL 87.

Clarke, Stephen Hardcastle, born at Barr, co. Stafford, 19 May, 1865; 5s. Frederick Führmann, gent. TRINITY, matric. 11 Oct., 84, aged 19 (from Westminster school), exhibitioner 84, B.A. 88, M.A. 91; HONOURS :—3 classical mods. 86, 4 classics 88.

Clarke, Thomas, born at Wootton Bassett, Wilts. 1850; 2s. John, cler. NON-COLLEGIATE, matric. 30 Oct., 82, aged 32.

Clarke, William John Turner, born at Newtown, Tasmania, 1863; 1s. Joseph, arm. CHRIST CHURCH, matric. 16 Jan., 83, aged 22, B.A. 89, M.A. 91; bar.-at-law, Inner Temple, 91.

Clarke, William Robert Cowley, born at Sambrook, Salop. 1870; 2s. Samuel, cler. CHRIST CHURCH, matric. 12 Oct., 88, aged 18 (from Shrewsbury school), B.A. 92.

Clarkson, rev. Charles Bruce, born at Caine, Wilts, July, 1865; 1s. Richard, gent. CHRIST CHURCH, matric. 31 May, 84, aged 18, B.A. 88, M.A. 91 (HONOURS :—3 history 88); rector of Ampton, Suffolk, 91.

Claughton, Alan Oswald, born at Colombo, Ceylon, 1866; 4s. Piers Calverley, bishop of Colombo. UNIVERSITY COLL., matric. 17 Oct., 85, aged 19 (from Repton school), B.A. 89; HONOURS :—4 history 89.

Clauson, Albert Charles, born at Paddington 1870; 2s. Charles, gen. ST. JOHN'S, matric. 15 Oct., 87, aged 17 (from Merchant Taylors' school), scholar 87, B.A. 91 (HONOURS :—1 classical mods. 89, 2 classics 91); bar.-at-law, Lincoln's Inn, 91.

Clauss, Bruno Geoffrey, born at Llangyfelach, co. Glam., 9 April, 1873; 1s. John Bruno, of Morriston, Swansea, gent. CORPUS CHRISTI, matric. 18 Oct., 92, aged 19, from Llandovery coll.

Clauss, Paul Robert Adolph, born at Glasgow 22 June, 1868; o.s. Miles, gen. NEW COLL., matric. 13 Oct., 88, aged 20 (from Loretto school), B.A. 93; HONOURS :—3 classical mods. 90, 3 classics 92.

Claxton, Alban Edmond, born at Frampton Cotterell, co. Glouc., July, 1874; 1s. Donald Maclean, cler., deceased. KEBLE, matric. 15 Oct., 92, aged 18, from Uppingham and Forest schools.

Clay, Arthur Joseph, born at Burton-on-Trent 29 April, 1870; 1s. Charles John, arm. NEW COLL., matric. 11 Oct., 89, aged 19 (from Harrow); (HONOURS :—3 classical mods. 91, 4 law 92); brother of Ernest and Wilfrid H.

Clay, Charles Leigh, born at Chepstow, co. Mon., 23 Feb., 1866; 2s. Henry, arm. NEW COLL., matric. 16 Oct., 85, aged 19 (from Winchester), B.A. 89, M.A. 92; HONOURS :—3 classical mods. 87, 3 classics 89.

Clay, Ernest Charles, born at Stapenhill, co. Derby, 2 Dec., 1872; 3s. Charles John, B.A., J.P. NEW COLL., matric. 16 Oct., 91, aged 18 (from Marlborough coll.); brother of Arthur J. and Wilfrid H.

Clay, Patrick Andrew, born at Berwick-upon-Tweed Nov., 1870; 1s. John, gen. KEBLE, matric. 17 Oct., 89, aged 18 (from Hereford school), B.A. 92.

Clay, Wilfrid Henry, born at Stapenhill, co. Derby, 13 Feb., 1874; 4s. John Charles, J.P. NEW COLL., matric. 14 Oct., 92, aged 18 (from Repton school); brother of Arthur J. and Ernest C.

Claye, rev. Arthur Needham, born at Stockport, Cheshire, 1863; 2s. William, gent. PEMBROKE, matric. 26 Oct., 81, aged 18 (from Lancing coll.), scholar 81-5, B.A. 85, M.A. 88 (HONOURS :—2 classical mods. 83, 2 classics 85); curate of St. James, Great Grimsby, 86.

Clayforth, Ernest William, born at Darfield, Yorks, 1864; 2s. Henry, cler. CHRIST CHURCH, matric. 12 Oct., 83, aged 19 (from York school), scholar 82, B.A. 87, M.A. 90; HONOURS :—1 classical mods. 85, 1 classics 87.

Clayforth, Henry Charles Bernard, born at Darfield, Yorks, 1863; 1s. Henry, cler. WORCESTER, matric. 26 Jan., 82, aged 19 (from York school), exhibitioner 81-5, B.A. 86, M.A. 90; HONOURS :—Abbott scholarship 82, 2 classical mods. 83, 3 classics 85.

Clayton, Frederick George Hugh, born at Wylamon-Tyne, Northumberland, 5 Jan., 1873; 1s. capt. Richard, banker. UNIVERSITY COLL., matric. 15 Oct., 92, aged 19, from Harrow.

Clayton, George Savile, born at Newcastle-on-Tyne 1870; 3s. Nathaniel George, arm. UNIVERSITY COLL., matric. 15 Oct., 87, aged 17; brother of John B.

Clayton, (rev.) George Stewart, born in London 2 Jan., 1869; 3s. Sands, gen. UNIVERSITY COLL., matric. 15 Oct., 87, aged 18, from (Cheltenham coll.), B.A. 91; HONOURS :—4 history 91.

Clayton, Horace Evelyn, M.A., BRASENOSE, where see.

Clayton, John, born at Wakefield, Yorks, 11 June, 1873; 3s. Joe, gent., deceased. PEMBROKE, matric. 28 Oct., 92, aged 19, from Q. Eliz. gr. school, Wakefield.

Clayton, John Bertram, born at Tynemouth, Northumberland, 1861; 1s. Nathaniel George, arm. UNIVERSITY COLL., matric. 16 Oct., 80, aged 19 B.A. 84 (HONOURS:—3 history 84); student Inner Temple, 82; brother of George S.

Clayton, Joseph, born in London 18 April, 1868; 2s. Francis, gen. NON-COLLEGIATE, matric. 15 Oct., 87, aged 19 (from North London collegiate school); migrated to WORCESTER 89.

Cleave, Ernest, born at S. Helier, Jersey, 27 May, 1873; 4s. William Ohe, LL.D., cler. EXETER, matric. 18 Oct., 92, aged 19, from Leatherhead school.

Cleave, John Kyrle Frederick, born at Hereford 17 June, 1861; 3s. John, arm. HERTFORD, matric. 19 Oct., 81, aged 20 (from Forest school), scholar 80-5, B.A. 85 (HONOURS:—2 classical mods. 82, 3 classics 85); bar.-at-law, Gray's Inn, 88.

Cleaver, rev. Charles William Euseby, born at Ealing, Middx., Oct., 1861; 1s. William Henry, cler. CHRIST CHURCH, matric. 15 Oct., 80, aged 19, B.A. 85, M.A. 87; curate of Hebden Bridge, Yorks, 86.

Cleaver, William Edward, born at Stoney Croft, near Liverpool, 1 Sept., 1871; 1s. Richard Stuart, arm. ORIEL, matric. 22 Oct., 90, aged 19 (from Haileybury); HONOURS:—2 classical mods. 92.

Cleaver, William Henry, M.A., student CHRIST CHURCH 5479, where see.

Cleaver, rev. William Wilfrid Mackworth, born at Brighton 1865; 1s. William Henry, cler. CHRIST CHURCH, matric. 10 Oct., 84, aged 19 (from Tonbridge school), B.A. 87, M.A. 92; curate of Hebden Bridge, Yorks.

Clegg, Ernest Bernulf, born at Altrincham, Cheshire, 30 Dec., 1870; 4s. Neville, gen. NEW COLL., matric. 11 Oct., 89, aged 18 (from Uppingham and Eastbourne); HONOURS:—3 classical mods. 92.

Clegg, Robert Bailey, born at Goosnargh, co. Lanc., 1865; 1s. John James, gent. BALLIOL, matric. 23 Oct., 82, aged 17 (from Manchester gr. school); head assistant to collector and magistrate Kistna, Madras c.s. 84.

Clegg, William Gavin, born at Altrincham, Cheshire, 29 June, 1869; 3s. Neville, arm. MAGDALEN, matric. 16 Oct., 88, aged 19 (from Winchester); HONOURS:—3 classical mods. 90.

Clements, Ernest, born at Camberwell, Surrey, 1873; 1s. Hugh, C.S. CHRIST CHURCH, matric. 16 Oct., 91, aged 18 (from Dulwich coll.), scholar 91; selected candidate Indian C.S. 91.

Clements, (rev.) George William, born at Liverpool 3 Feb., 1853; 1s. George, cler. NEW INN HALL, 17 Jan., 83, aged 19 (from University coll., London); migrated to NEW INN HALL, B.A. 87; curate of St. John, Walham Green, Middlesex, 90.

Clemons, John Singleton, born at St. Leonards, Jamaica, 1869; 1s. John Nicholas, gent. NON-COLLEGIATE, matric. 4 June, 81, aged 19 (from Launceston gr. school, Tasmania), B.A 86 (HONOURS:—3 classical mods. 83, 4 classics 85), in the Oxford eight 85; bar.-at-law, Lincoln's Inn, 86.

Cleveland, Charles Rait, born at Bombay 1867; 3s. Henry, gent. BALLIOL, matric. 24 Oct., 85, aged 18 (from Christ coll., Finchley); assist. commissioner central provinces, India, 87.

Cliffe, Frank Hobson (Hodson in *M.R.*), born at Lincoln 1866; 1s. William, gen. CHARSLEY'S HALL, matric. 19 Feb., 87, aged 21, B.A. 89.

Clifford, Alfred Nathaniel, born at Twickenham, Middx., 24 Dec., 1867; o.s. Nathaniel, arm. ST. MARY HALL, matric. 25 April, 87, aged 19, from Cheltenham coll.

Clifford, sir Charles Cavendish, D.C.L., fellow ALL SOULS' 43, where see.

Clifford, George Henry, born at Sheffield 25 Oct., 1870; 1s. Henry Marcus, cler. NEW COLL., matric. 11 Oct., 89, aged 18 (from Rugby); HONOURS:—2 classical mods. 91; died 20 Oct., 92.

Clifford, Henry Francis, born at Frampton-on-Severn, co. Glouc., 19 Aug., 1871; 4s. Henry Thomas, esq. CHRIST CHURCH, matric. 16 Oct., 91, aged 20, from Haileybury.

Clifton, Robert Bellamy, M.A., fellow MERTON 69, and fellow WADHAM 82, where see.

Clifton, Walter Bellamy, born at Oxford 12 Sept., 1871; 3s. Robert Bellamy, prof. of experimental philosophy. MERTON, matric. 15 Oct., 90, aged 19, from Marlborough coll.

Clinton, Henry Pelham Archibald Douglas Pelham (7th) duke of Newcastle, born 28 Sept., 1864; 1s. Henry Pelham Alexander Pelham-Clinton, duke of Newcastle. MAGDALEN, matric. 16 Oct., 84, aged 20, from Eton.

Clinton, Osbert Henry Fynes- born at Leyland, co. Lanc., 9 Nov., 1869; 2s. Osbert, rector of Barlow Moor, co. Lanc. ST. JOHN'S, matric. 17 Dec., 91, aged 21 (from Manchester gr. school); HONOURS:—3 classical mods. 92, Taylorian scholarship (Spanish) 92.

Clissold, George Augustus, born at Wrentham, Suffolk, 1864; 3s. Edward Mortimer, gent. EXETER, matric. 12 May, 83, aged 19, from Christ coll., N.Z.

Clissold, rev. Joseph Morris, born at Balham, Surrey, 1866; 1s. Joseph, gent. HERTFORD, matric. 27 Oct., 85, aged 19, B.A. 88; curate of Staple Fitzpaine, Somerset, 89; died 18 Oct., 90.

Clouston, Joseph Storer, born at Carlisle 23 May, 1870; 1s. Thomas Smith, of Edinburgh, D.Med. MAGDALEN, matric. 16 Oct., 88, aged 18 (from Merchiston castle school, Edinburgh), B.A. 92; HONOURS:—1 physiology 92.

Cluff, rev. William Charles, born at Walthamstow, Essex, 1859; o.s. Charles John, arm. ST. JOHN'S, matric. 16 Oct., 79, aged 21, B.A. 83, M.A. 87 (HONOURS:—4 history 83); curate of St. Thomas, Finsbury Park, Middlesex, 91.

Clutsom, rev. Arthur Davis, born in London 1863; 2s. Frederick, gent. WORCESTER, matric. 16 Oct., 80, aged 17, B.A. 83, M.A. 87; missioner of St. Andrew, Salisbury, 89.

Clutterbuck, rev. William Charlton, born at Clonmel, co. Tipperary, 30 June, 1868; 2s. William, of Newark Park, co. Glouc. WADHAM, matric. 19 Oct., 85, aged 17 (from Wootton-under-Edge gr. school), B.A. 89; curate of St. Matthias, Stoke Newington, Middx., 91.

Coaks, Herbert, born at Thorpe Hamlet 1863; 2s. Isaac Bluff, gent. BRASENOSE, matric. 15 Jan., 83, aged 20 (from Eton), B.A. 87.

Coates, (rev.) Allan, born at Rochester 1846; 2s. Robert Patch, gent. NON-COLLEGIATE, matric. 4 Oct., 85, aged 39, B.A. 88 (HONOURS:—4 classics 85); rector of Barsham, Norfolk, 89.

Cobb, Arthur Rhodes, born at Adderbury, Oxon, 12 March, 1864; 2s. Edward, arm. NEW COLL., matric. 18 Oct., 83, aged 19 (from Winchester) HONOURS:—3 classical mods. 85; in the University eleven 86; died 6 Nov., 86.

Cobb, Cecil Henry, born at Clifton, Yorks, 20 Dec., 1867; 2s. William Henry, solicitor. NEW COLL., matric. 15 Oct., 86, aged 18 (from Winchester), B.A. 89; HONOURS:—2 classical mods. 88, 3 law 89.

Cobb, rev. Charles Julius, born at New Romney, Kent, 1866; 1s. Charles cler. UNIVERSITY COLL., matric. 11 Oct., 84, aged 18 (from Rochester school), exhibitioner 84, B.A. 87; HONOURS :—3 theology 87.

Cobb, Cyril Stephen, born at Margate, Kent, 6 Oct., 1861; 2s. James Francis, arm. MERTON, matric. 5 Feb., 81, aged 19 (from Newton Abbot coll. so. Devon), B.A. 84, M.A. and B.C.L. 87 (HONOURS :—3 law 84, 3 civil law 86); bar.-at-law, Middle Temple, 87.

Cobb, Harold Wolstenholme, born at Clifton, Yorks, 1869; 3s. William Henry, solicitor. HERTFORD, matric. 17 Nov., 87, aged 18; 2nd lieut. the Duke of Wellington's West Riding Regt. 91.

Cobb, John Gerard, born in London 22 June, 1862; 1s. Thomas, arm. NEW COLL., matric. 15 Oct., 81, aged 19 (from Rugby), B.A. 84; HONOURS:—4 law 84; solicitor 88.

Cobb, William Henry, born at Clifton, Yorks, 22 March, 1863; 1s. William Henry, solicitor. NEW COLL., matric. 15 Oct., 81, aged 18 (from Winchester), B.A. 84, M.A. 93 (HONOURS :—3 law 84); bar-at-law, Inner Temple, 84, city magistrate, Lucknow.

Cobbett, Basil, born at Peckham, Middx., 1865; 3s. Pitt, cler. ST. EDMUND HALL, matric. 22 Oct., 84, aged 19.

Cobbett, Francis Keighley, born at Twickenham, Middx., 1869; 1s. Richard Stutely, cler. UNIVERSITY COLL., matric. 15 Oct., 87, aged 18.

Cobbett, Herbert Richard, born at Twickenham, Middx., 1870; 2s. Richard Stutely, cler. UNIVERSITY COLL., matric. 13 Oct., 88, aged 18, from Rottingdean and Shrewsbury schools.

Cochran, Peter Campbell, born at Aberdeen 1870; 2s. Alexander, gent. ORIEL, matric. 25 Oct., 89, aged 19 (from Loretto school), B.A. 92; HONOURS: —4 law 92.

Cochrane, Alfred Henry John, born in the Mauritius 1865; 2s. David Crawford, cler. HERTFORD, matric. 14 Oct., 84, aged 19 (from Repton school), scholar 83, B.A. 88, M.A. 91 (HONOURS :—2 classical mods. 86, 3 classics 88); in the University eleven 85, 6, 8.

Cochrane, Cecil Algernon, born at Seghill, Northumberland, April, 1869; 3s. William, gen. CHRIST CHURCH, matric. 3 June, 87, aged 18 (from Sherborne school), scholar 88, B.A. 92; HONOURS:—3 chemistry 92.

Cockayne, rev. Henry, born at Sheffield 1865; o.s. Henry, arm. UNIVERSITY COLL., matric. 11 Oct., 84, aged 19 (from Sheffield school), B.A. 88, M.A. 91 (HONOURS :—3 classical mods. 86, 2 theology 88); curate of Chichester St. Paul 89.

Cockburn, George Bertram, born at Birkenhead 8 June, 1872; 2s. George, gent. NEW COLL., matric. 14 Oct., 92, aged 20, from Loretto school.

Cockburn, Nathaniel Clayton, born in London 1866; 1s. William Yates, arm. CHRIST CHURCH, matric. 30 May 85, aged 19 (from Eton), B.A. 90.

Cockcroft, Edward Francis, born at Keighley, Yorks, 26 Feb., 1870; 1s. Thomas Howarth, D.Med. BRASENOSE, matric. 14 Oct., 89, aged 19, from Winchester.

Cockerell, Robert Rennie Pepys, born in London 29 Nov., 1869; 1s. Frederick Pepys, architect, deceased. NEW COLL., matric. 14 Oct., 87, aged 17 (from Winchester) (HONOURS :—3 classical mods. 89); bar-at-law, Middle Temple, 92.

Cockerton, rev. Henry George, born in London 1863; 1s. Andrew Henry, gent. WORCESTER, matric. 27 Jan., 81, aged 18, B.A. 83, M.A. 87; curate of Hertford St. Andrew's 89, and of Clothall, Herts., 93.

Cooks, Arthur Somers, born at Stockport, Cheshire, 1870; 2s. John, arm. ORIEL, matric. 20 Oct., 88, aged 18 (from Manchester gr. school), scholar 88, B.A. 92; HONOURS:—1 classical mods. 90, 3 classics 92.

Cooks, Reginald Howard, born in London 1 July, 1872; 3s. Stroud Lincoln, publisher. MERTON, matric. 22 Oct., 91, aged 19, from Repton school.

Cooks, Samuel William, born at Moston, co. Lancaster, 1868; 2s. Samuel William, g. n. PEMBROKE, matric. 28 Oct., 86, aged 18 (from Manchester gr. school), scholar 86, B.A. 91; HONOURS :—1 classical mods. 88, 2 classics 90.

Coddington, William Dudley, born at Blackburn, co. Lanc., 1874; o.s. Francis Henry, gen. ST. EDMUND HALL, matric. 11 Feb., 92, aged 18.

Codrington, Robert Henry, created D.D. 16 June, 85. See Al. Ox. 2nd series 271.

Coe, Frank Harris Kine, born at Bury St. Edmund's 1862; 3s. Thomas, gent. ST. EDMUND HALL, matric. 25 Oct., 81, aged 19, B.A. and M.A. 88.

Coghlan, Edward William, born in London 20 May, 1862; 1s. Edward, gent. UNIVERSITY COLL., matric. 15 April, 82, aged 19 (from Marlborough coll.), scholar 82-6, B.A. 85 (HONOURS :—2 classical mods. 83, 1 classics 85); bar.-at-law, Middle Temple, 89.

Coghlan, rev. William Luther Stanley, born at Hardwick, co. Lanc., Sept., 1867; 1s. William, cler. CHARSLEY'S HALL, matric. 18 Oct., 87, aged 20, from Manchester gr. school.

Cohen, Benjamin Arthur, born in London 24 Dec., 1862; 1s. Arthur, Q.C., M.P. BALLIOL, matric. 18 Oct., 81, aged 18 (from Rugby), B.A. 86 (HONOURS :—2 classical mods. 82, 2 classics 85); bar-at-law, Inner Temple, 87.

Cohen, Harold Albert, born in London 1872; 5s. Lionel Louis, arm. BALLIOL, matric. 14 Oct., 90, aged 18 (from Clifton coll.); HONOURS :—1 classical mods. 92.

Cohen, Henry Alfred, born in London 1870; 1s. Alfred Louis, arm. BALLIOL, matric. 18 Oct., 88, aged 18 (from Harrow), B.A. 92; HONOURS :—2 classical mods. 90, 3 history 92.

Cohen, Hermann Joseph, born at Ramsgate, Kent, 31 Oct., 1860; 1s. James Hermann, gen. JESUS COLL., matric. 19 Oct., 81, aged 20 (from University coll., London, and fellow 92), scholar 81, B.A. 85 (HONOURS:—1 classical mods. 83, 1 classics 85, Hebrew scholarships 83 and 86, Syriac prize 86, septuagint prize 87); bar.-at-law, Inner Temple, 91.

Cohen, Jacob Waley, born in London 30 Oct., 1873; 1s. Nathaniel Louis, stockbroker. MERTON, matric. 18 Oct., 92, aged 17, from Clifton coll.

Cohn, John Rougier, M.A., fellow JESUS COLL. 82-9, where see.

Cokayne, Francis Stewart, born at Putney 7 Aug., 1871; 4s. George Edward, Norroy king of arms. ORIEL, matric. 22 Oct., 90, aged 19, from the Charterhouse.

Cokayne, (rev.) Morton Willoughby, born in London 11 Oct., 1866; 2s. George Edward, Norroy king of arms. ORIEL, matric. 23 Oct., 85, aged 19 (from the Charterhouse), B.A. 89, M.A. 92 (HONOURS :—4 history 89); curate of Carshalton, Surrey, 92.

Coker, Cadwallader, M.A., fellow NEW COLL. 44-53, where see.

Coker, John, M.A., fellow NEW COLL. 39-56, where see.

Colby, Frederick Thomas, D.D., fellow EXETER 49-75, where see.

Coldwell, Reginald Charles, born at Longford, Norfolk, 1861; 4s. Frederick Edmund, arm. HERTFORD, matric. 19 Oct., 81, aged 20.

Cole, Alfred William Richardson, born at Mount Coke St. Vincent, W.I., 15 Aug., 1873; 1s. Ebenezer, Wesleyan minister. MERTON, matric. 22 Oct., 91, aged 18 (from Kingswood school), exhibitioner 91.

Cole, Ernest Henry, born at Woolwich, Kent, 1866; o.s. Thomas Henry, cler. CHRIST CHURCH, matric. 16 Jan., 85, aged 19.

Cole, Robert William, born at Heston, Middx., 1869; 2s. Sydney, gen. NON-COLLEGIATE, matric. 27 April, 89, aged 20 (from Eton); migrated to BALLIOL; HONOURS :—3 law 92.

Cole, Sydney John, born in London 17 July, 1870; o.s. John, of Portsmouth, gen. NON-COLLEGIATE, matric. 12 Oct., 89, aged 19 (from Portsmouth gr. school); migrated to BALLIOL.

Cole, Thomas Edwyn Cecil, born at Bath 1872; 1s. Thomas, D. Med. CHRIST CHURCH, matric. 10 Oct., 90, aged 18 (from Bath coll.), scholar 90; HONOURS :—2 classical mods. 92.

Cole, William Gordon, M.A., fellow TRINITY 59-70, where see.

Cole, (rev.) William John, born at Swansea, co. Glam., 1865; 2s. Frederick, gen. KEBLE, matric. 17 Jan., 87, aged 22 (from Lampeter coll., where senior scholar, Bates prizeman 84, and B.A. 86), B.A. 89, M.A. 92 (HONOURS :—2 mathematical mods. 86, 2 mathematics 89), math. master R. Instit. school, Liverpool, 89-91; curate of Christ Church, Toxteth Park, 89.

Colebrooke, Edward Arthur, born at Ottershaw Park, Surrey, 12 Oct., 1861; 1s. sir Thomas Edward, bart. CHRIST CHURCH, matric. 21 May, 80, aged 18.

Colefax, Henry Arthur, born at Pudsey, Yorks, 9 July, 1866; 1s. Joseph Samuel, gent. MERTON, matric. 24 Oct., 85, aged 19 (from Bradford gr. school), postmaster 85, B.A. 88; student CHRIST CHURCH 91, M.A. 92; HONOURS :—1 chemistry 88.

Colegrove, rev. William Edward, born at Oxford 1859; 1s. Joseph, gent. NON-COLLEGIATE, matric. 18 Oct., 80, aged 21 (from Wesleyan school, Oxford), B.A. 84, M.A. 88 (HONOURS :—2 natural science 84); curate of St. Paul, Princes park, Liverpool, 91.

Coleman, rev. Alexis Irenée Du Pont, born at Wilmington, Del. U.S.A., Dec., 1864; 1s. Leighton, D.D. KEBLE, matric. 17 Jan., 83, aged 18 (from isle of Wight coll.), B.A. 87 (HONOURS :—3 classical mods. 84); curate of St. John Evangelist, Boston, U.S.A., 88, minister of St. Michael missionary church, Wilmington, 88, and chaplain to bishop of Delaware 88.

Coleman, Percy, born at Malton, Yorks, 14 June, 1872; 1s. Edwin Octavius, gen. QUEEN's, matric. 24 Oct., 90, aged 18 (from Kingswood school), scholar 89; HONOURS :—1 mathematical mods. 91.

Coleridge, Edward Philip, born at Rokeby, Yorks, 2 Jan., 1863; 2s. Alfred James, cler. ORIEL, matric. 18 Oct., 81, aged 18 (from Denstone coll.), exhibitioner 81-6, B.A. 85; HONOURS :—1 classical mods. 82, 2 classics 85.

Coleridge, Henry James, M.A., fellow ORIEL 45-52, where see.

Coleridge, Hubert James, born at Bromham, Beds., 26 Nov., 1868; 6s. Alfred James, cler. NON-COLLEGIATE, matric. 16 Oct., 86, aged 17 (from Bloxham school), bible clerk ALL SOULS' 87; HONOURS : 4 classics 90.

Coleridge, John Duke, baron, M.A., D.C.L., lord chief justice of England; hon. fellow EXETER coll. 82, where see.

Coleridge, William Arthur Rokeby, born at Rokeby, Yorks, 12 March, 1864; 3s. Alfred James, cler. NON-COLLEGIATE, matric. 19 Jan., 84, aged 19 (from Denstone coll.), bible clerk ALL SOULS' 84, B.A. 88; HONOURS :—2 classical mods. 85, 3 history 87.

Coles, Alfred Horsman, born at Streatham, Surrey, 26 Sept., 1865; 5s. Timothy Horsman, arm. NEW COLL., matric. 10 Oct., 84, aged 19 (from Winchester), B.A. 88 (HONOURS :—3 classical mods. 86, 3 classics 88); twin with Edward H.

Coles, rev. Charles Herbert, born in London 8 May, 1867; 7s. Lewis, gent. WORCESTER, matric. 17 Oct., 84, aged 17 (from Southwark gr. school), B.A. 88 (HONOURS :—2 classical mods. 86, 2 classics 88, 1 theology 89); curate of Coulsdon, Surrey, 90.

Coles, Edward Horsman, born at Streatham, Surrey, 26 Sept., 1865; 4s. Timothy Horsman, arm. NEW COLL., matric. 10 Oct., 84, aged 19 (from Winchester), scholar 83, B.A. 88 (HONOURS :—1 classical mods. 86, 1 classics 88, 3 history 89); twin with Alfred H.

Coles, Percival, born at Eastbourne, Sussex, 2 May, 1865; 4s. John Henry Campion, arm. UNIVERSITY COLL., matric. 11 Oct., 84, aged 19 (from Rugby), B.A. 89; HONOURS :—4 law 88.

Coles, Reginald Edward, born at Bidderstone, Wilts., 1863; 4s. George Lewis, cler. NON-COLLEGIATE, matric. 18 Oct., 80, aged 17 (from St. Mark's school, Windsor and Canterbury); migrated to CHARSLEY HALL, B.A. and M.A. 87.

Coles, Thomas, born at Oxford 1857; 2s. Benjamin Lewis, gent. NON-COLLEGIATE, matric. 13 Oct., 83, aged 26 (from central school, Oxford, and Culham training coll.), B.A. 87.

Coles, rev. Vincent Stuckey Stration, M.A., BALLIOL, where see.

Coll, Anthony Michael, born at Gibraltar Nov., 1862; o.s. Michael, arm. EXETER, matric. 15 Oct., 81, aged 19 (from Haileybury), B.A. 85, M.A. 92, B.C.L. 88; HONOURS :—2 George Lewis, cler. NON-COLLEGIATE, 2 civil law 87; bar.-at-law, Inner Temple, 87.

Coller, Frank Herbert, born at King's Lynn, Norfolk, 26 Dec., 1866; 4s. Richard, arm. CHRIST CHURCH, matric. 16 Oct., 84, aged 17 (from Westminster school), scholar 85, B.A. 89, M.A. 92 (HONOURS :—1 classical mods. 87, 1 classics 89), librarian 89, and president of the Oxford union society 90.

Collett, John Etheridge, born at Brixton, Surrey, 11 May, 1871; 1s. Augustus, gen. ST. JOHN'S, matric. 17 Oct., 89, aged 18 (from Merchant Taylors' school), exhibitioner 89.

Collett, William Michael, M.A., fellow ORIEL 65-75, where see.

Colley, (rev.) Francis Oswald, born at Sheffield 1865; 2s. Jonathan, gen. ST. JOHN's, matric. 11 Oct., 84, aged 19, B.A. 88, M.A. 91; curate of St. Andrew, Manchester, 89.

Collie, Alexander Winkworth, born at Alderley, Cheshire, 29 June, 1864; 4s. John, gent. JESUS COLL., matric. 18 Oct., 83, aged 19 (from Clifton coll.), B.A. 87; HONOURS :—3 classical mods. 85, 4 classics 87.

Collier, William, gen. (1s.); B.A. from JESUS COLL., Camb., 1878, M.A. and B.Med. 81, D.Med. 85; incorporated NON-COLLEGIATE) 27 May, 87 (educated at Sherborne school), M.R.C.S. 80, M.R.C.P. 86, F.R.C.P. 92, now of EXETER COLL.

Collin, rev. Eben Walter, M.A., chaplain NEW COLL. 90, where see.

Collinge, William, born at Oldham, co. Lanc., 19 May, 1873; 1s. Edward, J.P., barrister-at-law. CHRIST CHURCH, matric. 14 Oct., 92, aged 19, from Eton.

Collingwood, John Carnaby, born at Cornhill-on-Tweed, Northumb., 1 Oct., 1870; 1s. John, esq. ST. MARY HALL, matric 17 May, 92, aged 21.

Collingwood, Stuart Dodgson, born at Southwick, co. Durham, Jan., 1870; 1s. Charles Edward Stuart, cler. CHRIST CHURCH, matric. 1 June, 88, aged 18, B.A. 91; HONOURS:—2 theology 92.

Collingwood, Walter Gordon, born at Brigg, Cumberland, 23 May, 1861; 2s. Robert Gordon, cler. TRINITY, matric. 16 Oct., 80, aged 19 (from Winchester), B.A. 84.

Collins, Archibald Edward, born at Boston, co. Lincoln, 1869; 3s. William, cler. UNIVERSITY COLL., matric. 15 Oct., 88, aged 19, B.A. 91; HONOURS:—law 92.

Collins, Brenton Robie, born at Halifax, Nova Scotia, Aug., 1870; 2s. Brenton Halliburton, gen. CHRIST CHURCH, matric. 11 Oct., 89, aged 19, from Eton.

Collins, Carteret Fitzgerald, born at Halifax, Nova Scotia, 1865; 1s. Brenton Halliburton, arm. CHRIST CHURCH, matric. 25 May, 83, aged 18 (from Eton); bar.-at-law, Inner Temple, 88.

Collins, George Gower, born at Calcutta 1857; 2. George, of the Bengal pilot service (uncovenanted). UNIVERSITY COLL., matric. 15 Oct., 92, aged 35.

Collins, rev. Henry Bernard Codrington, born at Towcester, Northants, 10 Oct., 1862; 1s. Robert, cler. MERTON, matric. 17 Oct., 82, aged 20 (from Coventry gr. school), B.A. 87.

Collins, James, born at Romsey, Hants, 11 Oct., 1867; 2s. William, cler. MERTON, matric. 19 Jan., 88, aged 20, (from Rossall school); brother of William F.

Collins, Sidney Herbert, born at Llanelly, co. Carmarthen, 20 July, 1870; 2s. Thomas, gen. NON-COLLEGIATE, matric. 17 Oct., 91, aged 21, from Llanelly school.

Collins, rev. Tom, born at Cleckheaton, Yorks, 1861; 7s. Rawdon, gen. NON-COLLEGIATE, matric. 15 Oct., 87, aged 26 (from Glasgow university); curate of Wortley, Leeds, 91.

Collins, Thomas Basil, born at Newport, Salop, 1873; o.s. Tom, gen. CHRIST CHURCH, matric. 16 Oct., 91, aged 18, from Newport school.

Collins, Vere Maunsell, born at Windsor 2 July, 1872; 1s. William Maunsell, of London, D.Med. BALLIOL, matric. 14 Oct., 90, aged 18 (from the Charterhouse); HONOURS:—2 classical mods. 92.

Collins, rev. William Escott, born at Towcester, Northants, 15 Feb., 1865; 2s. Robert Codrington, cler. NON-COLLEGIATE, matric. 13 Oct., 84, aged 19 (from K. Edward school, Birmingham, and K. Henry VIII. school, Coventry); migrated to LINCOLN, B.A. 87; curate of Castor, Northants, 91. |-

Collins, William Fellowes, born at Ramsey, Essex, , 1866; 1s. William, cler. UNIVERSITY COLL., matric. 24 Jan., 84, aged 18, B.A. 87; of Kirkman Bank, Knaresborough, lieut. and Dragoons (Royal Scots Greys), 90; brother of James 88.

Collinson, Edward de Lisle, born at Hornsey, Middx., 1865; 1s. John, gen. NEW COLL., matric. 10 Oct., 84, aged 19 (from Winchester), scholar 84, B.A. 88 (HONOURS:—2 classical mods. 86, 2 classics 88), librarian of Oxford union society 87; bar.-at-law, Inner Temple, 90.

Collinson, Thomas Harrison, born at Bowness, Cumberland, 18 March, 1865; 3s. John Harrison, arm. WORCESTER, matric. 22 Jan., 85, aged 19, as Harrison (from Windermere gr. school), B.A. 87 and M.A. 90, as T. H. Collinson.

Collis, Edgar Leigh, born at Old Swinford, co. Worc., 25 Nov., 1870; 4s. William Blow, gen. KEBLE, matric. 12 Oct., 89, aged 18, from the Charterhouse.

Collis, Frederick William, born at Croydon, Surrey, 6 Nov., 1871; 1s. Frederick, gen. WORCESTER, matric. 14 Oct., 90, aged 18, from Croydon gr. school.

Collis, Harold, born at Croydon, Surrey, 24 May, 1873; 2s. Frederick Collis, merchant. WORCESTER, matric. 18 Oct., 92, aged 19, from Croydon school.

Collinson, Harry, born at Wimbledon, Surrey, 5 March, 1868; o.s. Henry Clarke, gen. MERTON, matric. 22 Oct., 87; 1 aged 19 (from Uppingham), B.A. 91.

Collyns, John Martyn, M.A., student CHRIST CHURCH 46-68, where see.

Colman, Charles Stacey, born at Peterboro 11 Oct., 1871; 6s. Samuel Crackanthorp, gen. QUEEN'S, matric. 24 Oct., 90, aged 19 (from Peterborough and Stortford schools), scholar 91; HONOURS:—1 classical mods. 92.

Colomb, Rupert Palmer, born at Southsea 6 March, 1869; 1s. John Charles Ready, K.C.M.G., etc. NEW COLL., matric. 18 Oct., 87, aged 18, from Eton.

Colquhoun, Henry Archibald Colebrooke, born at Peshawur, India, 10 Jan., 1873; 2s. James Andrew Sutherland, lieut.-col., R.A. MERTON, matric. 22 Oct., 91, aged 18 (from Wellington coll.), postmaster 91.

Colquhoun, William Erskine, born at Crockham, Kent, 2 June, 1866; 1s. John Erskine, cler. TRINITY, matric. 17 Oct., 85, aged 19, from Harrow.

Colt, Ronald Sherwin Holden Stuart Rae, born at Old Monkland, co. Lanark, 23 March, 1869; 1s. George Frederick Russell, of Gartsherrie, N.B., arm. CHRIST CHURCH, matric. 1 June, 88, aged 19 (from Harrow), B.A. 92; HONOURS:—4 history 92.

Colthurst, Arthur Beadon, born at Westbury-on-Trym, co. Gloucester, 15 Sept., 1869; 2s. Edward, merchant. EXETER, matric. 19 Oct., 87, aged 18 (from St. Mark's school, Windsor), B.A. 90.

Colthurst, Edmund Jolliffe, born at Thurloxton, Somerset, 3 Jan., 1874; 2. Thomas Colmer, gen. ST. MARY HALL, matric. 27 Oct. 91, aged 18.

Colvile, Algernon Holland, born at Walton Park, Liverpool, 30 Nov., 1870; 1s. Henry Algernon, gen. MERTON, matric. 29 Oct., 91, aged 20, from M.T. school, Great Crosby.

Colyer, John Edmeades Cox, born at Drayton, co. Leic , 1859; 1s. John Edmeades, cler. NON-COLLEGIATE, matric. 17 Jan., 82, aged 22.

Combe, Ralph Molyneux, born at Rajeote, India, 2 Dec., 1872; 3s. James John, major general. EXETER, matric. 22 Oct., 91, aged 18, from Haileybury.

Combs, Cyril Webster, born in London 1862; 2s. John, arm. WADHAM, matric. 26 Jan., 81, aged 19, B.A. and M.A. 87.

Combs, Frank Henry, born at Henwick, co. Worc., 25 Dec., 1866; 1s. Robert, gen. NON-COLLEGIATE, matric. 23 Jan., 86, aged 19 (from Worcester cathedral school); academical clerk MAGDALEN 86.

Comfort, rev. Charles Abraham, born at Oxford 7 Nov., 1865; o.s. Abraham, gent. NON-COLLEGIATE, matric. 12 June, 86, aged 20 (from Oxford high school); migrated to EXETER 87, B.A. 89, M.A. 93; curate of Fenny Stratford, Bucks, 90.

Comper, Leonard William, born at Aberdeen 20 Oct., 1867; 2s. John, cler. WORCESTER, matric. 22 Jan., 89, aged 21 (from Aberdeen gr. school and university), B.A. 92; HONOURS:—2 theology 92.

Compston, Herbert Fuller Bright, born at Barnsley, Yorks, 17 Oct., 1866; 4s. John, cler. NON-COLLEGIATE, matric. 13 Oct., 86, aged 18 (from Ilminster gr. school); exhibitioner EXETER 90, B.A. 91; HONOURS :—1 theology 91.

Compton, Herdmore, M.A., fellow MERTON 41-52, where see.

Compton, Charles Henry, born at Minestead, Hants, March, 1870; 1s. John, hon. canon of Winchester. KEBLE, matric. 12 Oct., 89, aged 19 (from Sherborne school and the Charterhouse), B.A. 92.

Compton, Francis, D.C.L., fellow ALL SOULS' 46, where see.

Compton, John, born at Minestead, Hants, June, 1873; 2s. John, hon. canon of Winchester. KEBLE, matric. 15 Oct., 92, aged 19 (from Uppingham school).

Compton, Leonard William, born at Frome, Somerset, 1864; 2s. Thomas Hoyle, cler. KEBLE, matric. 14 Oct., 84, aged 20 (from Churdstock school), B.A. 89; HONOURS :—2 classical mods. 86.

Comyns, Frank, born at Newbury, Berks, 7 April, 1862; 1s. Francis, gen. NON-COLLEGIATE, matric. 14 Jan., 88, aged 25, B.A. 91; HONOURS :—2 chemistry 91.

Comyns, John Hext, born at Cannes 15 April, 1873; 1s. George Young, cler. TRINITY, matric. 17 Oct., 91, aged 18, from Newton Abbot coll.

Conacher, Hugh Morison, born at Ashwell, Herts, 15 Jan., 1874; 2s. James, of the civil service. CORPUS CHRISTI, matric. 18 Oct., 92, aged 18 (from Worcester cathedral school), scholar 91.

Condell, Clement Vallange, born at Sleaford, Notts, 1 Feb., 1870; o.s. William Vallange, arm. MERTON, matric. 19 Oct., 89, aged 19, from Harrow.

Conder, Edward Daines, born at Leeds 30 May, 1872; 2s. Eustace Rogers, congregational minister. WADHAM, matric. 20 Oct., 91, aged 19, from Liverpool gr. school.

Condy, Charles Eric Sewell, born at Wandsworth, Surrey, 1862; 3s. Henry Bellmann, gent. NON-COLLEGIATE, matric. 18 Oct., 80, aged 18 from St. Matthias choir school, Kensington.

Conford, George James, born at Carshalton, Surrey, 5 Dec., 1869; 2s. George William, gen. CHRIST CHURCH, matric. 12 Oct., 88, aged 18 (from Southwark gr. school), scholar 91, B.A. 92 ; HONOURS :— 2 physiology 92.

Congreve, Richard, M.A., hon. fellow WADHAM 91, where see.

Congreve, Walter Norris, born at Chatham, Kent, 1863; 1s. William, arm. PEMBROKE, matric. 30 Oct., 80, aged 17 (from Harrow); lieut. Rifle brigade 85.

Congreve, William Congreve Macintosh, born in Inverness 1861; 1s. John, arm. ORIEL, matric. 6 Feb., 80, aged 19, from the Charterhouse.

Connal, Benjamin Michael, born at Christchurch, New Zealand, 1861; 2s. Ebenezer, merchant, CORPUS CHRISTI, matric. 19 Oct., 82, aged 21 (from Canterbury coll., N.Z.), exhibitioner 82-6, B.A. 87, M.A. 89; HONOURS :—1 classical mods. 83, 1 classics 86.

Connell, Arthur Cuthbert, born at Glasgow 17 Sept., 1872; 4s. Charles, shipbuilder. NEW COLL., matric. 14 Oct., 92, aged 20, from Loretto school.

Conner, Daniel Henry, born at Alverstoke 5 April, 1867; 1s. Daniel, capt. R.M. NEW COLL., matric. 16 Oct., 85, aged 18 (from St. Edward's school, Summertown), B.A. 88 (HONOURS :—3 history 88); bar.-at-law, Inner Temple, 91.

Connolly, John Francis, born at Limerick 1869; 1s. John, gen. CHRIST CHURCH, matric. 12 Oct., 88, aged 19 (from Belvedere coll., Dublin) scholar 88; assist. commissioner, Punjab, 90.

Connop, Richard, born at Penton, Cornwall, 12 May, 1863; 4s. Newell, of King's Nympton Park, Devon, arm. NEW COLL., matric. 14 Oct., 82, aged 19, from the Charterhouse.

Conolly, William, born at Castlelar, co. Kildare, 29 Oct., 1872; 2s. Thomas, arm. CHRIST CHURCH, matric. 6 June, 90, aged 17.

Conroy, sir John, bart., M.A., fellow BALLIOL 90, where see.

Constable, Albert Edward Brown-, born at Cheltenham 13 March, 1863; 5s. Charles, lieut.-col. NON-COLLEGIATE, matric. 22 Oct., 81, aged 18, from Cheltenham coll.

Constantinidi, Anthony, born at Alexandria, Egypt, 27 Jan., 1867; 4s. Sophocles, of London, arm. MAGDALEN, matric 26 Jan., 86, aged 18, from St. Edward's school, Summertown.

Conway, Horace, born at Wimbledon, Surrey, 2 April, 1869; 2s. Thomas, gen. KEBLE, matric. 17 Oct., 87, aged 18 (from Haileybury), B.A. 91.

Conybeare, rev. Charles Henry, born at Itchin Stoke, Hants, 5 Sept., 1851; 2s. Charles Ranken, cler. CHRIST CHURCH, matric. 17 Oct., 81, aged 30 (from Rugby), B.A. 84, M.A. 89 (HONOURS :—3 natural science 84); vicar of Itchin Stoke 85.

Conybeare, Frederick Cornwallis, M.A., fellow UNIVERSITY COLL. 80-7, where see.

Conybeare, Henry Crawford Arthur, born in Bombay 16 Jan., 1853; 1s. Henry, arm. MERTON, matric. 21 April, 82, aged 29 (from Westminster school and King's coll., London), B.A. 88, M.A. 91; deputy commissioner Oudh.

Cook, Amos, born at Woodstock, Oxon, 1866; 2s. Amos, gent. NON-COLLEGIATE, matric. 13 Oct., 84, aged 18 (from Oxford high school), B.A. 87, M.A. 91; HONOURS :—3 history 87.

Cook, Arthur Wilstend, born at Portsmouth 28 Nov., 1873; 2s. Edmund John, merchant. PEMBROKE, matric. 26 Oct., 92, aged 17 (from Portsmouth gr. school), scholar 91.

Cook, rev. Edward Barnwell, born at Beckley, Oxon, 1864; 1s. Charles Leckey, gent. CHRIST CHURCH, matric. 12 Oct., 83, aged 19 (from Manchester gr. school), scholar 82, B.A. 87 (HONOURS :—1 chemistry 87); curate of St. Agnes, Bristol, 90.

Cook, Herbert Frederick, born in London 1869; 1s. Frederick Lucas, arm. BALLIOL, matric. 19 Oct., 86, aged 17 (from Harrow), B.A. 91; HONOURS :—3 classical mods 88, 3 classics 90.

Cook, Theodore Andrea, born at Exmouth, Devon, 28 March, 1867; 1s. Henry, head master Wantage gr. school. WADHAM, matric. 16 Oct., 86, aged 19 (from Radley coll.), scholar 85, B.A. 91 (HONOURS :—2 classical mods. 88, 2 classics 90), in the University eight 89.

Cook, Thomas Reginald Hague, born at Mirfield, Yorks, June, 1866; 1s. Thomas Hague, arm. CHRIST CHURCH, matric. 16 Oct., 85, aged 19, from Radley coll.

Cook, rev. Thomas William, born at Wellingborough, Northants, Dec., 1866; 1s. Thomas, gent. HERTFORD, matric. 22 Oct., 86, aged 19 (from Lancing coll.), B.A. 89 (HONOURS :—3 classical mods. 88); curate of Warrington, co. Lanc., 90.

Cooke, Arthur, born at Little Horton, Yorks, 2 May, 1868; 1s. Henry James, gen., deceased. NEW COLL., matric. 14 Oct., 87, aged 19 (from Giggleswick school), B.A. 91; HONOURS :—2 chemistry 91.

Cooke, Arthur George, born at Orchard Portman, Somerset, 4 June, 1872; 3s. George Frederick, cler. CORPUS CHRISTI, matric. 16 Oct., 90, aged 19 (from Bath coll.), scholar 90; HONOURS :—2 classical mods. 92.

Cooke, Frederick James, born at Bedminster, Somerset, 1865; 1s. George Frederick, cler. ORIEL, matric. 23 Oct., 84, aged 19 (from Bath coll.); assist. commissioner central provinces India 86.

Cooke, rev. George Albert, M.A., fellow MAGDALEN 92, where see.

Cooke, George Hay, born at Gt. Budworth, Cheshire, April, 1866; 1s. Samuel Hay, vicar. CHRIST CHURCH, matric. 26 Jan., 85, aged 18 (from Radley coll.), B.A. 88, M.A. 91 (HONOURS :—2 history 88); brother of Samuel A. and William.

Cooke, rev. George Kennedy, born at Athlone 1860; 1s. George, gent. ST. EDMUND HALL, matric. 25 Oct., 80, aged 20, B.A. 86; curate of Southampton St. Luke 86.

Cooke, George Theophilus, B.D., fellow MAGDALEN 55, where see.

Cooke, rev. John James Dunne, born at Brampton Bryan, Devon, 26 Oct., 1866; 1s. John Dunne, gent. ST. JOHN'S, matric. 17 Oct., 85, aged 18 (from Cheltenham coll.), B.A. 88, M.A. 92 (HONOURS :—4 history 88); curate of Coleford, co. Gloucester, 90.

Cooke, rev. John Roper, born at Berkeley, co. Glouc., 26 Aug., 1866; 1s. Henry, gent. WADHAM, matric. 19 Oct., 85, aged 19 (from Clifton coll.), scholar 84, B.A. 89 (HONOURS :—2 classical mods. 87, 3 classics 89); curate of Downham, Suffolk, 90.

Cooke, Philip Henry, born at Nibley, co. Gloucester, 1872; 3s. Henry, gen. KEBLE, matric. 11 Oct., 90, aged 18, from Malvern coll.

Cooke, Samuel Arthur, born in Northumberland 31 July, 1870; 3s. Samuel Hay, vicar of Gt. Budworth, Cheshire. WADHAM, matric. 13 Oct., 89, aged 18, from Radley coll.

Cooke, Selwyn Montagu, born at Ealing, Middx., 26 June, 1871; 2s. Edwin Charles, arm. ST. JOHN'S, matric. 11 Oct., 90, aged 19 (from Merchant Taylors' school), scholar 90; HONOURS :—Hebrew scholarship 91.

Cooke, Thomas Percy, born at Hull, Yorks, 9 June, 1868; 2s. James, gen. NEW COLL., matric. 14 Oct., 87, aged 19 (from Harrow), B.A. 90 (HONOURS : —3 law 90); bar.-at-law, Inner Temple, 91.

Cooke, William, born at Great Budworth, Cheshire, Aug., 1869; 2s. Samuel Hay, vicar. KEBLE, matric. 13 Oct., 88, aged 19 (from an Oxford school), B.A. 92; HONOURS :—4 history 91.

Cooke, rev. William Albert, born at Handsworth, co. Stafford, 1863; 1s. William, gent. WORCESTER, matric. 27 Jan., 81, aged 18, B.A. 84 (HONOURS : —3 theology 84); curate of Addlestone, Surrey, 90.

Cookes, Thomas Horace, M.A., fellow WORCESTER 49-67, where see.

Cookson, Bryan, born at Newcastle-upon-Tyne 23 April, 1874; 1s. Norman Charles, of Oakwood, Wylam, Northumberland, coal owner. MAGDALEN, matric. 18 Oct., 92, aged 18, from Harrow.

Cookson, Geoffrey Montagu, born at Dallington, Northants, 1868; 5s. Christopher, cler. BALLIOL, matric. 16 Oct., 89, aged 18 (from Clifton coll.), exhibitioner 85, B.A. 90 (HONOURS :—1 classical mods. 88, 2 classics 90); cistern cadetship 91.

Cookson, George Heinrich Frederic, born at Frome, Somerset, 1871; 1s. Edgar William de, captain R.N. LINCOLN, matric. 20 Oct., 90, aged 19 (from Clifton coll.), exhibitioner 90; HONOURS :—3 classical mods. 92.

Cookson, Harry Eustace, born at Dallington, Northants, 10 July, 1863; 3s. Christopher, cler. ORIEL, matric. 31 Oct., 82, aged 19 (from Clifton coll.), bible clerk 82-6, B.A. 86, M.A. 93; HONOURS : —2 classical mods. 84, 3 classics 86.

Cookson, Hugh Cecil, born at Dallington, Northants, 4 June, 1862; 2s. Christopher, cler. TRINITY, matric. 15 Oct., 81, aged 19 (from Clifton coll.), exhibitioner 81; selected candidate Indian C.S. 81; died 11 Oct., 91, at Mooltan, India.

Coolidge, William Augustus Brevoort, M.A., fellow MAGDALEN 75, where see.

Coombes, Arthur Henry, born at Oxford 20 Aug., 1862; o.s. Thomas Henry. ST. JOHN'S, matric. 14 Oct., 82, aged 20 (from Magdalen coll. school), scholar 82, B.A. 86, M.A. 89; HONOURS :—1 mathematical mods. 84, 2 mathematics 86.

Coop, rev. James Ogden, born at Ashton-under-Lyne 2 June, 1865; 1s. John Hague, gen. NON-COLLEGIATE, matric. 27 April, 89, aged 19 (from Manchester gr. school and Owens coll.); migrated to EXETER, B.A. 92; HONOURS :—3 history 92.

Cooper, Arthur, born at Manchester 1860; 2s. Daniel, gent. ST. JOHN'S, matric. 13 Jan., 83, aged 23.

Cooper, Cecil Henry Hamilton, born at Peyton Grange, Suffolk, Oct., 1871; 1s. Henry William, cler. KEBLE, matric. 11 Oct., 90, aged 18, from Pocklington and Daventry gr. schools.

Cooper, Charles D'Oyley, born at Trentham, co. Stafford, 7 June, 1871; 2s. Samuel Herbert, of Stone, co. Staff., arm. UNIVERSITY COLL., matric. 18 Oct., 90, aged 19.

Cooper, Edward Cherrill, born at St. Heliers, Jersey, 27 July, 1866; 2s. James, gent. QUEEN'S, matric. 22 Oct., 84, aged 18 (from Victoria coll., Jersey, and Cranbrook gr. school), scholar 84, B.A. 88, M.A. 91; HONOURS :—2 classical mods. 86, 1 classics 88, 2 history 89.

Cooper, Edward Herbert, born at Newcastle under Lyme, 6 Oct., 1867; 1s. Samuel Herbert, arm. UNIVERSITY COLL., matric. 18 Oct., 86, aged 19, B.A. 90; HONOURS :—3 history 89.

Cooper, Francis John, born at Oldbury, Salop, 14 March, 1867; 2s. Charles John, gent. CHRIST CHURCH, matric. 16 Oct., 85, aged 18 (from the Charterhouse), exhibitioner 85, B.A. 88.

Cooper, George Henry, born at Cheltenham 29 May, 1866; 1s. John Capps, gent. MAGDALEN, matric. 16 Oct., 84, aged 18 (from Bath coll.), demy 84, B.A. 88; HONOURS :—2 classical mods. 86, 3 classics 88.

Cooper, Harry, born at Constitution in Chili, 20 Dec., 1863; 2s. Henry, gent., deceased. QUEEN'S, matric. 23 Oct., 82, aged 18 (from Christ's coll., Finchley), B.A. 86; HONOURS :—2 classical mods. 84, 3 classics 86.

Cooper, Henry Dickersteth, born at Forncett St. Mary, Norfolk, 19 Aug., 1861; 4s. John Edward, cler. KEBLE, matric. 10 Oct., 80, aged 19 (from Radley coll.), scholar 80, B.A. 84, M.A. 87, and tutor 90; fellow HERTFORD 89-91; HONOURS :—1 classical mods. 82, 1 classics 84.

Cooper, Henry Gosse Winfield, born at Redhill, Surrey, 1 April, 1872; 1s. Winfield, vicar of Crawley, Sussex. ORIEL, matric. 27 Oct., 91, aged 19, from Haileybury.

Cooper, John, M.A., fellow WADHAM, 38-68, where see.

Cooper, Leonard, born at Leeds, 1866; o.s. Leonard, gent. CORPUS CHRISTI, matric. 23 Oct., 84, aged 18 (from Radley coll.), B.A. 88; HONOURS : —4 history 88.

Cooper, rev. Sydney, born at Bromley, Kent, 14 Jan., 1862; 3s. Henry, gent. NEW COLL., matric. 15 May, 80, aged 18 (from the Charterhouse), B.A. 84, M.A. 87 (HONOURS :—2 classical mods. 82, 1 history 84); curate of Cirencester 89.

Cooper, rev. Thomas, born at Windermere, Westmorland, July, 1863; 1s. Thomas John, cler. KEBLE, matric. 17 Oct., 82, aged 19 (from Marlborough), B.A. 85, M.A. 90; curate of Coddenham, Norfolk, 90.

Cooper, William Astley, born at Froyle, Hants, March, 1874; 1s. William Rickford Astley, cler. KEBLE, matric. 15 Oct., 92, aged 18, from Lancing coll.

Cooper, rev. William Henry Windle, born at Wolverhampton 1855; o.s. William, gent. ST. JOHN'S, matric. 16 Oct., 80, aged 25, B.A. 83, M.A. 87 (HONOURS:—3 theology 83); curate of Holy Trinity, Margate, 87.

Cooper, William Nathaniel Ball, born in Salop May, 1869; 1s. Nathaniel, cler. CHRIST CHURCH, matric. 12 Oct., 88, aged 19 (from Shrewsbury gr. school), B.A. 92; HONOURS :—3 history 92.

Coore, Alban, born at Brighton 21 May, 1872; 1s. Alfred Thomas, gov. and chaplain Shrewsbury hospital. BRASENOSE, matric. 22 Oct., 91, aged 19 (from Hereford cathedral school), scholar 91.

Coore, George Barnard Milbank, born at Scruton, Yorks, 28 Dec., 1865; 4s. Henry, arm. CORPUS CHRISTI, matric. 23 Oct., 84, aged 18 (from Bath coll.), scholar 84, B.A. 88 (HONOURS:—1 classical mods. 86, 2 classics 88); bar.-at-law, Middle Temple, 90, private sec. to right hon. James Bryce, chancellor of the duchy of Lancaster 92.

Coote, Arthur Bernard, born at St. Ives, Hunts, 25 March, 1872; 2s. Charles. EXETER, matric. 22 Oct., 91, aged 19, from Merchiston castle school, Edinburgh.

Coote, Stanley Victor, born at Southsea, Hants, 30 May, 1862; 1s. Robert, arm. ORIEL, matric. 18 Oct., 81, aged 19 (from Winchester), B.A. 85, M.A. 88; student of Lincoln's Inn 82.

Cooten, Harold Van, born at The Vale, Guernsey, 16 Sept., 1873; 6s. John Rodolphus, schoolmaster. JESUS COLL., matric. 18 Oct., 92, aged 19 (from Elizabeth coll., Guernsey).

Cope, Richard Crosse, born at New Windsor, Berks, July, 1872; 2s. Richard, arm. KEBLE, matric. 17 Jan., 91, aged 18, from St. Mark's, Windsor.

Copleston, John Henry Herbert, born at Kirkby Overblow, Yorks, 5 July, 1865; 1s. John Henry, cler. CORPUS CHRISTI, matric. 23 Oct., 84, aged 19 (from Malvern coll.), B.A. 88; HONOURS :—3 classical mods. 86, 2 classics 88.

Copleston, right rev. Reginald Stephen, D.D., bishop of Colombo; fellow ST. JOHN'S 69-75, where see.

Corbet, Hugh Dryden, born at Upton Magna, Salop, 3 June, 1873; o.s. George William, B.A. MAGDALEN, matric. 18 Oct., 92, aged 19, from Eton.

Corbett, Joseph, born at Barmouth, co. Merioneth, 27 Nov., 1862; 3s. Edward, of Longnor Hall, Salop, M.P. EXETER, matric. 28 Jan., 81, aged 18, from Cheltenham coll.

Corbett, Leonard Bagott, born at Oswestry, Salop, 1872; 1s. Elijah Bagott, cler. ALL SOUL'S, matric. 14 Oct., 90, aged 18 (from Malvern coll.), bible clerk 90; HONOURS :—3 classical mods. 92.

Corbett, Roger John, born at Dodderhill, co. Worcester, 10 Aug., 1862; 1s. John, arm. CHRIST CHURCH, matric. 4 June, 81; aged 17 (from Shrewsbury school), B.A. 84.

Corbould, Edward James, born at Newbury, Berks, 1861; 1s. Edward James, cler. HERTFORD, matric. 19 Oct., 81, aged 20 (from Canterbury school), scholar 80-5, B.A. 85; HONOURS :—2 classical mods. 83, 4 classics 85.

Cordeux, Godfrey Pigott, M.A., fellow WORCESTER 52-6, where see.

Cordiner, rev. Robert Charles, born at Porchester, Hants, 22 Sept. 1861; o.s. Robert, arm. KEBLE, matric. '19 Oct., 80, aged 19 (from Rugby), B.A. 84, M.A. 87; chaplain at Bologna 86-7, and of All Saints', Rome, 89-91, rector of Lonnay, co. Aberdeen, 91.

Corfe, Charles John, M.A. ALL SOULS', created D.D. 22 Oct., 89; bishop of Corea 89. See *Al. Ox.* and series 297.

Corfield, William Henry, M.A. D. Med., fellow PEMBROKE 65-76, where see.

Corner, rev. Horace Glasgow, born at Hereford, 1869; 2s. James, gen. BRASENOSE, matric. 20 Oct., 87, aged 18 (from Hereford cathedral school), B.A. 90.

Cornes, Archibald John, born at Teddington, Middx., 1873; 1s. Frederick, merchant, deceased. ORIEL, matric. 27 Oct., 91, aged 18, from Marlborough coll.

Cornes, Julian, born at Teddington, Middx., 1874; 3s. Frederick, merchant, deceased. CORPUS CHRISTI, matric. 18 Oct., 92, aged 18 (from Clifton coll.), exhibitioner 91.

Cornewall, Herbert, born at Moccas, co. Hereford, 16 Nov., 1871; 2s. rev. sir George Henry, bart. ST. JOHN'S, matric. 22 Oct., 91, aged 19, from Wellington coll.

Cornish, Basil Sidney, born at Harrow, Middx., 12 June, 1869; o.s. Edward Brooking, gent. BRASENOSE, matric. 20 Oct., 87, aged 18 (from Manchester gr. school), scholar 87, B.A. 91; HONOURS :—2 classical mods. 89, 2 classics 91.

Cornish, Charles John, born at Salcombe Regis, Devon, 1859; 1s. Charles John, M.A., rector of Childrey, Berks. HERTFORD, matric. 4 June, 81, aged 22 (from the Charterhouse), scholar 82-5, B.A. 86, M.A. 89; HONOURS :—2 classical mods. 83, 2 classics 91.

Cornish, Charles Landesborough, born at Sydney, Australia, 1863; 5s. Edward Brooking, gent. PEMBROKE, matric. 26 Oct., 81, aged 18 (from Sherborne school), B.A. 86.

Cornish, Francis Cole, born at Narberth, co. Pembroke, 1863; 3s. Charles, cler. WORCESTER, matric. 18 Jan., 83, aged 20, from Llandovery coll.

Cornish, rev. James George, born at Debenham, Suffolk, 25 May, 1860; 2s. Charles John, M.A., rector of Childrey, Berks. HERTFORD, matric. 14 Oct., 80, aged 29 (from Haileybury), exhibitioner 90, B.A. 83, M.A. 89; HONOURS :—1 history 92), a private tutor.

Cornish, Thomas Brooking, M.A., fellow ORIEL 40-7, where see.

Cornwall, Edward William, born at Midhurst, Sussex, May, 1866; 2s. Arthur Walton, cler. KEBLE, matric. 22 Oct., 85, aged 19 (from Bath coll.), scholar 85, B.A. 89; HONOURS :—2 classical mods. 87.

Cornwall, Walter Emerson, born at Midhurst, Sussex, 1865; 3s. Arthur Walter, cler. HERTFORD, matric. 18 Oct., 83, aged 18 (from Clergy orphan school, Canterbury), scholar 82, B.A. 87; HONOURS :—1 classical mods. 85, 2 classics 87.

Cornwell, Henry Brand, born at Geddington, Northants, Sept., 1869; 2s. Thomas Charles, cler. PEMBROKE, matric. 17 Oct., 88, aged 19, from Oundle school.

Corry, William Aubrey Bourne de Bentley, born at Birkenhead, 2 Feb., 1864; 1s. William Corry de Bentley, vicar of Bengeworth, co. Worc. QUEEN'S, matric. 23 Oct., 82, aged 18, from Abingdon gr. school.

Corser, John Lyon, born at Daventry, Northants, 5 March, 1860; 1s. George James, cler. NON-COLLEGIATE, matric. 10 April, 80, aged 20 (from Cheltenham coll.), B.A. 86; bar.-at-law, Inner Temple, 90.

Corser, William Blacklock Haden, born at Doddington, Salop, Oct., 1871; 1s. Haden, metropolitan magistrate. CHRIST CHURCH, matric. 11 Oct., 89, aged 17, from Eton.

Coscia, Carlo Felice, created M.A. 2 Feb., 1886, Taylorian teacher of Italian 86 (see page 10).

Cosens, (rev.) Edward Arthur, born in London 15 July, 1860; 2s. William Reyner, D.D. NON-COLLEGIATE, matric. 18 Oct., 80, aged 20 (from King's coll. school, London, and Derby school); migrated to MERTON, B.A. 83, M.A. 87; vicar of St. Augustine Holly Hall, Dudley, 88.

Cosier, Henry Bell, born in London 2 Aug., 1860; 2s. Robert, arm. CHRIST CHURCH, matric. 24 Jan., 81, aged 19.

Cossins, William Henry, born at Marsala, in Sicily, 1864; 2s. Richard Brown, gen. BALLIOL, matric. 16 Oct., 83, aged 19 (from K. William's coll., isle of Man); selected candidate Indian C.S. 83, killed 24 March, 91, at Manipur.

Coster, Martin Edwin, born in London 4 Oct., 1867; o.s. William Frederick, gen. MERTON, matric. 20 Jan., 87, aged 19 (from Westminster school); migrated to CHARSLEY HALL, B.A. 90; HONOURS:—4 law 90.

Cosway, Percy Lee, born at Dewsbury, Yorks, 1864; 3s. George, gent. HERTFORD, matric. 20 Nov., 84, aged 20.

Cotes, Everard Charles, born at Newington, Oxon, 1863; 1s. Septimus, cler. NON-COLLEGIATE, matric. 4 June, 81, aged 18 (from Clifton coll.); HONOURS:—3 mathematical mods. 83.

Cotes, Everard Digby, born at Brighton 15 April, 1862; 5s. Digby Henry, cler. CHRIST CHURCH, matric. 14 Oct., 81, aged 19 (from Cheltenham coll.), scholar 81-4, B.A. 90; HONOURS:—2 classical mods. 83.

Cotes, Kenelm Digby, M.A. ALL SOULS', where see.

Cotes, rev. William Charles, born at Highworth, Wilts, 1861; 1s. Charles, gent. PEMBROKE, matric. 30 Oct., 80, aged 19 (from Abingdon school), scholar 80-4, B.A. 84, (HONOURS:—3 classical mods. 82, 4 theology 84); curate of St. Mary Mornington, Dunedin, New Zealand, 91.

Cother, Edward Lorler, born at Salisbury Feb., 1863; 2s. Philip Pinckney, gent. KEBLE, matric. 17 Jan., 83, aged 19, from St. Edmund's school, Salisbury.

Cother, William, B.A., student CHRIST CHURCH 30-7, where see.

Cotman, Leonard, born at Preston, co. Lanc., 2 May, 1869; 5s. Frederick, gen. PEMBROKE, matric. 17 Oct., 88, aged 19 (from Preston gr. school); HONOURS:—1 classical mods. 90, 3 classics 92.

Cottam, rev. Samuel Elsworth, born at Manchester 1864; o.s. Samuel, accountant. EXETER, matric. 4 June, 81, aged 17, B.A. 85, M.A. 88 (HONOURS:—2 theology 85); curate of St. Barnabas, New Humberstone, co. Leic., 89.

Cotteril, Jocelyn, born at Winchfield, Sussex, 12 May, 1859; 1s. Joscelyn, gent. ST. MARY HALL, matric. 23 Oct., 82, aged 23.

Cotton Albert Louis, born in London 12 Sept., 1874; 3s. Henry John Stedman, C.S.I., chief sec. to government of Bengal. BALLIOL, matric. 18 Oct., 92, aged 18; brother of Harry and Julian.

Cotton, Alfred Ernest, born in London 1864; 3s. Henry, late lord justice of appeal and a knight, deceased. CHRIST CHURCH, matric. 12 Oct., 83, aged 19; bar.-at-law, Lincoln's Inn, 90.

Cotton, Harry Evan Auguste, born at Midnapore, E. Indies, 27 May, 1868; 1s. Henry John Stedman, C.S.I. Indian C.S. JESUS COLL., matric. 19 Oct., 87, aged 19 (from Sherborne school), scholar 87, B.A. 91 (HONOURS:—2 classical mods. 89, 2 history 91, 2 law 92); treasurer of Oxford union society 91; bar.-at-law, Lincoln's Inn, 93.

Cotton, Hugh Benjamin, born in London 11 May, 1871; 4s. Henry, late lord justice of appeal, and a knight, deceased. MAGDALEN, matric. 14 Oct., 90, aged 18 (from Eton), in the University eight 92.

Cotton, James Sutherland, M.A., fellow QUEEN'S 71-4, where see.

Cotton, Julian James, born at Krishnagar, E. Indies, 3 Oct., 1869; 2s. Henry John Stedman, C.S.I. Indian C.S. CORPUS CHRISTI, matric. 20 Oct., 88, aged 19 (from Sherborne gr. school), scholar 88, B.A. 92 (HONOURS:—2 classical mods. 90, Greek prose 91, Latin verse 92, 2 classics 92); selected candidate Indian C.S. 92.

Cotton, Richard William, M.A., student CHRIST CHURCH 47-61, where see.

Cottrill, Charles Alfred Watson, born at Stanwell, Middx., 11 Aug., 71; o.s. Robert Alfred, arm. MERTON, matric. 15 Oct., 90, aged 19, from Grosvenor school, Twickenham.

Couch, Arthur Thomas (Quiller-), born at Bodmin, Cornwall, 21 Nov., 1863; 1s. Thomas Quiller, gent. TRINITY, matric. 14 Oct., 82, aged 18 (from Newton Abbot, and Clifton colls.), scholar 82-6 (HONOURS:—1 classical mods. 84, 2 classics 85); novelist.

Couchman, rev. Ernest Henley, born at Henley in Arden, co. Warwick, 10 Oct., 1862; 3s. Thomas Barnes, gent. BALLIOL, matric. 18 Oct., 81, aged 19 (from Rugby), scholar 80-5, B.A. 86, M.A. 92 (HONOURS:—2 classical mods. 82, 2 classics 85); curate of Wollaston, co. Worc., 91.

Couchman, Malcolm Edward, born at Henley in Arden, co. Warwick, 1869; 6s. Thomas Barnes, gent. CHRIST CHURCH, matric. 12 Oct., 88, aged 19 (from Leamington coll.), scholar 88, B.A. 92 (HONOURS:—1 classical mods. 90, 2 classics 92); selected candidate Indian C.S. 92.

Couchman, Philip Holbeche, born at Henley in Arden, co. Warwick, 29 Sept., 1866; 5s. Thomas Barnes, arm. KEBLE, matric. 14 Oct., 84, aged 18 (from Rugby), B.A. 87; a tea planter in Ceylon.

Coulson, John Edmund, M.A., student CHRIST CHURCH 44-59, where see.

Coulthard, Richard, born at Brampton, Cumberland, 2 Oct., 1871; 2s. Richard, gen. QUEEN'S, matric. 27 Oct., 91, aged 20.

Counsell, Hugh Alfred, born in London 1868; 2s. Edward James, arm. HERTFORD, matric. 27 Oct., 87, aged 19 (from Worcester cathedral school), scholar 86, B.A. 90; HONOURS:—3 classical mods. 89.

Coupland, Herbert, born at Harrogate, Yorks, 22 Sept., 1872; 2s. Joseph, gen. CORPUS CHRISTI, matric. 19 Oct., 91, aged 19 (from Ripon school), scholar 91.

Court, Edward Darlington, born at Middlewich, Cheshire, 22 June, 1869; 3s. William Roylance, arm. NEW COLL., matric. 15 Oct., 81, aged 19 (from Rugby), B.A. 84; HONOURS:—3 classical mods. 82, 3 history 84.

Courthope, William George, born in London 28 Nov., 1871; 1s. William John, civil service commissioner. NEW COLL., matric. 11 Oct., 92, aged 20, from Eton.

Courtney, William Leonard, M.A., fellow NEW COLL. 76, where see.

Cousins, Clarence Wilfred, born at Antananarivo in Madagascar 1872; 4s. William Edward congregational missionary. NON-COLLEGIATE, matric. 17 Oct., 91, aged 19, from Oxford high school.

Cousins, Dennis Charles, M.A., NEW COLL., where see.

Cousins, Frederick Charles, born in London 24 March, 1864; 1s. Thomas, gent. WADHAM, matric. 16 Oct., 83, aged 19 (from Christ's coll. Finchley), exhibitioner 83, B.A. 87, B.C.L. and M.A. 91; HONOURS :—1 classical mods. 85, 2 classics 87.

Cousins, Herbert Henry, born at Antananarivo in Madagascar 15 April, 1869; 1s. William Edward, congregational minister. NON-COLLEGIATE, matric. 16 Oct., 86, aged 18 (from Blackheath missionary school), postmaster MERTON 87, B.A. 89; HONOURS : —1 chemistry 89.

Cousins, Walter James, born at Norwood, Surrey, 1863; 3s. Stephen, arm. BRASENOSE, matric. 26 Jan., 81, aged 18 (from Tonbridge school), B.A. 83.

Coventry, hon. Henry Thomas, born in London 3 May, 1868; 3s. George William, earl (of Coventry). NEW COLL., matric. 14 Oct., 87, aged 19, from Eton.

Coventry, hon. Reginald William, born at Croome, co. Worc., 29 Aug., 1869; 4s. George William, earl (of Coventry). NEW COLL., matric. 19 Oct., 89, aged 20 (from Eton); HONOURS :—3 mathematical mods. 90.

Coventry, Richard George Temple, born at Powick, co. Worc., 22 Oct., 1869; 2s. William George, bar.-at-law. BRASENOSE, matric. 16 Oct., 88, aged 18 (from Hereford cathedral school), scholar 88; HONOURS :—2 classical mods. 90, 3 history 92.

Covernton, Alfred Laurence, born in London 1872; 4s. Alfred Hennell, merchant. ST. JOHN'S, matric. 17 Oct., 91, aged 19 (from Merchant Taylors' school), exhibitioner 91.

Covernton, James Gargrave, born at Manchester 1868; 1s. Alfred Hennell, gent. ST. JOHN'S, matric. 15 Oct., 87, aged 19 (from Merchant Taylors' school), scholar 87, B.A. 91, senior scholar 92; HONOURS : —1 classical mods. 89, 1 classics 91.

Covey, Loftus Edward Rogers, born at Tiverton, Devon, 13 Jan., 1871; 2s. Charles Rogers, cler. EXETER, matric. 22 Oct., 91, aged 20 from Pocklington gr. school.

Cowan, Alexander, born at Newington, Midlothian, 20 April, 1873; 1s. Alexander Oswald, D.Med. and paper maker. TRINITY, matric. 15 Oct., 92, aged 19, from Sedbergh school.

Cowan, Alexander Gillespie, born at Westerlee, Murrayfield, Edinburgh, 28 Oct., 1873; 2s. John James, paper maker. TRINITY, matric. 15 Oct., 92, aged 18, from Loretto school.

Cowan, Charles Howard, born at Edinburgh 9 Oct., 1873; 1s. John James, paper maker. BRASENOSE, matric. 22 Oct., 91, aged 19, from Haileybury.

Cowan, Lachlan, born at Glasgow 19 Oct., 1862; 1s. Lachlan, solicitor. QUEEN'S, matric. 20 Oct., 88, aged 19, from Merchiston Castle school, Edinburgh.

Coward, Henry, born in Liverpool 1850; o.s. Henry, gen. QUEEN'S, matric. 29 Jan., 83, aged 39. B.Mus. 89.

Cowburn, George Herbert, born at Royton, co. Lanc., 1873; 1s. Robert, cler. ORIEL, matric. 27 Oct., 92, aged 19 (from Manchester gr. school), scholar 92.

Cowdell, Frank Leopold, born at Croydon, Surrey, 2 March, 1863; 2s. Alfred Burton, arm. TRINITY, matric. 15 Oct., 81, aged 18 (from King's coll. school, London); died 27 Dec., 1883.

Cowell, Sibert Forrest Antrobus, born in London 24 Sept., 1863; 3s. Thomas William, arm. UNIVERSITY COLL., matric. 14 Oct., 82, aged 19 (from Westminster school), B.A. 86; HONOURS :—3 classical mods. 84, 4 classics 86.

Cowie, Donald William Garden, born in London 24 May, 1865; 2s. Hugh, arm. BALLIOL, matric. 16 Oct., 83, aged 18 (from the Charterhouse), B.A. 86 ({HONOURS :—2 law 86); student Gray's Inn 89; head assistant to collector and magistrate Tanjore, Madras c.s., 85.

Cowie, George, Selborne, born at Shanghai, China, Sept., 1872; 1s. George James Webster, bar.-at-law, deceased. NEW COLL., matric. 16 Oct., 91, aged 19, from Harrow.

Cowley, Arthur Ernest, M.A., TRINITY, where see.

Cowlishaw, Francis Ion, born at Christ Church, Canterbury, New Zealand, 10 Sept., 1869; 2s. William George, solicitor. BRASENOSE, matric. 16 Oct., 88, aged 19 (from Rugby), B.A. 93; bar.-at-law, Inner Temple, 93.

Cowlishaw, William Bosley, born at Canterbury, New Zealand, 28 May, 1866; 1s. William Patton, arm. MERTON, matric. 24 Oct., 85, aged 19, from Canterbury coll., N.Z.

Cox, (rev.) Alfred Peachey, born at Hendon, Middx., 1862; o.s. Alfred Trelove, cler. NON-COLLEGIATE, matric. 18 Oct., 80, aged 18, B.A. 84, M.A. 87 (HONOURS :— 3 theology 84); curate of St. James, Paddington, 91.

Cox, rev. Arthur Gill, born at Long Buckley, Northants, 1861; 1s. Arthur, arm. HERTFORD, matric. 18 Oct., 80, aged 19 (from Bromsgrove school), scholar 79-84, B.A. 84, M.A. 87 (HONOURS :—2 classical mods. 82, 3 classics 84); curate of Orton, Cheshire, 87.

Cox, rev. Edward Hayter, born at Kennington 26 Aug., 1862; 1s. Edward Hayter, gen. WORCESTER, matric. 16 Oct., 88, aged 26 (from King's coll. school, London, and Auckland coll., N.Z. B.A. 91; curate of Kilve, Somerset, 91.

Cox, Hubert Henry, born at Monk Silver, Somerset, 1864; 5s. Thomas, cler. EXETER, matric. 18 Oct., 83, aged 19 (from Aldenham gr. school), exhibitioner 83-6, B.A. 86; HONOURS :—2 classical mods. 85, 4 theology 86.

Cox, John Hugh, born at Peshawur, East Indies, 1870; 4s. Charles Lindsay, arm. BALLIOL, matric. 18 Oct., 88, aged 18 (from Clifton coll.); assist. magistrate N.W. provinces, India, 90.

Cox, Philip Francis, born at Watford, Herts, 1869; 2s. Frederick, cler. ST. JOHN's, matric. 15 Oct., 87, aged 18, from Marlborough coll.

Cox, Wilfred Machell, born at Hazelwood, co. Derby, 1873; 1s. John Charles, cler. KEBLE, matric. 15 Oct., 92, aged 19 (from Tonbridge school), exhibitioner 92.

Cox, rev. William Kipling, born at Daventry, Northants, 1849; 8s. William, gent. NON-COLLEGIATE, matric. 4 June, 81, aged 32 (from Daventry gr. school and London college of divinity, Highbury), perpetual curate Christ Church, Coventry, 84.

Cox, William Spiller, born at Hampstead, Middx., 7 Sept., 1870; 1s. Edward Webster, gen. QUEEN's, matric. 22 Oct., 89, aged 19 (from Westminster school), exhibitioner 89; HONOURS :—3 classical mods. 91.

Coxe, Henry Reynell Holled, born at Abbottabad, East Indies, 9 Oct., 1863; 1s. Holled Wallace Henry, major-general. NEW COLL., matric. 14 Oct., 82, aged 19 (from Winchester), assist. magistrate and collector, Bengal, 84.

Crackanthorpe, Dayrell Eardley Montague, born in London 9 Sept., 1871; 2s. Montague Hughes (formerly Cookson), Q.C. MERTON, matric. 15 Oct., 90, aged 19. from St. Paul's school.

Crackanthorpe, Montague Hughes, D.C.L., fellow ST. JOHN's 50-69, where see.

Craddock, Reginald Henry, born at Dhurmgola, East Indies, March, 1864; y.s. William, gent. KEBLE, matric. 17 Oct., 82, aged 18 (from Wellington coll.), B.A. (NON-COLLEGIATE), 92; assist. commissioner central provinces, India, 84.

Craddock, Reginald William, born at Oxford 1869; 2s. John William, pleb. NON-COLLEGIATE, matric. 14 Dec., 88, aged 19.

Craft, rev. Richard Henry, born at Mold, Flints, 1865; 1s. Richard Henry, gent. NON-COLLEGIATE, matric. 22 Jan., 81, aged 20 (from King's school, Chester), B.A. 84, M.A. 87 (HONOURS:—3 theology 84); curate of Stoke-on-Trent 90.

Cragg, William Alfred, born at Spanby, co. Lincoln, 1 Nov., 1859; 1s. William, arm. LINCOLN, matric. 22 Jan., 80, aged 20, from Lancing coll.

Craggs, rev. George, born at Stockton-on-Tees, co. Durham, 1864; 3s. Thomas George, arm. MAGDALEN, matric. 24 Jan., 84, aged 19 (from Durham gr. school), B.A. 87, M.A. 90; curate of Halesowen, co. Worc., 88.

Craig, rev. Douglas Tudor, born at Dublin 1867; 3s. Herbert Tudor, cler. ST. JOHN'S, matric. 17 Oct., 85, aged 18 (from Elizabeth coll., Guernsey, and Dover coll.), B.A. 88, M.A. 92 (HONOURS:—3 classical mods. 87); curate of Battersea 90.

Craig, Edwin Stewart, born at Belfast 1865; 1s. Robert Smyth, arm. UNIVERSITY COLL., matric. 13 Oct., 83, aged 18 (from St. Mark's, Windsor), scholar 83, B.A. 87, M.A. 90; HONOURS:—1 mathematical mods. 84, 1 mathematics 87.

Craig, William Alban Cunningham, born at Edinburgh 15 Nov., 1872; 1s. Edward Cunningham, deceased. ST. JOHN'S, matric. 17 Oct., 91, aged 18, from university of Glasgow.

Craigie, William Alexander, born in Dundee 1869; 4s. James, gen. BALLIOL, matric. 18 Oct., 88, aged 19 (from St. Andrew's university), bible clerk ORIEL 89; HONOURS:—1 classical mods. 90, 1 classics 92.

Craik, James Bowstead, born in Edinburgh Aug., 1874; 1s. James, W.S. ORIEL, matric. 27 Oct., 92, aged 18, from Marlborough coll.

Crailsheim, Francis William, born at Glasgow 1863; 5s. Anselm, gent. CORPUS CHRISTI, matric. 19 Oct., 82, aged 19 (from Fettes coll.), B.A. 85; HONOURS:—2 classical mods. 83, 3 law 85.

Crake, Arthur Hamilton, born in Madras 1863; 3s. William Hamilton, arm. PEMBROKE, matric. 10 Nov., 81, aged 18, B.A. 85, M.A. 89; HONOURS:—4 history 85.

Crake, Ernest Edward, born at Lincoln 18 May, 1871; 2s. John William, schoolmaster. JESUS COLL., matric. 15 Oct., 90, aged 19 (from King's school, Chester), exhibitioner 90; HONOURS:—2 classical mods. 92.

Crake, John Houlsey, born at Morpeth, Northumberland, 14 Feb., 1869; 1s. John William, schoolmaster. JESUS COLL., matric. 16 Oct., 88, aged 19 (from King's school, Chester), scholar 88, B.A. 92; HONOURS:—2 classical mods. 90, 3 classics 92.

Cramer, Henry Ellis, M.A., student CHRIST CHURCH 41-54, where see.

Crampton, Francis Wilfred, born at Brentford, Middx., 17 Oct., 1865; 8s. Thomas James, gen. JESUS COLL., matric. 23 Oct., 85, aged 20 (from Merchant Taylors' school), B.A. 89; HONOURS:—3 history 89.

Cranage, George Edward Wakefield, born at Wellington, Salop, 2 Aug., 1862; 1s. Joseph Edward, arm. NON-COLLEGIATE, matric. 14 Oct., 82, aged 20 (from Shrewsbury school); migrated to TRINITY 83, B.A. 87, M.A. 92.

Crane, George Percy, born at Tettenhall, co. Stafford, 11 Nov., 1879; 4s. Charles Henry, gen. CHRIST CHURCH, matric. 29 May, 91, aged 18, from Cheltenham coll.

Crane, James Edward, born at Dorchester, Dorset, 1865; o.s. James, arm. EXETER, matric. 27 May, 82, aged 19 (from Radley coll.), B.A. 85.

Craven, Frederick Brooke, born at Kirsall, co. Lanc., 1860; o.s. Frederick, gent. EXETER, matric. 22 Oct., 80, aged 20, from Eton.

Craven, Hugh Bertie, born at Daventry, Northants, 1865; 2s. John, arm. CHRIST CHURCH, matric. 31 May, 84, aged 19 (from Radley coll.), B.A. 87, M.A. 92.

Crawford, Donald, M.A., fellow LINCOLN 61-82, where see.

Crawford, Ernest Edward, born at Brixton, Surrey, 13 June, 1870; 2s. George William Perrin, gen. ST. EDMUND HALL, matric. 28 Oct., 91, aged 21, from Warminster gr. school and Trinity coll. Harrogate.

Crawfurd, rev. Lionel Payne, born at East Grinstead, Sussex, 1864; 5s. Charles Walter Payne, cler. BALLIOL, matric. 16 Oct., 83, aged 19 (from Eton), exhibitioner 82, B.A. 88, M.A. 90 (HONOURS:—accessit Hertford scholarship 84, 1 classical mods. 84, 3 classics 87); curate of Gateshead St. Cuthbert 90.

Crawfurd, Raymond Henry Payne, born at East Grinstead, Sussex, 9 Nov., 1865; 6s. Charles Walter Payne, cler. NEW COLL., matric. 10 Oct., 84, aged 18 (from Winchester), B.A. 88, M.A. 91; HONOURS:—2 classical mods. 85, 2 classics 88.

Crawhall, rev. Edmund Isaac Laroche, born at Alston, Cumberland, 21 July, 1864; 2s. Thomas Wilson Crawhall-Wilson, gent. WADHAM, matric. 11 Oct., 84, aged 20 (from Sedbergh school), B.A. 88, M.A. 91; curate of Easington, co. Durham, 91.

Crawhall, Walter John, born at Greenock, co. Renfrew, 18 Aug., 1865; 1s. John (Bownas), arm. MAGDALEN, matric. 16 Oct., 84, aged 19 (from Cheltenham coll.), B.A. 88.

Crawhall, William Henry, born at Greenock 29 May, 1869; 2s. John Bownas, gent. WADHAM, matric. 13 Oct., 88, aged 19, from Repton school.

Crawley, George Herbert, born at Witham, Essex, 16 Nov., 1863; 3s. Robert Townsend, cler. CHRIST CHURCH, matric. 25 May, 83, aged 19, from Forest school.

Crawley, George Richard Eric, born at Lewisham, Kent, 5 Dec., 1873; 3s. Charles Edward, M.A. ORIEL, matric. 27 Oct., 92, aged 18, from Forest school, Walthamstow.

Crawley, Richard, M.A., fellow WORCESTER 66-80, where see.

Crawley, Vicary Gibbs, born at Nether Heyford, Northants, 9 May, 1868; 6s. Thomas William, cler. QUEEN'S, matric. 21 Oct., 87, aged 19 (from St. Paul's school), scholar 87; HONOURS:—1 classical mods. 89, 1 history 91.

Crawshay, rev. George Alfred, born at Honiton, Devon, 6 Aug., 1864; 2s. Richard, arm. EXETER, matric. 28 April 87, aged 22, B.A. 91.

Creak, Eutrick Havelock, born in London 1868; 1s. Etrick William, commander R.N., F.R.S. LINCOLN, matric. 22 Oct., 86, aged 18 (from Blackheath school); migrated to (New Inn Hall) BALLIOL, B.A. 89.

Creak, Walter Huntley, born at Charlton, Kent, 24 Oct., 1873; 2s. Etrick William, commander R.N., F.R.S. ST. JOHN'S, matric. 17 Oct., 91, aged 17.

Creaton, rev. William Henry, born at Billeston, co. Leic., 1862; 1s. Donald Humphrey, cler. NON-COLLEGIATE, matric. 15 Oct., 81, aged 19, B.A. 86, M.A. 89; curate of St. Stephen's, Paddington, London, 88.

Cree, Herbert Edward, born at Upper Tooting, Surrey, 1868; 1s. Edward David, cler. ST. JOHN'S, matric. 15 Oct., 87, aged 19 (from Newark school), B.A. 91; HONOURS:—4 history 91.

Cree, John Adams, B.D., fellow MAGDALEN 52-8, where see.

Creighton, right rev. Mandell, D.D., bishop of Peterborough; hon. fellow MERTON 89, where see.

Cresswell, Richard Henry, born at Lee, Kent, 22 July, 1870; 1s. Richard, of Mickleton, co. Glouc., surgeon. ST. JOHN'S, matric. 12 Oct., 89, aged 19, from Cheltenham coll.

Crew, Crew Jennings, born at Lewcombe, Dorset, 18 Dec., 1870; o.s. Charles, gent. WORCESTER, matric. 14 Oct., 89, aged 18, from Sherborne gr. school.

Crichton, Alan Henry, born at Wells 1867; 1s. Henry Benyon, arm. CHRIST CHURCH, matric. 30 May, 85, aged 18, from Radley coll.

Crichton, David Sprunt, born at Dundas, N.B., 3 Nov., 1869; 2s. James, of Barrow-in-Furness, gent. NON-COLLEGIATE, matric. 15 Oct., 92, aged 22, from Edinburgh university.

Crickmay, Thomas Francis, born at Herne Hill, Middx., 18 Jan., 1874; 1s. Cecil Edward, of the home office. HERTFORD, matric. 22 Oct., 92, aged 18, from Berkhampstead school.

Crichton, rev. William Llewelyn, born at Clyro, co. Radnor, 1866; 2s. Henry Benyon, arm. CHRIST CHURCH, matric. 16 Oct., 85, aged 19 (from Radley coll.), B.A. 89; curate of Roath, co. Glamorgan, 90.

Crickitt, Percy Scott Hill, born in London 15 Oct., 1865; o.s. Henry Blackwood, gent. MERTON, matric. 24 Oct., 85, aged 20, B.A. 89, M.A. 92; (HONOURS:—4 law 89); bar.-at-law, Inner Temple, 91.

Crimes, Charles Hambleton, born at Halton, Cheshire, 1871; 1s. Thomas Hankinson, gen. NON-COLLEGIATE, matric. 18 Jan., 90, aged 19, from Birmingham gr. school.

Cripps, (rev.) Arthur Shearly, born at Tunbridge Wells, Kent, 10 June, 1869; 2s. William Charles, arm. TRINITY, matric. 15 Oct., 87, aged 18 (from the Charterhouse), B.A. 91; HONOURS:—2 history 91.

Cripps, Charles Alfred, M.A., B.C.L., fellow ST. JOHN'S 75-81, where see.

Cripps, Henry William, M.A., fellow NEW COLL. 34-45, where see.

Cripps, Reginald, born at Mooltan, E. Indies, 20 Dec., 1868; 5s. John Matthew, arm. BRASENOSE, matric. 20 Oct., 87, aged 18 (from Winchester); scholar 87, B.A. 91; HONOURS:—1 classical mods. 89, 2 classics 91.

Crisall, James Stephen, born at Oxford 1872; 1s. James Stephen, pleb. NON-COLLEGIATE, matric. 12 Oct., 89, aged 17 (from Oxford high school); migrated to WADHAM 6 April, 91.

Critchley, John William, born at Upholland, co. Lanc., 28 Jan., 1869; 2s. John, gen., deceased. BALLIOL, matric. 14 Oct., 90, aged 21 (from Wigan high school and St. Andrew's university); HONOURS:—2 classical mods. 92.

Crocker, Reginald, born at Brandon, Suffolk, 16 Dec., 1866; 4s. William Poord, rector. QUEEN'S, matric. 25 Oct., 86, aged 19, from King's school, Ely.

Croft, Robert William, born at Holme, Westmorland, July, 1872; 2s. Thomas, cler. KEBLE, matric. 20 Oct., 91, aged 19, from Hammersmith school.

Crofton, Frederick Norris Lowther, born at Heavitree, Devon, 27 May, 1870; 1s. Gorges Lowther, arm. EXETER, matric. 17 Oct., 88, aged 18, from Winchester.

Crombie, Charles Horley, born at Sydenham, Surrey, 27 Aug., 1874; 5s. John Nicol, engineer. WORCESTER, matric. 18 Oct., 92, aged 18, from Cheltenham coll.

Crombie, Ernest John, born at Auckland, N.Z., 4 May, 1870; 2s. John Nicol, gen. WORCESTER, matric. 16 Oct., 88, aged 18 (from King's coll. school, London), B.A. 91; HONOURS:—4 history 89.

Cromie, Henry Palmer, born at Cheltenham 1858; o.s. William, cler. WORCESTER, matric. 29 April, 81, aged 43.

Crompton, Alfred, born at Bury, co. Lanc., 23 Feb., 1859; 2. Alfred, gent. ST. MARY HALL, matric. 18 Oct., 92, aged 33.

Crompton, Edward Arthur, born in London 22 Nov., 1871; 3s. George, arm. EXETER, matric. 13 Oct., 90, aged 18, from Marlborough.

Crompton, George William, born in London 11 Dec., 1863; 1s. George, arm. EXETER, matric. 18 Oct., 82, aged 18 (from Marlborough), B.A. 86, M.A. 89.

Crompton, James Shepherd, born at Rochdale, co. Lanc., Nov., 1866; o.s. Abel, gent. PEMBROKE, matric. 27 Oct., 83, aged 18 (from Repton school), B.A. and M.A. 90.

Crompton, John, born at Rochdale, co. Lanc., 22 April, 1866; 12. James, primitive-methodist minister, JESUS COLL., matric. 18 Oct., 84, aged 18 (from Wrexham school), B.A. 89; HONOURS:—2 mathematical mods. 86.

Cronshaw, George Bernard, born at Pennington, co. Lanc., 11 Dec., 1872; 2s. Christopher, cler. QUEEN'S, matric. 27 Oct., 91, aged 18 (from Manchester gr. school), exhibitioner 91.

Cronshaw, rev. Herbert Priestley, born at Manchester 1864; 1s. Christopher, cler. ALL SOULS', matric. 2 Feb., 82, aged 18 (from Manchester gr. school), bible clerk 82-5, B.A. 85, M.A. 88 (HONOURS: —2 classical mods. 83, 3 classics 85, 2 theology 86), Diocesan inspector Exeter, and chaplain at Killerton, Devon, 90.

Crook, Thomas Ashley, born at Bolton, co. Lanc., 3 April, 1862; 3s. Joseph, gent. BALLIOL, matric. 20 Jan., 81; aged 18 (from Clifton and Bolton schools), B.A. 84, M.A. 87; HONOURS:—1 history 84.

Crooke, John Walter Parry, born in London 1866; 1s. Douglas Parry, arm. HERTFORD, matric. 19 Oct., 81, aged 19; student Lincoln's Inn 83.

Crookenden, George Pelham, born at Woolwich, Kent, 13 April, 1868; 3s. Isaac Adolphus, gent. TRINITY, matric. 15 Oct., 86, aged 18 (from Marlborough coll.), B.A. 90; HONOURS:—2 history 90.

Crookenden, Harry Milton, born at Woolwich, Kent, 29 Jan., 1862; 1s. John, gent. WORCESTER, matric. 21 Oct., 80, aged 18 (from Marlborough), B.A. 83, M.A. 92.

Croom, Frederic Galsworthy, born at Hatcham, Surrey, 30 July, 1869; o.s. Edmund Frederic, gen. ST. EDMUND HALL, matric. 19 Oct., 92, aged 23, from Haberdashers school.

Croome, Arthur Capel Molyneux, born at Stroud, co. Glouc., 27 Feb., 1866; 1s. Thomas Myers, solicitor, deceased. MAGDALEN, matric. 23 Oct., 85, aged 19 (from Wellington coll.), demy 85, B.A. 89, M.A. 92 (HONOURS:—1 classical mods. 87, 3 classics 89), in the University eleven 88-9.

Croome, James Samuel, born at Brighton 1864; o.s. James Hobbes, gen. NON-COLLEGIATE, matric. 12 March, 81, aged 17, B.A. 84, M.A. 87.

Crosby, John Hawke, born at Spalding, co. Lincoln, 9 July, 1849; 1s. Thomas, gent. QUEEN'S, matric. 26 Jan., 85, aged 35.

Cross, Francis John Kynaston, born at Eccles, co. Lanc., 14 Nov., 1865; 2s. Edward, gent. NEW COLL., matric. 16 Oct., 85, aged 19 (from Harrow), B.A. 89; HONOURS:—2 classical mods. 87, 3 classics 89.

Cross, George Edmund Kynaston, born at Montreal 1863; 1s. Thomas, arm. ST. JOHN'S, matric. 15 Oct., 81, aged 18, B.A. 85, M.A. 89, in the University eight 88.

Cross, Henry, born at Isceles, Suffolk, 1865; 4s. William, arm. HERTFORD, matric. 14 Oct., 81, aged 19 (from Bedford school), scholar 83, B.A. 86, M.A. 92 (HONOURS:—2 classical mods. 86, 3 classics 88), in the University eight 88.

Cross, (rev.) Henry McIntosh, born at Brighton 4 June, 1863; 1s. John Henry, cler. PEMBROKE, matric. 26 Oct., 81, aged 18 (from Abingdon school), scholar 81-2, B.A. 86; curate of Lenton, Notts., 86-8, Brading, isle of Wight, 88-90, and master Wymondham gr. school 91.

Cross, Thomas Aubrey Shepherd Shepherd, born at Bolton, co. Lanc., 23 Aug., 1873; 1s. Herbert Shepherd, M.P. BRASENOSE, matric. 21 Oct., 92, aged 19, from Eton.

Cross, William James, born in London 1867; o.s. William, gen. ST. EDMUND HALL, matric. 20 Jan., 91, aged 24.

Crossfield, Talbot King, born at Hackney, Middx., 15 April, 1861; 1s. Abraham, gent. ST. MARY HALL, matric. 17 Nov., 83, aged 22; bar.-at-law, Lincoln's Inn, 89.

Crosskey, Ernest, born at Lewes, Sussex, April, 1862; 1s. Robert, arm. HERTFORD, matric. 18 Oct., 80, aged 18 (from Bradfield coll.), B.A. 84 (HONOURS: —4 history 83); bar.-at-law, Inner Temple, 88.

Crossley, Ernest, born at Ravenhead, co. Lanc., 1861; 3s. John, gent. UNIVERSITY COLL., matric. 22 Jan., 80, aged 19 (from Harrow), B.A. 84 (HONOURS:—3 classical mods. 81); bar.-at-law, Lincoln's Inn, 86.

Crossman, Charles Stafford, born at Winterbourne, co. Glouc., 8 Dec., 1870; 3s. Edward, D.Med. NEW COLL., matric. 11 Oct., 89, aged 18 (from Winchester), scholar 88; HONOURS:—Hertford scholarship 90, 1 classical mods. 91.

Crossman, Douglas, born at Surbiton, Surrey, 1871; 1s. Alexander, gent. ORIEL, matric. 25 Oct., 89, aged 18 (from the Charterhouse), B.A. 93.

Crossman, Robert, born at Anderton, Cornwall, 1862; 1s. William, arm. BRASENOSE, matric. 10 June, 81, aged 19, from Uppingham school.

Crosthwaite, Robert Hervey Baldwin, born in the East Indies 1870; s. Robert Joseph, C.S.I., Indian C.S. UNIVERSITY COLL., matric. 13 Oct., 88, aged 18, B.A. 92; HONOURS:—3 history 92.

Crowdy, William Mase, born at Torquay, Devon, 22 Aug., 1856; 3s. Alfred Southby, arm. BRASENOSE, matric. 23 Oct., 85, aged 19 (from the Charterhouse), exhibitioner 85, B.A. 89; HONOURS:—2 classical mods. 87, 2 history 89.

Crowfoot, John Henchman, M.A., fellow JESUS COLL. 66-73, where see.

Crowfoot, John Winter, born at Wiggington, Oxon, 28 July, 1873; 1s. John Henchman, cler. BRASENOSE, matric. 21 Oct., 92, aged 19 (from Marlborough coll.), scholar 92.

Crowther, Alfred Briant Nelson, born at Stockwell, Surrey, 12 Dec. 1869; 1s. Alfred Hallworth, gen. EXETER, matric. 22 Jan., 89, aged 19 (from King's coll. school and King's coll., London); HONOURS: —3 classical mods. 90.

Crowther, Arthur Henry, born at Stanwix, Cumberland, 17 Aug., 1866; 2s. George, gent. JESUS COLL., matric. 28 Oct., 85, aged 19 (from Carlisle gr. school), B.A. 89; HONOURS:—2 classical mods. 87, 2 classics 89.

Crowther, Henry Stewart, born at Claines, co. Worc., May, 1863; 6s. William, cler. KEBLE, matric. 17 Oct., 82, aged 19 (from Canterbury school), B.A. 87; HONOURS:—2 classical mods. 84, 4 classics 86.

Crowther, rev. James Herbert Lea, born at Plymouth Oct., 1865; 1s. James Addington, gent. KEBLE, matric. 14 Oct., 84, aged 19 (from Plymouth high school), B.A. 87 (HONOURS:—1 history 87); curate of Little Wymondley, Herts, 90.

Croxall, Edward Randolph Tongue-, born at Aldridge, co. Stafford, 1869; o.s. Vincent Tongue, arm. HERTFORD, matric. 19 Jan., 88, aged 19.

Cruft, William George, born at Nottingham 7 June, 1871; o.s. William John, cler. EXETER, matric. 21 March, 89, aged 17 (from Nottingham high school); B.A. 92; HONOURS:—2 theology 92.

Cruickshank, rev. Alfred Hamilton, born at Clapham, Surrey, 18 March, 1862; o.s. George, colonial banker, deceased. NEW COLL., matric. 9 Dec., 81, aged 19 (from Winchester), scholar 81-5, B.A. 85, fellow 85, M.A. 88, tutor 86-91 [HONOURS:—1 classical mods. 82, Hertford scholarship 83 (accessit 82), accessit Ireland scholarship 84, 1 classics 85], librarian of the Oxford union society 85; assistant master Harrow 91.

Cruickshank, John William, born at Cannanore, E. Indies, 15 Feb., 1863; 1s. Robert Dickson, governor of Oxford prison. LINCOLN, matric. 23 Oct., 82, aged 19 (from Magdalen coll. school), B.A. 86, M.A. 89; HONOURS:—1 history 86.

Cruickshank, Robert Dickson, born at Cannanore, E. Indies, 15 Nov., 1864; 2s. Robert Dickson, governor of Oxford prison. QUEEN'S, matric. 22 Oct., 83, aged 18 (from Magdalen coll. school), B.A. 89, M.A. 91; curate of Bristol St. Nicholas 90; brother of the last named.

Crum, John Macleod Campbell, born at Tabley, Cheshire, 12 Oct., 1872; 2s. William Graham, esq. NEW COLL., matric. 16 Oct., 91, aged 19, from Eton.

Crum, Walter Ewing, born at Capleric, Renfrewshire, 1865; 1s. Alexander, arm. BALLIOL, matric. 17 Oct., 84, aged 19 (from Eton), B.A. 88, M.A. 92; HONOURS:—2 history 88.

Crump, Charles George, born at Weymouth, Dorset, 1862; 1s. Charles, arm. BALLIOL, matric. 1 Nov., 80, aged 18, B.A. 83 (HONOURS:—3 law 83); selected candidate Indian C.S. 80.

Crump, Eldon Annesley, born at Walsall, co. Staff., 8 June, 1874; 1s. John Farrington, solicitor. EXETER, matric. 18 Oct., 92, aged 18, from Malvern coll.

Crump, Frederick Cuthbert, born at Ivybridge, Devon, 12 Nov., 1873; 2s. John, Wesleyan minister. MERTON, matric. 18 Oct., 92, aged 18 (from M.T. school, Great Crosby), postmaster 92.

Crump, Harry Ashbrooke, born at Yeohampton, Devon, 1864; 2s. Charles, arm. BALLIOL, matric. 17 Oct., 82, aged 18, B.A. 85 (HONOURS:—3 mathematics 85); assist. commissioner central provinces, India, 89.

Crump, Louis Charles, born at Paignton, Devon, 2 Jan., 1869; 4s. Charles Ashbrooke, arm. BALLIOL, matric. 18 Oct., 88 (aged 17 ?), assist. collector and magistrate Surat 90.

Crump, Robert Simpson, born at Rochdale, co. Lanc., 27 Jan., 1865; 2s. Simpson, gent. QUEEN'S, matric. 22 Oct., 83, aged 18 (from Bradford gr. school), exhibitioner 83, B.A. 87; HONOURS:—2 classical mods. 85, 2 history 87.

Crump, William Bunting, born at Scarborough 29 April, 1868; 3s. Simpson, gen. QUEEN'S, matric. 21 Oct., 87, aged 19 (from Bradford gr. school), scholar 87, B.A. 92; HONOURS:—1 chemistry 92.

Cruse, David Augustus, born at Leeds 1865; o.s. Frederick Augustus, gent. UNIVERSITY COLL., matric. 24 Jan., 84, aged 19 (from Leeds gr. school), exhibitioner 84, B.A. 88; HONOURS:—2 classical mods. 86, 3 classics 88.

Cruso, Henry Alfred Anthony, born at Ipswich 5 Jan., 1874; o.s. Henry Edmund Tilsley, M.A., vicar of Bramford, Suffolk. BALLIOL, matric. 18 Oct., 92, aged 18 (from Rugby), exhibitioner 91.

Cruttwell, Charles Thomas, M.A., fellow MERTON 70-85, where see.

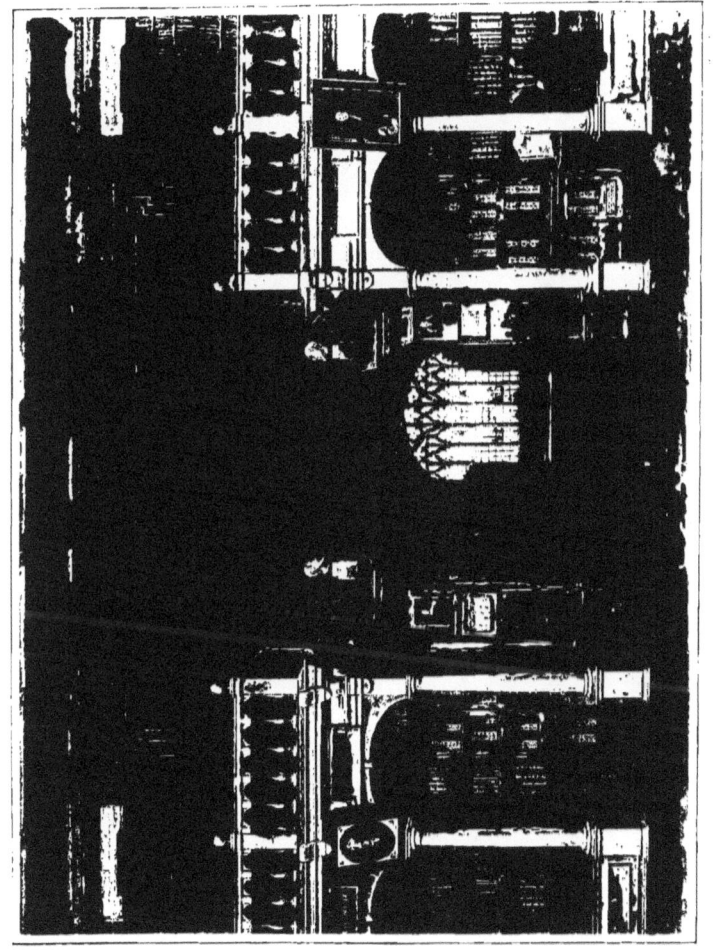

BODLEIAN LIBRARY.—By A. Pugin

Cruttwell, Hugh Macaulay, born at Winsley, Wilts, 27 Nov., 1871; 1s. Frederick Robert, arm. CHRIST CHURCH, matric. 10 Oct., 90, aged 18 (from Bath gr. school), exhibitioner 90; HONOURS:—2 classical mods. 92.

Cubbon, Henry, born at Douglas, isle of Man, 1864; 3s. Thomas, gen. NON-COLLEGIATE, matric. 22 Oct., 87, aged 23 (from K. William's coll. isle of Man), matriculated from ST. JOHN'S, CAMBRIDGE, 21 Oct., 84, B.A. 87, M.A. 89.

Cubitt, Bertram Blakiston, born at Thorpe, near Norwich, 20 Aug., 1869; 1s. Frank Astley, gent. BALLIOL, matric. 18 Oct., 81, aged 19 (from Rugby), B.A. 85; HONOURS:—2 classical mods. 82, 2 classics 85.

Cubitt, Thomas, born at Malvern, co. Worcester, 8 May, 1870; o.s. Lewis, arm. MERTON, matric. 19 Oct., 89, aged 19, from Eton.

Cullen, Thomas Frederick, born at Ballarat, Australia, 1857; 2s. Patrick, gent. NON-COLLEGIATE, matric. 15 April, 82, aged 25, from St. John's coll., Hurst-pierpoint.

Culley, John Henry, born at Horton, Northumberland, 1864; 3s. Matthew Tewart, arm. BRASENOSE, matric. 22 Oct., 83, aged 19, from Harrow.

Culshaw, rev. George Harold, born at Liverpool 18 Jan., 1864; 4s. William, architect, deceased. NON-COLLEGIATE, matric. 14 Oct., 82, aged 18 (from Rugby); migrated to EXETER 16 Oct., 83, B.A. 88, M.A. 89; curate of Hereford All Saints 90.

Cumberland, Charles Russell, born at Almorah, E. Indies, 1866; o.s. Charles Burrell, gent. ALL SOULS', matric. 13 Oct., 84, aged 18 (from Leamington coll.), bible clerk 84, B.A. 88; HONOURS:— 2 classical mods. 86, 3 classics 88.

Cuming, Francis Edward, born at Belfast 1864; 1s. James, D.Med. UNIVERSITY COLL., matric. 4 June, 81, aged 17, B.A. 85 (HONOURS:— 3 classics 85); bar.-at-law, Inner Temple, 93.

Cuming, Gordon, born at Gloucester April, 1870; 1s. John, cler. KEBLE, matric. 13 Oct., 88, aged 18 (from Clergy orphan school Canterbury); HONOURS: —4 history 91.

Cuming, John Shortridge, born at Gloucester, Jan., 1872; 2s. John, cler. KEBLE, matric. 21 Oct., 90, aged 18, from Hereford cathedral school.

Cumming, Alexander Robertson, born at Aberdeen 1871; 3s. Robert Scott, gen. BALLIOL, matric. 14 Oct., 90, aged 19 (from Aberdeen gr. school and university), selected candidate Indian c.s. 90.

Cumming, John Arthur, born at Aberdeen 1866; 2s. Robert Scott, gent. BALLIOL, matric. 24 Oct., 85, aged 19 (from Aberdeen university); assist. to collector and magistrate Kurnool, Madras c.s. 87.

Cumming, John Ghest, born at Houston, co. Renfrew, 1865; 1s. James Simpson, D.Med. BALLIOL, matric. 19 Oct., 87, aged 18 (from Glasgow university), B.A. 90; HONOURS:—2 Indian languages 99, Boden Sanskrit scholarship 90.

Cunliffe, Arthur Tabor, born at Woodford, Essex, 1872; 2s. Edward Shrubsole, arm. BALLIOL, matric. 14 Oct., 90, aged 18 (from Clifton coll.), exhibitioner 89; HONOURS:—1 classical mods. 92.

Cunliffe, Charles Pickersgill, born at Coulsdon, Surrey, 19 March, 1863; 4s. John, arm., deceased. MAGDALEN, matric. 15 Oct., 81, aged 18, from Eton.

Cunliffe, Heinrich James St. Benno, born at Munich 9 July, 1864; o.s. Henry, arm. EXETER, matric. 21 Oct., 86, aged 22, B.A. 91.

Cunningham, David John, D.Med. and prof. of anatomy and chirurgery in university of Dublin, created D.C.L. 22 June, 92.

Cunningham, George, born at Edinburgh 1867; 2s. George Miller, gent. BRASENOSE, matric. 28 Jan., 86, aged 19 (from Shrewsbury school), B.A. 90.

Cunningham, Joseph Thomas, B.A., fellow UNIVERSITY COLL. 82-9, where see.

Cunningham, Philip, born at Burgeo, Newfoundland, 1866; 7s. John, cler. ST. EDMUND HALL, matric. 23 Oct., 85, aged 19, B.A. 88, M.A. 92; HONOURS: 3 theology 89.

Cunningham, Thomas Joseph, born at Bristol 1855; 1s. John, arm. CHRIST CHURCH, matric. 15 Oct., 80, aged 25 (from Torre coll., Torquay), exhibitioner 80-4. B.A. 84, M.A. 87; HONOURS:—2 mathematical mods. 82, 3 classics 84.

Cupiss, rev. Herbert, born at Great Grimsby, co. Lincoln, 3 July, 1866; o.s. Francis Philip, gent. WORCESTER, matric. 20 Oct., 85, aged 19 (from Christ's hospital), scholar 84, B.A. 89; curate of Chaffcombe, Somerset, 89; died 2 June, 92, at Wimbledon.

Cure, Edward Henry Capel, born at Headington, Oxon, 27 June, 1866; 1s. Edward Capel, rector of St. George's, Hanover-square. NEW COLL., matric. 10 Oct., 84, aged 18 (from Winchester); HONOURS: —3 history 88.

Cure, Ernest Capel, born in London 29 Oct., 1861; 5s. Robert Capel, arm. UNIVERSITY COLL., matric. 16 Jan., 80, aged 18, from Eton.

Cure, Henry Capel, born at Bray, Berks, 1858; 1s. Laurence George Capel, cler. HERTFORD, matric. 27 Oct., 85, aged 27, scholar 86, B.A. 89; HONOURS:—2 classical mods. 87, 2 history 89.

Cure, Walter Robert Capel, born in London 6 Oct., 1870; 2s. Edward Capel, rector of St. George's, Hanover-square. MAGDALEN, matric. 14 Oct., 89, aged 19 (from Winchester); HONOURS:—3 law 92.

Curgenven, rev. Cecil Arthur, born at Lynne Regis, Dorset, 23 Feb., 1869; 1s. John, rector of Rousdon, Devon. WADHAM, matric. 15 Oct., 87, aged 18 (from Magdalen coll. school), B.A. 91; HONOURS: —4 history 91.

Curgenven, Francis Henry, M.A., fellow CORPUS CHRISTI 64-72, where see.

Curiel, Harold Worthington, born at Manchester 18 March, 1868; 2s. William, gen. EXETER, matric. 21 Oct., 86, aged 18 (from Warrington gr. school), scholar 86; B.A. 90; HONOURS:—1 mathematical mods. 87, 1 mathematics 90.

Curling, rev. Joseph James, born at Herne Hill, Surrey, 1844; o.s. Joseph, gent. ORIEL, matric. 19 Oct., 86, aged 42, B.A. 90 (HONOURS:— 2 theology 90); lieut. R.E. 65-72, yacht-master 82; incumbent of Bay of Islands 83-89, missionary 90-1, principal of theological college, St. John's (all) Newfoundland, 91.

Curling, Thomas Higham, born at Faversham, Kent, 25 Aug., 1872; 1s. John Harris, gen. WADHAM, matric. 20 Oct., 91, aged 19, from Faversham gr. school.

Currey, Cyril Curzon, born at Cape Town, 14 Nov., 1868; 3s. John Blades, arm. BRASENOSE, matric. 14 Oct., 89 (HONOURS:—2 law 92), bar.-at-law, Inner Temple, 93.

Currey, Edmund Samuel, born at Malling, Sussex, 1869; 6s. Edmund Charles, gen. MAGDALEN, matric. 20 Jan., 87, aged 18 (from the Charterhouse), B.A. 91.

Currey, rev. Reginald Henry Arthur, born at the Cape of Good Hope 1863; o.s. Robert Arthur, cler. HERTFORD, matric. 31 Jan., 84, aged 21 (from St. Paul's school), B.A. 89 (HONOURS:— 2 law 88); curate of All Saints', Upper Holloway, 91.

10

Currie, Charles Sibbald, born in Melbourne 1 Aug., 1866; 5s. John Lang, arm. CORPUS CHRISTI, matric. 26 Oct., 85, aged 19 (from Melbourne gr. school and university); scholar BRASENOSE 86, B.A. 90 (HONOURS:—a classical mods. 87, 3 classics 89); bar.-at-law, Middle Temple, 92.

Currie, Donald, born at Ayr, N.B., 23 March, 1874; 2s. Donald, J.P. UNIVERSITY COLL., matric. 15 Oct., 92, aged 18, from Ayr academy.

Currie, rev. Hugh Fenton, M.A., TRINITY, where see.

Currie, James, born at Edinburgh, 31 May, 1868; 1s. James, cler., LL.D. LINCOLN, matric. 18 Oct., 88, aged 20 (from Fettes coll. and Edinburgh university), scholar 88, B.A. 92; HONOURS:—3 classical mods. 90.

Currie, John MacMartin, born at Havre, France, 3 May, 1873; 2s. John Martin, shipowner. EXETER, matric. 22 Oct., 91, aged 18, from the Charterhouse.

Currie, John Ronald, born at Ayr, Scotland, 1870; 1s. Donald, arm. LINCOLN, matric. 20 Oct., 90, aged 20 (from Edinburgh university), scholar 90; HONOURS:— 1 classical mods. 92.

Currie, Leslie Batten, born at Parkend, co. Gloucester, 27 Feb., 1873; 2s. John, of Glasgow, D.Med. JESUS COLL., matric. 20 Oct., 91, aged 18 (from Newton Abbot coll., Devon), exhibitioner 91.

Currie, Lorne Campbell, born at Havre, France, 25 April, 1871; 1s. John Martin, gen. EXETER, matric. 16 Oct., 89, aged 18, from the Charterhouse.

Curry, Arthur Llewellyn, born at Tynemouth, Northumberland, 6 May, 1870; 4s. George, gen. NON-COLLEGIATE, matric. 15 Oct., 92, aged 22; matriculated from Corpus Christi, Cambridge, 22 Oct., 88, B.A. 92.

Curry, rev. William Dixon Blachford, M.A., EXETER, where see.

Curteis, Arthur Mapletoft, M.A., fellow TRINITY 57-9, where see.

Curteis, George Herbert, M.A., fellow EXETER 47-63, where see.

Curteis, Henry Herbert, born at Lichfield 8 Nov., 1863; 1s. George Herbert, canon. HERTFORD, matric. 18 Oct., 82, aged 18 (from Westminster and Rugby), B.A. 90.

Curtis, Alfred Cecil, born in London 27 March, 1862; 4s. John Charles, arm. ST. JOHN'S, matric. 16 Oct., 80, aged 18 (from Merchant Taylors' school), scholar 80-5, B.A. 84; HONOURS:—2 classical mods. 82.

Curtis, Edward Beaumont Cotton, born at Barnes, Surrey, 4 May, 1863; 2s. William Cotton, arm. TRINITY, matric. 21 May, 80, aged 17 (from Eton), B.A. 84; HONOURS:—classical mods. 82, a history 84.

Curtis, Frederick James, born at Handsworth, co. Stafford, 8 July, 1865; 2s. Samuel, gent. JESUS COLL., matric. 16 Oct., 84, aged 19 (from Birmingham gr. school), B.A. 88, B.C.L. 92; HONOURS:—2 classical mods. 86, 4 classics 88, 3 civil law 90.

Curtis, George Seymour, born at Southsea, Hants, 10 June, 1867; 1s. Seymour, arm. CHRIST CHURCH, matric. 15 Oct., 86, aged 19 (from Marlborough coll.), scholar 86; assist. collector and magistrate Ahmedabad, Bombay, 88.

Curtis, rev. Henry George Constable, born at Railton, co. Warwick, 26 Aug., 1865; 4s. Constable, arm. CHRIST CHURCH, matric. 12 June, 86, aged 20 (from Brighton coll.), B.A. 89; curate of Holy Trinity with St. Mary, Guildford, 90.

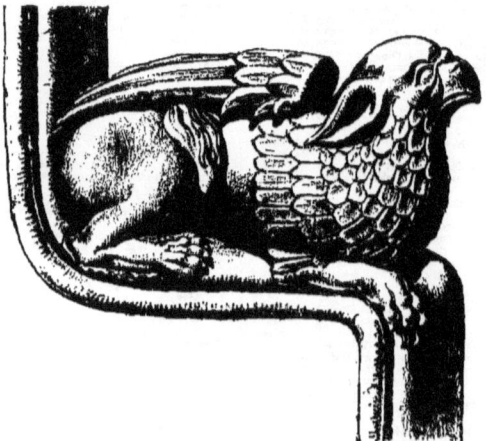

WOODEN STALL, ELBOW, BEAUCHAMP CHAPEL, WARWICK.—*Pugin*.

149   CURTIS. —— MATRICULATIONS, 1880 TO 1892. —— CZARNIKOW.   150

Curtis, Henry Eustace, born in London 30 April, 1863; 4s. Charles William, gent. EXETER, matric. 18 Oct., 82, aged 19, from Wellington coll.

Curtis, Lionel George, born at Derby 7 March, 1872; 3s. George James, rector of Coddington, co. Hereford. NEW COLL., matric. 16 Oct., 91, aged 19, from Haileybury.

Curtis, Walter Tennant, born at Islington 27 March, 1870; 3s. Charles Adrian, gen. UNIVERSITY COLL., matric. 12 Oct., 89, aged 19 (from Highgate school), scholar 89; HONOURS:—1 classical mods. 91.

Curtis, sir William Michael, born at Knowle Park, co. Glouc., 10 Nov., 1859; o.s. sir William Edmund, bart. CHRIST CHURCH, matric. 16 Jan., 80, aged 20; of Caynham Court, Ludlow, Salop, J.P., captain 4th batt. (militia) Gloucestershire regt. 82-4. See Foster's *Baronetage*.

Curtler, William Henry, M.A., fellow TRINITY 50-2, where see.

Curtler, William Henry Ricketts, born at Claines, co. Worcester, 28 Jan., 1862; o.s. Martin, gent. TRINITY, matric. 29 Jan., 81, aged 18, from Marlborough coll.

Curtois, Algernon, born at Branston, co. Lincoln, 5 Oct., 1865; 4s. Atwell, cler. WORCESTER, matric. 17 Oct., 84, aged 19 (from Marlborough coll.), scholar 84, B.A. 88, M.A. 91; HONOURS:— 2 classical mods. 86, 2 history 88.

Curtois, Rowland Sidney George Widdrington, born at Maidenhead, Berks, 19 Oct., 1868; o.s. Rowland Latimer Sidney, arm. TURRELL's HALL, matric. 15 May 86, aged 17 (from St. Kenelm's school, Cowley); migrated to WORCESTER, B.A. 91.

Curwen, Alan Delancy, born at Workington, Cumberland, 21 July, 1869; 2s. Henry Fraser, arm. CORPUS CHRISTI, matric. 1 Feb., 89, aged 19.

Curwen, Edward Darcy, born in London 26 Aug., 1864; 1s. Henry Fraser, arm. BRASENOSE, matric. 25 May, 83, aged 18 (from the Charterhouse), B.A. 90.

Curzon, hon. Francis Nathaniel, born 15 Dec., 1865; 3s. Alfred Nathaniel Holden, baron Scarsdale.

BALLIOL, matric. 22 Jan., 85, aged 19 (from Eton), B.A. 88; HONOURS:—2 classical mods. 86, 3 classics 88.

Curzon, hon. George Nathaniel, M.A., fellow ALL SOULS' 83-90 and 92, where see.

Cust, Arthur Perceval Purey, D.D., dean of York, fellow ALL SOULS' 50-4, where see.

Cust, Robert Henry Hobart, born at Hythe, Hants, 13 May, 1861; 2s. Robert Needham, bar.-at-law. MAGDALEN, matric. 27 April, 81, aged 19 (from Trinity coll., Cambridge, matric. 11 Nov., 79), B.A. 83, M.A. 86.

Custance, Arthur Frederick Musgrave, born at Hereford 28 Jan., 1866; 1s. George Musgrave, cler. BRASENOSE, matric. 14 Oct., 84, aged 18 (from Lancing coll.), exhibitioner 84; HONOURS:— 3 classical mods. 86.

Cutcliffe, (rev.) George, born at Dartmouth, Devon, 1870; 1s. George John, gen. NON-COLLEGIATE, matric. 17 Oct., 91, aged 21, from Teignmouth gr. school.

Cuthbert, Robert Howard, born at Oswestry, Salop, 1861; 3s. George, cler. NON-COLLEGIATE, matric. 8 Nov., 80, aged 19 (from Oswestry gr. school); migrated to HERTFORD, B.A. 86.

Cuthbertson, Clive, born at Shanghai, China, 1864; 6s. William Gilmour, arm. UNIVERSITY COLL., matric. 14 Oct., 82, aged 18 (from Glenalmond), B.A. 85 (HONOURS:—3 history 85); assist. magistrate and collector Bengal 84.

Cuthbertson, John Oswald, born at Shipley, Yorks, 11 April, 1870; 1s. John Montagu, surgeon, EXETER, matric. 17 Oct., 88, aged 18 (from Westminster school), B.A. 92.

Cutts, John Franklin Alexander, born at Hammersmith 6 Jan., 1869; 6s. Edward, cler. WORCESTER, matric. 14 Oct., 89, aged 20, from King's coll., London.

Cyprus, the archbishop of; created D.D. 27 June, 1889.

Czarnikow, Horace, born at Clapham, Surrey, 1865; 1s. Caesar, arm. BRASENOSE, matric. 22 April, 84, aged 19, from Harrow.

WOODEN STALL, ELBOW, BEAUCHAMP CHAPEL, WARWICK.—*Pugin*.

NORMAN ORNAMENT, ST. SAVIOUR'S CHURCH, SOUTHWARK.—*Pugin.*

D

Da-Costa, Kenneth Campbell, born in the Isle of Barbados 1864; 5s. David Campbell, arm. EXETER, matric. 18 Oct., 82, aged 18 (from Harrow), B.A. 87; bar.-at-law, Inner Temple, 88.

Dadley, Charles Carey, born at Nottingham 18 Jan., 1868; 3s. Elijah, gent. NON-COLLEGIATE, matric. 11 Oct., 90, aged 22, from Nottingham high school.

D'Aeth, Edward Knatchbull Hughes-, born at Wingham, Kent, 11 Sept., 1866; 5s. Narbrough Hughes, arm. ST. MARY HALL, matric. 24 Jan., 85, aged 18 (from Haileybury); migrated to LINCOLN 20 April following; settled in Florida, U.S.A.

D'Aeth, Henry Hughes-, born at Goodneston, Kent, , 1862; 3s. Narborough Hughes, arm. KEBLE, matric. 26 Jan., 82, aged 20, B.A. 86, M.A. 89.

Dakers, Hugh John, born at Hawick, Scotland, 5 Oct., 1863; 1s. John Rose, of Millport, Cumbrae, N.B., episcopalian minister. MAGDALEN, matric. 16 Oct., 82, aged 19 (from Bath coll.), demy 82, B.A. 87; HONOURS:—1 classical mods. 83, 2 classics 86.

Dale, Alfred Stanley, born at Rochester , 1869; 2s. George, gent. NON-COLLEGIATE, matric. 23 Jan., 86, aged 17 (from Rochester cathedral choir school); migrated to BRASENOSE 87, B.Mus. 89.

Dale, Charles William, born in London 15 May, 1851; 1s. James Charles, arm. NON-COLLEGIATE, matric. 24 Feb., 81, aged 29; migrated to WADHAM.

Dale, Frank Harry Busbridge, born in London 1872; 1s. Henry James, gen. BALLIOL, matric. 14 Oct., 90, aged 18 (from St. Paul's school), scholar 90; HONOURS:—1 classical mods. 92, accessit Hertford scholarship 91, Craven scholarship 91, Ireland scholarship 92.

Dale, George Richard, born at Rochester 1867; 1s. George, gent. UNIVERSITY COLL., matric. 17 Oct., 85, aged 18 (from Rochester school), exhibitioner 84, B.A. 89, M.A. 92; HONOURS:— 2 classical mods. 87, 2 classics 89.

Dale, Robert John, born at Liverpool 28 July, 1870; 4s. Robert Norris, arm. MERTON, matric. 17 Oct., 88, aged 19, from Harrow.

Dalebrook, John, born at the Cape of Good Hope May, 1868; 2s. John, arm. KEBLE, matric. 17 Oct., 87, aged 19 (from Hurstpierpoint coll.), B.A. 90; HONOURS:—3 history 90.

D'Alessio, Albert Patrick, born at Smyrna March 1872; 2s. John, arm. CHRIST CHURCH, matric. 10 Oct., 90, aged 18, from Radley coll.

Dalgado, Edwardo Avelino Patricio, born at Assazas Goa 8 March, 1867; 4s. Ambrose Louis, gen. NON-COLLEGIATE, matric. 12 Oct., 89, aged 22, from Dr. Wilson's coll., Bombay.

Dalgliesh, Charles Alfred, born at Newcastle-on-Tyne , 1868; 2s. Jonathan, M.R.C.S. TURRELL'S HALL, matric. 7 Dec., 91, aged 23.

Dalison, rev. Roger William Hammond, born at Plaxted, Kent, 1861; 3s. Maximilian Hammond, arm. MERTON, matric. 19 Jan., 80, aged 19, B.A. 84, M.A. 86; rector of Swyre, Dorset, 89.

Daller, Arthur George Henry, born at Kensington, 9 Sept., 1870; o.s. William, of H.M. office of works. BRASENOSE, matric. 14 Oct., 89, aged 19 (from Eastbourne coll.), exhibitioner 89; HONOURS:— 2 classical mods. 91.

Dallin, Francis Thomas, born at Oxford 15 Dec., 1873; o.s. Thomas Francis, fellow and tutor QUEEN'S, deceased. QUEEN'S, matric. 27 Oct., 92, aged 18 (from Rugby), scholar 92.

Dalrymple, rev. the hon. Robert Macgill, born 11 Oct., 1862; 4s. John Hamilton, earl of Stair. CHRIST CHURCH, matric. 13 Oct., 82, aged 20 (from Repton school), B.A. 87, M.A. 91; curate of St. Hilda, Leeds, 91.

Dalton, Fitzgerald Verity, born at Dean, Beds, Aug., 1862; 1s. Henry Robert, arm. CHRIST CHURCH, matric. 4 June, 81, aged 18, from Harrow.

Dalton, rev. Herbert Andrew, M.A., senior student CHRIST CHURCH 75-8, where see.

Dalton, Ormonde Maddock, born at Cardiff, co. Glamorgan, 3 Jan., 1866; 2s. Thomas Masters, arm. NEW COLL., matric. 10 Oct., 84, aged 18 (from Harrow), exhibitioner 84, B.A. 89; HONOURS: —1 classical mods. 86, 1 classics 88.

Dalton, Richard Charles, born at Birkin, Yorks, 1862; 1s. Richard, cler. NON-COLLEGIATE, matric. 18 Oct., 82, aged 20; migrated to BALLIOL.

Dalziel, Frederick Young, born at Islington 1869; 1s. William Alexander, arm. BRASENOSE, matric. 16 Oct., 88, aged 19, from Highgate school.

Daman, rev. Charles, M.A., fellow ORIEL 36-42, where see.

[151]   [152]

Daman, rev. Henry, M.A., fellow MAGDALEN 68-79, where see.

Daman, John Frederick Karl. See Dammann.

Dames, Edward Travers Longworth, born at Dublin 23 May, 1861; 1s. Francis Travers Longworth, Q.C. Ireland. NEW COLL., matric. 16 Oct., 80, aged 19 (from the Charterhouse), B.A. 85; (HONOURS:—2 classical mods. 81 (as D.L.), a law 84 (as L.D.)]; a student of Middle Temple 82 as E. T. Dames Longworth.

Dammann, John Frederick Karl, born at Edgbaston, co. Warwick, 16 Feb., 1865; 1s. Karl Christopher Ludwig, prof. of German in Mason coll., Birmingham. LINCOLN, matric. 17 Oct., 84, aged 19 (from K. Edward's school, Birmingham), B.A. 88, M.A. 92, as Daman; HONOURS:—4 history 88.

d'Angrogno-Pallavicino, Charles Alfred Alexander Manfred, marquis, born 1865; 2s. Alexander Manfred, marquis d'A-P. CHRIST CHURCH, matric. 6 Nov., 83, aged 18.

Daniel, Charles Henry Olive, M.A., fellow WORCESTER 63, where see.

Daniel, George William Trollope, born at Hulton, Essex, 8 Nov., 1865; 1s. William Mayow, cler. PEMBROKE, matric. 27 Oct., 84, aged 18, scholar 84, B.A. 88, M.A. 91; HONOURS:—2 classical schools, 86, 3 classics 88.

Daniel, Wilson Eustace, M.A., Grinfield lecturer 91-3, where see, p. 7.

Daniell, Edwyn Francis Staines, born at Devonport 1871; 1s. Frederick Francis, arm. ST. EDMUND HALL, matric. 24 Jan., 90, aged 19, from New Cross school.

Daniell, rev. Henry James, born at Aldingbourne, Sussex, 1866; 8s. George Frederick, cler. NON-COLLEGIATE, matric. 16 Oct., 86, aged 20 (from Kingsley coll., Westward Ho!), B.A. 89; curate of Rye, Sussex, 90.

Daniell, Reginald Allen, born at Lymington, Hants, 12 March, 1873; 1s. Henry, banker. UNIVERSITY COLL., matric. 17 Oct., 91, aged 18, from Winchester.

Daniels, Ernest Limbert, born at Walthamstow, Essex, 1864; 2s. James John, cler. HERTFORD, matric. 7 May, 89, aged 25 (from Magdalen coll. school), exhibitioner 90.

Daniels, rev. Frank Whitworth James, born in London 1862; 1s. James John, cler. NON-COLLEGIATE, matric. 15 Oct., 81, aged 19 (from Magdalen coll. and Worcester cathedral schools); migrated to HERTFORD, B.A. 85, M.A. 88; conduct of Eton coll. 90.

Daniels, Henry Oswald, born at Whalley Range, co. Lanc., 8 April, 1871; 9s. Thomas, cler. TRINITY, matric. 11 Oct., 90, aged 19, from Manchester gr. school.

Daniels, Sidney Reginald, born at Rodborough, co. Glouc., 18 Sept., 1873; 1s. Joseph, engineer. BALLIOL, matric. 20 Oct., 91, aged 18 (from Wycliffe coll., Stonhouse) (HONOURS:—Boden Sanskrit scholarship 93); selected candidate Indian C.S. 91.

Danks, Eric, born at Cheltenham 30 Sept., 1870; o.s. William, cler. QUEEN'S, matric. 20 Oct., 89, aged 19 (from Ripon gr. school), exhibitioner 89; HONOURS:—2 classical mods. 91.

Darbishire, Bernhard Vernon, born at Dygyfylchi, co. Carnarvon, 8 Aug., 1865; 1s. Vernon, arm. NON-COLLEGIATE, matric. 23 May, 85, aged 19 (from Dresden gymnasium); exhibitioner TRINITY 85, B.A. 89, M.A. 92 (HONOURS:—3 history 89); cartographer to Royal geographical soc. 93.

Darbishire, Francis Vernon, born at Glan-y-coed, co. Carnarvon, 1868; 1s. Vernon, arm. BALLIOL, matric. 19 Oct., 87, aged 19, B.A. 92; HONOURS:—4 chemistry 91.

Darbishire, Otto Vernon, born at Dygyfylchi, co. Carnarvon, 1870; 4s. Vernon, arm. BALLIOL, matric. 18 Oct., 88, aged 18 (from Dresden gymnasium and University coll. Bangor), B.A. 92; HONOURS:—2 botany 92.

Darley, Henry Sylvester, born at Sydney, Australia, 1864; 1s. Frederick Matthew, Q.C., M.L.C. EXETER, matric. 23 April, 84, aged 20, from Shrewsbury school.

Darlington, John, born in London 5 Dec., 1869; o.s. John, gen. LINCOLN, matric. 17 Oct., 89, aged 20 (from University coll. school, London), B.A. 93.

Dauglish, Maurice John, born in London 2 Oct., 1867; 6s. Henry William, gen. MAGDALEN, matric. 21 Oct., 86, aged 19 (from Harrow), B.A. 89 (HONOURS:—3 classical mods. 88), in the University eleven 89, 90.

D'Aumale, H.R.H. the duke, created D.C.L. 17 June, 91.

Daunt, rev. Achilles, born at Cork 20 Jan., 1867; o.s. Achilles, D.D. MERTON, matric. 24 Oct., 85, aged 18 (from Marlborough), B.A. 88 (HONOURS:—4 history 88); curate of St. John the Evangelist, Melcombe Regis, Dorset, 92.

Davenport, rev. Alexander Edward Fynes Clinton, born in Jersey 1862; 52. Charles Edgcombe, arm. NON-COLLEGIATE, matric. 15 Oct., 81, aged 19, B.A. 86, M.A. 89; curate of Porlock and Stoke Pero, Somerset, 91.

Davenport, rev. Francis, born at Skeffington, co. Leicester, 1861; 3s. John Charles, rector, deceased. NON-COLLEGIATE, matric. 14 April, 83, aged 22, B.A. 88, M.A. 90; rector of Maldwell, Northants, 91.

Davenport, John Davies, M.A., fellow BRASENOSE 64-76, where see.

Davenport, Ralph Tichborne, born in London Jan., 1873; 1s. George Horatio, cler. CHRIST CHURCH, matric. 9 April, 92, aged 19, from Eton.

Davenport, Thomas Marriott, M.A., PEMBROKE, where see.

Davenport, William Bromley, born in London 1862; 1s. William, M.P. NON-COLLEGIATE, matric. 20 Nov., 89, aged 18 (from Eton); migrated to BALLIOL; of Capesthorne, Cheshire, J.P., M.P. Cheshire (Macclesfield division) 86.

Davey, Charles Robert, born in Jersey 1849; 2s. James, gen. CHARSLEY'S HALL, matric. 24 April, 90, aged 41.

Davey, Ernest William Woods, born at Leyton, Essex, 1871; o.s. William Thomas, D.Med., M.R.C.S. LINCOLN, matric. 23 Oct., 91, aged 20, from Forest school.

Davey, sir Horace, Q.C., M.A., hon. fellow UNIVERSITY COLL., 84, where see, p. 31.

Davey, Horace Scott, born in London 25 April, 1865; 1s. sir Horace. ORIEL, matric. 27 Oct., 83, aged 18 (from Rugby); lieut. 18th Hussars 89.

David, Albert Augustus, born at Exeter 19 May, 1867; 2s. William, cler. QUEEN'S, matric. 30 Oct., 85, aged 18 (from Exeter gr. school), scholar 85, B.A. 89; HONOURS:—1 classical mods. 87, 1 classics 89.

David, rev. Arthur Evan, born at St. Fagans, Cardiff, co. Glam., 1 July, 1861; 3s. William, rector 57. NEW COLL., matric. 17 Jan., 80, aged 18 (from Magdalen coll. school), B.A. 83, M.A. 87 (HONOURS:—3 classical mods. 81, 3 classics 83), examining chaplain to bishop of Brisbane 91.

David, William, M.A., fellow JESUS COLL. 45-48, where see.

David, Harold Llewelyn, born at Laugharne, co. Carmarthen, 4 April, 1873; 2s. Samuel Sinclair, gent. QUEEN'S, matric. 27 Oct., 92, aged 19 (from Llandovery coll.), scholar 92.

Davidson, Andrew, born at Newcastle-on-Tyne 8 Aug., 1867; o.s. James, gen., deceased. NON-COLLEGIATE, matric. 17 Oct., 91, aged 24, from New coll. school Oxford.

Davidson, Edward Fitzwilliam, born at Chipping Sodbury, co. Gloucester, 22 June, 1868; 2s. Jonas Pascal, cler, NEW COLL., matric. 14 Oct., 87, aged 19 (from Winchester), scholar 87, B.A. 91; HONOURS :—1 classical mods. 89, 1 classics 91.

Davidson, Frederick Lewis Maitland, born at the Hague, Holland, 22 Dec., 1873; 1s. Frederick Maitland, of London, merchant. ST. JOHN'S, matric. 15 Oct., 92, aged 18 (from Winchester), scholar 92.

Davidson, George Gillies, born at Newhills, Aberdeenshire, 25 Nov., 1872; 1s. George, gen. NEW COLL., matric. 16 Oct., 91; aged 18, from Clifton coll.

Davidson, Lionel, born in London 1868; 3s. William, gent. BALLIOL, matric. 19 Oct., 86, aged 18 (from University coll. school, and University coll. London), B.A. 89 (HONOURS :— Indian languages 89); assist. collector and magistrate of North Arcot, Madras C.S. 88.

Davidson, Nigel George, born in London 29 Oct., 1873; 2s. Alexander, M.A., paper manufacturer. NEW COLL., matric. 14 Oct., 92, aged 18 (from the Charterhouse), exhibitioner 91.

Davidson, Norman James, born at Wortley, Yorks, 19 Dec., 1860; 1s. James, vicar of Christ Church, Chester. QUEEN'S, matric. 25 Oct., 80, aged 19 (from Royal institution school Liverpool), B.A. 88.

Davidson, Randall Thomas, M.A. TRINITY, D.D. by diploma 2 Dec., 1890, dean of Windsor 83-90, and bishop of Rochester 90. See *Al. Ox.* and series, 343.

Davidson, Robert Pringle, born at Inch, N.B., 1 July, 1872; 5s. John, gent. TRINITY, matric. 15 Oct., 92, aged 20 (from Edinburgh university), exhibitioner 90.

Davidson, William Dalzell, born at Kensington 18 Oct., 1871; 1s. Alexander, arm. MAGDALEN, matric. 14 Oct., 89, aged 18 (from the Charterhouse); HONOURS :—3 classical mods. 91.

Davie, Henry Augustus Ferguson-, born at Abbots Leigh, Somerset, 22 Aug., 1865; 2s. William Augustus, a clerk in House of Commons. NEW COLL., matric. 10 Oct., 84, aged 19, from Marlborough coll.

Davie, Henry Herrick Ferguson-, born at Yelverton, Norfolk, 26 June, 1867; 2s. Charles Robert, cler. ST. EDMUND HALL, matric. 18 Oct., 86, aged 19, from Marlborough coll.

Davies, rev. Arthur Edward, born at Kirk Andrews, Isle of Man, 8 Dec., 1866; 2s. Arthur, gent. QUEEN'S, matric. 30 Oct., 85, aged 18 (from Wem and Oswestry gr. schools), B.A. 89, M.A. 92 (HONOURS :—3 theology 88); curate of Great Marlow, Bucks, 90.

Davies, Arthur Picton Saunders-, born at l'entre, co. Pembroke, 1863; 1s. Arthur Henry Saunders, arm. CHRIST CHURCH, matric. 21 May, 80, aged 17 (from Eton); migrated to DOWNING COLL., CAMBRIDGE, 26 Jan., 83; of Pentre, co. Pembroke.

Davies, Charles Joseph, born at Llanwrin, co. Montgomery, 16 Oct., 1864; 2s. Thomas, rector, deceased. QUEEN'S, matric. 22 Oct., 83, aged 19, B.A. 91, M.A. 92.

Davies, Charles Robert, born in Virginia 1870; 1s. Thomas William, gen. HERTFORD, matric. 14 Oct., 89, aged 19 (from Worcester cathedral school), scholar 88 ; HONOURS :—3 classical mods. 91.

Davies, David Rhys, born at Llanilid, co. Glamorgan, 21 Aug., 1860; 3s. Thomas Morgan, rector. NEW COLL., matric. 17 Jan., 80, aged 19 (from Clifton coll.); migrated to NEW INN HALL, (BALLIOL), 87 (HONOURS :—3 classical mods. 81); student Inner Temple 82.

Davies, David Thomas, born at Lampeter, co. Cardigan, 2 May, 1867; 2s. Thomas, gen. NON-COLLEGIATE, matric. 13 Oct., 88, aged 21 (from St. David's coll. school Lampeter, and Christ coll. Brecon); migrated to JESUS COLL. 18 Oct., 90, B.A. 91.

Davies, Edward Owen, born at Bettwys, co. Merioneth, 1865; 1s. Robert, pleb. NON-COLLEGIATE, matric. 30 Jan., 90, aged 25, from University coll. Aberystwith.

Davies, Edward Read, born at Stratford, Wilts, 12 Jan., 1869; 1s. Edward, gen. BALLIOL, matric. 18 Oct., 88, aged 19 (from Westminster school); brother of Evan L.

Davies, Ernest Salter, born at Haverfordwest, 25 Oct., 1872; 4s. Thomas, principal of Baptist college, hon. D.D. America. JESUS COLL., matric. 20 Oct., 91, aged 18 (from University coll., Aberystwith), scholar 91.

Davies, Evan Lewis, born at Stratford-on-Avon, 16 June, 1870; 2s. Edward, of West Dulwich, Surrey, gen., deceased. BALLIOL, matric. 17 Oct., 89, aged 19 (from Westminster), B.A. 92; brother of Edward Read.

Davies, rev. Francis Parry Watkin-, born at Dolgelly, co. Merioneth, 15 Jan., 1862; 1s. David, rector of Llanchyddlad, Anglesey. JESUS COLL., matric. 29 Jan., 81, aged 19 (from Magdalen coll. school); migrated to NON-COLLEGIATE, Easter 82, and to MAGDALEN, Michaelmas 82, B.A. 84, M.A. 88; vicar of Llanfachreth, co. Merioneth, 88.

Davies, Gabriel Lloyd, born near Sandhurst, Berks, 3 Aug., 1864; 1s. Gabriel John, vicar of Bettws-y-Coed. LINCOLN, matric. 17 Oct., 84, aged 20 (from Derby school), exhibitioner 84, B.A. 88; HONOURS :—3 classical mods. 86, 4 classics 88.

Davies, George Sevier, born at Monmouth 28 April, 1868; 1s. Daniel George, cler. JESUS COLL., matric. 19 Oct., 87, aged 19 (from Rossall school), exhibitioner ORIEL 89, B.A. 92; HONOURS :—3 classical mods. 89.

Davies, Gilbert Hughes, born at Dolanog, co. Montgomery, 31 March, 1870; 5s. John, vicar of Llanynys, co. Denbigh. JESUS COLL., matric. 14 Oct., 89, aged 19 (from Ruthin gr. school), B.A. 93.

Davies, Griffith Ormond, born at Cardigan 1865; 2s. Thomas, gent. NEW INN HALL, matric. 19 Oct., 83, aged 19; of BALLIOL 87.

Davies, Herbert Mayo, born at Longhope, co. Gloucester, 18 Oct., 1864; 2s. Evan James, cler. MAGDALEN, matric. 24 Jan., 84, aged 19 (from Clifton coll.) (HONOURS :—3 classical mods. 85); bar.-at-law, Middle Temple, 88.

Davies, Isaac Redwood, born at Neath, co. Glamorgan, 2 Aug., 1870; 1s. Edward, arm. BRASENOSE, matric. 14 Oct., 89, aged 19, from Shrewsbury gr. school.

Davies, James Arthur, born at Bellamy, Madras, 1 June 1873; 1s. John Acworth, of Indian C.S. NEW COLL., matric. 14 Oct., 92, aged 19, from Rugby.

Davies, rev. John, born at Bolton. co. Lanc., 1866; o.s. David, arm. BRASENOSE, matric. 7 June, 84, aged 18 (from Manchester gr. school), B.A. 88, M.A. 91 (HONOURS :—3 theology 88); curate of St. Leonard, Bridgnorth, 89.

Davies, John, born at Tynfron, co. Cardigan, 27 Oct., 1868; 2s. Edwin, gen. JESUS COLL., matric. 16 Oct., 88, aged 19 (from Lampeter and Carmarthen gr. schools), exhibitioner 88, B.A. 91; HONOURS :— 3 classical mods. 90, 3 classics 92.

Davies, John Humphreys, born at Courtmawr, co. Cardigan, 15 April, 1871; 2s. Robert Joseph, gen. NON-COLLEGIATE, matric. 11 Oct. 90, aged 19 (from University coll. school, London, and Aberystwith coll.); migrated to LINCOLN Oct. 91.

Davies, rev. John Lodwick, born at Lampeter, co. Cardigan, 1864; 1s. Thomas, gent. NON-COLLEGIATE, matric. 13 Oct., 84, aged 20 (from Llandovery coll.), B.A. 89; curate of Portmadoc, co. Carnarvon, 89-91.
Davies, John Timothy, born at Llanachilyn, co. Merioneth, 25 May, 1869; 1s. John, vicar of Blaenau, co. Merioneth. WADHAM, matric. 17 Oct., 82, aged 20 (from Brecon coll.), scholar 82, B.A. 86, M.A. 89; HONOURS:—1 classical mods. 84, 2 classics.
Davies, John Wellington, born at Headington, Oxon, 19 July, 1873; 2s. Howell, gen. deceased. NON-COLLEGIATE, matric. 17 Oct., 91, aged 18, from St. John's school, Cowley, Oxford.
Davies, John William Saint Aubrey, born at Ramsden, Essex, , 1868; 1s. John Smallman, arm. BRASENOSE, matric. 14 Oct., 89, aged 21, from St. Edward's school, Summertown.
Davies, rev. John Wynne, born at Llanwrst, co. Denbigh, 13 Feb., 1865; 2s. John, cler. JESUS COLL., matric. 16 Oct., 84, aged 19, B.A. 88, M.A. 91.
Davies, rev. Joseph Sanger, born at Haverfordwest, co. Pembroke, , 1849; 1s. Thomas Wincher, gent. NON-COLLEGIATE, matric. 15 Oct., 81, aged 32 (from Highbury training college); migrated to QUEEN'S, B.A. 85, M.A. 88 (HONOURS:—2 theology 85); vicar of St. Matthias, Birmingham, 86-8, and of St. Mary Bredin, Canterbury, 88.
Davies, rev. Llewelyn Lloyd, born at Typicca, co. Carmarthen, , 1860; 3s. Henry, gen. JESUS COLL., matric. 19 Oct., 81, aged 21 (from Llandovery coll.), B.A. 85, M.A. 88; HONOURS:—3 mathematical mods. 83, 3 theology 85.
Davies, Maurice Llewellyn, born at Eardiston, co. Worc., 13 Sept., 1864; 4s. James Llewellyn, cler. BALLIOL, matric. 16 Oct., 83, aged 19 (from Marlborough coll.), scholar 82; HONOURS:—1 classical mods. 84, 2 classics 87.
Davies, Myles Fenton, born at Adlington, co. Lane., 1867; 2s. Benjamin, gent. NEW COLL., matric. 15 Oct., 86, aged 19 (from Winchester), B.A. 89; HONOURS:—1 law 89.
Davies, rev. Owen, born at Aberystwith 29 April, 1866; y.s. David, gen. JESUS COLL., matric. 20 Oct., 86, aged 20 (from University coll., Aberystwith), B.A. 90 (HONOURS:—3 mathematical mods. 88, 4 mathematics, 90); curate of Llanfair-Talhaiarn, co. Denbigh, 91.
Davies, rev. Reginald Aubrey de Vere Hart-, born at Gisburn, Yorks, , 1868; 1s. John Hart, cler. KEBLE, matric. 19 Oct., 86, aged 18 (from Clifton coll.), B.A. 90.
Davies, Robert, born at Llanbeblig, co. Carnarvon, 4 Nov., 1869; o.s. John, gent. NEW COLL., matric. 14 Oct., 92, aged 22, from University coll., North Wales.
Davies, Robert Bennet Wynne, born at Gwytherin, co. Denbigh, 18 Jan., 1873; 3s. David, vicar of Llansilin, Salop. UNIVERSITY COLL., matric. 17 Oct., 91, aged 18, from Oswestry gr. school.
Davies, Tabor, born at Melbourne, Victoria, Australia, , 1862; 6s. Charles, solicitor. NON-COLLEGIATE, matric. 17 Oct., 91, aged 29, from Melbourne university.
Davies, Thomas, born at Llansantfraid, co. Cardigan, 6 June, 1864; 9s. Evan, pleb. JESUS COLL., matric. 14 Oct., 89, aged 25, from Llanor school.
Davies, rev. Thomas Enoch Pritchard, born at Pembury, co. Carmarthen, 2 June, 1869; 3s. John, vicar of Llangurhen, co. Carmarthen. WADHAM, matric. 14 Oct., 89, aged 20 (from Shrewsbury gr. school), B.A. 92; HONOURS:—3 classical mods. 91.
Davies, Thomas Harold, born at Leeds , 1867; 2s. John, gent. UNIVERSITY COLL., matric. 18 Oct., 86, aged 19 (from Leeds gr. school), scholar 86, B.A. 90; HONOURS:—2 classical mods. 88, 2 classics 90.

Davies, Walter Harold, born at Bowdon, Cheshire, Aug., 1865; 1s. Walter, gent. NON-COLLEGIATE, matric.,13 Oct., 84, aged 19, from Harrow.
Davies, William, born at Llanelly, co. Carmarthen, 30 March, 1858; 5s. William, gen. NON-COLLEGIATE, matric. 6 Feb., 90, aged 31, from Carmarthen training coll.
Davies, William, born at Festiniog, co. Merioneth, 1872; y.s. William, esquire. ST. JOHN'S, matric. 17 Oct., 91, aged 19, from Rugby.
Davies, William Arthur, born at Colwyn, co. Carnarvon, 1869; 1s. Daniel Owen, cler. JESUS COLL., matric. 14 Oct., 89, aged 20.
Davies, William Crowther, born at Cloverly, Salop, 18 May, 1868; 2s. Edward, gen. EXETER, matric. 21 Oct., 86, aged 18 (from Wolverhampton gr. school), B.A. 89; HONOURS:—2 theology 89.
Davies, William Robert, born at Chorlton, co. Lanc., 27 June, 1870; 1s. William, of Bolton, gen., deceased. BALLIOL, matric. 20 Jan., 90, aged 19 (from Manchester gr. school), scholar 90; HONOURS:—2 mathematical mods. 91.
Davis, Arthur William, born at Burrington, Devon, 1861; 3s. Samuel, cler. BALLIOL, matric. 1 Nov., 80, aged 19 (from Rossall school); deputy commissioner, Assam, 82.
Davis, rev. Charles, born at Box, Wilts, 1851; 3s. John Poole, C.E. NON-COLLEGIATE, matric. 8 May, 82, aged 30 (from King's coll., London); migrated to EXETER 11 Oct., 84, B.A. 85, M.A. 88 (HONOURS:—2 theology 85); vicar of Holy Trinity, Hinckley, 88.
Davis, Charles Thomas, born at Brecon 1873; 1s. Thomas, engineer. BALLIOL, matric. 18 Oct., 92, aged 19 (from Brecon coll.), scholar 91.
Davis, Cyprian Corben, born at Reading, Berks, 8 Jan., 1873; 3s. Francis, gen. NON-COLLEGIATE, matric. 17 Oct., 91, aged 18 (from Reading school); brother of Francis N.
Davis, David, born at South Hylton, co. Durham, 1851; 2s. Thomas, gen. NON-COLLEGIATE, matric. 11 Oct., 90, aged 39 (from University coll., Manchester.
Davis, Edgar Crofts, born at Hinckley, co. Leicester, 24 Aug., 1869; 42. Samuel, arm. TRINITY, matric. 15 Oct., 87, aged 18 (from Rossall school), B.A. 92; HONOURS:—2 history 91.
Davis, Edward Arthur, born in London 1862; o.s. Edward May, arm. WADHAM, matric. 21 Oct., 80, aged 18, B.A. 83, M.A. 87.
Davis, Ernest de Graves, born at Melbourne Aug., 1867; 1s. Charles Percy, gen. BRASENOSE, matric. 20 Oct., 86, aged 19, from Wellington coll.
Davis, Francis Nevill, born at Reading, Berks, 4 May, 1867; 1s. Francis, gen. NON-COLLEGIATE, matric. 17 Oct., 91, aged 24.
Davis, Henry Desmond Fitzgerald, born at Sheffield 1871; 3s. Gronno, arm. ORIEL, matric. 22 Oct., 91, aged 19 (from Clifton coll.), scholar 90; HONOURS:—2 classical mods. 92.
Davis, Henry William Carless, born at Painswick, co. Glouc., 13 Jan., 1874; 1s. Henry Frederick Alexander, solicitor, deceased. BALLIOL, matric. 20 Oct., 91 aged 17 (from Weymouth coll.), scholar 90.
Davis, James, born at Leominster, co. Hereford, 26 Jan., 1869; 4s. James, manufacturer. JESUS COLL., matric. 18 Oct., 92, aged 24 (from University coll., Aberystwith), exhibitioner 92.
Davis, John Tyssul, born at Llandyssul, co. Cardigan, 12 June, 1869; 1s. David, gen. NON-COLLEGIATE, matric. 17 Oct., 91, aged 23, from University coll., Aberystwith.

Davis, Richard Cecil, born in London 9 June, 1873; 1s. Charles, gent. WORCESTER, matric. 18 Oct., 92 (from St. Paul's school), exhibitioner 92.
Davis, Robert Augustus, born at Bath 1861; o.s. Peter, gent. ST. EDMUND HALL, matric. 24 April, 84, aged 23; bar.-at-law, Middle Temple, 88.
Davis, Stanley Percy, born in London 23 Dec., 1866; 6s. Henry Newnham, arm. HERTFORD, matric. 14 Oct., 89, aged 22, from Wellington coll.
Davis, Stuart Gerald, born in London 1867; 7s. Henry, gent. PEMBROKE, matric. 1 Feb., 86, aged 19 (from Harrow), B.A. 89.
Davison, John Robert, born at Seal, Kent, Oct., 1869; 2s. John Robert, arm. CHRIST CHURCH, matric. 1 June, 88, aged 18, from Harrow.
Davison, William Henry, born at Ballymena, co. Antrim, Feb., 1872; 1s. Richard, arm. KEBLE, matric. 11 Oct., 90, aged 18, from Shrewsbury gr. school.
Davisson, James Weatherell, born at Welling, Kent, 1868; 1s. James, gent. UNIVERSITY COLL., matric. 18 Oct., 86, aged 18, exhibitioner 86; HONOURS:—3 classical mods. 88.
Davy, Francis Walter Hyne, born in London 13 Oct., 1871; o.s. Francis Hyne, gen. NON-COLLEGIATE, matric. 11 Oct., 90, aged 18, from Christ's hospital.

Davy, Henry Washington, born at Ringwood, Hants, 23 April, 1871; 3s. Henry Samuel, solicitor. MAGDALEN, matric. 14 Oct., 89, aged 18 (from Bradfield coll.); HONOURS:—3 classical mods. 91.
Davy, Herbert Tanner, born at Lynton, Devon, 11 June, 1865; 2s. William Tanner, cler. ST. MARY HALL, matric. 23 April, 84, aged 18 (from Winchester); migrated to EXETER, B.A. 87.
Dawbarn, Albert Yelverton, born at Liverpool 1862; 5s. William, gent. BALLIOL, matric. 15 Dec., 85, aged 23 (from Liverpool coll.); HONOURS: —2 mathematical mods. 87.
Dawes, James Arthur, born at Lee, Kent, 1866; o.s. Richard, gent. UNIVERSITY COLL., matric. 17 Oct., 85, aged 19, B.A. 88, M.A. and B.C.L. 92; HONOURS:—3 law 88, 3 civil law 90.
Dawkins, Horace Christian, born in London 1868; 5s. Clinton George, arm. BALLIOL, matric. 19 Oct., 86, aged 18, (from Eton), B.A. 92; HONOURS:—4 classics 90.
Dawkins, Thomas Frederic, born at Farmington, co. Glouc., 22 Aug., 1867; 4s. James Annesley, cler. BALLIOL, matric. 19 Oct., 86, aged 19 (from Rugby), B.A. 90; HONOURS:—3 classical mods. 88, a law 90.
Dawkins, William Boyd, M.A., hon. fellow JESUS COLL. 82, where see.

EAST GATE, NOW DEMOLISHED.—*From Skelton.*

Dawson, rev. Charles, born in Stafford 4 Nov., 1864; 3s. Edward John, gen. NON-COLLEGIATE, matric. 15 Jan., 87, aged 20 (from K. Edward's high school Stafford); migrated to EXETER 22 Jan., 89, B.A. 90.

Dawson, Geoffrey William, born at Gipsy Hill, Middx., 7 March, 1874; 4s. James, gen. TRINITY, matric. 17 Oct., 91, aged 19 (from the Charterhouse); selected candidate Indian C.S. 91.

Dawson, Wilfrid Finch, born at Uttoxeter, co. Stafford, 9 March, 1871; 3s. Arthur Finch, late capt. 6th Dragoon guards. NEW COLL., matric. 10 Oct., 90, aged 19 (from the Charterhouse); HONOURS:—2 classical mods. 92.

Day, rev. Arthur John, born at Wixoe, Essex, 1862; 5s. Edmund, cler. NON-COLLEGIATE, matric. 15 April, 82, aged 20; migrated to CHARSLEY HALL, B.A. 88; curate of West Gorton St. Mark, Lancashire, 89.

Day, rev. Charles John, born in Calcutta Aug., 1868; 1s. Charles Martin Hill, gent. ST. JOHN'S, matric. 15 Oct., 87, aged 19 (from Bedford school), B.A. 91; HONOURS:—4 theology 91.

Day, Charles Nevile, born at Easton, Northants, 10 July, 1871; 1s. Nevile, arm. TRINITY, matric. 11 Oct., 90, aged 19, from Rugby.

Day, Edward, born at Great Hale, co. Lanc., 1858; 3s. Edmund, cler. NON-COLLEGIATE, matric. 15 April, 82, aged 24, from High Wycombe gr. school.'

Day, rev. Ernest, born at Bredhurst, Kent, April, 1866; 2s. Hermitage Charles, cler. KEBLE, matric. 14 Oct., 84, aged 18 (from St. Leonard's-on-Sea, school), B.A. 88; vicar of Abbey Cwnihir, Radnor, 91.

Day, George, M.A., student CHRIST CHURCH 30-42, where see.

Day, George Ernest, born at Leyborn, Yorks, 18 April, 1868; 1s. George, cler. WORCESTER, matric. 17 Oct., 87, aged 19 (from Ripon gr. school), B.A. 91; HONOURS:—2 theology 91.

Day, rev. Gerard Cecil, born at Southsea, Hants,. March, 1864; 2s. Gerard James, gent. KEBLE, matric. 16 Oct., 83, aged 19 (from Norwich gr. school), B.A. 86, M.A. 91; curate of St. Michael and All Angel's, Northampton, 88.

Day, Henry George Cyril, born at Barnsley, Yorks, 2 March, 1872; o.s. Henry Josiah, M.A. cler. deceased. ST. JOHN'S, matric. 17 Jan., 91, aged 18 (from Merchant Taylors' school), exhibitioner 90.

PART OF LITTLE GATE, NOW DEMOLISHED.—*From Skelton.*

163   DAY. —— MATRICULATIONS, 1880 TO 1892. —— DELABERE.   164

Day, Horatio Edmund Valentine, born at Hackney, Middx., 14 Feb., 1871; 1s. Edward Stainton, arm. deceased. HERTFORD, matric. 14 Oct., 90, aged 19 (from St. Paul's school); HONOURS :— 3 classical mods. 92.

Day, Louis Ernest, born at Buckland, Devon, 4 March, 1866; 6s. George Hill, gent. ST. MARY HALL, matric. 24 Oct., 85, aged 19, B.A. 91.

Day, Percival Langston, born in London Sept., 1871; 2s. William Henry, D.Med. KEBLE, matric. 15 Oct., 92, aged 21, from King's coll., London.

Daymond, Herbert George, born at Brompton, Middx., 7 Dec., 1862; 1s. Albert, cler. KEBLE, matric. 18 Oct., 81, aged 18 (from Rugby), army tutor.

Deakin, Carrick Ransome, born at Ellen-How, Grange-over-Sands , 1872; 2s. Joseph, bar.-at-law. CORPUS CHRISTI, matric. 20 Oct., 91, aged 19, from Rugby.

Deakin, Charles Frederick, born at Cheadle, Cheshire, June, 1862; 5s. James Henry, arm. MERTON, matric. 18 Oct., 81, aged 19 (from Grange-over-sands school), B.A. 84, M.A. 89; bar.-at-law, Lincoln's Inn, 86.

Deakin, Ernest Newton, born at Sandbach, Cheshire, 26 Oct., 1865; 5s. James Henry, arm. MERTON, matric. 16 Oct., 84, aged 18, from Rugby.

Deakin, Francis Thomas, born at Wednesbury, co. Stafford, March, 1866; 1s. Thomas, gent. CHRIST CHURCH, matric. 12 June, 86, aged 19.

Deakin, Rupert, born at Birmingham, 10 July, 1852; 1s. Andrew, gent. BALLIOL, matric. 18 Oct., 81, aged 29 (from Handsworthbridge-trust school (NEW COLL., matric. 13 Oct., 88, aged 23), B.A. 88, M.A. 89; HONOURS :—2 mathematical mods. 82, 1 classical mods. 83, 2 classics 85.

Deakin, William Augustus, born at Moseley, co. Warwick, 1860; 1s. Francis, arm. MERTON, matric. 15 May, 80, aged 20.

Dean, Edward Brietzcke, D.C.L., fellow ALL SOULS' 36-55, where see.

Dean, Herbert Samuel, born in London 8 March, 1870; 1s. Samuel, gen. HERTFORD, matric. 25 Oct., 89, aged 19, from city of London school.

Dean, James Edward Troughton, born at Over Tabley, Cheshire, 10 Aug., 1870; 1s. Charles Kilshaw, arm. TRINITY, matric. 13 Oct., 88, aged 18 (from Marlborough coll.), B.A. 91.

Deane, Alfred Reginald, born at Queenstown, co. Cork, 26 Aug., 1864; 1s. Edward Pope, arm. QUEEN'S, matric. 21 Oct., 87, aged 23 (from Trinity coll., Dublin, matric. 11 Oct., 81, and B.A. 84.)

Deane, Charles Henry, M.A., fellow MAGDALEN, 55-63, where see.

Deane, rev. Edward Hugh, born at Ashen, Essex, Jan., 1862; 3s. William John, cler. KEBLE, matric. 18 Oct., 81, aged 19, B.A. 84 (HONOURS :— 2 history 84); curate of Boyton, Suffolk, 90.

Deane, Francis Hugh, M.A., fellow MAGDALEN 43-54, where see.

Deane, rev. Frederick Llewellyn, born at Stainton-le-Vale, co. Lincoln, Sept., 1868; 5s. Francis Hugh, cler. KEBLE, matric. 17 Oct., 87, aged 19 (from Rugby private school), B.A. 90 (HONOURS :— 2 theology 90); curate of Kettering 91.

Deane, Henry, B.D., fellow ST. JOHN'S 56-92, where see.

Deane, Horace Clifford, born in the Isle of Barbados 25 March, 1872; 1s. John Christie, sugar planter. ST. JOHN'S, matric. 11 Oct., 90, aged 18, from Harrison coll., Barbados.

Deane, right hon. sir James Parker, D.C.L., fellow ST. JOHN'S 29-41, where see.

Dear, Philip John, M.A., NON-COLLEGIATE 91, where see.

Dearden, John Lister, born at Horley, Yorks. 1865; 1s. John, gent. NON-COLLEGIATE, matric. 26 Oct., 85, aged 20, from Bradford gr. school.

Dearmer, rev. Percy, born in London 27 Feb., 1867; 2s. Thomas, gent. CHRIST CHURCH, matric. 12 June, 86, aged 19 (from Westminster school), B.A. 90 (HONOURS :— 3 history 90); curate of St. Anne, Lambeth, 91.

Deazeley, John Howard, M.A. MERTON, where see.

Debenham, Frank Bridgewater, born at Cheshunt, Herts, 25 Dec., 1865; 1s. Frank Gissing, gent. MAGDALEN, matric. 16 Oct., 84, aged 18 (from Winchester), B.A. 88.

Debenham, Horace Bentley, born at Cheshunt, Herts, 9 March, 1868; 2s. Frank Gissing, gent. MAGDALEN, matric. 22 Oct., 87, aged 19, from Winchester.

De-Bourbel, rev. Alard Charles, born in London 24 March, 1866; 1s. Augustus Alfred, arm. MERTON, matric. 16 Oct., 84, aged 18, B.A. 88, M.A. 91 (HONOURS :— 2 theology 88); vicar of Crowhurst, Surrey, 91.

De-Brett, Edward Adolphus, born at Meemaeeca, E. Indies, 21 June, 1867; 1s. Alfred, col. 18th N.I. NEW COLL., matric. 15 Oct., 86, aged 19 (from Winchester), assist. commissioner Narsinghpur, central province, 88.

De-Burgh, William George, born at New Wandsworth, Surrey, 24 Oct., 1866; o.s. William, arm. MERTON, matric. 24 Oct., 85, aged 18 (from Winchester), postmaster 85; B.A. 90; HONOURS :— 2 classical mods. 87, 1 classics 89.

De-Carteret, rev. George Frederick Cecil, born at New Wandsworth, Surrey, 19 March, 1866; 2s. Herbert Guille, late R.N. WADHAM, matric. 19 Oct., 85, aged 19, (from Western coll., Brighton), B.A. 89, M.A. 92; curate of St. Dunstan, Canterbury, 89.

De-Carteret, Reginald Malet, born in Jersey 25 March, 1865; 1s. Edward Charles Malet, arm. CHRIST CHURCH, matric. 25 May, 83, aged 18 (from Westminster school), B.A. 87 (HONOURS :— 3 law 87); bar.-at-law, Inner Temple, 88.

De-Castro, rev. Edward Henry Gilchrist, born at Putney, Surrey, Jan., 1868; o.s. Henry, gent. KEBLE, matric. 19 Oct., 86, aged 18 (from Brighton coll.); migrated to QUEEN'S, B.A. 90 (HONOURS :— 3 classical mods. 88, 2 history 90); curate of Beaminster, Wilts, 91.

De-Chair, rev. Frederick Beauchamp Cooper, born at Morley St. Botholph, Norfolk, 1 March, 1865; 1s. Frederick Blackett, rector. NEW COLL., matric. 88, M.A. 91 (HONOURS :— 2 classical mods. 86, 2 classics 88); curate of Weybridge 90.

Decie, Francis Edward Prescott, born in Corfu 19 July, 1861; 1s. Richard Prescott, arm. NEW COLL., matric. 16 Oct., 80, aged 19 (from Harrow), B.A. 84 (HONOURS :— 2 classical mods. 82, 3 law 85); bar.-at-law, Lincoln's Inn, 87.

Deedes, rev. Arthur Gordon, born at Heydour, co. Lincoln, 4 Feb., 1861; 3s. Gordon Frederick, cler. ORIEL, matric. 20 Jan., 80, aged 18 (from Halleybury), B.A. 83, M.A. 86 (HONOURS :— 3 theology 83); curate of St. John the Divine, Kennington, 86.

Delabere, John Baghot-, born at Prestbury, co. Glouc., 28 March, 1870; 3s. John, cler. WORCESTER, matric. 16 Oct., 88, aged 18 (from Brighton coll.), B.A. 91.

Delabere, rev. William St. John, born at Brixton, Surrey, 8 Sept., 1864; 2s. Henry Thomas, arm. TRINITY, matric. 15 Oct., 83, aged 19 (from Dulwich coll.), B.A. 87, M.A. 90 (HONOURS:—3 history 87); curate of Holy Trinity, Eltham, 91.

Delacour, Robert William, born at Cork 1862; 1s. Robert William, cler. CHARSLEY'S HALL, matric. 4 Nov., 84, aged 22.

De-la-Fosse, Claude Fraser, born in India 10 Feb., 1868; 2s. Henry Gordon, colonel, C.B. TRINITY, matric. 16 Oct., 86, aged 18 (from Bath coll.), B.A. 90; HONOURS:—3 law 90.

De-la-Hey, Edward William Martin Oldridge, born at Marple, Cheshire, 1868; 1s. Edward Oldridge, cler. UNIVERSITY COLL., matric. 17 Oct., 85, aged 17 (from Manchester gr. school), scholar 84, B.A. 91; HONOURS:—1 classical mods. 87, 1 classics 89, Aubrey Moore theological studentship 91.

De-la-Hey, Richard Willis, born at Woking, Surrey, 3 June, 1873; 1s. George, M.A., cler. UNIVERSITY COLL., matric. 15 Oct., 92, aged 19 (from Oundle school), scholar 92.

Delevingne, Malcolm, born in London 11 Oct., 1868; 2s. Ernest Thomas Shaw, gent. TRINITY, matric. 15 Oct., 87, aged 19 (from city of London school), scholar 86, B.A. 91 (HONOURS:—1 classical mods. 89, 1 classics 91); in home office.

De Lisle, Hirzell Frederick, born at Romford, Essex, 14 Dec., 1868; 1s. Hirzel Cary, vicar of Galleywood, Essex. LINCOLN, matric. 18 Oct., 88, aged 19, from Brentwood school.

Dell, Robert Edward, born at Marlborough, Wilts, 1 April, 1865; 1s. Robert, cler. UNIVERSITY COLL., matric. 11 Oct., 84, aged 19, from Birmingham school.

Demaüs, rev. Robert George Sutker, born at Chelsea 30 Oct., 1868; o.s. Robert, cler. LINCOLN, matric. 21 Oct., 87, aged 18 (from Edinburgh university), B.A. 90 (HONOURS:—2 history 90); curate of Waltham St. Lawrence, Berks, 91.

Dempsey, Henry Blundell, born at Walton, co. Lanc., 26 Dec., 1864; 3s. Arthur, of Wallasey, Cheshire, gent. MAGDALEN, matric. 10 Oct., 83, aged 18 (from the Charterhouse), B.A. 86; brother of the next-named.

Dempsey, rev. Hugh Paul, born at Walton, co. Lanc., 29 June, 1862; 2s. Arthur, gent. MAGDALEN, matric. 16 Oct., 80, aged 18 (from the Charterhouse), B.A. 84; curate of Sneinton, Notts, 91; brother of the last-named.

Dempster, Robert Hyder, born at Liverpool 22 Sept., 1869; 1s. Robert, gen. NON-COLLEGIATE, matric. 13 Oct., 88, aged 19 (from Liverpool institute), exhibitioner LINCOLN 89; HONOURS:—2 classical mods. 90.

Denbigh, John Halliday, born at Leeds 1868; 1s. John, gen. BRASENOSE, matric. 20 Oct., 87, aged 19 (from Bath coll.), scholar 86, B.A. 91; HONOURS:—1 mathematical mods. 89, 2 mathematics 91.

Dendy, Arthur, B.A., B.C.L., fellow UNIVERSITY COLL. 73, where see page 29

Dendy, Robert Arthur, born at Chichester 5 Sept., 1873; o.s. Charles Robert, late of East Grinstead, Sussex, banker, deceased. UNIVERSITY COLL., matric. 15 Oct., 92, aged 19, from Brighton coll.

Denham, Thomas, born in London 23 April, 1856; 4s. John Burden, gent. NON-COLLEGIATE, matric. 15 Oct., 81, aged 25 (from St. Mary's school, Islington); migrated to QUEEN'S Oct., 83, B.A. 85, M.A. 89; HONOURS:—2 history 85.

Denison, George Anthony, M.A., fellow ORIEL 28-39, where see.

Dennett, rev. Edward, born at Lymington, Hants, April, 1862; 1s. Edward, arm. KEBLE, matric. 19 Oct., 80, aged 18 (from Lymington school), B.A. 83, M.A. 87; curate of Hambleton, Hants, 91.

Dennett, Walker Marcus, born at Boston, U.S.A., 1870; o.s. Gideon Walker, gen. WORCESTER, matric. 14 Oct., 90, aged 20, from St. Austen's school, Staten Island, New York, U.S.A.

Dennis, Arthur James Herbert, born at Manchester 22 July, 1870; 2s. Meade Hodgson, surgeon-dentist, deceased. NON-COLLEGIATE, matric. 18 Feb., 92, aged 21, from Trinity coll. and gr. school, Stratford-on-Avon.

Dennis, George, H.B.M. consul at Smyrna, created O.C.L. 17 June, 85.

Dennis, Philip, born at Ingleby Harncliffe, Yorks, 1870; 1s. William, gen. ST. EDMUND HALL, matric. 22 Oct., 91, aged 21.

Denny, Edward Philip, born at Bergh Apton, Norfolk, Feb., 1868; 3s. Richard Cooke, cler. KEBLE, matric. 19 Oct., 86, aged 18 (from Haileybury), B.A. 89; (HONOURS:—3 classical mods. 88); a master at Maze Hill school, St. Leonard's, 90.

Denny, Ernest Wriothesley, born at Paddington 5 Feb., 1872; 3s. Thomas Anthony, arm. NEW COLL., matric. 10 Oct., 90, aged 18 (from Wellington coll.), passed into Sandhurst 92.

Dennys, Haddock James Lardner, born at Islington, Middx., 1861; o.s. Haddock, gent. NON-COLLEGIATE, matric. 15 Oct., 90, aged 29, from Ewell grange school.

Denrick, Francis Ernest, born at Islington 1850; 3s. William, gen. NON-COLLEGIATE, matric. 11 Oct., 90, aged 40.

Dent, Charles Henry, born at Wetherby, Yorks, 18 Oct., 84, 1865; 3s. John Dent, arm. BALLIOL, matric. 15 Oct., 84, aged 19 (from Harrow), B.A. 89; HONOURS: —3 history 88.

Dent, Frederick Thomas Lancey, born at Manningtree, Essex, 15 Jan., 1865; 1s. Frederick, gent. JESUS COLL., matric. 18 Oct., 83, aged 18, B.A. 87.

Denton, Henry St. Aubyn, born at Ashby-de-la-Zouch, co. Lincoln, 1862; 2s. John, cler. UNIVERSITY COLL., matric. 14 Oct., 82, aged 20, B.A. 87; HONOURS:—3 classics 86.

Dermer, Edward Conduitt, B.O., fellow ST. JOHN'S 61, where see.

Despard, rev. Arthur Vandeleur, born in London 11 Dec., 1861; 2s. George, cler. ST. JOHN'S, matric. 16 Oct., 80, aged 18 (from Merchant Taylors' school), B.A. 84, M.A. 88 (HONOURS:—3 classical mods. 82, 4 history 84); chaplain at Gothenburg 89.

Devenish, William Hammond, born at Pensford, Bristol, 19 June, 1861; 1s. Charles Weston, cler. BALLIOL, matric. 21 Oct., 80, aged 19 (from Winchester); scholar BRASENOSE 81-5, B.A. 84 (HONOURS:—3 classical mods. 82, 2 classics 84); librarian Oxford union society 82; bar.-at-law, Middle Temple, 90.

Devereux, hon. Robert Charles, born at Bassaleg, co. Mon., 11 Aug., 1865; 1s. Robert, viscount Hereford. NEW COLL., matric. 10 Oct., 84, aged 19 (from Eton), scholar 84, B.A. 88; HONOURS:—1 classical mods. 86, 3 classics 88.

Devonshire, Archibald, born at Bickley, Kent, June, 1868; 5s. Thomas Harris, arm. UNIVERSITY COLL., matric. 17 Jan., 91, aged 22, from Uppingham school.

Dew, Roderick, born at Tapsley, co. Hereford 21 Oct., 1872; 2s. Frederick Napleton, mayor. KEBLE, matric. 20 Oct., 91, aged 18, from Hereford school.

Dewar, Charles Gilbert, born at Middleton Stoney 3 Nov., 1865; 1s. William Wemyss, arm. BRASENOSE, matric. 22 Oct., 83, aged 18 (from Winchester), B.A. 87; bar.-at-law, Inner Temple, 89.

Dewar, David Erskine, M.A., B.C.L., fellow NEW COLL. 45-53, where see.

Dewar, George Albemarle Bertie, born in London 3 Nov., 1862; 2s. Albemarle, arm. NON-COLLEGIATE, matric. 6 Feb., 82, aged 19 (from Winchester), B.A. 86; HONOURS:—4 history 85.

Dewdney, Arthur John Bible, born at Dover 1872; 4s. Ann. NON-COLLEGIATE, matric. 15 Oct., 92, aged 20, from Dover coll.

Dewe, Thomas, born at Aldworth, Berks, 1865; 2s. Robert, arm. BRASENOSE, matric. 8 Dec., 83, aged 18 (from Reading school), scholar 83, B.A. 87, M.A. 92; HONOURS:—2 mathematical mods. 85, 2 mathematics 87.

Dewe, Wallace, born at Oxford 24 Dec., 1867; 1s. George, gent. TRINITY, matric. 16 Oct., 86, aged 18, from Bath coll.

Dewhurst, rev. Archibald, born at Walsall, co. Stafford, 1868; 2s. Lawrence, gen. NON-COLLEGIATE, matric. 12 Oct., 89, aged 21 (from model school, York), B.A. 92.

Dewhurst, rev. Lawrence, born at Walsall, co. Stafford, 1866; 1s. Lawrence, gen. NON-COLLEGIATE, matric. 16 Oct., 86, aged 20 (from York school), B.A. 89 (HONOURS:—2 law 89); curate of St. Jude, Plymouth, 90.

Dewhurst, Robert Paget, born at Clitheroe, co. Lanc., 1869; 1s. James, gen. BALLIOL, matric. 18 Oct., 88, aged 19 (from Clitheroe gr. school), scholar 87 (HONOURS:—2 classical mods. 90, 1 mathl. mods. 90, 2 maths. 92, junior mathl. exhibition 90); selected candidate Indian C.S. 92.

Dewhurst, William Arthur, born at Lymm, Cheshire, 21 Oct., 1871; 1s. John Dally, arm. BRASENOSE, matric. 15 Oct., 90, aged 18, from Marlborough coll.

Dewing, Maurice, born at Beyton, Suffolk, Jan., 1862; 5s. Edward May, arm. KEBLE, matric. 19 Oct., 80, aged 18 (from Bury St. Edmund's gr. school), B.A. 84; HONOURS:—3 classical mods. 82, 4 law 84.

Dews, Albert, born at Wakefield, Yorks, 1868; 1s. Ferdinand Baines, gent. BALLIOL, matric. 10 Feb., 86, aged 18 (from Rishworth gr. school), exhibitioner 85, B.A. 89; HONOURS:—2 classical mods. 87, 1 classics 89.

Dexter, Henry Aaron, born at Elmira Central, New York, U.S.A., 1861; 1s. John Milton, merchant. NON-COLLEGIATE, matric. 22 Oct., 91, aged 30, from Harvard coll., U.S.A.

Deykin, John Redfern, born at Edgbaston, co. Warwick, 1861; 1s. James, gent. PEMBROKE, matric. 30 Oct., 80, aged 19.

Dibb, Ashton Wilberforce, born at Tinnevelly district India, 29 Aug., 1861; 1s. Ashton, cler., deceased. NON-COLLEGIATE, matric. 17 Oct., 91, aged 30, from Marlborough coll. and King's coll., London.

Dibblee, George Binney, born at Trichinopoly, East Indies, 17 May, 1868; 1s. Frederick Lewis, gen. NON-COLLEGIATE, matric. 15 Oct., 87, aged 19 (from Haileybury); exhibitioner 88; fellow ALL SOULS' 90, B.A. 90; HONOURS:—1 history 90.

Dicey, Albert Venn, M.A., B.C.L., fellow ALL SOULS' 82, where see.

Dickenson, William George, born at Rise, near Hull, 1862; o.s. George, gent. ST. ALBAN HALL, matric. 28 Jan., 81, aged 19.

Dicker, Ernest Barratt, born at Newton Abbot, Devon, 16 Dec., 1871; o.s. John, gen. MERTON, matric. 19 Oct., 89, aged 17 (from Queen's coll., Taunton), postmaster 89; HONOURS:—1 classical mods. 91.

Dickerson, Richard Charles, M.A., fellow WORCESTER 61-6, where see.

Dickins, rev. Alan, born at Tardebig, co. Worcester, 11 Feb., 1862; 2s. Charles Allan, cler. ST. ALBAN HALL, matric. 9 Nov., 80, aged 18 (from Marlborough); migrated to EXETER, Oct., 82, B.A. 83; curate of St. Mary Magdalen, Bridgnorth, 88.

Dickins, Henry Compton, M.A., fellow NEW COLL., 57, where see.

Dickins, rev. William Arthur, born at St. Nicholas, Warwick, 18 April, 1861; 2s. Thomas Bourne, vicar of Emscote, co. Warwick. LINCOLN, matric. 22 Jan., 80, aged 18 (from Leamington coll.); curate of Penn, co. Stafford, 86.

Dickins, William Godfrey, born at Surbiton, Surrey, June, 1869; 1s. William Park, arm. ORIEL, matric. 20 Oct., 88, aged 19 (from Winchester), B.A. 91; HONOURS:—4 history 91.

Dickins, William Park, M.A., fellow MERTON 47-60, where see.

Dickinson, Charles Henry, born at Pietermaritzburg, Natal, 30 June, 1871; 1s. Charles Hammond, of Ilfracombe, arm. KEBLE, matric. 11 Oct., 90, aged 19, from Haileybury.

Dickinson, rev. Clement Wilberforce, born at Westerham, Kent, 1865; y.s. Francis, gent. NON-COLLEGIATE, matric. 20 Oct., 84, aged 19 (from Derby school), B.A. 88, M.A. 91 (HONOURS:—3 classical mods. 86, 2 theology 88, septuagint prize 87 and 90); curate of Masborough, Yorks, 91.

Dickinson, Oliver Horace, born at Shanghai, Siam, 13 Dec., 1866; 2s. Henry, gent. WORCESTER, matric. 17 Oct., 84, aged 18 (from Oundle school), B.A. 87; HONOURS:—2 law 87.

Dickinson, Thomas Loffill Dutton, born at St. Peter-at-Gowts, Lincoln, 13 Oct., 1866; o.s. Charles Sampson, arm. EXETER, matric. 28 Jan., 86, aged 19 (from Malvern coll.), B.A. 89, M.A. 92 (HONOURS: —3 law 89); bar.-at-law, Lincoln's Inn, 91.

Dickinson, rev. William John, born at Carlisle 25 Dec., 1864; o.s. Francis, gent. QUEEN'S, matric. 22 Oct., 83, aged 18 (from Carlisle high school and St. Bees gr. school), B.A. 87, M.A. 92 (HONOURS; —2 classical mods. 85); curate New Wortley, Leeds, 88.

Dickson, Arthur George Mitton, born at Athens 1870; o.s. Thomas George, arm. UNIVERSITY COLL., matric. 13 Oct., 88, aged 18 (from Bath coll.), scholar 88; HONOURS:—2 classical mods. 90.

Dickson, James William, born at Swansea 24 Aug., 1869; 2s. James, arm. EXETER, matric. 16 Oct., 89, aged 20, from St. Alban's gr. school.

Dickson, (sir) John Poynder of CHRIST CHURCH 85. See Poynder.

Digby, Everard Duffield, born in London 6 Oct., 1870; 3s. Henry, gen. NEW COLL., matric. 16 Oct., 91, aged 21, from King's coll. school, London.

Digby, rev. Frederick Wyldbore Wingfield, born at Coleshill, co. Warwick, July, 1865; 3s. John, arm. CHRIST CHURCH, matric. 31 May, 84, aged 18 (from Harrow), B.A. 88; M.A. 91; curate of Staple Fitzpaine, Somerset, 91.

Digby, George Hugh, born at Cottistock, Dorset, 21 Sept., 1867; 1s. John Almeric, arm. CHRIST CHURCH, matric. 23 Jan., 86, aged 18.

Digby, Hugh Mountjoy, born at Bath 22 Jan., 1864; 4s. Jeremiah Taylor, arm. ST. JOHN'S, matric. 13 Oct., 83, aged 19.

Digby, Kenelm Edward, M.A., fellow CORPUS CHRISTI 64-70, where see.

Digby, Kenelm Everard Joseph, born in London Nov., 1872; 1s. Kenelm Thomas, esq. CHRIST CHURCH, matric. 14 Oct., 92, aged 19.

Digby, Stephen Harold Wingfield, born at Astley, co. Warwick, Sept., 1872; 5s. John Digby, captain. CHRIST CHURCH, matric. 30 April, 92, aged 19, from Harrow.

Dighton, Richard, born at Coleford, co. Glouc.,
1860; 2s. John Henry, arm. NEW INN
HALL, matric. 22 Jan., 80, aged 20.

Dill, Samuel, M.A., fellow CORPUS CHRISTI 69-84,
where see.

Dimont, Charles Tunnacliff, born at Worcester 8 July,
1872; o.s. Charles Harding, cler. WORCESTER,
matric. 22 Oct., 91, aged 19 (from Worcester cathedral school), scholar 91.

Dingwall, Frederick Abercrombie, born at Edinburgh
20 Nov., 1862; 3s. Arthur, arm. ST. JOHN'S,
matric. 15 Oct., 81, aged 18 (from Merchant
Taylors' school), scholar 81-5, B.A. 86; HONOURS:
—2 classical mods. 83.

Dingwall, James, born at Logie Coldstone, co. Aberdeen, 1866; o.s. Robert. BALLIOL, matric. 19
Jan., 88, aged 22, from Aberdeen university.

Dinwoody, Frank Kenelm, born at Kirk Andrews,
Isle of Man, 1873; 4s. William Thomas,
cler. HERTFORD, matric. 14 Oct., 90, aged 17
(from clergy orphan school, Canterbury), scholar
89; HONOURS:—3 classical mods. 92.

Disbrowe, Charles Penrose, born at Raithby, co.
Lincoln, 2 Dec., 1866; 5s. Henry Sharp, cler.
QUEEN'S, matric. 1 Feb., 81, aged 18 (from Merchant
Taylors' school), B.A. 84, M.A. 89.

Disbrowe, Henry Sidney, born at Raithby, co.
Lincoln, 9 Oct., 1864; 6s. Henry Sharp, cler.
MERTON, matric. 19 Oct., 83, aged 19 (from Aldenham gr. school), B.A. 86, M.A. 91; HONOURS:—
4 history 86.

Disney, Edgar Norton, born at Southend, Essex,
1863; 1s. Edgar John, arm. PEMBROKE,
matric. 4 Feb., 81, aged 18, B.A. 86.

Disney, Robert Baxter, born at Ballymagellycot, co.
Kerry, 14 Sept., 1871; 4s. William Henry, cler.
WORCESTER, matric. 14 Oct., 90, aged 19 (from
Rossall school), scholar 89; HONOURS:—2 mathematical mods. 92.

Disraeli, Coningsby Ralph, born in London 25 Feb.,
1867; o.s. Ralph, late deputy clerk of the parliaments.
NEW COLL., matric. 16 Oct., 85, aged 18 (from the
Charterhouse); migrated to CHARSLEY HALL;
M.P. Altrincham division, of Cheshire, 92.

Dixey, Frederick Augustus, M.A., D.Med., fellow
WADHAM 85, where see.

Dixon, Alexander Nathaniel, born at Wadhurst,
Sussex, March, 1861; 2s. Henry, cler. CHRIST
CHURCH, matric. 15 Oct., 80, aged 19, B.A. 87.

Dixon, Arthur Lee, born at Pickering, Yorks, 27 Nov.,
1867; 2s. George Thomas, gent. WORCESTER,
matric. 22 Oct., 85, aged 17 (from Kingswood
school), scholar 84, B.A. 88; fellow MERTON 91,
M.A. 92; HONOURS:—1 mathl. mods. 86, 1 maths.
88, junior mathl. exhibition 86 and scholarship 87,
Herschel astronomical prize 89 and 90, proxime
accessit 90, and senior mathl. scholarship 91.

Dixon, Frederick Percival, born at Manchester 25
July, 1871; 1s. Percival Ridyard, arm. EXETER,
matric. 13 Oct., 90, aged 19 (from Manchester gr.
school), scholar 90; HONOURS:—2 classical mods.
92.

Dixon, rev. Henry Lancelot, born at Wolverhampton
1861; 1s. Godwin Hope, cler. PEMBROKE,
matric. 30 Oct., 80, aged 19 (from Sherborne school),
B.A. 83, M.A. 87 (HONOURS:—3 classical mods.
82); chaplain at Seville in Spain 87.

Dixon, Harold Bailey, M.A., fellow BALLIOL 86-7,
where see page 68.

Dixon, Mark William, born at Streatham, Surrey,
April, 1867; 1s. Mark Thomas, arm. CHRIST
CHURCH, matric. 6 May, 86, aged 19 (from Dover
coll.), B.A. 89; bar.-at-law, Inner Temple, 91.

Dixon, rev. William Hope, born at Leamington 14
Sept., 1863; 2s. Godwin Hope, cler. HERTFORD,
matric. 18 Oct., 82, aged 19 (from Sherborne school),
scholar 81-6, B.A. 86, M.A. 90 (HONOURS:—1
classical mods. 83, 2 classics 86); curate of Crewkerne, Wilts, 87.

Doane, William C., bishop of Albany, U.S.A., created
D.D. 26 May, 1891.

Dobbs, Henry Robert Conway, born in London 26
Aug., 1871; 2s. Robert Conway, arm. BRASENOSE,
matric. 15 Oct., 90, aged 19 (from Winchester),
scholar 90; selected candidate Indian civil service
90.

Dobell, Walter Duffield, born at Charlton Kings, co.
Glouc., March, 1873; 2s. Clarence Mason, gen.
MAGDALEN, matric. 22 Oct., 91, aged 19, from
Clifton coll.

Dobie, John Nicholson, born at Sowerby, Westmorland, 1866; 1s. William, D.Med. EXETER,
matric. 16 Oct., 84, aged 18 (from Bingley gr.
school), scholar 84-5; migrated to CAIUS COLL.,
Cambridge, 21 Oct., 85, B.A. 88; HONOURS:—3rd
class natural science Tripos (Cambridge) 88.

Dobie, Leonard Johnson, born in Cheshire 7 Jan., 1864;
3s. William Murray, D.Med. KEBLE, matric. 17
Jan., 83, aged 19 (from Marlborough), B.A. 87,
M.A. 90; HONOURS:—4 history 86.

Dobie, William Fullerton, born at Temple Sowerby,
Westmorland, 24 Dec., 1867; 2s. William, cler.
QUEEN'S, matric. 21 Oct., 87, aged 19 (from Bingley
and Bradford gr. schools), exhibitioner 87.

Dobinson, Henry Hughes, born at Carlisle
1864; 2s. Henry, arm. BRASENOSE, matric. 2 June,
82, aged 18 (from Repton school), B.A. 86, M.A.
89.

Doble, rev. Richard James, born at Falmouth, Cornwall, 1850; y.s. Richard, arm. HERTFORD,
matric. 27 Oct., 85, aged 18, B.A. 88, M.A. 92
(HONOURS:—4 history 88); chaplain and senior
classical master Trinity coll. Stratford-on-Avon 89.

Dobson, Christopher Masterman, born at Dromanby,
Yorks, Aug., 1863; o.s. Christopher Hill, D.Med.
CHRIST CHURCH, matric. 13 Oct., 82, aged 19, from
Harrow.

Dobson, John, born at Heversham, Westmorland, 11
Oct., 1874; 1s. George, gent. QUEEN'S, matric. 27
Oct., 91, aged 17 (from Heversham gr. school),
scholar 91.

Dobson, Louis Lempriere, born at Hobart, Tasmania,
10 June, 1872; 1s. Henry, solicitor. MAGDALEN,
matric. 22 Oct., 91, aged 19, from Oundle school.

Dodd, rev. William Herbert, born at Old Trafford,
co. Lanc. 12 June, 1860; o.s. William, gent. ST.
JOHN'S, matric. 16 Oct., 80, aged 20 (from Owens
coll., Manchester), B.A. 83, M.A. 88 (HONOURS:—
3 theology 83); curate of Almondbury, Yorks, 88.

Dodds, James Miller, born at Glasgow 1861;
2s. James, S.T.P. MERTON, matric. 18 Oct., 80,
aged 19 (from Glasgow university), postmaster 80-4,
B.A. 84; HONOURS:—2 classical mods. 81, 2 classics
84.

Dodds, Tom William, D.Mus., organist QUEEN'S 72,
where see.

Doderet, William, born at Madras 1862; 1s.
Frederick, gent. BALLIOL, matric. 1 Nov., 80,
aged 18 (from University coll. school, London);
special under-secretary, government of Bombay,
famine relief dept., and assistant collector and
magistrate Bombay C.S.

Dodgson, rev. Charles Lutwidge, M.A., student
CHRIST CHURCH 52, where see.

Dodgson, Campbell, born at Crayford, Kent, 13 Aug.,
1867; 7s. William Oliver, gent. NEW COLL.,
matric. 15 Oct., 86, aged 19 (from Winchester),
scholar 85, B.A. 90; HONOURS:—2 classical mods.
88, 1 classics 90, 2 theology 91.

Dodgson, Cyril George, born at Mymensing, E. Indies, 6 March, 1864; 1s. John Crawford, of Havre, arm. BALLIOL, matric. 18 Oct., 81, aged 17 (from Cheltenham coll.); and assistant collector and magistrate Khandish, Bombay, and forest settlement officer and Western Bhil agent 88.

Dodgson, Francis Hume, student CHRIST CHURCH 53-7, where see.

Dodson, hon. John William, born at Barcombe, Sussex, 22 Sept., 1869; 1s. John George, baron Monk Bretton. NEW COLL., matric. 12 Oct., 88, aged 19 (from Eton); HONOURS:—3 history 91.

Dodson, rev. Thomas Hatheway, born at Rotherham, Yorks, 11 May, 1862; 1s. George, gent. EXETER, matric. 20 Oct., 81, aged 19 (from Merchant Taylors' school), exhibitioner 81-5, B.A. 85, M.A. 88 (HONOURS:—3 classical mods. 83, 1 theology 85); principal S.P.G. coll., Trichinopoly, 89.

Dodson, rev. Walter Jeremiah, born at Dartmouth, Devon, 1869; o.s. William Frederick, LL.D. NON-COLLEGIATE, matric. 13 Oct., 88, aged 19 (from Dover coll.), B.A. 91.

Doherty, Arthur Henry, born at Kenilworth, co. Warwick, 11 March, 1868; 1s. William Butler, vicar of Cotham St. Matthew's. MAGDALEN, matric. 22 Oct., 87, aged 19 (from Bristol gr. school), demy 86, B.A. 92; HONOURS:—1 classical mods. 89, 2 classics 91.

Doherty, William Vernon, born at Wimbledon 4 June, 1871; 1s. William, arm. CHRIST CHURCH, matric. 8 June, 89, aged 18 (from Westminster school), B.A. 92.

Dolan, William John Joseph, born at Dublin 15 Sept., 1868; 1s. Henry, arm. NON-COLLEGIATE, matric. 16 Dec., 86, aged 18 (from Stonyhurst coll.); migrated to BALLIOL 87; died 29 Nov., 90, at Bath.

D'Ombrain, Cyril Wilberforce, born at Bournabat, Smyrna, 23 Aug., 1874; 4s. James, M.A., vicar of St. John's, Oldham. NON-COLLEGIATE, matric. 15 Oct., 92, aged 18, from Manchester gr. school.

Domeniohetti, rev. Richard Hippisley, born at Stoke Damerel, 21 April, 1863; 1s. Richard, of Louth, co. Linc., D.Med. ORIEL, matric. 31 Oct., 82, aged 19 (from Haileybury), B.A. 86 (HONOURS: —English verse 85), at the Brompton Oratory, 87.

Donald, Charles Stuart, born at Finchley, Middx., April, 1872; 1s. Charles Stuart, merchant. KEBLE, matric. 20 Oct., 91, aged 19, from Radley coll.

Donald, John Rowley, born at Kirkwall, isle of Orkney, 18 Dec., 1868; 1s. James, gen. WORCESTER, matric. 15 June, 88, aged 19 (from Hurstpierpoint coll.), scholar 87, B.A. 92; HONOURS:—2 mathematical mods. 90, 3 mathematics 92.

Donaldson, David Wardlaw, born at Hillhend, Glasgow, 22 Sept., 1872; 2s. William Anderson, merchant. NEW COLL., matric. 14 Oct., 92, aged 20, from Loretto school.

Donaldson, rev. Frederick George, born at Birmingham 10 Sept., 1860; 2s. Frederick William, gen. ST. ALBAN HALL, matric. 19 Oct., 80, aged 20; migrated to MERTON, B.A. 84, M.A. 88; curate of St. John Evangelist, Hammersmith, 89.

Donaldson, James Gordon, born at Staines, Middx., 18 March, 1873; 2s. Augustus Blair, cler. CHRIST CHURCH, matric. 14 Oct., 92, aged 19 (from Christ's hospital), exhibitioner 92.

Donaldson, William Lachlan, born at Staines, Middx., 17 April, 1872; 1s. Augustus Blair, cler. WORCESTER, matric. 20 Oct., 90, aged 18 (from Leatherhead school), scholar 90; HONOURS:—2 classical mods. 92.

Donaldson, William Patrick, born at Glasgow 4 March, 1871; 1s. William Anderson, merchant. BRASENOSE, matric. 22 Oct., 91, aged 20, from Loretto school.

Donkin, Arthur Edward, M.A., fellow EXETER 70-5, where see.

Donnell, rev. Charles Ernest Havelock, born at Staleybridge, co. Lanc, Jan., 1861; 7s. Joseph, arm. CHRIST CHURCH, matric. 21 May, 80, aged 19, B.A. 84 (HONOURS:—3 history 84); vicar of Ovingham, Northumberland, 91.

Donnithorne, Hugh Nicholas Mortimer, born at Fareham, Hants, 10 May, 1874; 1s. Nicholas, solicitor. HERTFORD, matric. 22 Oct., 92, aged 18, from Marlborough coll.

Donovan, Rev. Percy James, born at Croydon, Surrey, 1858; 3s. Joseph Bartram Axelby, cler. NON-COLLEGIATE, matric. 15 Oct., 81, aged 23; migrated to EXETER 20 April, 84, B.A. 85, M.A. 88 (HONOURS:—3 theology 85); vicar of Elmore, co. Glouc., 88-90, curate of Christchurch, Greenwich, 92.

Donovan, rev. Richard Henry, born at Southsea 1869; 1s. Richard Henry, cler. ST. EDMUND HALL, matric. 21 Jan., 87, aged 18, B.A. 89; curate of Walworth St. Paul, London, 91.

Donovan, rev. Sydney Charles, born at Dorking, Surrey, 1856; 2s. Joseph Bartram Axelby, cler. NON-COLLEGIATE, matric. 14 Oct., 82, aged 26, B.A. 89, M.A. 91; curate of All Saints, Rotherhithe, 90.

Dore, Walter Joseph, born at Chicago, U.S.A., 5 Jan., 1869; 1s. Edward Francis, gen. LINCOLN, matric. 17 Oct., 89, aged 20, from Harvard school, Chicago, and institute of technology, Boston.

Dott, William Patrick, born at Stepney, Middx., 26 Sept., 1867; 6s. James Forfar, arm. ST. MARY HALL, matric. 18 May, 89, aged 21.

Dougal, Charles Edward Roney-, born at Sunderland, co. Durham, 27 July, 1866; 4s. Richard, lieut.-col. MAGDALEN, matric. 16 Oct., 84, aged 18 (from Leamington coll.), demy 84, B.A. 90; HONOURS: —2 classical mods. 86.

Dougal, John Dougal Roney-, born at Swansea, co. Glam., 11 Sept., 1862; 3s. Richard, arm. TRINITY, matric. 27 Nov., 82, aged 20, from Leamington coll.

Doughty, Arthur George, born at Maidenhead, Berks, 1860; 2s. William James, arm. NEW INN HALL, matric. 3 May, 84, aged 24.

Douglas, lord Alfred Bruce, born at Ham Hill House, co. Wore., 22 Oct., 1870; 3s. John Sholto, marquis of Queensberry. MAGDALEN, matric. 14 Oct., 89, aged 18, from Winchester.

Douglas, Archibald William, born at Scaldwell, Northants, 3 June, 1870; 3s. hon. Arthur Gascoigne, bishop of Aberdeen and Orkney. KEBLE, matric. 11 Oct., 90, aged 20, from Glenalmond coll.

Douglas, Arthur Jeffreys, born at Salwarpe, co. Worcester, 1871; 6s. William Willoughby, rector. LINCOLN, matric. 20 Oct., 90, aged 19 (from Marlborough coll.), exhibitioner 90 (HONOURS:—3 classical mods. 92); brother of Robert G.

Douglas, rev. Daniel Greenhill, born at Workington, Cumberland, 1865; o.s. Thomas Sadler, D.Med. BRASENOSE, matric. 18 April, 83, aged 20 (from St. Bees gr. school), B.A. 86, M.A. 90 (HONOURS:—3 theology 86); curate of Distington, Cumberland, 90.

Douglas, Francis Edward, born at St. Heliers, Jersey, 17 Feb., 1871; 4s. Robert, English chaplain at Rouen. JESUS COLL., matric. 15 Oct., 92, aged 19, from Newcastle under Lyme high school.

Douglas, rev. Francis Sandford Keith, born in London 1858; 2s. John More, gent. NON-COLLEGIATE, matric. 22 Jan., 81, aged 23, [B.A. 83]; chaplain at Sao Paulo, and Santos, Brazil, 86-8; died 9 April, 92, in Brazil.

Douglas, James Archibald, born at Sheffield, Yorks, 7 March, 1866; 2s. Robert, cler. NON-COLLEGIATE, matric. 13 Oct., 83, aged 17; migrated to MERTON, B.A. 86, M.A. 91 (HONOURS :—4 history 86); lieut. Dorsetshire regiment 83, lieut. and squadron officer and Bengal lancers 86.

Douglas, rev. Robert Gresley, born at Salwarpe, co. Worc., March, 1860; 4s. William Willoughby, rector. KEBLE, matric. 19 Oct., 80, aged 18 (from Marlborough), B.A. 85, M.A. 87; vicar of Ladybrand with Ficksburg, Orange Free State, 90; brother of Arthur J.

Douglas, rev. Robert Langton, born at Davenham, Cheshire, 1 March, 1864; 1s. Robert, vicar of Kidsgrove, co. Staff. NON-COLLEGIATE, matric. 13 Oct., 83, aged 19 (from Sheffield collegiate school); migrated to NEW COLL., B.A. 86, M.A. 91 (HONOURS :—2 history 86); organizing sec. church of England temperance society 89.

Douglas, Sholto Osborne Gordon, born at St. Margarets, St. Andrew, co. Fife, 14 Sept., 1873; o.s. William Grant, commander R.N., retired. CHRIST CHURCH, matric. 4 June, 92, aged 19, from Fettes coll. and Portsmouth gr. school. See Foster's Peerage, E. MORTON.

Douglas, rev. Stair, born at Hardwick, co. Glouc., 23 May, 1867; o.s. William, cler. ORIEL, matric. 19 Oct., 86, aged 19 (from Clifton coll.), B.A. 89 (HONOURS :—3 history 89); curate of St. John the Evangelist, Clifton, Bristol, 91. See Foster's Peerage, M. QUEENSBERRY.

Douglass, Edward Wingfield, born at Hilton Albany, Cape Colony, June, 1873; 2s. Arthur, gent. KEBLE, matric. 15 Oct., 92, aged 19, from S. Andrew's, Grahamstown.

Douglass, rev. Frederick Wingfield, born at Market Harborough, co. Leicester, 1867; 2s. Edward S., cler. NON-COLLEGIATE, matric. 30 May, 85, aged 18 (from Oakham school), B.A. 89, M.A. 92; HONOURS :—4 theology 89); curate of St. Panoras, London, 89.

Doull, Alexander John, born at Halifax, Nova Scotia, 8 Sept., 1870; o.s. Alexander Keith, gen. ORIEL, matric. 29 Nov., 90, aged 20, from St. Edward's school Summertown.

Doulton, Hubert Victor, born in London 21 Jan., 1864; 4s. Frederick, gent. LINCOLN, matric. 23 Oct., 82, aged 18 (from Dulwich coll.), B.A. 86; HONOURS :—2 classical mods. 84, 2 history 86.

Dove, John, born at Birkenhead, Cheshire, 16 Nov., 1872; 2s. John Matthew, gen. NEW COLL., matric. 16 Oct., 91, aged 18, from Rugby.

Dover, rev. George, M.A., EXETER, where see.

Dowdall, Harold Chaloner, born at Croxteth, near Liverpool, 7 March, 1868; 2s. Thomas, arm. TRINITY, matric. 15 Oct., 87, aged 19 (from Rugby), scholar 87, B.A. 90 (HONOURS :—2 chemistry 90, 3 civil law 92); bar.-at-law, Inner Temple, 93.

Dowdall, Thomas Percy, born in Liverpool 14 Aug., 1866; 2s. Thomas, arm. CHRIST CHURCH, matric. 30 May, 85, aged 18, from Rugby.

Dowden, Edward, LL.D. Edinb., Erasmus Smith's prof. of oratory in university of Dublin 67, created D.C.L. 22 June, 92, 1st Taylorian lecturer 89; B.A. Trinity coll., Dublin, 63; HONOURS :—T.C.D. 1 philosophy 63, Wray metaphysical prize 63, English verse 64, English essay 64. See Men and Women of the Time.

Dowdeswell, Thomas Buckingham, born at Haresfield, co. Glouc., 1868; 1s. Thomas, gen. NON-COLLEGIATE, matric. 15 Oct., 87, aged 19 (from Worcester school for the blind); HONOURS :—3 theology 91.

Dowling, Henry Barré, born at Winchester 28 Sept., 1864; 1s. Barré Beresford, gent. TRINITY, matric. 11 Oct., 84, aged 20 (from Wellington coll.), B.A. 88; HONOURS :—4 law 88.

Down, rev. Edward Arthur, born at Dorking, Surrey, 4 Feb., 1862; 2s. James Dundas Sommers, solicitor. NEW COLL., matric. 15 May, 80, aged 18 (from the Charterhouse), B.A. 84, M.A. 87 (HONOURS :—3 classical mods. 81, 1 theology 84); curate of St. John the Divine, Kennington, 86.

Dowsett, John, born at West Ham, Essex, 1865; 2s. John, gent. EXETER, matric. 16 Oct., 84, aged 19 (from Christ's hospital), exhibitioner 84, B.A. 88; HONOURS :—2 classical mods. 86, 3 classics 88.

Dowson, Ernest Christopher(son), born at Lee, Kent, 2 Aug., 1867; 1s. Alfred Christopher, gen. QUEEN'S, matric. 25 Oct., 86, aged 19.

Dowson, Percy Enfield, born at Gee Cross, Cheshire, 24 July, 1873; 2s. Henry Enfield, B.A., unitarian minister. TRINITY, matric. 15 Oct., 92, aged 19 (from Rugby), scholar 91.

Doyle, John Andrew, M.A., fellow ALL SOULS' 69, where see.

Drage, rev. Evelyn William, born at Hatfield, Herts, 1868; 3s. Charles, D.Med. CHRIST CHURCH, matric. 12 June, 86, aged 18 (from Winchester), B.A. 89.

Drage, William Henry, born at Lincoln 22 March, 1871; 2s. Edward, gen. NON-COLLEGIATE, matric. 11 Oct., 90, aged 19, from Lincoln gr. school.

Drake, rev. Algernon Francis, born at Halestown, Cornwall, 19 Jan., 1864; 4s. William Hinton, rector of Bridestow, Devon. NON-COLLEGIATE, matric. 13 Oct., 84, aged 20 (from Truro gr. school); migrated to WADHAM, B.A. 87; curate of Winscombe, Somerset, 91.

Drake, Francis Courtney, born at Stratford, Essex, 30 Sept., 1868; 2s. Thomas, gen. NEW COLL., matric. 14 Oct., 92, aged 19 (from Winchester), scholar 87, B.A. 91 (HONOURS :—2 classical mods. 89, 2 classics 91), in Oxford University eight 89.

Drake, Frederick William, born at Woolwich 2 Aug., 1869; 3s. John Tippet, gen. PEMBROKE matric. 17 Oct., 88, aged 18 (from King's coll. school, London), scholar 88 (HONOURS :—2 classical mods. 90, 2 classics 92.

Drake, Herbert Lionel, born at Woolwich, Kent, 21 March, 1873; 4s. John Tippet, gen. ST. JOHN'S, matric. 17 Oct., 91, aged 18 (from Merchant Taylors' school), scholar 91; HONOURS :—Accessit Hertford scholarship 92, accessit Craven scholarship 92.

Drake, Herbert Mackworth, born at Veryan, Cornwall, April, 1870; 1s. Charles Mackworth, cler. KEBLE, matric. 13 Oct., 88, aged 18 (from Marlborough), B.A. 91; HONOURS :—3 history 91.

Draper, Warwick Herbert, born in London 4 April, 1873; 1s. Edward Herbert, M.A., bar.-at-law. UNIVERSITY COLL., matric. 15 Oct., 92, aged 19 (from Rugby), scholar 92.

Dredge, Joseph Alan, born at Hungerford, Berks, 1872; 2s. Joseph, gent. BALLIOL, matric. 18 Oct., 92, aged 20, from Hereford county school.

Drew, Frank Eric Charles, born at Great Malvern, co. Worc., 23 Sept., 1869; 1s. Francis Robert, cler. WORCESTER, matric. 16 Oct., 88, aged 19 (from Leamington coll.), exhibitioner 88; HONOURS :—3 classical mods. 90, 2 classics 92.

Drew, Herbert Bernard, born in London Aug. 1871; 1s. George Bernard, of Slenford, co. Linc., arm. KEBLE, matric. 11 Oct., 90, aged 19, from Haileybury.

Drewitt, John Arthur James, born at Patching, Sussex, 17 Oct., 1873; 1s. John, gen. MAGDALEN, matric. 22 Oct., 91, aged 18 (from Magdalen coll. school), demy 91.

Driffield, George Townshend, M.A., fellow BRASENOSE 39-45, where see.

Driver, Samuel Rolles, D.D., canon of CHRIST CHURCH 83, where see.
Drinkwater, William Edward, born in Antigua, West Indies, 28 Feb., 1869; 1s. Manoah John, cler. NON-COLLEGIATE, matric. 14 Dec., 88, aged 19, from Hurstpierpoint coll.
Druce, Alfred Ernest, born at Deanshanger, Stony Stratford, Bucks, , 1871; 1s. William Walter, gent. PEMBROKE, matric. 28 Oct., 92, aged 21.
Druce, Francis, born at Clapham, Surrey, 3 Jan., 1873; 4s. Alexander Devas, solicitor. MAGDALEN, matric. 9 Feb., 92, aged 19, from the Charterhouse.
Druce, George Claridge; created M.A. 4 June, 1889, an Oxford chemist, botanist and author of Oxfordshire "Flora."
Druce, William Havilland, born at Dover 5 Aug., 1867; 3s. Edward Read Nelson, C.E. EXETER, matric. 21 Oct., 86, aged 19, from Cheltenham coll.
Druitt, Arthur, born at Wimborne Minster, Dorset, 5 June, 1863; 4s. William, D.Med. NEW COLL., matric. 14 Oct., 82, aged 19 (from Marlborough coll.), B.A. 87, M.A. 91; HONOURS:—3 classical mods. 83, 3 history 86.
Druitt, Mayo, born at Christ Church, Hants, 13 Dec., 1869; 5s. James, arm. UNIVERSITY COLL., matric. 13 Oct., 88, aged 18 (from Westminster school); HONOURS:—Ægrotat history 92.
Druitt, rev. Philip, born at Christ Church, Hants, 4 Oct., 1865; 5s. James, arm. ST. MARY HALL, matric. 24 Jan., 84, aged 19 (from Westminster school); migrated to UNIVERSITY COLL., B.A. 88; HONOURS:—3 classics 88.
Drummond, Andrew Cecil, born in London 28 Jan., 1865; 1s. Edgar Atheling, arm. CHRIST CHURCH, matric. 16 Jan., 85, aged 19, from Eton.
Drummond, James, born at Dublin 14 May, 1835; 2s. William Hamilton, of Dublin, D.D., deceased. NON-COLLEGIATE, incorporated 21 Oct., 89, aged 54 (from Trinity coll., Dublin, B.A. 55, LL.D. 82, hon. D.Litt., 92; HONOURS:—1 classics 55, gold medal), M.A. Oxford 89, unitarian divine, professor of theology Manchester new college, London, 90, principal 85, and at Oxford 89. *See Men and Women of the Time.*
Drummond, Wingfield Fraser, born at Ardrollich, Perthshire, 22 Sept., 1861; 2s. Robert, arm. CHRIST CHURCH, matric. 31 Jan., 81, aged 19; migrated to NEW INN HALL (BALLIOL) 87.
Drury, John Frederick William, born at Brafferton, Yorks, 1859; 1s. William, gent. NEW COLL., matric. 18 Oct., 83, aged 24 (from St. David s coll., Carmarthen); migrated to CHRIST CHURCH, B.A. 87; HONOURS:—4 theology 87.
Drury, John William, born at Halifax, Yorks, 6 Oct., 1866; 2s. Mark Henry, arm. TRINITY, matric. 16 Oct., 86, aged 20 (from King's coll. school, London), B.A. 90.
Drury, Roger Mills, born at Helperhy, Yorks, 1863; 2s. William, gen. ST. EDMUND HALL, matric. 22 Oct., 87, aged 24.
Drysdale, William Docker, born in London 1866; o.s. Andrew, gent. ST. JOHN's, matric. 17 Oct., 85, aged 19 (from St. John's Wood school), B.A. 89, M.A. 92; HONOURS:—4 history 89.
Du-Boulay, rev. George Pascall Keble Houssemayne, born at Winchester 1 April, 1866; 3s. rev. James Thomas Houssemayne, a master at Winchester. EXETER, matric. 16 Oct., 84, aged 18 (from Winchester), B.A. 87, M.A. 91 (HONOURS:—3 history 87); curate of Sneinton, Notts, 89; brother of the next-named.
Du-Boulay, James Houssemayne, born at Winchester 15 April, 1868; 4s. rev. James Thomas Housse-

mayne, a master at Winchester. BALLIOL, matric. 19 Oct., 87, aged 19 (from Winchester); assist. collector and magistrate Belgaum, Bombay C.S., 89; brother of the last-named.
Du-Boulay, rev. James Thomas Houssemayne, M.A., fellow EXETER, 54-60, where see.
Du-Buisson, John Clement, born at Dreinton, co. Hereford, 12 Oct., 1871; 4s. Edmund, cler., deceased. MAGDALEN, matric. 14 Oct., 89, aged 18 (from Hereford cath. school), demy 89; HONOURS:—1 classical mods. 91.
Dubs, Frederick Ernest, born at Glasgow May, 1862; 4s. Henry, gent. NEW COLL., matric. 25 Jan., 83, aged 20 (from Glasgow university), B.A. 86, M.A. 90 (HONOURS:—2 classical mods. 84, 3 history 86); bar.-at-law, Inner Temple, 90.
Du-Cane, Arthur George, born at Rochampton, Surrey, 29 Sept., 1866; 3s. Richard, arm. ORIEL, matric. 8 Dec., 84, aged 18 (from the Charterhouse), B.A. 87; bar.-at-law, Inner Temple, 91.
Du-Cane, Edmund Arthur, born at Norbiton, Surrey, 25 June, 1872; 3s. sir Edmund Frederick, K.C.B., K.E., director of convict prisons, England. MAGDALEN, matric. 14 Oct., 90, aged 18 (from the Charterhouse); HONOURS:—3 classical mods. 92.
Ducat, Claude Tulloch, born at Bandon, E. Indies, 1861; 3s. Walter Marden, arm. WORCESTER, matric. 19 Oct., 82, aged 18 B.A. 87; student Middle Temple 83; lieut. Worcestershire Regt., 88, squadron officer 1st Bombay Lancers 89.
Duchesne, Alexander, born at Bombay in London 13 Dec., 1865; 1s. Robert, gent. WORCESTER, matric. 22 Oct., 85, aged 19, from Highbury park school.
Duck, William Birdsall, M.A., HERTFORD, where see.
Ducker, John Anthony, born at Wardle, co. Lanc., 1862; 1s. John, cler. BRASENOSE, matric. 21 May, 80, aged 18 (from Uppingham school), B.A. 83; HONOURS:—4 law 84.
Duckworth, Frederick Christopher, born at Tiverton, Devon, 22 March, 1864; 3s. Robert, cler. MAGDALEN, matric. 15 Oct., 81, aged 17 (from Blundell's and St. Peter's schools, Tiverton), demy 80-5, B.A. 85, M.A. 88 (HONOURS:—1 mathematical mods. 83, 1 mathematics 85); brother of William F.
Duckworth, Henry Thomas Forbes, born at Grassendale, co. Lanc., 29 Nov., 1868; 1s. Henry, gen. MERTON. matric. 22 Oct., 87, aged 18 (from Birkenhead school), postmaster 86, B.A. 91; HONOURS:—1 classical mods. 89, 1 classics 91, 2 theology 92.
Duckworth, Herbert Stratheden, born at Puttenham, Surrey, 4 Jan., 1872; 2s. William Arthur, cler. TRINITY, matric. 17 Oct., 91, aged 19, from Eton.
Duckworth, Rohinson, M.A., fellow TRINITY 60-76, where see.
Duckworth, William Feltrim, born at Tiverton, Devon, 20 Dec., 1862; 2s. Robert, cler. MAGDALEN, matric. 15 Oct., 81, aged 18 (from Tiverton school), scholar HERTFORD 82, B.A. 85, M.A. 88; HONOURS:—1 mathematical mods. 83, 1 mathematics 85; brother of Frederick C.
Duckworth, William Henry, born at Frome, Somerset, 1867; 1s. Russell, arm. NEW COLL., matric. 14 Oct., 87, aged 20 (from Harrow), B.A. 91; HONOURS:—2 classical mods. 89, 4 classics 91.
Dudding, Horatio Nelson, M.A., fellow EXETER 81-7, where see.
Dudley, George Fiske, born at Centreville Wayne, co. Indiana, U.S.A., 25 Sept., 1867; 2s. Willani Wade, attorney-at-law. NON-COLLEGIATE, matric. 22 Oct., 91, aged 24, from Kenyon coll., Ohio, U.S.A.
Dudman, James Lumsden Samuel, born at Pitney, Somerset, 9 Jan., 1866; 2s. Lumsden Shirreff, rector. WADHAM, matric. 16 Oct., 86, aged 20, from Newton Abbot coll.

Duff, Archibald Hay Gordon, born at Drummuir, Banffshire, 1864; 2s. Lachlan Duff, major, retired. EXETER, matric. 18 Jan., 83, aged 19 (from Eton), B.A. 86; HONOURS:—3 law 86.

Duff, Edward Gordon, born at Liverpool 17 Feb., 1863; 4s. Robert, gent. WADHAM, matric. 16 Oct., 83, aged 20 (from Cheltenham coll.), B.A. 87; librarian of the John Rylands library, Manchester, 93; brother of the next-named.

Duff, Harry, M.A., B.C.L., fellow ALL SOULS' 78-90, where see.

Duff, John Wight, born at Dundee 1866; o.s. William, gen. PEMBROKE, matric. 28 Oct., 86, aged 20 (from Aberdeen university), scholar 85, B.A. 90; HONOURS:—1 classical mods. 88, 1 classics 90.

Duff, Robert Harold Ambrose Gordon, born in London 1871; 1s. Alexander, major-general. LINCOLN, matric. 20 Oct., 90, aged 19 (from Sherborne school), scholar 90.

Duff, Robert William, born in London 18 March, 1873; 1s. Robert William, M.P. BRASENOSE, matric. 22 Oct., 91, aged 18, from Eton.

Dugard, George Frederick, born in London 10 Oct., 1866; 1s. Frederick, gent. JESUS COLL., matric. 23 Oct., 85, aged 19 (from Merchant Taylors' school), scholar 85, B.A. 89; HONOURS:—2 classical mods. 87, 3 classics 89.

Dugdale, Arthur, born at Moreton-in-the-Marsh, co. Glouc., Feb., 1869; 1s. James, arm. CHRIST CHURCH, matric. 1 June, 88, aged 19, from Winchester.

Dugdale, James Gordon, born at Burnley, co. Lanc., July, 1874; 2s. James, J.P. CHRIST CHURCH, matric. 14 Oct., 92, aged 18.

Dugdale, James Lionel, born at Pendleton, co. Lanc., Sept., 1862; 1s. John, arm. CHRIST CHURCH, matric. 4 June, 81, aged 18 (from Eton); of Crathorne, Yorks, and of Irwell Bank, Lancashire.

Dugdale, William Francis Stratford-, born at Merivale, co. Warwick, 20 Oct., 1872; 1s. William Stratford, arm. BALLIOL, matric. 20 Oct., 91, aged 19, from Eton.

Duggan, William Bottomley, M.A., LINCOLN, where see.

Duignan, Carl, born at Rushall, co. Stafford, 27 Nov., 1873; 2s. William Henry, solicitor. TRINITY, matric. 17 Oct., 91, aged 17, from Bromsgrove school.

Dumbleton, rev. Henry Francis, born at Swanmore, I.W., 1862; 2s. Edgar Norris, cler. HERTFORD, matric. 18 Oct., 80, aged 18, B.A. 83.

Dun, Finlay, born in Edinburgh, 19 April, 1862; 1s. John, arm. TRINITY, matric. 15 Oct., 81, aged 19 (from Loretto school); B.A. 84, M.A. 88; HONOURS: —4 law 84.

Dun, John Arthur, born in Edinburgh 1863; 2s. John, arm. BRASENOSE, matric. 19 Oct., 82, aged 19 (from Loretto school), B.A. 87, M.A. 89.

Dun, Robert Hay, born at Latchford, Cheshire, 5 July, 1870; 2s. John, banker. BRASENOSE, matric. 14 Oct. 89, aged 19 (from Loretto school), scholar 89; HONOURS:—2 classical mods. 91.

Dunbabin, Robert Leslie, born at Cambridge in Tasmania 1869; o.s. John, gen. CORPUS CHRISTI, matric. 20 Oct., 88, aged 19 (from Hobart Town school (Tasmania), exhibitioner 90, B.A. 92; HONOURS:—1 classical mods. 90, 1 classics 92.

Duncan, Andrew Jameson Matthews, born at Edinburgh 12 Nov., 1865; 3s. James Matthews, D.Med. NEW COLL., matric. 10 Oct., 84, aged 18 (from Fettes coll.), B.A. 87; HONOURS:—2 history 87.

Duncan, rev. Douglas Charteris, born at Liverpool Dec., 1862; 3s. Cairncross, gent. KEBLE, matric. 17 Oct., 82, aged 19 (from the Charterhouse), B.A. 85; curate of Kippax, Yorks, 88.

Duncan, rev. George, born in the Mauritius 8 Sept., 1860; 1s. John Corbett, of c.s. Mauritius. WADHAM, matric. 23 Jan., 80, aged 21, B.A. 84, M.A. 88; curate of Bladon, Oxon, 85.

Duncan, George Allan, born at Bournemouth, Hants, 1867; o.s. Alexander, gent. CORPUS CHRISTI, matric. 26 Oct., 85, aged 18, B.A. 89; HONOURS:— 3 physiology 89.

Duncan, rev. George Stewart, born at Turriff, co. Aberdeen, 1860; 2s. William, gen. NON-COLLEGIATE, matric. 11 Nov., 90, aged 30, from Princeton coll., U.S.A., M.A. and B.D.

Duncan, rev. James Collins, born at Brookville, co. Meath, 18 April, 1860; 1s. James Irwin, cler. QUEEN'S, matric. 24 Jan., 80, aged 19 (from Carlisle cathedral school), B.A. 83 (HONOURS:—2 theology 83); a secretary for church missionary society 90.

Duncan, rev. John Finlay Matthews, born in Edinburgh July 1868; 4s. James Matthews, D.Med. CHRIST CHURCH, matric. 3 June, 87, aged 18, B.A. 91.

Duncan, rev. Joseph, born in Liverpool 1844; 3s. John, gent. TURRELL'S HALL, matric. 5 June, 84, aged 40 (from St. Bees, gent. school); vicar of Dyker St. Silas, Northumberland, 89.

Duncan, Moir Brainnard, born at Kincardine, Scotland, 1866; y.s. Alexander, gen. NON-COLLEGIATE, matric. 3 Nov., 87, aged 21, from Glasgow university.

Duncan, Patrick, born at King Edward, co. Aberdeen, 21 Dec., 1870; 2s. John, gen. BALLIOL, matric. 17 Oct., 89, aged 18 (from Edinburgh university), scholar and Warner exhibitioner 88; HONOURS:— Craven scholarship 90, 1 classical mods. 91, necessit Ireland scholarship 91.

Duncan, Rashleigh Johnston, born at Bideford, Devon, 1862; 5s. Patrick, arm. PEMBROKE, matric. 30 Oct., 80, aged 18 (from Brighton coll.), B.A. 84, M.A. 87; HONOURS:—2 classical mods. 82, 3 classics 84.

Duncombe, Albert William Vander Horst, born at Allensmore, co. Hereford, 1864; o.s. William Duncombe Vander Horst, cler. BRASENOSE, matric. 18 April, 83, aged 19 (from Hereford school), B.A. 86.

Dundas, Charles Leslie, M.A., fellow JESUS COLL., 73-5, where see.

Dundas, Robert Nevill, born at Chelmsford, Essex, 14 Jan., 1867; 1s. Robert James, rector of Albury, Surrey. NEW COLL., matric. 18 Oct., 86, aged 19 (from Marlborough coll.), B.A. 89; HONOURS:—2 law 89.

Dunkin, rev. Henry, born in London 19 Oct., 1861; 1s. John, arm. NEW COLL., matric. 16 Oct., 80, aged 18 (from Haileybury), B.A. 84, M.A. 87 (HONOURS:—2 classical mods. 82, 3 classics 84); head master of Dorset county school, Charminster, 90.

Dunlap, Arthur Philip, B.D., fellow ST. JOHN'S 27-52, where see.

Dunlop, Charles Edward, born in Edinburgh 25 June, 1870; o.s. Charles, gen. WADHAM, matric. 19 Jan., 89, aged 18 (from Merchiston Castle school, Edinburgh), B.A. 93.

Dunn, Ernest Victor, born at Brierley Hill, co. Stafford, 1864; 3s. Thomas Mayor, cler. NON-COLLEGIATE, matric. 17 May, 80, aged 16, from Magdalen coll. school.

Dunn, James, born at Great Billing, Northants, Aug., 1865; 3s. George Matthew, gen. ST. EDMUND HALL, matric. 26 May, 90, aged 24, from Blind coll. Worcester.

Dunn, Stephen Troyte, born at Clifton, co. Gloucester, 26 Dec., 1868; 2s. James, cler. MERTON, matric. 21 Oct., 86, aged 17 (from Radley coll.), postmaster 86, B.A. 89; HONOURS:—3 chemistry 89. See Foster's *Baronetage*, ACLAND.

Dunn, William Stephens-, born in London 1870; 1s. William Henry, arm. BRASENOSE, matric. 14 Oct., 89, aged 19, from Winchester.

Dunne, rev. Charles Walter, born at Yarpole, co. Hereford, 13 May, 1863; 2s. Thomas, arm. CORPUS CHRISTI, matric. 19 Oct., 82, aged 19 (from Wellington coll.), B.A. 87; HONOURS:—2 classical mods. 83, 3 classes 86.

Dunne, Thomas Russell, born at Yarpole, co. Hereford, 1 Jan., 1861; 1s. Thomas, arm. BRASENOSE, matric. 18 Oct., 81, aged 20 (from Eton); of Bircher Hall and Gatley Park, co. Hereford, J.P.

Dunning, William, born in London 1864; o.s. Joseph William, arm. CHARSLEY'S HALL, matric. 16 Oct., 83, aged 19; migrated to EXETER 20 April, 84 (as Joseph William); bar.-at-law, Lincoln's Inn, 89.

Dunstan, Malcolm James Rowley, born in Cheshire 19 Aug., 1863; y.s. John, arm. MERTON, matric. 17 Oct., 82, aged 19 (from St. Paul's school), postmaster 81-5, B.A. 85, M.A. 91; HONOURS:—2 natural science 85.

Dunstan, Wyndham Rowley, lecturer in materia medica, professor of chemistry to the Pharmaceutical society in London, created M.A. 29 May, 88; brother of the preceding.

Du-Port, Arthur Durell, born at Reading; 1s. Charles Durell, M.A., inspector of schools. HERTFORD, matric. 22 Oct., 92, from St. Paul's school.

Du-Pontet, René Louis Alphonse, born in London 27 Aug., 1868; 1s. Marc Jules Henri, cler. TRINITY, matric. 15 Oct., 87, aged 19 (from St. Paul's school), scholar 86, B.A. 91 (HONOURS:—1 classical mods. 89, 2 classics 91, Hertford scholarship 88, Greek verse 89, Taylorian (French) scholarship 89, Latin verse 90, Craven scholarship 90, Latin essay 92, Derby scholarship 92); a master at Winchester.

Du-Pre, Arthur Michael Duncombe, born at Lower Guiting, co. Gloucester, 28 Aug., 1860; 2s. Michael T., cler. LINCOLN, matric. 22 Jan., 80, aged 19 (from Dulwich coll.), B.A. 82.

Durell, John Percy Lister Durell, born at Marchwood, Hants, 1864; o.s. John Durell, cler. EXETER, matric. 18 Oct., 82, aged 18 (from Winchester), B.A. 86, M.A. 89; HONOURS:—4 history 86.

Durell, Thomas Chaloner Durell, born at Warblington, Hants, 25 Aug., 1869; 1s. Frederick Thomas, arm. KEBLE, matric. 17 Oct., 87, aged 18 (from Portsmouth gr. school), B.A. 91; HONOURS:—3 classical mods. 89, 3 classics 91.

Durnford, right rev. Richard, D.D., bishop of Chichester, hon. fellow MAGDALEN 88, where see.

Durrant, Bernard Christian, born at Arretons. isle of Wight, 1872; 4s. Reginald Norman, cler. KEBLE, matric. 15 Oct., 92, aged 20, from Clifton coll.

Dutton, Frederic Hugh, born at Worcester, 1873; 3s. Samuel Telford, engineer. HERTFORD, matric. 22 Oct., 92, aged 19 (from Worcester cathedral school), scholar 91.

Duval, Stephen Peachey, born at Madras 12 Nov., 1870; 1s. Stephen Smith, arm. BRASENOSE, matric. 14 Oct., 89, aged 18 (from Highgate school), scholar 89; HONOURS:—2 classical mods. 91.

VIGNETTE USED BY THE UNIVERSITY PRESS 1517.—*From Ingram.*

Duxbury, rev. Anyon Herbert, born at Salford, co. Lanc., 13 June, 1867; 1s. Anyon, arm. WADHAM, matric. 16 Oct., 86, aged 19 (from Manchester gr. school), B.A. 89 (HONOURS :—2 theology 89); curate of Swinton, Yorks, 90.

Duxbury, Frederick Richmond, born at Salford, co. Lanc., 16 Feb., 1869; 2s. Anyon, gen. NON-COLLEGIATE, matric. 20 Oct., 88, aged 19 (from Manchester gr. school and Owens coll.); migrated to WORCESTER, B.A. 91.

Duxbury, William Samuel, born at Somerset East, Cape of Good Hope, 1864; 1s. William, gen. NON-COLLEGIATE, matric. 23 March, 89, aged 25, from Gill coll., Somerset East.

Dwight, rev. William Arthur, born at Cambridge, in America, June, 1867; o.s. William, arm. KEBLE, matric. 19 Oct., 86, aged 19 (from Radley coll.), B.A. 90 (HONOURS :—3 classical mods. 88, 3 classics 90); curate of Mells, Somerset, 91.

Dwyer, Michael Francis, born at Barrowstown, co. Tipperary, 1864; 2s. John William O'Neill, arm. BALLIOL, matric. 17 Oct., 82, aged 18 (from Tullabeg coll., Ireland, and Royal Irish university), B.A. 85 (HONOURS :—1 law 85); assist. commissioner, Punjab, 84.

Dyer, Arthur Edward, born in London 3 Oct., 1868; 2s. George Bailey, gen. QUEEN'S, matric. 21 Oct., 87, aged 19 (from Southwark gr. school), exhibitioner 87; died 1 April, 88.

Dyer, Arthur Victor, born at Stamford, co. Lincoln, 1865; o.s. Charles James, cler. NON-COLLEGIATE, matric. 15 April, 82, aged 17, from Bromsgrove gr. school.

Dyer, rev. Harry Joseph, born in Norwich 1862; o.s. Joseph, gent. ST. JOHN'S, matric. 21 Jan., 82, aged 20, B.A. 84, M.A. 88; vicar of Menstone-in-Wharfedale, Yorks, 90.

Dymond, Rev. Henry Newton, born in London , 1862; 1s. John Joseph, gent. CHRIST CHURCH, matric. 12 Oct., 83, aged 21 (from King's coll. school, London), B.A. 86, M.A. 90 (HONOURS :—3 classical mods. 84, 2 theology 86); vicar of Wootton, Berks, 90.

Dyne, John Bradley, D.D., fellow WADHAM, 32-8, where see.

Dyson, rev. Francis Julian, born at Rothley Temple, co. Leic., 7 April, 1864; 2s. Major Edwards, arm. TRINITY, matric. 21 Jan., 84, aged 19 (from Winchester), B.A. 89; chaplain of Wycliffe, Oxford, 90-2, vicar of Wymynswould 92.

Dyson, Reginald Joseph, born at Edgerton, Huddersfield, 24 Nov., 1873; 1s. Hiram, manufacturer. BALLIOL, matric. 18 Oct., 92, aged 18, from the Charterhouse.

Dyson, Thomas James, born at Netherton, Yorks, Dec., 1862; 1s. George, solicitor. CHRIST CHURCH, matric. 16 Jan., 80, aged 17, B.A. 83; HONOURS :— 3 law 83.

VIGNETTE USED BY THE UNIVERSITY PRESS 1585.—*From Ingram.*

STONE STRING COURSE, ST. ALBAN ABBEY.—*Pugin.*

E

Eady, Albert Arthur, born at Chertsey, Surrey, 1856; 4s. George John, of Sunbury, Middx., gent. NON-COLLEGIATE, matric. 22 Jan., 81, aged 25; migrated to WORCESTER, B.A. 85, M.A. 87.

Eady, William Henry, born at Chertsey, Surrey, 1857; 5s. George John, gent. NEW COLL., matric. 24 Jan., 81, aged 24, from Thanet collegiate school, Margate.

Eagleston, Arthur John, born at Oxford 29 Oct., 1870; o.s. Joseph, gent. BALLIOL, matric. 18 Oct., 88, aged 17 (from Oxford high school), scholar 87, Jenkyns exhibitioner 92; HONOURS :—1 classical mods. 90, 1 classics 92.

Ealand, rev. Frederick, born in London 1861; 1s. Frederick, gent. UNIVERSITY COLL., matric. 15 May, 80, aged 19, B.A. 84, M.A. 88 (HONOURS: —3 classical mods. 82, 3 history 84); curate of St. Anne, Holloway, 89.

Eales, rev. Arthur Richard Thomas, born in London 1864; 1s. Samuel, cler. NON-COLLEGIATE, matric. 23 Feb., 82, aged 18 (from Magdalen coll. school), B.A. 86, M.A. 88; curate of Romford, Essex, 91.

Eales, rev. Sidney Charles William, born at Moulmein in Burmah, 27 Jan., 1864; 2s. William Henry, R.N. LINCOLN, matric. 13 May, 86, aged 22 (from Dulwich coll. and King's coll., London), B.A. 90; curate of Lapley with Wheaton Aston, co. Staff. 90.

Eames, James Bromley, born at Bath 8 Dec., 1872; 3s. Frederick, gen. WORCESTER, matric. 22 Oct., 91, aged 18 (from Bath gr. school), exhibitioner 91.

Earle, Alfred, M.A., of MAGDALEN HALL, created D.D. (Hertford coll.) 26 Jan., 88; bishop suffragan of Marlborough 88, and rector of St. Michael's, Cornhill, 88. See *Al. Ox.* 2nd series, 402.

Earle, Archdale, born in London 12 March, 1861; 6s. Henry Edward, gent. QUEEN'S, matric. 25 Oct., 80, aged 19 (from Uppingham school), exhibitioner 80; joint magistrate and deputy collector, Bengal, 82.

Earle, Charles Chretien, born at Swanswick, Somerset, 24 Aug., 1865; 2s. rev. John, professor of Anglo-Saxon. NON-COLLEGIATE, matric. 13 Oct., 84, aged 19 (from Malvern coll.); migrated to LINCOLN 6 Jan., 87, B.A. 88; HONOURS :—2 classical mods. 86, 3 classics 88.

Earle, George Chester, born at Swanswick, near Bath, 24 May, 1870; 2s. rev. John, professor of Anglo-Saxon. KEBLE, matric. 13 Oct., 88, aged 18, B.A. 92; HONOURS :—2 classical mods. 90, 3 classics 92.

Earle, John, M.A., fellow ORIEL 48-58, where see, page 150.

Earle, John Rolleston, born at Swanswick, near Bath, 2 June, 1864; 1s. rev. John, professor of Anglo-Saxon. NON-COLLEGIATE, matric. 21 Jan., 82, aged 17, B.A. 85, M.A. and B.Med. 92; HONOURS: —4 natural science 85.

Earle, Lionel, born in London 1 Feb. 1866; 2s. Charles, late captain. MERTON, matric. 21 Oct., 86, aged 20 from Marlborough coll.

Earle, Percy Lovell, born at Kencott, Oxon, 1865; 2s. Robert Henry, cler. NON-COLLEGIATE, matric. 28 Jan., 84, aged 19, from St. Edward's school, Summertown.

Earnshaw, Albert, born at Netherton, Yorks, 1866; o.s. David, gen. PEMBROKE, matric. 25 Jan., 88, aged 22 (from Huddersfield school and Durham university), scholar 88, B.A. 91 (HONOURS: —1 classical mods. 89, 2 classics 91.

Eason, Benjamin Macfarlane, born in Dublin 11 Oct., 1868; 6s. Charles, gent. NON-COLLEGIATE, matric. 17 Jan., 91, aged 22.

East, Alfred Ernest, born in London Oct., 1867; 2s. Joshua, gent. TURRELL'S HALL, matric. 17 June, 86, aged 18 (from Harrow); migrated to NEW INN HALL (BALLIOL) 87.

Easton, rev. Harold Alfred, born at Taunton, Somerset, 29 July, 1865; 3s. William, gen. NON-COLLEGIATE, matric. 22 Oct., 87, aged 22 (from King's coll., Taunton); migrated to WADHAM, B.A. 90; curate of St. Francis, Ashton Gate, Bristol, 90.

Easton, James Marshall, born at Liverpool, 21 Apl., 1867; 2s. Thomas Ogilvy, gent. CORPUS CHRISTI, matric. 20 Oct., 86, aged 19 (from King William coll., isle of Man), B.A. 91 (HONOURS :—3 law 90); bar.-at-law, Inner Temple, 91.

Eastwick, James, M.A. and B.C.L., fellow TRINITY 73-6, where see.

Eastwood, Arthur, born at Chorlton-upon-Medlock, co. Lanc., 1858; 2s. Wright, gen. PEMBROKE, matric. 28 Oct., 86, aged 18 (from Manchester gr. school), scholar 86, B.A. 90; HONOURS :—1 classical mods. 88, 1 classics 90.

[183]   [184]

Eastwood, John Charles Basil, born at Camberwell, Surrey, 24 March, 1862; 3s. John Fisher, arm. NEW COLL., matric. 16 Oct., 80, aged 18 from Eton (HONOURS:—3 classical mods. 81); capt. 89 and adjutant 12th (Prince of Wales Royal) Lancers 91.

Eaton, John Richard Turner, M.A., fellow MERTON 47-65, where see.

Ebden, Frederick Rogers, born at Kensington 14 Feb., 1870; 2s. Richard Powney, arm. MAGDALEN, matric. 14 Oct., 89, aged 19 (from the Charterhouse); HONOURS:—2 classical mods. 91.

Eccles, Francis Yvon, born in London 1871; o.s. Ivon Richard, arm. CHRIST CHURCH, matric. 10 Oct., 90, aged 19, Westminster scholar 90.

Eck, rev. Herbert Vincent Shortgrave, born at Pinner, Middx., May, 1864; 1s. Augustus John, gen. KEBLE, matric. 16 Oct., 83, aged 19, B.A. 86, M.A. 90 (HONOURS:—2 theology 86); vice-principal Ely theological coll. 91.

Eckett, rev. Robert, born at Crouch End, Middx., 4 Aug., 1864; 2s. Henry, gent. QUEEN'S, matric. 22 Oct., 84, aged 20 (from King's coll., London), B.A. 89, M.A. 92; curate of Ottershaw, Surrey, 90.

Eddrup, Ernest Clement, born at Broomhill, Calne, Wilts, July, 1873; 5s. Edward Paroissien, cler. KEBLE, matric. 15 Oct., 92, aged 19, from St. Edward's school, Summertown.

Eddrup, rev. Theodore Basil, born at Bremhill, Wilts, 27 Nov., 1868; 5s. Edward Paroissien, cler. KEBLE, matric. 17 Oct., 87, aged 18 (from St. Edward's school, Summertown), B.A 90 (HONOURS:—3 theology 90); curate of Newchurch-in-Rossendale, co. Lanc., 91.

Eddy, Charles, M.A., fellow QUEEN'S 61-70, where see.

Edelsten, Ernest Alfred, born at Latchford, Cheshire, 13 Dec., 1861; 1s. John Molin, gent. NEW COLL., matric. 16 Oct., 80, aged 18 (from Warrington gr. school), B.A. 84, M.A. and B.Med. 89 (HONOURS:—3 classical mods. 82, 3 natural sciences 84.

Eden, Charles Garnet, born at Oxford 7 April, 1874; 3s. William, gen. MAGDALEN, matric. 18 Oct., 92, aged 18 (from Oxford high school), demy 92.

Eden, Frederick Charles, born at Brighton 6 March, 1864; 2s. Frederick Morton, arm. KEBLE, matric. 17 Oct., 82, aged 18 (from Wellington coll.), B.A. 86; HONOURS:—3 classical mods. 84, 3 history 86.

Eden, Frederick Morton, M.A., fellow ALL SOULS' 52-7, where see.

Eden, Robert, M.A., fellow CORPUS CHRISTI 30-3, where see.

Edersheim, rev. Alfred, M.A., 16 June, 1881, by decree of convocation, born 7 March, 1825, died 16 March, 89, at Mentone. See Al. Ox. 2nd series, 407.

Edgar, Campbell Cowan, born at Tongland, Kircudbright, 1871; 1s. Andrew, clergyman. ORIEL, matric. 27 Oct., 91, aged 20 (from Glasgow university), bible clerk 91.

Edgar, Wilfred Haythorne, born at East Sheen, Surrey, 9 Jan., 1864; 1s. Joseph Haythorn, arm. BALLIOL, matric. 17 Oct., 82, aged 18 (from Winchester), B.A. 85, M.A. 89 (HONOURS:—2 classical mods. 84, 3 classics 86); student Inner Temple, 84.

Edgcumbe, Piers Alexander Hamilton, viscount Valletort, born 2 July, 1865; 1s. William Henry, earl of Mount Edgcumbe. CHRIST CHURCH, matric. 12 Oct., 83, aged 18.

Edge, Andrew Fane, born at Naughton, Suffolk, 27 Jan., 1862; 5s. Charles Fane, rector, deceased. MAGDALEN, matric. 16 Oct., 80, aged 18, from Cranbrook gr. school.

Edgell, William Seymour, born at Roddon, Somerset, 2 Dec., 1861; 3s. Charles William, cler. ST. JOHN'S, matric. 23 Jan., 82, aged 20 (from Marlborough coll.), B.A. 86, M.A. 88.

Edgeworth, Ysidro Francis, M.A., Drummond professor of political economy 91, where see, p. 11.

Edgington, Arthur, born in London 4 Oct., 1870; 2s. Charles Nuttall, rector of March St. Peter. NEW COLL., matric. 11 Oct., 89, aged 19 (from the Charterhouse); HONOURS:—2 classical mods. 91.

Edginton, Charles, born at Reigate, Surrey, 17 Oct., 1869; 1s. Charles Nuttall, rector of March St. Peter. MAGDALEN, matric. 16 Oct., 88, aged 18 from the Charterhouse, B.A. 92; HONOURS:—2 classical mods. 90, 4 classics 92.

Edlin, Arthur Howard Colborne, born at Paddington, 18 June, 1866; 2s. Vernon, cler. NEW COLL., matric. 14 Jan., 90, aged 23, from Leatherhead school.

Edminson, Ernest Whalley, born at Sale, Cheshire, 3 Dec., 1865; 4s. Leonard Thomas, arm. MERTON, matric. 16 Oct., 86, aged 19, B.A. 89 (HONOURS:—2 history 89); curate of Powerstock, Dorset, 91.

Edminson, Leonard Herbert, born at Rusholme, co. Lanc., 4 Nov., 1856; 1s. Leonard Thomas, arm. NON-COLLEGIATE, matric. 22 Jan., 81, aged 24 (from Old Trafford school and University coll., London); migrated to NEW COLL., B.A. 84, M.A. 89.

Edmond, Theodore Orton Powell, born in London 11 March, 1867; 1s. John, solicitor. WADHAM, matric. 15 Oct., 87, aged 20, from Gosport school.

Edmonds, rev. Edward Pell, born at Oxford 1871; 4s. Richard Edward, cler. UNIVERSITY COLL., matric. 13 Oct., 88, aged 19, B.A. 91; HONOURS:—4 theology 91.

Edmondson, Frank, born at Liverpool 21 Sept., 1872; 3s. Edward, merchant. NEW COLL., matric. 16 Oct., 91, aged 19, from Winchester.

Edmonstone, Archibald, born at Woolwich, Kent, 30 May, 1867; o.s. Sir William, bart. CHRIST CHURCH, matric. 23 Jan., 86, aged 18.

Edmunds, Leslie Wynne, born at Solihull, co. Warwick, 29 Dec., 1872; o.s. Henry William, gen. QUEEN'S, matric. 9 Feb., 92, aged 19, from the Charterhouse and Radley coll.

Edmundson, George, M.A., fellow BRASENOSE 71-81, where see.

Edward, Allan Philip Kenrick, born at Capel, Surrey, 6 Dec., 1872; 1s. Allan, esq. EXETER, matric. 22 Oct., 91, aged 18, from Rugby.

Edwards, Alfred George, M.A. JESUS COLL., bishop of St. Asaph, 1889, D.D. by diploma 14 March, 89. See Al. Ox., 2nd series, 400.

Edwards, rev. Alfred Howell Grey, born at Llandinorwg, co. Carnarvon 1861; 2s. Henry, cler. HERTFORD, matric. 18 Oct., 80, aged 19, B.A. 84, M.A. 88; chaplain of St. Martin (Welsh church), Chester, 87.

Edwards, Arthur Charles, born at Peterborough 1870; o.s. Amos, gen. ST. EDMUND HALL, matric. 15 Jan., 91, aged 21, B.Mus. 92.

Edwards, Charles Harold, born at Bradford, Yorks, 31 Aug., 1868; 1s. Charles, vicar Holy Trinity, Bradford. TRINITY, matric. 15 Oct., 87, aged 19 (from Bradford gr. school); migrated to CAIUS COLL., CAMBRIDGE, 89.

Edwards, Charles Henry, born at Temple Sowerby, Westmorland, 1868; 3s. Anderson, vicar of Kirkland. QUEEN'S, matric. 21 Oct., 87, aged 19 (from St. Bees gr. school), exhibitioner 87, B.A. 92; HONOURS:—2 classical mods. 89, 3 law 91.

Edwards, Cyril Thomas Polhill, born at Orleton, co. Hereford, July, 1862; 3s. William Edward, cler. KEBLE, matric. 18 Oct., 81, aged 19 (from Shrewsbury school), B.A. 85, M.A. 91.

Edwards, David, M.A., student CHRIST CHURCH 47-84, where see.

Edwards, Evan, born at Blackheath, Kent, 1 Jan., 1869; 4s. Edward, gent. BRASENOSE, matric. 24 Jan., 89, aged 20 (from Haileybury), B.A. 93.

Edwards, Francis Harold, born at Liverpool 20 Jan., 1862; 2s. Thomas Grandage, arm. UNIVERSITY COLL., matric. 16 Oct., 80, aged 18 (from Rugby), B.A. 84; HONOURS :—2 classical mods. 82, 3 classics 84.

Edwards, Frank Llewellyn, born at Kington Magna rectory, Dorset, 13 Sept., 1873; 1s. Thomas Hyne, cler. NEW COLL., matric. 14 Oct., 92, aged 19 (from Bath coll.), scholar 91.

Edwards, Henry Passmore, born in London 1871; 1s. John Passmore, arm. CHRIST CHURCH, matric. 10 Oct., 90, aged 19, from Westminster school.

Edwards, Harry Victor, born at Sheriffhales, Salop, Jan., 1864; y.s. Edwin, gent. KEBLE, matric. 14 Oct., 84, aged 20 (from Newport school, Salop), B.A. 87.

Edwards, Herbert Edward Osman, born in Liverpool 18 Feb., 1864; o.s. Frederick, arm. MERTON, matric. 19 Oct., 83, aged 19 (from Christ's hospital), postmaster 82, B.A. 87, M.A. 91; HONOURS :— 1 classical mods. 85, 2 classics 87.

Edwards, James George, M.A., student CHRIST CHURCH 54-68, where see.

Edwards, Jervis de Gray Jervis-, born in London 23 April, 1863; 1s. Thomas, cler. ST. MARY HALL, matric. 30 April, 85, aged 21.

Edwards, John Henry Lilwall, born at Clodock, co. Hereford, Dec., 1867; 2s. James, KEBLE, matric. 13 Oct., 88, aged 20 (from Brecon coll.); HONOURS :—2 mathematical mods. 90, 3 theology 92.

Edwards, John Mansell Stuart, born at Condover, Salop, 18 May, 1861; 1s. Edward, gent. LINCOLN, matric. 22 Jan., 80, aged 18 (from Westminster school), B.A. and M.A. 86.

Edwards, John Morgan, born at Coed-y-pry, Llannwchllyn, Bala, co. Merioneth, 31 May, 1868; 4s. Owen, gent. JESUS COLL., matric. 18 Oct., 92, aged 24, from University coll., Bangor.

Edwards, John Rosindale Wynne-, born in Denbigh, 1864; 3s. John Copner, arm. CHRIST CHURCH, matric. 13 Oct., 82, aged 18 (from Giggleswick school), scholar 82, B.A. 85, M.A. 91; HONOURS :—1 mathematical mods. 84, 1 mathematics 85, 2 physics 87.

Edwards, Morrice Alfred, born at Buyukdere, in Turkey, 12 Sept., 1869; 3s. Richard, gen. WORCESTER, matric. 16 Oct., 88, aged 19 (from King's coll. school, London), exhibitioner 88, B.A. 92 (HONOURS :—3 classical mods. 90, 2 law 92); brother of Richard J. A. M.

Edwards, Owen Morgan, born at Bala, co. Merioneth, 1866; 1s. Owen, gent. BALLIOL, matric. 15 Oct., 84, aged 18 (from University coll., Aberystwith, and Glasgow university), scholar 84, B.A. 88; fellow LINCOLN 89, M.A. 91; HONOURS :—Stanhope essay 86, 1 history 87, Lothian essay 87.

Edwards, Reginald Dawson St. George, born at Rockorry, co. Fermanagh, 1873; 3s. Henry St. George, clerk, deceased. UNIVERSITY COLL., matric. 15 Oct., 92, aged 19, from Eastbourne coll.

Edwards, Richard Joseph Anthony Maria, born at Constantinople 1865; 1s. Richard, arm. EXETER, matric. 31 May, 84, aged 19 (from Woburn Park school), B.A. 88, M.A. 91 (HONOURS : —3 classical mods. 85, 2 law 88); bar.-at-law Lincoln's Inn, 89; died 10 April, 92, at Constantinople; brother of Morrice A.

Edwards, Robert Stephen, born at Brymbo, co. Denbigh, 1864; 1s. James, gent. JESUS COLL., matric. 23 Oct., 85, aged 21 (as Robert), B.A. 89 and M.A. 92; HONOURS :—4 chemistry 89.

Edwards, Thomas, born at Ystalyfera, co. Glamorgan, 1864; 1s. John, gen. MARCON'S HALL, matric. 23 April, 92, aged 28.

Edwards, William, M.A., fellow JESUS COLL. 74, where see.

Edwards, William, born at (St. Woolos), Newport, co. Monmouth, 23 Dec., 1871; 1s. William, congregational minister. JESUS COLL., matric. 18 Oct., 92, aged 20, from University coll., Cardiff.

Edwards, rev. William Alfred, born at Llandow, co. Glamorgan, 1 Dec., 1867; o.s. William Joseph, rector. NON-COLLEGIATE, matric. 15 Oct., 87, aged 19 (from Cowbridge gr. school); migrated to JESUS COLL., 12 Oct., 89, B.A. 90.

Egerton, Charles Cadwallader, M.A. fellow NEW COLL. 50-71, where see.

Egerton, Philip Reginald, M.A., B.C.L., fellow NEW COLL. 51-63, where see.

Egerton, William, born at Llangollen, 6 June, 1870; 5s. Philip Henry, arm. CORPUS CHRISTI, matric. 20 Oct., 88, aged 18 (from Rossall school); assist. magistrate and collector, Bengal, 90. See *Baronetage,* GREY-EGERTON.

Egerton, William Henry, M.A., fellow BRASENOSE 36-41, where see.

Eglin, William Hendee, born at Spencer co., U.S.A., 21 May, 1866; 1s. John, of Wellington, Ohio, farmer. NON-COLLEGIATE, matric. 18 Oct., 92, aged 26, from Ohio Wesleyan coll. and Drew theological seminary.

Eglington, Arthur, born at Surbiton, Surrey, 13 Feb., 1871; 2s. William, arm. LINCOLN, matric. 20 Oct., 90, aged 19, from Sherborne school.

Ehrhardt, Albert Frederick, born at Handsworth, co. Stafford, 1864; 4s. William, gent. WORCESTER, matric. 19 Oct., 82, aged 20 (from Birmingham school), B.A. 86 (HONOURS :—3 classical mods. 84, 3 classics 86); bar.-at-law, Inner Temple, 89.

Ehrke, Charles Edward Louis, born at Wedham, Essex, 20 Oct., 1871; 1s. Edward Paul Conrad, of Bath, gen. ST. JOHN'S, matric. 11 Oct., 90, aged 18 (from Bath college), exhibitioner 90; HONOURS :— 2 classical mods. 92.

Eichholz, Oreste, born at Chorlton on Medlock, 2 May, 1873; 2s. Adolphus, merchant. MAGDALEN, matric. 22 Oct., 91, aged 18 (from Manchester gr. school), demy 90.

Eisdell, John Warmington, born at Ipswich 1861; 2s. John Warmington, gent. MERTON, matric. 18 Oct., 80, aged 19.

Eland, (rev.) Edwin Harding, born at Market Harborough, co. Leic., 1862; 2s. William, arm. BALLIOL, matric. 1 March, 85, aged 23 (from University of London, B.A.), B.A. 89, M.A. 91 (HONOURS :—2 classical mods. 86, 2 classics 88); assistant master Radley coll. 89.

Eld, James Henry, B.D., fellow ST. JOHN'S 41-75, where see.

Eley, Charles Cuthbert, born at Hampstead, London, 4 Feb., 1873; 2s. William Thomas, manufacturer, deceased. BRASENOSE, matric. 21 Oct., 92, aged 19, from Rugby.

Elford, Percy, born at Exeter, 1867; 1s. Edwin, arm. CHRIST CHURCH, matric. 16 Oct. 85, aged 18 (from Exeter gr. school), scholar 84, B.A. 89, M.A. 92; fellow ST. JOHN'S 92; HONOURS:—1 chemistry 89.

Elgar, rev. Alfred Cassin, born at Bungay, Suffolk, 8 Oct., 1861; o.s. Alfred, gent. WORCESTER, matric. 20 Oct., 81, aged 20 (from Gloucester school), B.A. 85, M.A. 88 (HONOURS:—3 theology, 85) ; curate of Lee, Kent, 89.

Elger, Percival Charles, born in London 16 Nov., 1872; 2s. William Percival, captain. BRASENOSE, matric. 22 Oct., 91, aged 18, from Winchester.

Elger, Ronald Hayden, born at Kensington 16 Feb., 1870; 3s. George Gwyn, arm. TRINITY, matric. 13 Oct., 88, aged 18 (from Winchester school), B.A. 92; HONOURS:—4 law 92.

Elias, William Pritchard, born at Llansadwrn, isle of Anglesey, 7 April, 1870 ; 1s. Thomas, gen. ORIEL, matric. 25 Oct., 89, aged 19 (from Rossall school), scholar 89; HONOURS:—2 classical mods. 91.

Eliot, Charles Norton Edgecombe, fellow TRINITY 84, M.A. 89, where see.

Eliot, Claude Henry, born at Compton Abbas, Dorset, 18 Aug., 1869 ; 4s. William, canon of Worcester. MERTON, matric. 19 Oct., 89, aged 20 (from Haileybury); treasurer Oxford union society 92, president 93.

Eliot, Edward, B.C.L., fellow NEW COLL. 45-61, where see.

Eliot, Montague Charles, born 13 May, 1870 ; 2s. col. the hon. Charles George Cornwallis. EXETER, matric. 16 Oct., 89, aged 19 (from the Charterhouse), scholar 89 ; HONOURS:—2 classical mods. 91.

Eliot, Philip Frank, M.A. TRINITY, B. and D.D. 1891, dean of Windsor. See *Al. Ox.*, 2nd series, 490.

Eliot, rev. Philip Herbert, born at Calley, Scotland, (6 or 20?) Sept., 1862; 1s. Philip Frank, dean of Windsor. ORIEL, matric. 18 Oct., 81, aged 19, B.A. 85, M.A. 88; vicar of Winslow, Bucks, 89.

Elkington, rev. William Hardwicke Goodall, born in London 8 Jan., 1865; 3s. Arthur Guy, arm. ST. MARY HALL, matric. 14 April, 83, aged 18.

Ellaby, Ernest Ridsdale, M.A., fellow WADHAM 57, where see.

Ellaby, rev. George Alfred, born at Shirley, Hants, 28 April, 1868; 3s. George Watts, cler. WADHAM, matric. 16 Oct., 86, aged 18, B.A. 90; chaplain of St. Giles-in-the-Fields, London, 91.

Ellam, Arthur, born at Cheltenham 21 Aug., 1863; 1s. John, cler. QUEEN'S, matric. 23 Oct., 82, aged 19 (from King's coll. school London), B.A. 87, M.A. 92.

Ellerton, rev. Arthur John Bicknell, born at Crewe Green, Cheshire, 1866; 3s. John, cler. ST. JOHN'S, matric. 23 Jan., 86, aged 20 (from Merchant Taylors' school), B.A. 89 ; curate of Halifax, Yorks, 90.

Ellerton, rev. Francis George, born at Crewe Green, Cheshire, 19 Feb., 1861; 1s. John, rector of White Roothing, Essex. HERTFORD, matric. 18 Oct., 80, aged 19 (from Haileybury), scholar 79-84, B.A. 83, M.A. 92 (HONOURS:—2 classical mods. 82, 3 classics 84); curate of Bromborough 90-3, rector of Wirmingham, (hoth) Cheshire, 93.

Elles, Edmund Hardie, born at Wimbledon, Surrey, 12 Sept., 1867 ; 2s. Jameson, arm. NEW COLL., matric. 15 Oct., 86, aged 19 (from Winchester), scholar 85, B.A. 90 (HONOURS:—2 classical mods. 88, 3 classics 90) ; of the Indian civil service.

Elletson, Harry Chandos, born at Fleetwood, co. Lanc., 1868 ; 2s. Daniel Hope, arm. ST. JOHN'S, matric. 15 Oct., 87, aged 19 (from Rossall school), B.A. 92 ; HONOURS:—3 history 91.

Ellice, William Henry, born at Dover, Kent, 1866 ; 2s. sir Charles Henry, knight. CORPUS CHRISTI, matric. 23 Oct., 84, aged 18 (from Wellington coll.); HONOURS:—3 classical mods. 86.

Elliott, Charles James, bishop of Gloucester, created D.D. 16 June, 1885. See *Al. Ox.* and series, 418.

Elliott, Herbert, born at Wells, Somerset, Aug., 1871 ; 5s. Langford, arm. KEBLE, matric. 11 Oct., 90, aged 19, from Wells school.

Elliot, Gilbert John, born at Chetwynd, Salop, 6 May, 1864 ; 2s. William, vicar of Urinsop, co. Hereford. LINCOLN, matric. 19 Oct., 83, aged 19 (from Marlborough coll.), scholar 83, B.A. 87 (HONOURS:—1 classical mods. 85, 2 classics 87) ; assist. professor at Dundee.

Elliott, John Hugh Armstrong, born in London 14 May, 1861 ; 1s. John, arm. MAGDALEN matric. 16 Oct., 80, aged 19 (from Winchester), B.A. 84, M.A. 89 (HONOURS:—4 law 84); bar.-at-law, Inner Temple, 87.

Elliott, Adshead, born at Newton Heath, co. Lanc., Jan., 1869 ; 5s. John Matthews, arm. ORIEL, matric. 20 Oct., 88, aged 19 (from Manchester gr. school), B.A. 91.

Elliott, Edwin Bailey, M.A., fellow MAGDALEN 92, where see.

Elliott, rev. Edward James, born at Broadwater, Sussex, 1861 ; 2s. Edward King, cler. NON-COLLEGIATE, matric. 15 Oct., 81, aged 20 (from Brighton coll.) ; migrated to ST. JOHN'S, B.A. 85 ; curate of Cheltenham St. Mary 88.

Elliott, George Hugh, born at High Heskett, near Carlisle, 15 April, 1867 ; 1s. Isaac, gen. QUEEN'S, matric. 25 Oct., 86, aged 19 (from St. Bees gr. school), exhibitioner 86, B.A. 90 ; HONOURS:—3 mathematical mods. 88, 3 mathematics 90 ; curate of Hunslet, Yorks, 91.

Elliott, Joseph, M.A. QUEEN'S, where see.

Elliott, Richard Thomas, born at Camberwell, Surrey, 28 Sept., 1863 ; 2s. Richard, gent. WORCESTER, matric. 19 Oct., 82, aged 19 (from Southwark gr. school), exhibitioner 82-6, B.A. 86, M.A. 89 (HONOURS:—1 classical mods. 84, 2 classics 86).

Elliott, Robert Bernard, born at Poplar, Middx., 15 Dec., 1869 ; 1s. Robert John, vicar of St. Stephen's, Poplar. NON-COLLEGIATE, matric. 13 Oct., 88, aged 18, from Merchant Taylors' school.

Ellis, Arthur, born at Wigan, co. Lanc., 4 Dec., 1872 ; 2s. Thomas Ratcliffe, solicitor. TRINITY, matric. 17 Oct., 91, aged 18, from Rugby.

Ellis, Ernest Mostyn, born at Poole, Dorset, 23 June, 1871 ; 3s. Heber Dowling, D.Med. NEW COLL., matric. 10 Oct., 90, aged 19, from Eastbourne coll.

Ellis, Francis Henry Babington, born at Cranborne, Berks, 23 Feb., 1865 ; 2s. Conyngham, cler. BRASE-NOSE, matric. 14 Oct., 84, aged 19 (from Winchester), exhibitioner 84, B.A. 88, M.A. 91 ; HONOURS:—2 classical mods. 86, 3 classics 88.

Ellis, Godfrey Vines, born at Gloucester 13 July, 1864 ; o.s. Edmund Vines, gent. QUEEN'S, matric. 22 Oct., 82, aged 20, from Magdalen coll. school.

Ellis, Harold, born in London 10 April, 1874 ; 1s. Walter Lima Joel, solicitor. MERTON, matric. 28 Oct., 92, aged 18, from Clifton coll.

Ellis, Horace Telford, born at Maldon, Australia, 1864 ; 2s. Arthur Danvers, gent. WORCESTER, matric. 25 Jan., 83, aged 19 (from Sherborne school) ; HONOURS:—3 classical mods. 84.

Ellis, Philip James, born at Richmond, Surrey, 1867 ; 2s. Henry, arm. CORPUS CHRISTI, matric. 20 Oct., 86, aged 19 (from Forest school), B.A. 90 ; HONOURS:—2 classical mods. 88, 3 history 90.

Ellis, Robert Kingdon, born in London 4 July, 1861; 2s. George Henry, arm., deceased. MAGDALEN, matric. 16 Oct., 80, aged 19 (from Merchant Taylors' school), demy 80-4, B.A. 85, B.Med. 92; HONOURS:—3 natural science 84.

Ellis, Robinson, M.A. fellow TRINITY 58, where see.

Ellis, Thomas Edward, born at Llandissil, co. Merioneth, 16 Feb., 1859; 3s. Thomas, farmer. NEW COLL., matric. 16 Oct., 80, aged 21 (from University coll., Aberystwith), B.A. 85 (HONOURS: —3 classical mods. 82, 2 history 84); M.P. Merionethshire since 86, a junior lord of the treasury Aug., 92.

Ellis, Thomas Peter, born at Wrexham, co. Denbigh, 4 June, 1873; 2s. Peter, merchant. LINCOLN, matric. 23 Oct., 91, aged 18, from Oswestry high school.

Ellis, Walter Angus, born at Whitburn, co. Durham, 9 April, 1867; 12. Robert Keate, arm. TRINITY, matric. 16 Oct., 86, aged 19 (from Repton school), B.A. 89; HONOURS:—3 history 89.

Ellis, Walter Devonshire, born at Kings Norton, co. Worc., 21 Sept., 1871; 3s. Alexander Adcock, gen. NEW COLL., matric. 10 Oct., 90, aged 19 (from Winchester), scholar 89; HONOURS:—1 classical mods. 92, proxime accessit Hertford scholarship 91.

Ellison, Henry, M.A., fellow UNIVERSITY COLL. 43-53, where see.

Ellison, Henry Biomfield, born at Windsor 3 June, 1868; 4s. Henry John, cler. PEMBROKE, matric. 28 Oct., 86, aged 18 (from Radley coll.), scholar 86, B.A. 90; HONOURS:—2 classical mods. 88, 3 classics 90.

Elliston, Sydney Robert, born at Ipswich 1870; 2s. William Alfred, D.Med. PEMBROKE, matric. 17 Oct., 88, aged 18 (from Ipswich school), scholar 87, B.A. 92; HONOURS:—2 mathematical mods. 90, 3 mathematics 92.

Ellwood, Henry Whalley, born at Rangeworthy, co. Glouc., 1 Aug., 1873; 1s. Robert Gilbert, rector of Staunton-on-Wye, co. Hereford. BRASENOSE, matric. 21 Oct., 92, aged 19, from Christ's hospital and Hereford cathedral school.

Elphinstone, James Drummond, master of, born 16 April, 1865; 1s. William Buller, baron E. CHRIST CHURCH, matric. 16 Oct., 84, aged 19 (from Eton), B.A. 89; died Nov., 90, in South Africa.

Elrington, Nicholas, born at Saling, Essex, 1865; 3s. Thomas William, cler. WADHAM, matric. 11 Oct., 84, aged 19 (from Felsted school), B.A. 88; HONOURS:—2 classical mods. 86, 3 physiology 88.

Elton, Charles Isaac, B.A., fellow QUEEN'S 62-4, where see.

Elton, rev. George Goodenough, born at Ivor, Bucks, 1865; 1s. George, cler. ORIEL, matric. 27 Oct., 83, aged 18, B.A. 86, M.A. 90; curate of Sutton Coldfield, co. Warwick, 90.

Elton, (rev.) Herbert Gresley, born at Wheatley, Oxon, 22 Aug., 1865; 2s. Edward cler. ORIEL, matric. 27 Oct., 83, aged 18, B.A. 87, M.A. 90; curate of Grasmedale, co. Lanc., 90.

Elton, Oliver, born at Holt, Norfolk, 3 June, 1861; o.s. Charles Allen, cler. CORPUS CHRISTI, matric. 21 Oct., 80, aged 19 (from Marlborough coll.), scholar 80-5, B.A. 84; HONOURS:—2 classical mods. 81, 1 classics 84.

Elton, Walsingham Edmund Bourke, born at Clifton, co. Glouc., 19 Jan., 1862; 5s. Frederick, gent. QUEEN'S, matric. 23 Oct., 82, aged 20 (from Cheltenham coll.), B.A. 86.

Elvey, Charles Greville, born at Windsor, Berks, 2 Dec., 1863; 4s. sir George Job, knt. ST. JOHN'S, matric. 14 Oct., 82, aged 18, from Cheltenham coll.

Elwell, Clement Law Stewart, born at Long Ashton, co. Glouc., 18 July, 1869; 2s. Alfred Odell, cler. WORCESTER, matric. 16 Oct., 88, aged 19 (from Marlborough coll.), B.A. 91.

Elwell, James Dudley, born at Hove, Brighton, 19 July, 1872; 2s. Henry, M.A., vicar of Harlow, Essex. ST. JOHN'S, matric. 17 Oct., 91, aged 19, from Felsted school.

Elwes, Albert Cary, born at Bognor, Sussex, 24 Oct., 1868; 5s. Dudley George Cary, of Conway, Florida, U.S.A., arm. ST. JOHN'S, matric. 25 April, 90, aged 21, from Bedford gr. school.

Elwes, Dudley Frederick Cary, born at Bletchingley, Surrey, 14 Jan., 1864; 1s. Dudley George Cary, arm. KEBLE, matric. 16 Oct., 83, aged 19 (from Bedford gr. school), B.A. 86, M.A. 93; HONOURS: —3 chemistry 86.

Elwes, Gervase Henry Cary, born at Great Billing, Northants, 15 Nov., 1865; 1s. Valentine Dudley, arm. CHRIST CHURCH, matric. 30 May, 85, aged 18.

Elwin, Edgar Alfred, born at Dover, Kent, 1864; 1s. Edward, arm. BALLIOL, matric. 18 Oct., 81, aged 17 (from Dover coll.); senior assist. to collector and magistrate, and agent to the governor of Madras at Vizagapatam.

Elwin, Edmund Henry, born at Dover 18 Sept., 1871; 5s. Edmund, arm. MERTON, matric. 15 Oct., 90, aged 19, from Dover coll.

Elwin, Ernest Barnes, born at Dover 1870; 4s. Edward, gen. BALLIOL, matric. 18 Oct., 88, aged 18 (from Dover coll.); assist. to collector and magistrate Vizagapatam, Madras c.s.

Elworthy, Arthur Kershaw, born at Wellington, Somerset, 1867; 2s. Charles, gen. PEMBROKE, matric. 28 Oct., 86, aged 19.

Elworthy, Charles Kershaw, born at Wellington, Somerset, 16 Sept., 1865; 1s. Charles James, gent. MAGDALEN, matric. 16 Oct., 84, aged 19 (from Clifton coll.), B.A. 87.

Emanuel, Alfred Edward Lewis, born in London 15 June, 1873; 4s. Lewis, solicitor. TRINITY, matric. 15 Oct., 92, aged 19 (from St. Paul's school), scholar 91.

Emanuel, Charles Herbert Lewis, born in London 10 Jan., 1868; 2s. Lewis, solicitor. WADHAM, matric. 16 Oct., 86, aged 18 (from Harrow), B.A. 89; HONOURS:—3 law 89.

Emanuel, Montagu Rousseau, born in London 24 July, 1873; 1s. Joel, solicitor. BALLIOL, matric. 20 Oct., 91, aged 18, from Harrow.

Embry, James Hanks, born at Monmouth, 1862; o.s. James, gent. ST. EDMUND HALL, matric. 24 April, 84, aged 22.

Emeris, rev. William Charles, born at Gloucester 8 July, 1863; 2s. John, rector of Upton St. Leonard's, co. Glouc. NEW COLL., matric. 14 Oct., 82, aged 19 (from the Charterhouse), B.A. 86, M.A. 90 (HONOURS:—3 classical mods. 84, 3 history 86); curate of Kensington 90.

Emeris, William Robert, M.A., fellow MAGDALEN 39-43, where see.

Emmons, Hamilton, born in Boston, America, 1864; 1s. Robert Wales, arm. BALLIOL, matric. 16 Oct., 83, aged 19 (from Leamington coll.), B.A. 89; HONOURS:—3 chemistry 87.

Emmott, Charles, born at Oldham, co. Lanc., 1862; 5s. Thomas, gent. CHRIST CHURCH, matric. 13 Oct., 82, aged 20, B.A. 86 (HONOURS:—3 classical mods. 84, 3 classics 86); treasurer Oxford union society 85, president 86.

Empson, Cecil Annesley, born at Eydon, Northants, 14 June, 1868; 3s. Arthur John, cler. WORCESTER, matric. 17 Oct., 87, aged 19 (from Lancing coll.), B.A. 92; HONOURS:—3 classical mods. 89, 3 history 91.

193   EMTAGE. —— MATRICULATIONS, 1880 TO 1892. —— ETHERIDGE.   194

Emtage, Oliver de Courcy, born at Thornbury, isle of Barbados, 8 Feb., 1867; 4s. Edmund, gent. NON-COLLEGIATE, matric. 4 Nov., 86, aged 19 (from Harrison coll., Barbados), scholar WORCESTER 86, B.A. 90; HONOURS :—1 mathematical mods. 87, 2 mathematics 90, 4 physics 91.

Emtage, William Thomas Allder, born at St. James, Barbados, 1865; 2s. Edmund, gent. PEMBROKE, matric. 30 Oct., 80, aged 17 (from Harrison coll., Barbados), scholar 80, B.A. 83, M.A. 88; (HONOURS :—1 mathematical mods. 81, 1 mathematics 83, 1 natural science 85), examiner in natural science 90-1.

Engleheart, Clinton, born in London 30 May 1864; 3s. John Gardner Dillman, K.C.B. CHRIST CHURCH, matric. 12 Jan., 83, aged 18 (from Winchester), B.A. 87, M.A. 92.

Engleheart, Henry Lewis Dillman, born in London 2 Dec., 1860; 1s. John Gardner Dillman, K.C.B. CHRIST CHURCH, matric. 16 Jan., 80, aged 19, B.A. 83, M.A. 89 (HONOURS :—4 history 83); bar.-at-law, Lincoln's Inn, 88.

Engleheart, sir John Gardner Dillman, M.A., student CHRIST CHURCH 44-59, where see.

Engleheart, Victor Frederick, born at Frogmore, Berks, 4 March, 1867; 4s. John Gardner Dillman, K.C.B. NEW COLL., matric. 15 Oct., 86, aged 19 (from Rugby); HONOURS :—3 classical mods. 88.

English, Edward James, born at Edgbaston, co. Warwick, 5 Nov., 1867; 4s. Charles, gen. NON-COLLEGIATE, matric. 11 Oct., 90, aged 22 (from Birmingham gr. school); HONOURS :—2 classical mods. 92.

English, Fitzwilliam de Guadalupe, born at Brampton, Oxon, March, 1864; o.s. William Watson, cler. ST. MARY HALL, matric. 4 Nov., 80, aged 16 (from Lowestoft school), B.A. 84, M.A. 90.

Enraght, Hawtrey James, born at Brighton, Sussex, 1872; 2s. Richard William, cler. NON-COLLEGIATE, matric. 18 April, 91, aged 19, from Denstone coll.

Ensor, rev. Henry Hugh, born at Milborne Port, Somerset, 12 July, 1868; 1s. Francis Avery, arm. LINCOLN, matric. 21 Oct., 87, aged 19 (from Forest school), B.A. 90 (HONOURS :—2 history 90); curate of St. Bartholomew, Hyde, 92.

Enthoven, Reginald Edward, born at Hastings, Sussex, 23 Nov., 1869; 5s. James, gen. NEW COLL., matric. 14 Oct., 87, aged 17 (from Wellington coll.); assist. collector and magistrate Dharwar, Bombay 92.

Errington, Frederick Francis, born at Ashbourne, co. Derby, 30 July, 1861; 1s. John, cler. CHRIST CHURCH, matric. 24 Jan., 81, aged 20, from Radley coll.

Errington, Walter Alfred, born at Ashbourne, co. Derby, 24 Feb., 1868; 2s. John Richard, cler. PEMBROKE, matric. 17 Oct., 88, aged 20.

Erskine, Alan David, born at Cardross, co. Stirling, 26 Aug., 1872; 4s. Henry David, serj.-at-arms, house of commons. MAGDALEN, matric. 22 Oct., 91, aged 19, from the Charterhouse.

Erskine, rev. Charles, born in London 14 July, 1868; 1s. Charles, arm. ORIEL, matric. 18 Oct., 87, aged 19 (from Westminster school), B.A. 90 (HONOURS :—3 classical mods. 89.

Erskine, Henry Walter Coningsby, born at Edinburgh 11 May, 1872; 1s. hon. Augustus William. EXETER, matric. 13 Oct., 90, aged 18, from the Charterhouse.

Erskine, James Francis Henry St. Clair, 5th earl of Rosslyn, born 16 March, 1869; 1s. Francis Robert, 4th earl. MAGDALEN, matric. 16 Oct., 88, aged 19, from Eton.

Erskine, hon. William Augustus Forbes, born at Alloa, Scotland, 30 Oct., 1871; 2s. Walter Henry, earl of Mar and Kellie. MAGDALEN, matric. 14 Oct., 90, aged 18, from Eton.

Escombe, Frank, born at Blackheath, Kent, 20 Aug., 1874; 6s. Rowland, gent. EXETER, matric. 13 Feb., 92, aged 17, from Sevenoaks gr. school.

Escombe, Robert, born at Surbiton, Surrey, 13 June, 1865; 2s. Rowland, gent. EXETER, matric. 23 Oct., 85, aged 20, from Sevenoaks gr. school.

Escott, William Sydney Rhys Sweet, born at Carlton rectory, Beds, 10 Oct., 1867; 1s. William, cler. TRINITY, matric. 19 Jan., 87, aged 19 (from Coventry school), B.A. and M.A. 90; HONOURS :—3 law 90.

Espin, rev. Arthur Espinelle, born at Ashley Bridge, co. Lanc., June, 1865; o.s. William, cler. KEBLE, matric. 14 Oct., 84, aged 19, B.A. 87; curate of St. Woolos, Newport, co. Mon., 91.

Espin, Thomas Espinelle, D.D., fellow LINCOLN 49-54, where see.

Espin, William Mallam, born at Rondebosch, Cape of Good Hope, 1870; 1s. John, cler. ST. JOHN'S, matric. 13 Oct., 88, aged 18, from Natal.

Espinasse, rev. Richard Talbot, born at Wickham Bishops, Essex, 5 April, 1867; o.s. Richard, cler. NON-COLLEGIATE, matric. 18 Oct., 80, aged 18 (from the Charterhouse); migrated to BRASENOSE 22 Jan., 81, B.A. 84, M.A. 88; assist. master Ardingley coll. 84-90; curate of West Tarring, Sussex, 84-90.

Essery, Albert Golding, born at Kingswood, near Bristol, 23 Feb., 1867; o.s. Albert, gent. ST. JOHN'S, matric. 17 Oct., 85, aged 18 (from Bristol school), scholar 85, B.A. 89; HONOURS :—2 classical mods. 87, 3 classics 89.

Essex, Herbert James, born at Malvern Wells, co. Worc., 4 Aug., 1867; 1s. Thomas, schoolmaster. JESUS COLL., matric. 23 Oct., 85, aged 18 (from Clifton coll.), scholar 85, B.A. 89; HONOURS :—2 classical mods. 87, 3 classics 89.

Esson, William, M.A. fellow MERTON 60, where see.

Estcourt, Edmund Hiley Bucknall, M.A. fellow MERTON 26-31, where see.

Ethé, Hermann, created M.A. 5 June, 1888; examiner in oriental studies, 87,8,9, professor of oriental and modern languages at University coll., Aberystwith.

Ethelston, Arthur Anderson, born at Hinton, Salop, 14 Sept., 1861; 3s. Robert Peel, arm. CORPUS CHRISTI, matric. 1 Feb., 81, aged 19 (from Winchester), B.A. 84; HONOURS :—3 classical mods. 82, 4 law 84.

Ethelston, Hugh Wicksted, born at Whitchurch, Salop, 27 July, 1868; 5s. Robert Peel, arm. KEBLE, matric. 19 Oct., 86, aged 18 (from Winchester), B.A. 89.

Etheridge, Edward Harold, born at Haslemere, Surrey, Sept. 1872; 3s. Sanders, cler. KEBLE, matric. 20 Oct., 91, aged 19, from Marlborough coll.

Etheridge, Godfrey William, born at Farnham, Surrey, 16 May, 1870; 2s. Sanders, rector of Haslemere. KEBLE, matric. 12 Oct., 89, aged 19 (from Haileybury); HONOURS :—2 classical mods. 91.

Etheridge, rev. Leonard Sumner, born at Alresford, Hants, Feb. 1868; 1s. Sanders, cler. KEBLE, matric. 17 Oct., 87, aged 19 (from Marlborough coll.), B.A. 91 (HONOURS :—2 classical mods. 89, 3 history 91); curate All Saint's, Portsea, 92.

Etheridge, William Austin Gray, born at Oxford Oct., 1867; 1s. Austin Francis Gray, gent. KEBLE, matric. 19 Oct., 86, aged 19 (from Magdalen coll. school), exhibitioner 86, B.A. 90 (HONOURS :—1 history 90); schoolmaster.

13

Evans, rev. Alexander Cockburn, born at Cilgerran, co. Pemb., 24 April, 1868; 2s. David, cler. MERTON, matric. 22 Oct., 87, aged 19 (from Christ's coll. Brecon), B.A. 91 (HONOURS:—3 theology 91); curate of Abergavenny 91.

Evans, rev. Arnold Frederick, born at Brecon 1864; 1s. David Frederic, gent. NON-COLLEGIATE, matric. 13 Oct., 83, aged 19, B.A. 87 (HONOURS:—3 theology 87); curate of Pontnewynydd, co. Monmouth, 88.

Evans, Arthur Burroughes, born at Hull, Yorks, 28 March, 1874; 2s. Thomas Melancthon, surgeon. BALLIOL, matric. 18 Oct., 92, aged 18, from Clifton coll.

Evans, Arthur John, M.A., hon. fellow BRASENOSE, where see.

Evans, Charles James (Walbrand), born at Ross, co. Hereford, 27 Dec., 1859; 2s. Thomas, gen. ST. MARY HALL, matric. 18 Oct., 88, aged 28, B.A. 92.

Evans, rev. Charles Walter Lloyd, born at Frome, Dorset, July, 1867; o.s. Edward Lloyd, gen. ST. EDMUND HALL, matric. 22 Oct., 87, aged 20, B.A. 90; curate of Shireshead, co. Lanc., 91.

Evans, David Anwyl, born at Brondewynnant, near Barmouth, 1860; 2s. John, gent. NON-COLLEGIATE, matric. 18 Oct., 80, aged 20, B.A. 84.

Evans, David Joshua, B.D., fellow JESUS COLL. 41-66, where see.

Evans, David Richard, born at Wymondham, Norfolk, 1869; 1s. David, cler. NON-COLLEGIATE, matric. 25 Jan., 88, aged 19; HONOURS:—3 history 91.

Evans, David William, born at Merthyr Tydvil, co. Glam., 4 Nov., 1866; 1s. Thomas, gent. JESUS COLL., matric. 23 Oct., 85, aged 18 (from Llandovery coll.); HONOURS:—3 mathematical mods. 87.

Evans, rev. Ebenezer Williams, born at Llansantffraid, co. Merioneth, 1865; y.s. David, cler. NON-COLLEGIATE, matric. 17 Oct., 85, aged 20 (from King's school Chester); migrated to ST. EDMUND HALL, B.A. 88, M.A. 92; curate of Tarporley 89.

Evans, Edward Francis Herbert, born at co. Worc., Sept., 1873; 1s. Edward Wallace, gent. ORIEL, matric. 27 Oct., 92, aged 19, from Eton.

Evans, Francis Duntze, born at Cilgerran, co. Pembroke, 3 Aug., 1870; 2s. David, cler. BRASENOSE, matric. 14 Oct., 89, aged 19 (from Christ's coll. Brecon), scholar 89; HONOURS:—1 classical mods. 91.

Evans, Frank, born at Stamford, co. Lincoln, 1872; 2s. Daniel St. John, solicitor. ORIEL, matric. 27 Oct., 91, aged 19 (from Marlborough coll.), scholar 91.

Evans, Frank Jewel, born at Sculcoates, near Hull, July, 1872; 1s. Thomas Melancthon, arm. KEBLE, matric. 11 Oct., 90, aged 18, from Hull school.

Evans, rev. Frank Walbran Walbrand, born at Ross, co. Hereford, 29 Dec., 1864; 3s. Thomas, gen. MERTON, matric. 17 Oct., 88, aged 23 (from London university), B.A. 91 (HONOURS:—3 classical mods. 90); curate of Headingley, Leeds, 91.

Evans, Frederick Edmond, born at Llanelly, co. Carmarthen, 1859; 2s. Evan, gent. ST. ALBAN HALL, matric. 19 Oct., 80, aged 21 (from Llandovery coll.); migrated to EXETER, Lent term, 81 (and to NEW INN HALL 85, B.A. 86), M.A. 87.

Evans, Frederic James, born at Ouchan, parish of Douglas, I.o., 21 Oct., 1869; 1s. Frederic Hodgson, bar.-at-law, deceased. NON-COLLEGIATE, matric. 18 Oct., 92, aged 22, from Battersen gr. school, and Durham university.

Evans, George Henry Herbert, born at Woodchester, near Stroud, 17 Nov., 1860; 4s. George Henry, cler. NON-COLLEGIATE, matric. 17 Jan., 80, aged 19 (from Reading school and Marlborough coll.); scholar LINCOLN 80, B.A. 83, M.A. 89; HONOURS: —2 classical mods. 81, 2 classics 83.

Evans, rev. George Simon Tudor, born in London 1867; 4s. David, gen. ST. JOHN'S, matric. 15 Oct., 87, aged 20 (from University coll., Cardiff); HONOURS:—2 classical mods. 89, 3 classics 91.

Evans, Gerald, born at Eltham, Kent, 15 Oct., 1867; 1s. David, gen. EXETER, matric. 19 Oct., 87, aged 20 (from Blackheath school); died 31 Oct., 89, at Oxford.

Evans, Gilbert Luxmore, born at Oxford 4 March, 1866; 1s. Gilbert Henry of Pembroke coll. CORPUS CHRISTI, matric. 26 Oct., 85; aged 19 (from Eton), exhibitioner 84, B.A. 89; HONOURS:—2 classical mods. 87, 3 classics 89.

Evans, Harold Vivian, born at Huyton, co. Lanc., 1864; 1s. Llewellyn William, gent. NON-COLLEGIATE, matric. 14 Oct., 82, aged 18 (from Southport school); migrated to EXETER 83.

Evans, Henry Randell, born at Islington 1867; 1s. Frederick, gen. NON-COLLEGIATE, matric. 1 June, 88, aged 21 (from Abingdon gr. school); HONOURS: —2 classical mods. 90.

Evans, John, born at Llanfihangel-y-Creuddyn, co. Cardigan, 1861; 1s. William, cler. JESUS COLL., matric. 23 Oct., 80, aged 19 (from Swansea school), B.A. 87, M.A. 91; HONOURS:—2 classical mods. 82, 3 classics 84.

Evans, rev. John, born at Tregaron, co. Cardigan, 1867; 2s. William, pleb. NON-COLLEGIATE, matric. 13 Oct., 83, aged 28, B.A. 86, M.A. 91 (HONOURS: —1 theology 86); curate of Christ Church, West Bromwich, 91.

Evans, John Arthur, born at Rhosbedrwnal, co. Carnarvon, 8 Aug., 1859; 4s. Thomas, gent. NON-COLLEGIATE, matric. 17 Oct., 85, aged 26 (as John) (from Bottwnog gr. school); migrated to JESUS COLL., 30 April, 87, B.A. 88 (as John Arthur); HONOURS:—3 theology 88.

Evans, John Carbery, born at Brighton July, 1865; 1s. John Carbery, arm. CHRIST CHURCH, matric. 13 Oct., 82, aged 17 (from Eton), B.A. 85, M.A. 89; bar.-at-law, Inner Temple, 88.

Evans, John Gwenogvryn, created M.A. 7 June, 1887; a distinguished palæographer, joint-editor with prof. Rhys of the "Mabinogion," published by the Clarendon press.

Evans, John Howell, born at Wymondham, Norfolk, 13 March, 1871; 2s. David, vicar of Pont-Dolanog, Welshpool. NON-COLLEGIATE, matric. 17 Oct., 91, aged 21, from Christ coll., Brecon.

Evans, John Pughe, born at Llanfihangel, co. Montgom., 21 May, 1872; 1s. Edward, rector. JESUS COLL., matric. 20 Oct., 91, aged 19, from Oswestry gr. school.

Evans, John Young, born at Dowlais, co. Glamorgan, 1866; 1s. John Bennett, gen. CORPUS CHRISTI, matric. 20 Oct., 88, aged 22 (from University coll., Aberystwith), exhibitioner 88; HONOURS:— 1 classical mods. 90, 2 classics 92.

Evans, Lewis Herbert, born at Oxford 1871; 3s. Evan, master of Pembroke coll. PEMBROKE, matric. 26 Oct., 89, aged 18, from Rugby.

Evans, Martin Llewellyn, born in London 21 June, 1864; 1s. John Llewellyn, gent. TRINITY, matric. 15 Oct., 83, aged 19 (from Rugby), B.A. 86, M.A. 90; HONOURS:—3 classical mods. 85.

Evans, Pepyat Williams, born at Radyr, co. Cardiff, 7 May, 1862; 1s. Franklin George, gent. BALLIOL, matric. 18 Oct., 81, aged 19 (from University coll., Bristol), B.A. 86, M.A. and B.C.L. 88 (HONOURS: —3 classical mods. 83, 3 classics 85, 3 civil law 87); bar.-at-law, Inner Temple, 91.

Evans, Percy Bagnall, born at Edgbaston, co. Warwick, Jan. 1865; 1s. William, gent. CHRIST CHURCH, matric. 22 April, 84, aged 19 (from Eton), B.A. 87 (HONOURS:—2 history 87, 2 law 88); bar.-at-law, Inner Temple, 91.

Evans, Richard James, born at Oxford 1 Oct., 1871; o.s. Richard, gent. ST. MARY HALL, matric. 26 Oct., 92, aged 21.

Evans, rev. Samuel David, born at Cowbridge, co. Glamorgan, 10 Sept. 1862; 1s. Samuel David, pleb. JESUS COLL., matric. 19 Oct., 81 aged 19 (from Cowbridge school), B.A. 84; HONOURS:—4 law 84.

Evans, Theodore Robert John Norris, born at Ferryside, co. Carmarthen, 1863; 1s. Ernest, captain. EXETER, matric. 28 Jan., 81, aged 18, from a Clifton school.

Evans, Thomas Edward, born at Cowbridge, co. Glamorgan, 26 May, 1868; 4s. Samuel David, gen. JESUS COLL., matric. 19 Oct., 87, aged 19 (from Cowbridge gr. school), scholar 87 B.A. 91; HONOURS:—2 classical mods. 89, 2 classics 91.

Evans, Thomas Percival, born at Mordiford, co. Hereford, 1864; o.s. Thomas, gent. NON-COLLEGIATE, matric. 18 Oct., 83, aged 19, from Eton.

Evans, Walter, born at Little Somerford, Wilts, 1862; 2s. Arthur, cler. PEMBROKE, matric. 4 Feb., 81, aged 19.

Evans, Walter Rice, born at Tyr-Cymla, Llantwit, co. Glamorgan, 10 Sept., 1863; 2s. Edward, gen. JESUS COLL., matric. 18 Jan., 87, aged 23, from Cowbridge and Maidenhead schools.

Evans, William, born at Llanerch-y-medd, co. Anglesey, 20 March, 1867; o.s. William, gent. NON-COLLEGIATE, matric. 23 Jan., 86, aged 18 (from Beaumaris gr. school); migrated to JESUS COLL. 6 May, 86, B.A. 91.

Evans, William Franklen, M.A., fellow JESUS COLL. 90, where see.

Evans, William Hale, born at Ridgemour, Hants, 4 June, 1869; 1s. Joseph Russell, arm., deceased. NEW COLL., matric. 12 Oct., 88, aged 19 (from Tonbridge school), B.A. 92; HONOURS:—3 classical mods. 90, 3 classics 92.

Evans, William Melbourne, born at Farringdon-Gurney, Somerset, 13 May, 1871; 1s. John, Melbourne, gen. BRASENOSE, matric. 27 Jan., 91, aged 19, from St. Paul's school.

Eveleigh, William George, born at Northampton 1867; o.s. Henry, arm. QUEEN'S, matric. 25 Jan., 88, aged 21, B.Mus 91.

Evered, Philip, born at Otterhampton, Somerset, 1862; o.s. John Jeffrey Guy, arm. PEMBROKE, matric. 27 Oct., 83, aged 21; bar.-at-law, Inner Temple, 88.

Everington, Edgar Armstrong, born at East Dereham, Norfolk, Oct., 1870; 2s. William Devas, gen. KEBLE, matric. 12 Oct., 89, aged 18 (from Westminster school), B.A. 93; HONOURS:—2 law 92.

Everitt, Arthur Francis Graham, born at Paddington 27 Aug., ,1872; 1s. Francis William, Q.C. NEW COLL., matric. 17 Jan., 91, aged 18 (from Eton); HONOURS:—3 classical mods. 92.

Everitt, Arthur William Burch, born at Exmouth, Devon, 25 June, 1871; 1s. William John Wesley, cler. EXETER, matric. 14 Dec., 89, aged 18, from Exmouth school.

Everitt, Claude Arthur, born at Southsen, Hants, 1872; 1s. Herbert, lieut.-col. R.M.A. WADHAM, matric. 13 Oct., 90, aged 18, from Lanceing coll.

Everitt, Isaac Arthur Huskisson, born at Barlaston, co. Stafford. 7 May, 1872; 1s. Isaac Edward, WORCESTER, matric. 14 Oct., 90, aged 18, from Rugby.

Everitt, Nevill Henry, born at Edgbaston, co. Warwick, 1863; 3s. George Allen, gent. ST. EDMUND HALL, matric. 19 Oct., 82, aged 19.

Everitt, Walter Lewis Robbins Graham, born in London 1 March, 1874; 2s. Francis William Everitt-Everitt, Q.C. MERTON, matric. 18 Oct., 92, aged 18, from Eton.

Evershed, Edward, born at Burton-on-Trent, co. Derby, 1868; 5s. Sydney, gent. UNIVERSITY COLL. matric. 17 Oct., 85, aged 21, B.A. 88; HONOURS:—a history 88.

Evershed, Frank, born at Burton-on-Trent 1866; 4s. Sydney, gent. UNIVERSITY COLL., matric. 17 Oct., 85, aged 19, B.A. 88; HONOURS:—a history 88.

Every, Arthur George, born in London 1866; 1s. George Henry, gent. PEMBROKE, matric. 27 Oct., 85, aged 19 (from University coll. school, London), scholar 85, B.A. 89; HONOURS:—2 classical mods. 87, 1 classics 89.

Every, George Edmund, born in London 1869; 2s. George Henry, gen. NON-COLLEGIATE, matric. 13 Oct., 88, aged 19, from University coll. school, London.

Evetts, Percival Walter, born in Oxford 1867; 3s. Thomas, gent. CHARSLEY'S HALL, matric. 19 Jan., 89, aged 22.

Ewer, rev. Edward De, born in London 1841; 2.s. Frederick, gent. ST. MARY HALL, matric. 23 Jan., 82, aged 41; vicar of Longgrove, co. Hereford, 85-90, perpetual curate Welsh Newton 88-90.

Ewing, Guy Beaumont, born at West Mill, Herts, 28 June, 1863; 2s. John Aiken, cler. TRINITY, matric. 14 Oct., 82, aged 19 (from the Charterhouse), B.A. 89, M.A. 92.

Ewing, Malcolm Hart Orr, born in London 6 Jan., 1866; 6s. James, gent. deceased. QUEEN'S, matric. 30 Oct., 85, aged 19, from Christ's coll., Finchley.

Ewing, Robert, M.A., fellow ST. JOHN'S 70-6, where see.

Ewing, Wentworth Hugh Alexander, born at Shobden, Surrey, 3 Oct., 1864; 3s. John Aiken, cler. CHRIST CHURCH, matric. 12 Oct., 83, aged 19 (from the Charterhouse), exhibitioner 83, B.A. 87 (HONOURS: —2 classical mods. 85, 3 classics 87); bar.-at-law, Lincoln's Inn, 89.

Eyre, George Frederick, born in Devon 21 March, 1872; o.s. Frederick John, esq. TRINITY, matric. 17 Oct., 91, aged 19, from Lanceing coll.

Eyre, rev. John Richardson, born in London 1861; 2s. Richard Hodges, gent. NON-COLLEGIATE, matric. 21 Jan., 79, aged 21; migrated to MERTON, B.A. 85, M.A. 92 (HONOURS:—2 theology 85); vicar of All Saints, Finchley Road, London, 89; assumed the name of Eyre in lieu of Hodges.

STONE STRING COURSE, WESTMINSTER ABBEY.—*Pugin.*

F

Faber, Arthur Henry, M.A., fellow NEW COLL. 49-65, where see.

Faber, Arthur Traviss, born at Stockton-on-Tees 6 June, 1873; 6s. Henry Grey, solicitor. NEW COLL., matric. 14 Oct., 92, aged 19, from Shrewsbury school.

Fagan, James Bernard, born at Belfast, co. Antrim, 18 May, 1873; 1s. John, F.R.C.S. TRINITY, matric. 15 Oct., 92, aged 19, from Clongowes Wood coll., co. Kildare.

Fair, John St. Foyne, born in London 10 Aug., 1868; 2s. John arm. MAGDALEN, matric. 22 Oct., 87, aged 19 (from Harrow), B.A. 92; HONOURS:—3 law 91.

Fairbairn, Andrew Martin, D.D. Edinburgh 1878; created M.A. 17 May, 87; minister of the independent church, Bathgate, West Lothian, 60, and Aberdeen 72, principal of Airdale coll. 84, and of Mansfield coll., Oxford, 86, D.D. Yale 89, Muir lecturer in philosophy and history of religion, Edinburgh university, 78-83, chairman of congregational union of England and Wales 83; born 4 Nov., 38; father of Andrew and John.

Fairbairn, Andrew Martin, born at Bathgate, Scotland, Oct., 1870; 2s. Andrew Martin, D.D., principal of Mansfield coll. WADHAM, matric. 14 Oct., 89, aged 18 (from Oxford high school), B.A. 92.

Fairbairn, John Shields, born at Bathgate, Scotland, 21 Dec., 1868; 1s. Andrew Martin, D.D. principal of Mansfield coll. MAGDALEN, matric. 22 Oct., 87, aged 18 (from Bradford gr. school), demy 87, B.A. 91; HONOURS:—1 physiology 91.

Fairbrother, William Henry, born at Pendleton, co. Lanc., Dec., 1859; 1s. Henry, gent. KEBLE, matric. 18 Oct., 81, aged 21 (from Owens coll., Manchester), B.A. 85, M.A. 88 (HONOURS:—2 classical mods. 82, 1 classics 85), philosophy lecturer Lincoln coll.

[199]

Fairclough, William Robert, born at Moulmein, Burmah, 3 Feb., 1872; elder son of rev. John, of St. Augustine's mission, Burmah, HERTFORD, matric. 30 Jan., 91, aged 18 (from Forest school), exhibitioner 90; HONOURS:—3 classical mods. 92.

Fairfax, Geoffrey Evan, born at Sydney, Australia, 1862; 2s. James Reading, gent. BALLIOL, matric. 1 May, 82, aged 20 (from Sydney gr. school), B.A. 85 (HONOURS:—2 law 85); bar.-at-law, Inner Temple, 86.

Fairfax, Harold Walter, born at Sydney, Australia, 1869; 4s. James Reading, gent. BALLIOL, matric. 17 Oct., 89, aged 20 (from Sydney gr. school), B.A. 92; HONOURS:—3 law 92.

Fairfax, James Oswald, born at Sydney, Australia, 1863; 3s. James Reading, gent. BALLIOL, matric. 1 May, 82, aged 19 (from Sydney gr. school), B.A. 85 (HONOURS:—3 classical mods. 83, 3 classics 85); bar.-at-law, Inner Temple, 86.

Fairfax, John Mackenzie, born at Sydney, N.S. Wales, 16 Aug., 1870; o.s. Edward, gent. WADHAM, matric. 9 Feb., 92, aged 21.

Fairgrieve, James, born at Ardrossan, Ayrshire, 14 March, 1870; 1s. George, united presbyterian church minister. JESUS COLL., matric. 20 Oct., 91, aged 21 (from University coll., Aberystwith), exhibitioner 91.

Fairhurst, John William, born at Liverpool 1871; 1s. John, cler. ORIEL, matric. 20 Oct., 88, aged 17 (from Denstone coll.); HONOURS:—2 classical mods. 90, 2 classics 92.

Fairlie, rev. Hugh Macefield, born at Carlisle, 1865; 3s. John Macefield, gent. PEMBROKE, matric. 27 Oct., 85, aged 20, B.A. 88, M.A. 92 (HONOURS:—3 theology 88); curate of Christ church, Waterloo, 90.

Falcon, Charles Henry, born at Workington, Cumberland, Sept., 1870; 4s. Michael, solicitor. BRASENOSE, matric. 16 Oct., 88, aged 18, from Repton school.

[200]

Falcon, William Knightley, born at Mymensingh, East Indies, April, 1865; 2s. Anthony Benn, arm. PEMBROKE, matric. 27 Oct., 84, aged 19, from Lancing coll.

Fallows, John Arthur, born at Birmingham 22 Dec., 1864; o.s. Thomas Stratton, gent. QUEEN'S, matric. 22 Oct., 83, aged 18 (from Rugby), scholar 83, B.A. 87, M.A. 90; HONOURS :—2 classical mods. 84, 2 classics 87, 2 history 88.

Fanshawe, Arthur Adolphus, M.A., B.C.L., fellow NEW COLL. 49-55, where see.

Fanshawe, Henry Leighton, M.A., fellow NEW COLL. 51-7, where see.

Fanshawe, Reginald, M.A., fellow NEW COLL. 77-80, where see.

Farebrother, Thomas, M.A., QUEEN'S, where see.

Farlow, Sydney Charles (King-), born at Rusham, Surrey, 13 Dec., 1864; 3s. John King, arm. TRINITY, matric. 15 Oct., 83, aged 18 (from Harrow), B.A. 87, M.A. 91 (HONOURS :—2 classical mods. 85); bar.-at-law, Middle Temple, 89.

Farmer, Gabriel William Stahel, born at Harrow, Middx., 1865; 2s. John, organist of Balliol. BALLIOL, matric. 24 Oct., 85, aged 20 (from Harrow and University coll., London), exhibitioner 85, B.A. 88, B.Med. 90; HONOURS :—1 physiology 88.

Farmer, Henry Theodor Stahel, born at Harrow, Middx., 1869; 2s. John, organist of Balliol. BALLIOL, matric. 19 Oct., 87, aged 18 (from Harrow); HONOURS :—2 history 91.

Farmer, John Bretland, M.A., fellow MAGDALEN 89, where see.

Farmer, John Colton, born at Llyssin, Llanerfyl, North Wales, 9 Nov., 1873; 1s. James Urwick, schoolmaster. CHRIST CHURCH, matric. 14 Oct., 92, aged 18, from Newport school, Salop.

Farnell, Lewis Richard, M.A., fellow EXETER 80, where see.

Farnsworth, rev. Walter, born at Heaton Norris, co. Lanc., Dec. 1868; 1s. Joseph, gen. BRASENOSE, matric. 20 Oct., 87, aged 19 (from Manchester gr. school), scholar 87, B.A. 91 (HONOURS :—2 theology 91); curate of All Saints, Northampton, 91.

Farrar, Adam Storey, D.D., fellow QUEEN'S 52-63, where see.

Farrar, Henry Richard, M.A., fellow MERTON 43-53, where see.

Farquhar, Edward Taylor, born at (Rescobie ?), co. Forfar, May, 1863; 5s. William. KEBLE, matric. 17 Oct., 82, aged 19 (from Glenalmond coll.), B.A. 86.

Farquhar, James Edward Mainwaring, born at Devizes, Wilts, Aug., 1870; 1s. Edward Mainwaring, cler. CHRIST CHURCH, matric. 8 June, 89, aged 18, from Eton.

Farquhar, John Nicol, born at Aberdeen 1861; 1s. George, gent. CHRIST CHURCH, matric. 16 Oct., 85, aged 24 (from Aberdeen university), exhibitioner 84, B.A. 89; HONOURS :—1 classical mods. 87, 1 classics 89.

Farquharson, Alexander Haldane, born in London 12 March, 1867; 1s. James Ross, of Invercauld, co. Aberdeen, arm. CHRIST CHURCH, matric. 30 May, 85, aged 18, B.A. 88; HONOURS :—1 classical mods. 88.

Farquharson, Arthur Spencer Loat, born at Alverstoke, Hants, 22 Nov., 1871; 3s. Matthew Henry, col. late H.M.L.I. UNIVERSITY COLL., matric. 11 Oct., 90, aged 18 (from Rochester gr. school), exhibitioner 90; HONOURS :—1 classical mods. 92.

Farran, rev. George Erle, born at Surbiton, Surrey, 14 June, 1868; 1s. Francis Henry, arm. ORIEL, matric. 18 Oct., 87, aged 19 (from Rugby), B.A. 91; HONOURS :—4 history 91.

Farrant, Francis Westall, born at Llandudno, co. Carnarvon, 27 April, 1866; 3s. Robert, gent. TRINITY, matric. 17 Oct., 85, aged 19 (from Repton school), scholar HERTFORD 85, B.A. and M.A. 92; HONOURS :—3 classical mods. 87, 3 classics 89.

Farrant, Henry Gatchell, born at Llandudno, co. Carnarvon, 10 May, 1864; 2s. Robert, solicitor. NEW COLL., matric. 10 Oct., 84, aged 20 (from Repton school), B.A. 88 (HONOURS :—2 law 88); bar.-at-law, Inner Temple, 90.

Farrant, Percy Robert, born at Llandudno, co. Carnarvon, 25 April, 1868; 4s. Robert, arm, deceased. NEW COLL., matric. 18 Oct., 89, aged 19 (from Repton school), B.A. 91; HONOURS :—3 classical mods. 89, 2 law 90.

Farrar, rev. Charles Frederick, born at Chatteris, co. Cambr., 13 Sept., 1860; 4s. Charles, surgeon. LINCOLN, matric. 23 Oct., 80, aged 20 (from Bedford gr. school), scholar 80-4, B.A. 84, M.A. 87 (HONOURS :—2 classical mods. 82, 2 classics 84); assist. master Manchester gr. school and curate of St. Augustine, Pendlebury, 90.

Farrar Reginald Anstruther, born at Harrow, Middx., 14 May, 1861; 1s. Frederick William, archdeacon of Westminster. KEBLE, matric. 19 Oct., 80, aged 19 (from Marlborough coll.), B.A. 83, M.A. and B.Med. 89, D.Med. 90; HONOURS :—3 classical mods. 81.

Farrar, Walter, born in British Guiana April, 1865; 1s. Thomas, cler. KEBLE, matric. 16 Oct., 83, aged 18 (from Queen's coll., British Guiana), B.A. 87, M.A. 91; HONOURS :—3 theology 87.

Farrer, Frederick Edward, born in London 24 Oct., 1865; 4s. Frederic Willis, solicitor. NEW COLL., matric. 18 Jan., 84, aged 18 (from Winchester) (HONOURS :—2 history 87); bar.-at-law, Lincoln's Inn, 90.

Farrer, Henry Lefevre, born in London 24 March, 1862; 3s. William James, arm. BALLIOL, matric. 21 Jan., 80, aged 17 (from Eton); HONOURS :— 2 classical mods. 81.

Farrer Roland John, born in London 2 March, 1873; 7s. Frederick Willis, solicitor. BALLIOL, matric. 11 Feb., 92, aged 18, from Eton.

Farrer, rev. Oliver William, born in London 20 May, 1862; 4s. Oliver William, arm. BALLIOL, matric. 18 Oct., 81, aged 19 (from Eton), B.A. 85, M.A. 90 (HONOURS :—3 classical mods. 83, 3 history 85); curate of Wincanton, Somerset, 89.

Farrow, rev. Charles Bertram Darley, born at Tong, Yorks, 1868; 1s. Charles, cler. ORIEL, matric. 18 Oct., 87, aged 19 (from Bedford gr. school), B.A. 91; HONOURS :—3 classical mods. 89.

Fass, Adolph Henry, born in Natal, Africa, 22 Dec., 1866; 1s. Adolph, of London, gent. MAGDALEN, matric. 23 Oct., 85, aged 18 (from Bath coll.), B.A. 88; HONOURS :—3 history 88.

Fathers, George Henry, born at Oxford 1861; 3s. George, gent. NON-COLLEGIATE, matric. 13 Oct., 80, aged 23, B.A. 88, M.A. 91; HONOURS :— 3 history 88.

Faulkner, Thomas, born at Hinksey, Oxon, 1868; 3s. William Carey, gen. BRASENOSE, matric. 20 Oct., 86, aged 18, from Christ's coll., Finchley.

Fauntlethorpe, Bertram Platt, born at Battersea, Surrey, 30 May, 1871; 2s. John Pincher, of London, cler. KEBLE, matric. 15 Oct., 90, aged 19, from Rossall school.

Faunthorpe, John Champion, born at Wandsworth, Surrey, 30 Nov., 1872; 2s. John Pincher, of London, cler. BALLIOL, matric. 14 Oct., 92, aged 19 (from Rossall school); selected candidate Indian C.S. 92.

Faussett, Edward Philip Godfrey Godfrey-, born at Cheltenham 1863; o.s. Godfrey, cler. ST. JOHN'S, matric. 17 Oct., 85, aged 22, B.A. 89, M.A. 92 (HONOURS :—4 law 89); bar.-at-law, Inner Temple, 90.

Faussett, John Toke Godfrey, M.A., student CHRIST CHURCH 53-70, where see.

Faussett, Robert Godfrey, M.A., student CHRIST CHURCH 45, where see.

Fawcett, rev. Francis L'Estrange, born at Street, co. Longford, 29 Oct., 1859; y.s. Edward, cler. ST. MARY HALL, matric. 28 Jan., 80, aged 20, B.A. 84, M.A. 90; vicar of Luton St. Matthew 90.

Fawcett, right hon. Henry, created D.C.L. 9 June, 1880. *See Al. Ox.* and series, 451.

Fawcett, Henry Hargreave, born in Dublin 1861; 1s. Henry, arm. WORCESTER, matric. 21 Oct., 80, aged 19, from Dulwich coll.

Fawous, Louis Edward, born at Seaton Carew, co. Durham, 1864; 10s. Robert, gent. WORCESTER, matric. 19 Oct., 82, aged 18 (from King's coll. school, London), B.A. 85; HONOURS :—3 classical mods. 84.

Fawssett, rev. Humphrey Sandwith, born at Baumber, co. Lincoln, 1862; 3s. John, cler. EXETER, matric. 22 Oct., 80, aged 18 (from Newark school), B.A. 83 (HONOURS :—4 history 83); vicar of Great Sturton with Baumber, co. Linc., 91.

Fearenside, Charles Scott, born at Harrow Weald, Middx., 27 Feb., 1865; 2s. Charles Hebden, pleb. JESUS COLL., matric. 18 Oct., 83, aged 18 (from Oswestry gr. school), scholar 83, B.A. 87, M.A. 90; HONOURS :—2 classical mods. 85, 1 classics 87, 2 history 88.

Fearis, William Henry, born at Dewsbury, Yorks, 1869; o.s. William, gen. ST. JOHN'S, matric. 17 Oct., 91, aged 22.

Fearnside, Edward Lincoln, born at Leeds 1 May, 1865; 1s. Edwin, gent. QUEEN'S, matric. 22 Oct., 83, aged 18 (from Leeds gr. school), exhibitioner 83, B.A. 87, M.A. 92; HONOURS :—2 classical mods. 85, 3 classics 87.

Fearnsides, John William, born at Bradford, Yorks, 27 May, 1867; o.s. John, gent. MERTON, matric. 27 March, 86, aged 18 (from Mill Hill school), B.A. 89, M.A. and B.C.L. 92 (HONOURS :—2 law 89, 2 civil law 90); bar.-at-law, Inner Temple, 91.

Fearon, Robert Burton, born in London 1872; 2s. Francis, solicitor. KEBLE, matric. 9 Feb., 92, aged 20.

Fearon, William Andrewes, D.D., fellow NEW COLL. 64-80, where see.

Fedden, rev. Lorenzo Player, born in London 6 March, 1860; 2s. Olcher, arm. MERTON, matric. 27 April, 81, aged 21, B.A. 85, M.A. 87; curate of Stamford Hill St. Thomas, London, 90.

Feild, Edward Andrew, born at St. Petersburg, Russia, 1861; 2s. Edward Forbes, gen. KEBLE, matric. 20 Oct., 91, aged 30, from Uppingham school.

Feilden, Geoffrey Nelson, born at Witton, co. Lanc., 26 Nov., 1865; 2s. Robert, arm. KEBLE, matric. 22 Oct., 85, aged 19, from Newton Abbot coll., Devon.

Feilden, Randle Francis Campbell, born at Edinburgh 15 Jan., 1862 ; 1s. Randle Joseph, arm. CHRIST CHURCH, matric. 15 Oct., 80, aged 18.

Feilding, Percy Henry, born in London 23 Dec., 1867 ; 2s. lieut.-gen. the hon. Percy Robert. BALLIOL, matric. 19 Jan., 88, aged 21 (from Wellington), B.A. 89 ; curate of Buckland Newton, Dorset, 86-7.

Fell, Bryan Hugh, born at Ulverston 23 Nov., 1869 ; 5s. John, gen. QUEEN'S, matric. 20 Oct., 88, aged 18 (from Sedbergh school), exhibitioner 88 ; HONOURS :—2 classical mods. 90, 3 classics 92.

Fell, Edwin Frederick Berry, born at Withyham, Sussex, Sept., 1866 ; 2s. Edwin, arm. CHRIST CHURCH, matric. 30 May, 85, aged 18 (from Eton), B.A. 89.

Fell, George Hunter, D.D., fellow MAGDALEN 53-61, where see.

Fell, Godfrey Butler Hunter, born at Worldham, Hants., 22 April, 1872; 2s. George Hunter, D.D. MAGDALEN, matric. 22 Oct., 91, aged 19, from Eton.

Fellgate, Herbert Harry, born at Erith, Kent, 26 Sept., 1860 ; 2s. William David, gent. NONCOLLEGIATE, matric. 15 Oct., 81, aged 21 ; migrated to MERTON, B.A. 86, M.A. 88 ; HONOURS: —3 mathematical mods. 83 ; 4 mathematics 85.

Fellowes, Edmund Horace, born in London Nov., 1870 ; 2s. Horace Decimus, gen. ORIEL, matric. 25 Oct., 89, aged 18 (from Winchester), B.A. 92 ; HONOURS :—4 theology 92.

Fellowes, Evelyn Napier, born at Brighton, Norfolk, 3 June, 1862 ; 8s. Thomas Lyon, cler. TRINITY, matric. 15 Oct., 81, aged 19 (from Rugby), B.A. 84 ; HONOURS :—3 law 84.

Fellowes, Frederick, born in London 24 Aug., 1863 ; 1s. Horace Decimus, arm. ORIEL, matric. 30 Jan., 82, aged 18 (from Winchester), B.A. 85.

Fellowes, Walter, M.A., student CHRIST CHURCH 52-6, where see.

Felton, Ernest Edward, born at Milton, Kent, 8 April, 1864 ; 2s. William Valentine, gent. CHRIST CHURCH, matric. 25 May, 83, aged 19, from Eton.

Felton, Ernest Frederick, born in London 1862 ; 2s. William John, gent. HERTFORD, matric. 19 Oct., 81, aged 19.

Felton, rev. William Athill, born in Nottingham July, 1867 ; 1s. William, cler. CHRIST CHURCH, matric. 30 May, 85, aged 17 (from Nottingham high school), B.A. 89 ; curate of Thorpe Bassett, Yorks, 90.

Felton, William Frederic, born at Milton-juxta-Gravesend 1862 ; 1s. William Valentine, gent. CHRIST CHURCH, matric. 14 Oct., 81, aged 19, from Eton.

Fennell, Charles Henry, born at New Wandsworth, Surrey, 12 Dec., 1871 ; o.s. Charles John, fleet surgeon, deceased. MAGDALEN, matric. 24 Oct., 90, aged 18 (from St. Paul's school), demy 90.

Fenton, Albert Edward, born at Grappenhall, Cheshire, 1852 ; 1s. James, arm. NON-COLLEGIATE, matric. 13 Oct., 83, aged 31.

Fenton, Cornelius O'Connor, born at Birkenhead 30 Nov., 1866 ; 5s. Thomas, vicar of St. Peter's, Bkhd. QUEEN'S, matric. 27 Jan., 87, aged 20.

Fenton, Henry Banning, born at Weston, co. Gloucester, 1865 ; 3s. James, arm. HERTFORD, matric. 24 Oct., 84, aged 19.

Fenton, Samuel Llewellyn O'Connor, born at Birkenhead 11 Jan., 1863 ; 3s. Charles, cler. QUEEN'S, matric. 22 Oct., 83, aged 20 (from Trinity coll. Dublin, matric. Jan., 83), B.A. 86, M.A. 91 ; brother of Cornelius.

Fenwick, Bertram Emilius, born in London 1866 ; 2s. Henry, arm. BRASENOSE, matric. 21 Jan., 84, aged 18, from Eton.

Fenwick, rev. Cecil Owen Meynell, born at Needwood, co. Staff., 24 July, 1863 ; y.s. John Edward Addison, of Cheltenham, cler. BRASENOSE, matric. 2 June, 82, aged 18 (from Cheltenham coll.), B.A. 85, M.A. 89 ; curate of Buckland Newton, Dorset, 86-7.

Ferard, Henry Cecil, born at Winkfield, Berks, 25 July, 1864 ; 3s. Charles Cotton, bar.-at-law. UNIVERSITY COLL., matric. 13 Oct., 83, aged 19 (from Eton), assist. commissioner Oudh.

Ferard, John Edward, born at Vevey, Switzerland, 22 Jan., 1869; 2s. Charles Cotton, arm., deceased. MAGDALEN, matric. 22 Oct., 87, aged 18 (from Eton), demy 87, B.A. 92 (HONOURS :—1 classical mods. 89, 2 classics 91); passed for home civil service 93.

Ferard, Reginald Herbert, born at Winkfield, Berks, 21 June, 1866; 4s. Charles Cotton, bar.-at-law. EXETER, matric. 23 Oct., 85, aged 19 (from Eton), scholar 84, B.A. 89, M.A. 92; HONOURS :—1 classical mods. 87, 2 classics 89.

Ferguson, Arthur Foxton, born at Leeds 3 Jan., 1866; 2s. William, banker, deceased. NEW COLL., matric. 16 Oct., 85, aged 19 (from Sedbergh school); academical clerk MAGDALEN 87, B.A. 90.

Ferguson, rev. Edwin Augustus, born at Old Deer, Aberdeen, 24 Sept., 1864; 3s. George Arthur, lieut.-col. late Grenadier guards. MAGDALEN, matric. 19 Oct., 83, aged 19 (from the Charterhouse), B.A. 87, M.A. 91; curate of Shrivenham, Berks, 90.

Ferguson, George Pratt, born at Millerton in America, 1867; 1s. George Reid, cler. NON-COLLEGIATE, matric. 21 Oct., 89, aged 22.

Ferguson, John Grant, born at Edinburgh 1860; 2s. Alexander, gent. NON-COLLEGIATE, matric. 23 Oct., 80, aged 20.

Ferguson, Victor, born at Llandogo, co. Monmouth, 24 June, 1866; o.s. Richard Williams, cler. TRINITY, matric. 11 Oct., 84, aged 18 (from Cheltenham coll.); assumed the name of Ferguson in lieu of Williams, 2nd. lieut. South Wales borderers 87.

Ferguson, William Harold, born at Leeds 1874; 3s. William, deceased. KEBLE, matric. 15 Oct., 92, aged 18, from Magdalen coll. school.

Ferguson, John Carlyle, born at Leslie, co. Fife, 17 June, 1872; 1s. James, F.R.C.S. TRINITY, matric. 17 Oct., 91, aged 19 (from St. Paul's school), scholar 90.

Ferguson, Thomas Colyer, born in London 11 July, 1865; 1s. sir James Ranken, bart. CHRIST CHURCH, matric. 16 Oct., 85, aged 20 (from Harrow), B.A. 89.

Fernsby, Arthur Robert, born at Oxford 1868; 2s. Richard, gent. NON-COLLEGIATE, matric. 17 Oct., 85, aged 17 (from New coll. school, Oxford), chorister 78-83, B.A. 88.

Fernsby, Frederick Richard Elleson, born at Oxford 1867; 1s. Richard, gent. NON-COLLEGIATE, matric. 19 Jan., 85, aged 18, B.A. 87.

Ferrand, William Harris, born at Bingley, Yorks, 9 March, 1873; 1s. William, esq. CHRIST CHURCH, matric. 16 Oct., 91, aged 18, from Eton.

Ferrar, William John, born at Navestock, Essex, 1868; 1s. William Grey, arm. HERTFORD, matric. 29 Jan., 89, aged 21 (from Brentwood school); scholar 88, B.A. 92; HONOURS :—1 classical mods. 90, English verse 91, 2 classics 92.

ffarington, Henry Nowell, born at Wigan, co. Lanc. 21 March, 1869; o.s. Richard Atherton, gent. ST. EDMUND HALL, matric. 26 Jan., 89, aged 20.

ffinoh, rev. Kenneth Maule, born at Ludwell, Wilts, 1865; 1s. Matthew, cler. ST. EDMUND HALL, matric. 22 Oct., 83, aged 18, B.A. 87, M.A. 90; curate of St. John Divine, Chatham, 90.

ffinden, George Constantine Frederick Alexander Sketchley, born at Newport Pagnell, Bucks, 26 March, 1866; 1s. George, cler. ORIEL, matric. 23 Oct., 84, aged 18 (from Marlborough), B.A. 88, M.A. 91.

ffolkes, Harold Lewis Henry, born at Hillingdon, Norfolk, 20 Aug., 1873; 6s. Henry Edward Browne, cler. EXETER, matric. 22 Oct., 91, aged 18 (from Harpenden school); drowned 12 Feb., 92, near Oxford, in attempting to save a friend.

ffoulkes, Charles John, born in London 26 June, 1868; 2s. Edmund Salisbury, cler. ST. JOHN's, matric. 16 Oct., 86, aged 18, from Shrewsbury school.

ffoulkes, Edmund Salisbury, B.D., fellow JESUS COLL. 42-54, where see.

ffoulkes, John Wynne, born at Chester 8 Nov., 1861; 3s. William Wynne, county court judge. MAGDALEN, matric. 21 Jan., 82, aged 20 (from St. Edward's school, Summertown); migrated to BALLIOL, B.A. 88, M.A. 91.

ffrench, Le Bel Holbrooke Edward, born at Newton Tolney, co. Denbigh, 22 March, 1871; 4s. George, B.A., rector of Shinrone, King's co., Ireland. BALLIOL, matric. 14 Oct., 90, aged 19 (from Trent coll., Nottingham); HONOURS :—2 classical mods. 92.

Field, Alfred Ernest, born at Buckingham 31 July, 1864; 1s. Alfred Long, arm. TRINITY, matric. 14 Oct., 82, aged 18 (from Bedford modern school), scholar 81, B.A. 86, M.A. 90 (HONOURS :—1 mathematical mods. 84, 1 mathematics 86, 2 physics 87); master at Bedford grammar school.

Field, Cuthbert Arthur, born in London 1 May, 1868; 1s. George Hanbury, arm. NEW COLL., matric. 14 Oct., 87, aged 19, from Eton.

Field, George, born at Anfield, co. Lanc., 30 Sept., 1871; 2s. Samuel, arm. TRINITY, matric. 11 Oct., 90, aged 19 (from Uppingham school); HONOURS :—2 classical mods. 92.

Field, Oliver, born at Hampstead, Middx., 8 Feb., 1873; 3s. Walter, artist. TRINITY, matric. 17 Oct., 91, aged 18, from Clifton coll.

Field, Thomas M.A., fellow MAGDALEN 77-88, where see.

Field, Walter Paul Gray, born at West Rainton, Yorks, Jan., 1861; 4s. John, cler. KEBLE, matric. 19 Oct., 80, aged 19 (from Christ's hospital), scholar 79-84, B.A. 84, M.A. 87; HONOURS :—2 classical mods. 82, 2 classics 84.

Fiennes, Gerard York Twisleton-Wykeham, born at Leamington 18 July, 1866; 1s. hon. Wingfield Stratford, cler. NEW COLL., matric. 4 Dec., 82, aged 18 (from Winchester), B.A. 87; HONOURS :—3 law 85. See Foster's *Peerage*, baron SAYE and SELE.

Fiennes, rev. the hon. Wingfield Stratford Twisleton Wykeham, M.A., fellow NEW COLL. 52-64, where see.

Fillingham, rev. Robert Charles, born in London 5 May, 1861; o.s. Robert, arm. MERTON, matric. 16 Oct., 84, aged 23 (from a Tottenham school), B.A. 88 (HONOURS :—2 classical mods. 84, 3 classics 88); vicar of Hexton, Beds, 91.

Finoh, rev. Frederick Richard, born at Southport, co. Lanc., 1 Oct., 1871; 1s. Richard Brown, arm. BALLIOL, matric. 22 Oct., 90 (from Rugby), B.A. 91.

Finoh, Heneage Wynne, born in London 30 April, 1871; 1s. Edward Heneage Wynne, arm. NEW COLL., matric. 11 Oct., 89, aged 18 (from Eton), B.A. 92; HONOURS :—3 chemistry 92.

Finoh, Henry Charles, born at Chicheley, Bucks, 9 Dec., 1869; 1s. George, cler. UNIVERSITY COLL., matric. 13 Oct., 88, aged 18, B.A. 92; HONOURS :— 3 history 92.

Finoh, Hugh Earnshaw, born at Stafford March, 1871; 3s. Thomas Ross, cler. KEBLE, matric. 12 Oct., 89, aged 18, from Winchester.

Finoh, rev. Walter Ross, born at Sonning, Berks, 1867; 2s. Thomas Ross, cler. KEBLE, matric. 19 Oct., 85, aged 19 (from Winchester), B.A. 89 (HONOURS :—1 theology 89); curate of Longfleet, Dorset, 91.

Finch-Hatton, Murray Edward Gordon, earl of Winchelsea and Nottingham, M.A., fellow HERTFORD 75-6, where see.

Findlay, John, born at Much Woolton, co. Lanc., 27 Feb., 1871; 1s. John, gen. UNIVERSITY COLL., matric. 11 Oct., 90, aged 19.

Findlay, John Ritchie, born at Edinburgh 1866; 1s. John Ritchie, gent. BALLIOL, matric. 15 Oct., 84, aged 18 (from Harrow), B.A. 87; HONOURS:— 1 chemistry 87, 2 classics 89.

Fingland, Edward Dobbie, born at Wavertree, near Liverpool, 1859; 2s. James, gent. EXETER, matric. 22 Jan., 80, aged 21, from Edinburgh university and Liverpool coll.

Finn, Frank, born at Maidstone, Kent, 1869; 1s. Francis, gen. BRASENOSE, matric. 20 Oct., 86, aged 17 (from Maidstone school), scholar 86, B.A. 90 (HONOURS:—3 classical mods. 88, 2 classics 90), exhibitioner University Coll. 84.

Finney, William Arthur, born at Harborne, near Birmingham, 21 Nov., 1872; 1s. s. Thomas, gent. EXETER, matric. 29 Oct., 92, aged 19, from Mason coll. Birmingham.

Finney, rev. William Henry, born at Calverton, Notts., 28 Jan., 1868; 1s. William Henry, cler. QUEEN's, matric. 21 Oct., 87, aged 19 (from Owens coll. Manchester), exhibitioner 87, B.A. 91; HONOURS:—2 classical mods. 89, 2 classics 91.

Finzel, Conrad William Curling, born at Clevedon, Somerset, 7 July, 1869; 1s. Conrad William Curling, cler. EXETER, matric. 16 Oct., 89, aged 20, from Harrow.

Firminger, rev. John Herbert, born at Edmonton, Middx., 1866; 2s. Thomas Augustus Charles, cler. EXETER, matric. 16 Oct., 84, aged 18 (from Bath coll.), B.A. 88, M.A. 91 (HONOURS:— 3 theology 88); curate of St. Paul, Burton-on-Trent, 89.

Firminger, Walter Kelly, born at Edmonton, Middx., 28 Sept., 1870; 3s. Thomas Augustus, cler. MERTON, matric. 19 Oct., 89, aged 19, from Bury St. Edmund's school and Westfield school, Winchester.

Firmstone, Harold William, born at Hagley, co. Worcester, 28 May, 1868; 6s. William Charles, arm. HERTFORD, matric. 20 Oct., 87, aged 19 (from Rugby), scholar 86; HONOURS:—2 classical mods. 89; in the army.

Firmstone, Joseph Alexander Lockhart, born in London 21 Sept., 1869; o.s. Joseph, gen. LINCOLN, matric. 18 Oct., 88, aged 19, from Fettes coll.

Firth, Charles Harding, M.A. BALLIOL, where see.

Firth, Charles Henry Bramley, born at Ran-Moor, Yorks, 21 April, 1868; 5s. Mark, gent. CORPUS CHRISTI, matric. 20 Oct., 86, aged 18, from Rugby.

Firth, Edgar Beckwith, born at Malton, Yorks, 1863; 2s. George Arthur, cler. NON-COLLEGIATE, matric. 14 Oct., 82, aged 19, B.A. 86, M.A. 91.

Firth, rev. Edward Harding, born at Eccleshall, Yorks, 1 Dec., 1863; 5s. John, arm. TRINITY, matric. 15 Oct., 83, aged 19 (from Clifton coll.), B.A. 87, M.A. 90 (HONOURS:—2 theology 87); assist. master Clifton 87-90, rector of Micheldean, co. Glouc., 90.

Firth, Ernest Cecil Clark, born at Preston, co. Lanc., 1 Oct., 1866; 2s. Raymond, vicar of Christ church, Preston. LINCOLN, matric. 17 Oct., 84, aged 18 (from Marlborough coll.), scholar 84, B.A. 87, M.A. and B.C.L. 91 (HONOURS:—2 classical mods. 85, 3 classics 87, 2 civil law 89); bar.-at-law, Middle Temple, 90.

Firth, Henry Raywood, born at Preston, co. Lanc., 6 Feb., 1864; 1s. Raywood, cler. WORCESTER, matric. 19 Oct., 82, aged 18 (from Marlborough coll.), scholar 82; HONOURS:—1 classical mods. 83, 2 classics 86; died 8 Aug., 86.

Firth, Herbert Boiseau, born at Leeds 17 Jan., 1871; 4s. Frederick, gen., deceased. LINCOLN, matric. 20 Oct., 90, aged 19, from Leeds gr. school.

Firth, John Benjamin, born at Exeter 19 July, 1868; 2s. John Benjamin, gen. QUEEN's, matric. 21 Oct., 87, aged 19 (from Bradford gr. school), scholar 87, B.A. 91; HONOURS:—1 classical mods. 89, 1 classics 91.

Fisher, Albert Bulteel, M.A., fellow CORPUS CHRISTI 63-77, where see.

Fisher, Alfred Sellwood, born at Surbiton, Surrey, 19 April, 1873; 2s. John Alfred, of Kingston Hill, gen. NON-COLLEGIATE, matric. 17 Oct., 91, aged 18, from Kingston-on-Thames gr. school.

Fisher, Arthur Alexander, born at Brockenhurst, Hants, 1867; 2s. Herbert William, arm. CHRIST CHURCH, matric. 30 May, 85, aged 18, from Winchester.

Fisher, Cecil, born at Southsea, Hants, 18 July, 1868; 1s. John Arbuthnot, capt. R.N. MAGDALEN, matric. 22 Oct., 87, aged 19 (from the Charterhouse), B.A. 90 (HONOURS:—2 Indian languages 90); assist. magistrate and collector Bengal.

Fisher, Cecil Edward, M.A., student CHRIST CHURCH 57-62, where see.

Fisher, Charles, born at Doncaster, Yorks, 1863; 1s. Charles, gent. ST. EDMUND HALL, matric. 22 Oct., 83, aged 20 (from Doncaster school), B.A. 86, M.A. 90; HONOURS:—3 classical mods. 85.

Fisher, Charles Browning, born at Market Harborough, co. Leicester, 1863; 2s. Edward Knapp, arm. BRASENOSE, matric. 10 June, 81, aged 18, from Winchester.

Fisher, Charles Wilton, born at Surbiton, Surrey, 17 Oct., 1871; 1s. John Alfred, of Kingston Hill, gen. ST. EDMUND HALL, matric. 16 Oct., 90, aged 18, from Q. Elizabeth gr. school, Kingston-on-Thames.

Fisher, Frederick Anstis, born at Cardiff 1871; 6s. Robert Smith, gen. ST. EDMUND HALL, matric. 16 Oct., 90, aged 19.

Fisher, (rev.) Harold Fleming, born at Downham, co. Cambridge, 6 April, 1866; y.s. Frederick, rector. TRINITY, matric. 17 Oct., 85, aged 19 (from Haileybury), exhibitioner 85, B.A. 89, M.A. 92 (HONOURS:—2 classical mods. 87, 2 classics 89); curate of Seulcoates, Yorks, 90.

Fisher, Henry Warren, born 1847; 1s. Henry, cler. NON-COLLEGIATE, matric. 3 Nov., 83, aged 36; migrated to EXETER 11 Oct., 84, B.A. 87, M.A. 90.

Fisher, Herbert Albert Laurens, born in London 21 March, 1865; 1s. Herbert William, student CHRIST CHURCH 45-62, and grandson of William, student CHRIST CHURCH 15-23, great grandson of Philip, fellow UNIVERSITY COLL. NEW COLL., matric. 28 Oct., 84, aged 19 (from Winchester), scholar 83-8, fellow 88, B.A. 88, M.A. 91, tutor; HONOURS:— 1 classical mods. 86, 1 classics 88.

Fisher, Herbert Sealy, born at Bishops Itchington, co. Warwick, 1858; 2s. William, cler. NON-COLLEGIATE, matric. 18 Oct., 80, aged 22, from Chard gr. school.

Fisher, Herbert William, M.A., student CHRIST CHURCH 45-62, where see.

Fisher, Horace James, born at Oxford 1865; 2s. George, gent. ST. JOHN's, matric. 13 Jan., 83, aged 18, B.A. 86.

Fisher, James, M.A., fellow EXETER 27-37, where see.

Fisher, James Ernest Oakley, born at Dorchester, Dorset, 25 June, 1865; o.s. James, cler. EXETER, matric. 19 April, 82, aged 18 (from Harrow); died 13 March, 87.

Fisher, rev. John, D.D., fellow MAGDALEN 36, where see.

DIVINITY SCHOOL—By F. MACKENZIE

Fisher, John Cecil, born at Lytham, co. Lanc., 1868; 1s. Luke, D. Med. BRASENOSE, matric. 20 Oct., 87, aged 19 (from Warrington school and the Charterhouse), B.A. 91; HONOURS: —2 physiology 91.

Fisher, John Martyn, born at Taunton, Somerset, 26 Aug., 1873; 1s. Samuel P., merchant. WORCESTER, matric. 18 Oct., 92, aged 19, from King's coll., Taunton.

Fisher, Reginald Fleming, born at Downham, co. Cambr., July, 1864; 4s. Frederick, rector. KEBLE, matric. 16 Oct., 83, aged 19 (from Haileybury), B.A. 87; HONOURS :—3 classical mods. 85, 3 history 87.

Fisher, Reginald Wordsworth Cecil, born at Stoke Rochford, co. Lincoln, 17 April, 1872; 2s. Cecil Edward, vicar of Bournemouth St. Peter. KEBLE, matric. 20 Oct., 91, aged 19, from Haileybury.

Fisher, Richard, born at Blackpool, co. Lanc., 1861; 1s. John, gent. PEMBROKE, matric. 30 Oct., 80, aged 19, B.A. 84 (HONOURS :—3 law 84); bar.-at-law, Lincoln's Inn, 85.

Fisher, Stanley, born in London 12 Feb., 1867; 3s. George Henry Knapp, arm. BRASENOSE, matric. 15 Dec., 85, aged 18 (from Westminster school), B.A. 88, M.A. 92; bar.-at-law, Inner Temple, 90.

Fisher, rev. Steward Travers, born at Liston, Suffolk, 25 Sept., 1862; 2s. Thomas Ruggles, cler. ST. MARY HALL, matric. 19 Oct., 81, aged 19 (from Stratford-on-Avon school), B.A. 84, M.A. 88; curate of Dunston, co. Stafford, 90.

Fisher, Walter William, M.A., fellow CORPUS CHRISTI 71-4, where see.

Fisher, Wilfrid, M.A., student CHRIST CHURCH 53-62, where see.

Fiske, William Elwyn, born at Northleigh, Oxon, Feb., 1870; 2s. Robert White, cler. KEBLE, matric. 19 Oct., 89, aged 19 (from Sherborne school), B.A. 92.

Fisken, Archibald James, born at Ballarat, Australia, 25 June, 1866; 3s. Archibald, of Melbourne, arm. MAGDALEN, matric. 16 Oct., 84, aged 18, from Radley coll.

Fison, Francis Geoffrey, born at Ilkley, Yorks, 12 March, 1873; 1s. Frederick William, M.A. CHRIST CHURCH, matric. 14 Oct., 92, aged 19, from Harrow.

Fithian, Richard Barrett, born in New York, May, 1869; 1s. Joel Adams, arm. CHRIST CHURCH, matric. 13 Jan., 88, aged 18.

FitzGerald, lord George, born at Carton near Maynooth 16 Feb., 1862; 6s. Charles William, duke of Leinster. CHRIST CHURCH, matric. 21 May, 80, aged 18 (from Eton), B.A. 84.

Fitzgerald, Gerald Augustus Robert, M.A., fellow ST. JOHN'S 67-75, where see.

Fitz Gerald, Henry Purefoy, born at Preston Candover, Hants, 27 May, 1867; 2s. Richard Purefoy, lieut.-col. KEBLE, matric. 18 Oct., 89, aged 22, from Clifton coll., and some time a master there.

Fitz Gerald, rev. James Charles, born at Horkesley, Essex, 30 Oct., 1864; 1s. Charles, major-general. EXETER, matric. 31 May, 84, aged 19 (from Cheltenham coll), B.A. 88, M.A. 92; curate of Dolton, Devon, 90.

Fitz Gerald, John Foster Vesey, born in London Dec., 1864; o.s. John Foster Vesey, arm. KEBLE, matric. 17 Oct., 82, aged 18 (from St Mark's school, Windsor), B.A. 86, M.A. 89; bar.-at-law, Middle Temple, 92.

Fitzgerald, Michael Joseph, born at Dublin 1864; 5s. Thomas, arm. NON-COLLEGIATE, matric. 21 Jan., 82, aged 16.

Fitzgerald, Reginald Patrick, born at Castlemaine, Victoria, 12 March, 1874; 6s. hon. Nicholas, of St. Kilda; M.P. BALLIOL, matric. 18 Oct., 92, aged 18, from Downside coll., Bath.

FitzMaurice, Desmond, born in London 1874; 2s. John Gerald, inspector of schools. CHRIST CHURCH, matric. 14 Oct., 92, aged 18, (from Westminster school), scholar 92.

FitzMaurice, Henry Charles Keith Petty, (5th) marquis of Lansdowne, born 14 Jan., 1845; 1s. William Thomas, 4th marquis. BALLIOL, matric. 19 Oct., 63, aged 18 (from Eton), B.A. and M.A. 84 (HONOURS :—2 classical mods. 65, 2 classics 67), created D.C.L. 20 June, 88; governor-general of Canada 83, etc.; father of the next-named. See Foster's *Peerage.*

FitzMaurice, Henry William Edmund, earl of Kerry, born at Bowood, Wilts, 14 Jan., 1872; 1s. Henry Charles Keith, marquis (of Lansdowne). BALLIOL, matric. 1 Nov., 90, aged 18, from Eton.

FitzRoy, Cyril Duncombe, born in London 21 May, 1861; 3s. Francis Horatio, arm. ST. JOHN'S, matric. 5 Feb., 81, aged 19, from Wellington.

FitzRoy, Francis Horatio, B.A., fellow ALL SOULS' 47-50, where see.

Fitzwilliam, Edward Charles, born at Hurstpierpoint, Sussex, 1862; 1s. George, gent. NON-COLLEGIATE, matric. 14 Oct., 82, aged 20 (from Magdalen coll. school), B.A. 87, M.A. 92.

Flanagan, James Woulfe, born in Dublin 27 Jan., 1864; 4s. Stephen Woulfe, arm. TRINITY, matric. 11 Oct., 84, aged 20 (from Oscott coll.), B.A. 87, M.A. 91; bar.-at-law, Middle Temple, 91.

Flanagan, Richard John Woulfe, born at Killiney, Ireland, 1869; 5s. Stephen, arm. NON-COLLEGIATE, matric. 23 March, 87, aged 18.

Flatt, rev. Sidney Baker, born in Norwich 30 June, 1866; 5s. John, gent. WORCESTER, matric. 22 Oct., 85, aged 19 (from Norwich middle school), B.A. 88, M.A. 92; curate of St. Andrew, Croydon, 89.

Fleet, Algernon Massey, born at Hone, Kent, March, 1865; o.s. Thomas Horn, arm. CHRIST CHURCH, matric. 20 Jan., 82, aged 19 (from Eton), B.A. 86, M.A. 89.

Fleming, rev. Arthur Evelyn, born at East Retford, Notts, 8 July, 1864; 1s. Thomas Samuel, cler. QUEEN'S, matric. 22 Oct., 83, aged 19 (from Leeds gr. school), exhibitioner 83, B.A. 87, M.A. 91 (HONOURS :—2 classical mods. 85, 4 classics 87); a minor canon of Gloucester 91.

Fleming, Charles James Nicol, born in Edinburgh 5 April, 1868; 2s. James Nicol. QUEEN'S, matric. 21 Oct., 87, aged 19 (from Fettes coll.), scholar 87, B.A. 91; HONOURS :—2 classical mods. 89, 2 classics 91.

Fleming, Herbert James, born at Chipping Ongar, Essex, 1873; 5s. John, merchant. PEMBROKE, matric. 26 Oct., 91, aged 18 (from Dulwich coll.), scholar 91.

Fleming, John Edward Arthur Willis-, born in London 1872; o.s. John Browne, gen. PEMBROKE, matric. 10 Nov., 91, aged 19.

Fleming, Malcolm George, born at Bath Dec., 1866; 3s. James, S.T.B. ORIEL, matric. 5 Feb., 86, aged 19 (from Harrow), B.A. 89 (HONOURS :—3 history 89); bar.-at-law, Inner Temple, 92.

Fleming, Maxwell, born at Perth, N.B., 30 May, 1871; 3s. Archibald, B.A., cler. BALLIOL, matric. 18 Oct., 92, aged 21, from Edinburgh academy.

Fleming, William Kaye, born at Tunbridge, Kent, Dec., 1870; 1s. Isaac Plant, arm. TRINITY, matric. 11 Oct., 90, aged 19 (from Blackheath school), exhibitioner 87.

14

Flemmich, Arthur Helmuth, born at Roehampton, Surrey, 24 April, 1873; 3s. John Frederick, gen., deceased. BALLIOL, matric. 20 Oct., 91, aged 18, from Harrow.

Fletcher, rev. Albert, born at Accrington, co. Lanc., 1864; 4s. John Gascoigne, gent. ST. EDMUND HALL, matric. 22 Oct., 83, aged 19, B.A. 89; curate of St. Mark, Cheetham Hill, co. Lanc., 91.

Fletcher, Carteret Ernest, born at Oxford 24 Oct., 1868; 1s. Carteret John Halford, cler. TRINITY, matric. 16 Oct., 86, aged 17 (from Marlborough coll.), B.A. 89; HONOURS:—2 law 89, 2 civil law 90.

Fletcher, Carteret John Halford, M.A., WORCESTER, where see.

Fletcher, Charles Robert Leslie, M.A., fellow MAGDALEN 90, where see.

Fletcher, Ernest Edward, born at Gateshead-on-Tyne 25 May, 1869; 2s. Horace, gen. QUEEN'S, matric. 21 Oct., 87, aged 18 (from Magdalen coll. school, and Newcastle school of science), B.A. 90; bar.-at-law, Lincoln's Inn, 92.

Fletcher, Frank, born at Gloucester 1870; 3s. John, gent. BALLIOL, matric. 24 March, 86, aged 16 (from school), exhibitioner 86, B.A. 90; HONOURS:—2 classical mods. 87, 2 classics 89, Greek verse 88.

Fletcher, Frank, born at Atherton, co. Lanc., 3 May, 1870; 1s. Ralph, arm. BALLIOL, matric. 17 Oct., 89, aged 19 (from Rossall school), scholar 88; HONOURS:—accessit Hertford scholarship 90, Craven scholarship 92, 1 classical mods. 90, and of St. Mary Magdalen, ship 91; brother of Wilfrid.

Fletcher, Hamilton, born at Melbourne 15 Dec., 1868; 6s. John Frederick, gen., deceased. NON-COLLEGIATE, matric. 11 Oct., 90, aged 22 (from St. John-at-Hackney gr. school, London); migrated to PEMBROKE.

Fletcher, Lancelot Kohry, born at Richmond, Victoria, 1868; 2s. rev. William Roby, ex-vice-chancellor of Adelaide university. LINCOLN, matric. 20 Oct., 90, aged 22, from Adelaide university.

Fletcher, Lazarus, M.A., fellow UNIVERSITY COLL. 77-80, where see, page 33.

Fletcher, Wilfrid, born at Southport, co. Lanc., 23 Sept., 1873; 3s. Ralph, J.P., Lanarkshire, colliery owner, 27th wrangler, M.A. Cambridge. MERTON, matric. 18 Oct., 92, aged 19, from Rossall school.

Fletcher, William, D.D., fellow BRASENOSE 33-5, where see.

Fletcher, William Alfred Littledale, born at Childwall, co. Lanc., 1869; 1s. Alfred, arm. CHRIST CHURCH, matric. 12 Oct., 88, aged 19; stroke in University eight 90, rowed 91, 2.

Floersheim, Cecil Louis Ferdinand, born in London Jan., 1871; 1s. Louis Ferdinand, arm. CHRIST CHURCH, matric. 8 June, 89, aged 18, from Eton.

Floersheim, Walter Alfred, born in London 1873; 2s. Louis Ferdinand, arm. CHRIST CHURCH, matric. 6 June, 90, aged 17, from Eton.

Flower, Frederick Gerald, born at Addiscombe, Surrey, 1863; 1s. John, solicitor. EXETER, matric. 20 Oct., 81, aged 18, from Tonbridge.

Floyd, Charles Greenwood, M.A., student CHRIST CHURCH 49-67, where see.

Floyd, Ernest, born at Galleyden, Essex, 1s. George, rector of Frilsham, Berks. BRASENOSE, matric. 22 Oct., 83, aged 19, from Bradfield coll.

Floyd, George Alexander, born at Berkswell, co. Warwick, July, 1864; 2s. William, arm. KEBLE, matric. 14 Oct., 84, aged 20 (from Leamington coll.), exhibitioner 84, B.A. 88; HONOURS:—2 classical mods. 86, 4 classics 88.

Floyd, Thomas Owen, born at Frilford, Berks, 23 Jan., 1873; 1s. Thomas, gen. KEBLE, matric. 20 Oct., 91, aged 18, from Haileybury.

Floyer, rev. John Kestell, born at Marsh Chapel, co. Lincoln, 28 June, 1868; 4s. Ayscoghe, cler. WADHAM, matric. 19 Jan., 88, aged 22, B.A. 91.

Flux, rev. Alfred William, born in London 31 Oct., 1869; 2s. William, solicitor. NEW COLL, matric. 14 Oct., 82, aged 21 (from Marlborough), B.A. 85, M.A. 89 (HONOURS:—2 law 85); curate of Upper St. Leonards-on-Sea, Sussex, 91.

Flynn, Harold Frederick, born at Bradford, Yorks, 4 June, 1869; 2s. Thomas Henry, cler. ST. MARY HALL, matric. 22 Oct., 83, aged 21.

Foley, Blanchard, born in London 15 June, 1869; 2s. Joseph Benbrick, gen. MERTON, matric. 17 Oct., 88, aged 19 (from Highgate school), postmaster 88, B.A. 92 (HONOURS:—1 classical mods. 90, 1 classics 92), selected candidate Indian C.S. 92.

Foley, Edward Walwyn, M.A., fellow WADHAM 32-7, where see.

Follett, Charles John, C.B., M.A., B.C.L., fellow ST. JOHN'S 56-63, where see.

Follit, John Lucas, born at Crickhowell, co. Brecon, 31 May, 1867; 1s. John, gen. LINCOLN, matric. 22 Oct., 86, aged 19, from Hurstpierpoint coll.

Fookes, rev. Robert Goldstone, born at Gosfield, Essex, 1863; o.s. Thomas, gent. PEMBROKE, matric. 26 Oct., 81, aged 18, B.A. 84, M.A. 88, chaplain and divinity lecturer 90 (HONOURS:—3 mathematical mods. 83, 2 theology 85); curate of St. Giles 89 and 90, and of St. Mary Magdalen, Oxford, 90.

Footman, rev. John, born at Ipswich Nov., 1865; 3s. Henry, cler. KEBLE, matric. 14 Oct., 84, aged 18 (from Marlborough); migrated to CHARSLEY HALL, B.A. 88, M.A. 91; curate of Nocton, co. Linc., 91.

Footman, William Llewellyn, born at Laithdy, co. Carmarthen, 26 Aug., 1867; 1s. Robert, gen. JESUS COLL., matric. 20 Oct., 86, aged 19 (from Llandovery coll.), scholar 86, B.A. 90; HONOURS:—3 mathematical mods. 88, 3 mathematics 90.

Foottit, rev. Edward Hall, born at Cromwell, Notts, 26 Aug., 1867; 2s. Thomas Weightman, gent. NON-COLLEGIATE, matric. 15 Oct., 87, aged 20 (from Retford and Newark gr. schools); migrated to WORCESTER, B.A. 90 (HONOURS:—3 theology 90); curate of Newington, Hull, 91.

Forbes, Alexander Staats, born at Holloway, Middx., Nov., 1867; 1s. Alexander, arm. HERTFORD, matric. 30 Jan., 91, aged 23.

Forbes, Charles William, born at Falkirk in Scotland, Sept., 1871; 1s. William, arm. CHRIST CHURCH, matric. 16 Jan., 91, aged 19, from Eton.

Forbes, rev. Edward, born in London 18 Feb., 1867; 3s. Thomas Lawrence, gen. LINCOLN, matric. 22 Oct., 86, aged 19 (from city of London school), B.A. 89 (HONOURS:—3 theology 89); curate of St. Andrew, Peckham, 91.

Forbes, George Forrest Greenlaw, born at Dehra, East Indies, 1862; 2s. John Greenlaw, arm. BALLIOL, matric. 18 Oct., 81, aged 19 (from the Charterhouse); joint magistrate North West provinces, India, 89.

Forbes, rev. James, born in Carlisle 19 Aug., 1867; o.s. Archibald, gen. EXETER, matric. 16 Oct., 87, aged 19 (from Carlisle gr. school), scholar 87, B.A. 91 (HONOURS:—2 mathematical mods. 89, 3 mathematics 91); curate of Warrington, St. Paul, 91.

Forbes, Kenneth Brooks Donet, born in Jamaica 15 Sept., 1866; 5s. William, cler. ST. JOHN'S, matric. 17 Oct., 85, aged 19 (from Highgate school), scholar 85, B.A. 89, M.A. 92; HONOURS:—2 classical mods. 87, 2 classics 89.

Forbes, Reginald Arthur Villiers, born at Chatham, Kent, 31 Oct., 1865; o.s. Henry Villiers, of Somerton, Somerset, lieut.-col. R.M.L.I. MAGDALEN, matric. 16 Oct., 84, aged 18 (from the Charterhouse) demy 84, B.A. 89; HONOURS :—1 classical mods. 86, 3 classics 88.

Forbes, William Henry, M.A., fellow BALLIOL 73, where see.

Force, Charles Frank Bernard, born in London 1867; 1s. Frank Westway, gent. BRASENOSE, matric. 23 Oct., 85, aged 18 (from Lancing coll.), B.A. 90, M.A. 92.

Ford, Edward Wilton, born at Wootton, isle of Wight, 1859; 1s. Edward, cler. WORCESTER, matric. 26 Jan., 82, aged 23, B.A. 86, M.A. 88.

Ford, Harold Dodsworth, born at Carlisle 5 Aug., 1864; 3s. Henry Edmund, organist Carlisle cathedral. WADHAM, matric. 19 Jan., 85, aged 20, B.A. 88; HONOURS :—3 classical mods. 86, 3 history 88.

Ford, Herbert Graham, born at Carlisle 21 Aug., 1868; y.s. Henry Edmund, organist Carlisle cathedral. WADHAM, matric. 15 Oct., 87, aged 19 (from Sedbergh school), scholar 86, B.A. 91; HONOURS : —2 classical mods. 89, 2 classics 91.

Ford, James Arthur, born at Paddington 16 July, 1870; 1s. Edmund Salway, arm. BRASENOSE, matric. 16 Oct., 88, aged 18 (from Winchester), in the University eight 92.

Ford, William Lionel Joyce, born at Woodchester, co. Glouc., 7 June, 1874; 1s. William John, of Stroud, manufacturer, Sr. JOHN'S, matric. 15 Oct., 92, aged 18, from St. Mark's, Windsor, and Dean Close school, Cheltenham.

Forman, John Balls, born in London 1864; 2s. Archibald, gent. EXETER, matric. 18 Oct., 83, aged 19, B.A. 87, M.A. 90.

Formby, rev. Charles Wykeham, born at Latchingdon, Essex, March, 1865; y.s. Richard Edward, rector. KEBLE, matric. 16 Oct., 83, aged 18 (from Haileybury), B.A. 86; curate of Fawley 92.

Formby, Hugh Carlton, born at Latchingdon, Essex, Oct., 1863; 4s. Richard Edward, rector. HERTFORD, matric. 18 Oct., 83, aged 21, B.A. 86; capt. football eleven 86.

Foropoulos, Joachim Demetrius, born in the island of Chios 1859; o.s. Demetrius, gent. NON-COLLEGIATE, matric. 14 Oct., 82, aged 23.

Forrest, Ernest William, born at Gainsborough, co. Lincoln, 1 Aug., 1858; 1s. Richard William, gen. ST. MARY HALL, matric. 27 Oct., 91, aged 32.

Forrest, Henry Telford Stoner, born in London 11 April, 1870; 1s. Henry Vaughan, fleet-paymaster, R.N. NEW COLL., matric. 14 Oct., 92, aged 22 (from Plymouth coll.), selected candidate (6th) for Indian C.S. 92.

Forrest, Jabez Philip, born at Escurial in Spain, 1863; 4s. James, gent. NON-COLLEGIATE, matric. 13 Oct., 83, aged 20, from King's school, Chester.

Forrest, rev. Jacob Anastasio, born at Avila in Spain, 1861; 3s. James, gent. NON-COLLEGIATE, matric. 18 Oct., 80, aged 19 (from King's school, Chester); migrated to BALLIOL, B.A. 85, M.A. 89 (HONOURS: —4 classics 84); curate of Bishop Hatfield, Herts, 88.

Forrest, Robert William, born at Liverpool 20 Feb., 1863; 1s. Robert William, cler. QUEEN'S, matric. 7 Dec., 82 (from Westminster school), B.A. 86; died 88.

Forrest, Walter Porcy, born at Shrewsbury. CHRIST CHURCH, matric. 12 Oct., 83 (from Shrewsbury school), exhibitioner 83.

Forrester, Edward Ellis, born at Malmesbury, Wilts, 5 May, 1872; 3s. William, solicitor. BRASENOSE, matric. 22 Oct., 91, aged 19 (from Marlborough coll.), scholar 91.

Forshaw, Edward Roney, born at George Town, Demerara, 2 Aug., 1864; 1s. George Anderson, attorney.' WADHAM, matric. 23 April, 84, aged 19 (from King's coll. school, London); bar.-at-law, Lincoln's Inn, 89.

Forster, Claude William, born in London 13 July, 1873; 3s. William Stewart, solicitor. NON-COLLEGIATE, matric. 14 Oct., 92, aged 19, from Harrow school.

Forster, Henry William, born at Lewisham, Kent, 31 Jan., 1866; 1s. major John, of Southampton. NEW COLL., matric. 16 Oct., 85, aged 19 (from Eton), B.A. 89 (HONOURS :—3 law 89); in the University eleven 87, 8, 9; M.P. Sevenoaks division, Kent, 92.

Forster, John Gibson, born at Carlisle 20 April, 1872; 2s. John, gen. QUEEN'S, matric. 24 Oct., 90, aged 18 (from Carlisle gr. school), exhibitioner 90; HONOURS :—3 mathematical mods. 92.

Forster, Leonard Stewart, born in London 14 Sept., 1870; 2s. William Stewart, solicitor. NEW COLL., matric. 12 Oct., 88, aged 18 (from Harrow); died 29 May, 89, at Oxford.

Fort, Charles Leyland, born at Alderbury, Wilts, 12 May, 1870; 3s. George Munkhouse, arm. NEW COLL., matric. 15 Oct., 89, aged 19 (from Winchester), scholar 88, B.A. 92; HONOURS :— 1 chemistry 92.

Fort, George Seymour, born at Coopersale, Essex, 1859; 1s. Richard, cler. HERTFORD, matric. 10 April, 80, aged 21 (from Uppingham school), B.A. 83 (HONOURS :—3 history 83), in the Oxford eight 82-3.

Fort, Henry Richard Trecothick, born at Coopersale, Essex, 17 Feb., 1867; 2s. Richard, cler. WORCESTER, matric. 19 Oct., 86, aged 19 (from Radley coll.), B.A. 90.

Fort, Hugh, born at Whalley, co. Lane., 14 May, 1862; 4s. Richard, M.P. Clitheroe 63-8. NEW COLL., matric. 15 Oct., 81, aged 19 (from Winchester), scholar 81-5 (HONOURS :—1 classical mods. 83, 1 law 85); bar.-at-law, Inner Temple, 87.

Fortesoue, Chichester Samuel Parkinson, baron Carlingford and Clermont, hon. student CHRIST CHURCH 67, where see.

Fortey, Henry Comber, born at Bellary, E. Indies, 13 July, 1873; 1s. Henry, arm. BALLIOL, matric. 17 Oct., 82, aged 19, from Rossall school.

Forth, Thomas Francis, born at Melbourne, co. Derby, 1867; 1s. Thomas Petty, cler. NON-COLLEGIATE, matric. 19 Jan., 89, aged 22 (from Denstone coll.), B.A. 92; HONOURS:—4 theology 92.

Fortnum, Charles Drury Edward, created D.C.L. 26 June, 1889, hon. fellow QUEEN'S 92 (s. Charles, of London), born at Hornsey, Middx., March 1820; F.S.A. 58, a trustee of the British Museum 89, and a great benefactor to the university. See *Men and Women of the Time*.

Fosbery, Charles Sanderson, born at Worksop, Notts., 1866; 1s. rev. George William, M.A. Cantab. QUEEN'S, matric. 16 March, 92, aged 26.

Foskett, Herbert William, born at Annerley, Surrey, 15 Dec., 1864; 1s. John, arm. NEW COLL., matric. 10 Oct., 84, aged 19 (from Harrow), B.A. 88; HONOURS :—2 law 88.

Foster, Arthur, born in Camberwell, London, 29 July, 1869; 2s. George Devington, arm. MAGDALEN, matric. 16 Oct., 88, aged 19 (from the Charterhouse), B.A. 92; HONOURS :—2 classical mods. 90, 2 law 92.

Foster, Balthazar Stephen Sargant, born at Edgbaston, co. Warwick, 31 Aug., 1867; 1s. Balthazar Walter, knight. MAGDALEN, matric. 15 Oct., 86, aged 19 (from Uppingham school), B.A. 89; bar.-at-law, Inner Temple, 92.

Foster, Charles Bertram, born in London 14 July, 1868; 1s. Richard Betton, solicitor. MAGDALEN, matric. 22 Oct., 87, aged 19 (from the Charterhouse), B.A. 92; brother of Gerald Harinan.

Foster, Charles Cecil, born in Westminster 10 Dec. 1870; o.s. Charles Philip, solicitor. MERTON, matric. 12 Feb., 92, aged 21, from University coll. school, London.

Foster, rev. Charles Wilmer, born at Dalton, Yorks, 3 June, 1866; 1s. Charles William, vicar. ST. JOHN'S, matric. 16 Oct., 84, aged 18 (from Sheffield collegiate school), B.A. 87, M.A. 91; curate of St. Andrew, Great Grimsby, 91.

Foster, Ernest, born at North Curry, Somerset, 22 April, 1867; 4s. Charles Millett, solicitor. NEW COLL., matric. 15 Oct., 86, aged 19 (from King's coll. Taunton), B.A. 91; HONOURS :—2 classical mods. 88, 2 classics 90.

Foster, Francis Edward, born at Leintwardine, co. Hereford, 1865; 2s. Joseph, cler. NON-COLLEGIATE, matric. 17 Oct., 85, aged 20, from Clipping Campden gr. school.

Foster, Gerald Harman, born at Eastbourne, Sussex, 26 Sept., 1872; 2s. Richard Betton Charles Pulsford Manley, solicitor. MAGDALEN, matric. 22 Oct., 91, aged 19, from Haileybury.

Foster, Henry Knollys, born at Malvern 30 Oct., 1873; 1s. Henry, cler. TRINITY, matric. 15 Oct., 92, aged 18, from Malvern coll.

Foster, rev. Herbert Henry, born at Taunton, Somerset, 1864; o.s. William Lea, gent. PEMBROKE, matric. 27 Oct., 83, aged 19, B.A. 86, M.A. 90; HONOURS :—2 theology 86.

Foster, Herbert William, born at Melling near Liverpool, 2 Feb., 1861; 2s. Edwin, gent. BALLIOL, matric. 21 Oct., 80, aged 18 (from Liverpool institute); registrar high court Madras, and member of the board of examiners.

Foster, John Kenneth, born at Lightcliffe near Halifax, 1866; 1s. John, of Combe Park, Berks, arm. MAGDALEN, matric. 23 Oct., 85, aged 19, from Eton.

Foster, Joseph, M.A. 31 May, 1892 *(honoris causa)*, author of "Alumni Oxonienses," "The British Peerage," and many other genealogical works (1s. Joseph, of Sunderland, co. Durham, deceased), born 9 March, 44. See *Men and Women of the Time*.

Foster, Joseph Percy Thomasin, born at Barnston, Essex, 1866; 1s. James Thomasin, arm. CORPUS CHRISTI, matric. 23 Oct., 84, aged 18, B.A. 89; HONOURS :—3 classical mods. 86, 4 history 88.

Foster, Norris Tildasley, born at Bromsgrove 1856; 1s. Frederick Francis Forster, arm. NON-COLLEGIATE, matric. 17 Jan., 80, aged 24, as Forster (from K. Edward's school, and Queen's coll. Birmingham); migrated to TURRELL'S HALL, B.A. 88, as Foster, having altered the spelling of his name; bar.-at-law, Inner Temple, 91.

Foster, Philip Staveley, born at Halifax 11 July, 1865; 1s. Abraham Briggs, of Canwell Hall, Tamworth, arm. MAGDALEN, matric. 16 Oct., 84, aged 19 (from Eton), B.A. 89.

Foster, rev. Tom Horatio, born at Leeds, Yorks, 1862; 1s. Williamson, gent. NON-COLLEGIATE, matric. 13 Jan., 83, aged 21 (from Yorkshire coll., and St. John's school, Leeds); migrated to EXETER, B.A. 86 (HONOURS :—2 theology 86); domestic chaplain to bishop of Lichfield 91.

Foster, rev. William Hay, born in London 1862; o.s. Thomas, gent. NON-COLLEGIATE, matric. 17 Jan., 80, aged 18, B.A. 84, M.A. 87; curate of Margate, Kent, 90.

Foster, William Melville, born at Huddersfield Oct., 1871; 2s. John Edwin, surgeon. CHRIST CHURCH, matric. 6 June, 90, aged 18, from Dover coll.

Foster, William Footner, born in London 27 May, 1869; 1s. Richard, gen. NEW COLL., matric. 11 Oct., 89, aged 20 (from Winchester), B.A. 92.

Fothergill, Sydney Roden, born at Aberdare, co. Montgomery, 14 Oct., 1864; 1s. Richard, arm. NEW COLL., matric. 10 Oct., 84, aged 19 (from Eton), B.A. 89, M.A. 91 (HONOURS :—2 classical mods. 85, 2 classics 88); bar.-at-law, Lincoln's Inn, 91.

Fothergill, Theodore Roden, born at Tenby, co. Pemb., 24 Feb., 1869; 2s. Richard, arm, NEW COLL., matric. 12 Oct., 88, aged 19 (from Eton); HONOURS :—2 classical mods. 90.

Fotheringham, John Knight, born at Tottenham, Middx., 14 Aug., 1874; 2s. David, presbyterian minister. MERTON, matric. 18 Oct., 92, aged 18 (from city of London school), exhibitioner 91.

Foulkes, Arthur Glyndwr, born at Sale, Cheshire, 1864; o.s. Arthur David, gent. PEMBROKE, matric. 25 Jan., 83, aged 19 (from Harrow), B.A. 86, M.A. 89; student Inner Temple 84.

Fowkes, Henry Evett, born at Sydenham, Kent, 28 Nov., 1864; o.s. Henry Kaper George, gent. TRINITY, matric. 15 Oct., 83, aged 19 (from Dulwich coll.), scholar 83, B.A. 87, M.A. 90; HONOURS :—1 classical mods. 84, 2 classics 87.

Fowler, Arthur John, born at Tunbridge Wells, Kent, 29 Feb., 1868; 5s. Robert, of Tonbridge, Kent, cler. CORPUS CHRISTI, matric. 24 Oct., 87, aged 19 (from Rugby and Sedbergh schools), exhibitioner 87, B.A. 92 (HONOURS :—1 classical mods. 89, 3 classics 91); brother of Henry Watson, 77.

Fowler, Benjamin John Boyes, born at Plymouth 1863; o.s. Benjamin John, gent. PEMBROKE, matric. 23 Oct., 82, aged 19, B.A. 88.

Fowler, George Herbert, born at Lincoln Sept., 1861; o.s. John, cler. KEBLE, matric. 19 Oct., 80, aged 19 (from Eton), scholar 80-3, B.A. 84; HONOURS :—2 natural science 84.

Fowler, Gerald, born at Leytonstone, Essex, 27 July, 1866; 4s. William, (formerly M.P.). ORIEL, matric. 23 Oct., 85, aged 19 (from Clifton coll.), B.A. 88 (HONOURS :—3 classical mods. 87), in the University eleven 88.

Fowler, Henry de Galle Lewis, born at Point-du-Galle, Ceylon, 2 March, 1861; 1s. John Townsend, arm. BALLIOL, matric. 29 Jan., 81, aged 19 (from Rugby), B.A. 84 (HONOURS :—2 classical mods. 82, 2 classics 84); brother of Robert Clive, 86.

Fowler, Henry Ernest, born at Tittenhall, co. Stafford, April, 1870; 1s. Henry Hartley, arm. CHRIST CHURCH, matric. 8 June, 89, aged 19, from Begbrooke school.

Fowler, John Henry, born at Liverpool 3 Jan., 1861; 1s. Henry Piggin, cler. TRINITY, matric. 16 Oct., 80, aged 19 (from Manchester and York schools), scholar 80-5, B.A. 84, M.A. 87 (HONOURS :—1 classical mods. 81, 1 classics 84, English essay 86); assumed the name of Fowler in lieu of Piggin 84; a master at Manchester school.

Fowler, Robert Clive, born at Madras 20 Jan., 1868; 4s. John Townsend, of Madras c.s. EXETER, matric. 21 Oct., 86, aged 18, from Warwick school; brother of Henry, 81.

Fowler, Robert Copp, born at Ulting, Essex, 5 Nov., 1867; 1s. Newell Vicary, vicar 63. NEW COLL., matric. 15 Oct., 86, aged 18 (from Winchester), scholar 86, B.A. 89 (HONOURS :—1 mathl. mods. 87, 1 maths. 89, accessit junior mathl. exhibition 87 and 88, senior mathl. scholarship 93, accessit 91, and proxime accessit 92), Herschel astronomical prize 92.

Fowler, Thomas, D.D., president of CORPUS CHRISTI 81, where see.

Fowler, William Strode, born at Brighton 1862; o.s. William Strode, cler. MERTON, matric. 18 Oct., 81, aged 19.

Fowler, William Warde, M.A., fellow LINCOLN 72, where see.

Fownes, Arthur Galliver, born at All Cannings, Wilts, March, 1872; 2s. John Edward Curtis, cler. KEBLE, matric. 11 Oct., 90, aged 18, from Wantage school.

Fox, Armine Wodehouse, born at Weston-super-Mare 7 April, 1869; 2s. William Charles, cler. EXETER, matric. 17 Oct., 88, aged 19 (from Wellington coll.), exhibitioner 88; HONOURS :—3 classical mods. 90.

Fox, Arthur Cunliffe, born at Bolton-le-Moors, co. Lanc., 6 June, 1865; 1s. John, of Stourton Grange, Hunslet, Yorks, unitarian minister. NON-COL-LEGIATE, matric. 17 Oct., 91, aged 22, from Newark gr. school and Yorkshire coll. Leeds.

Fox, Edward Vaughan, born at Leonard Stanley, co. Glouc., 12 Sept., 1861; 1s. Vaughan Simpson, cler. LINCOLN, matric. 23 Oct., 80, aged 19 (from Haileybury), B.A. 84; HONOURS :—3 classics 84.

Fox, George Richard Lane, born in London 15 Dec., 1870; 1s. James Richard Lane, arm. NEW COLL., 11 Oct., 89, aged 19 (from Eton); HONOURS: —2 classical mods. 91.

Fox, rev. Gilbert Basil, born at Delamere, Cheshire, 1865; 7s. William Darwin, cler. ST. JOHN'S, matric. 13 Oct., 83, aged 18, B.A. 87, M.A. 91; curate of Eastbourne St. Anne 89.

Fox, Herbert Francis, M.A., fellow BRASENOSE 89, where see.

Fox, Herbert Hamilton, born at Padiham, co. Lanc., 11 Feb., 1868; 1s. Joseph Hamilton, gent. WOR-CESTER, matric. 19 Oct., 86, aged 18, from Westminster and Reading schools.

Fox, Hugh McElroy, born at Dinapore, Bengal, 1873; 2s. Michael Augustus, gen. CHRIST CHURCH, matric. 16 Oct., 91, aged 18.

Fox, Robert Barchiy, born at Falmouth 24 July, 1873; 1s. Robert, gent. MAGDALEN, matric. 18 Oct., 92, aged 19, from Winchester.

Fox, William Alexander, born at Wellington, Somst., 28 Dec., 1865; 3s. Thomas, gen. LINCOLN, matric. 21 Oct., 87, aged 21 (from Clifton coll.), exhibitioner 87; B.A. 91; HONOURS :—2 classical mods. 89, 2 classics 91.

Foxcroft, Cecil Talbot, born at Hinton Charterhouse near Bath, 24 Nov., 1868; 1s. Edward Talbot Day, arm. MAGDALEN, matric. 16 Oct., 88, aged 19 (from Eton); HONOURS :—4 history 92.

Frampton, Richard Ernest Edward, born at Burghclere, co. Glouc., 1864; 1s. Richard, cler. BRASENOSE, matric. 22 Oct., 83, aged 19 (from Malvern coll.), scholar 83, B.A. 87, M.A. 90; HONOURS :—1 classical mods. 85, 3 classics 87.

Francis, Earley Christopher, born at Thames Ditton, Surrey, 14 Oct., 1861; 4s. Robert, of Crofton Hall, Kent, arm. MAGDALEN, matric. 27 April 81, aged 19 (from Clifton coll.), B.A. 84, M.A. 88.

Francis, Hugh Albert, born at Bradwell Ash, Suffolk, Feb., 1866; 2s. John Grimwade, gent. EXETER, matric. 22 Oct., 85, aged 19 (from Bury St. Edmund's school), B.A. 89, M.A. 92; HONOURS :—2 classical mods. 87, 3 history 89.

Francis, Hugh Carwardine, born at Staunton, co. Glouc., 20 July, 1868; y.s. George Edward, late crown receiver Forest of Dean. EXETER, matric. 16 Oct., 89, aged 21.

Francis, Walter, born at South Church, Essex, 1869; 4s. Charles Wordley, arm. CORPUS CHRISTI, matric. 20 Oct., 88, aged 19 (from Repton school), assist. to collector and magistrate, Tanjore, 90.

Francke, Paul Mortimer, born at New York 24 May, 1866; 1s. Axel Patrick, gent. TRINITY, matric. 17 Oct., 85, aged 19 (from Westminster school), B.A. 88 (HONOURS :—3 classical mods. 87); bar-at-law, Inner Temple, 90.

Francke, Victor Ernest, born at Paddington 13 Jan., 1872; 3s. Axel Patrick, gent. TRINITY, matric. 11 Oct., 90, aged 18, from Bath coll.

Francombe, Henry Reynolds, born at Oxford 29 March, 1872; 2s. Samson, gen. QUEEN'S, matric. 24 Oct., 90, aged 18, from Oxford high school, etc.

Frankish, Harold, born at Kirmington, co. Linc., 12 March, 1873; 2s. William John, gent. WOR-CESTER, matric. 18 Oct., 91, aged 19.

Franklin, Abraham Henry, born in London 6 July, 1866; o.s. Abraham, gent. WADHAM, matric. 19 Jan., 85, aged 18 (from Real-schule at Frankfort-on-the-Maine), B.A. 88; HONOURS :—3 law 88.

Franklin, Francis Sidney Herbert, born at Knighton, ST. JOHN'S, matric. 11 Oct., 84, aged 19 (from city of London and King's coll. schools), B.A. 87, M.A. 92; HONOURS :—2 classical mods. 86, 4 law 87.

Franklin, Herbert Charles Temple, born Oct., 1865; 1s. Charles, arm. ORIEL, matric. 23 Oct., 84, aged 19 (from King's coll. school, London); scholar 84, D.A. 88; HONOURS :—1 classical mods. 86, 1 classics 88.

Franks, William Temple, born at Croydon, Surrey, 18 March, 1862; 2s. Joseph Fletcher, gent. WAD-HAM, matric. 15 Oct., 81, aged 19 (from Dulwich coll.), scholar 81-5, B.A. 85, Stowell fellow UNI-VERSITY COLL. 88, B.C.L. 89 (HONOURS :—2 classical mods. 83, 1 classics 85); bar.-at-law, Inner Temple, 90.

Fraser, rev. Alexander Campbell, born at Edinburgh 1860; 3s. Alexander Campbell (D.C.L.) ORIEL, matric. 19 Oct. 80, aged 20 (from Edinburgh university, M.A., 80), B.A. 83, M.A. 87; vicar of Bilton, Yorks, 89.

Fraser, Alexander Campbell, hon. LL.D. Glasgow 71, created D.C.L. 13 June, 1883, professor of logic and metaphysics in the University of Edinburgh 1856, dean of the faculty of arts 59; born at Ardchattan, co. Argyll, Sept., 1819. See *Men and Women of the Time*.

Fraser, Alexander Edmund, born at Edinburgh 1865; 1s. John, gent. CORPUS CHRISTI, matric. 27 Oct., 81, aged 18, B.A. 85, M.A. 88 (HONOURS : —4 history 85); student Inner Temple, 84.

Fraser, Charles James Roy, born at Inverness 1864; 1s. Charles Ross, arm. BALLIOL, matric. 16 Jan., 83, aged 18 (from Leamington coll.), B.A. 86; HONOURS :—3 classical mods. 84, 3 history 86.

Fraser, James Denholm, born at Demerara, B. Guiana, 10 Nov., 1870; 3s. James Denholm, arm. QUEEN'S, matric. 22 Oct., 89, aged 18 (from Christ's hospital), scholar 89; assist. commissioner Burma 89.

Fraser, James Nelson, born at Retford, Notts, 1867; 1s. James, gen. BALLIOL, matric. 18 Oct., 88, aged 18 (from Rossall school), exhibitioner 87; HONOURS :—1 classical mods. 90, 1 classics 92.

Fraser, Simon Joseph, (16th) lord Lovat, born at Beaufort Castle, near Inverness, 25 Nov., 1871; 2s. Simon, lord Lovat. MAGDALEN, matric. 14 Oct., 90, aged 18, from Fort Augustus school.

Fraser, Stuart Mitford, born at Berbice in Guiana, 1865; 2s. James Denholm, arm. BALLIOL, matric. 17 Jan., 83, aged 18 (from Tiverton school); assist. collector and magistrate Bombay C.S., employed as guardian and tutor to the Raja of Kolohapur, the chief of Kagal and the Kunwar Saheb of Iiharnagar.

Frazer, Evan Richards, born at Sydney, Australia, 1867; 1s. John, gent. BALLIOL, matric. 19 Oct., 87, aged 20 (from Sydney university), B.A. 92.

Frazer, rev. Joseph Robert Francis, born at Kensington 20 Feb., 1869; 1s. Joseph, arm. MERTON, matric. 22 Oct., 87, aged 18 (from Dulwich coll.), exhibitioner 87; HONOURS :—2 mathematical mods. 89, 3 mathematics 91.

Frazer, William Ray, born in London 23 Dec., 1873; 3s. Joseph, gent. LINCOLN, matric. 25 Oct., 92, aged 18 (from Dulwich coll.), scholar 92.

Free, Richard William, born at Southwark, Surrey, 1860; 1s. Richard William, gen. NON-COLLEGIATE, matric. 29 Oct., 91, aged 31.

Freeborn, John Charles Richard, M.A., EXETER, where see.

Freeman, Charles Lawrence, born in London 6 Oct., 1868; o.s. Robert, gent. UNIVERSITY COLL., matric. 18 Oct., 86, aged 18 (from Westminster school), B.A. 90; HONOURS :—2 classical mods. 88, 4 classics 90.

Freeman, Ernest Allen, born in London 1864; 2s. Henry Samuel, gent. NON-COLLEGIATE, matric. 29 Jan., 81, aged 17, from Amersham Hall school near Reading.

Freeman, Henry Herbert, born in London 1862; 1s. Henry Samuel, arm. NON-COLLEGIATE, matric. 20 Nov., 80, aged 18, from Benhilton park school, Sutton, Surrey.

Freeman, Horace, born at Newbury, Berks, 4 Feb., 1872; 7s. James, schoolmaster. BRASENOSE, matric. 22 Oct., 91, aged 19 (from Christ's hospital), exhibitioner 91.

Freeman, James Edward, born at Buxton, 20 March, 1871; 2s. Joseph Bray, gen. BRASENOSE, matric. 15 Oct., 90, aged 19 (from Huddersfield coll.), exhibitioner 90; HONOURS :—2 classical mods. 92.

Freeman, Robert Massie, born at High Leigh, Cheshire, 1866; 1s. Robert Marriott, cler. UNIVERSITY COLL., matric. 11 Oct., 84, aged 18 (from Stony Stratford coll. and Loretto school), scholar 84; HONOURS :—1 classical mods. 86.

Freer, (rev.) Arthur Savile Beresford, born at Hough ton, co. Leicester, 6 Feb., 1866; 3s. William Thomas, cler. TRINITY, matric. 11 Oct., 84, aged 18 (from Radley coll.), B.A. 88 (HONOURS :—1 history 88); curate of Chacewater, Cornwall, 90.

Freese, rev. Frederick Edmeston, born at Milton, Kent, 11 July, 1863; 1s. Frederick William, gen. TRINITY, matric. 15 Oct., 81, aged 18 (from Dulwich coll.), B.A. 85, M.A. 88 (HONOURS :—2 history 85); missionary in Japan 89.

Freke, Denis James Hussey, born at Hannington, Wilts, 25 Oct., 1866; 2s. Ambrose Denis, arm. MAGDALEN, matric. 23 Oct., 85, aged 18 (from Eton), demy 84, B.A. 89; HONOURS :—2 classical mods. 87, 3 classics 89.

Fremantle, Francis Edward, born in London 29 May, 1872; 2s. hon. William Henry, canon of Canterbury. BALLIOL, matric. 17 Jan., 91, aged 18, from Eton.

Fremantle, hon. Reginald Scott, born in London 11 Feb., 1863; 2s. Thomas Francis, and lord Cottesloe 90. BALLIOL, matric. 18 Oct., 81, aged 18 (from Eton), B.A. 86, M.A. 88; HONOURS :—2 classical mods. 83.

Fremantle, Selwyn Howe, born at Swanbourne, Bucks, 11 Aug., 1869; 1s. hon. Edmund Robert, rear admiral, C.B., C.M.G. MAGDALEN, matric. 16 Oct., 88, aged 19 (from Eton); assist. magistrate north west provinces of India.

Fremantle, hon. Thomas Francis, born in London 5 Feb., 1862; 1s. Thomas Francis, and lord Cottesloe 90. BALLIOL, matric. 28 April, 81, aged 19 (from Eton), B.A. 85, M.A. 89.

Fremantle, rev. William Archibald Culling, born in London 26 July, 1865; 1s. hon. William Henry, canon of Canterbury. BALLIOL, matric. 15 Oct., 84, aged 19 (from Eton), B.A. 88, M.A. 91; curate of Dorking St. Paul 90.

Fremantle, rev. the hon. William Henry, M.A., fellow BALLIOL 82, where see.

Fremantle, very rev. William Robert, D.D., dean of Ripon, fellow MAGDALEN 31-42, where see.

French, Lewis, born in London 26 Oct., 1873; 3s. David, of Eltham, Kent, merchant. ST. JOHN'S, matric. 15 Oct., 92, aged 18, from Merchant Taylors' school.

French, Walter Thomas, born at Oxford 1873; 1s. Sidney Walter, gent. BALLIOL, matric. 18 Oct., 92, aged 19.

Frend, Edwin George Clifford, born in London 30 May, 1871; 1s. Edwin, of Brighton, arm. WADHAM, matric. 13 Oct., 90, aged 19, from Haileybury.

Frere, Laurie, born in London 15 May, 1866; 1s. Bartle John Laurie, arm. BRASENOSE, matric. 23 Oct., 85, aged 19 (from Eton), B.A. 88.

Frere, rev. Leonard Hanbury, born at Horham, Suffolk, 1 Jan., 1861; 1s. Edward Hanbury, cler. NON-COLLEGIATE, matric. 3 Nov., 83, aged 23 (from Bradfield coll. and the chancellor's school Lincoln); university missionary to central Africa 85.

Frid, Ernest Wanless, born at Lewisham, Kent, 1861; o.s. William Saltonstall, gent. NON-COLLEGIATE, matric. 21 Jan., 82, aged 21 (from Dulwich coll.), B.A. 87.

Fripp, rev. Charles Edward Bowles, born at Portishead, Somerset, 1 Oct., 1866; o.s. Charles Spencer, cler. ST. MARY HALL, matric. 24 Oct., 85, aged 19 (from St. Edward's school Summertown), B.A. 89, M.A. 92; curate of Reddall Hill, co. Stafford, 91.

Fritche, Cheslyn Whiston Allan, born at Newton Regis 1867; o.s. George Cheslyn, rector. HERTFORD, matric. 5 Feb., 86, aged 19.

Frith, Frederick Wright Churchill, born at Allestree, co. Derby, Dec., 1866; 3s. Marischall Keith Smith, cler. KEBLE, matric. 22 Oct., 85, aged 18, from Canterbury school.

Froggatt, Henry, born at Bitterley, Salop, 1858; 2s. John, gent. CHARSLEY'S HALL, matric. 16 Oct., 86, aged 28, B.A. 89; HONOURS :—3 history 89.

Frost, Herbert Sells, born at Ashby near Bristol, 9 Feb., 1861; 4s. William Durant, gent. MERTON, matric. 18 Oct., 81, aged 20, B.A. 86, M.A. 88.

Frost, Percival Gildart, born at Pirton, Wilts, 24 March, 1867; 1s. Charles, arm., deceased. MAGDALEN, matric. 23 Oct., 85, aged 18 (from Winchester), B.A. 89.

Froude, Ashley Anthony, born in London 28 June, 1863; 1s. James Anthony, regius professor of history. ORIEL, matric. 18 Oct., 81, aged 18, (from Westminster school), B.A. 84; C.M.G. 92, secretary to Behring Sea commissioners.

Froude, John Anthony, M.A., D.C.L., fellow ORIEL 92, where see, page 151.

Fry, Bernard Cecil, born at Darlington 6 Aug., 1872; 4s. Theodore, M.P. NEW COLL., matric. 16 Oct., 91, aged 19 (from Clifton coll.), exhibitioner 92.

Fry, Charles Burgess, born at West Croydon, Surrey, 25 April, 1872; 1s. Lewis John, of C.S. WADHAM, matric. 20 Oct., 91, aged 19 (from Repton school), scholar 90; in the University eleven 92.

Fry, Gilbert Herbert, born at Clapham 1871; o.s. Thomas, arm. CHRIST CHURCH, matric. 11 Oct., 89, aged 18 (from Westminster school), scholar 90; HONOURS :— 2 classical mods. 91.

Fry, Henry John Blount, born at Aspley, Beds, 28 July, 1870; 2s. John Blount, of Esher, Surrey, D. Med. EXETER, matric. 16 Oct., 89, aged 19 (from Haileybury), B.A. 92; HONOURS :— 4 history 92.

Fry, Henry (Stackhouse Luther), M.A., ST. JOHN'S, where see.

Fry, Theodore Wilfrid, born at Blackwell, co. Durham, 6 May, 1868; 2s. Theodore, M.P. NEW COLL., matric. 18 Oct., 86, aged 18 (from Clifton coll.), exhibitioner 86, B.A. 89; HONOURS :— 1 history 89.

Fry, Walter Llewellyn, born at Darlington, co. Durham, 1866; 3s. Charles Rutter, gent. ST. JOHN'S, matric. 16 Jan., 85, aged 19, B.A. 87; HONOURS :— 2 law 87, 1 civil law 89.

Fryer, Percy John, born at Tiddenham, co. Gloucester, 1841; 8s. John, gent. NON-COLLEGIATE, matric. 29 Jan., 81, aged 40.

Fulda, Frederick Antony, born at Manchester Oct., 1869; o.s. Antony, arm. ORIEL, matric. 20 Oct., 88, aged 18 (from the Charterhouse), B.A. 92.

Fulford, John Loveband Langdon, born at Woodbury, Devon, 2 Jan., 1871; 1s. John Loveband, cler. EXETER, matric. 16 Oct., 89, aged 18 (from Exeter gr. school); HONOURS :— 3 classical mods. 91.

Fulford, Robert Philip Percival, born at Montreal 1863; 2s. Francis Drummond, arm. EXETER, matric. 20 Oct., 81, aged 18 (from Sherborne school), B.A. and M.A. 90.

Fullbrook, Parkinson Stanfield, born at Reading 1861; 5s. Stephen Round, arm. WADHAM, matric. 16 Jan., 80, aged 19 (from Reading school); died 81.

Fuller, Arthur Rose, born at Riding-Mill-on-Tyne, Northumberland, 2 Jan., 1874; 1s. Rose, registrar district probate court. MAGDALEN, matric. 18 Oct., 92, aged 18, from Eton.

Fuller, Frank Baden, born at Bath 11 June, 1863; 2s. Arthur, gent. MERTON, matric. 17 Oct., 82, aged 19 (from Christ coll., Finchley), postmaster 82-5, B.A. 86 (HONOURS :— 1 mathematical mods. 84, 2 mathematics 86); bar.-at-law, Inner Temple, 89.

Fuller, John Michael Fleetwood, born at Curnham, Wilts, 21 Oct., 1864; 1s. George Pargiter, gent. CHRIST CHURCH, matric. 25 May, 83, aged 18 (from Winchester); HONOURS :— 3 history 87.

Fullmer, rev. Charles Henry, born in London 1866; 2s. Christopher Wilkinson, cler. ST. EDMUND HALL, matric. 23 April, 85, aged 19, B.A. 88; curate of Salwarpe, co. Worcester, 92.

Fullmer, rev. Christopher William, born in London, , 1863; 1s. Christopher Wilkinson, cler. NON-COLLEGIATE, matric. 18 Oct., 83, aged 20 (from Wolverhampton gr. school); migrated to ST. EDMUND HALL, B.A. 87 (HONOURS :— Ægrotat theology 87); curate of West Felton, Salop, 87.

Fullmer, rev. Herbert Graham, born in London 1870; 3s. Christopher, cler. ST. EDMUND HALL, matric. 7 May, 89, aged 19, B.A. 92; HONOURS :— 4 theology 92.

Furneaux, Henry, M.A., fellow CORPUS CHRISTI 54-69, where see.

Furniss, Henry Sanderson, born at Paddington 1868; 1s. Thomas Sanderson, bar.-at-law. HERTFORD, matric. 14 Oct., 89, aged 21.

Furniss, Thomas Sanderson, born in London 11 May, 1872; 2s. Thomas Sanderson, bar.-at-law. MERTON, matric. 22 Oct., 91, aged 19, from Harrow.

Furnival, Anthony St. John, born at Tockenham, Wilts, 27 Dec., 1872; 3s. James, rector of Muston, Notts. NON-COLLEGIATE, matric. 17 Oct., 91, aged 18, from Repton school.

Furnival, Charles, born at Escott, Devon 1863; 3s. James, cler. NON-COLLEGIATE, matric. 15 Oct., 81, aged 18.

Furse, Michael Bolton, born at Staines, Middx., 12 Oct., 1870; 4s. Charles Wellington, canon of Westminster. TRINITY, matric. 12 Oct., 89, aged 19 (from Eton); HONOURS :— 3 classical mods. 91.

Fyers, Evan William Hamilton, born at Kingswood, Sussex, Sept., 1864; 2s. William Augustus, arm. CHRIST CHURCH, matric. 12 Oct., 83, aged 19, B.A. 87.

Fyfe, Andrew Johnstone, born in London 1873; o.s. Andrew, D. Med. CORPUS CHRISTI, matric. 16 Oct., 90, aged 17, from St. Paul's school.

STONE BOSS, ST. GEORGE'S AT ROUEN.— *Pugin.*

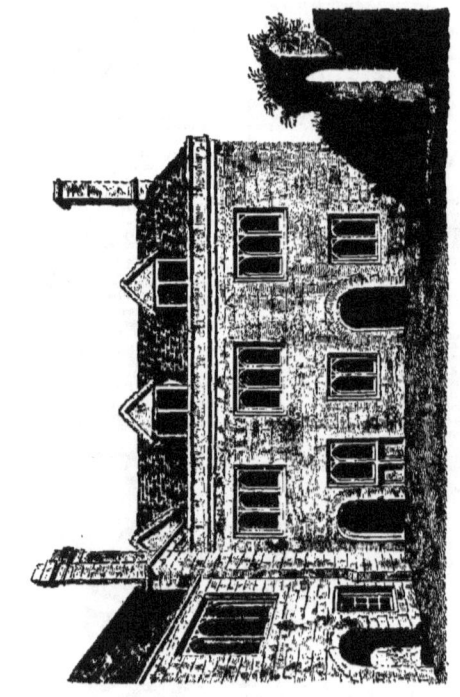

ST. GEORGE'S HALL, now demolished.—*From an engraving by Shelton.*

STONE STRING COURSE, ST. ALBAN ABBEY—*Pugin.*

G

Gaby, Ralph Hale, born in London 1861; 3s. Edward, gent. WORCESTER, matric. 20 Oct., 81, aged 20 (from Bath coll.), exhibitioner 81-4, B.A. 84, M.A. 88; HONOURS :—2 classical mods. 82, 4 law 84.

Gainsford, rev. George Bernard, born at Hitchin, Herts, 1868; 1s. George, cler. PEMBROKE, matric. 28 Oct., 86, aged 18 (from St Mark's school, Windsor), B.A. 90 (HONOURS :—3 theology 90); curate of Bedford St. Paul 91.

Gairdner, Harry Hamilton, born at Lisbeg, co. Galway, 10 July, 1873; 4s. John, gen. BRASENOSE, matric. 22 Oct., 91, aged 18, from Barnes and Woking school.

Gairdner, William Henry Temple, born at Ardrossan, co Ayr, N.B., 31 July, 1873; 2s. William Tennant, prof. of medicine. TRINITY HALL, matric. 15 Oct., 92, aged 19 (from Rossall school), exhibitioner 92.

Gaisford, Arthur, born in London 21 March, 1870; 2s. George, cler. CHRIST CHURCH, matric. 18 Jan., 89, aged 18 (from Eton), B.A. 92.

Gaisford, Ernest Charles, born in London Sept., 1874; 3s. George, cler., M.A. CHRIST CHURCH, matric. 14 Oct. 92, aged 18, from Eton.

Gaisford, George, M.A., student CHRIST CHURCH 45-59, where see.

Gaisford, Philip John, born at Broadwater, Sussex, Oct., 1868; 3s Thomas, arm. CHRIST CHURCH, matric. 3 June, 87, aged 18 (from Edglaston school), B.A. 90

Gaitskell, Arthur, born at Cheltenham 20 Aug., 1869; 5s. James, lieut.-col Indian army. NEW COLL., matric. 25 Jan., 88, aged 18 (from Cheltenham coll.), assist. commissioner Burma.

Galbraith, James Francis Wallice, born at Islington, 1869; 2s. Hugh James, arm. ORIEL, matric. 18 Oct., 87, aged 18 (from Blackheath school), scholar 87, B.A. 92 (HONOURS :—1 classical mods. 89, 2 classics 91, 2 law 92); librarian of Oxford union society 91, president 92.

Galbraith, William, born at Stirling 1872; o.s. Thomas, gent. BALLIOL, matric. 21 Oct., 80, aged 18 (from Winchester), B.A. 8, (HONOURS :— 1 classical mods. 82, 2 classics 84); student Lincoln's Inn 82.

Galbraith, William Lyle, born in London 19 July, 1869; 1s. William Robert, arm. MERTON, matric. 17 Oct., 88, aged 19 (from Winchester), postmaster 88, B.A. 92; HONOURS :—1 classical mods. 90, 1 classics 92.

Gale, Clement Rowland, born at Kew, Surrey, 1860; 1s. William Frederick, gent. EXETER, matric. 22 Oct., 80, aged 20, B.A. 86, B.Mus. 89.

Gale, James, born at Wantage, Berks, 1856; 2s. Henry, gent. NON-COLLEGIATE, matric. 18 Oct., 80, aged 24 (from Culham coll.), B.A. 87, M.A. 90.

Gale, rev. John Sadler, born at Bristol 1863; 1s. Isaac Sadler, cler. HERTFORD, matric. 18 Oct., 82, aged 19, B.A. 85; assist. chaplain Nice 90-1, and Grahamstown, South Africa, 91.

Gale, Norman Rowland, born at Kew, Surrey, 1862; 2s. William Frederick, gent. EXETER, matric. 22 Oct., 80, aged 18, B.A. 84.

Gale, Walter Augustus, born at Gernkiston in Australia, 1865; 6s. William, gent. EXETER, matric. 24 Jan., 84, aged 19.

Galer, Allan Maxey, born in London 24 Nov., 1867; 1s. John Maxey, gent. WORCESTER, matric. 19 Oct., 86, aged 18 (from Dulwich coll.), scholar 86, B.A. 91; HONOURS :—2 classical mods. 88, 3 classics 90.

Gales, Richard Lawson, born at Littlehampton, Sussex, 27 Dec., 1862; 1s. Richard Smith, ship owner, LINCOLN, matric. 17 Oct., 84, aged 21, B.A. 87; HONOURS :—English verse 86, 3 history 87.

Galfry, Lawrence, born at Sinfalva 1866; 2s. Thomas, gen. NON-COLLEGIATE, matric. 18 Jan., 90, aged 24.

Galloway, Lewis Stanley, born at Timperley, Cheshire, 3 Nov. 1866; 2s. William Lewis, gent. WADHAM, matric. 19 Oct., 85, aged 18.

Galloway, Thomas Percival, born at Gateshead-upon-Tyne 12 Nov., 1871; 2s. Thomas, gen. WADHAM, matric. 20 Oct., 91, aged 19, from Banister court school, Southampton.

Galpin, Francis Walter, born at Datchet, Bucks, 1866; 4s. Thomas Dixon, publisher. BALLIOL, matric. 15 Oct., 84, aged 18 (from the Charterhouse), B.A. 88; HONOURS :—2 classical mods. 86, 4 law 88,

[225]   [226]   15

Galpin, Henry Frank, born at Oxford 7 Jan., 1860; 6s. John, gent. QUEEN'S, matric. 22 Oct., 84, aged 24, B.A. 87, M.A. and B.C.L. 91 (HONOURS :— a civil law 89) ; a solicitor and proctor in vice-chancellor's court, Oxford.

Galsworthy, John, born at Kingston-on-Thames, Surrey, 14 Aug., 1867 ; 1s. John, gent. NEW COLL., matric. 18 Oct., 86, aged 19 (from Harrow), B.A. 89 (HONOURS :—2 law 89) ; bar.-at-law, Lincoln's Inn, 90.

Galt, William James, born at Hangchow, China, 8 July, 1872; 1s. James, surgeon. WADHAM, matric. 20 Oct., 91, aged 19 (from Hull and East Riding coll.), exhibitioner 90.

Galton, rev. Arthur Howard, born at Hadzor, co. Worc., 14 Dec., 1852 ; 1s. Herman Ernest, late capt. 60th Rifles. NEW COLL., matric. 15 Oct., 86, aged 33 (from Cheltenham coll. 68-70, and Clare coll., Camb., 73-5), B.A. 90 (HONOURS :—2 history 90) ; Roman Catholic priest, Oscott coll., near Birmingham.

Gambier, Michael Seymour Gore, born at Sharnbrook, Beds, 1862 ; 2s. Charles Gore, cler. BRASENOSE, matric. 26 Jan., 81, aged 19, from Wellington coll.

Gamble, Reginald Arthur, born at Auckland, N.Z., 1863 ; 2s. Dominick James, arm. BALLIOL, matric. 18 Oct., 81, aged 18, B.A. 84 ; under secretary to the government of India in the department of finance and commerce.

Games, Harold Games Wynn Hughes-, born at Castletown, isle of Man, 19 May, 1872; 3s. Joshua (H.-G.) archdeacon of the isle of Man. WORCESTER, matric. 22 Oct., 91, aged 19 (from K. William's coll., isle of Man), exhibitioner 90.

Games, rev. Stephen Herbert Wynn Hughes-, born at Liverpool 1862 ; 2s. Joshua, archdeacon of isle of Man. WORCESTER, matric. 20 Oct., 81, aged 19 (from K. William's coll., I.M.), scholar 81-5, B.A. 85 (HONOURS :—2 classical mods. 83, 2 classics 85) ; domestic chaplain to Bishop of Sodor and Man 88-9, curate of St. Giles, Cripplegate, London, 90.

Gamlen, Arthur George Loraine, born at Harrow, Middx., 15 March, 1871 ; 1s. Robert Heale, solicitor. NEW COLL., matric. 11 Oct., 89, aged 19 (from the Charterhouse), B.A. 92 ; HONOURS :—3 law 92.

Gamlen, William Blagdon, M.A., fellow of EXETER, where see page 129.

Gamon, John Percival, born at Chester 23 March, 1865 ; 1s. John, arm. TRINITY, matric. 15 Oct., 83, aged 18 (from Marlborough coll.), B.A. 86, M.A. 90 ; HONOURS :—3 law 86.

Gandell, Schomberg Frederick, born at Oxford 14 March, 1859; 3s. Robert, canon of Wells and Laudian prof. of Arabic. TRINITY, matric. 15 Oct., 83, aged 24 (from Haileybury and Kingsley coll. Westward Ho!), B.A. 87.

Gandell, Shirley Mark Kerr, born at Oxford 1866 ; 5s. Robert, canon of Wells and Laudian prof. of Arabic. HERTFORD, matric. 14 Oct., 84, aged 18 (from Uppingham school), scholar 83, B.A. 89 ; HONOURS :—3 classical mods. 86, 4 classics 88.

Gane, rev. Charles Moreton, born at Wootton Bassett 1860 ; o.s. Robert, gent. NON-COLLEGIATE, matric. 18 Oct., 80, aged 20 (from Chippenham gr. school) ; curate of St. Saviour's, with All Souls, Oxton, Cheshire, 90.

Garbett, Montague George Hubert, born at Colney Hatch, Middx., 15 Jan., 1862 ; y.s. Edward, cler. MERTON, matric. 18 Oct., 81, aged 19.

Garden, Huntly Charles, born at Simla, E. Indies, 1866 ; 1s. Archibald Macdonald, arm. BRASENOSE, matric. 23 Oct., 85, aged 19 (from Shrewsbury gr. school), B.A. 89 ; HONOURS :—2 classical mods. 87, 2 history 89.

Gardener, Edward William Axtell, born at Oxford 1869 ; o.s. Edward, gen. NON-COLLEGIATE, matric. 17 Dec., 87, aged 18 (from Bedford house, Oxford), B.A. 90.

Gardiner, Edward Norman, born at Buckingham 26 Jan., 1864 ; o.s. Edward Joshua, cler. CORPUS CHRISTI, matric. 19 Oct., 83, aged 19 (from Marlborough coll.), exhibitioner 83, B.A. 88, M.A. 90 ; HONOURS :—2 classical mods. 84, 2 classics 87.

Gardiner, Frederick George, born in London 1874 ; o.s. Edward Bennett, gent. KEBLE, matric. 14 Dec., 92, aged 18.

Gardiner, George Austin, born at Cole Orton, co. Leicester, 14 Oct., 1872 ; o.s. George Edward, vicar of Lyonsdown, H.T., New Barnet. NEW COLL., matric. 14 Oct., 92, aged 19, from the Charterhouse.

Gardiner, John, born at Oxford 1865 ; 2s. John Job, gent. NON-COLLEGIATE, matric. 23 May, 85, aged 20, B.A. 89 ; HONOURS :—4 history 89.

Gardiner, Samuel Rawson, M.A., hon. student CHRIST CHURCH 78 ; fellow ALL SOULS' 84, and of MERTON 92, where see page 95.

Gardner, Alan Hugh, born at Liverpool 1872 ; 1s. Henry, B.A., cler. NON-COLLEGIATE, matric. 17 Dec., 92, aged 20.

Gardner, rev. Charles Graham, born in London 1863 ; 1s. Charles, gent. NON-COLLEGIATE, matric. 18 Oct., 83, aged 20 (from Forest school), B.A. 86 (HONOURS :—3 theology 86); missionary at Tokyo, Japan.

Gardner, Ernest, born in London 25 Dec., 1864 ; o.s. William John, physician. LINCOLN, matric. 23 Oct., 82, aged 18 ; migrated to CHARSLEY HALL ; bar.-at-law, Lincoln's Inn, 89.

Gardner, Harold Ennis, born at West Chester, New York, U.S.A., 27 Jan., 1870 ; 1s. William Robert. NEW COLL., matric. 14 Oct., 87, aged 17 (from Grant Crosby school, and University coll. Liverpool), B.A. 91 ; HONOURS :—3 classical mods. 89, 2 law 91.

Gardner, rev. Herbert, born at North Meols, co. Lanc., 3 Jan., 1866 ; 1s. Joseph Sturdy, cler. MERTON, matric. 16 Oct., 84, aged 18 (from Tonbridge school), B.A. 88 (HONOURS :—4 theology 88) ; curate of St. John's, Waterloo, 90.

Gardner, John Addyman, born at Bradford, Yorks, 3 July, 1867 ; 1s. Thomas, accountant. MAGDALEN, matric. 21 Oct., 86, aged 19 (from Bradford gr. school), demy 86, B.A. 90 ; HONOURS :—1 chemistry 89.

Gardner, Percy, M.A., Christ's coll. Camb., fellow LINCOLN COLL., where see.

Gardner, Robert Cecil Dunn-, born in London 1871 ; 1s. Cecil, arm. EXETER, matric. 26 April, 88, aged 17 (from the Charterhouse), B.A. 92.

Gardner, rev. Walter Sturdy, born at Southport, co. Lanc., 29 Jan., 1868 ; 2s. Joseph Sturdy, clir. ST. MARY HALL, matric. 24 Oct., 85, aged 17, exhibitioner 85, B.A. 90 ; curate of Nantwich, Cheshire, 91.

Garforth, George Ernest, born at Northallerton, Yorks, 1863 ; 3s. Francis Willoughby, arm. CHRIST CHURCH, matric. 24 Jan., 81, aged 18, B.A. 85.

Garnett, James Harold, born at Pennington, co. Lanc., 7 Aug., 1872 ; 1s. James. LINCOLN, matric. 23 Oct., 91, aged 19, from Manchester gr. school.

Garnett, Theodore, born at Southport, co. Lanc., 23 June, 1867 ; 2s. Philip Frederick, solicitor. CHRIST CHURCH, matric. 21 May, 80, aged 18 (from K. Edward's school); migrated to NEW INN HALL, B.A. 84 (BALLIOL 87).

Garnier, John Trefusis Carpenter-, born at Rookesbury Park, Hants, 2 Feb., 1874; 1s. John C. G., of Rookesbury, M.A. and J.P. CHRIST CHURCH, matric. 4 June, 92, aged 18.

Garnier, Thomas Parry, M.A., fellow ALL SOULS' 63-73, where see.

Garnsey, Henry Edward Fowler, D.D., fellow MAGDALEN 51, where see.

Garrard, rev. William Austin, born at Dalston, London, 13 Sept., 1863; 3s. Thomas Edward, of Beckenham, gent. MAGDALEN, matric. 16 Oct., 82, aged 19 (from King's coll. school), B.A. 85, M.A. 89; HONOURS :—4 theology 85.

Garratt, Charles Eustace, born at Little Tew, Oxon, 20 March, 1861; 1s. Charles Foster, cler. ST. JOHN'S, matric. 13 April 80, aged 19.

Garratt, Walter Henry, born at Merifield, Cornwall, 19 Sept., 1868; 3s. Ludlow, cler. WORCESTER, matric. 17 Jan., 88, aged 19 (from a Tunbridge Wells school; died 6 Oct., 89.

Garrett, Abraham, born at Leiston, Suffolk, 11 Nov., 1871; 3s. Henry Newson, gen. BRASENOSE, matric. 15 Oct., 90, aged 18 (from Bath coll.), exhibitioner 90; HONOURS :—2 classical mods. 92.

Garrett, James Hugh Eliot, born at Weymouth, Dorset, 13 Nov., 1867; 1s. William Raymond, arm. NEW COLL., matric. 16 Oct., 85, aged 17 (from Clifton coll.); assist. magistrate and collector Bengal.

Garstang, Walter, born at Blackburn, co. Lanc., 9 Feb., 1868; 1s. Walter, D.Med. ST. EDMUND HALL, matric. 25 April, 84, aged 16; migrated to JESUS COLL., B.A. 88, M.A. 90; HONOURS :—2 morphology 88.

Garth, right hon. sir Richard, M.A., student CHRIST CHURCH 39-47, where see.

Garthwaite, Liston, born at Newcastle-on-Tyne, 1833; 2s. William Walker, gent. NON-COLLEGIATE, matric. 18 Oct., 80, aged 47, from London university.

Garvie, Alfred Ernest, born at Zyarden in Poland, 29 Aug., 1861; 3s. Peter, gen., deceased. NON-COLLEGIATE, matric. 12 Oct., 89, aged 28 (from Glasgow university, M.A.), B.A. 92; HONOURS :—1 theology 92.

Garwood, Redmond, born at Acomb, Yorks, 20 July, 1873; o.s. Clifton Ramsay, of Acomb, solicitor. QUEEN'S, matric. 27 Oct., 92, aged 19 (from York school), exhibitioner 92.

Gaskin, Leonard Edmund Palmer, born at Boulogne-sur-mer 8 Aug., 1872; 5s. Joseph, Wesleyan minister. CHRIST CHURCH, matric. 16 Oct., 91, aged 19 (from Kingswood and Bedford schools), selected candidate Indian C.S. 91.

Gates, Arthur Charles, born in London , 1871; 3s. Philip Chaschore, arm. CORPUS CHRISTI, matric. 25 Oct., 89, aged 18 (from Westminster school); HONOURS :—3 classical mods. 91.

Gates, Frank Campbell, born at Croydon, Surrey, 9 Nov., 1862; 4s. George, gent. BALLIOL, matric. 21 Oct., 80, aged 17 (from Cheltenham coll.); bar.-at-law, Lincoln's Inn, 91, junior secretary to civil commissioners, Burmah, 87.

Gaudet, George Herbert, born in London 1863; o.s. Julius, arm. BRASENOSE, matric. 18 Oct., 81, aged 18 (from Harrow); in the army.

Gaudin, Philip John, born at St. Heliers, Jersey, 1858; o.s. John Francis, merchant. NON-COLLEGIATE, matric. 15 Oct., 92, aged 24, from Victoria coll., Jersey.

Gauntlett, John Henry Lainson, born at Swansea 27 Oct., 1865; 1s. John George, cler. WORCESTER, matric. 17 Oct., 84, aged 18 (from Bromsgrove school); organist scholar 84.

Gautz, William Lewis, born at Calicut in Madras, Jan., 1873; o.s. William Sydenham, bar.-at-law. KEBLE, matric. 20 Oct., 91, aged 18, from Clifton coll.

Gay, Edward, M.A. (MAGDALEN HALL). See HERTFORD coll.

Gay, William, M.A., fellow PEMBROKE 50-4, where see.

Gayer, Charles Edward, born at Corowa, Australia, 11 May, 1864; 1s. Robert, arm. ST. MARY HALL, matric. 15 May, 86, aged 22.

Gayford, Sydney Charles, born at Wicken-Bonant, Essex, 26 Oct., 1871; 3s. John, gen. EXETER, matric. 13 Oct., 90, aged 18 (from Felsted school), scholar 90; HONOURS :—1 classical mods. 92.

Geake, Edward, born at St. Germans, Cornwall, 1866; 1s. Edward, arm. CHRIST CHURCH, matric. 10 Oct., 84, aged 18 (from Plymouth school); assist. magistrate and collector, Bengal.

Geddes, James, born at Camberwell, Surrey, 1874; o.s. James, gent. NON-COLLEGIATE, matric. 15 Oct., 92, aged 18, from King's coll. school, London.

Gedge, Henry Theodore Sydney, born in London Aug., 1870; 1s. John Wycliffe, cler. KEBLE, matric. 11 Oct., 90, aged 20, from Loretto school.

Gedge, John Denny, born at Brockford, Suffolk, Jan., 1868; 3s. John Denny, cler. KEBLE, matric. 19 Oct., 86, aged 18, B.A. 90; HONOURS :—2 classical mods. 88, 3 classics 90.

Gee, rev. Claude Valentine, born at Hope Mansel, co. Hereford, 1862; 2s. Thomas, arm. BRASENOSE, matric. 22 Oct., 80, aged 18 (from Hereford school); scholar 80-5, B.A. 84, M.A. 91 (HONOURS :—3 classical mods. 82, 3 classics 84); curate of St. Columba Southwick, Sunderland, 86-91, vicar of Castletown, Sunderland, 91.

Gee, Ernest Edward Gorham, born at Knighton, co. Leic., 1 April, 1871; 1s. Harry Simpson, arm. CHRIST CHURCH, matric. 10 Oct., 90, aged 19, from Oakham school.

Gee, Herbert Walter, born at Walcot, near Bath, 21 Sept., 1866; 2s. William, vicar of East Coker, deceased. NEW COLL., matric. 16 Oct., 85, aged 19 (from Sherborne school); assist. commissioner Punjab, 87.

Gee, rev. Richard Heron, born at Freshford, Somerset, 20 April, 1864; 4s. William, arm. NEW COLL., matric. 12 Oct., 83, aged 19 (from Bath coll. and King's coll., London), B.A. 87, M.A. 91 (HONOURS :—3 classical mods. 85, 2 theology 87); curate of St. Anne, Soho Square, 91.

Gee, William Henry, born at Oxford 17 April, 1871; 1s. William Henry, gen. MERTON, matric. 19 Oct., 89, aged 18 (from Oxford high school), exhibitioner 89; HONOURS :—2 classical mods. 91.

Gegg, Frank William, born at Wandsworth, Surrey, 14 Feb., 1866; 2s. Joseph, dean of Perth, Western Australia. QUEEN'S, matric. 22 Oct., 84, aged 17 (from Magdalen coll. school), B.A. 87, M.A. 92; brother of the next-named.

Gegg, rev. Walter Buchanan, born at Wandsworth, Surrey, 25 Jan., 1869; 1s. Joseph, dean of Perth, W.A. QUEEN'S, matric. 28 Oct., 81, aged 21 (from Bishop's coll., Perth, W.A.), B.A. 85, M.A. 89; curate of West with East Pulford, Devon, 89.

Geist, Alfred, born at Burdwan, East Indies, 1857; 2s. Bernard cler. NON-COLLEGIATE, matric. 13 Oct., 84, aged 27.

Geldart, Alfred Herbert, born at Thorpe Hamlet, Norfolk, 1864; 1s. Herbert Decimus, arm. UNIVERSITY COLL., matric. 13 Oct., 83, aged 19, B.A. 87; HONOURS :—4 history 87.

Geldart, William Martin, fellow ST. JOHN'S 92, M.A. 92, where see.
Gell, Ewen Alfred, born at Brighton 8 March, 1870; 1s. Alfred Freeman, solicitor, EXETER, matric. 22 Jan., 89, aged 18, from Wells coll.
Gell, Philip L.; Helton, M.A., BALLIOL, where see page 86.
Gellibrand, Thomas William, born at Hobart Town, Tasmania, 14 April, 1866; 1s. Thomas Lloyd, gent. deceased, QUEEN'S, matric. 22 Oct., 84, aged 18 (from Bradfield coll.), B.A. 87.
Gellibrand, Walter Tice, born at Hobart Town, Tasmania, 1871; 2s. Thomas Lloyd, of Frankfort-on-Main, gen. deceased. MAGDALEN, matric. 14 Oct., 89, aged 18 (from Bradfield coll.); HONOURS:—3 classical mods. 91.
Genge, Robert Sealy, born at Limington, Somerset, Oct., 1862; o.s. Richard, pleb. KEBLE, matric. 16 Oct., 83, aged 20 (from Bedford school), B.A. 86, M.A. 90; HONOURS:—3 theology 86.
Gennadius, John, created D.C.L. 21 Feb., 1882; Chargé D'Affaires, from the Hellenic Government in London.
Gent, John, M.A., fellow TRINITY 69-86, where see.
Gent, Lawrence Francis Mill, born at South Molton, Devon, Aug., 1868; 8s. Robert Abraham, cler. KEBLE, matric. 19 Oct., 86, aged 18 (from Perse school, Cambridge), B.A. 90.
Geoghegan, Richard Henry, born at Birkenhead, Cheshire, 1856; 1s. Richard Taylor, gent. NON-COLLEGIATE, matric. 19 Jan., 84, aged 18; HONOURS:—Chinese scholarship 86.
George, Francis William Brownlow, born at Holywell, Oxon., 7 Dec. 1873; 2s. Hereford Brooke, cler. NEW COLL., matric. 16 Oct., 91, aged 17, from Winchester coll. and Bedford school.
George, rev. Hereford Brooke, M.A., fellow NEW COLL. 56, where see page 205.
George, James Morgnn Tomkins, born at Bristol 1867; 1s. James, cler. BALLIOL, matric. 24 Oct., 85, aged 18 (from Malvern coll.), exhibitioner 84, B.A. 88 (HONOURS:—2 Indian languages 88); assist. commissioner, Burma.
George, William Edward, born at Aberdare, co. Glam., 24 July 1865; 1s. John Joseph, unitarian minister. NON-COLLEGIATE, matric. 18 Jan., 90, aged 24, from University coll., Cardiff.
Georgeson, James, born at Wick, co. Caithness, 20 Feb., 1869; 1s. William of Aberdeen, gen. PEMBROKE, matric 25 Oct., 90, aged 21 (from Aberdeen university), scholar 90; HONOURS:—2 classical mods. 92.
Gepp, Henry Dora, M.A., fellow NEW COLL. 53-75, where see page 215.
Gerrans, Henry Tresawna, M.A., fellow WORCESTER, 82, where see.
Gethen, rev. Percy, born at Hereford 20 Dec., 1862; 3s. Henry, gent. NON-COLLEGIATE, matric. 13 Oct., 83, aged 20 (from Merchant Taylors' school), scholar WADHAM 83; migrated to NEW COLL., B.A. 86, M.A. 90 (HONOURS:—2 theology 86); sub.-warden St. Thomas coll., Colombo, Ceylon, 88.
Gibbes, Frank Douglas, born in London 3 Sept., 1872; 2s. George Davison, stockbroker, BRASENOSE, matric. 22 Oct., 91, aged 19, from Winchester coll.
Gibbins, rev. Henry de Beltgens, born at Port Elizabeth, South Africa, 23 May, 1865; 1s. Joseph Henry, accountant. WADHAM, matric. 16 Oct., 83, aged 18 (from Bradford gr. school), scholar 83, B.A. 88, M.A. 90 (HONOURS:—2 classical mods. 85, 2 classics 87, Cobden prize 89.

Gibbins, Horace John, born at Brighton 24 July, 1870; 1s. John George, architect. EXETER, matric. 16 Oct., 89, aged 19 (from Brighton coll.), scholar 89; HONOURS:—1 classical mods. 91.
Gibbons, Arthur Christian, born at Lower Milton, co. Worcester, Dec., 1868; 7s. Benjamin, cler. KEBLE, matric. 17 Oct., 87, aged 19 (from Eton), B.A. 91.
Gibbons, Leonard Philip, born at Lower Milton, co. Worc., July, 1867; 6s. Benjamin, cler. KEBLE, matric. 19 Oct., 86, aged 18 (from Eton), B.A. 90.
Gibbons, Robert, born at Scend, Wilts, 15 June, 1866; o.s. Robert, cler. MERTON, matric. 24 Oct., 85, aged 19, from Harrow.
Gibbons, William John Brodrick Edgeworth, born at Walsall, co. Stafford, 12 May, 1870; 1s. William Edgeworth, gen. WORCESTER, matric. 16 Oct., 88, aged 18 (from Uppingham school).
Gibbs, Charles Herbert, born at Hensall, Yorks, 1869; o.s. Joseph James, vicar 67. ST. JOHN'S, matric. 15 Oct., 87, aged 18 (from Rossall school), B.A. 90; HONOURS:—3 classical mods. 89.
Gibbs, Francis Lomax, born at Clifton Hampden, Oxon, 28 Jan., 1869; 4s. John Lomax, cler. CHRIST CHURCH, matric. 13 Oct., 88, aged 18, B.A. 92.
Gibbs, George Abraham, born at Charlton House Nailsen, Somerset, 6 July, 1873; 1s. Antony, M.A. CHRIST CHURCH, matric. 14 Oct., 92, aged 19, from Eton.
Gibbs, Henry Lloyd, born in London 21 July, 1861; 5s. Henry Hucks, of Aldenham House, Herts., late M.P. CHRIST CHURCH, matric. 21 May, 80, aged 18.
Gibbs, Joseph Arthur, born at Belmont, Somerset, 25 Nov., 1867; 2s. George Louis Monck, arm. CHRIST CHURCH, matric. 14 Jan., 87, aged 19.
Gibbs, rev. Reginald, born at Clifton Hampden, Oxon, 29 June, 1867; 3s. John Lomax, gent. KEBLE, matric. 19 Oct., 86, aged 19 (from Lancing coll.), B.A. 91; HONOURS:—3 theology 90.
Gibbs, Stanley Vaughan, born in London 7 Jan., 1872; 3s. George Louis Monck, arm., deceased. NEW COLL., matric. 17 Jan., 91, aged 19, from the Charterhouse.
Gibbs, Villiers, born at South Kensington 20 June, 1871; 1s. Ben Thomas Brandreth, knight, deceased. ST. JOHN'S, matric. 12 Oct., 89, aged 18, from Oswestry gr. school.
Giblin, William Leslie, born at Hobart Town, Tasmania, 28 Feb., 1867; 1s. William Robert, arm. LINCOLN, matric. 22 Oct., 86, aged 19, from Christ's coll., Hobart Town.
Gibson, Alan Graeme, born at Pinner, Herts, 7 Feb., 1874; 1s. Edward Graeme, of Chislehurst, M.A., solicitor. UNIVERSITY COLL., matric. 15 Oct., 92, aged 18, from Haileybury.
Gibson, Arthur Edward, born at West Cowes, I.W., 10 June, 1863; 1s. John Edward, surgeon. EXETER, matric. 18 Oct., 82, aged 19 (from the Charterhouse), B.A. 87, M.A. 89; HONOURS:—2 classical mods. 84, 3 history 86.
Gibson, Bertram Robert, born at Dartford, Kent, 4 Dec., 1868; 2s. Charles Reginald, arm. TRINITY, matric. 15 Oct., 87, aged 18 (from Canterbury school), B.A. 91 (HONOURS:—3 law 91); bar.-at-law, Inner Temple, 92.
Gibson, Charles, born at Lancaster 30 July, 1867; 1s. Thomas, arm. UNIVERSITY COLL., matric. 18 Oct., 86, aged 19 (from Westminster school), B.A. 89; HONOURS:—2 law 89.
Gibson, Edgar Charles Sumner, M.A., select preacher 93-4, see page 6.
Gibson, Robinson Fooks, born at Sittingbourne, Kent, 2 Nov., 1861; 1s. Frederick George, gent. QUEEN'S, matric. 4 May, 81, aged 19 (from Q. Elizabeth gr. school, Faversham); bar-at-law, Middle Temple, 85.

Gibson, Wilfrid Graham, born at Angaston, Australia, 15 Dec., 1867; 1s. John, gent. BALLIOL, matric. 19 Oct., 86, aged 18 (from Warwick school), scholar 85; drowned 5 Aug., 87, at Warwick.

Gibson, hon. William, born in Dublin 16 Dec., 1868; 1s. Edward, baron Ashbourne. MERTON, matric. 29 April, 89, aged 20 (from Harrow school, and Trinity coll. Dublin), B.A. 92; HONOURS :—3 history 92.

Gibson, William Ralph Boyce, born in Paris 15 March, 1869; 2s. William, gen. QUEEN'S, matric. 20 Oct., 88, aged 19 (from Kingswood school), scholar 87, B.A. 92; HONOURS :—2 mathematical mods. 89, 2 mathematics 92.

Gidley, John, born at Exeter 1867; 1s. Bartholomew Charles, arm. ST. JOHN'S, matric. 20 April, 85, aged 18 (from Winchester), B.A. 88, M.A. 91; HONOURS :—4 law 88.

Giffard, Agnew Walter Giles, born in Guernsey 28 April, 1869; 3s. Agnew, gen. QUEEN'S, matric. 7 May, 89, aged 20, from Elizabeth coll., Guernsey.

Giffard, Alexander William, born in London 1872; 2s. Henry Alexander, Q.C. CHRIST CHURCH, matric. 16 Oct., 91, aged 19, from Harrow.

Giffard, Henry Alexander, M.A., senior student CHRIST CHURCH 62-6, where see.

Giffard, Hardinge Stanley, lord Halsbury, created D.C.L. 17 June, 1891. See *Al. Ox.*, and series, 522.

Giffard, Walter John Frederick, born in London March, 1870; 1s. Henry Alexander, Q.C. CHRIST CHURCH, matric. 12 Oct., 88, aged 18 (from Harrow), exhibitioner 90; HONOURS :— 2 classical mods. 90, 3 classics 92.

Gifford, Edwin Hamilton, D.D., ST. JOHN'S, CAMBRIDGE, 61 ; incorporated 30 Nov., 89, aged 68, from Pembroke coll., where see.

Gilbert, Frank, born at Hackney, Middx., 1871; 2s. Edward Gillett, D.Med. CHRIST CHURCH, matric. 10 Oct., 90, aged 19 (from Westminster school), exhibitioner 90; HONOURS :— 2 classical mods. 92.

Gilbert, Harry Upfield, born in London 13 Aug., 1872; 3s. Edward Gillett, D.Med. MERTON, matric. 22 Oct., 91, aged 19 (from Merchant Taylors' school), postmaster 91.

Gilbert, Joseph Henry, born at Hull 1 Aug., 1817; s. Joseph, cler. ; a member of MAGDALEN COLL., M.A. by decree of convocation 17 June, 84, Sibthorpian professor of rural economy 84, F.R.S. 60, royal medallist 67, F.L.S., F.R.Meteorl.S., LL.D. Glasgow 83, and Edinburgh 90, Ph.D. Giessen ; a member of the chemical society 41, president 82-3, etc. See *Men and Women of the Time*.

Gilbert, rev. Robert Henry, born at Penkridge, co. Stafford, 28 April, 1868 ; 1s. Edmund Colin, gen. NON-COLLEGIATE, matric. 13 Oct., 88, aged 20 (from Forebridge academy, Stafford); migrated to JESUS COLL. 28 April, 90, B.A. 91 (HONOURS :—3 theology 91); curate of Goole, Yorks, 91.

Gilbertson, Francis William, born at Llangwick, near Swansea, 11 April, 1873; 1s. Arthur, gen. MAGDALEN, matric. 19 Jan., 91, aged 17, from the Charterhouse.

Gilbertson, Lewis, B.D., fellow JESUS COLL. 40-71, where see.

Gildea, Harry Percival Simes, born at West Lulworth 29 Oct., 1872; 4s. William, vicar of Netherbury, Dorset. NON-COLLEGIATE, matric. 17 Oct., 91, aged 18, from Bromsgrove gr. school.

Gilderdale, Thomas Barlow, born at Walthamstow, Essex, June, 1868; 4s. John Smith, late chaplain at Dresden, deceased. KEBLE, matric. 13 Oct., 88, aged 20 (from Forest school), B.A. 92.

Giles, rev. Clement Douglas, born at Partney, co. Lincoln, 1864; 3s. Robert, cler. HERTFORD, matric. 18 Oct., 83, aged 19, B.A. 88, M.A. 90; curate of St. John, Bathwick, 89.

Giles, Robert Sidney, born at Cleveden, Somerset, 2 Dec., 1865; o.s. Richard William, of London, bar.-at-law. MAGDALEN, matric. 16 Oct., 84, aged 18 (from Clifton coll.), demy 84, B.A. 88, M.A. 91 (HONOURS :—2 chemistry 88); bar.-at-law, Middle Temple, 90.

Gill, rev. Henry Sutherland Dashwood, born at Stratford-on-Avon, Aug., 1862; 2s. Francis Turner, cler. KEBLE, matric. 18 Oct., 81, aged 19 (from St. Edward's school, Summertown), B.A. 85, M.A. 89 (HONOURS :—3 classical mods. 83, 4 history 85); curate of All Saints', Battersea Park, Surrey, 90.

Gill, John Henry, born at Radford, Notts., 26 May, 1869; o.s. John Henry, arm., deceased. NEW COLL., matric. 12 Oct., 88, aged 19 (from Harrow), B.A. 91; HONOURS :—aegrotat law 91.

Gill, William Arthur, fellow ORIEL 90, M.A. 90, where see page 150.

Gillespie, Charles Melville, born at Edinburgh 12 Oct., 1866; 2s. James Donaldson, D.Med. TRINITY, matric. 17 Oct., 85, aged 19 (from Edinburgh academy and university), scholar 84, B.A. 89, M.A. 92; HONOURS :—1 classical mods. 87, 1 classics 89.

Gillett, Charles Edwin, born at Banbury 13 Nov., 1861; 1s. Charles, a banker. NON-COLLEGIATE, matric. 17 Jan., 80, aged 18, from Scarborough school.

Gillett, rev. Charles Thomas, born at Clifton, co. Glouc., 15 Dec., 1857; o.s. Charles Thomas, gent. NON-COLLEGIATE, matric. 15 Oct., 81, aged 24 (from Bristol gr. school); migrated to QUEEN'S, B.A. 85, M.A. 92; curate of Handsworth, co. Staff., 86-9.

Gillett, George Gabriel Scott, born at Hawley, Hants., 1874; 1s. Edward Alfred, cler. KEBLE, matric. 15 Oct., 92, aged 18 (from Westminster school), scholar 92.

Gilliat, Charles Robert, born in London 2 March, 1868; 2s. Algernon, of Stoke Poges, Bucks., arm. MAGDALEN, matric. 22 Oct., 87, aged 19 (from Eton), B.A. 91; HONOURS :—3 history 90; brother of Walter E.

Gilliat, Frederick Hatfeild, born at Portsmouth 16 Jan., 1865; 3s. Alfred, arm. MAGDALEN, matric. 19 Oct., 83, aged 18 (from Haileybury), B.A. 87, M.A. 90; assistant master Bishop Stortford school 90.

Gilliat, John Babington, born in London 10 April, 1868; 1s. John Saunders, M.P. NEW COLL., matric. 15 Oct., 86, aged 18 (from Eton), B.A. 90; HONOURS :—3 history 89.

Gilliat, Walter Evelyn, born at Winkfield, Berks, 22 July, 1869; 3s. Algernon, of Stoke Poges, Bucks, arm. MAGDALEN, matric. 16 Oct., 88, aged 19 (from the Charterhouse), B.A. 93; brother of Charles R.

Gillmor, rev. Fitzwilliam John Carter, born at St. John's, Newfoundland, 1868; 1s. William, arm. NON-COLLEGIATE, matric. 14 Jan., 88, aged 20, B.A. 92; curate of Wantage, Berks, 92.

Gillott, Joseph Henry, born at Solihull 27 Sept., 1864; 2s. Joseph, of Birmingham, manufacturer. WADHAM, matric. 16 Oct., 83, aged 19.

Gillson, Maurice Puget, born at Malvern, co. Worc., 21 June, 1870; 3s. Henry Thomas, of Mudeford, Hants, general in the army. UNIVERSITY COLL. matric. 11 Oct., 90, aged 20, from Rugby.

Gilmour, Alexander Wallace, born at Darjeeling, East Indies, March, 1870; o.s. Wallace, arm. CHRIST CHURCH, matric. 18 Jan., 89, aged 18, from Harrow.

Gilpin, Bradney Wentworth, born at Plymouth 17 Sept., 1866; 2s. Bradney Todd, arm. WORCESTER, matric. 16 Oct., 88, aged 22 (from Brampton school, Hunts), B.A. 91.

Girdlestone, Arthur Henry, born at Jubbulpore in East Indies, 30 July, 1869; 1s. Francis Brooke, of Bristol, arm. NEW COLL., matric. 12 Oct., 88, aged 19, from Marlborough.

Girdlestone, Charles Richey, born at Wordsley, co. Stafford, 16 Jan., 1864; 1s. Robert Baker, cler. CHRIST CHURCH, matric. 12 Oct., 83, aged 19 (from the Charterhouse), exhibitioner 83-4, B.A. 88, M.A. 90; HONOURS:—3 classical mods. 85, 3 classics 87.

Girdlestone, rev. Henry, born at Penkridge, co. Stafford, 5 July, 1863; 1s. Henry, of Bathampton, cler. MAGDALEN, matric. 16 Oct., 82, aged 19 (from Bath coll.), B.A. 86, M.A. 89 (HONOURS:—3 mathematical mods. 83, 3 chemistry 86), stroke of the Oxford eight 85-6; chaplain Bath coll. 90.

Girdlestone, rev. James Hammond Le Breton, born at Hawkstone, Salop, 1865; o.s. Frederick Paddon, cler. ST. EDMUND HALL, matric. 22 Oct., 87, aged 22, B.A. 91; curate Brighton St. Paul 91.

Giveen, Henry Martley, born at Pimlico 9 April, 1869; 2s. Richard Lockwood, vicar of St. Mark, Clerkenwell. WADHAM, matric. 13 Oct., 88, aged 19 (from Marlborough coll.), scholar 87, B.A. 92; HONOURS:—1 classical mods. 90, 2 law 92, proxime accessit Vinerian law scholarship 93.

Giveen, Richard Lockwood, born in Westminster 10 May, 1872; 3s. Richard Lockwood, cler. UNIVERSITY COLL., matric. 11 Oct., 90, aged 18 (from Merchant Taylors' school), scholar 90; HONOURS: —2 classical mods. 92.

Giveen, Robert Fielding, born at Monkstown, co. Dublin, 1866; 1s. Richard Lockwood, cler. KEBLE, matric. 19 Oct., 86, aged 20, from Marlborough coll.

Gladstone, Charles Evelyn David, born at Loddington, Northants, 6 July, 1870; 2s. David Thomas, cler. KEBLE, matric. 12 Oct., 89, aged 19, from Eastbourne coll.

Gladstone, Robert, born at Wavertree, co. Lanc., 6 May, 1866; 3s. Robert, arm. NEW COLL., matric. 10 Oct., 84, aged 18 (from Eton), B.A. 88, M.A. and B.C.L. 91; HONOURS:—2 law 88, 1 civil law 90.

Gladstone, right hon. William Ewart, M.A., D.C.L., hon. student CHRIST CHURCH 59, where see.

Glancy, Reginald Isidore Robert, born in Dublin, 1874; 1s. Thomas Frank, lieut.-col. R.E., CHRIST CHURCH, matric. 14 Oct., 92, aged 18 (from Cheltenham coll.), scholar 92.

Glanville, Henry Carew, M.A., fellow EXETER 54-6, where see page 127.

Glasgow, Charles Ponsonby Robertson-, born at Kilwinning, co. Ayr, 26 Feb., 1870; 2s. Robert Bruce, arm. MAGDALEN, matric. 14 Oct., 89, aged 19 (from Uppingham school); HONOURS:—3 classical mods. 91.

Glasson, William John Wharton, M.A., bursar ST. JOHN'S 89, where see.

Gledhill, Walter Riley, born at Holmfirth, Yorks, · Dec. 1873; 6s. William, gen. KEBLE, matric. 20 Oct., 91, aged 18, from Huddersfield coll.

Glenday, rev. Edward Albert, born at Newcastle-under-Lyne, co. Stafford, 1865; 3s. John, gen. NON-COLLEGIATE, matric. 15 Oct., 87, aged 22 (from Newcastle-under-Lyne school); migrated to PEMBROKE, B.A. 92 (HONOURS:—2 theology 90); curate of St. John Evangelist, Blackburn, 91.

Glennie, rev. Herbert John, born at Bury St. Edmund's 22 Jan., 1860; 1s. John David, cler. KEBLE, matric. 22 Jan., 80, aged 19 (from Marlborough coll.), B.A. 83, M.A. 86 (HONOURS:—2 classical mods. 81, 4 classics 83; curate of Leeds 89.

Glennie, rev. Reginald Gerard, born at Blore Ray, co. Stafford, 11 Nov., 1864; 3s. John David, cler. KEBLE, matric. 16 Oct., 83, aged 18 (from Canterbury school), B.A. 87, M.A. 92 (HONOURS:—3 classical mods. 85, 2 theology 87); resident chaplain to archbishop of York 92.

Glennie, rev. William Bourne, born in London July 1866; 1s. William Rickards, arm. ORIEL, matric. 23 Oct., 85, aged 19 (from the Charterhouse), B.A. 89, M.A. 92; curate of Ely Holy Trinity 90.

Glenton, Frederick Richardson, born at South Mims, Middx., Aug., 1872; 1s. Frederick, gen. ST. MARY HALL, matric. 18 Jan., 90, aged 17.

Gloag, William Murray, born at Edinburgh 1865; 1s. William Ellis, gent. BALLIOL, matric. 16 Oct., 83, aged 19 (from Edinburgh academy), B.A. 88; HONOURS:—1 history 87.

Glossop, rev. Arthur George Barnard, born at Twickenham, Middx., 9 Nov., 1867; 3s. George Goodwin, cler. TRINITY, matric. 16 Oct., 86, aged 18 (from St. Mark's school, Windsor), B.A. 89 (HONOURS:—3 history 89); curate of St. Mary Virgin, Colchester, 91.

Glossop, John Francis Gilleroy, born at Twickenham, Middx., 29 Nov., 1869; 2s. Francis Henry Newland, arm. MAGDALEN, matric. 15 Oct., 81, aged 18 (from Tunbridge Wells), B.A. 84, M.A. 90.

Glover, Alfred Charles, born at Geneva Aug., 1868; o.s. Frederick, Indian judge, deceased. BRASENOSE, matric. 20 Oct., 87, aged 19 (from Eton), B.A. 91 (HONOURS:—4 law 91); bar.-at-law, Middle Temple, 92.

Glover, Arthur Leone, born at Hornsey, Middx., 1860; 1s. Robert Reaveley, arm. MERTON, matric. 18 Oct., 80, aged 20, B.A. 85, M.A. 88.

Glover, rev. Ernest Augustus, born at Shepton Mallet, Somerset, 5 April, 1867; 2s. Frederick Augustus, cler. EXETER, matric. 23 Oct., 85, aged 19 (from Christ's hospital), B.A. 88, M.A. 92; curate Quebec chapel 91.

Glover, rev. Harold Salisbury, born at Manchester 1869; 1s. William Henry, gen. ST. EDMUND HALL, matric. 22 Oct., 87, aged 18, B.A. 91; HONOURS:—2 theology 91.

Glubb, rev. John Matthew, born in London 1865; o.s. John Matthew, captain. EXETER, matric. 16 Oct., 84, aged 19 (from Bedford gr. school), B.A. 88, M.A. 91 (HONOURS:—2 theology 88); curate of Aylsham, Norfolk, 88.

Glyn, Arthur Plumptre, born at Wycliffe, Yorks, 16 May, 1864; 6s. Charles Thomas, cler. CHRIST CHURCH, matric. 25 May, 83, aged 19 (from Marlborough), B.A. 88.

Glyn, Carr John, M.A., student CHRIST CHURCH 1818-25, where see.

Glyn, Frederick, 4th lord Wolverton (88), born in London 24 Sept., 1864; 2s. hon. Henry Carr, admiral R.N. NON-COLLEGIATE, matric. 30 Oct., 82, aged 18, from Eton.

Glyn, (sir) Gervase Powell (bart.), born at Ewell, Surrey, 3 Oct., 1862; 2s. sir George, bart., vicar of Ewell. NEW COLL., matric. 15 Oct., 81, aged 19 (from Winchester), B.A. 85, M.A. 91; HONOURS: —3 history 85.

Glyn, Henry Thomas, B.A., student CHRIST CHURCH 41-5, where see.

Glyn, Hugh Douglas, born at Hampstead, Middx., 2 April, 1871; 1s. Richard Henry, gen. QUEEN'S, matric. 22 Oct., 89, aged 18 (from Merchant Taylors' school), scholar 89; HONOURS:—2 classical mods. 91.

Glyn, Lionel Claude, born at Hampstead, Middx., 4 Aug. 1873; 2s. Richard Henry, banker. MERTON, matric. 18 Oct., 92, aged 19 (from St. Paul's school), exhibitioner 92.

Glyn, Maurice George Carr, born in London 12 March, 1872; 2s. hon. Pascoe Charles, banker. NEW COLL., matric. 16 Oct., 91, aged 19, from Radley coll.

Glynn, Edward Francis, born in London 30 Oct., 1873; o.s. Edward, gen. MERTON, matric. 12 Feb., 92, aged 19, from Repton school.

Gmelin, Charles Henry Stuart, born at Krishnaghur, Bengal, 28 May, 1872; 3s. Frederick, cler. KEBLE, matric. 20 Oct., 91, aged 19 (from Magdalen coll. school), scholar 91.

Gmelin, rev. Frederick Edwin, born at Krishnagur 7 Dec., 1866; 1s. Frederick, cler. LINCOLN, matric. 22 Oct., 86, aged 19 (from Chipping Campden gr. school and Oxford high school), scholar 86, B.A. 90 (HONOURS:—1 classical mods. 88, 2 classics 90, 2 theology 91); curate of Stonehouse St. George, Devon, 91.

Goad, Alfred Arthur, born at Carshalton, Surrey, 29 May, 1871; 5s. Edwin Curtis, gen. EXETER, matric. 16 Dec., 90, aged 19 (from Eton); died 3 May, 91, at Oxford.

Goddard, Charles Henry, born in London 14 June, 1873; 1s. Charles, esq. HERTFORD, matric. 20 Oct., 91, aged 18, from the Charterhouse.

Goddard, Gerald Henry George, born at Acocks Green, co. Worc., 9 Oct., 1869; 5s. William Henry, M.A., late rector of East Mersen, Essex. ST. EDMUND HALL, matric. 20 Jan., 91, aged 21, from Denstone coll., Staffs.

Goddard, Henry Langton, born in Leicester 9 July, 1866; 1s. Joseph, architect. WADHAM, matric. 11 Oct., 84, aged 18 (from Haileybury), B.A. 87, M.A. 92, M.R.I.B.A.

Goddard, Nigel Ernle, born at Sutton Coldfield, co. Warwick, 16 June, 1870; 2s. Francis Aspinwall, vicar of Caverswall, co. Staff. JESUS COLL., matric. 14 Oct., 89, aged 19 (from Eton), scholar, exhibitioner 90; HONOURS:—3 classical mods. 91.

Goddard, William Charles Gilbert, born at Broad Chalk, Wilts, 20 Oct., 1869; o.s. William Gilbert, gen. BRASENOSE, matric. 27 Jan., 91, aged 21, from Sherborne school.

Godding, Francis Wallace, born in London Sept., 1866; 2s. John, cler. KEBLE, matric. 19 Oct., 86, aged 20, from Harrow.

Godding, James William Sleigh, born at Homerton, Middx., 1864; 1s. John, cler. HERTFORD, matric. 14 Oct., 84, aged 20 (from Eton), scholar 84, B.A. 88 (HONOURS:—2 classical mods. 86, 2 classics 88); bar.-at-law, Inner Temple, 89.

Godfray, Humphrey Marett, born at Jersey 1863; 6s. Walter Bertram, Greffier of the royal court of Jersey. EXETER, matric. 18 Oct., 83, aged 20 (from Victoria coll., Jersey), exhibitioner 82-5, B.A. 87 (HONOURS:—2 law 87); treasurer and president of Oxford union society 87; student of the Inner Temple 83, Greffier of Jersey; died there 17 Jan., 92.

Godfrey, Charles John Merivale, born in London 1863; 2s. Charles Richard, gent. HERTFORD, matric. 22 Oct., 81, aged 18 (from Magdalen coll. school); migrated to NEW INN HALL, B.A. 86 (Balliol 87).

Godfrey, Daniel Race, M.A., fellow QUEEN'S 38-40, where see page 177.

Godfrey, rev. George, born at Sheffield 30 July, 1866; 1s. George, cler. QUEEN'S, matric. 22 Oct., 84, aged 18 (from Doncaster gr. school), B.A. 87, M.A. 91 (HONOURS:—4 history, 87); curate of Church Langton, Northants, 89.

Godfrey, rev. John Talbot, born at Croxall, co. Derby, 1863; 2s. William, gent. NON-COLLEGIATE, matric. 10 April, 86, aged 23, B.A. 89, M.A. 92; curate of Dorking 89.

Godley, Alfred Denis, M.A., fellow MAGDALEN 83, where see.

Godley, sir John Arthur, K.C.B., M.A., fellow HERTFORD 74-81, where see.

Godley, John Cornwallis, born at Cootehill, co. Cavan, 9 Feb., 1861; 3s. James, cler. CORPUS CHRISTI, matric. 21 Oct., 80, aged 19 (from Marlborough coll.), scholar 80-5, B.A. 85; HONOURS:—1 classical mods. 81, accessit Hertford scholarship 81 and 82, 1 classics 84.

Godman, Sherard Haughton, born at Kirdford, Sussex, Jan., 1865; 2s. Joseph, arm. CHRIST CHURCH, matric. 27 May, 82, aged 17, from Eton.

Godson, Edward Alexander, born at Chipping Camden, co. Glouc., 26 Dec., 1870; 4s. William, gen. NON-COLLEGIATE, matric. 11 Oct., 90, aged 19, from Chipping Campden gr. school.

Godson, Edwin Augustus Marshall, born at Horsington, Somerset, 1865; 1s. Edwin, cler. NEW COLL., matric. 17 Oct., 85, aged 20, B.A. 88, M.A. 92.

Godson, rev. William Ernest, born at Redruth in Australia, 1865; 3s. William, gen. NON-COLLEGIATE, matric. 15 Oct., 87, aged 22 (from Chipping Campden gr. school), B.A. 90; curate of Rodditch, co. Worc., 91.

Godwin, George Harold, born at Merton, Surrey, 22 June, 1873; 1s. William Alfred, gent. BALLIOL, matric. 18 Oct., 92, aged 19 (from King's coll. school), exhibitioner 91.

Goe, Field Flowers, bishop of Melbourne, created D.D. 23 Nov., 1886. See Al. Ox., 2nd series, 534.

Goetz, Charles Edward, born in London 22 Jan., 1872; 2s. Edward, esq. BALLIOL, matric. 20 Oct., 91, aged 19, from Harrow.

Goff, Park, born at Bothwell, co. Lanark, 12 Feb., 1870; 9s. Bruce, D.Med. TRINITY, matric. 13 Oct., 88, aged 18 (from Marlborough coll.), B.A. 92; HONOURS:—4 law 92.

Goff, Thomas Clarence Edward, born in London 1867; 1s. Thomas, arm. CHRIST CHURCH, matric. 12 June, 86, aged 19, from Eton.

Gofton, John Ernest, born at Wartham Percy, Yorks, 1870; 1s. John, cler. ST. JOHN'S, matric. 13 Oct., 88, aged 18 (from York school), B.A.

Gold, Archibald Gilbey, born in London 1870; 5s. Charles, gen. CHRIST CHURCH, matric. 6 June, 90, aged 20, from Tavistock school.

Goldberg, Asher, born at Nijninovgorod, Russia, 1865; 2s. Jacob, merchant. NON-COLLEGIATE, matric. 17 Oct., 91, aged 26.

Goldie, Bruce Morton, born in Chelsea, Middx., 4 Jan., 1869; 1s. Bruce, gen. CHRIST CHURCH, matric. 14 Oct., 87, aged 18 (from Westminster school), scholar 87, B.A. 91; HONOURS:—2 classical mods. 89, 2 classics 91.

Goldner, Alfred Leopold, born in London 24 Dec., 1870; 1s. Samuel, gen. BALLIOL, matric. 1 May, 89, aged 18 (from the Charterhouse), B.A. 92; HONOURS:—2 law 92.

Goldschmidt, Charles Alfred, born in London 27 Nov., 1872; 1s. Maurice Adolf, gen. BALLIOL, matric. 20 Oct., 91, aged 18, from Harrow.

Goldstein, Isidor, born at Simno Tuvulski, Poland, 29 Sept., 1865; o.s. Abraham, gent. NON-COLLEGIATE, matric. 26 Jan., 85, aged 23, exhibitioner Exeter 85 (HONOURS:—Hebrew scholarship 85); drowned near Medley Lock, Oxford, 2 Dec., 85.

Gomes, Augusto José, born at Victoria, Hong Kong, 31 March, 1871; 2s. John Baptista, gen. TRINITY, matric. 17 Oct., 91, aged 20, from Xavier coll., Bombay, and Bombay university.

Gompertz, Henry Hesse Johnston, born at Mundial, E. Indies, 31 May, 1868; 1s. Henry James, arm. EXETER, matric. 13 Oct., 86, aged 19 (from Bedford gr. school), scholar 86, B.A. 90 (HONOURS :—2 classical mods. 88, 2 classics 90), passed for the army, 90.

Gondal, H.H. sir Bhugvut Sinh Jareja, K.C.I.E., LL.D. Thakore Saheb of; created D.C.L. 22 June, 1892; fellow of Bombay university.

Gonner, Edward Carter, born in London 5 March, 1862; 2s. Peter Kersey. LINCOLN, matric. 23 Oct., 80, aged 18 (from Merchant Taylors' school), B.A. 84, M.A. 87; HONOURS :—1 history 84.

Gooch, Charles Edmund, born in London 1870; 1s. Charles Cubitt, arm. BALLIOL, matric. 18 Oct., 88, aged 18 (from Eton), B.A. 92; HONOURS: —2 classics 92.

Good, rev. Edward Henry, born at Queensferry, Edinburgh 1863; 1s. Edward, cler. BRASENOSE, matric. 19 Oct., 82, aged 19 (from Durham gr. school), B.A. 85, M.A. 89 (HONOURS :—3 theology 85); curate of St. Stephen, Westbourne-park, London, 91.

Goodban, rev. Frederick William, born in London 1861; 1s. James Frederick, gent. NON-COLLEGIATE, matric. 15 Oct., 81; aged 20 (from King's coll. school, London), B.A. 84, M.A. 88; curate of St. Mary Haggerston, London, 89.

Goode, John, born at sea, 30 Aug., 1874; 3s. John Charles, gent. BRASENOSE, matric. 21 Oct., 92, aged 18, from Brentwood school.

Goodenough, rev. Leonard William Victor, born at Valetta, Malta, 25 Oct., 1865; 1s. James Graham, capt. R.N., deceased. NEW COLL., matric. 10 Oct., 84, aged 18 (from Winchester), B.A. 88, M.A. 91 (HONOURS :—4 history 88); curate of St. Mark, New Swindon, 89.

Goodger, Henry William, born at Barton, co. Stafford, 5 July, 1871; 1s. Henry, gen. LINCOLN, matric. 27 Jan., 90, aged 18.

Goodrich, Edwin Stephen, born at Weston-super-Mare, Somerset, 21 June, 1868; 2s. Octavius Pitt, vicar of Humber. MERTON, matric. 18 Oct., 92, aged 24, from University coll., London.

Goodrich, Thomas Bartlet, born at Hardmead, Bucks, 1873; 2s. Bartlet George, cler. NON-COLLEGIATE, matric. 17 Oct., 91, aged 18.

Goodrich, William John, born at Humbery, co Gloucester, 1867; 1s. Octavius, cler. BALLIOL, matric. 24 Oct., 85, aged 18 (from the Charterhouse), scholar 84, B.A. 89, M.A. 93; HONOURS :—proxime accessit Hertford scholarship 86, 1 classical mods. 87, accessit Craven scholarship 88, 1 classics 89.

Goodrich, Alfred Thomas Scrope, M.A., fellow ST. JOHN's 79-90, where see.

Goodwin, Arthur Charles, born at Ashbourne, co. Derby, June, 1869; 2s. Robert Docksey, D.Med. KEBLE, matric. 22 Oct., 88, B.A. 93; HONOURS :—2 classical mods. 90, 3 classics 92.

Goodwin, Arthur William, born in London March, 1872; 4s. Benjamin, gen. KEBLE, matric. 11 Oct., 90, aged 18, from King's coll. school, London.

Goodwin, Harry Smyth, born at Merthyr Tydfil, co. Glam., 30 Sept., 1870; 1s. Albert John, cler. QUEEN's, matric. 22 Oct., 89, aged 19 (from Rossall school), scholar 89; HONOURS :—2 classical mods. 91.

Goodwin, Harvey, bishop of Carlisle, created D.C.L. 17 June, 1885, died 25 Oct., 91. See *Al. Ox.*, and series, 539.

Goodwin, rev. John Howard, born at Worcester 26 May, 1868; 4s. Thomas Knott, gen. NON-COLLEGIATE, matric. 15 Oct., 87, aged 19 (from Bedford gr. school); migrated to WORCESTER, B.A. 92; curate of Barking.

Goodwin, William Watson, created D.C.L. 25 June, 1890, professor of Greek in Harvard university, hon. LL.D. Cambridge, 13 June, 83.

Goodwyn, Walter Meredith, born at Ilfracombe, Devon, 1871; 4s. Julius Edmund, arm. S. JOHN's, matric. 11 Oct., 90, aged 19 (from Tiverton school), passed for Sandhurst 93.

Goodyear, Charles Moncrieff, born at Manchester 26 July, 1867; 1s. Charles, gent. MERTON, matric. 24 Oct., 85, aged 18 (from Manchester gr. school), postmaster 85, B.A. 90; HONOURS :—2 mathematical mods. 87, 2 mathematics 89.

Gordon, Alexander Stillingfleet, born at Ryde, I.W., April, 1871; o.s. Cosmo Spencer, cler. KEBLE, matric. 12 Oct., 89, aged 18, from isle of Wight college, Ryde.

Gordon, Charles James Mackay, born at Tobago in East Indies, 1856; 5s. Robert, gen. BALLIOL, matric. 19 Oct., 87, aged 21 (from Glasgow university), exhibitioner 87, B.A. 92; HONOURS :—2 classical mods. 89, 2 classics 91.

Gordon, Frederick, solicitor. ORIEL, matric. 27 Oct., 2s. 92, aged 18, from Harrow. 1874;

Gordon, Edward, born at Manchester, co. Lanc., 9 Jan., 1867; 2s. Bernard, gen. QUEEN's, matric. 28 April, 91, aged 24, from Manchester gr. school.

Gordon, George, born at Hammerwich, co. Stafford, 11 Aug., 1863; 2s. Robert, rector. NEW COLL., matric. 14 Oct., 82, aged 19 (from Radley coll.), B.A. 85 (HONOURS :—3 law 85); assistant commissioner, Assam.

Gordon, George Vincent Hamilton, born at Pietermaritzburg, 1865; 2s. George Hamilton, co. R.E., ORIEL, matric. 23 Oct., 84, aged 19, from Canterbury gr. school.

Gordon, Henry Doddridge, M.A., fellow NEW COLL. 52-61, where see page 215.

Gordon, Hugh, born in London 7 Feb., 1863; 3s. John, a master in high court of judicature. NEW COLL., matric. 4 Dec., 82, aged 19 (from Westminster school and King's coll., London), B.A. 85, M.A. 90; HONOURS :—3 chemistry 86; brother of John Henry.

Gordon, James, born at Adderbury, Oxon, 25 July, 1861; 1s. Henry, vicar of Harting. NEW COLL., matric. 15 May, 80, aged 18 (from Malvern coll.), B.A. 84, M.A. and B.Med. 89; HONOURS :— 2 natural science 84.

Gordon, James Charles, born at Raisance in Guiana, 9 Jan., 1859; 1s. Thomas Robert, arm. ST. MARY HALL, matric. 24 Oct., 85, aged 26; bar.-at-law, Gray's Inn, 86.

Gordon, John Henry, born at Chelsfield, Kent, 1 May, 1865; 4s. John, arm. MAGDALEN, matric. 16 Oct., 84, aged 19 (from Bradfield coll.), B.A. 87; HONOURS: —3 mathematical mods. 86, 4 mathematics 87; died 27 Feb., 92; brother of Hugh.

Gordon, Mervyn Henry, born at Harting, Sussex, July, 1872; 4s. Thomas Doddridge, cler. KEBLE, matric. 11 Oct., 90, aged 18, from Marlborough coll.

Gordon, Percival Wilmot, born at Newtimber, Sussex, June, 1874; 2s. Arthur Pitman, M.A., rector. CHRIST CHURCH, matric. 4 June, 92, aged 18, from Winchester.

Gordon, Robert Whittaker, born at Newton Heath, co. Lanc., 3 Dec., 1863; 2s. James, cler. BRASENOSE, matric. 22 Oct., 83, aged 19 (from Manchester gr. school), exhibitioner 83, B.A. 87, M.A. 90; [HONOURS :—2 classical mods. 85, 3 classics 87.

Gordon, rev. William, born at Hammerwich, co. Stafford, 1865; 1s. Robert, cler. UNIVERSITY COLL., matric. 15 Jan., 87, aged 21 B.A. 90 (HONOURS :—4 theology 90]; curate of Strathfield Mortimer, Berks, 91; brother of George.

Gordon, William Alexander, born at Aberdeen 9 May, 1869; 3s. George Hamilton, arm. TRINITY, matric. 25 Oct., 87, aged 18 (from Canterbury school), B.A. 91; HONOURS :—4 history 91; brother of George V. H.

Gordon, William Pritchard, born at Oldbury, Salop, July, 1862; 1s. William Pierson, arm. CHRIST CHURCH, matric. 16 Jan., 80, aged 18 (from Eton), B.A. 83 (HONOURS :—3 history 83); bar.-at-law, Inner Temple, 87.

Gore, Charles, M.A., fellow TRINITY 75, where see.

Gore, Gerard Holmes, born at Leighton, Essex, 18 April, 1872; 3s. Thomas Holmes, solicitor. MAGDALEN, matric. 22 Oct., 91, aged 19, from Clifton coll.

Gore, hon. Seymour Fitzroy Ormsby, born 18 Jan., 1863; 3s. William Richard, baron Harlech. BRASENOSE, matric. 28 April, 81, aged 18 (from Eton), B.A. and M.A. 89.

Goring, Charles, born in London 12 Sept., 1862; 1s. John, cler. CHRIST CHURCH, matric. 14 Oct., 81, aged 19 (from Eton), B.A. 85, M.A. 89; brother of the next.

Goring, Walter, born at Wiston, Sussex, 21 Dec., 1863; 2s. John, cler. CHRIST CHURCH. matric. 27 May, 82, aged 18 (from Eton); brother of the last.

Gorton, Richard Hall, born at Manchester 16 Aug., 1868; o.s. Richard arm. ORIEL, matric. 18 Oct., 87, aged 19 (from Harrow), B.A. 90.

Goschen, right hon. George Joachim, M.A., created D.C.L. 22 June, 1881; hon. fellow ORIEL 82, where see page 151.

Goschen, George Joachim, born at Hastings 15 Oct., 1866; 1s. George Joachim, chancellor of the exchequer 87-92. BALLIOL, matric. 24 Oct., 85, aged 19, from Rugby.

Goschen, William Henry, born in London 7 June, 1870; 2s. George Joachim, chancellor of the exchequer 87-92. NEW COLL., matric. 11 Oct., 89, aged 19, from Rugby.

Gosling, George Bruce, born at Bath 3 Nov., 1869; 3s. George Frederick, arm. TRINITY, matric. 13 Oct., 88, aged 18 (from Harrow), B.A. 92; HONOURS :—3 history 92.

Gosling, Walter Charles, born at Newtown, Berks, 17 Sept., 1870; 2s. Francis Charles, cler. MERTON, matric. 15 Oct., 90, aged 20, from Eton.

Goss, William Nathaniel, born at Barrow-in-Furness 18 Jan., 1873; 3s. Thomas, vicar of Carlisle St. James. QUEEN'S, matric. 27 Oct., 92, aged 19 (from Carlisle school), exhibitioner 92.

Gossage, Alfred Milne, born at Garston, co. Lanc., 13 March, 1864; 2s. William, F.C.S., deceased. MAGDALEN, matric. 16 Oct., 82, aged 18 (from Clifton coll.), demy 82, B.A. 86, M.A. and B.Med. 91; HONOURS :—1 chemistry 86.

Gosselin, rev. Charles Carteret, born at St. Peter Port, Guernsey, 17 Oct., 1866; 1s. Charles Thomas, arm. LINCOLN, matric. 17 Oct., 84, aged 18 (from Elizabeth coll., Guernsey), B.A. 87, M.A. 91 (HONOURS :—3 theology 87); curate of St. Clement, Fulham, 89.

Gosset, Arthur Henry, M.A., fellow NEW COLL. 77-85, where see page 218.

Gosset, Percy Stuart Moncrieff, born in London 5 Feb., 1861; 2s. William Driscoll, major-general R.E. KEBLE, matric. 19 Oct., 80, aged 19 (from Cheltenham coll.), B.A. 83, M.A. 87; assistant master Bradfield coll.; perished in the burning of Exeter new theatre 5 Sept., 87.

Gotch, Francis; s. Francis W., non.-conf. divine, created M.A. 10 Nov., 1885; B.Sc. London University; assistant to the Waynflete professor of physiology, examiner in natural science, Oxford, 91-2; prof. of physiology at University coll., Liverpool, 91, F.R.S. 92.

Gotley, George Henniker, born at Sheen, Berks, 1860; 2s. James, gen. ORIEL, matric. 9 Dec., 89, aged 29.

Gotto, Donald, born in London 6 Aug., 1862; 5s. Henry Jenkins, gent. NEW, matric. 21 Jan., 82, aged 19 (from Westminster school), B.A. 87.

Goudge, rev. Henry Leighton, born in London 1867; 1s. Henry, gent. UNIVERSITY COLL., matric. 17 Oct., 85, aged 18 (from Blackheath school), scholar 84, B.A. 89 (HONOURS :—1 classical mods. 87, 1 classics 89); curate of St. Mark, Leicester, 90.

Goudge, Joseph Ernest, born at Swindon 22 April, 1869; 1s. Joseph, gen. PEMBROKE, matric. 17 Oct., 88, aged 19 (from Queen's coll., Taunton), scholar 88 (HONOURS :—2 classical mods. 90, 2 classics 92); selected candidate Indian C.S. 92.

Goudge, Thomas Sidney, born at Swindon, Wilts, 4 Dec., 1870; 2s. Joseph, gen. MERTON, matric. 15 Oct., 90, aged 19 (from Wesleyan coll., Sheffield), exhibitioner 90.

Gough, Alfred Bradley, born at Brixton, Surrey, 12 Jan., 1872; 1s. Henry, bar.-at-law. ST. JOHN'S, matric. 17 Oct., 91, aged 19, from King's coll.

Gough, rev. Alfred William, born at Hartshill, co. Stafford, 13 Dec. 1862; 3s. Howard England, cler. ST. JOHN'S, matric. 14 Oct., 82, aged 19 (from Merchant Taylors' school), B.A. 85, M.A. 89 (HONOURS :—2 classical mods. 84); vicar of St. Matthew Jersey, 90-2, and of Wakefield Holy Trinity, 92.

Gough, rev. Arthur Cecil, born at Malvern, co. Hereford, 8 June, 1866; 5s. Howard England Tunnicliffe, cler., deceased. WADHAM, matric. 19 Oct., 85, aged 19 (from Merchant Taylors' school), B.A. 89, M.A. 92; curate of Christ Church, South Mymms, Herts, 92.

Gough, Arthur Valentine, born at Houghton-le-Spring, co. Durham, 14 Feb., 1872; 3s. Robert Louis Henry, vicar of Chilton Moor. BRASENOSE, matric. 15 Oct., 90, aged 18 (from Durham gr. school), scholar 90; HONOURS :—2 classical mods. 92.

Gough, rev. Francis John, born at Oxford 8 June, 1865; 2s. Charles, gent. NON-COLLEGIATE, matric. 13 Oct., 83, aged 18 (from New coll., Oxford, chorister 75-81), B.A. 86, M.A. 90 (HONOURS :—3 history 86); curate of Nottingham St. Sephens 86.

Gough, Frederick Harrison, born at Manchester 1863; 1s. Robert Lewis Henry, vicar of Chilton Moor, co. Durham. ORIEL, matric. 31 Oct., 82, aged 19 (from Durham gr. school), B.A. 86, M.A. 89; HONOURS :—1 classical mods. 84, 2 classics 86.

Gough, John, born at Wolverhampton 1861; o.s. John, pleb. NON-COLLEGIATE, matric. 15 Oct., 81, aged 20, from Tettenhall coll., Staffs.

Gough, Reginald Melville, born at Oldham, co. Lanc., May, 1860; 2s. Robert Louis Henry, vicar of Chilton Moor, co. Durham. KEBLE, matric. 22 Oct., 85, aged 19.

Gough, William Charles, born at Oxford 9 April, 1864; 1s. Charles, gent. NON-COLLEGIATE, matric. 15 Oct., 81, aged 17 (from New coll. school, Oxford, chorister 76-9), exhibitioner EXETER 83-5, B.A. 85, M.A. 91; HONOURS :—2 classical mods. 83, 2 classics 85.

Gough, William Henry, born at Houghton-le-Spring, co. Durham, 1869; 4s. Robert Louis Henry, vicar of Chilton Moor. WADHAM, matric. 13 Oct., 88, aged 19, B.A 92; HONOURS :—3 law 91.

Goulbourn, very rev. Edward Meyrick, D.D., dean of Norwich 66-89, fellow MERTON 41-6, where see page 96.

Gould, Arthur Baring, born at Lew Trenchard, Devon, 15 Dec., 1865; 4s. Edward, arm., deceased. MAGDALEN, matric. 16 Oct., 84, aged 18 (from Winchester), B.A. 88 (HONOURS :—3 law 87); bar.-at-law, Inner Temple, 89.

Gould, rev. Charles Hamerton-, born at Sheffield, 1 March, 1865; 1s. Charles, bar.-at-law. NEW COLL., matric. 18 Jan., 84, aged 18 (from Harrow), B.A. 87, M.A. 90 (HONOURS :—3 history 87); curate of Portsea 89.

Gould, James Aubrey, M A., fellow NEW COLL. 46-56, where see page 213.

Gould, rev. Reginald Freestone, born at Kingham, Oxon, 1861 ; 2s. Richard Augustus, cler. ST. MARY HALL, matric. 19 Oct., 81, aged 20, B.A. 85, M.A. 91; curate of Peterborough St. Mary 84.

Goulden, Herbert Edward, born at Uckfield, Sussex, 3 Oct., 1871 ; 1s. Edward Baker, gen. TRINITY, matric. 11 Oct., 90, aged 19, from Canterbury school.

Gouldschmidt, Edmund Benoit Julian, born at Neuilly, near Paris, , 1864 ; o.s. Solomon, arm. CHRIST CHURCH, matric. 1 May, 83, aged 19.

Gouldsmith, Harold Salter, born at Clifton, co. Glouc., 1874 ; 2s. Samuel Salter, solicitor. BALLIOL, matric. 18 Oct., 92, aged 18, from Clifton coll.

Gouldsmith, rev. Herbert, born at Richmond, Surrey, 1863 ; 2s. Henry, gent. NON-COLLEGIATE, matric. 14 Oct., 82, aged 19 (from city of London school); migrated to EXETER, B.A. 86, M.A. 89 (HONOURS :—3 theology 86); church missionary society's incumbent of Old Church, Calcutta, 90.

Gourlay, William Edmund Crawfurd Austin-, M.A., fellow NEW COLL. 40-63, where see page 211.

Govett, Lionel Arthur, born at Richmond, Surrey, 19 March, 1863; 1s. Charles Albert, solicitor. NEW COLL., matric. 16 Oct., 81, aged 18 (from the Charterhouse), B.A. 85, M.A. 88; HONOURS:— 1 classical mods. 83, 2 classics 85.

Govett, rev. Robert, M.A., fellow WORCESTER 35-44, where see.

Gower, Frederick Archibald Gresham Leveson-, born at Titsey, Surrey, 20 Feb., 1871 ; 2s. Granville William Gresham (L.-G.), arm. MAGDALEN, matric. 14 Oct., 90, aged 19, from Winchester.

Gower, Granville Charles Gresham Leveson-, born at Limpsfield, Surrey, 25 Sept., 1865; 1s. Granville William Gresham (L.-G.), arm. BALLIOL, matric. 22 Jan., 85, aged 19 (from Eton), B.A. 90.

Gower, Henry Dudley Gresham Leveson-, born at Titsey Place, Surrey, 8 May, 1873; 4s. Granville Gresham, (L.-G.), esq. MAGDALEN, matric. 27 Oct., 92, aged 19, from Winchester.

Gower, Ronald William Gresham Leveson, born in London 22 Sept., 1863 ; 1s. Granville Leveson (L.-G.), arm. CHRIST CHURCH, matric. 4 June, 81, aged 17 (from Eton) ; died 21 July, 89.

Gowlland, Peter Yeames, born in London 1864 ; 1s. Peter Yeames, arm. BRASENOSE, matric. 10 June, 81, aged 17 (from Merchant Taylors' school), B.A. 85, M.A. and B.C.L. 90 (HONOURS :— 3 law 85) ; bar.-at-law, Inner Temple, 86; died 2 Jan., 92, in London.

Grace, Charles Millar, born at Wakefield, Yorks, 25 Jan., 1865 ; 2s. William, gent., deceased. QUEEN'S, matric. 22 Oct., 83, aged 18 (from Wakefield gr. school), exhibitioner 83, B.A. 88.

Grace, Granville Morton, born at Lampeter, co. Cardigan, 5 June, 1867 ; 1s. Allen Zachariah, cler. JESUS COLL., matric. 15 Oct., 90, aged 23 (from Lampeter coll.), exhibitioner 90, B.A. 92; HONOURS: —2 physics 92.

Graff, Edward Charles, born in London 1855 ; 3s. James, gent. CHARSLEY'S HALL, matric. 22 Oct., 85, aged 30.

Graff, Harold John, born in London 1872 ; 2s. Stephen John, supt. admiralty office. NON-COLLEGIATE, matric. 17 Oct., 91, aged 19, from King's coll., London.

Graham, Arthur Harington, born in London 17 July, 1867 ; 3s. Joseph, Q.C. MAGDALEN, matric. 22 March, 86, aged 18 (from Eton), B.A. 89, bar.-at-law, Middle Temple, 91.

Graham, Arthur Smith, born at Tulse Hill, Surrey, July, 1871 ; 4s. Christopher North, esquire. CHRIST CHURCH, matric. 16 Oct., 91, aged 20, from Tonbridge school.

Graham, Cecil William Noble, born at Langbanke, Renfrewshire, N.B., 19 Sept., 1872 ; 2s. John Hall Noble, of Drums house, Erskine parish, gent. TRINITY, matric. 13 Dec., 92, aged 20, from Eton.

Graham, George Cyril, born at Coventry 31 July, 1861 ; 6s. James John George, vicar of Much Cowarne, co. Worc. QUEEN'S, matric. 1 Feb., 81, aged 19.

Graham, rev. Ivor Charles, born at Arthuret, Cumberland, 1869 ; 3s. Malise Reginald, cler. ORIEL, matric. 18 Oct., 87, aged 18 (from the Charterhouse), B.A. 91.

Graham, James Dunsiervillc, born at Skelmorlie Castle, Ayrshire, 15 May, 1873 ; 1s. Donald, C.I.E., East India merchant, BRASENOSE, matric. 14 Oct., 92, aged 19, from Harrow.

Graham, Robert Arthur, born at Meerut, East Indies, 13 Dec., 1870 ; 1s. Thomas, arm. BRASENOSE, matric. 14 Oct., 89, aged 18 (from Winchester), scholar, 89; assist. collector and magistrate, South Canara, Madras, c.s.

Grahame, Alexander Hugh Erskine, born in London , 1867 ; 2s. John Anthony, arm. BALLIOL, matric. 24 Oct., 85, aged 18, from Harrow.

Grahame, John Buchanan, born at Dumblane, Perthshire, 21 Aug., 1861 ; 1s. John, arm. UNIVERSITY COLL., matric. 16 Oct., 80, aged 19 (from Rugby), B.A. 86.

Grahame, Walter, born in London 1872 ; 2s. John Anthony, gen. BALLIOL, matric. 20 Oct., 91, aged 19.

Gramshaw, Ernest Reginald, born at Brighton 19 Nov., 1870; 2s. Robert, solicitor. ST. JOHN'S, matric. 17 Jan., 90, aged 19, from Brighton coll.

Granet, William Grey, born at Genoa, Italy, 13 Oct., 1867; 2s. William Augustus, gent. BALLIOL, matric. 24 Oct., 85, aged 18 (from Rugby), B.A. 89; HONOURS:—2 history 89.

Grant, Alan St. George, born at Portsmouth 13 April, 1869 ; 3s. William, banker. NEW COLL., matric. 18 Oct., 87, aged 18, from Harrow.

Grant, Sir Alexander, bart., created D.C.L. 9 June, 80; died 30 Nov., 84. See Al. Ox., and series, 549.

Grant, Alexander, born at Bolton, co. Lanc., 5 Sept., 1866 ; 3s. Alexander, arm. MERTON, matric. 16 Oct., 84, aged 18 (from Manchester gr. school), postmaster 84, B.A. 90, fellow ALL SOULS' 90, M.A. and B.C.L. 91 ; HONOURS :—1 classical mods. 85, 1 classics 88, 1 law 89, 2 civil law 90, Eldon law scholarship 91.

Grant, Alfred Hamilton, born at Edinburgh 12 June, 1872; 3s. Alexander, baronet. BALLIOL, matric. 14 Oct., 90, aged 18 (from Fettes coll.); HONOURS: —2 classical mods. 92.

Grant, Arthur James, born at Mallegaum, East Indies, 1868; 2s. Henry Martin, of the Indian c.s. MAGDALEN, matric. 21 Oct., 86, aged 18 (from Dulwich coll.), exhibitioner 86, B.A. 89 (HONOURS:—1 Indian languages 89), junior sec. to financial commissioner Punjab.

Grant, Cecil, born at Lynton, Kent, 18 Aug., 1870; 5s. John, gent. WADHAM, matric. 14 Oct., 89, aged 19 (from Sutton Valence school), scholar 88; HONOURS:—2 classical mods. 91.

Grant, Charles Bathe, born at Poona, East Indies, 22 July, 1866; 1s. Henry Martin, gent. QUEEN'S, matric. 22 Oct., 84, aged 18 (from Burkhamstead gr. school), scholar 84, B.A. 88, fellow 91, M.A. 91; HONOURS:—1 classical mods. 86, 1 classics 88, 1 history 89.

Grant, Douglas Stewart, born at Patterson, America, 1865; o.s. David Beach, arm. CHRIST CHURCH, matric. 22 Jan., 83, aged 18.

Grant, Edmund Lennard Deacon, born in London 1861; 1s. Albert, arm. BRASENOSE, matric. 28 April, 81, aged 20 (from Eton), B.A. 85, M.A. 89, bar.-at-law, Inner Temple, 86.

Grant, Edward Pierce, M.A., fellow NEW COLL. 51-9, where see page 215.

Grant, Hugh Ibratazon, born at Southsea, Hants, 5 Oct., 1866; 2s. William, banker. NEW COLL., matric. 16 Oct., 85, aged 19 (from Winchester), B.A. 89, HONOURS:—3 law 89.

Grant, James Augustus, born at Julunda, E. Indies, March, 1867; 1s. James Augustus, arm. CHRIST CHURCH, matric. 15 Oct., 86, aged 19.

Grant, James George, born at Leith 16 Nov., 1864; o.s. James, capt. R.N. WADHAM, matric. 23 April, 84, aged 19 (from Sedbergh school), B.A. 87, M.A. 91.

Grant, rev. John Alexander, born at Rothsay, Bute, 27 Dec., 1866; 2s. William, arm. MERTON, matric. 17 Oct., 88, aged 21 (from Aberdeen or St. Andrews university), B.A. 92 (HONOURS:—3 history 92); curate of Cross Stone.

Grant, John Macpherson, born at Edinburgh 22 March, 1863; 1s. George Macpherson, bart. CHRIST CHURCH, matric. 14 Oct., 81, aged 18, from Eton.

Grant, (sir) Ludovic Janus (bart.), born in Bombay 4 Sept., 1862; 1s. sir Alexander, bart. BALLIOL, matric. 18 Oct., 81, aged 19 (from Fettes coll.), exhibitioner 80-6, B.A. 86 (HONOURS:—1 classical mods. 83, 2 classics 85); advocate, professor of public law at University of Edinburgh 90.

Grant, Matthew George, born at Halifax, Nova Scotia, 26 Feb., 1862; 1s. George, gent., deceased. NEW COLL., matric. 16 Oct., 80, aged 18 (from Liverpool coll.), exhibitioner 80, B.A. 84, M.A. 92; HONOURS: —2 mathematical mods. 82, 2 mathematics 84.

Grant, Patrick Charles Murray, born at Calicutt, E. Indies, 11 Aug., 1860; 2s. Patrick, arm. BALLIOL, matric. 21 Jan., 80, aged 19 (from Rugby), B.A. 84; HONOURS:—4 history 83.

Grant, William Frederick Forsyth, born at St. Cyres, co. Kincardine, 2 Aug., 1868; 1s. Frederick Grant, of Montrose, N.B., colonel. MAGDALEN, matric. 21 Oct., 89, aged 18, from Winchester.

Grant, William Thorold, born at Leamington April, 1862; 3s. Frederick Augustus, arm. CHRIST CHURCH, matric. 14 Oct., 81, aged 19 (from Eton); student Inner Temple 82.

Graves, Charles, bishop of Limerick, created D.C.L. 22 June, 1881. See *Al. Ox.*, and series, 551.

Graves, Henry, born at Kensington 1871; 1s. Algernon, gen. BALLIOL, matric. 17 Oct., 89, aged 18 (from Derby school), exhibitioner 88; HONOURS:—1 classical mods. 91.

Gray, Asa, foreign F.R.S., created D.C.L. 22 June, 1887; professor of botany at Harward 42-73; born 18 Nov., 1810, died 30 Jan., 88. See *Al. Ox.*, and series, 552.

Gray, Charles Herbert, born at Pateley Bridge, Yorks, 1869; 1s. Samuel, cler. UNIVERSITY COLL., matric. 15 Oct., 87, aged 18, B.A. 90; HONOURS:—3 mathematical mods. 88, 4 mathematics 90.

Gray, D'Arcy Philip Ashb'ton, born at South Kensington 7 Jan., 1873; 4s. William, of Farley Hill Place, Berks (colonel). UNIVERSITY COLL., matric. 17 Oct., 91, aged 18, from Wellington coll.

Gray, Edward Benjamin, M.A., D.Med. EXETER, where see page 129.

Gray, Edward Francis, born at Alwalton, Hunts, 15 Jan., 1871; 4s. Edward, cler. ORIEL, matric. 22 Oct., 90, aged 19 (from Haileybury); HONOURS:— 3 classical mods. 92.

Gray, Ernest Avling Simpson, born at Blandford, Dorset, 19 June, 1870; 3s. Benjamin, congregational minister. MAGDALEN, matric. 14 Oct., 89, aged 19 (from Silcoates school, and University coll., London), demy 89, B.A. 92; HONOURS:—2 mathematical mods. 90, 2 mathematics 92.

Gray, George Buchanan, born at Blandford, Dorset, 1865; 2s. Benjamin, congregational minister. NON-COLLEGIATE, matric. 13 Oct., 88, aged 23, B.A. 91; HONOURS:—Hebrew scholarship 89 and 91, septuagint prize 90, 1 Semitic studies 91.

Gray, Herbert Edward, born at Oxford 1 May, 1872; 1s. Edward Benjamin, D.Med. MAGDALEN, matric. 14 Oct., 90, aged 18, from Shrewsbury school.

Gray, James Black, D.D., fellow ST. JOHN'S 52-72, where see.

Gray, John Walter, born at Everton Bucks, 28 28 March, 1874; 1s. John Burdin, vicar. KEBLE, matric. 15 Oct., 92, aged 18, from Bromsgrove school.

Gray, Perceval, born at Oxford 1 Oct., 1873; 2s. Edward Benjamin, D.Med. NEW COLL., matric. 14 Oct., 92, aged 19, from Rugby.

Gray, Robert, born at Orcop, co. Hereford, 1878; 1s. Arthur, cler. NEW COLL., matric. 14 Oct., 83, aged 18.

Gray, William, born at Cheltenham Jan., 1864; 1s. Acheson, arm. EXETER, matric. 18 Jan., 83, aged 18, from Clifton coll.

Gray, William Anderson, born at Aberdeen 1867; 3s. Alexander, gent. BALLIOL, matric. 24 Oct., 85, aged 18 (from Aberdeen and Glasgow universities), exhibitioner 85, B.A. 89; HONOURS:—1 classical mods. 87, 1 classics 89; died 91.

Gray, William Royston, born at Wigton, Cumberland, 1867; 2s. William, cler. ST. JOHN'S, matric. 16 Oct., 86, aged 19 (from Merchant Taylors' school), scholar 86, B.A. 90; HONOURS:—1 classical mods. 88, 3 classics 90.

Grayson, Ernest Nowell, born at Rockferry, Cheshire, 1873; 2s. George Enoch, F.R.I.B.A. BALLIOL, matric. 18 Oct., 92, aged 19, from Sedbergh school.

Greatbatch, Arthur Mitchell, born at Oxford 1858; 2s. Levi. NON-COLLEGIATE, matric. 26 Oct., 85, aged 27, B.A. 89.

Greathed, Edward Archer, born at Rome 4 Feb., 1866; 1s. William Wilberforce, major-general. NEW COLL., matric. 10 Oct., 84, aged 18 (from Eton), B.A. 89; HONOURS:—4 history 88.

Greathed, Edward Wilberforce Osborn, born at Wimborne, Dorset, 7 July, 1870; 1s. genl. Edward Harris, K.C.B. CHRIST CHURCH, matric. 1 June, 88, aged 17 (from Eton), B.A. 91; HONOURS:—2 history 91.

Greatorex, Ronald Henry, born at Stapleton, co. Glouc., 18 May, 1862; 2s. Edward, arm. ST. JOHN'S, matric. 15 Oct., 81, aged 19 (from Bristol school), scholar 81, B.A. 84; HONOURS:—2 mathematical mods. 83, 3 mathematics 84, 4 physiology 86.

Greaves, Arthur Ivan, born at South Norwood, Surrey, Jan. 1873; 1s. James Henry, C.E. KEBLE, matric. 20 Oct., 91, aged 18, from Hurstpierpoint coll.

Greaves, rev. Edmund, born at Cosgrove, Northants, 24 June, 1867; 3s. John Albert, M.A., vicar of Billingborough. LINCOLN, matric. 13 May, 86, aged 18 (from University school, Pittsburg, Virginia U.S.A.), B.A. 89 (HONOURS:—2 theology 89); curate of St. Mary-the-less, Lambeth 91.

Greaves, James, born at Oldham, co. Lanc., 1864; 1s. John, gent. NON-COLLEGIATE, matric. 13 Oct., 83, aged 19 (from Chester training coll.), B.A. 88; HONOURS:—3 history 87.

Greaves, John Hall, born at Oldham, co. Lanc., 26 Dec., 1863; 2s. Hilton, gent. HERTFORD, matric. 18 Oct., 83, aged 19 (from Rugby), B.A. 87 (HONOURS:—1 law 87, 3 civil law 89); bar.-at-law, Lincoln's Inn, 89.

Greaves, Richard Ley, born at Cirencester 12 Sept., 1869; 1s. Richard Thomas, of East Carlton, Uppingham, gen. ST. EDMUND HALL, matric. 22 Oct., 91, aged 22, from Denstone coll.

Greaves, William Ernest, born at Shoreham, Sussex, Aug., 69; 1s. William, gen. KEBLE, matric. 13 Oct., 88, aged 19 (from Harrow), B.A. 92; HONOURS:—3 classical mods. 90, 3 classics 92.

Green, Alexander Henry, M.A., fellow GONVILLE AND CAIUS, Cambridge, 55-68, hon. fellow 92, professor of geology, Oxford, 88; incorporated from Christ Church 18 Jan., 89, aged 56, where see.

Green, rev. Arthur Daniel, born at Rainham, Kent, 1854; o.s. Daniel Graie, gent. NON-COLLEGIATE, matric. 15 April, 82, aged 28 (from Rochester gr. school); curate of St. Paul's cathedral mission, Calcutta, 91.

Green, Arthur Meredith Wilson, born at Seaforth, co. Lanc., 3 Aug., 1870; 1s. Henry Meredith, gen., deceased. NON-COLLEGIATE, matric. 12 Oct., 89, aged 19 (from Liverpool institute and Ellesmere coll., Salop); migrated to NEW COLL.; HONOURS: 2 history 92.

Green, rev. Charles Alfred Howell, born at Llanelly, co. Carmarthen, May, 1864; 1s. Alfred John Morgan, cler. KEBLE, matric. 16 Oct., 83, aged 19 (from the Charterhouse), scholar 83, B.A. 87, M.A. 92 (HONOURS:—2 classical mods. 84, 2 classics 87); librarian of Oxford union society 86, president 87; curate of Aberdare, co. Glam., 88.

Green, Claude Egerton, born at Leiden, Essex, 1863; 1s. Henry Egerton, arm. BALLIOL, matric. 17 Oct., 82, aged 19 (from Rugby), B.A. 86, M.A. 89; HONOURS:—1 classical mods. 84, 3 classics 86.

Green, rev. Edmund Tyrrell, born in London 1865; o.s. Charles Alexander, gent. NON-COLLEGIATE, matric. 13 Jan., 83, aged 18 (from Southwark gr. school), scholar ST. JOHN'S 86, B.A. 86, M.A. 89 (HONOURS:—1 theology 86, Denyer and Johnson theological scholarship 87); lecturer in theology and Hebrew St. David's coll., Lampeter, 90.

Green, Francis William, born 1865; 2s. Edward arm. CHRIST CHURCH, matric. 16 Jan., 80, aged 15.

Green, George Buckland, Fereday fellow ST. JOHN'S 88, M.A. 90, where see page

Green, Harry John, born at Mirfield, Yorks, 20 Dec., 1869; 1s. George, gen. NON-COLLEGIATE, matric. 18 Jan., 90, aged 20, from Mirfield and Bradford gr. schools.

Green, rev. Herbert Webster, born at Stoke-on-Trent 1867; 3s. Edward John, arm. UNIVERSITY COLL., matric. 13 Oct., 88, aged 21; HONOURS:—2 history 91.

Green, James Samuel, born in London 1861; o.s. James Richard Goring, arm. PEMBROKE, matric. 4 Feb., 80, aged 19, B.A. 83, B.C.L. and M.A. 86 (HONOURS:—2 law 83, 3 civil law 85); bar.-at-law, Lincoln's Inn, 85.

Green, rev. James William, born at Kidbrooke, Kent, Feb., 1866; 1s. Samuel, gent. ORIEL, matric. 23 Oct., 85, aged 19 (from Lancing coll.), B.A. 88, M.A. 92; curate of St. Mary, Woolwich, 89.

Green, John Edward, born at Erdington, co. Warwick, 1862; 1s. John Fowler, cler. CHRIST CHURCH, matric. 26 Jan., 85, aged 23.

Green, Marshall Yeoman, born at Byker, Northumberland, Jan., 1867; 1s. Thomas, cler. CHRIST CHURCH, matric. 30 May, 85, aged 18, B.A. 90.

Green, Martin Holdich, M.A., fellow TRINITY 72, where see.

Green, Percy Sleath, born in London 23 Jan., 1869; 2s. John, arm. EXETER, matric. 28 April, 87, aged 18, from Eton.

Green, Reginald Southwell Graham, born at Southwell, Notts, 14 Oct., 1865; 2s. Joseph, cler. QUEEN'S, matric. 22 Oct., 84, aged 19 (from Appleby gr. school, Westmoreland), exhibitioner 84, B.A. 88, M.A. 92; HONOURS:—2 classical mods. 86, 2 classics 88.

Green, Richard Harry, born at Rowley Regis, co. Stafford, 9 Aug., 1869; 2s. Richard, gen. WORCESTER, matric. 14 Oct., 89, aged 27, from Bromsgrove school.

Green, Theophilus Herbert, born at Dowdeswell, co. Gloucester, 1861; 1s. Theophilus, arm. BALLIOL, matric. 1 Nov., 80, aged 19 (from Leamington coll.), B.A. 84, M.A. 91; HONOURS:—3 classical mods. 82, 3 classics 84.

Greene, Charles Henry, born at Henley-on-Thames, 1865; 2s. William, gen. WADHAM, matric. 11 Oct., 84, aged 19 (from Bedford gr. school), B.A. 88, M.A. 91; HONOURS:—3 classical mods. 86, 2 history 88.

Greene, Herbert William, M.A., B.C.L., fellow MAGDALEN 88, where see.

Greene, Walter Raymond, born at Bury St. Edmund's 1870; 1s. Edward Walter. arm. ORIEL, matric. 27 Jan., 88, aged 18 (from Eton), B.A. 92.

Greenfield, James Lawrence, born at Reading 21 Aug., 1865; 1s. James, gent. WADHAM, matric. 19 Oct., 85, aged 20, from Reading gr. school.

Greenfield, Thomas Joseph (Martineau), born at Lewisham, Kent, 27 Feb., 1864; 2s. Thomas Joseph, bar.-at-law. NON-COLLEGIATE, matric. 14 Oct., 82, aged 18 (from St. Paul's school); exhibitioner MAGDALEN 83-6, B.A. 86; HONOURS:—3 classical mods. 84, 3 mathematics 86.

Greenham, Henry Warren Goodwin, born at Ludborough, co. Lincoln, 1871; 1s. Henry, cler. CHARSLEY'S HALL, matric. 19 Feb., 87, aged 16, B.A. 90.

Greenhow, Wilfred Harry, born in East Indies 17 Oct., 1872; 1s. Henry Martineau, army surgeon, retired. EXETER, matric. 13 Oct., 90, aged 17, from Marlborough coll.

Greenidge, Abel Hendy Jones, born at St. John, island of Barbados, 1866; 2s. Nathaniel, cler. BALLIOL, matric. 15 Oct., 84, aged 18 (from Harrison coll., Barbados), exhibitioner 85, B.A. 88, fellow HERTFORD 89, M.A. 91; HONOURS :— 1 classical mods. 86, 1 classics 88.

Greenish, Frederick Robert, born at Haverfordwest, co. Pembroke, 1856; 1s. Robert, gent. NEW COLL., matric. 24 Jan., 81, aged 25, B.Mus. 83, D.Mus. 91.

Greenland, Herbert Francis Flower, born at Selhurst, Surrey, 28 Sept., 1871; 1s. Charles Francis, of Sydenham, Kent, gen. ST. JOHN'S, matric. 17 Oct., 89, aged 18 (from Merchant Taylors' school), scholar 89; HONOURS :— 1 classical mods. 91.

Greenlees, Dan Colville, born at Campbeltown, co. Argyll, 5 March, 1869; o.s. Charles Colville, gen. QUEEN'S, matric. 21 Oct., 87, aged 18 from Merchiston Castle school, Edinburgh.

Greentree, Richard, born at Westmeon, Hants, 10 April, 1874; o.s. John. BALLIOL, matric. 18 Oct., 92, aged 18 (from Malvern coll.), scholar 92.

Greenway, George Cattell, born at Leamington 1866; 1s. George Cattell, arm. BRASENOSE, matric. 21 Jan., 84, aged 18, from Winchester.

Greenway, John Bralyn, born at Plymouth 1 Aug., 1866; 2s. John, arm. TRINITY, matric. 11 Oct., 84, aged 18 (from Plymouth coll.), B.A. 87, M.A. 91.

Greenway, Kelynge, born at Warwick 27 June, 1867; 1s. Kelynge, arm. BRASENOSE, matric. 26 Jan., 86, aged 18, from Harrow.

Greenway, rev. Lionel Croft Kelynge, born at Warwick 20 Nov., 1868; 2s. Kelynge, arm. TRINITY, matric. 15 Oct., 87, aged 18 (from Harrow), B.A. 91 (HONOURS :— 3 theology 91); curate of St. Giles, Reading

Greenwood, Arthur, born in Newcastle-under-Lyne 1833; 3s. George Wright, gent. ST. ALBAN HALL, matric. 5 July, 81, aged 28.

Greenwood, rev. Frederick William Thompson, born at Newark, Notts, 6 July, 1866 or 8; 1s. Thomas Frederick, surgeon-major. WADHAM, matric. 18 Jan., 87, aged 18 (from Newark gr. school), B.A. 89 (HONOURS :— 3 theology 89); curate of Gainsborough 90.

Greenwood, Hubert John, born at Swarcliffe, Yorks, Nov., 1867; 4s. John, arm. CHRIST CHURCH, matric. 30 May, 85, aged 17, from Eton.

Greenwood, John Arthur, born at Todmorden, Yorks, 13 Nov., 1867; o.s. Robert, gen. MERTON, matric. 22 Oct., 87, aged 19, from Forest school.

Greenwood, Thomas, born at Crayke, Yorks, 1862; 2s. Thomas, arm. CHARSLEY'S HALL, matric. 18 Oct., 81, aged 19 (from Wellington coll.); migrated to EXETER 31 Jan., 82, thence to BALLIOL, B.A. 88.

Greeven, Richard, born at Camberwell 1856; 2s. Hermann, arm. CHRIST CHURCH, matric. 16 Oct., 85, aged 19 (from Dulwich coll.), scholar 85, B.A. 86 (HONOURS :— 2 law 88); bar.-at-law, Inner Temple, 88, joint magistrate north-west provinces, India, 87.

Gregorie, Frank St. Barbe, born at Oxford 31 March, 1869; o.s George Wayne, com. R.N. CHRIST CHURCH, matric. 12 Oct., 88, aged 19, from Radley coll.

Gregory, Edward Denys Wyndl, born at Southampton 1875; 1s. Francis Maundy, M.A., cler. MARCON HALL, matric. 5 May, 92, aged 17.

Gregory, Herbert, born at Ardwick, co. Lanc., 25 Feb., 1861; 1s. Francis, gent. MAGDALEN, matric. 16 Oct., 80, aged 19 (from Owens college, Manchester), demy 80-5, B.A. 86; HONOURS :— 2 classical mods. 82, 2 classics 84, 1 history 85.

Gregory, Robert, M.A., CORPUS CHRISTI 46; dean of St. Paul's 91, D.D. by decree 21 March, 91. See *Al. Ox.* 2nd series, 561.

Gregson, rev. Francis Sitwell Knight, born at Low Lynn, Northumberland, 1865; 8s. Henry, arm. BRASENOSE, matric. 14 Oct., 84, aged 19 (from Durham gr. school), B.A. 87, M.A. 91; curate of Christ Church, Gateshead, 88.

Greig, Ronald Alister, born at Hong Kong 26 Jan., 1873; 3s. James, of Chislehurst, Kent, banker. UNIVERSITY COLL., matric. 15 Oct., 92, aged 19, from Highgate school.

Grenfell, Algernon George, born at Park Gate, Cheshire, 4 Nov., 1863; 1s. Algernon Sidney, cler. QUEEN'S, matric. 23 Oct., 82, aged 18 (from Repton, Marlborough and Clifton colls.), scholar 82, B.A. 86, M.A. 89; HONOURS :— 1 classical mods. 84, 2 classics 86.

Grenfell, Bernard Pyne, born at Birmingham 16 Dec., 1869; 1s. John Granville, a master at Clifton. QUEEN'S, matric. 20 Oct., 88, aged 18 (from Clifton coll.), scholar 88, B.A. 92; HONOURS :— 1 classical mods. 90, 1 classics 92.

Grenfell, Wilfred Thomason, born at Park Gate, Cheshire, 28 Feb., 1865; 2s. Algernon Sydney, cler. QUEEN'S, matric. 20 Oct., 88, aged 23 (from Marlborough coll. and London hospital), M.R.C.S. and L.R.C.P.

Gresham, rev. George Frederick Stanley, born in London, 1864; 1s. George, gent. ST. EDMUND HALL, matric. 23 Oct., 85, aged 21 (from King's college school, London), B.A. 89, M.A. 92 (HONOURS :— 2 theology 89); curate of St. Andrew, Bethnal Green, 89.

Gresson, Charles Richard Haygarth, born at Worthing, Sussex, Sept., 1869; 3s. John George, cler. HERTFORD, matric. 19 Oct., 88, aged 19, from Lancing coll.

Gresson, Francis Henry, born at Worthing, Sussex, 1868; 2s. John George, cler. ORIEL, matric. 2 Jan., 87, aged 18 (from Winchester), B.A. 92; in the Oxford eleven 88 and 89.

Grewing, Henry Johnstone, born at Sydenham July, 1873; 1s. Henry, foreign banker. CHRIST CHURCH, matric. 14 Oct., 92, aged 19, from Eton.

Grey, Alexander Harry, born at Embleton, Northumberland, 10 June, 1870; 3s. George Henry, arm. KEBLE, matric. 12 Oct., 89, aged 19, from Clifton coll.

Grey, Charles Edward, born at Bournemouth 16 Dec., 1866; 1s. Edward, arm. TRINITY, matric. 17 Oct., 85, aged 18 (from Harrow), B.A. 89 (HONOURS :— 3 classical mods 87); bar.-at-law, Lincoln's Inn, 92.

Grey, (sir) Edward (bart.), born in London 25 April, 1862; 1s. George Henry, arm. BALLIOL, matric. 21 Oct., 80, aged 18 (from Winchester); HONOURS : — 2 classical mods. 81, 3 law 84; M.P. Northumberland (Berwick-on-Tweed division) 85; under sec. foreign affairs 92.

Grey, Thomas Robinson, born at Gainford, co. Durham, 4 Nov., 1862; 2s. John, of The Parklands, Stonehouse, co. Glouc., arm. MAGDALEN, matric. 21 Jan., 82, aged 19 (from Eton), B.A. 85, M.A. 89; bar.-at-law, Inner Temple, 87.

Grey, William Edward, born at Hambledon, Bucks, 11 May, 1866; 6s. admiral the hon. George. TRINITY, matric. 11 Oct., 84, aged 18, from Bournemouth school.

Gribble, Francis Henry, born at Pilton, Devon, 15 July, 1862; 1s. Henry, banker. EXETER, matric. 1 Nov., 80, aged 18 (from Chatham House school, Ramsgate), scholar 80-4, B.A. 84; HONOURS :— 2 classical mods. 82, 1 classics 84.

Grier, John Charles, born in London 1864; 1s. William Magee, arm. WORCESTER, matric. 19 Oct., 82, aged 18.

Grierson, Douglas, born at Kensington 28 Feb., 1873; 4s. James, gen., deceased. NEW COLL., matric. 16 Oct., 91, aged 18, from Rugby.

Grierson, Herbert John Clifford, born at Lerwick in Shetland 1866; 2s. Andrew, arm. CHRIST CHURCH, matric. 11 Oct., 89, aged 23 (from Aberdeen university), exhibitioner 89; HONOURS:— 2 classical mods. 91.

Griess, Philip Henry Peters, born at Burton-on-Trent 29 July, 1871; 1s. John Peter, gen., deceased. NEW COLL., matric. 10 Oct., 90, aged 19 (from Epsom coll.); HONOURS:—2 classical mods. 92.

Griffin, George Griffin, M.A., student CHRIST CHURCH 48-61, where see.

Griffin, rev. John Parnell, born at Kemm, Somerset, 1 Nov., 1862; 2s. John, arm. MAGDALEN, matric. 15 Oct., 81, aged 18 (from Clifton coll.), B.A. 87, M.A. 86, student Inner Temple 84; curate of Rowbarton, Somerset, 90.

Griffith, Alexander, born at Stewardstown, co. Tyrone, 25 Jan., 1868; o.s. Alexander, cler. WADHAM, matric. 26 Oct., 86, aged 18 (from Tonbridge school), exhibitioner 86, B.A. 90; HONOURS:—2 classical mods. 88, 2 classics 90.

Griffith, Arthur Ernest, born at Llanrwst, co. Denbigh, July, 1863; 3s. John Robert, gent. KEBLE, matric. 17 Oct., 82, aged 19 (from Beaumaris school), B.A. 85 (HONOURS:—3 law 85); bar.-at-law, Inner Temple, 88.

Griffith, Arthur Troyte, born at Oxford 19 June, 1864; 1s. George, a master at Harrow. ORIEL, matric. 27 Oct., 83, aged 19, B.A. 87.

Griffith, rev. Charles Ashley, born at Bettws-y-coed, co. Carnarvon, Sept., 1861; 2s. Joseph William, cler. KEBLE, matric. 19 Oct., 80, aged 19 (from Magdalen coll. school), B.A. 84; curate of Limehouse St. Ann, London, 89.

Griffith, Clement William Haslewood, born at Oxford 1862; 2s. Samuel Young Naylor, cler, CORPUS CHRISTI, matric. 15 Feb., 83, aged 21, B.A. 86, M.A. 89; HONOURS:—3 classical mods. 84, 3 classics 86.

Griffith, Francis Llewellyn, born at Brighton 27 May, 1862; 6s. John, vicar of Sandridge, Herts. QUEEN'S, matric. 15 May, 80, aged 17 (from Sedbergh and Highgate schools), B.A. 84; HONOURS: —2 classical mods. 82.

Griffith, George Marshall, born at Eastbourne, Sussex, 18 Aug., 1866; 3s. Charles Marshall, Q.C., NEW COLL., matric. 16 Oct., 85, aged 19 (from Winchester), B.A. 88; HONOURS:—2 history 88.

Griffith, Llewellyn John Theophilus, born at Deal, Kent, 1864; y.s. Thomas Llewellyn, cler. UNIVERSITY COLL., matric. 13 Oct., 83, aged 19 (from Wellington coll.); HONOURS:—3 classical mods. 85.

Griffith, Thomas Henry, B.C.L., fellow NEW COLL. 48-64, where see page 213.

Griffith, Thomas Hugh, born at Putney 1859; 1s. Thomas, gent. NON-COLLEGIATE, matric. 15 Oct., 81, aged 22 (from Christ's hospital); migrated to BALLIOL 82, B.A. 85; HONOURS:—2 classical mods. 83, 3 classics 85.

Griffiths, Alban Lawrence, born at Llanelly, co. Brecon, 3 Dec., 1865; 1s. Arthur, cler. JESUS COLL., matric. 28 Oct., 85, aged 19 (from Christ's coll., Brecon), scholar 85, B.A. 89; HONOURS:— 3 classical mods. 87, 3 classics 89.

Griffiths, Albert Edward, born at Madras 2 Feb., 1871; 2s. John, lieut. Oxfordshire volunteers. NON-COLLEGIATE, matric. 17 Jan., 91, aged 19, from High Wycombe gr. school.

Griffiths, Charles Ernest, born at Maestcg, co. Glam, 21 Sept., 1873; 1s. John Thomas, B.D., vicar of Llanelwr. JESUS COLL., matric. 18 Oct., 92, aged 19, from Aberystwith gr. school and Christ's church coll., Brecon.

Griffiths, David Enoch, born at St. Dogmells, co. Pembroke, 26 March, 1872; o.s. Thomas. WORCESTER, matric. 22 Oct., 91, aged 19, from Oundle school.

Griffiths, rev. David Thomas, born at Kidwelly, co. Carmarthen, 17 Oct., 1868; 1s. David, gen. JESUS COLL., matric. 16 Oct., 88, aged 20, (from University coll. Aberystwith), scholar 89, B.A. 92 (HONOURS:—1 mathematical mods. 90, 1 mathematics 92); curate of St. Peter's, Carmarthen, 93.

Griffiths, John, M.A., fellow JESUS COLL. 63, where see.

Griffiths, rev. John, born at Llanfihangel, co. Cardigan, 1857; 1s. David, gent. NON-COLLEGIATE, matric. 18 Oct., 80, aged 23 (from the coll. Llandovery), migrated to ST. JOHN'S, B.A. 84, M.A. 87, (HONOURS:—3 theology 84); curate of Llandrillo-yn-Rhos with St. Paul, Colwyn Bay, North Wales, 86.

Griffiths, Maurice, born at Machynlleth, co. Montgomery, 20 June, 1863; 2s. John, gen. EXETER, matric. 21 Oct., 86, aged 23 (from University coll., Cardiff), B.A. 89; HONOURS:—3 theology 89.

Griffiths, Robert George, born at Birmingham 13 March, 1866; 2s. Francis Henry, gen., deceased. NON-COLLEGIATE, matric. 11 Oct., 90, aged 24, from K. Edward's school, Birmingham.

Griffiths, Trevor, born at Worcester 28 Feb., 1871; 3s. Frederick William, cler. WORCESTER, matric. 14 Oct., 89, aged 18, from Hereford cathedral school.

Griffiths, Walter Gould, born at Bristol 19 May, 1866; 1s. Walter William, gent. JESUS COLL., matric. 23 Oct., 85, aged 19 (from Bristol gr. school), B.A. 89, M.A. 92; HONOURS:—2 classical mods. 87, 2 classics 89.

Griffiths, William James, born at Port Elizabeth 20 April, 1868; 2s. Thomas 'Griff,' arm., deceased. HERTFORD, matric. 14 Oct., 90, aged 22, from Bowden coll., Cheshire, and St. Andrew's coll., Grahamstown.

Grimes, Leonard Avery, born at Toowoomba, Queensland, 31 May, 1869; 1s. James Watts, gen. WADHAM, matric. 19 Jan., 89, aged 19.

Grimley, Reginald Fearn, born at Mosely, co. Warwick, 24 April, 1870; 3s. John, arm. BALLIOL, matric. 17 Oct., 89, aged 19 (from K. Edward's high school, Birmingham); assist. to collector and magistrate Coimbatore, Madras C.S.

Grimshawe, Edmund Salisbury Vaughan, born at Apsley Guise, Beds, , 1863; 1s. Charles Livius, arm. EXETER, matric. 4 June, 81, aged 18, from Harrow.

Grindle, Edmund Samuel, M.A., QUEEN'S, where see page 184.

Grindle, Gilbert Edmund Augustine, born at Pokesdown, Hants, 28 May, 1869; 1s. Edward Samuel, arm. CORPUS CHRISTI, matric. 22 Oct., 87, aged 18 (from Kensington school), scholar 87, B.A. 91, fellow 91 (HONOURS:—1 classical mods. 89, 1 classics 91, English essay 90; passed for the Home C.S. 92.

Grindley, rev. Robert Dutton, born at Wandsworth, Surrey, 30 March, 1866; 2s. Robert Dutton, gent. TRINITY, matric. 17 Oct., 85, aged 19 (from Highgate school), B.A. 90, M.A. 92 (HONOURS:—2 classical mods. 87, 2 classics 89); curate of Monkwearmouth, co. Durham, 90.

Grindrod, rev. Francis Lloyd, born at Chester, 21 July, 1864; 1s. William, vicar of Alne, Yorks. LINCOLN, matric. 19 Jan., 84, aged 20 (from St. Peter's school, York), B.A. 87, M.A. 92; curate of Edgmond, Salop, 88.

Grindrod, George Herbert, born at Rochdale, co. Lane., 11 July, 1863; o.s. NON-COLLEGIATE, matric. 18 Oct., 87, aged 24 (from St. Mark's coll., Chelsea); migrated to NEW COLL., B.A. 90; HONOURS:—2 history 90.

Grindrod, William Harold, born at Chester Dec., 1865; 2s. William, cler. KEBLE, matric. 22 Oct., 85, aged 19 (from York school), B.A. 89; HONOURS: —3 history 88.

Grissell, Hartwell de la Garde, M.A., BRASENOSE, where see.

Griswold, Hervey de Witt, born at Dryden, U.S.A., 1860; 1s. Benjamin, gen. NON-COLLEGIATE, matric. 20 Oct., 88, aged 28 from Union coll., Schenectady, and Union theological seminary, New York city.

Gritten, Digby, born in London 30 Jan., 1863; 7s. Henry Frederick, of Brixton, gent. NON-COLLEGIATE, matric. 13 Jan., 83, aged 19 (from Elstree school), B.A. 92.

Gritten, William George Howard, born in London 1870; o.s. William, arm. BRASENOSE, matric. 14 Oct., 89, aged 19 (from Giggleswick and Manchester gr. schools), scholar 89; HONOURS:—2 classical mods. 91.

Grose, rev. Thomas Hodge, M.A., fellow QUEEN'S 70, where see page 174.

Grosvenor, Harry John, born at Ludlow, 1864; 1s. John, gent. CHRIST CHURCH, matric. 13 Oct., 82, aged 18 (from Shrewsbury school), exhibitioner 80-6; migrated to BALLIOL, B.A. 87.

Grosvenor, lord Henry George, born 23 June, 1861; 3s. Hugh Lupus, duke of Westminster. CHRIST CHURCH, matric. 21 May, 80, aged 18.

Grotrian, Harold Hunter, born at Hessle, Yorks, 12 June, 1871; 3s. Frederick Brent, M.P., etc. BRASENOSE, matric. 15 Oct., 90, aged 19, from the Charterhouse.

Grotrian, Herbert Brent, born at Hessle, Yorks, 29 March, 1870; 2s. Frederick Brent, M.P., etc. TRINITY, matric. 13 Oct., 88, aged 18 (from Rossall school), B.A. 92; HONOURS:—3 law 91, 3 civil law 92.

Grove, Henry, born at Tulse Hill, Surrey, 1863; 1s. Edward, arm. BRASENOSE, matric. 21 Jan., 82, aged 19, from Harrow.

Groves, Charles Nixon, born at Nottingham Feb., 1871; 1s. Charles Innocent, gen. KEBLE, matric. 12 Oct., 89, aged 18, from Bradfield coll.

Groves, Herbert Barton, born at Lincoln 30 Nov., 1871; 1s. Edward, gen. NEW COLL., matric. 10 Oct., 90, aged 19 (from Leeds gr. school), exhibitioner 90; HONOURS:—1 classical mods. 92.

Grubb, Lewis Henry, born at Clogheen, Ireland, 27 July, 1865; o.s. Henry Samuel, arm. TRINITY, matric. 22 Jan., 85, aged 19 (from Rugby), B.A. 88, M.A. 92.

Gruchy, George Le Maitre, born in Jersey 22 April, 1869; 1s. George, gen. WADHAM, matric. 13 Oct., 88, aged 19 (from Victoria coll., Jersey), B.A. 91.

Gruchy, rev. Sorel John, born at St. Heliers, Jersey, 1862; 1s. Sorel, gen. NON-COLLEGIATE, matric. 18 Oct., 80, aged 18, B.A. 84, M.A. 91; HONOURS: —2 classical mods. 82, 3 classics 84.

Grueber, Erwin, Hon. M.A. 83 reader in Roman law 81-93. See BALLIOL, page 69.

Grundy, Ernest Paul Richard Blackburne, born at Paignton, Devon, 6 Dec., 1873; 2s. Thomas Richard, M.A., cler. WADHAM, matric. 18 Oct., 92, aged 19, from St. Michael's coll. Lyme Regis.

Grundy, Frederick, born at Brecon 16 Jan., 1869; 4s. Frank, gen. JESUS COLL., matric. 16 Oct., 88, aged 19 (from Christ coll., Brecon), scholar 88; HONOURS:—3 classical mods. 90.

Grundy, George Beardoe, born at Wallasey, Cheshire, 1863; o.s. George Frederick, cler. BRASENOSE, matric. 21 April, 88, aged 27 (from Lichfield gr. school), B.A. 91; HONOURS:—2 classical mods. 90, 2 classics 91, geographical studentship 92.

Grut, Charles Frederick de Jersey, born at Greenouth, N.Z., 4 April, 1872; 1s. Alfred Charles, banker, deceased. EXETER, matric. 18 Oct., 92, aged 20, from Marlborough gr. school.

Gubbins, James Cornwallis, born at Upham, Hants, Feb., 1870; 2s. Richard Shard, cler. CHRIST CHURCH, matric. 11 Oct., 89, aged 19, from Winchester.

Guedalla, Florence Montefiore, born at Sydenham, Kent, 23 June, 1873; 1s. Joseph, solicitor. BALLIOL, matric. 18 Oct., 92, aged 19, from Rugby.

Guerrier, rev. William Joyson, born in London 1860; 1s. Henry John, gent. WORCESTER, matric. 27 Jan., 81, aged 21, B.A. 84 (HONOURS:—2 theology 84); curate of Oxford St. Clement 85.

Guest, rev. Edward Albert, born at Wem, Salop, 1865; 3s. John, cler. NON-COLLEGIATE, matric. 28 Jan., 84, aged 22 (from Tarporley gr. school); migrated to ST. EDMUND HALL, B.A. 87, M.A. 90; curate of Emanuel church, Paddington, 88.

Guille, rev. Hubert George de Carteret, born at Exeter 2 April, 1861; 3s. George, de Carteret, rector of Little Torrington, Devon. TRINITY, matric. 16 Oct., 80, aged 19 (from Cheltenham coll.), B.A. 84, M.A. 87 (HONOURS:—2 classical mods. 82, 3 classics 84); curate of Rampisham, Dorset, 85-7.

Guinness, Richard Noel, born at Stillorgan, co. Dublin, 22 Dec., 1870; 5s. Henry, arm. TRINITY, matric. 12 Oct., 89, aged 18 (from Uppingham school), B.A. 92; HONOURS:—3 history 92.

Gulley, Henry James, born at Horfield, co. Hereford, 1870; 4s. Henry Doddridge, cler. KEBLE, matric. 11 Oct., 90, aged 20, from King's school, Bristol.

Gully, James William Herschell, born in London 1869; 2s. William Court, Q.C. BALLIOL, matric. 19 Oct. 86, aged 19 (from Winchester), B.A. 90 (HONOURS:—3 classical mods. 88); bar.-at-law, Inner Temple, 92.

Gundry, Joseph, born at Bridport, Dorset, March 1868; 1s. Joseph Pearkes Fox, arm., deceased. HERTFORD, matric. 29 Oct., 87, aged 19.

Gunner, George Herbert, born at Bishops Waltham, Hants, 22 July, 1863; 7s. Charles James, solicitor, deceased. NEW COLL., matric. 14 Oct., 82, aged 19 (from Haileybury), B.A. 87, M.A. 92 (HONOURS: —3 classical mods. 84, 3 classics 86); bar.-at-law, Inner Temple, 90.

Gunnery, rev. Frederick Bernard, born in London Oct., 1866; 3s. Reginald, cler. CHRIST CHURCH, matric. 15 Oct., 86, aged 20, B.A. 90; curate of St. John Baptist, Moordown, Bournemouth 91.

Gunning, rev. Henry William Maude, born at Northampton 21 April, 1865; 4s. George William, arm. CHRIST CHURCH, matric. 18 May, 84, aged 19 (from Radley coll.), B.A. 88, M.A. 91; curate of Wigan, co. Lanc., 89.

Gunson, Herbert Edward, born at Leyton, Essex, 17 Aug., 1869; 1s. Edward Richard, gen. ST. EDMUND HALL, matric. 20 Jan., 91, aged 22, from St. Stephen's coll. Walthamstow, and King's coll.

Gunter, James Spencer St. Aubyn, born at Wetherby, Yorks, 1873; 2s. Robert, colonel in the army, M.P. MERTON, matric. 18 Oct., 92, from Eton.

Günther, Robert William Theodore, born at Surbiton, Surrey, 23 Aug., 1869; 1s. Albert Charles L. G., D. Med., F.R.S. MAGDALEN, matric. 16 Oct., 88, aged 19 (from University coll. school, London), demy 87, B.A. 92; HONOURS:—1 morphology 92, biological scholarship at Naples 93.

Gurney, Archer George Harptree, born at Wribbenhall, co. Worcester, 21 Feb., 1869; 2s. Augustus William, cler. WORCESTER, matric. 16 Oct., 88, aged 19 (from St. Michael coll., Tenbury), B.A. 91.

Gurney, Cyril, born in London March, 1868; 1s. Alfred, cler. CHRIST CHURCH, matric. 3 June, 87, aged 19 (from Winchester), B.A. 91; HONOURS:— 3 history 91.

Gurney, Edward Richmond, born at Wribbenhall, co. Worcester, 1868; 1s. Augustus William, cler. CHARSLEY'S HALL, matric. 2 Nov., 86, aged 18.

Gurney, Gerald, born in Paris 15 Feb., 1862; 1s. Archer Thompson, cler., deceased. MERTON, matric. 18 Oct., 81, aged 19; migrated to NEW INN HALL, B.A. 85 (BALLIOL 87), M.A. 89; HONOURS:—4 history 85.

Gurney, George Henry Goldsworthy, born at Uffington, Berks, 10 May, 1867; o.s. Henry, cler. WORCESTER, matric. 29 Jan., 86, aged 18 (from Bishop Stortford school), B.A. 88.

Gurney, William Hampden, born at Wraxall, Somerset, Jan., 1870; 2s. Alfred, cler. CHRIST CHURCH, matric. 1 May, 90, aged 20, from the Charterhouse.

Guthrie, David Charles, born in London 1861; 1s. James Alexander, arm. CHRIST CHURCH, matric. 12 Jan. 83, aged 21 (from Eton), M.P. South Northants 92.

Guthrie, William James, born at Edinburgh 1861; 2s. William, arm. BALLIOL, matric. 21 Oct., 80, aged 19 (from Glasgow university); selected candidate Indian civil service 80.

Guzman, Antonio Leocadio, born at Caracas, South America, 1870; 1s. Antonio. CHRIST CHURCH, matric. 18 Jan., 89, aged 18.

Guy, rev. Hugh, born at Walthamstow, Essex, 21 May, 1865; 6s. Frederick Barlow, cler. HERTFORD, matric. 14 Oct., 84, aged 19 (from Forest school), B.A. 87, M.A. 91 (HONOURS:—3 classical mods. 86); curate of St. John Evangelist, Bury St. Edmund's, 90.

Guy, rev. Ralph Courtenay, born at Walthamstow, Essex, 23 May, 1866; 7s. Frederick Barlow, cler. CORPUS CHRISTI, matric. 26 Oct., 85, aged 19 (from Forest school); scholar HERTFORD 85, B.A. 89, M.A. 92; HONOURS:—2 classical mods. 87, 3 classics 89.

Guyer, rev. Brett, born at Torquay, Devon, 21 April, 1864; 2s. James Brett, arm. TRINITY, matric. 11 Oct., 84, aged 20, B.A. 90, M.A. 91 (HONOURS:— 3 history 90); curate of St. John, Torquay, 90.

Gwilliam, George Henry, B.D., fellow HERTFORD 75, where see.

STONE ANIMAL, ROUEN CATHEDRAL.—*Pugin.*

Gwyn, Charles Jackson, born at Cardiff, co. Glamorgan, 1861; 2s. David, gent. PEMBROKE, matric. 26 Oct., 81, aged 20, B.A. 84, M.A. 88.

Gwyn, Walter John, born in London 11 Sept., 1856; 2s. George Boyce, gent. ST. MARY HALL, matric. 22 Oct., 85, aged 29, B.A. and M.A. 92.

Gwynn, rev. John, scholar TRINITY COLL., DUBLIN, 1848, B.A. 50, fellow 53-6, M.A. 51, B.D. 61, D.D. 80, (ad eundem 7 July 60, created D.C.L. 22 June 92), regius professor of divinity in the university of Dublin 88, warden of St. Columba's coll. 56-64, rector of Tullyaughnish 63-82, dean of Raphoe 73-82, dean of Derry and rector of Templemore, Derry, 82-3, etc. For list of work see *Crockford*; father of Stephen Lucius, next-named.

Gwynn, Stephen Lucius, born at St. Columb near Dublin, 13 Feb., 1864; 1s. John, dean of Raphoe. Columba coll., Dublin), B.A. 87; HONOURS:— 1 classical mods. 84, 1 classics 86.

Gwynn, William Boulton, born at Wem, Salop, 27 Sept., 1869; 2s. Samuel Hetton, surgeon, deceased. NON-COLLEGIATE, matric. 12 Oct., 89, aged 20, from Wem gr. school and Epsom coll.

Gwynne, (rev.) Andrew Betton, born at Whitchurch, Salop, Oct., 1861; 3s. Samuel Taylor, gent. ST. EDMUND HALL, matric. 25 Oct., 80, aged 19 (from Shrewsbury school), B.A. 85, M.A. 87; curate Richmond St. Matthias, Surrey, 87.

Gwynne, Henry Vaughan, born at Kilvey, co. Glamorgan, 12 Feb., 1869; 6s. Richard, gen. WORCESTER, matric. 22 Jan., 89, aged 20, from Swansea gr. school.

Gwynne, Reginald John, born in London 1863; 1s. James Eglinton Anderson, gent. PEMBROKE, matric. 27 Oct., 83, aged 20, from Lancing coll.

Gwyther, Edward Newill, born in London 8 Dec., 1873; 2s. Frederick George, banker. EXETER, matric. 18 Oct., 92, aged 18, from Rugby.

Gwyther, William Clements, born in London Sept., 1866; 1s. Frederick George, gen. KEBLE, matric. 20 Oct., 91, aged 25, from University coll. school, London.

Gygas, George, born at Maritz, Germany, 1869; 1s. George Charles, arm. NON-COLLEGIATE, matric. 21 Oct., 89 aged 20, from Wiesbaden, Bonn and Berlin schools.

STONE ANIMAL, ROUEN CATHEDRAL.—*Pugin*.

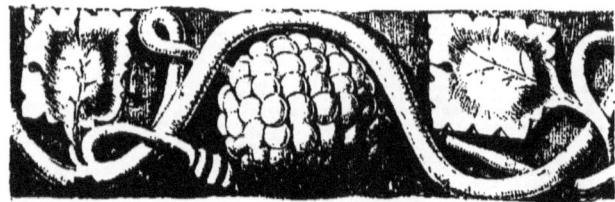

STONE ORNAMENT FROM BEDDINGTON CHURCH, SURREY.—*Pugin.*

H

Hack, Bertie Starmer, born at Leicester 29 March, 1872; 2s. Matthew, gen. CHRIST CHURCH, matric. 10 Oct., 90, aged 18, from Rugby.

Hacking, Alfred Joseph, born at Sheffield 1857; o.s. Thomas, gent. NON-COLLEGIATE, matric. 13 Oct., 83, aged 26; migrated to EXETER, B.A. 87; HONOURS :—4 law 87.

Hackney, Walter, born at Cottingham, Yorks, 1853; 4s. Nathan, gent. NON-COLLEGIATE, matric. 22 Jan., 81, aged 28, B.A. 86, M.A. 87.

Haddan, Arthur Francis, born in London 22 July, 1865; 1s. Thomas Henry, bar.-at-law, deceased. EXETER, matric. 18 Oct., 83, aged 18, from Winchester.

Hadden, Henry Alexander, born at Scarborough 1 Feb., 1864; 6s. Frederick John, gent. UNIVERSITY COLL., matric 13 Oct., 83, aged 19 (from Rugby), B.A. 83, M.A. 90; HONOURS :—4 history 87.

Hadley, Henry, born at Cheltenham 27 March, 1863; 1s. Henry, deputy inspector-gen. of military hospitals, NON-COLLEGIATE, matric. 17 Oct., 91, aged 28 (from Cheltenham coll.), lieut. 1st West India regt. 89-90.

Hadow, Frank Burness, born in London 24 Jan., 1874; 1s. John Lovell Gwatkin, rector of Melcombe Regis. TRINITY, matric. 15 Oct., 92, aged 18, from Repton school.

Hadow, Herbert Edgeumbe, born at South Cerney, co. Glouc., 2 June, 1872; 3s. William Elliot, vicar. NON-COLLEGIATE, matric. 11 Oct., 90, aged 18, from Malvern coll.

Hadow, William Henry, M.A., B.Mus., fellow WORCESTER 88, where see.

Hahn, Charles Theophilus, born at Wandsworth, Surrey, 1870; o.s. Theophilus Sigismund, gen. PEMBROKE, matric. 5 May, 88, aged 18, B.A. 92.

Hahn, Frederick Alexander, born at Zemipan, Mexico, 17 May, 1860; 2s. Frederick John, gent. EXETER, matric. 31 Jan., 82, aged 21 (from Rugby); bar.-at-law, Lincoln's Inn, 88.

Haig, Alfred Edward, born in London 3 June, 1866; 1s. Henry Alexander, arm. TRINITY, matric. 17 Oct., 85, aged 19 (from Winchester), lieut. Scottish Borderers.

Haig, Douglas, born at Wemyss, Fifeshire, 1861; 5s. John, arm. BRASENOSE, matric. 22 Oct., 80, aged 19 (from Clifton coll. and Limpsfield school); captain 91, and adjutant 7th (the Queen's own) Hussars 88.

Haigh, Arthur Elam, M.A., fellow HERTFORD 78-86, where see.

[259]

Haigh, Arthur Henry, born at Petersfield, Hants, Aug., 1864; 1s. Henry, cler. CHRIST CHURCH, matric. 25 May, 83, aged 18 (from Winchester and Owens coll., Manchester), B.A. 86; HONOURS :— 3 history 86.

Hailey, Hammett Reginald Clode, born at Newport Pagnell, Bucks, 1869; 1s. Hammett, D.Med. ST. JOHN'S, matric. 15 Oct., 87, aged 18 (from Merchant Taylors' school), scholar 91, B.A. 92; (HONOURS :—2 classical mods. 89, 2 classics 91); 1st selected candidate Indian c.s. 92.

Hailey, William Malcolm, born at Newport Pagnell, Bucks, 15 Feb., 1872; 3s. Hammett, D.Med. CORPUS CHRISTI, matric. 16 Oct., 90, aged 18 (from Merchant Taylors' school), scholar 90; HONOURS :— 1 classical mods. 92.

Haines, George Henry, born at Oxford 17 Aug., 1869; 3s. William, gent. MAGDALEN, matric. 16 Oct., 88; aged 19 (from Oxford high school), exhibitioner 88, B.A. 92; HONOURS :—2 mathematical mods. 90, 3 mathematics 92.

Haines, Harry Fowler, born at Gloucester 18 Oct., 1868; y.s. Herbert, cler., deceased. NON-COLLEGIATE, matric. 18 Jan., 90, aged 21, from Hutchin's school, Hobart.

Haines, James, born at Oxford 2 Jan., 1868; 4s. William, gent. KEBLE, matric. 19 Oct., 86, aged 18 (from Oxford high school), exhibitioner 86, B.A. 89; HONOURS :—2 history 89.

Haines, John Castle, born at Oxford 1865; 3s. William, gent. NON-COLLEGIATE, matric. 15 Dec., 85, aged 20, B.A. 89.

Haines, John Thomas Augustus, M.A., fellow UNIVERSITY COLL. 83-90, where see page 34.

Haines, rev. Percy Noel, born at Duntisbourne near Cirencester, 10 June, 1863; 7s. John Poole, arm. BRASENOSE, matric. 7 June, 84, aged 20 (from Cheltenham coll.), B.A. 88, M.A. 91; curate of Pewsey, Wilts, 89.

Haines, rev. Walter Charles, born at Oxford 1862; 2s. William, gent. NON-COLLEGIATE, matric. 17 May, 80, aged 18 (from Christ church cathedral school, chorister 72-8); B.A. 84, M.A. 87 (HONOURS :—3 history 84); curate of Bishop Stortford 85-7.

Haines, William Pritchett, born at Bellary, India, 3 June, 1871; 1s. Thomas, missionary, L.M.S. NON-COLLEGIATE, matric. 17 Oct., 91, aged 20, from Independent coll., Taunton.

Hainsselin, Montague Thomas, born at Devonport, Devon, 19 Nov., 1871; 4s. Thomas, gen., deceased. NON-COLLEGIATE, matric. 12 Oct., 89, aged 17, from Plymouth gr. school.

[260]

Hainsselin, Sydney, born at Devonport, Devon, 1867; 2s. Thomas, arm. CHARSLEY HALL, matric. 23 Jan., 90, aged 23.

Hair, Andrew Campbell, born at Bures, Suffolk, 5 May, 1867; 1s. James, gen. ST. EDMUND HALL, matric. 21 Jan., 87, aged 19 (from Woking school), B.A. 89.

Halcomb, Guy Worthington, born at North Adelaide, Australia, 9 July, 1870; 1s. Frederick, clerk of Parliaments. BRASENOSE, matric. 2 May, 90, aged 19, from Adelaide school.

Haldane, Henry Chicheley, born at Edinburgh 10 Aug., 1872; 3s. James, accountant. BRASENOSE, matric. 15 Oct., 90, aged 18, from the Charterhouse.

Haldane, James Brodrick Chinnery, born in Edinburgh 24 July, 1868; 1s. James Robert Alexander, bishop of Argyll and the Isles. CHRIST CHURCH, matric. 12 Oct., 88, aged 20 (from Loretto school), B.A. 92; HONOURS :—3 history 92.

Haldane, John Scott, B.Med. Edinb., Hon M.A. Oxon. 14 March, 1893, assist. physiological department University museum.

Haldane, Patrick Vernon Chinnery, born in Edinburgh Feb., 1870; 2s. James Robert Alexander, bishop of Argyll and the Isles. PEMBROKE, matric. 25 Oct., 90, aged 20, from Loretto school.

Haldinstein, Henry Hyman, born at Norwich 1863; 3s. Philip Victor, gent, BALLIOL, matric. 18 Oct., 81, aged 18 (from Norwich gr. school), B.A. 85, M.A. 89 (HONOURS :—3 classical mods. 82, 3 history 85); bar.-at-law, Inner Temple, 86.

Hale, David, born at Bath 1862; 1s. David, arm. EXETER, matric. 15 May, 80, aged 18 (from Sydney coll., Bath), B.A. 83.

Hale, Herbert Percy, born at Michael Troy, co. Monmouth, 1868; 1s. James Evans, gen. ST. EDMUND HALL, matric. 20 Jan. 91, aged 23.

Hale, James Rashleigh, born at Rusthall, Kent 1874; 1s. James Charles, cler. KEBLE, matric 15 Oct., 92, aged 18, from the Charterhouse.

Hales, Charles Lawrence, born in London April, 1873; 2s. John Arthur, solicitor. UNIVERSITY COLL., matric. 22 Oct., 92, aged 19, from St. Paul's school.

Hales, Herbert Marvielle Atherstone, born at Heywood, co. Lanc., May, 1870; 2s. William Atherstone, cler. KEBLE, matric. 13 Oct., 88, aged 18 (from Godolphin school), passed for the army.

Hales, James Elton, born at Brighton 23 July, 1872; 1s. Richard Cox, cler. UNIVERSITY COLL., matric. 17 Oct., 91, aged 19 (from Wellington coll.), scholar 91.

Halford, rev. George Douglass, born in London June, 1865; 3s. Edward, D.Med. KEBLE, matric. 14 Oct., 84, aged 19 (from Felsted school), B.A. 88 (HONOURS :—3 theology 88); curate of St. Peter, Jarrow-on-Tyne, 90.

Hall, Alexander Nelson, born at Dunslew, Oxon, 25 July, 1865; 1s. Alexander William, arm. ORIEL, matric. 8 Dec., 84, aged 19, from the Charterhouse.

Hall, Alfred Daniel, born at Rochdale, co. Lanc., 22 June, 1864; 1s. Edwin, gent. BALLIOL, matric. 18 Oct., 81, aged 17 (from Manchester gr. school), scholar 80-5, B.A. and M.A. 88; HONOURS :—1 natural science 84.

Hall, Bertie Ryman Ryman, born at Oxford 6 May, 1874; o.s. Edwin Alder R.-H., art publisher. ST. JOHN's, matric. 15 Oct., 92, aged 18, from Magdalen coll. school.

Hall, Bertram Alexander, born at Surat, E. Indies, 10 Nov., 1871; 1s. Alexander Charles, arm. CHRIST CHURCH, matric. 6 June, 90, aged 18, from Cheltenham coll.

Hall, rev. Cecil Gallopine, born at East Carlton, Notts, 13 May, 1868; 4s. Thomas Owen, cler. TRINITY, matric. 15 Oct., 87, aged 19 (from Rossall school), scholar 86, B.A. 91; HONOURS :—1 classical mods. 89, 2 classics 91.

Hall, Charles Oswin, born at Tynemouth, Northumbd., 4 Oct., 1864; 1s. James, arm. MAGDALEN, matric. 19 Oct., 83, aged 19 (from Eton), B.A. 87.

Hall, Douglas Bernard, born at Wavertree, co. Lanc., 1867; 4s. Bernard, arm. CHRIST CHURCH, matric. 15 Oct., 86, aged 19, from the Charterhouse.

Hall, rev. Edward Gage, born at Egham, Surrey, 1869; 2s. Frederick, cler. BRASENOSE, matric. 16 Oct., 88, aged 19 (from St. Edward's school, Summertown), B.A. 91; HONOURS :—3 theology 91.

Hall, Edward George, born at Coln St. Denis, co. Glouc., 1866; 2s. Edward Duncan, cler. KEBLE, matric. 11 Oct., 90, aged 24 (from Marlborough coll.); HONOURS :—2 classical mods. 92.

Hall, rev. Francis Henry, M.A., fellow ORIEL 73, where see page 150.

Hall, Frederick William, born in London 3 Dec., 1868; 1s. William, gent. TRINITY, matric. 16 Oct., 86, aged 18 (from St. Paul's school), scholar 85, B.A. 90; HONOURS :—Greek verse 87, accessit Craven scholarship 87, Greek prose 88, 1 classical mods. 88, 1 classics 90.

Hall, rev. George Mellish James, born at Merstham, Surrey, 1848; o.s. Charles, gent. NON-COLLEGIATE, matric. 13 Oct., 83, aged 35 (from city of London school and London coll. of divinity 69); migrated to EXETER 11 Oct., 84, B.A. 87, M.A. 90 (HONOURS :—4 classics 87); held various curacies 71-88, vicar of Pishill, Oxon, 88.

Hall, George William Louis Marshall, born in London 1863; 3s. Marshall, gent. NON-COLLEGIATE, matric. 11 Feb., 82, aged 19.

Hall, rev. Gilbert Montague, born at Cambridge 1868; 2s. William Crabbe, gen. ST. JOHN's, matric. 15 Oct., 87, aged 19 (from Felsted school), B.A. 91; HONOURS :—3 theology 91.

Hall, Harry Reginald Holland, born at Hornsey, Middx., 30 Nov., 1873; o.s. Sydney Prior, artist. ST. JOHN's, matric. 22 Oct., 91, aged 18 (from Merchant Taylors' school), scholar 91.

Hall, Harry Walter Winsloe, born at Secunderabad, 14 Jan., 1869; 4s. Louis Frederick, major-gen. late B.A. MAGDALEN, matric. 16 Oct., 88, aged 19 from Lancing coll.), academical clerk 91, B.A. 88.

Hall, rev. Henry Robert, born at Oxford 18 Nov., 1861; 2s. Henry, gent. NON-COLLEGIATE, matric. 15 Oct., 81, aged 19 (from the Central school, Oxford); migrated to PEMBROKE, B.A. 85, M.A. 90; sub-librarian Radcliffe library 86-90; curate of St. Peter-le-Bailey, Oxford, 86; and assistant master Oxford high school 90.

Hall, Henry William, born at Coln St. Denis, co. Glouc. 28 Feb., 1865; 1s. Edward Duncan, cler. HERTFORD, matric. 14 Oct., 84, aged 19, B.A. 88, M.A. 91; HONOURS :—3 classical mods. 86, 3 classics 88.

Hall, Hugh, M.A., MERTON, where see page 100.

Hall, Hugh Fergie, born at Liverpool 27 June, 1832; 1s. Charlton Robert, of Tan-y-Bryn, co. Carnarvon, gent. NON-COLLEGIATE, matric. 15 Oct., 92, aged 60, from Royal institution, Liverpool.

Hall, James, born at Cambridge Sept., 1870; y.s. George, gen. NON-COLLEGIATE, matric. 12 Oct., 89, aged 19, from Blackheath school.

Hall, John Dryden, born at Christ Church, New Zealand, 1865; 2s. sir John, knight. ST. JOHN's, matric. 11 Oct., 84, aged 19, B.A. 89; bar.-at-law, Inner Temple, 89; brother of Wilfred.

Hall, John Felix, born at Liverpool 1845; 3s. Charlton Robert, gent. NON-COLLEGIATE, matric. 4 June, 81, aged 36, from Liverpool institute.

Hall, rev. Joseph, born at Diddulph Moor, co. Glouc., 13 Feb., 1863; 3s. Joshua, gent. JESUS COLL., matric. 18 Oct., 82, aged 19 (from Brecon coll.), B.A. 86 (HONOURS :—2 classical mods. 84, 3 classics 86); curate of Llandenny, co. Mon., 89.

Hall, Mildmay Francis, born at Navenby, co. Lincoln, 11 July, 1866; 4s. Charles, cler. TRINITY, matric. 15 Oct., 87, aged 21 (from Perse school, Cambridge), B.A. 91; HONOURS :—3 history 90.

Hall, Thomas Aubrey Chappé, born at Woodley, Ruddington, Notts, 16 June, 1873; 1s. John Hall, D. Med., deceased. BRASENOSE, matric. 21 Oct., 92, aged 19, from Leamington coll. and Tonbridge school.

Hall, Walter Clarke, born at Hanley, co. Stafford, Oct., 1863; y.s. William, gent. CHRIST CHURCH, matric. 16 Jan., 85, aged 22, from Liverpool institute.

Hall, Wilfred, born at Christ Church, New Zealand, June, 1864; 1s. sir John, knight. KEBLE, matric. 16 Oct., 83, aged 19; B.A. 87; HONOURS :—4 history 87; brother of John D.

Hall, William, born in Edinburgh 11 Dec., 1872; o.s. Peter, merchant. PEMBROKE, matric. 28 Oct., 92, aged 19, from Rugby.

Hall, William Clarke, born at Durham May, 1866; 1s. William, cler. CHRIST CHURCH, matric. 16 Oct., 85, aged 19 from Folkestone school), B.A. 87 (HONOURS :—2 history 88); bar.-at-law, Gray's Inn, 89.

Hall, William Edward Scott-, born in London 11 Aug., 1863; 7s. Samuel, arm. ST. MARY HALL, matric. 18 May, 89, aged 25.

Hallack, Arthur, born at Port Elizabeth, Cape of Good Hope, Jan. Sept., 1868; o.s. George, gen. NON-COLLEGIATE, matric. 11 Oct., 90, aged 22, from South African coll., Cape Town.

Hallam, rev. John Matthew, born at Oxford 4 May, 1867; o.s. John Winfield, architect. EXETER, matric. 21 Oct., 86, aged 19 (from Magdalen coll. school), scholar 86, B.A. 90 (HONOURS :—2 classical mods. 88, 3 classics 90, 2 theology 91); curate of Upton, Bucks, 91.

Hallard, James Henry, born at Edinburgh 1861; 2s. Frederick, gent. BALLIOL, matric. 18 Oct., 81, aged 20 (from Edinburgh university), B.A. 84, M.A. 89; HONOURS :—2 classical mods. 83.

Hallett, Cecil Walter Charles, born at Ryde, I.W., 5 Nov., 1868; o.s. Walter Lecky, late a captain Indian army, deceased. MAGDALEN, matric. 22 Oct., 87, aged 18 (from Cheltenham coll.), demy 87, B.A. 91; HONOURS :—2 classical mods. 89, 3 classics 91.

Hallett, Cyril, born in London 1 May, 1864; 6s. James Alfred, gent. ORIEL, matric. 27 Oct., 83, aged 19 (from Westminster school), B.A. 86, M.A. 90.

Hallifax, Arthur George, born at Darjeeling, Bengal, 1869; 4s. Benjamin, tea-planter. BALLIOL, matric. 19 Oct., 87, aged 18 (from Tiverton school), B.A. 90 (HONOURS :—2 Indian languages 90); assist. magistrate and collector Bengal.

Hallifax, Charles Joseph, born at Darjeeling, Bengal, 1867; 3s. Benjamin, tea-planter. BALLIOL, matric. 24 Oct., 85, aged 18 (from Tiverton school), scholar 85, B.A. 88 (HONOURS :—1 Indian languages 88); assist. commissioner Punjab.

Hallifax, Edwin Richard, born at Darjeeling, Bengal, 1874; 7s. Benjamin, tea-planter. BALLIOL, matric. 18 Oct., 92, aged 18 (from Tiverton school), Blundell scholar 91.

Hallifax, Henry Francis, born at Moonda Kotee, Darjeeling, Bengal, 19 Sept., 1872; 6s. Benjamin, tea-planter. BALLIOL, matric. 20 Oct., 91, aged 19 (from Tiverton school), scholar 91; selected candidate Indian civil service 91.

Hallowes, rev. Brabazon Chambre, born at Mold, Flints, April, 1861; 3s. Brabazon, of Glapwell Hall, co. Derby, cler. EXETER, matric. 28 Jan., 81, aged 19 (from Haileybury), B.A. 86, M.A. 87; curate of H. T., Stroud, 87-8.

Hallowes, Walter Haffenden, born at Futtesgurh 3 June, 1873; 3s. William, late colonel 85th L.I., deceased. UNIVERSITY COLL., matric. 15 Oct., 92, aged 19, from Wellington coll.

Hallward, John, born at Frittenden, Kent, 21 Feb., 1870; 2s. Thomas William Onslow, cler. BRASENOSE, matric. 14 Oct., 89, aged 19 (from Winchester); exhibitioner 89, HONOURS :—2 classical mods. 91.

Hallward, Lancelot William, born in London 4 July, 1867; 3s. John Leslie, cler. ORIEL, matric. 19 Oct., 86, aged 19 (from Haileybury), B.A. 89 (HONOURS :—2 classical mods. 88); curate of Great Yarmouth 91.

Halsey, Frederick, born in London 29 Nov., 1870; 3s. Thomas Frederick, of Great Gaddesden, Herts, M.P. MAGDALEN, matric. 20 Jan., 90, aged 19 (from Eton); HONOURS :—3 classical mods. 91.

Halsey, Walter Johnston, born in London 1 June, 1868; 1s. Thomas Frederick, of Great Gaddesden, Herts, M.P. MAGDALEN, matric. 22 Oct., 87, aged 19 (from Eton), B.A. 91; HONOURS :—3 classical mods. 91, 2 law 91.

Hamer, Charles John, born in St. George's Hanover Square, Middx., 1857; 2s. John Edward Bridges, gen. TURRELL'S HALL, matric. 24 April, 91, aged 34.

Hamersley, Herbert, born at Nuffield, Oxon, 17 Sept., 1869; 2s. Arthur, cler., deceased. MAGDALEN, matric. 16 Oct., 88, aged 19 (from Sherborne gr. school), B.A. 92; HONOURS :—3 classical mods. 90, 4 history 92.

Hamerton, rev. Laurence Collingwood, born at Warwick 30 Jan., 1867; 1s. Samuel Collingwood, cler., deceased. MAGDALEN, matric. 21 Oct., 86, aged 19 (from Marlborough coll.), B.A. 89; curate of Highworth with Sevenhampton, Wilts, 91.

Hamerton, rev. Thomas Johnson, born at Londonderry, Ireland, 1846; 2s. William Henry, gent., ST. ALBAN HALL, matric. 4 June, 80, aged 40; migrated to NEW INN HALL (Balliol) 87; curate of St. Peter, Hunslet Moor, Leeds, 75-7, and of St. Agnes, Burmantofts, Leeds, 77-82, vicar of St. Alban, Leeds, 82.

Hamerton, William Frederic Mountgarrett, born at Stalybridge, co. Lanc., 11 July, 1872; 1s. Thomas Johnson, vicar of St. Alban, Leeds. ST. EDMUND HALL, matric. 20 Oct., 92, aged 20, from Leeds gr. school.

Hamilton, Alexander Chetwood, M.A., UNIVERSITY COLL., where see page 36.

Hamilton, Andrew, born at Edinburgh 18 March, 1870; 1s. James, merchant. NON-COLLEGIATE, matric. 17 Oct., 91, aged 21, from Watson's coll., Edinburgh.

Hamilton, Archibald Robert, born at Hastings 7 Aug., 1869; o.s. Archibald Robert, vicar of Greenham, Hants. KEBLE, matric. 12 Oct., 88, aged 19 (from Winchester); scholar 87; HONOURS :—3 mathematical mods. 90.

Hamilton, Charles Robert, born Aug., 1867; 1s. Charles, bishop of Quebec. KEBLE, matric. 22 Oct., 85, aged 18 (from Lennoxville school and Bishops coll. school, Quebec), B.A. 88; HONOURS :—2 history 88.

Hamilton, Edmund Hardy, born at Holywood, co. Down, 1 April, 1863; 4s. William Hardy, gent. LINCOLN, matric. 23 Oct., 82, aged 19 (from Royal school, Armagh), B.A. 85.

Hamilton, Edward Montague, born in Rosaria in the Argentine Republic July, 1870; 1s. Walter Adolphus, cler. KEBLE, matric. 12 Oct., 89, aged 19, from King's school, Chester.

Hamilton, Francis Sumner, born at Manchester 1865; 3s. Andrew, gent. BALLIOL, matric. 16 Oct., 83, aged 18 (from Manchester gr. school); assist. magistrate and collector, Bengal.

Hamilton, Gawayne Baldwin, born at Combe St. Nicholas, Somerset, 20 Aug., 1861; o.s. Hans, cler. BALLIOL, matric. 21 Oct., 80, aged 19 (from Winchester), B.A. 86 (HONOURS :—2 classical mods. 82, 2 classics 84); bar.-at-law, Inner Temple, 86.

Hamilton, George Francis Clements, born at Eglingham, Northumberland, 24 March, 1870; 2s. George Hans, archdeacon of Northumberland, D.D. TRINITY, matric. 12 Oct., 89, aged 19 (from the Charterhouse); HONOURS :— 2 classical mods. 91.

Hamilton, John Andrew, M.A., fellow MAGDALEN 82-9, where see.

Hamilton, Robert Clifton, born at Bath 1872; 5s. William Harding, gen. KEBLE, matric. 20 Oct., 91, aged 19 (from Christ's hospital), scholar 91.

Hamilton, Sidney Graves, M.A., fellow HERTFORD 78, where see.

Hamilton, rev. Thomas, born at Manchester 1866; 1s. Thomas, gent. NON-COLLEGIATE, matric. 23 Jan., 86, aged 20 (from city of London school), exhibitioner of EXETER 88, B.A. 89, M.A. 92 (HONOURS :—4 theology 89) ; curate of St. German Roath, co. Glamorgan, 90.

Hamilton, William, born in the East Indies 4 Dec., 1868; 1s. William, gent. WORCESTER, matric. 22 Jan., 89, aged 20, from Newton Abbot coll.

Hamilton, rev. William Richard Cecil, born at Monk Hopton, Salop, 14 June, 1868; 3s. John James, esq. MERTON, matric. 22 Oct., 87, aged 19 (from Dulwich coll.), B.A. 91 (HONOURS :—3 classical mods. 89, 4 classics 91); curate of St. Nicholas, Warwick.

Hamilton, William Stirling, born at Edinburgh 7 July, 1869; 1s. Hubert, advocate. MAGDALEN, matric. 16 Oct., 88, aged 19 (from Winchester), demy 88, M.A. 92; (HONOURS :—2 classical mods. 90, 2 classics 92); selected candidate (and) Indian civil service 92.

Hamlyn, Clarence Adolphus, born in London 13 April, 1861; 3s. Lesoufe, arm. ST. MARY HALL, matric. 25 April, 87, aged 26; bar.-at-law, Middle Temple, 87.

Hammans, Henry Christopher, born at Oxford Feb. 1864 ; o.s. Henry, gent. KEBLE, matric. 17 Jan., 83, aged 18 (from Honiton school), B.A. 86, M.A. 90; HONOURS :—2 classical mods. 84, 2 classics 86.

Hammick, Stephen Frederick, born at York-town, Surrey, 2 Feb., 1871; 1s. St. Vincent Alexander, bart. BRASENOSE, matric. 23 Jan., 91, aged 18 (from Marlborough coll.), passed into Sandhurst 92.

Hammond, Anthony, born at Priston near Bath, Nov., 1864 ; 1s. Henry Wansley, arm. KEBLE, matric. 14 Oct., 84, aged 19 (from Lancing coll.), B.A. 87; HONOURS :—2 classical mods. 86.

Hammond, Charles Edward, M.A. fellow EXETER 59-73, where see page 128.

Hammond, Egbert Laurie Lucas, born at Ipswich, Suffolk, 12 Jan., 1873; 2s. Joseph, canon of Truro. KEBLE, matric. 15 Oct., 92, aged 19, from Newton Abbot coll.

Hammond, George Amedée, born in London 1865; 1s. George Hutchinson, arm. BRASENOSE, matric. 14 Oct., 84, aged 19 (from Eton), B.A. 88 ; HONOURS :—2 history 88.

Hammond, Henry Edward Denison, born at Priston, Somerset, 26 Nov., 1866; 2s. Henry, arm. CORPUS CHRISTI, matric. 26 Oct., 85, aged 18 (from Lancing coll.), scholar 85, B.A. 92 ; HONOURS :—2 classical mods. 87, 3 classics 89.

Hammond, John Lawrence Le Breton, born at Drightlington, Yorks, 18 July, 1872 ; 2s. Vavasour Fitzhammond, cler. ST. JOHN'S, matric. 17 Oct., 91, aged 19 (from Bradford school), scholar 90.

Hammond, William Remington, born at Kensington 1869 ; 2s. George Hutchinson, arm. BRASENOSE, matric. 16 Oct., 88, aged 19, from Eton.

Hampden, rev. Alfred Bertie Hobart-, born at Ahmednuggar 9 July, 1860 ; 2s. hon. George Augustus, Indian judge. LINCOLN, matric. 22 Jan., 80, aged 19 (from Clifton coll.), B.A. 83, M.A. 87 (HONOURS :—3 classical mods. 81, 4 history 83); curate of Leytonstone, Essex, 90 ; twin with the next.

Hampden, Edward Hampden Hobart-, born at Ahmednuggar 9 July, 1860 ; 2s. hon. George Augustus, Indian judge. LINCOLN, matric. 22 Jan., 80, aged 19 (from Clifton coll.), scholar 79-83, B.A. 83, M.A. 87 (HONOURS :—3 classical mods. 81, 3 classics 83) ; died 24 Oct., 87 ; twin brother of the last-named.

Hampden, Ernest Miles Hobart-, born 21 Nov., 1864 ; 5s. hon. George Augustus, Indian judge. BRASENOSE, matric. 22 Oct., 83, aged 18 (from Clifton coll.), scholar 83-6, B.A. 88 ; HONOURS :—2 classical mods. 85.

Hampshire, Harry, born at South Ossett, Yorks, 25 Dec., 1873 ; o.s. Henry, esq. HERTFORD, matric. 22 Oct., 92, aged 18 (from St. Oswald's coll., Ellesmere), scholar 91.

Hampson, Edward James, born at Manchester 1864 ; 2s. James, gent. EXETER, matric. 18 Oct., 83, aged 19 (from Radley coll.), B.A. 87, M.A. 92.

Hampson, Henry Christian, born at Rusholme, co. Lanc., 27 Feb., 1872 ; 7s. Francis, arm. BRASENOSE, matric. 15 Oct., 90, aged 18 (from Manchester gr. school), scholar 90; HONOURS :—2 classical mods. 92.

Hampson, John Nicholl, born at Stubton, co. Lincoln, 17 Nov., 1866 ; 4s. William Seymour, cler. KEBLE, matric. 19 Oct., 86, aged 19 (from Haileybury), B.A. 90 (HONOURS :—4 history 90) ; brother of Thomas P.

Hampson, rev. Thomas Philip, born at Stubton, co. Lincoln, 6 April, 1864 ; 3s. William Seymour, cler. KEBLE, matric. 27 Jan., 81, aged 18 (from Winchester), B.A. 84, M.A. 87 ; curate of Clapham, Surrey, 86.

Hanbury, Anthony Ashley, born in London 4 Jan., 1861 ; 3s. Robert, gent. EXETER, matric. 2 Jan., 87, aged 19, from Eton.

Hanbury, Arthur Davenport, born at Scarborough 7 Oct., 1867 ; 1s. hon. Arthur Allan Bateman, cler. CHRIST CHURCH, matric. 16 Oct., 85, aged 18 (from Winchester), B.A. 89.

Hancock, Ernest Albert, born in London 1863 ; 3s. John, cler. KEBLE, matric. 17 March, 83, aged 20.

Hancock, Ernest Albert, born at Appleton, Berks, 1866; 2s. Alfred William, gent. KEBLE, matric, 17 March, 84, aged 18.

Handcock, hon. Thomas Albert Edward, born at Athlone, Ireland, 26 March, 1865 ; 1s. Richard, baron Castlemaine. CHRIST CHURCH, matric. 16 Oct., 81, aged 18, B.A. 85.

Hankey, Arthur, born at Chittagong, East Indies, 12 Sept., 1871 ; o.s. Herbert, B.C.S. NEW COLL., matric. 10 Oct., 90, aged 17 (from Winchester); HONOURS :—3 classical mods. 92.

Hankey, Norman Frederick, born in London 27 Nov., 1865 ; 1s. Frederick Alers, banker, M.P. deceased. MAGDALEN, matric. 16 Oct., 84, aged 18 (from Sherborne coll.), exhibitioner 84, B.A. 89 ; HONOURS :—2 classical mods. 86, 2 history 88.

Hankey, Spencer Taverner, born at Lyne, Surrey, 30 April, 1870; 2s. Frederick Alers, banker, M.P. deceased. MAGDALEN, matric. 14 Oct., 89, aged 19, Wellington coll.

Hankin, Julian de Kestel, born at Southampton 16 Sept., 1861; 1s. Charles Wright, arm. UNIVERSITY COLL., matric. 16 Oct., 80, aged 19 (from Highgate school), scholar 80-2; HONOURS:—3 classical mods. 82.

Hankin, St. John Emile Clavering, born at Southampton 25 Sept., 1869; 3s. Charles Wright, gen. MERTON, matric. 21 Oct., 86, aged 17 (from Malvern coll.), postmaster 86, B.A. 90; HONOURS: —2 classical mods. 88, 2 classics 90.

Hankins, Richard Frederick, born in London 17 May, 1867; o.s. Richard, gent. ST. JOHN'S, matric. 17 Oct., 85, aged 18 (from Highgate school), scholar 85, B.A. 89; HONOURS:—3 classical mods. 87, 3 history 90.

Hanmer, Wyndham Charles Henry, born at Woburn, Beds, 17 Sept., 1867; 1s. Edward Francis, bart. CHRIST CHURCH, matric. 24 April, 88, aged 20, from Eton.

Hannay, Robert Kerr, born at Glasgow 31 Dec., 1867; 1s. Thomas, of Bridge-of-Allan, N.B., gen. UNIVERSITY COLL., matric. 12 Oct., 89, aged 21 (from Glasgow university); HONOURS:—2 classical mods. 91.

Hannen, right hon. sir James, lord of appeal 91, and life peer as baron Hannen, of Burdock, Sussex; created D.C.L. 20 June 86 (1s. James, of Dulwich, Surrey), born 1821; educated at St. Paul's school and Heidelberg university; bar.-at-law, Middle Temple, 48, bencher 78, serjeant-at-law 68, and knighted 14 May, 68, Justice court of Queen's bench 68-72, P.C. 72, judge of probate court 72-5, president of the probate divorce and admiralty division of high court of judicature 75, ex-officio member of court of appeal 81-91, contested Shoreham 65. See Foster's *Men at the Bar*.

Hanning, rev. Rowland Foster, born at Maidenhead, Berks, 1863; 3s. James, arm. CHRIST CHURCH, matric. 25 May, 83, aged 19 (educated at Rome, B.A. 87, M.A. 91; curate of Southborough, Kent, 90.

Hanrott, Charles James, born at Abergavenny, co. Monmouth, 19 April, 1870; 1s. William Wilfrid, gen. QUEEN'S, matric. 22 Oct., 89, aged 19 (from Lampeter and Carmarthen gr. school), bible clerk 89; HONOURS:—2 classical mods. 91.

Hansard, Arnold Greaves, born in London 1867; 2s. Septimus Cox, cler. UNIVERSITY COLL., matric. 17 Oct., 85, aged 18, B.A. 89; HONOURS:—3 mathematical mods. 86, 3 history 89.

Hansard, Hugh Hasen, born in Colombo 1869; 3s. Arthur, arm. ORIEL, matric. 20 Oct., 88, aged 19 (from Malvern coll.), B.A. 91; HONOURS:—4 law 91.

Hansard, Richard Massey, born in Colombo, Ceylon, 16 Sept., 1867; 1s. Arthur, gen. ORIEL, matric. 21 Jan., 87, aged 19 (from Malvern coll.), B.A. 91.

Hansell, rev. Arthur Lloyd, born at Thorpe near Norwich, 21 June, 1865; 4s. Peter Edward, solicitor. MAGDALEN, matric. 16 Oct., 84, aged 19 (from the Charterhouse), B.A. 88, M.A. 92; curate of Wantage, Berks, 91.

Hansell, Henry Peter, born at Thorpe, near Norwich, 2 Nov., 1863; 3s. Peter Edward, architect. MAGDALEN, matric. 21 Oct., 82, aged 18 (from Malvern coll.), B.A. 85, M.A. 90; HONOURS:—2 history 85.

Hansell, Percy John, born at New Cross, Surrey, 1870; o.s. John Bell, cler. CHRIST CHURCH, matric. 11 Oct., 89, aged 19 (from Croydon school), exhibitioner 88; HONOURS:—2 mathematical mods. 91.

Hansell, Peter, M.A., fellow UNIVERSITY COLL. 29-36, where see page 31.

Hanson, Eric Dorville, born at Clapham, Surrey, 1860; 8s. Joseph, gent. NON-COLLEGIATE, matric. 15 Oct., 81, aged 21 (from Dulwich coll. and St. Augustine coll., Canterbury); exhibitioner CHRIST CHURCH 84-6, B.A. 85, M.A. 88; HONOURS: —2 theology 85.

Hanson, Philip Herbert, born at Bradford, Yorks, 18 Sept., 1871; 1s. Charles Henry, gen. BALLIOL, matric. 14 Oct., 90, aged 19 (from high school Edinburgh, and Edinburgh university), exhibitioner 89; HONOURS:—1 classical mods. 92, Greek prose 92.

Harcourt, Augustus George Vernon, M.A., a senior student CHRIST CHURCH 59, where see.

Harcourt, Henry, born at Forest Gate, Essex, 20 Sept., 1873; 3s. Robert Frederick Muller, B.A. Cambridge, and lecturer King's coll., London. PEMBROKE, matric. 28 Oct., 92, aged 19 (from Merchant Taylors' school), scholar 92.

Harcourt, Leveson William Vernon-, born at Monmouth 15 Oct., 1871; 1s. Leveson Francis, arm. BALLIOL, matric. 14 Oct., 90, aged 18 (from Winchester); HONOURS:—3 mathematical mods. 92.

Hardeman, Joseph Tilley, born at Alsager, Cheshire, 11 May, 1865; 1s. Charles Henry, gent. TRINITY, matric. 15 Oct., 83, aged 18 (from Clifton coll.), B.A. 87, M.A. 90; HONOURS:—2 classical mods. 85, 3 classics 87.

Harden, John Newman, born at Rushford Park, co. Lane., 1866; 1s. Michael, gent. BALLIOL, matric. 15 Oct., 84, aged 18 (from St. Paul's school); selected candidate Indian C.S. 84; died of cholera in India 87.

Harden, rev. Walter Frederic, born at Surbiton, Surrey, 1868; 1s. Frederick North, gen. ST. EDMUND HALL, matric. 22 Oct., 87, aged 19; curate of Probus, Cornwall, 91.

Harder, Alexander von, born at Achern in Baden 1862; o.s. Alexander. NON-COLLEGIATE, matric. 4 Nov., 80, aged 18.

Hardey, rev. Montague, born in London 26 Oct., 1862; 2s. Henry, gent., deceased. QUEEN'S, matric. 28 Oct., 81, aged 19 (from King's coll. London), B.A. 84, M.A. 88; priest-vicar of Lichfield and chancellor's vicar 90.

Hardie, Robert Purvis, born at Edinburgh 31 Aug., 1864; 2s. William Purvis, arm. MERTON, matric. 16 Oct., 84, aged 20 (from Edinburgh university), exhibitioner 83, B.A. 88; HONOURS:—1 mathematical mods. 85, 2 classics 88.

Hardie, William Ross, born in Edinburgh 1862; 1s. William, gent. BALLIOL, matric. 21 Oct., 80, aged 18 (from Edinburgh university), scholar 79-84, Jenkyns exhibitioner 83, fellow 84, B.A. 84, M.A. 87 [HONOURS:—1 classical mods. 81, proxime accessit Hertford scholarship 81, Hertford and Ireland scholarships 82, Greek verse 82, Greek prose 82, Latin verse 83, 1 classics 84, Craven scholarship 84, Derby scholarship 85); classical moderator 91-2, proctor 93-4.

Harding, George James Plumpton, born at Ness, Salop, 13 Jan., 1868; o.s. George Henry Tetlow, deceased. LINCOLN, matric. 21 Oct., 87, aged 19.

Harding, George Valentine, born at Rockfield, co. Monmouth, 14 Feb., 1865; 4s. John Taylor, vicar. NEW COLL., matric. 17 Dec., 83, aged 18 (from Marlborough coll.), B.A. 87; HONOURS:—2 classical mods. 85, 3 law 87.

Harding, Herbert Olive Denman, born at Ayott S. Lawrence 1865; 6s. John, D.D. BALLIOL, matric. 15 Oct., 84, aged 19 (from Forest school); assist. to collector and magistrate Coimbatore, Madras C.S.

Hardinge, Arthur Henry, M.A., fellow ALL SOULS' 81-9 and 91, where see page 273.
Hardman, Edward Trevor, born at Twickenham, Middx., 4 Feb., 1861; 3s. Charles Alexander, arm. UNIVERSITY COLL., matric. 28 Feb., 80, aged 19 (from the Charterhouse), B.A. 83, M.A. 86; HONOURS:—2 classical mods. 81, 4 history 83.
Hardman, Harold Fitzwilliam, born at Bristol 11 April, 1867; 1s. Joseph William, cler. MERTON, matric. 24 Oct., 85, aged 18 (from Radley coll.), B.A. 88 (HONOURS:—4 history 88); 2nd lieut. the Prince Albert's (Somersetshire light infantry), 90.
Hardman, James, born at Hey near Oldham, co. Lanc., March, 1867; 1s. Joseph; gent. ORIEL, matric. 23 Oct., 84, aged 17, B.A. 89, M.A. 91; HONOURS:—4 classics 88.
Hardwick, Francis William, born at Tewkesbury, co. Glouc., 11 Jan., 1861; o.s. Frederick Wilson, major 10th Bengal, N.I. NEW COLL., matric. 4 June, 81, aged 20 (from Eton), B.A. 84, M.A. 88; HONOURS:—2 history 84.
Hardy, Ernest George, M.A., fellow JESUS COLL. 75-8, where see.
Hardy, Frank Armitage, born at Umballa, East Indies, 7 June, 1866; 3s. Edmund Armitage, colonel. KEBLE, matric. 22 Oct., 85, aged 19 (from Clifton coll.), B.A. 89; HONOURS:—3 classical mods. 87, 3 classics 89.
Hardy, Gathorne Gathorne-, born at Staplehurst, Kent, 18 Dec., 1870; 2s. John Stuart, arm. CHRIST CHURCH, matric. 11 Oct., 89, aged 18.
Hardy, Guy Charles, born at Anstey Manor, Hants., 1 July, 1873; 1s. Herbert Carey, of Uckfield, Sussex, gent., deceased. MAGDALEN, matric. 18 Oct., 92, aged 19, from Eton.
Hardy, Harold, born at Kurrachee, East Indies, July, 1864; o.s. John Braithwaite, arm. KEBLE, matric. 16 Oct., 83, aged 19 (from Lancing coll.), B.A. 86 (HONOURS:—3 law 86); bar.-at-law, Gray's Inn, 91.
Hardy, Henry Ernest, born at Kussoulie, East Indies, Jan. 1869; 3s. Edward Armitage, arm. KEBLE, matric. 13 Oct., 88, aged 19 (from Clifton coll.), B.A. 92; HONOURS:—4 theology 91.
Hardy, John Francis Llewellyn, born at Cheltenham, 7 Dec., 1860; 1s. Edward Crocke, arm. HERTFORD, matric. 1 Feb., 81, aged 20 (from Marlborough coll.), scholar 80-4, B.A. 84, M.A. 92 (HONOURS:—2 classical mods. 82, 3 classics 84); bar.-at-law, Lincoln's Inn, 86.
Hardy, William Hepburn Cozens-, born at Kensington 20 March, 1868; 1s. Herbert, Q.C., M.P. NEW COLL., matric. 14 Oct., 87, aged 19 (from University coll. school, London), B.A. 91 (HONOURS:—2 classical mods. 89, 3 classics 91, geographical studentship 93); president of Oxford union society 91.
Hare, George Thompson, born at Wyke, Dorset, 1 May, 1861; 2s. Richard, solicitor, deceased. WADHAM, matric. 19 Oct., 81, aged 20, from Weymouth coll.
Hare, Percy Richard, born in London 2 April, 1870; 1s. hon. Hugh Henry, Queen's foreign service messenger. NEW COLL., matric. 2 May, 89, aged 19, from Eton.
Hare, Richard Granville, viscount Ennismore, born 12 Sept., 1866; o.s. William, earl of Listowel. CHRIST CHURCH, matric. 30 May, 85, aged 18, B.A. 88.
Hare, William Ernest Kent, born at Sandgate, Kent, 6 April, 1870; 1s. Richard William, arm. QUEEN'S, matric. 21 Oct., 87, aged 17 (from Haversham gr. school), exhibitioner 87, B.A. 90; HONOURS:—3 mathematical mods. 89, 4 mathematics 90.
Harford, Edward Bridges, born at Bathford, Somerset, 26 Dec., 1871; o.s. Edward John, cler. MERTON, matric. 22 Jan., 91, aged 19, from Eton.

Harford, Frederick Dundas, born at Stoke Bishop, Hants., Feb., 1862; 2s. John Battersby, arm. CHRIST CHURCH, matric. 15 Oct., 80, aged 18 (from Harrow), B.A. 84.
Harford, Hugh Wyndham Luttrell, born at Henbury, co. Glouc., 2 April, 1862; 3s. William Henry, arm. TRINITY, matric. 21 May, 80, aged 18, from Eton.
Harington, Edward, born at Hanwell, Middx., 25 Oct. 1863; 3s. sir Richard, bart. CHRIST CHURCH, matric. 13 Oct., 82, aged 18 (from Westminster school), B.A. 87 (HONOURS:—3 classical mods. 84, 4 history 86); bar.-at-law, Inner Temple, 89.
Harington, sir Richard, bart., student CHRIST CHURCH 53-60, where see.
Harker, rev. Ernest Gardner, born at Croydon, Surrey, 1868; 2s. George, gen. NON-COLLEGIATE, matric. 14 Jan., 86, aged 20 (from St. John's school, Cowley); migrated to EXETER, B.A. 92; curate of St. Paul, Burton-on-Trent, 93.
Harker, George Hodgson, born at Pateley Bridge, Yorks, 1866; 1s. George. ST. JOHN'S, matric. 17 Oct., 85, aged 19, from Harrogate school.
Harland, Cecil, born at Bridlington Quay, Yorks, 1863; 1s. Thomas, arm. ST. JOHN'S, matric. 15 Oct., 81, aged 18, B.A. 84, M.A. 88; HONOURS:—4 law 84.
Harley, John Hunter, born at Stirling 23 May, 1866; o.s. James, gen. NON-COLLEGIATE, matric. 17 Oct., 91, aged 26, from Glasgow university.
Harley, Robert, F.R.S. 1863 and F.R.A.S., created M.A. 23 Nov., 86, vice-master Mill Hill school 72-81, principal Huddersfield coll. 81-6, born 23 Jan., 28.
Harman, Lawrence William King-, born in London 23 Nov., 1863; o.s. Edward Robert, of Newcastle, co. Longford, M.P., arm. MAGDALEN, matric. 25 April, 83, aged 19 (from the Charterhouse); student Inner Temple 85; died 23 Oct., 86.
Harmsworth, Hildebrand Aubrey, born at Hampstead Heath, London, 15 March, 1872; 5s. Alfred, bar.-at-law. MERTON, matric. 18 Oct., 92, aged 20.
Harnett, rev. William Henry Lee, born at Wolverton, Bucks., 5 Oct., 1864; 2s. Francis William, cler. PEMBROKE, matric. 16 Oct., 83, aged 20 (from Cheltenham gr. school); scholar 81-5, B.A. 85, M.A. 88 (HONOURS:—3 classical mods. 83, 3 classics 85, 2 chemistry 86); lecturer of Watford, Herts, 91.
Harper, Arthur Paul, born at Canterbury, N.Z., 27 June, 1865; 1s. Leonard, arm. CHRIST CHURCH, matric. 10 Oct., 84, aged 19, B.A. 87; bar.-at-law, Inner Temple, 88.
Harper, rev. Charles Coleridge, born at Christchurch, Canterbury, N.Z., 30 Dec., 1866; 2s. Leonard, of Canterbury, N.Z., arm. KEBLE, matric. 19 Oct., 86, aged 19 (from Christchurch aforesaid), B.A. 89 (HONOURS:—3 history 89); curate of St. Matthew, Chapel Allerton, Yorks, 90.
Harper, Henry Guy, born at Oxford 5 Nov., 1866; o.s. Henry Smith, of the Bodleian. MAGDALEN, matric. 16 Oct., 84, aged 18, from Magdalen coll. school.
Harper, Hugo Daniel, D.D., principal of JESUS COLL. 77, where see.
Harper, rev. Walter Hugo, born at Sherborne, Dorset, 15 March, 1863; 2s. Hugh Daniel, principal of Jesus. UNIVERSITY COLL., matric. 14 Oct., 82, aged 19 (from Sherborne school), B.A. 86, M.A. 89 (HONOURS:—2 theology 86); curate of St. Mary the Virgin, Reading, 87.
Harpur, Eliot Caldwell, born at Spalford, Notts, 25 Feb., 1865; 2s. George, cler. NEW COLL., matric. 16 Oct., 85, aged 19 (from Winchester), scholar 84, B.A. 89; HONOURS:—2 classical mods. 87, 4 classics 89.

Harries, John Tyfaelog, born at Llandefaelog, co. Brecon 1861; 3s. Gilbert Charles Frederick, cler. MERTON, matric. 19 Jan., 80, aged 19, B.A. 84.

Harriott, Charles Warre, born at Arundall, N.S.W., 18 Jan., 1869; 1s. Thomas Warre, gen. MERTON, matric. 9 Dec., 89, aged 20 (from Sydney university); HONOURS :—3 law 92.

Harris, hon. Alexander Charles, born at Bally Edmond, near Rostrevor, co. Down, 18 Dec., 1872; 2s. Edward James, earl of Malmesbury. CHRIST CHURCH, matric. 29 May, 91, aged 18 (from Wimborne school); twin brother James Edward.

Harris, Alfred Herschell, born at Ootacamund in East Indies 29 Oct., 1863; 8s. George Anstruther, arm. TRINITY, matric. 11 Oct., 90, aged 27; HONOURS :—Chinese scholarship 92.

Harris, Arthur Butler, born at Edgbaston, co. Warwick, 1 June, 1865; 1s. Edward, cler. TRINITY, matric. 11 Oct., 84, aged 19 (from Clifton coll.), B.A. 88, M.A. and B.Med. 92; HONOURS :— a physiology 88.

Harris, Charles, born in London, 1864; 2s. John, gent. BALLIOL, matric. 17 Oct., 82, aged 18, scholar 81-6, B.A. 89; HONOURS :—1 mathematical mods. 83, accessit junior mathematical scholarship 84, 1 mathematics 86.

Harris, rev. Charles, born at Islington 20 July, 1865; 1s. Charles Richard, gent. LINCOLN, matric. 19 Oct., 83, aged 18 (from St. Olave's gr. school, Southwark), scholar WADHAM 83, B.A. 87, M.A. 90 (HONOURS :—1 classical mods. 85, 2 classics 87); assist. master Christ coll., Brecon, 90, assist. Ripon gr. school 90-1; curate of Kingsley, co. Stafford, 91.

Harris, Charles, born at Leamington, co. Warwick, 1865; 2s. Charles, gent. CHRIST CHURCH, matric. 20 Oct., 84, aged 19, B.A. 88, M.A. 92.

Harris, Charles Etheridge, born at Oxford 11 Feb., 1870; 1s. John, gen. NON-COLLEGIATE, matric. 13 Oct., 88, aged 18 (from Magdalen coll. school), B.A. 92; HONOURS :—3 classical mods. 90, 3 theology 92.

Harris, Frederick, born at Leeds 1862; 3s. Lewis, arm. CHRIST CHURCH, matric. 24 Jan., 81, aged 19, from London university.

Harris, Frederick Cowley, born in London March, 1863; 2s. Salem Constable, gent. KEBLE, matric. 17 Oct., 82, aged 19 (from St. Mark's school Windsor), B.A. 86, M.A. 89; HONOURS :—3 mathematical mods. 84.

Harris, Frederick William, born at Leicester 4 March, 1866; 2s. Samuel, solicitor. MAGDALEN, matric. 16 Oct., 84, aged 18 (from Harrow), B.A. 87, M.A. 91.

Harris, George Montagu, born at Torquay, Devon, 26 Nov., 1868; o.s. George Colyer, vicar of St. Luke's. NEW COLL., matric. 9 Dec., 87, aged 19 (from Winchester), B.A. 91; HONOURS :—2 law 91.

Harris, Henry, B.D., fellow MAGDALEN 50-8, where see.

Harris, Henry, born at Whitchurch, Hants, Sept., 1870; 1s. Henry, arm. CHRIST CHURCH, matric. 21 Jan., 90, aged 19, from Eton.

Harris, Hermann Gundert, born at Chittoor, Madras, 26 Jan., 1869; 3s. George Anstruther, late I.C.S. EXETER, matric. 3 Nov., 91, aged 32.

Harris, James Edward, viscount Fitzharris, born at Bally Edmond, co. Down, 18 Dec., 1872; 1s. Edward James, earl of Malmesbury. CHRIST CHURCH, matric. 29 May, 91, aged 18, from Wimborne school; twin brother Alexander C.

Harris, Leonard Tatham, born at Falmouth 1872; 1s. Arthur Den, D.Med. NEW COLL., matric. 16 Oct., 91, aged 19 (from Bath coll.); selected candidate Indian C.S. 91.

Harris, Richard, born at Oxford 1862; 4s. Charles Hawkins, gent. NON-COLLEGIATE, matric. 18 Oct., 80, aged 18, from Christ Church cathedral school.

Harris, Richard Julian, born at Plymouth 1861; 1s. John Oliver, cler. MERTON, matric. 18 Oct., 80, aged 19.

Harris, rev. Robert William, born in London 1863; 1s. Robert, gent. JESUS COLL., matric. 19 Oct., 81, aged 18 (from city of London school), scholar 80-5, B.A. 85, M.A. 88 (HONOURS :—2 classical mods. 83, 2 classics 85); assist. sec. 89-91, and sec. to East London church fund 91.

Harris, Samuel Collard, born at Taunton, Somerset, 19 April, 1869; y.s. Thomas, gen. NEW COLL., matric. 12 Oct., 88, aged 19 (from city of London school), B.A. 92; HONOURS :—3 classical mods. 90, 3 classics 92.

Harris, Thomas, B.D., fellow MAGDALEN 35-50, where see.

Harris, Thomas, born at Oxford 1868; 3s. Thomas Jarvis, gen. NON-COLLEGIATE, matric. 23 April, 87, aged 19 (from Mt. Radford school, Exeter), B.A. 91.

Harris, Thomas Whitmore, born at Sutton, Notts, 1865; 8s. John, gent. ST. JOHN'S, matric. 13 Jan., 83, aged 18, B.A. 86 (HONOURS :—3 law 86); bar.-at-law, Lincoln's Inn, 89.

Harris, Wilfrid, born at York 1866; 5s. John, gen. NON-COLLEGIATE, matric. 21 Oct., 89, aged 23, from Ripon gr. school and B.A. Durham.

Harris, William Birkbeck, born at Bradford, Yorks, 11 Nov., 1867; elder son William Wilson, arm. HERTFORD, matric. 27 Oct., 87, aged 19, from Shrewsbury gr. school.

Harris, William Frederick, born at Oxford 1863; 5s. Thomas, gent. NON-COLLEGIATE, matric. 15 Oct., 81, aged 18; migrated to ST. EDMUND HALL, B.A. and M.A. 90.

Harrison, Anthony Edward, born at Penrith, Cumberland, 1865; 1s. William, arm. ST. JOHN'S, matric. 13 Oct., 83, aged 18.

Harrison, rev. Arthur Leonard, born at Old Charlton, Kent, 2 Dec., 1862; 1s. Thomas Arthur John, arm. NEW COLL., matric. 14 Oct., 82, aged 19 (from Wellington coll.), B.A. 87, M.A. 90 (HONOURS :— 3 classical mods. 84); curate of Haslemere, Hants, 90.

Harrison, Arthur Selwyn, born at Rackheath, Norfolk, 5 Aug., 1866; 2s. Thomas, cler. UNIVERSITY COLL., matric. 15 Oct., 87, aged 19 (from Haileybury), exhibitioner 87, B.A. 91; HONOURS :—1 classical mods. 89, 2 classics 91.

Harrison, Bernard Oliver, born in London 1872; 1s. Frederick, arm. BALLIOL, matric. 17 Oct., 89, aged 17, from St. Paul's school.

Harrison, rev. Charles Bruce, born at Sherborne, Dorset, July, 1865; y.s. Charles Matthew, arm. NON-COLLEGIATE, matric. 17 Oct., 85, aged 20 (from Elizabeth coll., Guernsey); migrated to NEW COLL. 86, B.A. 88, M.A. 92 (HONOURS :—a theology 88); curate of Sherborne, Dorset, 91.

Harrison, Cuthbert Woodville, born at Liverpool 23 Jan., 1874; 1s. Cuthbert, of Dyrham, Wilts, gent. BALLIOL, matric. 17 Oct., 92, aged 18, from Clifton coll.

Harrison, rev. Cyril Harling, born at Oxford 1860; 1s. James, cler. NON-COLLEGIATE, matric. 17 Jan., 80, aged 20 (from the Charterhouse); migrated to MERTON, B.A. 84; curate of Chadwell St. Mary, Essex, 88.

Harrison, rev. Edward Hubert, born at Lahore, E. Indies, 1860; 1s. Richard Henry, cler. NON-COLLEGIATE, matric. 28 Jan., 84, aged 20, B.A. 89; curate of St. Paul Lorells, Handsworth, co. Stafford, 90.

INTERIOR OF ST MARY'S CHURCH—By F. Mackenzie.
Oxford Almanac, 1834.

Harrison, Francis, M.A., fellow ORIEL 52-68, where see page 153.

Harrison, Francis Capel, born at Calcutta 21 June, 1863; 2s. Edward Francis, arm. BALLIOL, matric. 23 Oct., 82, aged 19 (from Rugby); of the finance and commerce department, government of India.

Harrison, Frederick, M.A., fellow WADHAM 54-70, where see.

Harrison, Frederick, born at Carleton, Yorks, 9 Nov., 1865; 4s. Joseph, gent., deceased. NEW COLL., matric. 10 Oct., 84, aged 18 (from Giggleswick school), scholar 84, B.A. 87, M.A. 91 (HONOURS:—1 mathematical mods. 83, junior mathematical scholarship 86, 1 mathematics 87, 1 physics 89.

Harrison, Harrop William Abel, born at Stalybridge, co. Lanc., 1865; o.s. William Henry, arm. UNIVERSITY COLL., matric. 11 Oct., 84, aged 19. B.A. 87 (HONOURS:—4 law 87); bar.-at-law, Lincoln's Inn, 90.

Harrison, rev. Harry George, born in London 26 March, 1866; 8s. James William, gent. WORCESTER, matric. 17 Oct., 84, aged 18 (from Highgate school), B.A. 88, M.A. 91 (HONOURS:—2 classical mods. 86, 3 classics 88); curate of St. Matthew, Oakley Square, London, 91.

Harrison, Henry, born at Holywood, co. Down, 17 Dec., 1867; 2s. Henry, arm. BALLIOL, matric. 20 Jan., 87, aged 19, from Westminster school (HONOURS:—3 classical mods. 88); M.P. Mid Tipperary, May, 90-92.

Harrison, rev. Henry Lawrence, born at Buxton, co. Derby, 30 Oct., 1868; 1s. John Edwin, gen. WORCESTER, matric. 17 Oct., 87, aged 19 (from Uppingham school), B.A. 90 (HONOURS:—4 history 90); curate of West Kirby, Cheshire, 91.

Harrison, Herbert William Broadley, born at Ross, co. Hereford, 1867; 5s. Broadley, arm. BRASENOSE, matric. 28 Jan., 86, aged 19 (from the Charterhouse), B.A. 89.

Harrison, Hugh, born at Bray, Ireland, 27 May, 1870; 2s. Michael, an Irish judge. EXETER, matric. 16 Oct., 89, aged 17 (from Sherborne school); and lieut. the King's own Yorkshire light infantry 92.

Harrison, James Kay Maberly, born at Newby Bridge, co. Lanc., 29 March, 1869; 1s. James, cler. TRINITY, matric. 13 Oct., 88, aged 19 (from St. Mark's school, Windsor), B.A. 92; HONOURS:—3 classical mods. 90, a law 92.

Harrison, John Butler, M.A., fellow NEW COLL. 54-79, where see page 215.

Harrison, John Philip, born at Pendennis Castle, Cornwall, 20 June, 1872; 1s. William John Rose, capt. R.A., deceased. MERTON, matric. 18 Oct., 92, aged 20, from Beaumont coll.

Harrison, Lawrence Alexander, born in London 23 Oct., 1866; 1s. Lawrence, stockbroker. NEW COLL., matric. 16 Oct., 85, aged 18 (from Eton); HONOURS:—2 history 89.

Harrison, Lawrence Jackson, born at Penrith, Cumberland, 1867; y.s. William, gent. WADHAM, matric. 16 Oct., 86, aged 19, B.A. 92.

Harrison, Marmaduke Cecil Crofton, born at Cheltenham 14 July, 1864; 1s. Lawrence John, cler. EXETER, matric. 18 Oct., 82, aged 18 (from Rugby), B.A. 87, M.A. 89.

Harrison, Martin Gaston Swallow, born at Blythe, Northumberland, 1869; 1s. Alexander James, cler. ST. EDMUND HALL, matric. 19 Jan., 88, aged 19.

Harrison, Oliver Ormerod, born at Staveley, Kendal, 1873; 3s. Daniel, solicitor. ORIEL, matric. 27 Oct., 91, aged 18, from the Charterhouse.

Harrison, Spencer Henry, born at Old Wolverton, Bucks, 1872; o.s. Spencer Richard, gen. PEMBROKE, matric. 10 Nov., 91, aged 19.

Harrison, Theodore Edward, born in London 1863; 1s. Thomas, cler. EXETER, matric. 19 Oct., 82, aged 19 (from Uppingham school), B.A. NON-COLLEGIATE 86; HONOURS:—3 classics 86.

Harrison, Thomas, born at Bowness, Cumberland, 18 March, 1865; 3s. John, arm. WORCESTER, matric. 22 Jan., 85, aged 19, B.A. 87 as T. H. Collinson, where see page 127.

Harrison, Thomas, born at Liverpool 1867; 1s. Thomas, gen. CORPUS CHRISTI, matric. 20 Oct., 86, aged 19 (from Harrow), B.A. 89.

Harrison, Wilfred Baker, born at Alverthorpe, Yorks, 1870; 1s. Joseph, cler. NON-COLLEGIATE, matric. 17 Oct., 91, aged 21, from Wakefield collegiate school.

Harrison, rev. William Francis Lightfoot, born at Pontesbury, Salop, 20 Oct., 1863; o.s. William, cler. LINCOLN, matric. 17 Jan., 83, aged 19 (from Haileybury), B.A. 87, M.A. 91; curate of Holy Trinity, Stockton-on-Tees, 91.

Harrison, William Montagu, born at Old Charlton, Kent, 4 Feb., 1871; 3s. Arthur Thomas, capt. R.A., deceased. MAGDALEN, matric. 14 Oct., 90, aged 19 (from Wellington coll.), demy 90; HONOURS:—1 classical mods. 92.

Harrison, William Walker Estcourt, born at Skelton, Yorks, 9 Jan., 1862; 1s. William Estcourt, vicar of Sturton-le-Steeple, Lincoln. NEW COLL., matric. 15 Oct., 81, aged 19 (from Stony Stratford coll.); migrated to CHARSLEY HALL, B.A. 87.

Harry, Leslie Warlow, born in London 12 Aug., 1866; 2s. Ebenezer John, gent. LINCOLN, matric. 27 Oct., 85, aged 19 (from University coll. school), exhibitioner 85-6; exhibitioner BRASENOSE 86, B.A. 89, M.A. 92; HONOURS:—2 classical mods. 87, 3 classics 89.

Hart, Alfred John, born in London 6 April, 1862; 3s. Edward, arm. BALLIOL, matric. 18 Oct., 81, aged 19 (from Rugby), B.A. 85, M.A. 88 (HONOURS:—3 classical mods. 83); student of Inner Temple 84; a solicitor.

Hart, Charles Hopwood, born at Bolton, Cumberland, Feb., 1872; 2s. Peter Hopwood, cler. KEBLE, matric. 15 Oct., 92, aged 20, from Manchester gr. school.

Hart, Edgar Bruce, born at Pekin, China, 1873; 1s. sir Robert, G.C.M.G., inspector Chinese customs. UNIVERSITY COLL., matric. 17 Oct., 91, aged 18.

Hart, Henry D'Arcy, born in London, 1866; 1s. James, gent. BALLIOL, matric. 15 Oct., 84, aged 18 (from Clifton coll.), B.A. 88, M.A. 91 (HONOURS:—2 classical mods. 86, 3 classics 88); bar.-at-law, Lincoln's Inn, 92.

Hart, Herbert Leslie, born at Colton, co. Lanc., 31 March, 1870; o.s. Robert Slater, cler. PEMBROKE, matric. 29 Jan., 91, aged 20, from Cartmel gr. school.

Hart, John Joseph, born at Ashton-under-Lyne 1862; 1s. Thomas Ebenezer, gent. BALLIOL, matric. 18 Oct., 81, aged 19 (from Manchester gr. school), exhibitioner 82.

Hart, Robert Ernest Sperling, born at Takeley, Essex, 2 Jan., 1872; o.s. Robert, cler. MERTON, matric. 15 Oct., 92, aged 18 (from Marlborough coll.), postmaster 90; HONOURS:—1 classical mods. 92.

Hart, Walter Perry, born at Halstead, Essex, 1869; 3s. Josiah, cler. NON-COLLEGIATE, matric. 27 April, 89, aged 22.

Harte, Walter James, born at Wells, Somerset, 7 Aug., 1867; 2s. Edward, gen. WORCESTER, matric. 22 Oct., 85, aged 19 (from Bath coll.), B.A. 88, M.A. 92; HONOURS:—2 history 88.

Harter, Charles Beard Hatfield, born at Cranfield, Beds, Jan., 1861; 5s. George, cler. CORPUS CHRISTI, matric. 16 April, 80, aged 19 (from Harrow); migrated to NEW INN HALL, B.A. 83.

Hartley, Edward, born at Bury, co. Lanc., 1867; 2s. John, gen. UNIVERSITY COLL., matric. 11 Oct., 90, aged 23 (from Bury school); HONOURS: —3 classical mods. 92.

Hartley, rev. Robert, born at Halifax 1864; o.s. Robert, gent. EXETER, matric. 12 May, 83, aged 19, B.A. 87, M.A. 90 (HONOURS:—2 theology 87); curate of SS. Philip and James, Oxford, 88.

Hartley, rev. Salter Saint George John, born at Staveley, Yorks, June, 1867; 1s. Joseph, arm. ST. JOHN'S, matric. 16 Oct., 86, aged 19 (from Harrow), scholar 90, B.A. 90; HONOURS:—2 theology 90.

Hartnoll, Henry Sullivan, born at Exeter 17 June, 1862; 1s. Henry Thomas, arm. TRINITY, matric. 15 Oct., 81, aged 18, from Exeter school; student Inner Temple 82, deputy commissioner Burmah.

Harvey, Edward Nourse Rowley, born at Fawley, Hants, 20 Jan., 1864; o.s. Edward Nourse, magistrate. LINCOLN, matric. 3 Feb., 86, aged 22, from a Bournemouth school.

Harvey, Eustace John, born in London 25 Aug., 1866; 2s. Alfred Spelding, arm. CORPUS CHRISTI, matric. 26 Oct., 85, aged 19 (from University coll. school), scholar 85, B.A. 88, M.A. 92; HONOURS:— 2 classical mods. 87, a history 88.

Harvey, rev. Frank Northam, born at Southampton , 1865; 2s. Aaron, schoolmaster. EXETER, matric. 21 Jan., 85, aged 20 (from Handel coll., Southampton), B.A. 88, M.A. 91; curate of St. Denys, Southampton, 88-91; brother of Thomas H. and Walter R.

Harvey, Franklin, M.A., MAGDALEN, where see page 327.

Harvey, Hamilton Law, born in London , 1865; 1s. Robert Kibble, arm. BALLIOL, matric. 15 Oct., 84, aged 19 (from Giggleswick school); selected candidate Indian c.s. 84.

Harvey, Henry Auber, M.A., student CHRIST CHURCH 43-69, where see.

Harvey, Henry Herbert, born at Oxford , 1865; o.s. Henry, pleb. NON-COLLEGIATE, matric. 12 Oct., 89, aged 24 (from Cowley St. John's school), B.A. 92; HONOURS:—3 theology 92.

Harvey, Henry Paul, born in Paris 1 Oct., 1869; 1s. Henry, baron De Torquett, deceased. NEW COLL., matric. 12 Oct., 88, aged 19 (from Rugby), B.A. 93; HONOURS:—2 classical mods. 90, 1 classics 92; passed for home civil service 93.

Harvey, John, born at Glasgow , 1865; 1s. John, gen. BALLIOL, matric. 22 Oct., 83, aged 18 (from Edinburgh academy), B.A. 88; HONOURS:—2 classical mods. 85, 2 classics 87.

Harvey, John Musgrave, born in London 22 Dec., 1865; 2s. Charles Musgrave, cler. KEBLE, matric. 14 Oct., 84, aged 18 (from Marlborough coll.), scholar 84, B.A. 88; HONOURS:—2 classical mods. 86, 3 classics 88.

Harvey, Ralph Key, born at Strentham, Surrey, , 1865; o.s. Charles, gent. BRASENOSE, matric. 17 Dec., 84, aged 19, from Winchester.

Harvey, rev. Reginald, born at Berkhampstead, Herts, 16 May, 1865; 7s. Frederick Burn, cler. KEBLE, matric. 16 Oct., 83, aged 18 (from Halleybury), B.A. 87 (HONOURS:—2 theology 86); curate of Bakewell, co. Derby, 91.

Harvey, Reginald Henry, born at Bebington, Cheshire, Jan., 1858; 4s. Herbert, cler. CHRIST CHURCH, matric. 3 June, 87, aged 19 (from Radley coll.), B.A. 92.

Harvey, rev. Richard Charles Musgrave, born in London 6 Sept., 1864; 1s. Charles Musgrave, cler. KEBLE, matric. 24 Oct., 83, aged 19 (from Marlborough coll.), B.A. 87, M.A. 90 (HONOURS: —2 classical mods. 85, 3 classics 87); curate of Portsea, Hants, 88.

Harvey, Thomas, born at Londonderry , 1859; 1s. James, gent. NON-COLLEGIATE, matric. 28 Jan., 84, aged 25.

Harvey, rev. Thomas Herbert, born at Southampton 12 July, 1861; 1s. Aaron, gent. EXETER, matric. 20 Oct., 81, aged 20 (from Handel coll., Southampton), B.A. 84, M.A. 88 (HONOURS:—1 theology 84); missionary and master in Church missionary soc. coll., Ningpo, China, 88; died 19 Aug., 90, on his outward voyage; brother of Frank M. and of the next.

Harvey, Walter Roscoe, born at Southampton 1866; 3s. Aaron, gen. EXETER, matric. 1 May, 88, aged 22 (from All Saints' school, Southampton); died at Southampton 24 April, 1890.

Harvey, William Gaskell Long, born at Liverpool 15 Nov., 1865; o.s. William Gaskell. TRINITY, matric. 15 Oct., 83, aged 19 (from Wellington coll.); migrated to NEW INN HALL (Balliol 87), B.A. 89.

Harward, Alfred Edgar, born at Wirksworth, co. Derby, , 1865; 5s. Arthur, gent. BALLIOL, matric. 16 Oct., 83, aged 18 (from Rossall school); assist. magistrate and collector Bengal.

Harwood, Basil, M.A., organist CHRIST CHURCH 92, where see.

Haselfoot, Arthur Godfrey, born in London 4 March, 1870; 3s. Frederick Kneller, arm. CHRIST CHURCH, matric. 11 Oct., 89, aged 19 (from Winchester), scholar 89; died 27 May, 90.

Haselfoot, Charles Edward, born in London 2 Aug., 1864; 1s. Frederick Kneller, bar.-at-law. NEW COLL., matric. 16 Oct., 83, aged 19 (from Winchester), scholar 82, B.A. 87; fellow HERTFORD 88, M.A. 90; HONOURS:—1 mathematical mods. 84, 1 mathematics 86, accessit junior mathematical scholarship 85 and senior mathematical scholarship 87, Herschel astronomical prize 87, 1 physics 88.

Haselfoot, Frederick William, born in London 22 Sept., 1867; 2s. Frederick Kneller, bar.-at-law. NEW COLL., matric. 15 Oct., 86, aged 19 (from Winchester), scholar 85, B.A. 90; HONOURS:—1 mathematical mods. 87, 2 mathematics 89.

Haselfoot, Henry John, born in London 20 Feb., 1872; 4s. Frederick Kneller, bar.-at-law. HERTFORD, matric. 20 Oct., 91, aged 19 (from Honiton school), exhibitioner 91.

Haserick, Alfred Ernest, born at Manchester 30 July, 1862; 1s. Frederick Augustus, gent. CHRIST CHURCH, matric. 10 Oct., 84, aged 22 (from Old Trafford school), B.A. 90, M.A. 92.

Haskins, Henry Minshull, born at Ventnor, I.W., June, 1866; 2s. John, gent. CHRIST CHURCH, matric. 16 Oct., 85, aged 19, from Harrow.

Haslam, rev. John Park, born at Preston, co. Lanc., 1856; 1s. John, gent. UNIVERSITY COLL., matric. 4 June, 81, aged 25, B.A. 84, M.A. 88 (HONOURS:—3 theology 84); curate of Bolton-le-Sands 84-7, and of Haslingden, co. Lanc., 87.

Hassall, Arthur, M.A., student CHRIST CHURCH 84, where see.

Hassall, Arthur Edward, born at Leamington Aug., 1864; 1s. James Wright, arm. BALLIOL, matric. 16 Jan., 83, aged 18 (from Leamington coll.), B.A. 86; HONOURS:—2 classical mods. 84, 2 classics 86.

Hastings, Charles Paget, born at Areley, co. Worc., 23 March, 1865; 3s. John Parsons, cler. KEBLE, matric. 16 Oct., 83, aged 18 (from Rossall school), scholar 84, B.A. 87; HONOURS:—1 history 86.

Hastings, rev. James Francis, born at Areley Kings, co. Worc., 10 Jan., 1862; 2s. John Parsons, cler. CORPUS CHRISTI, matric. 26 Oct., 81, aged 19 (from Repton school), B.A. 85 (HONOURS:—4 history 85); curate of Hartley, co. Worc., 91.

Hastings, Thomas McMillan, born at Elland, Yorks, 23 Feb., 1863; 1s. Thomas, gent. NEW COLL., matric. 14 Oct., 82, aged 19 (from Winchester), B.A. 87; HONOURS:—2 classical mods. 84, 2 classics 86.

Haswell, Edward William, born at Rugby 3 March, 1866; 1s. William, gen. WADHAM, matric. 15 Oct., 87, aged 21 (from Rugby), B.A. (NON-COLLEGIATE) 91; HONOURS:—4 theology 91.

Hatch, Arthur Herbert, born at Quebec 1864; 1s. Edwin cler. BALLIOL, matric. 15 Oct., 84, aged 20 (from Malvern coll.), B.A. 92.

Hatch, Charles Wycliffe, born at Birmingham 12 Sept., 1867; 1s. Samuel Charles, gent. PEMBROKE, matric. 27 Oct., 85, aged 18, from Rugby.

Hatch, George Washington, born in London 1872; 4s. Henry, merchant. BALLIOL, matric. 20 Oct. 91, aged 19 (from St. Paul's school); selected candidate for Indian C.S. 91.

Hatch, rev. James Edgar, born at Camberwell, Surrey, 1859; o.s. James John, gent. ST. MARY HALL, matric. 23 Oct., 82, aged 23; migrated to KEBLE and afterwards to HERTFORD, B.A. and M.A. 90; curate of St. Matthew, Quebec, 88-9, and of Lapworth, co. Warwick, 90.

Hatch, Wilfrid Stanley, born at Quebec 11 Sept., 1865; 2s. Edwin, cler. ORIEL, matric. 17 Dec., 83, aged 18 (from Magdalen coll. school), exhibitioner TRINITY 84, B.A. 87, M.A. 90; HONOURS:—3 law 87.

Hatchard, Frank Sumner Utterton, born at Guildford, Surrey, 1861; 4s. Thomas Goodwyn, bishop of Mauritius. MERTON, matric. 18 Oct., 81, aged 20 (from the Charterhouse), B.A. and M.A. 88.

Hatchard, Frederick Harris, born at Wimborne, Dorset, 22 Jan., 1868; 1s. Henry, arm. LINCOLN, matric. 22 Jan., 87, aged 19, from Weymouth coll.

Hatfeild, Gilliat Edward, born in London 1865; 2s. Gilliat, gen. NON-COLLEGIATE, matric. 20 Jan., 83, aged 18, from Harrow.

Hathaway, Walter Lawrence, born at Bellary, Madras, 19 Aug., 1864; 3s. Arthur, of Indian C.S. NEW COLL., matric. 17 Dec., 83, aged 19 (from Clifton coll.) B.A. 87, M.A. 90; HONOURS:—3 classical mods. 85.

Hatherley, Arthur Wilfrid, born at Newport, co. Monmouth, 1872; 3s. Henry, gen. NON-COLLEGIATE, matric. 11 Oct., 88 (from Christ Church cathedral school and Wycliffe coll., Stonehouse); migrated to ST. JOHN'S, exhibitioner 93.

Hatherley, rev. Henry Bishop, born at Portsmouth 1866; 1s. Henry, gent. ST. EDMUND HALL, matric. 23 Oct., 85, aged 19, B.A. 89; curate of Lambeth Holy Trinity 90.

Hatton, John Leigh Smeathman, born at Aston, co. Warwick, 1865; s. John Leigh, cler. HERTFORD, matric. 27 Oct., 85, aged 20 (from Ashby-de-la-Zouch school); scholar 84, B.A. 89, M.A. 92; HONOURS:—accessit junior mathematical exhibition 87, 1 mathematical mods. 87, 1 mathematics 89, 2 physics 90.

Havell, Herbert Lord, born at Reading, Berks, 1867; 3s. Charles Richard gent. UNIVERSITY COLL., matric. 21 May, 80, aged 17 (from Reading school); scholar 80-4, B.A. 84; HONOURS:—1 classical mods. 82, 2 classics 84.

Haverfield, Francis John, M.A., student of CHRIST CHURCH 92, where see.

Havergal, rev. Ernest, born at Copie, Beds, 1861; 4s. Henry East, cler. ST. EDMUND HALL, matric. 28 Jan., 82, aged 21, B.A. 85, M.A. 88 (HONOURS:—3 theology 85); curate of Sedlescombe, Sussex, 91.

Havergal, rev. Eustace, born at Copie, Beds, 1857; 2s. Henry East, cler. ST. EDMUND HALL, matric. 19 April, 80, aged 23, B.A. 83, M.A. 86 (HONOURS:—4 history 83); a solicitor 78-83, held various curacies since 83, curate of Belvedere, Kent, 90.

Havers, Arthur Claude, born in London 7 Dec., 1871; 2s. John Cory, arm. TRINITY, matric. 11 Oct., 90, aged 18, from Shrewsbury school.

Havers, Henry Leslie, born at Bokingham, Surrey, 26 June, 1873; 3s. John Cory, merchant. TRINITY, matric. 15 Oct., 92, aged 19 (from Shrewsbury school.

Havers, William Joseph, born at Twickenham 16 Aug., 1870; 2s. John Cory, arm. TRINITY, matric. 13 Oct., 88, aged 18 (from Shrewsbury school), B.A. 92; HONOURS:—2 law 92.

Havilland, James Rainier de, born in Jersey Dec., 1870; 5s. James, arm. KEBLE, matric. 11 Oct., 90, aged 19, from a Blackheath school.

Havilland, Reginald Saunnares de, born at Paignton, Devon, 1861; 4s. John, arm. CORPUS CHRISTI, matric. 21 Oct., 80, aged 19 (from Eton), exhibitioner 80-4, B.A. 84, (HONOURS:—2 mathematical mods. 82, 3 classics 84); in the Oxford eight 82 and 83.

Hawes, Edward Burn, born at Richmond, Surrey, 16 Aug., 1871; 2s. Edward, arm. TRINITY, matric. 17 Jan., 91, aged 19 (from Canterbury school), Ford student 90.

Hawes, Ivon Henry Skipwith, born at Woolwich, Kent, 1869; 4s. Arthur Briscoe, arm. HERTFORD, matric. 29 Jan., 89, aged 20.

Hawes, Robert Porson, born at Richmond, Surrey, 22 June, 1868; 1s. Edward, arm. PEMBROKE, matric. 28 Oct., 86, aged 18 (from Canterbury school), B.A. 89.

Hawke, Edward George, born at Deptford 7 Nov., 1869; 1s. George Frederick Edward, gen. NON-COLLEGIATE, matric. 12 Oct., 89, aged 19 (from University coll. London); exhibitioner WADHAM 90, B.A. 92; HONOURS:—1 history 92.

Hawke, Harry Clifton Gladstone, born at Stonehouse, Devon, 21 May, 1861; 3s. John, artist. ST. MARY HALL, matric. 24 Jan., 84, aged 22 (as Harry Clifton Hawke); migrated to WADHAM 1 May, 86, B.A. 87, M.A. 91 (as Harry Gladstone Hawke); HONOURS:—4 history 87.

Hawke, John Anthony, born at Tolgulla, Cornwall, 1869; 2s. Edward Henry, gen. ST JOHN'S, matric. 15 Oct., 87, aged 18 (from Merchant Taylors' school), scholar 87, B.A. 91, M.A. 91 (HONOURS:—1 law 91); bar.-at-law, Middle Temple, 92.

Hawken, rev. Charles Sydney, born at Tamerton, Devon, 1863; 3s. Charles Thomas, arm. MERTON, matric. 19 Jan., 80, aged 17 (from Tiverton school), B.A. 83 (HONOURS:—3 history 83); assistant master Cheltenham coll. 85-7; incumbent of All Saints, Bodalla, N.S. Wales, 90.

Hawker, Henry Gore, born at Plymouth 1865; o.s. William Henry, arm. UNIVERSITY COLL., matric. 11 Oct., 84, aged 19 (from Winchester), B.A. 88; HONOURS:—2 classical mods. 86.

Hawkes, Samuel John, M.A., fellow QUEEN'S 61-9, where see page 182.

Hawkes, Thomas, born at Teignmouth, Devon, 12 July, 1869; o.s. John Joseph, gen. PEMBROKE, matric. 17 Oct., 88, aged 19 (from Queen's coll., Taunton), scholar 88, B.A. 92; HONOURS:—2 classical mods. 90, 3 classics 92.

Hawkesworth, Charles Edward Mackenzie, born at Sudborough, Northants, 25 June, 1868; 1s. John William, arm. QUEEN'S, matric. 21 Oct., 87, aged 19 (from Clifton coll.), scholar 87, B.A. 91; HONOURS:—2 classical mods. 89, 1 classics 91, 1 history 92.

Hawkin, Robert Crawford, born at Edmonton, Middx., 1 May, 1871; 2s. Edward, cler. PEMBROKE, matric. 28 Jan., 90, aged 18 (from Colwyn bay and Eastbourne schools), scholar 88; HONOURS :— 2 mathematical mods. 91.

Hawkins, Antony Hope, born in London 9 Feb., 1863; 2s. Edwards Comerford, cler. BALLIOL, matric. 18 Oct., 81, aged 18 (from Marlborough coll.), scholar 81-5, B.A. 85, Jenkyns exhibitioner 85, M.A. 89 (HONOURS :—1 classical mods. 82, 1 classics 85), president of the Oxford union society 86; bar.-at-law, Middle Temple, 87.

Hawkins, Charles Cæsar, born at Lamberhurst, Kent, 15 March, 1864; y.s. Robert, vicar. MAGDALEN, matric. 16 Oct., 82, aged 18 (from Eton), demy 82-6, B.A. 86, M.A. 90; HONOURS :—1 classical mods. 83, 1 classics 86.

Hawkins, Edgar, born at Birkdale, co. Lanc., 26 Sept., 1862; 1s. Frederick James, arm. MERTON, matric. 17 Jan., 83, aged 19 (from Westminster school), B.A. 86, M.A. 89; HONOURS :—4 chemistry 86.

Hawkins, Edward William, M.A., fellow PEMBROKE 60-70, where see.

Hawkins, Frank Hobart, born at Sumnertown, Oxon, 1865; 4s. Charles Titian, gent. ST. JOHN'S, matric. 14 Oct., 82, aged 19, B.A. 86, M.A. 89.

Hawkins, Henry Forshaw, born at Birkdale, co. Lanc., 16 June, 1864; 2s. Frederick James, solicitor. EXETER, matric. 18 Oct., 83, aged 19 (from Westminster school), B.A. 87, M.A. and B.C.L. 90; HONOURS :—3 classical mods. 85, 3 law 87, 2 civil law 88.

Hawkins, rev. sir John Cæsar, bart., M.A., ORIEL, where see page 153.

Hawksford, Cyril Vyvynn, born at St. Heliers, Jersey, 3 June, 1867; o.s. Francis, gen. MERTON, matric. 20 Jan., 87, aged 19 (from Victoria coll., Jersey), B.A. 90 (HONOURS :—4 law 90); bar.-at-law, Middle Temple, 92.

Hawley, Arthur, born in London July, 1870; 2s. Alfred, arm. CHRIST CHURCH, matric. 11 Oct., 89, aged 19 (from Uppingham school), B.A. 92; HONOURS :—3 history 92.

Hawley, Charles William, born at Leamington, co. Warwick, 27 Sept., 1863; 1s. John Hugh, schoolmaster. NON-COLLEGIATE, matric. 19 Jan., 85, aged 21 (from a Surbiton school); migrated to WADHAM 18 April, 85, B.A. 88, M.A. 91.

Haworth, rev. Albert Joseph Reginald, born at Pontish, Russia, 1/12 Dec. 1863; 2s. Joseph, arm. WORCESTER, matric. 22 Jan., 85, aged 21 (from Owens coll., Manchester), B.A. 88 (HONOURS :—4 theology 88); curate of St. Mary the virgin, Sedgley, co. Staff., 89.

Haworth, John Goodier, born at Altrincham, Cheshire, 1 Nov., 1870; 3s. Abraham, gen. NEW COLL., matric. 11 Oct., 89, aged 18 (from Rugby); HONOURS :—3 history 92.

Hawtrey, Charles Henry, born at Eton 21 Sept., 1858; 4s. John William, cler. PEMBROKE, matric. 4 Feb., 81, aged 22, from Rugby.

Hawtrey, Gilbert Henry Courtenay, born at Windsor June, 1869; 1s. Henry Courtenay, cler. ST. EDMUND HALL, matric. 18 Oct., 88, aged 19 (from St. Mark's school, Windsor), B.A. 91.

Hawtrey, John William, born at Rimpton, Somerset, 1869; 3s. Montague John Grigg, cler. KEBLE, matric. 14 Oct., 84, aged 19 (from St. Mark's school, Windsor), B.A. 87.

Hay, Henry Maurice Drummond, born at Seggieden, co. Perth, 22 Oct., 1869; 2s. Henry Maurice, arm. CHRIST CHURCH, matric. 14 Oct., 87, aged 17, from Winchester.

Hay, John James, born at Edinburgh 20 May, 1867; o.s. James, arm. UNIVERSITY COLL., matric. 25 April, 87, aged 19, from Rugby.

Hay, Marinnus, born at Glasgow 28 Nov., 1865; 3s. William, cler. NON-COLLEGIATE, matric. 13 Oct., 88, aged 22 (from St. John's school, Cowley), B.A. 92; HONOURS :—3 classical mods. 90, 4 classics 92.

Hay, Reginald Neville Ellis, born at Bognor, Sussex, , 1867 ; o.s. Arthur Hurldan, arm. BRASENOSE, matric. 20 Oct., 86, aged 19, from Eton.

Hay, rev. Richard Arthur Hay, born at Thames, Surrey, 1865; 2s. Richard Hay, arm. WORCESTER, matric. 18 Oct., 83, aged 18 (from St. Paul's school), scholar 82, B.A. 87, M.A. 91 (HONOURS :—2 classical mods. 84, 2 classics 87); curate of St. Werburgh, Derby, 89.

Haycock, rev. Trevitt Reginald Hine-, born at Old Charlton, Kent, 3 Dec., 1861; 2s. William, solicitor. NEW COLL., matric. 16 Oct., 80, aged 18 (from Wellington coll.), B.A. 85, M.A. 90 (HONOURS :—3 law 84), in the Oxford eleven 83 and 84; bar.-at-law, Lincoln's Inn, 86; curate of Rotherham, Yorks, 90.

Hayden, Charles Bertram, born at West Hendred, Berks, , 1875; 3s. Charles Frederick, vicar. NON-COLLEGIATE, matric. 23 April, 92, aged 17, from Christ Church cathedral school.

Hayden, Charles Frederick, M.A., fellow CORPUS CHRISTI 49-56, where see.

Hayden, Oswald Ernest, born at Helmdon, Northants, 30 June, 1872; 2s. Charles Frederick, cler. CHRIST CHURCH, matric. 18 Jan., 91, aged 18 (from Warwick school); HONOURS :—2 classical mods. 92.

Hayes, Edward Harold, M.A., fellow NEW COLL. 78, where see page 206.

Hayes, Thomas Herbert, born at Serayingham, Yorks, 3 Oct., 1870; 1s. Thomas, cler. WORCESTER, matric. 16 Oct., 88, aged 18 (from Marlborough coll.), B.A. 91.

Hayman, Henry, D.D., fellow ST. JOHN'S 41-55, where see.

Hayne, Robert, born at Fordington, Dorset, 1867; o.s. Robert, gent. BRASENOSE, matric. 23 Oct., 85, aged 18 (from Winchester), B.A. 88, M.A. 92.

Haynes, rev. Charles Edward, born at Fulwood, co. Lanc, , 1865; 1s. Edward Joseph, cler. NON-COLLEGIATE, matric. 16 Oct., 86, aged 21, migrated to HERTFORD, B.A. 89; HONOURS :—3 theology 89); curate of Broadwater, Sussex, 90.

Haynes, Everard Joseph, born at Caterick, Yorks, , 1869 ; 2s. Edward Joseph, cler. BALLIOL, matric. 18 Oct., 88, aged 19, B.A. 92; HONOURS : —3 classical mods. 90, 3 classics 92.

Haynes, Stanhope Henry Shekell, born at Romford, Essex, 22 Dec., 1873; 1s. Henry Shekell, solicitor. ORIEL, matric. 27 Oct., 92, aged 18, from Haileybury.

Hayter, William Goodenough, born in London 23 Jan., 1869; 4s. Henry Goodenough, gen. NEW COLL., matric. 12 Oct., 88, aged 19 (from Winchester), scholar 87, B.A. 92; HONOURS :—2 classical mods. 90, 2 classics 92.

Hayton, Edward Chadwick, born at Niton, I.W., 25 March, 1873; 1s. George, M.A., rector. MAGDALEN, matric. 18 Oct., 92, aged 19 (from Marlborough coll.), exhibitioner 91.

Hayton, George, M.A., fellow QUEEN'S 55-8, where see page 181.

Hayward, Charles John William, born at Rushall, Wilts, 16 Nov., 1869; 2s. John, gen. WORCESTER, matric. 16 Oct., 88, aged 18 (from Sherborne school), scholar 88, B.A. 92; HONOURS :—2 classical mods. 90, 3 law 92.

Hayward, Charles Spencer, born at Norwood, Surrey, 8 Nov., 1861; 2s. Walter William, arm., deceased. MAGDALEN, matric. 16 Oct., 80, aged 18 (from Christ's hospital, and King's coll., London), demy 80-4; HONOURS:—2 mathematical mods. 82, 3 mathematics 84.

Hayward, Charles Waterfield, born at Norwood, Australia, June, 1867; 1s. Edward Waterfield, gent. KEBLE, matric. 22 Oct., 85, aged 18 (from St. Peter's coll. school, Adelaide), B.A. 88, M.A. 92. (HONOURS:—2 law 88); bar.-at-law, Inner Temple, 90.

Hayward, Charles Wilters Andréa, born at Huntingdon, co. Hereford, 21 July, 1866; 2s. Johnson, arm. EXETER, matric. 21 Jan., 85, aged 18 (from Rugby school) (HONOURS:—3 law 88); bar.-at-law, Inner Temple, 90.

Hayward, Henry Rudge, M.A., fellow PEMBROKE 58-64, where see.

Hayward, Norman, born at Dartmouth, Devon, Sept., 1867; 2s. William, gent. KEBLE, matric. 19 Oct., 86, aged 19 (from Portsmouth gr. school), B.A. 90.

Hazell, Alfred Ernest William, born at West Derby, co. Lanc., 20 Feb., 1869; 1s. John, gent. JESUS COLL., matric. 16 Oct., 88, aged 19 (from K. Edward's school, Birmingham), scholar 88, B.A. 92; HONOURS:—1 classical mods. 90, 2 classics 92.

Hazell, Edgar, born in London 18 May, 1872; 3s. Joseph, gent. MAGDALEN, matric. 22 Oct., 91, aged 19, from the Charterhouse.

Hazledine, Frederick John, born at Kingsdon, Somerset, 20 May, 1864; 3s. William, cler. NON-COLLEGIATE, matric. 17 Jan., 91, aged 26 (from Shrewsbury gr. school), headmaster church of England gr. school, etc.

Hazledine, William Clough, born at Donington, Salop, March, 1870; 1s. John Rowland Levett, arm. ORIEL, matric. 25 Oct., 89, aged 19 (from Repton school), B.A. 92.

Head, Charles Henry, born in London 1866; 1s. Charles, gent. NON-COLLEGIATE, matric. 19 Jan., 84, aged 18, B.A. 87.

Head, Frederick Dewar, born at Dalston, Middx., 16 April, 1867; 4s. Timothy John, gent. QUEEN'S, matric. 30 Oct., 85, aged 18 (from Merchant Taylors' school), B.A. 89; HONOURS:—3 classical mods. 87, 3 law 89.

Head, Harry, born at Tunbridge Wells, Kent, 1864; 2s. Charles Henry, gent. BALLIOL, matric. 17 Oct., 82, aged 18 (from Bedford school); lieut. R.A. 86, as Harry Francis.

Head, Lewis William, born at Peasemore, Berks, 1868; 2s. William, gen. ST. EDMUND HALL, matric. 25 Jan., 91, aged 23.

Headlam, rev. Arthur Cayley, born at Whorlton, co. Durham, 2 Aug., 1862; 1s. Arthur William, vicar of Durham, St. Oswalds. NEW COLL., matric. 15 Oct., 81, aged 19 (from Winchester), scholar 81-5, B.A. 85; fellow ALL SOULS' 85, B.A. 88, chaplain 88 (HONOURS:—2 classical mods. 83, 1 classics 85); divinity lecturer ORIEL 88, and QUEEN'S 89; examining chaplain to bishop of Southwell 91; brother of Lionel W.

Headlam, Cecil, born in London 19 Sept., 1872; 5s. Edward, bar.-at-law, deceased. MAGDALEN, matric. 22 Oct., 91, aged 12 (from Rugby), demy 91.

Headlam, Francis John, M.A., fellow UNIVERSITY COLL. 54-73, where see page 32.

Headlam, Lionel William, born at Whorlton, co. Durham, 6 Jan., 1870; 3s. Arthur William, cler. NEW COLL., matric. 23 Nov., 89, aged 19 (from Eton), B.A. 92; HONOURS:—3 mathematical mods. 90, 4 classics 92; brother of Arthur C.

Headlam, Maurice Francis, born at Manchester 19 Oct., 1873; 1s. Francis John, M.A., J.P., stipendiary, Manchester. CORPUS CHRISTI, matric. 18 Oct., 92, aged 18 (from Eton), scholar 91.

Headlam, Morley Lewis Caulfield, born at Whorlton, co. Durham, 13 Feb., 1868; 2s. Morley, gen. ALL SOULS', matric. 19 Oct., 87, aged 19 (from Durham gr. school), bible clerk 87; HONOURS:—3 classical mods. 89, 4 classics 91.

Heal, Joseph John, born at Frome, Somerset, 1844; 2s. Joseph, gent. NON-COLLEGIATE, matric. 15 Oct., 92, aged 48, from Frome school.

Healey, Gerald Edward Chadwyck-, born in London 16 May, 1873; 1s. Charles Edward Heley-C-H., Q.C. TRINITY, matric. 15 Oct., 92, aged 19, from Eton.

Healey, John Edward, born at Leicester 1862; 2s. William, gent. NON-COLLEGIATE, matric. 17 Oct., 85, aged 23, B.A. 89.

Hearn, rev. Frank Basil, born at Roxwell, Essex, 23 Sept., 1865; 4s. Thomas John, rector of Wootton, Oxon. NEW COLL., matric. 15 Oct., 84, aged 19 (from Bradfield coll.), B.A. 88, M.A. 92 (HONOURS:—2 theology 88); curate of St. Mary the Virgin, Reading, 89; brother of James R.

Hearn, James, born in London 30 March, 1873; 2s. Arthur Ridley, gent., deceased. BRASENOSE, matric. 21 Oct., 92, aged 19 (from Christ's hospital), exhibitioner 92.

Hearn, James Ridgway, born at Roxwell, Essex, May, 1863; 2s. Thomas John, rector of Wootton, Oxon. KEBLE, matric. 17 Oct., 82, aged 19 (from Felsted school), B.A. 87, M.A. 92.

Hearn, Thomas John, M.A., fellow NEW COLL. 42-52, where see page 212.

Heath, John Everard, born at Newcastle-under-Lyne, co. Stafford, 29 May, 1866; 4s. Robert, gent. BRASENOSE, matric. 25 Oct., 85, aged 19, from Rugby.

Heathcote, Gilbert Wall, M.A., fellow NEW COLL. 24-38, where see page 209.

Heathcote, rev. Wyndham Selfe, born at Dorking, Surrey, 22 Jan., 1862; 7s. Thomas Jenkyns, arm. TRINITY, matric. 15 Oct., 81, aged 19 (from Clifton coll.), B.A. 85 (HONOURS:—3 theology 85); curate of Streatham St. Andrew 90.

Heather, Henry James Shedlock, born in London 9 May, 1863; 1s. James, arm. BALLIOL, matric. 17 Oct., 82, aged 19 (from St. Paul's school), B.A. 86, M.A. 91; HONOURS:—2 mathematical mods. 83, 2 mathematics 86.

Heaton, rev. Albert Edward, born at Birmingham April, 1867; 4s. James, gen. NON-COLLEGIATE, matric. 15 Oct., 87, aged 20 (from K. Edward VI. (high) school, Birmingham); migrated to KEBLE, B.A. 90 (HONOURS:—4 theology 90); curate of Llantillio-Pertholey, co. Mon., 91.

Heaton, Ernest, born at Bettwys-yn-Rhos, co. Denbigh, 21 May, 1861; 2s. Hugh Edward, cler. JESUS COLL., matric. 23 Oct., 80, aged 19 (from Marlborough coll.); migrated to UNIVERSITY COLL., B.A. 84.

Heaton, George, born at Milan 9 June, 1861; 1s. George, gent. MAGDALEN, matric. 16 Oct., 80, aged 19 (from Clifton coll.), demy 80-5, B.A. 85, B.Med. and M.A. 88; HONOURS:—1 natural science 83.

Heaton, Gilbert, born at Bettwys-yn-Rhos, co. Denbigh, 2 May, 1868; 6s. Hugh Edward, cler. WORCESTER, matric. 19 Oct., 86, aged 18 (from Marlborough coll.), B.A. 90.

Heaton, Guy, born at Hampstead, Middx., April, 1861; o.s. William Henniker, M.P. JESUS COLL., matric. 25 Oct., 80, aged 19 (from Reigate school); migrated to HERTFORD, B.A. 84, M.A. 87; HONOURS:—4 history 84.

Heaton, Hugh, born at Bettwys-yn-Rhos near Abergele, 4 Nov., 1865; 4s. Hugh Edward, cler. WORCESTER, matric. 17 Oct., 84, aged 18 (from Rossall school), B.A. 87; a master at Cheltenham coll. 89, died 1 May, 91.

Heawood, Allan Henry, born at Combs, Suffolk, 2 Oct., 1867; 3s. John Richard, cler. ST. MARY HALL, matric. 18 Jan., 87, aged 19, B.A. 92.

Heawood, Percy John, born at Newport, Salop, 8 Sept., 1861; 1s. John Richard, cler. EXETER, matric. 22 Oct., 80, aged 19 (from Ipswich gr. school), scholar 80-5, B.A. 83, M.A. 87; HONOURS:—1 mathematical mods. 81, 1 mathematics 83, 2 classics 85, junior 82, and senior mathematical scholarship 86, Herschel astronomical prize 86; of Durham university (ad eundem) 1 May, 88, mathematical lecturer 88.

Heazell, Francis Nicholson, born at Nottingham 1866; 2s. William Arthur, gent. WADHAM, matric. 19 Oct., 85, aged 19 (from University coll., Nottingham), B.A. 91.

Heberden, Charles Buller, M.A., principal BRASENOSE 89, where see.

Hecker, Henry Charles Paynham Teusch, born in Hawke Bay, New Zealand, 30 May, 1866; o.s. Henry Charles, schoolmaster, N.Z. WADHAM, matric. 15 Oct., 89; aged 21, from Cheltenham coll.

Hecksoher, Edward John, born at Manchester 23 Aug., 1869; 3s. Martin Bernard, D.Med. NEW COLL., matric. 12 Oct., 88, aged 19 (from Giggleswick school), scholar 88, B.A. 91; HONOURS:—1 mathematical mods. 89, 2 mathematics 91.

Hedgeland, Harold Charles, born at Exeter 13 Sept., 1872; 1s. John White, cler., deceased. MAGDALEN, matric. 22 Oct., 91, aged 19, from Exeter gr. school.

Hedger, rev. Ernest, born in London Dec., 1867; 2s. Frederick, arm. ST. JOHN'S, matric. 16 Oct., 86, aged 18 (from King's school, Canterbury), B.A. 89; (HONOURS:—4 theology 89); curate of Aberford, Yorks, 90.

Hedley, Basil, born at Beckley, Sussex, 17 Jan., 1863; 1s. William, rector. BALLIOL, matric. 17 Oct., 82, aged 19 (from Clifton coll.), B.A. 87, M.A. 91; HONOURS:—3 classical mods. 84, 4 classics 86.

Hedley, George Wald, born at Langho, co. Lanc., 23 May, 1871; 1s. Matthew, cler. MERTON, matric. 15 Oct., 90, aged 19 (from Manchester gr. school), exhibitioner 90; HONOURS:—3 mathematical mods. 92.

Hedley, William Henry, born at Medomsley, co. Durham, 1867; 1s. William Henry, gent. HERTFORD, matric. 22 Oct., 86, aged 19.

Heelas, rev. William Denton, born at Reading 20 May, 1862; 1s. Daniel, gent. WADHAM, matric. 15 Oct., 81, aged 19 (from Reading gr. school); B.A. 84, M.A. 88; curate of St. George, Newcastle-on-Tyne, 91.

Heelis, rev. Thomas, born at Long Marton, Westmorland, Aug., 1867; 4s. John, cler. KEBLE, matric. 19 Oct., 86, aged 19 (from Appleby gr. school), B.A. 89; curate of Kirkby Thore, Westmorland, 91.

Heginbottom, George Astheton, born at Ashton-under-Lyne, co. Lanc., 20 Jan., 1871; 5. Thomas, gen. PEMBROKE, matric. 28 Jan., 90, aged 19, from Rugby.

Heilgers, Frank Fehrman, born in London 26 March, 1869; 4s. Frederick William, late of Champion Hill, Surrey, arm., deceased. MAGDALEN, matric. 22 Oct., 87, aged 18, from Dulwich coll.

Heineman, Edmund Lewis, born at Dresden 1866; 2s. Lewis, arm. CHRIST CHURCH, matric. 31 May, 84, aged 18 (from Datchet school), B.A. 87.

Helbert, Lionel Helbert, born at Brighton 13 June, 1870; 3s. Frederick John, arm. ORIEL, matric. 25 Oct., 89, aged 19 (from Winchester), scholar 89; HONOURS:—2 classical mods. 91.

Hele, John Calvert, born at Ridgeway, Devon, 1861; 2s. George, gen. NEW COLL., matric. 15 March, 92, aged 31.

Hellier, rev. Henry Griffin, born at Bristol 1854; 1s. Henry, gent. NON-COLLEGIATE, matric. 13 Oct., 83, aged 29; migrated to NEW INN HALL 85, and to BALLIOL 87; vicar of St. Michael and All Angels', North Kensington, 86-91, and of Billingshurst, Sussex, 91.

Helme, Ernest, born at Walthamstow June, 1873; 1s. Richard, gent. CHRIST CHURCH, matric. 14 Oct., 92, aged 19, from Winchester.

Helme, Francis Mashiter, born at Folkestone, Kent, Sept., 1861; 7s. Thomas, arm. CHRIST CHURCH, matric. 10 April, 80, aged 18, from Eton.

Hemans, Philip Wynne, born in London 1862; 2s. Henry William, gent. ST. EDMUND HALL, matric. 30 April, 84, aged 22.

Hemmerde, Charles Louis, born at Peckham, Surrey, 24 June, 1867; 3s. James Godfrey Locke, of Blackheath, arm. MAGDALEN, matric. 21 Oct., 86, aged 19 (from Winchester), B.A. 89; HONOURS:—2 law 89.

Hemmerde, Edward George, born at Peckham, Surrey, , 1872; y.s. James Godfrey Locke, arm. UNIVERSITY COLL., matric. 11 Oct., 90, aged 18 (from Winchester); scholar 90; HONOURS:—1 classical mods. 92.

Hemmings, Theophilus, born at Salisbury 1841; 1s. Theophilus, pleb. NEW COLL., matric. 12 Feb., 83, aged 42, B.Mus. 85.

Hemsley, Alfred Macartney, born at Ealing, Middx. 20 July, 1860; 3s. Alexander, gent. ST. MARY HALL, matric. 28 Jan., 80, aged 19 (from Westminster school), B.A. 82.

Hemsley, George Herbert, born at Harlaxton, co. Lincoln, 11 Aug., 1869; 3s. Henry, gen. MERTON, matric. 15 Oct., 90, aged 21, from Bedford modern school.

Hemsley, William James, born at Ely, co. Camb., 9 Oct., 1864; 1s. John, gent. JESUS COLL., matric. 18 Oct., 83, aged 19 (from Marlborough coll.), scholar 83, B.A. 87; HONOURS:—2 classical mods. 85, 3 classics 87.

Henderson, Bernard William, born at Islington 1872; 2s. John Thomas, arm. LINCOLN, matric. 20 Oct., 90, aged 18 (from University coll. school, London); scholar 89; HONOURS:—1 classical mods. 92.

Henderson, Edward Lowry, born in London June 1873; y.s. Peter Lindsay, shipowner. ORIEL, matric. 27 Oct., 92, aged 19, from Radley coll.

Henderson, Harold Edmund, born at Leeds Aug., 1867; 7s. William George, D.D., dean of Carlisle. KEBLE, matric. 17 Oct., 87, aged 20, from Leeds gr. school.

Henderson, Nelson Faviell, born at Dulwich, Surrey, 24 Sept., 1865; 2s. James, gent. MAGDALEN, matric. 19 Oct., 83, aged 18 (from Dulwich coll.), B.A. 87, M.A. 90.

Henderson, Patrick Arkley Wright, M.A., fellow WADHAM 67, where see.

Henderson, Peter, born at Bradford, Yorks, 15 July, 1872; 1s. Andrew, gen. QUEEN'S, matric. 22 Oct., 89, aged 17 (from Bradford gr. school), exhibitioner 89; HONOURS:—a chemistry 92.

Henderson, Robert Arthur, born at Leeds, March, 1870; 8s. William George, D.D., dean of Carlisle. KEBLE, matric. 11 Oct., 90, aged 20, from Carlisle gr. school.

Henderson, rev. Wilfred, born 30 Jan., 1865; 5s. William George, D.D., dean of Carlisle. KEBLE, matric. 22 Oct., 85, aged 20 (from Leeds gr. school), B.A. 88 (HONOURS :—3 theology 88) ; curate of Christ church, Albany-street, London, 89.

Henderson, William George, D.D., dean of Carlisle, fellow MAGDALEN 46-52, where see page 322.

Hendry, Frederic, born at Abelour, co. Banff, 1867 ; 7s. William, gen. CHRIST CHURCH, matric. 12 Oct., 88, aged 21 (from Aberdeen university), scholar 89.

Hendy, Ernest William, born at Trowbridge, Wilts, 23 Nov., 1872 ; 2s. James Wadman, woollen merchant, deceased. BALLIOL, matric. 18 Oct., 90, aged 19 (from Tiverton school), exhibitioner 92.

Henlé, Frederick Thomas Henry, born in London 2 March, 1874 ; 1s. Louis Anthony, merchant. BALLIOL, matric. 18 Oct., 92, aged 18, from Clifton coll.

Henley, hon. Anthony Morton, born in London 4 Aug., 1873 ; 3s. Anthony Eden, lord Henley. BALLIOL, matric. 20 Oct., 91, aged 18, from Eton.

Henley, Arthur Keith, born at Putney, Surrey, 12 April, 1863; 2s. hon. Robert, vicar. NEW COLL., matric. 14 Oct., 82, aged 19 (from the Charterhouse), B.A. 86, M.A. 90 ; HONOURS :—2 classical mods. 84, 3 theology 86.

Henley, Edward Cornish, born 9 June, 1871 ; 2s. Henry Cornish, colonel. LINCOLN, matric. 19 Jan., 91, aged 19, from Lancing coll.

Henley, rev. Robert Eden, born at Putney, Surrey, 10 Sept., 1861 ; 1s. hon. Robert, vicar. ST. MARY HALL, matric. 21 Jan., 81, aged 19 (from King's coll.), B.A. 84, M.A. 87 ; curate of Chester Holy Trinity 84-91, vicar of Wharton, Cheshire, 91.

Henly, Launcelot Millner, born at Ruscombe, Berks, Oct., 1868 ; 4s. John, cler. KEBLE, matric. 17 Oct., 87, aged 18 (from Leatherhead school), B.A. 91.

Henn, Charles Cooper, born at Chorlton-on-Medlock, co. Lanc., 1863; 4s. John, cler. WORCESTER, matric. 19 Oct., 82, aged 19 (from Christ's hospital), scholar 81-6, B.A. 86 ; HONOURS :—2 classical mods. 83, 3 classics 86 ; died 25 Sept., 91.

Henn, rev. Percy Umfreville, born at Greenhays, near Manchester, 21 Jan., 1865; 5s. John, cler. WORCESTER, matric. 6 Dec., 83, aged 18 (from Christ's hospital), scholar 83, B.A. 87, M.A. 90 (HONOURS : 2 classical mods. 85, 3 classics 87) ; assist. master St. John's coll., Hurstpierpoint, 90.

Henniker, Frederick Chandos, born at South Charlton, Northumberland, 2 Sept., 1866 ; 3s. Robert, cler. BALLIOL, matric. 24 Oct., 85, aged 19 (from St. Paul's school) ; assist. commissioner Assam.

Henniker, John Granville, born at Alnwick, Northumberland, 11 Jan., 1862 ; 1s. Robert, cler. TRINITY, matric. 16 Oct., 80, aged 18 (from Marlborough coll.), B.A. 84 (HONOURS :—2 classical mods. 82, 3 classics 84) ; of Calcott Somers, and of Mayfurlong, co. Stafford.

Henniker, Percy George Vincent, born at Maidstone, Kent, 1867 ; 1s. Thomas Faulkner, gen. NEW COLL., matric. 18 Jan., 87, aged 20.

Henniker, Robert Percy, born at South Charlton, Northumberland, 14 Dec., 1863; 2s. Robert, cler. NON-COLLEGIATE, matric. 13 Oct., 83, aged 19, from St. Paul's school.

Henning, Edward Nares, born in London 16 Dec., 1871 ; o.s. Edward Nares, of Sherborne, Dorset, arm., deceased. CORPUS CHRISTI, matric. 16 Oct., 90, aged 18, from Sherborne school.

Henriques, Henry Straus Quixano, born at Broughton, co. Lanc., 8 Nov., 1866 ; 1s. Edward Michells, gent. WORCESTER, matric. 22 Oct., 85, aged 18 (from Manchester gr. school), scholar 8., B.A. 89 (HONOURS :—1 classical mods. 87, 2 classics 89; 1 law 90, Vinerian law scholarship 91, 2 civil law 91) ; bar.-at-law, Inner Temple, 92.

Henriques, Quentin Quixano, born at Broughton, co. Lanc, 16 March, 1874 ; 5s. Arthur Quixano, merchant. CORPUS CHRISTI, matric. 18 Oct., 92, aged 18 (from Manchester school), scholar 91.

Henry, rev. Douglas William, born at Brading, isle of Wight, 1861 ; s. Jeremiah, arm. NON-COLLEGIATE, matric. 16 Oct., 86, aged 25 (from Rochester cathedral gr. school); migrated to EXETER 22 Jan., 89, B.A. 89 (HONOURS :—3 mathematical mods. 88) ; curate of St. Michael's, Battersea, 90.

Henry, George Stuart, born at Coates, co. Gloucester, 3 Dec., 1871 ; 2s. Thomas Allan, arm. MERTON, matric. 15 Oct., 90, aged 18, from Harrow.

Henry, William Howard, born at Stillorgan, co. Dublin, 29 July, 1861 ; 1s. William, gen. ; of TRINITY, Dublin, incorporated from WADHAM 9 Dec., 86, aged 25 (educ. at Leamington coll.), B.A. 87.

Hensley, Cyril Wolferstan, born at Haileybury coll. 31 May, 1872 ; 2s. Augustus de Morgan, cler. ORIEL, matric. 27 Oct., 91, aged 19, from Haileybury.

Henson, rev. Herbert Hensley, born in London 8 Nov., 1863; 4s. Thomas, gen. NON-COLLEGIATE, matric. 15 Oct., 81, aged 17 (from Broadstairs school), B.A. 84 ; fellow ALL SOULS' 84-91, M.A. 88 (HONOURS :—1 history 84,) ; head of the Oxford house, Bethnal Green, 87-8, vicar of Barking, Essex, 88.

Henson, John, born at Burton Field, co. Leicester, 29 June, 1873 ; 2s. William, gent. WORCESTER, matric. 22 Oct., 91, aged 18 (from Leamington coll. and Tonbridge school), scholar 91.

Hepburn, Arnold, born at Ramsbotham, co. Lanc., 1869 ; 4s. Archibald, gen. BALLIOL, matric. 19 Oct., 87, aged 18 (from Leamington coll.), exhibitioner 87, B.A. 92 ; HONOURS :—3 history 91.

Hepher, Cyril, born at Leeds 28 Oct., 1872 ; 1s. John, cler. NEW COLL., matric. 16 Oct., 91, aged 18, from Leeds gr. school.

Hepper, Charles Henry, born in York 1872 ; 1s. William, gen. NON-COLLEGIATE, matric. 13 Oct., 88, aged 16.

Herald, John Lungair, born at Arbroath, co. Fife, 1862; 1s. John, gent. BALLIOL, matric. 18 Oct., 81, aged 19 (from Arbroath school) ; assist. commissioner Assam.

Herapath, Alfred Edward, born at Penleigh near Bristol, 16 Feb., 1869 ; 3s. Alfred Newton, arm. MERTON, matric. 17 Oct., 88, aged 19, from Rugby.

Herbert, hon. Auberon Edward William Molyneux, fellow ST. JOHN'S 55-69, where see.

Herbert, Dennis Henry, born at Hemingford Abbotts, Hunts, 25 Feb., 1869 ; 1s. Henry, rector. WADHAM, matric. 13 Oct., 88, aged 19 (from Ely cathedral school), B.A. 92 ; HONOURS :—3 history 92.

Herbert, Edward William, born at Gateshead, co. Durham, 14 Nov., 1866 ; 2s. Samuel Asher, cler. JESUS COLL., matric. 10 June, 85, aged 18 (from Crediton school), B.A. 89 ; HONOURS :—3 classical mods. 87, 2 mathematical mods. 87, 2 mathematics 89.

Herbert, rev. George, born at Vauxhall, Surrey, June 1866 ; o.s. George William, vicar of Vauxhall St. Peter. NEW COLL., matric. 28 Oct., 84, aged 18 (from Eton), B.A. 89 ; curate of Lower Gornall, co. Stafford, 90.

Herbert, Henry Beresford, born at Gateshead, co. Durham, 19 Jan., 1869; 3s. Samuel Asher, cler. EXETER, matric. 19 Oct., 87, aged 18 (from Leamington coll.), exhibitioner 87, B.A. 91; HONOURS:—2 mathematical mods. 89, 3 mathematics 91.

Herbert, sir Robert George Wyndham, G.C.B., C.M.G., D.C.L., fellow ALL SOULS' 54, where see page 271.

Herdman, Emerson Crawford, born at Belfast Jan., 1869; 1s. John, gent. CHRIST CHURCH, matric. 12 June, 86, aged 17.

Hereford, James Tudor, born at Mordiford, co. Hereford, 1869; 1s. Richard James, arm. ST. JOHN'S, matric. 13 Oct., 88, aged 19, from Wellington coll.

Herford, Ulric Vernon, born at Greenheys, co. Lanc., 1867; 3s. William Henry. NON-COLLEGIATE, matric. 21 Oct., 89, aged 22.

Herford, rev. William Llewellyn, born at Lancaster Jan., 1858; 1s. William Henry, gent. KEBLE, matric. 22 Oct., 85, aged 27 (from Owens college, Manchester), B.A. 88 (HONOURS:—3 theology 88); curate of Dury St. Mark, co. Lanc., 90.

Hering, Maurice George, born at Shipley, Yorkshire, 11 Nov., 1866; 2s. William Ernest Augustus, gen., deceased. QUEEN'S, matric. 25 Oct., 86, aged 19 (from Bradford gr. school', exhibitioner 86, B.A. 91; HONOURS:—2 classical mods. 88, 3 history 90.

Heriot, Everard Alexander, born at Blackheath, Kent, 2 April, 1872; 3s. Robert, arm. BRASENOSE, matric. 15 Oct., 90, aged 18, from Harrow.

Herkomer, Hubert, M.A., 29 June, 1886, by decree of convocation, hon. fellow ALL SOULS' 87, where see page 275.

Heron, Francis Arthur, born at Chorley, co. Lanc., 3 Dec., 1864; 1s. Arthur Penson, arm. NEW COLL., matric. 12 Oct., 83, aged 18 (from the Charterhouse), B.A. 87; HONOURS:—2 morphology 87.

Herridge, Decimus, born at New Swindon, Wilts, 1863; 2s. James, cler. NON-COLLEGIATE, matric. 13 Oct., 88, aged 25, from a Banbury school.

Herron, Herbert George Whitby, born at Twickenham, Middx., 6 Jan., 1866; 1s. George Oliver, gent. EXETER, matric. 23 Oct., 85, aged 19 (from Rugby); assist. magistrate and collector Bengal.

Herschel, Arthur Edward Hardcastle, born at Hawkhurst, Kent, 5 Oct., 1873; 2s. sir William James, bart. CHRIST CHURCH, matric. 4 June, 92, aged 18, from Winchester.

Herschel, John Charles William, born at Dacca in East Indies, 22 May, 1869; 1s. sir William James, bart. CHRIST CHURCH, matric. 18 Jan., 89, aged 19 (from Winchester), B.A. 92; HONOURS:—4 physics 92.

Herschell, Farrer, lord Herschell, created D.C.L. 30 June, 1886. See *Al. Ox.* and series 649.

Hervey, lord Arthur Charles, bishop of Bath and Wells, created D.D. 16 June, 1885. See *Al. Ox.* and series 649.

Hervey, lord Francis, M.A., fellow HERTFORD 74, where see.

Hesketh, Marsh, born at Burslem, co. Stafford, 1874; 1s. William, gen. CHRIST CHURCH, matric. 16 Oct., 91, aged 17 (from Newcastle-under-Lyne school), scholar 90; HONOURS:—2 mathematical mods. 92.

Heslop, William Owen Clayton, born at Preston, co. Lanc., 4 Sept., 1865; 1s. Ralph Clayton, D. Med. EXETER, matric. 23 Oct., 85, aged 20.

Hessey, James Dodson, born at Basing, Hants, 3 July, 1867; 1s. Robert Falkner, vicar. MAGDALEN, matric. 21 Oct., 86, aged 19, from Rugby.

Hessey, Robert Falkner, M.A., fellow MAGDALEN 53-64, where see page 323.

Heurtley, Archibald Charles, born at Frant, Sussex, 1872; 5s. Charles Abel, cler. CHRIST CHURCH, matric. 10 Oct., 90, aged 18 (from Shrewsbury school); HONOURS:—3 classical mods. 92.

Heurtley, Charles Abel, D.D., canon of CHRIST CHURCH 53, where see.

Heurtley, Claud, born at Frant, Kent, 1874; 2s. Charles Abel, cler. KEBLE, matric. 15 Oct., 92, aged 18, from Tiverton.

Hewart, Gordon, born at Bury, co. Lanc., 1870; 1s. Giles, gen. UNIVERSITY COLL., matric. 15 Oct., 87, aged 17 (from Manchester gr. school), scholar 87, B.A. 92; HONOURS:—2 classical mods. 89, 2 classics 91.

Hewby, Louis John, born in London 21 March, 1871; 3s. John Pitch, surgeon. MAGDALEN, matric. 14 Oct., 89, aged 18 (from St. Paul's school), demy 89; HONOURS:—1 classical mods. 91.

Hewetson, James, born at Measham, co. Derby, 28 Sept., 1872; 5s. John, cler. TRINITY, matric. 15 Oct., 92, aged 20, from Repton school.

Hewetson, rev. Joseph, M.A., WORCESTER, where see.

Hewetson, rev. Joseph Brown, born at Maryport, Cumberland, 9 March, 1861; 3s. John, gent. QUEEN'S, matric. 6 Nov., 80, aged 19 (from Carlisle and Shrewsbury gr. schools), B.A. 84, M.A. 87; curate of Christ Church cathedral, Victoria, Vancouver, 91.

Hewetson, rev. William, born at Measham, co. Derby, 1862; 3s. John, cler. WORCESTER, matric. 19 Oct., 82, aged 20, B.A. 86, M.A. 89 (HONOURS:—3 theology 86); curate of St. Paul 87-8, and of St. Matthias, Birmingham, 88-90, and of Aston-by-Birmingham 90.

Hewett, Henry Victor, born at Bombay 15 Jan., 1868; 3s. Thomas Douglas, arm., deceased. QUEEN'S, matric. 30 Oct., 85, aged 17, from Ludlow gr. school.

Hewett, Herbert Tremenheere, born at Norton Fitzwarren, Somerset, 25 May, 1864; o.s. William Henry, gent. TRINITY, matric. 15 Oct., 83, aged 19 (from Harrow school), B.A. 87; in Oxford university eleven 86; bar-at-law, Inner Temple, 91; captain of Somersetshire county cricket club.

Hewett, John, born at Babbicombe, Devon, 1865; 4s. John, cler. UNIVERSITY COLL., matric. 13 Oct., 83, aged 18 (from King's coll., London), B.A. 87; HONOURS:—3 classical mods. 85.

Hewett, John Arthur Binford, born at Bicknoller, Somerset, 1869; 2s. John Prowse, cler. ST. JOHN'S, matric. 13 Jan., 83, aged 20, B.A. 87, M.A. 89.

Hewett, Mervyn William, born at Birkenhead, Cheshire, 1861; 2s. William Henry, cler. WORCESTER, matric. 21 Oct., 80, aged 19 (from Bromsgrove school), scholar 80-2.

Hewett, William Arthur Steains, born at Sydenham 1869; 1s. William, arm. UNIVERSITY COLL., matric. 13 Oct., 88, aged 19, B.A. 92 (HONOURS:—4 history 92), in Oxford University eight 92.

Hewins, William Albert Samuel, born at Wolverhampton 1865; 2s. Samuel, gent. PEMBROKE, matric. 27 Oct., 84, aged 19 (from Wolverhampton school), scholar 84, B.A. 87, M.A. 93; HONOURS:—1 mathematical mods. 85, 2 mathematics 87.

Hewitt, Copley Delisle, born at Walton-on-Thames 28 Oct., 1871; 2s. Thomas, bar.-at-law. MAGDALEN, matric. 22 Oct., 91, aged 19, from the Charterhouse.

Hewitt, rev. James Bradley, born at Leysters, co. Worcester, 6 Dec., 1863; 3s. Thomas Swinton, vicar. WADHAM, matric. 17 Oct., 82, aged 18 (from Lancing coll.), B.A. 87; curate of Dunchurch, co. Warwick, 89.

Hewitt, James Francis, B.A., student CHRIST CHURCH 54-60, where see.

Hewlett, George, born at Wick St. Laurence, Somerset, 1874; 1s. Joseph, esq. HERTFORD, matric. 22 Oct., 92, aged 18 (from Bristol gr. school), scholar 91.

Hewlett, Sydney Gerald, born at Hastings 1862; y.s. Alfred Stephen, cler. KEBLE, matric. 11 Oct., 90, aged 28, from Harrow.

Hext, Edward Francis Amyas, born at St. Veep, Cornwall, 20 Aug., 1867; 2s. George, vicar. TRINITY, matric. 16 Oct., 86, aged 19 (from Haileybury), B.A. 89; HONOURS:—4 history 89.

Hext, George, B.D., fellow CORPUS CHRISTI 47-58, where see.

Hext, George Kendall, born at St. Veep, Cornwall, 20 Oct., 1864; 1s. George, vicar. CORPUS CHRISTI, matric. 19 Oct., 82, aged 18 (from Harrow), B.A. 86; HONOURS:—3 law 86.

Hext, Thomas James Kitson, born at King's Teignton, Devon, May, 1861; 5s. John Hawkins, vicar. HERTFORD, matric. 3 Feb., 82, aged 20.

Hexter, William Vardon Paterson, born at Cothelstone, Salop, 25 Feb., 1872; s. William, vicar 70. NON-COLLEGIATE, matric. 17 Oct., 91, aged 19, from Warwick gr. school.

Heycock, rev. Francis Wheaton, born at Pytchley, Northants, 28 July, 1868; 2s. Charles Henseman, capt. 75th regt. NEW COLL., matric. 18 Oct., 87, aged 19 (from Cheltenham coll.), B.A. 90 (HONOURS:—3 history 90); curate of Ealing, Middlesex, 91.

Heygate, Arthur Conolly (Gage), born at Londonderry 18 Aug., 1862; 3s. Frederick William, bart. CHRIST CHURCH, matric. 14 Oct., 82, aged 20 (from Eton), scholar 82, B.A. 86; migrated to ST. JOHN'S, M.A. 91; HONOURS:—1 classical mods. 83, 1 classics 86.

Heywood, John Henry, born at Oldham, co. Lanc., 1869; 3s. George, arm. UNIVERSITY COLL., matric. 15 Oct., 87, aged 18, B.A. 91.

Heywood, William Rowe, born at Forest Hill, Kent, 24 Jan., 1868; 1s. Samuel, arm. TRINITY, matric. 15 Oct., 87, aged 19 (from Merchant Taylors' school), B.A. 90 (HONOURS:—2 law 90); bar.-at-law, Middle Temple, 92.

Hibbert, Bernard Roland, born at Shrewsbury Nov., 1868; 2s. Samuel, gen. KEBLE, matric. 13 Oct., 88, aged 19 (from Ellesmere coll., Salop), B.A. 91.

Hibbert, Gerald Kenway, born at Neath, co. Glamorgan, 1 Feb., 1872; 1s. Walter Griffiths, gen. JESUS COLL., matric. 15 Oct., 90, aged 18 (from University coll., Aberystwyth), exhibitioner 90; HONOURS:—2 classical mods. 92.

Hibbert, Norman Burrell, born at Staveley, co. Derby, 8 March, 1868; 4s. William, gen. QUEEN'S, matric. 25 Jan., 88, aged 19, from Staveley school.

Hichens, rev. Arthur Smythe, born at Speldhurst, Kent, 21 Jan., 1868; 2s. Frederick Harrison, vicar of Canterbury St. Stephen's. MAGDALEN, matric. 21 Oct., 86, aged 18 (from Clifton coll.), B.A. 89 (HONOURS:—3 history 89); curate of Potter's Bar, Middlesex, 91.

Hichens, rev. Baron Henry Paull, born at St. Ives, Cornwall, 3 Aug., 1863; 4s. William, solicitor. EXETER, matric. 23 Oct., 85, aged 22 (from Cheltenham coll.), B.A. 89, M.A. 92; curate of Holy Trinity, Weymouth, 91.

Hichens, Basil Snaith, born at Guilsborough, Northants, 21 June, 1873; 3s. Thomas Sikes, vicar. HERTFORD, matric. 14 Oct., 90, aged 17.

Hichens, James Byrn, born in London 16 Oct., 1872; 1s. John Knill Jope, stockbroker. MAGDALEN, matric. 22 Oct. 91, aged 19 (from Winchester), exhibitioner 91.

Hichens, John Ley, born at Lichfield 4 July, 1872; 1s. John Ley, late of St. Ives, Cornwall, physician, deceased. BALLIOL, matric. 18 Oct., 92, aged 20, from Winchester.

Hichens, John Oldham, born at Guilsborough, Northants, 23 Nov., 1870; 2s. Thomas Sikes, vicar. TRINITY, matric. 12 Oct., 89, aged 18 (from Winchester), B.A. 92; HONOURS:—4 history 92.

Hichens, Peverell Smythe, born at Speldhurst 27 June, 1870; 3s. Frederick Harrison, rector of Canterbury St. Stephen. MAGDALEN, matric. 16 Oct., 88, aged 18 (from Clifton coll. and King's school, Canterbury), B.A. 92; HONOURS:—1 physiology 92.

Hichens, Richard Arthur James, born at Colchester, Essex, 13 Aug., 1871; 3s. Richard, cler. EXETER, matric. 21 Jan., 91, aged 18, from Marlborough.

Hickes, George, born at Hursley, Hants, March, 1874; 1s. Thomas Harold Frederick, cler. KEBLE, matric. 15 Oct., 92, aged 18, from Malvern coll.

Hickey, Godfrey Michael Vincent, born at Cawnpore, India, 28 Sept., 1872; 1s. Robert Walter Hunter Guest, cler. QUEEN'S, matric. 27 Oct., 91, aged 19 (from Magdalen coll. school), bible clerk 91.

Hickley, Charles Lushington, born at Ham, Surrey, , 1863; 2s. Thomas Allen, gent. PEMBROKE, matric. 26 Oct., 81, aged 18 (from Winchester), B.A. 84; bar.-at-law, Inner Temple, 87.

Hickley, John George, B.D., fellow TRINITY 43-51, where see.

Hickman, Henry Richard Belcher, born in London 11 April, 1866; o.s. William, gent. CHRIST CHURCH, matric. 10 Oct., 84, aged 18 (from Westminster school), B.A. 88; HONOURS:—3 physiology 88.

Hickox, rev. Sidney Ernest, born at Bromley-by-Bow March, 1867; o.s. Walter, gen. KEBLE, matric. 90 (HONOURS:—2 theology 90); curate of Grimsby St. James 90.

Hicks, Edward Lee, M.A., fellow CORPUS CHRISTI 66-74, where see.

Hicks, Francis Baptist, born at Plymouth 1869; 1s. Francis, gen. UNIVERSITY COLL., matric. 15 Oct., 87, aged 18 (from Sherborne school), B.A. 91; HONOURS:—3 classical mods. 89, 3 classics 91.

Hicks, Frederick Cyril Nugent, born at Dunstable, Beds, 28 June, 1872; o.s. Charles Cyril, of Wokingham, Berks, D.Med. BALLIOL, matric. 20 Oct., 91, aged 18 (from Harrow), scholar 90.

Hicks, George Dawes, born at Shrewsbury 1863; 1s. Christopher, gen. NON-COLLEGIATE, matric. 21 Oct., 89, aged 26.

Hickson, Sydney John, scholar DOWNING, Cambridge, 79, B.A. 82, M.A. 85, fellow 87, D.Sc. (HONOURS:—1 class natural science tripos 88); created M.A. (Oxon) 29 May, 88; deputy Linacre professor of human and comparative anatomy; educated at University coll. school and University coll., London, and St. Bartholomew's hospital.

Higgins, Alfred Charles, born at Cheltenham 1858; 3s. John, gent. NON-COLLEGIATE, matric. 19 Jan., 84, aged 26, from Cheltenham gr. school.

Higgins, Francis Tyringham, born in London 22 July, 1864; 1s. Joseph Napier, Q.C. CHRIST CHURCH, matric. 12 Oct., 83, aged 19 (from Westminster school), scholar 83, B.A. 87, M.A. 90 (HONOURS:—2 classical mods. 85, 2 history 87); bar.-at-law, Lincoln's Inn, 89.

19

Higgins, Henry Llewellyn, born at Peel, isle of Man, 1862; 1s. Henry, D.Med. EXETER, matric. 20 Oct., 81, aged 19 (from K. William's coll., isle of Man), scholar 81-5, B.A. 85, M.A. 88; HONOURS: —2 mathematical mods. 83, 3 natural science 85.

Higgins, William, born at Stamford, co. Lincoln, 1861; o.s. William, arm. MERTON, matric. 18 Oct., 80, aged 19 (from Shrewsbury gr. school), B.A. 84, M.A. 91.

Higgs, Arthur Gerald, born at Handborough, Oxon, 1859; y.s. Richard William, rector, deceased. NEW INN HALL, matric. 18 Jan., 82, aged 23.

Higgs, Arthur Hibble, M.A. BALLIOL, where see page 70.

Higham, James, born at Faversham, Kent, 29 July, 1865; 6s. James, gent. WADHAM, matric. 11 Oct., 84, aged 19 (from Faversham gr. school), B.A. 88, M.A. 92; HONOURS:—2 classical mods. 86, 2 classics 88.

Highfield, John Carrick, born at Blencogo, Cumberland, 17 Dec., 1865; 1s. George, gent. QUEEN'S, matric. 30 Jan., 84, aged 18 (from Sedbergh gr. school), B.A. 86.

Highton, Gerard Arthur, born at Podymore, Somerset, 27 Sept., 1863; 3s. Alfred, vicar of Great Bourton. NON-COLLEGIATE, matric. 15 Oct., 81, aged 18, from Marlborough.

Highton, Hugh Percy, born at Podymore, Somerset, 24 Aug., 1865; 4s. Alfred, vicar of Great Bourton. MAGDALEN, matric. 16 Oct., 84, aged 19 (from Marlborough coll.), exhibitioner 84, B.A. 88; HONOURS:—1 chemistry 88.

Hignell, Sidney Robert, born at Thornbury, co. Glouc., 3 June, 1873; 2s. Thomas Evans, gent. EXETER, matric. 18 Oct., 92, aged 19 (from Malvern coll.), scholar 92.

Hignett, Edward Ashmore, born at Walthamstow, Essex, 1872; 1s. George Edward, cler. NON-COLLEGIATE, matric. 19 Jan., 89, aged 17 (from Manchester gr. school); migrated to BALLIOL 90, B.A. 92; HONOURS:—2 history 92.

Hignett, Geoffrey, born at Liverpool Dec., 1871; 4s. John, gent. CHRIST CHURCH, matric. 14 Oct., 92, aged 20, from University coll., Liverpool.

Hignett, Henry Reginald, born at Ringway, Cheshire, 29 Jan., 1870; 1s. Henry Alfred, cler. WADHAM, matric. 14 Oct., 89, aged 19 (from Denstone coll.), B.A. 92; HONOURS:—3 history 92.

Higson, George Lewis, born at Lytham, co. Lancs., 23 Sept., 1868; 3s. Peter, accountant. JESUS COLL., matric. 14 Oct., 89, aged 21 (from Manchester gr. school), B.A. 92.

Higson, Thomas Atkinson, born at Stockport, Cheshire, 18 Nov., 1873; 2s. Jacob, C.E. NEW COLL., matric. 16 Oct., 91, aged 17, from Rossall school.

Higson, William, born at Allerton, co. Lancs., 1863; 1s. John, arm. CHRIST CHURCH, matric. 27 May, 82, aged 19, from Eton.

Hildersheim, Paul, born at Dundee 1866; 2s. David, gent. ST. JOHN'S, matric. 17 Oct., 85, aged 19 (from King's coll. school), B.A. 89, M.A. and B.C.L. 92; HONOURS:—a law 89, 3 civil law 91.

Hildersheimer, Alfred Abraham, born at Chorlton-upon-Medlock, co. Lancs., 1873; 1s. Albert, gent. PEMBROKE, matric. 28 Oct., 92, aged 19 (from University coll. school London), scholar 92.

Hildyard, rev. Lyonel D'Arcy, born at Bury, co. Lancs., 5 Feb., 1861; 3s. Charles Frederick, cler. MAGDALEN, matric. 19 Oct., 83, aged 22 (from Birmingham gr. school), clerk 83, B.A. 87, M.A. 90; in Oxford university eleven 84, 85.

Hildyard, Robert Thoroton, born at Yorktown, Surrey, Oct., 1873; 1s. Robert Charles Thoroton, capt. R.E. CHRIST CHURCH, matric. 14 Oct., 92, aged 19.

Hill, right hon. Alexander Staveley, D.C.L., Fereday fellow ST. JOHN'S 54-65, where see.

Hill, rev. Arthur, born at Neath, co. Glamorgan, 21 Aug., 1864; 1s. John, gent. JESUS COLL., matric. 18 Oct., 83, aged 19 (from Llandovery coll.), scholar 83, B.A. 88; HONOURS:—1 classical mods. 85, 2 classics 87.

Hill, rev. Charles Sydney, born at St. Winnow, Cornwall, Jan., 1869; 3s. George, cler. KEBLE, matric. 17 Oct., 87, aged 18 (from Winchester), B.A. 91 (HONOURS:—2 history 90); curate of Llangynwyd 93.

Hill, Ebenezer Brown, born at Dollar, co. Clackmannan, 1863; 2s. Ebenezer Brown, cler. NON-COLLEGIATE, matric. 20 Oct., 90, aged 27.

Hill, Edward, M.A., student CHRIST CHURCH 27-50, where see.

Hill, Edward, fellow ST. JOHN'S 51-7, where see.

Hill, Edward Maurice born in London 8 Jan., 1862; 1s. George Birkbeck, D.C.L. BALLIOL, matric. 21 Oct., 80, aged 18 (from Haileybury), exhibitioner 79-85, B.A. 84 (HONOURS:—1 classical mods. 81, 1 classics 84); bar.-at-law, Inner Temple, 88.

Hill, Ernest, born at Ickford, Bucks, 6 March, 1867; 2s. Walter, cler. PEMBROKE, matric. 27 Oct., 85, aged 18 (from Uppingham and Sherborne schools), scholar 85; HONOURS:—2 classical mods. 87.

Hill, Ernest George, born at Oxford 26 Feb., 1872; 1s. George, baptist minister. MAGDALEN, matric. 22 Oct., 91, aged 19 (from Leeds gr. school), demy 90.

Hill, Eustace St. Clair, born in Honiton, Devon, Sept., 1873; 4s. James Turner, major-general in the army. CHRIST CHURCH, matric. 14 Oct., 92, aged 19, from Lancing coll.

Hill, Francis John, born at Timsbury, Somerset, 1 Oct., 1862; 2s. Richard, cler. EXETER, matric. 4 June, 81, aged 18, from Marlborough.

Hill, George Birkbeck Norman, D.C.L., hon. fellow PEMBROKE 72, where see.

Hill, George Francis, born at Berhampore, East Indies, 22 Dec., 1867; 4s. Samuel John, gen. MERTON, matric. 15 March, 88, aged 20 (from University coll. school and University coll., London), exhibitioner 88, B.A. 92; HONOURS:—1 classical mods. 89, 1 classics 91.

Hill, Gerard Robert, born at Milverton, co. Warwick, 19 Feb., 1872; 1s. Henry, of Thornton Dale, Pickering, gen. BALLIOL, matric. 20 Oct., 91, aged 17 (from Eton), exhibitioner 90.

Hill, Henry Staveley, born in London 22 May, 1865; o.s. Alexander Staveley, M.P., D.C.L. ST. JOHN'S, matric. 11 Oct., 84, aged 19 (from Westminster school); bar.-at-law, Inner Temple, 91.

Hill, Hugh Percy, born in London 6 Sept., 1864; 4s. Charles, gent. LINCOLN, matric. 19 Oct., 83, aged 19 (from University coll. school, London), B.A. 87, M.A. 92 (HONOURS:—2 law 87); bar.-at-law, Inner Temple, 89.

Hill, James Pennell, born at Ahmundabad, East Indies, 8 Nov., 1861; 1s. James Turner, arm. BALLIOL, matric. 29 Jan., 81, aged 19 (from Lancing coll.), B.A. 84 (HONOURS:—3 classical mods. 82); lieut. E. Yorkshire regt. 84, Wing-officer 20th Bombay N.I. 87.

Hill, James Robert, born at Dollar, co. Clackmannan, 1862; s. Ebenezer Brown, cler. ST. JOHN'S, matric. 15 Jan., 87, aged 25 (from Glasgow university), B.A. 90.

Hill, John Latty, born at Aylesbury, Bucks, 1871; 3s. Walter, cler. ST. EDMUND Hall, matric. 1 May, 90, aged 19, from Selwyn coll., Cambridge (matric. 22 Oct., 88).

Hill, Matthew Davenport, born in London 17 Jan., 1872; 2s. Matthew Berkeley, surgeon, deceased. NEW COLL., matric. 10 Oct., 90, aged 18 (from Eton), scholar 90.

Hill, Reginald Duke, born in London Jan., 1866; 1s. James Duke, arm. BRASENOSE, matric. 7 June, 84, aged 18, from Eastbourne coll. and Harrow.

Hill, Rowland Torrens, born in London 9 Oct., 1866; 1s. Pearson, arm. ORIEL, matric. 23 Oct., 85, aged 19 (from Haileybury), B.A. 88 (HONOURS :—4 law 88); bar.-at-law, Inner Temple, 92.

Hill, Stanley Paris, born at Croughton, Oxon, 1867; o.s. John Stanley, cler. NON-COLLEGIATE, matric. 13 May, 84, aged 17, from Llandaff cathedral school.

Hill, Vernon Tickell, born at Llandaff 1871; 2s. Edward Stock, col., C.B., M.P. ORIEL, matric. 25 Oct., 89, aged 18 (from Winchester); in Oxford university eleven 92.

Hill, Walter Francis, born at Redminster, co. Glouc., 1870; 1s. Benjamin Walter, accountant. NON-COLLEGIATE, matric. 4 June, 92, aged 22, from Bristol cathedral school.

Hill, William Ellis, born at Glasgow 1862; 1s. Julius, arm. BALLIOL, matric. 21 Jan., 80, aged 18 (from Eton), B.A. 83, M.A. 86 (HONOURS:—3 classical mods. 81, 1 history 83); bar.-at-law, Inner Temple, 85.

Hill, William Henry, born at Swindon, Wilts, 1872; 2s. Henry, gen. LINCOLN, matric. 23 Oct., 91, aged 19 (from Worcester cathedral school), exhibitioner 91.

Hill, rev. William Pollock-, born at Upper Norwood, Surrey, Aug., 1866; 1s. William Thompson, D.Med. KEBLE coll. school, London), B.A. 90 (HONOURS :—4 theology 90); curate of Lambourne, Berks, 90.

Hillard, Abraham, born at Eastington, co. Glam., 10 July, 1858; 4s. Charles, Wesleyan minister, deceased. NON-COLLEGIATE, matric. 21 Jan., 91, aged 32, from Kingswood school and Eastbourne coll.

Hillard, rev. Albert Ernest, born at New Swindon, Wilts, 8 Dec., 1865; 6s. Charles, cler. CHRIST CHURCH, matric. 16 Oct., 85, aged 19 (from Kingswood school and University coll., London), scholar 85, B.A. 89, M.A. 92 (HONOURS :—1 classical mods. 87, 1 classics 89); chaplain Clifton coll. 90.

Hillard, Frederick Arthur, born at Swindon, Wilts, 27 June, 1868; 7s. Charles, cler. NON-COLLEGIATE, matric. 17 Jan., 91, aged 22, from New coll., Eastbourne.

Hillard, Edward, born at Croydon, Surrey, 20 Nov., 1867; 1s. George Edward Anstruther, late captn. in the arm., deceased. MAGDALEN, matric. 22 Oct., 87, aged 19 (from Malvern coll.), B.A. 91; HONOURS :—2 history 91.

Hilliard, Francis Porteus Tyrrell, born at Ealing, Middx., 17 Nov., 1872; 4s. Joseph Stephen, cler. MAGDALEN, matric. 22 Oct., 91, aged 18, from Lancing coll.

Hilliard, Robert Osborne, born at Dublin 1869; o.s. Vandeleur, gen. BALLIOL, matric. 18 Oct., 88, aged 19 (from Clifton coll.), B.A. 92; HONOURS :—4 history 91.

Hillier, Arthur Cecil, born at Calais 1858; o.s. George Edward, arm. WORCESTER, matric. 26 Jan., 82, aged 24. B.A. 85; HONOURS :—4 law 85, 3 history 86.

Hills, Charles Robe, born 30 June, 1874; 1s. Charles Tilburne, solicitor. TRINITY, matric. 15 Oct., 92, aged 18, from Haileybury coll.

Hills, Charles Lilburne, born at Holyhead 7 May, 1871; 2s. Charles Stevens, arm. TRINITY, matric. 11 Oct., 90, aged 19 (from Christ's hospital), scholar 89; HONOURS :—1 classical mods. 92.

Hills, Eustace Gilbert, born at Kirkby Fleetham, Yorks, 1868; 3s. Herbert Augustus, a judge in India. BALLIOL, matric. 19 Oct., 87, aged 19 (from Eton), B.A. 91; HONOURS :—3 history 91.

Hills, rev. Henry Gardner, born in London Dec., 1866; 4s. John, gent. KEBLE, matric. 22 Oct., 85, aged 18 (from Marlborough coll.), B.A. 88, M.A. 92 (HONOURS :—3 history 88); curate of Ramsgate 90.

Hills, John Waller, born in London 1867; 2s. Herbert Augustus, a judge in India. BALLIOL, matric. 24 Oct., 85, aged 18 (from Eton); HONOURS: —2 classical mods. 87, 2 classics 89.

Hinchliff, Henry Mountain Weston, born at Cavendish, Essex, 11 Dec., 1869; 4s. Chamberlain Henry, major in the army. LINCOLN, matric. 17 Oct., 89, aged 19, from U.S. coll. Westward Ho!

Hinckley, Richard Arthur, born at Lichfield 25 March, 1867; 1s. Arthur, gen. WORCESTER, matric. 21 Jan., 87, aged 19 (from Uppingham school), B.A. 92.

Hind, Edward, born at Bolton-le-Moors, co. Lanc., 13 Jan., 1871; 4s. Charles, rector of Ferns, co. Wexford. KEBLE, matric. 11 Oct., 90, aged 19, from Rossall school.

Hind, rev. Henry Norman, born at Plymouth 10 Aug., 1861; 1s. Robert, cler. LINCOLN, matric. 80, aged 19 (from Durham school), B.A. 84, M.A. 89; curate of Liversedge, Yorks, 84.

Hind, Jesse William, born at Nottingham 20 Aug., 1866; 1s. Jesse, arm. TRINITY, matric. 17 Oct., 85, aged 19 (from Clifton coll.), B.A. 88; HONOURS :—4 law 88.

Hindley, Godfrey John Douglas, born at Lambeth 17 Nov., 1872; 4s. Charles Hugh, arm. CHRIST CHURCH, matric. 16 Jan., 91, aged 18 (from Dulwich coll.), scholar 89.

Hinds, Allen Banks, born at Ramsgate 4 Dec., 1867; 2s. Henry, gen. BALLIOL, matric. 21 Jan., 89, aged 18 (from Vale academy, Ramsgate), scholar of CHRIST CHURCH 89, Dixon student 92, B.A. 92; HONOURS: —1 history 92, Stanhope essay prize 92.

Hine, rev. John Edward, born at Nottingham 1867; 2s. Benjamin, gent. NON-COLLEGIATE, matric. 14 Oct., 82, aged 21 (from University coll. school, and University coll., London), B.A. 86, M.A. 90; senior resident officer Radcliffe infirmary, Oxford, 80-2, B.Med. Lond. 79, D.Med. 83; University missionary central Africa and priest in charge of pro-cathedral Zanzibar 91.

Hingley, Alfred Edward, born at Cradley, co. Worcester, 1868; 3s. Samuel, gen. UNIVERSITY COLL., matric. 15 Oct., 87, aged 19, B.A. 91; HONOURS :—2 classical mods. 89, 3 classics 91.

Hinkson, Ernest Augustus, born in Isle of Barbados 1870; o.s. Augustus Briggs, gen. ST. JOHN's, matric. 12 Oct., 89, aged 19, from Harrison coll., Barbados.

Hinshelwood, Alfred Ernest, born at High Broughton, co. Lanc., 6 March, 1867; 4s. George Frederick, gent. TRINITY, matric. 17 Oct., 91, aged 24, from Melbourne and Sydney universities.

Hinton, George Stephen, born at Harmondsworth, Middx., 1859; 2s. George Stephen, cler. ST. EDMUND HALL, matric. 25 Oct., 81, aged 22.

Hinton, Rayner Winterhotham, born at Roborough, co. Glouc., 1867; 1s. William Henry, arm. BALLIOL, matric. 24 Oct., 85, aged 18 (from Tiverton school), scholar 85.

Hipwood, Charles, born in London 22 July, 1869; 1s. Lacy Charles Thomas, solicitor. WADHAM, matric. 13 Oct., 88, aged 19 (from Christ's hospital), scholar 87, B.A. 93; HONOURS :—2 classical mods. 90, 1 classics 92.

Hird, David, born at Arbroath, N.B., 8 May, 1871; 5s. Alexander of Inchenpe, N.B., gent. NON-COLLEGIATE, matric. 15 Oct., 92, aged 21 (from Arbroath high school), M.A. Edinburgh university.

Hirsch, Ernest Leonard, born at Moseley, co. Warwick, 14 May, 1871; 2s. Solly, merchant. LINCOLN, matric. 23 Oct., 91, aged 20, from K. Edward's school, Birmingham.

Hirst, Francis Wrigley, born at Dalton, near Huddersfield, 10 June, 1873; 2s. Alfred, gent. WADHAM, matric. 18 Oct., 92, aged 19 (from Clifton coll.), scholar 91.

Hirst, Henry Denne, born at Canterbury 1 July, 1865; 1s. Thomas, rector of Bishopsbourne, Kent. KEBLE, matric. 14 Oct., 84, aged 19 (from Haileybury), B.A. 87, M.A. 93.

Hirst, Hugh Taylor, born at Saddleworth, Yorks, 1864; 3s. John, gent. BALLIOL, matric. 17 Oct., 82, aged 18 (from Wakefield gr. school), B.A. 87.

Hirst, James Croasland, born at Shipley, Yorks, 1871; 2s. John, gen. QUEEN'S, matric. 15 Jan., 90, aged 19.

Hirst, John Lee, born at Plumpton, Yorks, 25 Sept., 1863; o.s. Robert Baines. gent., deceased. QUEEN'S, matric. 27 May, 82, aged 18, B.A. 86; HONOURS :—3 law 86.

Hirst, Philip Leslie, born at Moldpun, in Huddersfield, 1 July, 1863; 5s. William Edward, gent. BALLIOL, matric. 23 Oct., 82, aged 19 (from Rugby); selected candidate Indian C.S. 82.

Hirst, William Alfred, born at Huddersfield 5 Aug., 1870; 1s. Alfred, gen. WORCESTER, matric. 14 Oct., 89, aged 19 (from Clifton coll.), scholar 89; HONOURS :—2 classical mods 91.

Hirst, William Edward, born at Deighton, Yorks, 8 Oct., 1870; 1s. William Henry, gen. EXETER, matric. 13 Oct., 90, aged 20 from Rossall school.

Hirtzel, Frederic Arthur, born at Selhurst, Surrey, 14 May, 1870; 1s. Frederick, arm. TRINITY, matric. 12 Oct., 89, aged 19 (from Dulwich coll.), scholar 88; HONOURS :—proxime accessit Hertford scholarship 90, accessit Craven scholarship 90, 1 classical mods. 91, Craven scholarship 91.

Hitchcock, Thomas, born at New York, America, Nov., 1860; 3s. Thomas, arm. BRASENOSE, matric. 12 April, 80, aged 19, B.A. 84.

Hitchings, Gerard, born in London 24 June, 1869; 2s. Richard Neville, gen. TRINITY, matric. 13 Oct., 88, aged 19 (from Clifton coll.), B.A. 92.

Hives, Charles Vesey, born at Dublin 14 May, 1872; 1s. Charles John, of London, lieut. R.N., deceased. CORPUS CHRISTI, matric. 16 Oct., 90, aged 18, from U.S. coll., Westward Ho!

Hoare, Edward Brereley, born at Jesmond, near Newcastle-on-Tyne, 25 July, 1872; 2s. Robert Gurney, banker. MAGDALEN, matric. 14 Oct., 90, aged 18, from Elstree and Harrow schools.

Hoare, Wilfred Ernest, born at Lincoln 6 Dec., 1864; 2s. Herbert, cler. MERTON, matric. 17 Oct., 82, aged 17 (from Kingswood school), exhibitioner 82, B.A. 86, M.A. 92; HONOURS :—2 mathematical mods. 84.

Hobbs, Francis Walter, born at Ryde, isle of Wight, 20 March, 1863; 3s. Benjamin, gent. WORCESTER, matric. 17 Oct., 84, aged 21 (from St. Paul's school), B.A. 89.

Hobhouse, Charles Edward Henry, born at East Grinstead, Sussex, 30 June, 1862; 1s. sir Charles, bart. CHRIST CHURCH, matric. 21 May, 80, aged 17 (from Eton); M.P. Wilts 92.

Hobhouse, right rev. Edmund, D.D., assistant to bishop of Lichfield; fellow MERTON 41-57, where see page 96.

Hobhouse, Leonard Trelawney, born at St. Ives, Cornwall, 8 Sept., 1864; 3s. Reginald, archdeacon of Bodmin. CORPUS CHRISTI, matric. 19 Oct., 83, aged 19 (from Marlborough coll.), scholar 83; fellow MERTON 87, B.A. 88, M.A. 90; HONOURS :—1 classical mods. 84, 2 classics 87.

Hobhouse, rev. Walter, born at Nelson, New Zealand, 5 or 6 April, 1862; 2s. Edmund, bishop of Nelson, N.Z., 58-65. NEW COLL., matric. 16 Oct., 80, aged 18 (from Eton), scholar 80-4, B.A. 84; fellow HERTFORD 84-7, M.A. 87; student CHRIST CHURCH 87; HONOURS :—1 classical mods. 81, accessit Hertford scholarship 82, proxime accessit Ireland scholarship 83 and 84, 1 classics 84, English essay 85, Latin essay 86.

Hockley, Guy Wittenoom, born at Malden, Surrey, 1869; 2s. Julius Joseph, arm. BALLIOL, matric. 19 Oct., 87, aged 18 (from Tiverton school), scholar 87, B.A. 91; HONOURS :—2 classical mods. 89, 2 classics 91.

Hockliffe, Ernest, born at Bedford 17 Feb., 1863; y.s. Frederick, gent. LINCOLN, matric. 23 Oct., 82, aged 19 (from Bedford gr. school), scholar 81-6, B.A. 86, M.A. 89; HONOURS :—1 classical mods. 83, 2 classics 86.

Hockmeyer, rev. Johannes, born in Manchester 30 April, 1863; 4s. Otto, gent. QUEEN'S, matric. 23 Oct., 82, aged 19 (from Manchester gr. school), bible clerk 82, B.A. 87, M.A. 92 (HONOURS :—2 history 86); curate of East Grafton, Wilts, 89.

Hodge, Harold, born in London 1862; 3s. Edward Grose, gent. PEMBROKE, matric. 26 Oct., 81, aged 19 (from St. Paul's school), scholar 81-5, B.A. 86, M.A. 88, HONOURS :—2 classical mods. 83, 3 classics 85.

Hodge, John Barwick, born in London 5 Sept., 1863; 3s. William Barwick, arm. CHRIST CHURCH, matric. 13 Oct., 82, aged 19 (from Westminster school), scholar 82, B.A. 86; HONOURS :—1 classical mods. 84, 1 classics 86, 1 history 87.

Hodge, Thomas Williams, born at Hawarden, Flints, 1869; 4s. Hugh, gen. NON-COLLEGIATE, matric. 22 Oct., 87, aged 27, B.A. 90; HONOURS :—3 theology 90.

Hodge, William Ritchie, born at Leyton, Essex, 26 May, 1866; 1s. Charles, gent. TRINITY, matric. 15 Oct., 92, aged 26, from King's coll., London.

Hodges, rev. Edward James, born at Wentworth, Yorks, 1854; 2s. William, cler. NON-COLLEGIATE, matric. 13 Oct., 84, aged 30, B.A. 88.

Hodges, Edward Noel, M.A. QUEEN's, created D.D. 27 June, 89; bishop of Travancore and Cochin 90. See Al. Ox., and series, 670.

Hodges, Frederick George, born at Suramungmum, Madras, 14 Feb., 1874; y.s. William Henry, major 1st Madras infantry. WADHAM, matric. 18 Oct., 92, aged 18, from Warminster gr. school.

Hodges, rev. Herbert Arthur, born at Wentworth, Yorks, 1861; 4s. William, cler. NON-COLLEGIATE, matric. 21 Jan., 82, aged 21, B.A. 85, M.A. 89 (HONOURS :—3 theology 85); vicar of Long Lane, co. Derby, 90.

Hodges, John Richardson. NON-COLLEGIATE, 1882. See EYRE, page 196.

Hodges, William Herbert, born at Sherwood, Notts, 13 Oct., 1873; 1s. William Abraham, banker. WADHAM, matric. 18 Oct., 92, aged 19 (from Banister court school, Southampton), exhibitioner 92.

Hodges, William Richardson, born in St. Pancras, London, May, 1873; 7s. Richard, gen. WADHAM, matric. 17 March, 91, aged 18.

Hodgkin, Thomas, created D.C.L. 30 June, 1886; of Newcastle-upon-Tyne, banker [s. John, of Tottenham, Middx.], born 29 July, 31; fellow University coll., London, 64, hon. D.C.L. Durham, hon. D.Litt. Dublin 92; author of "Italy and her Invaders," edited the "Letters of Cassiodorus," etc., for the Clarendon press.

Hodgkin, William, born at Treales, co. Lanc., July, 1870; 2s. Joseph, perpetual curate of. KEBLE, matric. 29 Jan., 89 aged 18 (from Kirkham gr. school), B.A. 92.

Hodgkinson, Frank Austin Langton, born at Gainsborough, co. Lincoln, 27 July, 1872; 4s. George Langton, clerk. BRASENOSE, matric. 22 Oct., 91, aged 19, from Harrow.

Hodgkinson, rev. Frederick Karslake, born at Wells, Somerset, 25 May, 1861; 4s. William Sampson, of Folkestone, esq., deceased. MAGDALEN, matric. 16 Oct., 80, aged 19 (from Winchester), B.A. 84, M.A. 87; vicar of Worsley, co. Lanc., 90.

Hodgson, Archibald Sanford, born at Esher, Surrey, 26 Nov., 1873; 2s. William Sanford, deceased. NEW COLL., matric. 14 Oct., 92, aged 18, from Eton.

Hodgson, Brian Houghton, F.R.S., created D.C.L. 26 June, 1889, corresponding member of the institute of France, late of the Bengal c. s. and British minister in Nepal.

Hodgson, Charles Greaves, born at Buxton, co. Derby, 14 March, 1869; 1s. Francis Greaves, clerk. ORIEL, matric. 20 Oct., 88, aged 19 (from Rugby school), B.A. 92.

Hodgson, Charles Henry, born at Bromfield, Salop, 23 Sept., 1868; o.s. Charles Hodgetts, gen. BRASENOSE, matric. 20 Oct., 87, aged 19 (from Hereford cathedral school), scholar 87, B.A. 91; HONOURS: —3 classical mods. 89, 3 classics 91.

Hodgson, Christopher Anthony Rowlandson, born at Sydenham, Surrey, 27 Dec., 1873; 2s. Arthur Pemberton, Madras c.s., retired. WORCESTER, matric. 18 Oct., 92, aged 18, from St. Paul's school.

Hodgson, Henry Bernard, M.A., senior student of CHRIST CHURCH 78-85, where see.

Hodgson, Shadworth Hollway, M.A., hon. fellow CORPUS CHRISTI 82, where see.

Hodgson, Timothy, born at Bongate, Appleby, Westmorland, 20 Jan., 1874; 2s. John, of Heights, near Appleby, gent. QUEEN'S, matric. 27 Oct., 92, aged 18 (from Appleby school), scholar 92.

Hodgson, rev. William, born at Colne, co. Lanc., 17 June, 1863; 1s. William, clerk. NON-COLLEGIATE, matric. 13 Oct., 84, aged 21 (from Clergy orphan school, Canterbury); migrated to MERTON, B.A. 87, M.A. 91 (HONOURS: —1 theology 87); curate of Christ Church, Claughton, 90.

Hodgson, William Frederick Sanford, born at Esher, Surrey, 26 July, 1869; 1s. William Sanford, arm: NEW COLL., matric. 12 Oct., 88, aged 19 (from Eton), B.A. 91; HONOURS: —3 history 91.

Hodsdon, rev. Victor Henry, born at High Wycombe, Bucks, 1867; o.s. Henry, arm. CHARSLEY'S HALL, matric. 22 Jan., 84, aged 17, B.A. 87, M.A. 90; curate of Bristol St. Simon 89-90.

Hodsoll, Charles Wilfred Pollock, born at Loose, Kent, 1874; 5s. Charles Maxfield, esq. UNIVERSITY COLL., matric. 15 Oct., 92, aged 18 (from Maidstone school), exhibitioner 92.

Hodson, Albert Edgar, born at Dalston, Middx., 30 March, 1867; 5s. William, gent. WORCESTER, matric. 8 May, 86, aged 19 (from Dalston school), B.A. 90; brother of William.

Hodson, Thomas Callan, born at Moulsey, Middx., 12 Dec., 1871; 7s. Arthur, gen. QUEEN'S, matric. 24 Oct., 90, aged 18 (from Christ's hospital), scholar 90.

Hodson, Thomas Wortley, born at Wortley, Yorks, 13 Sept., 1869; 1s. Thomas, clerk. QUEEN'S, matric. 20 Oct., 88, aged 19 (from St. Bees gr. school), B.A. 92.

Hodson, Vincent Sutherland, born at Stoke Newington 1874; 2s. Arthur, R.N., retired. MARCON'S HALL, matric. 5 May, 92, aged 18.

Hodson, William, born at Dalston 27 April, 1862; 1s. William, gen. QUEEN'S, matric. 1 March, 87, aged 24; an architect; brother of Albert E.

Hogarth, David George, born at Barton-on-Humber, co. Lincoln, 23 May, 1862; 1s. George, vicar. MAGDALEN, matric. 15 Oct., 81, aged 19 (from Winchester), demy 81-5, B.A. 85, M.A. 88, fellow 86; classical tutor 86; HONOURS: —1 classical mods. 82, 1 classics 85, Craven travelling fellowship 86.

Hogg, Adam Spencer, born in London 9 March, 1870; 3s. Adam, arm. TRINITY, matric. 13 Oct., 88, aged 18 (from Cheltenham coll.), B.A. 92; HONOURS: —3 law 92.

Hogg, Guy Weir, born at Calcutta 24 Oct., 1861; 1s. Charles Swinton, arm. CHRIST CHURCH, matric. 21 May, 80, aged 18, from Eton.

Hogg, John Ewer Jefferson, born at Norton-on-Tees, co. Durham, 6 July, 1860; 1s. John, arm. MAGDALEN, matric. 19 Jan., 80, aged 19 (from Somerset coll., Bath), B.A. 84; bar.-at-law, Lincoln's Inn, 87.

Holbrooke, Sidney William Briscoe, born at Cheltenham, co. Glouc., 1 Nov., 1873; o.s. Thomas, gent. WADHAM, matric. 18 Oct., 88, aged 18 (from Pocklington gr. school).

Holcroft, Arthur, born at Bilston, co. Stafford, 1863; 4s. Thomas, gent. ST. JOHN'S, matric. 15 Oct., 81, aged 18, B.A. 92.

Holden, Edward Charles Shuttleworth, born Dam., 1865; o.s. Charles, arm. CHRIST CHURCH, matric. 25 May, 83, aged 18, from Eton.

Holden, Ernest Harrington, born at Middleton, Yorks, 5 Sept., 1869; 1s. Harrington William, clerk. NON-COLLEGIATE, matric. 13 Oct., 88, aged 19 (from Whitchurch gr. school and Denstone coll.), B.A. 92 (HONOURS: —2 classical mods. 90, 2 classics 92); brother of John C.

Holden, Hyla, born at Durham 14 Sept., 1867; 5s. Henry, D.D., headmaster Durham school. BALLIOL, matric. 19 Oct., 86, aged 19 (from Durham gr. school), B.A. 92; HONOURS: —2 classical mods. 88, 3 classics 92.

Holden, Hyla Henry, born at Weymouth, Dorset, 9 Sept., 1873; 3s. William Rose, bar.-at-law. WORCESTER, matric. 18 Oct., 92, aged 19, from Dover coll.

Holden, John, born at Blackburn, co. Lanc., 2 Sept., 1866; 1s. James, gen. NON-COLLEGIATE, matric. 13 Oct., 88, aged 22 (from Blackpool gr. school), B.A. 92.

Holden, John Clement, born at Searby-cum-Ownby, co. Lanc., 28 Feb., 1872; 2s. Harrington William, of Doncaster, clerk. NON-COLLEGIATE, matric. 17 Oct., 91, aged 19 (from Whitchurch gr. school and Denstone coll.); brother of Ernest H.

Holden, Joshua, born at Todmorden, Yorks, 30 Dec., 1870; 2s. William, gen. TRINITY, matric. 11 Oct., 90, aged 19 (from Manchester central school and Normal college of science, South Kensington, and royal school of mines), scholar 89.

Holder, Jabez Henry, born at Homerton, Middx., 1854; 3s. Benjamin, clerk. NON-COLLEGIATE, matric. 3 Nov., 83, aged 29, from a Manchester school.

Holding, rev. John, of St. David's coll., Lampeter. NON-COLLEGIATE, Cambridge; matric. 21 Oct., 84; migrated to CORPUS CHRISTI, Camb., B.A. 84, M.A. 88 (HONOURS: —24th junior optime 84); vicar of Bottisham, co. Camb., 82.

Holding, William, D.C.L., fellow ST. JOHN's 55-69, where see.

Holding, William Septimus, born at Tunbridge, Kent, Sept., 1866; o.s. William Sextus, arm. CHRIST CHURCH, matric. 8 June, 89, aged 22 (from Tonbridge school), B.A. 92; HONOURS:— 3 history 92.

Holdship, Arthur Herbert, born at Auckland, New Zealand, 26 June, 1873; 3s. George, esquire. EXETER, matric. 22 Oct., 91, aged 18, from Cheltenham coll.

Holdsworth, Francis Lewis, born at Surbiton, Surrey, 1863; 2s. George Lewis, gent. CHRIST CHURCH, matric. 20 Jan., 82, aged 19, from Winchester.

Holdsworth, William Searle, born at Beckenham, Kent, 7 May, 1871; 1s. Charles Joseph, solicitor. NEW COLL., matric. 10 Oct., 90, aged 19 (from Dulwich coll.), exhibitioner 89.

Hole, Hugh Marshall, born at Tiverton, Devon, 1865; 1s. Charles Marshall, gent. BALLIOL, matric. 16 Oct., 83, aged 18 (from Tiverton school), exhibitioner 83-5, B.A. 88; HONOURS :—4 law 87.

Hole, John Mackenzie, born at Broadwood Kelly, Devon, 1863; 1s. Nathaniel, cler. ST. JOHN's, matric. 15 Oct., 81, aged 18.

Holland, Alfred, born at Ashbourne Hall, co. Derby, 14 Aug., 1859; 4s. Frederick, arm. CHRIST CHURCH, matric. 20 Jan., 80, aged 22, B.A. 84, M.A. 89; student, Inner Temple, 83.

Holland, Charles, born at Sherwood, Notts, 14 Sept., 1864; 3s. William Henry, gent. NON-COLLEGIATE COLL., matric. 13 Jan., 83, aged 18 (from Hurstpierpoint); migrated to MERTON, B.A. 86, M.A. 89; HONOURS :—2 classics 86.

Holland, rev. Charles Henry, born at London, Canada, 1860; 1s. Charles, arm. WADHAM, matric. 26 Jan., 81, aged 21, B.A. 84; HONOURS :— 3 history 84; curate of Kirkby Misperton, Yorks, 88.

Holland, rev. Edgar Rogers, born at Prestwich, co. Lanc., 1865; 2s. Joseph, D.Med. PEMBROKE, matric. 23 Oct., 82, aged 18 (from Leamington coll.), scholar 82-4, B.A. 86, M.A. 90; HONOURS :—2 classical mods. 84.

Holland, rev. George Edmund, born at Bury St. Edmund's 24 May, 1867; 1s. Stewart, cler. NON-COLLEGIATE, matric. 16 Oct., 86, aged 19 (from Rivington and Blackrod gr. school, Bolton); migrated to EXETER, B.A. 89; curate of Coventry, St. Mark, 90.

Holland, Henry Scott, M.A., senior student CHRIST CHURCH 70-85, where see.

Holland, Herbert Conway, born at Bury St. Edmund's 5 March, 1871; 2s. Steward, cler. WORCESTER, matric. 14 Oct., 89, aged 18 from Dudley gr. school.

Holland, Leonard Duncan, born at Leeds 16 Jan., 1874; 2s. Henry Wilkinson, late Wesleyan methodist minister. MERTON, matric. 18 Oct. 92, aged 18 (from Kingswood school), exhibitioner 92.

Holland, Percy, born in London 28 Oct., 1862; 4s. Stephen George, arm. TRINITY, matric. 21 Jan., 82, aged 19, scholar 82-6, B.A. 85, M.A. 91 (HONOURS :—2 classical mods. 83, 2 law 85); bar.-at-law, Lincoln's Inn, 87.

Holland, Robert Erskine, born in London 29 June, 1873; 2s. Thomas Erskine, professor of international law, Oxford, ORIEL, matric. 27 Oct., 92, aged 19 (from Winchester), scholar 92.

Holland, Robert Martin, born in London 10 Oct., 1872; 1s. Frederick Whitmore, cler. TRINITY, matric. 17 Oct., 91, aged 19, from Eton.

Holland, Thomas Erskine, M.A., D.C.L., fellow ALL SOULS' 75, where see page 272.

Holland, William Edward Sladen, born at Leeds 8 July, 1873; 1s. William Lyal, cler. MAGDALEN, matric. 22 Oct., 91, aged 18 (from Durham gr. school 85-91), exhibitioner 91.

Holland, William Francis Claude, born in London 1866; 1s. William James, gent. BRASENOSE, matric. 28 Jan., 86, aged 20 (from Eton), B.A. 90; in the University eight 87, 8, 9, 90, stroke 89.

Hollings, Henry de Burgh, M.A., B.C.L., fellow CORPUS CHRISTI 70, where see.

Hollis, Algernon Edward, born at Keale, co. Stafford, 3 July, 1874; 3s. Henry William, of Darlington, J.P., engineer. ST. JOHN's, matric. 13 Oct., 92, aged 18 (from Tonbridge school), scholar 92.

Hollis, George Arthur, born at Osmaston, co. Derby, 1868; 1s. Henry William, gen. KEBLE, matric. 12 Oct., 89, aged 21 (from Repton school), B.A. 92; HONOURS :—1 theology 92, Liddon theological studentship 92.

Holloway, Algernon James, born at Wells, Somerset, 12 July, 1871; 2s. John Henry, arm. CHRIST CHURCH, matric. 10 Oct., 90, aged 17, from Bath coll.

Holloway, George, born at Thame, Oxon, 1870; 3s. Benjamin George, gent. TURRELL's HALL, matric. 3 Feb., 85, aged 15, B.A. 88.

Holloway, John Everett, born at Wells, Somerset, 12 Aug., 1865; 2s. John Henry, gent. QUEEN's, matric. 23 Jan., 83, aged 19 (from Wells gr. school), B.A. 86, M.A. 89; HONOURS :—4 law 86.

Holloway, William John, born at Wootton, Oxon, 1869; 2s. Christopher, gen. NON-COLLEGIATE, matric. 13 Oct., 88, aged 19, B.A. 92; HONOURS :—2 theology 92.

Holme, rev. George Frederick, born at Nanthead, Cumberland, 23 Feb., 1860; 3s. Thomas, cler. NON-COLLEGIATE, matric. 17 Jan., 80, aged 19 (from Appleby gr. school); migrated to QUEEN's, B.A. 82, M.A. 86; curate of Hulme Holy Trinity, co. Lanc., 91.

Holme, Gerald Ptoler, born at Cheltenham, co. Glouc., 1873; 2s. George Jackson, dentist. NON-COLLEGIATE, matric. 23 April, 92, aged 19, from Malvern coll.

Holme, Randle Fynes Wilson, born at Beckenham, Kent, 4 July, 1864; 2s. James Wilson, arm. CORPUS CHRISTI, matric. 19 Oct., 83, aged 19 (from Sherborne school), B.A. 87; HONOURS:— 2 classical mods. 85, 1 law 87.

Holme, Robert Francis Lyon, born at Lee, Kent, 28 Nov., 1870; 1s. Robert, cler. QUEEN's, matric. 22 Oct., 89, aged 18 (from Winchester), scholar 88, B.A. 93; HONOURS :—2 mathematical mods. 91, 4 mathematics 92.

Holme, rev. Robert Weston Metcalfe, born at Saddleworth, Yorks, 3 June, 1866; 4s. Thomas, vicar of Moorside, Oldham. NON-COLLEGIATE, matric. 17 Oct., 85, aged 19 (from Owens coll. Manchester); migrated to LINCOLN 87, B.A. 88.

Holmes, Charles John, born at Preston, co. Lanc., July, 1868; 1s. Charles Rivington, cler. BRASENOSE, matric. 20 Oct., 87, aged 18 (from Eton), scholar 87; HONOURS :—2 classical mods. 89.

Holmes, Francis William Reginald, born at Stroud, co. Glouc., 1870; 2s. Frank, gen. BALLIOL, matric. 18 Oct., 88, aged 18 (from Blundell's school, Tiverton); HONOURS :—3 classical mods. 90, 4 classics 92.

Holmes, Harry, born at Harwood Hall, Essex, 1865; 1s. Henry, arm. BRASENOSE, matric. 15 Jan., 83, aged 18, from Harrow.

Holmes, rev. Herbert Cecil, born at Wakerley, Northants, 1866; 3s. Edward, cler. ST. MARY HALL, matric. 24 Oct., 85, aged 19 (from Coventry school), B.A. 90; curate of Peterborough St. Mark 91.

Holmes, Joseph William Mountenay, born at Lewisham, Kent, 26 July, 1870; 2s. William, solicitor. MAGDALEN, matric. 14 Oct., 89, aged 19 (from a Blackheath school, and King's coll., London), demy 89; HONOURS:—1 history 92.

Holmes, Oliver Wendell, created D.C.L. 30 June, 1886, LL.D. Cambridge 17 June, 86, and Edinburgh 86 (son of rev. Abiel Holmes), D.Med. 35, professor of anatomy and physiology in Dartmouth coll. 38-40, and in Harvard coll. 47-82, author of the "Autocrat of the Breakfast-Table," etc., and a collection of poems ; born 29 Aug., 1809.

Holmes, Richard Ellis, born at Pontefract, Yorks, 20 March, 1863; 1s. Richard Hind, gent. NONCOLLEGIATE, matric. 14 Oct., 82, aged 19 (from Wakefield gr. school); migrated to TRINITY Jan., 84, B.A. 85, M.A. 89; HONOURS:—3 history 85.

Holmes, William, born at Dublin , 1871; 1s. Hugh, an Irish judge. ORIEL, matric. 25 Oct., 89, aged 18 (from the Charterhouse); HONOURS: —3 history 92.

Holms, John Mitchell, born at Ibrox, near Glasgow, 23 June, 1863; 1s. James, gent. BALLIOL, matric. 18 Oct., 81, aged 18 (from a Glasgow school); joint magistrate N.W. provinces, India.

Holroyd, George William Fraser, born at Wimbledon, Surrey, 31 March, 1871; 1s. William, colonel. CHRIST CHURCH, matric. 11 Oct., 89, aged 18 (from Winchester), exhibitioner 91.

Holt, Alwyn Ernest, born at Farnley, Yorks, 6 Sept., 1867; 3s. Edward, arm. NEW COLL., matric. 15 Oct., 86, aged 19 (from Bedford school), B.A. 90; HONOURS:—3 classical mods. 88, 3 law 90.

Holt, Harold Edward Sherwin, born at Harrogate, Yorks, 10 Oct., 1862; o.s. Joseph, of Ogbeare Hall, N. Devon, arm. MAGDALEN, matric. 17 April, 82, aged 19 (from Eton), B.A. 86.

Holt, Henry Spawforth, born at Dewsbury, Yorks, Aug., 1860; 1s. Elias, arm. KEBLE, matric. 19 Oct., 80, aged 20 (from Rossall school), exhibitioner 80-3, B.A. 83, M.A. and B.C.L. 87 (HONOURS :— 3 mathematical mods. 80, 1 civil law 86); of London, solicitor.

Holt, James William, born at Farnley, Yorks, 1872; 2s. Edward, arm. UNIVERSITY COLL., matric. 28 April, 92, aged 20.

Holt, Richard Durning, born at Liverpool 13 Nov., 1868; 1s. Robert Durning, arm. NEW COLL., matric. 14 Oct., 87, aged 18 (from Winchester); HONOURS:—2 classical mods. 89.

Holt, rev. Vernon, born at Brooklands, near Manchester, 10 July, 1866; 1s. Daniel, gent. EXETER, matric. 23 Oct., 85, aged 19 (from Bedford school), exhibitioner 84, B.A. 88, M.A. 92 (HONOURS :— 4 history 88) ; curate of Deddington, Oxon, 89.

Holton, Sydney Harcourt Dunsford, born at Kingstown, Dublin, 7 Dec., 1869; 3s. Francis Holton, late surgeon-general, A.M.S. EXETER, matric. 22 Oct., 91, aged 21 (from Bradfield coll.), exhibitioner 91.

Holyoak, Amandus William, born at Ardwick, co. Lanc., 1867; 2s. Henry, gent. BRASENOSE, matric. 23 Oct., 85, aged 18 (from Manchester gr. school), scholar 85, B.A. 89 ; HONOURS:—2 classical mods. 87, 3 classics 89.

Home, Charles Cospatrick Archibald Douglas, lord Dunglass, born at Newton Don, Berwickshire, 29 Dec., 1873; 1s. Charles Alexander, earl of Home, M.A. CHRIST CHURCH, matric. 4 June, 92, aged 18, from Eton.

Home, Robert, born in London 29 Oct., 1872; 2s. John Stuart, gen. QUEEN'S, matric. 27 Oct., 91, aged 18 (from Swansea gr. school), exhibitioner 91.

Homer, John Keelinge, born at Bridgnorth, Salop, 20 March, 1863; 2s. Thomas Keelinge, gent. LINCOLN, matric. 23 Oct., 82, aged 19 (from Malvern coll.), B.A. 86, M.A. 89; HONOURS:— 2 classical mods. 84.

Homfray, Francis Richards, born at Cowbridge, co. Glam., '17 Feb., 1863; 2s. John Richards, arm. BRASENOSE, matric. 21 Jan., 82, aged 18, from Eton.

Homfray, Frederick Charles, born at Ashley Abbots, Salop, Jan., 1864; 1s. Henry Edmund. CHRIST CHURCH, matric. 27 May, 82, aged 18, from Shrewsbury gr. school.

Hone, Edward Richard, born at Longsight, Manchester, 13 Sept., 1873; 1s. Evelyn Joseph, M.A., vicar of S. John's, Deptford. WADHAM, matric. 18 Oct., 92, aged 19 (from Blackheath prop. school), exhibitioner 92.

Hood, Henry Fuller Acland, born at Bridgwater, Somerset, 12 Dec., 1865; 3s. sir Alexander Acland, bart. BALLIOL, matric. 17 Oct., 82, aged 18 (from Eton), B.A. 86; HONOURS:—3 classical mods. 84, 3 history 86.

Hood, Robert Fuller Acland, born at West Quantoxhead, Somerset, 7 Sept., 1866; 4s. sir Alexander Periam, bart. NEW COLL., matric. 16 Oct., 85, aged 19 (from Eton), B.A. 90 (HONOURS:—2 theology 89) ; Universities missionary at Zanzibar 91.

Hooke, George, born at Higher Broughton, co. Lanc., 23 April, 1872; o.s. Richard, artist. NEW COLL., matric. 16 Oct., 91, aged 19, from Manchester gr. school.

Hoole, rev. Charles Holland, M.A., senior student CHRIST CHURCH 61, where see.

Hooper, Francis Alfred Cochmay, M.A., fellow TRINITY 59-71, where see.

Hooper, Gerald Huntley, born at Leamington 23 Oct., 1873; 2s. Edmund Huntley, M.A. CHRIST CHURCH, matric. 16 Oct., 91, aged 17, from Winchester.

Hooper, Herbert Ross, born at Brighton April, 1864; 5s. Robert Poole, cler. HERTFORD, matric. 19 Oct., 81, aged 17, B.A. 86, M.A. 88.

Hooper, James John, M.A., fellow ORIEL 48-84, where see page 153.

Hooson, Thomas John, born at Rhos-Llanerch-rugog, co. Denbigh, 28 Feb., 1873; 1s. Edward, gen. JESUS COLL., matric. 15 Oct., 92, aged 17 (from Ruabon gr. school); exhibitioner UNIVERSITY COLL., 1893.

Hope, Adrian Charles, born at Rhyl, Flints, 1863; 2s. Samuel Pearce, arm. PEMBROKE, matric. 2 May, 82, aged 19.

Hope, Charles Douglas, born at Drayton, Middx., 15 April, 1867; 3s. William, lieut-col. V.C. TRINITY, matric. 17 Oct., 85, aged 18 (from Bloxham school), exhibitioner 85, B.A. 90; HONOURS:—3 mathematical mods. 87, 2 history 89.

Hope, Charles William Weobley, born at Tenby, co. Pemb., 9 Aug., 1864; 1s. Charles Weobley, admiral R.N. BALLIOL, matric. 16 Oct., 83, aged 18 (from Mannamead school, Plymouth); joint magistrate N.W. prov., India.

Hope, Frederick Beresford, born at Kunnan-Kulam, Cochin, 20 Feb., 1872; 2s. William, cler. EXETER, matric. 21 Jan., 91, aged 18, from Exeter gr. school ; twin with Henry T.

Hope, Godfrey Dawson Taylor, born at Oxford 31 March, 1868 ; 2s. Sackett, vicar of Chedworth. QUEEN'S, matric. 25 Oct., 86, aged 18 (from Lancing coll.), scholar 86, B.A. 89.

Hope, Henry Green, born at Chester 9 Jan., 1867; 1s. James Green, gent. NON-COLLEGIATE, matric. 26 Oct., 85, aged 18 (from Chester school), B.A. 89, M.A. 92; HONOURS :—3 classical mods. 87, 3 law 89.

Hope, Henry Townsend, born at Kunnan-Kulam, Cochin, 20 Feb., 1872; 3s. William, cler. EXETER, matric. 21 Jan., 91, aged 18, from Exeter gr. school; twin brother of Frederick D. ; died 4 Jan., 92.

Hope, James Fitzalan, born in London 11 Dec., 1870; 1s. James Robert Hope-Scott, Q.C., deceased. CHRIST CHURCH, matric. 8 June, 89, aged 18.

Hope, James Henry Francis, born in London 1854; 1s. James Butterfield, gent. NON-COLLEGIATE, matric. 17 Oct., 85, aged 31 (from King's coll., London), B.A. 89, M.A. 92; HONOURS :—3 law 89.

Hope, Robert Philip, born at Darwick in Elmet, Yorks, 29 June, 1873; 2s. Charles Augustus, rector. MERTON, matric. 18 Oct., 92, aged 19 (from Eton), postmaster 92.

Hope, rev. Walter Muirhend, born in London 1859; o.s. Ashfield Church, gent. HERTFORD, matric. 18 Oct., 82, aged 23, B.A. 85, M.A. 89 ; curate of Hailey 91.

Hoper, Thomas Loveday, born at Beeding, Sussex, 1 Aug., 1869; 2s. Henry, gen. WORCESTER, matric. 14 Oct., 89, aged 20 (from Oundle school), B.A. 92.

Hopkins, rev. Alexander Henry, born at Pangbourne, Berks, 10 June, 1862; 3s. Robert John, arm. HERTFORD, matric. 3 Feb., 80, aged 18; migrated to BALLIOL, B.A. and M.A. 89.

Hopkins, rev. Charles Edward, born at Widnes, co. Lanc., 3 May, 1861; 1s. David, gent. NON-COLLEGIATE, matric. 15 Oct., 81, aged 20 (from Farnworth and Edgbaston gr. schools); migrated to QUEEN'S, B.A. 86, M.A. 90 (HONOURS :—4 history 85) ; curate of Alverstoke, Hants, 88.

Hopkins, Ernest Threlfall, born at Edgbaston, co. Warwick, 12 Sept., 1861 ; 1s. John Satchell, arm. BALLIOL, matric. 21 Oct., 80, aged 19 (from Rugby), B.A. 84 (HONOURS :—2 classical mods. 82, 2 history 84) ; a brewer.

Hopkins, Francis Henry, born at Worthing 18 July, 1871; 2s. Henry, arm. MERTON, matric. 19 Oct., 89, aged 18.

Hopkins, Henry Mayne Reid, born at Cheshunt 11 March, 1867; 3s. David, arm. TRINITY, matric. 17 Oct., 85, aged 18 (from Dulwich coll.); assist. magistrate N.W. province, India.

Hopkins, John Wilson, born at Cheltenham March, 1865; 4s. Francis William, arm. NON-COLLEGIATE, matric. 4 Nov., 84, aged 19 from Cheltenham gr. school.

Hopkins, Joseph Evan, born at Merthyr-Tydvil, co. Glam., 1861 ; 2s. Joseph, gent. EXETER, matric. 18 Oct., 83, aged 19, B.A. 86, M.A. 90.

Hopkins, William Hustler, born in London May, 1866 ; 2s. William Innes, arm. ORIEL, matric. 23 Oct., 85, aged 19 (from Canterbury school), B.A. 89.

Hopkinson, Alfred (Hume), M.A., B.C.L., Stowell fellow UNIVERSITY COLL. 73-80, where see page 34.

Hopkinson, Emilius, born in London 31 March, 1869; 1s. Jonathan, arm. TRINITY, matric. 15 Oct., 87, aged 18 (from Haileybury), B.A. 91 ; HONOURS :—3 physiology 91.

Hopkinson, John Henry, born at East Stoke, Notts., 15 Dec., 1863 ; 1s. Henry, gent. LINCOLN, matric. 23 Oct., 82, aged 18 (from Newark gr. school), B.A. 85, M.A. 89 ; HONOURS :—2 classical mods. 84.

Hopwood, Walter, born at Louth, co. Lincoln, 4 Sept., 1872; 2s. Walter William, cler. MAGDALEN, matric. 22 Oct., 91, aged 19, from Louth school, and Bradfield coll.

Hordern, rev. Hugh Maudsley, born at Throwley, Kent, Sept., 1868 ; 3s. Herbert Loveday, arm. CHRIST CHURCH, matric. 3 June, 87, aged 18 (from Winchester), B.A. 91.

Hore, Leslie Fraser Standish, born at Munree in East Indies, 5 Aug., 1870; 2s. Frederick Standish, lieut.-col. (retired). CORPUS CHRISTI, matric. 25 Oct., 89, aged 19 (from Wellington) ; HONOURS :—3 classical mods. 91.

Horley, Richard Rothwell, born at Sefton, Liverpool, 6 Jan., 1874 ; 1s. Engelbert, cler. QUEEN'S, matric. 26 April, 92, aged 18, from the Charterhouse.

Horn, Henry, M.A., fellow MAGDALEN 31-4, where see page 321.

Hornby, Charles Harry St. John, born at Much Dewchurch, co. Hereford, 24 June, 1867 ; 1s. Charles Edward, vicar of Elyington, co. Glouc. NEW COLL., matric. 15 Oct., 86, aged 19 (from Harrow), exhibitioner 86, B.A. 91 (HONOURS :—1 classical mods. 88, 3 classics 90), in Oxford eight 90 ; bar.-at-law, Inner Temple, 92.

Hornby, Gerald Frederick, born at Muirtree, co. Lanc., 9 June, 1862 ; 3s. Henry Hugh, gent. CORPUS CHRISTI, matric. 27 Oct., 81, aged 19 (from Winchester), B.A. 86, M.A. 89; HONOURS : —2 classical mods. 83, 2 law 85 ; died 9 Feb., 90.

Hornby, John James, D.D., fellow BRASENOSE 49-69, where see page 353.

Hornby, Richard, born at Long Preston, Yorks, 17 Aug., 1869; 2s. Thomas, gen. QUEEN'S, matric. 20 Oct., 88, aged 19 (from Giggleswick school), exhibitioner 88, B.A. 91 ; HONOURS :—1 chemistry 91, Burdett-Coutts scholarship 92.

Hornby, William Meysey, born at Ebrington, co. Glouc., 18 Jan. or July, 1870; 2s. Charles Edward, vicar, NEW COLL., matric. 18 Oct., 88, aged 18, from Harrow.

Horndon, David, born at Bodmin, Cornwall, 1864 ; 2s. David William John Hicks, arm. EXETER, matric. 31 Jan., 82, aged 18 (from Winchester), B.A. 85.

Horne, Alderson Burrell, born in London 20 Nov., 1863 ; 2s. Edgar, gent. PEMBROKE, matric. 30 Jan., 82, aged 20 (from Westminster school), a solicitor 87.

Horne, rev. Charles Silvester, born at Cuckfield, Sussex, 1865; 3s. Charles, arm. NON-COLLEGIATE, matric. 23 Oct., 86, aged 21 (from Newport gr. school, Salop, and Glasgow university) ; minister Kensington congregational church.

Horne, rev. Edward Hastings, born at Benares, E. Indies, 20 Sept., 1862 ; y.s. Charles, arm., E.I.C.S. TRINITY, matric. 15 Oct., 83, aged 21 (from Clifton and King's coll., London), B.A. 87, M.A. 90 (HONOURS :—2 chemistry 87) ; curate of St. Peter-le-Bailey, Oxford, 91.

Horne, Frederick William, born at Drinkstone, Suffolk, 16 Jan., 1866 ; 1s. Frederick Edward, cler. CHRIST CHURCH, matric. 16 Jan., 85, aged 19, from the Charterhouse.

Horne, John William, born at Rawmarsh, Yorks, 1865 ; 3s. William, pleb. NON-COLLEGIATE, matric. 16 May, 91, aged 26, from Battersea training coll.

Horne, William Ogilvie, born at Wick, Caithness, 1 Nov., 1862 ; 3s. James, arm. TRINITY, matric. 16 Oct., 80, aged 17 (from Clifton coll.); head assist. to collector and magistrate, South Arcot, Madras C.S.

Horner, John Fitz Lloyd, born at Cheltenham 6 April, 1861 ; 1s. John, arm. CHRIST CHURCH, matric. 31 Jan., 81, aged 19, from Malvern coll.

Hornsby, Matthew, born at Silloth, Cumberland, 18 April, 1868 ; 4s. Isaac, a master at St. Kenelms, Cowley. QUEEN'S, matric. 27 Oct., 91, aged 23, from St. Bees gr. school.

Horsley, Harold Richard, born at Headington, Oxon, 1873; 1s. Richard, gen. NON-COLLE-GIATE, matric. 9 June, 90, aged 17, from Oxford high school.

Horton, Robert Forman, M.A., fellow NEW COLL. 79-87, where see page 218.

Horwill, Herbert William, born at Sandown, I.W., 14 May, 1864; 1s. James, bible christian minister. NON-COLLEGIATE, matric. 14 Oct., 82, aged 18 (from Shebbear school, and Victoria coll., Jersey); scholar WADHAM 82, B.A. 86; HONOURS :—1 classical mods. 84, 2 classics 86, English essay 87.

Horwood, Charles Harry Russell, born at Broadwater, Sussex, 20 Nov., 1867; 1s. Charles, arm. BRASE-NOSE, matric. 16 Oct., 88, aged 20, from Highgate gr. school.

Horwood, rev. Faulkner Russell, born at Maldon, Essex, 1869; o.s. Edward Russell, cler. BRASENOSE, matric. 22 Oct., 80, aged 18, B.A. 84, M.A. 87; vicar of Aldermaston, Berks, 88.

Hose, Frederick Thomas Goodfellow, born at Harpenden, Herts, 1863; 1s. Thomas, cler. HERTFORD, matric. 3 Feb., 82, aged 19.

Hose, John Walter, born at Camberwell, Surrey, 25 Oct., 1865; 1s. John Walker, gent. TRINITY, matric. 11 Oct., 84, aged 18 (from Dulwich coll.), scholar CHRIST CHURCH 84-6; joint magistrate N.W. province of India.

Hoskyns, sir John Leigh, bart., M.A., fellow MAGDALEN 43-5, where see page 321.

Hoste, Evelyn Clinton, born at Dinan in France 19 March, 1860; 4s. James Richard Philip, cler. NON-COLLEGIATE, matric. 15 Jan., 87, aged 26, B.A. 89. See Foster's *Baronetage*.

Hoste, rev. James William, born at Heigham, near Norwich, 4 Nov., 1861; 2s. George Charles, rector of Hoxton, Suffolk. MAGDALEN, matric. 24 Jan., 81, aged 19 (from Haileybury), B.A. 84, M.A. 91 (HONOURS:—2 theology 84); curate of Holy Trinity, Twickenham, 91.

Hoste, Philip, born at Stanhoe, Norfolk, 23 April, 1858; 3s. James Richard Philip, cler. NON-COLLEGIATE, matric. 23 April, 87, aged 29, B.A. 90; HONOURS : —4 history 90.

Hotson, John Herbert, born at Long Stratton, Norfolk, Oct., 1872; 2s. John, solicitor. KEBLE, matric. 20 Oct., 91, aged 19, from Beccles school.

Hough, Walter Robert, born at Carlisle 1864; 4s. Edwin, gent. PEMBROKE, matric. 3 May, 83, aged 19, B.A. 86.

Houghton, Arthur Villiers, born at Boston Spa, Yorks, 1870; 2s. Edward James, cler. HERTFORD, matric. 14 Oct., 90, aged 20 (from Eton), exhibitioner 90; HONOURS :—Abbotts scholarship 91, 1 classical mods. 92.

Houghton, rev. Edward John Walford, born at Alvechurch, co. Worcester, 11 Aug., 1867; 1s. Edward James, cler. NON-COLLEGIATE, matric. 22 Oct., 87, aged 20 (from Sherborne and Swansea gr. schools); migrated to CHRIST CHURCH, B.A. 91; HONOURS:—2 classical mods. 89, 2 classics 91.

Houghton, rev. Thomas, born at Tranmere, Cheshire, 1851; 2s. Thomas, gent. ST. JOHN'S, matric. 16 Oct., 80, aged 29, B.A. 83, M.A. 92 (HONOURS:—3 history 83); curate of St. Paul's 83-7, and vicar of St. John, Sheffield, 87.

Houldsworth, Henry Hamilton, born at Coltness House, co. Lanark, Sept., 1867; 1s. William, arm. CHRIST CHURCH, matric. 3 June, 87, aged 19 (from Eton), B.A. 91.

Houlton, sir Edward Victor Lewis, G.C.M.G., fellow of ST. JOHN'S 42-54, where see.

House, Harry Hammond, born at Anderson, Dorset, 27 July, 1863; 1s. Thomas Hammond, rector, deceased. CORPUS CHRISTI, matric. 19 Oct., 82, aged 19 (from Sherborne gr. school), scholar 82-6, B.A. 87, M.A. 93 (HONOURS:—1 classical mods. 83, Greek verse 84, 2 classics 86); a master at Malvern coll.

House, Henry Frederick, born at Bristol 1864; 1s. Richard, gent. BALLIOL, matric. 17 Oct., 82, aged 18 (from Bristol gr. school); joint magistrate N.W. provinces, India.

House, William, born at Taunton, Somerset, 1859; y.s. John, gent. NON-COLLEGIATE, matric. 13 Oct., 84, aged 25, from Stoke St. Gregory and King's coll. London.

House, William Joseph, born at Abingdon, Berks, 13 March, 1870; o.s. Joseph, schoolmaster. WADHAM, matric. 14 Oct., 89, aged 19 (from city of London school), exhibitioner 89; HONOURS :—1 classical mods. 91.

Household, Horace West, born at King's Lynn Jan., 1870; 1s. Robert Henry, arm. CHRIST CHURCH, matric. 12 Oct., 88, aged 18 (from Shrewsbury gr. school), scholar 89, B.A. 92; HONOURS :—2 classical mods. 90, 2 history 92.

Houseman, rev. John, born at Hollywell, Northants, 24 Dec., 1866; o.s. John, cler. WORCESTER, matric. 29 Jan., 86, aged 19 (from Haileybury), B.A. 90; curate of Leatherhead, Surrey, 91.

Houston, Henry Spiers, born at Frome, Somerset, 16 Jan. or May, 1870; 1s. Henry Carey, gen. WADHAM, matric. 14 Oct., 89, aged 18 (from Tettenhall coll. Wolverhampton), B.A. 92.

How, Archibald Barwell, M.A., fellow EXETER 86, where see page 123.

How, Francis Ambrose Walsham, born at Whittington, Salop, 25 Jan., 1870; 5s. William Walsham, bishop of Wakefield. KEBLE, matric. 12 Oct., 89, aged 19 (from Uppingham), B.A. 92.

How, John Hall, born at Castletown, Yorks, 31 March, 1871; o.s. John, gen. WADHAM, matric. 14 Oct., 89, aged 18 (from Berkhamstead school), scholar 88; HONOURS :—1 classical mods. 91.

How, Walter Wybergh, born at Narwell, near Shrewsbury, 28 May, 1861; 3s. Thomas Maynard, solicitor. NEW COLL., matric. 16 Oct., 80, aged 19 (from Winchester), scholar 80-4, B.A. 84, fellow MERTON 85, M.A. 87; HONOURS :—2 classical mods. 81, 1 classics 84.

Howard, Charles James Stanley, viscount Howard of Morpeth, born in London 8 March, 1867; 1s. George James, earl of Carlisle. BALLIOL, matric. 10 Feb., 86, aged 18 (from Rugby), scholar 86, B.A. 89; HONOURS :—1 history 89.

Howard, Frederick Thomas, born at Sudbury, co. Derby, 1868; 2s. Charles, gen. NON-COLLEGIATE, migrated to BALLIOL 88, B.A. 90; HONOURS :—2 geology 90, Burdett-Coutts scholarship 90.

Howard, hon. Hubert George Lyulph, born 3 April, 1871; 2s. George James, earl of Carlisle. BALLIOL, matric. 20 Jan., 90, aged 18.

Howard, Robert, born at Stamford Hill, Middx., 30 Jan., 1872; 2s. David, gen. TRINITY, matric. 11 Oct., 90, aged 18, from Marlborough coll.

Howard, Stanley Heddon, born at Fordcombe, Kent, 1869; 3s. Henry Charles, cler. NON-COLLEGIATE, matric. 11 Oct., 90, aged 21, from Warminster gr. school.

Howard, Stanley McKnight, born at Hales Owen, co. Worc., 14 Feb., 1872; 1s. Henry, arm. NEW COLL., matric. 10 Oct., 90, aged 18, from Eton.

Howe, George Richard Penn Curzon-, viscount Curzon, born 28 April, 1861; 1s. Richard William Penn, earl Howe. CHRIST CHURCH, matric. 5 March, 81, aged 19 (from Eton); M.P. Wycombe division, Bucks, 85.

Howe, rev. Henry Arnold, born at Cheetham Hill, co. Lanc., 1864; 1s. George Guest, arm. UNIVERSITY COLL., matric. 14 Oct., 82, aged 18, B.A. 85, M.A. 90; HONOURS :—4 history 85.

Howe, Newton Ebenezer, born at Lewisham, Kent, 1849; 3s. Thomas Heslope, gent. of MAGDALEN COLL., CAMBRIDGE, incorporated 10 June, 86, aged 37, from MERTON.

Howe, Rupert Bohun Blunt, born at Lewisham, Kent, 1866; 2s. Thomas Heslope, gent. CHRIST CHURCH, matric. 16 Oct., 85, aged 19, from Harrow; brother of Newton and Thomas.

Howe, Thomas Harris Manners, born at Lewisham, Kent, 1864; 1s. Thomas Heslope, gent. CHRIST CHURCH, matric. 16 Oct., 85, aged 21, from Harrow.

Howe, William Norton, born at Castleton, co. Lanc., 5 Oct., 1870; 1s. Alfred, arm. EXETER, matric. 16 Oct., 89, aged 19.

Howell, Alan George Ferrers, born in London 1856; 7s. Thomas Jones, arm. LL.B., from TRINITY COLL., CAMBRIDGE, 79, LL.M. 82 (HONOURS :—8th in 3rd class law tripos 78), of NEW COLL. 29 Jan., 89, aged 33; bar.-at-law, Inner Temple, 81.

Howell, Arthur John William James, born at Merthyr Tydvil, co. Glam., 1861; 1s. John, cler. ST. JOHN'S, matric. 4 June, 81, aged 20.

Howell, Arthur Pearse, M.A., Fereday fellow ST. JOHN'S 54-63, where see.

Howell, Cecil Bertram, born at Dunmow, Essex, 1871; 2s. Horace Sidney, of London, D.Med. CHARSLEY'S HALL, matric. 2 Nov., 86, aged 15.

Howell, Daniel Lewis, born at Much-y-Rallt, co. Montgomery, 15 Nov., 1864; 2s. David, solicitor. MAGDALEN, matric. 24 Jan., 84, aged 19 (from Shrewsbury gr. school), B.A. 87; HONOURS :—3 history 87.

Howell George James, born in London 13 Dec., 1859; 2s. George, solicitor. ST. MARY HALL, matric. 27 Oct., 87, aged 27 (from Greycotes school); migrated to JESUS COLL., B.A. 92.

Howell, John Cyril, born at Surbiton, Surrey, 1873; 1s. Edgar Hedley, merchant. CHRIST CHURCH, matric. 14 Oct., 92, aged 19, from Radley coll.

Howell, William Tudor, born at Pwllheli, co. Carnarvon, 15 Oct., 1862; 4s. David of Wrexham. NEW COLL., matric. 15 Oct., 81, aged 19 (from Shrewsbury gr. school), B.A. 85, B.C.L. 89 (HONOURS :—3 classical mods. 83, 3 law 85, 3 civil law 86); bar.-at-law, Inner Temple, 87.

Howes, Percy Graham, born at Stoke Dannarel, Devon, Nov., 1873; 3s. Frederick Augustus, major-general, R.E. KEBLE, matric. 15 Oct., 92, aged 18.

Howkins, John Drysdale, born at Hartlepool 30 May, 1873; o.s. John, C.E. TRINITY, matric. 15 Oct., 92, aged 19, from Fettes coll.

Howse, George Frederick, born at Ilford, Essex, 1868; o.s. Walter, arm. BALLIOL, matric. 17 Oct., 89, aged 21, scholar 88; HONOURS :—1 mathematical mods. 91, junior mathematical scholarship 91.

Howson, Thomas Henry, born at Oxford 1868; 1s. James, gent. NON-COLLEGIATE, matric. 16 Oct., 86, aged 18, B.A. 91; HONOURS :—3 history 90.

Hudleston, rev. Cuthbert, born at Madras 26 March, 1863; 4s. William, member of Madras council. NEW COLL., matric. 14 Oct., 82, aged 19 (from Wellington), B.A. 86 (HONOURS :—4 history 86); curate of Stepney St. Dunstan 87.

Hudson, Arthur, born at Wisbeach, co. Cambridge, 1861; 2s. Henry, gent. TURRELL'S HALL, matric. 20 May, 86, aged 25 (from Barton school, Wisbeach); migrated to BALLIOL, B.A. 90; bar.-at-law, Inner Temple, 92.

Hudson, Arthur Ernest Ledgar, born at Manchester 8 April, 1865; o.s. William, gent. LINCOLN, matric. 19 Oct., 83, aged 18 (from Manchester gr. school), scholar 83, B.A. 91; HONOURS :—2 classical mods. 85.

Hudson, rev. Charles Henry Bickerton, born at Wick St. Laurence, co. Worc., 5 Aug., 1861; 3s. Charles Smith, arm. MAGDALEN, matric. 19 Oct., 83, aged 22 (from Cheltenham coll.), B.A. 86, M.A. 90; curate of St. Barnabas, Oxford, 86.

Hudson, rev. Ernest Roberts, born at Cambridge 1865; 5s. Philip Samuel, arm. HERTFORD, matric. 14 Oct., 83, aged 19 (from Felsted school), scholar 83, B.A. 88 (HONOURS :—3 classical mods. 86, 3 classics 88); curate of Wednesbury St. James 89.

Hudson, rev. Henry Arnold, born at Manchester April, 1863; 2s. Thomas Barrow, gent. KEBLE, matric. 14 Oct., 84, aged 21 (from Macclesfield gr. school), B.A. 87, M.A. 92 (HONOURS :—3 theology 87); curate of Northfield, co. Worc., 91.

Hudson, Herbert Kynaston, born in London 10 Sept., 1864; 2s. Edward Taylor, cler, and 3rd master St. Paul's school, deceased. NON-COLLEGIATE, matric. 13 Oct., 84, aged 20 (from Christ's hospital); migrated to WADHAM 19 Oct., 85, B.A. 92.

Hudson, James Frank, born at Champion Hill, Surrey, 19 Sept., 1872; 1s. James, gen. JESUS COLL., matric. 20 Oct., 91, aged 19 (from St. Paul's school), exhibitioner 91.

Hudson, John Keble, born at Chorlton-on-Medlock, co. Lanc., 7 Dec., 1867; 3s. Thomas Barrow, gent. KEBLE, matric. 19 Oct., 86, aged 18 (from Macclesfield gr. school); scholar WADHAM 85, B.A. 90; HONOURS :—2 classical mods. 88, 1 classics 90.

Hudson, Walter, born at Briarfield, co Lanc., 22 Oct., 1866; elder son of John, gen. EXETER, matric. 16 Oct., 89, aged 23 (from University coll., Liverpool), exhibitioner 89, B.A. 92; HONOURS :—1 history 92.

Hudson, William Henry, born at Christchurch, Hants, 7 Jan., 1871; 1s. Samuel, gen. HERTFORD, matric. 14 Oct., 89, aged 18 (from Portsmouth school), scholar 87; HONOURS :—2 classical mods. 91.

Huggett, Edgar Vaux, born in London 30 May, 1869; 1s. Thomas, arm. LINCOLN, matric. 20 Oct., 81, aged 19 (B.A. from CHARSLEY HALL 86), M.A. 88; bar.-at-law, Middle Temple, 88; died 30 Jan., 92.

Hughes, Arthur, born at Barnet, Herts, 1861; 1s. Arthur, arm. ST. JOHN'S, matric. 16 Oct., 80, aged 19 (from Merchant Taylors' school), scholar 80, B.A. 87; HONOURS :—1 classical mods. 82, 2 classics 84.

Hughes, Arthur, born in London March, 1863; 3s. Thomas, Q.C. ORIEL, matric. 31 Oct., 82, aged 19 (from Haileybury); a solicitor.

Hughes, Arthur James, born at Rochdale, co. Lanc., 2 June, 1872; 8s. James, gen. QUEEN'S, matric. 24 Oct., 90, aged 18 (from Colwyn Bay school), scholar 90; HONOURS :—1 classical mods. 92.

Hughes, Arthur Montague D'Urban, born at Worthing, Sussex, 3 Nov., 1873; 1s. Edwin Montague Martin, cler. ST JOHN'S, matric. 17 Oct., 91, aged 17 (from Clergy orphan school, Canterbury), scholar 90.

Hughes, Charles Ernest, born at Maidstone, Kent, June, 1867; 3s. Henry, gent. KEBLE, matric. 19 Oct., 86, aged 19 (from Canterbury school), B.A. 89; HONOURS :—3 history 89.

Hughes, rev. Edward Basil Armstrong, born at Kegworth, co. Leicester, 21 Feb., 1866; 2s. Nathaniel Thomas, cler. WORCESTER, matric. 22 Oct., 85, aged 19 (from Marlborough), B.A. 90; curate of St. Augustine, Holly Hall, Dudley, 91.

Hughes, George Dickson Marshall, born at Dover 1867; 2s. Edward Carter, arm. ORIEL, matric. 19 Oct., 86, aged 19, from Canterbury school.

Hughes, Herbert Alfred, born at Liverpool 21 May, 1863; 5s. Joseph, gent. BALLIOL, matric. 18 Oct., 81, aged 18 (from Liverpool Institute); sometime I.C.S.; hon. captain and riding master and Dragoon guards (Queen's bays) 89.

Hughes, James Roydon, M.A., fellow NEW COLL. 27-43, where see page 209.

Hughes, Jasper Nicolls, born at Laugharne, co. Carm., Dec., 1871; 1s. John, cler. KEBLE, matric. 11 Oct., 90, aged 18 (from St. Edward's school, Summertown), passed into Sandhurst 92.

Hughes, rev. John Prytherch Poole-, born at Aberayron, co. Cardigan, Aug., 1864; 1s. William, gent. WORCESTER, matric. 18 Oct., 83, aged 19 (from Llandovery coll.), B.A. 87; curate of Ruabon, co. Denbigh, 91.

Hughes, rev. Leonard, born at Coventry, co. Warwick, 15 July, 1868; 1s. Andrew, cler. CORPUS CHRISTI, matric. 22 Oct., 87, aged 19 (from Coventry school), B.A. 91; HONOURS:—3 classical mods. 89, 3 history 91.

Hughes, rev. Octavius Rutherford Foster, born at Bangor 15 Dec., 1864; 4s. Hugh Robert, D.Med. CHARSLEY'S HALL, matric. 5 Feb., 86 aged 21 (from Friars school and Christ coll., Bangor); migrated to EXETER, B.A. 90, M.A. 92.

Hughes, Ralph Buller, born at Whimple, Devon, 1871; 2s. William Temple, arm. BALLIOL, matric. 14 Oct., 90, aged 19 (from Marlborough coll.); selected candidate Indian C.S. 90.

Hughes, Robert Edward, born at Wandsworth 19 June, 1866; 1s. Edward William, gen. JESUS COLL., matric. 21 Jan., 90, aged 23 (from Oswestry and University coll.), Aberystwith); scholar 89; HONOURS:—1 chemistry 92.

Hughes, Rowland Thomas Armstrong, born at Kegworth, co. Derby, 16 Feb., 1864; 1s. Nathaniel Thomas, cler. CHARSLEY'S HALL, matric. 30 Oct., 82, aged 18 (from Marlborough); migrated to KEBLE, B.A. 85, M.A. 92; HONOURS:—3 law 85.

Hughes, William Alexander, born at Blackheath, Kent, 1869; 2s. George Martin, solicitor. PEMBROKE, matric. 28 Oct., 90, aged 23.

Hughes, rev. William Hawker, M.A., fellow JESUS COLL. 72, where see.

Hughes, rev. William Worthington Poole-, born at Aberayron, co. Cardigan, 1866; 2s. William, gent. BALLIOL, matric. 15 Oct., 84, aged 18 (from Llandovery coll.), scholar 84, B.A. 89 (HONOURS:—1 mathematical mods. 86, 2 mathematics 88); assist. master Sherborne school 91.

Hugonin, Edgar, born at Worthing, Sussex, Dec., 1863; 5s. Francis James, arm. BRASENOSE, matric. 25 May, 83, aged 19 (from Carshalton), B.A. 87.

Hulbert, Henry Harper, born at Corsham, Wilts, 12 April, 1863; 1s. Thomas, arm. MAGDALEN, matric. 15 Oct., 81, aged 18 (from Bath coll.), B.A. 84.

Hulbert, John, born at Great Stanmore, Middx., 12 Sept., 1866; 4s. John Henville, solicitor. NEW COLL., matric. 16 Oct., 85, aged 19 (from Marlborough coll.), B.A. 89; HONOURS:—3 classical mods. 87, 4 history 89.

Huleatt, rev. Charles Housfield, born at Potter's Bar, Middx., 19 Oct., 1863; 2s. Hugh, vicar of St. John's, Bethnal Green. MAGDALEN, matric. 16 Oct., 82, aged 18 (from St. Paul's school), demy 81-5, B.A. 88, M.A. 92 (HONOURS:—2 classical mods. 84, 3 classics 86); chaplain at Luxor, Egypt, 90; curate of St Mark, Broadwater Down, 92.

Hulkes, Cecil James Gladdish, born at Frindsbury, Kent, 6 Nov., 1863; o.s. James, arm. CHRIST CHURCH, matric. 13 Oct., 80, aged 18 (from the Charterhouse), B.A. 85; HONOURS:—3 history 85.

Hulme, Frank Howell, born at Stratford, Essex, 8 May, 1867; 1s. Frederick Edward, gen. WORCESTER, matric. 22 Jan., 91, aged 23, from Marlborough.

Hulse, sir Edward, bart, M.A., fellow ALL SOULS' 29-53, where see page 277.

Hulse, Hamilton John, born in London 21 Feb., 1864; 3s. sir Edward, bart. BALLIOL, matric. 17 Oct., 82, aged 18 (from Harrow); HONOURS:—2 classical mods. 83; bar.-at-law, Inner Temple, 89.

Hulse, Richard Lamplough, born at Withington, co. Lanc., 15 Jan., 1867; 2s. William Wilson, C.E. MAGDALEN, matric. 26 Jan., 86, aged 19, from Uppingham school.

Hulton, Charles Copley, born at Emberton, Bucks, 12 Jan., 1850; 6s. Campbell Bassett Arthur Grey, rector. MERTON, matric. 24 Oct. 85, aged 25 (from Cheltenham coll.), B.A. 89.

Hulton, Samuel Fletcher, born at Emberton, Bucks, 20 Feb., 1862; 7s. Campbell Bassett Arthur Grey, rector. NEW COLL., matric. 15 May, 80, aged 18 (from the Charterhouse), B.A. 84 (HONOURS:—3 classical mods. 81, 2 law 84); bar.-at-law, Inner Temple. 88.

Humble, William Eustace Emerson, born at Spalding, co. Lincoln, 4 March, 1873; 1s. John Ralph, cler. QUEEN'S, matric. 27 Oct., 91, aged 18, from Richmond gr. school.

Hume, Martin Wheler, born in London 18 Aug., 1873; 1s. Edward, bar.-at-law. TRINITY, matric. 15 Oct., 92, aged 19, from Winchester.

Humfrey, Lebbeus Charles, born at Cubley, co. Derby, Oct., 1871; 2s. Cave, cler. KEBLE, matric. 20 Oct., 91, aged 20, from Brecon coll.

Humphery, Francis William, M.A., B.Med. CHRIST CHURCH, where see.

Humphreys, Alfred Thomas, born at Coneron, near Nantes, France, 20 Oct., 1868; 9s. Thomas Williams, gen. JESUS COLL., matric. 20 Oct., 91, aged 22 (from Lampeter coll.), scholar 91; HONOURS:—3 mathematical mods. 92.

Humphreys, Francis Joseph, born at Camberwell, Surrey, 1862; 1s. Edward, arm. BRASENOSE, matric. 18 Oct., 81, aged 19 (from Eton), B.A. 85; cox of the University eight 84 and 85.

Humphreys, Humphrey Richard, born at Ruabon, co. Denbigh, 1871; 1s. Humphrey, cler. KEBLE, matric. 12 Oct., 89, aged 18 (from Christ's hospital), scholar 88; HONOURS:—2 classical mods. 91.

Humphreys, Isaac, born at Llanfechell, isle of Man, 1863; 1s. John, pleb. NON-COLLEGIATE, matric. 14 Oct., 82, aged 19, from Friars school, Bangor.

Humphreys, William Edward, born at Beaumaris, isle of Anglesea, 10 Jan., 1861; 1s. Edward, gent. JESUS COLL., matric. 15 Oct., 80, aged 19 (from Beaumaris school), scholar 80-5, B.A. 84, M.A. 87; HONOURS:—3 mathematical mods. 82, 2 natural science 84.

Hunebelle, Jules Charles Alfred, born at Chalôns-sur-Marne 1861; 2s. Edward, gen. BALLIOL, matric. 20 Feb., 89, aged 28, from Paris university.

Hunt, Albert Thorley Gignac, born at Dinton, Bucks, Aug., 1863; 1s. William Thorley, cler. KEBLE, matric. 18 Oct., 81, aged 18 (from Sutton Valence school), exhibitioner 81-4, B.A. 85 (HONOURS:—3 classical mods. 83); brother of George R.

Hunt, rev. Alfred Ezra, born at Bath 1 March, 1863; 1s. Ezra, surgeon, deceased. WADHAM, matric. 23 Jan., 82, aged 18 (from Somersetshire coll., Bath), B.A. 85, M.A. 88 (HONOURS:—4 history 85); curate of Birmingham St. George 86; brother of Reginald C.

Hunt, Alfred William, M.A., hon. fellow CORPUS CHRISTI 82, where see page 380.

Hunt, Arthur Surridge, born at Romford, Essex, 1 March, 1871; 1s. Alfred Henry, gent. QUEEN'S, matric. 22 Oct., 89, aged 18 (from Eastbourne coll.), scholar 89; HONOURS:—1 classical mods. 91.

Hunt, Charles D'Arcy, born in London 12 April, 1870; 2s. Edmund D'Arcy, colonel. EXETER, matric. 16 Oct., 89, aged 19, from Radley coll.

Hunt, Charles William, born at New Alresford, Hants, 1867; 1s. William Henry, gent. BALLIOL, matric. 24 Oct., 85, aged 18 (from Trent coll., Notts.), B.A. 89.

Hunt, Donald Robert Chalmers-, born at Ware, Herts. 23 Nov., 73; 2s. Joseph Chalmers, solicitor. TRINITY, matric. 17 Oct., 91, aged 17, from Haileybury.

Hunt, George Rupert, born at Bathwick, Somerset, 23 March, 1873; 4s. William Thorley Gignac, cler. KEBLE, matric. 15 Oct., 92, aged 19 (from Sutton Valence school); brother of Albert T. G.

Hunt, Joseph, M.A., fellow QUEEN'S 47-53, where see page 178.

Hunt, Leonard Kenrick Chalmers-, born at Chadwell, Ware, Herts, 29 Jan., 1871; 1s. Joseph, gen. EXETER, matric. 16 Oct., 89, aged 18, from Haileybury.

Hunt, rev. Reginald Coombs, born at Bath 23 Dec., 1865; 2s. Ezra, surgeon, deceased. WADHAM, matric. 11 Oct., 84, aged 18 (from Somersetshire coll., Bath), B.A. 87, M.A. 91 (HONOURS:—2 classical mods. 86); curate of Beckenham Holy Trinity 92; brother of Alfred E.

Hunt, Reginald Kenrick Cyril, born at Kensington, Middx., May, 1872; 3s. Edmund D'Arcy, arm. CHRIST CHURCH, matric. 29 May, 91, aged 19, from Radley coll.

Hunt, Robert Wallis, born at Clapham, Surrey, 1869; 6s. Henry Wallis, arm. CORPUS CHRISTI, matric. 24 Oct., 87, aged 18 (from Dover coll.), HONOURS:—2 classical mods. 89, 3 classics 91.

Hunt, rev. Robert Walter Carew, born at Clapham, Surrey, 19 Feb., 1861; 1s. Joseph, arm. MERTON, matric. 25 Jan., 84, aged 18 (from St. Edward's school, Summertown), B.A. 87, M.A. 91; (HONOURS:—3 history 87); curate of Littlemore, Oxon, 90.

Hunt, Thomas Henry, M.A., student CHRIST CHURCH 47-53, where see.

Hunt, Wilfrid Mortimer, born at Kensington 1871; 1s. John Mortimer, arm. BALLIOL, matric. 17 Oct., 89, aged 18 (from Harrow), B.A. 92; HONOURS:—1 law 92, Vinerian law scholarship 93.

Hunt, William Thorley Gignac, M.A., student CHRIST CHURCH 56-62, where see.

Hunter, Broughton Sheridan, born at Calcutta Jan., 1865; 1s. sir William Wilson, K.C.S.I. NON-COLLEGIATE, matric. 17 Oct., 85, aged 20; migrated to BALLIOL; died at Durban, South Africa, 18 Oct., 88.

Hunter, Henry Charles Vicars, born at Horsley, co. Derby, 1861; 1s. Henry Frotheringham, arm. CHRIST CHURCH, matric. 15 Oct., 80, aged 19, from the Charterhouse.

Hunter, John Leslie, born at Newmains-House, co. Lanark, 1873; 1s. James, gen. BALLIOL, matric. 11 Feb., 92, aged 19, from Harrow.

Hunter, John Mark Somers, born at Laurence Kirk, co. Kincardine, 1865; 1s. Joseph, cler. ST. EDMUND HALL, matric. 21 Jan., 85, aged 19 (from Denstone coll.), B.A. 88; HONOURS:—2 history 88.

Hunter, Matthew, born at Canside, near Settle, Yorks, 30 Dec., 1863; 3s. William, gent. QUEEN'S, matric. 23 Oct., 82, aged 18 (from Giggleswick school), exhibitioner 82, B.A. 85, M.A. 90; HONOURS:—2 natural science 85, Burdett-Coutts scholarship 88.

Hunter, Norman Macleod, born at Halifax, Nova Scotia, 1869; 1s. James, gen. ST. JOHN'S, matric. 18 April, 91, aged 22.

Hunter, Patrick Francis, born at Roden, Salop, 14 Jan., 1870; 1s. Patrick, gen., deceased. UNIVERSITY COLL., matric. 12 Oct., 89, aged 19, from Rugby.

Hunter, Robert Holmes, born in London 1870; 1s. Robert Holmes, arm. CHARSLEY'S HALL, matric. 2 Nov., 86, aged 16.

Hunter, Robert Scott, born at Coonoor, East Indies, Sept., 1870; o.s. James, in the army. NEW COLL., matric. 12 Oct., 88, aged 18 (from Fettes coll.), B.A. 91 (HONOURS:—3 law 91); bar.-at-law, Inner Temple, 92.

Hunter, William, B.D., fellow ST. JOHN'S 31-46, where see.

Hunter, William Chevers, born at Calcutta 1870; 2s. William Wilson, K.C.S.I. BALLIOL, matric. 18 Oct., 88, aged 18 (from Eton); HONOURS: —3 classical mods. 90.

Hunter, sir William Wilson, K.C.S.I., C.I.E., born 15 July, 1840; s. A. Galloway, of Denholm. M.A. by decree of convocation 29 Jan., 89; examiner in oriental studies 89-90, hon. LL.D. Cambridge 20 June, 1887, and Glasgow, late vice-chancellor of Calcutta; Indian C.S. since 61, director-general of statistics to government of India 71, member of viceroy's legislative council 81, president of the education commission in India 82, father of Broughton S. and William E. For list of his works see *Men and Women of the Time*.

Huntingford, Edward, D.C.L., fellow NEW COLL. 38-48, where see page 211.

Huntingford, George William, M.A., fellow NEW COLL. 33-50, where see page 211.

Huntington, rev. Henry Edward, born at Leghorn, Italy, 1861; 1s. Henry John, cler. KEBLE, matric. 26 Oct., 80, aged 18 (from Malvern coll.), B.A. 85, M.A. 88 (HONOURS:—Taylorian scholarship in Italian 82, 2 classical mods. 83, 2 classics 85); assist. master Wellington coll. 85-9, and of Malvern 89, where he died 5 March, 93.

Hurry, Arnold Eardley, born at Bournemouth, Hants, 1861; 2s. Nicholas, gent. BALLIOL, matric. 21 Oct., 80, aged 19 (from city of London school), student Inner Temple 80; assist. commissioner, Punjab.

Hurst, Arthur Reginald, born at Horsham, Sussex, 20 June, 1867; 2s. Robert Henry, arm. CHRIST CHURCH, matric. 18 Jan., 89, aged 21 (from Westminster school), B.A. 92.

Hurst, Herbert, born at Temple Cowley, Oxon, 17 May, 1833; 4s. John, pleb. NON-COLLEGIATE, matric. 21 Jan., 82, aged 48, B.A. 86.

Husbands, Edmund Thomas, born in London 1871; 1s. Edmund Thomas Tibbetts, gen. NON-COLLEGIATE, matric. 16 May, 91, aged 20, from Cathedral school, Hereford.

Hussey, George, born at Ringstend, Norfolk, 4 Feb., 1865; 5s. William Law, hon. canon of Manchester. KEBLE, matric. 16 Oct., 83, aged 18 (from Haileybury), B.A. 90.

Hussey, Henry Percy, born at Lamberhurst, Sussex, 17 April, 1865; 4s. Edward, arm. NEW COLL., matric. 12 Oct., 83, aged 18 (from Eton), B.A. 87 (HONOURS:—3 classical mods. 85, 4 classics 87); bar.-at-law, Inner Temple, 91.

Hussey, rev. John, born at Ringstead, Norfolk, 4 Nov., 1866; 6s. William Law, hon. canon of Manchester. KEBLE, matric. 22 Oct., 85, aged 18 (from Haileybury), B.A. 87, M.A. 92 (HONOURS:—3 classical mods. 87, 3 theology 89) ; curate of Tidenham, co. Mon., 90.

Hussey, Victor Edwin George, born at Melcomb Regis, Dorset, 16 June, 1873 ; 1s. John Fraser, M.R.C.S. EXETER, matric. 18 Oct., 92, aged 19 (from St. Paul's school), scholar 92.

Hussey, William Law, M.A., student CHRIST CHURCH 31-53, where see.

Hutchings, Arthur Edward, born at Bristol 1864; 1s. William Henry, cler. ST. EDMUND HALL, matric. 26 Jan., 84, aged 20.

Hutchings, Ernest Peter, born at Clewer, Berks, , 1871 ; 7s. William Henry, cler. ST. JOHN'S, matric. 11 Oct., 90, aged 19, from Lancing coll.

Hutchings, rev. George Cyril, born at Monkton Wyld, Dorset, 9 July, 1864; 4s. Robert Sparke, cler. KEBLE, matric. 16 Oct., 83, aged 19 (from Winchester), B.A. 86, M.A. 90 (HONOURS :—2 history 86); curate of Melksham 91.

Hutchins, rev. Horace George Mackenzie Chester, born at Nutley, Sussex, 18 Oct., 1864 ; 1s. William Horace, cler. ST. MARY HALL, matric. 16 April, 83, aged 18, B.A. 89 ; curate of St. Aidan, South Shields, 90.

Hutchins, Thomas Lee, born at Oxford 1868 ; 1s. Thomas, gent. NON-COLLEGIATE, matric. 13 Oct., 88, aged 20, B.A. 91.

Hutchinson, Arthur, born at Pitstone, Herts, 19 Feb., 1871 ; 2s. Charles, cler. WORCESTER, matric. 14 Oct., 90, aged 19 (from Bedford gr. school), exhibitioner 90 ; (HONOURS:—3 classical mods. 92.

Hutchinson, rev. Charles Alleyne, born at Forton, Hants, 11 June, 1867 ; 1s. Charles Pierrepont, cler. QUEEN'S, matric. 25 Oct., 86, aged 19 (from Lancing coll.), scholar 86, B.A. 89 (HONOURS :—3 classical mods. 88, 4 theology 89); curate of St. Michael and All Angels, Northampton, 90.

Hutchinson, Francis Ernest, born at Forton, Hants, 17 Sept , 1871 ; 3s. Charles Pierrepont, cler. TRINITY, matric. 11 Oct., 90, aged 19 (from Lancing coll.); HONOURS :—2 classical mods 92.

Hutchinson, Frederick William, born at Harrogate, Yorks, Aug., 1870 ; 4s. William Illion, cler. KEBLE, matric. 12 Oct., 90, aged 19 (from Haileybury), scholar 88 ; HONOURS:—2 classical mods. 91.

Hutchinson, Robert Hamilton, born at Tiddington, co. Warwick, 13 Jan., 1868 ; 2s. Alexander Ross Elliott, arm. MERTON, matric. 23 March, 87, aged 19, from Haileybury.

Hutchinson, Standish Grady John Parker, born at Castletown, co. Tipperary, 9 Jan., 1870 ; 1s. Anthony, arm. MAGDALEN, matric. 28 Jan., 89, aged 17 (from St. Columba academy, Dublin); HONOURS:—3 history 92.

Hutchison, rev. Ernest Alexander, born at Runcorn, Cheshire, 1865 ; 1s. John, arm. S. JOHN'S, matric. 13 Oct., 83, aged 18 (from Warrington school), B.A. 87, M.A. 90 (HONOURS :—4 theology 87) ; curate of Shrewsbury S. Mary 90.

Hutt, James, born at Oxford 11 May, 1870 ; 2s. Charles, deceased. NON-COLLEGIATE, matric. 15 Oct., 92, aged 22, from Oxford high school.

Hutton, rev. Gerard Motham, born at Brighton 1863 ; 4s. Joseph Henry, cler. UNIVERSITY COLL., matric. 14 Oct., 82, aged 19 (from Bristol gr. school), exhibitioner 82-6, B.A. 86, M.A. 89 (HONOURS:—2 classical mods. 84, 2 classics 86); assist. master Leeds gr. school 90.

Hutton, Henry Leonard, born at Stilton, Hunts, 5 Oct., 1867 ; 4s. Thomas, rector. NEW COLL., matric. 15 Oct., 86, aged 19 (from Haileybury), B.A. 90 ; HONOURS:—2 classical mods. 88, 2 classics 90.

Hutton, Maurice, M.A., fellow MERTON 79-86, where see page 99.

Hutton, Reginald Cecil, born at Barnet, Herts, 1868 ; 6s. Robert Rossiter, cler. ST. JOHN'S, matric. 14 Jan., 87, aged 19 (from Merchant Taylors' school), B.A. 91.

Hutton, rev. William Holden, M.A., fellow ST. JOHN'S 84, where see.

Hutton, rev. William Richmond, born at Brighton 1 Oct., 1861 ; 3s. Joseph Henry, cler. ST. JOHN'S, matric. 16 Oct., 80, aged 19 (from Bristol school), scholar 80-5, B.A. 85, M.A. 89 (HONOURS :—2 classical mods. 82, 3 classics 84); curate of Kirkstall, Yorks, 90 ; died 20 Feb., 93 ; brother of Gerard M.

Huxham, George Trevor, born at Birkenhead, Cheshire, 21 July, 1862 ; 1s. Vavasour, gen. WORCESTER, matric. 17 Oct., 87, aged 25 (from Birkenhead school), B.A. 90.

Huxley, rev. John, born in Cheshire 1857 ; 1s. John, gent. NON-COLLEGIATE, matric. 17 Jan., 80, aged 23; migrated to ST. JOHN'S, B.A. 82, M.A. 87 ; curate of Southwell 83.

Huxley, Leonard, born in London 1861 ; 1s. right hon. Thomas Henry, professor. BALLIOL, matric. 21 Jan., 80, aged 19 (from University coll. school and St. Andrew's university), exhibitioner 80-4, B.A. 83 (HONOURS:—1 classical mods. 81, 1 classics 83); student Inner Temple 82 ; a master at the Charterhouse 84.

Huxley, right hon. Thomas Henry, president royal society 83, created D.C.L. 17 June, 85; surgeon in the navy 46-50, F.R.S. 50 ; lord rector of Aberdeen university 72-4, professor natural history royal school of Mines 54, Copley medallist (royal society) 88, Romanes lecturer 93, etc., born, Ph.D. Breslau, hon. D.Med. Wurzburg, and hon. LL.D. Edinburgh, Dublin 78 and Cambridge 79, fellow royal coll., surgeons 84, privy councillor 92, born at Ealing 4 May, 1825. See *Men and Women of the Time*.

Hyatt, Ernest Edward, born at Queensbury, Yorks, 11 Feb., 1865 ; 1s. John Carter, M.A., vicar. NON-COLLEGIATE, matric. 13 Oct., 88, aged 23, from Pannall coll., Harrogate.

Hyde, Charles Frederick, born at Gillingham, Dorset, 1855 ; 1s. Charles Frederick, cler. NON-COLLEGIATE, matric. 21 Jan., 80, aged 27, from St. Michael's coll., Tenbury ; died 17 March, 93.

Hyde, John Garmston, born at Worcester 1865 ; 1s. Thomas Garmston, solicitor. EXETER, matric. 18 Oct., 84, aged 18 (from Winchester), B.A. 86.

Hydes, rev. Thomas Arnold, born at Sheffield 1865 ; 1s. Thomas, gent. NON-COLLEGIATE, matric. 1 May, 86, aged 21, B.A. 89 ; curate of Gorleston, Norfolk, 91.

STONE STRING COURSE, WINCHESTER CATHEDRAL.—*Pugin.*

I

Ilbert, Courtenay Peregrine, C.S.I., C.I.E., M.A., fellow BALLIOL 64-74, where see page 67.

Iliff, rev. Kenneth Durnford, born at Bishop Wearmouth, co. Durham, 1865; 4s. George, cler. NON-COLLEGIATE, matric. 16 Oct., 86, aged 21 (from a Sunderland school), B.A. 90 (HONOURS:— 3 theology 90); curate of St. Austell, Cornwall, 90.

Iliffe, Frederick, D.Mus., organist ST. JOHN'S 83, where see.

Illingworth, Alfred Clarence, born at Leominster, co. Hereford, 1867; 2s. Eli, methodist minister. LINCOLN, matric. 23 Oct., 91, aged 24 (from Lampeter coll.), exhibitioner 90.

Illingworth, John Richardson, M.A., fellow JESUS COLL. 72-84, where see.

Ince, William, D.D., canon of CHRIST CHURCH 78, where see.

Ind, Charles Edward, born at Westbury, Salop, 29 Jan., 1869; 3s. William, schoolmaster. JESUS COLL., matric. 19 Oct., 87, aged 18 (from Brecon coll.), B.A. 90; HONOURS:—3 chemistry 90.

Inderwick, Walter Andrew, born in London 14 Feb., 1870; 4s. Frederick Andrew, Q.C. MAGDALEN, matric. 14 Oct., 89, aged 19, from Winchester.

Inge, Charles Cuthbert, born at Crayke, Yorks, 2 May, 1868; 2s. William, D.D., provost of Worcester coll. MAGDALEN, matric. 22 Oct., 87, aged 19 (from Eton), demy 87; B.A. 91; HONOURS:—1 classical mods. 89, 2 classics 91, archæological studentship at Athens 91.

Inge, rev. William, D.D., provost of WORCESTER 81, where see.

Inge, William Ralph, M.A., fellow HERTFORD 88, where see.

Ingham, Ernest Graham, bishop of Sierra Leone, created D.D. 20 Feb., 1883. See *Al. Ox.* and series 786.

Ingham, George, born at Barwick-in-Elmete, Yorks, 28 Jan., 1871; 3s. James, arm. MERTON, matric. 19 Oct., 89, aged 18 (from Bradford gr. school), postmaster 89; HONOURS:—1 chemistry 92.

Ingham, rev. William, born at Todmorden, Yorks, 1862; 3s. John Arthur, gent. ST. JOHN'S, matric. 4 June, 81, aged 19, B.A. 84, M.A. 89; vicar of Old Malton, Yorks, 92.

Ingilby, sir Henry Day, bart., M.A., fellow MAGDALEN 48-55, where see page 322.

Ingledew, Alfred Edward, born at Tynemouth, Northumberland, 18 Jan., 1869; 2s. James, gen. WORCESTER, matric. 17 Jan., 88, aged 18, from Richmond gr. school.

Ingledew, Hugh Murray, born at Cardiff 23 Oct., 1865; 3s. John Pylus, arm. MERTON, matric. 16 Oct., 84, aged 18 (from St. Edward's school, Summertown), B.A. 87; HONOURS:—4 law 87.

Inglis, John Alexander, born at Worcester 3 Feb., 1873; 1s. Alexander, of Cheltenham, D.Med. CHRIST CHURCH, matric. 16 Oct., 91, aged 18 (from Cheltenham coll.), scholar 91.

Inglis, John Campbell, born at Edinburgh 4 May, 1867; 3s. Thomas, R.I.C. medical service. NEW COLL., matric. 16 Oct., 85, aged 18 (from Wellington coll.), B.A. 89; HONOURS:—2 classical mods. 87, 1 history 89.

Inglis, rev. Rupert Edward, born in London 17 May, 1863; 4s. sir John, knight. UNIVERSITY COLL., matric. 21 Jan., 82, aged 18 (from Rugby), B.A. 85; (HONOURS:—3 history 85); curate of Helmsley, Yorks, 89-90.

Ingold, Edwin George, born at Bishop's Stortford, Herts, 4 June, 1869; 1s. George, gen. TRINITY, matric. 17 Oct., 91, aged 22 (from Bishop Stortford school, King's coll. London, and City Guilds institute, South Kensington), scholar 90.

Ingram, Alfred Winnington-, born at Stanford, co. Worc., 15 Sept., 1861; 6s. Edward Winnington, cler. KEBLE, matric. 18 Oct., 81, aged 20 (from Bromsgrove), B.A. 85, M.A. 89.

Ingram, Arthur David, born at Westminster 3 March, 1869; 5s. Henry Manning, cler. KEBLE, matric. 3 Oct., 88, aged 19 (from Radley coll.), B.A. 92; HONOURS:—3 classical mods. 90, 3 law 92.

Ingram, Ernest Arthur, born at Cardiff, co. Glam. 16 April, 1873; 1s. John Robotham, gen. JESUS COLL., matric. 15 Oct., 90, aged 17, from Monmouth gr. school.

Ingram, Francis Manning, born in London 6 Nov., 1864; 3s. Henry Manning, cler. MAGDALEN, matric. 19 Oct., 83, aged 18 (from Winchester), exhibitioner 83, B.A. 87, M.A. 90; HONOURS:— 3 classical mods. 85, 3 classics 87.

Ingram, Gerald Constantine Winnington-, born at Stanford-on-Teme, co. Worc., 26 June, 1869; 7s. Edward, rector. NEW COLL., matric. 18 Oct., 87, aged 18 (from Bromsgrove gr. school); scholar 86, B.A. 91; (HONOURS:—accessit Hertford scholarship 87, accessit Craven scholarship 87, 1 classical mods. 89, 2 classics 91); selected candidate Indian c.s. 92.

Ingram, rev. Henry Hugh, born in London 17 May, 1861; 1s. Henry Manning, cler. BRASENOSE, matric. 26 Jan., 81, aged 19 (from Westminster school), B.A. 90, M.A. 92; curate of Hebden Bridge, co. Lanc. 90.

Ingram, Horace Walpole, born in London 25 March 1863; o.s. Frederick, bar.-at-law. QUEEN'S, matric. 2 May, 82, aged 19, from the Charterhouse.

Ingram, Robert Antony, born in London 11 Feb., 1866; 4s. Henry Manning, cler. CHRIST CHURCH, matric. 10 Oct., 84, aged 18 (from Westminster school), B.A. 88, M.A. 92.

Ingram, William Findlay, born at Moss head, near Aberdeen, 1867; 1s. John, schoolmaster. ORIEL, matric. 18 Oct., 87, aged 20 (from King's coll. Aberdeen); bible clerk 87, B.A. 92; HONOURS: —1 classical mods. 89, 2 classics 91.

Inman, Arnold, born at Hatheaton, Somerset, 3 Nov., 1867; o.s. Thomas Frederick, of Bath, solicitor. MAGDALEN, matric. 21 Oct., 86, aged 18 (from Clifton coll.), demy 86, B.A. 90 (HONOURS: —2 chemistry 90); bar.-at-law, Inner Temple, 92.

Innes, Arthur Donald, born at Simla, East Indies, 15 Sept., 1863; 2s. James John McLeod, arm. ORIEL, matric. 1 Nov., 82, aged 19 (from Marlborough coll.), scholar 82-6, B.A. 87, M.A. 89; HONOURS: —2 classical mods. 83, 2 classics 86.

Innes, Edward Alfred Mitchell-, born at Edinburgh 21 Dec., 1863; 5s. Gilbert, arm. BALLIOL, matric. 16 Oct., 83, aged 19 (from Wellington coll.), exhibitioner 83; HONOURS:—2 classical mods. 85, 4 classics 87.

Innes, Gilbert Plantagenet Mitchell-, born at Edinburgh June, 1863; o.s. Alexander Mitchell, arm. CHRIST CHURCH, matric. 16 Oct., 85, aged 22.

Innes, Reginald Heath Long, born at Sydney, Australia, 1869; 3s. George, puisne judge N.S.W., and a knight. NEW COLL., matric. 10 Dec., 88, aged 19 (from Malvern coll.), B.A. 91 (HONOURS:—2 history 91); bar.-at-law, Lincoln's Inn, 93.

Ionides, Constantine Albert, born at Constantinople 1864; 2s. Constantine, arm. BALLIOL, matric. 1 Feb., 82, aged 18 (from Radley coll.), B.A. 86, M.A. 91 (HONOURS:—3 history 85); bar.-at-law, Inner Temple, 86.

Ireland, William Edward, born at Birmingham 10 Jan., 1869; 1s. William Soame, gen. NON-COLLEGIATE, matric. 13 Oct., 88, aged 19, B.A. 91; HONOURS:—3 theology 92.

Iremonger, William George, born in London Feb., 1875; 1s. William Henry, esq. KEBLE, matric. 15 Oct., 92, aged 17, from Winchester school.

Irish, Harold John Henry, born at Barnstaple, Devon, 9 Aug., 1870; o.s. Thomas Braund, arm. BRASENOSE, matric. 14 Oct., 89, aged 19, from Sherborne gr. school.

Irvine, John Dods Pringle, born at King Williams Town, Cape of Good Hope, 9 May, 1871; 1s. John James, gen., deceased. MAGDALEN, matric. 14 Oct., 89, aged 18, from the Charterhouse; died 20 Feb., 92, at Bedford.

Irvine, rev. William George, born at Westbourne, Sussex, 13 June, 1866; 1s. William Henry, cler. WORCESTER, matric. 22 Oct., 85, aged 19 (from St. Mark's school, Windsor), B.A. 89, M.A. 92; curate of Icklesham, Sussex, 89.

Irving, Edward Eccles, born at Walton, co. Lanc., 3 March, 1873; 1s. Robert, M.A., vicar Christ Church, Sefton Park, Liverpool. HERTFORD, matric. 22 Oct., 92, aged 19 (from Liverpool coll.), scholar 91.

Irving, Henry Brodribb, born in London 5 Aug., 1870; 1s. John Henry Brodribb (tragedian). NEW COLL., matric. 12 Oct., 88, aged 18 (from Marlborough), B.A. 91 (HONOURS:—2 history 91); a student of the Inner Temple; his father assumed the additional surname of Irving.

Irwell, Laurence, born at Headingley, Yorks, 25 Nov., 1861; o.s. Isaac, gent. WADHAM, matric. 17 Oct., 82, aged 20, from Christ's coll., Cambridge, where he matriculated 9 Nov., 80.

Irwin, Acheson, born at Leeds 1863; 1s. George, gent. HERTFORD, matric. 18 Oct., 82, aged 19.

Irwin, rev. Edmund Alexander, born at Newtown, co. Warwick, Aug., 1869; 4s. Henry, cler. KEBLE, matric. 13 Oct., 88, aged 19 (from St. Edward's school, Summertown); HONOURS:—2 history 91.

Isaac, Arthur Whitmore, born at Powick Court, co. Worcester, 1871; 1s. John Swinton, of Broughton Park, Worcester, bar.-at-law. ORIEL, matric. 27 Oct., 90, aged 19, from Harrow.

Isaac, Edward Swinton Wodehouse, born at Dewsbury, Yorks, 1871; 1s. Edmund Whitmore, cler. ORIEL, matric. 22 Oct., 90, aged 19, from the Charterhouse.

Isaac, John Farmer Vivian, born at Hinton Charterhouse, near Bath, 1868; 1s. Thomas William, arm. ST. JOHN'S, matric. 20 Oct., 87, aged 19 (from Harrow), B.A. 91; HONOURS:—a chemistry 91.

Ismay, James Hainsworth, born at Waterloo, co. Lanc., 4 March, 1867; 2s. Thomas Henry, gent. EXETER, matric. 23 Oct., 85, aged 18 (from Harrow), B.A. 90, M.A. 92.

Ive, Olive, born at Guiseley, Yorks, 1866; 4s. David, gen. QUEEN'S, matric. 15 Jan., 91, aged 25.

Izard, Herbert Crawford, born at Woodmancote, New Zealand, 18 Nov., 1869; 4s. Charles Beard, gen. TRINITY, matric. 12 Oct., 89, aged 19, from Lancing coll.

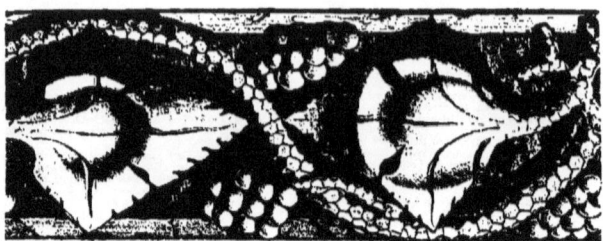

[WOODEN ORNAMENT FROM ROUEN CATHEDRAL.—*Pugin*.]

J

Jackman, Joseph Allan, born at St. Michael, isle of Barbados, , 1862; 2s. Joseph, gent, PEMBROKE, matric. 4 June, 81, aged 19 (from Codrington coll., Barbados), scholar 81, B.A. 85; HONOURS :—2 classical mods 83, 3 classics 85

Jackson, Alfred, born at Hull, Yorks, 28 Jan., 1873; 10s. Samuel Brock, shipowner. WADHAM, matric. 20 Oct., 91, aged 18, from the Hull and East Riding coll.

Jackson, Archibald, born at Chesterton, co. Stafford, 1 May, 1867; 3s. William Henry, rector of Thorpe Arch, Yorks. MAGDALEN, matric. 18 Jan., 88, aged 20 (from St. Michael's coll., Tenbury), academical clerk 88, B.A. 91.

Jackson, rev. Arthur Aubert, born at Wormley, Herts, 17 June, 1864; 7s. Thomas, of Ware Hill House, Herts, arm. MAGDALEN, matric. 19 Oct., 83, aged 19 (from the Charterhouse), clerk 83, B.A. 88, M.A. 90, chaplain 91; curate of South Hinksey, Oxon, 91-2, vicar of Horspath, Oxon, 92.

Jackson, Arthur Mason Tippetts, born in London 30 Dec., 1866; 1s. Mason, gent. BRASENOSE, matric. 14 Oct., 84, aged 17 (from Westminster school), scholar 84, B.A. 88 (HONOURS :—1 Indian languages 88, Boden sanskrit scholarship 88); bar.-at-law, Inner Temple, 88, assist. collector and magistrate (entered Indian c.s. 85).

Jackson, Charles James, born at Wrexham, co. Denbigh, 7 Dec., 1872; 1s. Thomas Evans, merchant, deceased. WADHAM, matric. 18 Oct. 91, aged 19.

Jackson, Clement Nugent, M.A., fellow HERTFORD 81-6, where see.

Jackson, Cyril, born in London 6 Feb., 1863; 1s. Lawrence Morris, gent. NEW COLL., matric. 4 June, 81, aged 18 (from the Charterhouse), B.A. 85, M.A. 88 (HONOURS :—2 classical mods 83, 2 classics 85.

Jackson, Cyril Hugh, born in London 24 July, 1868; 2s. Arthur, solicitor. NEW COLL., matric. 15 Oct., 86, aged 18 (from Lancing coll. and Dresden), B.A. 89 (HONOURS :—3 law 89); brother of Edward M.

Jackson, Edward, born at Headingley, Yorks, 1866; 1s. William Thomas, gent. ORIEL, matric. 8 Dec., 84, aged 19, B.A. 89, M.A. 91 (HONOURS : —3 classics 88); bar.-at-law, Inner Temple, 93.

Jackson, Edward Mackenzie, born in London 27 May, 1867; 1s. Arthur, solicitor. NEW COLL., matric. 16 Oct., 85, aged 18 (from Lancing coll. and Dresden), B.A. 88 (HONOURS :—2 law 88); bar.-at-law, Lincoln's Inn, 89; brother of Cyril H.

[319]

Jackson, Elphinstone, born in Calcutta 1868; 2s. Elphinstone, arm. ORIEL, matric. 18 Oct., 87, aged 19 (from Lancing coll.), B.A. 91.

Jackson, Francis Ernest, born at Sydney, New South Wales, 20 Feb., 1872; 3s. Alfred William, gen. NEW COLL., matric. 16 Oct., 91, aged 19 (from city of London school); selected candidate Indian c.s. 91.

Jackson, Frederick Huth, born in London 26 April, 1863; 1s. Thomas Hughes, arm. BALLIOL, matric. 28 Jan., 84, aged 20 (from Harrow), B.A. 87, M.A. 91 (HONOURS :—2 history 87); student Lincoln's Inn 84.

Jackson, George Erskine, born at Allyghur, India, 13 March, 1872; 1s. James Rawlinson, late of Indian medical department, deceased. CORPUS CHRISTI, matric. 19 Oct., 91, aged 19, from Haileybury.

Jackson, rev. Harry Hamilton, born at Caverham, Suffolk, Nov., 1865; 1s. Henry, gent. CHRIST CHURCH, matric. 30 May, 85, aged 19 (from Blackheath school), B.A. 88, M.A. 92 (HONOURS :—2 theology 88); curate of St. Luke's, Bromley Common, Kent, 91.

Jackson, John, born at Macclesfield, Cheshire, 24 Dec., 1862; 1s. John, gent. HERTFORD, matric. 19 Oct., 81, aged 18 (from Macclesfield school), scholar 80-0, B.A. 86, M.A. 88 (HONOURS :—1 classical mods. 82, 2 classics 85.

Jackson, John Henry, born at Southport, co. Lancs., 6 June, 1866; 1s. John Henry, arm. CHRIST CHURCH, matric. 30 May, 85, aged 18 (from Westminster school), B.A. 89; bar.-at-law, Inner Temple, 91.

Jackson, Samuel, born at Dorking, Surrey, 24 Sept., 1861; 3s. William, cler. MERTON, matric. 18 Oct., 80, aged 19 (from Kingswood school and Eastbourne coll.), postmaster 80-3, B.A. 85, M.A. 87; HONOURS :—2 mathematical mods. 81, 2 mathematics 84.

Jackson, Thomas Chalice, born at Otley, Yorks, 19 Aug., 1868; 3s. Josiah, gen. LINCOLN, matric. 18 Oct., 88, aged 20, from Yorkshire coll., Leeds.

Jackson, Thomas Graham, M.A., hon. fellow WADHAM 80, where see.

Jackson, Thomas Hughes, born at Birkenhead, Cheshire, 1871; 4s. Thomas Hughes, arm. BALLIOL, matric. 14 Oct., 90, aged 19, from Harrow.

Jackson, Thomas Watson, M.A., fellow WORCESTER 64, where see.

[320]

Jackson, William, M.A., fellow WORCESTER 44-8, where see.

Jackson, William, born at Rock Ferry, Cheshire, 16 Jan., 1862; 3s. William, of Floetham House, St Bees, esq., deceased. QUEEN'S, matric. 28 Oct., 81, aged 19 (from St. Bees gr. school), B.A. 85, M.A. and B.C.L. 89; HONOURS:—2 classical mods. 83, 2 law 85, 3 civil law 87.

Jackson, William Hatchett, M.A. NEW COLL. 76, see page 219, and tutor KEBLE, where see.

Jackson, William Walrond, D.D., rector of EXETER 87, where see page 122.

Jacob, Charles William, born at Basingstoke, Hants, Oct., 1871; 2s. Charles Joseph, gen. KEBLE, matric. 12 Oct., 89, aged 17, from Basingstoke school.

Jacob, rev. Harry, born at Basingstoke, Hants, May, 1866; 1s. Charles Joseph, gent. KEBLE, matric. 14 Oct., 84, aged 18 (from Queen's school, Basingstoke), B.A. 87, M.A. 92 (HONOURS:—3 history 87); curate of Kidlington, Oxon, 89.

Jacob, rev. John Attwood, born at Horningham, Wilts, 1866; 3s. James John, cler. KEBLE, matric. 22 Oct., 85, aged 19 (from Lancing coll.), B.A. 88, M.A. 92 (HONOURS:—4 theology 88); curate of Salisbury St. Edmund 90.

Jacob, rev. William, born at Horningham, Wilts, 1862; 1s. James John, cler. KEBLE, matric. 18 Oct., 81, aged 19 (from Lancing coll.), B.A. 85; curate of Branksome, Dorset, 88.

Jacobs, Henry, D.D., dean of Christ Church, New Zealand, fellow QUEEN'S 48-51, where see page 178.

Jacobs, Maurice, born at Sheffield, Yorks, 6 Feb., 1864; y.s. Michael, gent. WADHAM, matric. 16 Oct., 83, aged 19 (from St. Paul's school), scholar 82, B.A. 87, M.A. 90; HONOURS:—2 classical mods. 85, 3 classics 87.

Jacobson, Alfred Charles Barker, born at Liverpool 1867; 1s. Isidore, gen. NON-COLLEGIATE, matric. 27 April, 89, aged 22 (from Liverpool coll.); migrated to ST. MARY HALL, B.A. 92.

Jacques, William Baldwin, born at Leyland, co. Lanc., 1864; 1s. Kenton, cler. BRASENOSE, matric. 2 June, 82, aged 18 (from Shrewsbury gr. school), B.A. 85, M.A. 89.

Jacson, Owen Fitzherbert, born at Thruxton, co. Hereford, 4 April, 1861; 4s. Edward Rogers, cler. CHRIST CHURCH, matric. 15 Oct., 80, aged 19, from Marlborough coll.

Rolin-Jaequemyns, Gustave, created D.C.L. 8 Sept., 1880; legal adviser to the king of Siam 92, Belgian advocate, some time minister of the interior for Belgium, president of the institute of international law 73.

Jago, John Darell, born at Brunswick, Canada, 1866; y.s. Darell, lieut.-col. EXETER, matric. 31 May, 84, aged 18, from Newton Abbot coll., South Devon.

James, Alfred Henry Cotes, born at Cotham, Bristol, 30 Oct., 1873; 1s. Alfred Bartlett, gen. MERTON, matric. 12 Feb., 92, aged 18, from Sherborne school.

James, rev. Arthur Harold, born at Winkfield, Berks, 1865; 3s. Samuel Benjamin, cler. HERTFORD, matric. 27 Oct., 87, aged 22, B.A. 90; curate of North Marston, Bucks, 91.

James, Benjamin, born in Llangadock, co. Carmarthen, 14 Jan., 1874; 1s. John, gent. MERTON, matric. 18 Oct., 92, aged 18 (from Llandovery coll.), postmaster 92.

James, Charles Ashworth, B.A., fellow HERTFORD 81, where see.

James, Charles Wilford, born at Coatham, Yorks, 1 Jan., 1874; 2s. Thomas, iron master. LINCOLN, matric. 25 Oct., 92, aged 18, from Russall school.

James, hon. Cuthbert, born in London 29 Feb., 1872; 2s. Walter Henry, lord Northbourne. MAGDALEN, matric. 14 Oct., 90, aged 19 (from Harrow); brother of Walter John.

James, David, born at Llaneynfelyn, co. Cardigan, 14 April, 1857; 1s. John, gent. NON-COLLEGIATE, matric. 15 Oct., 92, aged 35, from St. David's, Lampeter.

James, Ernest Edward, born at Peakirk, Northants, 1862; 1s. Edward, cler. ST. JOHN'S, matric. 16 Oct., 80, aged 18 (from the Charterhouse), B.A. (NON-COLLEGIATE) 85.

James, Eustace Lindsey Haweis, born at Bolarum, East Indies, 29 Feb., 1872; 1s. Walter Haweis, capt. R.E., deceased. NEW COLL., matric. 10 Oct., 90, aged 18, from Eton.

James, Francis Edward, born at Bray, near Dublin, 21 May, 1861; 3s. Francis Edward, arm. MERTON, matric. 18 Oct., 80, aged 19, from Cheltenham coll.

James, Francis Fuller, born in London 14 Oct., 1863; o.s. Benjamin Fuller, cler. CHRIST CHURCH, matric. 13 Oct., 82, aged 18 (from Westminster school); HONOURS:—2 classical mods. 84; student Inner Temple 84; died 11 Feb., 85.

James, George Fitzhugh Bush, born at Clifton, co. Glouc., 19 or 26 Sept., 1873; 1s. Stephen George, of Hanover. MERTON, matric. 18 Oct., 92, aged 19, from Uppingham school.

James, Henry, born at Truro, Cornwall, 21 Aug., 1856; 4s. William, gen., deceased. NON-COLLEGIATE, matric. 11 Oct., 90, aged 32, from St. Mary's school, Truro.

James, Henry George Humphry, born at Morton, co. Stafford, 1871; 1s. George, gen. UNIVERSITY COLL., matric. 11 Oct., 90, aged 19.

James, Henry Lewis, born at Newcastle Emlyn, co. Cardigan, 18 March, 1864; 2s. Peter, gent. JESUS COLL., matric. 18 Oct., 82, aged 18 (from Brecon coll.), scholar 82-6, B.A. 86, M.A. 91; HONOURS:—2 classical mods. 84, 2 classics 86.

James, Henry Rosher, born 28 Sept., 1873; 1s. George Coulson, gen. CHRIST CHURCH, matric. 14 Oct., 81, aged 18 (from Westminster school), scholar 82-6, B.A. 85, M.A. 88 (HONOURS:—1 classical mods. 83, 1 classics 85); professor at Patna coll., Bombay; brother of Lionel.

James, Herbert Armitage, B.D., fellow ST. JOHN'S 69-87, where see.

James, Herbert Richard, born at Oxford 1873; 1s. Thomas, gen. NON-COLLEGIATE, matric. 18 Oct., 90, aged 17 (from Bedford House school, Oxford); brother of Philip J.

James, rev. Herbert Thomas Herbert, born at Pontypridd, co. Glamorgan, 21 May, 1865; o.s. Herbert, gent. QUEEN'S, matric. 30 Jan., 84, aged 18 (from Winchester), B.A. and M.A. 90.

James, Hugh Somers, born at Croydon, Surrey, 19 Oct., 1871; 2s. Henry, arm. TRINITY, matric. 11 Oct., 90, aged 18, from Marlborough coll.

James, James, born at Alltglaies, Llangorwen, co. Cardigan, 6 Sept., 1863; 3s. David. JESUS COLL., matric. 18 Oct., 92, aged 89.

James, John Henry, M.A., fellow BRASENOSE 48-53, where see page 355.

James, John Henry, born at Rock, co. Worcester, 8 July, 1863; 1s. Alfred, cler. ORIEL, matric. 2 June, 82, aged 18 (from Shrewsbury gr. school); died 28 Jan., 92.

James, rev. John Lovell, born at Prestatyn, near Rhyl, 1863; 1s. Enoch Rhys, cler. NON-COLLEGIATE, 14 Oct., 82, aged 19 (from St. Paul's coll., Stony Stratford), B.A. 87; curate of St. Mary the Less, Lambeth, 88.

James, rev. John Robert, born at Athlone, Ireland, 4 Dec., 1864; s. Matthew Hopkins, vicar of St. Thomas, Hull. LINCOLN, matric. 17 Oct., 84, aged 19 (from Hull school and East Riding coll.); migrated to CHARSLEY HALL, B.A. 89; curate of Dearham, Cumberland, 90.

James, Leonard, born at Clifton, co. Glouc., 27 Oct., 1865; o.s. William Morris, arm. TRINITY, matric. 11 Oct., 84, aged 18 (from Highgate school), B.A. 89, M.A. 91; bar.-at-law, Inner Temple, 90.

James, Lionel, born in London 11 July, 1868; 3s. George Coulson, arm. CHRIST CHURCH, matric. 14 Oct., 87, aged 19 (from Westminster school), scholar 87, B.A. 91 (HONOURS:—1 classical mods. 89, 2 classics 91); brother of Henry R.

James, Montague Vidal, born at Guernsey 19 Aug., 1802; 9s. William Rhodes, gent. LINCOLN, matric. 23 Oct., 82, aged 20 (from Eton), B.A. 86, M.A. 89; died 6 May, 91.

James, Philip John, born at Oxford 17 Aug., 1874; 2s. Thomas, gent. NON-COLLEGIATE, matric. 20 Oct., 90, aged 16 (from Bedford House school, Oxford); brother of Herbert R.

James, Richard Lloyd Langford-, born at Llanfairisgner, co. Carnarvon, 1873; 1s. Francis Lloyd, L.-J. in the army. KEBLE, matric. 15 Oct., 92, aged 19 (from Shrewsbury school), scholar 92.

James, St. John Baskerville, born at Winkfield, Berks, 1868; 4s. Samuel Benjamin, cler. HERTFORD, matric. 14 Oct., 90, aged 22, from Schorne coll.

James, hon. Walter John, born in London 2 Sept., 1869; 1s. Walter Henry, lord Northbourne. MAGDALEN, matric. 22 Oct., 87, aged 18 (from Harrow), B.A. 91 (HONOURS:—3 history 91); brother of Cuthbert.

James, William Edward, born at Cardigan 16 Sept., 1867; o.s. Levi, gen. CORPUS CHRISTI, matric. 20 Oct., 86, aged 19 (from Rugby), B.A. 89; HONOURS:—3 classical mods. 88, 3 law 89.

Jameson, Ernest Augustus, born at Edinburgh 1868; 1s. Augustus Grant, gen. NON-COLLEGIATE, matric. 13 Oct., 88, aged 18 (from G. Watson's coll., Edinburgh); migrated to EXETER, B.A. 93; HONOURS:—3 theology 92.

Jamieson, James Murray Auldjo, born at Edinburgh 9 July, 1871; a.s. James Auldjo, w.s. NEW COLL., matric. 10 Oct., 90, aged 19, from Fettes coll.

Jamieson, John Christian, born at Berwick-on-Tweed 23 Jan., 1871; 1s. William Allan, of Edinburgh, D.Med. BALLIOL, matric. 14 Oct., 90, aged 19, from Edinburgh academy.

Jannings, George Edward, born at Fishlake, Yorks, 19 June, 1870; 1s. Edward, gen. TRINITY, matric. 12 Oct., 89, aged 19 (from the Charterhouse), B.A. 92; HONOURS:—4 law 92.

Jansen, rev. Francis Charles Theodore, born at Gloucester 1865; o.s. Charles Theodore, gent. NON-COLLEGIATE, matric. 13 Oct., 84, aged 19, B.A. 88, M.A. 91 (HONOURS:—3 theology 88); curate of Clifton, Bristol, 88.

Jaques, John Harforth, born at Bishopwearmouth, co. Durham, 13 Aug., 1870; o.s. John Gartin, gen. TRINITY, matric. 12 Oct., 89, aged 19 (from Tonbridge school); HONOURS:—3 classical mods. 91.

Jardine, Hugh Raoul, born at Allahabad, in East Indies, 1870; 3s. William, arm. BALLIOL, matric. 17 Oct., 89, aged 19 (from Fettes coll.), B.A. 92; HONOURS:—4 law 92.

Jardine, John Inglis Fenke, born in London 1864; 1s. John, arm. BRASENOSE, matric. 15 Jan., 83, aged 19, from Eton.

Jardine, Malcolm Robert, born at Simla, East Indies, 4 June, 1869; 2s. William, arm. BALLIOL, matric. 18 Oct., 88, aged 19 (from Fettes coll.), B.A. 93 (HONOURS:—2 classical mods. 90, 3 classics 92), in the University eleven 89, 90, 1, 2.

Jarain, H.H. (sir) Bhugvut Sinh, K.C.I.E., LL.D., Thakore Saheb, of Gondal, created D.C.L. 22 June, 1892; LL.D., fellow Bombay university.

Jayne, Basil John, born at Llanelly, co. Brecon, 6 March, 1871; 1s. Basil, arm. WADHAM, matric. 5 May, 90, aged 19, from St. David's coll. school, Lampeter.

Jayne, right rev. Francis John, D.D., bishop of Chester, fellow JESUS COLL. 68-79, where see.

Jeans, rev. George Edward, M.A., fellow HERTFORD 85, where see.

Jebb, Richard Claverhouse, D.Litt, Regius professor of Greek, University of Cambridge 1889, M.P. Cambridge university 91, created D.C.L. 17 June, 91; 1s. Robert; scholar TRINITY COLL., CAMB., 60, B.A. 62, M.A. 65, fellow 63-76 and 89, tutor 72-4, hon. fellow 88-9 (HONOURS:—Porson scholarship 59, Greek verse 59, Craven scholarship 60, senior classics 61, public orator 69-76); prof. Greek, Glasgow, 75-89; born 27 Aug., 41. See *Men and Women of the Time*.

Jeffcock, Charles Augustus Castleford, born at Wolstanton, co. Stafford, April, 1872; 2s. John Thomas, vicar. KEBLE, matric. 14 Oct., 92, aged 18, from the Charterhouse.

Jefferies, Arthur Charles, born at Newbay, co. Wexford, 1869; 1s. Thomas, gen. BRASENOSE, matric. 1 May, 89, aged 20 (from Harrow), B.A. 92.

Jefferson, Gordon, born at Egremont, Cumberland, 6 Sept., 1868; 4s. Henry, arm. MERTON, matric. 17 Oct., 88, aged 20, from Harrow.

Jeffery, Edward John, born at Falmouth, Cornwall, 1868; 2s. Elias, gent. CHARSLEY'S HALL, matric. 3 Nov., 83, aged 25.

Jeffery, Francis Augustus Peyton, born at Oxford 1867; 2s. Edward, gent. NON-COLLEGIATE, matric. 17 April, 80, aged 18.

Jeffery, William James, born at Falmouth 1856; 1s. Elias, gent. NON-COLLEGIATE, matric. 13 Jan., 83, aged 27, from Kimberley gr. school, Falmouth.

Jeffrey, Alexander Niven, born at Edinburgh 1863; 2s. John, arm. BRASENOSE, matric. 8 Dec., 83, aged 20, from Fettes coll.

Jeffrey, Percy Shaw, born at Cheltenham 1863; 1s. Thomas Ashby, gent. QUEEN'S, matric. 30 Jan., 84, aged 21, B.A. 87, M.A. 90; HONOURS: —3 mathematical mods. 85.

Jeffrey, Peter, born at Edinburgh 1870; 1s. David, gen. BALLIOL, matric. 17 Oct., 89, aged 19 (from Harrow); HONOURS:—3 history 92.

Jeffrey, Robert, born at Edinburgh 1871; 2s. David, gen. BALLIOL, matric. 14 Oct., 90, aged 19, from Harrow.

Jeffrey, Russell Henry, born at Cheltenham 12 July, 1867; 2s. Thomas Ashby, gen. NON-COLLEGIATE, matric. 13 Oct., 88, aged 21 (from Cheltenham mod. school), B.A. 92.

Jeffreys, Arthur Henry, born at Bournemouth, Hants, Jan., 1873, or Nov., 1872; 1s. John, gen. CHRIST CHURCH, matric. 29 May, 91, aged 18, from Radley coll.

Jeffreys, Henry Anthony, M.A., student CHRIST CHURCH 1848, where see page 407.

Jeffreys, Herbert Castleman, born at Taunton, Somerset, 27 Nov., 1864; o.s. Herbert Castleman, squatter. NEW COLL., matric. 11 Oct., 89, aged 24, from university of Melbourne.

Jeffreys, Marmaduke Robert, M.A., student CHRIST CHURCH 1895-38, where see page 413.

Jelf, Charles Richard, born at Putney, Middx., Dec., 1873; 2s. Arthur Richard, Q.C. M.A. CHRIST CHURCH, matric. 14 Oct., 92, aged 18 (from Eton), scholar 92.

Jelf, Ernest Arthur, born at Putney, Surrey, 3 Oct., 1868; 1s. Arthur Richard, Q.C. NEW COLL., matric. 14 Oct., 87, aged 19 (from Haileybury), B.A. 91 (HONOURS:—2 classical mods. 89, 3 classics 91); bar.-at-law, Inner Temple, 93.

Jelf, George Edward, M.A., student CHRIST CHURCH 52-61, where see page 420.

Jelf, George Edward, born at Clapton, Surrey, 13 March, 1865; 1s. George Edward, cler. ORIEL, matric. 23 Oct., 84, aged 19 (from Haileybury), B.A. 87.

Jellett, John Hewitt, D.D., created U.C.L. 22 June, 1887; provost of Trinity coll., Dublin; born 25 Dec., 17, died 19 Feb., 88. See *Al. Ox.* 2nd series, 747.

Jellie, William, born at Moneyrea, co. Down, 1865; 1s. Robert, gen. NON-COLLEGIATE, matric. 21 Oct., 89, aged 24, from Belfast academical institute.

Jelly, Frank Edward, born at Middleton, co. Lanc., 20 March, 1870; 3s. James, cler., deceased. MAGDALEN, matric. 16 Oct., 88, aged 18 (from Manchester gr. school), demy 88, B.A. 92; HONOURS:—1 mathematical mods. 89, 1 mathematics 91.

Jelly, rev. John Edgar, born at Middleton, co. Lanc., 18 March, 1865; 2s. James, cler. WADHAM, matric. 16 Oct., 83, aged 18 (from Manchester gr. school), exhibitioner 82, B.A. 88 (HONOURS:— Abbott scholarship 83, 1 mathematical mods. 84, 2 mathematics 87); curate of St. George, Chorley, 90.

Jenkins, Charles M., of Lampeter; HONOURS:—3 mathematical mods. 86.

Jenkins, David, born at Henfars, co. Carmarthen, 1861; 1s. David, gent. JESUS COLL., matric. 23 Oct., 80, aged 19, from Llandovery coll.

Jenkins, Dudley Melville, born at Michaelstow-y-Vedw, co. Monmouth, 5 Oct., 1861; 1s. William, rector. JESUS COLL., matric. 19 Jan., 80, aged 18 (from Cheltenham coll.), B.A. 84, M.A. 88.

Jenkins, rev. Griffith Wight, born at Blakesley, Northants, 28 June, 1866; 2s. James, vicar. WADHAM, matric. 16 Oct., 86, aged 20 (from Leamington coll.), B.A. 89 (HONOURS:—2 classical mods. 98); curate of St. John's, Eastover, Bridgwater, 90.

Jenkins, rev. Howell William, born at Dowlais, co. Glamorgan, 6 Dec., 1859; 2s. Thomas, gent. LINCOLN, matric. 22 Jan., 80, aged 20 (from Llandovery coll.); migrated to NEW INN HALL, B.A. 86; curate of Aberdare, co. Glam., 89.

Jenkins, Richard Arthur, born in London 2 Nov., 1874; o.s. Richard Jonathan, C.E. BRASENOSE, matric. 21 Oct., 92, aged 18 (from Highgate school), scholar 92.

Jenkins, Richard Morgan, born at Llanfihangil-y-Creuddyn, co. Cardigan, 24 Jan., 1862; 2s. Richard, gent. NON-COLLEGIATE, matric. 15 Oct., 81, aged 20, from Ystradmeurig school.

Jenkins, Thomas, born at Swansea, co. Glam., 1869. QUEEN'S, matric. 14 Jan., 90, aged 21.

Jenkins, rev. Thomas Leoline, born at Hoyland, Yorks, Oct., 1860; o.s. Llewellyn, gent. NON-COLLEGIATE, matric. 15 Oct., 81, aged 21 (from Denstone coll.); migrated to HERTFORD, B.A. 85, M.A. 88 (HONOURS:—4 theology 89); curate of Pulliam St. Mary Magdalene 85.

Jenkins, William James, M.A., fellow BALLIOL 40-52, where see page 67.

Jenkins, William Owen, born at Treherbert, co. Glam., 1864; o.s. William, gent. JESUS COLL., matric. 20 Oct., 81, aged 17, B.A. 85, M.A. 89; HONOURS:—2 classical mods. 83, 2 classics 85.

Jenkins, rev. William Skinner, born at Galashiels, Selkirk, April, 1867; 3s. Alfred Augustus, cler.

Keble, matric. 19 Oct., 86, aged 19 (from Sedbergh school), B.A. 89 (HONOURS:—4 theology 89); curate of Sunderland Holy Trinity 91.

Jenkins, William Turbeville Llewellyn, born at St. Mellons, co. Monmouth, 1859; 3s. Edward, cler. BRASENOSE, matric. 12 April, 80, aged 21.

Jenkinson, John Wilfrid, born at Norwood, Surrey, 31 Dec., 1871; 2s. William Wilberforce, gen. EXETER, matric. 13 Oct., 90, aged 18 (from Bradfield coll.), scholar 90; HONOURS:—2 classical mods. 92.

Jenks, Thomas Henry, born at Penn, co. Stafford, 1868; 1s. William, gen. NON-COLLEGIATE, matric. 20 Jan., 83, aged 15 (from St. Kenelm school, Cowley); migrated to CHARSLEY HALL, B.A. 87.

Jenner, Arthur Charles William, born in London 27 Feb., 1864; 3s. William, bart. CHRIST CHURCH, matric. 12 Jan., 83, aged 18 (from Marlborough coll.), B.A. 86 (HONOURS:—1 history 86); bar.-at-law, Lincoln's Inn, 89.

Jenner, Gilbert, born at Low Catton, co. Derby, 5 Oct., 1872; 3s. Edmund Francis, rector, deceased. NON-COLLEGIATE, matric. 19 Oct., 90, aged 17 (from Magdalen coll. school); HONOURS:—3 classical mods. 92; brother of Robert C.

Jenner, Hugh Cecil Robert Francis, born at Woodville, Sutton, co. Hereford, 13 July, 1872; 1s. Hugh, esquire. ORIEL, matric. 27 Oct., 91, aged 19, from Haileybury.

Jenner, Louis Leopold Charles Albert, born in London 2 Dec., 1865; 4s. sir William, bart. TRINITY, matric. 11 Oct., 83, aged 18 (from Marlborough coll.), B.A. 89; HONOURS:—3 physiology 88.

Jenner, rev. Robert Christopher, born at Catton, Yorks, 4 Jan., 1868; 2s. Edmund, cler. WORCESTER, matric. 22 Jan., 85, aged 17 (from Newark gr. school), B.A. 89, M.A. 91; curate of Stamfordham, Northumberland, 91; brother of Gilbert.

Jenner, William Slark Baden, born at Baldock, Herts, July, 1870; 1s. William, D. Med. KEBLE, matric. 11 Oct., 90, aged 20, from Uppingham school.

Jennings, James George, born at Seacombe, Cheshire, 14 June, 1866; o.s. James, gen. LINCOLN, matric. 18 Oct., 88, aged 22 (from Ashby de la Zouch gr. school), B.A. 92; HONOURS:—2 history 92.

Jennings, William Harnett, born at Palamcotta, Southern India, 1873; 1s. Harnett Ellison, cler. KEBLE, matric. 20 Oct., 91, aged 18, from Dulwich coll.

Jennison, George, born at Manchester 13 Jan., 1872; 1s. George, merchant, deceased. BALLIOL, matric. 11 Feb., 92, aged 20, from Manchester gr. school.

Jephson, William Vincent, born at Ayot St. Peter, Herts, 6 Oct., 1873; 1s. Henry, rector. KEBLE, matric. 15 Oct., 92, aged 19, from Haileybury coll.

Jepson, Edgar Alfred, born in London 1864; 1s. Alfred, gent. BALLIOL, matric. 16 Oct., 83, aged 19 (from Leamington coll.), B.A. 89; HONOURS:—2 classical mods. 85, 3 classics 87.

Jersey, Edward Muriel de, born at Aslacton, Norfolk, 17 July, 1866; 1s. Peter Rivers, vicar of Empshott. NEW COLL., matric. 16 Oct., 85, aged 19 (from Haileybury), B.A. 92; HONOURS:—2 classical mods. 87, 4 classics 89.

Jervis, rev. Edward, born in London 22 Aug., 1868; 4s. Thomas, D. Med. CHRIST CHURCH, matric. 12 June, 86, aged 17 (from Westminster school), B.A. 89; curate of All Saints, South Acton, Middlesex, 91.

Jervoise, Francis Henry Tristram, born at the Moat, Bridford, Wilts, Dec., 1872; 1s. Francis Michael Ellis, M.A., J.P. CHRIST CHURCH, matric. 14 Oct., 92, aged 19, from Winchester.

Jervoise, col. John Purefoy Ellis, bursar, KEBLE, where see.

Jessel, Albert Henry, born in London 1865; 2s. Henry, arm. BALLIOL, matric. 16 Oct., 83, aged 18 (from Clifton coll.), B.A. 87, M.A. 91 (HONOURS :—3 classical mods. 85, 3 classics 87) ; bar.-at-law, Inner Temple, 89.

Jessel, Frank Herbert, born in London 1861 ; 2s. Edward, arm. MERTON, matric. 18 May, 80, aged 19 ; migrated to CHARSLEY HALL 84.

Jessel, Herbert Merton, born at Brighton 27 Oct., 1866; 2s. sir George, knt., master of the rolls. NEW COLL., matric. 10 Oct., 84, aged 17, from Rugby.

Jesson, William Arthur, born at Awbridge, Hants, 1862 ; 3s. Thomas, arm. NON-COLLE-GIATE, matric. 15 Oct., 81, aged 19 (from Harrow) ; migrated to BALLIOL 82 ; died 20 May, 1884.

Jeudwine, George Wynne, M.A., fellow QUEEN'S 70-6, where see page 182.

Jeune, right hon. sir Francis Henry, president probate court, &c., hon. fellow HERTFORD 91, where see.

Jevons, rev. Henry Hamon, born at Willenhall, co. Stafford, 20 Feb., 1869 ; o.s. Henry, gent. UNIVERSITY COLL., matric. 18 Oct., 86, aged 19 (from Rugby), B.A. 89 ; (HONOURS :—4 theology 89) ; curate of St. Paul, Burton-on-Trent, 90.

Jex-Blake, Arthur John, born at Cheltenham, co. Gloucester, 31 July, 1873; 2s. Thomas William, dean of Wells. MAGDALEN, matric. 18 Oct., 92, aged 19 (from Eton), demy 91.

Jex-Blake, Thomas Bowen, born at Cheltenham 4 Feb., 1872 ; 1s. Thomas William, D.D., dean of Wells. BALLIOL, matric. 17 Jan., 91, aged 18 (from Eton) ; HONOURS :—Latin verse 91, 2 classical mods. 92.

Jex-Blake, Thomas William, D.D., dean of Wells, fellow QUEEN'S 55-8, where see page 181.

Joachim, Harold Henry, born in London 1868 ; o.s. Henry, arm. BALLIOL, matric. 19 Oct., 86, aged 18 (from Harrow), scholar 85, Jenkyns exhibitioner 90, fellow MERTON 90, B.A. 91 ; HONOURS :—1 classical mods. 88, 1 classics 90.

Joachim, (professor) Joseph, created D.Mus. (Ox.) 14 Feb., 1888 ; the celebrated violinist ; born at Kitsee, near Presburg in Hungary, 15 July, 31 ; master of the chapel royal at Hanover 53 ; created D.Mus. Cambridge 8. March, 77 ; conductor royal academy of music in Berlin 82, and musical director of the royal academy of arts. See *Men and Women of the Time*.

Jobling, George Cruddas, born at Newcastle-upon-Tyne 17 Aug., 1871 ; 1s. Frederick Richard, cler. EXETER. matric. 13 Oct., 90, aged 19, from Haileybury.

Jobson, William Henry Oswald Stewart, born at Derby 1861 ; 3s. John, gent. WORCESTER, matric. 21 Oct., 80, aged 19 (from Malvern coll.), exhibitioner 80-3, B.A. 83 ; HONOURS :—2 mathematical mods. 82.

Jodrell, Philip Neville, born at Wood-Dalling, Norfolk, 1862 ; 2s. Charles Philip, cler. PEMBROKE, matric. 26 Oct., 81, aged 19 (from Bishop Stortford school), B.A. 86 (HONOURS :—3 history 85) ; bar.-at-law, Middle Temple, 88.

John, Edward Ernest Seymour Hutchinson, born at Londonderry 21 March, 1871 ; o.s. William Thomas, cler. QUEEN'S, matric. 24 Oct., 90, aged 19 (from Richmond gr. school), exhibitioner 91 ; HONOURS :—3 mathematical mods. 92.

Johns, Edward Francis, born at Ricknansworth, Herts, 15 April, 1861 ; 2s. Charles Alexander, cler. EXETER, matric. 15 May, 80, aged 19 (from Bradfield coll.), exhibitioner 80-5, B.A. 84, M.A. 87 ; HONOURS :—Abbott scholarship 81, 2 classical mods. 82.

Johnson, Archibald, born at St. George, Isle of Bermuda, 1 Aug., 1859 ; 1s. Alexander, gent. ST. MARY HALL, matric. 3 May, 84, aged 25.

Johnson, Arthur Basil Noel, born 5 April, 1861 ; 3s. George Henry Sacheverell, dean of Wells. MAGDALEN, matric. 16 Oct., 80, aged 19 (from Malvern coll.), clerk 80-3, B.A. 84 ; HONOURS :—a classical mods. 82.

Johnson, Arthur Exton, born at Grafton, in Australia, 20 Nov., 1871 ; 1s. James Hart, cler. NON-COLLEGIATE, matric. 17 Dec., 89, aged 18, from St. John's coll. school, Cowley, Oxford.

Johnson, Arthur Henry, M.A., fellow ALL SOULS' 69-73, where see page 282.

Johnson, Charles, born at Newcastle-on-Tyne 2 May, 1870 ; o.s. Edmund White, arm. TRINITY, matric. 13 Oct., 88, aged 18 (from Giggleswick school), scholar 87, B.A. 92 (HONOURS :—2 classical mods. 90, 1 classics 92) ; passed for the home C.S. 93.

Johnson, Charles Bailey, M.A. PEMBROKE, where see.

Johnson, Charles Blois, born at Liverpool 30 Aug., 1862 ; 1s. William Thomas, arm. WORCESTER, matric. 22 Jan., 85, aged 22, from Merchant Taylors' school.

Johnson, Edward Mayott, born at Shenfield, Essex, 1865 ; 1s. Matthew Warton, gent. ORIEL, matric. 27 Oct., 83, aged 18 (from Lancing coll.), B.A. 86, M.A. 90 ; HONOURS :—3 history 86.

Johnson, Ernest, born at Prestwich, co. Lanc., 1870 ; 2s. John Thewlis, arm. BRASENOSE, matric. 16 Oct., 88, aged 18 (from Winchester), B.A. 91 (HONOURS :—4 law 91) ; bar.-at-law, Inner Temple, 93.

Johnson, Ernest Wright, born at Abingdon, Berks, 1865 ; 3s. James Lacey, gent. PEMBROKE, matric. 23 Oct., 82, aged 17 (from Abingdon school), scholar 82-6, B.A. 86, M.A. 89 ; HONOURS :—1 classical mods. 84.

Johnson, Francis Edward, born at Tonbridge, Kent, 11 Aug., 1868 ; 4s. John Henry, solicitor. MAGDALEN, matric. 22 Oct., 87, aged 19, from Winchester.

Johnson, rev. Gifford Henry, born at Buckingham 30 Nov., 1869 ; o.s. Henry, gent. MERTON, matric. 18 Oct., 81, aged 21, B.A. 85, M.A. 88 (HONOURS :— 3 theology 84) ; curate of St. Mary, Kilburn, 90.

Johnson, Harold William, born at Preston, co. Lanc., 17 Aug., 1864 ; 1s. Thomas, vicar of Eastrington, Yorks. LINCOLN, matric. 19 Oct., 83, aged 19 (from Forest school), B.A. 86 ; HONOURS :— 3 history 86.

Johnson, Henry John, born at Oxford 1869 ; 1s. Henry, gent. NON-COLLEGIATE, matric. 17 Oct., 85, aged 16 (from Bedford house school, Oxford), B.A. 88, M.A. 92.

Johnson, rev. Herbert Mark, born at Cardiff, co. Glam., 25 April, 1868 ; 5s. George, arm. WORCESTER, matric. 19 Oct., 86, aged 18 (from St. Edward's school, Summertown), B.A. 89.

Johnson, Horace Lawrence, born at Hackney, Middx., 1869 ; 3s. Lawrence Hawkins, gent. ST. JOHN'S, matric. 13 Oct., 88, aged 19 (from Merchant Taylors' school), scholar 88 ; drowned 16 Feb., 89, in the Isis at Oxford.

Johnson, Horace Maxwell, born at Mitcham, Surrey, 3 Jan., 1869 ; y.s. Mary Henry, arm. EXETER, matric. 21 Oct., 86, aged 17 (from Haileybury) ; bar.-at-law, Inner Temple, 92.

Johnson, Ivor Lowthian, born at Llandaff, co. Glamorgan, 31 July, 1873 ; 4s. Walter, of Rounton Grange, Yorks, esq. MAGDALEN, matric. 18 Oct., 92, aged 19, from Winchester coll.

Johnson, John Frederick, born at Canterbury 22 Oct., 1870 ; 4s. George, brewer. LINCOLN, matric. 25 Oct., 92, aged 22.

Johnson, John Robson, born at North Sunderland, Northumberland, 1855; 2s. John, gent. WORCESTER, matric. 24 Jan., 80, aged 25, B.A. 85, M.A. 86.

Johnson, John Tysilio, born at Rock-Ferry, Cheshire, 11 July, 1862; 1s. Tysilio, arm. MAGDALEN, matric. 15 Oct., 81, aged 19 (from Brecon coll.), demy 81-3, B.A. 85; HONOURS :—2 natural science 85.

Johnson, Joseph, born at Lambeth, Surrey, 1854; 1s. Joseph, gent. NON-COLLEGIATE, matric. 13 June, 85, aged 31, from St. Jude's school, Southwark.

Johnson, Ledru Rollin, born at Collinsville, Illinois, 27 June, 1859; 2s. Jackson Maddison, arm. QUEEN'S, matric. 24 Jan., 80, aged 20 (from Washington University, St. Louis), B.A. 83.

Johnson, Leslie Bradyll, born in London 18 Nov., 1871; 1s. William, deceased. ST. MARY HALL, matric. 18 Oct., 92, aged 20.

Johnson, Lionel Pigot, born at Broadstairs, Kent, 15 March, 1867; 1s. William Victor, a captain in the army, NEW COLL., matric. 15 Oct., 86, aged 19 (from Winchester), scholar 85, B.A. 90; HONOURS: —2 classical mods. 88, 1 classics 90.

Johnson, Oswald Carnegy, born at Flore, Rutland, 16 Aug., 1867; o.s. Frederick Pigot, rector of Oakney, Wilts, deceased. NEW COLL., matric. 15 Oct., 86, aged 19 (from Haileybury), B.A. 90; HONOURS :—3 theology 90.

Johnson, Percy Marr, born in London 13 Dec., 1868; 1s. Thomas Marr, arm. MERTON, matric. 21 Oct., 86, aged 17 (from Radley coll.), B.A. 90; HONOURS: —3 law 90.

Johnson, Robert, born at Warwick 15 Dec., 1866; 2s. Robert, gent. JESUS COLL., matric. 23 Oct., 85, aged 18 (from Warwick gr. school), scholar 85, B.A. 89, M.A. 92; HONOURS :—1 classical mods. 87, 2 classics 89.

Johnson, Robert Baines, born in London 1862; 1s. Robert, arm. ST. JOHN'S, matric. 16 Oct., 80, aged 18, B.A. 85, M.A. 88.

Johnson, Robert Thorley, born at Hindley, co. Lanc., 1865; 4s. James Henry, arm. UNIVERSITY COLL., matric. 11 Oct., 84, aged 19 (from Wakefield school), exhibitioner 84, B.A. 88, M.A. 91; HONOURS :—2 classical mods. 86, 3 classics 88.

Johnson, Ronald Frederic Godolphin, born at Torrington, Devon, 1864; 1s. John George, arm. BRASENOSE, matric. 21 Jan., 82, aged 18, from Eton.

Johnson, Stuart Henry James, born in London 1867; o.s. Edmund Charles, D.Med. CHRIST CHURCH, matric. 3 June, 87, aged 19 (from Eton), B.A. 92.

Johnson, Thomas Ernest Reeve, born at Runcorn, Cheshire, 8 Jan., 1862; o.s. Thomas, arm. WADHAM, matric. 17 Oct., 82, aged 19, from Kensington gr. school.

Johnson, Walter Lyulph, born at Washington, co. Durham, 15 July, 1872; 1s. Walter, iron-master. NEW COLL., matric. 16 Oct., 91, aged 19, from Leeds gr. school and Eton.

Johnson, William Knox, born at Monkstown, co. Dublin, 26 Feb., 1868; 1s. Henry, cler. MERTON, matric. 22 Oct., 87, aged 19 (from R.N. school, New Cross), B.A. 91; HONOURS :—1 history 91.

Johnston, George Arthur, born at Bath 15 Feb., 1872; o.s. George, lieut.-col. TRINITY, matric. 12 Oct., 89, aged 18 (from Wellington coll.), B.A. 92; HONOURS :—3 law 92.

Johnston, Henry George, born at Magherlin, Ireland, 1860; 1s. Walter, cler. NON-COLLEGIATE, matric. 18 Oct., 80, aged 20 (from Merchant Taylors' school), exhibitioner EXETER 80-4, B.A. 84; HONOURS :— 3 classical mods. 82, 3 classics 84.

Johnston, James Arranloe, born at Hornsey, Middx., 7 Nov., 1866; 3s. John Alexander, gent. BALLIOL, matric. 24 Oct., 85, aged 18 (from Mill Hill school), D.A. 90 (HONOURS :—2 classical mods. 87, a law 89); bar.-at-law, Inner Temple, 92.

Johnston, John Goring, born at Wellington, New Zealand, 2 Aug., 1870; 1s. (hon.) Walter Woods. WADHAM, matric. 13 Oct., 88, aged 18 (from Stonyhurst), B.A. 92; bar.-at-law, Inner Temple, 92; brother of Walter G.

Johnston, rev. John Octavius, M.A., LINCOLN, where see page 246.

Johnston, Prideaux Selby William, born at Edgbaston, co. Warwick, 9 April, 1870; 2s. William Henry, arm. CORPUS CHRISTI, matric. 25 Oct., 89, aged 19 (from Clifton coll.), exhibitioner 89; HONOURS :—3 classical mods. 91.

Johnston, Walter Goring, born at Wellington, New Zealand, 13 May, 1873; 4s. (hon.) Walter Woods. EXETER, matric. 21 Jan., 91, aged 17 (from Stonyhurst); brother of John G.

Johnston, rev. William Cranley, born at Cranley, Surrey, 1867; 1s. William Boys, cler. ST. EDMUND HALL, matric. 21 Oct., 86, aged 19, B.A. 89; curate of Dudley St. James 91.

Johnstone, Arthur Gifford Whitside, born at Colton, co. Stafford, Dec., 1861; 2s. Edward, cler. KEBLE, matric. 19 Oct., 80, aged 18 (from Radley coll.); migrated to NEW INN HALL (Balliol 88), B.A. 89.

Johnstone, Charles Edward, born at Wareham, Kent, Aug., 1865; 2s. Edward, cler. KEBLE, matric. 14 Oct., 84, aged 19 (from Radley coll.), B.A. 88; HONOURS :—2 classical mods. 86, 4 classics 88.

Johnstone, Francis Herbert, born at Didsbury, co. Lanc., 16 Jan. 1867; 2s. Herbert Allison, schoolmaster. WADHAM, matric. 19 Oct., 85, aged 18 (from Manchester gr. school), scholar 84, B.A. 89; HONOURS :—2 classical mods. 87, 3 classics 89.

Johnstone, Henry Beresford, born at Alva, co. Stirling, 26 Jan., 1871; 3s. James, arm. MERTON, matric. 19 Oct., 89, aged 18 (from Wellington coll.), B.A. 92; HONOURS :—3 history 92.

Johnstone, James, M.A., fellow ST. JOHN'S 57-66, where see.

Johnstone, James, born 21 Dec., 1873; o.s. James, bar.-at-law, MERTON, matric. 22 Oct., 91, aged 17, from Lancing coll.

Johnstone, Oscar Rudolph Bernard, born in London Jan., 1868; 2s. Karl Bernard, arm. KEBLE, matric. 13 Oct., 88, aged 20, from Glenalmond coll. and Birmingham gr. school.

Johnstone, rev. Philip Marmaduke Cramer, born at Aden, Arabia, 28 June, 1866; 3s. Robert Maxwell, arm. KEBLE, matric. 22 Oct., 85, aged 19 (from Bath gr. school), B.A. 88 (HONOURS :—2 history 88); curate of Kenwyn, Cornwall, 89.

Johnstone, Robert Souley, born at Forfar 1862; 1s. Robert Souley, gent. BRASENOSE, matric. 18 Oct., 81, aged 19 (from Wolverhampton school), scholar 81-4, exhibitioner 84, B.A. 85 (HONOURS :—1 classical mods. 83, 1 classics 85); died Nov., 86.

Johnstone, Verney Lovett, born at Belgaum in East Indies 4 July, 1868; 4s. Robert Maxwell, arm. MERTON, matric. 22 Oct., 86, aged 19 (from Wellington), postmaster 87, B.A. 91; HONOURS :—1 classical mods. 89, 1 classics 91, Liddon theological studentship 91.

Joicey, James John, born at Jesmond, Newcastle-on-Tyne, 1871; o.s. William James, esq. HERTFORD, matric. 20 Oct., 91, aged 20, from Aysgarth school.

Jolley, Charles Edward, born at Higham Ferrers, Northants, , 1860; 1s. Charles, gen. NEW COLL., matric. 18 Jan., 87, aged 27, B.Mus. 88.

Jolley, William Spry, born at Osborne, I.W., 1881; 2s. William Rowe, cler. HERTFORD, matric. 4 May, 81, aged 19.

Jolliffe, Arthur Ernest, born at Oxford 23 Jan., 1871; 4s. Henry, of Oxford. BALLIOL, matric. 18 Oct., 88, aged 17 (from Oxford high school), scholar 87, B.A. 91; fellow CORPUS CHRISTI 91; HONOURS :— 1 mathematical mods. 89, 2 mathematics 91, junior 89 and senior mathematical scholarship 92.

Jolliffe, hon. Hylton George Hylton, born in London 10 Nov., 1862; o.s. Hedworth, lord Hylton. ORIEL, matric. 1 June, 82, aged 19 (from Eton), B.A. 85, M.A. 91; HONOURS :—a history 85.

Jolly, William Arnold, born at Charlcombe, Somerset, 1 May, 1869; 4s. William Cruckwell, gen. NEW COLL., matric. 12 Oct., 88, aged 19 (from Clifton coll.); HONOURS :—1 history 91.

Jones, Alfred Clement, born at Cheltenham 16 April, 1871; o.s. John Thomas, cler. BRASENOSE, matric. 15 Oct., 90, aged 19 (from Cheltenham gr. school), scholar 89; HONOURS :—1 mathematical mods. 91.

Jones, Alfred Inwood, born at Brighton April, 1871; 2s. Alfred, cler. KEBLE, matric. 11 Oct., 90, aged 19, from Leamington coll.

Jones, Arthur Ernest, born at Llandudno, co. Carnarvon, 28 May, 1873; 1s. John, curate. JESUS COLL., matric. 18 Oct., 92, aged 19, from Ruthin school.

Jones, Arthur Grant, born at Westbury-on-Severn , 1868; 3s. Christopher Jay, cler. ORIEL, matric. 19 Oct., 86, aged 18 (from Marlborough coll.), B.A. 90; HONOURS :—3 mathematical mods. 88, 2 mathematics 90.

Jones, Arthur John, born at Aberdervyn, co. Denbigh, 27 Jan., 1871; 2s. John Morice, cler. LINCOLN, matric. 20 Oct., 90, aged 19, from Ruthin school.

Jones, Arthur Mervyn, born at Bromley, Kent, 13 Oct., 1874; 2s. Alfred Orlando, of Harrogate, D.Med. UNIVERSITY COLL., matric. 15 Oct., 92, aged 18, from the Charterhouse.

Jones, Arthur Trevor Richardson, born at Llanyblodwell, Salop, , 1869; o.s. Richard, cler. NON-COLLEGIATE, matric. 13 Oct., 88, aged 19, from Oswestry gr. school.

Jones, Arthur Wentworth, born at Mottram-en-Longdendale, Cheshire, 26 Nov., 1862; 1s. William Henry, vicar. BALLIOL, matric. 17 Oct., 82, aged 19 (from Kingswood school and Clifton coll.), exhibitioner 82-4; migrated to QUEEN'S, B.A., M.A. 92; HONOURS :—2 natural science 85.

Jones, Benjamin, born at Llangeinwen, isle of Anglesey, , 1865; y.s. Thomas, pleb. NON-COLLEGIATE, matric. 13 Oct., 88, aged 23.

Jones, Cecil Joseph, born at Nantwich, Cheshire, 11 May, 1873; 3s. William, J.P., D.L., BRASENOSE, matric. 21 Oct., 92, aged 19, from Malvern coll.

Jones, rev. Charles Ambrose Sturges, born at Chichester, Oct., 1867; 3s. Charles, gen. KEBLE, matric. 20 Oct., 88, aged 21 (from Magdalen coll. school), B.A. 91; brother Thomas O. 81.

Jones, rev. Charles Frederick, born at Llanidloes, co. Montgomery, 30 June, 1849; y.s. John, cler. NON-COLLEGIATE, matric. 13 Oct., 83, aged 34 (from Llandovery collegiate school, and St. David's coll., Lampeter, B.A. 73); migrated to WADHAM 17 Oct., 85; held various curacies 74-82.

Jones, Charles Lerigo, born at Ardwick, co. Lancaster, 13 March, 1872; 1s. Charles Henry. WORCESTER, matric. 22 Oct., 91, aged 19, from St. George's coll., Harrogate.

Jones, Charles Percy, born at Biggleswade, Beds, 7 Jan., 1868; 1s. Charles, gen. WORCESTER, matric. 21 Jan., 87, aged 19, from Willesden high school.

Jones, Charles Sydney, born at Wavertree, near Liverpool, 7 Feb., 1872; 1s. Charles William, arm. MAGDALEN, matric. 14 Oct., 90, aged 18, from the Charterhouse.

Jones, David, born at Llanelly, co. Carmarthen, 22 Sept., 1871; 5s. Charles, gen. JESUS COLL., matric. 15 Oct., 90, aged 19 (from Oswestry gr. school), exhibitioner 90; HONOURS :—2 mathematical mods. 92.

Jones, rev. David Akrill, born at Hinley, Somerset, 11 April, 1867; 1s. Samuel Rowland, cler. MERTON, matric. 21 Oct., 86, aged 19 (from Cowbridge gr. school and Brecon coll.), B.A. 90; (HONOURS :— Ægrotat theology 90); curate of Caudon, co. Glam., 90.

Jones, rev. David Alexander, born at Ash, co. Glam., March, 1869; 1s. David, cler. KEBLE, matric. 17 Oct., 87, aged 18 (from Oswestry gr. school), B.A. 90; HONOURS :—3 theology 90.

Jones, David Ambrose, born at Cilcennin, co. Cardigan, 3 June, 1869; 2s. Timothy John, arm., deceased. CORPUS CHRISTI, matric. 16 Oct., 90, aged 21, from University coll. of Wales.

Jones, rev. David Evans, born at Llansantffread, co. Cardigan, 14 Jan., 1866; 1s. Thomas, vicar of Rhoslanerchrugog, co. Denbigh. JESUS COLL., matric. 20 Oct., 86, aged 20 (from Ruabon gr. school and Brecon coll.), B.A. 89 (HONOURS :— 3 classical mods. 88); curate of Pickering, Yorks, 90.

Jones, David John, born at Treherbert, co. Glamorgan, 31 Dec., 1870; 1s. William, pleb. JESUS COLL., matric. 14 Oct., 89, aged 18 (from Carmarthen gr. school), exhibitioner 89; HONOURS :—2 mathematical mods. 92.

Jones, rev. David Morgan, born at Llangadock, co. Carmarthen, , 1863; 1s. David, gent. WORCESTER, matric. 19 Oct., 82, aged 19 (from Llandovery coll.), scholar 81-6, B.A. 86, M.A. 93; sub-librarian (HONOURS :—2 classical mods. 84, 3 classics 86); curate of SS. Philip and James, Leckhampton, 88.

Jones, rev. David Saunders, born at Llanybyther, co. Carnarvon, , 1859; 2s. Henry, cler. NON-COLLEGIATE, matric. 17 Oct., 81; aged 22 (from Llandovery coll.); migrated to WORCESTER, B.A. 85, M.A. 88; rector of Llanfrynach, co. Brecon, 90.

Jones, Edgar, born in London 13 Jan., 1874; 1s. William, accountant. BRASENOSE, matric. 21 Oct., 92, aged 18 (from Merchant Taylors' school), scholar 92.

Jones, Edgar Montague, born at Bristol 1 June, 1866; 4s. William, arm. NEW COLL., matric. 16 Oct., 85, aged 19 (from Bristol gr. school), scholar 85, B.A. 89; HONOURS :—a mathematical mods. 86, 1 mathematics 89.

Jones, rev. Edgar Philip, born in London 1861; 2s. Benjamin, gent. NON-COLLEGIATE, matric. 12 June, 86, aged 25, B.A. 90, M.A. 92; curate of Bath (Holy Trinity) 91.

Jones, Edmund Herbert, born in London 25 April, 1870; 4s. Richard, gen. WORCESTER, matric. 14 Oct., 90, aged 20, from Malvern coll.

Jones, Edward Coley Burne, D.C.L., hon. fellow EXETER 82, where see page 124.

Jones, Edward Herbert, born at Chipstead, Surrey, 1870; 2s. Herbert Wright, arm. CHRIST CHURCH, matric. 14 Oct., 87, aged 17, B.A. 91.

Jones, Edward Maxwell, born at Devauxden, co. Monmouth, 29 Nov., 1873; 3s. George, M.A. Camb., clerk, deceased. EXETER, matric. 18 Oct., 92, aged 18.

Jones, Edward Owen, born at Machynlleth, co. Merioneth, 16 Oct., 1870; 3s. Hugh, rector of Llangynllo. NON-COLLEGIATE, matric. 11 Oct., 90, aged 19 (from St. David's coll., Lampeter, B.A.); migrated to JESUS COLL. 19 Oct., 92.

Jones, Edward Rhys, M.A., fellow BRASENOSE 43-51, where see page 352.

Jones, rev. Edward William, born at Thames Ditton, Surrey, 1867; 3s. Thomas Evans, gent. BRASENOSE, matric. 23 Oct., 85, aged 18 (from Hereford school), scholar 85, B.A. 89 (HONOURS:—2 classical mods. 87, 3 classics 89); curate of Connah's Quay, Flints, 90.

Jones, Edward Wynne, born at Llangadfan, co. Montgomery, 1859; 3s. John Matthew, cler. JESUS COLL., matric. 23 Oct., 80, aged 21.

Jones, Ernest Henry Vaughan, born at Tewksbury 10 July, 1866; o.s. Henry, gen. ST. MARY HALL, matric. 18 Jan., 87, aged 22.

Jones, Ernest Yarrow, born at Fairfield, Liverpool, 1872; 2s. Edward, merchant. PEMBROKE, matric. 26 Oct., 91, aged 19 (from Liverpool coll.), scholar 91.

Jones, Evan Bowen, born at Ynysfor, co. Merioneth, 1868; 2s. John, arm. CORPUS CHRISTI, matric. 22 Oct., 87, aged 19 (from Shrewsbury school), B.A. 91; HONOURS:—3 classical mods. 89, 4 law 90.

Jones, Evan Thomas, born at Bala, co. Merioneth, 1871; 1s. John, gen. NON-COLLEGIATE, matric. 29 Oct., 90, aged 19, from Bala gr. school.

Jones, Francis Adolphus, born in London 1862; 3s. Charles Edward, arm. UNIVERSITY COLL., matric. 16 Jan., 80, aged 18, B.A. 83, M.A. 87 (HONOURS:—3 classical mods. 81, 3 history 83); bar.-at-law, Lincoln's Inn, 86.

Jones, Francis Emilius Fletcher, born at Chester 31 Aug., 1868; 2s. Richard, cler. WORCESTER, matric. 24 April, 88, aged 19, from Rossall school.

Jones, Francis Thomas, born at Dalston, Middx., 7 Feb., 1867; 4s. John Humphreys, gent. WORCESTER, matric. 14 March, 85, aged 18, B.A. 88; HONOURS:—1 law 87.

Jones, Frank Edward Thorp, born at Ambleside, Westmorland, 23 April, 1869; 1s. Frank Maud Taylor, arm. MAGDALEN, matric. 16 Oct., 88, aged 19 (from Eton); HONOURS:—3 classical mods. 90, 3 history 92.

Jones, Frederick William, born at Oundle, Notts, 20 Dec., 1871; 1s. William Morgan, rector of Marks Tey, Essex. MAGDALEN, matric. 14 Oct., 90, aged 18 (from St. Paul's school); HONOURS:— 2 classical mods. 92.

Jones, George Stanley Owen, born at Hartley Mawditt, Hants, 29 Sept., 1871; 1s. George, cler. EXETER, matric. 16 Oct., 90, aged 19, from Marlborough coll.

Jones, Gilbert Maule, born in London 17 Dec., 1867; 5s. Charles Edward, solicitor. NEW COLL., matric. 15 Oct., 86, aged 18 (from Winchester), B.A. 89; HONOURS:—3 law 89.

Jones, Gillat Herbert, born in Surrey 12 March 1868; 1s. Herbert Wright, gen. WORCESTER, matric. 17 Jan., 88, aged 19 (from Newport gr. school), B.A. 92.

Jones, Harry, born at Wellington, Salop, 1865; 2s. Edward, arm. NEW INN HALL, matric. 20 Oct., 86, aged 21; of BALLIOL 87.

Jones, Harry Vernon, born at Farnham, Surrey, 28 April, 1862; 2s. William Thomas, gent. EXETER, matric. 20 Oct., 81, aged 19 (from Haileybury); farming in Florida, U.S.A.

Jones, Henry James Church, born at Aberforth, co. Cardigan, 30 Nov., 1870; o.s. John, cler., deceased. ST. JOHN'S, matric. 12 Oct., 89, aged 19, from Christ coll., Brecon.

Jones, Henry Maxwell, born at Thornes, Yorks, 7 Dec., 1864; 4s. Henry, vicar. NEW COLL., matric. 15 Oct., 84, aged 19 (from Merchant Taylors' school), B.A. 88, M.A. 91; HONOURS:—3 history 88.

Jones, Henry Owen, born at Llanfechain, co. Montgomery, 1874; 3s. David, cler. KEBLE, matric. 15 Oct., 92, aged 18, from Oswestry gr. school.

Jones, Henry Stuart, born in Leeds 15 May, 1867; 1s. Henry William, cler. BALLIOL, matric. 19 Oct., 86, aged 19 (from Rossall school), scholar 85, Jenkyns exhibitioner 90, fellow TRINITY 90, B.A. 90; HONOURS:—accessit Craven scholarship 86, Hertford scholarship 86, Ireland and Craven scholarships 88, 1 classical mods. 88, Greek prose 90, 1 classics 90, Craven travelling fellowship 90, Derby scholarship 91.

Jones, Herbert Morice, born at Rhosllanerch-rugog, co. Denbigh, 3 Feb., 1870; 1s. John Morice, cler. JESUS COLL., matric. 15 Oct., 90, aged 20, from Ruthin gr. school.

Jones, Howell, born at Cape Town, South Africa, 1861; 1s. Thomas Griffith, gent. PEMBROKE, matric. 10 May, 82, aged 20 (from Brecon school), B.A. 85; (HONOURS:—4 law 85); bar.-at-law, Middle Temple, 86.

Jones, Hugh, M.A., fellow JESUS COLL. 39-45, where see.

Jones, Hugh, born at Williamstown, Victoria, Australia, 1862; 1s. Thomas, gen. NON-COLLEGIATE, matric. 17 Oct., 91, aged 29, from Melbourne university.

Jones, James, born at Aberdaron, co. Carnarvon, 1858. NON-COLLEGIATE, matric. 12 Oct., 89, aged 31 (from Bala school and Lampeter); HONOURS:—3 mathematical mods. 89, as of Lampeter.

Jones, James John, born at Llanfair Dufferin-Clwyd, co. Denbigh, 4 June, 1867; 1s. Richard, gen. JESUS COLL., matric. 15 Oct., 90, aged 19 (from Ruthin gr. school), scholar 90 (HONOURS:—3 mathematical mods. 92); Wesleyan minister.

Jones, John Arthur, born at Tregarth, co. Carnarvon, 2 June, 1867; 1s. Hugh, gent. JESUS COLL., matric. 23 Oct., 85, aged 18 (from Kingswood school Bath, and Wesleyan coll., Sheffield), B.A. 89; HONOURS:—3 classical mods. 87, 3 history 89.

Jones, John David, born at Tailey, co. Carmarthen, 7 Sept., 1871; 1s. David, gen. QUEEN'S, matric. 22 Oct., 89, aged 16 (from Llandovery coll.), scholar 89; HONOURS:—2 classical mods. 91.

Jones, John Edward, born at Llanegwad, co. Carmarthen, 20 Jan., 1867; 1s. David, gen. JESUS COLL., matric. 19 Oct., 87, aged 20 (from Llandovery coll.); HONOURS:—2 classical mods. 89, 4 history 91.

Jones, John Eyton-, born at Llangollen, co. Denbigh, 1863; 1s. Hugh, pleb. JESUS COLL., matric. 18 Oct., 82, aged 19 (from Llandovery coll.); HONOURS:—3 classical mods.

Jones, rev. John Gower, born at Llanelly, co. Carmarthen, 21 Jan., 1864; 1s. Thomas, gen. NON-COLLEGIATE, matric. 13 Oct., 88, aged 24 (from University coll. Bangor); migrated to JESUS COLL. 21 Jan., 89, B.A. 91; curate of Tredegar, co. Monmouth, 91.

Jones, John Griffith, born at Llwynffynon, co. Carm., 1865; o.s. Griffith, gen. NON-COLLEGIATE, matric. 28 Jan., 82, aged 18.

Jones, rev. John Hugh Watkins, born at Carmarthen, 1862; 1s. Titus Lewis, gent. NON-COLLEGIATE, matric. 12 Oct., 82, aged 20; migrated to WORCESTER, B.A. 86, M.A. 89; curate of Christ Church, Swansea, 89.

Jones, John Morris, born at Llandrygan, isle of Anglesey, 17 Oct., 1864; 1s. Morris, gent. JESUS COLL., matric. 18 Oct., 83, aged 19 (from Brecon school); scholar 83, B.A. 87, M.A. 90; HONOURS: —2 mathematical mods. 85, 3 mathematics 87.

Jones, John Puleston, born at Llanbedr, co. Denbigh, 1862; 1s. Evan, gent. BALLIOL, matric. 15 Oct., 84, aged 22 (from the Blind coll., Worcester), B.A. 88, M.A. 92; HONOURS:—1 history 88.

Jones, rev. John Rees, born at Carmarthen 1870; 1s. John, gen. NON-COLLEGIATE, matric. 27 April, 89, aged 19 (from Brecon coll.), B.A. 89.

Jones, John Reginald, born at Bunbury, Cheshire, 24 May, 1872; 1s. James, arm. TRINITY, matric. 11 Oct., 90, aged 18, from the Charterhouse.

Jones, rev. John Thomas, born at Lampeter, co. Cardigan, 17 Aug., 1866; 2s. David, gent. WADHAM, matric. 3 Nov., 86, aged 20 (from Lampeter coll.), B.A. 89 (HONOURS:—3 classical mods. 86, 4 classics 89); curate of Penarth, Cardiff, 89.

Jones, Lancelot James Napier, born at Magherafelt, co. Londonderry, 8 Aug., 1870; 2s. David, cler. JESUS COLL., matric. 14 Oct., 89, aged 19 (from Oswestry gr. school), scholar 90 (HONOURS:—2 classical mods. 91); died 9 Sept., 92.

Jones, Leifchild Stratton, born in London 16 Jan., 1862; 4s. Thomas, bar.-at-law, deceased. TRINITY, matric. 15 Oct., 81, aged 19 (from Scotch coll., Melbourne), scholar 81-5, B.A. 86 (HONOURS:—1 mathematical mods. 82, 1 mathematics 85); contested Westminster 92.

Jones, Leycester Hudson Leslie-, born at Camborne, Cornwall, 13 Feb., 1872; 1s. Hudson, D.Med. BRASENOSE, matric. 15 Oct., 90, aged 18 (from Hereford cathedral school; scholar 90; HONOURS: —2 classical mods. 92.

Jones, rev. Maurice, born at Trawsfynydd, co. Merioneth, 1869; 2s. William, pleb. JESUS COLL., matric. 18 Oct., 89, aged 19 (from Brecon coll.), B.A. 86 (HONOURS:—1 mathematical mods. 84, 1 theology 86); curate of Carnarvon 86-88, Welshpool 89-90.

Jones, rev. Nathaniel, born at Wootton, Salop, 1861; 1s. John, pleb. NON-COLLEGIATE, matric. 11 Oct., 82, aged 21 (from Oswestry school), B.A. 86 (HONOURS:—1 theology 86); minister of Tarragulla, Victoria, 88.

Jones, Nathaniel, born at Cefn, co. Brecon, Oct., 1870; 1s. Thomas, cler. NON-COLLEGIATE, matric. 6 Feb., 92, aged 21, from Cardigan collegiate school and Llandovery coll.

Jones, rev. Percy Herbert, born at Warblington, Hants, 1865; 2s. James Owen, arm. CHRIST CHURCH, matric. 10 Oct., 84, aged 19 (from Christ's hospital), exhibitioner 84, scholar 87, B.A. 88, M.A. 92 (HONOURS:—1 mathematical mods.86, 2 mathematics 88); assist. master Weymouth coll. and curate of Upwey, Dorset, 90.

Jones, Philip Burne, born in London 2 Oct., 1861; o.s. Edward Coley, A.R.A. UNIVERSITY COLL., matric. 15 May, 80, aged 18, from Marlborough coll.; artist.

Jones, Rees David, born at Clynere, co. Brecon, 1859; 1s. John, gent. JESUS COLL., matric. 19 Oct., 81, aged 22 (from Aberystwith coll.), B.A. 85; HONOURS:—2 classical mods. 83.

Jones, Reginald Bence, born at Kilnacross, co. Cork, 1866; 2s. William, arm. ST. JOHN'S, matric. 11 Oct., 84, aged 18.

Jones, Reginald Heber, born at Newport, co. Mon., 1867; o.s. Morgan Middleton, arm. MERTON, matric. 15 Dec., 83, aged 16 (from Brighton coll.); migrated to ORIEL, B.A. 86, M.A. 91; bar.-at-law, Inner Temple, 87.

Jones, rev. Richard Charles Stuart, born in London 12 Dec., 1865; 1s. Richard, gent. WORCESTER, matric. 17 Oct., 84, aged 18 (from Malvern coll.), B.A. 88, M.A. 91 (HONOURS:—3 classical mods. 86, 2 theology 88); curate of Cirencester 89.

Jones, Richard Davis, born at Berlin, Wisconsin, U.S.A., 1855; 1s. John A., congregational minister. NON-COLLEGIATE, matric. 22 Oct., 91, aged 36, from Iowa coll., U.S.A.

Jones, rev. Richard Edmunds, born at Bangor 1862; 1s. John, cler. JESUS COLL., matric. 19 Oct., 81, aged 19 (from Brecon school); scholar 82-5, B.A. 86, M.A. 89 (HONOURS:—1 classical mods. 83, 3 classics 85); assist. master King Edward school, Bromsgrove, 91; headmaster of the Lodge school, island of Barbados, 92.

Jones, Richard Tyrrell, born at Llansillin, Salop, 27 June, 1871; 1s. John, arm. NEW COLL., matric. 1 May, 90, aged 18 (from Eton); in the University eleven 92.

Jones, Richard William Hyndman, born at George Town, British Guiana, 14 June, 1864; o.s. Hugh Hyndman, cler. QUEEN'S, matric. 22 Oct., 83, aged 19, from Marlborough and Brighton colls.

Jones, Robert Aylward, born at Leeds 16 June, 1870; 5s. Evan Miller, gen. QUEEN'S, matric. 22 Oct., 89, aged 19 (from Leeds gr. school), exhibitioner 89; HONOURS:—2 classical mods. 91.

Jones, rev. Robert Morris, born at Llanfairtalhaiarn, co. Denbigh, 8 Oct., 1862; o.s. Elias, gent. NON-COLLEGIATE, matric. 23 Jan., 86, aged 23; migrated to JESUS COLL., 20 Jan., 88, B.A. 89; curate of Llanllechid 90.

Jones, Thomas Bowen, born at Dinas, co. Brecon, 11 Dec., 1869; 2s. Roderick, gen., deceased. LINCOLN, matric. 20 Oct., 90, aged 20 (from Llandovery coll.); HONOURS:—3 classical mods. 92.

Jones, rev. Thomas Jesse, born at Abergele 28 April, 1856; 1s. Jesse, pleb. NON-COLLEGIATE, matric. 6 Feb., 80, aged 25; migrated to MERTON 81, B.A. 82, M.A. 87; vicar of Pontlottyn 87-90, and rector of Gelligaer, co. Glam., 90.

Jones, Thomas Oliver Sturges, born at Chichester June, 1862; 1s. Charles Sturges, gent. KEBLE, matric. 18 Oct., 81, aged 19 (from the Charterhouse); brother of Charles A. 88.

Jones, Walter Hugh, born at Bunbury, Cheshire, 12 Dec., 1873; 2s. James, gent. MERTON, matric. 18 Oct., 92, aged 18, from Marlborough coll.

Jones, William Basil, D.D., bishop of St. Davids, fellow UNIVERSITY COLL. 51-7, where see page 32.

Jones, William Eccles, M.A., fellow JESUS COLL. 59-81, where see.

Jones, William Griffith, born at Neath, co. Glamorgan, July, 1866; 3s. Elias William, arm. ST. MARY HALL, matric. 24 Oct., 87, aged 21 (from a Neath school), B.A. 91.

Jones, William Monk, born at Camberwell 24 Aug., 1858; 3s. Charles Theodore, gen. NON-COLLEGIATE, matric. 17 Oct., 91, aged 33, from Cheshunt coll. and University coll., London.

Jones, William Morris, born at Llanddeiniolen, co. Carnarvon, 1861; 1s. Morris Hoskin, pleb. JESUS COLL., matric. 19 Oct., 81, aged 20 (from Brecon coll.), scholar 81-4; drowned at Ifsley 3 March, 82.

Jones, William Silvanus, born at Machynlleth, co. Montgomery, 2 Oct., 1856; 2s. David, gent. LINCOLN, matric. 23 Oct., 80, aged 24 (from Aberystwith coll.), B.A. 84, M.A. 88; HONOURS:— 4 classics 84.

Jones, right rev. William West, D.D., fellow ST. JOHN'S 56-79, where see.

Jordan, Arthur Edward North, born at Glanworth, co. Cork, 18 Sept., 1872; o.s. Percival Walsh, cler. MERTON, matric. 22 Oct., 91, aged 19, from Monkton-Combe school, Bath.

Jordan, Ernest Daniel, born at Dudley, co. Worcester, , 1861; 1s. Joseph, cler. HERTFORD, matric. 20 Nov., 80, aged 19; migrated to WADHAM, B.A. 85; HONOURS :—3 classical mods. 82.

Jordan, Henry, born at Southsea, Hants, 11 April, 1868; 2s. Joseph, colonel. KEBLE, matric. 17 Oct., 87, aged 19 (from Cheltenham coll.), exhibitioner 87, B.A. 90; HONOURS :—2 history 90, 3 civil law 92.

Jordan, James Herbert, born at Prestwich, co. Lanc., , 1870; 6s. Thomas Hudson, arm. UNIVERSITY COLL., matric. 13 Oct., 88, aged 18 (from Manchester gr. school); HONOURS :—3 law 92.

Jordan, Louis Henry, born at Halifax, N.S., 27 July, 1855; yst. son of William, merchant, deceased. NON-COLLEGIATE, matric. 22 Oct., 92, aged 37 from Dalhousie university, Halifax, B.A. 75, M.A. 78, of Edinburgh university, D.D. 81, etc., etc.; has also studied at Princeton theological seminary, N.J., Union theological seminary, N.Y. city, also at Leipzig, and at Berlin.

Joscelyne, rev. Albert Ernest, born at Chelmsford, Essex, 8 April, 1866; 2s. Frederick, gent. JESUS COLL., matric. 16 Oct., 84, aged 18 (from Merchant Taylors' school), scholar 84, B.A. 89, M.A. 91 (HONOURS :—2 classical mods. 86, 3 classics 88); curate of St. George in the East, London, 90.

Joscelyne, Herbert Cathcart, born at Oxford 1864; 2s. Henry, cler. NON-COLLEGIATE, matric. 28 Jan., 82, aged 18, B.A. 87.

Jose, Arthur Wilberforce, born at Clifton, co. Glouc., 4 Sept., 1863; 1s. William Wilberforce, gent. BALLIOL, matric. 18 Oct., 81, aged 18 (from Clifton coll.), scholar 80-2.

Joseland, Frank Pursell, born at Worcester 1863; 1s. Alfred, gent. NON-COLLEGIATE, matric. 22 Oct., 86, aged 23, from Worcester gr. school.

Joseph, Horace William Brindley, born at Chatham, Kent, 28 Sept., 1867; 2s. Alexander, cler. NEW COLL., matric. 15 Oct., 86, aged 19 (from Winchester), scholar 85-91, B.A. 90, fellow 91; HONOURS :—1 classical mods. 88, Greek testament prize 89, 1 classics 90, Arnold essay 92.

Jotcham, Charles Molyneaux Moody, born at Wantage, Berks, 17 Dec., 1870; 2s. Llewellyn, solicitor. ST. JOHN'S, matric. 11 Oct., 90, aged 17, from Bristol gr. school.

Jotcham, William Clarke, born at Wantage, Berks, 1866; 1s. Llewellyn, solicitor. ST. JOHN'S, matric. 14 Oct., 82, aged 16, B.A. 87, M.A. 91.

Jourdain, rev. Francis Charles Robert, born at Manchester 4 March, 1865; 1s. Francis, vicar. MAGDALEN, matric. 19 Oct., 83, aged 18 (from Ashburne gr. school), B.A. 87, M.A. 90; curate of Great Thurlow, Suffolk, 90.

Jourdain, Reginald Towle, born at Brixton, Surrey, Dec., 1868; 2s. Nevill, arm. KEBLE, matric. 17 Oct., 87, aged 18 (from Haileybury), exhibitioner 87, B.A. 92; HONOURS :—3 history 91.

Jowers, Bertram Stretton, born at Brighton 1867; 4s. Frederick William, arm. BRASENOSE, matric. 22 Jan., 85, aged 18, from Winchester and King's coll. school, London.

Jowers, Harold, born at Brighton 20 March, 1870; 5s. Frederick William, surgeon. NEW COLL., matric. 11 Oct., 89, aged 19 (from Shrewsbury gr. school); assist. commissioner central provinces India.

Jowett, Albert, born at Saltaire, Yorks, 1867; 5s. Thomas, gen. QUEEN'S, matric. 15 Jan., 91, aged 23, B.Mus. 91.

Jowett, Benjamin, M.A., master of BALLIOL 70, where see page 62.

Jowett, John Henry, born at Halifax, Yorks, 1863; 3s. Josiah, gen. NON-COLLEGIATE, matric. 3 Nov., 88, aged 25, from Edinburgh university.

Jowitt, John Herbert, born at Leeds 16 July, 1866; 1s. Robert Benson, of Harehills, Leeds, gent. HERTFORD, matric. 27 Oct., 85, aged 19.

Joy, Edward Bedford, born at Leeds 12 Jan., 1865; 2s. George Outhwaite, arm. NEW COLL., matric. 10 Oct., 84, aged 19 (from Uppingham school), B.A. 88, M.A. 92; HONOURS :—2 classical mods. 86, 4 classics 88.

Joy, George Frederick, born at Bampton, Oxon, 18 July, 1871; 2s. Henry, D.D. WORCESTER, matric. 14 Oct., 89, aged 18 (from Worthing and Stamford schools), B.A. 92; HONOURS :—3 law 92.

Joy, Henry Archibald Robert, born at Bampton, Oxon, 24 March, 1870; 1s. Henry, D.D., WORCESTER, matric. 16 Oct., 88, aged 18 (from Worthing school), B.A. 91; HONOURS :—2 theology 91.

Joy, Percy Claud, born at Ambleside, Westmorland, Sept., 1867; 2s. Samuel, cler. ORIEL, matric. 19 Oct., 86, aged 19 (from Winchester), B.A. 90; HONOURS :—3 theology 89.

Joy, Richard Eustace, born in Leeds 9 Sept., 1866; 3s. George Outhwaite, gent. WORCESTER, matric. 22 Oct., 85, aged 19 (from Uppingham school), B.A. 89, M.A. 92; HONOURS :—4 law 89.

Joyce, Francis Hayward, M.A., student CHRIST CHURCH 48-63, where see page 417.

Joyce, rev. George Hayward, born at Harrow on the Hill, Middx., 13 Nov., 1864; 2s. Francis Hayward, vicar. ORIEL, matric. 27 Oct., 83, aged 18 (from the Charterhouse), scholar 83, B.A. 88 (HONOURS: —2 classicl mods. 85, 2 classics 87); curate of Holy Trinity, Shrewsbury, 89.

Joyce, rev. Gilbert Cunningham, born at Harrow, Middx., 8 April, 1867; 3s. Francis Hayward, vicar. BRASENOSE, matric. 14 Oct., 84, aged 18 (from Harrow), scholar 84, B.A. 88, M.A. 92; HONOURS: —1 classical mods. 86, 1 classics 88.

Joyce, Robert Barclay, born at Harrow, Middx., 25 Sept., 1863; 1s. Francis Hayward, vicar. KEBLE, matric. 17 Oct., 82, aged 19 (from Wellington), B.A. 87; HONOURS :—3 classical mods. 84, 3 classics 86.

Joyce, Sidney, M.A., student CHRIST CHURCH 52-65, where see page 418.

Joynes, Richard, D.D., fellow CORPUS CHRISTI 47-52. where see page 383.

Jozam, Nicholas, born at Tur, Hungary, 6 Dec., 1869; 2s. Alexius, organist, deceased. NON-COLLEGIATE, matric. 3 Nov., 92, aged 22, from Rolorsvai, Hungary, Unitarian coll.

Judge, Thomas, born at Brackley 1872; 1s. Thomas, gent. NON-COLLEGIATE, matric. 15 Oct., 92, aged 20, from Magdalen coll. school.

Jukes, rev. Joseph Hordern, M.A. WADHAM, where see.

Julius, right rev. Churchill, M.A., bishop of Christ Church, New Zealand, D.D. (*honoris causa*), 23 March, 1893. See *Al. Ox.* 2nd. series, 778.

STONE STRING COURSE, CROYDON CHURCH, SURREY.—*Pugin.*

K

Kallsch, Alfred, born in London 13 March, 1863; o.s. Mark, gent. BALLIOL, matric. 18 Oct., 81, aged 18 (from King's coll. school, London), exhibitioner 80-6, B.A. 86 (HONOURS:—2 classical mods. 82, 3 classics 85); bar.-at-law, Middle Temple, 87.

Kane, Henri Brevoort, born at New York 1867; 2s. Peter, lieut.-col. U.S. army. WADHAM, matric. 19 Jan., 85, aged 18.

Karslake, rev. Henry John Withington, born at Westcott, Surrey, 28 Nov., 1868; 2s. William Henry, vicar. MERTON, matric. 22 Oct., 87, aged 18 (from Eastbourne coll.), B.A. 92.

Karslake, John Burgess Preston, born in London 10 Feb., 1868; o.s. Preston, arm. TRINITY, matric. 16 Oct., 86, aged 18 (from Eton), B.A. 89 (HONOURS: —a law 89); bar.-at-law, Middle Temple, 90.

Karslake, William Henry, M.A., fellow MERTON 51-63, where see page 97.

Karslake, William Reginald, born at Westcott, Surrey, April, 1867; 1s. William Henry, vicar. ORIEL, matric. 19 Oct., 86, aged 19 (from Eastbourne coll.), B.A. 90; (HONOURS:—3 history 90.

Kay, Alfred Reginald, born at Oakley, co. Lanc., June, 1869; 2s. Samuel, arm. ORIEL, matric. 20 Oct., 86, aged 17, from Fettes coll.

Kay, Andrew Cassels, born at Alexandria, Egypt, 1 April, 1862; 1s. Henry Cassels, arm. NEW COLL., matric. 24 Jan., 81, aged 19 (from Fettes coll.), scholar 81-5, B.A. 85 (HONOURS:—1 classical mods. 82, 1 classics 85); bar.-at-law, Inner Temple, 87.

Kay, Arthur Faulkner, born at Pendleton, co. Lanc., 24 May, 1863; 5s. Robert Henry, gent. WADHAM, matric. 22 April, 82, aged 18.

Kay, Harold, born at Stockport, Cheshire, 31 Aug., 1867; 1s. Thomas, gen. EXETER, matric. 21 Oct., 86, aged 19, from Uppingham school, and Owens coll., Manchester.

Kay, Henry Mosley, born at Manchester 1864; 3s. Samuel, gent. ORIEL, matric. 25 Jan., 83, aged 19, B.A. 86, M.A. 89.

Kaye, Cecil William, born at Potters Bar, Middx., 1866; 4s. James, arm. UNIVERSITY COLL., matric. 19 Jan., 85, aged 19 (from Marlborough), B.A. 88, M.A. 91; (HONOURS:—3 classical mods. 86, 2 classics 88.

Kaye, rev. John, born at Cawthorne, Yorks, 1 July, 1865; 1s. Joshua, of Dean Hill, Barnsley, arm. MAGDALEN, matric. 24 Jan., 84, aged 18 (from Uppingham school); migrated to BALLIOL, B.A. and M.A. 90; curate of Westbury, Wilts, 91.

Kaye, William Astell, born in London 16 July, 1871; 1s. Joseph, a master of the high court of justice. MAGDALEN, matric. 14 Oct., 90, aged 18, from Winchester.

Kaye, William John Pottit, born at Cambridge 4 April, 1864; o.s. Astley Edward, arm. QUEEN's, matric. 22 Oct., 83, aged 19 (from York school), exhibitioner 83-5; lieut. F., Kent regt. 85, and 30th Bengal N.I. 87, deputy assist. commissary general Indian staff corps 88.

Kealy, Charles Gonvil, born at Gosport, Hants, 2 July, 1867; 3s. John Robert, D.Med. TRINITY, matric. 16 Oct., 86, aged 19 (from Epsom coll.), B.A. 90.

Kealy, Edward Herbert, born at Gosport 7 June, 1873; 4s. John Robert, D.Med. UNIVERSITY COLL., matric. 15 Oct., 92, aged 19, from Felsted school.

Kearns, John Willis, born at Aldershot, Hants, 7 Sept., 1862; 9s. James, gen. NON-COLLEGIATE, matric. 23 April, 87, aged 24 (from Malvern coll.); migrated to WADHAM 24 Jan., 88, B.A. 91.

Kearsley, Charles Edward, born at Halliwell, co. Lanc., 1848; 4s. James, gent. NON-COLLEGIATE, matric. 6 Feb., 80, aged 32, from Chetham collegiate school.

Keates, Edmund Lyon, born at Liverpool 21 May, 1861; 1s. Joseph Andrew, arm. NEW COLL., matric. 24 Jan., 81, aged 19 (from Uppingham school), B.A. 84 (HONOURS:—3 law 84); bar.-at-law, Inner Temple, 87.

Keates, rev. Herbert Andrew, born at Liverpool 1 Oct., 1865; 3s. Joseph Andrew, gent. NEW COLL., matric. 10 Oct., 84, aged 19 (from Uppingham school), B.A. 88 (HONOURS:—3 classical mods. 86, 2 history 88); curate of St. Matthias, Malvern Link, 89.

Keatinge, Maurice Walter, born at Monkstown, co. Dublin, 25 Feb., 1867; 2s. Maurice, arm. EXETER, matric. 21 Oct., 86, aged 19 (from St. Mark's school, Windsor), exhibitioner 86, B.A. 90; HONOURS:—2 classical mods. 88, 2 classics 90.

Keays, Edward Henry, born at Stoke Newington 28 Aug., 1872; 1s. Frederick Lovell, solicitor. NON-COLLEGIATE, matric. 17 Oct., 91, aged 19 (from the Charterhouse) ; migrated to TRINITY 91.

Kebby, Alfred Hodges, born at Oxford 16 May, 1868; o.s. Charles Henry Hodges, NON-COLLEGIATE, matric. 15 Oct., 92, aged 25, from central school, Oxford.

Keble, Richard James, born at Bussage, co. Gloucester, June, 1870; 4s. Thomas, cler. KEBLE, matric. 12 Oct., 89, aged 19, from Lancing coll.

Keble, Thomas, M.A., fellow MAGDALEN 46-51, where see page 322.

Keble rev. Thomas Charles, born at West Ilsley, Berks, Feb., 1864; 3s. Thomas, cler. KEBLE, matric. 17 Oct., 82, aged 18 (from Lancing coll.), B.A., M.A. 92; curate of collegiate church, Wolverhampton, 88.

Keck, Thomas Charles Leicester Powys-, born at Adelaide, South Australia, 12 Aug., 1871; 1s. Thomas Banco (P-K), lieut. 60th Royal rifles. BRASENOSE, matric. 22 Oct., 91, aged 20, from the Charterhouse.

Keeling, Albert Stanley, born in London 1863; 3s. Alfred, gent. KEBLE, matric. 18 Oct., 81, aged 18 (from the Charterhouse and Marlborough coll.), B.A. 85, M.A. 90; HONOURS:— a history 85.

Keeling, rev. Ernest William Philipps, born at Adston, Northants, 22 Oct., 1866; o.s. Francis, vicar. NON-COLLEGIATE, matric. 17 Oct., 85, aged 18 (from Northleach gr. school); migrated to WADHAM 16 April 88, B.A. 91; curate of High Wycombe, Bucks, 91.

Keeling, John Henry, born at Hackney, Middx., 1862; o.s. John Clough, arm. BRASENOSE, matric. 29 Oct., 83, aged 21; migrated to BALLIOL, B.A. and M.A. 90; bar.-at-law, Middle Temple, 87.

Keene, Henry George, of Wadham coll., created M.A. 14 June, 1887; fellow of Calcutta university. See *Al. Ox.* and series, 782.

Keene, rev. Rees, born at English Bicknor, co. Glouc., 1861; 1s. Roger, gent. JESUS COLL., matric. 23 Oct., 80, aged 19, B.A. 83, M.A. 87 (HONOURS:—2 theology 83); lecturer St. Bees college, and curate of St. Bees, Cumberland, 86.

Keer, rev. William Brown, M.A., NON-COLLEGIATE, where see.

Keerl, Eversfield Fraser, born at Baltimore 1863; o.s. Thomas Mundell, gent. NON-COLLEGIATE, matric. 14 Oct., 82, aged 19; migrated to CORPUS CHRISTI, B.A. 86; HONOURS:—3 classics 86.

Keevil, Edward, born at Road, Somerset, 1855; 6s. James, gent. NON-COLLEGIATE, matric. 17 Jan., 82, aged 25, from Bath coll.

Keilor, rev. John Danby Downing, born at East Dulwich, Surrey, 1867; 1s. John Clark, arm. BRASENOSE, matric. 20 Oct., 87, aged 20 (from King's coll. school, and King's coll., Lond.), B.A. 90 (HONOURS:—3 theology 90); curate of St. Mary-le-more, Wallingford, 90.

Kekewich, sir Arthur, Q.C., M.A., a Justice High Court, fellow EXETER 54-8, where see page 127.

Kekewich, Arthur Langston, born in London 14 Sept., 1862; 2s. sir Arthur, UNIVERSITY COLL., matric. 15 Oct., 81, aged 19, B.A. 85, M.A. 88 (HONOURS:—3 history 85); curate of All Saints', Wellingborough, 86-7, and of St. Bartholomew, Dover, 88, until he died 31 Dec., 91.

Kelcey, rev. Edward Foord-, born at Smeeth, Kent, 29 Jan., 1859; 2s. William, gent. PEMBROKE, matric. 2 May, 84, aged 25, B.A. 87, M.A. 92; HONOURS:—3 theology 87.

Kellett, Ernest Edward, born at Maidstone, Kent, 23 Aug., 1864; 2s. Featherstone, Wesleyan minister. WADHAM, matric. 17 Oct., 82, aged 18 (from Kingswood school), scholar 81, B.A. 86, M.A. 89 HONOURS:—1 mathematical mods. 83, 2 classics 86; Ellerton theological essay 87.

Kelly, Alfred Davenport, born at Ashton-under-Lyne, co. Lanc., 5 April, 1872; 4s. James Davenport, canon of Manchester. NEW COLL., matric. 16 Oct., 91, aged 19, from Manchester gr. school.

Kelly, rev. Arthur, born at Shipley, Yorks, 3 Jan., 1861; 2s. William, cler. QUEEN'S, matric. 25 Oct., 80, aged 19 (from Bradford school), exhibitioner 80-4, B.A. 84, M.A. 87 (HONOURS:—2 classical mods. 82, 3 classics 84); curate of Wensley, Yorks, 85.

Kelly, William Fraser Claughton, born at Neuera Ellia, Ceylon, Aug., 1865; o.s. William Frederick, cler. KEBLE, matric. 14 Oct., 84, aged 19 (from Uppingham school), B.A. 87 (HONOURS:—4 history 87); bar.-at-law, Inner Temple, 92.

Kelsall, rev. Henry James, born at Stafford Feb., 1862; 2s. John, arm. WORCESTER, matric. 21 Oct., 80, aged 18 (from King Edward's school, Stafford), B.A. 84, M.A. 87; curate of Tutbury 85-7, of Horningglow, co. Stafford, 87-91.

Kelsall, rev. John Edward, born at Fareham, Hants, 5 Jan., 1864; 1s. William, gent. BALLIOL, matric. 17 Oct., 82, aged 18 (from Rugby), B.A. 85, M.A. 89; curate of Wavertree (H.T.) 89.

Kemans, Herbert Nassau, born in London 1872; 1s. Henry, gen. BALLIOL, matric. 1 May, 90, aged 18, from Dulwich coll.

Kemble, Hulton Henry, born at Hesket in the Forest, Cumberland, 21 Sept., 1868; y.s. Nicholas Freese (?) Young, vicar. ST. MARY HALL, matric. 24 Oct., 87, aged 19, B.A. 91.

Kemmis, Edward Bernhard, born at Plumstead, Kent, June, 1873; 4s. William, col. late R.A. WADHAM, matric. 13 Oct., 90, aged 17, from St. Edward's school, Summertown.

Kemmis, Gilbert, born at Woolwich, Kent, 4 June, 1875; 5s. William, of Ballinacor, co. Wicklow, D.L., late colonel R.A. ST. JOHN'S, matric. 15 Oct., 92, aged 17, from St. Edward's school, Summertown.

Kemmis, Lewis George Nicholas, born at Plumstead, Kent, 21 Nov., 1870; 3s. William, late col. R.A. WADHAM, matric. 15 Oct., 87, aged 16 (from Magdalen coll. school), B.A. 90; HONOURS:— 3 law 90.

Kemmis, rev. Marcus Steinman, born at Southend, Kent, 1868; 2s. William, late col. R.A. MAGDALEN, matric. 25 March, 85, aged 17, B.A. and M.A. 91; curate of Plusmoor (Christ Church), near Sheffield, 91.

Kemp, Francis David, born at Polton, Midlothian, March, 1872; 1s. David, lieut.-col. KEBLE, matric. 20 Oct., 91, aged 19, from Durham gr. school.

Kemp, George, born at Rochdale, co. Lanc., 1867; George Fowke, gent. BALLIOL, matric. 13 April, 83, aged 16, from Shrewsbury gr. school.

Kemp, Manley Colchester, born at Forest Hill, Surrey, 1861; 2s. Charles Fitch, arm. HERTFORD, matric. 18 Oct., 80, aged 19 (from Harrow), scholar 79-84, B.A. 84 (HONOURS:—2 classical mods. 81, 3 classics 84]; in the University eleven 81, 2, 3, 4.

Kemp, William Cayzer, born at Redhill, Surrey, 1865; 1s. William Joel, gent. WORCESTER, matric. 20 Oct., 82, aged 16 (from Reigate school), exhibitioner 81-3, scholar 83-5, B.A. 85; HONOURS:— a mathematical mods. 83, 2 mathematics 85.

Kemp, William Edelman, born at Kensington 29 Nov., 1870; 4s. Alexander Davidson, gen. WORCESTER, matric. 16 Oct., 88, aged 17 (from King's coll. school, London), B.A. 92.

Kempson, rev. Edwin Hone, born at Hales Owen, co. Worcester, 16 April, 1862; 1s. Edwin Alfred, cler. CHRIST CHURCH, matric. 14 Oct., 81, aged 19 (from Rugby school), scholar 81-6, B.A. 85, M.A. 88 (HONOURS:—1 mathematical mods. 83, 1 mathematics 85); assist. master Clifton coll. 87-8, and Harrow 88.

Kempson, Henry, born at Claverdon, co. Warwick, 15 July, 1866; 3s. Edwin Alfred, cler. CHRIST CHURCH, matric. 16 Oct., 85, aged 19 (from Malvern coll.), B.A. 89; HONOURS:—2 classical mods. 87.

Kendall, rev. Henry George Ommaney, born at Richmond, Surrey, 14 April, 1866; 1s. Henry John Broughton, of Bush Hall, Hatfield, Herts. MAGDALEN, matric. 16 Oct., 84, aged 18 (from the Charterhouse), B.A. 88; curate of Cheshunt, Herts, 91.

Kendall, John Frederick (William), born at Skipton-on-Swale, Yorks, 15 July, 1865; o.s. John, arm. HERTFORD, matric. 28 Oct., 85, aged 20 (from Rugby), B.A. 89.

Kendall, Leigh, born at Southsea, Hants, 1863; o.s. George Adolphus, arm. NON-COLLEGIATE, matric. 28 Jan., 84, aged 21, from St. Helen's coll., Southsea.

Kendall, Nevill, born at Ewell, Surrey, 2 Jan., 1871; 2s. Henry John Broughton, of Hatfield, Herts, gen. PEMBROKE, matric. 26 Oct., 89, aged 18 (from Eton), scholar 89; HONOURS :—2 classical mods. 91.

Kendall, Percy John, born at Exeter 9 Sept., 1866; 1s. John, solicitor. EXETER, matric. 21 Oct., 86, aged 20, B.A. 90 (HONOURS: 2 law 90, 3 civil law 92); bar.-at-law, Lincoln's Inn, 92.

Kendrick, Walter Ernest, born at Birmingham 12 Nov., 1860; 1s. Walter, gent. LINCOLN, matric. 23 Oct., 80, aged 19 (from King Edward's school, Birmingham), B.A. 83 (HONOURS :—3 law 83); admitted a solicitor.

Kennard, Auberon Claud Hegan, born in London 20 May, 1870; 1s. Edmund Hegan, arm. NEW COLL., matric. 24 Oct., 88, aged 18 (from Eton), B.A. 92 (HONOURS :—3 classical mods. 90, 4 classics 92); passed into Sandhurst 93.

Kennard, Charles Heywood, born in London 18 May, 1872; 3s. Adam, esquire. BRASENOSE, matric. 22 Oct., 91, aged 19, from Winchester.

Kennedy, Arnold, born at Stepney Green, Middx., 1853; 3s. John, M.A. and D.D. Edinburgh, congregational minister. QUEEN'S, matric. 16 March, 92, aged 39.

Kennedy, Bennet Christian Huntington Calcraft, born at Lucea, in Italy, 8 June, 1871; 4s. Bennet Sherard, cler. QUEEN'S, matric. 22 Oct., 89, aged 18 (from Dulwich coll.), scholar 89; assist. magistrate and collector (junior civilian) Ahmedabad, Bombay c.s. 91.

Kennedy, Henry, born at Bradford, Yorks, 1 Dec., 1860; 5s. Richard, gent. NON-COLLEGIATE, matric. 18 Oct., 80, aged 19 (from Bradford gr. school); migrated to MERTON, B.A. 84.

Kennedy, Mervyn Le Bas, born at Kilmore, Ireland, 25 May, 1858; 1s. Thomas Le Ban, cler. LINCOLN, matric. 29 Jan., 81, aged 22 (from Armagh royal school and scholar Trinity coll., Dublin, 80), scholar 80-1.

Kennedy, Pitt Shadwell Portalés, born at Dublin 6 May, 1868; 3s. Tristram, bar.-at-law, deceased, M.P. co. Louth. WADHAM, matric. 15 Oct., 87, aged 19, from Westminster school.

Kennedy, Robert Harborough Sherard, born at Putney, Surrey, 1862; 5. Bennet, cler. NEW COLL., matric. 16 Oct., 80, aged 18, from Windermere coll.

Kennerley, Charles Vincent, born at Leamington, 1866; o.s. James, gen. LINCOLN, matric. 24 Jan., 89, aged 22.

Kennion, George Wyndham, bishop of Adelaide; created D.D. 7 Nov., 82. See *Al. Ox.* and series, 767.

Kenny, Thomas Meikle, born at Glasgow 1852; 3s. Thomas, gen. UNIVERSITY COLL., matric. 11 Oct., 90, aged 38.

Kenrick, Cyril Cranmer Curteis, born at Newbury, Berks, 6 July, 1872; 3s. William Mascall, MERTON, matric. 22 Oct., 91, aged 19, from the Charterhouse.

Kenrick, Wilfred Byng, born at Birmingham 4 Dec., 1872; 1s. William, of Harborne, gen. BALLIOL, matric. 20 Oct., 91, aged 18, from Rugby.

Kensington, Theodore, M.A., fellow NEW COLL. 69-86, where see page 216.

Kent, Albert Frank Stanley, born at Stratford Tony, Wilts, 26 March, 1863; 6s. George Davies, rector, deceased. MAGDALEN, matric. 16 Oct., 82, aged 19 (from Magdalen coll. school), B.A. 86, M.A. 90; HONOURS :—2 physiology 86.

Kent, Arthur Reginald, born at Ludlow 1867; 3s. Charles, cler. WORCESTER, matric. 19 Oct., 86, aged 19, from Swansea gr. school.

Kent, rev. Charles Archer, born at Ryde, I.W., 1864; o.s. Benjamin Archer, D.Med. EXETER, matric. 23 April, 83, aged 19 (from Harrow), B.A. 86, M.A. 91 (HONOURS :—3 theology 86); incumbent of Laura St. John, South Australia, 88-91; curate of Mount Sorell, co. Leic., 91.

Kent, Charles Harry, born at Ludlow, Salop, 14 March, 1868; 2s. Charles, cler. EXETER, matric. 19 Oct., 87, aged 19, from Stratford-on-Avon school.

Kent, Henry Edwin Hunter, born at Portland, Dorset, 1866; 5s. Hunter, arm. ST. JOHN'S, matric. 21 April, 84, aged 18 (from Sherborne school), B.A. 87.

Kent, Irving, born at Hobart Town, Tasmania, 17 June, 1866; 3s. William, arm. NEW COLL., matric. 16 Oct., 85, aged 19 (from Rugby), B.A. 89, M.A. and B.C.L. 92 (HONOURS :—2 classical mods. 87, 2 classics 89, 2 law 90, 2 civil law 91); bar.-at-law, Inner Temple, 92.

Kent, Sidney Joseph Frederick, born at Portsmouth 7 Aug., 1870; 1s. Frederick, gen. WADHAM, matric. 11 Oct., 89, aged 19 (from Park House school, Exeter); B.A. 92.

Kent, Thomas Parkes, born at Charlestown, East Indies, 5 May, 1869; 1s. Alfred, gen. CHRIST CHURCH, matric. 14 Oct., 87, aged 18 (from Kingswood school), scholar 86, B.A. 90; HONOURS :—1 mathematical mods. 88, accessit junior mathematical exhibition 89, 1 mathematics 90, 2 physics 91.

Kent, William Charles, born at Hazelhurst, Surrey, 1866; 2s. Francis Jackson, gen. BRASENOSE, matric. 20 Oct., 85, aged 20 (from Blackheath school and Brighton coll.), B.A. 90; stroke University eight 91.

Kenyon, Frederic George, born in London 15 Jan., 1863; 4s. John Robert, Q.C., D.C.L. NEW COLL., matric. 14 Oct., 82, aged 19 (from Winchester), scholar 82-6, B.A. 86; fellow MAGDALEN 88, M.A. 89; HONOURS :—1 classical mods. 83, proxime accessit Hertford scholarship 84, Greek testament prize 85, 1 classics 86, English essay 89.

Kenyon, rev. Gerald, born in London 7 Aug., 1864; 5s. John Robert, Q.C., D.C.L. WORCESTER, matric. 25 April, 84, aged 19 (from Winchester), B.A. 89, M.A. 92; curate of Peterborough St. Paul 90.

Kenyon, Lloyd, 4th baron, born in London 5 July, 1864; o.s. hon. Lloyd. CHRIST CHURCH, matric. 27 May, 82, aged 17, from Eton.

Ker, William Paton, M.A., fellow ALL SOULS' 79-86 and 88, where see page 273.

Kerr, George Baillie, born at Dundee 27 Aug., 1866; 1s. William, arm. MERTON, matric. 24 Oct., 85, aged 19, from St. Edward's school, Summertown.

Kerr, Mark, born in isle of Barbados 1866; 2s. Thomas, gent. NON-COLLEGIATE, matric. 20 Jan., 87, aged 17, from Harrison coll., Barbados.

Kerr, Russell James, born in London 23 Jan., 1863; 5s. Russell James, arm. CHRIST CHURCH, matric. 4 June, 81, aged 18 (from Eton), B.A. 84 (HONOURS :— 4 history 84); bar.-at-law, Inner Temple, 87. See Foster's *Peerage*, M. LOTHIAN.

Kerr, Walter Hume, born at Dunse, co. Berwick, 1862; 2s. Daniel, cler. NON-COLLEGIATE, matric. 21 Jan., 82, aged 20.
Kerr, William Walter Schomberg, earl of Ancram, born 29 March, 1867; 1s. Schomberg, marquis of Lothian. NEW-COLL., matric. 15 Oct., 86, aged 19 (from Eton), capt. 3rd. batt. Royal Scots (Lothian regt.), A.D.C. to governor of New South Wales, accidentally shot near Bomlasla, N.S.W., 17 June, 92. See Foster's *Peerage.*
Kerry, Alfred Parmenter, born in London 23 June, 1862; 4s. William, vicar of Bristol St. Judes. NEW COLL., matric. 19 Nov., 80, aged 18 (from Marlborough), B.A. 83, M.A. 87; HONOURS:—4 history 83.
Kerry, Arthur Frank, born at Oxford 28 July, 1862, 3s. Henry, gent. EXETER, matric. 18 Oct., 82, aged 20 (from Wesleyan school, Oxford); scholar 81-6, B.A. 87, M.A. 90; HONOURS:—2 physiology 86.
Kershaw, John Bowers, born at Prescot, co. Lanc., 6 Sept., 1865; 1s. Thomas, gent. BRASENOSE, matric. 22 Oct., 83, aged 18 (from Great Crosby school), junior Hulme exhibitioner 83-6 and senior 86; B.A. 88, M.A. 90; HONOURS:—2 classical mods. 85, 2 classics 87, 4 history 88.
Kershaw, John Felix, born in London , 1874; 1s. Louis Addin, B.A., bar.-at-law. BALLIOL, matric. 18 Oct., 92, aged 18, from Shrewsbury.
Kershaw, Leonard William, born at Walton-le-Dale, co. Lanc., 18 Nov. 1864; 2s. James Clegg, vicar. QUEEN'S, matric. 23 Oct., 82, aged 17 (from Rossall school), B.A. 85 (HONOURS:—3 law 85); bar.-at-law, Inner Temple, 86.
Kersley, Stewart Roper, born at Middleton, Norfolk, , 1866; o.s. Thomas Henry, cler. NON-COLLEGIATE, matric. 17 Oct., 85, aged 19 (from Magdalen coll. school), B.A. 88, M.A. 92.
Kessler, Charles Sigismund, born at Berlin 1858; y.s. Julius, of Marineschein by Teplitz in Bohemia, D.Med. NON-COLLEGIATE, matric. 20 Oct., 84, aged 26, B.A. 87, M.A. 92; HONOURS:—3 classical mods. 86.
Ketchlee, Thomas Wild, born at Peckham, Surrey, 1869; 4s. Benjamin, gent. NON-COLLEGIATE, matric. 19 Jan., 89, aged 19 (from King's coll. London); migrated to EXETER two days after.
Ketchley, rev. Harry Ernest, born at Hull 26 May, 1866; 3s. Walter Grey, cler. ST. MARY HALL, matric. 29 Jan., 86, aged 19 (from Densione coll.); migrated to CHRIST CHURCH, B.A. 89; curate of Romsey, Hants. 90.
Kettle, rev. Alfred Cooke, born at Wolverhampton , 1865; 3s. Rupert Alfred, knt. ST. JOHN'S, matric. 11 Oct., 84, aged 19, B.A. 87, M.A. 92 (HONOURS:—3 theology 87); curate of St. Columba, Sunderland, 88.
Kettle, William Henry Herman Arundell, born at Battle, Sussex, June, 1863; 1s. William Arundell, cler. KEBLE, matric. 18 Oct., 81, aged 18, B.A. 85, M.A. 88; HONOURS:—3 mathematical mods. 83, 3 mathematics 85.
Kettlewell, Arthur Bradley, born at Cheltenham 30 Sept., 1871; 1s. Thomas, colonel in the army. NEW COLL., matric. 10 Oct., 90, aged 19 (from Cheltenham coll.); selected candidate for Indian C.S. 90.
Kettlewell, Arthur Midgley, born at Stanley, Yorks, Oct., 1862; 3s. William Christian, gent. ST. JOHN'S, matric. 14 Oct., 82, aged 20, from Uppingham school.
Kettlewell, Percy William Henry, born at Rock Ferry, Cheshire, Dec., 1868; 1s. William John, gen. KEBLE, matric. 13 Oct., 88, aged 19 (from Chigwell school), B.A. 92; HONOURS:—3 classical mods. 90, 3 classics 92.

Kewley, Arthur George, born at Thorpe, co. Derby, 22 April, 1863; 4s. Joseph William, rector. NON-COLLEGIATE, matric. 13 Jan., 83, aged 19; migrated to MERTON, B.A. 86.
Key, Arthur, born at Hempahill, Notts, 1858; 3s. Edward, pleb. NON-COLLEGIATE, matric. 16 May, 91, aged 33, from Battersea training coll.
Key, admiral sir Astley Cooper, K.C.B., created D.C.L. 9 June, 1880; died 3 March, 88. See *Al. Ox.* and series, 792.
Key, Kingsmill James, born at Strentham, Surrey, 11 Oct., 1864; 2s. sir Kingsmill George, bart. ORIEL, matric. 27 Oct., 83, aged 19 (from Clifton coll.), B.A. 88, in University eleven 84, 5, 6, 7.
Kidd, rev. Beresford James, born at Birmingham 10 Nov., 1863; 1s. James, cler. KEBLE, matric. 17 Oct., 81, B.A. 86, M.A. 89 (HONOURS:—3 classical mods. 83, 2 classics 86, 1 theology 87), theological tutor to non-collegiate students 86; curate of SS. Philip and James, Oxford, 87.
Kiddle, Arthur William, born at Coventry 15 Aug., 1871; 2s. John William, congregational minister. MAGDALEN, matric. 14 Oct., 90, aged 19 (from Manchester gr. school), demy 90; HONOURS:—2 classical mods. 92.
Kidson, John Henry, born at Amblecote, Stourbridge, co. Worcester, 11 Dec., 1872; o.s. John, gen. QUEEN'S, matric. 27 Oct., 91, aged 18 (from Stourbridge school), scholar 90.
Kidston, George Jardine, born at Dalnottar, Old Kilpatrick, co. Dumbarton, 25 Jan., 1873; 2. George Jardine, shipowner. NEW COLL., matric. 16 Oct., 91, aged 18, from Eton.
Kilburn, Burleigh Dunbar, born in London 1869; o.s. William Edward, arm. CHRIST CHURCH, matric. 16 Jan., 80, aged 19, B.A. 83; bar.-at-law Inner Temple, 85.
Kilburn, rev. Ernest Edward, born at Hampstead, Middx., 1864; 3s. Henry Ward, gen. NON-COLLEGIATE, matric. 13 Oct., 88, aged 24 (from Merchant Taylors' school); migrated to ST. JOHN'S, B.A. 91 (HONOURS:—2 theology 91); curate of Hoxton St. Saviour, London, 92.
Kilby, Reginald George, born at Musaphapoor, India, 1873; 1s. George Charles, bar.-at-law. PEMBROKE, matric. 18 Oct., 92, aged 19 (from Winchester); scholar 92.
Kimber, Charles Dixon, born at Wandsworth, Surrey, Oct., 1863; 2s. Henry, solicitor. MERTON, matric. 19 Oct., 83, aged 19 (from Epsom coll.), B.A. 86.
Kimber, Henry Dixon, born at Wandsworth, Surrey, 8 Nov., 1862; 1s. Henry, solicitor LINCOLN, matric. 20 Oct., 81, aged 18 (from Epsom coll.), B.A. 84, M.A. 88; HONOURS:—3 law 84.
Kincaid, Charles Augustus, born at Indore in East Indies 1870; 2s. William, arm. BALLIOL, matric. 17 Oct., 89, aged 19 (from Sherborne school); assistant collector and magistrate Karachi, Bombay C.S., 90.
Kindersley, John Molesworth, born at Paddington 1869; 1s. Edward Nassau Molesworth, late capt. 19th regt. HERTFORD, matric. 29 Oct., 87, aged 18 (from Repton school), scholar 86 (HONOURS:—2 classical mods. 89, 3 classics 91); passed eastern cadet ship 92.
Kindersley, William Eustace, born at Brampford Spoke, Devon, 7 Sept., 1868; 6s. Richard Cockburn, cler. EXETER, matric. 17 Oct., 87, aged 19 (from Marlborough), scholar 86, B.A. 92 (HONOURS:—2 classical mods. 89, 3 classics 91); and for eastern cadet ship 92.
King, Bryan, M.A., fellow BRASENOSE 35-43, where see page 352.
King, Charles Edward, born at Durham 1858; 2s. Charles William, cler. ORIEL, matric. 31 Oct., 82, aged 19 (from Clifton coll.), B.A. 87, M.A. 90; HONOURS:—2 history 86.

King, Charles Kirwan, born at Camberwell, Surrey, 14 April, 1860; 1s. Thomas William, D.Med. EXETER, matric. 19 Oct., 87, aged 18, from Dulwich coll.

King, Charles Montague, born at Calcutta 1872; 2s. Henry Oakes, arm. BALLIOL, matric. 14 Oct., 90, aged 18 (from St. Paul's school), scholar 89; selected candidate Indian C.S. 90.

King, right rev. Edward, D.D., bishop of Lincoln, canon of CHRIST CHURCH 73-85, where see page 404.

King, Edward Septimus, born at Little Glemham, Suffolk, April, 1864; 7s. Richard Henry, cler. KEBLE, matric. 16 Oct., 83, aged 19 (from Ipswich gr. school), B.A. 86, M.A. 93.

King, Edwin Cruickshank, born in London July, 1871; o.s. Edwin Hollurow Green, esq. CHRIST CHURCH, matric. 16 Oct., 91, agrd 20, from Bradfield coll.

King, George Chatfield, born at Wirloomorleros, in Australia, 28 Oct., 1866; o.s. Robert John, gen. MERTON, matric. 26 April, 88, aged 21 (from Sydney university, N.S.W., B.A.), B.A. 90 (HONOURS :—3 law 90); bar.-at-law, Lincoln's Inn, 91.

King, George Cyril Meade-, born at Henbury, co. Glouc., 19 Sept., 1869; 2s. Herbert, arm. MERTON, matric. 22 Oct., 87, aged 18 (from Clifton coll.), exhibitioner 87, B.A. 91; HONOURS :—2 classical mods. 89, 1 history 91.

King, rev. George Eden, born at Cantley, Yorks, April, 1869; 4s. Samuel, cler. CHRIST CHURCH, matric. 1 June, 88, aged 19 (from the Charterhouse), B.A. 91.

King, Gerald Mohun, born at Limpley Stoke, Somerset, 1868; 4s. John Webb, gen. LINCOLN, matric. 19 Feb., 87, aged 19, from Clifton coll.

King, Godfrey James, born at Oxford 29 Oct., 1870; 1s. John Richard, cler. ORIEL, matric. 25 Oct., 89, aged 18, from Haileybury; brother of Hugh C.

King, Horace Shirley Freeman, born at Little Braxted, Essex, 1 Aug., 1869; 2s. John Freeman, cler. TRINITY, matric. 13 Oct., 88, aged 19 (from Haileybury), B.A. 91; HONOURS :—3 classical mods. 90.

King, Hugh Charles, born at Holywell, Oxford, 26 Oct., 1872; 3s. John Richard, cler. ORIEL, matric. 27 Oct., 91, aged 19, from Rossall school.

King, Jabez, born at Ashby-de-la-Zouch 1866; 3s. Thomas, gent. NON-COLLEGIATE, matric. 16 Oct., 86, aged 20 (from Ashby school), B.A. 91.

King, John Edward, M.A., fellow LINCOLN 82-92, where see page 242.

King, John Richard, M.A., fellow ORIEL 76, where see page 150.

King, rev. Louis Henry, born at Newcastle-under-Lyne, co. Stafford, 1856; o.s. Richard, gent. ST. EDMUND HALL, matric. 25 Oct., 80, aged 24, B.A. 83, M.A. 87; curate of Creech, Somerset, 91.

King, Philip Virtue, born at Brighton 1870; 1s. Alfred, gen. ST. EDMUND HALL, matric. 22 Oct., 91, aged 20.

King, Robert Curzon Henry Moss, born at Lucknow, East Indies, 26 July, 1871; 2s. Robert Moss, of I.C.S. MERTON, matric. 15 Oct., 90, aged 19 (from Eton); HONOURS :—3 classical mods. 92.

King, Robert Stuart, born at Leigh, Essex, April, 1862; 5s. Walker, rector. HERTFORD, matric. 19 Oct., 81, aged 19 (from Felstend school), B.A. 85.

King, rev. William Arthur, born at Durham June, 1864; 3s. Charles William, cler. deceased. KEBLE, matric. 16 Oct., 83, aged 19 (from Durham gr. school), B.A. 87, M.A. 90 (HONOURS :—3 theology 87); curate of Hunslet St. Cuthbert, Yorks, 88.

King, William James, born at Glasgow 1864; 2s. James, gent. CORPUS CHRISTI, matric. 19 Oct., 83, aged 19 (from Loretto school), B.A. 87; HONOURS :—3 classical mods. 85, 4 law 87.

King, William Richard Cambridge, born at Carham, Northumberland, 21 March, 1867; 1s. John Richard, rector. ORIEL, matric. 23 Oct., 85, aged 18 (from Haileybury), B.A. 89, M.A. 92; HONOURS :—3 classical mods. 87, 3 history 89; brother of Godfrey and Hugh.

Kingdon, George Holman, born at Exeter 3 May, 1872; o.s. George Canning, gen. MERTON, matric. 22 Oct., 91, aged 19, from Exeter gr. school.

Kingdon, Gilbert Kniveton, born at Ashburne, co. Derby, 1866; 1s. Clement Boughton, arm. PEMBROKE, matric. 29 Jan., 85, aged 19, B.A. 90, M.A. 92.

Kingdon, Paul Augustine, M.A., fellow EXETER 41-54, where see page 125.

Kingdon, rev. Reginald Arthur, born at Whiteston, Devon, July, 1868; 4s. Robert Hawker, rector. KEBLE, matric. 17 Oct., 87, aged 19 (from Leatherhead school), B.A. 91; HONOURS :—2 theology 90.

Kingsbury, Henry Walter, born at Washington, America, 1863; o.s. Henry Walter, arm. NON-COLLEGIATE, matric. 14 Oct., 82, aged 19.

Kingsbury, William Evelyn, born in London 7 May, 1866; 1s. William Joseph, arm. TRINITY, matric. 17 Oct., 85, aged 19 (from Marlborough coll.), B.A. 88; HONOURS :—4 theology 88.

Kingscott, Alexander Fitzhardinge, born in East Indies 1869; 2s. Fitzhardinge, arm. ST. EDMUND HALL, matric. 24 Jan., 90, aged 21.

Kingsford, Charles Lethbridge, born at Ludlow, Salop, 1863; 3s. Sampson, cler. ST. JOHN'S, matric. 15 Oct., 81, aged 18 (from Rossall school), scholar 81-5, B.A. 85, M.A. 88; HONOURS :—2 classical mods. 82, 1 classics 85, 2 history 86, Arnold essay 88.

Kingsford, rev. Edward Lethbridge, born at Atherston, co. Warwick, 1868; 5s. Sampson, cler. CORPUS CHRISTI, matric. 20 Oct., 86, aged 18 (from Rossall school), B.A. 90 (HONOURS :—3 history 90); curate of Gt. Malvern, co. Worc., 91.

Kingsley, rev. Basil Herbert, born at Stratford-on-Avon 1862; 2s. Robert, D.Med. MERTON, matric. 18 Oct., 80, aged 18 (from Shrewsbury gr. school and Clifton coll.), B.A. 86, M.A. 88; curate of Wantage, Berks, 88.

Kingston, rev. Walter Park, born at Northampton, 1868; 6s. William, gen. NON-COLLEGIATE, matric. 12 Jan., 89, aged 21, B.A. 92; HONOURS : —3 theology 92.

Kinloch, Francis, born at Edinburgh 6 Oct., 1863; 3s. sir Alexander, bart. NEW COLL., matric. 14 Oct., 82, aged 19 (from Eton), B.A. 86; HONOURS:— 3 history 86. See Foster's *Baronetage*.

Kinnersley, John, born at Castel, Guernsey, 2 March, 1873; 3s. William Thomas, gen. MERTON, matric. 19 Feb., 92, aged 18, from Elizabeth coll., Guernsey.

Kinsman, Frederick Joseph, born at Warren, Trumbull co., Ohio, U.S.A., Sept., 1868; 1s. Frederick, gen. KEBLE, matric. 20 Oct., 91, aged 23, from St. Paul's school, Concord, N.H., U.S.A.

Kippen, William James, born at Edinburgh 20 March, 1866; o.s. James Hill, arm. TRINITY, matric. 11 Oct., 84, aged 18 (from Clifton coll.), B.A. 88 (HONOURS :—3 history 87); advocate 90.

Kirby, rev. Edward, born at Darlington, co. Durham, 10 April, 1863; 1s. Robert Lisle, arm. CORPUS CHRISTI, matric. 19 Oct., 81, aged 19 (from Durham gr. school), scholar 82-5, B.A. 86, M.A. 89 (HONOURS :—2 classical mods. 84, 2 classics 86); curate of St. John Evangelist, Darlington, 87.

Kirby, Walter Reginald, born in London 5 March, 1872; 2s. Thomas Frederick, bar.-at-law. EXETER, matric. 3 Nov., 91, aged 19 (from the Charterhouse), scholar 91.

Kirby, William Henry, born at Genoa 1872; 1s. Henry Grosvenor, arm. BALLIOL, matric. 14 Oct., 90, aged 18, from Winchester.

Kirkby, rev. John Henry, born at Leeds 1860; 3s. Charles, gent. QUEEN'S, matric. 15 May, 80, aged 20, B.A. 84, M.A. 87; curate of Menawood, Yorks, 89.

Kirkby, rev. Marsh, M.A.; see ST. MARY HALL.

Kirkby, Paul Jerome, born at Wandsworth 1869; 4s. William, cler., deceased. HERTFORD, matric. 19 Oct., 88, aged 19 (from clergy orphan school, Canterbury), scholar 87, B.A. 91; HONOURS :—1 mathematical mods. 89, junior mathematical scholarship 90, 1 mathematics 91.

Kirkby, William, born at Wandsworth, Surrey, 1864; 3s. William, cler., deceased. NON-COLLEGIATE, matric. 3 Nov., 83, aged 19 (from Magdalen coll. school); died 29 June, 92.

Kirkham, rev. Charles Thomas, born at Manchester 16 Sept., 1869; 2s. Thomas, cler. QUEEN'S, matric. 20 Oct., 88, aged 19 (from Bradford gr. school), B.A. 91.

Kirkham, rev. John Brooke, born at Ashover, co. Derby, 5 Aug., 1868; 1s. Thomas, cler. QUEEN'S, matric. 20 Oct., 88, aged 20 (from Bradford gr. school and King's coll., London); HONOURS :—3 history 91.

Kirkman, Frederick Bernulf Beever, born at Umzinto, Natal, 16 Feb., 1869; 1s. John, gen. LINCOLN, matric. 18 Jan., 88, aged 18 (from Beaumaris gr. school), B.A. 91; HONOURS :—3 history 91.

Kirkpatrick, Henry Pownall, born at Prestwich, co. Lanc., 1862; 1s. Edward, arm. BRASENOSE, matric. 10 June, 81, aged 19 (from Uppingham school.

Kirkpatrick, William, born at Monks Horton, Kent, 1861; 1s. John, arm. ST. JOHN'S, matric. 15 Oct., 81, aged 20, from the Charterhouse.

Kirton, William Ferdinand, born at St. Croix in West Indies 18 Oct., 1870; 3s. William Ferdinand, of Grenada, gen. CORPUS CHRISTI, matric. 25 Oct., 89, aged 19 (from Royal coll., Trinidad); HONOURS :—3 mathematical mods. 91, 3 history 92.

Kirwan, rev. Ernest Cecil, born at Gittisham, Devon, Sept., 1867; 2s. Richard, cler. KEBLE, matric. 19 Oct., 86, aged 19 (from Forest school), B.A. 90 (HONOURS :—3 theology 89): curate of Bracknell, Berks, 91.

Kirwan, rev. Robert Mansel, born at Gittisham, Devon, 13 March, 1861; 1s. Richard, cler. KEBLE, matric. 19 Oct., 80, aged 19 (from St. Paul's school), B.A. 85; curate of Westbury, Wilts, 88-91; assist. chaplain Allahabad, India, 91.

Kitcat, Aubrey Paul, born at Charlton, co. Glouc., 15 May, 1863; 2s. David, rector of Weston Birt, co. Glouc. NEW COLL., matric. 15 Oct., 81, aged 18 (from Bradfield coll.), B.A. 84; HONOURS :— 4 law 84.

Kitcat, Cecil James, born at Swallowfield, Berks, 12 Oct., 1864; 3s. John, vicar. MAGDALEN, matric 15 Jan., 83, aged 18 (from St. Mark's school, Windsor), B.A. 85; died 3 March, 88.

Kitcat, rev. Henry James, born at Waltham Abbey, Essex, March 1860; 1s. James Harris, gent. KEBLE, matric. 22 Jan., 80, aged 19 (from Bradfield coll.), B.A. 84 (HONOURS :—3 classical mods. 81, 2 history 83); curate of Holy Trinity, Upper Chelsea, London, 91.

Kitchin, very rev. George William, D.D., dean of Winchester, student CHRIST CHURCH 46-63, where see page 414.

Kitchin, Hugh Bridges, born at Brantwood, Cumberland, Oct., 1867; 2s. George William, dean of Winchester. CHRIST CHURCH, matric. 15 Oct., 86, aged 18 (from Shrewsbury gr. school), B.A. 90.

Kitchingman, William Ernest, born at Wolverhampton 26 Jan., 1870; o. s. John, rector of Bonsall, co. Derby. ST. JOHN'S, matric. 12 Oct., 89, aged 19, from Canterbury school.

Kitson, James Butler, born at Antony, Cornwall, 1870; 1s. John Francis, cler. PEMBROKE, matric. 26 Oct., 89, aged 19 (from Shrewsbury school), scholar 88; HONOURS :—2 classical mods. 91.

Kitson, John Francis, cler. KEBLE, matric. 15 Oct., 92, aged 19, from Haileybury.

Kitto, Harold, born at Poplar, Middx., 4 July, 1870; 2s. John Fenwick, cler. MERTON, matric. 19 Oct., 89, aged 19 (from Marlborough), postmaster 89; HONOURS :—2 classical mods. 91.

Kitto, Robert Collingwood Middleton, born at Fryerstown, Australia, 1864; 2s. Richard, arm. NEW COLL., matric. 23 Oct., 84, aged 20, from Loretto school; HONOURS :—3 classical mods. 86.

Knapp, Arthur Rowland, born at Woolston, Hants, 1871; 2s. Charles Barrett, arm. CHRIST CHURCH, matric. 11 Oct., 89, aged 18 (from Westminster school), scholar 89; assist. collector and magistrate at Malabar, Madras c.s., 91.

Knapp, Charles, born at Kingston-on-Thames 1867; 4s. Russell George Atkinson, gen. NON-COLLEGIATE, matric. 17 Oct., 88, aged 21, B.A. 92; HONOURS :—2 theology 91.

Knapp, Henry John, M.A. (MAGDALEN HALL), see Hertford coll.

Knapp, Herbert Henry George, born at Rouen, in France, 3 Feb., 1870; 1s. Henry John, of Oxford, cler. NON-COLLEGIATE, matric. 24 May, 88, aged 18 (from Q. Elizabeth gr. school, Ipswich), B.A. 92; HONOURS :—1 theology 92.

Knapp, John Matthew, born at Newport Pagnell, Bucks, 8 April, 1868; 1s. Matthew Grenville, of Linford Hall, Bucks, arm. MAGDALEN, matric. 18 Oct., 86 (from Haileybury), B.A. 90; HONOURS :—2 history 90.

Knatchbull, rev. Henry Dalrymple, born at Jersey 11 June, 1864; 2s. Reginald Edward, M.A. ST. JOHN'S, matric. 13 Oct., 83, aged 19, B.A. 87, M.A. 91; curate Great Berkhamstead, Herts, 91.

Knaus, Charles Theodore, born in London 16 April, 1865; 1s. Theodore, arm. TRINITY, matric. 15 Oct., 87, aged 24 (from Dulwich and University coll. London); treasurer and president of Oxford union society 89.

Knight, Andrew Greville Boughton-, born at Ludlow, Salop, Feb., 1868; 2s. Andrew, arm. CHRIST CHURCH, matric. 14 Oct., 87, aged 19.

Knight, Angus Clifton, born at Keswick, Cumberland, 18 Dec., 1873; o.s. Alexander Angus Halley, D.Med. QUEEN'S, matric. 27 Oct., 91; aged 17 (from Aberdeen school and Epsom coll.), scholar 91.

Knight, Charles Nell, born in London 1866; 2s. John Burgess, gent. ST. JOHN'S, matric. 24 Jan., 84, aged 18, B.A. 88, M.A. 91; HONOURS : 3 history 87.

Knight, Charles Stacey, born at St. Brides, co. Glamorgan, 25 June, 1862; 3s. Charles Rumsey, vicar. WADHAM, matric. 23 Jan., 82, aged 18, from St. Edward's school, Summertown.

Knight, Francis Henry Greville, born at Broad Hayes, Devon, 3 April, 1871; 1s. Thomas Henry, cler. BRASENOSE, matric. 20 Oct., 86, aged 21, from Appuldurcombe school, I.W., and Winchester.

Knight, George, born at Morland, Westmorland, 1 Sept., 1872; 2s. Joseph, cler. QUEEN'S, matric. 27 Oct., 91, aged 19 (from Appleby gr. school), exhibitioner 91.

Knight, Herbert Arthur, born at Chawton, Hants, 16 June, 1871; 4s. Edward Bridges, cler., deceased. UNIVERSITY COLL., matric. 11 Oct., 90, aged 19, from Wellington coll.

Knight, Herbert Theodore, born at Dundee 23 March, 1869; o.s. William Angus, LL.D. and professor. EXETER, matric. 17 Oct., 88, aged 19 (from Fettes coll.), exhibitioner 88, B.A. 92; HONOURS:—3 classical mods. 90, 4 classics 92.

Knight, Hubert, born at Twickenham, Middx., 28 Dec., 1866; 3s. William Henry, gen. QUEEN'S, matric. 21 Oct., 87, aged 19, from King's coll. school, London.

Knight, Hugh Coleraine, born at St. Brides, co. Glamorgan, 1861; 2s. Charles Rumsey, vicar. QUEEN'S, matric. 25 Oct., 80, aged 19 (from Bromsgrove gr. school), exhibitioner 80-2, scholar 82-4, B.A. 84; HONOURS:—3 classical mods. 82, 4 law 84.

Knight, John Walker, M.A., fellow MAGDALEN 49-66, where see page 322.

Knightley, Rainald Edward, born at Tulse Hill, Surrey, 14 Dec., 1867; 1s. Thomas Edward, arm. EXETER, matric. 23 Oct., 85, aged 18 (from the Charterhouse), B.A. 90.

Knipe, Christopher, born at Dublin June, 1870; 1s. William, arm. ORIEL, matric. 25 Oct., 89, aged 19, from Winchester.

Knowlden, William John, born in London 1863; 2s. Thomas Richard, gent. HERTFORD, matric. 18 Oct., 83, aged 20, B.A. 87, M.A. 90; HONOURS:—3 theology 87.

Knowles, Edward Hadarezer, M.A., fellow QUEEN'S 44-50, where see page 178.

Knowles, Herbert Bottomley, born at Bradford, Yorks, 1867; 1s. David, gent. CHRIST CHURCH, matric. 15 Oct., 86, aged 19 (from Bradford school), scholar 85, B.A. 90; HONOURS:—3 mathematical mods. 88, 2 physics 90.

Knowles, rev. John George, born at Manchester 1865; 1s. Robert, gent. BRASENOSE, matric. 14 Oct., 84, aged 19 (from Manchester gr. school), scholar 84, B.A. 88 (HONOURS:—2 classical mods. 86, 4 classics 88); curate of Prestwich, co. Lanc., 92.

Knowles, John Halliley, born at Chester 19 July, 1869; o.s. William Ellis, of Oxford, gen. QUEEN'S, matric. 22 Oct., 89, aged 18, from Choristers school.

Knowles, John Haslam, born at Turton, co. Lanc., July, 1869; 1s. Robert Millington, arm. CHRIST CHURCH, matric. 3 June, 87, aged 17 (from Eton), B.A. 90; drowned 15 Aug., 90.

Knowles, rev. Maurice Mason, born at Boston, co. Lincoln, June, 1864; 3s. John Mason, gent. NON-COLLEGIATE, matric. 23 Jan., 86, aged 21 (from Boston school); migrated to CHRIST CHURCH, B.A. 89.

Knox, Charles Edward Leslie, born at Drumsrath, co. Down, 14 Aug., 1864; 1s. Charles Beresford, cler. KEBLE, matric. 16 Oct., 83, aged 19 (from Rossall school), B.A. 86; HONOURS:—3 theology 86.

Knox, Edmund Arbuthnot, M.A., fellow MERTON 68-84, where see page 98.

Knox, Edmund Francis Vesey, born at Newcastle, co. Down, 23 Jan., 1865; 1s. Vesey Edmund, arm. KEBLE, matric. 16 Oct., 83, aged 18 (from St. Columba coll., Dublin), scholar 83, B.A. 86; fellow ALL SOULS' 86, M.A. 90 (HONOURS:—1 history 86); of Shinnah House, co. Down, M.P. W. Cavan, 90; bar.-at-law, Grays Inn, 89. See Foster's *Peerage*, E. RATHDONNELL.

[STONE BOSS, ST. GEORGE NEAR ROUEN.—*Pugin*.]

Knox, Harry, born in Trinidad 1867; 2s André Blasini, arm. BALLIOL, matric. 19 Oct., 86, aged 19 (from the Oratory school, Edgbaston), B.A. 90 (HONOURS :—2 law 90); bar.-at-law, Inner Temple, 92, brother of Howard V.

Knox, rev. Herbert Carnegie, born at Sonning, Berks, 1863; 3s. Henry George Augustus, arm. BALLIOL, matric. 29 Jan., 81, aged 18 (from Eton), B.A. 84, M.A. 87 (HONOURS :—3 classical mods. 82, 2 theology 84); missionary in China 89; brother of Stuart.

Knox, Howard Vincent, born at Trinidad 7 Dec., 1868; 4s. André Blasini, bar.-at-law. EXETER, matric. 21 Oct., 86, aged 17, passed for the army.

Knox, Stuart Carnegie, born at Sonning, Berks, 19 April, 1870; 4s. Henry George Augustus, arm. NEW COLL., matric. 11 Oct., 89, aged 19 (from Eton), B.A. 92; (HONOURS :—2 law 92); brother of Herbert.

Knox, Thomas Carey, born in East Indies 10 Aug., 1862; 1s. Thomas John, of the Madras C.S. EXETER, matric. 4 June, 81, aged 18 (from Winchester), B.A. 85, M.A. 88.

Knox, rev. William Ferguson, born at Urney, Ireland, 8 Sept., 1861; 1s. Andrew Ferguson, arm. HERTFORD, matric. 8 Nov., 80, aged 19, B.A. 84, M.A. 88; of Urney, co. Tyrone, curate of Burnley St. Paul, co. Lanc., 90.

Koe, Alfred Pemberton, born at Hampton Wick, Middx., 1866; 1s. Ralph, gent. UNIVERSITY COLL., matric. 17 Oct., 85, aged 19 (from Haileybury), B.A. 88; HONOURS :—3 law 88.

Koe, Digby Latimer Francis, born at Blackheath, Kent, 5 March, 1865; 1s. Frederick Pemberton, arm. MERTON, matric. 19 Oct., 83, aged 18; migrated to MERTON, B.A. 86.

Koecher, John Edgar, born at Manchester 10 Jan., 1869; 2s. John Michael, gen. NEW COLL., matric. 9 Dec., 87, aged 18, from Manchester gr. school.

Kooller, Franz, born at Antwerp , 1858; 1s. Francis, arm. NEW COLL., matric. 27 Jan., 86, aged 28, B.Mus. 11 Nov., 86.

Krebs, Heinrich, PH.D., M.A., Taylorian librarian, see page 4.

Kunz, Raoul de Dreux, born at Edinburgh 1870; 2s. Jules Antony Louis, gen. NEW COLL., matric. 25 Jan., 88, aged 18, B.Mus. 90.

Kyffin, John, born at Tremadoc, co. Carnarvon, Feb., 1866; 1s. Thomas Lloyd, cler. KEBLE, matric. 16 Oct., 83, aged 17, from St. Mark's school, Windsor.

Kyle, Henry Greville, born at Clifton, co. Glouc., 18 April, 1869; 1s. Robert, cler. MERTON. matric. 17 Oct., 88, aged 19, from Cheltenham coll.

Kynaston, rev. Tewkesbury Henry, born at Wincanton, Somerset, , 1848; 4s. Joseph, gent. KEBLE, matric. 5 Nov., 84, aged 36 (from Gloucester theological coll.); rector of Bushey, Herts, 85.

Kynnersley, Edmund McKenzie Sneyd, M.A., Fereday fellow ST. JOHN'S 65-79, where see.

Kyrle, rev. Cecil Leigh Money-, born at Tupsley, co. Hereford, 20 Jan., 1868; 3s. John Erle, lieut.-col. ORIEL, matric. 21 Jan., 87, aged 19 (from Winchester), B.A. 90; curate of Snelston St. Matthias, Notts, 91.

Kyrle, rev. Rowland Tracy Ashe Money-, born at Tupsley, co. Hereford, 2 Aug., 1866; 2s. John Erle, lieut.-col. NEW COLL., matric. 16 Oct., 85, aged 19 (from Winchester), scholar 84, B.A. 89, M.A. 92 (HONOURS :—classical mods. 87, 2 history 89); curate of Portsea, Hants, 90.

[STONE BOSS, ST. GEORGE NEAR ROUEN.—*Pugin*.]

WOODEN ORNAMENT, ROUEN CATHEDRAL.—*Pugin.*

L

Labat, Christopher de Burgh de, born at Williamstown, co. Dublin, 1870; 4s. Andrew Tyrrell, cler. NON-COLLEGIATE, matric. 13 Oct., 88, aged 18 (from St. Edward's school, Summertown), B.A. 92; HONOURS :—3 classical mods. 90, 3 theology 92.

Labilliere, Charles Edgar Delacour de, born in London 20 Aug., 1869; 1s. Francis Peter, arm. EXETER, matric. 17 Oct., 88, aged 19 (from Harrow), B.A. 92.

Labouchere, Arthur Maxwell, born at Brighton 1874; 2s. Arthur, gent. ORIEL, matric. 27 Oct., 92, aged 18, from Wellington coll.

Labouchere, John Arthur, born at Brighton Feb., 1870; 1s. Arthur, arm. CHRIST CHURCH, matric. 21 Jan., 90, aged 19, from Wellington coll.

Lace, Edgar Crofts, born at Wells, Somerset, 1865; 2s. John William, cler. ST. EDMUND HALL, matric. 22 Oct., 84, aged 19, B.A. 88, M.A. 91.

Lace, Francis Walter, born at Pill, Somerset, Sept., 1871; 8s. John William, vicar. KEBLE, matric. 17 Jan., 91, aged 19, from Bristol gr. school.

Lach-Szyrma, Philip I., see Szyrma.

Lade, James, born at Port Glasgow, co. Renfrew, 22 Feb., 1869; 2s. Alexander, solicitor, deceased. UNIVERSITY COLL., matric. 12 Oct., 89, aged 20 (from Glasgow university); HONOURS :—1 law 92.

Lainé, Harold George, born at St. Saviour's, Guernsey, 21 Oct., 1872; 3s. John de Jersey, gen. JESUS COLL., matric. 20 Oct., 91, aged 18 (from Elizabeth coll., Guernsey), exhibitioner 91.

Laing, Charles Miskin, born at Rosherville, London, 8 Feb., 1863; o.s. Charles, deceased. MAGDALEN, matric. 15 Oct., 81, aged 18, B.A. 85, B.C.L. and M.A. 88 (HONOURS :—3 history 85, 2 law 86, a civil law 87); bar.-at-law, Inner Temple, 89.

Laing, Philip Mathison Tovey, born at Colchester matric. 15 Oct., 81, aged 17 (from Bedford school); migrated to ST. JOHN'S, B.A. 86.

Laing, Samuel, born at Richmond, Surrey, 11 Sept., 1870; 1s. Samuel, arm., deceased. BALLIOL, matric. 17 Oct., 89, aged 19 (from St. Andrew's university); HONOURS :—1 classical mods. 91.

Lake, Arthur Brabazon, born at Wrexham, Flints, Feb., 1869; 1s. Arthur, major. UNIVERSITY COLL., matric. 15 Oct., 87, aged 18, from Haileybury.

Lake, Kenneth Alexander, born at Monkton, Kent, 22 June, 1871; 3s. James, gen. MAGDALEN, matric. 14 Oct., 90, aged 19 (from Bromsgrove school); HONOURS :—3 classical mods. 92.

Lake, Kirsopp, born at Southampton 1872; o.s. George Anthony Kirsopp, D.Med. LINCOLN, matric. 23 Oct., 91, aged 19 (from St. Paul's school), exhibitioner 91.

Lake, William Charles, M.A., fellow BALLIOL 38-59, where see page 67.

Lamb, Charles William, born at Islington, London, 1866. NON-COLLEGIATE, matric. 17 Oct., 91, aged 25, from Holloway high school.

Lamb, Edmund George, born at Dublin 8 July, 1863; s. Richard Westbrook, arm. MERTON, matric. 17 Oct., 82, aged 19, B.A. 86, M.A. 89; HONOURS :— 3 history 86.

Lamb, Loftus Gerard Willum, born at Whitehaven, Cumberland, 23 Sept., 1867; 2s. James, gen. QUEEN'S, matric. 21 Oct., 87, aged 20, from Uppingham.

Lamb, Maurice, born at Basingstoke, Hants, 5 April, 1869; 4s. John Workman, gen. QUEEN'S, matric. 21 Oct., 87, aged 18 (from Haileybury), B.A. 90; HONOURS :—4 theology 90.

Lamb, Percy Stewart, born at Aldridge, co. Stafford, Feb., 1865; 2s. Francis William, cler. WORCESTER, matric. 18 Oct., 83, aged 18, from St. Edward's school, Summertown.

Lambert, Francis John, born at Fordingbridge, Hants, 23 Nov., 1866; 1s. Edward Henry George, capt. R.N. PEMBROKE, matric. 27 Oct., 85, aged 18 (from Cheltenham coll.), B.A. 89; curate of Halling, Kent, 90; died 13 Jan., 92.

Lambert, George Bancroft, born at Newlyn, Penzance, 28 Oct., 1873; 1. Thomas Thornton, nonconformist minister. MAGDALEN, matric. 18 Oct., 92, aged 19 (from Kingswood school), demy 91.

Lambert, Henry Charles Miller, born in London 7 Dec., 1868; 1s. Henry Thomas, arm., deceased. NEW COLL., matric. 14 Oct., 87, aged 18 (from Eton), exhibitioner 87, B.A. 92; HONOURS :—1 classical mods. 89, 1 classics 91.

Lambert, Hugh Biddulph, born at Ledbury, co. Hereford, 21 Nov., 1867; 1s. William Henry, cler. MERTON, matric. 24 Oct., 85, aged 17, from Winchester coll. and Hereford cathedral school.

Lambert, Lionel, born in London 25 May, 1869; 2s. Alan, gen. CHRIST CHURCH, matric. 18 Jan., 89, aged 19 (from Winchester), B.A. 92; HONOURS: —Ægrotat history 92.

Lambert, Perceval, born at Leeds 9 Aug., 1860; 2s. William, gent. LINCOLN, matric. 23 Oct., 80, aged 20 (from Leeds gr. school), B.A. 83; HONOURS: —3 law 83.

Lambley, Richard Henry, born at Norton, co. Gloucester, 1858; y.s. William, gen. NON-COLLEGIATE, matric. 13 Oct., 83, aged 25 (from Carmarthen coll.); migrated to UNIVERSITY COLL., B.A. 87, M.A. 90.

Lambton, hon. Claud, born 4 Jan., 1865; 7s. John George, earl of Durham. BALLIOL, matric. 28 Jan., 84, aged 19 (from Eton), B.A. 89; HONOURS: —4 history 87. See Foster's *Peerage*.

Lamont, Donald Mackay, born at Reay, Caithness, 26 Nov., 1852; 1s. Malcolm, gen. MERTON, matric. 22 Oct., 87, aged 24 (from King's coll., Old Aberdeen), exhibitioner 87; HONOURS:—2 classical mods. 89.

La-Motte, Digby Holden Rose Harwick, born in London 22 Oct., 1861; 1s. George Crespigny, cler. TRINITY, matric. 16 Oct., 80, aged 18 (from Rugby), B.A. 85, M.A. 91 (HONOURS:—1 classical mods. 82, Latin verse 84); a master at St. Paul's school, London.

Lamprill, Edward Arthur, born at Brighton, Tasmania, 1866; 1s. Frederick, arm. CORPUS CHRISTI, matric. 20 Oct., 86, aged 20, B.A. 90; HONOURS: —3 classical mods. 88, 4 history 90.

Lance, Philip, born at Kuch, Behar, India, 28 Sept., 1869; 3s. William Henry Joseph, lieut.-col. EXETER, matric. 17 Oct., 88, aged 19 (from Victoria coll., Jersey), scholar 88, B.A. 92; HONOURS: —3 classical mods. 90.

Lancelot, rev. John Bennett, born at Gresford, co. Denbigh, 11 Feb., 1864; 1s. Abraham, gent. JESUS COLL., matric. 18 Oct., 83, aged 19 (from Wrexham and Chester schools), B.A. 87, M.A. 90 (HONOURS:—1 classical mods. 85, 2 classics 87); assist. master Manchester gr. school 90; curate of Christ Church, Dudsbury, 90.

Lancy, rev. Walter Graham de (now Walter Graham), born in London 1864; 2s. William Jonathan Smith, gent. NON-COLLEGIATE, matric. 22 Jan., 81, aged 17, B.A. 85, M.A. 87 (HONOURS:—4 theology 84, Taylorian scholarship in Spanish 84), chaplain in Burma 86-90.

Landels, Thomas Durley, born at St. Marylebone, London, 1862; 4s. William, D.D., baptist minister. NON-COLLEGIATE, matric. 17 Oct., 91, aged 29, from University coll., London.

Landon, rev. Guy, born at Eastbourne, Sussex, 24 Nov., 1865; 1s. Edward Henry, cler. LINCOLN, matric. 27 Oct., 85, aged 19 (from King's coll. school, London), scholar 85, B.A. 89, M.A. 92 (HONOURS:—2 classical mods. 87, 2 classics 89); curate of Midhurst 89.

Landon, John Chichester Crewe, born at Ashford, Devon, 2 April, 1868; o.s. Charles Whittington, cler. WORCESTER, matric. 17 Jan., 88, aged 19, (from Sherborne school), B.A. 92.

Landon, Perceval, born at Hastings 29 March, 1869; 3s. Edward Henry, cler., deceased. HERTFORD, matric. 19 Oct., 88, aged 19 (from Forest school), scholar 87; HONOURS:—3 classical mods. 90, 3 law 92.

Landon, Thomas Hamlyn Whittington, born at Pernambuco 1869; 2s. Ernest Whittington, gen. WORCESTER, matric. 14 Oct., 89, aged 20, from St. Austen's school, Staten Island, N.Y.

Lane, Arthur Edward Cecil, born at Kings Bromley Manor, co. Stafford, Aug., 1871; 2s. John Henry Bagot, late colonel Coldstream guards, deceased. CHRIST CHURCH, matric. 16 Oct., 91, aged 20, from Shrewsbury school and the Charterhouse.

Lane, Charles James, born at Douglas, co. Cork, 17 June, 1869; 3s. James, arm. ST. JOHN'S, matric. 13 Oct., 88, aged 19 (from Bath coll.), scholar 88; HONOURS:—1 classical mods. 90.

Lane, Charles Middleton Robert Douglas, born at Kemp Town, Sussex, 1864; 4s. Richard Douglas Hay, arm. PEMBROKE, matric. 3 May, 83, aged 19.

Lane, Ernald, M.A., fellow ALL SOULS' 60-79, where see page 281.

Lane, Richard Ouseley Blake, born in London 23 Sept., 1868; 1s. Richard Ouseley Blake, Q.C. TRINITY, matric. 16 Oct., 86, aged 18 (from Marlborough coll.), B.A. 91 (HONOURS:—3 history 90); bar.-at-law, Inner Temple, 92.

Lane, Robert Charlton, born in London 26 Jan., 1873; 1s. Charles Thomas, solicitor. NEW COLL., matric. 14 Oct., 92 (from Winchester), exhibitioner 91.

Lane, Sidney Ernald Ralph, born in London 1861; o.s. Sidney Leveson, arm. BRASENOSE, matric. 2 June, 82, aged 18 (from Eton), B.A. 86; bar.-at-law, Inner Temple, 87.

Lanfear, rev. Carl Silvius Viereck, born at Cassel, Germany, 1857; 1s. John Viereck, gent. WORCESTER, matric. 4 June, 81, aged 24, B.A. 84 (HONOURS:—2 theology 84); curate of Letcombe Regis, 84.

Lang, Andrew, M.A., hon. fellow MERTON 89, where see page 95.

Lang, rev. Cosmo Gordon, born at Fyvie, co. Aberdeen, 1865; 2s. John Marshall, gent. BALLIOL, matric. 17 Oct., 82, aged 17 (from Glasgow university), scholar 82-6, B.A. 86 (HONOURS:—2 classics 85, M.A. 89 (HONOURS:—2 classics 85, 1 history 86), president Oxford union society 84; student, Inner Temple, 84; curate Leeds 90.

Lang, rev. Robert Lowman, born at Fawley, Hants, 1868; 1s. Robert Lowman, gent. NON-COLLEGIATE, matric. 20 Jan., 83, aged 15 (from Christ Church cathedral school, chorister 78-83), B.A. 86, M.A. 90 (HONOURS:—Ægrotat theology 86), assist.-master St. Paul's cathedral choir school 90.

Lang, William Andrew, born at Melbourne 23 Jan., 1863; 1s. William, gent. ORIEL, matric. 2 June, 82, aged 18 (from Clifton coll.), B.A. 85; bar.-at-law, Inner Temple, 87.

Langdon, Arthur Mervyn, born at High Beckington, Devon, 16 Dec., 1870; 2s. Alfred, vicar of Slanford, co. Linc. NEW COLL., matric. 19 Oct., 89, aged 15 (from Winchester), scholar 88; HONOURS:—1 mathematical mods. 91.

Lange, Frederick Louis Christian, born at St. Kilda, Melbourne, 8 May, 1871; 1s. s. Frederick Louis Christian, gent., deceased. BALLIOL, matric. 18 Oct., 92, aged 21, from church of England gr. school, Melbourne.

Langenberg, James Arthur van, born at Kandy, Ceylon, 2 March, 1866; 2s. James, arm. MERTON, matric. 28 Jan., 86, aged 19 (from Forest school, Walthamstow); bar.-at-law, Inner Temple, 88.

Langhorne, rev. Alexander Reginald, born at Broughton, Wilts, 7 Nov., 1863; 2s. Alexander Grant Smith, gent. NON-COLLEGIATE, matric. 4 Nov., 84, aged 20 (from Claremont school, Birkenhead, and Loretto); curate to LINCOLN, B.A. 88; curate of St. Mary, Somers Town, London, 89.

Langley, Alexander, born at Barnet, Herts, 1871; o.s. Dankwaerts John, gen. PEMBROKE, matric. 25 Oct., 90, aged 19 (from Christ's hospital), scholar 89; HONOURS:—2 classical mods. 92.

Langley, Reginald Hubert, born at Bristol June, 1872; o.s. Aaron, gen. NEW COLL., matric. 18 Oct., 90, aged 18, from Dover coll.

Langridge, Arthur Bincy, born in London 24 Dec., 1865; 2s. Henry, gent. CORPUS CHRISTI, matric. 23 Oct., 84, aged 18 (from the Charterhouse), scholar 84, B.A. 88 (HONOURS:—accessit Hertford scholarship 85, 1 classical mods. 86, 2 classics 88); bar.-at-law, Middle Temple, 90.

Langsdorf, William Bell, born at Carlisle, Pen., U.S.A., 1866; o.s. A. S., gent. NON-COLLEGIATE, matric. 15 Oct., 92, aged 26, from Leipsic university, etc.

Langsford, rev. Sydney William, born at South Norwood, Surrey, 17 Feb., 1865; 2s. Richard Turner, gent. LINCOLN, matric. 17 Oct., 84, aged 19 (from South Norwood coll.), B.A. 88, M.A. 91 (HONOURS:—3 classical mods. 86, 3 history 88); curate of Walworth St. Peter, Surrey, 89.

Langston, Frederick William, born in London 7 June, 1859; 1s. Frederick William, gen. NON-COLLEGIATE, matric. 12 Oct., 89, aged 30, from Philological school, London.

Langton, Algernon William Stephen Gore-; lord Langton, born in London 9 Nov., 1871; 1s. William Stephen, earl Temple. CHRIST CHURCH, matric. 16 Oct., 91, aged 19, from Eton.

Langworthy, Geoffrey Parker, born in London 9 Oct., 1872; 4s. James William, arm. CHRIST CHURCH, matric. 29 May, 91, aged 18, from Rugby.

Langworthy, Richard, born in London 25 Nov., 1868; 3s. James William, arm. CORPUS CHRISTI, matric. 16 Oct., 88, aged 19 (from Marlborough), B.A.

Lankester, Edwin Ray, M.A., hon. fellow EXETER 89, and hon. fellow MERTON 92, where see page 95.

Larken, Hubert, born at Lincoln 15 March, 1874; 1s. Francis Roper, solicitor. MAGDALEN, matric. 18 Oct., 92, aged 18, from the Charterhouse.

Larkins, John Russell, born at Greenwich, Kent, 1866; 1s. Frederick, gen. EXETER, matric. 16 Oct., 84, aged 18 (from Auckland school, N.Z., and King's coll., London), scholar 84-6; died at Auckland, N.Z., 31 May, 86.

Lascelles, hon. Daniel Henry, born 1 Aug., 1862; 2s. Henry Thynne, earl of Harewood. CHRIST CHURCH, matric. 14 Oct., 81, aged 19, from Eton. See Foster's *Peerage*.

Lascelles, Edwin John Moore, born at Brighton 1863; 1s. Edwin, cler. PEMBROKE, matric. 24 Jan., 82, aged 19.

Lascelles, Harold, born at Graffham, Sussex, 18 Aug., 1873; 2s. Rowley, B.A. rector of Lavington, Sussex. ST. JOHN'S, matric. 15 Oct., 92, aged 19, from Marlborough.

Laski, Alexander de, born at Brighton 27 July, 1865; 1s. Alexander, arm. MERTON, matric. 24 Oct., 84, aged 20.

Lassetter, rev. Leslie Beauchamp, born at Sydney, Australia, Jan., 1865; 4s. Frederic, of London, arm. MAGDALEN, matric. 16 Oct., 84, aged 19 (from Eton), B.A. 87; HONOURS:—3 history 87.

Latham, Alexander Mere, born at Sandbach, Cheshire, 20 Aug., 1862; 1s. George Williani, M.P., deceased. BRASENOSE, matric. 10 June, 81, aged 18 (from Wellington), B.A. 85 (HONOURS:—4 law 85); bar.-at-law, Inner Temple, 90.

Latham, Arderne Mere, born in London 5 Dec., 1872; 1s. Philip Arderne, M.A. BRASENOSE, matric. 3 Feb., 91, aged 18, from St. Mark's school, Windsor.

Latham, Arthur Carlyle, born at Cambridge 1 Dec., 1867; 3s. Peter Wallbrook, Downing professor of medicine at Cambridge. BALLIOL, matric. 19 Oct., 87, aged 19 (from Fettes coll, and Edinburgh university), B.A. 90 (HONOURS:—2 chemistry 90, 1 physiology 92); incorporated B.A. at King's coll., Cambridge, 90.

Latham, John, born at Liverpool 10 Feb., 1865; y.s. William, gent. WADHAM, matric. 16 Oct., 83, aged 18 (from Owens coll., Manchester, and Christ coll., Cambridge, matric. 29 Jan., 83), B.A. 86; HONOURS:—3 mathematical mods. 84, 4 history 86.

Latham, rev. John Alfred, born at Northwich, Cheshire, 27 Sept., 1863; o.s. William, arm. MERTON, matric. 16 Oct., 84, aged 19, B.A. 87, M.A. 92; curate of Whalley, co. Lanc., 89.

Latham, rev. John Mere, born in London 22 June, 1866; 1s. Francis Law, bar.-at-law. CORPUS CHRISTI, matric. 26 Oct., 85, aged 19 (from Rugby), exhibitioner 86, B.A. 89, M.A. 92 (HONOURS:—2 classical mods. 87, 3 law 89); curate of All Saints', South Lambeth, 91.

Lathy, Maurice Frederick, born at Tillington, Sussex, 3 Jan., 1869; 2s. Thomas, gent., deceased. NON-COLLEGIATE, matric. 16 Oct., 86, aged 17 (from Portsmouth gr. school), B.A. 90.

Latimer, rev. Roynon Charles Washington, born at Headington, Oxon, 1860; 3s. Frederick, gent. ST. ALBAN HALL, matric. 4 Feb., 81, aged 21; curate of Wilsford with Woodford, Wilts, 90.

Latter, Algernon, born at Pirfield, Kent, 26 Nov., 1870; 5s. Robinson, arm. TRINITY, matric. 12 Oct., 89, aged 18 (from Canterbury school), HONOURS:—2 classical mods. 91.

Latter, Hugh, born at North Mimms, Herts, 8 Jan., 1868; 4s. Arthur Simon, cler. CORPUS CHRISTI, matric. 20 Oct., 86, aged 18 (from Marlborough), scholar 86, B.A. 90; HONOURS:—1 classical mods. 88, 2 classics 90.

Latter, Oswald Hawkins, born at Fulham, Middx., 7 Aug., 1864; 2s. Arthur Simon, vicar. KEBLE, matric. 16 Oct., 83, aged 19 (from the Charterhouse), B.A. 87, tutor 89, M.A. 90; HONOURS:—1 morphology 87.

Lattimer, Robert Binney, born at Carlisle 3 Feb., 1863; 3s. William, gent. QUEEN'S, matric. 28 Oct., 81, aged 18 (from Carlisle and Durham gr. schools), exhibitioner 81-2, scholar 82-5, B.A. 85, M.A. 89; HONOURS:—2 classical mods. 83, 3 classics 85.

Laughlin, Henry Ernest Everett, born in London 1867; 3s. Frederick Hamilton, M.A. cler. NON-COLLEGIATE, matric. 15 Oct., 90, aged 25, from Denstone coll.

Laughton, Leonard George Carr, born at Southsea, Hants, 23 Dec., 1871; 1s. John Knox, professor of modern history, King's coll., London. ST. JOHN'S matric. 17 Oct., 91, aged 19 (from Eastbourne coll.), exhibitioner 91.

Laurence, Henry Hamilton, born at East Chaylton, Bucks, 23 Feb., 1864; 3s. Percival, rector of Walesby, co. Lincoln. NEW COLL., matric. 12 Oct., 83, aged 19 (from Forest school), scholar 83, B.A. 87; HONOURS:—2 classical mods. 85, 3 classics 87.

Laurence, Thomas Ernest de Vere, born at Beckenham, Kent, 25 May, 1867; 1s. Thomas Herbert, gen. NON-COLLEGIATE, matric. 20 Oct., 90, aged 23 (from Hurstpierpoint coll.); migrated to TRINITY 91.

Laurie, Allan James, born in Edinburgh 29 Oct., 1873; 1s. James Dundas, stockbroker. TRINITY, matric. 15 Oct., 92, aged 18, from Fettes coll.

Laurie, Henry Montague, born in London 1866; 4s. David Crawford, D.Med. BALLIOL, matric. 15 Oct., 84, aged 18, B.A. 87 (HONOURS:—2 law 87); bar.-at-law, Middle Temple, 87; assist. commissioner central provinces India.

Laurie, Oscar Sydney, born at Burntisland, co. Fife, 23 Aug., 1863; 1s. William Alexander, W.S. and keeper H.M.'s gazette, Scotland. BRASENOSE, matric. 23 Jan., 90, aged 24, from Burntisland school.

Laurie, Ranald Macdonald, born in London July, 1869; 1s. Robert Peter, arm. CHRIST CHURCH, matric. 14 Oct., 87, aged 18 (from Eton), B.A. 92.

Lavender, Charles Ernest, born at Canterbury 1864; 2s. Thomas, gent. ST. EDMUND HALL, matric. 5 Nov., 85, aged 21; curate of Barkingside, Essex, 89-90, chaplain at Tangier 90; died 17 March, 92.

Laverty, Wallis Hay, M.A. fellow QUEEN'S 69-73, where see page 182.

Lavie, rev. Cecil Tudor, born at Vizianagram, East Indies, Aug., 1864; 1s. Tudor, of the Indian office. NEW COLL., matric. 10 Oct., 84, aged 20 (from Wellington), exhibitioner 84, B.A. 89, M.A. 91; HONOURS :—2 classical mods. 86, 2 classics 88.

Lavie, Germain, M.A., student CHRIST CHURCH 54-61, where see page 419.

Lavie, Germain, born in London 20 June, 1862; 1s. Germain, arm. CHRIST CHURCH, matric. 14 Oct., 81, aged 19 (from Westminster school), B.A. 86; HONOURS :—4 history 85.

Lavies, Robert Sherwood, born in London 1866; 10s. Joseph Samuel, D.Med. ST. MARY HALL, matric. 20 Oct., 84, aged 18.

Law, Cecil Arbuthnot, born in London 25 June, 1872; 1s. Patrick Francis, arm. ORIEL, matric. 22 Oct., 90, aged 18 (from Winchester), scholar 90; HONOURS :—2 classical mods. 92.

Law, Hugh Alexander, born at Dublin 28 July, 1872; 2s. Hugh, Q.C., M.P., lord chancellor of Ireland 81-3. UNIVERSITY COLL., matric. 11 Oct., 90, aged 18, from Rugby.

Law, Robert Arbuthnot, born at North Repps, Norfolk, 1842; 3s. Patrick Comerford, cler. ST. ALBAN HALL, matric. 1 Nov., 81, aged 39; rector of Larling, Norfolk, 69-70, and of Gunthorpe with Bale 70, until he died 11 Dec., 89.

Law, rev. Robert Hartley, born at Padiham, co. Lanc., 1 June, 1862; o.s. Thomas Charles, arm. BRASENOSE, matric. 18 Oct., 81, aged 19 (from Rossall school), scholar 81-5, B.A. 85 (HONOURS :—3 classical mods. 83, 3 classics 85); curate of Windermere St. John 91.

Law, rev. William Smalley, born at Northampton 1865; 2s. William, gent. NON-COLLEGIATE, matric. 17 Oct., 85, aged 20 (from a Northampton school); migrated to KEBLE, B.A. 88, M.A. 92 (HONOURS :—2 theology 88); curate of Belgrave, co. Leic., 88.

Lawes, Edward Thornton Hill, born at Bristol 26 Dec., 1860; 1s. Henry Fricker, bar.-at-law. CORPUS CHRISTI, matric. 25 Oct., 89, aged 19 (from Clifton coll.), B.A. 92; HONOURS :—3 classical mods. 91, 3 law 92.

Lawes, Percy Charles Willoughby, born at Islington 21 Jan., 1870; 2s. Joseph Christopher, gen. WADHAM, matric. 28 Jan., 90, aged 20.

Lawford, Herbert Bowring, born at Wandsworth, Surrey, 13 April, 1864; 4s. George, arm. TRINITY, matric. 29 Jan., 83, aged 18 (from Marlborough), B.A. 86.

Lawless, Joseph Aymar Charles, born at Monkstown, co. Dublin, Feb., 1868; 3s. William Hampden, arm. NON-COLLEGIATE, matric. 19 Feb., 87, aged 19, from Bath coll.

Lawley, hon. Francis Charles, B.C.L., fellow ALL SOULS' 48-53, where see page 279.

Lawrance, Henry, born at Barbados 23 Sept., 1863; 1s. Edward, arm. EXETER, matric. 18 Oct., 82, aged 19 (from Westminster school), B.A. 86, M.A. 89.

Lawrance, Thomas Dalton, born at Dunsby, co. Lincoln, 26 Jan., 1865; 1s. John Compion, Q.C. ORIEL, matric. 27 Oct., 83, aged 18 (from Rugby), B.A. 87; M.A. 90; bar.-at-law, Inner Temple, 91.

Lawrence, Henry, born at Alnmouth, Northumberland, 17 Sept., 1871; 1s. Major. QUEEN'S, matric. 24 Oct., 90, aged 19 (from East Retford and Richmond gr. schools); HONOURS :—3 classical mods. 92.

Lawrence, Henry Staveley, born at Culdaff, co. Donegal, 20 Oct., 1870; 2s. George Henry, of Eastbourne, late R.C.S. MAGDALEN, matric. 16 Oct., 88, aged 17 (from Haileybury); assist. collector and magistrate Kaira, Bombay C.S. 90.

Lawrence, Hubert Carlton, born at Wolverhampton , 1862; 4s. Thomas Reginald, gen. WORCESTER, matric. 20 Oct., 81, aged 19 (from Wolverhampton school), scholar 80-5, B.A. 85, M.A. 90; HONOURS :—2 classical mods. 83, 3 classics 85.

Lawrence, Hugh Mullineux, born at Manchester 1866; 1s. Hugh Mullineux, gent. NON-COLLEGIATE, matric. 26 Jan., 85, aged 19, from Thorpe Arch school, Yorks.

Lawrence, James Frederic Nathaniel, born in London , 1874; o.s. Nathaniel Tertius, solicitor. BALLIOL, matric. 20 Oct., 91, aged 17, from Eton.

Lawrence, William, born at Blackrock, Dublin, , 1872; 5s. William Mervin, gen. NON-COLLEGIATE, matric. 26 April, 90, aged 18, from Wesley coll. Dublin.

Lawrence, William Matthew Trevor, born 17 Sept., 1870; 1s. James John Trevor, baronet, M.P. NEW COLL., matric. 11 Oct., 89, aged 19, from Shrewsbury gr. school.

Lawrence, rev. Zante Webb, born at Wandsworth, Surrey, , 1861; 1s. James Eli, gent. EXETER, matric. 22 Oct., 80, aged 19, B.A. 83, M.A. 87 (HONOURS :—4 history 83); curate of Southbourne, Hants, 88.

Lawrie, Nevill Shute, born at Boxley, Kent, 11 Oct., 1868; 4s. John, arm. QUEEN'S, matric. 20 Oct., 88, aged 20, from Bury St. Edmund's school and Marlborough.

Lawson, rev. George Mervyn, born in London 7 May, 1865; 2s. George, gent. PEMBROKE, matric. 29 Jan., 85, aged 19 (from Westminster school and King's coll., London), B.A. 89; Universities missionary to Central Africa 92.

Lawson, Harry Lawson Webster, born in London 18 Dec., 1862; 1s. Edward Levy, bart. BALLIOL, matric. 20 Jan., 81, aged 18 (from Eton), B.A. 84, M.A. 88 (HONOURS :—2 classical mods. 82, 1 history 84); bar.-at-law, Inner Temple, 91; M.P. west St. Pancras Nov., 85, to July, 92, and for Cirencester division of Gloucestershire 93.

Lawson, right hon. James Anthony, created D.C.L. 17 June, 1885. See *Al. Ox.*, and series, 826.

Lawson, Richard, born at Aldborough, Yorks, 9 March, 1864; 3s. Andrew, arm. CHRIST CHURCH, matric. 27 May, 82, aged 18, from Harrow.

Lawson, Robert, M.A., student CHRIST CHURCH 42-9, where see page 414.

Lawson, Wilfrid, born at Netherhall, Cumberland, 21 Oct., 1862; 1s. sir Wilfrid, bart., M.P. TRINITY, matric. 15 Oct., 81, aged 18 (from Harrow), B.A. 85; student Inner Temple 83. See Foster's *Baronetage*.

Lawton, Edward, born at Manchester 1 Jan., 1873; 2s. Edward, accountant. CORPUS CHRISTI, matric. 18 Oct., 92, aged 19, from Manchester gr. school.

Layton, Thomas Charles Litchfield, M.A., fellow PEMBROKE 54-6, where see.

Lea, Edward Thomas, born at Falmouth, Isle of Jamaica, Sept., 1864; 2s. Thomas, cler. ST. EDMUND HALL, matric. 22 Oct., 83, aged 19, B.A. 86; HONOURS :—3 theology 87.

Lea, Ernest Edward, born at Wribbenhall, co. Worc., 1871; 4s. John Wildman Thomas, gen. ORIEL, matric. 25 Oct., 89, aged 18, from Bradfield coll.

Lea, Frederick Simcox, M.A., fellow BRASENOSE 53-6, where see page 355.
Lea, James Herbert, born at Tezpur, East Indies, 27 April, 1867; 1s. Richard, arm. BALLIOL, matric. 16 Oct., 86, aged 19 (from Rugby); assist. magistrate and collector Bengal 88.
Lea, John Walter, born in London May, 1873; o.s. Walter, cler. KEBLE, matric. 20 Oct., 91, aged 18, from Clergy orphan school, Canterbury.
Lea, St. John Wildman, born at Wribbenhall, co. Worc., March, 1869; 3s. John Wildman Thomas. ORIEL, matric. 18 Oct., 87, aged 18, from Malvern coll.
Lea, Stephen Henry, born at Far Forest, Bewdley, co. Worcester, June, 1868; 2s. Josiah Turner, cler. KEBLE, matric. 17 Oct., 87, aged 19 (from Lancing coll.), B.A. 90.
Lea, William, born at Ribbesford, co. Worcester, Aug., 1862; 1s. Josiah Turner, cler. KEBLE, matric. 18 Oct., 81, aged 19 (from the Charterhouse), B.A. 85, M.A. 88; HONOURS :—3 classical mods. 83, 2 theology 85.
Leach, Arthur Francis, M.A., fellow ALL SOULS' 74-82, where see page 282.
Leach, Godfrey, born at South Hampstead, Middx., 24 Aug., 1870; 1s. Francis, arm. TRINITY, matric. 12 Oct., 89, aged 19 (from Marlborough), B.A. 92; HONOURS :—3 law 92.
Leach, Kenneth Henry, born in London 15 May, 1863; 1s. John Henry, rector of Cosson, co. Leic. NEW COLL., matric. 9 Dec., 81, aged 18 (from the Charterhouse), B.A. 85 (HONOURS :—3 classical mods. 83, 3 law 85); bar.-at-law, Lincoln's Inn, 88.
Leadam, Edward Arthur, born at Iver, Bucks, 10 March, 1865; o.s. William Ward, D.Med. TRINITY, matric. 15 Oct., 84, aged 18 (from Shrewsbury school), B.A. 91; HONOURS :—4 law 91.
Leadam, Isaac Saunders, M.A., fellow BRASENOSE 72-6, where see page 356.
Leage, Richard William, born in London 1869; 1s. Richard William, gen. EXETER, matric. 17 Jan., 88, aged 18 (from Merchant Taylors' school), B.A. 91; HONOURS :—1 law 91, Vinerian scholarship 92.
Leah, Ernest, born at Stockport, Cheshire, 4 Aug., 1870; 1s. George, arm. QUEEN'S, matric. 27 Jan., 90, aged 19, from Harpenden school and three years at a Cambridge school.
Lear, Herbert Nelson, born at Bishopstone, Wilts, Jan., 1862; 2s. Francis, archdeacon of Sarum. KEBLE, matric. 19 Oct., 80, aged 18 (from Winchester), B.A. 84.
Lear, James Percy, born at Cheltenham 1871; 2s. William, gen. NON-COLLEGIATE, matric. 17 Oct., 91, aged 20, from Wind coll., Powyke.
Leary, James Walter, born at St. Augustus in Africa, Feb., 1871; 5s. William, gen. KEBLE, matric. 11 Oct., 90, aged 19, from Hurstpierpoint coll.
Leather, Percival Charles du Sautoy, born at Cramond near Edinburgh, 28 March, 1867; 2s. Frederick John, J.P. Yorks, deceased. NEW COLL., matric. 23 Jan., 86, aged 18 (from Winchester), B.A. 89; HONOURS :—1 history 89.
Leathes, Carteret de Mussenden, born at Herringfleet, Suffolk, 19 Sept., 1869; 3s. Hill de Mussenden, arm. HERTFORD, matric. 19 Jan., 88, aged 18.
Leathes, John Herbert, born in London 5 Nov., 1864; 2s. Stanley, D.D., prof. Hebrew, K. coll., London. NEW COLL., matric. 10 Oct., 84, aged 19 (from Winchester), scholar 84, B.A. 90; HONOURS :—2 classical mods. 86, 2 classics 88.

Leathes, Thomas Denton Stanger, born in London 8 Feb., 1871; 1s. Leonard, solicitor. BRASENOSE, matric. 15 Oct., 90, aged 19 (from Sherborne school); HONOURS :—2 classical mods. 92.
Lecky, William Edward Hartpole, historian, created D.C.L. 20 June, 88; born near Dublin 26 March, 38; educated at Cheltenham coll., B.A. TRINITY COLL., Dublin, 59, M.A. 63, LL.D., and of St. Andrew's university, hon. D.Litt. Cambridge 16 June, 91. See *Men and Women of the Time*.
Le-Cornu, Charles Lambert Hillor, born at St. Peter's, Jersey, 2 Dec., 1865; o.s. Charles Philip, arm. MERTON, matric. 25 Jan., 84, aged 20, B.A. 89, M.A. 90.
Ledlie, James Crawford, born at Calcutta 29 April, 1860; o.s. Alexander Homer, gent. LINCOLN, matric. 29 April, 81, aged 21 (from the Johanneum, Hamburg, and Queen's coll., Belfast); scholar 81-5, B.A. 85, B.C.L. 87, M.A. 89 (HONOURS :—1 classical mods. 82, Taylorian exhibition Italian 82, Taylorian scholarship in German 83, 1 classics 84, 3 law 85, 2 civil law 86), bar.-at-law, Middle Temple, 90.
Ledsam, Edward Alfred Goddington Salt, born at Edgbaston 1870; 5s. Joseph, gen. NON-COLLEGIATE, matric. 11 Oct., 90, aged 20, from King Edward school, Birmingham.
Ledward, Robert Harold, born at Liverpool 1856; 3s. Charles Orit, gent. UNIVERSITY COLL., matric. 24 Jan., 84, aged 18, B.A. 87 (HONOURS :—4 law 87); died 15 Nov., 88.
Lee, Alexander Johnson, born at Hartlebury, co. Worc., 23 May, 1870; 3s. John Walter, cler. NON-COLLEGIATE, matric. 15 Oct., 87, aged 17 (from Westminster school), B.A. 90.
Lee, Charles Poole, born at Broseley, Salop, May, 1871; 3s. Henry, cler. KEBLE, matric. 11 Oct., 90, aged 19, from Stratford-on-Avon school; brother of Henry P.
Lee, Frank Herbert, born at Stepney, Middx., 1868; 2s. Richard, cler. KEBLE, matric. 17 Oct., 87, aged 19 (from St. Edward's school, Sumnertown), B.A 90; HONOURS :—3 history 90.
Lee, Frederick Reginald Benedict Duncan, born at Aberdeen 1862; 1s. Frederick George, cler. ST. EDMUND HALL, matric. 24 April, 84, aged 22, B.A. 87, M.A. 91.
Lee, rev. Godfrey Bolles, M.A., fellow NEW COLL. 36-61, where see page 211.
Lee, Harold Ernest, born at Chester 1 March, 1871; 1s. Charles, accountant. EXETER, matric. 13 Oct., 90, aged 19.
Lee, Hector Edward, born in London 1867; 6s. William, gent. ST. JOHN'S, matric. 17 Oct., 85, aged 18 (from Merchant Taylors' school), scholar 85, B.A. 89; HONOURS :—1 mathematical mods. 87, 3 physics 89.
Lee, Henry, born at Upper Clapton, Middx., 1 Feb., 1861; 1s. George gent. TRINITY, matric. 17 Jan., 80, aged 18 (from Haileybury), B.A. 82; HONOURS: —3 law 82.
Lee, Henry Kenneth, born at Christ Church, New Zealand, 9 July, 1871; 1s. Henry William, of Torquay, arm. NEW COLL., matric. 10 Oct., 90, aged 19, from Cheltenham coll.
Lee, rev. Henry Philips, born at Broseley, Salop, May, 1865; 1s. Henry, cler. KEBLE, matric. 16 Oct., 83, aged 18 (from Stratford-on-Avon), B.A. 89, M.A. 91; curate of Tettenhall Wood, co. Staff.; brother of Charles P. and of the next-named.
Lee, Herbert, born at Broseley, Salop, 1873; y.s. Henry, cler. KEBLE, matric. 14 Dec., 92, aged 19.
Lee, John, born at Roxburgh manse, Scotland, 1860; 3s. William, S.T.P. BALLIOL, matric. 21 Oct., 80, aged 20 (from Fettes coll. and Glasgow university), exhibitioner 80-5, B.A. 85; HONOURS: —2 classical mods. 82, 2 classics 84.

Lee, John Edwards Vaughan, born at Llanharan, co. Glamorgan, 27 Sept., 1863; 2s. Vaughan Hanning, of Dillington Park, Somerset, M.P. NEW COLL., matric. 15 Oct., 81, aged 18, from Harrow.

Lee, John Wollen, born at Broseley, Salop, 1867; 2s. Henry, cler. KEBLE, matric. 17 Jan., 87, aged 20, B.A. 89.

Lee, Lancelot John, M.A., fellow NEW COLL. 52-74, where see page 215.

Lee, rev. Percy Thomas, born at Brampton 1864; 8s. John, arm. HERTFORD, matric. 18 Oct., 82, aged 18, B.A. 85, M.A. 89; curate of Alston, Cumberland, 88.

Lee, Robert Warden, born at Hanmer, Flints, 1869; 3s. Matthew Henry, vicar. BALLIOL, matric. 19 Oct., 87, aged 18 (from Kossall school), scholar 86, B.A. 91 (HONOURS:—1 classical mods. 89, 1 classics 91), passed for eastern cadetship 91.

Lee, William Herbert, born in London 1865; 5s. William, arm. ST. JOHN'S, matric. 13 Oct., 83, aged 18 (from Merchant Taylors' school), scholar 83, B.A. 87 (HONOURS:—2 Indian languages 87); assist. commissioner Assam 86.

Leo, William Lauriston Melville, born at Bridport, Dorset, 8 Oct., 1865; 1s. Melville Lauriston, cler. MAGDALEN, matric. 16 Oct., 84, aged 19, from Wellington coll. and Forest school, Essex.

Lee, William Stevens, born in London 5 Oct., 1871; 3s. John Bennett Littlewood, gen. WADHAM, matric. 13 Oct., 90, aged 19 (from Dover coll.), exhibitioner 90 (HONOURS:—2 classical mods. 92); assumed the name of Lee in lieu of Littlewood.

Lee-Warner, James, M.A., fellow UNIVERSITY COLL. 66-72, where see page 33.

Leech, Samuel Chetwynd, born at Derby 13 Aug., 1872; 2s. Samuel, solicitor, deceased. NEW COLL., matric. 16 Oct., 91, aged 19, from the Charterhouse.

Leech, Stephen, born at Reddish, co. Lanc., 8 July, 1864; 2s. John, arm. MAGDALEN, matric. 19 Oct., 83, aged 19, from Eton.

Leech, William Henry Bragg, born at Timperley, Cheshire, 21 July, 1870; 2s. Peter, of Whitehaven, gen. NON-COLLEGIATE, matric. 6 Feb., 92, aged 21 (from Owens coll., Manchester, and London University, B.A.); migrated to QUEEN'S Oct., 92.

Leechman, Alleyne, born in Ceylon 16 April, 1869; 2s. William Carey, gen. CORPUS CHRISTI, matric. 20 Oct., 88, aged 19 (from St. Paul's school), scholar 87.

Leeder, Forrest Bertram, born at Swansea, co. Glam., 19 Jan., 1865; 3s. John Mack, gent. ST. MARY HALL, matric. 18 Oct., 82, aged 17.

Leeds, William Henry Arthur St. John, born at Rancoon 3 March, 1864; 2s. Henry, arm. NEW COLL., matric. 18 Oct., 83, aged 19 (from Cheltenham coll.); assist. commissioner Burma 85.

Leeman, William, born at Liverpool 2 Nov., 1868; 2s. Henry James. EXETER, matric. 18 Oct., 92, aged 23, from Liverpool Institute.

Lees, Edward, born at Great Bridge, Tipton, co. Stafford, 16 July, 1873; 1s. Edward, draper. EXETER, matric. 18 Oct., 92, aged 19, from Wolverhampton gr. school.

Lees, Kenneth Maxwell, born at Torquay, Devon, 15 Aug., 1872; 1s. Richard, gent. TRINITY, matric. 17 Oct., 91, aged 19, from Bristol school.

Lees, William Gilbert Hyde, born at Southport, co. Lanc., 21 Dec., 1865; 2s. Charles, gent. WADHAM, matric. 19 Oct., 85, aged 19, from Eton.

Leete, Henry Baird, born at Newton-le-Willows, co. Lanc., , 1865; 1s. Edward Stokes, gent. WORCESTER, matric. 18 Oct., 83, aged 18 (from Epsom coll.), exhibitioner 83, B.A. 87, M.A. 90; HONOURS:—2 classical mods. 85, 2 history 87;

Leetham, Arthur Richard, born at Margate, Kent, 18 March, 1864; 1s. William, gent. ST. MARY HALL, matric. 20 Oct., 83, aged 19 (from Thanet coll., Margate); migrated to QUEEN'S.

Le-Fanus, Henry Frewen, born at Dublin 1 April, 1870; 6s. William Richard, commissioner public works, Ireland. KEBLE, matric. 12 Oct., 89 (from Haileybury), B.A. 90; HONOURS:—2 history 92.

Lefroy, rev. Charles Edward Cottrell, born at Fremantle, Australia, Oct., 1862; 2s. Henry Maxwell, gent. KEBLE, matric. 18 Oct., 81, aged 18 (from Bradfield coll.), B.A. 86, M.A. 90 (HONOURS:—3 classical mods. 83, 3 classics 85); assist. master Dulwich coll. 89, and curate of St. Giles, Camberwell, 89.

Lefroy, Walter John Magrath, born in Guernsey April, 1870; 1s. Benjamin, of Littlehampton, capt. R.N. QUEEN'S, matric. 21 Oct., 87, aged 17, from R.N. coll., New Cross, and Giggleswick school.

Legard, D'Arcy, born at Stokesley, Yorks, 5 June, 1873; O.S. Francis Digby, rector, deceased. NEW COLL., matric. 16 Oct., 91, aged 18, from Winchester.

Legg, rev. Richard Wickham, born at West Farleigh, Kent, 29 July, 1867; 1s. William, rector of Hawkinge, Kent. NEW COLL., matric. 14 Oct., 87, aged 20 (from Harrow), B.A. 92; HONOURS:—2 classical mods. 89.

Legg, William Alexander Hannay, born in London 20 Aug., 1868; 1s. David, gen. NON-COLLEGIATE, matric. 12 Oct., 89, aged 21 (from University coll. school, London, and Mansfield coll., Oxford), B.A. 92.

Leggatt, Edward Owen Every, born at Chingleput, East Indies, 2 March, 1862; 1s. William Benjamin, C.E. LINCOLN, matric. 20 Oct., 81, aged 17 (from St. Paul's school), scholar 81-5, B.A. 85 (HONOURS:—3 law 85); joint magistrate N.W. provinces, India, 84.

Leggatt, Ernest Home, born at Ootacamund, East Indies, 23 May, 1870; 3s. William Benjamin, arm. KEBLE, matric. 12 Oct., 89, aged 19 (from St. Paul's school); assist. collector and magistrate Surat Bombay C.S. 91.

Legge, right rev. the hon. Augustus, M.A. CHRIST CHURCH, bishop of Lichfield 1891, D.D. by diploma 11 July, 91. See Al. Ox. and series, 834.

Legge, Hugh, born in London 27 April, 1870; y.s. hon. George Barrington, cler. TRINITY, matric. 12 Oct., 89, aged 19 (from Haileybury), in Oxford eight 93.

Legge, rev. James, M.A., professor of the Chinese language and literature 1876. See Corpus Christi page 387.

Legge, James Granville, born at Hong-Kong, Siam, 17 Aug., 1861; 1s. James, Chinese professor. QUEEN'S, matric. 15 May, 80, aged 18 (from city of London school), scholar 80-5, B.A. 84; HONOURS:—2 classical mods. 82, 2 classics 84.

Legge, Robert George, born at Leamington 3 Aug., 1864; 2s. hon. George Barrington, cler. KEBLE, matric. 16 Oct., 83, aged 19 (from Haileybury), B.A. 87; HONOURS:—2 history 88.

Legge, Thomas Morison, born at Hong-Kong, Siam, 6 Jan., 1863; 2s. James, Chinese professor. NON-COLLEGIATE, matric. 14 Oct., 82, aged 19 (from Magdalen coll. school); migrated to TRINITY 84, B.A. 86, M.A. and B.Med. 90; HONOURS:—2 physiology 86.

Legge, Walter Douglas, born at North Elmham, Norfolk, 31 Oct., 1865; 1s. Augustus George, vicar. CHRIST CHURCH, matric. 31 May, 84, aged 18, from the Charterhouse.

Legh, Edmund Willoughby, born at Leigh, Surrey, 1874; 1s. Henry Edmund, vicar. UNIVERSITY COLL., matric. 15 Oct., 92, aged 18, from Malvern coll.

Legh, John Arthur, born at Shrewsbury 13 July, 1864; y.s. Robert. arm. NEW INN HALL, matric. 3 May, 84, aged 19, from Shrewsbury gr. school.

Leigh, Arthur Henry Austen, B.D., fellow ST. JOHN'S 59-76, where see.

Leigh, Cholmeley Austen, M.A., fellow TRINITY 52-64, where see page 451.

Leigh, hon. Edward Chandos, M.A., fellow ALL SOULS' 55-71, where see page 260.

Leigh, Francis William, born in London 4 July, 1860; 1s. William, arm. NON-COLLEGIATE, matric. 18 Oct., 80, aged 19, from Oratory school, Birmingham.

Leigh, Henry Devenish, born at Southampton 21 Dec., 1863; 5s. Frederick, solicitor. NEW COLL., matric. 15 Oct., 81, aged 17 (from Oundle school), scholar 80-6, B.A. 85; fellow CORPUS CHRISTI 86, M.A. 88 (HONOURS:—1 classical mods. 83, accessit Hertford scholarship 83, 1 classics 85); student Lincoln's Inn 84.

Leigh, rev. John Rowland, born at Llanivono, co. Glam., 12 May, 1864; 1s. Daniel, cler. ORIEL, matric. 1 Nov., 81, aged 19 (from Marlborough coll.), B.A. 85, M.A. 88; curate of Gargrave, Yorks, 90.

Leigh, Richard Edward, born at Aberdare, co. Glam., Sept., 1867; 3s. Daniel, cler. BRASENOSE, matric. 20 Oct., 87, aged 20 (from Llandovery coll.), exhibitioner 87, B.A. 92; HONOURS:—2 classical mods. 89, 4 classics 91.

Leighton, Bryan Baldwin, born in London 26 Nov., 1868; 1s. Baldwin, bart. CHRIST CHURCH, matric. 13 Jan., 88, aged 19.

Leith, Walter Alexander, born in London 24 Sept., 1869; 1s. Walter, gen. BRASENOSE, matric. 23 April 88, aged 18, from Brighton coll.

Lely, Hugh Mountency, born at Norwich 1 March, 1869; 1s. William Grinfield Ostler, arm., afterwards Lely. UNIVERSITY COLL., matric. 15 Oct., 87, aged 18.

Le Maistre, rev. Alexander Philip, born at St. Brelads, Jersey, 21 Dec., 1860; 3s. George John, cler. LINCOLN, matric. 23 Oct., 80, aged 19 (from Brighton and Cheltenham colls.), B.A. 84, M.A. 87 (HONOURS:—3 theology 84); minor canon and sacristan, Peterborough, 91.

Le Maistre, rev. Sylvester John James Sullivan, born at Ingham, co. Lincoln, 1860; 2s. James. cler. KEBLE, matric. 22 Jan., 80, aged 20 (from York school), B.A. 83, M.A. 87 (HONOURS:—3 classical mods. 81, 3 theology 83); rector of Everingham, Yorks, 91.

Le Maistre, William de Villencufre, born in Jersey 24 Aug., 1863; 4s. George John, cler. KEBLE, matric. 16 Oct., 83, aged 20 (from Cheltenham and Brighton colls.), B.A. 87, M.A. 90; HONOURS:—3 classical mods. 85.

Le Maitre, Alfred George, born at Twickenham, Middx., 1866; 1s. Alfred William, gent. ST. JOHN'S, matric. 17 Oct., 85, aged 19 (from Merchant Taylors' school), exhibitioner 85, B.A. 89, M.A. 92; HONOURS:—3 classical mods. 87, 3 history 89.

Lemarchand, Frederick Payne, born in Ceylon 23 July, 1862; 1s. Francis Wharton, gent. MERTON, matric. 12 Nov., 80, aged 18 (from Malvern coll.), B.A. 86.

Le Marchant, William Gaspard, born in London 10 Nov., 1873; 3s. sir Henry Denis, bart. M.A. EXETER, matric. 18 Oct., 92, aged 18, from Eton.

Le-Mesurier, Havilland, born at Genoa, Italy, 22 June, 1866; 1s. Edward Algernon, arm. BALLIOL, matric. 17 Oct., 84, aged 18 (from Rugby); personal assistant to chief commissioner Assam, 86.

Le-Mesurier, John Cortlandt Williams, born In London April, 1869; 1s. John cler. CHRIST CHURCH, matric. 1 June, 88, aged 19 (from the Charterhouse), B.A. 93.

Le-Mesurier, John Henry, born at Guernsey 1863; 1s. John Henry, arm. JESUS COLL., matric. 19 Oct., 81, aged 18 (from Elizabeth coll. Guernsey), scholar 81-5, B.A. 86; HONOURS:—3 classical mods. 83, 3 classics 85.

Le-Mesurier, Sydney, born at Chatham, Kent, 29 June, or July, 1869; 2s. Frederick Augustus, LL.D. EXETER, matric. 17 Oct., 88, aged 19 (from St. Mark's school, Windsor), B.A. 92.

Lemon, Arthur Henry, born at Blackheath, Kent, 23 Aug., 1864; 3s. William George, bar.-at-law. EXETER, matric. 18 Oct., 83, aged 19 (from Merchant Taylors' school), scholar 83, B.A. 87; HONOURS:—2 classical mods. 85, 3 classics 87.

Lemonius, Basil Clare, born in Liverpool 9 July, 1868; 3s. Augustus Henry, arm. EXETER, matric. 19 Oct., 87, aged 18.

Lempriere, Charles, D.C.L., fellow ST. JOHN'S 37, where see.

Lempriere, Charles Cyril, born at Hull 19 April, 1870; 1s. Percy Reid, captain. WORCESTER, matric. 14 Oct., 89, aged 19 (from Radley coll.), exhibitioner 89; HONOURS:—2 classical mods. 91.

Lempriere, Lancelot Raoul, born at Leeds, Yorks, 30 Aug., 1872; 2s. Percy Reid, captain. WORCESTER, matric. 22 Oct., 91, aged 19, from Haileybury.

Lempriere, William, M.A., fellow EXETER 43-4, where see page 126.

Lennox, Charles Gordon, lord Settrington, born 30 Dec., 1870; 1s. Charles Henry Gordon, earl of March. CHRIST CHURCH, matric. 1 June, 88, aged 19, from Eton.

Lennox, hon. Charles Spencer Bateman Hanbury Kincaid, M.A., fellow ALL SOULS, 48-62, where see page 279.

Lennox, Cosmo Charles Gordon, born in London 17 Aug., 1868; o.s. lord Alexander Gordon, M.P. CHRIST CHURCH, matric. 14 Oct., 87, aged 19, from Woburn gr. school.

Lennox, lord Walter Charles Gordon, born 29 July, 1865; 4s. Charles Henry, duke of Richmond, CHRIST CHURCH, matric. 31 May, 84, aged 18 (from Eton); M.P. South West Somerset 88. See Foster's *Peerage*.

Lepard, Arthur George Campbell, born at Canterbury 1863; 1s. Samuel Campbell, cler. WORCESTER, matric. 19 Oct., 82, aged 19 B.A. 85, M.A. 89; HONOURS:—2 theology 86.

Leslie, Archibald Richard Stewart, born at Tunbridge Wells 7 Oct., 1873; 2s. lieut.-col. Archibald Young. TRINITY, matric. 17 Oct., 91, aged 18, from Inverness coll.

Leslie, Charles Frederick Henry, born in London 8 Dec., 1861; 3s. Henry David, arm. ORIEL, matric. 19 Oct., 80, aged 18 (from Rugby) in the University eleven 81, 2, 3.

Leslie, David, born in London 3 Nov., 1873; 1s. George Dunlop, artist. WADHAM, matric. 20 Oct., 91, aged 17, from Marlborough coll.

Leslie, rev. Edward Charles, born at Little Hothfield, Essex, 15 July, 1858; 1s. Thomas, arm. NONCOLLEGIATE, matric. 29 April, 81, aged 22 (from Wiesbaden and Bedford gr. schools), B.A. 84, M.A. 88 (HONOURS:—4 theology 84); curate of St. Paul, Wokingham, 88.

Lester, rev. George Mackenzie Lester, born at Swanage, Dorset, 7 Dec., 1861; 2s. Lester, cler. UNIVERSITY COLL., matric. 16 Oct., 80, aged 18 (from Sherborne school), B.A. 83, M.A. 90 (HONOURS:—3 history, 83); incumbent of Mutnibarra 85-9, and of Gayndah, (both) Queensland, 89-90, curate of St. Andrew, Bethnal Green, 90.

Lester, Henry Arthur, born at Birmingham 1869; 1s. Edward, engineer. NON-COLLEGIATE, matric. 15 Oct., 92, aged 23, from Bedford mod. school.

THE STATUE GALLERY.—By W. WESTALL

Lester, John Bingley Garland, born at Swanage, Dorset, 11 Feb., 1865; 3s. Lester, cler. UNIVERSITY COLL., matric. 11 Oct., 84, aged 19 (from Sherborne school), B.A. 90; HONOURS:—2 history 88.

Lester, Lester Vallis, M.A., fellow ST. JOHN'S 86-9, where see.

Lester, Percy Holland, born at Kirkdale, co. Lanc., 20 Jan., 1871; 2s. Edward, arm. EXETER, matric. 16 Oct., 89, aged 18 (from Great Crosby school), scholar 89; HONOURS:—2 mathematical mods. 91.

L'Estrange, Percival Hastings, born at Charlton, Kent, 27 July, 1871; 2s. Paget Walter, col. R.A., retired. QUEEN'S, matric. 24 Oct., 90, aged 19 (from Sedbergh school), exhibitioner 90; HONOURS: —2 classical mods. 92.

Le-Sueur, Peter, born at St. Heliers, Jersey, 1871; 1s. Peter, merchant. NEW COLL., matric. 15 March, 92, aged 21

Le-Sueur, rev. Reginald, born in Jersey 1868; 3s. Joshua, cler. ST. JOHN'S, matric. 16 Oct., 86, aged 18 (from Victoria coll., Jersey), B.A. 91; HONOURS:—2 theology 90.

Lethbridge, Edward Galton Haron, born at Lanenrth, Cornwall, 12 Aug., 1867; 1s. John. ST. JOHN'S, matric. 14 Jan., 87, aged 18, from the Charterhouse.

Lethbridge, Francis Washington, born at Wood Green, Middx., 3 Feb., 1867; 1s. sir Roper, knt., late M.P., etc. EXETER, matric. 28 Jan., 86, aged 18.

Lethbridge, William, born at Hornby, co. Lanc., 1864; o.s. Charles Henry, gent. BRASENOSE, matric. 19 Oct., 82, aged 18 (from Rossall school), B.A. 88, M.A. 89.

Letts, Harold Arthur, born at Sydenham, Kent, 28 June, 1861; 6s. Thomas, gent. MERTON, matric. 18 Oct., 81, aged 20 (from St. Edward's school, Summertown); postmaster 81, until his death 27 Aug., 84.

Leuchars, William Wood, born at Wandsworth, Surrey, 8 Nov., 1872; 1s. William, gent. NEW COLL., matric. 16 Oct., 92, aged 18, from St. Leonard's and Clifton colls.

Leudesdorf, Charles, M.A., fellow PEMBROKE 73, where see.

Lever, Albert Stuart, born in London 1 July, 1873; 2s. Charles Baldwin, lawyer, deceased. EXETER, matric. 18 Oct., 92, aged 19, from Haileybury coll.

Lever, Harrie Reginald, born in London 19 Nov., 1872; o.s. Richard Croft, surgeon major, army medical staff. NEW COLL., matric. 10 Oct., 90, aged 19 (from Harrow); HONOURS:—3 classical mods. 92.

Leverton, rev. Henry Lewis, born at Truro, Cornwall, 29 May, 1861; 2s. Henry Spry, arm. ST. MARY HALL, matric. 28 Jan., 80, aged 18 (from Sherborne school), scholar 80-1; migrated to ORIEL, 81, B.A. 84; curate of Wrawby, co. Linc., 89.

Levick, Lionel Tudway, born at Hunters Hill, N.S.W., 7 Dec., 1872; 4s. James Armstrong, merchant, deceased. PEMBROKE, matric. 26 Oct., 91, aged 18 (from Cheltenham coll.), scholar 91.

Levinge, Edward Vere, born at Cuttack, E. Indies, 24 May, 1867; 2s. Henry Corbyn, gent. BALLIOL, matric. 24 Oct., 85, aged 18 (from Cheltenham coll.), B.A. 88 (HONOURS:—2 law 88); assist. magistrate and collector Bengal 87.

Lewarne, rev. Nathaniel Nicholas, born at S. Columb, Cornwall, 22 June, 1858; 1s. Nicholas, gent. NON-COLLEGIATE, matric. 16 Oct., 86, aged 28 (from a Tregoney school); migrated to EXETER, B.A. 89 (HONOURS:—3 theology 89); curate of Christ Church, Plymouth, 89.

Lewes, Arthur Harold, born in London 25 Nov., 1869; 5s. John Tayer, of London, arm. CHRIST CHURCH, matric. 12 Oct., 88, aged 18 (from New Cross school), scholar 87; B.A. 92; HONOURS:— 2 mathematical mods. 90, 3 mathematics 92.

Lewin, Frederick Ellerker, born at Clapham, Surrey, 10 July, 1862; 4s. Thomas Ellerker, arm. CHRIST CHURCH, matric. 14 Oct., 81, aged 19 (from Westminster school), scholar 81, B.A. 85; HONOURS:— 3 classical mods. 83.

Lewis, Arthur Bowen Wolseley, born at Llanwrst, co. Denbigh, 23 Sept., 1866; 1s. Thomas Wolseley, cler. TRINITY, matric. 16 Oct., 86, aged 20 (from Cheltenham coll.), B.A. 90, M.A. 88 — 3 history 90.

Lewis, Arthur Edward, born at Wrexham, co. Denbigh, 17 May, 1861; 2s. John, arm. CHRIST CHURCH, matric. 24 Jan., 81, aged 19 (from Shrewsbury gr. school), B.A. 84.

Lewis, Arthur King, born in Isle of Ascension 21 Jan., 1867; 3s. James, gent. TRINITY, matric. 16 Oct., 86, aged 19 (from Christ's hospital), exhibitioner 85, scholar 86; HONOURS:—2 classical mods. 88, 3 classics 90.

Lewis, Charles Edward Llewellyn, born at Guilsfield, co. Montgomery, 6 May, 1865; 5s. David Phillips, cler. MERTON, matric. 16 Oct., 84, aged 19 (from Brecon coll.); migrated to TURRELL'S HALL, B.A. 89; HONOURS:—3 classical mods. 86.

Lewis, Charles Frank, born at Aston near New York, 1 June, 1869; o.s. Robert Wardell, cler. EXETER, matric. 17 Oct., 88, aged 19, from a Lyme Regis school.

Lewis, David Lancelot Peter, born at Bayswater, Middx., 8 March, 1868; 1s. David Jones, of Llwynoelyn, co. Carmarthen, arm. CHRIST CHURCH, matric. 3 June, 87, aged 19 (from Westminster school), B.A. 91.

Lewis, rev. David, M.A., fellow JESUS COLL. 39-46, where see.

Lewis, Edward Pilcher, born at Exeter 1864; 2s. Charles, arm. NON-COLLEGIATE, matric. 15 April, 82, aged 18 (from Clifton coll.); migrated to EXETER 21 Oct., 82, B.A. 87, M.A. 90.

Lewis, Francis Samuel, born at Corsham, Wilts, 6 Feb., 1858; 1s. Samuel, gent. NON-COLLEGIATE, matric. 15 Oct., 81, aged 30 (from London university); migrated to QUEEN'S, B.A. 84, M.A. 86; some time assist. Bodleian; librarian at the Cape.

Lewis, Frank Ball, born in London 18 May, 1863; 1s. Francis Theodore, gent. QUEEN'S, matric. 28 Oct., 81, aged 18 (from Merchant Taylors' school), B.A. 84; HONOURS:—3 law 84.

Lewis, Frank Warburton, born at Broseley, Salop, 11 Jan., 1871; 3s. George W., of Handsworth, gen. NON-COLLEGIATE, matric. 17 Jan., 91, aged 22, from University of London, B.A. 90.

Lewis, rev. George, born at Monmouth 25 Feb., 1848; 1s. George, gent. BALLIOL, matric. 18 Oct., 81, aged 33 (from Monmouth school, and B.A. 69, and M.A. 79, university Lond.), B.A. 84, M.A. 88 (HONOURS:—2 classical mods. 82, 1 theology 84), served various curacies 72-88, vicar of Dodderhill, co. Worcester, 88.

Lewis, George Harold, born at Ripon, Yorks, 1862; 2s. Walter Sunderland, cler. CORPUS CHRISTI, matric. 27 Oct., 81, aged 19 (from Brighton coll.), B.A. 86; HONOURS:—Abbott scholarship 81; 2 classical mods. 83, 2 classics 85.

Lewis, George James, born in London 1868; o.s. George Henry, arm. BALLIOL, matric. 19 Oct., 87, aged 19, from Harrow.

Lewis, Gwilym, born at Llanfihangel Esgeifiog, isle of Anglesey, 21 Nov., 1871; 1s. William, cler. JESUS COLL., matric. 15 Oct., 90, aged 18, from Beaumaris gr. school.

Lewis, Herbert Theodore, born at Bristol 1864; 3t. George, arm. CHRIST CHURCH, matric. 17 Feb., 83, aged 19. B.Mus. 86.

Lewis, Hugh Mitchell, born in London 1867; 3t. Robert Benjamin, gent. UNIVERSITY COLL., matric. 18 Oct., 86, aged 19 (from Marlborough), scholar 86, B.A. 92; HONOURS:—2 mathematical mods. 87, 2 mathematics 90.

Lewis, John Guy Robert, born at Paddington 1869; 1s. John French, gent. PEMBROKE, matric. 17 Oct., 88, aged 19 (from Birmingham school), scholar 88, B.A. 92; HONOURS:—2 classical mods. 90, 2 classics 92.

Lewis, rev. John Herbert Wightman, born at Shrewsbury 1862; 2s. John, cler. WORCESTER, matric. 19 Oct., 82, aged 20, B.A. 85, M.A. 89; curate of High Ongar, Essex, 90.

Lewis, John Howard, born at Llandilo, co. Carmarthen, 1865; 2s. David, gent. NON-COLLEGIATE, matric. 28 Jan., 84, aged 19 (from Llandovery coll.), B.A. 87; HONOURS:—3 theology 87.

Lewis, John Wilfred, born at Briton Ferry, co. Glamorgan, 16 April, 1873; 2s. David, M.A., cler. JESUS COLL., matric. 18 Oct., 92, aged 19.

Lewis, Lewis Elwyn, born at Mersham, Kent, 1858; 1s. Lewis Woodward, cler. NON-COLLEGIATE, matric. 20 Nov., 80, aged 22.

Lewis, Reginald Heathcote Somers-, born in London 18 Aug., 1873; 1s. Reginald, solicitor. UNIVERSITY COLL., matric. 17 Oct., 91, aged 18, from the Charterhouse.

Lewis, Richard Percy, born in London 10 March, 1874; 1s. Richard, bar.-at-law, deceased. UNIVERSITY COLL., matric. 15 Oct., 92, aged 18, from Winchester.

Lewis, Thomas John, born at Grenville, Bucks, 28 Jan., 1870; 1s. John, gent. JESUS COLL., matric. 15 Oct., 90, aged 20 (from Llandovery coll), exhibitioner 90.

Lewis, William, born at Leesfield, co. Lanc., 30 Dec., 1864; 2s. Thomas, of Oldham, gent. NON-COLLEGIATE, matric. 14 Jan., 88, aged 23, B.A. 92.

Lewis, William Augustus, born at Henllan, co. Denbigh, 14 April, 1865; 1s. William, schoolmaster. JESUS COLL., matric. 23 Oct., 85, aged 20 (from Ruthin gr. school), B.A. 88.

Lewis, William Henry, born at Oystermouth, co. Glam., 17 May, 1869; 1s. William George, supdt. of customs. JESUS COLL., matric. 15 Oct., 90, aged 21 (from University coll., Aberystwith), scholar 90.

Lewis, William James, M.A., fellow ORIEL 69, where see page 149.

Lewthwaite, George, born in Cumberland Dec., 1868; 3s. George, arm. KEBLE, matric. 17 Oct., 87, aged 18 (from Giggleswick gr. school), B.A. 90.

Ley, Edward Charles Hay, born in London 1869; o.s. Edward, gen. PEMBROKE, matric. 26 Oct., 91, aged 22.

Ley, Jacob, born at "Algoninc" in Canada 3 Dec., 1863; o.s. George, gent. CHRIST CHURCH, matric. 12 Jan., 83, aged 19, from Tonbridge school.

Liberty, Stephen, born in London 26 Nov., 1871; 1s. Nathaniel, cler. CHRIST CHURCH, matric. 10 Oct., 90, aged 18 (from Westminster school), exhibitioner 90; HONOURS:—2 classical mods. 92.

Liddell, Charles Lyon, born in London 1861; o.s. Charles, arm. CHRIST CHURCH, matric. 15 Oct., 80, aged 19 (from the Charterhouse), B.A. 85; HONOURS:—4 history 84.

Liddell, Frederick Francis, born 7 June, 1865; 2s. Henry George, D.D. and dean of Christ Church, Oxford. CHRIST CHURCH, matric. 31 May, 84, aged 18 (from Eton), scholar 88, B.A. 88, fellow ALL SOULS' 91, M.A. 92; HONOURS:—2 classical mods. 86, 2 mathematical mods. 86, 1 classics 88, Eldon scholarship 92.

Liddell, George William, born at Sutton, Yorks, 29 Jan., 1867; o.s. George William Moore, arm., deceased. MAGDALEN, matric. 26 Jan., 86, aged 18 (from Eton); died 17 Nov., 88, at Oxford.

Liddell, very rev. Henry George, D.D., dean of CHRIST CHURCH 1855-91, where see page 404.

Liddell, Lionel Charles, born 22 May, 1868; 3t. Henry George, D.D., dean of Christ Church, Oxford. CHRIST CHURCH, matric. 15 Oct., 86, aged 18 (from Winchester), B.A. 90.

Lidderdale, Edward Wadsworth, born in London 30 April, 1869; 1s. William, governor of Bank of England, P.C. NEW COLL., matric. 12 Oct., 88, aged 19 (from Winchester), B.A. 91; HONOURS:—2 history 91.

Liddon, Edward Parry, born at Taunton Dec., 1871; 1s. Edward, D.Med. CHRIST CHURCH, matric. 16 Oct., 91, aged 19, from Winchester.

Le Lievre, Frederick William Stamp, born at St. Peter Port, Guernsey, 1863; o.s. Frederick, gent. PEMBROKE, matric. 4 Feb., 81, æg.d 18 (from Elizabeth coll., Guernsey), scholar 81-3, B.A. 85, M.A. 87; HONOURS:—3 classical mods. 82.

Ligertwood, Thomas George, born at Aberdeen Nov., 1870; 2s. John, gen. KEBLE, matric. 11 Oct., 90, aged 19 (from Ripon gr. school); HONOURS:—3 classical mods. 92.

Lightfoot, Henry Le Blanc, M.A., bursar CORPUS CHRISTI 92, where see page 387.

Lightfoot, rev. John Alfred, born at Maryport, Cumberland, 1861; 1s. George, gent. NON-COLLEGIATE, matric. 18 Oct., 80, aged 19 (from Merchant Taylors' school); migrated to HERTFORD, B.A. 83, M.A. 87 (HONOURS:—3 theology 83); tutor and assist. chaplain, London college of divinity 85; afternoon lecturer Christ Church, Highbury, London, 86.

Lightfoot, Thomas William(s), born at Valetta, Malta, 1866; 2s. Thomas, arm. NON-COLLEGIATE, matric. 4 Nov., 84, aged 18 (from Doncaster gr. school); lieut. south Wales borderers 90, wing officer 8th Bengal N.I. 92.

Lillingston, rev. Septimus Ernest Luke (Spooner), born at Edgbaston, co. Warwick, 1863; 7s. Edward, cler. CHARSLEY HALL, matric. 15 Oct., 81, aged 18; migrated to HERTFORD 84, B.A. 86, B.Mus. 86, M.A. 89; curate of Paignton, Devon, 89-91.

Lillingston, Walter Percy, pleb. (1s.), born at Oxford 1864. NON-COLLEGIATE, matric. 18 April, 91, aged 27.

Lillingstone, Cecil George Campbell, born at Yass in New South Wales, Australia, 28 July, 1871; 4s. Frederick Arthur Cecil, vicar of St. James, Clapham, HERTFORD, matric. 30 Jan., 91, aged 19 (from Merchant Taylors' school and the Charterhouse), exhibitioner 90.

Lindeman, Alfred Sanderson, born in London 4 May, 1864; 6s. Sidney Alfred, gent. ST. MARY HALL, matric. 12 Oct., 87, exhibitioner 81-5, B.A. 86, M.A. 92.

Linden, Edmund count von, born at Nurnberg in Bavaria, 1864; 1s. count Henry. CHARSLEY HALL, matric. 30 Oct., 80, aged 18.

Lindesay, Robert Thomas Mauleverer, born at Loughry, co. Tyrone, 9 May, 1870; 4s. Frederic, arm. TRINITY, matric. 13 Oct., 88, aged 18, from Manchester school.

Lindley, Francis Oswald, born in London 12 June, 1872; 4t. sir Nathaniel, lord justice of appeal. MAGDALEN, matric. 14 Oct., 90, aged 18, from Winchester.

Lindley, Lennox Henry, born in London 14 May, 1868; 3t. sir Nathaniel, lord justice of appeal. MAGDALEN, matric. 21 Oct., 86, aged 18 (from Winchester), B.A. 90.

Lindley, Walter Barry, born in London 31 Dec., 1861; 2s. sir Nathaniel, UNIVERSITY COLL., matric. 16 Oct., 80, aged 18 (from Winchester), B.A. 83, M.A. 87 (HONOURS:—2 history 83); bar.-at-law, Lincoln's Inn, 87.

Lindley, Walter Delmar, born at Mansfield, Notts, 24 Jan., 1864; 5s. Robert Charles, of Culverthorpe, co. Linc., gent. MAGDALEN, matric. 19 Oct., 83, aged 19 (from Eton), B.A. 86, M.A. 90.

Lindo, Frank Charles, born at Paddington 1872; o.s. Charles, arm. ORIEL, matric. 22 Oct., 90, aged 18, from Clifton coll.

Lindow, Isaac William Burns, born at Cleator, Cumberland, June, 1868; 1s. James Lindow, arm. CHRIST CHURCH, matric. 13 Jan., 88, aged 19, from St. Leonard's school.

Lindow, Samuel Lindow Burns, born at Cleator, Cumberland, Oct., 1869; 2s. James Lindow, arm. BALLIOL, matric. 18 Oct., 88, aged 19 (from Harrow); migrated to BRASENOSE, B.A. 91.

Lindsay, David Alexander Edward, lord Balcarres, born at Dunecht House, Aberdeen, 10 Oct., 1871; s. James Ludovick, earl of Crawford and Balcarres. MAGDALEN, matric. 14 Oct., 90, aged 19 (from Eton), treasurer Oxford union society 93.

Lindsay, George Campbell, born at Edinburgh 3 Jan., 1863; 2s. Thomas Sturn, underwriter at Lloyds. WADHAM, matric. 17 Oct., 82, aged 19, from Loretto school.

Lindsay, Patrick Charles Nugent, born at North Shields, Northumberland, 1872; 3s. Henry, collector of customs. PEMBROKE, matric. 26 Oct., 91, aged 19, from King's coll. school, London.

Lindsay, Wallace Martin, M.A., fellow JESUS COLL. 82, where see.

Lindsell, rev. Henry Bayly, born at Holme, Beds, 15 Nov., 1862; 4s. Charles Samuel, arm. TRINITY, matric. 15 Oct., 81, aged 18 (from Harrow), B.A. 85 (HONOURS:—2 classical mods. 83, 1 theology 85, Denyer and Johnson theological scholarship 88); curate at Birmingham 85-6, and at Arreton, I.W., 86-7; died 20 May, 90.

Linford, Arthur Howard, born in London 17 Sept., 1861; 2s. William Thomas, actuary. MAGDALEN, matric. 16 Oct., 80, aged 19 (from Q. Elizabeth gr. school, Cranbrook), B.A. 86 (HONOURS:—4 history 84); student Inner Temple 84.

Lingard, Frank Charlton, born at Manchester 1862; 2s. John Rowson, solicitor, deceased. EXETER, matric. 22 Oct., 80, aged 18, from Brighton coll.

Lingen, sir Ralph Robert Wheeler baron Lingen, K.C.B., M.A., created D.C.I. 22 June 81; (see *Al. Ox.* and series, 854); hon. fellow TRINITY 86, where see.

Linnell, William, born at Ashton, Northants, Aug., 1869; 1s. William, gen. KEBLE, matric. 13 Oct., 88, aged 19 (from Guilsborough gr. school), B.A. 93; HONOURS:—2 classical mods. 90, 3 classics 92.

Linsley, William Hessell, born at Sydney 1861; o.s. John Richard, gen. BALLIOL, matric. 18 Oct., 81, aged 20 (from Sydney university); B.A. 85, M.A. 91 (HONOURS:—3 classical mods. 83, 4 classics 85); bar.-at-law, Inner Temple, 87.

Linton, Sydney, bishop of Riverina, created D.D. 4 March, 1884. See *Al. Ox.* and series, 854.

Linzee, Charles Arthur, born at Jermyns, near Romsey, 1862; y.s. Robert George, arm. CHRIST CHURCH, matric. 15 Oct., 80, aged 18.

Lipscomb, Charles Burton, born at Temple Ewell, Kent, 1864; 1s. Charles Henry, rector, WORCESTER, matric. 18 Jan., 83, aged 19; migrated to ST. MARY HALL, B.A. 92.

Lipscombe, Maurice John, born at Canterbury 27 Oct., 1869; 2s. John Streatfeild, arm, deceased. MAGDALEN, matric. 23 Oct., 85, aged 18 (from the Charterhouse), B.A. 89.

Lipsett, Henry Caldwell, born at Dominica, West Indies, 15 Nov., 1868; 2s. Henry Caldwell, gen. LINCOLN, matric. 18 Oct., 88, aged 19 (from Christ's hospital), scholar 88, B.A. 92; HONOURS:—2 classical mods. 90, 3 classics 92.

Lister, Alfred James, born at North Shields, Northumberland, 1871; 1s. James Maxfield, cler. PEMBROKE, matric. 25 Oct., 90, aged 19.

Lister, Edward, born at Sheffield 15 July, 1871; 3s. George, gen., deceased. WADHAM, matric. 14 Oct., 89, aged 18 (from Sheffield gr. school), scholar 88; HONOURS:—1 classical mods. 91.

Lister, James, born at Seaforth, co. Lanc., 1863; 1s. James, gent. UNIVERSITY COLL., matric. 13 Oct., 83, aged 20; migrated to CHARSLEY HALL, B.A. 88.

Little, Andrew George, born at Marsh Gibbon, Bucks, 1863; 2s. Thomas, cler. BALLIOL, matric. 17 Oct., 82, aged 19 (from Clifton coll.), B.A. 87, M.A. 89; HONOURS:—2 classical mods. 83, 1 history 86.

Little, Arthur Henry Alban Knox, born at Sherborne, Dorset, 17 June, 1867; 1s. William John K.-L., canon of Worcester. CHRIST CHURCH, matric. 14 Jan., 87, aged 19, from Winchester.

Little, Bryan Padgett Gregson, born at Stewartstown, co. Tyrone, 2 March, 1862; 1s. Samuel, gent. ST. EDMUND HALL, matric. 16 Jan., 83, aged 20; died 8 Sept., 87.

Little, Charles William, born at Tonbridge, Kent, 22 May, 1870; 3s. Joseph Russell, cler. and assist. master Tonbridge school. NEW COLL., matric. 11 Oct., 89, aged 19 (from Winchester), scholar 88; HONOURS:—2 classical mods. 91.

Little, James, born at Dublin 4 Aug., 1872; 1s. James, D.Med. NEW COLL., matric. 18 Oct., 90, aged 18 (from Radley coll.); HONOURS:—3 classical mods. 92.

Little, John David George, born at Blackrock, co. Dublin, 24 Feb., 1868; o.s. Henry Alexander, arm. MERTON, matric. 21 Oct., 86, aged 18 (from Eton); HONOURS:—3 classics 90.

Little, John Francis Gore, born at Tullaghan, co. Sligo, 8 Jan., 1870; 1s. Francis Gore, major, late B.A., and chief constable of Preston. TRINITY, matric. 11 Oct., 90, aged 18 (from Magdalen coll. school); exhibitioner EXETER 91; HONOURS 1—2 classical mods. 92.

Little, William, M.A., fellow CORPUS CHRISTI 71, where see page 379.

Littlebury, Walter Sydney Herbert, born at Worcester 1869; 3s. Joseph, gen. NON-COLLEGIATE, matric. 13 Oct., 88, aged 19 (from Worcester cathedral school), B.A. 91; HONOURS: —2 theology 91.

Littledale, John Bolton, born at Weaverham, Cheshire, June, 1868; 2s. John Bolton, arm. CHRIST CHURCH, matric. 13 Jan., 88, aged 19 (from Eton), B.A. 92.

Littledale, Thomas Bolton, born at Weaverham, Cheshire, Sept., 1869; 3s. John Bolton, arm. CHRIST CHURCH, matric. 18 Oct., 88, aged 19, from Eton.

Littlehales, Alfred Morgan, born at Wimbledon, Surrey, 1870; 4s. Frederick, arm. CHRIST CHURCH, matric. 1 June, 88, aged 18.

Littlehales, Charles Gough, born at Bulvan, Essex, 20 May, 1871; 1s. Walter Gough, rector 70. EXETER, matric. 16 Oct., 89, aged 18, from Forest school, Walthamstow.

Littlewood, Alfred Sydney, born at Turnsworth, Dorset, 8 Feb., 1867; o.s. Alfred Samuel, cler. UNIVERSITY COLL., matric. 18 Oct., 86, aged 19 (from Sherborne school), scholar 86, B.A. 90; HONOURS:—1 classical mods. 88, 2 classics 90.

Littlewood, Reginald Basil, born at Stoke Newington 14 May, 1871; 2s. Arthur, gent. WADHAM, matric. 13 Oct., 90, aged 19 (from Merchant Taylors' school), exhibitioner 85; HONOURS:—2 classical mods. 92.

Littlewood, Thomas Henry, born at Hipperholme, Yorks, 4 July, 1862; 2s. William Edensor, cler. CORPUS CHRISTI, matric. 27 Oct., 81, aged 19 (from Clifton coll.), exhibitioner 81-2, scholar 82-6, B.A. 86, M.A. 90; HONOURS:—1 mathematical mods. 82, 2 classical mods. 83, 1 mathematics 85, 1 physics 86.

Litton, Edward Arthur, M.A., fellow ORIEL 36-44, where see page 152.

Litton, George John Letablere, born at Dublin 1867; o.s. John Letablere, arm. ORIEL, matric. 14 Dec., 85, aged 18 (from Eton), B.A. 90; (HONOURS: —1 history 88, 1 law 89), passed and for eastern cadetship 91.

Liversidge, Howard Willmott, born at Dalston, Middx., 1869; 1s. William Henry, gen. HERTFORD, matric. 26 Oct., 88, aged 19 (from St. John-at-Hackney gr. school), B.A. 92 (HONOURS:— 1 history 92); librarian Oxford union society 92.

Livesey, rev. Harold, born at Knotty Ash, co. Lanc., 1866; 2s. Thomas, gent. NON-COLLEGIATE, matric. 17 Oct., 85, aged 19 (from Hereford school), B.A. 88, M.A. 92; curate of St. John, Cubitt town, London, 89.

Livesey, John Cort, born at Worthen, Salop, 29 Jan., 1864; 1s. Thomas Alexander, cler. WORCESTER, matric. 25 Jan., 84, aged 19 (from Owens coll., Manchester), B.A. 87, M.A. 90; HONOURS:—3 theology 87.

Livesey, William Baldwin, born at Stafford 1861; 1s. William Harrison, gent. NON-COLLEGIATE, matric. 18 Oct., 80, aged 19, from St. Edward's school, Summertown, and St. Paul's coll., Stony Stratford.

Livingstone, Arthur Claude, born at Birkenhead, Cheshire, 1873; 3s. George Ramsay, gent. ORIEL, matric. 27 Oct., 92, aged 19, from Shrewsbury school.

Livingstone, George Frederick James Fenton, born at Edinburgh 1869; 3s. Thomas Livingstone, arm. MERTON, matric. 18 Oct., 80, aged 20.

Livingstone, James Eld Brancker, born at Claughton, Cheshire, July, 1871; 2s. George Ramsay, arm. ORIEL, matric. 22 Oct., 90, aged 19, from Shrewsbury gr. school.

Livingstone, rev. Robert George, M.A. fellow PEMBROKE 66, where see.

Livingstone, rev. William Ramsay, born at Birkenhead 11 June, 1868; 1s. George Ramsay, arm. ORIEL, matric. 18 Oct., 87, aged 19 (from Rugby), B.A. 90; curate of St. Paul's, Sculcoates, Hull, 93.

Llewellin, Thomas Johnes, born at Abercarn, co. Monmouth, 10 July, 1862; 2s. William, arm. UNIVERSITY COLL., matric. 26 Jan., 81, aged 18 (from Cheltenham coll.), B.A. 84; HONOURS:—3 classical mods. 82, 3 law 84.

Llewellyn, Charles Leysham Dillwyn, born at Cadoxton, co. Glam., 29 June, 1870; 2s. John Talbot Dillwyn, bart. NEW COLL., matric. 11 Oct., 89, aged 19, from Eton.

Llewellyn, John Connop Thirlwall, born at Clifton, co. Glouc., 26 March, 1868; 1s. John Griffith, gen. WADHAM, matric. 19 Jan., 89, aged 20, from Repton school.

Llewelyn, William Dillwyn, born at Ynisygerwn, co. Glam., 1 April, 1868; 1s. John Talbot Dillwyn, bart. NEW COLL., matric. 14 Oct., 87, aged 19 (from Eton), B.A. 91; HONOURS:—4 law 91, in Oxford eleven 90-1.

Lloyd, rev. Arthur Gittins, born at Newbridge, co. Denbigh, 28 Jan., 1865; 4s. John, gent. QUEEN'S, matric. 22 Oct., 83, aged 18 (from Bromsgrove collegiate school), B.A. 86, M.A. 90; curate of Edgbaston 91.

Lloyd, Charles Harford, M.A., D.Mus., CHRIST CHURCH, where see page 426.

Lloyd, right rev. Daniel Lewis, M.A. JESUS COLL., bishop of Bangor 1890, D.D. by diploma 27 May, 90. See Al. Ox. and series, 860.

Lloyd, David, born at Tynllyn, co. Cardigan, 1861; 4s. James, gent. KEBLE, matric. 17 Oct., 82, aged 21 (from Lampeter coll.); HONOURS:— 3 classical mods. 82, 3 classics 84.

Lloyd, Ernest Sampson, born at Wednesbury, co. Staff., 26 May, 1870; 2s. Sampson Zachary, gen. LINCOLN, matric. 17 Oct., 89, aged 19 (from Clifton coll.), scholar 89, B.A. 92; HONOURS:— 1 history 92.

Lloyd, rev. George Frederick, born at Ludlow, Salop, 1866; 1s. John Charles, gent. CHRIST CHURCH, matric. 16 Oct., 85, aged 19 (from Shrewsbury school), exhibitioner 85, B.A. 89, M.A. 92 (HONOURS: —3 theology 89); curate of Dursley, co. Gloucester, 90.

Lloyd, Henry Frederic, born at Exeter 1860; 1s. Horace Charles, arm. ORIEL, matric. 16 April, 80, aged 20.

Lloyd, Howard Lloyd, burn at King's Heath near Birmingham, 27 Sept., 1868; 1s. Howard, arm. UNIVERSITY COLL., matric. 15 Oct., 87, aged 19, B.A. 91; HONOURS:—3 history 91.

Lloyd, John Barclay, born in London 29 June, 1864; 1s. Frederick Giesler, arm. MAGDALEN, matric. 19 Oct., 83, aged 19 (from Highgate school), exhibitioner 84, B.A. 87; HONOURS:—2 classical mods. 84, 2 classics 87.

Lloyd, John Edward, born in Liverpool 5 May, 1861; 1s. Edward, arm. LINCOLN, matric. 20 Oct., 81, aged 20 (from Chatham institute Liverpool, and University coll. Aberystwith), B.A. 86, M.A. 88; HONOURS:—1 classical mods. 83, 1 history 85.

Lloyd, Llewelyn Foster, born at Prestwich, co. Lanc., 1862; 2s. col. Lloyd, of Thornhill, West Cowes, I.W. CHRIST CHURCH, matric. 24 Jan., 81, aged 19.

Lloyd, Oswald, born at Rand, co. Lincoln, 1863; 3s. Charles Albert, rector. NON-COLLEGIATE, matric. 18 Oct., 83, aged 20, B.A. 86; HONOURS: —3 history 86.

Lloyd, Percy Robert, born at Walthamstow, Essex, 1868; 10s. Edward, gen. PEMBROKE, matric. 25 Oct., 87, aged 19 (from Eastbourne coll.), B.A. 91.

Lloyd, Richard Morgan, born at Llanrhystid, co. Cardigan, 1861; o.s. John, cler. JESUS COLL., matric. 10 Jan., 80, aged 19.

Lloyd, Theodore Howard, born at Bletchingley, Surrey, 2 Oct., 1872; 1s. Alfred Howard, gen. CHRIST CHURCH, matric. 29 May, 91, aged 18, from Eton.

Lloyd, Thomas Owen, born at Olton Hall, co. Warwick, 16 June, 1873; 1s. Sampson Samuel, B.A., Cambridge, and of the Priory, Warwick, J.P. BRASENOSE, matric. 21 Oct., 92, aged 19, from Eton.

Lloyd, Walter Edwin, born at Newport, co. Monmouth, July, 1869; 2s. John Lewis, gen. CHRIST CHURCH, matric. 1 June, 88, aged 18 (from Sherborne school), B.A. 91; HONOURS :—3 chemistry 91.

Lloyd, William, born at Sysyllt, co. Cardigan, 1862; 2s. John, gent. NON-COLLEGIATE, matric. 19 Jan., 85, aged 23, from Ystradmeurig gr. school, and University coll. Aberystwith.

Lloyd, rev. William Stowe, born at West Smethwick, co. Stafford, 23 Aug., 1866; 2s. Thomas, gent. NON-COLLEGIATE, matric. 16 Oct., 86, aged 20; migrated to WORCESTER, B.A. 89 (HONOURS :—3 theology 89); curate of St. Columba, Southwick, Sunderland, 91.

Lloyd, William Wellesley Gordon, born at Beaumaris 1868; 1s. Evan Garnons, arm. ST. JOHN'S, matric. 13 Oct., 88, aged 20 (from Harrow), B.A. 93.

Lock, Ernest Seppings Cardew, born at Headington, Oxon, 8 Sept., 1871; 3s. Edward Seppings, gen. NON-COLLEGIATE, matric. 11 Oct., 90, aged 19, from King's coll. Taunton.

Lock, rev. George Rideal, born at Fareham, Hants, 1850; o.s. George, gent. WORCESTER, matric. 27 Jan., 81, aged 31, B.A. 84, M.A. 87; curate of Hawkhurst, Kent, 88.

Lock, Walter, M.A., fellow MAGDALEN 69, where see page 312, and sub-warden KEBLE 81, where see also.

Locke, Albert Walter, born at Neuilly, near Paris, 1869; 3s. George, gen. BRASENOSE, matric. 24 Jan., 89, aged 20, from Dover coll.

Locke, Alexander George, arm. (3s.), born at Teignmouth, Devon, 23 Aug, 1862. CHRIST CHURCH, matric. 15 Oct., 80, aged 18 (from Eton), B.A. 90.

Locker, William Algernon, born in London 31 Dec., 1863; y.s. Arthur, arm. MERTON, matric. 17 Oct., 82, aged 18 (from the Charterhouse), B.A. 86; HONOURS :—3 history 85.

Locker, William Jervis, born at Aston Stoney, co. Stafford, 1874; 2s. William Thomas, J.P. ORIEL, matric. 27 Oct., 92, aged 18, from Repton school.

Lockett, Harry Duncan, born at Mount Ward, co. Cornwall, Jamaica, 22 Nov., 1873; 4s. George, Wesleyan methodist. MERTON, matric. 18 Oct., 92, aged 18, from High school, Jamaica.

Lockhart, Alexander Francis Maxwell, B.A., fellow HERTFORD 78-89, where see.

Lockhart, James Somerville, M.A., fellow HERTFORD 75, where see.

Locock, Charles Dealtry, born at Brighton 27 Sept., 1862; 1s. Alfred Henry, cler. UNIVERSITY COLL., matric. 15 Oct., 81, aged 19 (from Winchester), B.A. 86; HONOURS :—2 classical mods. 83, 3 classics 85. See Foster's *Baronetage*.

Locock, Henry Thornton, born at Brighton 26 April, 1864; 2s. Alfred Henry, cler. TRINITY, matric. 15 Oct., 83, aged 19 (from Winchester), B.A. 87; HONOURS :—2 classical mods. 84.

Lodge, Frederick, born at Queenborough, Tasmania, 20 Nov., 1862; 2s. Lorenzo, accountant, deceased. NEW COLL., matric. 14 Oct., 82, aged 19 (from Hobart high school), B.A. 85 (HONOURS :—3classical mods. 83, 3 classics 85); bar.-at-law, Inner Temple, 87.

Lodge, Richard, M.A., fellow BRASENOSE 78, where see page 349.

Lofthouse, Benjamin, born at Tadcaster, Yorks, 1868; 5s. Thomas, gen. QUEEN'S, matric. 16 March, 92, aged 24.

Lofthouse, William Frederick, born at Norwood, Surrey, 6 Sept., 1871; o.s. William Beet, arm. TRINITY, matric. 11 Oct., 90, aged 19 (from city of London school), scholar 89; HONOURS :— Greek verse 91, 1 classical mods. 92

Logan, Balfour, born at Hoylake, Cheshire, 3 Oct., 1868; 2s. Edward, arm. TRINITY, matric. 15 Oct., 87, aged 19 (from Radley coll.), B.A. 92; lieut. the Devonshire regt. 91.

Logan, Ewen Reginald, born in London 30 Dec., 1869; 2s. Francis, bar.-at-law. EXETER, matric. 17 Oct., 88, aged 19, from the Charterhouse.

Lomax, Cyril, born at Marton, Cheshire, 8 June 1871; 3s. John, cler. KEBLE, matric. 20 Oct., 91, aged 20, from Rossall school.

Lomax, Ernest William, born at Lincoln 1854; 1s. William, gen. NON-COLLEGIATE, matric. 19 Jan., 89, aged 35, from gr. school and theological coll., Lincoln.

Lomax, John Acton, born at Stibbard, Norfolk, 1861; 1s. John, cler. BRASENOSE, matric. 22 Oct., 80, aged 19, from Manchester gr. school.

Long, rev. Charles Newell, born at Leamington, co. Warwick, Feb., 1868; o.s. Charles Edward, cler. KEBLE, matric. 19 Oct., 86, aged 18 (from Leamington coll.), exhibitioner 86, B.A. 91 (HONOURS :—2 classical mods. 88, 2 classics 90); curate of Hoxton St. Saviour 91.

Long, rev. Francis, born at Ashford, Kent, 1861; 2s. Michael, gent. NON-COLLEGIATE, matric. 22 Jan., 81, aged 20; exhibitioner UNIVERSITY COLL. 81-5, B.A. 84, M.A. 87 (HONOURS :— 3 classical mods. 82, 3 classics 84); curate of St. Margaret, Dunham Massey, Cheshire, 85-90.

Long, rev. Frank, born at New Wandsworth, Surrey, 28 Jan., 1864; 2s. William Edward, gen. MAGDALEN, matric. 21 Oct., 86, aged 22, B.A. 89; curate of Bamborough, Northumberland, 89.

Long, Frederick Percy, born at Wells, Norfolk, 13 Jan., 1868; 1s. Frederick, gen. WORCESTER, matric. 17 Oct., 87, aged 19 (from Epsom coll.), exhibitioner 87, B.A. 91; HONOURS :—1 classical mods. 89, 1 classics 91.

Long, Henry Charles, born at Ferry Hill, co. Durham, 29 July, 1867; 1s. Frederick, cler. LINCOLN, matric. 22 Jan., 87, aged 19 (from Horspath school, Oxford); migrated to CHARSLEY HALL Sept. 87, and to QUEEN'S in 89.

Long, Maurice St. Clare, born in London 2 Aug., 1862; 2s. Edwin, R.A. MERTON, matric. 18 Oct., 81, aged 19 (from Somersetshire coll., Bath), B.A. 85, M.A. 88 (HONOURS :—2 classical mods. 83, 4 classics 85); killed Sept. 91, in Burgos railway accident, Spain.

Long, Richard Seymour, born at Liverpool, 31 Oct., 1862; 1s. Richard England, gent. NON-COLLEGIATE, matric. 29 Jan., 81, aged 18 (from Liverpool institute), exhibitioner BALLIOL 82-5, B.A. 84; HONOURS :—2 classical mods. 82, 2 history 84.

Long, Samuel Charles, born at Setcrington, Yorks, 29 Sept., 1869; 1s. Samuel, capt. R.A. MAGDALEN, matric. 18 Jan., 88, aged 18 (from Winchester), B.A. 91.

Long, Thomas Henry Douglas, born at Dudley, co. Worc., 10 April, 1872; o.s. Henry, of Worcester, gen. ST. EDMUND HALL, matric. 19 Oct., 92, aged 20, from West Bromwich school.

Long, rev. William Edward, born at Battersea, Surrey, 20 Feb., 1862; elder son of William Edward, arm. MAGDALEN, matric. 16 Oct., 80, aged 18 (from King's coll. school, London), demy 79-84, B.A. 84; fellow QUEEN'S 85-91, M.A. 87 (HONOURS :— 1 classical mods. 81, Greek prose 83); 1 classics 84, rector of Holwell, Dorset, 90; fellow University coll., London, 92.

Long, William Edward, born at Congresbury, Somerset, 21 Feb., 1873; o.s. William, colonel, ORIEL, matric. 22 Oct., 91, aged 19, from Eton.

Long, William Edward, M.A., fellow QUEEN'S 85-91, where see page 182.

Longden, Wilfred Maurice Murray, born at Fawkham, Kent, Oct., 1870; 4s. Charles, arm. WORCESTER, matric. 14 Oct., 89, aged 19, from St. Edward's school, Summertown.

Longdon, John Smith, born at Llanginehc, co. Glam., 22 Feb., 1867; 4s. David. JESUS COLL., matric. 19 Oct., 87, aged 20, from Brecon school.

Longe, Francis Edward Guy, born at Tuddenham, Suffolk, 8 May, 1871; 6s. John, rector of Sternfield, Suffolk. KEBLE, matric. 11 Oct., 90, aged 19, from Haileybury.

Longe, Herbert Davy, born at Sidmouth, Devon, 18 March, 1862; 3s. John, cler. PEMBROKE, matric. 26 Oct., 81, aged 19, from Ipswich gr. school.

Longland, rev. Charles Boxall, born at Rotherfield Greys, Oxon, 1862; 1s. Charles Pitman, cler. WORCESTER, matric. 27 June, 81, aged 19, B.A. 85, M.A. 88 (HONOURS:—4 theology 85); curate of Tranmere, Cheshire, 90.

Longley, sir Henry, K.C.B., M.A., B.C.L., student CHRIST CHURCH 53-61, where see page 420.

Longley, John Augustine, born at Lambeth, Surrey, 28 Aug., 1866; o.s. Henry. K.C.B. (89). CHRIST CHURCH, matric. 30 May, 85, aged 18 (from Eton), B.A. 89; HONOURS:—3 classical mods. 87, 3 classics 89.

Longmore, Philip Raynsford, born at All Saints, Hertford, , 1873; 2s. Matthew Skinner, solicitor. MAGDALEN, matric. 22 Oct., 91, aged 18, from Clifton coll.

Longsdon, John Wilson, born at Seacroft, Yorks, 6 July, 1861; 3s. Henry John, cler. ST. JOHN'S, matric. 15 Oct., 81, aged 20 (from Merchant Taylors' school), B.A. 87, M.A. 90.

Longson, Edward Harold, born at Stretford, co. Lanc., 28 July, 1872; 1s. James Edward, gen. NEW COLL., matric. 16 Oct., 91, aged 19, from Southport school.

Longworth, Edward Travers Dames, B.A. NEW COLL. 1885, see DAMES, page 355.

Lonsdale, John Pemberton Heywood Heywood, born at Brewood, co. Stafford, 2 Aug., 1869; y.s. Arthur Pemberton, arm. NEW COLL., matric. 19 Jan., 89, aged 19 (from Eton); cox of university eight 89, 90, 1, 2.

Lonsdale, Walter Henry, born at Hessle, Yorks, , 1865; y.s. , gen. NEW COLL., matric. 15 Jan., 91, aged 26.

Loosemore, Alfred, born at Tiverton, Devon, 27 Jan., 1873; o.s. Robert Francis, solicitor, J.P. BRASENOSE, matric. 21 Oct., 92, aged 19, from Blundell's school, Tiverton.

Lopes, George de Arroyoave, born in London 9 Jan., 1872; 1s. George Ludlow, arm. BALLIOL, matric. 14 Oct., 90, aged 18, from Eton. See Foster's *Baronetage*.

Lopes, Henry Ludlow, born at Maristow, Devon, 30 Sept., 1865; 1s. sir Henry, lord justice of appeal. BALLIOL, matric. 22 Jan., 85, aged 19 (from Eton), B.A. 89 (HONOURS:—2 history 88); bar.-at-law, Inner Temple, 90. See Foster's *Baronetage*.

Loraine, Wilfrid Howard, born at Waterloo, co. Lanc., 1865; 2s. Nevison, cler. CHARSLEY'S HALL, matric. 10 May, 83, aged 18 (from International coll., London); migrated to BRASENOSE 84, B.A. 89; bar.-at-law, Middle Temple, 89.

Lord, rev. David William, born at Lochlie, co. Forfar, , 1864; 1s. David, gen. NON-COLLEGIATE, matric. 14 Oct., 82, aged 18 (from Rishworth gr. school); migrated to HERTFORD 82, B.A. 86, M.A. 89 (HONOURS:—2 theology 86); curate of Leicester St. Peter 88.

Lord, John Goodair, born at Crewe, Cheshire, Feb., 1860; 1s. Richard, D.Med. KEBLE, matric. 22 Oct., 85, aged 16 (from King's coll. school, London), B.A. 89; HONOURS:—1 morphology 89.

Lord, Reginald Stevens, born at Monton, co. Lanc., 27 April, 1873; 1s. William Chuley, lawyer. EXETER, matric. 18 Oct., 92, aged 19, from the Charterhouse.

Lord, Robert Harley, born at Bradford, co. Lanc., , 1859; 1s. Joshua, gen. NON-COLLEGIATE, matric. 15 Oct., 87, aged 28 (from Manchester school and Owens coll.); HONOURS:—2 theology 90.

Lord, Robert John Cornwallis, born at Portrush, co. Antrim, Sept., 1871; 1s. Robert Gillman, D.Med. CHRIST CHURCH, matric. 10 Oct., 90, aged 19, scholar 90; selected candidate Indian C.S. 90.

Lord, rev. William Pritchard, born at Oldham, co. Lanc., 21 Feb., 1859; 1s. Samuel, gen. WORCESTER, matric. 17 Oct., 87, aged 28 (from Manchester gr. school), B.A. 91.

Lorimer, Charles, born at Toorak, near Melbourne, , 1862; 3s. James, arm. EXETER, matric. 19 Oct., 82, aged 20 (from Hawthorne gr. school, Melbourne), B.A. 87; bar.-at-law, Inner Temple, 87.

Lorimer, James, born in Victoria, Australia, 1860; 2s. James, gent. NON-COLLEGIATE, matric. 14 Oct., 82, aged 22.

Lorimer, John Gordon, born at Glasgow 1870; 1s. Robert, cler. CHRIST CHURCH, matric. 11 Oct., 89, aged 19 (from Edinburgh university); assist. commissioner Punjab 91.

Lough, rev. Edward Inglis, born at St. George's, isle of Bermuda, 7 Aug., 1861; 1s. John Francis Burnaby Lumley, cler. TRINITY, matric. 16 Oct., 80, aged 19 (from Sherborne school), B.A. 84, M.A. 87; curate of Hebden Bridge, co. Lanc., 84.

Love, rev. John Garton William, born in London 23 Jan., 1858; 1s. George Alfred, deceased. WADHAM, matric. 19 Oct., 85, aged 19, B.A. 88, M.A. 92 (HONOURS:—2 theology 88); curate of St. Agnes, Toxteth Park, 91.

Lovegrove, Edwin William, born at Wilford, Notts, 2 June, 1868; 1s. Edwin, cler. and schoolmaster. NEW COLL., matric. 14 Oct., 87, aged 19 (from Gt. Crosby school), scholar 87, B.A. 91; HONOURS:—1 mathematical mods. 89, 1 mathematics 91.

Loveland, John Douglas Errington, born in London 1866; 1s. Richard Loveland, arm. ST. JOHN'S, matric. 13 Oct., 83, aged 17.

Lovell, Charles Petre, born in London 1863; 1s. Samuel, gent. ST. JOHN'S, matric. 15 Oct., 81, aged 18 (from Merchant Taylors' school), scholar 81-5, B.A. 88, M.A. and B.Med. 91; HONOURS:—3 natural science 85.

Lovell, Samuel Walter, born in London 6 Oct., 1866; 3s. Samuel, gent. LINCOLN, matric. 3 Feb., 86, aged 19 (from Christ's hospital); HONOURS:—2 classical mods. 87; died 7 April, 87.

Lovett, Harrington Verney, born at Exeter 1864; 2s. Robert, cler. BALLIOL, matric. 17 Oct., 82, aged 18 (from Sherborne gr. school); assist. commissioner Oudh 84.

Lovett, rev. Thomas, born at Whittington, Salop, 15 Aug., 1865; 2s. John Hamilton, captain in the army. MAGDALEN, matric. 19 Oct., 83, aged 18, B.A. 87, M.A. 91; curate of Woolley, Wakefield, 90.

Lovibond, rev. George Matthew, born at Blackford, Somerset, 19 March, 1869; 1s. Robert Matthew, arm. ST. MARY HALL, matric. 25 April, 87, aged 18, B.A. 90.

Low, Charles Ernest, born at Walton, Cumberland, 29 Nov., 1869; 1s. Charles, cler. WADHAM, matric. 13 Oct., 88, aged 18 (from Rugby), scholar 87, B.A. 92 (HONOURS:—1 classical mods. 90, 3 classics 92); selected candidate Indian c.s. 92.

Low, Walter Edgar, born in London 25 Nov., 1872; 4s. George, arm. BRASENOSE, matric. 15 Oct., 90, aged 17 (from Merchant Taylors' school), scholar 90; HONOURS:—2 classical mods. 92.

Low, William Mackay, born at Newport, America, 1862; o.s. Andrew, arm. BRASENOSE, matric. 22 Jan., 80, aged 19, from Winchester.

Lowe, Cecil Henry, born at Great Dunmow, Essex, 1863; 2s. George William, cler. CHRIST CHURCH, matric. 12 Oct., 83, aged 20, B.A. 87; HONOURS:—4 theology 87.

Lowe, Henry Parker, born at Norwood, Surrey, 21 Oct., 1866; 2s. William, gent. CHRIST CHURCH, matric. 16 Oct., 85, aged 19 (from Westminster school), scholar 84, B.A. 89, M.A. and B.C.L. 92; HONOURS:—1 classical mods. 87, 2 classics 89; bar.-at-law, Middle Temple, 90.

Lowe, Horace Gordon, born at New Beckenham, Norfolk, 1868; 3s. Edward Jackson, cler. NON-COLLEGIATE, matric. 15 Oct., 87, aged 19, from Trent and Grantham schools.

Lowe, Joseph Peter, born at Salford, co. Lanc., 3 Dec., 1867; o.s. Joseph, arm. MERTON, matric. 21 Oct., 86, aged 18 (from Manchester gr. school), exhibitioner 86; HONOURS:—2 classical mods. 88, 3 classics 90.

Lowenthal, Sidney Joseph, born at Lindley, Yorks, 24 Aug., 1871; 4s. Joseph, of Huddersfield, Yorks, J.P. CORPUS CHRISTI, matric. 16 Oct., 90, aged 19 (from Rugby); HONOURS:—2 classical mods. 92.

Lower, Henry, born at St. Johns, Newfoundland, 22 March, 1862; o.s. Henry Martyn, rector of Foulmire, co. Camb. NEW COLL., matric. 15 Oct., 81, aged 19 (from Winchester), B.A. 85, M.A. 88; HONOURS:—2 classical mods. 82, 3 classics 85.

Lowndes, Charles Arthur, born at Windermere, Westmorland, 1864; 1s. Charles Clayton, cler. BRASENOSE, matric. 19 Oct., 82, aged 18 (from King's school Canterbury), exhibitioner 82-6, B.A. 86; HONOURS:—3 history 86.

Lowndes, Edward Arthur Selby-, born in London 22 May, 1873; o.s. William Seymour, late capt. in the army. EXETER, matric. 17 Oct., 92, aged 19 (from Merchant Taylors' school), scholar 92; HONOURS:—Hebrew scholarship 92.

Lowndes, Frederick Sawrey Archibald, born at Windermere 22 Jan., 1868; 2s. Charles Clayton, cler. TRINITY, matric. 15 Oct., 87 (from Canterbury school), Ford student 86, B.A. 92; HONOURS:—2 Abbott scholarship 88, classical mods. 89, 3 classics 91.

Lowndes, George Rivers, born at Poole Keynes, co. Glouc., 1 Jan., 1862; 3s. Richard, vicar of Sturminster Newton. NEW COLL., matric. 16 Oct., 80, aged 18 (from Winchester), scholar 80-5 (HONOURS:—3 classical mods. 82, 3 classics 84); bar.-at-law, Lincoln's Inn, 90.

Lowndes, rev. Harold Norman, born at Wallasey, Cheshire, 1869; 4s. Francis Dobson, arm. ST. JOHN'S, matric. 13 Oct., 88, aged 19 (from Rossall school), B.A. 91.

Lowndes, Richard, born in London Jan., 1866; 4s. Richard, cler. KEBLE, matric. 14 Oct., 84, aged 18 (from Sherborne gr. school); HONOURS:—3 classical mods. 86.

Lowry, Arthur Belmore, born at Northleach, co. Glouc., 7 Aug., 1868; 5s. Charles Henry, cler. TRINITY, matric. 15 Oct., 87, aged 19 (from Eton), exhibitioner 86, B.A. 91 (HONOURS:—2 classical mods. 89, 2 classics 91); local gov. department London.

Lowry, Charles Henry, M.A., fellow QUEEN's 49-55, where see page 178.

Lowry, Henry Dawson, born at Truro, Cornwall, 22 Feb., 1869; 1s. Thomas Shaw, gen. NON-COLLEGIATE, matric. 14 Jan., 88, aged 18 (from Queen's coll., Taunton), B.A. 91; HONOURS:—3 chemistry 91.

Lowsley, Horace Adiel, born at Hampstead Norreys, Berks, 1 June, 1870; 4s. Luke, gen. WADHAM, matric. 14 Oct., 89, aged 19 (from Cheltenham coll.), B.A. 92.

Luard, Charles Eckford, born at Farnham, Surrey, Aug., 1866; 2s. Charles Henry, col. R.E. CHRIST CHURCH, matric. 13 Jan., 88, aged 18 (from Marlborough), B.A. 90 (HONOURS:—2 chemistry 90); and lieut. the Prince of Wales own (West Yorkshire regt.) 92.

Luard, John Godfrey, born at Olveston, co.' Glouc., 13 Dec., 1862; o.s. John Godfrey, gent. EXETER, matric. 20 Oct., 81, aged 18 (from Marlborough), B.A. 87, M.A. 91; student Inner Temple 85.

Lubbock, Cecil, born at Northaw, Herts, 15 Feb., 1872; 2s. Frederick, merchant. TRINITY, matric. 21 Oct., 91, aged 19 (from Eton), scholar 90. HONOURS:—accessit Hertford scholarship 92.

Lubbock, Charles Western, born at North Cray, Kent, 5 June, 1862; 1s. Nevile, arm. BALLIOL, matric. 1 Feb., 82, aged 19 (from Eton); died 16 April, 90. See Foster's *Baronetage*.

Lubbock, Geoffry, born in London 18 May, 1873; 2s. Henry James, banker. TRINITY, matric. 15 Oct., 92, aged 19, from Eton.

Lucas, Arthur, born at Darlington, co. Durham, 24 Jan., 1863; 1s. Arthur solicitor. TRINITY, matric. 15 Oct., 81, aged 18 (from Clifton coll.); and assist. collector and magistrate Khandesh 83.

Lucas, rev. Henry Jesse Andrewes, born at Redland, near Bristol, 9 April, 1862; 3s. George William, gent. WORCESTER, matric. 19 Oct., 86, aged 24 (from Clifton coll.), B.A. 89 (HONOURS:—3 theology 89); curate of St. John, Bury St. Edmund's, 90.

Lucas, Hugh Nathaniel, born at Reigate, Surrey, 5 Aug., 1871; 2s. Horace Joseph, arm., deceased. NEW COLL.; HONOURS:—3 classical mods. 92.

Lucas, Ponsonby Tottenham, born at Rhossili, co. Glam., 1869; 3s. John Ponsonby, cler. ORIEL, matric. 20 Oct., 88, aged 19 (from Llandovery coll.), B.A. 92; HONOURS:—2 classical mods. 90.

Lucas, rev. Vincent William, M.A., CHRIST CHURCH, where see page 426.

Lucas, William Henry, M.A., fellow BRASENOSE 44-52, where see page 352.

Lucas, William Henry, born at Darlington, co. Durham, 18 Feb., 1867; 3s. Arthur, solicitor. NEW COLL., matric. 15 Oct., 86, aged 19 (from Clifton coll.); assist. collector and magistrate Sind.

Lucena, Stephen Lancaster, born at Enfield, Middx., Sept., 1869; 1s. Stephen Lancaster, arm. CHRIST CHURCH, matric. 30 May, 88, aged 19, from Harrow.

Lucey, rev. Algernon Charles, born at Biddenden, Kent, 15 Sept., 1860; o.s. Ebenezer Curling, cler. MAGDALEN, matric. 16 Oct., 80, aged 18 (from Tonbridge school), B.A. 83, M.A. 87 (HONOURS:—3 history 83); curate of St. James Norlands, London, 87.

Luckie, Edgar George Fraser, born in London 1862; 1s. David Fraser, arm. BALLIOL, matric. 18 Oct., 81, aged 19 (from a London school); selected candidate Indian C.S. 81.

Luckman, Arthur Weston, born at Mortlake, Surrey, 1870; 1s. Samuel, gent. CHARSLEY'S HALL, matric. 2 Nov., 86, aged 16.

Ludlow, Henry John, born at Hastings, Sussex, 22 Jan., 1862; o.s. John, major-general. EXETER, matric. 27 April, 81, aged 19 (from Rugby); died at sea in 84.

Ludlow-Bruges, Henry Hungerford, M.A., ST. JOHN'S, where see.

Luffman, Samuel, born at Milborne Port, Somerset, 1865; 6s. John, gent. NON-COLLEGIATE, matric. 10 April, 80, aged 25, from Didsbury coll., Manchester.

Lummis, Edward William, born at Kingston-on-Hull, Yorks, 23 March, 1867; 1s. William, gent. WORCESTER, matric. 22 Oct., 85, aged 18 (from Birmingham school), scholar 84, B.A. 89; HONOURS:—2 classical mods. 87, 3 classics 89.

Lumsdaine, Edwin Robert John Sandys, born at Canterbury June, 1864; 1s. Francis Gordon, cler. CHRIST CHURCH, matric. 18 Jan., 84, aged 19, B.A. 87.

Lund, Reginald William, born at Sutton, Yorks, 9 Dec., 1869; 3s. James, arm. CORPUS CHRISTI, matric. 20 Oct., 88, aged 18 (from Rugby); HONOURS:—3 law 92.

Lungley, James, born at Southampton 1863; o.s. Peter, gent. NON-COLLEGIATE, matric. 15 Oct., 81, aged 18 (from Magdalen coll. school); migrated to ST. JOHN'S, B.A. 86; HONOURS:—4 history 85.

Lupton, Hugh, born at Roundhay, near Leeds, 11 May, 1861; 5s. Francis, gen. UNIVERSITY COLL. matric. 15 May, 80, aged 19 (from Rugby), B.A. 84; HONOURS:—3 history 84; a civil engineer.

Lupton, Walter James Edwin, born at Clapham, Surrey, 30 May, 1871; 2s. William, arm. NEW COLL., matric. 10 Oct., 90, aged 19, from city of London school.

Lury, Harford Elton, born at Hythe, Hants, 1868; 1s. John Elton, arm. HERTFORD, matric. 29 Jan., 89, aged 21.

Lush, Roland Gerald, born at Southsea 1868; y.s. Joseph, gent. NON-COLLEGIATE, matric. 23 Oct., 86, aged 18, from Appuldurcombe coll., I.W.

Lushington, Charles, M.A., student CHRIST CHURCH 22-55, where see page 413.

Lushington, Franklyn Guy, born at Elstead, Surrey, 1862; 5s. James Law, arm. BALLIOL, matric. 18 Oct., 81, aged 19 (from Highgate school), B.A. 85, M.A. 90; HONOURS:—2 classical mods. 83, 4 classics 85.

Lushington, sir Godfrey, K.C.B., M.A., fellow ALL SOULS' 51-62, where see page 280.

Lushington, Guy, born in Calcutta 10 Sept., 1861; 3s. Edward Harbord, arm. UNIVERSITY COLL., matric. 16 Oct., 80, aged 19, from Eton (HONOURS: —2 law 84); bar.-at-law, Middle Temple, 87. See Foster's *Baronetage*.

Luttman, Walter Charles, born at High Wycombe, 1876; 1s. Charles Edwin, gen. QUEEN'S, matric. 14 Jan., 90, aged 20.

Luttrell, Claude Mohun Fownes-, born at Kilton, Somerset, 9 Sept., 1867; 4s. George, of Dunster Castle, Somerset, arm. MAGDALEN, matric. 21 Oct., 86, aged 19 (from Eton), B.A. 90.

Luxmoore, John Stonhouse, born at Ashford, co. Derby, 1 Aug., 1863; 1s. John Reddaway, vicar. EXETER, matric. 18 Jan., 83, aged 19 (from Stratford-on-Avon school), B.A. 88.

Luxmoore, William Cyril, born at Ashford, co. Derby, 13 July, 1871; 2s. John Reddaway, vicar. KEBLE, matric. 20 Oct., 91, aged 20, from Winton house school, Winchester.

Luxmoro, Launcelot Alford, born at Torquay, Devon, 17 Feb., 1871; elder son of Charles Noble, arm. NEW COLL., matric. 10 Oct., 90, aged 19, from Eton.

Luxton, rev. Ernest William, born at Hatherleigh, Devon, 13 June, 1859; 5s. Thomas, gent. LINCOLN, matric. 23 Oct., 80, aged 21 (from Taunton Wesleyan coll.), B.A. 83, M.A. 90 (HONOURS:—3 theology 83); curate of St. George 83-7, and of St. Mark, Portsea, 87; died at Corfu Feb., 92.

Lyall, sir Alfred Comyns, K.C.B., K.C.I.E. (2. Alfred, cler.), born at Coulsdon, Surrey, 3 May, 1835 (from Eton); created D.C.L. 26 June, 89, hon. LL.D. Camb. 10 June, 91, sec. for India 73, foreign sec. 78, lieut. gov. N.W. provinces 82, a member of the council of India 88, secretary to the order of the star of India and to the order of the Indian empire, Rede lecturer Cambridge 91, K.C.B. 24 May, 81, K.C.I.E. 15 Feb., 87. See *Men and Women of the Time*.

Lyall, Francis Frederick, born at Dacca, India, 12 June, 1872; 3s. David Robert, I.C.S., etc. BALLIOL, matric. 20 Oct., 91, aged 19 (from Edinburgh academy); selected candidate Indian C.S. 91.

Lydall, Cecil Wykeham, born in London 9 Jan., 1873; 2s. Wykeham Hawltone, D.Med. WORCESTER, matric. 18 Oct., 92, aged 19 (from Bradfield coll.), exhibitioner 91.

Lyde, Lionel William, born at Wigton, Cumberland, 28 March, 1863; 1s. William, cler. QUEEN'S, matric. 23 Oct., 82, aged 19 (from Sedbergh gr. school), exhibitioner 82-6, B.A. 86, M.A. 89; HONOURS:—2 classical mods. 83, 3 classics 86.

Lygon, William, 7th earl Beauchamp, born in London 20 Feb., 1872; 1s. Frederick, 6th earl Beauchamp. CHRIST CHURCH, matric. 10 Oct., 90, aged 18 (from Eton); president Oxford union society 93.

Lynam, Alfred Edmund, born at Stoke-upon-Trent, 29 March, 1873; 7s. Charles, F.R.I.B.A. EXETER, matric. 18 Oct., 92, aged 19 (from Rossall school), scholar 92.

Lynam, Charles Cotterill, M.A., HERTFORD, where see.

Lynam, Robert Garner, born at Stoke-on-Trent, co. Stafford, 15 Aug., 1859; 2s. Charles, architect. NON-COLLEGIATE, matric. 11 Oct., 90, aged 31, from K. William coll., I.M., and King's coll., Lond.

Lynch, John Finnis, born nr. Bagdad Oct., 1865; 1s. Stephen, gent. BRASENOSE, matric. 14 Oct., 84, aged 18 (from Harrow); bar.-at-law, Inner Temple, 88.

Lynch, Mark Wilson, born at Renmore, co. Galway, July, 1866; 1s. Wilson, major. CHRIST CHURCH, matric. 18 Jan., 83, aged 17, B.A. 87 (HONOURS:— 2 classics 87, 2 history 88); of Durns, co. Galway, died 21 Dec., 92. See Foster's *Our Noble and Gentle Families*.

Lyne, Richard Fernandez, born at St. David's, Exeter, 9 Dec., 1872; 1s. Charles Richard Nunez, M.A., cler. NON-COLLEGIATE, matric. 7 Dec., 91, aged 18, from Cheltenham coll.

Lyon, Edmund Herbert, born at East Stratton, Hants, 1861; o.s. Samuel Edmund, cler. HERTFORD, matric. 18 Oct., 80, aged 19 (from the Charterhouse); cox University eight 81, 2, 3; student Inner Temple 83.

Lyon, Francis Gardner, born in London 3 Feb., 1873; o.s. s. William, of Finchampstead, Berks, late of war office, UNIVERSITY COLL., matric. 15 Oct., 92, aged 19, from Wellington coll.

Lyon, George Herbert, born at Valparaiso, Chili, 19 June, 1873; 2s. William, stockbroker. BRASENOSE, matric. 21 Oct., 92, aged 19, from Wellington coll.

Lyon, Herbert, born at St. Hellers, Jersey, 1867; 5s. William, gen. CORPUS CHRISTI, matric. 20 Oct., 86, aged 19 (from Winchester), B.A. 92; HONOURS:—3 classical mods. 88, 2 history 90.

Lyon, Hugh Fraser, born at Oborne, Dorset, 23 Feb., 1867; 3s. William Hector, vicar of Sherborne. TRINITY, matric. 12 Oct., 89, aged 22 (from Sherborne school), B.A. 92; HONOURS:—3 history 92.

Lyon, James, born at Salford, co. Lanc., 25 Oct., 1872; 1s. James, gen. QUEEN'S, matric. 27 Oct., 91, aged 19, from Ormskirk gr. school.

Lyon, hon. Kenneth Bowes, born 26 April, 1867; 6s. Claude, earl Strathmore. CHRIST CHURCH, matric. 23 Jan., 86, aged 18.

Lyon, Leopold Playfair, born at Rossall 20 Feb., 1872; 1s. James Tennant, arm. HERTFORD, matric. 14 Oct., 90, aged 18 (from Harrow); HONOURS:—2 classical mods. 92.

Lyon, Percy Comyn, born in St. Heliers, Jersey, 1862; 4s. William, arm. ORIEL, matric. 18 Oct., 81, aged 19 (from Bruton school); joint magistrate and deputy collector, Bengal, 83.

Lyons, Gerald, born in Lowestoft, Suffolk, 1870; 1s. John Edward, capt. in the army. BRASENOSE, matric. 24 Jan., 89, aged 19, from Beaumont coll., Windsor.

Lys, Francis John, born at Bere Regis, Dorset, 13 July, 1863; 1s. Francis Daniel, gent. WORCESTER, matric. 19 Oct., 82, aged 19 (from Sherborne school), scholar 82-6, B.A. 86, M.A. 89; HONOURS:—1 classical mods. 84, 2 classics 86, Latin verse 85.

Lys, William, born at Bere Regis, Dorset, 12 Jan., 1870; 4s. Francis Daniel, arm. BRASENOSE, matric. 16 Oct., 88, aged 18 (from Weymouth and Bath colls.), scholar 88, B.A. 91; HONOURS:—2 classical mods. 90); selected candidate Indian C.S. 92.

Lysaght, Frederick Percy, born at Backwell, Somerset, April, 1863; 3s. John, C.E. EXETER, matric. 31 Jan., 82, aged 18 (from Abingdon gr. school), B.A. 88; bar.-at-law, Middle Temple, 90.

CANDELABRA, RADCLIFFE LIBRARY.—*From Lascelles.*

STRING COURSE IN BEAUCHAMP CHAPEL., WARWICK.—*Pugin.*

M

McAlester, Charles Godfrey Somerville, born at Kilmaurs, co. Ayr, 21 Jan., 1868; 1s. Charles, colonel. BALLIOL, matric. 19 Oct., 87, aged 19, from Cheltenham coll. (HONOURS:—3 classical mods. 89, 4 classics 91); bar.-at-law, Inner Temple, 92.

Macan, Reginald Walter, M.A., fellow UNIVERSITY COLL. 84, where see page 29.

McArthur, James Fowler, born at Glasgow 1864; 1s. James, gen. BALLIOL, matric. 17 Oct., 82, aged 18 (from Manchester gr. school); scholar 81-6, B.A. 86; HONOURS:—2 natural science 85.

McArthur, Malcolm Stewart Hannibal, born at Chatham, Kent, 10 March, 1872; 4s. Charles, general, R.M. QUEEN'S, matric. 17 Oct., 91, aged 19 (from Tavistock school), exhibitioner 91.

McArthur, William Lyon, born at Paisley, co. Renfrew, 3 Dec., 1870; 3s. James, gen. WORCESTER, matric. 14 Oct., 89, aged 18 (from Manchester gr. school); scholar 89; HONOURS:—1 classical mods. 91.

Macaulay, Denzil Ibbetson Michael, born at Bankoora, 1871; 2s. Colman Patrick Louis, arm. UNIVERSITY COLL., matric. 12 Oct., 89, aged 18.

Macaulay, rev. George Robert, born in London 11 Oct., 1865; o.s. James, D.Med., editor of "The Leisure Hour," etc. QUEEN'S, matric. 22 Oct., 84, aged 19 (from St. Paul's school), B.A. 88, M.A. 91; HONOURS:—3 theology 88.

McBarnet, Alexander Cockburn, born in London 1868; 1s. Alexander Cockburn, arm. BALLIOL, matric. 19 Oct., 87, aged 19 (from Fettes coll.), B.A. 90 (HONOURS:—3 law 90); bar.-at-law, Inner Temple, 92.

McCance, John Stouppe Finlay, born at Belfast 1865; o.s. Finlay, arm. BRASENOSE, matric. 22 April, 84, aged 19 (from Academical institute, Belfast), B.A. 87 (HONOURS:—3 law 87); of Suffolk, co. Antrim.

McCandlish, Edward John, born at Edinburgh 8 May, 1867; 1s. John McGregor, arm. MERTON, matric. 21 Oct., 86, aged 19 (from Loretto school), B.A. 89; HONOURS:—4 history 89.

McCann, Hugh O'Donoghue, born at Belfast 18 March, 1861; 1s. Hugh O'Donoghue, gent. QUEEN'S, matric. 25 Oct., 80, aged 19 (from Bedford gr. school); scholar 80-4, B.A. 84, M.A. 87; HONOURS:—3 mathematical mods. 82, 2 natural science 84.

McCheane, Arthur Henry Owen, born at Keynston, Dorset, Sept., 1870; 1s. William Hiley, arm. KEBLE, matric. 18 Jan., 90, aged 19.

McClintock, Henry Foster, born at Dublin 11 Aug., 1871; 1s. Francis Leopold, knight, and admiral R.N. NEW COLL., matric. 10 Oct., 90, aged 19, from Winchester.

MacColl, Dugald Sutherland, born at Glasgow 10 March, 1859; o.s. Dugald, presbyterian minister. LINCOLN, matric. 20 Oct., 81, aged 22 (from University coll., London); scholar 81-5, B.A. 84 (HONOURS:—English verse 82, 2 classics 84); B.A. University of London 79, M.A. 81, fellow University coll., London, 82.

McComb, Samuel, born in Londonderry, Ireland, 1862; 2s. Samuel, gen. NON-COLLEGIATE, matric. 24 May, 90, aged 28, from Academical institute, Derry.

McConnell, Ronald Stafford, born at Wolverton, Bucks, 1860; 4s. James Edward, arm. MERTON, matric. 18 Oct., 80, aged 20.

McCorquodale, Harold, born at Newton-le-Willows, co. Lanc., 1866; 4s. George, arm. CHRIST CHURCH, matric. 18 Jan., 84, aged 18.

McCorquodale, Norman, born at Newton-le-Willows, co. Lanc., 1867; 5s. George, gent. PEMBROKE, matric. 23 Oct., 82, aged 18.

McCowan, Walter, born at Walton-on-Thames, Surrey, July, 1866; o.s. Thomas James Craig, cler. KEBLE, matric. 19 Oct., 86, aged 20, from Brighton coll.

McCulloch, Ikirgeny, born at Cambo, Fifeshire, 2 Dec., 1863; 1s. William, cler., LL.D. NEW COLL., matric. 18 Oct., 83, aged 19 (from Cheltenham coll.), B.A. 87 (HONOURS:—3 classical mods. 85, 4 law 87); died at Davos Platz 21 Jan., 91.

McCurdy, Edward Alexander Coles, born at Nottingham 1871; s. Alexander, cler. BALLIOL, matric. 17 Oct., 89, aged 18, from Loughborough school.

MacDermot, Edward Terence, born at Bath 11 June, 1873; o.s. Edward Deane, D.Med. MAGDALEN, matric. 9 Feb., 92, aged 18, from Downside coll., Bath.

McDermott, Cornelius William, born at Portsmouth 1863; 1s. Cornelius William, arm. CHRIST CHURCH, matric. 27 May, 82, aged 19, B.A. 86, M.A. 89.

Macdona, Egerton Milne Cumming, born at West Derby, co. Lanc., 25 Feb., 1867; o.s. John Cumming, arm. NEW COLL., matric. 15 Oct., 86, aged 19 (from Eton), B.A. 90 (HONOURS :—2 classical mods. 88, 2 history 90); bar.-at-law, Middle Temple, 91.

Macdonald, Alexander, born in London 30 Aug., 1862; 1s. Alexander, artist. CORPUS CHRISTI, matric. 27 Oct., 81, aged 19 (from Magdalen coll. school), exhibitioner 82-5, B.A. 86, M.A. 88; HONOURS :—1 classical mods. 83, 3 classics 85.

Macdonald, Alexander, created M.A. 24 April 1883, born 18 Feb., 39; Mr. Ruskin's, master of drawing, Oxford, 66; keeper of the University galleries 90; father of the preceding.

Macdonald, Alexander Herbert, born at Marlborough, Wilts, 12 Nov., 1870; 1s. William, arm. KEBLE, matric. 18 Jan., 90, aged 19 (from Marlborough), exhibitioner 89.

McDonald, Archibald, born at Strathfieldsaye, Hants, 1869; 1s. Donald, gen. ST. JOHN'S, matric. 15 Oct., 87, aged 18 (from Hurstpierpoint coll.), B.A. 91; HONOURS :—3 history 91.

Macdonald, Charles John, born in East Indies Oct., 1865; 1s. Laehlan, gen. ST. JOHN'S, matric. 16 Oct., 86, aged 20.

Macdonald, rev. Frederick Charles, born at Nottingham 22 March, 1860; 4s. Thomas Mosse, cler. NON-COLLEGIATE, matric. 18 Oct., 80, aged 20 (from Merchant Taylors' school); migrated to ORIEL 81, B.A. 83, M.A. 87; curate of Bishopwearmouth 84-9, and of St. Mark, Millfield, 89.

Macdonald, George, born at Elgin, co. Moray, 1862; 3s. James, D.D., BALLIOL, matric. 6 May, 84, aged 22 (from Edinburgh university), B.A. 87, M.A. 91; HONOURS :—1 classical mods. 85, 1 classics 87.

Macdonald, Herbert Lindsay, born at Wallabadah, N.S.W., 10 Oct., 1872; 1s. J. M. L. J.P. MERTON, matric. 22 Oct., 91, aged 19, from Rugby and Sydney university.

Macdonald, rev. James Middleton, born at Melbourne 7 Feb., 1857; 3s. David, D.D., minister church of Scotland. NON-COLLEGIATE, matric. 15 Jan., 87, aged 29 (from Scottish coll. Melbourne, B.A. 77, and Sydney university, M.A. 79); migrated to EXETER, B.A. 89, assistant chaplain and precentor 89-90 (HONOURS :—Syriac prize 88, 2 theology 89); chaplain at Hourah, Bengal, 91.

Macdonald, John Ronald Moreton-, born at Largie, Argyllshire. N.B., 25 May, 1873; 1s. Charles M.-M., D.L., deceased. MAGDALEN, matric. 18 Oct., 92, aged 19 from Eton.

Macdonald, Kenneth Lachlan, born in East Indies 1868; 2s. Lachlan, gent. ST. JOHN'S, matric. 16 Oct., 86, aged 18, B.A. 90; bar.-at-law, Inner Temple, 91.

Macdonald, Patrick Ogilvy, born at Montrose, Forfarshire, 20 Sept., 1862; 2s. Patrick, gent. LINCOLN, matric. 17 Oct., 84, aged 22 (from St. Andrews, and Edinburgh university), scholar 84, B.A. 88; HONOURS :—2 classical mods. 86, 3 classics 88.

Macdonald, Robert Stewart, born at Cardiff 1854; 2s. Alexander, gen. NON-COLLEGIATE, matric. 8 June, 80, aged 35 (from Cardiff school); migrated to ST. JOHN'S, B.A. 92.

Macdonald, Ronald, born in London 27 Oct., 1860; 2s. George, LL.D. (the novelist). TRINITY, matric. 14 Oct., 82, aged 21, B.A. 85; HONOURS :—3 history 85.

McDonell, Angus, born at Lower Broughton, co. Lanc., 1867; 3s. Æneas Ronald, arm. UNIVERSITY COLL., matric. 17 Oct., 85, aged 18.

Macdonell, Arthur Anthony, M.A., deputy professor of Sanskrit 88, etc., where see page 9.

Macdonell, Philip James, born in London 10 Jan., 1873; 1s. James, gen. BRASENOSE, matric. 15 Oct., 90, aged 17 (from Clifton coll.), exhibitioner 90; librarian of Oxford union society 93.

McDougall, Dugald Gordon, born at Hawthorn, near Melbourne, 28 March, 1867; 2s. Dugald, gen. BALLIOL, matric. 18 Oct., 88, aged 21 (from Melbourne university, M.A.), exhibitioner 89, B.A. 92 (HONOURS :—1 classical mods. 90, 1 law 92); bar.-at-law, Inner Temple, 92.

McDowall, Charles Robert Loraine, born at Malvern, co. Worcester, 9 June, 1872; 1s. Charles, D.D., head master of Highgate school. EXETER, matric. 22 Oct., 91, aged 19 (from Marlborough coll.), scholar 91.

Mace, Arthur Cruttenden, born at Glenorchy, Tasmania, 1874; 2s. John Cruttenden, cler. KEBLE, matric. 15 Oct., 92, aged 18, from St. Edward's school, Summertown.

Mace, J.hn Henry Bromby, born at Hobart, in Tasmania, March, 1870; 1s. John Cruttenden, cler. KEBLE, matric. 12 Oct., 89, aged 19 (from St. Edward's school, Summertown); HONOURS :—4 history 92.

Macfadyen, Alfred Newth, born at Manchester 3 Nov., 1869; 4s. John Allison, D.D., congregational minister. WADHAM, matric. 15 Oct., 88, aged 18 (from Manchester gr. school), exhibitioner 87, B.A. 92; HONOURS :—2 classical mods. 90, 2 classics 92.

Macfadyen, Dugald, born at Whalley Range, co. Lanc., 25 Dec., 1867; 3s. John Allison, D.D. MERTON, matric. 21 Oct., 86, aged 18 (from Manchester gr. school), exhibitioner 86, B.A. 90; HONOURS :—2 history 89, 1 theology 91.

McFadyen, John Edgar, born at Glasgow 17 July, 1870; 1s. James Hemphill, gen. BALLIOL, matric. 14 Oct., 90, aged 20 (from Glasgow university), exhibitioner 90; HONOURS :—1 classical mods. 92, septuagint prize 93.

Macfadyen, William Allison, born at Manchester 1865; 1s. John Allison, D.D. BRASENOSE, matric. 22 Oct., 83, aged 18 (from Manchester gr. school), scholar 83, B.A. 88; HONOURS :—2 classical mods. 85, 2 classics 87, 2 history 88.

McFarlane, Alfred James, born 20 June, 1870; 4s. Samuel, cler. NON-COLLEGIATE, matric. 12 Oct., 89, aged 19 (from Bradford modern school); migrated to MERTON, B.A. 92; HONOURS :—3 history 92.

McGilchrist, John, born at Kilarrow, co. Argyll, 1866; 1s. John, cler. BALLIOL, matric. 16 Oct., 86, aged 20 (from Glasgow university), exhibitioner 88, 2 classics 90.

McGrath, George Robert Blake, born at Alderley Edge, Cheshire, 30 Nov., 1871; 1s. William Valentine Blake, of Manchester, arm. MAGDALEN, matric. 14 Oct., 90, aged 18, from Harrow.

McGregor, Alexander John, born at Robertson, Cape of Good Hope, 1865; 1s. Andrew, cler. ORIEL, matric. 26 Jan., 84, aged 19, exhibitioner 85, B.A. 87 (HONOURS :—1 history 87), librarian 86, and president of Oxford union society 88; bar.-at-law, Inner Temple, 89.

Macgregor, Peter Balderston, born at Helidon, Australia, 1866; 1s. Alexander Balderston, gen. NON-COLLEGIATE, matric. 2 June, 84, aged 18 (from Ipswich gr. school, Queensland); migrated to BALLIOL 85, B.A. 88; HONOURS :—3 mathematical mods. 86.

Machell, Walter Leonard, born at Auckland, N.Z., 6 Feb., 1866; 2s. Robert Scott, capt. 82nd regt. EXETER, matric. 23 Oct., 85, aged 19 (from Westward Ho! coll.), B.A. 90, M.A. 92.

Machen, rev. Richard Dighton, born at Staunton, co. Glouc., Sept., 1868; 3s. Edward, cler. KEBLE, matric. 17 Oct., 87, aged 19 (from Rossall school), B.A. 90; HONOURS:—3 theology 90.

MacHutchin, Arthur, born at Talke, co. Stafford, 12 March, 1863; 1s. Mark Wicks, rector. CHARSLEY'S HALL, matric. 13 Oct., 81, aged 18 (from K. William coll. I.M.); migrated to QUEEN'S 82.

McIntire, Ninian Edward, born at Barton Leonard, Yorks, 9 May, 1862; 1s. Travis, cler. QUEEN'S, matric. 25 Oct., 80, aged 18 (from Giggleswick gr. school), exhibitioner 80-4, B.A. 84, M.A. 67; HONOURS:—3 mathematical mods. 82, 3 maths. 84.

McIntosh, Henry James, born at Edinburgh 1865; 2s. George, arm. CHRIST CHURCH, matric. 10 Oct., 84, aged 19 (from Edinburgh university); assist. magistrate and collector Bengal 86.

McIntyre, James Lewis, born at Edinburgh 1868; 3s. James, gen. UNIVERSITY COLL., matric. 15 Oct., 87, aged 19 (from Edinburgh university), scholar 87, B.A. 91; HONOURS—2 classical mods. 89, 1 classics 91.

Macirone, Francis Peter, born in London 1 Aug., 1871; o.s. George Augustus, of the Admiralty. ST. JOHN'S, matric. 11 Oct., 90, aged 19 (from Felsted school), exhibitioner 92; HONOURS:—3 classical mods. 92.

MacIver, David, born in London 31 Oct., 1873; o.s. John, gen., deceased. QUEEN'S, matric. 27 Oct., 92, aged 19 (from Radley coll.), scholar 92.

Mack, Arthur Paston, born at Paston Hall, Norfolk, 1863; 6s. John, gent. WORCESTER, matric. 20 Oct., 81, aged 18.

Mackall, John William, M.A., fellow BALLIOL 82-91, where see page 68.

Mackarness, Arthur John Coleridge, born 30 April, 1865; 3s. John Fielder, bishop of Oxford. TRINITY, matric. 15 Oct., 83, aged 18 (from Winchester), B.A. 86.

McKay, Harold, born at Rumboldswyke, Sussex, 4 Feb., 1873; 3. John, gen. NON-COLLEGIATE, matric. 17 Oct., 91, aged 18, from Central school, Chichester.

Mackay, rev. Henry Falconer Barclay, born at Milford Haven, co. Pembroke, 24 March, 1864; 1s. Alexander Eugene, D.Med. MERTON, matric. 12 Oct., 83, aged 19, B.A. 87, M.A. 90 (HONOURS:—1 theology 87); curate of All Saints, Clifton, Bristol, 91.

Mackay, John Archibald, born at Rothesay 1861; 1s. John, gent. CHRIST CHURCH, matric. 30 Oct., 85, aged 24 (from Glasgow university), exhibitioner 85; HONOURS:—1 classical mods. 87, 3 classics 89.

Mackay, John William, born in San Francisco 12 Aug., 1870; 1s. John William, U.S. senator for Nevada. WADHAM, matric. 29 April, 89, aged 18, from Beaumont coll. near Windsor.

Mackay, Malcolm, born at Shepton Mallet, Somerset, May, 1873; 3s. George, solicitor. KEBLE, matric. 15 Oct., 92, aged 19, from Lancing coll.

Mackay, Robert John, born at Edinburgh 1859; o.s. Robert Gordon, gen. UNIVERSITY COLL., matric. 15 Oct., 81, aged 22 (from Edinburgh university), scholar 81-3.

McKean, John Fairbairn, born at Edinburgh; 5s. Andrew, esquire. HERTFORD, matric. 20 Oct., 91, aged (from Watson's coll. and Edinburgh university), scholar 92; HONOURS:—1 mathematical mods. 92, junior mathematical exhibition 93.

McKee, rev. John Reginald, born at Belfast 2 June, 1865; o.s. John, EXETER, matric. 28 Jan., 86, aged 20, B.A. 89, M.A. 92 (HONOURS:—2 theology 89); curate of Melbourne, co. Derby, 90.

McKee, William John, born at Clogherney, co. Tyrone, 30 March, 1866; 1s. John, gen. JESUS COLL., matric. 1 Nov., 87, aged 21, from Queen's coll., Galway.

McKenzie, Alexander Gordon, born at Bishop Wearmouth, co. Durham, 23 June, 1871; 1s. Alexander George, solicitor. CHRIST CHURCH, matric. 6 June, 90, aged 18, from Rugby.

Mackenzie, Farquhar John Conrad, born at Edinburgh April, 1861; 3s. Donald, gent. KEBLE, matric. 19 Oct., 80, aged 19 (from Loretto school); scholar 80-4, B.A. 84; HONOURS:—2 classical mods. 82, a classics 84.

Mackenzie, Francis Granville, born in London 31 Aug., 1865; 2s. sir Kenneth Smith (sol-disant), bart. NEW COLL., matric. 10 Oct., 84, aged 19 (from Wellington coll.); bar.-at-law, Inner Temple, 89.

Mackenzie, Hector Graham Gordon, born at Leamington 11 Aug., 1869; 4s. Gordon Gates, arm., deceased. MAGDALEN, matric. 16 Oct., 88, aged 19 (from Winchester), B.A. 92; HONOURS:—3 classical mods. 90, 3 history 92.

Mackenzie, John George Kenneth, born in London 7 Sept., 1863; 1s. John Henry, solicitor, deceased. NEW COLL., matric. 14 Oct., 82, aged 19 (from Winchester), scholar 82-6, B.A. 86, M.A. 90; HONOURS:—1 classical mods. 84, 2 classics 86.

Mackenzie, rev. Kenneth, born at Edinburgh June, 1865; 6s. Donald, arm. KEBLE, matric. 16 Oct., 83, aged 20 (from Loretto school), B.A. 87 (HONOURS: —2 classical mods. 85, 3 history 87); curate of St. Mary, Redcliffe, Bristol, 90.

Mackenzie, Kenneth John, born at Edinburgh 6 Oct., 1861; 1s. sir Kenneth Smith (sol-disant), bart. NON-COLLEGIATE, matric. 21 May, 80, aged 18 (from Charterhouse and Rugby); lieut. 4th batt. (Prince Consort's Own) rifle brigade.

Mackenzie, Martin Edward, born at Dissington, Cumberland, Sept. 1863; 1s. Hugh Munro, gent. KEBLE, matric. 17 Oct., 82, aged 19 (from Glenalmond coll.), B.A. 85.

Mackenzie, Samuel Kenneth, born in London 1869; 2s. Samuel, gen. HERTFORD, matric. 19 Oct., 88, aged 19, from Highgate school.

Mackenzie, William Kenneth Seaforth, born at Sydney, N.S.W., 1872; 2s. Walter Fawkes, D.Med. ST. JOHN'S, matric. 17 Oct., 91, aged 19, from Sydney university.

Mackenzie, William Roderick Dalziel, born at Harpsden, near Henley, Oxon, Sept., 1864; 1s. William Dalziel, arm. CHRIST CHURCH, matric. 22 April, 84, aged 19.

Mackesy, Thomas Lewis, born at Waterford Aug., 1862; 1s. Henry, arm. KEBLE, matric. 18 Oct., 81, aged 19 (from Wellington), scholar 81-5, B.A. 85; HONOURS:—2 classical mods. 83, 3 classics 85.

Mackie, Edmund St. Gascoigne, born at Cotham, co. Glouc., Jan., 1867; 5s. John, cler. KEBLE, matric. 19 Oct., 86, aged 19, chorister Magdalen 76-18 (from Sedbergh gr. school), exhibitioner 86, B.A. 89; HONOURS:—3 classical mods. 88, 2 theology 89.

Mackinder, Halford John, born at Gainsborough 18 Feb., 1861; 1s. Draper, D.Med. CHRIST CHURCH, matric. 15 Oct., 80, aged 19 (from Epsom coll.), scholar 80-5, B.A. 83, M.A. 87, student 92 (HONOURS:—1 natural science 83, 2 history 84, Burdett-Coutts scholarship 83, treasurer 82, and president of Oxford union society 84, university reader in geography 87; bar.-at-law, Inner Temple, 86.

Mackinder, Lionel Everard, born at Gainsborough 1868; 3s. Draper, D.Med. NON-COLLEGIATE, matric. 15 Oct., 92, aged 24, from Epsom coll.

Mackinnon, Frank Douglas, born at Hornsey, Middx., 11 Feb., 1871; 1s. Benjamin Thomas, gen. TRINITY, matric. 11 Oct. 90, aged 19 (from Highgate school), exhibitioner 89; HONOURS :—1 classical mods. 92.

Mackintosh, Neil Donald, born at Raigmore, Inverness, 31 Dec., 1866; 1s. Æneas William, arm. CHRIST CHURCH, matric. 1 June, 88, aged 21, from Eton.

Mackintosh, William Eneas, born at Edinburgh March, 1870; 1s. William, arm. CHRIST CHURCH, matric. 18 Jan., 89, aged 18 (from Harrow), B.A. 92; HONOURS :—4 history 92.

Mackintosh, William Lachlan, born at Inverness 1860; 1s. Eneas, arm. ST. MARY HALL, matric. 23 Oct., 82, aged 22; migrated to PEMBROKE, B.A. 86, M.A. 90.

Mackonochie, Charles Alexander, born at Marlow, Bucks, Jan., 1870; 4s. James, arm. CHRIST CHURCH, matric. 11 Oct., 89, aged 19 (from Lancing coll.), B.A. 93.

Mackonochie, rev. James Alison, born in London 1861; 2s. James, arm. CHRIST CHURCH, matric. 21 May, 80, aged 19, B.A. 84, M.A. 92; chaplain to earl of Home 91.

McLachlan, Angus, born at Darlington, co. Durham, Oct., 1861; 4s. Thomas, arm. KEBLE, matric. 19 Oct., 86, aged 25 (from Loretto school), B.A. 89; HONOURS :—4 history 89.

Maclachlan, rev. Archibald Campbell, born at Newton Valence, Hants, 11 April, 1864; 1s. Archibald Neil, vicar. MAGDALEN, matric. 16 Oct., 84, aged 20 (from Eton), B.A. 90.

McLachlan, Donald, born at Darlington 4 Oct., 1873; 1s. Thomas Hope, artist. NEW COLL., matric. 14 Oct., 92, aged 20, from Loretto school.

Maclagan, Edward Douglas, born at Murri, East Indies, 25 Aug., 1864; 4s. Robert, general R.E. NEW COLL., matric. 12 Oct., 83, aged 19 (from Winchester), B.A. 86, M.A. 90 (HONOURS :—2 classics 86); assist. commissioner Punjab 85.

McLaren, rev. Douglas, born in London Jan., 1866; 3s. John Wingate, arm. ORIEL, matric. 23 Oct., 85, aged 19 (from King's coll., London), B.A. 89, M.A. 92 (HONOURS :—2 theology 89); curate of Micheldean, co. Glouc., 91.

MacLaren, John Wallace Hozier, born at Summertown, near Oxford, 16 July, 1861; 3s. Archibald, gen. MAGDALEN, matric. 16 Oct., 80, aged 19 (from Wellington), exhibitioner 83-4, B.A. 85, M.A. 87 (HONOURS :—2 classical mods. 82, 3 classics 84); master of preparatory school at Summertown.

McLaughlin, John Fletcher, born at Cartwright, Ontario. 17 July, 1863; 4s. John, esq., deceased. NON-COLLEGIATE, matric. 15 Oct., 92, aged 29, from Victoria university, Ontario.

McLaughlin, Vivian Guy Ouseley, born at Woolwich, Kent, 25 Sept., 1865; 4s. Edward, col. R.A. LINCOLN, matric. 27 Oct., 85, aged 20, from Clifton coll.

Maclean, Alexander, born in London 15 Aug., 1867; 1s. Henry, gent. CHRIST CHURCH, matric. 16 Oct., 85, aged 18 (from Westminster school), B.A. 90; bar.-at-law, Middle Temple, 91.

McLean, Alexander, born in Bavaria 1869; 2s. Lachlan, gen. BRASENOSE, matric. 20 Oct., 87, aged 18, from Blackheath school and King's coll., London.

McLean, Douglas Hamilton, born at Sydney, N.S.W., 18 March, 1863; 2s. John Donald, gent., deceased. NEW COLL., matric. 14 Oct., 82, aged 19 (from Eton), B.A. 87 (HONOURS :—4 history 86), in the Oxford eight 83, 4, 5, 7.

Maclean, Francis John, born in London 1872; 3s. Henry, gent. CHRIST CHURCH, matric. 10 Oct., 90, aged 18, from Westminster school.

McLean, Hector, born at Sydney, N.S.W., 5 Nov., 1864; 3s. John Donald, arm. NEW COLL., matric. 26 Jan., 85, aged 20 (from Eton), in the University eight 85, 6, 7, president of the University boat club; died 20 Jan., 1888.

MacLean, John Alexander, born at Sydney, Australia, 14 July, 1866; 4s. John Donald, arm., deceased. NEW COLL., matric. 16 Oct., 85, aged 19, from Eton.

McLean, Malcolm Parker Millar, born at Hampstead, Middx., 27 March, 1867; 2s. Thomas Millar, gen. WORCESTER, matric. 16 Dec., 87, aged 20, B.A. 91.

McLean, Norman, born at Hawthornden, N.S.W., 2 April, 1861; 1s. John Donald, arm., deceased. NEW COLL., matric. 24 Jan., 81, aged 19 (from Eton), B.A. 84; HONOURS :—4 history 84.

Macleane, rev. Douglas, M.A., fellow PEMBROKE 82-92, where see.

Macleay, James William Ronald, born in Edinburgh 1870; 1s. Alexander, arm. BALLIOL, matric. 17 Oct., 89, aged 19 (from the Charterhouse); HONOURS :—3 history 92.

Macleod, Norman Cranstoun, born at Invergordon castle, Ross-shire, 1866; 3s. Robert Bruce Æneas, commander R.N. NEW COLL., matric. 16 Oct., 85, aged 19 (from Wellington), B.A. 89 (HONOURS :—2 law 88); bar.-at-law, Inner Temple, 90.

Maclure, Edward St. John, born at Burnley, co. Lanc., April, 1864; 1s. Edward Craig, dean of Manchester. KEBLE, matric. 16 Oct., 83, aged 19 from Rossall school (HONOURS :—3 theology 86) died 2 Sept., 87.

McMaster, Kenneth Hovil, born at Lambeth 12 Jan., 1870; 2s. Joseph, arm. BRASENOSE, matric. 1 Oct., 89, aged 19 (from Dulwich coll.), exhibitioner 89; HONOURS :—3 classical mods. 91.

Macmillan, Alexander, created M.A. 25 March, 1881, late publisher to the university.

Macmillan, Alexander, born at Shallock, co. Ayr, 3 Aug., 1866; 1s. Alexander, arm. LINCOLN, matric. 20 Oct., 90, aged 24 (from Glasgow university), scholar 90; HONOURS :—3 classical mods. 92.

McMillan, rev. Charles Duncan Horatio, born at Keynsham, near Bristol, 24 March, 1864; o.s. Charles, gent. NON-COLLEGIATE, matric. 13 Oct., 84, aged 20 (from Bruton gr. school and Bristol coll.); migrated to WADHAM 29 Jan., 86, B.A. 88, M.A. 92 (HONOURS :—2 history 88); curate of Wakefield 91.

McMillan, James, born at Dumfries 28 Oct., 1859; o.s. Robert, gent. QUEEN'S, matric. 10 Nov., 85, aged 26 (from Dumfries school and Glasgow university); bible clerk 85.

McMullen, Alan, born at Hertford 28 May, 1872; 6s. Alexander Peter, arm. BALLIOL, matric. 14 Oct., 90, aged 18 (from Rugby), scholar 89.

McMullen, rev. Richard Gell, B.D., fellow CORPUS CHRISTI 35-46, where see page 981.

Macnab, Arthur Alexander, born at Halifax, Canada, 1867; 2s. Alexander, of London, gent. UNIVERSITY COLL., matric. 17 Oct., 85, aged 18 (from St. Edward's school, Summertown), B.A. 88; HONOURS :—3 history 88.

Macnaghten, Terence Charles, born at Allahabad, India, 3 Dec., 1872; 3s. Elliot, M.A. Bengal C.S. HERTFORD, matric. 22 Oct., 92, aged 19 (from the Charterhouse), scholar 91.

McNair, Arthur Wyndham, born at Norwood, London, 23 Aug., 1872; 4s. John Frederick Adolphus, C.M.G. major R.A., retd., sometime governor of Penang. BALLIOL, matric. 20 Oct., 91, aged 19 (from St. Paul's school); selected candidate Indian C.S. 91.

McNeile, Hector, M.A., fellow ST. JOHN'S 65-71, where see page 487.

McNeill, Alexander, born at Edinburgh 19 Dec., 1862; 4s. Alexander, arm. TRINITY, matric. 15 Oct., 81, aged 18 (from Loretto school), B.A. 85; HONOURS:—2 history 85.

McNeill, Duncan, born in London 19 Aug., 1864; 1s. Malcolm, arm. CORPUS CHRISTI, matric. 19 Oct., 83, aged 19 (from the Charterhouse), scholar 83, B.A. 87 (HONOURS:—2 classical mods. 84, 2 classics 87); bar.-at-law, Inner Temple, 89.

McNeill, Ronald John, born at Torquay, Devon, 1862; o.s. Edmund John, gent. CHRIST CHURCH, matric. 2 Feb., 82, aged 20, B.A. 86 (HONOURS:— 2 history 84); of Craigdunn, co. Antrim; bar.-at-law, Lincoln's Inn, 88.

Maconochie, Alexander Francis, born at Mitcham 16 Nov., 1862; 1s. Alexander, of Wimbledon, gent. BALLIOL, matric. 21 Oct., 80, aged 17 (from Westminster school); and assist. collector and magistrate Baroda 82.

Maconochie, Evan, born at Edinburgh 8 July, 1868; 3s. Alexander, of C.S., deceased. NEW COLL., matric. 14 Oct., 87, aged 19 (from Sherborne school); assist. collector and magistrate Panch Mahals, and assist. political agent Narukut, Bombay c.s.

Macphail, Edmund Whittingstall St. Maur, M.A., JESUS COLL., wh ire see.

Macpherson, Arthur Hoste, born at Calcutta 4 Jan., 1857; 2s. sir Arthur George, K.C.I.E. TRINITY, matric. 17 Oct., 83, aged 19 (from Marlborough coll.), B.A. 88, M.A. and B.C. L. 92; HONOURS:— 3 law 88, a civil law 90.

Macpherson, Ewan Francis, born at Bernera, Australia, 1864; 5s. Allan, arm. BRASENOSE, matric. 22 Oct., 83, aged 19 (from Winchester), scholar 83-6, exhibitioner 86, B.A. 88 (HONOURS:—1 classical mods. 85, 2 classics 87, 2 law 88); an advocate, Edinburgh.

Macpherson, Ewen, born at Calcutta 1 Sept., 1872; 4s. sir Arthur George, K.C.I.E., a judge of high court, India. TRINITY, matric. 17 Oct., 91, aged 19, from Haileybury.

McPherson, Hugh, born at Paisley, co. Renfrew, 1870; 1s. Duncan, gen. BALLIOL, matric. 17 Oct., 89, aged 19 (from Paisley gr. school and Glasgow university), exhibitioner 89; assist. magistrate and collector Bengal 91.

McPherson, Joseph William, born at Brislington, Somerset, 1866; 6s. Donegal, gen. CHRIST CHURCH, matric. 14 Oct., 87, aged 21 (from Dublin coll. of science), scholar 86, B.A. 90; HONOURS:—1 chemistry 90.

McPherson, Robert William, born at St. Andrews, Scotland, 1864; 3s. John, gen. BALLIOL, matric. 16 Oct., 83, aged 19 (from St. Andrews university); selected candidate Indian c.s. 83.

Macpherson, William Charteris, born in London 1862; 2s. William, arm. ORIEL, matric. 18 Oct., 81, aged 19 (from the Charterhouse), student Middle Temple 83.

McPherson, William Hay, born at St. Andrews, Fife, 10 March, 1868; 4s. John, gen. LINCOLN, matric. 21 Oct., 87, aged 19 (from St. Andrews university), exhibitioner 88; HONOURS:— 2 classical mods. 89, 2 classics 91.

Macqueen, Archibald, born at St. Bees, Cumberland, 23 June, 1867; 1s. John, a master at St. Bees. QUEEN'S, matric. 25 Oct., 86, aged 19 (from St. Bees gr. school), exhibitioner 86, B.A. 90; HONOURS: —2 classical mods. 88, 3 classics 90.

Macran, Henry Stewart, born at Dublin 1867; 2s. Henry Edward, cler. BALLIOL, matric. 1 May 89, aged 22, scholar Trinity coll. Dublin, 86, and fellow 90; HONOURS:—1 classics and 1 modern literature at Dublin university 88.

Macray, Walter Robert, born at Bletchington, Oxon, 1863; 4s. William Dunn, rector of Ducklington. NON-COLLEGIATE, matric. 30 Oct., 82, aged 19 (from Sutton Valence school), B.A. 86, M.A. 90; HONOURS:—3 classical mods. 84, 3 classics 86.

Macray, William Dunn, M.A., fellow MAGDALEN 91, where see page 316.

Macrorie, Basil Francis Newall, born at Accrington, co. Lanc., 11 March, 1867; 1s. William Kenneth, bishop of Maritzburg. BRASENOSE, matric. 20 Oct., 86, aged 19, from Winchester.

Macvey, Thomas, born at Edinburgh 16 July, 1871; 1s. John, gen. WADHAM, matric. 20 Oct., 91, aged 20 (from Edinburgh university), scholar 89.

Macvicar, Charles Robert, born at Weybridge, Surrey, 4 June, 1868; 1s. Joseph Duncan, cler. TRINITY, matric. 13 Oct., 88, aged 20 (from Marlborough coll.), exhibitioner 88, B.A. 92; HONOURS:—2 classical mods. 90, 4 classics 92.

MacVicar, Herbert Montgomerie, born at Rayleigh, Essex, 18 Dec., 1871; 2s. Joseph Duncan, cler. BRASENOSE, matric. 22 Oct., 91, aged 19 (from Marlborough coll. and Tiverton gr. school), exhibitioner 91.

McVicker, John William, born at Londonderry 1861; 1s. Alexander, gent. WORCESTER, matric. 18 Oct., 83, aged 22 (from Queen's coll., Belfast), exhibitioner 83-4.

Macy, rev. Vincent Travers, born at Oxhill, co. Warwick, 1868; 5s. Vincent Hardwicke, cler. NON-COLLEGIATE, matric. 23 Jan., 86, aged 18 (from Merchant Taylors' school), B.A. 89, M.A. 92; curate of St. Thomas, Portman Square, London, 91.

Madan, Arthur Cornwallis, M.A., senior student CHRIST CHURCH 69, where see page 407.

Madan, Falconer, B.A., fellow BRASENOSE 76-81 and 86, where see page 350.

Madan, Henry George, M.A., fellow QUEEN'S 61, where see page 173.

Madan, Spencer, born at Torquay, Devon, April, 1867; 12. Spencer, cler. deceased. PEMBROKE, matric. 28 Oct., 86, aged 19, from St. Mark's school, Windsor.

Maddock, Philip Harington, born at Trowbridge, Wilts, 21 April, 1863; o.s. Philip Bainbridge, cler. LINCOLN, matric. 23 Oct., 82, aged 19 (from Marlborough coll.), scholar 82-6, B.A. 86, M.A. 89; HONOURS:—1 classical mods. 84, 3 classics 86, 3 history 87.

Maddox, Stuart Lockwood, born at Aleppo, East Indies, 3 June, 1866; 2s. Ralph Henry, cler. WORCESTER, matric. 22 Oct., 85, aged 19 (from Fettes coll.), exhibitioner 85, B.A. 88, M.A. 92 (HONOURS: —3 law 88); assist. magistrate and collector Bengal.

Madeley, Walter, born at Handsworth, co. Stafford, 2 June, 1865; 1s. Frederick, gent. NEW COLL., matric. 10 Oct., 84, aged 19 (from Rugby), B.A. 89, M.A. 91; HONOURS:—1 classical mods. 86, 2 classics 88.

Magee, rev. John Arthur Victor, born 8 Oct., 1869; 3s. William Connor, bishop of Peterborough (after archbishop York), MERTON, matric. 22 Oct., 87, aged 18 (from Haileybury), B.A. 90 (HONOURS:—3 history 90), president of the Oxford union society 92.

Magnus, Laurie, born in London 5 Aug., 1872; 1s. Philip, B.A. and B.SC. Lond. MAGDALEN, matric. 22 Oct., 91, aged 19 (from St. Paul's school), demy 91.

Magor, Richard Martin, born at Penzance, Cornwall, 1865; 3s. Martin, gent. WORCESTER, matric. 18 Oct., 83, aged 18.

Magrath, John Richard, D.D., provost of QUEEN'S 78, where see page 172.
Maguire, James Rochefort, M.A., fellow ALL SOULS' 79-86, where see page 285.
Mahaffy, Arthur William, born at Howth, co. Dublin, 22 Oct., 1869; 1s. John Pentland, D.D. MAGDALEN, matric. 16 Oct., 88, aged 18 (from Trinity coll., Dublin, and Marlborough); demy 88 (HONOURS:—3 classical mods. 90); passed for the army.
Mahaffy, John Pentland, D.D., hon. fellow QUEEN'S 1882; created D.C.L. 22 June, 92, prof. ancient history in university of Dublin 71, scholar Trinity coll., Dublin, 58, B.A. 59, M.A. 62, fellow 64, D.D. 86, senior moderator in classics and philosophy 59, Donnellan lecturer 73, examiner and lecturer in classics, philosophy, music and modern languages, Dublin university; born near Vevay 26 Feb., 39. For list of his works see *Men and Women of the Time*.
Mahon, Edward, born at Rawmarsh, Yorks, 11 June, 1862; 4s. William Vesey, bart. EXETER, matric. 4 June, 81, aged 18 (from Marlborough coll.), B.A. 84; HONOURS:—3 law 84.
Mahon, Foster McMahon, born at Aspley Guise, Beds, 1873; 1s. William Henry Cortlandt, solicitor. UNIVERSITY COLL., matric. 15 Oct., 92, aged 19, from Dulwich coll.
Mahon, rev. George Edward, born at Leighton Mendip, Somerset, July, 1861; 2s. George Augustus, cler. KEBLE, matric. 19 Oct., 80, aged 19 (from Lancing coll.), B.A. 83, M.A. 88 (HONOURS:— 3 theology 83); curate of New Clee, co. Linc., 85.
Maidlow, John Mott, M.A., fellow QUEEN'S 62-75, where see page 182.
Maidment, Horace James, born at Henstridge, Somerset, 11 Jan., 1865; 2s. Thomas, gent. JESUS COLL., matric. 18 Oct., 83, aged 18; migrated to NON-COLLEGIATE, B.A. 88, M.A. 91; HONOURS:—3 classical mods. 85, 3 classics 87.
Maillard, Jonas Daniel, born at South Petherton, Somerset, 5 Oct., 1864; 2s. Daniel Galland, Wesleyan minister. NON-COLLEGIATE, matric. 15 Oct., 87, aged 21 (from Kingswood school, Bath, and University coll., Cardiff), scholar JESUS COLL. 88, B.A. 91; HONOURS:—1 classical mods. 89, 2 classics 91.
Main, James, born at Burghead near Elgin, 1855; 7s. William, pleb. NON-COLLEGIATE, matric. 15 Oct., 81, aged 26, from Glasgow university.
Mainwaring, Charles Egerton Forbes Milman, born in the Mauritius 20 Feb., 1867; 1s. Egerton Miles, arm. MAGDALEN, matric. 20 Oct., 85, aged 18 (from Eton), B.A. 89.
Mair, Robert Bird Robertson, born at Barranagore, Calcutta, 12 May, 1870; 4s. William, of Knowehead, Crieff, co. Perth, C.E. QUEEN'S, matric. 27 Oct., 92, aged 22, from St. Andrews university.
Maitland, David Baxter, born at Dundee 12 April, 1872; 1s. Edward Francis, of Hazel Hall, Dundee. MAGDALEN, matric. 11 Oct., 90, aged 18, from Eton.
Majendie, Lionel Robert, born at Elvetham, Hants, Sept., 1871; 1s. Arthur, cler. CHRIST CHURCH, matric. 6 June, 90, aged 18 (from Winchester); HONOURS:—2 classical mods. 92.
Majendie, rev. William Richard Stuart, born at Tipperary Jan., 1869; 1s. William Francis, arm. KEBLE, matric. 17 Oct., 87, aged 18 (from Honiton school), B.A. 90.
Makins, Ernest, born at Kensington 14 Oct., 1869; 1s. Henry Francis, arm. CHRIST CHURCH, matric. 19 Oct., 88, aged 18, from Winchester.

Malan, Walter de Merindol, born at Wimbledon, Surrey, 20 Sept., 1873; 1s. Arthur Noel, cler. NEW COLL., matric. 14 Oct., 92, aged 19 (from Winchester), scholar 91.
Malcolm, Ian Zachary, born in Quebec, Canada, 3 Sept., 1868; 1s. Edward Donald, col. R.E. NEW COLL., matric. 14 Oct., 87, aged 19, from Eton.
Malcolm, James Aratoon, born at Bushera, Persia, 1867; 4s. Aratoon, arm. BALLIOL, matric. 10 Feb., 86, aged 18, from Cliftonville school, Margate.
Malcolm, Napier, born at Ranley Grange, near Worcester, 17 March, 1870; 4s. George, C.C.S., general in the army. NEW COLL., matric. 11 Oct., 89, aged 19 (from Halleybury); HONOURS:—2 classical mods. 91.
Malcolm, William Rolle, M.A., fellow ALL SOULS' 64-75, where see page 281.
Malcolmson, Joseph, born at Waterford, Ireland, 12 May, 1862; 0. s. David, arm. NEW COLL., matric. 23 Jan., 82, aged 19, from Eton.
Malden, Alfred William, born at Biggleswade, Beds, 31 Oct., 1868; 1s. Joshua John, gen. QUEEN'S, matric. 21 Oct., 87, aged 18 (from Felsted school), B.A. 91; HONOURS:—4 law 91.
Malden, rev. Percy, born at Pattingham, co. Stafford, June, 1863; 2s. Ringham Sibthorpe, cler. CHARSLEY'S HALL, matric. 31 Oct., 82, aged 19 (from Canterbury school); migrated to KEBLE, B.A. 87; curate of St. John the Divine, Kennington, Surrey, 88.
Malet, Leonard de Carteret, born at Riccarton in New Zealand 1870; 1s. Frederick de Carteret, gen. CHRIST CHURCH, matric. 11 Oct., 89, aged 19.
Maling, Arthur Freville, born at Sunderland 29 July, 1872; 1s. Edward Allan, D.Med. EXETER, matric. 22 Oct., 91, aged 19, from Rossall school.
Maling, rev. Henry Bromley, born at Christ Church, N.Z., June, 1864; 1s. Thomas James, gent. KEBLE, matric. 16 Oct., 83, aged 19 (from Christ Church gr. school, N.Z.), B.A. 86, M.A. 89 (HONOURS:— 3 history 86); curate Holy Trinity, Ely, 87.
Malins, Herbert, born at Cradley, co. Stafford, 17 Sept., 1869; 2s. Edward, arm. EXETER, matric. 17 Oct., 88, aged 19 (from Malvern coll.); migrated to MARCON'S HALL, B.A. 92.
Mallam, Arthur Phosphor, born at Oxford 6 March, 1872; 3s. George, gen. TURRELL'S H LL, matric. 27 Jan., 88, aged 15 (from Leamington and Eastbourne colls.); migrated to WORCESTER, B.A. 92.
Mallam, Ernest, born at Oxford 1 Jan., 1870; 2s. Henry Parr, surgeon. MAGDALEN, matric. 16 Oct., 88, aged 18 (from Clifton coll.), B.A. 92; HONOURS: —1 physiology 92.
Mallam, Herbert Edward, born at Poole Keynes, Wilts, 10 Dec., 1873; 3s. Benjamin, M.A., rector. HERTFORD, matric. 22 Oct., 92, aged 18, from Royss's school, Abingdon.
Malleson, Cecil George, born at Melbourne 1866; o. s. Alfred Brooks, gen. PEMBROKE, matric. 27 Oct., 85, aged 19, from Harrow.
Malleson, rev. Herbert Harry, born at Birkenhead April 1864; 1s. Frederick Amadée, cler. KEBLE, matric. 14 Oct., 82, aged 20 (from royal institution, Liverpool), B.A. 88 (HONOURS:—2 history 88); curate of Longbridge-Deverill, Wilts, 90.
Malleson, Rodbard, born at Wimbledon, Surrey, 1867; o. s. Francis Rodbard, gen. HERTFORD, matric. 27 Oct., 85, aged 18.
Mallet, Charles Edward, born in London 2 Dec., 1862; 1s. Charles, gent. BALLIOL, matric. 18 Oct., 81, aged 18 (from Harrow), B.A. 85 (HONOURS:— 2 classical mods. 83, 1 history 85), librarian Oxford union soc. 85; bar.-at-law, Middle Temple, 89.

Mallet, Louis Dupan, born in London 10 July, 1864; 3s. sir Louis. BALLIOL, matric. 16 Oct., 83, aged 19, from Clifton coll.

Mallett, George Herbert Wippell, born at Jaunpore, Bengal, Feb., 1872; 2s. William George, cler. EXETER, matric. 13 Oct., 90, aged 18, from Exeter gr. school.

Malpas, Theodore Fitz Henry, born at Bishops Waltham, Hants, 1872; 8s. Henry, cler. NON-COLLEGIATE, matric. 27 April, 89, aged 17, from Denstone coll.

Manby, Arthur Francis, born at Cockren, Yorks, 1861; 2s. Aaron, vicar of Nidd. WADHAM, matric. 16 Oct., 80, aged 19, B.A. 84.

Mangin, Robert Rattray, born at Howick, Northumberland, 1 Oct., 1863; 3s. Edward Nangreave, cler., deceased. NEW COLL., matric. 4 Dec., 82, aged 19 (from Marlborough), B.A. 86, M.A. 90; HONOURS :—3 classics 85.

Mann, Archibald Henry, born at Milford, co. Pembroke, 1869; 3s. Gother Frederick, arm. JESUS COLL., matric. 19 Oct., 81, aged 18 (from Elizabeth coll. Guernsey), B.A. 87; HONOURS :— 3 classical mods. 83, 3 classics 85.

Mann, Gerard Noel Cornwallis, born at Falmouth 28 Oct., 1872; 3s. Charles Noel, cler. TRINITY, matric. 17 Oct., 91, aged 18, from Marlborough coll.

Mann, James Saumarez, M.A., fellow TRINITY 79-88, and 89-90, where see page 454.

Manning, Percy, born at Leeds, Yorks, 24 Jan., 1870; 3s. John gent., deceased. NEW COLL., matric. 12 Oct., 88, aged 18 (from Clifton coll.); HONOURS :— 3 classical mods. 90.

Manoukian, Orshag Sarkis Senekerim, born at Guedik, near Constantinople, 1864; 3s. Senekerim. BALLIOL, matric. 17 Oct., 84, aged 18 (from Roberts coll. Constantinople); migrated to NEW INN HALL 85.

Mansel, Algernon Lascelles, born at Affpuddle, Dorset, 6 Sept., 1868; 1s. Arthur Edmund, of Dorchester, arm. MAGDALEN, matric. 22 Oct., 87, aged 19 (from Winchester), B.A. 92; HONOURS: —3 classical mods. 89.

Manson, Alexander, born at Buxton, Notts, 18 Sept., 1844; 1s. Alexander Thomas Grist, cler., deceased. NON-COLLEGIATE, matric. 25 Oct., 90, aged 46, from Cholmeley school, Highgate.

Manston, rev. Augustus Constantine, born at Liverpool 13 April, 1861; 1s. Augustus. gent. NON-COLLEGIATE, matric. 18 Oct., 80, aged 19 (from Liverpool institute); migrated to MERTON, B.A. 84 (HONOURS: —4 classics 84); curate of Christ Church, Marylebone, 87.

Mant, Reginald Arthur, born at Gegoomgan, Queensland, 27 Sept., 1870; 3s. George, gen. TRINITY, matric. 12 Oct., 89, aged 19 (from Maryborough school, Queensland); HONOURS :—2 classical mods. 91.

Mantell, John Charles, born at Swinton Park, Manchester, 20 Oct., 1871; o.s. sir John Iles, kt. WORCESTER, matric. 9 Feb., 92, aged 20.

Manvell, rev. Arnold Edward William, born at Dover, Kent, 1868; 1s. William, gen. NON-COLLEGIATE, matric. 13 Oct., 88, aged 20, B.A. 91.

Mapleton, Harvey William, born at Badgworth, Somerset, 1865; 1s. Harvey Mallory, rector. ST. JOHN'S, matric. 11 Oct., 84, aged 19, B.A. 88; HONOURS :—4 theology 88.

Mapleton, Henry Banbury, born in London 1863; o.s. Henry, D.Med., inspect.-genl. EXETER, matric. 19 Oct., 82, aged 19 (from Clifton coll.), B.A. 86, M.A. 91.

Mapleton, Reginald Bree, born at Badgworth, Somerset, 1869; 2s. Harvey Mallory, rector. ST. JOHN'S, matric. 13 Oct., 88, aged 19 (from St. Mark's school, Windsor), B.A. 91.

Marcon, Cecil Thomas, born at Edgefield, Norfolk, 14 July, 1866; y.s. Walter Hubert, cler. WORCESTER, matric. 17 Dec., 88, aged 22, from Holt gr. school, Norfolk.

Marcon, Charles Abdy, M.A., of ST. MARY HALL, where see.

Marett, Robert Ranulph, born at St. Brelade, Jersey, 13 June, 1866; o.s. sir Robert Pipon, knt. BALLIOL, matric. 22 Jan., 85, aged 18 (from Victoria coll. Jersey), exhibitioner 84, B.A. 89; fellow EXETER 91, M.A. 91 (HONOURS :—1 classical mods. 86, accessit Hertford scholarship 86, Latin verse 87, 1 classics 88); student Inner Temple 85.

Margesson, rev. William Anthony, born at Mountfield, Sussex, 6 Oct., 1866; 3s. Reginald Whitehall, cler. KEBLE, matric. 19 Oct., 86, aged 20 (from Wellington), B.A. 90 (HONOURS :—3 history 89); curate of Harrow Green 91.

Margetts, Francis Edward, born at Duxford, co. Camb., 1860; 2s. Francis Thomas, cler. NON-COLLEGIATE, matric. 18 Oct., 80, aged 20.

Margoliouth, David Samuel, M.A., fellow NEW COLL. 81, where see page 206.

Marindin, Arthur Henry, born at Calcutta 12 Aug., 1868; 1s. Henry Colville, bar.-at-law, NEW COLL., matric. 14 Oct., 87, aged 19 (from Eton and King's coll. London), B.A. 90.

Marjoribanks, hon. Archibald John, born 25 Nov., 1861; 4s. Dudley Coutts, lord Tweedmouth. ORIEL, matric. 12 March, 81, aged 19, from Eton.

Markby, sir William, K.C.I.E., M.A., D.C.L., fellow BALLIOL 83 (where see page 64), and fellow ALL SOULS' 83.

Markheim, Henry William Gegg, M.A., fellow QUEEN'S 71, where see page 175.

Marks, Hugh, born at Croydon, Surrey, May, 1863; 2s. John George, gent. KEBLE, matric. 18 Oct., 83, aged 20 (from Croydon school), B.A. 86, M.A. 90; HONOURS :—2 history 86.

Marples, George Jobson, born at Sheffield 27 July, 1845; 1s. George, arm. ST. MARY HALL, matric. 18 Oct., 88, aged 43; bar.-at-law, Inner Temple, 82.

Marrable, Arthur George, born in London 26 April, 1863; 1s. George, arm. UNIVERSITY COLL., matric. 14 Oct., 82, aged 19, from Rugby (HONOURS: —3 classical mods. 83); of the Staff college, Sandhurst; lieut. King's Own Yorkshire light infantry 85, served in the Burmese expedition 86-7, medal with two clasps.

Marriner, John Sumner, born at Shalford, I.W., 20 April, 1867; o.s. William, cler. TRINITY, matric. 16 Oct., 89, aged 19 (from Wellington), B.A. 89; HONOURS :—3 history 89.

Marriott, Arthur Edward, born at Stockport, Cheshire, 6 April, 1871; 2s. Joshua, gen. ST. JOHN'S, matric. 12 Oct., 89, aged 18, from Rossall school.

Marriott, Charles Bertrand, born at Leicester 1 Oct., 1868; 1s. Charles Hayes, D.Med. TRINITY, matric. 16 Oct., 86, aged 18 (from Uppingham school), B.A. 90 (HONOURS :—3 history 89); bar.-at-law, Inner Temple, 92; brother of John R.

Marriott, Cyril Humphrey White, born at Withersfield, Essex, 15 Feb., 1866; 1s. Humphrey Richard George, of Abbots Hall, Essex, arm. MAGDALEN, matric. 16 Oct., 84, aged 18, from Harrow.

Marriott, Douglas, born at Bowdon, Cheshire, 7 April, 1865; 3s. Francis, solicitor. NEW COLL., matric. 15 Oct., 84, aged 19 (from Repton), B.A. 87; HONOURS :—2 history 87.

Marriott, Ernest Theodore, born at Bowdon, Cheshire, 27 April, 1867; 4s. Francis, gen. MERTON, matric. 25 Oct., 89, aged 22, from Repton.

Marriott, rev. Frank Ransome, born at Bowdon, Cheshire, 1861; 2s. Francis, arm. NEW COLL., matric. 16 Oct., 80, aged 19 (from Repton), B.A. 84, M.A. 87 (HONOURS:—4 law 83); curate 88-90, and vicar of Warlingham, Surrey, 90.

Marriott, John Arthur Ransome, M.A., NEW COLL., where see page 219.

Marriott, John Reginald, born at Leicester 20 Oct., 1871; 3s. Charles Hayes, D.Med. TRINITY, matric. 11 Oct., 90, aged 18, from Eton (HONOURS:—2 classical mods. 92); brother of Charles B.

Marriott, William Edmund, born at Eton 15 Dec., 1863; 3s. Wharton Booth, cler. PEMBROKE, matric. 25 Jan., 83, aged 19 (from Bradfield coll.), scholar 82-5, B.A. 89, M.A. 93; HONOURS:—2 classical mods. 84.

Marriott, William Smith-, born at Sydling, Dorset, 5 Aug., 1865; 1s. John Bosworth, arm. CHRIST CHURCH, matric. 12 Oct., 83, aged 18, B.A. 87, M.A. 90; bar.-at-law, Lincoln's inn, 90.

Marsden, Benjamin Anderton, born at Burstow, Surrey, 23 April, 1872; y.s. Thomas, rector 55-74. NON-COLLEGIATE, matric. 6 Feb., 92, aged 19, from King's coll. school and King's coll., London.

Marsden, Daniel Owen, born in Pen-y-byn, co. Cardigan, 2 July, 1868; 5s. John George, gen. JESUS COLL., matric. 14 Oct., 89, aged 21 (from St. David's coll., Lampeter), scholar 89, B.A. 92; HONOURS:—2 history 92.

Marsh, Bower, born at Rochester 25 Jan., 1866; 2s. Bower, solicitor. EXETER, matric. 23 Oct., 85, aged 19 (from Christ's hospital), scholar 85, B.A. 89; HONOURS:—2 mathematical mods. 87, 2 history 89.

Marsh, Edward Caldecot, born at Belgaum, E. Indies, 17 May, 1865; 1s. Edward Newnham, arm. MERTON, matric. 19 Oct., 83, aged 18 (from Malvern coll.), B.A. 87.

Marsh, Hubert Henry Lovatt Lloyd, born at Sheerness, Kent, 24 Sept., 1870; 1s. Henry, staff paymaster R.N. BRASENOSE, matric. 22 March, 90, aged 19, from Kelly coll., Tavistock.

Marsh, James Ernest, M.A., BALLIOL, where see page 70.

Marsh, John Bishop, born at Plaistow, Essex, 1865; 1s. Richard William, cler. QUEEN'S, matric. 14 Jan., 90, aged 27.

Marsh, rev. William, born at Clayton, Yorks, 1863; o.s. William Hobson, gent. EXETER, matric. 24 Jan., 84, aged 21 (from Hemsworth gr. school and Durham university), scholar 83, B.A. 87, M.A. 91 (HONOURS:—Septuagint prize 85 and 89, Greek testament prize 87, 1 theology 87); vice-principal Gloucester theological college 90.

Marshall, Alfred, M.A., fellow BALLIOL 65-77, where see page 68.

Marshall, Alfred, born at Liverpool May, 1863; y.s. Henry, gent. KEBLE, matric. 18 Oct., 81, aged 18 (from Bedford school), B.A. 84, M.A. 88.

Marshall, Arthur, born in London 1863; 2s. Robert, chief clerk of the rolls. EXETER, matric. 4 June, 81, aged 18, from the Charterhouse.

Marshall, Arthur William Montague, born at Great Barr, co. Stafford, 13 Oct., 1868; 4s. John, ironmaster, late of Cheltenham, deceased. MAGDALEN, matric. 22 Oct., 87, aged 19 (from Harrow), B.A. 91 (HONOURS:—2 classical mods. 89, 3 classics 91); brother of John H. A.

Marshall, Charles Cecil, born at Hartford, Cheshire, 1872; 6s. Thomas Horatio, esq. ORIEL, matric. 27 Oct., 91, aged 19, from Radley coll.

Marshall, Charles Henry Derham, born at Blakemore, co. Hereford, 9 Feb., 1872; 1s. Henry Barnard Derham, cler. KEBLE, matric. 20 Oct., 91, aged 19, from Hereford cathedral school.

Marshall, Cyril Baker, born at Hedenham, Suffolk, 28 Aug., 1868; 1s. Robert Manning, rector. NEW COLL., matric. 14 Oct., 87, aged 19 (from Winchester), B.A. 90; HONOURS:—2 history 90.

Marshall, Douglas Hamilton, born at Wells, Somerset, 23 June, 1867; 5s. Hugh Graham, gen. WORCESTER, matric. 19 Oct., 86, aged 19 (from Fettes coll.), exhibitioner 86, B.A. 91; HONOURS:—2 classical mods. 88, 2 classics 90.

Marshall, Edmond, born at High Wycombe 25 Nov., 1871; 2s. Thomas, gen. NON-COLLEGIATE, matric. 18 Jan., 90, aged 18 (from St. Mark's school, Windsor); migrated to ST. EDMUND HALL, B.A. 92.

Marshall, Edward, M.A., fellow CORPUS CHRISTI 36-46, where see page 381.

Marshall, Ernest Theodore, born at Dundalk 1866; 1s. Henry, arm. CHARSLEY HALL, matric. 15 Oct., 84, aged 18 (from Winchester); migrated to BRASENOSE 85; lieut. the East Yorkshire regt. 91, academical clerk MAGDALEN 89, B.A. 90.

Marshall, Francis Denham, born at Peckham Rye, Surrey, 30 Jan., 1860; 2s. Arthur, arm. EXETER, matric. 28 Oct., 87, aged 18 (from Highgate school).

Marshall, Francis Eden, born at Westcott Barton, Oxon, 1863; 2s. Joiner, cler. ST. JOHN'S, matric. 15 Oct., 81, aged 18 (from the Charterhouse), B.A. 84, M.A. 88.

Marshall, rev. Gerald Keith Stirling, born at Farnham Royal, Bucks, 1866; 3s. Stirling Frederick, cler. HERTFORD, matric. 27 Oct., 85, aged 19, B.A. 89; curate of Barking, Essex, 90.

Marshall, Horace, born at Allerton, Yorks, 23 May, 1868; 1s. Thomas, of Leeds, solicitor. TRINITY, matric. 15 Oct., 87, aged 19 (from Eton), exhibitioner 86, B.A. 91; HONOURS:—2 classical mods. 89, 2 classics 91.

Marshall, rev. James McCall, M.A., fellow BRASENOSE 63-6, where see page 356.

Marshall, John, born at West Derby, co. Lanc., 10 Sept., 1862; 2s. John Whitebread, arm. NEW COLL., matric. 15 Oct., 81, aged 19 (from Liverpool coll. and Edinburgh university), B.A. 85, M.A. 89; HONOURS:—1 classical mods. 83, 1 classics 85.

Marshall, John Herbert Allen, born at Great Barr, co. Warwick, Aug., 1863; 1s. John, arm. UNIVERSITY COLL., matric. 14 Oct., 82, aged 19 (from Clifton coll.), B.A. 92; brother of Arthur W. M.

Marshall, Louis, born at Denia in Spain 9 Dec., 1870; 1s. Henry, gen. BALLIOL, matric. 17 Oct., 89, aged 18 (from Rugby); assist. magistrate N.W. provinces, India.

Marshall, Reginald, born at Hartford, Cheshire, 8 Dec., 1870; 5s. Thomas Horatio, arm. WADHAM, matric. 20 Jan., 91, aged 20, from Radley coll.

Marshall, Thomas Wilfrid, born at High Wycombe, Bucks, 6 Nov., 1869; 1s. Thomas, solicitor. LINCOLN, matric. 24 Jan., 89, aged 19 (from St. Mark's school, Windsor); HONOURS:—3 law 91.

Marshall, rev. Walter Langley, born at Pyrton, Oxon, 22 Dec., 1864; 2s. George, cler. CHRIST CHURCH, matric. 12 Oct., 83, aged 18 (from Westminster school), B.A. 87, M.A. 92 (HONOURS: —1 history 87); assist. chaplain Genoa 90-1, curate of St. Saviour, Hoxton, 91.

Marsham, Charles George Bullock, born in London 3 Dec., 1872; 1s. Robert Henry Bullock, London police magistrate. MERTON, matric. 22 Oct., 91, aged 18, from Eton.

Marsland, Philip Rickards, born at Blackheath, Kent, 1869; 1s. Robert Wood, gen. CHRIST CHURCH, matric. 11 Oct., 89, aged 20 (from St. Paul's school), scholar 88.

Marsland, Reginald Price Wood, born at Lee, Blackheath, Kent, 29 July, 1873; 2s. Robert Wood, solicitor. NEW COLL., matric. 14 Oct., 92, aged 19, from St. Paul's school.

Marston, John Harold, born at Wolverhampton 29 Sept., 1868; 2s. John, arm. MERTON, matric. 22 Oct., 87, aged 19 (from Wolverhampton school), postmaster 87, B.A. 92 (HONOURS :—2 mathematical mods. 88, 2 history 91); bar.-at-law, Middle Temple, 92.

Marston, Sidney, born at Longton, co. Stafford, 17 June, 1873; 3s. John, manufacturer. WORCESTER, matric. 18 Oct., 92, aged 19, from Longton gr. school.

Marston, William John Edward, born at Kersal, co. Lanc., 7 June, 1869; 5s. Charles Dallas, cler. LINCOLN, matric. 18 Oct., 88, aged 19 (from Bedford school), exhibitioner 88; HONOURS:—2 classical mods. 90, 4 classics 92.

Marten, Clarence Henry Kennett, born in London 28 Oct., 1872; 2s. Alfred George, Q.C. BALLIOL, matric. 20 Oct., 91, aged 18, from Eton.

Marten, John Thomas, born at Blackheath, Kent, 28 Sept., 1872; 2s. Charles Henry, stockbroker. NEW COLL., matric. 16 Oct., 91, aged 19, from Clifton coll.

Martin, Bradley, born at New York 1873; 2s. Bradley, arm. CHRIST CHURCH, matric. 10 Oct., 90, aged 17.

Martin, Charles, M.A., senior-student CHRIST CHURCH 64-9, where see page 493.

Martin, Charles Robert Hesketh, born at Killegar, Ireland, 11 Oct., 1863; 1s. Henry, rector of Agher, co. Meath. TRINITY, matric. 14 Oct., 82, aged 19 (from Cheltenham coll.), exhibitioner 82; died 8 March, 84, at Cyprus.

Martin, Clifford Henry Williams, born at Weston-super-Mare 1161; 3s. Edward arm. NON-COLLEGIATE, matric. 19 Jan., 84, aged 22 (from a Clifton school), B.A. and M.A. 92; HONOURS :—3 history 87.

Martin, Douglas Eycott, born at Rochester 10 Aug., 1866; 1s. William Eycott, cler. TRINITY, matric. 17 Oct., 85, aged 19 (from Marlborough coll.), B.A. 88.

Martin, George Herbert, born at Exeter 12 March, 1872; 4s. John May, arm. MERTON, matric. 22 Oct., 90, aged 18 (from Exeter gr. school), postmaster 90; HONOURS:—2 mathematical mods. 92.

Martin, Harold, born at Aughton, co. Lanc., 3 Nov., 1867; 3s. Thomas, gent. LINCOLN, matric. 17 Oct., 84, aged 16 (from royal institute, Liverpool), B.A. 88, M.A. 91; HONOURS:—3 law 88.

Martin, Henry, born at Altrincham, Cheshire, 1870; 5s. John, gen. NON-COLLEGIATE, matric. 15 Oct., 87, aged 17 (from Edinburgh institute), B.A. 90; HONOURS:—2 history 90.

Martin, Henry Basil, born at Folkestone, Kent, 1866; 2s. Hezekiah, cler. BRASENOSE, matric. 23 Oct., 85, aged 19, from Lancing coll.

Martin, Horace Eccles, born at Lisbon 24 Dec., 1873; 1s. Thomas, of Oxford, merchant, deceased. NON-COLLEGIATE, matric. 15 Oct., 92, aged 18, from Portsmouth gr. school.

Martin, John, born at Coventry, co. Warwick, 1856; 1s. William, cler. HERTFORD, matric. 18 Oct., 83, aged 19 (from Worcester cathedral school), scholar 81-6, B.A. 86, M.A. 90.

Martin, John Brooks, born at Sandford-on-Thames 1867; 1s. John, gen. NON-COLLEGIATE, matric. 27 Jan., 87, aged 30, B.A. 90.

Martin, John Pearson, born at Maryport, Cumberland, 5 Dec., 1864; 1s. John, gent. QUEEN'S, matric. 22 Oct., 84, aged 19 (from Blair Lodge school, Stirlingshire), B.A. 90, M.A. 91.

Martin, John Sturges, born at Radley coll., Abingdon, 2 May, 1874; 2s. Charles, M.A., warden of Radley coll. CHRIST CHURCH, matric. 14 Oct., 92, aged 18, from Winchester.

Martin, Reginald Hnes, born in London 6 May, 1872; 1s. William Hugh, gen. LINCOLN, matric. 17 Oct., 89, aged 17, from a Littlehampton school.

Martin, Robert Hall, born at Altrincham, Cheshire, June, 1871; 1s. Robert, D.D. KEBLE, matric. 20 Oct., 91, aged 20.

Martin, Stephen Burfield, born at Hailsham, Sussex, 1867; 1s. Robert Thomas, gent. NON-COLLEGIATE, matric. 23 Jan., 86, aged 19, from Worcester cathedral school.

Martin, Thomas Henry, born at York 1865; 2s. Daniel, gen. NON-COLLEGIATE, matric. 1 Feb., 89, aged 24, from St. Peter's school, York, and ST. JOHN'S COLL., Cambridge, matric. 21 Oct., 85, B.A. 88; HONOURS :—3 history 88.

Martin, William, born at St. Austell, Cornwall, 1862; 1s. William Langdon, gent. HERTFORD, matric. 19 Oct., 81, aged 19.

Martineau, James, D.D., created D.C.L. 20 June, 1888; hon. D.Litt., Dublin, 92. See *Al. Ox.* 2nd series, page 922.

Martius, Alexander Carl Edward Wilhelm, born at Berlin 6 Sept., 1874; 1s. Dr. Carl Alexander. TRINITY, matric. 15 Oct., 92, aged 18, from a Berlin gymnasium.

Martley, Henry Lancelot, born at Dublin 1868; o.s. Robert Henry, gen. ST. EDMUND HALL, matric. 21 Oct., 86, aged 18 (from Dulwich coll.), B.A. 91.

Martley, rev. William Gibson, born at Dublin 21 Nov., 1859; 2s. Francis Blackburne, arm. BALLIOL, incorporated 31 Jan., 85, aged 22 (from Rugby and scholar Trinity coll., Dublin, 79), B.A. 86, M.A. 89 (HONOURS :—2 classical mods. 83, 1 theology 85); curate of Aylesbury 85-7; B.A. Dublin 81, M.A. 85, senior moderator in classics and in modern literature, vice-chancellor's Latin medallist and Berkeley's Greek medallist 82.

Marton, George Henry Powys, born at Brighton 11 April, 1869; 1s. George Blucher Heneage, arm. CHRIST CHURCH, matric. 18 Jan., 89, aged 19, from Eton.

Martyn, Charles Harrison, born at Palgrave Priory, Norfolk, 1862; 1s. Charles John, cler. CHRIST CHURCH, matric. 15 Oct., 88, aged 18.

Martyn, John Darke, born at Ibberton, Dorset, 10 Oct., 1871; 2s. John, cler. EXETER, matric. 22 Oct., 91, aged 20, from Sherborne gr. school.

Martyn, Samuel Symons, born in isle of Man 1855; o.s. Samuel Symons, arm. KEBLE, matric. 26 Jan., 86, aged 31, B.Mus. 88.

Martyn, William Turnavine, born at Saltash 8 May, 1863; 1s. William, gent. QUEEN'S, matric. 23 Oct., 82, aged 19 (from Stoke school, Devonport), B.A. 85.

Martyn-Linnington, Richard Linnington, born at Bridge, Devon, 28 Aug., 1868; 2s. Richard Martyn, gen. PEMBROKE, matric. 25 Oct., 87, aged 19 (from Rugby); assumed the additional name of Linnington.

Marvin, Francis Sydney, born in London 1863; 1s. Francis Benthani, gent. ST. JOHN'S, matric. 14 Oct., 82, aged 19 (from Merchant Taylors' school), scholar 81-6, B.A. 86, senior scholar 87, M.A. 89 (HONOURS:—1 classical mods. 84, 1 classics 86, 2 history 87); inspector of schools 92.

Marygold, Francis Henry, born in Oxon 1856; 1s. George, gen. NON-COLLEGIATE, matric. 28 May, 87, aged 31, B.A. 90.

Maskelyne, Mervin Herbert Nevil Story, M.A., hon. fellow WADHAM 73, where see page 530.

Mason, Alfred Edward Woodley, born at Camberwell, Surrey, 7 May, 1865; 2s. William Woodley, gent. TRINITY, matric. 11 Oct., 84, aged 19 (from Dulwich coll.), B.A. 88; (HONOURS:—2 classical mods. 86, 3 classics 88.

Mason, Alfred Victor, born at Colne, co. Lanc., 5 Oct., 1867; 2s. Thomas, gen. MERTON, matric. 22 Oct., 87, aged 20 (from Uppingham), B.A. 92; HONOURS:—3 classical mods. 89, 3 classics 91.

Mason, Edmund Merest, born at Wem, Salop, Oct., 1870; o.s. Peter Pearson, cler. CHRIST CHURCH, matric. 11 Oct., 89, aged 18 (from Shrewsbury school), exhibitioner 89.

Mason, Henry Williams, M.A. student CHRIST CHURCH 47-76, where see page 416.

Mason, Richard Shires-, born at Gargrave, Yorks, 21 Dec., 1860; o.s. Richard Shires, gent., deceased. QUEEN'S, matric. 28 Oct., 81, aged 20 (from Giggleswick gr. school), B.A. 85 (HONOURS:—3 theology 85); assumed the additional name of Shires.

Mason, Sydney, born at Pietermaritzburg, 6 April, 1867; 3s. Frederick, gen. MERTON, matric. 21 Oct., 86, aged 19 (from Kingswood school, Bath), postmaster 86, B.A. 90; HONOURS:—2 mathematical mods. 88, 2 history 90.

Maspero, Gaston, created D.C.L. 22 June, 1887, hon. fellow QUEEN'S 87, where see page 176.

Masse, Edgar Francis Hubert Joseph, born at Sydenham, Kent, 1861; 2s. Joseph Francis Paul, gent. WORCESTER, matric. 21 Oct., 80, aged 19, B.A. 86.

Massey, Arnold Stuart, born in London Nov., 1872; 1s. Thomas Massey, barrister-at-law. ORIEL, matric. 27 Oct., 91, aged 19, from the Charterhouse.

Massie, John, born at Newton-le-Willows, co. Lanc., 1843; 1s. Robert, arm. scholar ST. JOHN'S, CAMBRIDGE, 64 (from Atherstone school), B.A. 66, M.A. 70 (HONOURS:—2nd class in Cambridge classical tripos 66), incorporated 9 Dec., 86, from CORPUS CHRISTI, vice-principal (?) of Mansfield coll. 85.

Master, Arthur Gilbert, born in London 1867; 4s. Charles Gilbert, arm. EXETER, matric. 21 Oct., 86, aged 19, B.A. 89.

Master, Richard Chester, born at the Abbey, Cirencester, 28 Aug., 1870; 1s. Thomas William Chester, arm. CHRIST CHURCH, matric. 11 Oct., 89, aged 19, from Harrow.

Masterman, John Story, M.A., fellow BRASENOSE 73-7, where see page 356.

Mather, Frederick Henry Vaughan, born at Clifton 1872; 6s. Frederick Vaughan, cler. KEBLE, matric. 17 Jan., 91, aged 19, from Bristol university coll.

Mather, rev. John Cyril Vaughan, born at Clifton, co. Glouc., Sept., 1869; 1s. Frederick Vaughan, cler. KEBLE, matric. 17 Oct., 82, aged 20 (from Clifton coll.), B.A. 85; curate of St. John Evangelist, Upper Norwood, 86.

Mather, Walter Stanley, born at Waterloo, co. Lanc., 4 June, 1872; 2s. Arthur Stanley, solicitor and notary. TRINITY, matric. 15 Oct., 92, aged 20, from Rugby.

Mathers, John Shackleton, born at Leeds 1868; 1s. John Shackleton, gen. NON-COLLEGIATE, matric. 11 Oct., 90, aged 22, from Lancaster gr. school and Christ's coll., Cambridge, matric. 21 Oct., 87, B.A.

Matheson, Alan, born at Hong Kong, China, 1860; o.s. Colin, gen. NON-COLLEGIATE, matric. 12 Oct., 89, aged 26, from University coll. school, London, and Edinburgh university B.Med.

Matheson, Alexander, born in London 1872; 2s. Ewing, C.E. BALLIOL, matric. 20 Oct., 91, aged 19, from St. Paul's school.

Matheson, rev. Charles, M.A., fellow ST. JOHN'S 50-6, where see page 460.

Matheson, Percy Ewing, M.A., fellow NEW COLL. 81, where see page 206.*

Mathew, Edward Jermyn, born in London 1860; o.s. Edward Fisher Ruggles, gen. ST. EDMUND HALL, matric. 7 May, 87, aged 27; migrated to TRINITY HALL, Cambridge (matric. 21 Oct., 89), exhibitioner 90, B.A. 90; HONOURS:—2nd class in history tripos 90, English essay 90, 3rd class in law tripos 91, Harness prize 92.

Mathew, Francis Bernard, born at Richmond, Surrey, 5 Dec., 1868; 1s. justice sir James Charles Mathew. TRINITY, matric. 16 Jan., 85, aged 18 (from Birmingham oratory school), B.A. 88 (HONOURS:—2 history 88); bar.-at-law, Lincoln's Inn, 90.

Mathews, Charles Arnold Frank, born at Laughton, co. Linc., 27 May, 1868; 2s. William Arnold, hon. canon Carlisle. QUEEN'S, matric. 25 Oct., 87, aged 18 (from Carlisle and Appleby gr. schools), exhibitioner 86, M.A. 91; HONOURS:—2 classical mods. 88, 3 classics 90.

Mathews, Charles Joseph, born at Cirencester 1863; 2s. Joseph, gen. QUEEN'S, matric. 15 Jan., 91, aged 28.

Mathias, rev. Hugh Henry, born at Canterbury, New Zealand, Nov., 1862; 10s. Octavius, cler. KEBLE, matric. 14 Oct., 84, aged 21 (from Christ Church, N.Z.), B.A. 87 (HONOURS:—2 theology 87); curate of Knaipoi, Canterbury, N.Z., 90.

Mathie, David William, born at Rothesay 1867; o.s. David, arm. NON-COLLEGIATE, matric. 13 Oct., 88, aged 21, B.A. 92.

Maton, Osbert Stephen Matson Poolman, born at Southampton 1867; 1s. Stephen, gen. NON-COLLEGIATE, matric. 27 Jan., 87, aged 20 (from a Salisbury school); migrated to EXETER, B.A. 90; HONOURS:—2 law 90.

Maton, William Clifford, born at Great Cheverell, Wilts, 1871; 3s. Stephen, gen. QUEEN'S, matric. 16 March, 92, aged 21.

Matson, rev. Robert Bidwell, born at Wilby, Northants, 31 March, 1867; 1s. Robert, cler. NON-COLLEGIATE, matric. 18 Oct., 80, aged 29 (from St. John's coll., Hurstpierpoint, and Culham coll.); migrated to MERTON, B.A. 89 (HONOURS:—3 history 83); curate of Busbridge, Surrey, 84-6.

Matterson Robert de Mowbray, born at Aldershot 4 May, 1873; 1s. William Key, late major in the army, deceased. CORPUS CHRISTI, matric. 18 Oct., 92, aged 19, from Sherborne school.

Matthew, Gerald Walter, born at Calcutta 25 Oct., 1871; o.s. Henry James, bishop of Lahore. TRINITY, matric. 11 Oct., 90, aged 18, from Haileybury.

Matthews, Arthur Percy, born at North Coates, co. Lincoln, July, 1869; 4s. Timothy Richard, cler. NON-COLLEGIATE, matric. 17 Oct., 91, aged 22.

Matthews, Charles Edward, born at Newark, Notts, 1862; 3s. Thomas, gen. EXETER, matric. 22 Oct., 80, aged 19 (from Newark gr. school), B.A. 83, M.A. and B.Med. 88, D.Med 92.

Matthews, Ernest Lewis, born at Gloucester 12 April, 1871; 4s. John Albert, gen. BALLIOL, matric. 20 Jan., 1990, aged 18 (from King's coll. London), B.A. 92; HONOURS:—2 history 92.

Matthews, Frank Herbert, born in London 1861; 2s. George Augustus, gen. CORPUS CHRISTI, matric. 21 Oct., 80, aged 19 (from Dulwich coll.), scholar 80-5, B.A. 84, M.A. 89 (HONOURS:—2 classical mods. 82, 1 classics 84); headmaster Bolton gr. school 92.

Matthews, George Fielding, born at North Coates, co. Lincoln, June, 1862; 2s. Timothy Richard, cler. WORCESTER, matric. 18 Oct., 83, aged 21, B.A. 87, M.A. 90; brother of Richard N. and Wilfred N.

Matthews, Henry Webster, born at Charlton on Medlock, co. Lanc., 10 June, 1869; 2s. James Edward, gen. JESUS COLL., matric. 16 Oct., 88, aged 19 (from Manchester gr. school); exhibitioner 88, B.A. 92; HONOURS:—1 classical mods. 90, 2 classics 92.

Matthews, rev. Richard Northon, born at North Coates, co. Lincoln, July, 1860; 1s. Timothy Richard, cler. KEBLE, matric. 18 Oct., 81, aged 21, B.A. 84, M.A. 88; curate of Roxby with Risby, co. Lincoln, 91; brother of George F. and of the next.

Matthews, Wilfred Noel, born at North Coates, co. Lincoln, Nov., 1870; 5s. Timothy Richard, cler. NON-COLLEGIATE, matric. 15 Oct., 92, aged 21; brother of George F. and Richard N.

Matthey, Percy St. Clair, born in London Oct., 1863; 2s. George, F.R.S. EXETER, matric. 18 Oct., 82, aged 18 (from Eton), B.A. 86.

Maud, Arthur Roland, born at Ancaster, co. Lincoln, 9 Sept., 1866; 4s. John Primatt, vicar. KEBLE, matric. 19 Oct., 86, aged 20, from Leamington coll.

Maud, Henry George, born at Assington, Suffolk, 31 Jan., 1867; 5s. Henry Landon, cler. UNIVERSITY COLL., matric. 18 Oct., 86, aged 19 (from Leamington coll.), scholar 86; HONOURS:— 2 classical mods. 88, 3 classics 90.

Maud, John Primatt, LL.B., student CHRIST CHURCH 42-4, where see page 414.

Maude, Charles Edmund, born at Canterbury 16 May, 1865; 2s. Thomas William, arm. MERTON, matric. 16 Oct., 84, aged 19 (from Christ Church coll., N.Z.), B.A. 87.

Maude, Eustace Addison, born at Wallasey, Cheshire, 5 Jan., 1863; 1s. Robert Eustace, capt. in army. TRINITY, matric. 17 April, 82, aged 19 (from Wellington coll.); lieut. royal Scots Greys 89.

Maude, rev. Joseph Hooper, M.A., fellow HERTFORD 75-84 and 87, where see.

Maude, Thomas, born at Christ Church, New Zealand, 1864; 1s. Thomas William, arm. HERTFORD, matric. 18 May, 83, aged 19, B.A. 87; bar.-at-law, Inner Temple, 88.

Maude, Walter, born at Rugby 1866; 8s. Thomas James, gent. BALLIOL, matric. 18 Oct., 81, aged 19 (from Highgate school); under sec. general revenue and statistical departments, Bengal.

Maudsley, Joshua, born at Settle, Yorks, 17 Nov., 1873; 1s. John, of Settle, Yorks, gent. QUEEN'S, matric. 27 Oct., 92, aged 18 (from Giggleswick school), exhibitioner 92.

Maudson, rev. Arthur Henry, born at Leeds 1867; 2s. Richard Thomas, gen. BRASENOSE, matric. 20 Oct., 86, aged 19 (from Bath coll.), scholar 86, B.A. 90 (HONOURS:—1 mathematical mods. 88, 3 mathematics 90); curate of Kimberworth, Yorks, 91.

Maughan, David, born at Sydney, N.S.W., 5 Feb., 1873; 1s. John, gen. BALLIOL, matric. 20 Oct., 91, aged 18, from King's school, Parramatta, N.S.W.

Maughan, Veargitt William, born at Clapton, Middx., 1863; o.s. Veargitt, gent. ST. JOHN'S, matric. 11 Oct., 84, aged 21; died at Oxford 29 May, 88.

Maunsell, Frederick Baker Laing, born at Shroton, Dorset, 15 Nov., 1872; 3s. Frederick Webster, cler. BRASENOSE, matric. 21 Oct., 91, aged 18, from Sherborne school.

Maunsell, Richard Cecil, born at Iwerne Courtney, Dorset, 2 Dec., 1866; 2s. Frederick Webster, rector of Symondsbury, Dorset. WADHAM, matric. 16 Oct., 86, aged 19 (from Sherborne school), B.A. 92; HONOURS:—2 classical mods. 88, 2 classics 90.

Maurice, Frank Lyttleton Powys, born at Bletchingley, Surrey, 10 Sept., 1870; o.s. Lyttleton Henry Powys, rector of Northover, Somerset. ST. JOHN'S, matric. 17 Jan., 91, aged 20.

Maurice, John Meredith, born at Brighton 1865; 4s. Pries, arm. BRASENOSE, matric. 29 April, 82, aged 17.

Maurice, Robert Baskerville, born at Marlborough, Wilts, 13 Aug., 1868; 2s. James Blake, D.Med. LINCOLN, matric. 21 Oct., 87, aged 19 (from Marlborough coll.), scholar 87; B.A. 92; HONOURS:—2 classical mods. 89, 2 classics 91.

Mavrogordato, Anthony Emanuel, born in London 10 Dec., 1873; 2s. Emanuel Anthony, merchant. TRINITY, matric. 15 Oct., 92, aged 18, from the Charterhouse.

Mavrogordato, Eustratius Emanuel, born in London 21 Feb., 1870; 1s. Emanuel, arm. NEW COLL., matric. 11 Oct., 89, aged 18, from Winchester.

Mavrojani, Spyridion Alexander, born in London 23 Sept., 1866; o.s. Alexander, arm. TRINITY, matric. 17 Oct., 85, aged 19 (from Harrow), B.A. 88, M.A. and B.C.L. 92 (HONOURS:—3 law 88, 3 civil law 90); bar.-at-law, Inner Temple, 90.

Mawdesley, Arthur Leyland, born at Liverpool Sept., 1866; o.s. John Leyland, gent. ST. EDMUND HALL, matric. 29 Jan., 86, aged 19, from New Brighton school.

Mawdsley, Alfred Archibald, born at Eaglefield, Flints, 6 July, 1864; 1s. Peter Alfred, gent. LINCOLN, matric. 18 Oct., 83, aged 19 (from Shrewsbury gr. school), B.A. 86; HONOURS:—3 history 86.

Mawson, William Willmott, born at Manchester 13 Jan., 1873; 1s. William Willmott, lieut.-col. MERTON, matric. 18 Oct., 92, aged 19, from Eton.

Max-Müller, Friedrich, Ph.D., M.A., fellow ALL SOULS', 58, where see page 271.

Max-Müller, Wilhelm Grenfell, born at Oxford 9 June, 1867; 1s. Friedrich Max, prof. comp. philology. UNIVERSITY COLL., matric. 17 Oct., 85, aged 18 (from Eton), B.A. 89; HONOURS:—2 classical mods. 87, 3 law 89.

Maxse, Reginald Edgar Berkeley, born at Hamburg 1870; y.s. Henry Fitzhardinge, equitis. ST. JOHN'S, matric. 17 Jan., 91, aged 21.

Maxted, Basil Eden, born at Hessle, Yorks, 1863; 2s. Edward Philip, arm. PEMBROKE, matric. 4 Feb., 80, aged 17 (from Eton), B.A. 82, M.A. 86.

Maxwell, Charles Frederick Maitland, born at Holywych, Hartfield, Sussex, 15 Feb., 1874; 1s. William Henry, rear-admiral R.N. CORPUS CHRISTI, matric. 18 Oct., 92, from the Charterhouse.

Maxwell, Frederick Mackenzie, born in Turk's Island 1860; 4s. Joseph, rector of St. Matthew, Nassau, New Providence, Bahamas, deceased. BALLIOL, matric. 17 Oct., 82, aged 22 (from London university); B.A. 85, M.A. 91 (HONOURS:—1 law 85); bar.-at-law, Lincoln's Inn, 84.

Maxwell, Thomas Doveton, born at Worthing, Sussex, 6 July, 1873; 8s. William, late major-gen. royal Bengal artillery, deceased. BALLIOL, matric. 18 Oct., 92, aged 19 (from Tiverton school); Blundell scholar 92.

May, Alston James Weller, born at Stoke-on-Trent, co. Stafford, 5 Nov., 1869; 1s. Samuel, arm. ORIEL, matric. 20 Oct., 88, aged 18 (from Leeds gr. school); scholar 88, B.A. 92; HONOURS:—1 classical mods. 90, 2 classics 92.

May, Arthur Sigfrid, born in London 1866; 2s. Frederick Schiller, cler. ST. JOHN'S, matric. 11 Oct., 84, aged 18 (from Merchant Taylors' school), B.A. 88 (HONOURS:—2 history 88); bar.-at-law, Gray's Inn, 92.

May, Arthur William, born at Worle, Somerset, 1862; 1s. Samuel, gen. NON-COLLEGIATE, matric. 13 Oct., 83, aged 21, B.A. 87, M.A. 90.

May, Edward Henry Fox, born at West Allington, Devon, 14 Aug., 1867; 1s. Edward William, cler. EXETER, matric. 21 Oct., 86, aged 19, from Exeter gr. school.

May, Edward Lupton, born in London 15 June, 1872; o.s. Edward Henry, surgeon. ST. JOHN'S, matric. 17 Oct., 91, aged 19 (from Merchant Taylors' school), scholar 91.

May, George Charles, born at Uxbridge, Middx., 1867; 1s. Henry William, arm. ST. JOHN'S, matric. 16 Oct., 86, aged 19 (from Malvern coll.), B.A. 90; HONOURS:—3 history 90.

May, Henry Thomas, M.A., fellow NEW COLL. 33-51, where see page 210.

May, rev. Herbert Hine, born at Frome, Somerset, 1861; 4s. William Hine, arm. WADHAM, matric. 16 Oct., 80, aged 19 (from Sherborne school), scholar 79-84, (B.A. 84, M.A. 88 (HONOURS:—2 classical mods. 82, 2 classics 84); curate of St. Paul's, Oxford, 90.

May, Paul Herman, born at Frankfort-on-Main 1872; 3s. Julius, formerly Belgian consul at San Francisco. NON-COLLEGIATE, matric. 22 Nov., 1892, aged 20.

May, Robert Augustus, born at Purwich, co. Derby, 23 Jan., 1865; 5s. Edmund, cler. MERTON, matric. 19 Oct., 83, aged 18 (from Cheltenham coll.), B.A. 87, M.A. 90.

May, Thomas Edward, born at Devizes, Wilts, 18 Jan., 1870; 7s. Edmund, rector of All Cannings. LINCOLN, matric. 18 Oct., 88, aged 18, from Radley coll.

May, William, born at Reading, Berks, 4 May, 1863; 1s. George, D. Med. NEW COLL., matric. 4 June, 81, aged 18 (from the Charterhouse), B.A. 84; HONOURS:—2 classical mods. 83, 4 history 84.

Maycock, Herbert William, born at Coventry 6 Oct., 1863; 3s. James, arm. MERTON, matric. 19 Oct., 83, aged 20 (from Coventry gr. school), B.A. 86, M.A. 90.

Mayes, Herbert Frederick, born at Dover 1869; 1s. Frederick, arm. BALLIOL, matric. 18 Oct., 88, aged 19 (from Dover coll.); assist. commissioner central provinces, India, 90; bar.-at-law, Inner Temple, 90.

Mayhew, rev. Anthony Lawson, M.A., chaplain WADHAM 80, where see page 533.

Mayhew, rev. Cyril, born at Tornio 1863; o.s. William Augustus John, arm. NON-COLLEGIATE, matric. 21 Jan., 82, aged 18 (from Brighton coll.), chaplain on Bombay estnb. 92.

Maynard, Herbert John, born at Wandsworth, Surrey, 1865; 2s. Frederick Waite, gent. ST. JOHN'S, matric. 13 Oct., 83, aged 18, from Merchant Taylors' school (HONOURS:—Stanhope essay prize 85, 1 history 86), under sec. revenue depart. Punjab.

Maynard, James Douglas, born at Hornsey, Middx., 1871; 2s. Robert Russell, gent. NON-COLLEGIATE, matric. 17 Dec., 92, aged 21.

Maynard, Walter Edward, born at Oxford, Suffolk, Sept., 1865; 1s. Walter Fawkes, cler. EXETER, matric. 12 May, 83, aged 17 (from Haileybury), B.A. 86; cox. of Oxford university eight 86; died at Jubbulpore 2 Aug., 87.

Mayne, Frank, born at Wotton-under-Edge, co. Glouc., 1868; 3s. Charles Downe, gen. NON-COLLEGIATE, matric. 15 Oct., 87, aged 19, from Colston's school, Bristol.

Mayne, Jonathan Webster Coryton, born at Gloucester April, 1868; 1s. Jonathan, cler. KEBLE, matric. 17 Oct., 87, aged 19 (from Tonbridge school), B.A. 90; HONOURS:—2 classical mods. 89.

Mayo, Charles Joseph, born at Corsham, Wilts, 8 April, 1866; 1s. Charles Thomas, arm. TRINITY, matric. 11 Oct., 84, aged 18 (from Clifton coll.), B.A. 88; HONOURS:—4 law 88.

Mayo, Edmund Godfrey, born at Corsham, Wilts, 26 April, 1867; 2s. Charles Thomas, gent. TRINITY, matric. 17 Oct., 85, aged 18 (from Clifton coll.), B.A. 89; HONOURS:—2 classical mods. 87, 3 classics 89.

Mayo, rev. Francis Benjamin, born at Melrose, Scotland, June, 1862; 3s. Benjamin, gen. WORCESTER, matric. 18 Jan., 83, aged 20 (from Birmingham school), B.A. 86, M.A. 89 (HONOURS:—2 theology 86); chaplain and assist. master Blackheath proprietary school 90.

Mayo, John Pym, born at Corsham, Wilts, 31 Jan., 1872; 4s. Charles Thomas, gen. BALLIOL, matric. 20 Oct., 91, aged 19, from Clifton coll.

Mayow, Mayow Wynell, M.A., student CHRIST CHURCH 1829-37, where see page 413.

Mead, Charles Clement, born at Cyn, East Indies, 1865; 2s. Clement John, arm. BALLIOL, matric. 16 Oct., 83, aged 18 (from Eton), selected candidate Indian c.s. 83; died at Calcutta 31 May, 88.

Mead, Charles Walter, born at Scarborough on Hudson, America, 1862; 3s. Edward, cler. NON-COLLEGIATE, matric. 21 Jan., 82, aged 20, B.A. 86, M.A. 88; bar.-at-law, Middle Temple, 88.

Mead, George Robert Stow, born in London 1863; 2s. Robert, arm. NON-COLLEGIATE, matric. 15 Oct., 87, aged 24, from Rochester school.

Meade, Charles Augustine, born at Bradford, Yorks, 2 June, 1872; 4s. Harry, M.R.C.S. Eng. ST. JOHN'S, matric. 15 Oct., 92, aged 20, from Bradford gr. school.

Meade, Charles Hippisley, born at Binegar, Somerset, 23 May, 1866; 3s. William, cler. TRINITY, matric. 11 Oct., 84, aged 18 (from Bath coll.), B.A. 87; HONOURS:—3 theology 88.

Meade, Francis Henry, born at Wylye, Wilts, 6 Dec., 1870; 1s. rev. the hon. Sidney, of Bradford-upon-Avon. MAGDALEN, matric. 14 Oct., 89, aged 18, from Eton.

Meade, George Hamilton, born at Binegar, Somerset, 9 Oct., 1870; 4s. William, cler. TRINITY, matric. 12 Oct., 89, aged 19 (from Bath coll.), B.A. 92.

Meares, Noel Edgar, born in London 1867; 1s. Thomas, arm. EXETER, matric. 16 Oct., 84, aged 17, from Winchester.

Mears, Edward, born at West Hartlepool, co. Durham, 10 Nov., 1865; o.s. Edward, gen. QUEEN'S, matric. 20 Oct., 83, aged 18 (from Dronfield school, Sheffield), scholar 83, B.A. 87; HONOURS:—2 mathematical mods. 85, 2 chemistry 87.

Mears, Edward Grimwood, born at Winchester 21 Jan., 1869; s. William, schoolmaster. NON-COLLEGIATE, matric. 15 Jan., 87, aged 17, from Queen's school, Basingstoke.

Medd, Charles Septimus, M.A., fellow UNIVERSITY COLL. 64-74, where see page 32.

Medd, Peter Goldsmith, M.A., fellow UNIVERSITY COLL. 52-77, where see page 32.

Medley, Dudley Julius, born in London 1861; 2s. Julius George, arm. KEBLE, matric. 19 Oct., 80, aged 19 (from Wellington), B.A. 83, M.A. 87 (HONOURS:—1 history 83); modern history lecturer 84.

Medlicott, Arthur Lewis, born at Chirra Soonji, E. Indies, 1858; 3s. Henry Bennet, arm. BALLIOL, matric. 19 Oct., 87, aged 19 (from Clifton coll.); assist. commissioner Assam 89.

Medlicott, Robert Sumner, born in Buriton, Hants, 2 May, 1869; 1s. Walter Edward, vicar of Swanmore, Hants. MAGDALEN, matric. 16 Oct., 88, aged 19 (from Winchester), B.A. 92; HONOURS:—3 classical mods. 90, 4 history 84.

Mee, Edward Melford, M.A., fellow QUEEN'S 79-86, where see page 183.

Mee, Frederick Franklin, born at Redcliffe, Bristol, 1 Feb., 1869; 1s. James, of Northampton, gen. NON-COLLEGIATE, matric. 17 Oct., 91, aged 22, from Bristol gr. school.

Mee, John Henry, M.A., D.Mus., fellow MERTON 75-9, where see page 99.

Meeres, Eustace William Marriott, born at Horsmonden, Kent, 12 Oct., 1867; 1s. Horace, vicar of Bradwell, Wilts. NEW COLL., matric. 15 Oct., 86, aged 19 (from Marlborough coll.), B.A. 91; HONOURS :—2 classical mods. 88, 3 classics 90.

Meggy, Douglas Henry, born at Chelmsford, Essex, May, 1872; 1s. Frederick Henry, gen. CHRIST CHURCH, matric. 6 Feb., 92, aged 19, from Felsted school.

Meiklejohn, Max John Christian, born at Bowdon, Cheshire, 1866; 1s. John Miller Dow, arm. ORIEL, matric. 23 Oct., 84, aged 18 (from Fettes coll.), exhibitioner 84, B.A. 88; HONOURS :—2 classical mods. 86, 4 classics 88.

Mellen, Chase Hugo, born at Cincinnati, America, 1864; 2s. William Proctor, arm. BRASENOSE, matric. 21 Jan., 84, aged 20, B.A. 87.

Mellen, Clark Victor, born at Cincinnati, America, June, 1865; 3s. William Proctor, arm. BRASENOSE, matric. 22 April, 84, aged 18.

Mellersh, William Lock, born at Cheltenham, co. Glouc., 21 July, 1872; 1s. William Henry, solicitor. CHRIST CHURCH, matric. 29 May, 91, aged 18, from Cheltenham coll.

Melliar, Robert Aubrey Foster-, born at Redgrave, Suffolk, Sept., 1870; 2s. Andrew, cler. KEBLE, matric. 12 Oct., 89, aged 19, from Uppingham.

Mellish, Peter Bertie, born at Orton, Notts, 25 Nov., 1866; 2s. William John, cler. CORPUS CHRISTI, matric. 26 Oct., 85, aged 18 (from Rossall school), exhibitioner 85, B.A. 89; HONOURS :—2 classical mods. 87, 4 classics 89.

Mellone, Sidney Herbert, born at Crosson, in America, 13 May, 1869; 1s. William Edward, of Bessells Green, Kent, dissenting minister, NON-COLLEGIATE, matric. 6 Dec., 90, aged 21, from University coll., London.

Mellor, Cecil, born at Bolton, co. Lanc., 1865; 1s. Joseph, arm. ORIEL, matric. 23 Oct., 84, aged 19 (from Harrow), B.A. 87.

Melvill, Harry Edward, born in London 3 Jan., 1866; 1s. William Henry, arm. UNIVERSITY COLL., matric. 11 Oct., 84, aged 18, B.A. 88 (HONOURS :—4 history 88); bar.-at-law, Inner Temple, 92.

Melville, Beresford Valentine, born at Shelsley, co. Worc., 30 Sept., 1857; 2s. David, arm. BRASENOSE, matric. 26 Jan., 81, aged 23 (from Marlborough coll.), B.A. 85; HONOURS :—3 classical mods. 82.

Melville, Frank, born at Leeds 9 Jan., 1870; 3s. Charles, gen. NON-COLLEGIATE, matric. 11 Oct., 90, aged 20, from Leeds gr. school.

Menabrea, general count, created D.C.L. 22 June, 1881. See *M. Ox.* and series, 942.

Mendl, Sigismund Ferdinand, born in London 1866; 1s. Ferdinand, gent. UNIVERSITY COLL., matric. 24 Jan., 84, aged 17, B.A. 87, M.A. 90 (HONOURS :—2 law 87); bar.-at-law, Inner Temple, 88.

Menneer, Frank Blackmore, born at Torre, Devon, 27 April, 1873; 2s. Nicholas Tonkin, gen. NON-COLLEGIATE, matric. 29 Oct., 91, aged 18, from Torre coll., Torquay.

Menteath, Charles Granville Stuart, born at Malvern, co. Worcester, 26 Nov., 1868; 1s. Granville Thorold, arm. ST. JOHN'S, matric. 13 Oct., 88, aged 19. B.A. 91; HONOURS :—4 theology 91.

Menzies, Alfred Irvine, born at Lambeth 20 Dec., 1863; 2s. James Irvine, of Blackfriars, physician. MERTON, matric. 17 Oct., 82, aged 18 (from St. Paul's school), postmaster 82, B.A. 86, M.A. 91; HONOURS :—3 chemistry 86.

Menzies, Frederick, M.A., fellow BRASENOSE 37-67, where see page 352.

Menzies, Frederick Charles Graham, born at Edinburgh Nov., 1872; 4s. Graham, arm. CHRIST CHURCH, matric. 16 Jan., 91, aged 18.

Menzies, George Kenneth, born in London 1869; 2s. James Martin, arm. BALLIOL, matric. 17 Oct., 89, aged 20, from St. Andrews university.

Menzies, John Herbert, born at Tittensor, co. Stafford, 5 April, 1871; 2s. George, gen. EXETER, matric. 13 Oct., 90, aged 19 (from Newcastle-under-Lyme high school); brother of the next.

Menzies, Robert, born at Trentham, co. Stafford, 22 Oct., 1865; 1s. George, gent. EXETER, matric. 23 Oct., 85, aged 19 (from Newcastle-under-Lyme high school), B.A. 88, M.A. 92.

Menzies, William, born at Weem, Perthshire, 1868; 1s. Robert, gent. BALLIOL, matric. 18 Oct., 92, aged 24 (from St. Andrews and Edinburgh universities), exhibitioner 91.

Mercer, Charles Alexander, born at Gainsborough, co. Linc., 19 Feb., 1870; 2s. Fletcher, gen. LINCOLN, matric. 27 Jan., 90, aged 19, from Gainsborough gr. school.

Mercer, Edward Gilbert, born at Walcot, Somerset, 26 Jan., 1873; 1s. Edward John Bush, of Bath, gent. MAGDALEN, matric. 18 Oct., 92, aged 19 (from King's school, Gloucester); clerk 92.

Mercer, Fletcher James, born at Gainsborough, co. Lincoln, 22 June, 1861; 1s. Fletcher, gen. MERTON, matric. 18 Oct., 80, aged 19 (from Gainsborough gr. school), B.A. 84, M.A. 87; HONOURS :—4 history 84.

Mercer, rev. Richard, born at Kirkby, near Liverpool, 1860; 1s. Henry, gent. HERTFORD, matric. 18 Oct., 80, aged 20, B.A. 83, M.A. 87 (HONOURS :—4 theology 83); curate of St. Peter, Everton, 84-8; died (? May), 89.

Merchant, rev. George Lawson, born at Bury, co. Lanc., 12 July, 1868; 3s. Charles Martin, gen. TRINITY, matric. 15 Oct., 87, aged 19 (from Shrewsbury school), B.A. 91.

Meredith, rev. John Llewellyn, born at Worcester 22 March, 1868; 1s. Jonathan, gen. WORCESTER, matric. 17 Oct., 87, aged 19 (from Malvern Link school), B.A. 90.

Merk, Frederick Holland, born at Dhurmsala, East Indies, 1853; 4s. John Nepomuk, cler. BALLIOL, matric. 17 Oct., 82, aged 19 (from Christ's hospital), scholar 82, Jenkyns exhibitioner 86, B.A. 87; HONOURS :—1 classical mods. 83, 1 classics 86.

Merk, Walter Henry, born at Dhurmsala, East Indies, 27 April, 1861; 3s. John Nepomuk, cler. BALLIOL, matric. 21 Oct., 80, aged 19 (from Christ's hospital), scholar 79-82; selected candidate India C.S. 80; died May or June, 84, in India.

Merriken, William Good, born at Hull, Yorks, 1863; 1s. William Smith, gen. NEW COLL., matric. 24 Jan., 81, aged 33, B.Mus. 83.

Merry, Theodore Arthur, born at Guilden Morden, co. Cambridge, 1861; 3s. Robert, cler. BRASENOSE, matric 22 Jan., 80, aged 19.

Merry, rev. Walter Mansell, born at Oxford 23 April, 1863; 1s. William Walter, rector of Lincoln coll. EXETER, matric. 31 Jan., 80, aged 16 (from Malvern coll.), B.A. 85, M.A. 88 (HONOURS :—2 classical mods. 83); curate of St. Cross, Winchester, 90.

Merry, William Joseph Collings, born at Oxford 29 June, 1867; 2s. William Walter, rector of Lincoln coll. MAGDALEN, matric. 6 May, 86, aged 18 (from Marlborough), B.A. 89; HONOURS :—2 physiology 89.

Merry, William Walter, D.D., rector of LINCOLN 84, where see page 240.

Merryweather, Harry Hill, born at Sheffield, 27 Oct., 1862; o.s. Henry, D.Med. NON-COLLEGIATE, matric. 27 May, 82, aged 19 (from Sheffield collegiate school); migrated to WADHAM 19 April, 84, B.A. 86, M.A. 88.

Mertens, Arthur Lewin de Mounteney, born at Shoreham, Sussex, 1869; 1s. Frederick Mounteney Dirs, cler. ST. JOHN'S, matric. 12 Oct., 89, aged 20, from Lancing coll.

Mertens, Lionel George, born at Lucerne, Switzerland, 1866; 3s. Herman Dirs, arm. UNIVERSITY COLL., matric. 17 Oct., 85, aged 19 (from Bruton gr. school), B.A. 88 (HONOURS:—2 history 88); assist. master at Herga, Westgate-on-Sea.

Mertens, Rowland Denne, born at Lucerne, Switzerland, 1867; 5s. Herman Dirs, arm. ST. JOHN'S, matric. 16 Oct., 86, aged 19 (from Bruton gr. school and King's coll., London), B.A. 90 (HONOURS:—3 theology 89); assist. master at Walton lodge, Clevedon, Somerset.

Messer, Allan Ernest, born at Reading, Berks, 1865; 4s. John, gent. ST. JOHN'S, matric. 13 Oct., 83, aged 18 (from Reading school), scholar 83, B.A. 87; HONOURS:—1 mathematical mods. 85, 2 law 87.

Meston, James Scorgie, born at Old Machar, co. Aberdeen, 1865; 1s. James, gen. BALLIOL, matric. 16 Oct., 83, aged 18 (from King's coll., Aberdeen); joint magistrate N.W. provinces India 85.

Metcalfe, rev. Edmund Lionel, born in London 1868; o.s. Edmund, D.Med. CHRIST CHURCH, matric. 3 June, 87, aged 19 (from Eton), B.A. 91; HONOURS:—4 history 91.

Metcalfe, Edward, born at Burnley, co. Lanc., 24 April, 1861; 2s. Edward, gen. ST. MARY HALL, matric. 28 April, 92, aged 30.

Methuen, James, born at Leith, near Edinburgh, 1862; 1s. James, gen. BRASENOSE, matric. 2 June, 82, aged 20 (from Fettes coll.), B.A. 86.

Metzler, George Richard, born in London May, 1869; 1s. George Thomas, arm. CHRIST CHURCH, matric. 13 Jan., 88, aged 18 (from Harrow), B.A. 92.

Meyer, Charles Julius, born at Wavertree, near Liverpool, 1869; y.s. Frederick Adolphus, gen. BALLIOL, matric. 18 Oct., 88, aged 19 (from Rossall school), B.A. 92; HONOURS:—2 mathematical mods. 90, 3 law 92.

Meyler, Hugh Harries, born at Ambleston, co. Pemb., 28 July, 1865; 2s. Eleazar, calvinistic methodist minister. JESUS COLL., matric. 16 Oct., 84, aged 19 (from Haverfordwest gr. school), scholar 84-6, B.A. 91; HONOURS:—3 history 88.

Meyrick, Frederick, M.A., fellow TRINITY 47-60, where see page 450.

Meyrick, Frederick James, born at Blickling, Norfolk, 11 Dec., 1871; 1s. Frederick, rector. NEW COLL., matric. 10 Oct., 90, aged 18 (from Felsted school); HONOURS:—3 classical mods. 92.

Michael, Walter Henry, born in London 1866; 1s. Walter Amos, gen. BALLIOL, matric. 24 Oct., 85, aged 19 (from Newark gr. school); assist. to collector and magistrate, and agent to the governor of Madras at Vizagapatam.

Michell, Francis Bernard, born at Chantry, Somerset, 28 March, 1870; y.s. William, rector of Dinder, WADHAM, matric. 13 Oct., 88, aged 18 (from Wells cathedral school), B.A. 91; HONOURS:—3 theology 91.

Michell, James Edward, born at Truro, Cornwall, 1864; 4s. Slyman, arm. CORPUS CHRISTI, matric. 19 Oct., 82, aged 18 (from Sherborne school), B.A. 85, M.A. 89.

Michell, rev. Percy Turner, born at Hulston, Cornwall, 13 Nov., 1866; 2s. Samuel Vincent Pryce, gent. QUEEN'S, matric. 30 Oct., 85, aged 18 (from Epsom coll.), B.A. 88, M.A. 92; curate of Barnstaple 90.

Michell, Walter Cecil, born in London 9 Aug., 1864; 2s. William Marwick, arm. MERTON, matric. 19 Oct., 83, aged 19 (from Hammersmith school), B.A. 87 (HONOURS:—2 classical mods. 85, 4 history 86); brother of the next.

Michell, William Walton, born in London 4 April, 1863; 1s. William Marwick, arm. MERTON, matric. 19 Oct., 83, aged 20 (from Hammersmith school), B.A. 89 (HONOURS:—3 classical mods. 85); brother of the last named.

Michelmore, Philip, born at Painsford, Devon, 22 Oct., 1866; 1s. Philip, arm. TRINITY, matric. 17 Oct., 85, aged 18 (from Clifton coll.), B.A. 88, M.A. 92; HONOURS:—2 law 88.

Micklem, Edward Godfrey, born at Billingbear, Berks, 17 Aug., 1873; 2s. Edward, major-general in the army. NEW COLL., matric. 14 Oct., 92, aged 19 (from Eton), scholar 91.

Micklethwait, St. John Gore, born at Stratford-on-Avon 29 April, 1870; 1s. John Pollard, of Penheim, co. Mon., barrister-at-law. UNIVERSITY COLL., matric. 12 Oct., 88, aged 19 (from Clifton coll.), B.A. 92; HONOURS:—2 law 92.

Middleton, Frederick Sholto, born at Tiverton, Devon, 1862; 1s. Sholto, cler. BRASENOSE, matric. 21 May, 80, aged 18 (from Rossall school), migrated to Sidney coll., Cambridge.

Middleton, Frederick Thomas, born at Wallasey, Cheshire, 9 Dec., 1864; 1s. Frederick Dobson, arm. ORIEL, matric. 1 June, 82, aged 18, B.A. 92.

Middleton, Gerald Courtney, born at Bruton, Somerset, June, 1867; 4s. Sholto, cler. NON-COLLEGIATE, matric. 13 Oct., 88, aged 21 (from Blundell's school, Tiverton); migrated to LINCOLN Oct., 90.

Middleton, John Henry, born at York 5 Oct., 1846; 1s. John, of Cheltenham, esq. EXETER, matric. 8 June, 65, aged 18 (from Cheltenham coll.), M.A. by decree of convocation 8 Feb., 87, hon. M.A. Cambridge 11 Nov., 86, and fellow KING'S 88, D.Litt. 92, examiner in classics Cambridge, 88-9, 90, Slade prof. of fine art 86, and keeper of Fitzwilliam museum, Cambridge, 89, D.C.L. Bologna, an architect at Cheltenham F.S.A. 79, author of ancient Rome, etc. See *Men and Women of the Time.*

Midgley, John Metcalfe, born at Burley, Leeds, 1873; 2s. James, solicitor. ST. JOHN'S, matric. 17 Oct., 91, aged 18.

Miers, Reginald Hanbury, born at Little Dean, co. Glouc., 1864; 1s. Richard Hanbury, arm. BALLIOL, matric. 17 Oct., 82, aged 18.

Miéville, Lewis, born in London 12 Nov., 1866; 2s. John Lewis, gent. EXETER, matric. 23 Oct., 85, aged 18 (from Harrow); bar.-at-law, Inner Temple, 90.

Milburn, Robert Gordon, born at Tulse Hill, Surrey, 30 May, 1870; 1s. Robert, arm. TRINITY, matric. 12 Oct., 89, aged 19 (from Tonbridge school), HONOURS:—3 classical mods. 91.

Mildmay, Arundell Charles St. John, M.A., fellow MERTON 44-9, where see page 96.

Mildmay, rev. Aubrey Nevill St. John, born at Long Marston, Yorks, 14 Feb., 1865; 6s. Charles Arundell, rector of Denton, Norfolk. NEW COLL., matric. 10 Oct., 84, aged 19 (from Winchester), scholar 83, B.A. 88 (HONOURS:—2 classical mods. 86, 3 classics 88); curate of St. Paul's, Truro.

Mildmay, Paulet Bertram St. John, born at Lapworth, co. Warwick, 27 June, 1862; 5s. Arundel Charles St. John, cler. KEBLE, matric. 19 Oct., 80, aged 18, from Winchester.

Miles, Edward Falconer Sam Adair, born at Fizabad, India, 14 Feb., 1865; 1s. Thomas George, late major in the army, deceased. NON-COLLEGIATE, matric. 15 Oct., 92, aged 27, from a Norwood school.

Miles, John Charles, born in London 29 Aug., 1870; 1s. John, solicitor. EXETER, matric. 16 Oct., 89, aged 19 (from Shrewsbury gr. school), scholar 89; HONOURS:—2 classical mods. 91.

Miles, John Thomas, born at Merthyr Tydvil, co. Glam., 7 June, 1871; 1s. Job, congregational minister. WADHAM, matric. 18 Oct., 92, aged 21, from University coll., Aberystwith.

Miles, Philip Napier, born at Westbury, co. Glouc., 1865; o.s. Philip William Skinner, arm. ORIEL, matric. 26 April, 84, aged 19, B.A. 87, M.A. 90; HONOURS:—4 history 87.

Milford, Archibald Lock, born at Exeter 1864; 4s. Frederick, gent. PEMBROKE, matric. 2 May, 82, aged 18, from Sherborne school.

Milford, Reginald Stewart, born at Brightwell, Berks, 12 Oct., 1865; 3s. Robert Newman, rector of East Knoyle, Wilts. NEW COLL., matric. 10 Oct., 84, aged 18 (from Winchester), scholar 84, B.A. 88 (HONOURS:—3 classical mods. 86, 3 law 88); brother of the two following.

Milford, Robert Theodore, born at Brightwell, Berks, 21 Jan., 1862; 2s. Robert Newman, cler. NEW COLL., matric. 16 Oct., 80, aged 18 (from Haileybury), B.A. 84, M.A. 88; HONOURS:—2 classical mods. 82, 2 classics 84.

Milford, Walter Seymour, born at Knoyle, Wilts, 5 April, 1869; 4s. Robert Newman, cler. MAGDALEN, matric. 16 Oct., 88, aged 19 (from Haileybury), B.A. 92; HONOURS:—3 classical mods. 90, 3 law 92.

Mill, James, born at Arbroath, co. Forfar, 16 May, 1862. TRINITY, matric. 17 Oct., 85, aged 23 (from Edinburgh university), B.A. 89; HONOURS:—2 classical mods. 87, 2 classics 89.

Mill, James Edward, born at Rivière-du-Loup, near Quebec, 1868; 2s. James, gen. UNIVERSITY COLL., matric. 25 Oct., 87, aged 19, B.A. 90; HONOURS:—3 law 90.

Millain, sir John Everett, bart., R.A., created D.C.L. 9 June, 1880. See *Al. Ox.* and series, 955.

Millar, Arthur David, born at Abernethy, co. Perth, 8 July, 1867; 1s. David, gen. QUEEN'S, matric. 21 Oct., 87, aged 20 (from Glasgow academy and university), bible clerk 87; HONOURS:—2 classical mods. 89, 2 classics 92.

Millar, rev. Frederick George, born in London 4 Dec., 1868; 1s. Frederick Charles James, arm. UNIVERSITY COLL., matric. 15 Oct., 87, aged 18 (from Westminster), B.A. 91; HONOURS:—3 classical mods. 89, 3 classics 91.

Millar, John Hepburn, born at Edinburgh 1864; 1s. John, lord Craighill, of Session. BALLIOL, matric. 17 Oct., 82, aged 18 (from Edinburgh academy), B.A. 87 (HONOURS:—1 classical mods. 83, 1 classics 86); advocate.

Millar, Thomas, born at Liverpool 1872; 1s. Samuel, gen. CHRIST CHURCH, matric. 16 Oct., 92, aged 19 (from Liverpool coll.), scholar 91; selected candidate Indian C.S. 91.

Millard, Christopher Sclater, born at Basingstoke, Hants, 7 Nov., 1872; 2s. James Elwin, D.D. KEBLE, matric. 11 Oct., 90, aged 17, from Basingstoke school.

Millard, rev. Frederick Luke Holland, born at St. Kitts, West Indies, 1866; 1s. Frederick, cler. ST. EDMUND HALL, matric. 26 Jan., 84, aged 18, B.A. 87, M.A. 90 (HONOURS:—2 theology 87), of Durham university (M.A. *ad eundem* 90); vice-principal Durham training coll. 89-91, lecturer Warrington training coll., and curate of Warrington 92.

Millard, Frederick Maule, M.A., fellow MAGDALEN 67-70, where see page 324.

Millard, James Elwin, D.D., fellow MAGDALEN 53-65, where see page 323.

Miller, Edward, M.A., fellow NEW COLL. 44-57, where see page 212.

Miller, Edward Mansell, M.A., fellow MAGDALEN 62, where see page 311.

Miller, Francis, born at St. Vincent, Cape de Verd, 1867; 5s. Thomas, gent. PEMBROKE, matric. 27 Oct., 85, aged 18 (from Clifton coll.), B.A. 89.

Miller, George, M.A., fellow EXETER 57-65, where see page 127.

Miller, George Charles, born at Stranraer, co. Wigtown, 1869; 1s. John, gen. NEW COLL., matric. 25 Jan., 88, aged 19.

Miller, George Russell, born at Horley, Surrey, 1860; s. William Oliver, arm. BRASENOSE, matric. 21 May, 80, aged 20, from Harrow.

Miller, John, born in London 2 Jan., 1867; y.s. George, gent. WADHAM, matric. 16 Oct., 86, aged 19 (from Lancing coll.), B.A. 90.

Miller, John Coube, born in London 10 June, 1869; 1s. George, sec. education depart. NEW COLL., matric. 12 Oct., 88, aged 19 (from Haileybury), B.A. 92; HONOURS:—3 classical mods. 90, 3 history 92.

Miller, John Henry, born at Blackheath, Kent, 9 Nov., 1869; 1s. John Nicholas, D.Med. MERTON, matric. 17 Oct., 88, aged 18 (from Forest Hill school), B.A. 92; HONOURS:—3 classical mods. 90, 3 law 92.

Miller, John Robert Charlesworth, M.A., fellow CORPUS CHRISTI 65-6, where see page 384.

Miller, Percy Alexander, born at Liverpool 1870; o.s. Alexander, gen. PEMBROKE, matric. 28 Jan., 89, aged 19.

Miller, Taverner Barrington, born in London 16/18 Aug., 1872; 1s. George Taverner, merchant. ST. JOHN'S, matric. 15 Oct., 92, aged 20.

Miller, Thomas Frederick Dawson, born at Gateshead, co. Durham, 20 Dec., 1868; 2s. Thomas Robson, (from Durham school), B.A. 90 (HONOURS:—2 law 90); bar.-at-law, Inner Temple, 91.

Miller, William, born at Wigton, Cumberland, 6 Dec., 1864; 1s. William, gent. HERTFORD, matric. 18 Oct., 83, aged 18 (from Rugby), scholar 83, B.A. 87, M.A. 90 (HONOURS:—1 classical mods. 84, accessit Hertford and Ireland scholarships 85, 1 classics 87); bar.-at-law, Inner Temple, 89.

Miller, William Duppa, born at Tupsley, co. Hereford, 1868; 1s. William, arm. HERTFORD, matric. 17 Nov., 86, aged 18 (from St. Edward's school, Summertown), exhibitioner 86, B.A. 89; HONOURS:—3 classical mods. 88.

Miller, William Sanderson, M.A., fellow NEW COLL. 40-6, where see page 212.

Millett, Harold Wake, born at Southsea, Hants, 6 March, 1872; 4s. Hamlet William, cler. PEMBROKE, matric. 25 Oct., 90, aged 18 (from Faversham gr. school), scholar 90; HONOURS:—2 classical mods. 92.

Milliken, Ernest, born at Derby 1863; 1s. Ernest, arm. BRASENOSE, matric. 10 June, 81, aged 18 (from the Charterhouse), B.A. 85, M.A. 88.

RADCLIFFE OBSERVATORY — By F. Mackenzie
From Ackermann

Milliken, Kenneth Edward, born at Derby Feb., 1867; 2s. Ernest, arm. CORPUS CHRISTI, matric. 26 Oct., 85, aged 17 (from Somerset coll., Bath), B.A. 89, M.A. 93 (HONOURS :—3 classical mods. 87, 4 classics 89); bar.-at-law, Middle Temple, 92.

Millington, Herbert Lionel, born at Leamington Nov., 1864; 4s. Thomas Street, cler. KEBLE, matric. 16 Oct., 83, aged 18 (from Leamington coll.), B.A. 87; HONOURS :—3 classical mods. 85, 4 classics 87.

Millington, Thomas Ernest, born at Loughborough, co. Leic., 22 Dec., 1863; 3s. Thomas Street, cler. NON-COLLEGIATE, matric. 17 Oct., 81, aged 17 (from Leamington coll. and Rugby); migrated to QUEEN'S, B.A. 85.

Millington, William Algernon, born at Penge, Surrey, 19 April, 1870; 1s. William, cler. WORCESTER, matric. 14 Oct., 89, aged 19 (from Rossall school), scholar 89; HONOURS :—2 classical mods. 91.

Mills, rev. Arthur John, born at Leicester 1860; o.s. Thomas, gent. NON-COLLEGIATE, matric. 4 Nov., 80, aged 20, B.A. 90, M.A. 92; curate of Hinckley 91.

Mills, Clarence Michael de Verinne, born in India 30 April, 1873; 3s. Michael Edward, cler. NON-COLLEGIATE, matric. 17 Oct., 91, aged 18, from Cheltenham coll.

Mills, Edward Francis James, born at Bhangalpore, East Indies, 28 Dec., 1863; 1s. Michael Edward, cler. ST. MARY HALL, matric. 22 Oct., 83, aged 19.

Mills, hon. Egremont John, born at Ramsay, Kent, 4 Sept., 1866; 3s. sir Charles Henry, bart., after lord Hillingdon. CHRIST CHURCH, matric. 31 May, 84, aged 17, from Eton.

Mills, Henry Percival, born at Aylmerton, Norfolk, 3 Oct., 1870; 1s. William Woodward, rector. KEBLE, matric. 12 Oct., 89, aged 19, from Haileybury.

Mills, Philo Laos, born at Hartford in America Sept., 1870; 3s. Lawrence Heyworth, D.D. HERTFORD, matric. 19 Oct., 88, aged 18, from All Saints school, Bloxham.

Mills, Thomas Ross, born at Berwick-on-Tweed 13 Nov., 1869; 4s. David, arm. WADHAM, matric. 13 Oct., 86, aged 18 (from Berwick gr. school and Edinburgh university), scholar 87; HONOURS :— 1 classical mods. 90, 1 classics 92.

Mills, Walter Wilgress, born at Eltham, Kent, 1867; o.s. Thomas Wilgress, arm. UNIVERSITY COLL., matric. 18 Oct., 86, aged 19, B.A. 89; HONOURS :—3 history 89.

Milman, Arthur, M.A., student CHRIST CHURCH 46-60, where see page 415.

Milman, Henry Clayton, born at Shoeburyness, Suffolk, 21 April, 1864; 3s. George Alderson, arm. KEBLE, matric. 16 Oct., 83, aged 19 (from Eton), B.A. 87; HONOURS :—3 chemistry 87.

Milman, Henry Salusbury, M.A., fellow ALL SOULS' 44-58, where see page 278.

Milman, William Henry, M.A., student CHRIST CHURCH 43-58, where see page 414.

Milne, rev. Ernest Arthur, born at Monken-Hadley, Herts, 13 May, 1862; y.s. Frank, arm. KEBLE, matric. 18 Oct., 81, aged 19 (from the Charterhouse and Winchester), B.A. 86, M.A. 88; curate of St. Paul's, Hemel Hempstead, 87-9, etc.

Milne, Joseph Grafton, born at Bowdon, Cheshire, 23 Dec., 1867; 3s. William, gen. CORPUS CHRISTI, matric. 20 Oct., 86, aged 18 (from Manchester gr. school), scholar 86, B.A. 90; HONOURS :—1 classical mods. 88, 2 classics 90, archæological studentship at Athens 90.

Milne, William Herbert, born at Bowdon, Cheshire, 1864; 1s. William, gen. BALLIOL, matric. 21 April, 82, aged 18, from Manchester gr. school (HONOURS :—1 classical mods. 83); scholar 82 until his death 16 Nov., 84.

Milner, Alfred, M.A., fellow NEW COLL. 76, where see page 205.

Milner, rev. George Ernest John, born at Frating, Essex, 1864; 1s. John, cler. NON-COLLEGIATE, matric. 14 Oct., 82, aged 19 (from the Charterhouse); migrated to HERTFORD, B.A. 85, M.A. 92 (HONOURS :—3 theology 85); curate of Milford, Godalming, 88-90.

Milner, Herbert Wilson, born at Liverpool 1870; 3s. James Walker, cler. BALLIOL, matric. 14 Oct., 90, aged 20; HONOURS :—3 classical mods. 92.

Milner, James Arthur, born at Liverpool 1867; 2s. James Walker, cler. ST. JOHN'S, matric. 11 Oct., 90, aged 23.

Milner, Thomas, born at Liverpool 1865; 1s. James Walker, cler. BALLIOL, matric. 24 Oct., 85, aged 20 (from Shrewsbury gr. school), B.A. 89.

Milns, William Robert, born at Alford, co. Lincoln, 1865; 3s. John Coupland, gen. KEBLE, matric. 17 Jan., 91, aged 26.

Milroy, Edward Andrew Wallace, born in London 6 May, 1873; 1s. Andrew Wallace, M.A., vicar of St. Mary, W. Cowes, isle of Wight. BALLIOL, matric. 18 Oct., 92, aged 19, from Winchester.

Milward, William Courtenay, born at Cardiff 15 Dec., 1871; 3s. James, D.Med. JESUS COLL., matric. 14 Oct., 89, aged 17, from Cardiff collegiate school.

Minchin, Edward Alfred, born at Weston-super-Mare Feb., 1866; 2s. Charles Nicholl, gent. KEBLE, matric. 19 Oct., 86, aged 20 (from Bishop's coll., Bangalore), exhibitioner 88, B.A. 90; HONOURS :— 1 morphology 90, biological scholarship at Naples 91, Radcliffe fellowship 92.

Minchin, Harry Christopher Montague, born at Wootton St. Mary, co. Gloucester, 16 Dec., 1861; 3s. Henry Charles, cler. WADHAM, matric. 15 Oct., 81, aged 19 (from Malvern coll.), scholar 80-5, B.A. 86, M.A. 91; HONOURS :—1 classical mods. 83, 2 classics 85.

Minchin, Lawrence Harry Jackson, born at Wormley, Herts, 17 Aug., 1863; 1s. Harry Holdsworth, rector. CHRIST CHURCH, matric. 13 Oct., 82, aged 19 (from Malvern coll.), exhibitioner 82-3.

Minns, Walter Hardwick Christopher, born at Egham, Surrey, 29 Jan., 1870; 1s. George William, rector. NEW COLL., matric. 11 Oct., 89, aged 19 (from Marlborough); assistant commissioner Burma 91.

Minshull, rev. Thomas Freer, born at Castle-Bromwich, co. Warwick, 1861; 4s. Thomas Evans, cler. ST. EDMUND HALL, matric. 25 Oct., 81, aged 20, B.A. 88, M.A. 90; curate of Sculcoates, Yorks, 89.

Minton, Harry Herbert, born at Ryton, Salop, 1861; 3s. Samuel, cler. NON-COLLEGIATE, matric. 17 Oct., 81, aged 20; migrated to ST. JOHN'S, B.A. 86.

Minty, Henry Oliver, born at Cheltenham 1863; 1s. Oliver, gent. EXETER, matric. 18 Oct., 83, aged 20 (from Dublin coll. of science), exhibitioner 82-6, B.A. 87, M.A. 90; HONOURS :—1 chemistry 86.

Mirehouse, Henry George, born at Easton in Gordano, Somerset, 1862; 1s. Henry John, arm. MERTON, matric. 18 Oct., 80, aged 18, B.A. 85; HONOURS :—4 history 84.

Mirrlees, Charles Alexander Duchanan, born in Stirlingshire 26 Sept., 1868; 3s. James Duchanan, gen. MERTON, matric. 19 Oct., 89, aged 20, from Loretto school.

27

Miskin, Alfred Hills, born at Dartford, Kent, 28 April, 1869; 2s. William, arm. WADHAM, matric. 13 Oct., 88, aged 19 (from Canterbury school); HONOURS:—4 law 91.

Mitchell, Alexander, born at Sauchie, co. Clackmannan, 1871; 1s. Alexander, arm. BALLIOL, matric. 17 Oct., 89, aged 18, from Harrow.

Mitchell, Alexander Ian, born at Mixbury, co. Glouc., 13 April, 1869; 1s. Thomas John, capt. King's Dragoon Guards. NEW COLL., matric. 12 Oct., 88, aged 19, from Eton.

Mitchell, Alfred Ernest, born at Edgbaston, co. Warwick, 17 July, 1869; 2s. Aurelius Bruce, arm. MERTON, matric. 17 Oct., 88, aged 19 (from Uppingham school); HONOURS:—3 law 91.

Mitchell, Andrew Alexander, born at Glasgow 1860; o.s. Andrew, solicitor, deceased. EXETER, matric. 22 Jan., 80, aged 20, from Harrow.

Mitchell, Charles Ainsworth, born at Thetford, Norfolk, 20 Nov., 1867; s. Thomas Robinson, D.Med., deceased. NON-COLLEGIATE, matric. 15 Jan., 87, aged 19 (from K. William coll., I.M.); migrated to EXETER 22 Jan., 89, B.A. 89.

Mitchell, Charles Forbes Dignum, born in London 15 Sept., 1870; o.s. Charles Forbes Bowerbank, arm. QUEEN'S, matric. 22 Oct., 89, aged 18, from Maidstone gr. school.

Mitchell, Edward, B.D., fellow ST. JOHN'S 46-78, where see page 480.

Mitchell, rev. John Thomas, born at Glasgow 1863; o.s. Thomas, arm. CORPUS CHRISTI, matric. 19 Oct., 82, aged 19, B.A. 87, M.A. 91 (HONOURS: —3 classical mods. 83, 3 classics 86); curate of West Ham, Essex, 88.

Mitchell, rev. Lancelot, born at Herne Bay, Kent, 1868; o.s. Thomas Davis, arm. UNIVERSITY COLL., matric. 18 Oct., 86, aged 18 (from Maidstone gr. school), exhibitioner 86, B.A. 89 (HONOURS:—3 theology 89); curate of Yiewsley St. Mathew 91.

Mitchell, Peter Chalmers, born at Dunfermline, co. Fife, 1865; 1s. Alexander, D.D. CHRIST CHURCH, matric. 10 Oct., 84, aged 19 (from Aberdeen university), exhibitioner 84, B.A. 88, M.A. 93; HONOURS:—1 morphology 88.

Mitchell, Richard St. John, born at Oakham 5 May, 1871; 5s. Richard, of Toronto, Canada, D.D., of Dublin university. HERTFORD, matric. 20 Oct., 91, aged 20, from Christ's hospital and Banister court school, Southampton.

Mitchell, Robert Andrew, born at Bradford, Yorks, 20 Dec., 1869; 7s. John Harper, arm. MAGDALEN, matric. 16 Oct., 88, aged 18 (from Bradford gr. school), B.A. 92; HONOURS:—2 history 92.

Mitchell, Walter Rankin, born at Airdrie, co. Lanark, N.B., 29 Aug., 1873; 5s. David, writer. EXETER, matric. 18 Oct., 92, aged 19, from Blair Lodge school.

Mitcheson, Richard Edmund, M.A., B.C.L., student CHRIST CHURCH 83-92, where see page 424.

Mitchinson, right rev. John, M.A., D.C.L., hon. fellow PEMBROKE 84, where see page 553.

Moat, William, born at Montreal 9 Oct., 1867; 1s. Robert, gen. EXETER, matric. 28 April, 87, aged 19 (from Trinity coll. school, Stratford on Avon), B.A. 91.

Moberly, Arthur Norman, born at New Alresford, Hants, 1874; 3s. John Cornelius, solicitor. CHRIST CHURCH, matric. 4 June, 92, aged 18.

Moberly, George Herbert, M.A., fellow CORPUS CHRISTI 64-70, where see page 383.

Moberly, George Keble, born on the Rhine 28 Feb., 1871; 1s. George Herbert, cler. WORCESTER, matric. 14 Oct., 89, aged 18, from Winchester.

Moberly, rev. Gerald Edward, born at Winchester 20 July, 1864; 2s. Henry Edward, vicar of Heckfield, Hants. NEW COLL., matric. 11 Dec., 82, aged 18 (from Winchester), B.A. 85 (HONOURS:—4 history 85); curate of St. George, Portsea, 89.

Moberly, Henry Edward, M.A., fellow NEW COLL. 41-60, where see page 212.

Moberly, Robert Campbell, D.D., canon of CHRIST CHURCH 92, where see page 404.

Mocatta, Henry Elias, born at St. Heliers, co. Lanc., Jan., 1862; 1s. William Abraham, cler. PEMBROKE, matric. 4 Feb., 81, aged 19, D.A. 85, M.A. 87.

Mocatta, rev. Maurice John, born at Eccleston, co. Lanc., 4 April, 1864; 2s. William Abraham, vicar. NEW COLL., matric. 12 Oct., 83, aged 19 (from Magdalen coll. school and Haileybury), B.A. 87, M.A. 90; curate of Wednesbury St. James 87.

Moffat, William Kennedy, born at Carlisle 1873; o.s. Thomas, gent. PEMBROKE, matric. 28 Oct., 92, aged 19.

Moffatt, John Anderson Stanley Paget, born at Kilmore, Ireland, 1854; 1s. Christopher William, cler. NON-COLLEGIATE, matric. 4 Nov., 84, aged 30 (from Lond. university, K.A.); migrated to EXETER 22 April, 85, B.A. 88, M.A. 91.

Moger, George Ernest, born at Widcombe, near Bath, 16 May, 1864; 3s. Horace, arm. TRINITY, matric. 15 Jan., 83, aged 18 (from Bath coll.), B.A. 86, B.C.L. 89 (HONOURS:—2 law 86, 3 civil law 88); a solicitor 89.

Moir, Frank John, born at Jedburgh, co. Roxburgh, Oct., 1868; 3s. John, dean of Glasgow. KEBLE, matric. 17 Oct., 87, aged 18 (from Glenalmond); brother of James W.

Moir, George Herbert Cecil, born at Clifton 1870; o.s. George, arm. EXETER, matric. 20 Jan., 90, aged 20.

Moir, James William, born at Jedburgh, co. Roxburgh, June, 1864; 2s. John, dean of Glasgow. KEBLE, matric. 17 Oct., 87, aged 23 (from Glenalmond), B.A. 90; brother of Frank J.

Molesworth, Arthur Hilton, born at Bettershanger, Kent, 1 June, 1860; 4s. Rennell Francis Wynn, cler. PEMBROKE, 4 Feb., 80, aged 19; migrated to NEW INN HALL 84; bar.-at-law, Inner Temple, 85.

Molesworth, Lionel Charles, born at Highlea, Cheshire, 18 March, 1873; 2s. Richard, major in the army. UNIVERSITY COLL., matric. 15 Oct., 92, aged 19, from Westminster school.

Molineux, William, born at Preston, co. Lanc., 19 June, 1867; 2s. John, gen. WORCESTER, matric. 17 Oct., 87, aged 20 (from Preston gr. school), B.A. 90.

Moll, Frederick Henry Leopold, born in London 4 Feb., 1865; 1s. Henry, gent. WORCESTER, matric. 19 Oct., 86, aged 20, as Frederick (from Blind coll., Worcester), B.A. 89.

Molyneux, Philip, M.A., HERTFORD, where see.

Monahan, Francis John, born at Dublin 1865; 2s. James Henry, arm. BALLIOL, matric. 16 Oct., 83, aged 18 (from Birmingham oratory school), assist. commissioner, Assam 85.

Monckton, Harewood Lascelles, born at Goole, Yorks, 6 June, 1861; o.s. Marshall, surgeon. NON-COLLEGIATE, matric. 27 May, 82, aged 17; migrated to WADHAM 10 May, 89.

Monckton, Herbert Haden, born at Coren, near Wolverhampton, 28 July, 1861; 1s. Inglis George, cler. WADHAM, matric. 16 Jan., 80, aged 18, B.A. 83.

Monckton, John Lionel Alexander, born in London Dec., 1861; 1s. sir John Braddick, knt. ORIEL, matric. 19 Oct., 80, aged 18 (from the Charterhouse), B.A. 85, M.A. 88; bar.-at-law, Lincoln's Inn, 85.

Monckton, Ralph Granville, born at Boxted, Kent, 1868; 6s. Walter, gen. ST. EDMUND HALL, matric. 21 Oct., 86, aged 18.

Moncreiff, James Arthur Fitz Herbert, born at Somersal-Herbert, co. Derby, 19 July, 1872; 1s. Hon. Robert Chichester, cler. NEW COLL., matric. 16 Oct., 91, aged 19, from Repton school.

Money, Noel Ernest, born at Montreal, Canada, May, 1867; 1s. Albert William, arm. CHRIST CHURCH, matric. 31 May, 84, aged 17, from Radley coll.

Money, Walter McLachlan, born in London 1866; 1s. Walter, arm. NEW COLL., matric. 16 Oct., 85, aged 19 (from Bradfield coll.), B.A. 89, M.A. and B.C.L. 92 (HONOURS:—3 classical mods. 87, 3 law 89); barrister-at-law, Inner Temple, 91.

Monier-Williams, sir Monier, K.C.I.E., D.C.L., hon. fellow UNIVERSITY COLL. 92, where see page 31.

Monro, Claude Frederick Hugh, born in London 29 April, 1863; 1s. Frederick Thomas, arm. HERTFORD, matric. 19 Oct., 81, aged 18; migrated to NEW INN HALL (Balliol 87), B.A. and M.A. 88.

Monro, David Binning, M.A., provost of ORIEL 82, where see page 146.

Monro, Tregonwell, born at Bournemouth, Hants, Aug., 1867; 2s. Hector, arm. ST. JOHN'S, matric. 17 Oct., 85, aged 18, from Radley coll.

Monson, hon. sir Edmund John, G.C.M.G., M.A. fellow ALL SOULS' 58-82, where see page 281.

Monson, William John, born at Croft vicarage, co. Lincoln, 12 Sept., 1873; 1s. hon. Evelyn John, M.A., cler., deceased. MAGDALEN, matric. 18 Oct., 92 (from Eton), demy 92.

Montagnon, Louis Langlois, born at Cheltenham 10 March, 1873; 1s. Louis William, gent. HERTFORD, matric. 22 Oct., 92, aged 19 (from Cheltenham coll.), scholar 92.

Montagu, hon. John Walter Edward Douglas-Scott-, born 10 June, 1866; 1s. Henry James, Baron Montagu. NEW COLL., matric. 27 Jan., 86, aged 19, from Eton.

Montagu, hon. Robert Henry Douglas-Scott-, born 30 July, 1867; 2s. Henry John, Baron Montagu. NEW COLL., matric. 15 Oct., 86, aged 19, from Eton.

Montague, Charles Edward, born at Ealing, Middx., 1867; 3s. Francis, gent. BALLIOL, matric. 24 Oct., 85, aged 18 (from city of London school), exhibitioner 84; HONOURS:—1 classical mods. 87, 2 classics 89.

Montague, Francis Charles, M.A., fellow ORIEL 81-8, where see page 154.

Montefiore, rev. Durbin Brice, born at Charmouth, Dorset, 20 Oct., 1860; 3s. Thomas Law, cler. ST. ALBAN HALL, matric. 19 Oct., 80, aged 21; migrated to EXETER Oct., 82, B.A. 83, M.A. 89; rector of Spaxton, Somerset, 91.

Montgomerie, Charles Waterton Edmonstone, born at Sydenham, Kent, 1866; 2s. Hugh, gent. CHRIST CHURCH, matric. 16 Oct., 85, aged 19 (from Copenhagen); in settlement depart. central provinces, India.

Montgomerje, Hastings Seton, born at Oeyra, in E. Indies, 6 Jan., 1872; 1s. Thomas George, arm. TRINITY, matric. 11 Oct., 90, aged 18, from Winchester.

Montgomery, Arthur Hope, born at Longsight, co. Lanc., 1867; 2s. Robert, gent. PEMBROKE, matric. 27 Oct., 85, aged 18 (from Manchester gr. school), scholar 85-6, B.A. 89, M.A. and B.C.L. 92 (HONOURS:—3 classical mods. 87, 2 history 89, 3 civil law 91); bar.-at-law, Inner Temple, 91.

Montgomery, Charles James, born at Chester 30 May, 1871; 2s. John Knowles, cler. LINCOLN, matric. 20 Oct., 90, aged 19 (from Chester gr. school); HONOURS:—2 classical mods. 92.

Montgomery, Robert Mortimer, born at Chester 2 Dec., 1869; 1s. John Knowles, cler. NON-COLLEGIATE, matric. 13 Oct., 88, aged 18 (from Chester gr. school), B.A. 92; HONOURS:—3 classical mods. 90, 3 history 92.

Montgomery, William, born at Christ Church, New Zealand, 1866; 1s. William, gen. BALLIOL, matric. 24 Oct., 85, aged 19 (from Canterbury coll., N.Z.), B.A. 88 (HONOURS:—1 law 88); bar.-at-law, Inner Temple, 90, as William Hugh.

Montgomery, William Percy, born at Manchester 20 Feb., 1867; 1s. Robert, arm. MERTON, matric. 16 Oct., 84, aged 17 (from Manchester gr. school), postmaster 84, B.A. 87, M.A. 92; HONOURS:—3 chemistry 87.

Montmorency, William Geoffrey Bouchard de, 6th viscount Mountmorres, born 23 Sept., 1872; 1s. William Browne, viscount Mountmorres. BALLIOL, matric. 14 Oct., 90, aged 18 (from Radley coll.), exhibitioner 89.

Monypeny, William, born at Portadown, co. Armagh, 1867; 2s. William, gen. BALLIOL, matric. 21 Jan., 89, aged 22 (from Dungannon royal school, and scholar Trinity coll., Dublin, 86), exhibitioner 88; HONOURS:—3 classical mods. 89.

Moody, John Frederick Badger, born at Derby 28 July, 1865; 1s. John, solicitor. EXETER, matric. 18 Jan., 83, aged 18 (from Rugby), fellow royal veterinary association.

Moon, rev. Cecil Graham, born at Fetcham, Surrey, 7 June, 1867; 4s. sir Edward Graham, bart., and cler. MAGDALEN, matric. 21 Oct., 86, aged 19 (from Eton); curate of Mistley with Bradfield, Essex, 91.

Moon, Robert Oswald, born in London 17 March, 1865; 3s. Robert, bar.-at-law. EXETER, matric. 10 Oct., 84, aged 19 (from Winchester), B.A. 90, M.A. 92; HONOURS:—2 classical mods. 86, 2 classics 88.

Moor, Cresacre George, born at Canterbury 26 March, 1851; 1s. Allen Page, cler. CHRIST CHURCH, matric. 3 June, 87, aged 19, from Westminster school.

Moor, Philip, born at Ampfield, Hants, May, 1863; 4s. John Frewen, cler. KEBLE, matric. 17 Oct., 82, aged 19, B.A. 86 (HONOURS:—4 theology 86); died 20 June, 87.

Moore, Alfred, born at Bishopwearmouth, co. Durham, 1864; 5s. John, arm. EXETER, matric. 18 Oct., 83, aged 19 (from Wellington coll.), B.A. 87.

Moore, Arthur Collin, born at Rome 18 March, 1866; 3s. John Collingham, gent. QUEEN'S, matric. 20 Oct., 85, aged 19 (from Bradfield coll.), B.A. 88; HONOURS:—2 classical mods. 87.

Moore, Arthur Stephens Withers, born at Kelvedon Hatch, Essex, 27 Aug., 1868; 1s. John Lucas, late chaplain R.N., deceased. MAGDALEN, matric. 22 Oct., 87, aged 19 (from Lancing coll.), demy 87; HONOURS:—2 classical mods. 89, 2 classics 91.

Moore, Charles Henry Dodwell, born at Honington, co. Lincoln, 3 Feb., 1872; 3s. Henry Dodwell, M.A., vicar. PEMBROKE, matric. 26 Oct., 92, aged 20, from Newark school.

Moore, Claude, born at Princetown, Devon, 1864; 3s. James Richard, arm. CHARSLEY'S HALL, matric. 11 Oct., 90, aged 18, from Winchester.

Moore, Edward, D.D., principal of ST. EDMUND HALL 64, where see page 619.

Moore, Edward Alfred Livingstone, born at Oxford 13 Nov., 1870; 1s. Edward, D.D., principal of St. Edmund hall. CHARSLEY'S HALL, matric. 25 Oct., 89, aged 18 (from Marlborough coll.), scholar 89; HONOURS:—1 classical mods. 91.

Moore, Edward James, born at Crawley, co. Stafford, 1 May, 1862. CHRIST CHURCH, matric. 14 Oct., 81, aged 19 (from Epsom coll.), B.A. 87, M.A. and B.Med. 91.

Moore, Edward William, born at East Moulsey, Surrey, 3 May, 1866; 1s. William Ferniclough, gent. NON-COLLEGIATE, matric. 26 Oct., 85, aged 19 (from Canterbury school), scholar CHRIST CHURCH 85, B.A. 89; HONOURS :—a classical mods. 87, 2 classics 89.

Moore, Ernest Andrew, born in London 18 May, 1869; 2s. John Collingham, gen. QUEEN'S, matric. 21 Oct., 87, aged 18 (from Bradfield coll.); selected candidate Indian C.S. 87.

Moore, Francis Bell Grant, born at Barbados 14 April, 1863; y.s. Henry Willoughby, cler. TRINITY, matric. 2 Feb., 82, aged 18 (from Harrison and Codrington colls., Barbados), B.A. 86; HONOURS : —3 classical mods. 83, 4 classics 85.

Moore, Frederick Dalgety, born at Invercargill, N.Z., 22 April, 1867; 1s. Frederick Henry, gen. EXETER, matric. 22 Jan., 89, aged 21, from Christ Church, N.Z.

Moore, Geoffrey Stuart, born at Greenhithe, Kent, 23 June, 1871; 2s. Stuart Archibald, arm. QUEEN'S, matric. 27 Jan., 90, aged 18, from Westminster school.

Moore, George Ralph, born at Duffield, co. Derby, 1859; 3s. Francis Wellington, cler. NON-COLLEGIATE, matric. 22 Jan., 81, aged 22 (from Derby school), B.A. 89.

Moore, rev. Halhed Sydney, born at Lovington, Somerset, 28 Dec., 1861; 3s. Peter Halhed, cler. KEBLE, matric. 27 Jan., 81, aged 19 (from Marlborough coll.), exhibitioner 82-4, B.A. 84, M.A. 88 (HONOURS :—3 classical mods. 82, 3 classics 84); missionary Calcutta 88.

Moore, Harold Broadbent, born at Stretford, co. Lanc., 1867; 3s. William, gen. BRASENOSE, matric. 20 Oct., 86, aged 19 (from Manchester gr. school), scholar 86, B.A. 90; HONOURS :—1 classical mods. 88, 2 classics 90.

Moore, Harry Christopher, born at Kensington 28 Oct., 1872; 3s. John Collingham, portrait painter, deceased. BALLIOL, matric. 14 Oct., 90, aged 17 (from Bradfield coll.), exhibitioner 89; HONOURS :— 1 classical mods. 92.

Moore, Harry Wilkinson, born at Drumcondra, Dublin, 1857; 1s. Daniel, gent. TURRELL'S HALL, matric. 24 Jan., 84, aged 33.

Moore, rev. Henry, M.A., fellow WORCESTER 65, where see page 573.

Moore, rev. Herbert, born at Pill, Somerset, Dec., 1863; 4s. Peter Halhed, cler. KEBLE, matric. 17 Oct., 82, aged 18 (from Clifton coll.), exhibitioner 82, B.A. 87, M.A. 90 (HONOURS :—1 classical mods. 84, 2 classics 86); priest of St. Andrew mission, Tokyo, Japan, 91.

Moore, rev. Herbert Augustine, born at Camberwell, Surrey, 1860; 3s. Daniel, cler. UNIVERSITY COLL., matric. 16 Oct., 80, aged 20 (from St. Paul's school), B.A. 84, M.A. 87; HONOURS :—4 history 84.

Moore, Hubert Stuart, born at Greenhithe, Kent, 29 July, 1869; 1s. Stuart Archibald, barrister-at-law, QUEEN'S, matric. 25 Jan., 88, aged 18, from Westminster school.

Moore, rev. John Henry, born at Clapham, Surrey, 1853; o.s. Henry John, gent. EXETER, matric. 25 Oct., 82, aged 29, from Lancing coll.

Moore, Joseph Henry Hamilton, M.A., fellow HERTFORD 75-88, where see page 601.

Moore, Lewis Grenville, born at Trichinopoly in East Indies 24 Nov., 1871; 1s. Lewis, judge Indian C.S. WORCESTER, matric. 14 Oct., 90, aged 18 (from Cheltenham coll.), scholar 90; selected candidate Indian C.S. 90; brother of Pierce.

Moore, Oswald Allen, born at Hulland, co. Derby, 19 June, 1864; o.s. Robert Stephen, vicar of Mickley, Yorks. MAGDALEN, matric. 19 Oct., 83, aged 19 (from Repton school), B.A. 87, M.A. 90.

Moore, Pierce Langrishe, born at Trichinopoly, Madras, 29 June, 1873; 2s. Lewis, judge Indian C.S. CHRIST CHURCH, matric. 14 Oct., 92, aged 19 (from Cheltenham coll.), scholar 92.

Moore, Ralph Headley, born in London 9 April, 1870; 1s. Thomas, arm. BRASENOSE, matric. 23 Jan., 90, aged 19, from Leamington coll.

Moore, Reginald Bowerman, born at Lyme Regis, Dorset, 1851; 1s. William Walling, gent. NEW COLL., matric. 27 Jan., 85, aged 34, B.Mus. 3 Dec., 85.

Moore, Reginald William Ilickerton, born at Ilfracombe, Devon, 1865; 1s. William Clark, cler. HERTFORD, matric. 18 Oct., 83, aged 18 (from King's coll. school), B.A. 86, M.A. 90.

Moore, Richard Clarke, born at Ringway, Cheshire, 1865; 1s. Joseph, gen. NON-COLLEGIATE, matric. 17 Oct., 91, aged 26, from Owens coll. and Unitarian coll., Manchester.

Moore, Walter Francis, born in London 1862; 6s. John, gen. NON-COLLEGIATE, matric. 12 Oct., 89, aged 17, from Bradford gr. school.

Moore, William, M.A., fellow MAGDALEN 72-9, where see page 325.

Moore, William Maxwell Scott, born at Moleman near Londonderry 1862; 2s. Robert Lyon, arm. BRASENOSE, matric. 16 Oct., 80, aged 18 (from Winchester), B.A. 91.

Moorsom, Launcelot Richard Purton, born at Sadberge, co. Durham, 2 Aug., 1866; 2s. Robert Maude, cler. EXETER, matric. 21 Oct., 86, aged 20.

Moran, rev. Walter Isidore, born at Cheetham, co. Lanc., 9 June, 1865; 3s. Patrick Thomas, arm. MERTON, matric. 16 Oct., 84, aged 19 (from Manchester gr. school), postmaster 84, B.A. 89, M.A. 92 (HONOURS :—1 mathematical mods. 85, 2 mathematics 88); lecturer St. Stephen's, Canonbury, etc., 91.

Morant, Robert Lawrie, born in London 7 April, 1863; 1s. Robert, artist. NEW COLL., matric. 15 Oct., 81, aged 18 (from Winchester), B.A. 85, M.A. 89; HONOURS :—2 classical mods. 82, 1 theology 85.

Mordaunt, Gerald John, born at Staple Hill, Weilsbourne, co. Warwick, 20 Jan., 1873; 3s. John Murray, of Bromley, Kent., esq. UNIVERSITY COLL., matric. 15 Oct., 92, aged 19, from Rugby or Wellington.

Moreland, Christopherson Hudson, born at Belfast 1867; 2s. William Harrison, gen. LINCOLN, matric. 22 Oct., 86, aged 19 (from Clifton coll.), scholar 87, B.A. 90; HONOURS :—1 classical mods. 88, 2 classics 90.

Moreton, rev. Arthur Cyprian Moreton, born in the island of Labuan, Borneo, 1867; 2s. Julian, cler. NON-COLLEGIATE, matric. 15 Jan., 87, aged 20 (from Forest and Hurstpierpoint schools), B.A. 90; assist. master St. John's coll., Hurstpierpoint, 90.

Moreton, rev. Tudor Phillips, born at Labuan, Borneo, 1865; 1s. Julian, cler. NON-COLLEGIATE, matric. 23 Jan., 86, aged 21 (from Merchant Taylors' school), B.A. 89 (HONOURS :—3 theology 89); curate of Hughenden, Bucks, 91.

Morfill, William Richard, M.A., ORIEL, where see page 153.

Morgan, Charles Edgar, born at Ystrad-Dyfodwy, co. Glamorgan, 1860; 1s. William Henry, cler. KEBLE, matric. 16 Oct., 83, aged 23 (from Lampeter coll.); HONOURS :—3 classical mods. 85, 3 classics 86.

Morgan, David Hughes, born at Llandovery 16 Aug., 1871; 1s. David, gen. QUEEN'S, matric. 24 Oct., 90, aged 19, from Christ's coll., Finchley.

Morgan, Edward Henry Elers, born at Tunbridge Wells 1865; 1s. Edward, arm. UNIVERSITY COLL., matric. 11 Oct., 84, aged 19, B.A. 88; HONOURS :—3 classical mods. 86, 4 classics 88.

Morgan, Edwin Vernon, born at Aurora Cayuga lake, N.Y., U.S.A., 1866; 1s. Henry Augustine, gen. NON-COLLEGIATE, matric. 28 April, 92, aged 26, from Harvard University, U.S.A.

Morgan, Frank, born at Carmarthen March, 1869; 2s. William James, gen. KEBLE, matric. 13 Oct., 88, aged 19 (from Llandovery coll.), exhibitioner 88, B.A. 92; HONOURS :—3 classical mods. 90, 1 history 92.

Morgan, Frederick Stuart, born in London 1871; 1s. Frederick, arm. HERTFORD, matric. 19 Oct., 88, aged 17, from Uppingham.

Morgan, sir George Osborne, bart., M.A., Stowell fellow UNIVERSITY COLL. 50-7, where see page 34.

Morgan, Harington, born in Madras 1865; 4s. sir Walter, knt. PEMBROKE, matric. 27 Oct., 83, aged 18; bar.-at-law, Middle Temple, 87.

Morgan, Harry John, born at Portmadoc, co. Carnarvon, 16 Nov., 1871; 1s. John, cler. BRASENOSE, matric. 22 Oct., 91, aged 19, from Brecon coll.

Morgan, Henry Tilson, born at Walcot, Somerset, 22 May, 1871; 2s. Francis Augustine, cler. NEW COLL., matric. 17 Oct., 90, aged 19 (from Bath coll.), scholar 90; HONOURS:—1 classical mods. 92.

Morgan, John Arthur, born at Llanllechid, co. Carnarvon, 1873; 2s. John, cler. ST. JOHN'S, matric. 15 Oct., 92, aged 19, from Llandovery coll.

Morgan, rev. John Percy, born at Pontnewynydd, co. Monmouth, Oct., 1863; 1s. John, cler. KEBLE, matric. 18 Oct., 81, aged 17 (from Cowbridge), B.A. 84 (HONOURS:—3 history 84); curate of St. Woolos, Newport, co. Monmouth, 90.

Morgan, Theodore Whittingham Pughe, born at Newtown, co. Montgomery, 26 June, 1872; 1s. John Pughe, vicar of Dolfor, co. Montgomery. JESUS COLL., matric. 20 Oct., 91, aged 19, from St. Oswald's coll., Ellesmere.

Morgan, Thomas, born at Letterston, co. Pembroke, 1864; o.s. George, gent. JESUS COLL., matric. 19 Oct., 81, aged 19.

Morgan, Thomas Holmes, born at Swansea, co. Glam., 1867; 1s. Thomas Edward, cler. CHARSLEY'S HALL, matric. 16 Oct., 86, aged 19.

Morgan, Thomas Westlake, born at Congresbury, Somst., 1870; o.s. Thomas Miles, gen. QUEEN'S, matric. 15 Jan., 91, aged 21.

Morgan, William Frederick Taylor, born in London 11 Jan., 1866; 1s. William Taylor, D.Med. PEMBROKE, matric. 27 Oct., 84, aged 18 (from Brecon school), B.A. 88; HONOURS:—2 classical mods. 86, 2 classics 88.

Morgan, William Seldon, born at Newport, co. Pembroke, 13 Feb., 1872; o.s. James, gen. QUEEN'S, matric. 24 Oct., 90, aged 18 (from Cardigan school and Llandovery coll.), scholar 90; HONOURS:—2 classical mods. 92.

Moriarty, Gerald Patrick, born at Dieppe, France, 1863; y.s. Stephen Stack, gen. BALLIOL, matric. 18 Oct., 81, aged 18 (from Brighton coll.), B.A. 85; HONOURS :—2 classical mods. 83, 1 history 85, Arnold essay prize 86.

Morice, rev. Francis David, M.A., fellow QUEEN'S 71, where see page 174.

Morice, rev. Harry Chalmers Gray, born at Brixton, Surrey, 1866; 4s. James, gent. EXETER, matric. 16 Oct., 84, aged 18 (from Bedford gr. school), scholar 83, B.A. 89, M.A. 91 (HONOURS:—1 classical mods. 86, 2 classics 88); curate of Churchstow, Devon, 90.

Morice, rev. Thomas Richards, M.A., fellow JESUS COLL. 52, where see page 509.

Morier, right hon. sir Robert Burnett David (G.C.B., G.C.M.G.); born in Paris 1827; o.s. David Richard, arm. BALLIOL, matric. 5 March, 45, aged 18 (HONOURS :—2 classics 49), B.A. 50; created D.C.L. 26 June, 89; a student of Inner Temple 47; entered diplomatic service 53, envoy extraordinary, etc., Portugal 76-81, Spain 81-4, ambassador extraordinary and minister plenipotentiary at the court of St. Petersburg 84, P.C., G.C.M.G., 13 Feb., 86, G.C.B. 30 Sept., 87.

Morier, Victor Albert Louis, born at Darmstadt 18 Feb., 1867; o.s. right hon. sir Robert Burnett, G.C.B. BALLIOL, matric. 11 May, 86, aged 19; died 27 May, 92, at sea.

Morison, Lennox James, born at Lewisham, Kent, 6 Sept., 1872; o.s. William Lennox, merchant, deceased. PEMBROKE, matric. 26 Oct., 91, aged 19 (from King's coll. school), scholar 91.

Morkill, John William, born at Seacroft, Yorks, Nov., 1861; 1s. John, arm. ORIEL, matric. 21 May, 80, aged 19 (from Radley coll.), B.A. 84, M.A. 87; HONOURS :—3 law 84.

Morland, Arthur Bell, born at Abingdon, Berks, 1869; 4s. John Thornhill, arm. PEMBROKE, matric. 17 Oct., 88, aged 19 (from Abingdon school), scholar 88, B.A. 92; HONOURS :—2 classical mods. 90, 3 classics 92.

Morland, Philip Hugh, born at Abingdon, Berks, 14 April, 1873; 5s. John Thornhill, M.A., solicitor. ST. JOHN'S, matric. 15 Oct., 92, aged 19, from Abingdon school.

Morland, Servante, born at Montreal June, 1869; 3s. Thomas, arm. CHRIST CHURCH, matric. 18 Jan., 89, aged 19, from Portsea school.

Morley, George, born at Bradford, Yorks, 17 Nov., 1873; 1s. William James, architect. WORCESTER, matric. 22 Oct., 91, aged 17 (from Bradford gr. school), scholar 91.

Morley, Henry Lawrence, born at Edenbridge, Kent, 12 April, 1868; 6s. George, vicar of Astwood, Bucks. NON-COLLEGIATE, matric. 15 Oct., 87, aged 19 (from Marlborough coll.); HONOURS:—2 classical mods. 89, 4 classics 91.

Morley, Reginald Arthur, born at Hever, Kent, 8 Aug., 1870; 7s. George, vicar of Astwood, Bucks. NON-COLLEGIATE, matric. 21 Oct., 89, aged 19 (from Dunchurch school and Malvern coll.); HONOURS:—3 classical mods. 91.

Morley, Sidney Frederick, born at Hever, Kent, 1866; 5s. George, cler. UNIVERSITY COLL., matric. 17 Oct., 85, aged 19 (from Dulwich coll.), exhibitioner 85, B.A. 88; HONOURS :—3 history 88.

Morphew, Henry Leslie, born at Wrotham, Kent, 20 March, 1866; 3s. William George, gen. WORCESTER, matric. 29 Jan., 86, aged 19.

Morrah, Herbert Arthur, born at Winchester 22 Sept., 1870; 1s. James Arthur, col. late 60th rifles. ST. JOHN'S, matric. 11 Oct., 90, aged 20, from Highgate school.

Morrell, Frederic Parker, M.A., steward ST. JOHN'S 83, where see page 492.

Morrell, George Herbert, M.A., B.C.L., EXETER, where see page 130.

Morrell, Herbert Hugh, born at Hay, co. Radnor, May, 1866; 4s. Hopewell Baker, arm. ST. JOHN'S, matric. 11 Oct., 84, aged 18, from St. Edward's school, Summertown.

Morrell, Philip Edward, born at Oxford 4 June, 1870; 1s. Frederic Parker, solicitor to the university. BALLIOL, matric. 17 Oct., 89, aged 19 (from Eton); HONOURS:—3 classical mods. 91.

Morrell, William John, born at Tiverton, Devon, 6 April, 1868; 1s. William. gent. BALLIOL, matric. 24 Oct., 85, aged 17 (from Tiverton school), scholar 84, B.A. 90; HONOURS:—1 classical mods. 87, 2 classics 89, 2 history 90.

Morres, Edward Redmond, born at Wokingham, Berks, 3 Sept., 1873; 1s. Hugh Redmond, cler., M.A., deceased. MAGDALEN, matric. 18 Oct., 92, aged 19, from Winchester.

Morris, Alfred Tudor, born at Oakwood, co. Glam., 19 April, 1863; 2s. James, vicar of Cwm, Flints. JESUS COLL., matric. 18 Oct., 82, aged 19 (from Beaumaris gr. school), B.A. 86 ; HONOURS:—3 classical mods. 84.

Morris, Arthur John, born at Lambeth 1862; 1s. Henry, cler. BRASENOSE, matric. 16 Oct., 80, aged 18 (from Merchant Taylors' school), exhibitioner 88, B.A. 92 ; HONOURS:—3 classical mods. 90, 3 history 92.

Morris, Charles John, born at Shrewsbury 1863; 1s. Charles John, arm. CHRIST CHURCH, matric. 14 Oct., 81, aged 18 (from Eton); migrated to NEW INN HALL 85.

Morris, Edgar Ford, born at Withington, co. Lanc., 20 May, 1874; 3s. Joseph, of Southport, merchant. BALLIOL, matric. 18 Oct., 92, aged 18 (from Rugby), scholar 91.

Morris, rev. Edward Henry, born at Carleton, Yorks, 12 Aug., 1862; 1s. Thomas Edward, vicar. CHRIST CHURCH, matric. 4 June, 81, aged 18 (from Westminster school), B.A. 86; curate of Holy Trinity, Gainsborough, co. Linc., 92.

Morris, Francis John Albert, born at Balwharrie, co. Perth, 1869; 5s. Albert John Thomas, cler. BALLIOL, matric. 18 Oct., 88, aged 19 (from Dulwich coll.); HONOURS:—3 classical mods. 90.

Morris, George Ernest, born at Bicton, Salop, Feb., 1874; 6s. Charles John, B.A. CHRIST CHURCH, matric. 4 June, 92, aged 18, from Harrow.

Morris, rev. Herbert Forster, born at Stretford, co. Lanc., 23 Dec., 1866; 2s. John, gent. WORCESTER, matric. 19 Oct., 86, aged 19 (from Old Trafford school), B.A. 90; curate of Wetherby, Yorks, 92.

Morris, Joseph Ernest, born at Beddington, Surrey, 1866 ; 3s. Joseph, gent. UNIVERSITY COLL., matric. 11 Oct., 84, aged 18, B.A. 88 (HONOURS:—2 classical mods. 86, 3 classics 88); bar.-at-law, Lincoln's Inn, 90.

Morris, Lewis, M.A., hon. fellow JESUS COLL. 77, where see page 124.

Morris, William, M.A., hon. fellow EXETER 82, where see page 124.

Morris, William, born at Cowley St. John, near Oxford, 1869; o.s. William, gen. NON-COLLEGIATE, matric. 20 Oct., 92, aged 21, from SS. Philip and James boys school, Oxford.

Morris, William John, M.A., JESUS COLL., where see page 514.

Morris, Wyndham Vassall Bush, born at Fishponds, Bristol, 21 Nov., 1869; 2s. Alfred George, B.A., rector of Roglet, co. Mon. NON-COLLEGIATE, matric. 1 Nov. 92, aged 22, from Hereford county coll.

Morrison, James Archibald, born at Fonthill Gifford, Wilts, 18 Sept., 1873; 2s. Alfred, gen. NEW COLL., matric. 14 Oct., 92, aged 18 (from Eton); in Oxford eight 93.

Morrison, William Rae, born at Aston, near York, 4 Sept., 1871 ; 1s. William Hiram, arm. CHARSLEY'S HALL, matric. 18 Oct., 89, aged 18, from Phillip's academy, Andover, Mass., U.S.A.

Morshead, Edmund Doidge Anderson, M.A., fellow NEW COLL. 74-9, where see page 217.

Morshead, Frederick, M.A., fellow NEW COLL. 53-66, where see page 215.

Morshead, Leonard Frederick, born at Winchester 5 Sept., 1868 ; 1s. Frederick, arm. BALLIOL, matric. 19 Oct., 87, aged 19 (from Winchester), assist. magistrate and collector Bengal 89.

Mort, rev. Ernest, born at St. Marks, Sydney, 1862; 5s. Thomas Sutcliffe, arm. CHRIST CHURCH, matric. 16 Jan., 80, aged 18, B.A. 83 (HONOURS:—3 theology 83); curate of Holy Trinity, Greenwich, 87.

Mort, George Frederick, born at Fenton, co. Stafford, 22 Nov., 1873; 2s. George Drewry, gent. NEW COLL., matric. 14 Oct., 92, aged 19, from Aldenham gr. school.

Mortimer, Edwin John, born at Stanwellmore, Middx., 1870; 1s. Eli George, gen. NON-COLLEGIATE, matric. 17 Oct., 91, aged 21, from St. Frideswide's school, Oxford.

Mortimer, Frank, born at Orford, co. Lanc., 21 July, 1872; 2s. William, gen. EXETER, matric. 13 Oct., 90, aged 18, from Leigh high school.

Mortimer, George Frederic Lloyd, born at Walthamstow, Essex, 1866; 3s. Mortimer Lloyd, cler. BALLIOL, matric. 24 Oct., 85, aged 19 (from Birkenhead school), B.A. 89, M.A. 92 (HONOURS: —2 classical mods. 87, 1 classics 89), librarian 88, and president 89 of Oxford union society ; bar.-at-law, Inner Temple, 91.

Mortimer, Harry Percival, born at Warrington 19 Aug., 1870; 1s. William, arm. TRINITY, matric. 13 Oct., 86, aged 18 (from Marlborough coll.), B.A. 92; HONOURS:—3 law 92.

Mortimer, Hugh Carstairs Jones, born at St. Asaph, co. Denbigh, 6 Feb., 1867 ; 1s. Hugh Maurice, arm. MERTON, matric. 21 Oct., 86, aged 19, B.A. 89.

Mortimer, John Hamilton, born at Wimbledon, Surrey, 13 Aug., 1872 ; 1s. Percy, stockbroker. MAGDALEN, matric. 22 Oct., 91, aged 19, from Eton.

Mortimer, Leonard, born at Redhill, Surrey, 1872 ; 2s. Charles, gen. EXETER, matric. 20 Jan., 90, aged 18 from Clifton coll.

Mortimer, Mansel Witherby Jones, born at Tranmere, Cheshire, 1868 ; 4s. Mortimer Lloyd Jones, cler. BALLIOL, matric. 19 Oct., 87, aged 19 (from Birkenhead school); HONOURS:—4 law 90.

Mortimer, rev. Percy, born at Swansea, co. Glam., 7 Dec., 1862 ; 1s. Francis William, gen. JESUS COLL., matric. 18 Oct., 82, aged 19 (from Llandovery coll), B.A. 86, M.A. 89; curate of St. Saviour, Iuth, 88.

Morton, rev. D'Arcy Strangways, born at Malton, Yorks, 21 July, 1861 ; 2s. Edwin, arm. NON-COLLEGIATE, matric. 23 Oct., 80, aged 19 (from Hedford gr. school) ; migrated to WORCESTER, B.A. 84 (HONOURS:—4 law 84) ; vicar of North Dalton, Yorks, 91.

Morton, Francis Arthur, born at Wakefield, Yorks, 1866 ; 3s. Charles, arm. UNIVERSITY COLL., matric. 11 Oct., 84, aged 18 (from Wakefield school), exhibitioner 83, B.A. 90 ; bar.-at-law, Lincoln's Inn, 92.

Moscardi, Alexander Francis George, born at Bath 18 Oct., 1874; 3s. Lucio Donato, late teacher of languages, deceased. BALLIOL, matric. 18 Oct., 92, aged 18 (from Bath coll.), exhibitioner 91, scholar 92 ; HONOURS:—accessit Hertford scholarship 92.

Moseditchian, Haroutune Nisham, born at Cresarea in Asia Minor 1861 ; y.s. Nisham. BALLIOL, matric. 18 Oct., 81, aged 20 (from Robert's coll, Constantinople), B.A. 85 ; HONOURS:—4 law 85.

Moseley, Herbert Harvey, born at Holt, Wilts, 3 April, 1873 ; 1s. Herbert Henry, cler. WORCESTER, matric. 5 Dec., 90, aged 17, from Marlborough coll.

Moseley, James Fairclough, born at Manchester 1864; 2s. Joseph, gent. PEMBROKE, matric. 23 Oct., 82, aged 18, B.A. 86, M.A. 89.

Moseley, Oswald Grange, born at Levenshulme, co. Lanc., 1868; 3s. Joseph, gen. PEMBROKE, matric. 12 May, 87, aged 19.

Mosenthal, Joseph, born in London 24 Feb., 1863; 6s. Adolphus, gent. MERTON, matric. 18 Oct., 81, aged 18 (from King's coll. school, London), B.A. 84; bar.-at-law, Lincoln's Inn, 86.

Moses, Samuel, born in London 21 April, 1864; 2s. Sylvester, gent. TRINITY, matric. 14 Oct., 82, aged 18 (from city of London school), scholar 82-6, B.A. 86, M.A. 89 (HONOURS :—2 mathematical mods. 83, 1 classical mods. 84, 3 classics 86); bar.-at-law, Inner Temple, 88.

Mosley, Godfrey, born at Egginton, co. Derby, 15 Jan., 1863; 2s. Rowland, rector. CORPUS CHRISTI, matric. 19 Oct., 82, aged 19 (from Repton school), B.A. 86; HONOURS:—3 classical mods. 84, 3 history 86.

Mosley, Henry, born at Newcastle, co. Stafford, Dec., 1868; o.s. Henry, gen. KEBLE, matric. 17 Oct., 87, aged 18 (from Newcastle-under-Lyme high school), B.A. 90; HONOURS :—3 history 90.

Moss, Arthur Spence, born at Hull, 9 June, 1853; 5s. William Henry, gen. NON-COLLEGIATE, matric. 22 Oct., 87, aged 34 (from Rugby), civil engineer.

Moss, Cyril Raymond, born at Huyton, near Liverpool, Oct., 1870; 3s. Charles Bradbury, gen. KEBLE, matric. 11 Oct., 90, aged 19, from Tenbury school.

Moss, Reginald Heber, born at Huyton, co. Lanc., 24 Feb., 1868; 2s. Charles Bradbury, gen. KEBLE, matric. 17 Jan., 87, aged 18 (from Radley coll.), B.A. 90 (HONOURS :—3 history 90); in Oxford University eleven 89.

Mossman, Martin Dawson, born at Calverley, Yorks, Sept., 1872; 1s. William, gen. KEBLE, matric. 20 Oct., 91, aged 19, from Bradford gr. school.

Mossop, Leonard, born at Chelsea, Middx., 1 May, 1869; 1s. Charles, arm. TRINITY, matric. 15 Oct., 87, aged 18 (from Bath coll.), B.A. 91 (HONOURS :—2 law 91); bar.-at-law, Lincoln's Inn, 93.

Mostyn, Sydney Gwenfrwd, born at Bramton, Essex, 1866; 2s. John, minister. EXETER, matric. 16 Oct., 84, aged 18 (from Ipswich gr. school), scholar 84, B.A. 88, M.A. 92; HONOURS :—1 mathematical mods. 86, accessit junior mathematical exhibition 86, 1 mathematics 88, 1 physics 89.

Mothersill, Frank, born at Whalley Range, co. Lancaster, 1865; 2s. Christopher, gen. PEMBROKE, matric. 27 Oct., 85, aged 20, from Uppingham school.

Mott, Charles Egerton, born at Birkenhead, Cheshire, Feb., 1871; 2s. Charles Grey, arm. ORIEL, matric. 20 Oct., 88, aged 17 (from Uppingham school), B.A. 92; HONOURS :—2 history 92.

Mottram, Joshua, born in London 1851; 1s. Joshua, cler. EXETER, matric. 4 June, 81, aged 30 (from Merchant Taylors' school), B.A. 85, M.A. 88.

Moubray, John James, M.A., hon. fellow ST. JOHN'S 89, where see page 478.

Moulder, Edwyn Richard Denys, born at St. Paul, Demerara, 9 Oct., 1873; 2s. Thomas Jordan, cler. MERTON, matric. 22 Oct., 91, aged 18, from Queen's coll., Demerara.

Moulder, Thomas Henry Knight, born at Georgetown, Demerara, 25 May, 1872; 1s. Thomas Jordan, cler. NEW COLL., matric. 16 Oct., 91, aged 19, from Oxford high school and Queen's coll., British Guiana.

Moulder, rev. Thomas Jordan, born at St. Lawrence, Kent, 1848; 2s. Cornelius, gen. NEW INN HALL, matric. 12 June, 86, aged 38; father of the two preceding.

Moullin, Charles William Mansell, M.A., D.Med. fellow PEMBROKE 77-86, where see page 555.

Moulton, rev. Thomas William, born at Kidgrove, co. Stafford, 1861; 1s. Levi, gen. NON-COLLEGIATE, matric. 24 Jan., 82, aged 21 (from Cobridge coll. Stoke-upon-Trent, and Ardingly coll., Hayward's Heath), B.A. 87.

Moultrie, rev. Austin, born at Barrow Gurney, Somerset, Dec., 1867; 4s. Gerard, cler. KEBLE, matric. 22 Oct., 85, aged 17 (from Radley coll.), B.A. 89 (HONOURS :—3 classical mods. 87); curate of East Thorpe, Mirfield, Yorks, 91.

Moultrie, rev. John, born at Bright Waltham, Berks, 3 Feb., 1860; 2s. Gerard, vicar of South Leigh. NEW COLL., matric. 17 Jan., 80, aged 19, B.A. 83 (HONOURS:—3 classical mods. 81, 4 history 83); curate of Christ Church, Doncaster, 88.

Mount, Charles Bridges, M.A., fellow NEW COLL. 45-66, where see page 212.

Mount, Francis, born in London 8 July, 1872; 2s. William George, of Wasing, Berks, M.P. NEW COLL., matric. 16 Oct., 91, aged 19, from Eton; brother of the next named.

Mount, George Talbot, born at Reading 28 Nov., 1870; 3s. William George, M.P. NEW COLL., matric. 11 Oct., 89, aged 18 (from Eton); HONOURS : —2 classical mods. 91.

Mount, William Arthur, born at Hartley Court, Berks, 3 Aug., 1866; 1s. William George, of Wasing Place, Berks, M.P. NEW COLL., matric. 16 Oct., 85, aged 19 (from Eton), B.A. 89, M.A. 92; HONOURS :— 3 classical mods. 87, 2 history 89.

Mountford, John Arthur Mannering, born at Congleton, Cheshire, 1872; 1s. John Wollaston, arm. BALLIOL, matric. 14 Oct., 90, aged 18 (from Ludlow school), exhibitioner 90.

Mourant, Archibald Gervase, born in Jersey 20 Dec., 1871; 2s. Edward, Queen's receiver for Jersey. WADHAM, matric. 13 Oct., 90, aged 18, from Victoria coll., Jersey.

Mourilyan, Charles Thomas, born at Sheerness, Kent, 16 Aug., 1870; 1s. Thomas Longley, staff-commander, R.N. WADHAM, matric. 20 Oct., 91, aged 21, from isle of Wight coll., Ryde.

Mowat, John Lancaster Gough, M.A. fellow PEMBROKE 71, where see page 553.

Mowatt, Frank Herbert, born in London 1867; 1s. Frank, arm. CORPUS CHRISTI, matric. 20 Oct., 86; aged 19 (from Harrow), B.A. 89; HONOURS :— 3 history 89.

Mowbray, Archibald John Holme, born at Surbiton, Surrey, 13 Sept., 1869; 1s. Charles Cochrane, of Glasgow, ironmaster. MAGDALEN, matric. 16 Oct., 88, aged 19 (from Radley coll.), demy 87, B.A. 92; HONOURS:—2 chemistry 91.

Mowbray, sir John Robert, bart., hon. student CHRIST CHURCH 76, where see page 412.

Mowbray, Robert Gray Cornish, M.A., fellow ALL SOULS' 73, where see page 272.

Moxon, Archibald James, born at Grandborough, co. Warwick, 3 March, 1872; 1s. William, arm. KEBLE, matric. 11 Oct., 90, aged 18, from Rugby.

Moxon, Ernest Henry, born at Sherborne, Yorks, 1867; 4s. Francis Henry, gen. ST. EDMUND HALL, matric. 29 Jan., 86, aged 19.

Moyle, John Baron, M.A., D.C.L., fellow NEW COLL. 76, where see page 206.

Moyle, Robert Edward, born at Chudleigh, Devon, 30 May, 1872; 5s. George, cler. CHRIST CHURCH, matric. 14 Oct., 1872; 1s. William, arm. B.A. 85, M.A. 88; HONOURS :— 1 natural science 85.

Moyle, Vyvyan Henry Copley, born at Eston, Yorks, 29 April, 1872; o. s. Vyvyan Henry, vicar of Ashampstead, Berks. LINCOLN, matric. 23 Oct., 91, aged 19.

Moyles, Thomas Henry Cave, born at Birmingham 29 Dec., 1870; 1 s. Thomas, D.Med. LINCOLN, matric. 20 Oct., 90, aged 19, from Birmingham school.

Mozley, Thomas, M.A., fellow ORIEL 29-37, where see page 152.

Muckleston, Rowland, M.A., fellow WORCESTER 37-56, where see.

Muddiman, Joseph George, born at Leighton Buzzard, Beds, 1862; 1s. Alexander Phillips, gent. EXETER, matric. 28 Jan., 81, aged 19 (from University coll. school), B.A. 85, M.A. 89.

Mugliston, Francis Udall, born at Cheltenham 23 Aug., 1870; 2s. John, cler., and a master at Cheltenham. TRINITY, matric. 11 Oct., 90, aged 20 (from Cheltenham coll.); HONOURS :—3 classical mods. 92.

Muir, Kenneth, born at St. Petersburgh 28 May, 1867; 2s. Andrew, arm. TRINITY, matric. 17 Oct., 85, aged 18, from Uppingham school.

Muir, sir William, K.C.S.I., created D.C.L., 14 June, 1882. See *Al. Ox.* and series, 996.

Muir, William Edward, born at Effingham 21 Jan., 1872; 1s. Francis. TRINITY, matric. 11 Oct., 90, aged 18, from Merchiston Castle school.

Muir-Mackenzie, Montague Johnstone, B.A., fellow HERTFORD 74-89, where see page 601.

Mullens, Richard Carey, born at East Pennard, Somst., 5 March, 1862; o. s. Richard, gen. NEW INN HALL, matric. 29 Oct., 81, aged 19 (from Pennard school); migrated to JESUS COLL. 23 April, 83.

Mullings, Frank Tudway, born at Cirencester 28 July, 1871; 1s. John, gen. EXETER, matric. 13 Oct., 90, aged 19, from Malvern coll.; died 16 Feb., 93.

Mullins, Charles Herbert, born at Grahamstown, Cape of Good Hope, June, 1869; 2s. Robert John, canon of Grahamstown. KEBLE, matric. 13 Oct., 88, aged 19 (from St. Andrew's coll. Grahamstown), B.A. 92; HONOURS :—3 law 91.

Mullins, George James Herbert, born at Uppingham, Rutland, 1868; 1s. George Henry, cler. KEBLE, matric. 17 Oct., 87, aged 19 (from Canterbury school); lieut. royal marines L.I. 90.

Mullins, Hugh Willoughby, born at Brixton, Surrey, 26 July, 1867; 4s. John, major-gen. R.E. MAGDALEN, matric. 23 Oct., 85, aged 18 (from the Charterhouse), B.A. 89.

Mullins, Reginald Cuthbert, born at Grahamstown, Cape of Good Hope, 6 June, 1873; 3s. Robert John, canon of Grahamstown. KEBLE, matric. 20 Oct., 91, aged 18, from St. Andrew's coll., Grahamstown.

Mullins, rev. Robert George, born at Grahamstown, Cape of Good Hope, April, 1867; 1s. Robert John, canon of Grahamstown. KEBLE, matric. 19 Oct., 86, aged 19 (from St. Andrew's coll. Grahamstown), B.A. 89; HONOURS :—3 history 89, 3 theology 90.

Mulvany, Charles Mathew, born at Dunville, Ontario, Canada, 28 Aug., 1867; s. John, of London, D.Med. MAGDALEN, matric. 21 Oct., 86, aged 19 (from St. Paul's school), demy 86, B.A. 90, fellow 92; HONOURS :—accessit Hertford scholarship 87, 1 classical mods. 88, Craven scholarship 88, accessit Ireland scholarship 89, 1 classics 90.

Mumford, rev. John Thwaites, born at Lee, Kent, 14 Feb., 1868; 1s. Peter, gen. WADHAM, matric. 13 Oct., 88, aged 20 (from King's coll. school, Lond.), B.A. 91.

Mumford, Robert Philip Arthur, born at Tattenhill, co. Stafford, 1869; 1s. Robert Francis, cler. PEMBROKE, matric. 26 Oct., 89, aged 20, B.A. 92.

Münch, Oscar Charles de, Free Baron, born at Wurtemberg 1865; 1s. Charles. BALLIOL, matric. 11 March, 85, aged 20, from Stüttgart gymnasium.

Munday, John Augustus, born at Southsea, Hants, 1864; o.s. John, gen. QUEEN'S, matric. 15 Jan., 91, aged 27.

Mundy, Benjamin Henry Hutton, born at Oxford 7 May, 1872; y.s. James, gen., deceased. NON-COLLEGIATE, matric. 8 June, 89, aged 17 (from New coll. school, Oxon), B.A. 92.

Mundy, Charles Drayner Massingberd, born at South Ormsby, co. Lincoln, July, 1867; 2s. Charles Francis, arm. CHRIST CHURCH, matric. 18 Oct., 86, aged 19, from St. Mark's school, Windsor.

Mundy, Ernest William Mundy, born at Weston-super-Mare 26 June, 1869; 2s. James Terry, cler. (formerly J. T. Patch, see *Al. Ox.* and series, page 1077). EXETER, matric. 17 Oct., 88, aged 19, from Exeter gr. school.

Mundy, Godfrey Bertram Massingberd, born at Bolinbroke, co. Lincoln, 1872; 2s. Charles Francis, arm. UNIVERSITY COLL., matric. 17 Oct., 91 aged 19.

Mundy, Walter, born at Upper Tooting, Surrey, 1864; 4s. Thomas Clement, gent. EXETER, matric. 18 Oct., 82, aged 18, from Christ's coll., Finchley.

Munk, William Geoffrey, born at Exeter 12 Oct., 1865; 1s. Edwin Isaac, gen. WORCESTER, matric. 17 Oct., 84, aged 19 (from St. Edward's school, Summertown), B.A. 87, M.A. 91; HONOURS :—3 theology 87.

Munn, rev. John Turner, born at Newchurch, co. Lanc., 1863; 2s. Robert, gent. UNIVERSITY COLL., matric. 14 Oct., 82, aged 19, B.A. 86, M.A. 89 (HONOURS :—1 theology 86); curate of Aylesbury, Bucks, 87.

Munns, Hugh Lumpners, born at Snaresbrook, Essex, 1860; 3s. Arnold Lumpners, arm. UNIVERSITY COLL., matric. 13 Oct., 88, aged 18, B.A. 91; HONOURS :—3 law 91.

Munns, Thomas Deason, born at Sydenham, Kent, 1863; 2s. Arnold Sumners, gen. NON-COLLEGIATE, matric. 22 Jan., 81, aged 18; migrated to EMANUEL COLL., CAMBRIDGE, 24 May, 81; bar.-at-law, Middle Temple, 87.

Munro, Alexander Richard Bowman, born at Melrose 18 Feb., 1871; o.s. Alexander Begg, gen. QUEEN'S, matric. 24 Oct., 90, aged 19 (from Bradford gr. school), exhibitioner 90; HONOURS :—1 classical mods. 92.

Munro, Henry Acland, born in London 18 Nov., 1865; 2s. Alexander, sculptor. NEW COLL., matric. 10 Oct., 84, aged 18 (from the Charterhouse), B.A. 88 ; HONOURS :—2 physiology 88.

Munro, Hugh, born at Totteridge, Herts, 7 March, 1863; 1s. David, gent. CHRIST CHURCH, matric. 14 Oct., 81, aged 18 (from Westminster school), scholar 81, B.A. 85, M.A. 88; HONOURS :—2 classical mods. 83, 3 classics 85.

Munro, Hugh St. John Stewart, born at Monte Video 22 Oct., 1865; 1s. James St. John, arm. TRINITY, matric. 11 Oct., 84, aged 18 (from Clifton coll.), B.A. 87; HONOURS :—3 classical mods. 86.

Munro, John Arthur Ruskin, born in London 1864; 1s. Alexander, sculptor, deceased. EXETER, matric. 18 Oct., 82, aged 16 (from the Charterhouse), scholar 82-6, B.A. 86; fellow of LINCOLN 88, M.A. 89; HONOURS :—1 classical mods. 83, 1 classics 86.

Munro, Kenneth, born at Totteridge, Herts, 1869; 3s. David, gen. HERTFORD, matric. 12 May, 88, aged 21.

Munro, rev. MacDonald, born at Lynn, Norfolk, 1850; 2s. Alexander, gen. NON-COLLEGIATE, matric. 17 Oct., 81, aged 31 (from Headingley coll., Leeds); migrated to EXETER 7 Nov., 83, B.A. 84, M.A. 88; HONOURS :—3 theology 84.

Munro, Malcolm, born at Hendon, Middx., 1868; 4s. David, gen. NON-COLLEGIATE, matric. 30 March, 89, aged 20, B.A. 92.

Munroe, George Peabody, born in Paris 1864; 4s. John, arm. BALLIOL, matric. 16 Oct., 83, aged 19.

Muntz, Duncan Albert, born at Kersley, co. Warwick, 1867; 2s. Philip Albert, M.P. CORPUS CHRISTI, matric. 20 Oct., 86, aged 19 (from Eton); HONOURS :—3 law 90.

Muntz, Ronald Aylett, born at Hockley Heath, co. Warwick, 3 June, 1872; 4s. George Frederick, of Umberslade, gen. PEMBROKE, matric. 25 Oct., 90, aged 18, (from Westward Ho ! coll.

Murdoch, Charles Edward Gambier, born in London 12 May, 1865; 1s. Charles Townsend, of Buckhurst, Wokingham, Berks, late lieut. rifle brigade. MAGDALEN, matric. 29 Jan., 85, aged 19 (from Eton), B.A. 87.

Murdoch, George Cuthbert, born in Edinburgh March, 1872; o.s. Alexander D., cler. KEBLE, matric. 20 Oct., 91, aged 19, from Glenalmond coll.

Murdock, William, born at Barrow-in-Furness, co. Lanc., 12 Nov., 1871; 2s. William Mallabey, of Gilwern, near Abergavenny, C.E. NON-COLLEGIATE, matric. 17 Oct., 91, aged 19, from Cowbridge gr. school.

Mure, James Edward Lockhart-, born at Balmaghie, Scotland, 25 July, 1864; 1s. James Oehterlony, arm. BALLIOL, matric. 16 Oct., 83, aged 19 (from Ayr academy), B.A. 88 (HONOURS :—2 classical mods. 85, 2 law 87); of Livingstone, co. Kirkcudbright ; died at Sandiago, California, 22 Oct., 90.

Murphy, Herbert, born at Preston, co. Lanc., 4 Dec., 1860; 1s. Joseph Patrick, cler. BALLIOL, matric. 21 Oct., 80, aged 19 (from Uppingham school), B.A. 84; HONOURS :—2 history 84.

Murphy, James Kotupna, born at St. Kilda, Melbourne, 15 Nov., 1869; 1s. James, gent. MAGDALEN, matric. 21 Oct., 92, aged 23, from Melbourne university.

Murray, rev. Barrington Boyle, born at Shrivenham, Berks, Feb., 1868 ; 1s. George William, cler. KEBLE, matric. 19 Oct., 86, aged 18 (from Haileybury), B.A. 89.

Murray, right hon. sir Charles Augustus, K.C.B., M.A., fellow ALL SOULS' 27-51, where see page 277.

Murray, Edward, born in London, Oct., 1869; 2s. Charles Frederick, arm. ORIEL, matric. 20 Oct., 88, aged 18, from Eton.

Murray, Edward Mackenzie, born at Cargill, Perthshire, 3 June, 1874; o.s. Mackenzie, B.LL.S. ORIEL, matric. 27 Oct., 92, aged 18, from Rugby.

Murray, rev. Frederick Auriol, born at Stone, Kent, 22 Nov., 1865; 1s. Frederick William, rector. KEBLE, matric. 14 Oct., 84, aged 18 (from Lancing coll.), B.A. 87 (HONOURS :—4 history 87); curate of St. Mark, Surbiton, 91.

Murray, George Gilbert Aimé, born at Sydney, Australia, 2 Jan., 1866 ; 3s. sir Terence Aubrey, knt. ST. JOHN'S, matric. 11 Oct., 84, aged 18 (from Merchant Taylors' school), scholar 84, B.A. 88, fellow NEW COLL. 88, M.A. 91 (HONOURS : —1 classical mods. 85, Hertford and Ireland scholarship 85, Latin verse 86, Greek verse 86, Craven scholarship 86, Greek prose 87, 1 classics 88, Derby scholarship 89); professor of Greek at Glasgow university 89.

Murray, George Henry Lygon, born in London May, 1871; 2s. George Joseph, gen. KEBLE, matric. 12 Oct., 89, aged 18 (from Radley coll.), B.A. 92 ; HONOURS :—4 law 92.

Murray, George Keith, born at Aberturret, Crieff, Perthshire, July 1873 ; 2s. sir Patrick Keith, bart. ORIEL, matric. 27 Oct., 92, aged 19, from Harrow.

Murray, George Sholto Douglas, M.A., senior student CHRIST CHURCH 68-73, where see page 424.

Murray, Harold James Ruthven, born at Peckham, Surrey, 1869 ; 1s. James Augustus Henry, hon. M.A. BALLIOL, matric. 20 Jan., 87, aged 18 (from Mill Hill school), exhibitioner 86, B.A. 90 (HONOURS :— 2 mathematical mods. 88, 1 mathematics 90.

Murray, Herbert Harley, C.B., M.A., student CHRIST CHURCH 48-59, where see page 419.

Murray, James Augustus Henry, LL.D., created M.A. 10 Nov., 85. See All. Ox. 2nd series 1000.

Murray, John Hubert Plunkett, born at Sydney, Australia, 29 Dec., 1861 ; 2s. sir Terence Aubrey, knt., deceased. MAGDALEN, matric. 15 Oct., 81, aged 19 (from Brighton coll., and University coll., London), demy 81-5, B.A. 86 (HONOURS :— 1 classical mods. 82, 1 classics 85); bar.-at-law, Inner Temple, 86.

Murray, John Rigby, born at Ardwick, co. Lanc, 13 March, 1857 ; 2s. Benjamin Rigby, arm. NON-COLLEGIATE, matric. 17 Jan., 80, aged 22 (from Eton); migrated to TRINITY 80, B.A. 83, M.A. 86 ; bar.-at-law, Inner Temple, 84.

Murray, Maurice William, born at Stone, Kent, 14 July, 1870 ; 3s. Frederick William, rector. QUEEN'S, matric. 22 Oct., 89, aged 19, from Lancing coll.

Murray, Oswyn Alexander Ruthven, born at Mill Hill, Middx., 17 Aug., 1873 ; 4s. James Augustus Henry, hon. M.A., etc. EXETER, matric. 22 Oct., 91, aged 18 (from Oxford high school), scholar 91.

Murray, Wilfred George Ruthven, born at Hendon, Middx., 20 Oct., 1871 ; 3s. James Augustus Henry, of Oxford, hon. M.A. BALLIOL, matric. 14 Oct., 90, aged 18 (from Oxford high school), exhibitioner 89.

Murray, William, born at Edinburgh 31 Oct., 1865 ; 1s. John, commander R.N., deceased. MAGDALEN, matric. 23 Oct., 85, aged 19 (from Edinburgh university), B.A. 90 ; HONOURS :—2 history 89.

Murray, William Charles, born in London Dec., 1865 ; 1s. Charles Frederick, arm. ORIEL, matric. 23 Oct., 84, aged 18 (from Eton), B.A. 87.

Murton, Charles Duncan, born in London 1866 ; 2s. Walter, arm. UNIVERSITY COLL., matric. 11 Oct., 84, aged 18, B.A. 88 ; HONOURS :—2 law 88.

Muschamp, Evelyn George, born at Westbury-on-Trym, co. Gloucester, 18 Feb., 1872 ; 2s. John George Sowerby, M.A. Camb. NON-COLLEGIATE, matric. 15 Oct., 92, aged 19, from Bristol gr. school.

Musgrave, Arthur George, born at Mold, Flints, 1869 ; 3s. Francis, arm. UNIVERSITY COLL., matric. 13 Oct., 88, aged 19, B.A. 92 ; HONOURS :— 3 classical mods. 90, 2 history 92.

28

Musgrave, Harold Sanderson, born at Hascombe, Godalming, Surrey, Dec., 1870; 4s. rev. Vernon Musgrave, M.A. CHRIST CHURCH, matric. 15 Oct., 92, aged 21, from Lancing coll.

Musgrave, Herbert Wenman Wykeham-, born in London 26 March, 1871; 1s. William Aubrey, arm. NEW COLL., matric. 10 Oct., 90, aged 19, from Eton.

Myburgh, Alexander Macdonald, born in London 4 Nov., 1869; 1s. Philip Albert, arm. CHRIST CHURCH, matric. 13 Jan., 88, aged 18, from Eton.

Myer, Walden, born at Lake View, Erie co., New York, 17 March, 1866; 2s. Albert James, general officer U.S. army. NON-COLLEGIATE, matric. 17 Oct., 91, aged 25 (from Harvard university, U.S.A., B.A.); migrated to EXETER 18 Oct., 92.

Myers, Ernest James, M.A., fellow WADHAM 68-83, where see page 532.

Mylne, Thomas Herbert, born at Brisbane, Australia, 1869; 2s. Graham, arm. BALLIOL, matric. 19 Oct., 87, aged 18, from Sydney university.

Mynors, rev. Aubrey Baskerville, born at Llanware, co. Hereford, 1866; 2s. Walter Baskerville, cler. ORIEL, matric. 26 Jan., 84, aged 18 (from Malvern coll.); B.A. 87, M.A. 90; curate of Portsea, Hants, 89.

Myres, John Linton, born at Preston, co. Lanc., 3 July, 1869; 1s. William Miles, vicar of Swanbourne, Bucks, 79. NEW COLL., matric. 12 Oct., 88, aged 19 (from Winchester); scholar 87; fellow MAGDALEN 92, B.A. 92; HONOURS :—1 classical mods. 90, 1 classics 92, Burdett-Coutts scholarship 92, Craven travelling fellowship 92.

Myrtle, Frederick Septimus, born at West Derby, co. Lanc., 7 Oct., 1862; 7s. William, gent. CORPUS CHRISTI, matric. 27 Oct., 81, aged 19, from Rugby.

STONE ANIMAL, ROUEN CATHEDRAL. - *Pugin*.

WOODEN ORNAMENT, NORTH TRANSEPT (DOOR), ROUEN CATHEDRAL.—*Pugin.*

N

Naef, Conrad James, born in London 28 July, 1871; 1s. Conrad, gen. MERTON, matric. 15 Oct., 90, aged 19 (from city of London school), postmaster 90; HONOURS :—1 classical mods. 92.

Nagel, David Henry, born at Dundee 10 Nov., 1862; 1s. Henry, gen. TRINITY, matric. 17 Oct., 82, aged 19 (from Dundee institute and St. Andrews university), scholar 82, B.A. 86, M.A. 89, fellow 90 (HONOURS :—Taylorian (German) exhibition 83, 1 chemistry 86); Millard demonstrator Trinity and Balliol, and natural science lecturer Jesus coll.

Nall, rev. George Herbert, born at Yarmouth 1861; 2s. George, gen. QUEEN'S, matric. 15 May, 80, aged 19 (from Shrewsbury school), scholar 80-5, B.A. 84, M.A. 87 (HONOURS :—2 classical mods. 81, 2 classics 84); a master Westminster school 86.

Nance, Ernest Morton, born at Cardiff, co. Glamorgan, 15 Aug., 1868; 1s. William Edwin, gen. JESUS COLL., matric. 20 Oct., 91, aged 23 (from University coll., Cardiff), scholar 91.

Nance, James Trengrove, B.D., fellow ST. JOHN'S 76-87, where see page 488.

Nankivell, Robert William Day, born at Bournemouth, Hants, 10 Dec., 1872; 2s. Herbert, D.Med., Edinburgh. HERTFORD, matric. 20 Oct., 91, aged 18 (from the Charterhouse), scholar 90.

Nanson, rev. Arthur Cecil, born at Carlisle 11 Sept., 1861; 3s. John, arm. NON-COLLEGIATE, matric. 18 Oct., 80, aged 19 (from Sedbergh school); migrated to TRINITY 82, B.A. 84, M.A. 91 (HONOURS :—4 history 84); curate of St. Mary de Crypt, Gloucester, 91.

Napier, Arthur Sampson, M.A., fellow MERTON 85, where see page 94.

Napier, Arthur Wilson, born at Stoke Damarel, Devon, Jan., 1871; 5s. Gerald John, arm. KEBLE, matric. 17 Oct., 89, aged 18, from Westward Ho! coll.

Napier, Bertram Harold, born in London Feb., 1861; 1s. William Donald, F.R.S. CHRIST CHURCH, matric. 15 Oct., 80, aged 19.

Napier, Charles Frederick, born in London 24 Feb., 1862; 2s. hon. William. KEBLE, matric. 19 Oct., 80, aged 18 (from Tonbridge school), B.A. 83 (HONOURS :—3 law 83); bar.-at-law, Middle Temple, 85.

Napier, Edward Berkeley, born at Shepton Mallet, Somerset, 1862; 3s. Edward Berkeley, arm. MERTON, matric. 18 Oct., 80, aged 18, from Bradfield coll.

Nash, Arthur George, born at Tulse Hill, London, 29 May, 1862; 2s. Frederick John, gent. ST. EDMUND HALL, matric. 19 Oct., 82, aged 20 (from Oundle school); re-entered at EXETER 18 Oct., 92.

Nash, rev. Edward Henry, born at Banbury 7 May, 1868; o.s. Henry Allden, cler. NON-COLLEGIATE, matric. 16 Oct., 86, aged 18 (from Birmingham school); migrated to EXETER 17 Oct., 88, B.A. 90, M.A. 93 (HONOURS :—3 classical mods. 88); curate of Brighton 91.

Nash, Edward Jackson, born at Weston, Notts, 12 Jan., 1863; 3s. George, cler. LINCOLN, matric. 23 Oct., 80, aged 17 (from Louth gr. school), scholar 80-4, B.A. 85, M.A. 87; HONOURS :—3 classical mods. 82, 4 classics 84.

Nash, rev. Francis Peel, born at Old Sodbury, co. Glouc., 27 June, 1861; 7s. Robert Seymour, cler. EXETER, matric. 22 Oct., 80, aged 19 (from Marlborough), B.A. 84, M.A. 87; curate of Swinton, co. Lanc., 85.

Nash, George Lloyd, M.A., student CHRIST CHURCH 48-53, where see page 419.

Nash, rev. Henry Allden, born in London 1838; o.s Charles, gent. NON-COLLEGIATE, matric. 29 April, 81, aged 43 (from London coll. of divinity); vicar of St. Margaret, Birmingham, 75-90, and of Ogley-Hay 90; father of Edward Henry.

Nash, Henry Egerton, born at Hardwicke, co. Glouc., Aug., 1873; 1s. Alexander, cler. KEBLE, matric. 15 Oct., 92, aged 19, from Marlborough coll.

Nash, rev. James Okey, born at Pernambuco 1863; 2s. Thomas, arm. HERTFORD, matric. 19 Oct., 81, aged 18 (from King William coll., I.M.), scholar 80-5, B.A. 86, M.A. 89 (HONOURS :— 1 classical mods. 83, 2 classics 85); curate of St. Andrew's, Bethnal Green, 86-9.

Nash, Spencer Hampden, born at Clifton, co. Glouc., 1863; 6s. Charles, gent. BALLIOL, matric. 18 Oct., 81, aged 18 (from Clifton coll.), exhibitioner 80, until his death 85; HONOURS :— 1 classical mods. 82.

Nash, rev. Thomas Clifford, born at Great Chesterford, Essex, 1851; o.s. Thomas Frederick, gen. CHRIST CHURCH, matric. 12 Jan., 83, aged 32 B.A. 85, M.A. 89; chaplain at Teneriffe 87.

Nash, William Devereux Gregory, born at Bellean, co. Lincoln, 23 July, 1869; 1s. William, cler. NEW COLL., matric. 12 Oct., 88, aged 19 (from Winchester), scholar 87; HONOURS:—1 classical mods. 90, 3 classics 92.

Naters, rev. Edward Herbert, born at Horsforth, Oxon, 1864; 2s. Charles John, cler. NON-COLLEGIATE, matric. 13 Oct. 81, aged 20, B.A. 89; curate of Epworth, co. Lincoln, 80.

Nathan, Geoffrey, born at Rome 27 Feb., 1874; 1s. Ernest, gent. WORCESTER, matric. 18 Oct., 92, aged 18, from Dover coll.

Naylor, Henry Paul Todd- (C.I.E. 90); born at Hartford Grange, Cheshire, 1861; 3s. William Todd, gen. UNIVERSITY COLL., matric. 16 Oct., 80, aged 19 (from Shrewsbury school), deputy commissioner Burma, C.I.E., 90.

Naylor, rev. William Smethurst, born at Longton, co. Lanc., 1863; 1s. William, gen. WORCESTER, matric. 19 Oct., 82, aged 19, B.A. 85, M.A. 89; curate of St. Andrew's, Burnley, 91.

Neal, John Richmond, born at Moseley, co. Warwick, 1870; 2s. James, D.Med. ST. JOHN'S, matric. 12 Oct., 89, aged 19 (from Epsom coll.), exhibitioner 91, B.A. 92; HONOURS:—3 theology 92.

Neale, Charles Montague, born at Cirencester, co. Glouc., 1856; 0.s. Charles, gen. NON-COLLEGIATE, matric. 23 April, 91, aged 35 (from King's coll., London); bar.-at-law, Middle Temple, 85.

Neale, Edgar, born at Bromsgrove, co. Worcester, 6 Dec., 1872; 4s. Jonathan William, gen. WORCESTER, matric. 22 Oct., 91, aged 18 (from Bromsgrove gr. school), scholar 91.

Neale, Thomas, born at Bromsgrove, co. Warwick, 1 Feb., 1867; 1s. Jonathan William, gen. WORCESTER, matric. 19 Oct., 86, aged 19 (from Bromsgrove gr. school), scholar 85, B.A. 90; HONOURS:—1 mathematical mods. 87, 2 mathematics 90.

Neave, John Alexander, born in London 1854; 0.s. John, gen. NON-COLLEGIATE, matric. 10 April, 80, aged 26, from a Greenock school.

Neck, Arthur Percy Van, born at Paddington 1870; o.s. John Grant, gen. BALLIOL, matric. 18 Oct., 88, aged 18 (from University coll. school, London); HONOURS:—3 classical mods. 90, 1 law 92.

Negus, Albert Edward, born at Cambridge 27 Nov., 1868; 2s. Saunders Road, gen. LINCOLN, matric. 18 Oct., 88, aged 19 (from Perse school, Cambridge), B.A. 92; HONOURS:—4 history 92.

Neighbour, Thomas Frank, born at Brixton, Surrey, 18 Nov., 1869; o.s. Blandford, arm. EXETER, matric. 17 Oct., 88, aged 18 (from Marlborough coll.

Neil, Archibald Alexander, born at Glasgow 15 July, 1872; 3s. Alexander, gen. MERTON, matric. 22 Oct., 91, aged 19 (from Manchester gr. school), postmaster 91.

Neish, Edward William, born in London 1865; 6s. William, arm. UNIVERSITY COLL., matric. 13 Oct., 83, aged 18 (from Glenalmond coll.), B.A. 89; HONOURS:—2 classical mods. 85, 3 classics 87.

Nelson, Alfred Leonard, born at Kenilworth, co. Warwick, 13 Nov., 1872; 5s. Charles, gent. MERTON, matric. 15 Oct., 90, aged 18, from Radley coll.

Nelson, Charles Meikle, born at Waddington 1865; o.s. Charles, D.Med. HERTFORD, matric. 14 Oct., 84, aged 19, B.A. 88, M.A. 91; bar.-at-law, Inner Temple, 91.

Nelson, rev. Edward John, born at Sandford, Wilts, 4 Oct., 1867; 2s. Maurice Horace, arm. HERTFORD, matric. 22 Oct., 86, aged 19 (from Sherborne school), exhibitioner 86, B.A. 90 (HONOURS:—2 history 90); curate of Portsea 92.

Nelson, John Percival, born at Hill Kenilworth, co. Warwick, 5 March, 1874; 6s. Charles, gent. MERTON, matric. 18 Oct., 92, aged 18, from Radley coll.

Nelson, Oswald Thomas Pemberton, born at Feckenham, co. Worc., March, 1873; 2s. William, cler. KEBLE, matric. 15 Oct., 92, aged 19, from Clifton coll.

Nepean, Evan Alcock, born at Mitcham, Surrey, 13 Sept., 1865; 1s. Evan Colville, gent. UNIVERSITY COLL., matric. 11 Oct., 84, aged 19 (from Sherborne school), scholar 84-6, B.A. 88 (HONOURS:—3 classical mods. 86, 1 law 88), in University eleven 87-88; bar.-at-law, Inner Temple, 91.

Nesbitt, Alan Chancellor, born at Liverpool 1874; 2s. Robert Henry, gent. CHRIST CHURCH, matric. 14 Oct., 92, aged 18 (from Westminster school), scholar 92.

Nesbitt, Walter John, born at Clapham, Surrey, 16 Oct., 1867; 2s. Robert Henry, gen. MERTON, matric. 22 Oct. 91, aged 24, from Newton Abbot coll.

Nettlefold, Frederick John, born at Hastings, Sussex, 1865; 1s. Frederick. CORPUS CHRISTI, matric. 22 Oct., 87, aged 20, from Eastbourne coll.

Nettleship, Henry, M.A., fellow CORPUS CHRISTI 73. where see page 370.

Nettleton, George Alfred Travers, born at Weymouth 30 March, 1871; 2s. Harry Thomas, M.R.C.S.E. (R.N.) EXETER, matric. 16 Oct., 89, aged 18 (from Merchant Taylors' school), exhibitioner 89; HONOURS:—2 classical mods. 91.

Neubauer, Adolph, M.A. hon. fellow EXETER 90, where see page 125.

Neve, Edward John, born at Onken, co. Stafford, 26 April, 1870; 1s. John, solicitor. NEW COLL., matric. 11 Oct., 89, aged 19 (from Winchester); and lieut. Princess Charlotte of Wales (Royal Berkshire) regiment 92.

Nevile, Charles Swainston, born at Fledborough, Notts, 5 July, 1864; 2s. Charles, cler. KEBLE, matric. 16 Oct., 83, aged 19 (from Budleigh Salterton), B.A. 86, M.A. 92.

Nevill, Charles Thomas Harvey, born at Yarmouth, Norfolk, 17 March, 1869; 3s. Henry Ralph, canon of Norwich and archdeacon of Norfolk. WADHAM, matric. 15 Oct., 87, aged 18, from Haileybury.

Nevill, Dudley Frederic, born at Bolehull, co. Warwick, 2 Nov., 1872; 2s. Robert Whately, solicitor. NEW COLL., matric. 16 Oct., 91, aged 18 (from Rugby), exhibitioner 91.

Nevill, rev. Edmund Robert, born 6 June, 1862; 1s. Samuel Tarratt, bishop of Nottingham and Dunedin, N.Z. LINCOLN, matric. 17 Jan., 83, aged 19 (from Lancing coll.), B.A. 86 (HONOURS:—3 theology 86); curate of St. Pancras 87-90, chaplain to bishop of St. Albans 90.

Nevill, rev. Ralph Williams, born at Yarmouth 10 June, 1863; 1s. Henry Ralph, archdeacon of Norfolk, KEBLE, matric. 17 Oct., 82, aged 19 (from Haileybury), B.A. 86, M.A. 89; domestic chaplain to bishop of Winchester 88-90, vicar of Hook, Hants, 90.

Newbald, Clement Arthur, born at Pontefract, Yorks, 15 July, 1867; o.s. Samuel Wilherforce, cler. WADHAM, matric. 16 Oct., 86, aged 19 (from Bromsgrove gr. school), B.A. 89.

Newbery, Stobart Bryce, born at Ottery St. Mary, Devon, 24 Feb., 1870; 1s. Joseph Vickers, arm. NEW COLL., matric. 19 Jan., 89, aged 19 (from Rugby), B.A. 92; HONOURS:—3 law 92.

Newbold, Arthur Henry Drakeford Stonehewer, born at Preston, Cheshire, 2 Sept., 1870; o.s. Edward, D.Med. CHRIST CHURCH, matric. 16 Jan., 91, aged 20, from Eastbrook school, Wokingham.

Newbolt, Francis George, born at Bilston, co. Stafford, 1863; 2s. Henry Francis, cler. BALLIOL, matric. 16 Oct., 83, aged 20 (from Clifton coll.), B.A. 87, M.A. 90 (HONOURS :—3 chemistry 87); bar.-at-law, Inner Temple, 90.

Newbolt, Henry John, born at Bilston, co. Stafford, 1862; 1s. Henry Francis, cler. CORPUS CHRISTI, matric. 27 Oct., 81, aged 19 (from Clifton coll.), scholar 81-5, B.A. 85, M.A. 88 (HONOURS : —1 classical mods. 82, 2 classics 85); bar.-at-law, Lincoln's Inn, 87.

Newby, Thomas Hardy, born at Mears Ashby, Northants, 1873; 4s. Henry, vicar, deceased. KEBLE, matric. 15 Oct., 92, aged 19, from Hurstpierpoint coll.

Newcomb, rev. Clement Ernest, born at Kidderminster 16 June, 1857; 6s. William, gen. QUEEN'S, matric. 22 Oct., 84, aged 27 (from Bedford gr. school), B.A. 87, M.A. 91 (HONOURS :—4 theology 87); curate of St. George's, Kidderminster, 87.

Newcomb, Frederick Baker, born at Kidderminster 13 March, 1856; 5s. William, gen. QUEEN'S, matric. 28 Oct., 81, aged 25 (from Bedford gr. school), B.A. 84, M.A. 91.

Newcomb, rev. John Edward Waldron, born in London 1866; o.s. John, gen. ST. JOHN'S, matric. 17 Oct., 85, aged 19 (from Merchant Taylors' school), exhibitioner 85, B.A. 89 (HONOURS :—3 classical mods. 87, 4 theology 89); curate of Billingshurst, Sussex, 90.

Newcome, Henry Neville, born at Leavesden, Herts, April, 1865; 1s. Edward William, cler. CHARSLEY'S HALL, matric. 1 Nov., 83, aged 18 (from Haileybury); migrated to KEBLE, B.A. 86.

Newenham, rev. Arthur O'Brien, born at York 15 Feb., 1862; 3s. Bagenal Burdett, vicar of Bilton, Yorks. QUEEN'S, matric. 4 June, 81, aged 19 (from Rossall school), B.A. 84, M.A. 93; curate of Beverley minster, Yorks, 91.

Newman, Arthur Philip Stillingfleet, born in London 1869; 1s. Philip, gen. BALLIOL, matric. 18 Oct., 88, aged 19 (from Leamington coll.), B.A. 92; HONOURS :—2 classical mods. 90, 3 classics 92.

Newman, Denis, born at Barnsley, Yorks, 4 June, 1874; 4s. J. J., of Oundle, Northants, solicitor. UNIVERSITY COLL., matric. 15 Oct., 92, aged 18, from Wellington coll.

Newman, Francis William, B.A., hon. fellow WORCESTER 83, where see page 574.

Newman, James Steer, born at Emsworth, Hants, 1861; 3s. William, cler. NON-COLLEGIATE, matric. 10 April, 80, aged 19, from Harlow coll., Essex.

Newman, Richard, born at New Mills, co. Derby, 7 April, 1871; 1s. Frederick William, cler. BRASENOSE, matric. 14 Oct., 89, aged 18 (from Hereford cathedral school), scholar 89; HONOURS :—2 classical mods. 91.

Newman, William Arthur, born at Canterbury 21 Oct., 1865; 1s. William Alexander, cler. TRINITY, matric. 11 Oct., 84, aged 18 (from Sherborne school), B.A. 88; HONOURS :—3 classical mods. 86.

Newman, William Frederick Wyndham, born at Bradninch, Devon, 19 Dec., 1872; 1s. William Frederick, M.A., vicar of Hockworthy, Somerset. ST. JOHN'S, matric. 6 April, 92, aged 19, from Blundell's school, Tiverton.

Newman, William Lambert, M.A., fellow BALLIOL 54, where see page 63.

Newnham, George William, M.A., fellow CORPUS CHRISTI 31-3, where see page 381.

Newsholme, Joseph Wilkinson, born at Settle, Yorks, 1867; 7s. John Wilkinson, arm. MERTON, matric. 21 Oct., 86, aged 19.

Newsom, George Ernest, born at Blundell Sands, co. Lanc., 24 May, 1871; 1s. George, arm. MERTON, matric. 22 Oct., 90, aged 19 (from Great Crosby school), exhibitioner 90; HONOURS :—2 classical mods. 92.

Newsom, John Alexander, born at Curragh, co. Kildare, 29 Jan., 1861; 2s. John, gent. CHRIST CHURCH, matric. 15 Oct., 80, aged 19 (from Christ's hospital), exhibitioner 80-4, B.A. 84, M.A. 88; HONOURS :—a classical mods. 82, 3 classics 84.

Newton, Arthur Edward, born at Corfe, Somerset, 1862; 2s. Francis Wheat, arm. PEMBROKE, matric. 26 Oct., 81, aged 19 (from Eton), B.A. 84 (HONOURS :—3 classical mods. 82), in Oxford university eleven 85.

Newton, Benjamin Willis, B.A., fellow EXETER 26-32, where see page 125.

Newton, Cecil Elsdale, born at Combe, Devon, 20 May, 1871; 1s. Joseph Knight, cler. BALLIOL, matric. 17 Oct., 89, aged 18 (from St. Edward's school, Summertown); migrated to BALLIOL; HONOURS :—Abbott scholarship 89.

Newton, Charles Farley, born at Croydon, Surrey, Aug., 1861; o.s. Charles, gent. CHRIST CHURCH, matric. 13 Oct., 82, aged 21 (from Lancing coll.); migrated to BALLIOL, B.A. 89, M.A. 92.

Newton, sir Charles Thomas, K.C.B., M.A., D.C.L., hon. fellow WORCESTER 74, where see page 574.

Newton, Charles William, born at Liverpool 1 Jan., 1867; 1s. James Banner, arm. TRINITY, matric. 17 Oct., 85, aged 18 (from the Charterhouse), B.A. 89, M.A. 92.

Newton, rev. George Herbert, born at Leeds 29 March, 1867; 4s. Francis, cler. NON-COLLEGIATE, matric. 16 Oct., 86, aged 19 (from Leeds gr. school); migrated to EXETER 20 Oct., 88, B.A. 90 (HONOURS: —3 classical mods. 88, 3 history 90); curate of Hackney, London, 90.

Newton, rev. Henry, born in Victoria, Australia, 5 Jan., 1866; 1s. Frederick Robert. MERTON, matric. 19 Oct., 89, aged 23 (from Sydney university), B.A. 89 (HONOURS :—2 mathematical mods. 90, 3 mathematics 91); curate of St. John at Hackney 91.

Newton, Hugh Goodwin, born at Barrells Park, Henley-in-Arden, co. Warwick, 14 March, 1873; 1s. Thomas Henry Goodwin, M.A. UNIVERSITY COLL., matric. 15 Oct., 92, aged 19, from Repton school.

Newton, John Horton, born at Barnet, Middx., 8 Aug., 1862; 1s. John, gen. EXETER, matric. 19 April, 82, aged 19 (from Rugby), B.A. 85, M.A. 88.

Newton, William Latham, born at Whorlton, Yorks, 13 Jan., 1862; 3s. John Fendall, of Sandybrooke Hall, co. Derby, arm. deceased. MAGDALEN, matric. 16 Oct., 80, aged 18, from Richmond gr. school.

Niblett, Harry Edward, born at Cheltenham 25 July, 1866; 3s. Charles, gen. TRINITY, matric. 16 Oct., 86, aged 20 (from Dublin coll. of science), scholar 85, B.A. 90; HONOURS :—1 chemistry 90.

Nichol, Henry Ernest, born at Hull, Yorks, 1863; o.s. George Henry, gen. NEW COLL., matric. 18 Jan., 87, aged 24, B.Mus. 88.

Nichol, John Pringle, born at Glasgow 1863; 1s. John, prof. of English literature at Glasgow university. BALLIOL, matric. 22 Oct., 83, aged 20 (from Clifton coll. and Glasgow university), scholar 83-6, B.A. 89; HONOURS :—3 history 86.

Nicholas, Tom Ferdinand, born at Newport, co. Mon., 26 Sept., 1857; 2s. Thomas Walter, gen. UNIVERSITY COLL., matric. 10 Feb., 92, aged 34; from Chipping Campden gr. school.

Nicholetts, John, born at Chipstable, Somerset, 1862; o.s. William, cler. PEMBROKE, matric. 26 Oct., 81, aged 19, B.A. 86, M.A. 88.

Nicholl, Christopher Edward, born at Llandough, co. Glam., 1871; 2s. Stephen Harry Foxden. ORIEL, matric. 22 Oct., 90, aged 19 (from Bradfield coll.), exhibitioner 90.

Nicholl, George Frederick, M.A., hon. fellow BALLIOL. 88, where see page 67.

Nicholl, John Illyd Dilwyn, born at Merthyr Maur, co. Glamorgan, May 1861; 1s. John Cole, arm. CHRIST CHURCH, matric. 21 May, 80, aged 19 (from Eton), B.A. 84 (HONOURS:—4 history 84); bar.-at-law, Inner Temple, 89.

Nicholls, Benjamin Ernest, born at Ryfleet, Surrey, 4 Oct., 1864; 1s. Henry, of Oxford, arm. MAGDALEN, matric. 24 Jan., 84, aged 19 (from Winchester), B.A. 86; in the University eleven 84.

Nicholls, Charles Henry, born at Kindford, Sussex, 30 Dec., 1866; 2s. Henry, M.A., London. NEW COLL., matric. 18 Oct., 86, aged 19 (from Winchester), B.A. 90; HONOURS:—3 botany 90.

Nicholls, Henry, M.A., WADHAM, where see page 534.

Nichols, Francis Morgan, M.A., fellow WADHAM 49-56, where see page 532.

Nichols, Samuel Uriah, born at Manchester 23 Dec., 1861; o.s. Samuel, gen. ST. MARY HALL, matric. 24 Oct., 87, aged 25.

Nicholson, Arthur Carlton, born in London 1865; 3s. William, gen. CHRIST CHURCH, matric. 27 May, 82, aged 17 (from Winchester), B.A. 85; HONOURS:—4 history 85.

Nicholson, Charles Archibald, born in London 27 April, 1867; 1s. Charles, bart. NEW COLL., matric. 15 Oct., 86, aged 19 (from Rugby), B.A. 90 (HONOURS:—3 history 89); an architect.

Nicholson, rev. Claude Humphrey de Bohun, born at Forest Hill, ESSEX, 3 March, 1868; 1s. Horace, D.D. CHRIST CHURCH, matric. 15 Oct., 86, aged 18 (from Portsmouth gr. school), B.A. 89, M.A. 93; curate of Walcot St. Swithin, Bath, 91.

Nicholson, Edward Williams Byron, M.A. TRINITY, Bodley's librarian 82, where see page 456.

Nicholson, Harold, born at Plymouth 18 June, 1874; 4s. Francis Alfred, merchant, deceased. EXETER, matric. 18 Oct., 92, aged 18, from Sedbergh school.

Nicholson, Hugh Blomfield, born in London 13 Nov., 1866; 5s. William, M.P. Petersfield. NEW COLL., matric. 16 Oct., 85, aged 18 (from Harrow); lieut. the King's Royal Rifle Corps 90.

Nicholson, rev. Hugh Smith, born at Windermere, Westmorland, 27 Oct., 1860; 6s. John, arm. TRINITY, matric. 16 Oct., 80, aged 19 (from the Charterhouse), B.A. 84, M.A. 87 (HONOURS:—3 history 84); curate of Roath, co. Glamorgan, 85.

Nicholson, John Henry, born at St. Heliers, Jersey, 3 Sept., 1871; 1s. Robert, gen. ST. MARY HALL, matric. 27 Jan., 91, aged 20, from St. Edward's school, Retford.

Nicholson, Richard Thomas, born at Maidstone, Kent, 1864; 1s. Richard Thomas, gen. UNIVERSITY COLL., matric. 14 Oct., 82, aged 18 (from Maidstone school), exhibitioner 82-6, B.A. 86, M.A. 91; HONOURS:—2 classics 86.

Nicholson, Tom Marshall, born at Leeds 4 Jan., 1867; 2s. William, gen. QUEEN'S, matric. 10 Nov., 85, aged 18 (from Grantham school), B.A. 89.

Nicholson, William Glaister, born in London 1870; 1s. Henry, arm. ORIEL, matric. 20 Oct., 88, aged 18, from St. Paul's school.

Nickalls, Guy, born at Sutton, Kent, 12 Nov., 1866; 3s. Tom, arm. MAGDALEN, matric. 21 Oct., 86, aged 19 (from Eton), B.A. 90; in the University eight 87, 8, 9, 90-1; Wingfield sculls 87, 8, 9, 91.

Nickalls, Hugh Patteson, born at Bromley, Kent, 1865; 2s. Tom, arm. PEMBROKE, matric. 27 Oct., 84, aged 19.

Nickalls, Norman Tom, born at Holmesdale, Kent, 3 April, 1864; 1s. Tom, arm. NEW COLL. matric. 12 Oct., 83, aged 19, from Eton.

Nickalls, Vivian, born at Holmesdale, Kent, 3 Sept., 1871; 4s. Tom, arm. MAGDALEN, matric. 14 Oct., 90, aged 19 (from Eton); in the University eight 91, 2, 3.

Nicol, Arthur Patrick, born at Liverpool 25 Jan., 1873; 3s. William, shipowner. NEW COLL., matric. 14 Oct., 92, aged 19, from Harrow.

Nicol, rev. Harold Doull, born at Birmingham 6 Jan., 1868; 2s. William Doull, gen. NON-COLLEGIATE, matric. 15 Oct., 87, aged 19 (from Birmingham school), B.A. 91; HONOURS:—3 classical mods. 89, 3 classics 91.

Nicolle, Francis George Stainforth, born at St. Heliers, Jersey, 15 May, 1871; 1s. Francis de Gruchy, gen. PEMBROKE, matric. 26 Oct., 89, aged 18 (from Victoria coll., Jersey), scholar 89.

Nicolson, Arthur Badenach, born at Glenbervie, Scotland, 1865; 1s. James Badenach, arm. UNIVERSITY COLL. matric. 11 Oct., 84, aged 19, B.A. 87; HONOURS:—3 history 87.

Nicolson, Edward Badenach, born at Glenbervie, co. Kincardine, 1868; 2s. James Badenach, arm. BALLIOL, matric. 19 Oct., 86, aged 18 (from Fettes coll.), B.A. 90; HONOURS:—3 classical mods. 88, 2 law 90.

Ninis, rev. Richard Duncan, born at Stockport, Cheshire, April, 1867; 1s. George Wyatt, cler. KEBLE, matric. 19 Oct., 86, aged 19 (from Ellesmere coll.), B.A. 89; curate of Leicester St. Matthew 90.

Nix, John Stanley, born at Holwood House, Somersham, Hunts. 28 Dec., 1868; 1s. John, arm. TRINITY, matric. 15 Oct., 87, aged 18 (from Cheltenham coll.), B.A. 90; HONOURS:—3 classical mods. 89, 3 history 90.

Nixon, Harry Vidal, born at Norwood, Surrey, 1865; 2s. Henry, gen. BRASENOSE, matric. 23 Oct., 85, aged 20, from Eton.

Nixon, Leigh Hunter, born in Madras 1872; 1s. Robert Bell, merchant. KEBLE, matric. 9 Feb., 92, aged 20.

Nixon, Rowland Thomas de Miller, born at Stresa, in Italy, 28 Sept., 1871; 12s. Francis Russell, bishop of Tasmania. WADHAM, matric. 13 Oct., 90, aged 19 (from Pocklington school), exhibitioner 90.

Noble, John Henry Brunel, born at Newcastle-upon-Tyne 1865; 3s. Andrew, capt., C.B. BALLIOL, matric. 15 Oct., 84, aged 19 (from Eton), B.A. 89, M.A. 91; HONOURS:—2 history 88.

Noble, Philip Ernest, born at Newcastle-upon-Tyne 23 Nov., 1870; 4s. Andrew, capt., C.B. TRINITY, matric. 18 Jan., 90, aged 19, from Eton.

Noel, Montague Henry, M.A., CHRIST CHURCH, where see page 426.

Noel, rev. Wyndham, born at Llanvabon, co. Glamorgan, 29 Aug., 1865; 1s. David, cler. NON-COLLEGIATE, matric. 13 Oct., 84, aged 19 (from Brecon coll.); migrated to EXETER, B.A. 87; curate of Holy Trinity, Bradford-on-Avon, 87;

Noott, rev. Edgar Frank Cornwallis, born at Poole, Dorset, 1860; 2s. Francis Harry, arm. MAGDALEN, matric. 19 Jan., 80, aged 20, B.A. 83, M.A. 86, chaplain 86-90, and of St. John's 87-8; private chaplain to countess of Craven 87, rector of Barley, Herts, 91.

Norden, Theodore Langdon Van, born at New Orleans, U.S.A., 26 Feb., 1869; 1s. Warner, of New York, banker. NON-COLLEGIATE, matric. 22 Oct., 92, aged 23, from Columbia coll. and union theological seminary, New York.

Norgate, Gerald Le Grys, born at East Dereham, Norfolk, 1866; 1s. Charles, gen. NON-COLLEGIATE, matric. 13 Oct., 84, aged 18 (from Felsted school), exhibitioner BRASENOSE 86, B.A. 88; HONOURS:—3 history 88.

Norman, rev. William Eglesfield Bathurst, born at Kingston, Canada, 21 Nov., 1860; 3s. George Lewis, solicitor. EXETER, matric. 16 April, 80, aged 19 (from Westminster school and King's coll., Lond.), B.A. 83, M.A. 88; chaplain at Dyculla, Bo. 86-7, vicar of Biddenham, Beds, 90.

Norrie, John Adam, born at Edinburgh 1872; 2s. John Robert, gen. BALLIOL, matric. 14 Oct., 90, aged 18 (from Edinburgh university), scholar 88 (HONOURS:—Boden scholarship 92); selected candidate Indian C.S. 90.

Norris, rev. Charles Leslie, born at Highbury, Middx., 28 April, 1862; 1s. Edward Samuel, M.P., Limehouse. NEW COLL., matric. 16 Oct., 80, aged 18 (from Eastbourne coll.), B.A. 84, M.A. 87 (HONOURS:—3 law 84); student Inner Temple 81, curate of St. Saviour, Eastbourne, 85.

Norris, Edward Greville, born at Clapton, Middx., 24 Feb., 1871; 2s. Edward Samuel, M.P. NEW COLL., matric. 12 Oct., 89, aged 18 (from Eastbourne coll.); HONOURS:—1 classical mods. 91.

Norris, Henry Robert, born at Salford, co. Lanc., 1871; 1s. Charles Edward, cler. BRASENOSE, matric. 15 Oct., 90, aged 19 (from Manchester gr. school), scholar 90; HONOURS:—a classical mods. 92.

Norris, Hugh Littleton, born in London 28 March, 1863; 3s. John Pilkington, archdeacon and canon of Bristol, B.D. TRINITY, matric. 1 June, 81, aged 18 (from the Charterhouse), B.A. 85 (HONOURS:—4 history 85); an artist.

Norris, William, born at Alverstoke, Hants, 1872; 3s. William, captain Rifle Brigade. BRASENOSE, matric. 22 Oct., 91, aged 19, from Uppingham school.

North, Eustace Herbert (Guest), born at Dartmouth, Kent, 1869; 3s. Isaac William, cler. KEBLE, matric. 17 Oct., 87, aged 18 (from Blackheath school), scholar 87, B.A. 91; HONOURS:—1 classical mods. 89, 2 classics 91.

North, James William, born at Campfield, co. Lanc., 1864; 1s. William, arm. NON-COLLEGIATE, matric. 16 Oct., 86, aged 22 (from Hardwick school); migrated to EXETER, B.A. 89.

Northcote, hon. Amyas Stafford, born 25 Oct., 1864; 5s. sir Stafford, bart., 1st earl of Iddesleigh. UNIVERSITY COLL., matric. 14 Oct., 82, aged 17.

Northcote, George Russell, born at Monk Oakhampton, Devon, 10 Oct., 1869; 8s. Henry Moubray, cler. NEW COLL., matric. 12 Oct., 88, aged 19 (from Winchester), scholar 82-6, fellow 86, B.A. 86, M.A. 89 [HONOURS:—1 classical mods. 83, Hertford scholarship 84 (accessit 83), Ireland scholarship 85, 1 classics 86, Derby scholarship 87, Eldon law scholarship 88]; bar.-at-law, Lincoln's Inn, 91.

Northcote, Stafford Harry, viscount St. Cyres, born at Little Ouseburne, Yorks, 23 Aug., 1869; 1s. Walter Stafford, earl of Iddesleigh. MERTON, matric. 17 Oct., 88, aged 19 (from Eton), exhibitioner 89; student CHRIST CHURCH 93, B.A. 93; HONOURS:—1 history 92.

Northey, Charles Henry, born at Chaddesden vicarage, co. Derby, 26 April, 1873; 2s. Edward William, M.A., of Wootton House, Surrey, J.P., cler. MAGDALEN, matric. 18 Oct., 92, aged 19, from Eton.

Norton, Arthur William Fox, born at Camberwell, Surrey, 1866; 2s. Frank Douglas, gen. EXETER, matric. 19 Oct., 87, aged 21, from Denstone coll.

Norton, Cecil Grafton, born at Great Missenden, Bucks, 1867; 3s. David Evans, cler. KEBLE, matric. 22 Oct., 85, aged 18 (from Bruton school), B.A. 88; HONOURS:—2 history 88.

Norton, David Evans, born at Dover 4 Jan., 1863; 2s. David Evans, cler. KEBLE, matric. 18 Oct., 81, aged 18 (from Bruton school), B.A. 85, M.A. 88 (HONOURS:—2 classical mods. 83, 2 classics 85); headmaster Bruton go.

Norton, James Leas, born at Carmarthen 1865; 7s. Henry, gent. NEW COLL., matric. 10 Oct., 84, aged 19 (from Bruton school), B.A. 88; HONOURS:—3 classical mods. 86, 3 classics 88.

Norton, William Alfred, born at Exeter 13 May, 1870; o.s. William, gen. EXETER, matric. 16 Oct., 89, aged 19 (from Exeter school); HONOURS:—3 classical mods. 91.

Nott, Frederick Richard Harding, born at Barnstaple, Devon, 1864; o.s. Richard, cler. EXETER, matric. 18 Oct., 83, aged 19.

Nott, Gilbert Harwood, born at Bristol 1867; 2s. William, gent. NEW COLL., matric. 17 Oct., 85, aged 18 (from Probus school); migrated to BALLIOL, B.A. 89; HONOURS:—3 mathematics 89.

Nowell, Thomas Whitaker, M.A., fellow BRASENOSE 48-62, where see page 355.

Nowell, Walter Salmon, born at Sudyah, East Indies, 1867; 2s. Ralph, arm. BRASENOSE, matric. 20 Oct., 86, aged 19 (from Harrogate school), B.A. 89.

Nugent, Anthony Frederick, 11th earl of Westmeath, born at Furbough, co. Galway, 11 Jan., 1870; 1s. William, earl of Westmeath. CHRIST CHURCH, matric. 10 Oct., 90, aged 20.

Nugent, Claud, born in London 1866; 1s. Edmund Charles, arm. CHRIST CHURCH, matric. 16 April, 86, aged 18, B.A. 91.

Nugent, rev. Edmund Frederick, born in London 4 Feb., 1866; 2s. Edmund Charles, arm. CHRIST CHURCH, matric. 16 April, 86, aged 20, B.A. 90, M.A. 92; curate of Finningham, Suffolk, 90.

Nunn, Harold, born at Ripon, Yorks, 10 Aug., 1873; 1s. Henry Drury Cust, M.A., hon. canon of Ripon, etc. MAGDALEN, matric. 18 Oct., 92, aged 19 (from Ripon gr. school), demy 92.

Nussey, Cecil Anthony, born at Richmond, Surrey, 4 March, 1872; 1s. Anthony Foxcroft, solicitor. KEBLE, matric. 20 Oct., 91, aged 19, from Haileybury.

Nuthall, John Frederick, born at Kingston-on-Thames, Surrey, 3 June, 1872; 1s. John Frederick, of Eastbourne, arm. ST. EDMUND HALL, matric. 22 Oct., 91, aged 23, from Ardingly gr. school.

Nutt, George, M.A., fellow EXETER 69-77, where see page 128.

Nutt, George Arthur, born in London 1866; o.s. Josiah, gen. QUEEN'S, matric. 25 Oct., 80, aged 19 (from Birmingham school), scholar 80-4, B.A. 85; HONOURS:—2 mathematical mods. 82, 2 mathematics 84.

Nutt, rev. Horace Young, born at Stourbridge, co. Worcester, 1864; 1s. Horace, gent. ST. JOHN'S, matric. 16 Oct., 86, aged 22 (from Sherborne school), B.A. 89; curate of St. Dunstan, Edge Hill, Liverpool, 90.

Nutt, John William, M.A., fellow ALL SOULS' 58-75, where see page 281.

Nuttall, Charles Ewen, born at Kingston in Jamaica, 1871; 2s. Enos, bishop of Jamaica. NON-COLLEGIATE, matric. 12 Oct., 89, aged 18 (from Ramsgate school), migrated to MERTON, B.A. 92; HONOURS:—4 history 92.

Nuttall, rev. Ebenezer Appleby, born at Barnoldswick, Yorks, 1861; y.s. James, gent. WORCESTER, matric. 21 Oct., 80, aged 19, B.A. 83 (HONOURS:—3 history 83); curate of Burton-on-Trent 86.

Nuttall, Thomas Kirkpatrick, born at Liverpool 23 Nov., 1863; o.s. Thomas, gent. PEMBROKE, matric. 26 Oct., 81, aged 17 (from Liverpool coll.), B.A. 85 (HONOURS:—1 theology 85); bar.-at-law, Lincoln's Inn, 90.

Nutter, Alfred Barrett, born at Bedford 18 May, 1870; o.s. John Frederick, arm. BRASENOSE, matric. 14 Oct., 89, aged 19 (from Bedford school), scholar 89; HONOURS:—2 classical mods. 91.

STONE ANIMAL, ROUEN CATHEDRAL.—*Pugin*.

FONT, FORMERLY IN ST. PETER-IN-THE-EAST, OXFORD.—From an engraving by *Skelton*.

O

Oakden, Ralph, born at Helensburgh, Scotland, 12 July, 1871; 1s. Roger, vicar of Sutton, Salop, NON-COLLEGIATE, matric 11 Oct., 90, aged 19 (from Cranbrook gr. school); HONOURS :— 2 classical mods. 92.

Oake, Robert Christopher, born at Leeds, Yorks, 1853; 2s. Thomas Christopher, C.E. MARCON'S HALL, matric. 24 Oct., 91, aged 38.

Oakeley, Edward de Clifford William, born in London 21 Nov., 1864; o.s. William Edward, arm. CHRIST CHURCH, matric. 25 May, 83, aged 18.

Oakeley, William Ingnall, M.A., fellow JESUS COLL. 46-54, where see page 512.

Oakeshott, Francis Benjamin, born at Dalston, Middx. 1864; 3s. Jonathan, gen. JESUS COLL., matric. 18 Oct., 82, aged 18 (from city of London school), scholar 82-6, B.A. 86, M.A. 91; HONOURS :— 2 mathematical mods. 83, 2 mathematics 86.

Oakley, rev. Roland Edward George, born in London 1868; 2s. John, D.D. and dean of Manchester. ST. JOHN'S, matric. 13 Oct., 88, aged 20 (from Brighton coll.), B.A. 92; HONOURS :— 4 history 92.

Oakley, William John, born at Shrewsbury 1873; 1s. William, gent. CHRIST CHURCH, matric. 14 Oct., 92, aged 19, from Shrewsbury school.

Oakshott, rev. George Herbert, born at New Ferry, Cheshire, 18 July, 1868; 4s. Thomas William, arm. CORPUS CHRISTI, matric. 22 Oct., 87, aged 19 (from Rugby), B.A. 90.

O'Beirne, Hugh James, born in Dublin 1866; 2s. Hugh, arm. BALLIOL, matric. 15 Oct., 84, aged 18 (HONOURS :— 2 Indian languages 87); selected candidate Indian c.s. 84.

O'Brien, Patrick William, born at Dalhousie, East Indies, 14 May, 1868; 3s. Patrick, arm. BALLIOL, matric. 19 Oct., 87, aged 19 (from Malvern coll.); selected candidate Indian c.s. 87.

O'Brien, Peter Henry, born at Mooltan, East Indies, 1863; 1s. Patrick, arm. BALLIOL, matric. 21 Oct., 80, aged 17 (from Malvern coll.); deputy commissioner, Assam, 82.

O'Brien, Ranald Martin, born at Mooltan, East Indies, 1865; 2s. Patrick, arm. BALLIOL, matric. 19 Oct., 86, aged 20 (from Malvern coll.); HONOURS :— 3 classical mods. 88; died 13 Aug., 89.

O'Brien, Timothy Carew, born at Dublin 1862; 1s. Timothy, arm. NEW INN HALL, matric. 3 May, 84, aged 22; in the University eleven 84-5. See Foster's *Baronetage*.

Occleston, Sydney Vernon, born at Ashton-on-Mersey, Cheshire, 1869; 2s. John James, gen. EXETER, matric. 17 Oct., 88, aged 19, from Radley coll.

O'Connor, Edward, born at Marchtown, co. Cambridge, 9 April, 1864; 6s. Thomas, gen. LINCOLN, matric. 23 Oct., 82, aged 18 (from Oundle school), scholar 82-4, B.A. 87; HONOURS :— 3 classical mods. 84, 4 classics 86.

Oddie, John William, M.A., fellow CORPUS CHRISTI 67, where see page 379.

O'Dell, Thomas Smyth, born at Dublin 1867; elder son of Thomas Scruton, arm. HERTFORD, matric. 27 Oct., 87, aged 20.

Odgers, Arthur William, born at Bridgewater, Somerset, 1871; 2s. James Edwin, cler. LINCOLN, matric. 20 Oct., 90, aged 19, from Sedbergh school.

Odgers, Charles Edwin, born at Bridgewater, Somerset, 17 Jan., 1870; 1s. James Edwin, cler. LINCOLN, matric. 17 Oct., 89, aged 19 (from Bath coll. and Owens coll.), scholar 89; HONOURS :— 2 classical mods. 91.

Odling, George Smee, born at Oxford 25 May, 1873; 1s. William, M.A., professor of chemistry. MAGDALEN, matric. 18 Oct., 92, aged 19, from Cowley military coll.

Odling, William, M.A., fellow WORCESTER 72, where see page 573.

O'Donohoe, James Patrick, born at Shutford, Oxon, 1861; 1s. Martin, gen. UNIVERSITY COLL., matric. 16 Oct., 80, aged 19 (from Wakefield school), exhibitioner 80-3, B.A. 84, M.A. 91.

O'Donovan, Morgan William, born at Cork, Ireland, 1861; 1s. Henry Winthrop, arm. MAGDALEN, matric. 29 Oct., 81, aged 20, B.A. 86.

O'Dwyer, Charles Philip Firmin, born at Chatham, Kent, 23 July, 1866; o.s. Charles Archer O'Rourke, gen. PEMBROKE, matric. 27 Oct., 85, aged 19 (from Portsmouth school), scholar 85, B.A. 91; HONOURS :— 2 classical mods. 87.

Oescher, Henri, born in Paris 1858; o.s. Lewis, gent. NON-COLLEGIATE, matric. 18 Oct., 80, aged 22.

O'Flaherty, Alfred Ernest, born at Liverpool 1869; 2s. Philip, cler. ORIEL, matric. 22 Oct., 90, aged 21 (from Edinburgh university), scholar 90; HONOURS :— 3 classical mods. 92.

Ogden, Alexander McRitchie, born at Bangor 1864; 3s. George Henry, gent. JESUS COLL., matric. 18 Oct., 82, aged 18 (from Bangor school), B.A. 86, M.A. 89; HONOURS :— 2 mathematical mods. 84, 3 mathematics 86.

Ogilvie, William Frederick, born at Sydney, Australia, 1869; 1s. Edward David Stewart, arm. NON-COLLEGIATE, matric. 23 May, 85, aged 23 (from Sydney university); migrated to BALLIOL, B.A. 88; HONOURS :— 3 history 88.

Ogilvy, Gilbert Francis Molyneux, born at Auchterhouse, co. Forfar, 9 April, 1868 ; 4s. Reginald Howard, arm. UNIVERSITY COLL., matric. 13 Oct., 88, aged 20, B.A. 92 ; HONOURS :—4 history 92.

Ogle, Ambrose Addington, born at Sutton, co. Derby, 26 June, 1866; 6s. James Ambrose, cler. KEBLE, matric. 22 Oct., 85, aged 19 (from Haileybury), B.A. 89 ; HONOURS :—2 classical mods. 87, 3 classics 89.

Ogle, Arthur, born at Liverpool 19 May, 1871 ; 1s. John, gen. MAGDALEN, matric. 14 Oct., 90, aged 19 (from Gt. Crosby school), exhibitioner 90.

Ogle, Cyril, born in London 19 April, 1861 ; 3s. John William, D.Med. TRINITY, matric. 21 May, 80, aged 19 (from Westminster school), B.A. 84, M.A. and B.Med. 90 (HONOURS :—2 natural science 84) ; L.R.C.P., M.R.C.S. 88.

Ogle, John Gilbert, born at Sedgeford, Norfolk, 17 Jan., 1862 ; 5s. James Ambrose, cler. KEBLE, matric. 19 Oct., 80, aged 18 (from Haileybury), B.A. 84, M.A. and B.Med. 89, D.Med. 91 ; HONOURS :—2 natural science 84.

Ogle, Octavius, M.A., fellow LINCOLN 52-9, where see page 242.

Ogle, William, M.A., D.Med., fellow CORPUS CHRISTI 47-64, where see page 382.

Ohren-Ovington, Cecil, born at Longton, co. Stafford, 30 March, 1866; 1s. John Ohren, gent. UNIVERSITY COLL., matric. 17 Oct., 85, aged 19 (from Rugby), B.A. 89 (HONOURS : — 3 classical mods. 87, 2 history 89); assumed the additional name of Ovington.

Oldaker, Francis Allcock, born at Kingston, Surrey, 2 June, 1871 ; o.s. Francis Allcock, of Epsom, artist. BALLIOL, matric. 14 Oct., 90, aged 19 (from Epsom coll.) ; HONOURS :—3 classical mods. 92.

Oldfield, Charles Bayley, born at East Woodhay, Hants, 21 Nov., 1866 ; 1s. George Biscoe, cler. NEW COLL., matric. 16 Oct., 85, aged 18 (from Haileybury), B.A. 89 (HONOURS :—4 law 88) ; bnr.-at-law, Inner Temple, 89, practising in India.

Oldfield, Edmund Prescot, born at Calcutta 1862 ; 1s. Henry Ambrose, gen. KEBLE, matric. 19 Oct., 80, aged 18 (from the Charterhouse), B.A. 83, M.A. 88.

Oldfield, Frederick Biscoe, born at Motcombe, Dorset, 7 April, 1871 ; 2s. George Biscoe, cler. NEW COLL., matric. 23 Nov., 89, aged 18 (from Haileybury); student Inner Temple.

Oldfield, Josiah, born at Ryton, Salop, 1863 ; 2s. David, gen. NON-COLLEGIATE, matric. 15 April, 82, aged 19, B.A. 85, M.A. and B.C.L. 88 (HONOURS :—2 theology 85, 2 civil law 87); bar.-at-law, Lincoln's Inn, 92.

Oldham, Charles Evelyn Arbuthnot William, born at Galway 1869 ; 3s. Charles Emilius, arm. BALLIOL, matric. 18 Oct., 88, aged 19 (from Galway school) ; assist. magistrate and collector Bengal.

Oldham, George Ernest, born in Dublin 1867 ; 3s. James, gen. NON-COLLEGIATE, matric. 15 Oct., 87, aged 20 (from Bristol school), B.A. 90.

Oldham, Henry Yule, born at Dusseldorf 14 Dec., 1862 ; 5s. Thomas, LL.D. JESUS COLL., matric. 18 Oct., 82, aged 19 (from Rugby), B.A. 86, M.A. 90 (HONOURS :—2 morphology 86), a master at Harrow.

Oldham, Joseph Houldsworth, born at Bombay, India, 20 Oct., 1874 ; 1s. G. , W lieut.-col. R.E. TRINITY, matric. 15 Oct., 92, aged 17, from Edinburgh academy.

Oldham, Walter Frederick, born at Rathmines, Dublin, 20 Jan., 1869 ; 4s. James, gen., deceased. BALLIOL, matric. 17 Oct., 89, aged 20 (from Tonbridge school), exhibitioner 89, B.A. 92 ; HONOURS :—2 history 92.

Oliver, rev. Alfred Creswick, born at Prestbury, Cheshire, 1863 ; 1s. Thomas, gen. EXETER, matric. 19 Oct., 87, aged 24 (from Newcoll., Eastbourne), B.A. 90 (HONOURS :—3 history 90); curate of Pilling, co. Lanc., 90.

Oliver, Arthur Pope, born at Bollington, Cheshire, 1864 ; 3s. William Thomas, gen. EXETER, matric. 18 Jan., 83, aged 19.

Oliver, rev. Arthur West, born at New Orleans 1859 ; 6s. George Washington, arm. QUEEN'S, matric. 24 Jan., 80, aged 21, B.A. 83, M.A. 86 (HONOURS :—3 theology 83); vicar of Bootle St. Mathew 91.

Oliver, Ernest Scales, born at Farnley, Yorks, 1871 ; 1s. George, gen. ORIEL, matric. 22 Oct., 90, aged 19 (from Leeds school), scholar 90; HONOURS :—2 classical mods. 92.

Oliver, Frederick William, M.A., student CHRIST CHURCH 53-61, where see page 420.

Oliver, George Frederick, born at Ashton-on-Mersey 1862 ; o.s. George, arm. EXETER, matric. 18 Jan., 83, aged 21.

Oliverson, Cecil Henry, born in London 1868 ; 1s. Richard, arm. CHRIST CHURCH, matric. 15 Oct., 86, aged 18, B.A. 92.

Oliverson, Harold Arthur, born in London 1872 ; 2s. Richard, arm. CHRIST CHURCH, matric. 6 June, 90, aged 18, from Eton.

Olivier, Gerard Kerr, born at Frensham, Surrey, 1869 ; 4s. Henry Arnold, cler. MERTON, matric. 17 Oct., 88, aged 19, from Winchester.

Olivier, rev. Henry Eden, born at Wilton, Wilts, 16 Feb., 1866 ; 3s. Dacres, rector. NEW COLL. matric. 16 Jan., 85, aged 18 (from Marlborough coll.), B.A. 89 (HONOURS :—2 history 88); curate of St. John the Evangelist, Westminster, 91.

Olivier, Reginald Ernest, born at Wilton, Wilts, 1871 ; 6s. Dacres, rector. CHRIST CHURCH, matric. 11 Oct., 89, aged 18 (from Westminster school) ; HONOURS :—3 classical mods. 91.

Ollard, Sidney Leslie, born at Wisbeach, co. Cambridge, 26 Sept., 1875 ; 1s. Sidney, of Leighton Buzzard, Beds, solicitor. ST. JOHN'S, matric. 15 Oct., 92, aged 17.

O'Malley, Bryan Francis Keppel, born at Hitcham, Norfolk, 2 Feb., 1873 ; 1s. Bryan, cler. HERTFORD, matric. 20 Oct., 91, aged 18 (from Norwich gr. school), scholar 90.

Oman, Charles William Chadwick, M.A., fellow ALL SOULS' 83, where see page 274.

Ommanney, Walter Fabian, born at Chew Magna, Somerset, 20 Jan., 1868 ; 2s. Edward, vicar. EXETER, matric. 22 Oct., 80, aged 19.

Omond, Thomas Stewart, M.A., fellow ST. JOHN'S 72-8, where see page 486.

O'Neill, Frank Bernard, born at Willesley, Kent, 31 Oct., 1869 ; 2s. George Bernard, arm. TRINITY, matric. 13 Oct., 88, aged 18 (from Haileybury), cahibitioner 88, B.A. 92 ; HONOURS :— 3 classical mods. 90, 4 history 92.

O'Neill, William Henry, born at Lee, Kent, 25 Oct., 1867 ; 2s. William, arm. JESUS COLL., matric. 20 Oct., 86, aged 18 (from Haileybury), scholar 86, B.A. 90 (HONOURS : — 2 classical mods. 88, 3 classics 90); assistant schoolmaster.

Onslow, Henry Phipps, born at Snpey, co. Hereford, 2 April, 1869 ; o.s. Phipps, rector. KEBLE, matric. 17 Oct., 87, aged 18 (from Haileybury), B.A. 90.

Oppé, Albert Tanvil, born at Lyons 1869 ; 1s. Sigmund Ormia. UNIVERSITY COLL., matric. 13 Oct., 88, aged 19, B.A. 92 ; HONOURS :—4 law 92.

Oppenheim, Edwin Camillo, born at Alexandria, in Egypt, 1868 ; o.s. Gustavus Adolphus, arm. CHRIST CHURCH, matric. 14 Oct., 87, aged 19 ; migrated to CHARSLEY HALL, B.A. 91 ; HONOURS :—3 law 91.

Oppenheim, Frederick Sigismund, born at Manchester 26 Jan., 1873 ; 1s. Sigismund, gen. TRINITY matric. 17 Oct., 91, aged 18, from Rugby.

Oppenheim, Henry James, born in London 28 March, 1869; 1s. Henry, arm. CHRIST CHURCH, matric. 24 April, 88, aged 19, B.A. 92.

Oppenheim, Rudolph, born at Berlin 1871; 1s. Benoit, arm. BALLIOL, matric. 1 May, 90, aged 19.

Oppenheimer, Francis Charles, born in London 17 Dec., 1870; 1s. sir Charles, B.B.M. consul general Frankfort-on-Maine. BALLIOL, matric. 14 Oct., 90, aged 19, from Frankfort gymnasium.

Orange, Hugh William, born at Broadmoor, Berks, 14 April, 1866; o.s. William, D.Med. NEW COLL., matric. 16 Oct., 85, aged 19 (from Winchester); scholar 84, B.A. 91; HONOURS :—1 classical mods. 87, 1 classics 89.

Orchard, John, born at Ryde, I.W., 27 Dec., 1874; 2s. Richard, of Bridgewater, nonconformist minister. NON-COLLEGIATE, matric. 15 Oct., 92, aged 17, from Shebbear coll.

Orchardson, William Quiller, A.R.A. 1868, R.A. 1877, created D.C.L. 25 June, 90. See *Men and Women of the Time.*

Ord, Arthur Burrell, born at Nisbet, co. Roxburgh, 29 Sept., 1870; 6s. John, arm. MAGDALEN, matric. 14 Oct., 89, aged 19 (from Monkton Combe and Rossall schools), demy 89; selected candidate Indian C.S. 89; died at Madras 11 March, 92.

Ord, Christopher Cameron, born at Charlton, Kent, 1869; o.s. Christopher Knox, D.Med. MAGDALEN, matric. 16 Oct., 88, aged 19 (from Blackheath school), exhibitioner 88, B.A. 92; HONOURS :—2 classical mods. 90, 3 classics 92.

Orde, Thorley Launcelot Maximilian, born at Chathill, Northumberland, 1865; 2s. Henry Powlett Shafto. BALLIOL, matric. 15 Oct., 84, aged 19 (from Richmond gr. school), B.A. 88; HONOURS :—4 history 88.

O'Regan, John Rowan Hamilton, born at Dunlavin, co. Wicklow, 29 May, 1870; 1s. John, archdeacon of Kildare 69-79. BALLIOL, matric. 17 Oct., 89, aged 19 (from Clifton coll.), scholar 88; HONOURS :—1 classical mods. 91.

O'Reilly, William Edmund, born at Laurencetown, co. Down, 1873; 1s. William Edward, solicitor. NEW COLL., matric. 16 Oct., 91, aged 18 (from Harrow), scholar 91.

Orlebar, Edward Yarde. born at Willington, Beds, 1872; 4s. Augustus, vicar. NEW COLL., matric. 16 Oct., 91, aged 19, from Radley coll.

Orme, William Platt, born at Leeds, Yorks, 18 Aug., 1860; 1s. John, nonconformist minister. LINCOLN, matric. 29 Jan., 81, aged 20, from Shrewsbury gr. school.

Ormerod, Arthur Latham, born at Brighton 14 July, 1870; 2s. Edward Latham, D.Med. NEW COLL., matric. 11 Oct., 89, aged 19 (from Rugby), scholar 89, B.A. 92; HONOURS :—1 chemistry 92.

Ormerod, Edward, born at Westbury-on-Trym, co. Glouc., 10 Sept., 1868; 2s. Henry, gen. KEBLE, matric. 13 Oct., 88, aged 20 (from Bristol school), B.A. 91; HONOURS :—4 theology 91.

Ormerod, Joseph Arderne, M.A., D.Med., fellow JESUS COLL. 71-5, where see page 513.

Ormiston. Henry Lee, born at Camberwell, London, 12 Jan., 1874; 3s. Thomas, C.I.E., civil engineer. NEW COLL., matric. 14 Oct., 92, aged 18 (from Dulwich coll.), exhibitioner 92.

Ormiston, Thomas Lane, born at Malabar Hill, Bombay, 20 May, 1867; 3s. Thomas, arm. TRINITY, matric. 16 Oct., 86, aged 19 (from Dulwich coll.), B.A. 89; selected candidate for Indian C.S. 86; and lieut. King's own Scottish borderers 90, and of Indian staff corps 26th Madras infantry.

Ormond, Arthur William, born at Melbourne 1864; y.s James, gen. BRASENOSE, matric. 14 Oct., 84, aged 20, B.A. 87.

Ormond, Ernest William, born at Brighton 1863; 2s. John, cler. NEW COLL., matric. 15 Oct., 81, aged 18, B.A. 86; HONOURS :—3 law 85, bar.-at-law, Inner Temple, 87.

Ormond, John, M.A., fellow PEMBROKE 56-7, where see page 554.

Orpwood, Harry Charles, born at Oxford 1869; 2s. William, gen. NON-COLLEGIATE, matric. 13 Oct., 88, aged 19.

Orr, Charles Gathorne Edmund, born at Salehurst, Sussex, 1862; 2s. Alexander, vicar. ORIEL, matric. 24 Nov., 80, aged 18 (from the Charterhouse), B.A. 83, M.A. 87.

Osborn, Edward Bolland, born in London 1867; 1s. Edward Haydon, arm. MAGDALEN, matric. 6 Feb., 85, aged 18 (from Rossall school), exhibitioner 85, B.A. 90; HONOURS :—2 mathematical mods. 86, 3 mathematics 88.

Osborn, rev. Francis Wilfrid, born at Kibworth, co. Leicester, 26 April, 1862; 1s. Montagu Francis Finch, rector. KEBLE, matric. 27 Jan., 81, aged 18 (from Uppingham school), exhibitioner 81-5, B.A. 84, M.A. 92 (HONOURS :—2 classical mods. 83, 3 classics 84,); curate of St. Michael, Camdentown, 89.

Osborn, Montagu Francis Finch, M.A., fellow MERTON 47-52, where see page 97.

Osborn, Montagu John, born at Kibworth, co. Leicester, 19 Feb., 1869; 2s. Montagu Francis, rector. KEBLE, matric. 13 Oct., 88, aged 19, B.A. 91; HONOURS :—3 classical mods. 90.

Osborn, Nathaniel Francis Banner, born in London 1872; 3s. Charles Edward, gen. ST. JOHN'S, matric. 11 Oct., 90, aged 18 (from Merchant Taylors' school), scholar 90; HONOURS :—accessit Hertford scholarship 92, and proxime accessit 91, 1 classical mods. 92, and 2 mathematical mods. 92.

Osborn, Percy Lancelot, born at Blackburn, co. Lanc., 1870; 3s. Edward Haydon, arm. MAGDALEN, matric. 14 Oct., 89, aged 19 (from Manchester gr. school), demy 88; HONOURS :—1 classical mods. 91.

Osborne, lord Albert Edward Godolphin, born 10 April, 1866; s. George, duke of Leeds. BALLIOL, matric. 28 May, 85, aged 19.

Osborne, Algernon Willoughby-, born at Schole, East Indies, 1865; 2s. Willoughby, arm. HERTFORD, matric. 20 Jan., 83, aged 18, B.A. 86, M.A. 92 (law 86.

Osborne, rev. George Edward Caulfield, born at Fleetwood, co. Lanc., 4 Sept., 1866; o.s. George Yarnold, cler. TRINITY, matric. 17 Oct., 85, aged 19 (from Rossall school), B.A. 89, M.A. 92 (HONOURS :—2 history 89); curate of Botley, Hants, 90.

Osborne, Henry Bryan Godfrey Godfrey Faussett, born at Littleton, co. Worcester, 1865; 1s. Henry Godfrey Godfrey Faussett, cler. CHRIST CHURCH, matric. 25 May, 83, aged 18, B.A. 87, M.A. 91.

Osmond, Percy Herbert, born at Calcutta 22 July, 1872; 2s. Walter Marsh, of Salisbury, architect. ST. JOHN'S, matric. 17 Oct., 91, aged 19 (from Berkhampstead school), scholar 90.

O'Sullivan, Vincent James, born at New York, U.S.A., 28 Nov., 1868; 2s. Eugene, merchant. EXETER, matric. 3 Dec., 92, aged 24.

Oswell, Frank, born at Groombridge, Sussex, 1863; 2s. Benjamin. CHRIST CHURCH, matric. 14 Oct., 81, aged 18 (from Eastbourne coll.), B.A. 85; HONOURS :—3 classical mods. 83.

Oswell, rev. Harrison, born at Withyham, Sussex, 27 Sept., 1866; 3s. William Cotton, arm. CHRIST CHURCH, matric. 30 May, 85, aged 18 (from Eastbourne coll.), B.A, 88; curate of St. John Evangelist, Bethnal Green, 90.

Otter, Francis, M.A., fellow CORPUS CHRISTI 61-75, where see page 383.

Ottley, Robert Laurence, M.A., fellow MAGDALEN 86, where see page 316.

Otto, John Ellison, born at Jedmwuk, co. Roxburgh, 1872; 1s. William Ellison, gen. MAGDALEN, matric. 14 Oct., 90, aged 18, from Harrow.

Ould, Robert, born at York 1872; 6s. Fielding Frederick, cler. KEBLE, matric. 11 Oct., 90, aged 18, from clergy orphan school, Canterbury.

Ouvry, Ernest Carrington, born at Wing, Bucks, 1866; 2s. Peter Thomas, cler. WADHAM, matric. 19 Oct., 85, aged 19, from Marlborough coll.

Overend, Frederick Laurence, born at Manchester 1864; 1s. Robert, gen. JESUS COLL., matric. 18 Oct., 83, aged 19 (from Manchester gr. school), B.A. 87; HONOURS:—3 chemistry 86.

Overend, Walker, born at Keighley, Yorks, 1859; 1s. Thomas, gent. BALLIOL, matric. 16 Oct., 83, aged 24 (from royal school of mines and St. Bartholomew hospital), scholar 82, B.A. 86; HONOURS:—1 physiology 86, Radcliffe travelling fellowship 87.

Overend, Wilkinson, born at Keighley, Yorks, 1862; 2s. Thomas, gen. KEBLE, matric. 16 Oct., 83, aged 19 (from Yorkshire coll., Leeds), scholar 83, B.A. 88; HONOURS:—3 physiology 87, Radcliffe travelling fellowship 88.

Overton, rev. Frederick Arnold, born at Hackness, Yorks, 15 July, 1852; 1s. Samuel Charlesworth, cler. NON-COLLEGIATE, matric. 13 Oct., 84, aged 22 (from King's coll., London); exhibitioner EXETER 84, B.A. 87, M.A. 91 (HONOURS:—2 theology 87); assist. chaplain 90; curate of Headington, Oxon, 87-93, vicar of High Cross, Herts, 93.

Owen, rev. Arthur Frank Cowley, born at East Dulwich, Surrey, 1861; 3s. Edward, arm. WADHAM, matric. 26 Jan., 81, aged 20, B.A. 83, M.A. 87; chaplain at Genoa 89-91; vicar of Swanscombe All Saints, Kent, 91.

Owen, Arthur Synge, born at Cheltenham 22 Aug., 1871; o.s. James Albert, cler. NEW COLL., matric. 10 Oct., 90, aged 19 (from Cheltenham coll.), scholar 90; HONOURS:—1 classical mods. 92.

Owen, rev. Charles Frederick, born at Ystalyfera, co. Glamorgan, 1855; 2s. Eleazer, pleb. NON-COLLEGIATE, matric. 21 Jan., 82, aged 27, B.A. and M.A. 90; curate of Llandebie, co. Carmarthen, 90.

Owen, Donald Millman, B.D., fellow BALLIOL 52-66, where see page 67.

Owen, rev. Edward Charles Everard, M.A., fellow NEW COLL. 84-91, where see page 218.

Owen, Edward Cunliffe, born at Oxford 9 Feb., 1860; 2s. Sidney James, reader in Indian history. PEMBROKE, matric. 25 Jan., 88, aged 18 (from Haileybury), scholar 88, B.A. 92; HONOURS:—2 classical mods. 89, 1 classics 91.

Owen, Edward Tudor-, born at Rhyl, Flints, 1871; 1s. Edward, cler. CHRIST CHURCH, matric. 11 Oct., 89, aged 18 (from Shrewsbury school), scholar 89; HONOURS:—1 classical mods. 91.

Owen, Edwin James, born at Llanllechid, co. Carmarthen, 1859; 1s. Elias, cler. NON-COLLEGIATE, matric. 18 Oct., 80, aged 21.

Owen, Fearnley Wells, born in London 1870; 1s. George, arm. BRASENOSE, matric. 16 Oct., 88, aged 18 (from Marlborough coll.), B.A. 91 (HONOURS:—2 law 91, 3 civil law 92); bar.-at-law, Inner Temple, 92.

Owen, Henry Percy, born at Sydney, Australia, 1860; 4s. Robert, gen. CHRIST CHURCH, matric. 8 May, 80, aged 20, B.A. 83; bar.-at-law, Inner Temple, 85.

Owen, Herbert Dorset, born at Hindringham, Norfolk, 14 March, 1863; 2s. John Maurice Dorset, vicar. WADHAM, matric. 17 Oct., 82, aged 19 (from Haileybury), scholar 81, B.A. 86 (HONOURS:—1 classical mods. 84, 2 classics 86), assistant schoolmaster.

Owen, James Albert, M.A., fellow UNIVERSITY COLL. 68-71, where see page 33.

Owen, John, born at Tall-y-llyn, co. Merioneth, 1855; 2s. Evan, gen. CHARSLEY'S HALL, matric. 20 Oct., 80, aged 25.

Owen, John, born at Nevin, co. Carnarvon, 1864; 1s. James, pleb. NON-COLLEGIATE, matric. 12 Oct., 89, aged 25 (from Bala school), B.A. 92; HONOURS:—2 classics 92.

Owen, Langer (Mende Loftus), born at Sydney, Australia, 1863; 1s. William, arm. NEW COLL., matric. 4 June, 81, aged 18 (from the Charterhouse), B.A. 86 (HONOURS:—2 classical mods. 83, 3 classics 85); bar.-at-law, Lincoln's Inn, 88.

Owen, rev. Loftus Mende, born at Liverpool 1861; 2s. Loftus, cler. CORPUS CHRISTI, matric. 19 Oct., 83, aged 19 (from Rossall school), B.A. 87 (HONOURS:—2 classical mods. 85, 4 history 87); curate of Leeke, co. Staff, 91.

Owen, Michael Roberts, born at Llanrug, co. Carnarvon, 1861; 3s. Michael, gen. CHARSLEY'S HALL, matric. 8 Feb., 90, aged 25.

Owen, Reginald Solly, born at Hooton, Cheshire, 6 Nov., 1861; 3s. John, cler. CHRIST CHURCH, matric. 15 Oct., 80, aged 18 (from Westminster school), scholar 80, B.A. 84, M.A. 87 (HONOURS: —2 classical mods. 82, 2 classics 84.

Owen, Richard, born at Bryneglwys, co. Denbigh, 14 Jan., 1872; 2s. Richard, rector of Erryrys 86. NON-COLLEGIATE, matric. 15 Oct., 92, aged 20, from Ellesmere coll.

Owen, Richard Edward, born at Aberystwith, co. Cardigan, 1868; 1s. Edward, pleb. JESUS COLL., matric. 14 Oct., 89, aged 21 (from Lampeter coll), exhibitioner 89; HONOURS:—3 classical mods. 91.

Owen, Robert, M.A., fellow JESUS COLL. 45-64, where see page 512.

Owen, Rupert Kenneth Wilson, born at Burstow, Surrey, 3 April, 1853; 3s. Octavius Freire, M.A., rector 48-55. ST. JOHN'S, matric. 17 Jan., 90, aged 36, from Merchant Taylors' school.

Owen, Sidney George, M.A., student CHRIST CHURCH 91, where see page 410.

Owen, Sidney James, M.A., student CHRIST CHURCH 83, where see page 408.

Owen, Thomas Griffith, born at Caerwys, co. Montgomery, 1860; 2s. David, gen. NON-COLLEGIATE, matric. 28 Jan., 82, aged 21; migrated to EXETER, B.A. 88, M.A. 91; HONOURS:—4 theology 87.

Owtram, rev. Cuthbert Ellidge, born at Surbiton, Surrey, 1864; 2s. Robert Hermon, gent. WORCESTER, matric. 18 Oct., 83, aged 19 (from the Charterhouse), B.A. 87, M.A. 90 (HONOURS:—3 theology 87); curate of Jimbourne, Kent, 88.

Oxley, James Charles Stewart, born at Secunderabad, India, 15 Nov., 1872; 1s. Charles Rawson, colonel in the army. CHRIST CHURCH, matric. 14 Oct., 92, aged 17.

Ozanne, James Duncan, born at Launceston, Tasmania, 1864; 3s. Joseph, gen. ST. EDMUND HALL, matric. 18 May, 83, aged 19, B.A. 86, M.A. 90.

Ozanne, Robert John Thorpe, born at St. Peter Port, Guernsey, 1863; 5s. John, D.Med. CORPUS CHRISTI, matric. 1 Feb., 80, aged 18 (from Elizabeth coll., Guernsey), scholar 81-5, B.A. 84, M.A. 89; HONOURS:—3 classical mods. 82, 2 classics 84.

STONE STRING COURSE, WINCHESTER CATHEDRAL.—*Pugin.*

P

Packard, Edward Turner, born at Bramford, Suffolk, 2 May, 1868; 1s. Edward, arm. TRINITY, matric. 15 Oct., 87, aged 19 (from Ipswich school), Ford student 86, B.A. 91 (HONOURS :—3 law 91); bar.-at-law, Inner Temple, 92.

Packe, rev. Hornce, born at Shangton, co. Leicester, 25 March, 1866; 4s. Henry Vere, rector. WORCESTER, matric. 22 Oct., 85, aged 19 (from St. Edward's school, Summertown), B.A. 90, M.A. 92.

Packer, James, born at Barbados 1874; 1s. James, planter. LINCOLN, matric. 25 Oct., 92, aged 18.

Packer, rev. Leonard Frederick, born in London 1865; 6s. John Graham, cler. MAGDALEN, matric. 19 Oct., 83, aged 18, B.A. 87, M.A. 91; curate of St. Helier's, Jersey, 91.

Paddison, Charles Edward, born at Stapleford, co. Lincoln, 1872; s. Charles Foster, gen. BRASENOSE, matric. 22 Oct., 91, aged 19, from Richmond gr. school.

Paddison, George Frederick, born at Stapleford, co. Lincoln, 7 June, 1873; 2s. Charles Foster, of Ingleby, co. Linc., gent. QUEEN'S, matric. 27 Oct., 92, aged 19 (from Richmond gr. school), hon. scholar and exhibitioner 92.

Paddison, Richard, born at Hampton, Middx., 1863; 1s. Howard, arm. BALLIOL, matric. 17 Oct., 82, aged 19 (from Tiverton school), Blundell scholar 82-6, B.A. 87, M.A. 90 (HONOURS :—2 classical mods. 84); bar.-at-law, Lincoln's Inn, 89.

Padley, Henry Madeley, born at Retford, Notts, 1862; o.s. John Charles, gent. NON-COLLEGIATE, matric. 14 Oct., aged 20, B.A. 86.

Page, Alfred Finch, born at Derby 2 Sept., 1873; 2s. Alfred Thomas, gent. MAGDALEN, matric. 18 Oct., 92, aged 19 (from Bradford gr. school), demy 91.

Page, Charles, born at Harrow, Middx., 1868; 1s. David, gen. ORIEL, matric. 19 Oct., 86, aged 18 (from King's coll. school), scholar 86; HONOURS :—1 classical mods. 88, 3 classics 90.

Page, Cyril John Noble, born in London 23 Oct., 1867; 5s. William Emanuel, D.Med. TRINITY, matric. 16 Dec., 87, aged 20, from Westminster school.

Page, Herbert Vivian, born at Lancaster 30 Oct., 1862; 3s. Alexander Shaw, vicar of Selsey, co. Glouc. WADHAM, matric. 17 Oct., 82, aged 19 (from Cheltenham coll.), exhibitioner 81, B.A. 87, M.A. 90 (HONOURS :—2 classical mods. 84, 3 classics 86). in the University eleven 83, 4, 5, 6, captain 85, University Rugby football XV. 84-5; assist.-master Blundell's school, Tiverton, 86-8, and Cheltenham coll. 88.

Page, rev. John Ernest, born at Bilston, co. Stafford, 1862; 2s. John William, gen. WADHAM, matric. 17 Oct., 82, aged 20, B.A. 88, M.A. 89; curate of St. Luke, Maidenhead, 89.

Page, Robert Henry Frederick, born at Sidmouth, Devon, 1855; 1s. Robert Hyde, arm. WADHAM, matric. 16 April, 83, aged 28, student Middle Temple 83.

Page, Sidney Herbert, born at Tettenhall, co. Staff., 28 Feb., 1870; 5s. John, gen. TRINITY, matric. 12 Oct., 89, aged 19 (from Wolverhampton school); HONOURS :— 2 classical mods. 91.

Paget, Francis, D.D. dean of CHRIST CHURCH 92, where see page 404.

Paget, Richard Arthur Surtees, born at Shepton Mallet, Somerset, 1869; 1s. Richard Horner, bart. MAGDALEN, matric. 22 Oct., 87, aged 18 (from Eton); HONOURS :—3 chemistry 91.

Pain, rev. Frederick William Goodyer, born at Kolapur, East Indies, 1858; 2s. Charles, gen. ST. ALBAN HALL, matric. 16 Oct., 80, aged 22; curate of All Saints', Manchester, 85-8, curate of Sacred Trinity, Salford, 88.

Paine, rev. Ernest Charles, born at Forest Hill, Kent, 1865; 2s. George William, gen. WADHAM, matric. 19 Oct., 85, aged 20 (from King's coll. school), B.A. 89 (HONOURS :—4 classics 89); curate of Berwick-upon-Tweed 91.

Paize, Gerald, born at Blackheath, Kent, 1865; 4s. Hannon, gent. CHRIST CHURCH, 1867; 4s. Herbert, arm. MAGDALEN, matric. 25 May, 83, aged 18.

Paine, Herbert Norman, born at Addlestone, Surrey, matric. 26 Jan., 86, aged 19, from Bradfield coll.

Paine, Marshall Harcourt, born at Addlestone, Surrey, 1863; 3s. John Marshall, arm. MERTON, matric. 3 June, 81, aged 18 (from Bradfield coll.), B.A. 84; bar.-at-law, Inner Temple, 87.

[457]   [458]

Paine, William Henry, born in London 1864; 15. William Stephen, arm. MAGDALEN, matric. 21 Jan., 82, aged 18 (from Winchester), B.A. 85; HONOURS:—3 history 85.

Paine, William Worship, born in London 2 Nov., 1861; 35. Thomas, arm. NEW COLL., matric. 16 Oct., 80, aged 18 (from Rugby), B.A. 84; HONOURS:—a classical mods. 8a, 1 law 84.

Painter, Harold Liscombe, born at Ryde, I.W., 21 Dec., 1872; 2s. Richard, gen. BALLIOL, matric. 11 Feb., 92, aged 19, from Clifton coll.

Paitson, Leonard William, born at Nether Wasdale, Cumberland, 6 April, 1863; o.s. John, cler. LINCOLN, matric. 20 Oct., 81, aged 18, from Rossall school.

Pakenham, Thomas, 4th earl of Longford (87), born in Dublin 19 Oct., 1864; 15. William Lygon, earl of Longford. CHRIST CHURCH, matric. 14 Oct., 81, aged 16 (from Winchester), B.A. 85, M.A. 89 (HONOURS:—2 history 85); lieut. and Life guards 88.

Pakenham, Thomas Cecil, born at Emsworth, Hants, 18 Sept., 1864; 3s. Thomas Alexander, arm. NEW COLL., matric. 12 Oct., 83, aged 19 (from Winchester), B.A. 86; bar.-at-law, Inner Temple, 91.

Palairet, Lionel Charles Hamilton, born at Grange-Over-Sands, co. Lanc., 1870; 1s. Henry Hamilton, arm. ORIEL, matric. 25 Oct., 89, aged 19 (from Repton school), in university eleven 90, 1, 2, captain 92-3.

Palairet, Richard Cameron North, born at Grange-Over-Sands, co. Lanc., 1871; 2s. Henry Hamilton, arm. ORIEL, matric. 22 Oct., 90, aged 19 (from Repton school), in University association football XI. 91.

Palgrave, Augustin Gifford, born at Reigate, Surrey, 1866; o.s. sir Reginald Francis Douce, K.C.B., clerk of the parliaments. MERTON, matric. 21 April, 85, aged 19, B.A. 89, M.A. 92; HONOURS:—4 law 88.

Palgrave, rev. Francis Milnes Temple, born in London 7 Jan., 1865; o.s. Francis Turner, professor of poetry. TRINITY, matric. 15 Oct., 83, aged 19 (from Winchester), B.A. 87, M.A. 92 (HONOURS:—3 classical mods. 85, 3 theology 87); curate of Hetton-le-Hole, co. Durham, 90.

Palgrave, Francis Turner, M.A., fellow EXETER 47-62, where see page 126.

Palin, Edward, B.D., fellow ST. JOHN'S 43-66, where see page 180.

Palin, Edward Watson, born at Linton, co. Hereford, 1868; 1s. Edward, vicar. CHRIST CHURCH, matric. 6 Dec., 87, aged 19 (from Shrewsbury school), B.A. 91; HONOURS:—2 physiology 91.

Palmer, Clement Charlton, born at Barton-under-Needwood, co. Stafford, 1872; 2s. Clement. NON-COLLEGIATE, matric. 15 Jan., 91, aged 19.

Palmer, ven. Edwin, D.D., canon CHRIST CHURCH 77, where see page 425.

Palmer, Edwin James, born in Oxford 10 Jan., 1869; 1s. Edwin, archdeacon of Oxford. BALLIOL, matric. 19 Oct., 87, aged 18 (from Winchester), scholar 86, jenkyns exhibitioner 19, fellow 91, B.A. 91; HONOURS:—accessit Hertford scholarship 88, 1 classical mods. 89, Craven scholarship 89, accessit Ireland scholarship 90, 1 classics 91.

Palmer, Gerard Walker, born at Langharne, co. Carmarthen, June, 1885; 3s. William James, arm. KEBLE, matric. 16 Oct., 83, aged 18 (from St. Edward's school, Summertown), B.A. 86, M.A. 91.

Palmer, Herbert, born at Bradfield, Berks, 31 May, 1867; 1s. James Howard, cler. MAGDALEN, matric. 21 Oct., 86, aged 19 (from Haileybury), B.A. 89 (HONOURS:—3 history 89), assistant schoolmaster.

Palmer, Hubert Greville, born in London 15 April, 1872; 1s. Greville Horsley, B.A., banker. BRASE-NOSE, matric. 21 Oct., 92, aged 20, from Eton.

Palmer, John Howard, born at Lincoln 1863; 2s. John, gent. EXETER, matric. 18 Oct., 82, aged 19 (from Christ's hospital), B.A. 86; HONOURS:—1 mathematical mods. 84, 2 mathematics 86.

Palmer, Roundell, earl of Selbourne, M.A., D.C.L., hon. fellow MAGDALEN 62, where see page 319.

Palmer, William Jackson, born at Lincoln 1871; 1s. George, pleb. NON-COLLEGIATE, matric. 13 Oct., 88, aged 17, B.A. 91.

Panioty, Constantine Demetrius, born at Calcutta 1859; 3s. Demetrius, assist. private sec. to viceroy of India. EXETER, matric. 15 May, 80, aged 20; bar.-at-law, Lincoln's Inn, 84.

Pannell, Arthur Pidgeon, born at Cullompton, Devon, 27 Oct., 1870; 4s. John Pidgeon, gent. ST. MARY HALL, matric. 18 Oct., 92, aged 21; assumed the additional name of Pannell by deed poll.

Pantin, Robert Gerald, born at Blackheath, Kent, 29 March, 1871; 3s. Charles, gen. deceased. WADHAM, matric. 14 Oct., 89, aged 18 (from Bradfield coll.), scholar 88; HONOURS:—2 classical mods. 91.

Pantin, William Edward Pinder, born in London 11 Dec., 1862; 1s. Charles, gen. LINCOLN, matric. 29 Jan., 81, aged 18 (from Blackheath school), scholar 80-4, B.A. 85, M.A. 89; HONOURS:—2 classical mods. 82, 2 classics 84.

Panting, Lawrence Christopher, born at Chebsey, co. Stafford, 1869; 2s. Lawrence, cler. BALLIOL, matric. 18 Oct., 88, aged 19 (from Shrewsbury gr. school), scholar 87, B.A. 91; HONOURS:—2 chemistry 91.

Pape, Clarence Jackson, born at Keswick, Cumberland, 3 Jan., 1872; 4s. David, gen. QUEEN'S, matric. 24 Oct., 90, aged 18 (from St. Bees gr. school), exhibitioner 89.

Papillon, Edward Thomas, born at Oxford 24 May, 1873; o.s. Thomas Leslie, vicar of Writtle, Essex. NEW COLL., matric. 14 Oct., 92, aged 19 (from Marlborough), scholar 92.

Papillon, Godfrey Keppel, born at Colchester 24 Sept., 1867; 3s. Philip Oxenden (late M.P.). MERTON, matric. 21 Oct., 86, aged 19, from Marlborough.

Papillon, Pelham Rawstorne, born in London 22 June, 1861; 1s. Philip Oxenden, late M.P. UNIVERSITY COLL., matric. 13 Oct., 83, aged 19 (from Winchester), B.A. 87, M.A, and B.C.L. 90 (HONOURS:—2 classical mods. 85, 2 law 87, 1 civil law 88); bar.-at-law, Inner Temple, 91.

Papillon, Richard, born at Reading, Berks, 1863; 2s. Alexander Frenk William, major R.A. EXETER, matric. 18 Oct., 82, aged 19 (from Basingstoke), B.A. 85, M.A. 89.

Papillon, Thomas Leslie, M.A., fellow MERTON 65-9 (page 98), and fellow NEW COLL. 69-84, where see page 217.

Paravicini, Francis de, M.A., fellow BALLIOL 78, where see page 63.

Pargiter, rev. Alfred Arthur, born at Taunton, Somerset, 10 Oct., 1867; 7s. Robert, cler. JESUS COLL., matric. 20 Oct., 86, aged 19 (from Cheltenham coll.), scholar 86, B.A. 90; HONOURS:—2 classical mods. 88, 3 classics 90.

Park, Atherton Charles, born in London Oct., 1870; 1s. Alexander Waldegrave, arm. CHRIST CHURCH, matric. 12 Oct., 88, aged 17, from Harrow.

Parke, Edmond, born at Plymouth 1871; 1s. Richard, arm. NON-COLLEGIATE, matric. 12 Oct., 89, aged 18, from Newton Abbot coll.

Parke, William Alcock Whitbeck, born at Piddletown, Dorset, 1866; 1s. William, arm. CHRIST CHURCH, matric. 16 Oct., 85, aged 19, B.A. and M.A. 92.

Parker, Alfred John, born at Wednesbury, co. Stafford, 1866; 1s. George Ellis Ley, gen. NON-COLLEGIATE, matric. 23 Oct., 86, aged 20, from a Sedgeley school.

Parker, Arthur Percy, born at Newcastle-upon-Tyne 1867; 2s. Henry, arm, deceased. MAGDALEN, matric. 21 Oct., 86, aged 19, B.A. 90; in the Oxford eight 88.

Parker, Charles Arthur, born at Claxby, co. Lincoln, 1863; 6s. Richard, cler. NON-COLLEGIATE, matric. 4 June, 81, aged 18, from Bradfield coll.

Parker, Charles John, M.A., NON-COLLEGIATE, where see page 638.

Parker, Charles John Ernest, born at Grantham, co. Lincoln, 21 May, 1864; 1s. Charles John Bullivant, lieut.-col. MAGDALEN, matric. 16 Oct., 84, aged 20 (from Wellington), B.A. 89.

Parker, rev. Charles Lewis Edward, born in London 4 March, 1861; 1s. Charles Lewis, solicitor. NEW COLL., matric. 16 Oct., 80, aged 19 (from Charterhouse and Harrow), B.A. 84, M.A. 87 (HONOURS: —2 classical mods. 82, 4 history 84); assist. master Cordwalles, Maidenhead, 85-9, headmaster St. James coll., South Leigh, 89.

Parker, Charles Sandbach, born at Aigburth, co. Lanc., 1 Nov., 1864; 1s. Samuel Sandbach, arm. UNIVERSITY COLL., matric. 13 Oct., 83, aged 18, B.A. 87; HONOURS:—4 history 87.

Parker, Charles Sharpe, born in London 10 Jan., 1831; 4s. Reginald Amphlett, solicitor. WADHAM, matric. 17 Dec., 89, aged 38, B.A. 92.

Parker, Charles Stuart, M.A., fellow UNIVERSITY COLL. 54-69, where see page 32.

Parker, rev. Claud Campbell, born at Putney April, 1868; 2s. Joseph, gen. KEBLE, matric. 17 Oct., 87, aged 19, B.A. 90; HONOURS:—3 history 90.

Parker, Cyril Robert Holme, born at Carlisle 7 Nov., 1869; 3s. Thomas Holme, gen. WORCESTER, matric. 16 Oct., 88, aged 18, from Harrow.

Parker, Ernest Julius, born at Rowledge, Surrey, 20 Oct., 1872; 1s. Arthur William, cler. BRASENOSE, matric. 22 Oct., 92, aged 19 (from Marlborough coll.), scholar 92.

Parker, Evelyn Stuart, born at Childwall, co. Lanc., 22 June, 1869; 1s. Alfred Traill, arm. NEW COLL., matric. 12 Oct., 88, aged 19 (from Eton), B.A. 91; HONOURS:—3 classical mods. 90, 3 law 91.

Parker, Francis Henry Mervyn, born at Temple Sowerby, Westmorland, 4 Jan., 1873; 1s. Travers, esq. TRINITY, matric. 15 Oct., 92, aged 19, from Sedbergh school.

Parker, Francis William, born at Grantham, co. Lincoln, 26 March, 1868; 3s. Charles John Bullivant, lieut.-col. MAGDALEN, matric. 22 Oct. 87, aged 19 (from Wellington coll.); HONOURS:— 3 history 91.

Parker, Frederic Moore Searle, born at East Barnet, Herts, 9 Oct., 1870; 1s. Frederick Searle, arm. MERTON, matric. 19 Oct., 89, aged 17 (from Eton), postmaster 89; HONOURS:—2 classical mods. 91.

Parker, hon. Geoffrey Lawrence, born in London 24 May, 1874; 2s. Lawrence, earl of Rosse, K.P. BALLIOL, matric. 18 Oct., 92, aged 18, from Winchester.

Parker, George Bertie, born at Oxford 1867; o.s. George, gent. QUEEN'S, matric. 26 Jan., 85, aged 18.

Parker, George Edward, born at Oxford 1869; 1s. George, gen. NON-COLLEGIATE, matric. 27 Jan., 87, aged 18 (from New coll.), B.A. 90.

Parker, Henry Burkitt, born at Dublin 27 Oct., 1870; 1s. Henry Richard, LL.D. Dublin, headmaster Campbell coll., Belfast. HERTFORD, matric. 20 Oct., 91 (from Methodist coll., Belfast), scholar 90.

Parker, Henry Royster, born at Newcastle-upon-Tyne 1866; 1s. Henry, arm. BRASENOSE, matric. 22 Jan., 85, aged 19 (from Eton), B.A. 88; in the University eight 87, 8, 9.

Parker, John Clement, born at High Wycombe, Bucks, 19 Feb., 1871; 1s. John, solicitor. CHRIST CHURCH, matric. 17 Oct., 89, aged 18, from Uppingham school.

Parker, Richard William England, born at Shidfield, Hants, 1863; 1s. Richard, cler. CHRIST CHURCH, matric. 13 Oct., 82, aged 19 (from Clifton coll.), exhibitioner 82-6, B.A. 86; HONOURS: —2 classical mods. 84, 3 classics 86.

Parker, rev. Robert John Crompton, born at York 17 Feb., 1861; o.s. John, solicitor. WADHAM, matric. 11 Oct., 84, aged 23 (from Merchiston castle, Edinburgh), B.A. 88, M.A. 91; curate of Drighton 89.

Parker, Thomas, born at Sunderland, co. Durham, 1867; 1s. Thomas, gent. BRASENOSE, matric. 23 Oct., 85, aged 18 (from Durham gr. school), B.A. 89, M.A. 92 (HONOURS:—3 law 89), in University Rugby football xv. 88.

Parker, rev. Thomas Brownbill James, born at Stockport, Cheshire, 1 Dec., 1859; 2s. Joseph, gent. WORCESTER, matric. 21 Oct., 80, aged 20 (from Manchester gr. school); B.A. 83 (HONOURS:— 3 theology 83); rector of Whitfield, Northants. 89.

Parker, William Herbert, born at Iffley, near Oxford, 15 Aug., 1859; 1s. James Smith, arm. NON-COLLEGIATE, matric. 23 Oct., 80, aged 21, from Rugby.

Parkes, Alfred Joseph, born at Sheffield 20 April, 1862; 3s. David, professor. EXETER, matric. 17 Oct., 88, aged 26, from Firth coll.

Parkes, rev. Alfred Marshall, born at Chester 1866; o.s. Alfred, gent. ST. JOHN'S, matric. 11 Oct., 84, aged 18, B.A. 87, M.A. 91; curate of St. Matthew, Newcastle-upon-Tyne, 91.

Parkes, Harry Rutherford, born in London 18 Nov., 1862; 1s. sir Henry, K.C.B., G.C.M.G., etc. BRASENOSE, matric. 17 March, 81, aged 18 (from Halleybury), B.A. 84; a solicitor 88.

Parkes, William Herbert, born at Willenhall, co. Stafford, 30 Oct., 1870; 1s. Samuel, gen. EXETER, matric. 18 Oct., 90, aged 19, from Wolverhampton school.

Parkhurst, Lewis Evan, born at Pontymoil, co. Monmouth;—n, gent. JESUS COLL., matric. 18 Oct., 82, aged 19 (from Magdalen coll. school), scholar 82-6, B.A. 86, B.A led. 91; HONOURS:—2 chemistry 86.

Parkhurst, William Horatio, born at Ebbw Vale, co. Monmouth, 1861; 1s. Horatio John, gen. JESUS COLL., matric. 23 Oct., 80, aged 19.

Parkin, George Lewis, arm. ST. JOHN'S, matric. 15 Oct., 81, aged 19 (from Eton), B.A. 85.

Parkin, William Hugh, born at Elswick, Northumberland, July, 1869; o.s. William Hugh, major. BRASENOSE, matric. 24 Jan., 89, aged 19 (from Nedbergh gr. school), in University Rugby football XV. 91.

Parkinson, Claude Lewis James Musgrave, born at Carmarthen 30 Jan., 1870; 1s. Robert, cler. JESUS COLL., matric. 14 Oct., 89, aged 19 (from Manchester gr. school), exhibitioner 89, B.A. 92; HONOURS:—3 chemistry 92.

Parkinson, Frederick Wilton, born at Nymet Rowland, Devon, May, 1872; o.s. Richard, cler. KEBLE, matric. 11 Oct., 90, aged 18, from Crewkerne school.

Parlby, Walter Coventry Hall, born at Plymouth 1862; 3s. John Hall, cler. ST. JOHN'S, matric. 15 Oct., 81, aged 19, B.A. 85, M.A. 89.

Parlett, Leonard Montague, born at Huntingdon 28 May, 1870; 1s. John, arm. KEBLE, matric. 30 Jan., 90, aged 19 (from Bradfield coll.); assist. commissioner, Burma, 91.

Parmiter, Spurrier Clavell, born at Winchester 1867; 1s. John Spurrier, gen. BALLIOL, matric. 24 Oct., 85, aged 18 (from Ely school); exhibitioner ORIEL 85, B.A. 89, M.A. 92 (HONOURS :—2 classical mods. 87, 1 classics 89); president of the Oxford union society 88.

Parnell, rev. Arthur Henry, born in London 20 March, 1861; 2s. Richard, cler. ST. MARY HALL, matric. 19 Oct., 81, aged 20 (from St. Paul's school); migrated to MERTON, B.A. 85 (HONOURS :—4 theology 85); curate of Harlow, Essex, 85.

Parnell, Thomas Augustus, B.A., fellow ST. JOHN'S 40-5, where see page 479.

Parody, Augustus Lyon, born at Gibraltar 20 Feb., 1860; 2s. Richard, gen. BALLIOL, matric. 17 April, 80, aged 20.

Parr, John Walter, born at Swinton, co. Lanc., 1864; 1s. John Robert, cler. NON-COLLEGIATE, matric. 13 Oct., 83, aged 19, from Oakham school, Rutland.

Parr, Thomas Henning, born at Parkstone, Dorset, 12 Nov., 1864; 1s. John, cler. WORCESTER, matric. 18 Oct., 83, aged 18 (from Marlborough coll.), exhibitioner 83, B.A. 88, M.A. 90 (HONOURS :— 1 classical mods. 85, 2 classics 87); bar.-at-law, Inner Temple, 92.

Parry, Charles Hubert Hastings, M.A., D.Mus., choragus 84, see page 12.

Parry, Frederick Sydney, born at Hackney, Middx., 5 June, 1861; 2s. Edward, bishop of Dover. BALLIOL, matric. 21 Oct., 80, aged 19 (from Winchester), B.A. 85; HONOURS :—2 classical mods. 82, 2 classics 84.

Parry, Herbert Thomas, born at Ashton, Cheshire, 19 Aug., 1869; 2s. Henry, gen. NON-COLLEGIATE, matric. 12 Oct., 89, aged 20 (from Ellesmere coll.); migrated to WORCESTER, B.A. 92.

Parry, John Edward, born at Blackwood, co. Monmouth, 1859; 2s. John, cler. NON-COLLEGIATE, matric. 4 May, 81, aged 22.

Parry, John Jeffreys Bulkeley Jones-, born at Torpoint, Cornwall, 12 Dec., 1865; 1s. John Parry, capt. R.N. MAGDALEN, matric. 16 Oct., 82, aged 18 (from St. Mark's school, Windsor); lieut. duke of Cornwall's light infantry 86.

Parry, rev. John Morgan, born at Wolverhampton 9 Nov., 1867; 2s. John, cler. WORCESTER, matric. 22 Oct., 85, aged 17 (from Wolverhampton gr. school), B.A. 90, M.A. 92; curate of Bangor-Monachorum, co. Denbigh, 90.

Parry, Methold Sidney, born at Putney 23 Sept., 1863; 1s. Sidney, lieut.-col. R.H.A., deceased. UNIVERSITY COLL., matric. 28 April, 90, aged 26, from Cheltenham coll.

Parry, Morris Vivian, born at Wolverhampton 24 Oct., 1865; 1s. John, cler. WADHAM, matric. 17 Oct., 82, aged 16 (from Wolverhampton gr. school), B.A. 86, M.A. 89; lieut. the Hampshire regt. 90.

Parry, Oswald Hutton, born at Clifton, co. Glouc., 18 Nov., 1868; 8s. Edward St. John. cler. MAGDALEN, matric. 22 Oct., 87, aged 18 (from the Charterhouse), exhibitioner 88; HONOURS : —2 classical mods. 89, 3 classics 91.

Parry, Owen Glyndwr, born at Dobithuen, co. Montgomery, 1868; o.s. William, D.Med. MERTON, matric. 22 Oct., 87, aged 19, B.A. 91; HONOURS :—2 classical mods. 89.

Parry, Samuel Pryce, born at Oswestry, Salop, 30 May, 1866; 2s. Thomas Pryce, gen. QUEEN'S, matric. 22 Oct., 84, aged 18 (from Oswestry gr. school), B.A. 88, M.A. 91; HONOURS :—2 theology 88.

Parry, Thomas Parry Jones-, born at Keswick, Cumberland, 1869; elder son of Thomas Parry, ann. HERTFORD, matric. 27 Oct., 87, aged 18, from Sherborne school.

Parson, William Campbell, born at Finchampstead, Bucks, 21 June, 1871; 1s. John Campbell, cler. TRINITY, matric. 11 Oct., 90, aged 19, from Marlborough coll.

Parsons, Gerald Augustus Moutray, born at Lewes, Sussex, 20 March, 1870; 3s. Augustus James, cler. WORCESTER, matric. 16 Oct., 88, aged 18, from St. Paul's choir school.

Parsons, Harold George, born at Blackheath, Kent, 8 March, 1867; 1s. George, gen. WADHAM, matric. 16 Oct., 86, aged 19 (from Melbourne gr. school), scholar 85, B.A. 90 (HONOURS :—2 classical mods. 88, 2 classics 90); bar.-at-law, Inner Temple, 92.

Parsons, Henry Francis Crane, born at Bridgewater, Somst., 17 June, 1874; 1s. Henry James, Indian judge. EXETER, matric. 13 Feb., 92, aged 18, from Cheltenham coll.

Parsons, John Francis, born at Oxford 19 March, 1872; 1s. John, banker. MERTON, matric. 22 Oct., 91, aged 19 (from Rugby).

Parsons, Octavius Sydney, born at Simla, East Indies, 18 July, 1870; 7s. James Edmund Bacon, arm. QUEEN'S, matric. 22 Oct., 89, aged 19 (from Dulwich coll.), scholar 89; assist. commissioner, Burma, 91.

Parsons, William Edward, Lord Oxmantown, born in London 14 June, 1873; 1s. Laurence, earl of Rosse. CHRIST CHURCH, matric. 16 Oct., 91, aged 18, from Eton.

Purtington, Henry, M.A., student CHRIST CHURCH 26-34, where see page 413.

Partington, William Charles Mackenzie, born at Manchester 15 Sept., 1858; 2s. William Henry, gen., deceased. QUEEN'S, matric. 30 Oct., 85, aged 20.

Partridge, Aubrey Arthur Hungerford, born at Handsworth, co. Stafford, 1860; 1s. Arthur, arm. BALLIOL, matric. 21 Oct., 80, aged 20 (from Birmingham gr. school), B.A. 84, M.A. 92; HONOURS :—2 history 84.

Partridge, Lionel Stroud, born at Castle Bromwich, co. Warwick, 17 April, 1865; 2s. Joseph Arthur, of Oxford, arm. MAGDALEN, matric. 16 Oct., 84, aged 19 (from Magdalen coll. school), B.A. 88.

Partridge, Walter Ernest Clarke, born at Upper Rickinghall, Suffolk, 9 Nov., 1873; 1s. Walter Henry, cler. KEBLE, matric. 15 Oct., 92, aged 18, from High school, Oxford, and Haileybury coll.

Pascoe, rev. Wellington Renton, born at Philipstown, Ireland, 25 May, 1856; y.s. Thomas, gen. LINCOLN, matric. 19 Jan., 85, aged 28 (from King Williamstown gr. school, so. Africa), B.A. 90, M.A. 91; curate of St. Barnabas, Oxford, 90.

Passmore, William Philip, born at North Molton, Devon, 3 June, 1851; y.s. Francis Burdett, arm. NON-COLLEGIATE, matric. 23 May, 85, aged 33 (from Totnes school); migrated to EXETER, B.A. 88, M.A. 92.

Pater, Walter Horatio, M.A., fellow BRASENOSE 64, where see page 347.

Paterson, Alexander Macdonald, born at Rock Ferry, Cheshire, 25 Aug., 1867; 4s. Thomas Simpson, gen., deceased. NEW COLL., matric. 14 Oct., 87, aged 20 (from Loretto school), B.A. 91 (HONOURS :—2 classical mods. 89, 3 classics 91), in university Rugby football XV. 89, 90.

Paterson, Arthur Bourne, born at Coulter, co. Lanark, 1861; 1s. Robert, arm. HERTFORD, matric. 18 Oct., 80, aged 19 (from the Charterhouse), B.A. 83; HONOURS :—3 mathematical mods. 81, 3 history 83.

Paterson, rev. Gordon Walker, born at St. Andrews, N.B., 4 July, 1856; 4s. John, gen. TRINITY, matric. 11 Oct., 82, aged 19 (from St. Andrew's university, M.A. 82), B.A. 85, M.A. 90; examining chaplain diocese of Gibraltar 89.

From Ingram's Memorial.

Paterson, rev. Leslie Rimmer, born at Rock Ferry, Cheshire, Feb., 1866; 3s. Thomas Simpson, gen. KEBLE, matric. 22 Oct., 85, aged 19 (from Loretto school), B.A. 88, M.A. 92 (HONOURS:—4 theology 88); curate of St. Margaret, Walton-on-the-Hill, co. Lanc., 90.

Paterson, Marwood, born at Edgbaston 29 Nov., 1872; 1s. Thomas Walter, merchant. NON-COLLEGIATE, matric. 17 Oct., 91, aged 18 (from Highbury Park school); migrated to EXETER 18 Oct., 92.

Paton, Alfred Vaughan, born at Sheffield, Yorks, 18 Nov., 1861; 1s. John Brown, D.D., nonconformist minister. TRINITY, matric. 16 Oct., 80, aged 18 (from Nottingham school and Clifton coll.), scholar 80-4, B.A. 87, M.A. 80 (HONOURS:—2 classical mods. 82); lecturer in the college of science University of Durham, a student of the Middle Temple 83.

Paton, Frederick Henry Victor, born at Ragusa, Austria, 24 May, 1869; 2s. Archibald Andrew, arm. LINCOLN, matric. 18 Oct., 88, aged 19 (from Fettes coll.), B.A. 92; HONOURS:—4 history 91.

Paton, rev. John Duguid, born at Tuddenham, Suffolk, 1857; 3s. Alexander, cler. ST. EDMUND HALL, matric. 22 Jan., 80, aged 23, B.A. 81; curate of St. Mary, Southampton, 87.

Paton, Morton Brown, born at Nottingham 24 June, 1871; 4s. John Brown, M.A. London, D.D. Glasgow, nonconformist minister. BALLIOL, matric. 14 Oct., 90, aged 19, from Nottingham high school.

Paton, Thomas Lyall, born in parish of Liff and Benvie, co. Forfar, 29 Oct., 1868; y.s. William Mudie, gen. WADHAM, matric. 15 Oct., 87, aged 18 (from Fettes coll.), scholar 86, B.A. 90; HONOURS:—2 classical mods. 89.

Le Patourel, Harry Francis Garnier, born at St. Peter Port, Isle of Guernsey, 1872; 2s. Mesurier, gen. PEMBROKE, matric. 25 Oct., 90, aged 18 (from Elizabeth coll., Guernsey), exhibitioner 90.

Le Patourel, rev. Wallace Mackenzie, born at St. Peter Port, isle of Guernsey, 1865; 1s. Mesurier, arm. BALLIOL, matric. 19 Oct., 86, aged 21 (from Elizabeth coll., Guernsey), B.A. 90; HONOURS:—4 classics 90.

Patten, Alexander, born at Edinburgh June, 1863; 6s. James, arm. ORIEL, matric. 31 Oct., 82, aged 19, from Clifton coll.

Patterson, James Bruce, born at Southwark, Surrey, 23 Feb., 1871; 3s. Alexander, pleb. JESUS COLL., matric. 14 Oct., 89, aged 18 (from Southwark gr. school), scholar 89; HONOURS:—2 classical mods. 91.

Patterson, Melville Watson, born at Birkenhead 1873; 3s. William, merchant. NEW COLL., matric. 14 Oct., 92, aged 19 (from Winchester), scholar 91.

Patterson, Sutton, born at Newcastle-on-Tyne 1849; o.s. Robert, gen. NON-COLLEGIATE, matric. 6 Feb., 80, aged 31, from Nether Hall school, Doncaster.

Patterson, William Caine, born at Birkenhead 1868; 1s. William, arm. BALLIOL, matric. 19 Oct., 87, aged 19 (from Clifton coll.); selected candidate Indian c.s. 87.

Pattinson, Reginald, born at Edge Hill, Liverpool, 11 April, 1873; 1s. John Richard, gen. ORIEL, matric. 27 Oct., 91, aged 18, from Harrow.

Patton, rev. Thomas Lionel, born at Taunton, Somerset, 17 July, 1862; 1s. Lionel, gen. QUEEN'S, matric. 28 Oct., 81, aged 19 (from Newton Abbot coll.), B.A. 85, M.A. and B.C.L. 92; curate of All Saints, Gloucester, 86-8, and of St. Luke, Berwick St., 88-90.

Pattrick, Arthur Henry Saint, M.A., QUEEN'S, where see page 184.

Paul, Edward Clifford, born at Llanbadarnfawr, co. Cardigan, 1863; 3s. Theodore, gen. JESUS COLL., matric. 23 Oct., 80, aged 17 (from Hammersmith school), B.A. 84, M.A. 87.

Paul, rev. Frederick Campbell, born at Waltham Cross, Herts, 1861; 2s. William, gen. MERTON, matric. 18 Oct., 80, aged 19 (from Stortford school), postmaster 80-4, B.A. 84, M.A. 87 (HONOURS:—2 classical mods. 82, 2 classics 84); rector of St. Peter, Bristol, 92.

Paul, George Woodfield, M.A., fellow MAGDALEN 42-8, where see page 321.

Paulet, Gerald Hammerton, born at Kirk Hammerton, Yorks, 22 March, 1864; 2s. Charles Newton, vicar. MERTON, matric. 22 Jan., 89, aged 24, B.A. 92.

Paulson, Richard Elwyn, born at Addington, Kent, Aug., 1860; 4s. George Robert, rector. HERTFORD, matric. 1 Feb., 81, aged 20.

Pauw, Edward Klaas, born at Dumblane, co. Perth, 1871; 2s. Klaas, arm. BALLIOL, matric. 17 Oct., 89, aged 18 (from Rye coll., Peckham Rye); assist. commissioner Oudh 91.

Pavey, Alfred Katenbeck, born at Bingham, Notts, 1865; 1s. Alfred, cler. HERTFORD, matric. 18 Oct., 83, aged 20, B.A. 86, M.A. 90.

Paxton, Henry Arthur, born at Bangalore, East Indies, Sept., 1864; 2s. George, arm. CHARSLEY'S HALL, matric. 22 Jan., 84, aged 19, from Cowley school.

Payler, Frederic Trafford Morgan, born at Leamington 15 Sept., 1872; 1s. Frederick Payler Morgan, cler. BRASENOSE, matric. 22 Oct., 91, aged 19.

Payne, Charles Herbert, born at Abingdon, Berks, 9 Jan., 1869; o.s. Charles Edward, gen. MERTON, matric. 22 Oct., 87, aged 18 (from Abingdon school), B.A. 91, M.A. 92; HONOURS:—3 mathematical mods. 89, 4 theology 91.

Payne, Edward John, M.A., fellow UNIVERSITY COLL. 72, where see page 29.

Payne, Joseph Frank, D.Med., fellow MAGDALEN 63-83. where see page 324.

Payne, Julius Delmege, born at Weymouth, Dorset, 30 Oct., 1870; 1s. Samuel Ward, rector of Delamere, Cheshire. ST. JOHN'S, matric. 12 Oct., 89, aged 18 (from Merchant Taylors' school), scholar 89; HONOURS:—2 classical mods. 91.

Payne, Peter George Stanhope, born at Woburn, Beds, 16 July, 1860; 3s. Salusbury Gillies, sol-disant, bart. UNIVERSITY COLL., matric. 15 May, 80, aged 19 (from Rugby), B.A. 84 (HONOURS:— 2 law 83); bar.-at-law, Inner Temple, 85.

Payne, Robert Sidney, born at Wallingford St. Mary, Berks, May, 1874; 1s. Sidney, J.P. ORIEL, matric. 27 Oct., 92, aged 18, from Lancing coll.

Payne, Robert Whitworth, born at Frome, Somerset, 3 July, 1871; 1s. Robert, arm. CHRIST CHURCH, matric. 10 Oct., 90, aged 19 (from Shrewsbury gr. school), scholar 89.

Peacey, rev. William John, born in London 29 July, 1860; 3s. Arthur Thomas, gen. NON-COLLEGIATE, matric. 15 Oct., 81, aged 21; migrated to MERTON, B.A. 84, M.A. 88 (HONOURS:— 3 history 84); curate of Tankersley, Yorks, 88.

Peache, Gilbert Alan, born at Mangotsfield, co. Glouc., 30 Jan., 1868; 4s. Alfred, cler. PEMBROKE, matric. 28 Oct., 86, aged 18, from Haileybury.

Peachey, Gilbert Peverell, born in London 9 June, 1874; 2s. James Pearse, bar.-at-law. QUEEN'S, matric. 9 Feb., 92, aged 17, from Bradfield coll.

30

Peachey, James Herbert, born in London 18 Feb., 1868; 1s. James Pearso, bar.-at-law. QUEEN'S, matric. 25 Oct., 86, aged 18 (from Bradfield coll.), scholar 86, B.A. 90 (HONOURS:—3 classical mods. 88, 2 history 90, Arnold essay 92), librarian of Oxford union society 90.

Peacock, Arthur Braithwaite, born at Barnsley, Yorks., 15 Aug., 1864; 3s. William Harrison, solicitor. NON-COLLEGIATE, matric. 13 Oct., 88, aged 24 (from Barnsley high school), B.A. 92; HONOURS:—2 history 92.

Peacock, Basil Wilkinson, born at Stamford, co. Lincoln, 7 Sept., 1869; 4s. William Henry, arm. MERTON, matric. 17 Oct., 88, aged 19 (from Wellington), B.A. 91; HONOURS:—4 theology 91.

Peacock, Charles Alfred, born at Bosbury, co. Hereford, 19 Feb., 1868; 1s. Edwin, vicar of Nether Exe, Devon. NON-COLLEGIATE, matric. 11 Oct., 90, aged 22, from Pynes house school, Thorverton.

Peacock, Francis, born at Sunderland 18 Jan., 1869; 6s. James, shipbroker. ST. EDMUND HALL, matric. 20 Oct., 90, aged 23, from a Sunderland school.

Peacock, Frederick, born at Mentone, France, 20 Dec., 1867; o.s. Frederick Barnes, of the Indian c.s. NEW COLL., matric. 18 Jan., 87, aged 19 (from Eton); bar.-at-law, Inner Temple, 89.

Peacock, Mark Beauchamp, born at Brighton 2 March, 1860; 1s. Mark Beauchamp, bar.-at-law. TRINITY, matric. 17 Jan., 80, aged 19, from Wellington coll), B.A. 83, M.A. 86 (HONOURS:—3 law 83); student Lincoln's Inn 82.

Peake, Arthur Samuel, born at Leek, co. Stafford, 1866; 2s. Samuel, gen. ST. JOHN'S, matric. 13 Oct., 83, aged 17 (from Coventry school), scholar 83-5, B.A. 87; fellow MERTON 90, M.A. 91; HONOURS:—3 classical mods. 85, 1 theology 87, Denyer and Johnson theological scholarship 85, Ellerton theological essay 90.

Peake, Charles William, born at Tonbridge, Kent, 25 Oct., 1863; 1s. Charles Richard, banker. MAGDALEN, matric. 19 Oct., 83, aged 19 (from Magdalen coll. school), scholar HERTFORD 84, B.A. 87; HONOURS:—1 mathematical mods. 85, 2 mathematics 87, 3 physiology 88.

Peake, Edward, born at Chepstow, co. Monmouth, 1861; 2s. Richard, arm. ORIEL, matric. 20 Jan., 80, aged 19 (from Marlborough coll.), B.A. 83, M.A. 86 (HONOURS:—4 history 83), in the University eleven 81, 2, 3.

Peall, George Thomas, born in London 13 Dec., 1873; 1s. George Thomas, governor of 'Truant' school, London. NON-COLLEGIATE, matric. 15 Oct., 92, aged 18, from Stationers' school, Fleet Street.

Pearce, John William Ernest, born at Bristol 4 April, 1864; 1s. Henry Edwin, gen. MERTON, matric. 18 Oct., 81, aged 17 (from Manchester gr. school), postmaster 81-5, B.A. 85, M.A. 88; HONOURS:—1 classical mods. 83, 2 classics 85.

Pearce, Wilson Bennie Manley, born in London 1872; 5s. Stephen, artist. LINCOLN, matric. 23 Oct., 91, aged 19, from St. Paul's school.

Peareth, John Lennox, born at Edyll, co. Forfar, 1867; 3s. William, arm. BRASENOSE, matric. 20 Oct., 86, aged 19 (from Wellington), B.A. 90.

Pearkes, rev. William André, born at Watford, Herts, 1864; 4s. Edward, gen. ST. EDMUND HALL, matric. 22 Oct., 87, aged 23, B.A. 91.

Pearse, Alexander Joseph, born in Madagascar 8 Jan., 1869; 1s. Joseph, foreign missionary. NON-COLLEGIATE, matric. 17 Oct., 91, aged 22, from Blackheath missionary school and Edinburgh university.

Pearse, George Wingate, M.A., fellow CORPUS CHRISTI 49-51, where see page 382.

Pearse, rev. Reginald Vincent Devill, born at Barcheston, co. Warwick, 1862; 1s. Vincent, cler. ST. EDMUND HALL, matric. 2 June, 80, aged 18; migrated to NEW INN HALL, B.A. 85 (Balliol 87), M.A. 89; vicar of Charlton-Horethorn, Dorset, 89.

Pearson, Alexander, born at Edinburgh 1865; 1s. David Alexander, W.S. BRASENOSE, matric. 7 June, 84, aged 19 (from Loretto school), B.A. 89.

Pearson, Andrew, born at Laurence Kirk, co. Kincardine, 1866; 2s. David Alexander, arm. BRASENOSE, matric. 23 Oct., 85, aged 19, from Loretto school.

Pearson, Charles Henry, M.A., fellow ORIEL 54-73, where see page 153.

Pearson, rev. Charles William, born at Whitehaven 1848; 1s. William, gen. NON-COLLEGIATE, matric. 14 Oct., 82, aged 34 (from Church Missionary coll., Islington), B.A. 86, M.A. 89 (HONOURS: —2 theology 86); has served various curacies since 77, curate of Christ Church, Stanford, 91.

Pearson, Edgar Crosfield, born in Liverpool 28 July, 1873; 1s. Samuel, minister. TRINITY, matric. 15 Oct., 92, aged 19, from Manchester and Highgate schools.

Pearson, Frederic William, born at Wrenthorpe, Yorks, 28 March, 1873; 1s. William, gen. EXETER, matric. 22 Oct., 91, aged 18 (from Wakefield gr. school), scholar 92.

Pearson, George Allen Fisher, born at Combe, Hants, 29 Sept., 1869; 1s. George, cler. ST. MARY HALL, matric. 14 Oct., 89, aged 20.

Pearson, George Howard, born at Handsworth, co. Staff., 15 Jan., 1873; 7s. Joseph Hichman, ironmaster. ST. JOHN'S, matric. 22 Oct., 91, aged 18, from Shrewsbury gr. school.

Pearson, Harry, born at Gainsborough, co. Lincoln, 22 Jan., 1874; 2s. Isaac, merchant. TRINITY, matric. 15 Oct., 92, aged 18, from Repton school.

Pearson, John Henry, born at Surbiton, Surrey, 1858; 1s. Henry Daniel, cler. CHRIST CHURCH, matric. 21 May, 80, aged 22.

Pearson, Robert Barclay, born at Laurence Kirk, N.B., 20 Nov., 1871; 4s. David Alexander, W.S. BRASENOSE, matric. 22 Oct., 91, aged 19, from Loretto school.

Pearson, Roland George, born at Gainsborough, co. Lincoln, 1867; 2s. Edward arm. HERTFORD, matric. 22 Oct., 86, aged 19, B.A. 89.

Pearson, Thomas, M.A., fellow QUEEN'S 33-41, where see page 177.

Pease, Cyril Arthington, born at Westbury, co. Glouc., 16 June, 1868; 6s. Thomas, late of Westbury on Trym, gen. LINCOLN, matric. 21 Oct., 87, aged 19 (from Clifton coll.), exhibitioner 87, B.A. 91; HONOURS:—2 classical mods. 89, 3 classics 91.

Pease, Howard, born at Saltwell, co. Durham, 12 July, 1863; 1s. John William, of Newcastle-on-Tyne banker. BALLIOL, matric. 17 Oct., 82, aged 19 (from Clifton coll.), B.A. 87; HONOURS:— 2 classical mods. 84, 3 classics 86.

Pease, John William Beaumont, born at Pendower, Northumberland, 4 July, 1869; 2s. John William, of Newcastle-upon-Tyne, banker. NEW COLL., matric. 12 Oct., 88, aged 19 (from Marlborough coll.), B.A. 91; HONOURS:—3 history 91.

Pease, Joseph Robinson, born at Raywell, Cotting banker, Yorks, 27 Jan., 1873; 1s. Henry Joseph, banker. PEMBROKE, matric. 18 Oct., 91, aged 18, from Harrow.

Peachey, Richard Francis, born at Leytonstone, Essex, 1872; 2s. John Thomas Primrose, arm. HERTFORD, matric. 14 Oct., 90, aged 18 (from Repton); HONOURS:—3 classical mods. 92

Peck, Henry Cecil, born at Notton, Wilts, 11 Sept., 1865; 2s. Jasper Kenrick, bar.-at-law. UNIVERSITY COLL., matric. 11 Oct., 84, aged 19 (from Westminster school), B.A. 87, M.A. 91; HONOURS:— 4 law 87.

Peck, William Awdry, born in London 6 Aug., 1861; 1s. Jasper Kenrick, bar.-at-law. CHRIST CHURCH, matric. 15 Oct., 80, aged 19 (from Westminster school), scholar 80, B.A. 84, M.A. 89 (HONOURS:— 2 classical mods. 82, 2 history 84); bar.-at-law, Lincoln's Inn, 87.

Peckitt, Reginald Godfrey, born at Carlton Huthwaite, Yorks, 4 April, 1868; 1s. Reginald William, of the 84th regt. WADHAM, matric. 18 Jan., 87, aged 18 (from K. William coll., I.M.), B.A. 90.

Pedder, Arthur Lionel, born at Tamerton Folliott, Devon, 8 Feb., 1868; o.s. William Henry, late H.B.M. consul, China. MAGDALEN, matric. 21 Oct., 86, aged 18 (from Reading gr. school), demy 86, B.A. 90; HONOURS:—1 mathematical mods. 87, 1 mathematics 90, Herschel astronomical prize 91.

Pedder, John, born at Bath 1869; 2s. John, cler. ORIEL, matric. 18 Oct., 87, aged 18 (from Bath coll.), scholar 87, B.A. '92; HONOURS:—1 classical mods. 89, 2 classics 91.

Pedder, Thomas, born at Garstang, co. Lanc., June, 1861; 2s. Wilson, vicar. NON-COLLEGIATE, matric. 18 Oct. 80, aged 19 (from Rossall school); migrated to BRASENOSE 22 Jan., 81.

Peebles, Lewis Hay Irving, born at Falkirk, Scotland, 7 Dec., 1868; 2s. David Matthew, gen. WADHAM, matric. 13 Oct., 88, aged 19 (from Blair Lodge school, Edinburgh), exhibitioner 88, B.A. 92; HONOURS:—2 classical mods. 90, 2 classics 92.

Peel, Alfred Henry, born at Torquay, Devon, 31 March, 1864; 3s. Frederick, cler. ST. ALBAN HALL, matric. 28 Jan., 82, aged 17, from the Charterhouse.

Peel, Arthur George Villiers, born in London 27 Feb., 1868; 2s. Arthur Wellesley, speaker House of Commons. NEW COLL., matric. 15 Oct., 86, aged 18 (from Harrow), B.A. 91 (HONOURS:— 2 classical mods. 88, 1 classics 90), treasurer of the Oxford union society 88, and president 90.

Peel, right hon. Arthur Wellesley, speaker, created D.C.L. 22 June, 1887. See *Al. Ox.* 2nd series 1088.

Peel, Frederick, born at Watford, Herts, 1870; 3s. Frederick, B.Mus. NON-COLLEGIATE, matric. 11 Oct., 89, aged 19 (from York school), B.A. 92.

Peel, John Douglas, born at Alderley, Cheshire, 12 Dec., 1871; 4s. Charles, of North Rode, Cheshire, deceased. MAGDALEN, matric. 14 Oct., 90, aged 18 (from Eton); HONOURS:—2 classical mods. 92.

Peel, John Graham, born at Manchester 24 Jan., 1872; 1s. Gerald, arm. NEW COLL., matric. 20 Oct., 90, aged 18 (from Harrow); HONOURS:— 3 classical mods. 92.

Peel, Maurice Berkeley, born in London 23 April, 1873; 4s. Arthur Wellesley speaker House of Commons. NEW COLL., matric. 16 Oct., 91, aged 18, from Winchester.

Peel, Robert, born in London 12 April, 1867; 1s. Robert, baronet. TRINITY, matric. 16 Oct., 86, aged 19 (from Harrow); migrated to BALLIOL 87.

Peel, Samuel, born at Godalming, Surrey, 1866; 1s. Frederick, cler. NON-COLLEGIATE, matric. 16 Oct., 86, aged 20, from Magdalen coll. school, chorister 74-80.

Peel, Sidney Cornwallis, born in London 3 June, 1870; 3s. Arthur Wellesley, speaker House of Commons. NEW COLL., matric. 11 Oct., 89, aged 19 (Eton), scholar 89; HONOURS:—accessit Hertford scholarship 90, 1 classical mods. 91.

Peel, William Frederick, born in London 20 March, 1861; 1s. Archibald, arm. BALLIOL, matric. 4 March, 83, aged 21.

Peel, William Robert Wellesley, born in London 7 Jan., 1867; 1s. Arthur Wellesley, speaker House of Commons. BALLIOL, matric. 24 Oct., 85, aged 18 (from Harrow), B.A. 89 (HONOURS:—2 classical mods. 87, 2 classics 89), treasurer of the Oxford union society 87.

Peele, Richardson, born at Durham 1869; 4s. John Edward, gen. BRASENOSE, matric. 20 Oct., 87, aged 18 (from Durham gr. school), scholar 87.

Peers, rev. Herbert James, born at Mossley Hill, co. Lanc., 1865; 1s. Henry Robert, gen. WORCESTER, matric. 18 Oct., 83, aged 18, B.A. 87, M.A. 90 (HONOURS:—4 law 87); curate of Christ Church, Stone, co. Staff., 91.

Peet, Henry Herbert, born at Shanklin, I.W., 4 Sept., 1867; 1s. John, surgeon-major Indian army. NEW COLL., matric. 15 Oct., 86, aged 19 (from the Charterhouse); HONOURS:—4 law 90.

Pelle, James Hamilton Francis, born at Gogha, East Indies, 2 Aug., 1863; 1s. sir James Braithwaite, K.C.S.I. CORPUS CHRISTI, matric. 19 Oct., 82, aged 19 (from Harrow), scholar 82-6, B.A. 86, M.A. 90 (HONOURS:—2 classical mods. 83, accessit Hertford scholarship 83, 2 classics 86); headmaster Bury St. Edmund's school 90.

Peirce, John, born at Lambourne, Berks, 1 Dec., 1867; 1s. John, gen. ST. JOHN'S, matric. 16 Oct., 86, aged 18 (from Faversham school), scholar 86 (HONOURS:—1 classical mods. 88); died 88.

Pelham, Henry Francis, M.A., fellow BRASENOSE 89, where see page 350.

Pell, Albert Julian, born at Ickenham, Middx., 19 Nov., 1863; 1s. Beauchamp Henry St. John, cler. MERTON, matric. 17 Oct., 82, aged 19 (from Winchester), B.A. 86 (HONOURS:—2 classical mods. 84, 2 law 86); bar.-at-law, Lincoln's Inn, 87.

Pellatt, Thomas, born at Banbury, Oxon, 22 Feb., 1863; 2s. Daniel Parker, solicitor. TRINITY, matric. 17 Oct., 81, aged 18 (from Lancing coll.), B.A. 87, M.A. 90 (HONOURS:—1 history 87); a master at Marlborough coll.

Pelly, sir Harold, 4th bart., born at Warnham Court, Sussex, 28 Feb., 1863; 1s. sir George Henry, bart. CHRIST CHURCH, matric. 20 Jan., 82, aged 18 (from Harrow), B.A. 86.

Pember, Edward Henry, M.A., student CHRIST CHURCH 54-61, where see page 421.

Pember, Francis William, born at Hatfield, Herts, 1862; 1s. Edward Henry, Q.C. BALLIOL, matric. 21 Oct., 80, aged 18 (from Harrow), scholar 78-84; fellow ALL SOULS' 84-91, B.A. 84, M.A. 87 (HONOURS:—1 classical mods. 81, proxime accessit 81 and accessit Hertford scholarship 82, 1 classics 84, Ireland scholarship 84 (accessit 81 and 82), Craven scholarship 85, Eldon scholarship 87); bar.-at-law, Lincoln's Inn, 89.

Pember, Howard Edward, born at Hatfield, Herts, 1865; 2s. Edward Henry, Q.C. BALLIOL, matric. 15 Oct., 84, aged 19 (from Harrow), exhibitioner 84, B.A. 89 (HONOURS:—1 classical mods. 86, 2 classics 88); died 28 Nov., 91.

Pemberton, Bertram Roper Stote, born at Sunderland, co. Durham, 20 Jan., 1868; 3s. Rich. Laurence, arm. NEW COLL., matric. 25 Nov., 86, aged 18, B.A. 90; HONOURS:—4 law 90.

Pemberton, Francis Reginald, born at Little Hallingbury, Herts, Aug., 1863; 5s. Stanley, cler. KEBLE, matric. 17 Oct., 82, aged 19 (from Felsted school), B.A. 85, M.A. 90.

Pemberton, John Stapylton Grey, born at Bishopwearmouth, co. Durham, 23 Dec., 1860; 1s. Richard Laurence, of Hawthorne Tower, arm. NEW COLL., matric. 16 Oct., 80, aged 19 (from Eton), B.A. 84; fellow ALL SOULS' 85-92, M.A. 88 (HONOURS:—2 classical mods. 81, 1 classics 84); librarian 82, president of the Oxford union society 83; bar.-at-law, Middle Temple, 89, contested Sunderland 92.

Pemberton, Ralph Hylton, born at Sunderland 17 July, 1864; 2s. Richard Laurence, arm. JESUS COLL., matric. 18 Oct., 83, aged 19, from Eton.

Pemberton, rev. Robert, born in Calcutta 1868; 1s. Robert Charles Boileau, arm. UNIVERSITY COLL., matric. 18 Oct., 86, aged 18, B.A. 91; HONOURS: —3 classical mods. 88, 2 history 90.

Pembrey, Marcus Seymour, born at Oxford 1868; 2s. John Crips, gent. CHRIST CHURCH, matric. 16 Oct., 85, aged 17 (from Oxford high school), exhibitioner 88, B.A. 89, M.A and B.Med. 92; HONOURS:—1 physiology 89, Radcliffe travelling fellowship 90, Johnson astronomical essay prize,91.

Pendlebury, William Henry, born at Bolton, co. Lanc., 7 May, 1862; 1s. Thomas, merchant. CHRIST CHURCH, matric. 13 Oct., 82, aged 20 (from Manchester school), scholar 82, B.A. 85, M.A. 90; HONOURS:—2 natural science 85.

Penley, Horace Octavius, born at Cam, co. Glouc., 16 April, 1874; 4s. Francis Thorpe, M.A., cler. LINCOLN, matric. 25 Oct., 92, aged 18 (from Warwick school), exhibitioner 92.

Penlington, Edmund Tom, born in London 11 Oct., 1865; 2s. Thomas, arm. NEW COLL., matric. 16 Jan., 85, aged 19 (from Marlborough coll.), B.A. 88; HONOURS:—3 classical mods. 86, 2 classics 88.

Penn, Llewellyn Mayson, born at Bangor 30 June, 1870; 1s. Mayson, wesleyan minister. JESUS COLL., matric. 14 Oct., 89, aged 19 (from Kingswood school), scholar 89; HONOURS:—2 classical mods. 91.

Penn, rev. William Charles, born at Birmingham 1863; 1s. William Stone, gen. EXETER, matric. 16 Oct., 83, aged 21 (from university of London, B.A. 87), B.A. 88, M.A. 91 (HONOURS: —3 history 88); curate of West Ham, Essex, 91.

Pennant, Claud Douglas, born in London 12 Nov., 1867; 2s. col. the hon. Archibald Douglas. NEW COLL., matric. 15 Oct., 86, aged 18 (from Eton), B.A. 91; HONOURS:—3 classical mods. 88.

Pennefather, William de Montmorency, born at Geneva 27 Aug., 1869; o.s. Richard Daniel, col. east Kent regt. LINCOLN, matric. 17 Oct., 89, aged 20 (from Sherborne school), B.A. 92.

Pennell, Aubrey Percival, born at Minster, Kent, 1865; 1s. Charles, arm. CHRIST CHURCH, matric. 12 Oct., 83, aged 18, scholar 83-6, B.A. 86, M.A. 91 (HONOURS:—1 law 86, Boden sanskrit scholarship 86); student Middle Temple 83; deputy commissioner Burma.

Penney, Johnston, born in London 15 Sept., 1866; 2s. David Johnston Eckford, arm. TRINITY, matric. 17 Oct., 85, aged 19 (from Sherborne school); assist. magistrate north west provinces India.

Penney, rev. William Campbell, born at Bombay 1861; 1s. David Johnston Eckford, gent. HERTFORD, matric. 19 Oct., 81, aged 20 (from Sherborne school), scholar 80-5, B.A. 84, M.A. 89 (HONOURS:—1 classical mods. 83, 2 classics 85); assist. master Blundell's school, Tiverton, 87-9, headmaster Elizabeth coll., Guernsey, 89.

Pennington, Frederick, born at Alderley Edge, Cheshire, 1864; o.s. Frederick, M.P. EXETER, matric. 18 Jan., 83, aged 19, from University coll. school, London.

Pennington, Hugh, born at Forest Hill, Surrey, 12 June, 1870; 2s. Richard, gen. TRINITY, matric. 12 Oct., 89, aged 19, from Clifton coll.

Penny, rev. Fraser Hislop, M.A., ST. JOHN'S, where see page 491.

Pennyman, William Geoffrey, born at Ormesby, Yorks, 3 May, 1870; 3s. James Stovin, arm. BRASENOSE, matric. 23 Jan., 90, aged 19, from the Charterhouse.

Penrhyn, Arthur Leycester Leycester, born at East Sheen, Surrey, 10 March, 1866; 1s. Edwin Hugh Leycester, arm. BALLIOL, matric. 24 Oct., 85, aged 19 (from Eton), B.A. 89, M.A. 92 (HONOURS:— 3 classical mods. 87, 2 classics 89); bar.-at-law, Inner Temple, 92.

Penruddocke, John Powys, born at Wilton, Wilts, Sept., 1861; 1s. John Hungerford, cler. CHARSLEY'S HALL, matric. 18 April, 82, aged 20 (from Lancing coll.); migrated to WORCESTER, B.A. 89, M.A. 92.

Penruddocke, rev. William Fielding, born at South Newton, Wilts, Oct., 1866; 4s. John Hungerford, cler. KEBLE, matric. 19 Oct., 86, aged 20, B.A. 89; curate of Stretham, Norfolk, 90.

Penson, Edward Allen, born at Hascombe, Surrey, 23 Nov., 1870; 2s. Richard, of Armscote, Shipston-on-Stour, arm. UNIVERSITY COLL., matric. 12 Oct., 89, aged 18, from Marlborough.

Pentreath, rev. Arthur Godolphin, born at Market Rasen, co. Lincoln, 14 July, 1866; 1s. Frederick Richard, D.D., rector of Dodbrooke, south Devon. MAGDALEN, matric. 16 Oct., 84, aged 18 (from Henley gr. school and Radley coll.), demy 84, B.A. 88, M.A. 91 (HONOURS:—2 classical mods. 86, 3 classics 88); curate of St. Gabriel, Pimlico, 91.

Pentreath, Leonard Norbourne, born at Market Rasen, co. Lincoln, 17 Dec., 1868; 2s. Frederick Richard, D.D. etc. NON-COLLEGIATE, matric. 15 Oct., 87, aged 18 (from Henley gr. school); migrated to EXETER, B.A. 92.

Peppin, Arthur Hamilton, born at Wells, Somerset, 4 Jan., 1865; 1s. Stephen Francis Bedford, cler. WORCESTER, matric. 19 March, 84, aged 19, B.A. 87; HONOURS:—3 classical mods. 85.

Peppin, Gerald Francis Codrington, born at Horsington, Somerset, 1867; 2s. Stephen Francis Bedford, vicar. NON-COLLEGIATE, matric. 13 Oct., 88, aged 21, from Bath coll.

Peppin, Talbot Sydenham, born at Horsington, Somerset, Sept., 1868; 3s. Stephen Francis Bedford, vicar. KEBLE, matric. 17 Oct., 87, aged 19 (from Bath coll.), scholar 87; HONOURS:—2 classical mods. 89, 3 classics 91.

Pepys, George Digby, born in London 7 June, 1868; 1s. hon. George. ORIEL, matric. 18 Oct., 87, aged 19 (from Winchester), B.A. 90; HONOURS:— 3 history 90.

Pepys, Kenelm Charles Edward, earl of Cottenham, born in London 18 May, 1874; 1s. William John, earl of Cottenham. CHRIST CHURCH, matric. 14 Oct., 92, aged 18, from Eton.

Perceval, Cyril Ambrose, born at Woolfardisworthy, Devon, 27 Nov., 1866; 3s. Arthur Bernard, cler. NON-COLLEGIATE, matric. 13 Oct., 83, aged 16; migrated to QUEEN'S, B.A. 86, M.A. 90.

Percival, Aubrey Philip, born at Quainton, Northants, 13 May, 1868; 4s. James Stanley, arm. EXETER, matric. 19 Oct., 87, aged 18 (from Marlborough coll.), B.A. 91.

Percival, John, M.A., president TRINITY 78-87 where see page 448.

Percival, John Guthrie, born at Clifton, co. Glouc.,
10 Aug., 1866; 2s. rev. John, headmaster of Rugby.
MAGDALEN, matric. 21 Oct., 86, aged 20 (from
Clifton coll.), B.A. 89 (HONOURS :—2 chemistry 89);
of London, publisher.

Percival, Lancelot Jefferson, born at Clifton, co.
Glouc., 22 May, 1869; 3s. rev. John, headmaster of
Rugby. TRINITY, matric. 13 Oct. 88, aged 19, from
Clifton coll.

Percival, Philip Edward, born at Tibberton, co.
Glouc., 11 Nov., 1872; 2s. Edward Hope, Bo. C.S.,
retired. BALLIOL, matric. 20 Oct., 91, aged 18,
from the Charterhouse.

Percy, Henry Algernon George, Baron Warkworth,
born 21 Jan., 1871; 1s. Henry George, earl
Percy. CHRIST CHURCH, matric. 11 Oct., 89, aged
18 (from Eton); HONOURS :—1 classical mods. 91,
English verse 91.

Percy, hon. Josceline, born 26 Jan., 1872; 2s. Henry
George, earl Percy. CHRIST CHURCH, matric. 8
June, 89, aged 17, from Eton.

Perkin, John Arthur, born at Surbiton, Surrey,
1862; 3s. Robert, gent. EXETER, matric. 20
Oct., 81, aged 19 (from the Charterhouse), B.A. 86,
M.A. 88.

Perkins, Edward Algernon, born in London Feb.,
1868; 2s. George Frederick, arm. CHRIST CHURCH,
matric. 22 Oct., 89, aged 20, from Eton.

Perkins, Jocelyn Henry Temple, born at Hendon,
Middx., 5 Aug., 1870; 1s. John Robert, surgeon.
MAGDALEN, matric. 14 Oct., 89, aged 19 (from
Bedford school), exhibitioner 89, B.A. 92;
HONOURS :—2 history 92.

Perkins, Robert Cyril Layton, born at Badminton,
co. Glouc., 15 Nov., 1866; 2s. Charles Matthew,
cler. JESUS COLL., matric. 23 Oct., 85, aged 18
(from Merchant Taylors' school), scholar 85,
B.A. 89; HONOURS :—4 morphology 89.

Perks, Bernard, born at Wolverhampton 17 May,
1866; 2s. Samuel Hollis, arm. MAGDALEN, matric.
23 Oct., 85, aged 19 (from Repton), B.A. 89
(HONOURS :—3 history 89); bar.-at-law, Inner
Temple, 92.

Perks, Edwin Hollis, born at Newbridge, co. Stafford,
2 Nov., 1862; 1s. Samuel Hollis, arm. MAGDALEN,
matric. 16 Oct., 82, aged 19 (from Repton), B.A. 87.

Perrins, Frederick William Dyson, born at Worcester
25 May, 1864; o.s. James Dyson, gen. QUEEN'S,
matric. 23 Oct., 82, aged 18, from the Charterhouse.

Perris, Harry Shaw, born at Egremont, Cheshire, 1
Feb., 1870; 3s. Henry Woods, unitarian minister.
NON-COLLEGIATE, matric. 15 Oct., 92, aged 22,
from Norwich and Hull gr. schools and Owens
coll., Manchester.

Perry, Charles Elliott, born at Carlton, near Melbourne, Victoria, 19 May, 1871; 2s. Charles, incumbent of St. Jude's, Carlton, deceased. NON-COLLEGIATE, matric. 3 Feb., 91, aged 19, from
Church of England gr. school, Melbourne.

Perry, Frederick, born at Lilleshall, Salop,
1862; 1s. Isaac, gen. CHRIST CHURCH, matric. 14
Oct., 81, aged 19 (from Shrewsbury gr. school),
exhibitioner 81-4.

Perry, Frederick Samuel, born at Neilpo, Australia,
1861; o.s. George Murray, arm. EXETER,
matric. 22 Oct., 80, aged 19, from Brighton coll.

Perry, George Gresley, M.A., fellow LINCOLN 42-52,
where see page 242.

Perry, Herbert Louis, born in London 1865;
3s. William Robert, arm. HERTFORD, matric. 14
Oct., 84, aged 19. B.A. 87, M.A. 91.

Perry, John Frederick, born at Aston, co. Warwick,
3 or 8 Sept., 1873; 1s. John, gent. MAGDALEN,
matric. 22 Oct., 91, aged 18 (from Wolverhampton
school), demy 91.

Perry, Uvey George, born at Cirencester, co. Glouc.,
5 Jan., 1872; 3s. James. WORCESTER, matric. 22
Oct., 91, aged 19, from Weymouth coll.

Perry, William Stevens, bishop of Iowa, U.S.A., 1876;
created D.D. 21 June, 88; educated at Harvard;
born 22 Jan., 32; American church historian. See
Al. Ox. and series 1201.

Perryn, Richard George Henry, born at Venland
Conyers, co. Lanc., 25 Dec., 1864; 1s. Richard
Henry, arm. EXETER, matric. 21 Jan., 85, aged
20 (from Rugby), B.A. 88; practising as a barrister
in Canada.

Perse, Henry Seymour, born at Rahoon, co. Galway,
17 June, 1869; 2s. Henry Sadleir, arm. BRASENOSE,
matric. 14 Oct., 89, aged 20, from Cheltenham coll.

Peters, rev. Arthur Edward George, born at Wellington, Somerset, 12 Feb., 1866; 2s. Thomas, cler.
WORCESTER, matric. 22 Oct., 85, aged 19 (from
Christ's hospital), B.A. 89 (HONOURS :—2 theology
89); curate of Gillingham, Dorset, 91.

Peters, Frank Hesketh. M.A., fellow UNIVERSITY
COLL. 74, where see page 29.

Peters, Thomas Joseph, born at Great Berkhampstead, Herts, 1873; o.s. Thomas Joseph,
schoolmaster. PEMBROKE, matric. 28 Oct., 92,
aged 19 (from Berkhampstead school), scholar 92.

Peters, William Harold Stilwell, born at Rochester
Oct., 1866; 2s. Joseph, arm. CHRIST CHURCH,
matric. 30 May, 85, aged 18 (from Malvern coll.),
B.A. 88, M.A. 92.

Peterson, Franklin Sievewright, born at Edinburgh
1862; 7s. John, gen. NEW COLL.,
matric. 18 Jan., 87, aged 25, B.Mus. 92.

Petit, Oliver Stanley, born at Handsworth, co.
Warwick, 20 June, 1872; 2s. Joseph Lettiere, pen
manufacturer. LINCOLN, matric. 23 Oct., 92, aged
20, from Heathfield school, Handsworth.

Petre, Oswald Henry Philip, born in London 27
May, 1862; 1s. Edward, arm. CHRIST CHURCH,
matric. 4 June, 81, aged 19, exhibitioner 84-5, B.A.
86; HONOURS :—3 classical mods. 83, 3 history 85.

Petrie, William Matthew Flinders, created D.C.L.
22 June, 1892; professor of Egyptology, university
coll., London, Nov., 92; born 3 June, 1853. See
Men and Women of the Time.

De Peyster, Clermont Livingston, born at Clermont,
New York, 12 June, 1864; o.s. Frederick, gen.
WORCESTER, matric. 22 Jan., 89, aged 21, from
Harvard coll., U.S.

Pheasant, Frederick Charles, born at Southampton
1867; 5s. John, surveyor. NON-COLLEGIATE, matric. 17 Dec., 92, aged 25.

Phelps, Hugh Richard, born at Weymouth 6
Jan., 1869; 1s. Robert Hoskyns, major-general.
QUEEN'S, matric. 29 Jan., 89, aged 20, from
Weymouth coll.

Phelps, Edwin Ashby, born at Clifton, Bristol, 9
Jan., 1873; 1s. Philip Ashby, cler. MAGDALEN,
matric. 22 Oct., 91, aged 18 (from Clifton coll.),
demy 91.

Phelps, Ernest James, born at Waterpark, co. Limerick, 5 Aug., 1867; 2s. John Lecky, arm.,
deceased. MAGDALEN, matric. 23 Oct., 85, aged
18 (from Harrow), B.A. 89; bar.-at-law, Inner
Temple, 92.

Phelps, rev. Francis Robinson, born in Newfoundland
1863; 1s. Joseph Francis, cler. KEBLE,
matric. 18 Dec., 89, aged 26 (HONOURS :—3 mathematical school), B.A. 86, M.A. 89 (HONOURS :—3 mathematical mods. 84, 4 history 86); curate of St. John
Evangelist, Westminster, 90.

Phelps, John Henry Dixon, born at Houghton,
Carlisle, 4 Jan., 1872; 1s. John, cler. QUEEN'S,
matric. 27 Oct., 91, aged 19 (from Carlisle gr.
school), exhibitioner 91.

Phelps, Joseph Harold, born at St. Kilda, Melbourne, Victoria, 12 March, 1874; 4s. John Leeky, of Waterpark, co. Limerick. MAGDALEN, matric. 18 Oct., 92, aged 18, from Harrow.
Phelps, rev. Lancelot Ridley, M.A., fellow ORIEL 77 (where see page 150), and vice-principal ST. MARY HALL 85, where see page 609.
Pheysey, rev. Percy Wootton, born at Sefton, co. Lanc., 31 May, 1868; 1s. Richard, gen. WADHAM, matric. 16 Oct., 86, aged 18 (from Great Crosby school), B.A. 89 (HONOURS:—4 theology 89); curate of Northam, Devon, 91.
Philcox, Charles, born at Preston, near Brighton, 1868; 1s. James, arm. HERTFORD, matric. 22 Oct., 86, aged 18, from Wellington coll.
Philipps, William Lewis, born at Clyngwynne, co. Carmarthen, 1867; 1s. William Lewis, arm. CHRIST CHURCH, matric. 31 May, 84, aged 17, B.A. 88.
Philips, Arthur Dodsworth, born in London 16 Sept., 1869; 4s. John, arm. NEW COLL., matric. 19 Jan., 89, aged 19 (from Winchester); HONOURS:—3 classical mods. 90.
Philipson, Hylton, born at Tynemouth, Northumberland, 8 June, 1866; 3s. Hilton, solicitor. NEW COLL., matric. 16 Oct., 85, aged 19 (from Eton), B.A. 91, M.A. 92 (HONOURS:—4 history 89); in the University eleven 87, 8, 9.
Philipson, Ralph Hilton, born at Tynemouth, Northumberland, 17 Sept., 1861; 1s. Hilton, solicitor. NEW COLL., matric. 15 Oct., 81, aged 20, from Eton (HONOURS:—3 law 85); bar.-at-law, Lincoln's Inn, 89.
Phillimore, Charles Augustus, born at Dropmore, Bucks, 11 Aug., 1871; 3s. vice-admiral sir Augustus, K.C.B. CHRIST CHURCH, matric. 10 Oct., 90, aged 19 (from Westminster school), scholar 91; HONOURS:—2 classical mods. 92.
Phillimore, George Greville, born at Lostwithiel, Cornwall, 28 Oct., 1867; 2s. vice-admiral sir Augustus, K.C.B. CHRIST CHURCH, matric. 15 Oct., 86, aged 18 (from Westminster school), scholar 86, B.A. 90 (HONOURS:—1 classical mods. 88, 1 classics 90); bar.-at-law, Middle Temple, 91.
Phillimore, John Swinnerton, born at Boconnoc, Cornwall, 26 Feb., 1873; 4s. vice-admiral sir Augustus, K.C.B. CHRIST CHURCH, matric. 16 Oct., 91, aged 18 (from Westminster school), scholar 91; HONOURS:—Hertford scholarship 92 (accessit 91), Craven scholarship 92.
Phillimore, Robert Charles, born in London 19 Aug., 1871; 1s. sir Walter George Francis, bart. CHRIST CHURCH, matric. 11 Oct., 89, aged 18 (from Westminster school), president Oxford union society 92.
Phillimore, sir Walter George Francis, bart., D.C.L., fellow ALL SOULS' 67-71, where see page 262.
Phillipps, Henry Martyn, born at Deptford, Kent, 24 April, 1864; 4s. William, gen. LINCOLN, matric. 2 May, 89, aged 25, from Repton school.
Phillips, Christopher James, born at Deal, Kent, 13 Sept., 1873; 6s. Stephen, D.D., reader of Gray's Inn. BRASENOSE, matric. 16 Oct., 92, aged 19 (from St. Paul's school), scholar 92.
Phillips, Ernest Augustine, born at Wiveliscombe, Somerset, 1869; 2s. Abel, cler. ST. EDMUND HALL, matric. 18 Oct., 88, aged 19, B.A. 92.
Phillips, Ernest Spencer, born at Ickleford, Herts, 5 March, 1869; 1s. Spencer William, cler. TRINITY, matric. 13 Oct., 88, aged 19, B.A. 92; HONOURS:—3 theology 92.
Phillips, Francis Ashley, born at Crumlin, co. Monmouth, 11 April, 1873; 2s. Philip Samuel, gent. EXETER, matric. 3 Nov., 91, aged 18 (from Rossall school); in the University eleven 92.

Phillips, Frank Henry, M.A., MERTON, where see page 100.
Phillips, George Ingleton, born at Chesham, Bucks, 1866; 1s. John Samuel, gen. ST. EDMUND HALL, matric. 18 Oct., 88, aged 22.
Phillips, George Waller, born at Broughton, co. Lanc., 1862; 3s. George Allcroft, arm. BRASENOSE, matric. 22 Jan., 80, aged 18.
Phillips, Harry Edward William, born at Earls Coln, Essex, 26 Aug., 1867; 1s. Harry, of Handsworth, gen. NON-COLLEGIATE, matric. 6 Feb., 92, aged 24, from Birmingham gr. school.
Phillips, John Carey, born at Moughtrey, co. Montgomery, 26 April, 1866; 2s. George, baptist minister. JESUS COLL., matric. 28 April, 87, aged 21, from Oxford county and Presteign gr. schools.
Phillips, John Lort, born at Clanarberth, co. Cardigan, 21 April, 1867; 2s. Arthur Lort, arm. EXETER, matric. 17 Oct., 88, aged 21, from Harrow.
Phillips, Laurence Arthur, born at Calcutta 14 July, 1870; 1s. Arthur, arm. TRINITY, matric. 12 Oct., 89, aged 19 (from the Charterhouse), exhibitioner 88; HONOURS:—Accessit Hertford scholarship 90, 1 classical mods. 91.
Phillips, Leonard Richard Brewer, born at Beaufort, Brecon, 7 Aug., 1869; o.s. John Rhys, arm. deceased. LINCOLN, matric. 17 Oct., 89, aged 20 (from University coll., Aberystwith), B.A. 92.
Phillips, Martin Luther, born at Llangynwid, near Bridgend, 13 Sept., 1855; o.s. David, gen. NON-COLLEGIATE, matric. 22 Jan., 81, aged 25 (from Normal coll., Swansea, and commercial coll., Trevees, Brecon); migrated to QUEEN'S, B.A. 84, M.A. 87; HONOURS:—3 theology 84.
Phillips, Percival Stanton, born at Stowmarket, Suffolk, Aug., 1870; 2s. John, gen. EXETER, matric. 22 Jan., 89, aged 18, from Clifton coll.
Phillips, Richard Baxter, born at Margate, Kent, 4 Nov., 1869; 2s. John Edward, gent., deceased. ST. MARY HALL, matric. 26 Oct., 92, aged 22.
Phillips, St. John Knox Rickards, born at St. John's, Newfoundland, 1863; 1s. Andrew Knox, gen. WORCESTER, matric. 18 Oct., 83, aged 20.
Phillips, Sydney Archer, born at New Hampton, Middx., 27 Feb., 1865; 1s. William, gen. CORPUS CHRISTI, matric. 23 Oct., 84, aged 19 (from Croydon school), scholar 84, B.A. 88; HONOURS:—2 mathematical mods. 86, 3 mathematics 88.
Phillips, Theodore Evelyn Reece, born at Kibworth, co. Leic., 1868; 1s. Abel, cler. ST. EDMUND HALL, matric. 22 Oct., 87, aged 19, B.A. 91.
Phillips, Thomas Falkner, born at Broughton, co. Lanc., 1861; 2s. George Allcroft, arm. BRASENOSE, matric. 22 Jan., 80, aged 19 (from Uppingham), B.A. 84, M.A. 88.
Phillips, Walter Alison, born at Blackheath, Kent, 1865; y.s. John, arm. MERTON, matric. 17 Oct., 82, aged 17 (from Merchant Taylors' school), exhibitioner 82-6, B.A. 86; Merchant Taylors' senior scholar ST. JOHN'S 86 (HONOURS:—1 history 85); president of Oxford union society 86.
Phillips, William Watkin, born at Jubbulpore, in East Indies, 21 March, 1870; 4s. George Robert, major-general Madras cavalry. NEW COLL., matric. 12 Oct., 88, aged 18 (from Winchester); assist. to collector and magistrate North Arcot, Madras c.s.
Phillips, rev. Wilmot, born at Newmarket, co. Cambridge, 8 May, 1864; 1s. Henry Stephen, solicitor. WADHAM, matric. 11 Oct., 84, aged 20 (from Lancing coll.), B.A. 88 (HONOURS:—3 theology 88); curate of St. James, Edgbaston, 91.
Phillpot, William Edwin, born at Cheltenham 1863; o.s. Edwin, gen. NON-COLLEGIATE, matric. 17 Oct., 81, aged 18 (from Derby school); migrated to WORCESTER, B.A. 87.

Phillpotts, rev. Barrington Henry Arthur, born at Plymouth 30 March, 1860; 1s. Octavius, arm. ST. MARY HALL, matric. 22 Jan., 83, aged 22, B.A. 86, M.A. 89; missioner of society St. Peter, Exeter, 90.

Phillpotts, Henry John, M.A., student CHRIST CHURCH 52-62, where see page 420.

Phillpotts, rev. Henry Robertson, born at Lamerton, Devon, 12 Oct., 1867; 1s. Henry John, cler. KEBLE, matric. 19 Oct., 86, aged 19 (from Rugby), B.A. 90 (HONOURS:—3 history 89); curate of Barking, Essex, 92.

Phillpotts, James Surtees, M.A., B.C.L., fellow NEW COLL. 58-69, where see page 216.

Phillpotts, Owen Surtees, born at Rugby 9 Oct., 1870; 1s. James Surtees, arm. WORCESTER, matric. 14 Oct., 89, aged 19 (from Bedford gr. school), exhibitioner 89; HONOURS:—2 classical mods. 91.

Phillpotts, Ralegh Buller, born at Kensington 22 Oct., 1871; 1s. William Francis, of Englefield Green, Surrey, bar.-at-law. BALLIOL, matric. 14 Oct., 90, aged 18, from Winchester coll.

Phillpotts, William Francis, M.A., fellow NEW COLL. 55-71, where see page 216.

Phipps, Edmund Bampfylde, born at Valetta, Malta, 29 Dec., 1869; 1s. Ramsay Weston, col. R.A. NEW COLL., matric. 12 Oct., 88, aged 18 (from Winchester), B.A. 92; HONOURS:—2 classical mods. 90, 3 classics 92.

Phipps, George, born at Oxford 7 Jan., 1853; 2s. Stephen, pleb., deceased. NON-COLLEGIATE, matric. 21 Oct., 89, aged 36, from Thorogood's school, Oxford.

Phipps, John Capel Barré, born at Abergavenny, co. Mon., 1863; y.s. Barré, arm. BRASENOSE, matric. 2 June, 82, aged 19, from Clifton coll.

Phipps, John Lewis, born at Paddington April, 1872; o.s. Richard Leckonby Hothersal, arm. CHRIST CHURCH, matric. 16 Jan., 91, aged 18, from Harrow.

Phipps, Pickering, born at Collingtree, Northants, 28 July, 1861; o.s. Pickering, M.P. NEW COLL., matric. 16 Oct., 80, aged 19 (from Harrow), B.A. 85.

Pickard, rev. Henry Adair, M.A., student CHRIST CHURCH 51-68, where see page 419.

Pickering, James Bennett, born at Kearsley, co. Lanc., 26 Oct., 1863; 1s. Richard, gen. ST. MARY HALL, matric. 23 Oct., 82, aged 18.

Pickering, Thomas Edward, born at Abbots Bromley, co. Stafford, 1861; 1s. Thomas, arm. UNIVERSITY COLL., matric. 15 Oct., 81, aged 20 (from Shrewsbury school), scholar 81-6, B.A. 85, M.A. 90; HONOURS:—1 classical mods. 83, 2 classics 85.

Pickford, rev. Francis Newland, born at Newland, Yorks, 16 June, 1863; 6s. John, cler. NON-COLLEGIATE, matric. 15 Oct., 81, aged 18 (from Trent coll.); migrated to MERTON, B.A. 84 (HONOURS:—3 history 84); curate of Roma, Queensland, 90.

Picton, Lionel James, born at Bebington, Cheshire, 20 Feb., 1874; 2s. William Henry, architect. MERTON, matric. 18 Oct., 92, aged 18 (from Great Crosby school and University coll., Liverpool).

Pidcock, Charles Spencer, born at Leek, co. Stafford, Aug., 1869; 1s. Benjamin, cler. NON-COLLEGIATE, matric. 12 Oct., 89, aged 20, from Honiton gr. school.

Pierantoni, Augusto, created D.C.L. 19 May, 1885. See *Al. Ox.* 2nd series 1114.

Pierce, Thomas Herbert, born at Cowley, Oxon, 1871; 1s. Thomas, gen. NON-COLLEGIATE, matric. 19 Jan., 89, aged 18, from New coll. school, Oxon.

Piggin, John Henry, of TRINITY, 1880. See FOWLER, page 216.

Piggott, Henry Frederick, born at Guildford 1863; 2s. John William Mose, gen. NON-COLLEGIATE, matric. 1 May, 86, aged 23, B.A. 89, M.A. 92 (HONOURS:—3 law 89); brother of John W. M. B.

Piggott, Henry Howard, born at Padua 13 Sept., 1871; 2s. Henry James, cler. CORPUS CHRISTI, matric. 16 Oct., 90, aged 19 (from Kingswood school), scholar 88; HONOURS:—1 mathematical mods. 91, junior mathematical scholarship 92.

Piggott, John William Mose Benjamin, born at Guildford, Surrey, 1868; 3s. John, gen. NON-COLLEGIATE, matric. 13 Oct., 84, aged 16 (from Guildford gr. school), B.A. 88; brother of Henry F.

Piggott, Theodore Caro, born at Padua, Italy, 26 Oct., 1867; 2s. Henry James, cler. CHRIST CHURCH, matric. 10 Oct., 84, aged 16 (from Kingswood school), scholar 84, B.A. 88 (HONOURS: —2 classical mods. 86); assist. magistrate N.W. provinces India.

Pigot, rev. Edward Charles, born at Wigan, co. Lanc., 21 Oct., 1860; 3s. Octavius Frederick, chaplain Kirkdale prison. QUEEN'S, matric. 28 Oct., 81, aged 21 (from royal institution school, Liverpool), B.A. 84, M.A. 89; curate of Shifnal, Salop, 89.

Pigot, Montague Horatio Mostyn Turtle, born in London 9 Aug., 1865; 1s. Robert Turtle, ann. UNIVERSITY COLL., matric. 11 Oct., 84, aged 19 (from Westminster school), B.A. 88, M.A. and B.C.L. 92 (HONOURS:—2 classical mods. 86, 2 law 88); bar.-at-law, Middle Temple, 90.

Pigot, Raymond Melville, born at Hardingham, Norfolk, 26 Sept., 1868; 1s. William Melville, vicar. WADHAM, matric. 15 Oct., 87, aged 19, from Haileybury.

Pigott, Henry A'Court, born at Bemerton, Wilts, Feb., 1870; 2s. Wellesley Pole, cler. CHRIST CHURCH, matric. 12 Oct., 88, aged 18 (from Wellington), B.A. 91.

Pigou, Frederick Hugo, born at Dartford, Kent, 1867; 1s. Frederick Alexander Preston, gen. NON-COLLEGIATE, matric. 13 May, 84, aged 17 (from Harrow); lieut. the Hampshire regt. 89, officiating wing officer 1. infantry, Hyderabad contingent.

Pike, Herbert Watson, born at Weyhill, Hants. 9 Aug., 1863; 1s. Thelwell, D. Med. NEW COLL., matric. 14 Oct., 82, aged 19 (from Winchester), B.A. 85 (HONOURS:—2 law 85); under secretary to government N.W. provinces and Oudh.

Pike, Warburton Mayer, born at Wareham, Dorset, 25 Sept., 1861; 4s. John William, arm. BRASENOSE, matric. 22 Oct., 80, aged 19, from Rugby.

Pilcher, Alexander Munsey Warton, born at Virginia Water, Surrey, 3 March, 1870; 2s. John, arm. MAGDALEN, matric. 14 Oct., 89, aged 19, from Eton.

Pilcher, Cecil Westland, born at Boston, co. Lincoln, 1871; 2s. William, gen. KEBLE, matric. 12 Oct., 89, aged 19 (from Bath coll.), exhibitioner 88, B.A. 93; HONOURS:—3 classical mods. 91.

Pilcher, Francis, M.A., ORIEL, where see page 154.

Pilcher, John Harry Warton, born at Egham, Surrey, 16 June, 1865; 1s. John Giles, arm. MAGDALEN, matric. 16 Oct., 84, aged 19 (from Eton), B.A. 88, M.A. and B.C.L. 91 (HONOURS:—2 civil law 88); bar.-at-law, Inner Temple, 91.

Pile, George Henry Hudson, born in the Barbados Aug., 1871; o.s. Archibald Jones, speaker Ho. Reps. NEW COLL., matric. 13 Oct., 90, aged 19, from Winchester.

Pilgrim, Donnell Maynard, born in Barbados 26 Sept., 1869; 5s. Francis Vidgett, gen. QUEEN'S, matric. 25 Jan., 88, aged 18, from Clifton coll.

Pilkington, Charles Henry, M.A., fellow NEW COLL. 54-69, where see page 216.

Pilkington, Claude William Egerton Milborne Swinnerton, born at Chevet Park, Yorks, 11 May, 1863; 3s. Lionel, bart. CHRIST CHURCH, matric. 13 Oct., 82, aged 19 (from Eton), B.A. 85, M.A. 90.

Pilkington, Ernest Sinclair, born at St. Helens, co. Lanc., 12 March, 1869; 1s. Richard, of Rainsford Hall, co. Lanc., gen. MAGDALEN, matric. 22 Oct., 87, aged 18 (from Clifton coll.), B.A. 91; HONOURS: —4 history 90.

Pilkington, Henry William, born at St. Helens, co. Lanc., Feb., 1871; 1s. William Windle, gen. CHRIST CHURCH, matric. 11 Oct., 89, aged 18 (from Shrewsbury gr. school), B.A. 93; twin with Richard A.

Pilkington, Herbert Walter Malony, born at Rathdowney, Ireland, 1862; 4s. William, arm. WORCESTER, matric. 19 Oct., 82, aged 20.

Pilkington, Malcolm Carlisle, born at Merlewood, near Windermere, Cumberland, 20 Sept., 1873; 3s. George, of Stoneleigh, co. Lanc., J.P. MAGDALEN, matric. 18 Oct., 92, aged 19, from Eton.

Pilkington, Richard Arthur, born at St. Helens, co. Lanc., Feb., 1871; 2s. William Windle, gen. CHRIST CHURCH, matric. 11 Oct., 89, aged 18 (from Shrewsbury gr. school), B.A. 93; twin with Henry W.

Pilkington, Sidney, born at Windle Hall, co. Lanc., Nov., 1872; 3s. William Windle, gen. CHRIST CHURCH, matric. 16 Oct., 91, aged 18 (from Shrewsbury school); brother of Henry W. and Richard A.

Pilling, Frederick, born at East Dereham, Norfolk, 1871; 6s. John Henry Rushworth, cler. NON-COLLEGIATE, matric. 12 Oct., 89, aged 18, from Felsted school.

Pilling, Octavius Frank, born at Longham, Norfolk, 1867; 7s. John Henry Rushworth, cler. NON-COLLEGIATE, matric. 17 Oct., 85, aged 18 (from Lynn school), B.A. 92.

Pilsbury, Ernest Howard, born in London 13 Feb., 1868; 2s. Wilmot, gen. WORCESTER, matric. 17 Oct., 87, aged 19 (from Birmingham gr. school), scholar 87, B.A. 92; HONOURS :—1 classical mods. 89, 2 classics 91.

Pilson, Arthur Ashfield, born at Birts Morton, co. Worc., 19 Sept., 1873; 1s. Robert, rector. EXETER, matric. 18 Oct., 92, aged 19, from Dean Close memorial school, Cheltenham.

Pim, rev. Henry Bedford, born in London 25 Dec., 1862; 1s. Bedford Clapperton, R.N., the Arctic explorer. MERTON, matric. 22 Oct., 83, aged 20 (from Dulwich coll.), B.A. 86, M.A. 90 (HONOURS: —2 law 86); chaplain UNIVERSITY COLL. 88-9; curate of St. Andrew, Wells-street, London, 90.

Pimblett, rev. Charles Bradburn, born at Burton-upon-Trent 14 Jan., 1866; 1s. James, vicar of St. Matthews, Preston. WADHAM, matric. 19 Jan., 84, aged 18 (from Preston gr. school), exhibitioner QUEEN'S 84, B.A. 87, M.A. 90 (HONOURS :—3 theology 87); curate of Hadley, Salop, 91.

Pimblett, James Blundell, born at Tattenhill, co. Staff, 11 Aug., 1869; 3s. James, cler. WADHAM, matric. 21 Oct., 89, aged 20 (from Preston gr. school), B.A. 92; HONOURS :—3 theology 92.

Pimbury, George Cam Wellington, born at Brinscombe, co. Glouc., 22 May, 1867; 1s. George Cam, gen. TRINITY, matric. 13 Oct., 88, aged 21, from Cheltenham coll. and Monmouth school.

Pinchin, rev. Hugh Tennent, born at Southsea 1867; y.s. John, gent. NON-COLLEGIATE, matric. 23 Jan., 86, aged 19 ((from Salisbury gr. school), B.A. 89, M.A. 92 (HONOURS :—3 theology 89); curate of Paignton 91.

Pinchin, John Robert, born at Lamport, Hants, Feb., 1865; 1s. John, gen. NON-COLLEGIATE, matric. 17 Oct., 85, aged 20, from Salisbury gr. school.

Pinckney, Erlysman Charles, born at Bath, Somerset, Dec., 1871; 1s. Erlysman, arm. CHRIST CHURCH, matric. 29 May, 91, aged 19, from Wellington coll.

Pinckney, George, born at Milford Hill, near Salisbury, 1864; 1s. William, arm. EXETER, matric. 27 May, 82, aged 18, from Radley coll.

Pinder, North, M.A., fellow TRINITY 51-61, where see page 451.

Pinel, Arthur Risebrough, born at St. Heliers, Jersey, 19 Sept., 1873; 3s. John, captain. JESUS COLL., matric. 18 Oct., 92, aged 19 (from Victoria coll., Jersey), scholar 92.

Ping, rev. Andrew, born at Rotherham, Yorks, 1857; 5s. John, arm. NON-COLLEGIATE, matric. 23 May, 85, aged 28, B.A. 88 (HONOURS: —3 chemistry 88); curate of Nottingham (St. Ann) 90.

Pinhey, Arthur Francis, born at Surat, East Indies, 28 Oct., 1865; 3s. Robert Hill, kt. TRINITY, matric. 14 Oct., 82, aged 18 (from Clifton coll. and the Charterhouse) ; student Inner Temple 82; head-assist. to collector and magistrate Madura, Madras. c.s.

Pinhey, Henry Pellew Douglas, born at Poona, East Indies, Nov., 1872 ; 8s. sir Robert Hill, kt., sometime judge of high court of Bombay. KEBLE, matric. 20 Oct., 91, aged 18, from Lancing coll.

Pinhorn, Ralph Henry, born at Gillingham, Dorset, 1872 ; 1s. Charles Avery, cler. KEBLE, matric. 9 Feb., 92, aged 20.

Pink, Leopold Lucien, born at Catherington, Hants, Jan., 1870 ; 4s. William, gen. ST. EDMUND HALL, matric. 18 Oct., 88, aged 18, from Portsmouth gr. school.

Pinniger, James Wilkinson, born at Westbury, Wilts, 8 Dec., 1870 ; y.s. Henry William, solicitor. WADHAM, matric. 14 Oct., 89, aged 18 (from Lancing coll.) ; B.A. 92.

Pitcairn, David, M.A., fellow MAGDALEN 59-71, where see page 324.

Pitman, Charles Murray, born at Edinburgh 8 Jan., 1872 ; 7s. Frederick, W.S. NEW COLL., matric. 16 Oct., 91, aged 19 (from Eton) ; stroke of University eight 92, in the eight 93.

Pitman, Harry Anderson, born at North Berwick 4 Aug., 1866 ; 5s. Frederick, arm. NEW COLL., matric. 15 Dec., 85, aged 19 (from Eton), B.A. 89, M.A. 92 ; HONOURS :—2 morphology 89.

Pitman, Horace, born at Richmond, Surrey, 1870 ; 3s. George Frederick, arm. ORIEL, matric. 20 Oct., 88, aged 18 (from Blackheath school), scholar 88, B.A. 92 ; HONOURS :—1 classical mods. 90, 2 classics 92.

Pitman, James Campbell, born at Edinburgh 1 Dec., 1864 ; 4s. Frederick, W.S. NEW COLL., matric. 8 Dec., 83, aged 19 (from Eton), B.A. 87, M.A. 91 ; HONOURS :—3 history 87.

Pitman, William Edward, born at Southsea, Hants, 1864 ; 1s. William, arm. KEBLE, matric. 12 Feb., 83, aged 19.

Pitt, Vernon Herbert, born at Southsea, Hants, 12 April, 1867 ; 1s. Herbert, gen., deceased. NON-COLLEGIATE, matric. 13 Oct., 88, aged 21 (from R.N. school, New Cross), scholar of HERTFORD 88, B.A. 91 ; HONOURS :—1 mathematical mods. 89, 2 mathematics 91.

Pittar, Charles William Erskine, born at Khidderpore, East Indies, 1864; 2s. Charles Frederick, gent. BALLIOL, matric. 17 Oct., 82, aged 18 (from Bedford school); assist. commissioner Assam.

Pitter, John Edwin, born at Wonston, Hants, 10 Dec., 1868; 1s. John, gen. QUEEN'S, matric. 21 Oct., 87, aged 18 (from Haileybury), B.A. 92.

Pittman, Joseph Matthew, born at Hawthorne, near Melbourne, 1864; 2s. Joseph, arm. BALLIOL, matric. 21 Oct., 80, aged 16 (from Tiverton school), Blundell scholar 80-4, B.A. 84; HONOURS:— 1 classical mods. 82, 2 classics 84.

Plant, George Ralph, born at Weston-on-Trent, co. Staff., 1865; 5s. Samuel, cler. ST. EDMUND HALL, matric. 22 Oct., 84, aged 19, B.A. 87, M.A. 91.

Plant, Henry Francis, born at Weston-on-Trent, co. Staff., Nov., 1863; 4s. Samuel, cler. ST. EDMUND HALL, matric. 14 June, 83, aged 19, from Oundle gr. school.

Plarr, Victor Gustavus, born at Strasburg 21 June, 1863; o.s. Gustavus. NON-COLLEGIATE, matric. 14 Oct., 82, aged 19 (from Tonbridge school); migrated to WORCESTER 86; HONOURS:— 2 history 86.

Platel, John Joseph, born at Heurah in East Indies 23 March, 1870; 1s. Joseph, arm., deceased. BALLIOL, matric. 1 Nov., 90, aged 20 (from St. Xavier's coll., Calcutta); selected candidate Indian C.S. 92.

Platt, rev. Charles Henry, born at Withick, Yorks, 8 April, 1868; 1s. George Moreton, cler. KEBLE, matric. 17 Oct., 87, aged 19 (from Leeds gr. school), B.A. 90; HONOURS:— 3 theology 90.

Platt, Hugh Edward Pigott, M.A., fellow LINCOLN 68, where see page 241.

Platts, John Thompson, born in Calcutta 1830; 2s. Robert, gent. BALLIOL, 1 Feb., 81, aged 50 (from Bedford school); created M.A. 27 June, 81, teacher of Persian 80.

Plaxton, John William, born at Beverley, Yorks, 1873; 1s. William. NON-COLLEGIATE, matric. 15 Oct., 92, aged 19.

Playfair, Arthur Grace, born at Salterton, Devon, 1866; 3s. George William, arm. NON-COLLEGIATE, matric. 28 Jan., 84, aged 18, from an Edinburgh school.

Playfair, rev. Charles Stuart Macdonald, born at Edinburgh 1861; 2s. George William, arm. NON-COLLEGIATE, matric. 4 Nov., 80, aged 19, B.A. 83, M.A. 89 (HONOURS:— 3 theology 83); curate of Buckingham 84.

Playfair, Nigel Ross, born in London 1 July, 1874; 1s. William Smoult, D.Med. UNIVERSITY COLL., matric. 22 Oct., 92, aged 18, from Harrow.

Playne, Herbert Clement, born at Minchinhampton, co. Glouc., 25 Nov., 1870; 1s. Edward, gen. UNIVERSITY COLL., matric. 12 Oct., 89, aged 18 (from Clifton coll.), scholar 89; HONOURS:— 2 mathematical mods. 91.

Playne, William Heyworth, born at Minchinhampton, co. Glouc., 24 Oct., 1870; o.s. Arthur, arm. NEW COLL., matric. 11 Oct., 89, aged 18 (from Winchester); HONOURS:— 4 law 92.

Plum, Harry Victor, born at Worcester 1868; 2s. Robert Bagshaw, gent. HERTFORD, matric. 27 Oct., 87, aged 19 (from Worcester free school), scholar 86, B.A. 91; HONOURS:— 1 mathematical mods. 88, 2 mathematics 91.

Plumb, Charles Edward, born at Wisbech, co. Cambridge, 3 May, 1864; 1s. Abraham, cler. WORCESTER, matric. 22 Oct., 91, aged 27.

Plummer, Alfred, M.A., fellow TRINITY 65-75, where see page 433.

Plummer, rev. Charles, M.A., fellow CORPUS CHRISTI 73, where see page 379.

Plummer, William Edward, created M.A. 12 Nov., 1889, assistant observer at the Radcliffe observatory.

Plumptre, Arthur Huntingdon, born at Nonington, Kent, 30 Oct., 1869; 2s. Charles John, arm. TRINITY, matric. 13 Oct., 88, aged 18 (from Harrow), B.A. 92; HONOURS:— 3 classical mods. 90, 3 theology 92.

Plumptre, Francis Fitzherbert, born at Goodneston, Kent, 1864; 3s. John Bridges, arm. ORIEL, matric. 23 Oct., 85, aged 21, from Haileybury.

Plumptre, Henry Fitzwalter, born at Goodneston, Kent, 1871; 1s. John Bridges, arm. UNIVERSITY COLL., matric. 16 Oct., 80, aged 19 (from Limpsfield school), B.A. 85.

Plumptre, Henry Pemberton, born at Freville, near Dover, 24 Oct., 1870; 3s. Charles John, arm. TRINITY, matric. 12 Oct., 89, aged 18 (from Harrow); HONOURS:— 3 classical mods. 91.

Plumptre, Henry Western, born at Nonington, Kent, 3 Nov., 1867; 1s. Charles John, arm. NEW COLL., matric. 15 Oct., 86, aged 18 (from Harrow); scholar HERTFORD 86, B.A. 90; HONOURS:— 2 classical mods. 88, a third in 89.

Plumptre, John Bridges, born at Goodneston, Kent, 1863; 2s. John Bridges, arm. ORIEL, matric. 31 Oct., 82, aged 19 (from Monkton Combe school), B.A. 87, M.A. 89; HONOURS:— 4 theology 86.

Plumptre, John Vallis Nicholl, born at Corfe Mullen, Dorset, 1868; 2s. Robert William, cler. NON-COLLEGIATE, matric. 15 Jan., 87, aged 19 (from Malvern school and King's coll., London); migrated to UNIVERSITY COLL., B.A. 90; HONOURS:— 3 law 90.

Plumptre, Robert Garland, born at Corfe Mullen, Dorset, 8 June, 1865; 1s. Robert William, rector. EXETER, matric. 16 Oct., 84, aged 19 (from Winchester), scholar 84, B.A. 88, M.A. 91 (HONOURS:— 2 classical mods. 86, 3 classics 88, 1 theology 89); vice-principal of St. Edmund Hall 89, where see page 620.

Pocock, Nicholas, M.A., fellow QUEEN'S 38-48, where see page 177.

Pocock, Richard Lawrence, born at Sydenham, Kent, 1871; o.s. William Archbutt, bar.-at-law. PEMBROKE, matric. 28 Oct., 92, aged 18.

Pocock, Theodore Innes, born at Clifton, co. Glouc., 28 Feb., 1869; 2s. Nicholas, cler. CORPUS CHRISTI, matric. 20 Oct., 88, aged 19 (from Clifton coll.), scholar 87, B.A. 92; HONOURS:— 1 mathematical mods. 89, 1 mathematics 91.

Pode, Arthur Crawley, born in London 4 July, 1870; 3s. John Duke, of Slade, Devon, arm. KEBLE, matric. 12 Oct., 89, aged 19 (from Winchester coll.); migrated to WORCESTER.

Pode, Cyril Augustus, born in London 29 April, 1866; 2s. John Duke, of Slade, Devon, arm. WORCESTER, matric. 17 Oct., 87, aged 21 (from Forest school, Walthamstow), B.A. 93.

Pode, Ernest Duke Yonge, born in London 2 Aug., 1862; 1s. John Duke, arm. (from Winchester), B.A. 87 (HONOURS:— 3 natural science 84); M.R.C.S., L.R.C.P., scholar 87, B.A. 91, lost in the s.s. Bokhara off Renadores island 10 Oct., 92.

Pode, John Duke, M.A., fellow NEW COLL. 53-61, where see page 215.

Podmore, Claude, born at Elstree, Herts, April, 1868; 3s. Thompson, cler. KEBLE, matric. 19 Oct., 86, aged 18 (from Eastbourne coll.), B.A. 90.

Podmore, rev. Thompson, M.A., fellow ST. JOHN'S 42-57, where see page 480.

Pole, Herbert, born at Taunton, Somerset, 1866; 1s. George, gen. NON-COLLEGIATE, matric. 21 Oct., 89, aged 23, from Independent coll., Taunton.

Polehampton, Charles Arthur, born at Ross, co. Hereford, 18 Aug., 1864; 1s. Thomas Stedman, British chaplain, Oporto. ST. MARY HALL, matric. 23 April, 84, aged 19 (from Malvern coll.); migrated to MERTON, B.A. 87 (HONOURS:—3 classics 87); died 1 April, 89.

Polehampton, rev. Edward Henry, born at Ellel, co. Lanc., 25 Oct., 1866; 2s. Thomas Stedman, British chaplain, Oporto. QUEEN'S, matric. 30 Oct., 85, aged 19 (from Malvern coll.), B.A. 89 (HONOURS:—2 classical mods. 87, 1 classics 89); curate of St. Matthew, Walworth, Walsall, 91.

Polehampton, Herbert Edward, born at Dover 1863; 3s. John, cler. PEMBROKE, matric. 23 Oct., 82, aged 19.

Polehampton, rev. John, born at Leigh, near Tunbridge, 1861; 2s. John, cler. PEMBROKE, matric. 26 April, 80, aged 19, B.A. 83, M.A. 88; vicar of Woodlands St. Katherine, Somerset, 91.

Polehampton, Thomas Stedman, M.A., fellow PEMBROKE 57-63, where see page 555.

Pollard, Albert Frederick, born at Ryde, I.W., 16 Dec., 1869; 3s. Henry Hindes, gen. JESUS COLL., matric. 19 Oct., 87, aged 17 (from Felsted and Portsmouth schools), exhibitioner 87, B.A. 91; HONOURS:—2 classical mods. 89, 1 history 91; Lothian essay prize 92.

Pollard, Arthur Erskine St. Vincent, born at Pomeroy, Devon, 1869; 2s. Edwin John, admiral, R.N. ORIEL, matric. 20 Oct., 88, aged 19 (from Repton school); and lieut. the Border regt. 91.

Pollard, Henry Bargman, born at Ryde, I.W., 27 Nov., 1868; 1s. Henry Hindes, gen. CHRIST CHURCH, matric. 15 Oct., 86, aged 17 (from Portsmouth school), scholar 86, Dixon scholar 91; HONOURS:—1 morphology 90, biological scholarship at Naples 92.

Pollard, William Joseph, born at Swansea, co. Glam., 28 May, 1858; 2s. Joseph, gen. NON-COLLEGIATE, matric. 14 Oct., 82, aged 23 (from collegiate school, Swansea); migrated to QUEEN'S.

Pollen, Arthur Joseph Hungerford, born in London 13 Sept., 1866; 6s. John Hungerford, arm. TRINITY, matric. 16 Jan., 85, aged 18 (from Birmingham Oratory school), B.A. 88 (HONOURS:— 2 history 88); bar.-at-law, Lincoln's Inn, 93.

Pollen, John Hungerford, M.A., fellow MERTON 42-52, where see page 96.

Pollock, Frank, born in London 12 Aug., 1857; 4s. James Edward, D.Med. TRINITY, matric. 21 May, 80, aged 22 (from the Charterhouse), B.A. and M.A. 87.

Pollock, sir Frederick, bart., M.A. 27 Feb., 1883, by decree of convocation, and fellow CORPUS CHRISTI, see page 380.

Pollock, Harold Arthur, born at Hampstead, Middx., 10 Dec., 1869; 6s. Alfred Atkinson, arm. KEBLE, matric. 12 Oct., 89, aged 19, from Radley coll.

Pollok, Allan George, born at Ayr, N.B., 1872; 3s. Robert Morris, landowner. ST. JOHN'S, matric. 17 Oct., 91, aged 19, from Harrow.

Pollok, John Buchanan, born at Edinburgh 1860; 2s. Robert Morris, arm. ST. JOHN'S, matric. 13 Oct., 88, aged 18 (from Harrow); and lieut. the Black Watch (royal highlanders) 91.

Pollok, William Pollok Morris, born at Glasgow 12 March, 1867; 1s. Robert Morris, arm. TRINITY, matric. 16 Jan., 85, aged 17 (from Harrow school); lieut. 18th Hussars.

Pomeroy, hon. Ralph Legge, born 31 Dec., 1869; 2s. James Spencer, viscount Harberton. BALLIOL, matric. 23 April, 88, aged 18 (from the Charterhouse), B.A. 91 (HONOURS:—3 history 91); passed into Sandhurst 93.

Ponsonby, Arthur Augustus William Harry, born at Windsor 16 Feb., 1871; 3s. genl. sir Henry. BALLIOL, matric. 14 Oct., 90, aged 19, from Eton.

Ponsonby, Charles George Talbot, born at Goldington Bury, Beds, 1 May, 1874; 3s. Charles William Talbot, late R.N. ORIEL, matric. 27 Oct., 92, aged 18, from Harrow.

Pontifex, Edmund Charles, born at Vale, co. Glouc., 15 Nov., 1871; 1s. Alfred, rector. BRASENOSE, matric. 15 Oct., 90, aged 18, from Winchester.

Poole, Arthur William, bishop of Japan, created D.D. 20 Oct., 1883. See *Al. Ox.* and series 1129.

Poole, Francis Oswald, born at West Rainton, co. Durham, 17 Dec., 1870; 8s. Robert Henry, cler. KEBLE, matric. 20 Oct., 91, aged 20, from Cheltenham coll.

Poole, Reginald Lane, M.A. BALLIOL, where see page 70.

Poole, Sydney Henry, born at Folkestone 5 June, 1867; 2s. Edward John, gen. NON-COLLEGIATE, matric. 15 Oct., 87, aged 20, from a Folkestone school.

Poole, William Mansfield, born at Clifton, co. Glouc., 6 April, 1871; 2s. Robert Burton, D.D. MAGDALEN, matric. 14 Oct., 90, aged 19, from Bedford modern school (HONOURS:—3 mathematical mods. 92), in University eight 91.

Poore, Roger Alvin, born at Bath 8 July, 1870; 3s. Robert, arm. HERTFORD, matric. 14 Oct., 89, aged 19, from Sherborne school.

Pope, Ambrose, born at Newcastle-under-Lyme, co. Stafford, 25 May, 1865; 3s. Robert Wilson, pleb. NON-COLLEGIATE, matric. 12 Oct., 89, aged 24 (from University coll., Aberystwith); migrated to JESUS COLL. 15 Oct., 90; HONOURS:—3 classical mods. 91.

Pope, George Uglow, created M.A. 2 Feb., 1886, teacher of Tamil and Telugu 86, chaplain of Balliol 88, D.D. Lambeth 64, fellow University of Madras 59, etc. See Crockford's *Clerical Directory*.

Pope, Philip Joseph, born at Edgbaston, co. Warwick, 1870; 4s. Richard Vercoe, B.A. Lond. BALLIOL, matric. 18 Oct., 92, aged 22 (from Putney school); selected candidate Indian C.S. 92.

Pope, rev. Reginald Henry, born at Exeter 28 July, 1863; y.s. John, arm. BRASENOSE, matric. 19 Oct., 82, aged 19 (from Rugby), B.A. 86, M.A. 89; curate of Northchurch, Berkhamstad, 90.

Pope, Richard William Massy, B.D., censor of Non-Collegiate students 87, where see page 636.

Pope, Samuel, born in New Jersey, America, 23 Aug., 1868; 1s. William Rushton, arm. TRINITY, matric. 15 Oct., 87, aged 19, B.A. 91 (HONOURS:—3 law 91); bar.-at-law, Middle Temple, 92.

Pope, William Raymond, born at Barnstone, Notts, 1867; 1s. William John Pitfield, cler. TURRELL'S HALL, matric. 15 Oct., 86, aged 19.

Popham, Francis William Leybourne, born in London 1872; 1s. Francis Leybourne, arm. BRASENOSE, matric. 10 June, 81, aged 19, from Harrow.

Popham, Hugh Francis Arthur Leybourne, born in London 1864; 2s. Francis Leybourne, arm. BRASENOSE, matric. 19 Oct., 82, aged 18 (from the Charterhouse), B.A. 87, M.A. 89.

Popkin, John Llewellyn Traherne, born at St. Helier's, Jersey, 1869; 3s. Dan William Bassett, druggist. NON-COLLEGIATE, matric. 4 June, 92, aged 23, from Maesteg British school.

Portal, Spencer John, born at Malshanger, Hants, 14 May, 1864; 2s. Wyndham Spencer, arm. CHRIST CHURCH, matric. 13 Oct., 82, aged 18, from Winchester.

Porter, John Scott, born at Dublin 18 July, 1871; 1s. Andrew Marshall, LL.D. BRASENOSE, matric. 15 Oct., 90, aged 19 (from the Charterhouse), scholar 90; HONOURS:—2 classical mods. 92.

Porter, rev. Robert Waltham, born at Lower Norwood, Surrey, 1868; 1s. Thomas, gen. BRASENOSE, matric. 20 Oct., 86, aged 18 (from Dulwich coll.), scholar 86, B.A. 90 (HONOURS:—1 classical mods. 88, 1 classics 90); curate of All Saints', Poplar, 91.

Porter, Wilfrid King, born at Cheltenham 29 Dec., 1864; 9s. Robert Tindal, arm. BALLIOL, matric. 16 Oct., 83, aged 18 (from Cheltenham coll.), B.A. 88 (HONOURS:—a law 87, a civil law 88); selected candidate Indian C.S. 83; bar.-at-law, Gray's Inn, 88.

Porter, William Haldane, born at Belfast 15 May, 1867; y.s. Josiah, D.D., president Q. coll., Belfast. LINCOLN, matric. 21 Oct., 87, aged 20 (from Queen's coll., Belfast), scholar 87, B.A. 90; HONOURS:— a classical mods. 89, a classics 91.

Portman, Alan Berkeley, born at Corton, Dorset, 17 Feb., 1872; 1s. Thomas Walter Berkeley, cler. UNIVERSITY COLL., matric. 11 Oct., 90, aged 18, from Wellington coll.

Portman, hon. Edwin Berkeley, B.C.L., fellow ALL SOULS' 50-7, where see page 279.

Portman, Lionel, born at Corton Denham, Somerset, 26 Dec., 1873; 2s. rev. and hon. Walter Berkeley, B.A. UNIVERSITY COLL., matric. 15 Oct., 92, aged 18 (from Wellington coll.), cox. of the University eight 93.

Postance, rev. Charles Groves, born at Liverpool 28 March, 1865; 5s. Henry, cler. ST. MARY HALL, matric. 20 Oct., 84, aged 19, B.A. 88, M.A. 91; curate of West Kirby, Cheshire, 91.

Poste, Edward, M.A., fellow ORIEL 46, where see page 149.

Postlethwaite, George, born at Furness, co. Lanc., 1861; 6s. John, gen. NON-COLLEGIATE, matric. 17 Oct., 81, aged 21, B.A. 86; HONOURS:— 2 theology 84, septuagint prize 84, 2 classics 86.

Pott, Alfred, B.D., archdeacon of Berks, fellow MAGDALEN 53-5, where see page 323.

Pott, Alfred Francis Vaughan, born at Kennington, London, 10 June, 1873; 5s. Alfred, archdeacon of Berks. NEW COLL., matric. 14 Oct., 92, aged 19, from Eton.

Pott, Charles Stanley, born in London 11 Jan., 1869; 3s. Robert, gen. EXETER, matric. 17 Oct., 88, aged 19 (from Haileybury), B.A. 92.

Pott, George Stanley, born at Kennington, Surrey, 13 Aug., 1870; 4s. Alfred, archdeacon of Berks. MAGDALEN, matric. 14 Oct., 89, aged 19 (from Radley coll.), B.A. 93.

Pott, John Alfred, born in London 17 Nov., 1865; 2s. Alfred, archdeacon of Berks. KEBLE, matric. 14 Oct., 84, aged 18 (from Haileybury), B.A. 88; HONOURS:—3 classical mods. 86, 4 classics 88.

Potter, Edward Arthur Smalley, born at Ryde, I.W., 30 July, 1868; 1s. Edward Smalley, arm. EXETER, matric. 21 Oct., 86, aged 18, from Eton.

Potter, Henry, D.D., bishop of New York, created D.D. 24 May, 1892.

Potter, Walter Bertram, born at South Kensington 14 March, 1872; o.s. Rupert, bar.-at-law. MAGDALEN, matric. 14 Oct., 90, aged 18 (from the Charterhouse); HONOURS:—3 classical mods. 92.

Pottinger, Henry Allison, M.A., fellow WORCESTER 83, where see page 574.

Potts, rev. Frederick Arthur, born in London 26 May, 1862; o.s. Frederick, of Horsley Hall, co. Denbigh, arm. MAGDALEN, matric. 14 Jan., 81; aged 18, B.A. 84, M.A. 87 (HONOURS:—3 theology 84); curate of Bournemouth St. Peter 92.

Potts, Robert Ullock, born in London 16 June, 1866; 1s. Robert Alfred, gen. ORIEL, matric. 23 Oct., 84, aged 18 (from Ashby-de-la-Zouche school), B.A. 88; HONOURS:—3 classical mods. 86, 3 classics 88.

Potts, Thomas Radford, M.A., D.C.L., LINCOLN, where see page 246.

Poulter, Brownlow, M.A., fellow NEW COLL. 44-51, where see page 212.

Poulter, rev. Donald Francis Ogilvy, born at Blackheath, Kent, 17 Aug., 1862; 1s. Brownlow, gen. LINCOLN, matric. 23 Oct., 82, aged 20 (from Winchester), exhibitioner 84, B.A. 87, M.A. 90 (HONOURS:—1 classical mods. 84, 3 classics 86); curate of St. George, East Stonehouse, Devon, 87.

Poulton, Edward Bagnall, M.A., JESUS COLL., where see page 514.

Pountney, Arthur Meek, born at Clapham, Surrey, 30 Dec., 1873; 3s. William Henry, of Caversham, near Reading, artist. UNIVERSITY COLL., matric. 17 Oct., 91, aged 17 (from Reading gr. school), scholar 91; HONOURS:—1 mathematical mods. 92.

Powell, Alfred Thomas, born at East Stonehouse, Devon, 19 April, 1869; 2s. William, R.M. EXETER, matric. 17 Oct., 88, aged 19 (from Paignton coll.), scholar 88, B.A. 92; HONOURS:—1 mathematical mods. 90, 2 mathematics 92.

Powell, Arthur Marriott, born in London 31 May, 1869; 1s. Arthur Crofts, gen. NEW COLL., matric. 12 Oct., 88, aged 19 (from the Charterhouse 82-8), B.A. 93; HONOURS:—3 classical mods. 90, 4 history 92.

Powell, Claude Tringham Graham, born in London 18 July, 1869; 1s. Francis Graham, arm. ST. JOHN'S, matric. 13 Oct., 88, aged 19 (from Westminster school); HONOURS:—4 theology 92.

Powell, Edward Athelstane Lewis, born at Aberystwith, co. Cardigan, 12 Nov., 1870; 1s. William Beauclerc, arm. UNIVERSITY COLL., matric. 14 Oct., 89, aged 18, from Rugby.

Powell, Evan Worthington, born at Newton, co. Montgomery, 13 Nov., 1871; 1s. Evan, gen. BALLIOL, matric. 14 Oct., 90, aged 18 (from Winchester); HONOURS:—3 classical mods. 92.

Powell, Frederick Walter, born at Kempsay, co. Worcester, 17 April, 1854; 1s. Alfred, gen. LINCOLN, matric. 18 Oct., 83, aged 29 (from Mason coll., Birmingham), B.A. 86; HONOURS:—4 history 86.

Powell, Frederick York, M.A., student CHRIST CHURCH 84, where see page 408.

Powell, George Gordon, born at Croydon 21 May, 1865; 1s. George Thompson, gen. NON-COLLEGIATE, matric. 20 Oct., 84, aged 19 (from Wellington coll.); migrated to MERTON, B.A. 88; HONOURS:—4 law 88.

Powell, Henry Townsend, born at All Saints, Dorset, 19 April, 1861; 1s. Henry Clark, rector of Wylye, Somerset. MAGDALEN, matric. 23 Oct., 85, aged 19 (from Leamington coll.), B.A. 89 (HONOURS:—2 classical mods. 87, 3 classics 89); drowned Aug., 91, in Newfoundland.

Powell, Herbert Andrews, born at Charlton, Kent, 1863; 3s. Thomas Wilde, gen. CORPUS CHRISTI, matric. 26 Oct., 81, aged 18 (from Uppingham school), B.A. 85, M.A. and B.Med. 90, D.Med. and M.Ch. 92; HONOURS:—a classical mods. 82, 2 classics 85.

Powell, John Undershell, born at Bonham, Wilts, 4 Oct., 1865; 1s. John, cler. BALLIOL, matric. 15 Oct., 84, aged 19, fellow ST. JOHN'S 90, M.A. 91; HONOURS:—Greek verse 85, accessit Hertford scholarship 85, 1 classical mods. 86, Craven scholarship 87, proxime accessit 86, 2 classics 88, Latin essay 89.

Powell, Legh Richmond, born at Anglesea, Hants, 25 Aug., 1840; 3s. Henry Folliott, of Brandlesome Hall, co. Lanc., arm. NON-COLLEGIATE, matric. 10 April, 80, aged 39, from Lancing coll. and Ashbourne, co. Derby.

Powell, rev. Morgan Jones, born at Swansea, co. Glam., 1863; 1s. Thomas, gen. BALLIOL, matric. 17 Oct., 82, aged 19 (from Swansea gr. school), B.A. 86, M.A. 89 (HONOURS :—2 classical mods. 84, 3 classics 86); curate of St. John with St. Mary, Brecon, 89.

Powell, Thomas Linden, born at Newick, Sussex, 2 Jan., 1864; elder son of William, rector. NEW COLL., matric. 15 Oct., 84, aged 20 (from Bradfield coll. 77-9), B.A. 88 (HONOURS :—1 law 88); of Newick, Sussex.

Powell, Thomas Percy Prosser, born in London 26 Dec., 1869; 1s. Thomas Prosser, cler. ORIEL, matric. 20 Oct., 88, aged 18 (from the Charterhouse), B.A. 93.

Powell, William Geoffrey Lambert, born at Streatham, Surrey, 3 Dec., 1869; 4s. James Heslop, gen. HERTFORD, matric. 19 Oct., 88, aged 18 (from Lancing coll.), B.A. 92.

Powell, William George, born at Newick, Sussex, 25 Jan., 1865; 2s. William, cler. EXETER, matric. 16 Oct., 84, aged 19, from Bradfield coll. 77-82.

Powell, William Hawkins, born at Bristol 14 Feb., 1867; 1s. Septimus, gen. MERTON, matric. 21 Oct., 86, aged 19 (from Clifton coll.), B.A. 90; HONOURS :—3 history 90.

Power, Philip Ernest le Poer, born at Worthing, Sussex, 1 Nov., 1860; 1s. Philip Bennett, cler., M.A., Dublin. NEW COLL., matric. 16 Oct., 80, aged 19 (from Uppingham school), B.A. 84; HONOURS :—3 classical mods. 82.

Powers, George Wightman, born at Barwell, co. Leic., 9 May, 1864; 1s. George, gen. NEW COLL., matric. 12 Oct., 83, aged 19 (from Highgate school), scholar 83, B.A. 87, M.A. 91; HONOURS: —1 classical mods. 84, 1 classics 87, 1 history 88.

Powles, rev. Ernest, born at Liverpool 18 April, 1867; 1s. Kenneth, gen. WORCESTER, matric. 19 Oct., 86, aged 19 (from Dulwich coll.), B.A. 89; curate of St. Mark, Lakenham, Norfolk, 91.

Powles, Frederick James Endell, born at Rodmarton, co. Glouc., 25 Feb., 1867; 3s. Henry Charles, cler. MERTON, matric. 21 Oct., 86, aged 19, from Marlborough.

Powles, George Lewin, born at Liverpool March, 1868; o.s. George, cler. KEBLE, matric. 17 Oct., 87, aged 19 (from Kirkham school); migrated to ST. EDMUND HALL, B.A. 91.

Powles, Richard Cowley, M.A., fellow EXETER 42-50, where see page 125.

Powley, rev. Arthur Thomas, born at Langworthy, Cumberland, 26 July, 1860; 2s. John, gen. QUEEN'S, matric. 28 Oct., 81, aged 21 (from Penrith and Reading gr. schools), B.A. 84, M.A. 90 (HONOURS :—4 history 84); curate of Tarporley, Cheshire, 88.

Powning, Frederick Edmonds, born at Totnes, Devon, 1862; 2s. James, cler. ST. ALBAN HALL, matric. 28 Jan., 82, aged 20; migrated to MERTON, B.A. 87.

Powys, Francis Arthur, B.D., fellow ST. JOHN'S 51-70, where see page 483.

Powys, hon. John, born at Lilford Hall, Salop, 12 Jan., 1863; 2s. Thomas Lyttleton, lord Powys. NON-COLLEGIATE, matric. 21 Jan., 82, aged 19 (from Marlborough); migrated to BRASENOSE 82, B.A. 86.

Poynder, Frederick Cecil, born in London 18 April, 1862; o.s. Frederick, cler. ST. JOHN'S, matric. 16 Oct., 80, aged 18 (from Cheltenham coll.), scholar 80-4, B.A. 84, M.A. 87; HONOURS :—1 classical mods. 82, 2 classics 84.

Poynder, sir John Poynder Dickson, bart., born at Ryde, I.W., 31 Oct., 1866; 1s. John Bourmaster, rear-admiral R.N., C.B. CHRIST CHURCH, matric. 30 May, 85, aged 18 (from Harrow); 6th bart. (1884), assumed the additional name of Poynder on attaining his majority 12 Jan., 88, high sheriff, Wilts, 90, late lieut. 3rd royal Scots, M.P. Wiltshire, Chippenham division, 92.

Poynting, John Whitfield Elford, born at Fallowfield, near Manchester, 10 Oct., 1873; 1s. Charles Thomas, B.A., nonconformist minister. BALLIOL, matric. 18 Oct., 92, aged 19, from Sedbergh school.

Poynton, Arthur Blackburne, born at Kelston, Somerset, 28 June, 1867; 4s. Francis John, cler. BALLIOL, matric. 24 Oct., 85, aged 18 (from Marlborough coll.), scholar 84, B.A. 89; fellow HERTFORD 89, M.A. 92; HONOURS :—Hertford scholarship 85, 1 classical mods. 87, Craven scholarship 87 (accessit 86), 1 classics 89.

Poynton, Ernest Walter, born in London 22 March, 1872; 6s. Francis John, cler. EXETER, matric. 16 March, 91, aged 18 (from Marlborough); HONOURS :—3 classical mods. 92.

Poynton, Henry Hopwood, born at Kelston, Somerset, March, 1866; 3s. Francis John, cler. NON-COLLEGIATE, matric. 13 Oct., 84, aged 18 (from Clifton coll.

Prall, Richard Evans, born at Rochester 1864; 1s. Richard, arm. CHRIST CHURCH, matric. 27 May, 82, aged 18 (from Cranbrook school), B.A. 86 (HONOURS :—3 classical mods. 84, 3 history 86); bar.-at-law, Lincoln's Inn, 87.

Prance, Charles Herbert Gouldsmith, born at Plymouth 13 July, 1869; 1s. Charles Rooke, D.Med. MERTON, matric. 17 Oct., 88, aged 19, from Plymouth coll.

Prankerd, Archibald Arthur, M.A., D.C.L., WORCESTER, where see page 378.

Pratt, Charles Ernest, born at Cawthorne, Yorks, Aug., 1867; o.s. Charles Tiplady, cler. KEBLE, matric. 19 Oct., 86, aged 19 (from Rossall school); migrated to MARCON'S HALL, B.A. 92.

Pratt, Frederick Greville, born in Bombay 1870; 4s. Edward, arm. HERTFORD, matric. 19 Oct., 88, aged 18 (from Dulwich coll.), scholar 87 (HONOURS: —1 classical mods. 90); assist. collector and magistrate Thana, Bo. c.s.

Pratt, rev. George Edward Haslop, born at Kidderminster 1862; 1s. Edward Haslop, arm. ST. JOHN'S, matric. 26 Oct., 81, aged 19, B.A. 85 (HONOURS :—2 classical mods. 83, 3 theology 85); curate of Much Wenlock, Salop, 90.

Pratt, Henry Sheldon, born at Warwick 26 Jan., 1873; 1s. Henry, town councillor. LINCOLN, matric. 25 Oct., 92, aged 19, from Warwick school.

Pratt, Jacob (Vivour), born at Freetown, Sierra Leone, 1857; 3s. Robert, gen. CHRIST CHURCH, matric. 14 Oct., 81, aged 24, B.A. 87.

Preedy, William Webber, born at Stonehouse, Devon, 1869; 1s. George William, arm. KEBLE, matric. 17 Oct., 87, aged 18 (from Westward Ho! coll.), B.A. 90; HONOURS :—4 theology 90.

Prentice, Noel, born in Kent 25 Aug., 1870; o.s. George, gen. UNIVERSITY COLL., matric. 13 Oct., 88, aged 18 (from Maidstone school), exhibitioner 87, B.A. 91; HONOURS :—1 law 91.

Prescot, Kenrick, M.A., fellow MERTON 53-64, where see page 97.

Prescott, Henry Frederick, born at Sydenham, Kent, 19 March, 1866; 1s. Edgar Grote, organist. QUEEN'S, matric. 22 Oct., 84, aged 18 (from Dulwich coll.), B.A. 87; HONOURS :—3 classical mods 86.

Prescott, Herbert Grote, born at Lewisham, Kent, 3 Sept., 1872; 2s. Edward Grote, organist, B.A. Oxon. JESUS COLL., matric. 20 Oct., 91, aged 19 (from Merchant Taylors' school); scholar 91.

Prescott, Thomas Leigh, born at Caddington, Beds, 1870; 2s. Thomas, cler. BALLIOL, matric. 17 Oct., 89, aged 19 (from Marlborough coll.); assist. commissioner Punjab 91.

Pressey, rev. William James, born in London 1859; 2s. Arthur, gen. WADHAM, matric. 26 Jan., 81, aged 22, B.A. 84, M.A. 87 (HONOURS: —3 history 84); curate of Foxearth, Essex, 90.

Prestage, Edgar, born at Manchester 1869; 1s. John Edward, arm. BALLIOL, matric. 19 Oct., 87, aged 18 (from Radley coll.), B.A. 91; HONOURS: —2 history 91.

Preston, Charles Sansome, born in London 4 April, 1865; 1s. Thomas Sansome, solicitor. NEW COLL., matric. 10 Oct., 84, aged 19 (from Marlborough), B.A. 88, M.A. and B.C.L. 92 (HONOURS: —3 classical mods. 86, 2 history 88); bar.-at-law, Inner Temple, 91.

Preston, rev. Charles William Antony, born at Warcop, Westmorland, March, 1865; 1s. Charles, cler. CHRIST CHURCH, matric. 16 Oct., 85, aged 20 (from Felsted school), B.A. 89; curate of Keelby and Immingham, co. Lincoln, 91.

Preston, George Reginald Preston, born in London 18 March, 1869; 2s. Reuben, arm. MERTON, matric. 17 Oct., 88, aged 19 (from Blackheath school), B.A. 92; HONOURS: —3 classical mods. 90, 4 classics 92.

Preston, Percy Herbert, born in Worcester 1869; 2s. William Carnall, cler. NON-COLLEGIATE, matric. 14 Feb., 90, aged 21, from a Norwich school.

Preston, Percy Rawson, born at Norwood, Surrey, 10 Jan., 1870; 3s. Rawson, gen. EXETER, matric. 2 May, 89, aged 19 (from Harrow), B.A. 92; HONOURS: —4 theology 92.

Preston, Robert William Pigot Clarke Campbell, born at Culross, Perthshire, 1866; 1s. William Colin, cler. CHRIST CHURCH, matric. 31 May, 84, aged 18, from Eton.

Preston, rev. Roland D'Arcy, born at Sandgate, Kent, 1 July, 1867; 3s. John D'Arcy Warcop, vicar. EXETER, matric. 21 Oct., 86, aged 19 (from Marlborough), scholar 86, B.A. 90 (HONOURS: —2 classical mods. 88, 2 classics 90, 2 theology 91.

Prestwich, Joseph, born in London 12 March, 1812; 1s. Joseph, gent. CHRIST CHURCH, matric. entry dated 3 Nov., 1874, aged 62, M.A. by decree 11 Nov., 74, created D.C.L. 20 Nov., 88, university professor of geology 74-87, F.R.S. and vice-president 70-1, F.G.S., president geological society 70-2. See *Men and Women of the Time*.

Pretyman, Frederick, B.D., fellow MAGDALEN 42-58, where see page 321.

Previté, Henry Francis, born at Weedon, Kensington, 24 Jan., 1870; 2s. Joseph, arm. MERTON, matric. 17 Oct., 88, aged 18 (from Clifton coll.), exhibitioner 88, B.A. 92; HONOURS: —2 history 92.

Prevost, Charles Thomas Keble, born at Southsea, Hants, 19 July, 1866; 1s. Charles, lieut.-col. KEBLE, matric. 22 Oct., 85, aged 19 (from Sherborne school), B.A. 88; HONOURS: — 3 theology 88.

Priaulx, Osmond, born at Sydney, Australia, 1866; 1s. Osmond de Lancy, arm. CHRIST CHURCH, matric. 16 Jan., 84, aged 18.

Price, Arthur Long, born at Titley, co. Hereford, 1 May, 1865; 5s. David, cler. ST. MARY HALL, matric. 27 April, 89, aged 23.

Price, Arthur Radcliffe, born at Glenelg, Australia, 1863; o.s. Henry Strong, gent. PEMBROKE, matric. 23 Oct., 82, aged 19.

Price, Aubrey Charles, B.A., fellow NEW COLL. 49-57, where see page 214.

Price, Bartholomew, D.D., master of PEMBROKE 92, where see page 552.

Price, Bartholomew George, born at Oxford 7 May, 1870; 2s. Bartholomew, master of Pembroke. CHRIST CHURCH, matric. 12 Oct., 88, aged 18, from Winchester.

Price, Charles James Coverley, M.A., fellow EXETER 64-81 and 82, where see page 123.

Price, rev. Cyril, born at Selly Oak, near Worcester, 12 March, 1866; 6s. Thomas, cler. WORCESTER, matric. 22 Oct., 85, aged 19 (from Birmingham school), B.A. 89; curate of Stratford-on-Avon, co. Worcester, 90.

Price, Edwin Lessware, born at Bow, Middx., 1875; 1s. Edwin Alfred, gen. CHARSLEY'S HALL, matric. 3 Feb., 91, aged 16.

Price, George Frederic, D.D., fellow NEW COLL. 51-73, where see page 214.

Price, George Herbert, born at Somerton, Middx., 30 Aug., 1863; 3s. Henry Stephen, gen. BRASENOSE, matric. 19 Oct., 82, aged 19 (from Berkhamstead school), exhibitioner 82, B.A. 87; HONOURS: — 2 classical mods. 84, 3 classics 86.

Price, Henry, born at Muestey, co. Glam., 22 March, 1872; 3s. John. BRASENOSE, matric. 22 Oct., 91, aged 19 (from Llandovery coll.), scholar 90.

Price, Hugh, born at Edgbaston, co. Warwick, 1861; 4s. Thomas, cler. WORCESTER, matric. 19 Oct., 82, aged 21, B.A. 87.

Price, Hugh Hankes, born at Lampeter, co. Cardigan, 1865; 1s. William, gen. CHRIST CHURCH, matric. 10 Oct., 84, aged 19 (from Brecon school), B.A. 88 (HONOURS: —3 chemistry 88); brother of Llewelyn B.

Price, John, B.A., fellow NEW COLL. 34-45, where see page 211.

Price, John, born at Talley, co. Carmarthen, 10 Jan., 1870; 1s. David Long, doctor. LINCOLN, matric. 24 Jan., 89, aged 19.

Price, John Arthur, born at Shrewsbury 1862; o.s. John, gent. BALLIOL, matric. 18 Oct., 81, aged 19 (from Shrewsbury school), B.A. 86 (HONOURS: —2 classical mods. 83, 2 classics 85, 2 history 86); bar.-at-law, Lincoln's Inn, 90.

Price, Langford Lovell Frederic Rice, born in London 20 July, 1862; 2s. Aubrey Charles, cler. TRINITY, matric. 15 Oct., 81, aged 19 (from Dulwich coll.), scholar 81-5, B.A. 85; fellow of ORIEL 88, M.A. 88, treasurer 88; HONOURS: —1 classical mods. 82, 1 classics 85.

Price, Lewis Herbert, born at Titley, co. Hereford, 1864; 4s. David, cler. NON-COLLEGIATE, matric. 13 Jan., 83, aged 19 (from Abingdon gr. school); migrated to ST. MARY HALL, B.A. 86, M.A. 89.

Price, Llewelyn Bankes, born at Dolau, co. Cardigan, 16 Dec., 1867; 2s. William, gen. JESUS COLL., matric. 20 Oct., 86, aged 18 (from Brecon coll.), scholar 86, B.A. 89 (HONOURS: —3 chemistry 89); brother of Hugh B.

Price, Marmaduke Gwynne, born at Brecon 1860; 1s. Rees, cler. NON-COLLEGIATE, matric. 17 Oct., 80, aged 20 (from Christ's coll., Brecon), migrated to WORCESTER, B.A. 84; HONOURS: — 3 law 85.

Price, Owen Talbot, born at Surbiton, Surrey, 13 April, 1868; 1s. Charles John, gen. EXETER, matric. 21 Oct., 86, aged 18 (from Haileybury), B.A. 91.

Price, rev. Thomas Ralph, born at Cardigan 29 Nov., 1863; 2s. Charles, vicar of Pennal Machynlleth. JESUS COLL., matric. 15 Oct., 90, aged 26 (from St. John's, Leatherhend, and non.-coll., Cambridge, matric. 22 Oct., 88), B.A. 91.

Price, William Brinton, born at Margate, Kent, 1868; 1s. William Preston, D.Med. CHRIST CHURCH, matric. 15 Oct., 86, aged 18.

Price, William George, born at Newport, Essex, 1865; 1s. William James, gen. QUEEN'S, matric. 4 Feb. 84, aged 19, B.Mus. 86.
Price, rev. William Henry, born at Gloucester 21 April, 1859; 1s. William Farmer, gen. B.A. from ST. JOHN'S, CAMB., 80, M.A. 83; chaplain TRINITY, OXFORD, 84, incorporated 20 Feb., 88, aged 28 (from Hereford school); curate of St. Mary Magdalen with St. George the Martyr, Oxford, 85.
Price, William Hughes Bankes-, born at Marshfield, co. Glouc., 1862; 1s. John, cler. JESUS COLL., matric. 29 Jan., 81, aged 19, B.A. 84.
Prichard, Bertie Coppinger, born at Clifton, co. Glouc., 1869; 3s. Charles John Collins, gen. ORIEL, matric. 2 Feb., 87, aged 18.
Prichard, Harold Arthur, born at Kilburn, London, 30 Oct., 1871; 1s. Walter Stennett, solicitor. NEW COLL., matric. 10 Oct., 90, aged 18 (from Clifton coll.), scholar 90; HONOURS:—1 mathematical mods. 91, junior mathematical exhibition 92.
Prichard, Herbert William, born at Leeds 1873; o.s. William Joseph, gent. KEBLE, matric. 15 Oct., 92, aged 19 (from Leeds school), scholar 92.
Prichard, Matthew Stewart, born at Brislington, Somerset, 4 Jan., 1865; 3s. Charles Henry, gent., deceased. NEW COLL., matric. 8 Dec., 83, aged 18 (from Marlborough), B.A. 87 (HONOURS:—2 law 87, 2 civil law 89); bar.-at-law, Inner Temple, 91.
Prickard, Arthur Octavius, M.A., fellow NEW COLL. 66, where see page 205.
Prickard, Harry Seddon, born at Llandrindod, co. Radnor, 1866; 1s. William Edward, cler. ORIEL, matric. 23 Oct., 84, aged 18 (from Winchester); lieut. the Prince of Wales (north Staffordshire regt.) 90.
Prickett, rev. Marmaduke Alan, born in London 1 Oct., 1864; 1s. Thomas, cler. NEW COLL., matric. 10 Oct., 84, aged 20 (from Harrow and Cheltenham coll.); scholar HERTFORD 84, B.A. 89, M.A. 92 (HONOURS:—1 classical mods. 86); curate of Holy Trinity, Worthing, 90-1.
Pridham, Arthur, born at Taunton, Somerset, 20 July, 1871; 2s. John, gen. WORCESTER, matric. 14 Oct., 90, aged 19, from Taunton coll.
Pridmore, William Henry, born at Kenilworth, co. Warwick, 30 Oct., 1871; 2s. John, gen. NON-COLLEGIATE, matric. 12 Oct., 89, aged 17 (from Rugby); migrated to JESUS COLL. 20 Jan., 91, B.A. 92; HONOURS:—2 history 92.
Priestley, Albert Wesley, born at Thornton, Yorks, 5 July, 1865; 2s. Midgley, gen. QUEEN'S, matric. 30 Oct., 85, aged 20 (from Bradford gr. school), exhibitioner 85, B.A. 89, M.A. 92; HONOURS:—3 classical mods. 87, 3 classics 89.
Prince, Arthur, born at Manchester 15 April, 1864; 4s. John Franklin, gen. JESUS COLL., matric. 21 Jan., 85, aged 20 (from Christ coll., Brecon, and Itain school), B.A. 88, M.A. 91; HONOURS:—2 theology 88.
Prince, Harry Forth Wicksteed, born at Bonsall, co. Derby, Oct., 1863; o.s. Samuel, arm. CHRIST CHURCH, matric. 20 Oct., 82, aged 19, from Eton.
Prince, rev. Henry Rhodes, born at Taunton, Somerset, 1864; o.s. Henry, gen. NON-COLLEGIATE, matric. 17 Oct., 85, aged 21 (from Taunton school), B.A. 89; curate of St. Saviour's, Pimlico, 89.
Prince, rev. John Henry, born at Birmingham 1868; 1s. John, gen. NON-COLLEGIATE, matric. 15 Jan., 87, aged 19 (from Birmingham school), B.A. 90; curate of St. Matthew, Stonehouse, Devon, 90.

Pringle, James Lewis, born at Scarborough 1870; 2s. James Thomas, arm. ORIEL, matric. 8 May, 90, aged 20, from Radley coll.
Pringle, John Christian, born at Edinburgh 27 Aug., 1872; 2s. Robert, W.S. EXETER, matric. 22 Oct., 91, aged 19 (from Winchester), scholar 91.
Prinsep, rev. Harry Stewart, born at Lucknow 1863; 1s. Henry Auriol, arm. ORIEL, matric. 31 Oct., 82, aged 19 (from the Charterhouse), B.A. 87, M.A. 89; curate of old St. Pancras, London, 90.
Prioleau, Richard Trenholm, born at Liverpool Feb., 1865; 3s. Charles Kuhn, arm. CHRIST CHURCH, matric. 10 Oct., 84, aged 19 (from St. Edward's school, Summertown), B.A. 87; HONOURS:—4 law 87.
Prior, George Thurland, born at Oxford 16 Dec., 1862; 1s. George Thomas, gen. MAGDALEN, matric. 15 Oct., 81, aged 18 (from Magdalen coll. school), demy 81-6, B.A. 85, M.A. 88; HONOURS:—2 mathematical mods. 83, 1 natural science 85, 1 physics 86.
Prior, Sydney Herbert, born at Faringdon, Berks, 12 Oct., 1872; 1s. Henry Neville, gen. EXETER, matric. 16 Oct., 90, aged 18, from Oxford high school.
Pritchard, Arthur, born at Twickenham, Middx., 1863; 3s. William Tarn, gen. BALLIOL, matric. 17 Oct., 82, aged 19 (from Clifton coll.), B.A. and M.A. 90 (HONOURS:—2 classical mods. 84, 3 classics 86); bar.-at-law, Inner Temple, 90.
Pritchard, rev. Arthur, born at Everton, co. Lanc., 1861; 1s. Samuel, gen. NON-COLLEGIATE, matric. 13 Oct., 88, aged 27, B.A. 91.
Pritchard, Charles, D.D., fellow NEW COLL. 83, where see page 206.
Pritchard, George Eric Campbell, born at Freshwater, I.W., 1865; o.s. rev. Charles, Savilian professor of astronomy. HERTFORD, matric. 31 Jan., 84, aged 19 (from Clifton coll.), B.A. 87, M.A. and B.Med. 92; HONOURS:—1 physiology 87.
Pritchard, Godfrey, born at Putney, Surrey, 1862; 2s. Robert Albion, D.C.L. UNIVERSITY COLL., matric. 15 Oct., 81, aged 19 (from Clifton coll.); migrated to NEW INN HALL, B.A. 86.
Pritchard, rev. Lorenzo Alfred, born at Wednesbury, co. Staff., 23 Nov., 1862; 4s. Thomas, gen. WADHAM, matric. 11 Oct., 84, aged 21 (from Ruabon gr. school), B.A. 87, M.A. 91; curate of St. Cross (or the Abbey), Shrewsbury, 91.
Pritchard, Rowland, born at Ciltwilan, co. Carnarvon, 24 July, 1863; y.s. William, pleb. NON-COLLEGIATE, matric. 14 Oct., 92, aged 19 (from Friars school), Bangor; migrated to
Pritchitt, rev. John Frederick Stephen, born at Southwark 23 Aug., 1858; 2s. James John Joseph, arm. ST. MARY HALL, matric. 11 May, 81, aged 22; curate of St. Matthias, Malvern Link, co. Worcester, 89.
Probert, William Geoffrey, born at Bedford 1 May, 1864; 2s. capt. William Richard. LINCOLN, matric. 27 Oct., 85, aged 21 (from Melbourne university), B.A. 89; HONOURS:—4 history 89.
Probyn, Hugh Edmund Hamilton, born at Florence 11 Feb., 1871; 1s. John Holt, arm. MAGDALEN, matric. 14 Oct., 89, aged 18, from Haileybury.
Probyn, Percy Clifford, born in London 13 Nov., 1868; 1s. Clifford, gen. MAGDALEN, matric. 22 Oct., 87, aged 18 (from Westminster school), B.A. 90 (HONOURS:—4 law 90); bar.-at-law, Inner Temple, 92.
Probyn, Wilfred Julian Noel, born at St. Leonards, Sussex, 29 June, 1872; 2s. John Webb, of Mitcheldean, co. Glouc., esq. UNIVERSITY COLL., matric. 17 Oct., 91, aged 19, from Haileybury.

Procter, Francis Henry, born at Aldborough Hatch, Essex, 1890; 2s. John Mathias, rector of Thorley, Herts. NEW COLL., matric. 14 Oct., 87, aged 18 (from Merchant Taylors' school); HONOURS: —3 theology 90; brother of John E.

Procter, rev. John Edward Ingleby, born at Aldborough Hatch, Essex, 10 Sept., 1865; 1s. John Mathias, rector of Thorley. NEW COLL., matric. 16 Jan., 85, aged 19 (from Merchant Taylors' school), B.A. 88, M.A. 91 (HONOURS:—2 history 88); curate of Thorley 91; brother of Francis H.

Procter, John Mathias, M.A., fellow JESUS COLL. 59-65, where see page 513.

Procter, rev. Gordon Percy, born at Cheltenham 1866; 1s. Francis Bartlett, cler. NON-COLLEGIATE, matric. 17 Oct., 85, aged 19 (from King's coll. school and Aldenham gr. school); migrated to ST. MARY HALL, B.A. 91; HONOURS:—3 classical mods. 87.

Procter, Owen Francis, born at Pentonville, London, 1870; 2s. Francis Battell, D.D. NON-COLLEGIATE, matric. 15 Oct., 87, aged 17 (from Aldenham gr. school); migrated to ST. EDMUND HALL, B.A. 90; HONOURS:—4 theology 90.

Procter, Robert George Collier, born at East Budleigh, Devon, 13 May, 1868; o.s. Robert, arm. CORPUS CHRISTI, matric. 20 Oct., 86, aged 18 (from Bath coll. school), scholar 86, B.A. 90; HONOURS: —1 classical mods. 88, 2 classics 90.

Procter, William Henry, born at Heversham, Westmorland, 6 Nov., 1864; 3s. Edward, gen. QUEEN'S, matric. 23 Oct., 82, aged 17 (from Heversham gr. school), exhibitioner 81-6; HONOURS:—2 mathematical mods. 84, 3 mathematics 86.

Prosser, rev. David Lewis, born at Llangunnor, co. Carmarthen, June, 1868; 1s. David, gen. KEBLE, matric. 13 Oct., 88, aged 20 (from Llandovery coll.), scholar 88, B.A. 91; HONOURS:—3 history 91.

Prosser, Louis Anthony, born in London 1862; 2s. Henry, gen. NON-COLLEGIATE, matric. 17 Oct., 80, aged 18.

Prothero, Rowland Edmund, M.A., fellow ALL SOULS' 75-92, where see page 283.

Proudfoot, Robert Letalle, born at Leuchars, co. Fife, N.B., 10 Oct., 1871; 4s. Peter, schoolmaster. BALLIOL, matric. 18 Oct., 92, aged 21, from St. Andrew's university.

Prout, Thomas Jones, M.A., student CHRIST CHURCH 42, where see page 407.

Prowse, Richard Orton, born at Woodbridge, Suffolk, 22 July, 1862; 1s. Richard Hopkins, cler. BALLIOL, matric. 18 Oct., 81, aged 19 (from Cheltenham coll.), B.A. 85, M.A. 88; HONOURS:—3 classical mods. 83.

Prowse, William Byass, born at Wallingford, Berks, 1854; 2s. James, gent. PEMBROKE, matric. 10 Nov., 92, aged 38.

Pryce, Arthur Ivor, born at Bangor, co. Carnarvon, 15 Jan., 1867; 2s. John, cler. UNIVERSITY COLL., matric. 17 Oct., 85, aged 18 (from Westminster school), B.A. 89; HONOURS:—3 classics 89.

Pryce, rev. John Roland, born at Bangor 2 Dec., 1864; 1s. John, canon of Bangor. JESUS COLL., matric. 18 Oct., 83, aged 18 (from Westminster school), B.A. 87, M.A. 90 (HONOURS:—2 classical mods. 85, 3 classics 87); curate of St. Bridget, Chester, 91.

Pryor, Michael, born at St. Agnes, Cornwall, 1863; 6s. William, gen. NON-COLLEGIATE, matric. 13 Oct., 83, aged 20 (from Tredarth and Truntun gr. school); migrated to CHRIST CHURCH, B.A. 87, M.A. 90.

Pryor, Percival Arthur Leonard, born at Bennington, Herts, 27 Aug., 1865; 1s. John Eade, cler. MAGDALEN, matric. 19 Oct., 83, aged 18 (from Haileybury), B.A. 87, M.A. 91.

Pryse, Henry Louis Vanneck, born at Hall Green, co. Wore., 1864; o.s. Charles, gen. ST. JOHN'S, matric. 14 Oct., 82, aged 18, B.A. 86; HONOURS:— 3 law 86.

Pryse, Lewis Thomas Loveden, born at Llanbadarn Fawr, co. Cardigan, 5 Feb., 1864; 3s. sir Pryse, bart. EXETER, matric. 18 Oct., 83, aged 19, from Winchester.

Puckle, Horace, born in London 1865; 2s. James, arm. NON-COLLEGIATE, matric. 13 Oct., 84, aged 19 (from Brighton coll. and a Blackheath school); migrated to HERTFORD 87, B.A. 87, M.A. 92.

Pugh, David Humphrey, born at Bermondsey, Surrey, 1874; 3s. David, A.K.C., cler. NON-COLLEGIATE, matric. 15 Oct., 92, aged 18, from Lampeter coll.

Pugh, rev. David Richard, born at Llanbadarn, co. Cardigan, 19 Aug., 1866; 1s. John, cler. JESUS COLL., matric. 20 Oct., 86, aged 20 (from Brecon coll.), B.A. 89; HONOURS:—3 classical mods. 88.

Pugh, Henry George Bockett, born at Winchester 1870; 1s. Henry Pugh, arm. HERTFORD, matric. 14 Oct., 89, aged 19, B.A. 92; HONOURS:— 3 classical mods. 91.

Pugh, John Humphrey, born at Llanbadarn, co. Cardigan, 27 July, 1868; 2s. John, vicar of Llanbadarn Fawr (B.D. St. Davids coll., Lampeter). JESUS COLL., matric. 16 Oct., 88, aged 20 (from Brecon coll.), scholar 88, B.A. 92; HONOURS:—3 classical mods. 90, 3 theology 92.

Pugh, Lewis Pugh Evans-, born at Calcutta 1865; 1s. Lewis Pugh, late M.P. CORPUS CHRISTI, matric. 23 Oct., 84, aged 19 (from Winchester), B.A. 88 HONOURS:—2 classical mods. 86, 1 law 88); bar.-at-law, Lincoln's Inn. 89.

Pugh, David, A.K.C., cler. NON-COLLEGIATE, matric. 15 Oct., 92, aged 20, from Cowbridge gr. school and Lampeter coll.

Pughe, Arthur Owen, born at Llantrissant, Isle of Anglesey, 1864; 7s. Evan, cler. CHRIST CHURCH, matric. 12 Oct., 83, aged 19 (from Christ's hospital), scholar 83, B.A. 88, M.A. 90; HONOURS:—2 mathematical mods. 85, 2 mathematics 87.

Pullan, rev. Leighton, born at Lewisham, Kent, 3 March, 1865; 2s. Charles, gent. CHRIST CHURCH, matric. 10 Oct., 84, aged 19 (from Blackheath school), scholar 83, B.A. 88, lecturer in theology ST. JOHN'S 88, librarian 90, M.A. 91, and fellow 92; HONOURS:—1 classical mods. 86, 1 classics 88, Denyer and Johnson theological scholarship 91.

Pullan, Percy Dighton, born at Lewisham, Kent, Sept., 1870; 5s. Charles, gen. CHRIST CHURCH, matric. 8 June, 89, aged 18 (from Blackheath school), exhibitioner 91; HONOURS:—1 classical mods. 91.

Pullen, John, born at Wargrave, Berks, 28 Jan., 1874; 1s. Robert, gen., deceased. NON-COLLEGIATE, matric. 11 Oct., 90, aged 16, from Bedford House school, Oxford.

Pulleyne, Colet Cresswell, born at Hendingley, Leeds, 3 Nov., 1872; 1s. Benjamin Colet Pullan, solicitor. NEW COLL., matric. 14 Oct., 92, aged 19, from the Charterhouse.

Pulling, Charles William Pulling-, born at Cheetham Hill, co. Lanc., 1862; o.s. Charles James, cler. BRASENOSE, matric. 15 Jan., 83, aged 21, B.A. 88.

Pulling, rev. Edward Herbert Langley, born at Modbury, Devon, 23 Jan., 1859; 3s. Frederick, arm. NON-COLLEGIATE, matric. 18 Oct., 80, aged 21 (from Gosport royal academy); chaplain to the forces at Aldershot 91.

Pulling, Henry George, born at Eastnor, co. Hereford, 31 May, 1862; 3s. William, cler. WORCESTER, matric. 20 Oct., 81, aged 19 (from Marlborough school), scholar HERTFORD 80-6, B.A. 85, M.A. 92; HONOURS:—2 classical mods. 83, 3 classics 85.

Pulling, William, M.A., fellow BRASENOSE 36-52, where see page 352.

Pullinger, Frank, born at Oldham, co. Lanc., 19 March, 1866; 1s. William, gen. CORPUS CHRISTI, matric. 23 Oct., 84, aged 18 (from Manchester gr. school), scholar 84, B.A. 88, M.A. 91; HONOURS:—1 chemistry 87, Burdett-Coutts scholarship 89.

Pullinger, William, born at Oldham, co. Lanc., 1869; 2s. William, gen. BALLIOL, matric. 16 Dec., 87, aged 18 (from Manchester gr. school), scholar 86, B.A. 92; HONOURS:—1 chemistry 90.

Pulteney, Keppel, born in London 29 July, 1869; 1s. John Granville, arm. CHRIST CHURCH, matric. 14 Oct. 87, aged 18 (from Winchester), B.A. 92; HONOURS:—3 classical mods. 89, 3 history 91.

Purcell, Augustus Henry D'Olier, born at Sydenham Damarel, Devon, 12 Aug., 1865; 2s. William, cler. KEBLE, matric. 14 Oct., 84, aged 19 (from Marlborough); HONOURS:—2 classical mods. 86.

Purcell, rev. Edward, M.A., B.C.L., LINCOLN, where see page 246.

Purcell, Gilbert Kenelm Treffry, born at Fowey, Cornwall, 12 May, 1867; 1s. Handfield Noel, vicar. EXETER, matric. 23 Oct., 85, aged 18 (from St. Mark's school, Windsor), B.A. 88, M.A. 92; bar.-at-law, Lincoln's Inn, 90.

Purcell, Stephen Verner, born at Fowey, Cornwall, 18 Sept., 1873; 4s. Handfield Noel, M.A., vicar. CORPUS CHRISTI, matric. 18 Oct., 92, aged 19, from Bath coll.

Purchase, Edward James, born at Rending, Berks, 28 Oct., 1868; o.s. James, chief constable, Reading. WADHAM, matric. 15 Oct., 87, aged 18 (from Kendrick school, Reading), B.A. 91; HONOURS:—4 history 91.

Purves, William Alexander, born at Marypoint, Cumberland, 5 June, 1865; 3s. Richard, gen., deceased. QUEEN'S, matric. 22 Oct., 83, aged 18 (from Derby school), scholar 83, B.A. 88; HONOURS:—2 classical mods. 85, 4 classics 87.

Puxley, Edward Lavallin, born at Beerhaven, co. Cork, 10 June, 1861; 2s. Henry Lavallin, arm. BRASENOSE, matric. 22 Oct., 80, aged 19 (from Eton); in the university eight 83; student Inner Temple 81.

Puxley, Frank Lavallin Lavallin, born at Limerick 1866; 1s. Edward, cler. BRASENOSE, matric. 20 Oct., 86, aged 18 (from Eton), B.A. 89.

Puxley, Henry Edmund Lavallin, born at Cork 14 Feb., 1866; 3s. Henry Lavallin, arm. CORPUS CHRISTI, matric. 20 Oct., 88, aged 20 (from Eton); (HONOURS:—3 classical mods. 88), in the University eight 89, 90.

Puxley, Herbert Horace Edward Lavallin, born at St. Albans, Herts, 4 Jan., 1870; 2s. Edward Lavallin, cler. NON-COLLEGIATE, matric. 12 Oct., 89, aged 19, from Eton.

Puxley, Herbert Lavallin, born at Cockermouth, Cumberland, 23 Nov., 1872; 2s. Herbert Lavallin, cler. QUEEN'S, matric. 27 Oct., 91, aged 18 (from Eton), scholar 91.

Puxley, John Lavallin, born at Limerick 21 Dec., 1859; 1s. Henry Lavallin, arm. BRASENOSE, matric. 21 May, 80, aged 20, from Eton.

Pyatt, Henry Robert, born at Nottingham 1870; 1s. Henry William, gen. HERTFORD, matric. 25 Oct., 89, aged 19 (from Harrow), scholar 87; HONOURS:—1 classical mods. 91.

Pyddoke, Henry Whately, born at Cheltenham 5 Jan., 1866; 1s. Edward, cler. NEW COLL., matric. 16 Oct., 85, aged 19 (from Winchester), scholar 84, B.A. 88, M.A. 93; HONOURS:—1 mathematical mods. 86, 2 mathematics 88.

Pyne, Francis William, born in London 15 March, 1866; y.s. William, cler. WORCESTER, matric. 17 Dec., 84, aged 18 (from Bromsgrove gr. school), B.A.

Q

Quarrell, Thomas Read, born at Bransford, co. Worc., 1862; 1s. Thomas Chance, arm. EXETER, matric. 22 Jan., 80, aged 18, B.A. 82, M.A. 86; HONOURS:—3 history 82.

Quarrell, William Henry, born at Leigh, co. Worc., 1864; 2s. Thomas Chance, arm. EXETER, matric. 15 May, 80, aged 15, B.A. 83, M.A. 87 (HONOURS:—2 law 83); bar.-at-law, Lincoln's Inn, 85.

De Quetteville, William, M.A., fellow PEMBROKE 51-62, where see page 554.

De Quetteville, William Frederick Ludlow, born at Bath 9 Dec., 1864; o.s. William, cler. ORIEL, matric. 27 Oct., 83, aged 18 (from Harrow), B.A. 88, M.A. 92 (HONOURS:— 2 classical mods. 84, 2 history 87); bar.-at-law, Inner Temple, 92.

Quibell, James Edward, born at Newport, Salop, 1868; 1s. John, gen. CHRIST CHURCH, matric. 10 Oct., 84, aged 16 (from Newport school), exhibitioner 84, B.A. 88; HONOURS:—3 classical mods. 86, 3 chemistry 88.

Quicke, John Mintern, born at Ashbrittle, Somst., 6 Sept., 1865; 1s. Charles Penrose, cler. HERTFORD, matric. 27 Oct., 85, aged 20 (from Eton), scholar 83, B.A. 89; HONOURS:— 2 classical mods. 87, 2 classics 89.

Quilter, Hugh Henry, born at Leyton, Essex, 2 Nov., 1871; 5s. Frederick William, vicar of Kempsey, co. Worcester, D.D. HERTFORD, matric. 20 Oct., 91, aged 19 (from Worcester Cathedral school), exhibitioner 91.

ROMAN ORNAMENT, ST. SAVIOUR'S, SOUTHWARK.—*Pugin.*

R

Raboteau, Claude, born at St. Joseph, Missouri, U.S.A., 1862; 4s. Junius B., merchant. NON-COLLEGIATE, matric. 17 Oct., 91, aged 29, from Chester theological seminary, U.S.A.

Rackham, rev. Hanworth Hart, born at Liverpool 10 Aug., 1860; 2s. Matthew, gen. WORCESTER, matric. 19 Oct., 86, aged 26 (from Liverpool coll. and Ely school, etc.), B.A. 89; curate of Kidderminster 90.

Rackham, rev. Richard Belward, born at Liverpool 1863; 3s. Matthew, gen. WORCESTER, matric. 19 Oct., 82, aged 18 (from Ely school), exhibitioner 82, B.A. 86, M.A. 89 (HONOURS :—1 classical mods. 84, 1 classics 86, 1 theology 87); curate of Gt. Budworth, Cheshire, 89.

Radcliffe, Alan Fenwick, born at Milston, Wilts, 1868; 1s. Frederick Adolphus, cler. CORPUS CHRISTI, matric. 20 Oct., 86, aged 18 (from the Charterhouse), scholar 86, B.A. 90; HONOURS :—2 classical mods. 88, 2 classics 90.

Radcliffe, Arthur Henry Delmé, born at South Tidworth, Hants, 23 Nov., 1870; 1s. Henry Eliot Delmé, cler. EXETER, matric. 16 Oct., 89, aged 18 (from Sherborne school), B.A. 92.

Radcliffe, Cecil Frederick, born at Milston, Wilts, Jan., 1869; 2s. Frederick Adolphus, cler. HERTFORD, matric. 27 Oct., 87, aged 18, from the Charterhouse.

Radcliffe, Francis Reynolds Yonge, M.A., fellow ALL SOULS' 74-82, where see page 282.

Radcliffe, Harry Sydney, born in London 1867; 4s. David, equitis. EXETER, matric. 20 Jan., 90, aged 22, from Liverpool coll.

Radcliffe, Henry Eliot Delmé, M.A., fellow QUEEN'S 58-63, where see page 180.

Radcliffe, Joseph Greaves, born at Blackburne, co. Lanc., 1867; 1s. Robert Carr, arm. ORIEL, matric. 23 Oct., 85, aged 18, from Tadcaster.

Radcliffe, Norman Cyril Wilmot, born in London 10 May, 1863; 4s. John Alexander, solicitor. MAGDALEN, matric. 16 Oct., 82, aged 19 (from Eton), B.A. 87, M.A. 89.

Radermacher, John Edgar, born at Montreal 24 Feb., 1875; o.s. Jeremiah, gent. TRINITY, matric. 15 Oct., 92, aged 17.

Radford, Francis Vaughan, born at Fermoy, Ireland, 12 Aug., 1870; 1s. Frederick, late capt. 1st dragoons. EXETER, matric. 13 Oct., 90, aged 20, from Bedford gr. school.

Radford, Percival Charles, born at Downe St. Mary 1863; 2s. William Tucker Arundel, rector. UNIVERSITY COLL., matric. 15 Oct., 81, aged 18 (from Radley coll.); died 28 March 85.

Radford, William Tucker Arundel, born at Downe St. Mary, Devon, 1862; 1s. William Tucker Arundel, rector. EXETER, matric. 22 Jan., 80, aged 18 (from Radley coll.), B.A. 85, M.A. 86.

Radice, Charles Albert, born at Naples 1868; 2s. Albert Hampden, arm. UNIVERSITY COLL., matric. 15 Oct., 87, aged 19, from Bedford school (HONOURS :—3 mathematical mods. 88); assist. magistrate and collector Bengal.

Radice, Evasio Hampden, born at San Georgio, near Naples, 1866; 1s. Albert Hampden, arm. UNIVERSITY COLL., matric. 11 Oct., 84, aged 18, from Bedford school (HONOURS :—3 law 87); joint magistrate Oudh.

Radley, Charles Poole, born at Liverpool 1868; 3s. James, arm. UNIVERSITY COLL., matric. 15 Oct., 87, aged 19, B.A. 91 (HONOURS :—3 law 91); bar.-at-law, Inner Temple, 93.

Radley, Edward Yelf, born at Liverpool 28 April, 1867; 2s. James, gen. ST. JOHN'S, matric. 17 Oct., 85, aged 18 (from Rugby), B.A. 89.

Radley, Harold Yelf, born at Liverpool 12 Dec., 1873; 5s. James, gent., deceased. BRASENOSE, matric. 21 Oct., 92, aged 18, from Stratford-on-Avon school.

Radley, James French, born at Liverpool 3 Sept., 1865; 1s. James, gen. ST. JOHN'S, matric. 11 Oct., 84, aged 19 (from Rugby), B.A. 89.

Radley, John Allan, born at Uttoxeter, co. Stafford, 2 Oct., 1871; 1s. John Hawker, gen. KEBLE, matric. 11 Oct., 90, aged 19 (from Uttoxeter school); HONOURS :—3 classical mods. 92.

Radley, Stewart French, born at Liverpool 1871; 4s. James, arm. UNIVERSITY COLL., matric. 12 Oct., 89, aged 18.

Rae, Alfred Norman, born at Liverpool 26 April, 1872; 4s. Ebenezer, vicar of Emanuel church, West Dulwich. HERTFORD, matric. 20 Oct., 91, aged 19, from Cliftonville school near Margate.

Rae, Hugh Maples, born at Cheltenham 16 Oct., 1868; 2s. William Maples, arm. MERTON, matric. 19 Jan., 88, aged 19 (from Magdalen coll. school and Cheltenham coll.), B.A. 92.

Rae, John Clayton, born at Aberdeen 1865; 1s. John, gen. JESUS COLL., matric. 23 Oct., 85, aged 20; B.A. from ST. EDMUND HALL 88.

Ragg, rev. Lonsdale, born at Wellington, Salop, 1867; 5s. Thomas, cler. CHRIST CHURCH, matric. 16 Oct., 85, aged 18 (from Shrewsbury school), exhibitioner 85, B.A. 89, M.A. 92 (HONOURS :—2 classical mods. 87, 1 classics 89, 1 theology 90, Aubrey, Moore and Liddon theological studentships 91); curate of All Saints', Oxford, 90.

Ragg, Maurice Wilfred, born at Lawley, Salop, Aug., 1871; 6s. Thomas, cler. CHRIST CHURCH, matric. 14 Oct., 92, aged 21, from Great Yarmouth school.

Ragg, Philip Melancthon, born at Wellington, Salop, 1868; 4s. Thomas, cler. CHRIST CHURCH, matric. 15 Oct., 86, aged 18 (from Shrewsbury school), exhibitioner 86.

Ragg, Robert Stewart, born at Lawley, Salop, 26 Oct., 1869; 6s. Thomas, cler. QUEEN'S, matric. 20 Oct., 88, aged 18 (from Ripon gr. school), exhibitioner 88, B.A. 92; HONOURS :—2 classical mods. 90, 2 classics 92.

Raikes, Ernest Barkley, born at Carleton Forehoe, Norfolk, 18 Nov. 1863; 2s. Francis, rector. KEBLE, matric. 17 Oct., 82, aged 18 (from Haileybury), scholar 81, B.A. 87, M.A. 89 (HONOURS :—2 classical mods. 84, 2 classics 86); bar.-at-law, Inner Temple, 88.

Raikes, Frederick Munro, born in London 1 April, 1872; 1s. Robert Taunton, solicitor. UNIVERSITY COLL., matric. 19 Oct., 91, aged 19, from Radley coll.

Raikes, George Barkley, born at Carlton Forehoe, Norfolk, 14 March, 1873; 4s. Francis, of Hedenham Hall, Suffolk, cler., deceased. MAGDALEN, matric. 18 Oct., 92, aged 19, from Shrewsbury school.

Raleigh, Thomas, M.A., fellow ALL SOULS' 76, where see page 273.

Ram, Edward Digby Stopford-, born at Highgate, Middx., 29 Dec., 1868; 1s. George, cler. ST. JOHN'S, matric. 13 Oct., 88, aged 19, from Marlborough.

Rammell, Thomas Easton, born at Sturry, Kent, 8 April, 1867; 1s. William Lake, arm. TRINITY, matric. 16 Oct., 85, aged 19 (from Canterbury school), Ford student 85, B.A. 90; HONOURS :— 2 classical mods. 88, 4 classics 90.

Ramsay, rev. Henry Havelock, born in London 1864; 2s. Joseph, gent. EXETER, matric. 18 Oct., 82, aged 18 (from King's coll., London), B.A. 85, M.A. 90 (HONOURS :—1 theology 85); fellow St. Augustine's coll., Canterbury, 89, vice-principal Well's theol. coll. 93.

Ramsay, sir James Henry, bart., M.A., student CHRIST CHURCH 54-61, where see page 142.

Ramsay, James Stuart, born at Edinburgh 1870; o.s. James, gen. ORIEL, matric. 20 Oct., 88, aged 18 (from Edinburgh high school), scholar 88, B.A. 92; HONOURS :—2 classical mods. 90, 2 history 92.

Ramsay, Malcolm Graham, born at Glasgow 3 Feb., 1871; 2s. George Gilbert, professor of humanity at Glasgow. NEW COLL., matric. 10 Oct., 90, aged 19 (from Winchester), exhibitioner 90; HONOURS : —2 classical mods. 92.

Ramsay, rev. Norman Robert, born at Llannington 28 Feb., 1860; o.s. William Fermor, arm. NEW COLL., matric. 15 Oct., 81, aged 19 (from Harrow), B.A. 85, M.A. 90 (HONOURS :—2 classical mods. 84, 3 classics 85); curate of St. Mary, Redcliffe, Bristol, 86.

Ramsay, William Alexander, born at Glasgow 26 Jan., 1868; 1s. George Gilbert, professor of humanity at Glasgow. CORPUS CHRISTI, matric. 22 Oct., 87, aged 19 (from Winchester), B.A. 91; HONOURS : —2 history 90.

Ramsay, William Mitchell, M.A., fellow EXETER 82-7, where see page 128.

Ramsbotham, Alexander, born at Leeds 28 June, 1870; 2s. Samuel Henry, D.Med. EXETER, matric. 16 Oct., 89, aged 19 (from the Charterhouse), scholar 89; HONOURS :—2 classical mods. 91.

Ramsden, rev. Charles, born at Royton, co. Lanc., 1 Oct., 1863; 1s. Walter Henry Fox, surgeon. NON-COLLEGIATE, matric. 13 Oct., 84, aged 21 (from Manchester gr. school); migrated to WADHAM 21 April, 85, B.A. 87, M.A. 92; curate of Gisborough, Yorks, 89; brother of Walter.

Ramsden, Frederick Plumptre, born at Shirland, co. Derby, 8 March, 1863; 1s. Frederick Selwyn, cler. ST. JOHN'S, matric. 13 Jan., 83, aged 19, B.A. 86; HONOURS :—4 history 86.

Ramsden, Samuel Henry, born at Melbourne, Victoria, 23 June, 1871; 1s. George, gent. CHRIST CHURCH, matric. 14 Oct., 92, aged 21, from High school, Kew.

Ramsden, Walter, born at Saddleworth, Yorks, Oct., 1868; 4s. Walter Henry Fox, surgeon. KEBLE, matric. 13 Oct., 88, aged 20 (from Manchester gr. school), exhibitioner 88, B.A. 92; HONOURS :—1 physiology 92, Radcliffe fellowship 93; brother of Charles.

Rand, Walter Charles, born at Walton, Suffolk, 1863; 1s. John, gen. BALLIOL, matric. 18 Oct., 81, aged 18 (from Dulwich coll.); and assist. collector and magistrate Bombay 83.

Randall, rev. James Leslie, fellow NEW COLL, 48-56, created D.D. 22 Oct., 89; hon. canon Christ Church 78, archdeacon of Buckingham 80, suffragan bishop of Reading 89. See page 213.

Randall, Onesiphorus, born in London 1862; o.s. Onesiphorus, gen. WORCESTER, matric. 20 Oct., 81, aged 19, from Ipswich gr. school.

Randell, Thomas, born at Stottesden, Salop, 1849; 1s. George, pleb. NON-COLLEGIATE, matric. 6 Feb., 80, aged 31 (from St. Mark's coll., Chelsea, and B.A. University of London 71, M.A. 77); exhibitioner ST. JOHN'S 81, B.A. 82, M.A. 86, B.D. 89 (HONOURS :—Syriac prize 81, S:ptuagint prize 82, 1 theology 82, Greek testament prize 83, Denyer and Johnson theological scholarship 83, Hebrew scholarship 84); D.D. Durham university 92, examiner in theology 86, and principal Durham training college for masters (Bede coll.) 85-91, rector of Sunderland 92.

Randolph, Edward John, M.A., student CHRIST CHURCH 32-14, where see page 413.

Randolph, Francis Piram Randolph Hingeston-, born at Ringmore, Devon, 15 June, 1861; 1s. Francis Charles Hingeston, cler. KEBLE, matric. 18 Oct., 81, aged 20 (from Bromsgrove gr. school), B.A. 84; HONOURS :—3 classical mods. 83.

Randolph, John James, M.A., fellow MERTON 40, where see page 43.

Randolph, Joseph Randolph, born at Torre, Devon, 9 Oct., 1867; 1s. Arthur Randolph, capt., deceased. MAGDALEN, matric. 21 Oct., 86, aged 19 (from Radley coll.), B.A. 90 (HONOURS :—3 classical mods. 88, 2 law 90, 2 civil law 91); bar.-at-law, Inner Temple, 92.

Randolph, rev. William Frederick Herbert, born at Dunnington, Yorks, Nov., 1862; 4s. Edward John, rector. CHRIST CHURCH, matric. 15 Oct., 80, aged 17 (from the Charterhouse), scholar 83-5, B.A. 84, M.A. 88 (HONOURS :—2 history 84, 2 theology 85); vicar of Croydon St. Andrew 89.

Randolph, William Henry, born at Milverton, Somerset, April, 1873; 1s. Charles, surgeon. KEBLE, matric. 20 Oct., 91, aged 18, from Sherborne school.

Ranken, William Henry, M.A., fellow CORPUS CHRISTI 62-9, where see page 383.
Rankin, Daniel, born at Greenock, Renfrewshire, 1858; 3s. Daniel, gen. BALLIOL, matric. 17 Oct., 82, aged 24 (from Glasgow university), exhibitioner 82, B.A. 86; HONOURS:—2 classical mods. 84, 2 classics 86.
Rankin, James Reginald Lea, born at Bryngwyn, co. Hereford, 1871; 1s. James, M.P. CORPUS CHRISTI, matric. 19 Oct., 91, aged 20 (from Eton), exhibitioner 91.
Rannie, David Watson, born at Kinfauns, co. Perth, 1858; o.s. John Walker. ORIEL, matric. 20 Oct., 88, aged 30 (from Edinburgh university), B.A. 92 (HONOURS:—Stanhope essay 90, 1 history 92); of Conheath, Dumfriesshire, bar.-at-law, Inner Temple, 88.
Ransom, Harry Alexander Vincent, born in London 1868; o.s. Henry Spearman, gen. ST. JOHN'S, matric. 16 Oct., 86, aged 18 (from Tonbridge school), scholar 89, B.A. 91; HONOURS:—2 classical mods. 88, 4 classics 90.
Ransome, Bernard Vincent Charles, born at Toowoomba, Australia, 17 May, 1862; 1s. Bernard Vincent Frederick, cler. WADHAM, matric. 26 Jan., 81, aged 18 (from Cowbridge school), B.A. 84.
Ransome, Walter Henry Alford, born at Chetnole, Dorset, Nov., 1865; 2s. Vincent Frederick, cler. KEBLE, matric. 17 Oct., 82, aged 16 (from Reading gr. school); migrated to CHARSLEY'S HALL, B.A. 86.
Raper, Edward Bell, born at Ulverston, co. Lanc., 11 Jan., 1864; 1s. Joseph, gen. PEMBROKE, matric. 17 Oct., 83, aged 19 (from Shrewsbury school), scholar 83-5, B.A. 87; HONOURS:—1 classical mods. 84, 2 classics 86.
Raper, Robert William, M.A., fellow TRINITY 71, where see page 449.
Raphael, Richard Henry, born at Brighton 29 Aug., 1872; 3s. George Charles, banker. MAGDALEN, matric. 22 Oct., 91, aged 19, from Wellington coll.
Rashdall, rev. Hastings, M.A., fellow HERTFORD 88, where see page 598.
Rashleigh, Edward Stanhope, born at Edmonton, Middx., 22 April, 1865; 2s. Stanhope, cler. CORPUS CHRISTI, matric. 23 Oct., 84, aged 19 (from Clifton coll.), exhibitioner 85, B.A. 89; HONOURS:—3 classical mods. 86.
Rashleigh, rev. William, born at Farningham, Kent, 7 March, 1867; 2s. William Boys, gen. BRASENOSE, matric. 23 Oct., 85, aged 18 (from Tonbridge school), B.A. 89 (HONOURS:—3 classical mods. 87, 3 classics 89), in the University eleven 86, 7, 8, 9.
Ratcliff, Frederick Rawlinson, born at Liverpool 1873; 2s. Daniel Rawlinson, of London, gent. ORIEL, matric. 27 Oct., 92, aged 19.
Ratcliff, Sidney Charles, born at Hackney, Middx., 22 Jan., 1873; 1s. Sidney Charles, merchant. WADHAM, matric. 18 Oct., 92, aged 19 (from city of London school), exhibitioner 92.
Ratcliff, William Milner, born at Morley Hill, near Liverpool, 12 May, 1868; 1s. Daniel Rawlinson, of Great Alne Hall, Alcester, arm. ORIEL, matric. 18 Oct., 87, aged 19 (from Rugby), B.A. 91.
Ratford, Isaac Sherwood, born at St. Albans, Herts, 1872; o.s. Isaac Sherwood, arm. WADHAM, matric. 20 Jan., 91, aged 19, from Berkhamstead school.
Rathbone, Herbert Reynolds, born at Liverpool 28 March, 1862; 5s. Philip Henry, arm. NEW COLL., matric. 15 Oct., 81, aged 19 (from Clifton coll.), B.A. 85; HONOURS:—2 law 84.
Rattigan, Alan Mansell, born at Lahore, Punjab, 1871; 3s. William Henry, bar.-at-law. BALLIOL, matric. 20 Oct., 91, aged 20.

Rattigan, Henry Adolphus Boyden, born at Delhi, East Indies, 1864; 1s. William Henry, arm. BALLIOL, matric. 15 Oct., 84, aged 20 (from Harrow), B.A. 88 (HONOURS:—2 classical mods. 85, 2 law 88); bar.-at-law, Lincoln's Inn, 88.
Raupert, rev. Johannes Gottfried Ferdinand, born at Stettin, Germany, 29 Sept., 1858; 3s. Carl Wilhelm, merchant, deceased. NON-COLLEGIATE, matric. 22 Oct., 92, aged 34, from Leipzig.
Ravenshaw, John, born at Whitchurch, Salop, 2 July, 1867; 1s. Arthur, gen., deceased. MERTON, matric. 18 Oct., 92, aged 25, from St. Andrews university.
Ravenshaw, Thomas, born at Whitchurch, Salop, 30 Dec., 1868; 2s. Arthur, gen. LINCOLN, matric. 18 Oct., 88, aged 19 (from Denstone coll.), exhibitioner 89, B.A. 92; HONOURS:—2 classical mods. 90, 4 classics 92.
Rawling, John, born at Cockermouth 20 March, 1869; 3s. Thomas, gen. QUEEN'S, matric. 20 Oct., 88, aged 19 (from St. Bees gr. school), exhibitioner 88, B.A. 92; HONOURS:—1 classical mods. 90, 2 classics 92.
Rawlings, Gerald Francis, born at Romford, Essex, 13 June, 1870; 4s. Charles Joseph, solicitor. WORCESTER, matric. 18 Oct., 92, aged 22, from King's coll. school.
Rawlins, Arthur William, born at Clifton Campville, co. Stafford, July, 1871; 3s. Thomas Samuel Fraser, rector. KEBLE, matric. 11 Oct., 90, aged 19, from West Malvern school.
Rawlins, rev. Thomas Fraser Pye, born at Denchworth, Berks, 15 Oct., 1865; 1s. Thomas Samuel Fraser, cler. KEBLE, matric. 14 Oct., 84, aged 19 (from the Charterhouse), B.A. 87; M.A. 93; curate of Fulham St. James 89.
Rawlins, Thomas Samuel Fraser, M.A., fellow WORCESTER 53-62, where see page 575.
Rawlinson, George, M.A., fellow EXETER 40-6, where see page 125.
Rawlinson, Gerald Christopher, born at Whitehaven, Cumberland, 30 May, 1868; 2s. Robert, arm. EXETER, matric. 15 Oct., 84, aged 16 (from Malvern coll.), B.A. 92; HONOURS:—2 history 91.
Rawlinson, John Baldwin, born at Whitehaven, Cumberland, 1 May, 1867; 1s. Robert, arm. BRASENOSE, matric. 23 Oct., 85, aged 18 (from Malvern coll.), B.A. 88.
Rawlinson, Lionel Seymour, born at Oxford 21 May, 1864; 2s. George, canon of Canterbury. NON-COLLEGIATE, matric. 28 Jan., 82, aged 17, from Lancing coll.
Rawson, Philip Heathcote, born at Aigburth, co. Lanc., 1864; 2s. Philip, arm. UNIVERSITY COLL., matric. 13 Oct., 83, aged 19 (from Eton), B.A. 86, M.A. 90 (HONOURS:—3 law 86); bar.-at-law, Inner Temple, 87.
Rawson, Richard Hamilton, born at Aigburth, co. Lanc., 1862; 1s. Philip, arm. BRASENOSE, matric. 10 June, 80, aged 18, from Eton.
Rawstorne, Edward Buckley, born at Penwortham, co. Lanc., 13 July, 1870; 3s. William Edward, vicar. BALLIOL, matric. 20 Oct., 89, aged 19 (from Rugby); HONOURS:—2 classical mods. 91.
Rawstorne, Robert Edward, born at Penwortham, co. Lanc., May, 1861; 2s. William Edward, vicar. CHRIST CHURCH, matric. 13 Oct., 82, aged 18 (from Winchester), B.A. 86.
Rawstorne, William, born at Penwortham, co. Lanc., Sept., 1862; 1s. William Edward, vicar. BRASENOSE, matric. 10 June, 81, aged 18, from Winchester.
Rawstorne, William Edward, M.A., student CHRIST CHURCH 41-6, where see page 416.

Ray, Robert Amyatt, born in London 20 Dec., 1873; o.s. Amyatt Edmund, of C.S. UNIVERSITY COLL., matric. 15 Oct., 92, aged 18, from Wellington coll.

Raymond, William Maynard, born at Coggeshall, Essex, Feb., 1868; o.s. Charles Andrewes, cler. KEBLE, matric. 17 Oct., 87, aged 19 (from Lancing coll.), B.A. 91; HONOURS :—3 classical mods. 89, 3 history 91.

Raynes, rev. Herbert Alfred, born at Greenwich, Kent, 1864; 1s. Alfred Thomas, cler. CHRIST CHURCH, matric. 14 Oct., 81, aged 17 (from St. Paul's school), exhibitioner 81-5, B.A. 85, M.A. 89 (HONOURS :—2 mathematical mods. 83, 3 mathematics 85); curate of Christ Church, Hampstead, 92.

Raynsford, Henry Arthur, born at Bareilli, N.W.P. India, 11 Aug., 1873; 1s. Edward Charles William, late lieut.-col. R.H.A., deceased. UNIVERSITY COLL., matric. 15 Oct., 92, aged 19, from the Charterhouse.

Rea, Carleton, born at Worcester 7 May, 1861; 1s. Robert Tomkins, solicitor. MAGDALEN, matric. 19 Jan., 80, aged 18 (from Worcester cathedral school), B.A. 83, M.A. and B.C.L. 86 (HONOURS :—2 law 83, 2 civil law 85); bar.-at-law, Inner Temple, 84.

Rea, rev. James Thomas Roberts, born at Pembridge, co. Hereford, 1864; o.s. Thomas, gen. ST. JOHN'S, matric. 14 Oct., 82, aged 18, B.A. 86, M.A. 89 (HONOURS:—3 theology 86); curate of Bourda St. Barnabas, Georgetown, British Guiana, 90.

Read, Archibald, born at Glastonbury, Somerset, 15 April, 1867; 3s. Robert Arthur, gen. TRINITY, matric. 16 Oct., 86, aged 19 (from Clifton coll.), B.A. 90 ; HONOURS :—2 classical mods. 86, a history 90.

Read, Edmund Arthur Algernon, born at Blackheath, Kent, 1864 ; 2s. Edmund, gen. NON-COLLEGIATE, matric. 13 Oct., 84, aged 20 (from Harrow and St. Boniface coll., Warminster), B.A. 87 ; HONOURS :— 4 theology 87.

Read, Ernest Charles, born at Honiton, Devon, 2 April, 1861 ; 1s. Charles, arm. NEW COLL., matric. 16 Oct., 80, aged 19 (from Winchester), scholar 80-5, B.A. 84 (HONOURS :—2 classical mods. 81, 1 classics 84) ; died 13 July, 86.

Read, Francis Powell, born in London 23 April, 1872 ; 1s. Frederick George, esq. HERTFORD, matric. 20 Oct., 91, aged 19, from Forest school, Walthamstow, and Highgate school.

Read, Herbert James, born at Honiton, Devon, 1863 ; 2s. Charles, arm. BRASENOSE, matric. 18 Oct., 81, aged 18 (from Honiton school), scholar 80-3, exhibitioner 83, B.A. 84, M.A. 89 (HONOURS: —1 mathematical mods. 82, accessit junior mathematical scholarship 83, 3 mathematics 84, Herschel astronomical prize 85) ; and class clerk colonial office 89.

Read, William Inskip Digby Shuttleworth, born at Dartmouth 18 April, 1871 ; 2s. George Matthew, naval instructor, EXETER, matric. 27 May, 90, aged 19 (from Tiverton school), scholar 90 ; HONOURS :—2 classical mods. 92.

Reade, Herbert Vincent, born at Haileybury, Herts, 30 April, 1870 ; 1s. Henry St. John, cler. CORPUS CHRISTI, matric. 25 Oct., 89, aged 19 (from Haileybury), scholar 89 ; HONOURS :—2 classical mods. 91.

Reade, Joseph, born at Shipton-under-Wychwood, Oxon, 1863 ; o.s. Joseph, arm. BRASENOSE, matric. 22 Oct., 80, aged 17 (from Magdalen coll. school), B.A. 84, M.A. 88 ; bar.-at-law, Lincoln's Inn, 87.

Reade, William Henry Vincent, born at Beccles, Suffolk, 13 Jan., 1872; 2s. Henry St. John, cler. BALLIOL, matric. 20 Oct., 91, aged 19 (from Oundle gr. school); exhibitioner 90.

Reason, William, born at Clerkenwell, London, 1865; 2s. Henry Fletcher, gen. NON-COLLEGIATE, matric. 13 Oct., 88, aged 23, B.A. 91 ; HONOURS :—1 theology 91.

Reay, Lionel Edward, born at Birmingham 11 June, 1873 ; 2s. Lionel Dodds, Wesleyan minister. QUEEN'S, matric. 27 Oct., 92, aged 19 (from Kingswood school), scholar 91.

Recaño, Henry Felix Lawrence, born at Gibraltar 1871 ; 1s. Henry Felix, Q.C. UNIVERSITY COLL., matric. 19 Oct., 91, aged 20.

Redfern, John Lemon, born at Penrith, Cumberland, 25 June, 1862 ; o.s. Tom, gen. QUEEN'S, matric. 28 Oct., 81, aged 19 (from Penrith and Sedbergh gr. schools), B.A. 84, M.A. 88.

Redhead, Arthur Cecil Milne, born at Seedley, co. Lanc., 1866 ; 2s. Richard, gen. BRASENOSE, matric. 28 Jan., 86, aged 20 (from Wellington), B.A. 91, M.A. 92.

Redmayne, Martin, born at Chorlton-upon-Medlock, co. Lanc., 13 Nov., 1871; 1s. George Tunstall, gen. TRINITY, matric. 11 Oct., 90, aged 18 (from Peties coll.) ; HONOURS :—2 classical mods. 92.

Redmayne, Tunstall Fitzgerald, born at Tynemouth, Northumberland, 1863 ; 3s. John Morriner, gen. NON-COLLEGIATE, matric. 4 June, 81 (from Malvern col.), B.A. and M.A. 89.

Reece, George Henry Walton, born in London 30 Aug., 1862 ; 4s. Richard, arm. UNIVERSITY COLL., matric. 21 Jan., 82, aged 20 (from Westminster school), B.A. 85 ; HONOURS :—3 history 85.

Rees, Daniel, born at Llanfihangel, co. Carmarthen, 1865 ; 2s. John, gen. NON-COLLEGIATE, matric. 21 Oct., 89, aged 24, from Carmarthen school and Aberystwith coll.

Rees, David, born at Llanarth, co. Cardigan, 26 Sept., 1872 ; 1s. Rice. JESUS COLL., matric. 18 Oct., 92, aged 20, from Christ's coll., Brecon, and University coll., Aberystwith.

Rees, George, born at Llangendeirne, co. Carmarthen, 1867 ; 3s. Henry gen. NON-COLLEGIATE, matric. 23 April, 92, aged 25, from St. David's school, Lampeter.

Rees, John Conway, born at Llandovery, co. Carm., 13 Jan., 1870 ; 1s. Thomas, gen. JESUS COLL., matric. 15 Oct., 91, aged 20, from Llandovery coll.

Rees, rev. John Henry, born at Pontypool, co. Monmouth, 1865 ; o.s. Thomas Major, cler. NON-COLLEGIATE, matric. 16 Oct., 86, aged 21 (from Brecon school), B.A. 91 ; curate of Oswestry H.T. 90.

Rees, Richard Jenkin, born at Cyfoethybrenin, co. Cardigan, 1868 ; 1s. John, pleb. NON-COLLEGIATE, matric. 12 Oct., 89, aged 21 (from City of London school and Aberystwith coll., and B.A. Lond.), B.A. 92 ; HONOURS :—1 theology 92.

Rees, rev. Robert Montgomery, born at Morleetown, Devonport, Devon, 19 March, 1853 ; 1s. Robert, wesleyan minister, deceased. NON-COLLEGIATE, matric. 18 Oct., 92, aged 39, from Kingswood school.

Rees, William, born at Swansea, co. Glamorgan, 12 July, 1869 ; 1s. Thomas, gen. JESUS COLL., matric. 14 Oct., 89, aged 20, from Swansea gr. school.

Rees, William Goodman Edwards, born at Llanelly, co. Carmarthen, 24 Aug., 1859 ; 1s. Henry, gen. JESUS COLL., matric. 14 Oct., 89, aged 30 (from Glasgow university and from Emmanuel coll., Cambridge, matric. 30 April, 83, exhibitioner 85), B.A. 92 ; HONOURS :—2 classics 92.

Reeve, William George, born at Nyon, Switzerland, 12 Oct., 1867 ; 4s. Charles, arm. TRINITY, matric. 13 Oct., 88, aged 19 (from St. Mark's, Windsor) ; HONOURS :—3 mathematical mods. 90.

Reeves, Herbert Kempson, born at Richmond, Surrey, 16 Nov., 1865; 2s. Herbert Williams, arm. ORIEL, matric. 27 Oct., 83, aged 17 (from Cheltenham coll.), B.A. 86, M.A. 90; HONOURS:—3 law 86.

Reeves, Thomas Somerville, born at Kilfagnabeg, co. Cork, 1873; 1s. Isaac Morgan, D.D., dean of Ross. ORIEL, matric. 5 May, 92, aged 19, from Malvern coll.

Reichel, Henry Rudolph, M.A., fellow ALL SOULS' 80, where see page 273.

Reid, David Kenneth, born in London 8 May, 1870; 1s. David, arm., deceased. MAGDALEN, matric. 16 Oct., 88, aged 18 (from Winchester), B.A. 92; HALLOURS:—3 classical mods. 90, 2 history 92.

Reid, George Benvenuto, born at St. Kitts, West Indies, 29 June, 1865; 2s. William, arm. EXETER, matric. 24 Jan., 84, aged 18 (from Edinburgh institution), B.A. 87.

Reid, James Stafford, born at Belfast 24 Feb., 1861; 4s. James, gen. LINCOLN, matric. 23 Oct., 82, aged 21 (from Queen's coll., Belfast), scholar 82-3.

Reid, William Bruce, born at Newcastle-upon-Tyne, 13 Feb., 1871; o.s. William Bruce, gen. EXETER, matric. 16 Oct., 89, aged 18, from St. George's school, Harrogate.

Reinold, Arnold William, M.A., fellow MERTON, 66-70, and senior student CHRIST CHURCH 70-3, where see page 424.

Reiss, Charles Julius, born at Swinton, co. Lanc., 1873; 2s. Fitz, merchant. CHRIST CHURCH, matric. 14 Oct., 92, aged 19, from Harrow.

Reiss, James Arthur, born at Eccles, co. Lanc., 10 Nov., 1870; 2s. George Emil, arm. NEW COLL., matric. 12 Oct., 88, aged 17 (from Marlborough), B.A. 92; HONOURS:—2 classical mods. 90, 3 law 91.

Reiss, Leopold, born at Rock, co. Worc., 5 Sept., 1872; 1s. Frederick Augustus, rector. TRINITY, matric. 17 Oct., 91, aged 19, from Marlborough.

Remnant, James Farquharson, born in London 13 Feb., 1862; 4s. Frederick William, arm. MAGDALEN, matric. 16 Oct., 80, aged 18 (from Harrow), B.A. 83; of Southwold, Suffolk, bar.-at-law, Lincoln's Inn, 86.

Renaud, George, M.A., fellow CORPUS CHRISTI 38-9, where see page 381.

Rendall, Godfrey Arthur Harding, born at Great Rollright, Oxon, 30 June, 1867; 5s. Henry, rector. CORPUS CHRISTI, matric. 20 Oct., 86, aged 19 (from Rugby), scholar 86, B.A. 90; HONOURS:— 1 classical mods. 88, 3 classics 90, 2 law 91.

Rendall, Henry, M.A., fellow BRASENOSE 40-56, where see page 352.

Rendall, John, M.A., fellow EXETER 41-54, where see page 125.

Rendall, Seymour Henry, born at Great Rollright, Oxon, 4 Jan., 1870; 8s. Henry, rector. HERTFORD, matric. 14 Oct., 80, aged 19 (from Rugby), scholar 88; HONOURS:—2 classical mods. 91.

Rendle, Charles Edmund Russel, born at Plymouth 16 Jan., 1862; 1s. Edmund Marchman Russel, D.Med. NEW COLL., matric. 15 Oct., 81, aged 19 (from Glenalmond coll.), B.A. 86; HONOURS:— 2 classical mods. 83, 4 history 84.

Rennie, Ernest Amelius, born in London 12 Sept., 1868; 1s. George Banks, C.E. NEW COLL., matric. 14 Oct., 87, aged 19 (from Eton), B.A. 90; HONOURS:—3 history 90.

Renouf, Winter Charles, born at St. Heliers, Jersey, 1868; 4s. Francis George, arm. CHRIST CHURCH, matric. 14 Oct., 87, aged 19 (from Victoria coll., Jersey), scholar 87; assist. commissioner Punjab 89.

Rensselar, James Taylor Van, born at New York 1862; 2s. Maunsell, S.T.P. NEW COLL., matric. 27 Jan., 86, aged 24, from Hobart coll., Geneva, N.Y.

Renton, James Hall, born at Muswell Hill, Middx., 1863; 2s. James Hall, gen. PEMBROKE, matric. 4 Feb., 81, aged 18 (from Wellington), B.A. 84, M.A. 87.

Renwick, Arthur, born at Sydney, Australia, 31 Oct., 1869; 1s. Arthur, D.Med. WORCESTER, matric. 14 Oct., 90, aged 20, from Sydney university.

Renwick, Thomas Hilton, born at Shorwell, I.W., July, 1873; 2s. Thomas, vicar. CHRIST CHURCH, matric. 16 Oct., 91, aged 18, from Winchester.

Repton, Guy George, born in London 16 Aug., 1861; o.s. George, arm. BALLIOL, matric. 21 Jan., 80, aged 18 (from Eton), B.A. 84.

Revell, Charles John, born at Charlton, Kent, 1862; 2s. George Richard, gen. NEW COLL., matric. 4 Feb., 84, aged 22, B.Mus. 87.

Rew, John, born in London July, 1868; 1s. Quincey, gen. HERTFORD, matric. 28 Jan., 90, aged 21, from Malvern coll.

Reynolds, Cecil Arthur, born at Halton, Cheshire, 1873; 1s. Henry, arm. KEBLE, matric. 17 Jan., 91, aged 18 (from the Charterhouse), scholar 91.

Reynolds, Charles Tom, born at Ross, co. Hereford, 1866; 1s. Tom, gen. NEW COLL., matric. 14 Jan., 90, aged 24, B.Mus. 91.

Reynolds, George Reynold, born at South Hykeham, co. Lincoln, 1869; 3s. James, rector. ST. JOHN'S, matric. 12 Oct., 89, aged 19 (from Lancing coll.); HONOURS:—3 classical mods. 91.

Reynolds, James William, born at Lincoln 1849; 1s. William, gen. NON-COLLEGIATE, matric. 18 Oct., 80, aged 31 (from Queen's coll., Liverpool); migrated to WORCESTER, B.A. 83.

Reynolds, John, born at Latchford, Cheshire, 13 Dec., 1873; 4s. Sylvanus, capt. in militia, deceased. EXETER, matric. 18 Oct., 92, aged 18, from Clifton coll.

Reynolds, Leonard William, born at Haslemere, Bucks, 26 Feb., 1874; 4s. Thomas John, solicitor. EXETER, matric. 18 Oct., 92, aged 18, from Bradfield coll.

Reynolds, Richard Williams, born at Liverpool 1867; 1s. Daniel, gen. BALLIOL, matric. 19 Oct., 86, aged 19 (from Birmingham school), exhibitioner 85, B.A. 90; HONOURS:—2 classical mods. 88, 1 classics 90.

Reynolds, Samuel Harvey, M.A., fellow BRASENOSE 55-72, where see page 356.

Reynolds, rev. Sydney Montgomery, born at Southwick, co. Stafford, Jan., 1864; 4s. Thomas Leetham, gen. KEBLE, matric. 17 Oct., 82, aged 18 (from Portsmouth gr. school), B.A. 86, M.A. 89 (HONOURS:—2 morphology 86); curate of St. Ignatius, Hendon, Sunderland, 90.

Reynolds, Thomas Wilfrid, born at High Wycombe, Bucks, 7 Nov., 1870; 2s. Thomas, solicitor. ST. JOHN'S, matric. 17 Oct., 89, aged 18, from Lancing coll.

Rhenius, Charles Ernest Max, born at Edinburgh 15 May, 1869; 1s. James Robert, gen. MERTON, matric. 19 Oct., 89, aged 19 (from Edinburgh academy), B.A. 92.

Rhodes, Willoughby Westropp, born at Rugby March, 1866; o.s. Edward James, cler. PEMBROKE, matric. 27 Oct., 85, aged 19, from Haileybury.

Rhodes, Alfred Henry, born at Birmingham 1864; o.s. Alfred Dunston, arm. CHRIST CHURCH, matric. 18 Oct., 83, aged 19 (from Shrewsbury school), exhibitioner 83, B.A. 87, M.A. 90; HONOURS:—3 classical mods. 85, 4 classics 87.

Rhodes, Charles Arthur, born at Dewsbury, Yorks, 1865; 1s. Charles Edward, gen. EXETER, matric. 16 Oct., 84, aged 19 (from Giggleswick gr. school), B.A. 88, M.A. 91; bar.-at-law, Inner Temple, 90.

Rhodes, Frank, born at Hawkes Bay, New Zealand, 7 Sept., 1862; 5s. Joseph, arm. ST. MARY HALL, matric. 11 May, 81, aged 18, B.A. 85, M.A. 88; bar.-at-law, Inner Temple, 87.

Rhodes, Frederick John Madgwick, born at Camberwell, Surrey, 1863; 3s. Arthur Charles, arm. BRASENOSE, matric. 21 May, 80, aged 17, from Dulwich coll.

Rhodes, George Edward, born at Canterbury, New Zealand, 1866; 2s. Robert Henton, arm. BRASENOSE, matric. 14 Oct., 84, aged 18, from Christ coll., Christchurch, N.Z.

Rhodes, Herbert Alexander, born at Uttoxeter, co. Staff., 1869; 1s. Thomas, arm. CHRIST CHURCH, matric. 12 Oct., 88, aged 19 (from Shrewsbury school), B.A. 92; HONOURS:—2 classical mods. 90, 4 classics 92.

Rhodes, Hugh William, born at Ripon 11 Feb., 1866; 1s. John, gen. WORCESTER, matric. 22 Oct., 85, aged 19 (from York school), exhibitioner 85, B.A. 89, M.A. 92; HONOURS:—2 classical mods. 87, 4 law 89.

Rhodes, Robert Heaton, born in New Zealand 1861; 1s. Robert Heaton, arm. BRASENOSE, matric. 22 Oct., 80, aged 18 (from Hereford school), B.A. 85, M.A. 87; bar.-at-law, Inner Temple, 87.

Rhodes, William Heaton, born at Elmwood, Christchurch, N.Z., 2 May, 1870; 3s. Robert Heaton, gen. BRASENOSE, matric. 15 Oct., 90, aged 20, from Rugby.

Rhys, rev. Daniel Llewellin, born at Cardiff, co. Glam., 1864; o.s. Daniel, gen. BRASENOSE, matric. 22 Oct., 83, aged 19 (from Hereford cathedral school), scholar 83, B.A. 87, M.A. 92 (HONOURS:—2 mathematical mods. 85, 3 mathematics 87); assist. master Sutton Valence gr. school 89.

Rhys, John, M.A., fellow JESUS COLL. 81, where see page 509.

Ricardo, Clement Stuart, born in London Dec., 1870; 2s. Francis, gen. CHRIST CHURCH, matric. 6 Feb., 92, aged 21, from Eton.

Rice, Charles Columba, born at St. Columba, near Dublin, 1870; 1s. Robert, cler. CHRIST CHURCH, matric. 24 April, 88, aged 18, B.A. 91; HONOURS:—3 mathematical mods. 89.

Rice, Charles Hobbes, B.D., fellow ST. JOHN'S 51-68, where see page 483.

Rice, Hugh Goodenough, born at Hampnett, co. Glouc., 23 Aug., 1865; 3s. Richard, cler. PEMBROKE, matric. 27 Oct., 84, aged 19 (from Abingdon school), scholar 84, B.A. 88; HONOURS:—3 classical mods. 86, 3 classics 88.

Rice, John Morland, B.D., fellow MAGDALEN 47-64, where see page 322.

Rice, Percival Stanley Pitcairn, born in London 10 Dec., 1869; 2a. Robert, LL.D. NEW COLL., matric. 12 Oct., 88, aged 18 (from Winchester); assist. to collector and magistrate of Ganjam, Madras C.S., 90.

Rice, Reginald William, born at Tewkesbury, co. Glouc., 14 Nov., 1868; 1s. William, gen. JESUS COLL., matric. 20 Oct., 91, aged 22 (from University coll., Bristol, and Cardiff), scholar 92.

Rice, Walter Francis, born at Edenwood, co. Fife, Aug., 1872; 3s. Edward, arm. BALLIOL, matric. 14 Oct., 90, aged 18 (from Perth academy and Eton); selected candidate Indian C.S. 90.

Rice, rev. the hon. William Talbot, born at Fairford, co. Glouc., 24 March, 1861; 3s. Francis William, baron Dinevor. CHRIST CHURCH, matric. 21 May, 80, aged 19 (from Eton), B.A. 84, M.A. 87 (HONOURS:—3 classical mods. 82, 2 theology 84); vicar of Plumstead All Saints, Essex, 88.

Rich, Edward John William Henry, M.A., fellow NEW COLL. 37-51, where see page 211.

Rich, John, M.A., student CHRIST CHURCH 44-62, where see page 415.

Rich, rev. Leonard James, born at Manchester Sept., 1863; 2s. Jabez Davidge, gen. KEBLE, matric. 17 Oct., 82, aged 19 (from Liverpool institute), B.A. 85, M.A. 89 (HONOURS:—2 history 85); curate of Anfield St. Margaret, Liverpool, 86.

Rich, William Gordon, B.A., student CHRIST CHURCH 47-55, where see page 416.

Rich, William Joseph Dafter, born at Clifton, Bristol, 1873; 1s. William, officer of police. ST. JOHN'S, matric. 15 Oct., 91, aged 18 (from Bristol school), scholar 92.

Richards, Albert More Orlando, born at Kensington 1869; o.s. Samuel More, arm. ST. JOHN'S, matric. 14 Jan., 88, aged 19.

Richards, Bernard Stonhouse, born at Winchester 12 Aug., 1871; 7s. Henry Manning, cler. NEW COLL., matric. 10 Oct., 90, aged 19 (from Honiton school); HONOURS:—2 classical mods. 92.

Richards, Charles Reynell, born at Grays, Essex, 1863; 1s. William Henry, cler. EXETER, matric. 20 Oct., 81, aged 18, from Winchester.

Richards, Cyril James Ridding, born at Andover, Hants, July, 1870; 5s. Henry Manning, cler. EXETER, matric. 14 Dec., 89, aged 19, from Lancing coll.

Richards, rev. David, born at Ponterwyd, co. Cardigan, 5 May, 1862; 2s. John, arm. MERTON, matric. 18 Oct., 81, aged 19 (from Brecon coll.), postmaster 81-5, B.A. 85 (HONOURS:—1 mathematical mods. 82, 1 mathematics 85); curate Plymouth Holy Trinity 90-1, senior mathematical and and master Plymouth coll. 87.

Richards, Edward Daubeny Griffith, born at Weston-super-Mare 17 Oct., 1863; 2s. Edward Griffith, gen. CHARSLEY'S HALL, matric. 16 Oct., 1883, aged 19 (from Cheltenham coll.); lieut. south Staffordshire regt. 86.

Richards, Francis Augustus, born at Geneva 9 Aug., 1873; 2s. Solomon Augustus, esq. NEW COLL., matric. 14 Oct., 92, aged 19, from Harrow.

Richards, Franklin Thomas, M.A., fellow TRINITY 70-2 and 82, where see page 449.

Richards, George Chatterton, born at Churchover, near Rugby, 24 Aug., 1867; 3s. John, gen. BALLIOL, matric. 24 Oct., 85, aged 18 (from Rugby), scholar 83, B.A. 89; fellow HERTFORD 89-92, M.A. 92 (HONOURS:—proxime accessit Hertford scholarship 85, Ireland scholarship 87 (accessit 85), Craven scholarship 87 (accessit 86), 1 classical mods. 87, 1 classics 89, Craven travelling fellowship 89, Derby scholarship 90); professor of Greek University coll., South Wales, Cardiff.

Richards, Gerald Gurney, born at Ventnor, I.W., 29 July, 1870; 3s. Warwick Oben Gurney, arm. MERTON, matric. 15 Oct., 90, aged 20, from isle of Wight coll., Ryde.

Richards, Harold Cotton, born at Grays, Essex, 27 Feb., 1867; 3s. William Henry, cler. QUEEN'S, matric. 30 Oct., 85, aged 18 (from Winchester); lieut. 18th Hussars 91.

Richards, Henry Eric, born at Isleworth, Middx., 6 Dec., 1861; 1s. Henry William Parry, canon of St. Paul's. NEW COLL., matric. 16 Oct., 1880, aged 18 (from Eton), B.A. 85 (HONOURS:—2 law 84 1) bar.-at-law, Inner Temple, 87.

Richards, Henry Maunsell, born at Landour in the East Indies 1870; 2s. Joseph, cler. ST. JOHN'S, matric. 13 Oct., 88, aged 18 (from Merchant Taylors' school), exhibitioner 88, B.A. 92; HONOURS :—2 history 92.

Richards, Herbert Paul, M.A., fellow WADHAM 70, where see page 529.

Richards, John, born at Cookham, Berks, 1867; o.s. John, arm. CHRIST CHURCH, matric. 15 Oct., 86, aged 19 (from Radley coll.), B.A. 90.

Richards, John Cooper Allen, born at Martock, Somerset, 1 May, 1867; 1s. Edward England, arm. MERTON, matric. 21 Oct., 86, aged 18 (from Repton school), B.A. 90.

Richards, Morley John Beaver, born at Palaveram, Madras, 29 Dec., 1872; 1s. William Joseph, cler. LINCOLN, matric. 23 Oct., 91, aged 18 (from Marlborough.

Richards, Owen William, born at Isleworth, Middx., 30 Sept., 1873; 2s. Henry William Parry, canon of St. Paul's. NEW COLL., matric. 14 Oct., 92, aged 19, from Eton.

Richards, Richard Edward Lloyd, born at Caerymwch, co. Merioneth, 11 Aug., 1865; 1s. Richard Merydith, bar.-at-law, late of Dolgelly. MAGDALEN, matric. 24 Jan., 84, aged 18 (from Winchester), B.A. 88; bar.-at-law, Inner Temple, 90.

Richards, rev. Thomas Parry, born at Merthyr Tydvil, co. Glam., 1858; 1s. David, gen. JESUS COLL., matric. 23 Oct., 80, aged 22 (from Ystradmeurig school), B.A. 85 (as Thomas), M.A. 90, as Thomas Parry (HONOURS :—3 classical mods. 82, 4 classics 84); assist. chaplain Guild chapel and assist. master K. Edward gr. school, Stratford-on-Avon, 89.

Richards, rev. William Lewis Jones, born at Cardigan 3 Feb., 1861; 1s. William, gen. NON-COLLEGIATE, matric. 17 Oct., 81, aged 20 (from Christ's coll., Brecon); migrated to MERTON, B.A. and M.A. 88 (HONOURS :—3 classical mods. 83, 3 theology 85); missionary at Alleppey, India, 84, curate of Llandudno 90.

Richardson, Albert Ernest, born at Oxford 18 Aug., 1868; 4s. Joseph, gen. NON-COLLEGIATE, matric. 8 June, 89, aged 20 (from Wesleyan school, Oxford, etc.); migrated to WADHAM 13 Oct., 90, B.A. 92; HONOURS :—2 chemistry 92.

Richardson, rev. Albert Thomas, born at Darnford, co. Stafford, 20 Feb., 1862; 1s. James Cope, gen. HERTFORD, matric. 19 Oct., 81, aged 19 (from Walsall school), scholar 80-5, B.A. 85, M.A. 90; HONOURS :—1 mathematical mods. 82, 1 mathematics 85.

Richardson, Alfred Madeley, born at Southend, Essex, 1869; 1s. Alfred, D.D., KEBLE, matric. 26 Jan., 86, aged 17, organ scholar 85, B.Mus. 88, B.A. 90, M.A. 92.

Richardson, Arthur, born at Bollington, Cheshire, 1865; 2s. Frederick, cler. HERTFORD, matric. 20 Jan., 83, aged 18, B.A. 86, M.A. and B.C.L. 91; HONOURS :—3 classical mods. 84, 4 law 86.

Richardson, Arthur James, born at Clifton, co. Glouc., 1863; 3s. John, cler. HERTFORD, matric. 18 Oct., 82, aged 19 (from Harrow), scholar 81-6, B.A. 87, M.A. 89; HONOURS :—2 classical mods. 84, 3 history 86.

Richardson, Ernald Edward, born at Sketty-juxta, Swansea, July, 1869; 1s. John Crow, arm. CHRIST CHURCH, matric. 10 Oct., 90, aged 21, from Eton.

Richardson, Frank Collins, born at Paddington Aug., 1870; 1s. George, arm. CHRIST CHURCH, matric. 1 June, 88, aged 17 (from Marlborough); bar.-at-law, Inner Temple, 91.

Richardson, Gerald, born at Warwick 8 Sept., 1866; 2s. John, cler. ST. JOHN'S, matric. 17 Oct., 85, aged 19 (from Warwick school), B.A. 89; HONOURS :—Abbott scholarship 86, 2 classical mods. 87, 2 classics 89.

Richardson, Gilbert, born at Oxford 17 May, 1870; 5s. Joseph, gen. NON-COLLEGIATE, matric. 13 Oct., 88, aged 18, from Oxford high school.

Richardson, Godfrey Noel, born at Bolton-le-Moors, co. Lanc., 18 Oct., 1865; 3s. Henry Mason, of Barnsley, Yorks, gen. NON-COLLEGIATE, matric. 13 Oct., 83, aged 18 (from Barnsley high school), B.A. 87, M.A. 90 (HONOURS :—1 history 87); mod. history tutor NON-COLLEGIATE, and mod. history lecturer ORIEL.

Richardson, James Bernard, born at Glasgow 1862; 1s. David, arm. UNIVERSITY COLL., matric. 16 Jan., 80, aged 18 (from Harrow); lieut. 5th (Royal Irish) Lancers 83, killed near Suakim 26 March, 85; HONOURS :—3 classical mods. 81.

Richardson, John Walter, born at Swatow in China 6 April, 1867; 3s. Thomas William, gen. BALLIOL, matric. 24 May, 87, aged 20 (from Cheltenham coll.); HONOURS :—3 classical mods. 88.

Richardson, Oscar, born in London 1857; 2s. Richard, gen. WORCESTER, matric. 21 Oct., 80, aged 23.

Richardson, Thomas, M.A., fellow JESUS COLL. 49-52, where see page 513.

Richardson, Thomas William, born at Swatow in China 16 Jan., 1865; 2s. Thomas William, gen. NEW COLL., matric. 18 Oct., 83, aged 18 (from Brighton and Cheltenham colls.); assist. magistrate and collector Bengal 87.

Richardson, rev. William Cockin, born at Wolverhampton 27 March, 1865; 3s. John, cler. ST. MARY HALL, matric. 24 Oct., 85, aged 20 (from Coventry school), B.A. 89, M.A. 92; curate of St. Asaph, Birmingham, 90.

Richardson, William King, born at Boston, U.S.A., 1859; 1s. Henry, gen. BALLIOL, matric. 1 Nov., 80, aged 21 (from Harvard coll., U.S.A.), B.A. 84; HONOURS :—1 classical mods. 81, 1 classics 84.

Richardson, William Ryder, born at Manchester Sept., 1861; 1s. William Ryder, gen. NON-COLLEGIATE, matric. 22 Oct., 81, aged 20, from Manchester gr. school.

Richmond, Bruce Lyttelton, born in London 12 Jan., 1871; 1s. Douglas Close, charity commissioner. NEW COLL., matric. 10 Oct., 90, aged 19 (from Winchester), scholar 89; HONOURS :—1 classical mods. 92. See Foster's *Peerage*, ABERDARE.

Richter, Hans, created D.Mus. 25 April, 1885; a well-known composer.

Rickard, rev. Herbert, born at Derby 1864; 1s. John, gent. JESUS COLL., matric. 18 Oct., 82, aged 18 (from Derby school and King's coll. school, London), scholar 82-6, B.A. 85, M.A. 89 (HONOURS :—1 classical mods. 83, 2 classics 86); assist. organizing sec. addl.-curates society 90.

Rickards, Edward, born at Beckingham, co. Linc., 31 May, 1870; 2s. John, major-general. BRASENOSE, matric. 14 Oct., 89, aged 19, from Wellington.

Rickards, Robert Windsor, born in Cheshire 5 Oct., 1865; 1s. Robert, arm. NEW COLL., matric. 23 Oct., 85, aged 20, from Marlborough.

Ricketts, George William, born at Allahabad, East Indies 1864; 1s. George Henry Mildmay, arm. ORIEL, matric. 27 Oct., 83, aged 19 (from Winchester), scholar 83, B.A. 88 (HONOURS :— 2 classical mods. 85, 3 classics 87); in University eleven 87; bar.-at-law, Inner Temple, 89.

Rickman, rev. William Francis, born in Col de Tenebre, Italy, 25 June, 1868; 2s. William Charles, gen. WORCESTER, matric. 21 Jan., 87, aged 18 (from Haileybury coll.), B.A. 90 (HONOURS :— 3 history 90); curate of Clerkenwell St. John 91.

Riddell, Edward Francis, born in London 1865; 1s. Francis, arm. CORPUS CHRISTI, matric. 19 Oct., 83, aged 18, B.A. 88; HONOURS :— a law 87.

Riddell, Oswald Charles, born in London 27 Jan., 1871; 3s. Francis Henry, esq. TRINITY, matric. 17 Oct., 91, aged 20, from Birmingham Oratory school.

Riddelsdell, Harry Joseph, born at Hackney, Middx., 25 July, 1866; 2s. William Martin, gen. JESUS COLL., matric. 25 Oct., 88, aged 22 (from Edmonton school), exhibitioner 88, B.A. 92; HONOURS :— 1 classical mods. 90, 1 classics 92, Liddon theological studentship 92.

Ridding, Charles Henry, M.A., fellow MAGDALEN 56-66, where see page 323.

Ridding, right rev. George, D.D., bishop of Southwell, hon. fellow EXETER 90, where see page 125.

Ridding, William, M.A., B.C.L, fellow NEW COLL. 48-56, where see page 213.

Ridding, rev. William Caldecott, born at Winchester 22 Feb., 1864; 2s. William, cler. EXETER, matric. 18 Oct., 82, aged 19 (from Winchester), scholar 83, B.A. 87, M.A. 90 (HONOURS :— 2 classical mods. 84, 2 classics 87); curate of East Retford 89.

Ridgeway, Charles Lennox, born at Sternfield, Suffolk, 10 Sept., 1872; 1s. William Henry, rector, deceased. LINCOLN, matric. 20 Oct., 90, aged 18, from Westward Ho 1 coll.

Ridgeway, Charles Spencer Churchill Fitzgerald, born at Malvern, co. Worc., 4 July, 1872; o.s. Charles John, cler. NEW COLL., matric. 16 Oct., 91, aged 19, from Harrow.

Ridley, Edward, M.A., fellow ALL SOULS' 66-83, where see page 282.

Ridley, Francis Colborne, born at Worthing, Sussex, 16 Dec., 1864; 5s. Oliver Matthew, cler. NEW COLL., matric. 12 Oct., 83, aged 18 (from the Charterhouse), B.A. 87; HONOURS :— 3 classical mods. 85, 4 law 87.

Ridley, rev. Herbert, born at Ipswich Oct., 1861; 2s. Henry, gen. NON-COLLEGIATE, matric. 17 April, 80, aged 19 (from Ipswich school); migrated to NEW COLL., B.A. 83, M.A. 87 (HONOURS :— 3 classical mods. 81, 4 classics 83); curate of Plaistow St. Andrew 88.

Ridley, right hon. sir Matthew White, bart., M.A., fellow ALL SOULS' 63-74, where see page 282.

Ridpath, rev. Thomas Alan Johnson, born at Hampstead, Middx., May, 1867; 1s. Thomas Alexander, gen. KEBLE, matric. 19 Oct., 85, aged 18 (from Bradfield coll.), B.A. 89 (HONOURS :— 3 history 89); curate of Chester St. Paul's 91.

Ridsdale, Charles Henry, born at Clapham, Surrey, 2 March, 1873; 2s. Francis James, solicitor. TRINITY, matric. 15 Oct., 92, aged 19, from Malvern coll.

Rieu, Jean Louis, born in London 23 Nov., 1872; 1s. Charles Pierre Henri, Ph.D., professor of Arabic and Persian, University coll., Lond., and Lsk keeper of the Oriental MSS. at the British Museum. BALLIOL, matric. 20 Oct., 91, aged 18 (from University coll, Lond.); selected candidate for Indian c.s. 91.

Rigby, rev. Allan Danson, born at Liverpool 6 June, 1862; 4s. James Winstanley, gen. WADHAM, matric. 15 Oct., 81, aged 19 (from Liverpool coll.), scholar 80-5, B.A. 85 (HONOURS :— 1 classical mods. 83, 2 classics 85); curate of St. Peter, Regent Square, 87-90, and of St. Neots, Cornwall, 90-1.

Rigby, rev. Henry William, born at Doncaster 27 March, 1864; 1s. James, gen. QUEEN'S, matric. 4 June, 81, aged 19 (from Doncaster gr. school), B.A. 84, M.A. 88; vicar of Flamborough, Yorks, 90.

Rigg, Arthur Edmund, born at Trincomalee, in Ceylon, 12 Nov., 1870; 1s. Edmund, cler. CORPUS CHRISTI, matric. 25 Oct., 89, aged 18 (from Kingswood school), scholar 89; HONOURS :— 2 classical mods. 91.

Rigg, John, born at Shrewsbury 16 July, 1863; 1s. John, cler. CHRIST CHURCH, matric. 13 Oct., 82, aged 19 (from Shrewsbury school), exhibitioner 82, B.A. 86, M.A. 89; HONOURS :— 3 classics 86.

Rigge, Herbert Miles, born at Shirehampton, co. Glouc., 1856; 1s. John Morton, gen. ST. EDMUND HALL, matric. 25 Oct., 80, aged 24.

Rimmer, rev. Sydney Richard, born at Sectapore, E. Indies, 1867; o.s. John Whittle, arm. BRASENOSE, matric. 23 Oct., 85, aged 18 (from St. Bees gr. school), B.A. 88, M.A. 92; curate of Pudsey, Yorks, 90.

Ringrose, rev. Francis Davies, born at Swanland, near Hull, 14 April, 1863; 4s. Robert Boyes, arm. MERTON, matric. 19 Oct., 83, aged 20 (from Wellington coll.), B.A. 87, M.A. 90 (HONOURS :— 3 classical mods. 84, 2 theology 87); curate of Frodsham, Cheshire.

Ringrose, rev. Ronald Dugdale, born at Ferriby, Yorks, 3 May, 1868; y.s. Robert Boyes, arm. MERTON, matric. 22 Oct., 87, aged 19 (from Wellington), B.A. 91; HONOURS :— 2 theology 91.

Rintoul, Charles Randolph, born at Bothwell, Lanark, N.B., 9 Aug., 1871; 1s. Andrew, esq. ORIEL, matric. 27 Oct., 91, aged 20, from Sherborne school.

Ripley, Archibald Edmund, born at Eastham, Norfolk, 31 Dec., 1866; 4s. William Nottidge, cler. TRINITY, matric. 15 Oct., 87, aged 20 (from Norwich school), B.A. 91 (HONOURS :—ægrotat chemistry 91); treasurer 90, president of Oxford union society 91.

Rippon, Claude, born at Tiverton, Devon, 28 June, 1866; o.s. George, of Oxford, journalist. MERTON, matric. 20 Jan., 87, aged 20 (from Tiverton school), B.A. 90; HONOURS :— 3 chemistry 90.

Risley, John Shuckburgh, born at Hildenborough, Kent, 22 Dec., 1867; 2s. Shuckburgh Norris, bar.-at-law. MAGDALEN, matric. 21 Oct., 86, aged 18 (from Marlborough), exhibitioner 86, B.A. 90; HONOURS :— 2 classical mods. 88, 2 law 90, 2 civil law 91.

Ritchie, Charles, born at Woodford Bridge, Essex, 18 Nov., 1866; 2s. Charles Thompson, privy councillor. TRINITY, matric. 11 Oct., 84, aged 17 (from Westminster school), B.A. 88.

Ritchie, Charles Edward, born at Glasgow 5 Feb., 1866; 3s. William, of Stonehaven, gen. MAGDALEN, matric. 19 Oct., 83, aged 17 (from Aberdeen university), B.A. 86.

Ritchie, Charles Foster, born at Bickley, Kent, 7 March, 1865; 1s. Robert, architect. NEW COLL., matric. 12 Oct., 83, aged 18 (from Winchester), B.A. 88 (HONOURS :— 2 classical mods. 85, 2 history 87); bar.-at-law, Lincoln's Inn, 90.

Ritchie, Christopher, born at Clapham, Surrey, 30 Oct., 1870; o.s. Henry Scott, gen. WORCESTER, matric. 14 Oct., 90, aged 19, from the Charterhouse.

Ritchie, David, born at Glasgow 17 March, 1864; 2s. William, of Stonehaven, gen. MAGDALEN, matric. 19 Oct., 83, aged 19 (from Aberdeen university), B.A. 86.

Ritchie, David George, M.A., fellow JESUS COLL. 78, where see page 509.

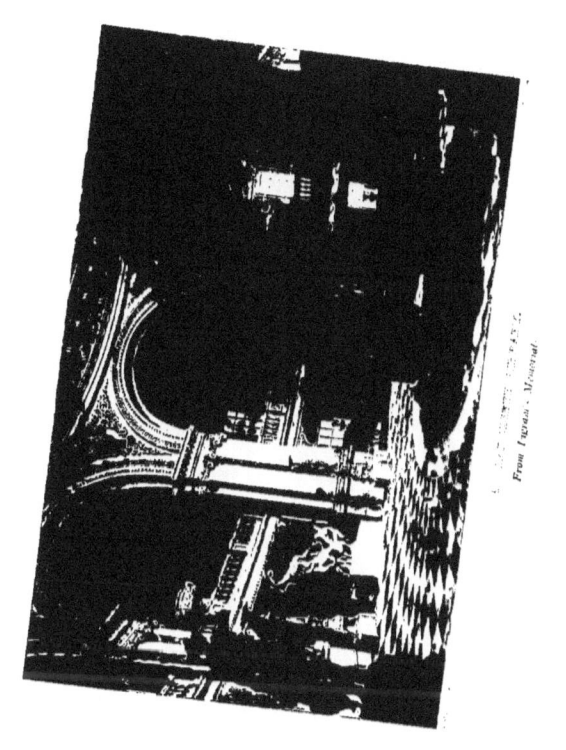

From Harper's Monthly.

Ritchie, Frederick, born at Dunottar, co. Kincardine, 8 Nov., 1869; 5s. William, arm. MERTON, matric. 19 Jan., 88, aged 18 (from Rugby), B.A. 90; brother of the next.

Ritchie, Harry Oliphant, born at Dunottar, co. Kincardine, 18 Aug., 1867; 4s. William, arm. MERTON, matric. 21 Oct., 86, aged 19 (from Rugby), B.A. 90; brother of the last.

Ritchie, James William, born at Buckhurst Hill, Essex, 7 Aug., 1868; 1s. James Thompson, arm. LINCOLN, matric. 22 Oct., 86, aged 18, from Westminster school.

Ritchie, William Hamilton, born at Glasgow 1862; 1s. William, arm. EXETER, matric. 18 Jan., 85, aged 21 (from Aberdeen university), B.A. 85; bar.-at-law, Inner Temple, 90.

Ritson, Frederick William, born at Sunderland 12 Feb., 1869; 2s. William, gen. WADHAM, matric. 13 Oct., 88, aged 19, from Durham gr. school.

Ritson, John Holland, born at Bolton, co. Lanc., 1868; 3s. Caleb, gent. BALLIOL, matric. 19 Oct., 86, aged 18 (from Manchester gr. school), scholar 85, B.A. 90; HONOURS :—2 mathematical mods. 88, 1 chemistry 90.

Rivers, rev. Arthur Rivers Nunn-, born at Windsor, Berks, 24 Nov., 1864 ; o.s. John Parkinson Till, cler. WADHAM, matric. 19 Jan., 84, aged 19, B.A. 89, M.A. 90 ; curate of Grimsby St. Andrew 91.

Rivers, lieut.-gen. Augustus Henry Lane Fox Pitt-, born 14 April, 1827, created D.C.L. 30 June, 86. See *Al. Ox.* 2nd series 1903.

Rivers, Charles Edmund, born at Wynberg, Cape Town, Feb., 1863; 2s. Josiah Charles, arm. ORIEL, matric. 18 Oct., 81, aged 18 (from Marlborough), B.A. 85 ; HONOURS :—3 classical mods. 82.

Riviere, Briton, born in London 14 Aug., 1840 ; o.s. William, artist, deceased. ST. MARY HALL, matric. 31 Jan., 63, aged 22 (from Cheltenham coll.), B.A. 66, M.A. 73, created D.C.L. 17 June, 1891, R.A. 81; the celebrated animal painter. See *Men and Women of the Time*.

Rivington, Henry Gibson, born in London 13 Oct., 1872; 2s. Walter, surgeon. WORCESTER, matric. 22 Oct., 91, aged 19 (from Haileybury), exhibitioner 91.

Roach, Frederick Norman, born at Barbados 1864; 5s. Joseph Waterman, gen. ST. JOHN'S, matric. 13 Oct., 83, aged 19.

Roach, William Griffiths, born at ffynongron, co. Penills., 3 May, 1870 ; o.s. Nathaniel. QUEEN'S, matric. 22 Oct., 89, aged 19, from St. Davids coll., Lampeter.

Roberts, Charles Henry, M.A., fellow ALL SOULS' 64, where see page 271.

Roberts, Harry Octavius Warwick, born at Mirzapore, East Indies, 1 Sept., 1869; 1s. Harry, gen. BALLIOL, matric. 18 Oct., 88, aged 19 (from Tiverton school), Blundell scholar 88 ; assist. magistrate N.W. provinces India 90.

Roberts, John, born in London 10 June, 1872 ; 3s. Abraham John, banker. CHRIST CHURCH, matric. 16 Oct., 91, aged 19, from Eton.

Robb, George Alexander, born at Keith, co. Banff, 1871 ; 3s. James, gen. NON-COLLEGIATE, matric. 17 Jan., 91, aged 20 (from Aberdeen gr. school); migrated to PEMBROKE coll.

Robberds, rev. Walter John Forbes, born at Burhampton, East Indies, Sept., 1863; 1s. Frederick Walton, cler. KEBLE, matric. 17 Oct., 82, aged 19 (from Glenalmond coll.), B.A. 86, M.A. 89 (HONOURS :—3 history 85) ; chaplain Cuddesdon coll., Oxford, 91.

Robbins, John William Everitt, born in London 1870 ; 2s. John, D.D. ORIEL, matric. 25 Oct., 89, aged 19, from the Charterhouse.

Robbs, Charles Haldane Denny, born at Grantham, co. Lincoln, 21 Feb., 1874; 1s. Charles Henry Denny, D.Med. MERTON, matric. 18 Oct., 92, aged 18 (from Dulwich coll.), postmaster 92.

Robbs, rev. Lewis, born at Stamford, co. Leic., 1868 ; 5s. William Edward, arm. BRASENOSE, matric. 20 Oct., 86, aged 18 (from Merchant Taylors' school), exhibitioner 86, B.A. 90 (HONOURS :—2 classical mods. 88, 3 classics 90) ; curate at Balham Hill 90.

Robert, Arthur Remington, born in New York 1869; 2s. Christopher Rheinlander, arm. CHRIST CHURCH, matric. 8 June, 89, aged 20.

Robert, Charles Lee, born at Newport in America 1872 ; 3s. Christopher Rheinlander, arm. CHRIST CHURCH, matric. 8 June, 89, aged 17.

Roberts, Archibald Cameron, born in London 11 Feb., 1865 ; 1s. Thomas Archibald, bar.-at-law. JESUS COLL., matric. 18 Oct., 83, aged 18 (from St. Paul's school), R.A. 87 ; HONOURS :—2 classical mods. 85, 4 classics 87.

Roberts, Arthur Carson, born at Frodsham, Cheshire, 1864 ; 1s. Thomas Howel Kyffin, gen. BALLIOL, matric. 17 Oct., 84, aged 18 (from Norwich gr. school), B.A. 88 (HONOURS :—3 mathematical mods. 84, 4 chemistry 86); bar.-at-law, Inner Temple, 89.

Roberts, Arthur Douglas, born at Wrexham, co. Denbigh, 6 Sept., 1872 ; 4s. Robert, gen. JESUS COLL., matric. 20 Oct., 91, aged 19 (from Wrexham school), scholar 91.

Roberts, Arthur Wilson, born at Mallignam, Bombay, 1874; 2s. Wilson Aylesbury, cler. C.M.S. NEW COLL., matric. 14 Oct., 92, aged 18, from Rossall school.

Roberts, Charles Henry, born at Tidebrook, Sussex, 22 Aug., 1865; 1s. James, cler. BALLIOL, matric. 15 Oct., 84, aged 19 (from Marlborough coll.), scholar 83, B.A. 90 (HONOURS :—1 classical mods. 86, 1 classics 88, 2 history 89) ; fellow of EXETER 90-91.

Roberts, David Henry Bancroft, born at Mold, Flints, 18 Feb., 1867 ; 1s. Henry, cler. LINCOLN, matric. 22 Oct., 86, aged 19 (from Christ's hospital), scholar 86 (HONOURS :—2 classical mods. 88, 3 classics 90, English verse 89); journalist, died 27 Nov., 92.

Roberts, Edward, born at Malligaum, Khandeish, Bombay, 30 June, 1872 ; 1s. Wilson Aylesbury, cler. C.M.S. NEW COLL., matric. 16 Oct., 91, aged 19, from Rossall school.

Roberts, rev. Ellis Gregory, born at St. Davids, near Festiniog, 1859 ; 3s. Ellis, cler. JESUS COLL., matric. 19 Jan., 80, aged 20 (from Ruthin school), scholar 81-3, B.A. 83, M.A. 88 (HONOURS :—2 classical mods. 81, 2 classics 83); curate of Langwm 89.

Roberts, Ernest Marling, born at Rodborough, co. Glouc., July, 1873 ; 3s. James Albin, gen. KEBLE, matric. 20 Oct., 91, aged 18, from Marlborough.

Roberts, Francis Edmund Villeneuve Russell, born in London 11 Jan., 1869 ; 1s. Edward, solicitor. NEW COLL., matric. 17 Oct., 87, aged 19 (from Clifton coll.), B.A. 92 ; HONOURS :—3 classical mods. 90, 2 law 92.

Roberts, general sir Frederick Sleigh, bart., V.C., G.C.B., G.C.I.E., created D.C.L. 8 Feb., 1881, lord Roberts 1892 ; See *Al. Ox.* 2nd series 1906.

Roberts, George Alexander, born at Oxford 1872 ; 2s. William, gen. NON-COLLEGIATE, matric. 11 Oct., 90, aged 18, from Oxford high school.

Roberts, George Edmund, born at Llanwrst, co. Denbigh, 19 July, 1865 ; 1s. Owen, arm. MERTON, matric. 16 Oct., 84, aged 19 (from Radley coll.), migrated to CHARSLEY HALL, B.A. 90.

Roberts, Hugh Thomas, born at Chester 3 March, 1862; 1s. Hugh, gen. CHRIST CHURCH, matric. 14 Oct., 81, aged 19, from St. Edward's school, Summertown.

Roberts, John Arthur, born at St. Asaph, Flints, 1863; o.s. Robert, gen. NON-COLLEGIATE, matric. 13 Oct., 83, aged 20, B.A. 86; HONOURS:—4 theology 86.

Roberts, John Drew, born at Kingstown, co. Dublin, 1864; 2s. Michael, fellow Trinity coll., Dublin, and professor of mathematics of Dublin university. HERTFORD, matric. 15 Feb., 87, aged 23 (from Sherborne school and Sidney Sussex college, Cambridge, matric. 22 Oct., 83), scholar 86.

Roberts, John Llewellyn, M.A., fellow QUEEN'S 50-63, where see page 179.

Roberts, rev. John Richard, born at Rhosymedre, co. Denbigh, 10 Oct., 1865; y.s. Ellis, cler. MERTON, matric. 16 Oct., 84, aged 19 (from Ruthin gr. school), postmaster 84, B.A. 88 (HONOURS:—2 classical mods. 86, 3 classics 88); curate of St. James, and cathedral, Bangor, 90.

Roberts, John Varley, D.Mus., organist MAGDALEN 82, where see page 328.

Roberts, Laurence Guilderdale, born at Wadsley, Yorks, 1863; 3s. Augustus Morton, D.Med. NON-COLLEGIATE, matric. 14 Oct., 82, aged 19, from Harlow coll., Essex.

Roberts, Lewis Jones, born at Aberayron, co. Cardigan, 25 May, 1866; 2s. Lewis, pleb. EXETER, matric. 7 Dec., 89, aged 23 (from St. Davids coll., Lampeter), exhibitioner 89; HONOURS:—2 history 92.

Roberts, Owen Owen, born at Gosphwysfa, co. Carnarvon, 10 Jan., 1865; 1s. Edward, gen. NON-COLLEGIATE, matric. 21 April, 88, aged 23, from Bangor coll.

Roberts, Paul Ernest, born at Ryde, I.W., 20 May, 1873; 1s. Paul, M.A., cler. WORCESTER, matric. 18 Oct., 92, aged 19 (from Bromsgrove school), scholar 92.

Roberts, Thomas Somerville, born at Llansaintffraid, co. Denbigh, 19 Jan., 1869; o.s. John, gen. JESUS COLL., matric. 19 Oct., 87, aged 18, from Llanrwst gr. school.

Roberts, William Augustus, born at Oxford 1864; 1s. William, gen. NON-COLLEGIATE, matric. 18 Oct., 83, aged 19 (from Magdalen coll. school), B.A. 86, M.A. 91; HONOURS:—2 chemistry 87.

Roberts, William Corbett, born in London 7 Nov., 1873; 1s. Richard, gent. ST. JOHN'S, matric. 15 Oct., 92, aged 18 (from Merchant Taylors' school), scholar 92.

Roberts, William David, born at Caron, co. Cardigan, 23 Feb., 1861; 2s. David, gen. JESUS COLL., matric. 21 Jan., 85, aged 23 (from St. Davids coll., Lampeter), B.A. 91; HONOURS:—3 classical mods. 84, 4 classics 87.

Roberts, Wilson Aylesbury, born at Ledbury, co. Hereford, 12 Feb., 1846; 1s. Wilson Aylesbury, gen. QUEEN'S, matric. 26 April, 83, aged 37, B.A. 86, M.A. 89; church missionary chaplain Bombay 69; father of Arthur W. and Edward.

Robertson, Alan Maxwell, born at Torquay, Devon, 1861; 5s. Robert, arm. EXETER, matric. 22 Oct., 80, aged 19, from Trinity coll., Stratford-on-Avon.

Robertson, rev. Archibald, M.A., fellow TRINITY 76-86, where see page 454.

Robertson, Benjamin, born at Dunphall, co. Morny, 1864; 1s. Benjamin, s.p. BALLIOL, matric. 16 Oct., 83, aged 19 (from Aberdeen university); assist. collector and magistrate serving under the government of India, etc.

Robertson, Charles Grant, born at Nynee Tal, East Indies, 1869; 2s. John, arm. HERTFORD, matric. 19 Oct., 88, aged 19 (from Highgate school), scholar 87, B.A. 92; HONOURS:—2 classical mods. 90, Stanhope essay 91, 1 classics 92; perhaps brother of John Herbert.

Robertson, Duncan Macpherson, born at Victoria, Australia, July, 1863; 4s. William, gen. NEW INN HALL, matric. 23 April, 83, aged 19.

Robertson, Edmund, M.A., fellow CORPUS CHRISTI 70, where see page 379.

Robertson, Edward Hercules, born at Forfar, N.B., 24 Jan., 1867; 1s. Alexander, sheriff substitute. NEW COLL., matric. 16 Oct., 85, aged 18 (from Marlborough), B.A. 88; HONOURS:—2 history 88.

Robertson, George Stuart, born in London 25 May, 1872; 1s. John Abel, merchant. NEW COLL., matric. 16 Oct., 91, aged 19 (from Winchester), scholar 90; HONOURS:—Greek testament prize 92, proxime accessit Hertford scholarship 92.

Robertson, James Hunter, born at Childwall, co. Lanc., 29 Nov., 1868; 2s. George Hunter, arm. EXETER, matric. 17 Oct., 88, aged 18, B.A. 92.

Robertson, John Ernest, born at Melbourne 10 Jan., 1868; 2s. William, gen. WADHAM, matric. 25 April, 88, aged 20 (from Geelong gr. school, Australia); brother of William St. Leonards.

Robertson, John Herbert, born at Ekah, in East Indies, 1868; 1s. John Grant, arm. BALLIOL, matric. 19 Oct., 87, aged 19 (from Highgate school); special assist. to collector and magistrate Cuddapah 89.

Robertson, Lawrence, born at Glasgow 1871; 4s. William Alexander, gent. BALLIOL, matric. 18 Oct., 92, aged 21 (from Glasgow academy); selected candidate, Indian C.S. 92.

Robertson, Percy Tindal, born at Nottingham 10 July, 1869; 4s. sir William Tindal, M.P. NEW COLL., matric. 19 Oct., 89, aged 20 (from Brighton coll.), B.A. 92; HONOURS:—2 classics 92.

Robertson, Robert Dannerman Fraser, born at Muchalls, co. Kincardine, 14 Feb., 1873; 1s. James Patrick Bannerman, lord justice general, Scotland. CHRIST CHURCH, matric. 16 Oct., 91, aged 18, from Winchester.

Robertson, William Alexander, born at Camberwell, Surrey, Aug., 1871; 1s. William, gen. CHRIST CHURCH, matric. 11 Oct., 91, aged 18 (from Westminster school), scholar 92.

Robertson, William Hope, born at Benholme Lodge, co. Forfar, 26 Aug., 1868; 2s. Alexander, advocate. NEW COLL., matric. 14 Oct., 87, aged 19 (from Marlborough), B.A. 90; HONOURS:—3 law 90.

Robertson, William St. Leonards, born at Hobart, Tasmania, 6 March, 1864; 1s. William, gen. WADHAM, matric. 22 Oct., 84, aged 20 (from Geelong gr. school); in university eight 86; brother of John Ernest.

Robertson, William Theodore Melvill, born at Berwick-on-Tweed 24 July, 1862; 3s. Alexander, gen. LINCOLN, matric. 23 Oct., 80, aged 18, from St. Edward's school, Summertown.

Robeson, Arthur Hemming, born at Forthampton, co. Glouc., 11 April, 1863; 1s. Hemming, archdencon of Bristol. UNIVERSITY COLL., matric. 15 Oct., 81, aged 18 from Haileybury (HONOURS:—2 classical mods. 83); capt. 1st batt. the King's (Shropshire light infantry) 92.

Robeson, Frederick Eden, born at Forthampton, co. Glouc., 14 Feb., 1870; 3s. Hemming, archdeacon of Bristol. MERTON, matric. 17 Oct., 88, aged 18 (from Eton), postmaster 88 (HONOURS:—2 classical mods. 90, 2 classics 92), in university eight 92.

Robeson, rev. Herbert Edward, born at Forthampton, co. Glouc., 21 Aug., 1866; 2s. Hemming, archdeacon of Bristol. ORIEL, matric. 23 Oct., 85, aged 19 (from Haileybury), B.A. 89 (HONOURS :— 4 history 89); curate of St. Mary, Redcliffe, Bristol, 91.

Robin, John William, born at Naples 1868; 4s. John Nicholas, gen. PEMBROKE, matric. 28 Oct., 86, aged 18, from Victoria coll., Jersey.

Robin, Leonard Philip, born at Barnston, Cheshire, 1863; 2s. Philip Raulin, cler. HERTFORD, matric. 4 June, 81, aged 18.

Robins, Stafford Denison, born at Caterham, Surrey, 1863; 2s. Arthur, cler. ST. EDMUND HALL, matric. 17 May, 80, aged 17.

Robins, William Aubrey, born at Bishopstone, co. Hereford, 23 Sept., 1868; 4s. George Augustus, rector. TRINITY, matric. 15 Oct., 87, aged 19 (from Harrow), B.A. 91; HONOURS:—4 history 91.

Robinson, Alfred, M.A., fellow NEW COLL. 65, where see page 205.

Robinson, Arthur Bradley, born at Florence 4 May, 1870; 1s. Arthur, arm. NEW COLL., matric. 12 Oct., 88, aged 18, from Marlborough; HONOURS: —3 classical mods. 90, 3 law 91.

Robinson, Arthur Taylor, born at Hull 1859; o.s. William Nicholas, gen. QUEEN'S, matric. 14 Jan., 90, aged 30.

Robinson, rev. Charles Ernest Russell, born at Hollinswood, co. Lanc., 1865; 1s. John, cler. NON-COLLEGIATE, matric. 13 Oct., 83, aged 18, B.A. 88; curate of Holt, co. Worcester, 91.

Robinson, Edmund Allen, born at Reedley Bank, co. Lanc., 1873; 3s. William, esq. UNIVERSITY COLL., matric. 17 Oct., 91, aged 18.

Robinson, Ernest Keene, born at Erith, Kent, 29 Jan. or June, 1864; 2s. William Owen, stockbroker. LINCOLN, matric. 23 Oct., 82, aged 18 (from Hillside school, Elstree), B.A. 85, M.A. 89; HONOURS:—3 law 85.

Robinson, rev. Francis Douglas, born at Wymondham, co. Leic., 1866; 1s. William Kay, cler. JESUS COLL., matric. 23 Oct., 85, aged 19, B.A. 89, M.A. 92 (HONOURS:—3 theology 89); curate of Christ Church, Isle of Dogs, London, 90.

Robinson, Francis John, born at Appleton, Berks, 22 Dec., 1873; 3s. Francis Edward, M.A., rector of Drayton, Berks. NON-COLLEGIATE, matric. 9 Dec., 91, aged 17, from Abingdon gr. school and Oxford high school.

Robinson, Frederick, born at Rochdale, co. Lanc., 1862; 7s. John, arm. EXETER, matric. 28 May, 85, aged 23 (from Clifton coll.); migrated to MARCON'S HALL, B.A. 91; M.A. from EXETER 92.

Robinson, Frederick, born at Liverpool 5 June, 1872; 2s. Arthur, gen. NEW COLL., matric. 16 Oct., 91, aged 19 (from Marlborough), exhibitioner 91.

Robinson, Frederick Sydney, born in London 30 Sept., 1862; 3s. John Charles, gen. LINCOLN, matric. 23 Oct., 80, aged 20 (from Marlborough), scholar 82-6, B.A. 86; HONOURS:—2 classical mods. 84, 2 classics 86.

Robinson, rev. George, born at Bedford 6 Dec., 1861; 2s. George, vicar of St. Matthew, Hull. NON-COLLEGIATE, matric. 19 Jan., 84, aged 22 (from Hull gr. school); migrated to WADHAM, B.A. 88; curate of Littleport, Ely, 91; brother of Hedley.

Robinson, George Croke, M.A., student CHRIST CHURCH 57-70, where see page 422.

Robinson, Harold, born at Leicester June, 1869; 2s. Stephen, arm. CHRIST CHURCH, matric. 12 Oct., 88, aged 19 (from Oakham gr. school), B.A. 92; HONOURS:—3 law 92.

Robinson, Harry Tavernor, born at Buckingham 1868; 2s. John, gen. ST. JOHN'S, matric. 17 Oct., 91, aged 23, from Berkhamstead school.

Robinson, Hedley Vicars, born at Bedford 1859; 1s. George, cler. NON-COLLEGIATE, matric. 17 Jan., 80, aged 21 (from Hull and East Riding coll.); brother of George.

Robinson, Henry, born at Gravesend, Kent, 1868; 2s. Charles, gen. PEMBROKE, matric. 28 Oct., 86, aged 18 (from Felsted school), B.A. 89.

Robinson, James Edward, born at Grassendale, co. Lanc., 27 Oct., 1865; 1s. John Park, gen. NEW COLL., matric. 11 Dec., 84, aged 19 (from Rugby), B.A. 87; HONOURS:—3 classical mods. 86, 2 law 87.

Robinson, John Alvaro, born at Portalepe, Portugal, 1861; 2s. George, gen. NON-COLLEGIATE, matric. 22 Oct., 86, aged 25 (from Edinburgh university); died April (?) 92, in Portugal.

Robinson, John Gorges, born at Lancaster 29 June, 1866; 2s. William, arm. CORPUS CHRISTI, matric. 26 Oct., 85, aged 19 (from Rugby), B.A. 90; HONOURS:—2 classical mods. 87, 4 classics 89.

Robinson, Percy, born at Lower Broughton, co. Lanc., 26 Feb., 1863; 2s. Jonathan, gen. CORPUS CHRISTI, matric. 19 Oct., 82, aged 19 (from Chorlton and Owens coll., Manchester), exhibitioner 82-6, B.A. 86; HONOURS:—2 classical mods. 84, 2 classics 86; 1 classics at London 81.

Robinson, Raphael, born at Cheetham, co. Lanc., 1866; 3s. Esholl, gen. BRASENOSE, matric. 23 Oct., 85, aged 19 (from Manchester gr. school), scholar 85, B.A. 89; HONOURS:—2 classical mods. 87, 4 classics 89.

Robinson, Roger Hayes-, born at Bath 29 June, 1871; 2s. Richard Hayes, cler. MERTON, matric. 15 Oct., 90, aged 19 (from Hermitage school, Bath); brother of Theodore.

Robinson, Sydney Maddock, born at Kurrachee, East Indies, 1865; 1s. Walter Allen, gen. NON-COLLEGIATE, matric. 13 Oct., 84, aged 18 (from Hereford cathedral school); migrated to BRASENOSE 86, B.A. 88; bar.-at-law, Middle Temple, 89.

Robinson, Theodore Hayes, born at Bath 22 June, 1870; 1s. Richard Hayes, cler. EXETER, matric. 16 Oct., 89, aged 19 (from Bath coll.), scholar 89 (HONOURS:—2 classical mods. 91); brother of Roger H.

Robinson, Thomas Chambers, born at Blackburn, co. Lanc., 1873; y.s. Arthur Ingram, solicitor. ORIEL, matric. 27 Oct., 91, aged 18, from Repton school.

Robinson, Thomas Hollick, born at Nuneaton, co. Warwick, 25 Nov., 1868; o.s. Rowland, gen. QUEEN'S, matric. 21 Oct., 87, aged 18 (from Malvern coll.), B.A. 92.

Robinson, Thomas William, born at Oxford 1861; 1s. William, merchant. NON-COLLEGIATE, matric. 14 Oct., 82, aged 21, B.A. 85.

Robinson, rev. Thomas Wood, born at Llanymynech, Salop, 1865; 2s. Thomas, gen. BALLIOL, matric. 16 Oct., 83, aged 18 (from Llandowery coll.), scholar 82, B.A. 88 (HONOURS:—1 mathematical mods. 85, 2 mathematics 87); assist. master Crediton gr. school 89.

Robinson, rev. Walter, born at Swansea, co. Glam., 1868; 3s. Thomas, gen. EXETER, matric. 22 Oct., 80, aged 18 (from Bishop Gore's school, Swansea), B.A. 83, M.A. 93; curate of Alveston, co. Warwick, 90.

Robinson, Walter Croke, M.A., fellow NEW COLL. 58, where see page 205.

Robinson, William Arthur, born at Long Marton, Westmorland, 9 Sept., 1872; 4s. William, gen. QUEEN'S, matric. 27 Oct., 91, aged 17 (from Appleby gr. school), exhibitioner 91.

Robinson, William Edward, born at Appleton, Berks., 1870; 1s. Francis Edward, cler. NON-COLLEGIATE, matric. 15 Oct., 87, aged 17 (from Abingdon school), B.A. 90.

Robinson, William Hammond, born at Manchester 24 Jan., 1868; o.s. William, cler. QUEEN'S, matric. 25 Oct., 86, aged 18 (from Manchester gr. school), scholar 86, B.A. 89; HONOURS :—1 chemistry 89, 2 history 91.

Robinson, William Peart, born at Burnley, co. Lanc., 22 Oct., 1861; 1s. William, arm. BALLIOL, matric. 4 June, 81, aged 19 (from Rugby), B.A. 86 (HONOURS :—3 classical mods. 82, 4 classics 85); of Reedley bank, Lancashire.

Robson, John, born at Edinburgh 29 Jan., 1872; 1s. William, solicitor. TRINITY, matric. 17 Oct., 91, aged 19, from Edinburgh academy.

Roche, Alexander Adair, born at Ipswich 24 July, 1871; 2s. William Brook, D.Med. WADHAM, matric. 13 Oct., 90, aged 19 (from Ipswich gr. school), scholar 89; HONOURS :—1 classical mods. 92.

Roddon, Robert Lindsay, born in London May, 1866; 2s. Robert Henry, gen. KEBLE, matric. 19 Oct., 86, aged 20 (from Cranleigh school), B.A. 90; HONOURS :—2 morphology 90.

Roderick, Edward Thomas, born at Pontadulais, co. Glam., 31 Oct., 1870; 1s. Daniel, cler. LINCOLN, matric. 17 Oct., 89, aged 19, from Llandovery coll.

Rodgers, John Edward, born in London 1863; 1s. John, cler. NON-COLLEGIATE, matric. 18 Oct., 80, aged 17, from Merchant Taylors' school.

Rodwell, rev. George Edward Chippendale, born at High Laver, Essex, June, 1865; 6s. Robert Mandeville, rector. KEBLE, matric. 14 Oct., 84, aged 19 (from St. Edward's school, Summertown), B.A. 87 (HONOURS :—3 classical mods. 86, 4 theology 87); curate of Boxley, Kent, 91.

Roe, rev. Charles Edward, born at Cambridge Jan., 1862; 2s. Robert, gen. ST. EDMUND HALL, matric. 22 Oct., 84, aged 25 (from Perse school, Cambridge), B.A. 91.

Roe, Francis Reginald, born at Umritzur, East Indies, 5 Aug., 1869; 2s. Charles Arthur, B.C.S. NEW COLL., matric. 12 Oct., 88, aged 19 (from Winchester) ; assist. magistrate and collector, Bengal, 90.

Rofe, Henry John, born at Rochdale, co. Lanc., 19 Feb., 1871; 1s. Henry, of Sherwood, Notts, C.E. BALLIOL, matric. 24 Oct., 90, aged 19, from Shrewsbury gr. school.

Roffey, John, born at Ditchling, Sussex, 1861; o.s. John, gen. NON-COLLEGIATE, matric. 17 Oct., 81, aged 21, B.A. 84, M.A. 88; HONOURS :— 3 history 84.

Rogers, Arthur, born at Swansea, co. Glamorgan, 15 Aug., 1868; 3s. Philip, gen. JESUS COLL., matric. 19 Oct., 87, aged 19 (from Swansea gr. school), scholar 87, B.A. 92; HONOURS :—a classical mods. 89.

Rogers, Arthur Charles, born at Shere, Surrey, Feb., 1871; 3s. Henry, cler. KEBLE, matric. 12 Oct., 89, aged 18 (from Mansfield school), B.A. 92.

Rogers, Arthur Edward, born at Sevenoaks, Kent, 18 July, 1871; 2s. John Thornton, arm. NEW COLL., matric. 11 Oct., 89, aged 18 (from Harrow), B.A. 92; HONOURS :—2 history 92.

Rogers, Arthur George Liddon, born at Oxford 18 Dec., 1864; 3s. James Edwin Thorold, late M.P., professor of political economy. BALLIOL, matric. 28 Jan., 84, aged 19 (from Westminster school), B.A. 87, M.A. 92 (HONOURS :—1 classical mods. 85, 2 history 87); secretary national liberal federation.

Rogers, Arthur Strangways, born in London 24 Jan., 1873; 2s. Arundel, a judge of county courts. TRINITY, matric. 17 Oct., 91, aged 18, from Cheltenham coll.

Rogers, Benjamin Bickley, M.A., fellow WADHAM 52-61, where see page 532.

Rogers, Bertram Mitford Heron, born at Oxford 25 Aug., 1860; 2s. James Edwin Thorold, late M.P., professor of political economy. NON-COLLEGIATE, matric. 17 Jan., 80, aged 19 (from Westminster school); migrated to EXETER, B.A. 83, B.Med. 89, D.Med. 92 (HONOURS :— 2 natural science 83) ; M.R.C.S.Eng. 89, practising medicine at Clifton.

Rogers, rev. Clement Francis, born at Oxford 25 Oct., 1866 ; 5s. James Edwin Thorold, late M.P., professor of political economy. JESUS COLL., matric. 23 Oct., 85, aged 19 (from Westminster school), B.A. 89, M.A. 92 (HONOURS :—2 mathematical mods. 87, 2 theology 89) ; curate of Pudsey St. Paul, Yorks, 90.

Rogers, Edgar, born at West Derby, Liverpool, 26 Feb., 1873 ; 1s. John Frederic, merchant. ST. JOHN'S, matric. 15 Oct., 92, aged 19, from Liverpool coll.

Rogers, Ernest, born at Enys, Cornwall, 10 Nov., 1865 ; 3s. Henry, capt. R.N. NEW COLL., matric. 10 Oct., 84, aged 18 (from Bedford school), B.A. 87 (HONOURS :—2 Indian languages 87) ; joint magistrate N.W. provinces, India.

Rogers, Francis Basset, born at Porthleven, Cornwall, 7 July, 1862 ; 8s. John Jope, M.P., deceased (see *Alumni* 2nd series p. 1220). MAGDALEN, matric. 15 Oct., 81, aged 19 (from Winchester), B.A. 85, M.A. 89 (HONOURS :—3 classical mods. 82, 2 theology 85); brother of Frederick Evelyn, etc., etc.

Rogers, Francis Edward Newman, born at Kensington 26 Dec., 1868 ; 1s. Walter Lacy, barrister, deceased. BALLIOL, matric. 19 Oct., 87, aged 18 (from Eton), B.A. 91; HONOURS :—3 classical mods. 89, 2 classics 91.

Rogers, Frederick Evelyn, born at Penrose, near Helstone, Cornwall, 30 Dec., 1860 ; 7s. John Jope, M.P. TRINITY, matric. 17 Jan., 80, aged 19 (from Eton), B.A. 83, M.A. 86 (HONOURS :—2 natural science 83) ; brother of Francis B., etc., etc.

Rogers, George Herbert, born at Batheaston, Somerset, 17 June, 1872 ; 4s. Thomas Percival, vicar. MAGDALEN, matric. 22 Oct., 91, aged 19 (from Lancing coll.), demy 91.

Rogers, Harry Spearing, born at Maidstone, Kent, 1860; 3s. William, gen. NON-COLLEGIATE, matric. 23 Oct., 80, aged 20, B.A. and M.A. 87.

Rogers, Herbert Lionel, born at Richmond, Surrey, 1871 ; 2s. John Robert Fydell, arm. CHRIST CHURCH, matric. 10 Oct., 90, aged 19 (from Leatherhead school), scholar 90; HONOURS : —1 classical mods. 92.

Rogers, John, born at Wrexham 1856 ; 1s. David, pleb. NON-COLLEGIATE, matric. 12 Oct., 89, aged 33, from Welsh presbyterian coll.

Rogers, John Davenport, M.A., B.C.L., Stowell fellow UNIVERSITY COLL. 86-7, where see page 34.

Rogers, Kenneth St. Aubyn, born at Plymouth 7 March, 1869; 6s. Henry, capt. R.N. WADHAM, matric. 13 Oct., 88, aged 19 (from Newton Abbot coll., S. Devon), exhibitioner 88, B.A. 92; HONOURS :— 1 mathematical mods. 90, 2 mathematics 92.

Rogers, Leonard James, born at Oxford 30 March, 1862; 2s. James Edwin Thorold, late M.P., professor of political economy. BALLIOL, matric. 21 Oct., 80, aged 18, scholar 79-84, B.Mus. and B.A. 84, M.A. 87 (HONOURS : — 2 mathematical mods. 81, 2 classical mods. 82, 1 mathematics 84, junior 81 and senior mathematical scholarship 85), mathematical moderator 89-90, professor of mathematics at Yorkshire college, Leeds.

Rogers, Philip Harold, born at Oswestry, Salop, 3 Nov., 1871; 2s. William Fletcher, gen. BRASENOSE, matric. 15 Oct., 90, aged 18, from Uppingham school.

Rogers, Ralph Baron, born at Mawnan, Cornwall, 1862; 1s. William, cler. EXETER, matric. 22 Oct., 80, aged 18 (from Eton), B.A. 84, M.A. 87; HONOURS :—a natural science 84.

Rogers, Thomas Englesby, M.A., fellow CORPUS CHRISTI 44-6, where see page 381.

Rogers, Tracy Percival, born at Clifton, near Bristol, 1870; 2s. William John, gen. BALLIOL, matric. 17 Oct., 89, aged 19, from Harrow.

Rogers, Walter, born at Penrose, Cornwall, 17 April, 1864; y.s. John Jope, M.P., deceased. TRINITY, matric. 15 Oct., 83, aged 19 (from Clifton coll.), scholar 83, B.A. 89, M.A. 92; HONOURS :—2 classical mods. 85, 2 classics 87.

Rogers, Walter, born at Peterborough, Ontario, Canada, 23 July, 1864; 1s. Henry Cassidy, of the Canadian, C.S., lieut.-col. MERTON, matric. 22 Oct., 91, aged 27; from Trinity coll., Toronto, and B.A. 85.

Rogers, William Owen Boulivant, born at Oswestry, Salop, 16 May, 1870; 1s. William Fletcher, gen. NEW COLL., matric. 11 Oct., 89, aged 19 (from Uppingham), B.A. 92; HONOURS :—3 law 92.

Rogerson, Thomas Cooper, born at Cheetham, co. Lanc., 5 Dec., 1870; 2s. Edward, gen. EXETER, matric. 22 Oct., 91, aged 20, from Cheetham school.

Rolfe, Benedict Hugh, born at Reading 21 March, 1874; o.s. Clapton Crabbe, architect. MERTON, matric. 22 Oct., 91, aged 17, from Magdalen coll. school.

Rolfe, Eugene Alfred, born at Brixton, Surrey, 1869; 3s. James Parham, arm. UNIVERSITY COLL., matric. 13 Oct., 88, aged 19 (from Christ's hospital), scholar 88, B.A. 92; HONOURS :—1 classical mods. 90, 3 classics 92.

Rolleston, Frederick Christopher Lawrence, born at Scraptoft, co. Leic., 29 July, 1866; 3s. William Lancelot, cler. ST. MARY HALL, matric. 24 Jan., 84, aged 18, from Repton school.

Rolleston, John Davy, born at Oxford 25 Feb., 1873; 4s. George, late professor of anatomy. BRASENOSE, matric. 22 Oct., 91, aged 18 (from Marlborough), scholar 91.

Rolleston, Samuel Vilett, born at Eythorne, Kent, 23 April, 1869; 1s. William Vilett, arm. CHRIST CHURCH, matric. 12 Oct., 88, aged 19 (from Westminster school), scholar 88, B.A. 91; HONOURS :—2 classical mods. 90.

Rolleston, William, born at Oxford 3 Sept., 1868; 3s. George, late professor of anatomy. MERTON, matric. 22 Oct., 87, aged 19 (from Marlborough), B.A. 91; HONOURS :—2 classical mods. 89, 3 classics 91.

Rolls, hon. Henry Allen, born in London 5 Aug., 1869; 2s. John Allen, baron Llangattock. CHRIST CHURCH, matric. 16 Oct., 91, aged 20, from Eton.

Rolls, hon. John Maclean, born in London 25 April, 1870; 1s. John Allan, baron Llangattock. CHRIST CHURCH, matric. 11 Oct., 89, aged 19 (from Eton), B.A. 93.

Rolt, rev. Cecil Henry, born at Limpsfield, Surrey, 10 May, 1865; 3s. Henry George, cler. NEW COLL., matric. 12 Oct., 83, aged 18 (from Winchester), B.A. 87, M.A. 90 (HONOURS :—3 history 87); curate South Shields 91.

Rolt, Francis Wardlaw, born at Limpsfield, Surrey, 24 Dec., 1861; 1s. Henry George, cler. ORIEL, matric. 30 Jan., 82, aged 20 (from Haileybury); HONOURS :—3 classical mods. 83.

Romanes, George John, born at Kingston, Canada, 20 May, 1848; 3s. George, cler. Scholar CAIUS COLL., Cambridge, 70, B.A. 71, M.A. 74, hon. fellow 92 (HONOURS :—a natural science 70, Hurney prize 73), Rede lecturer 85; of CHRIST CHURCH, Oxford, and incorporated 13 June, 90, aged 42; F.R.S. 79, and Croonian lecturer 75 and 81, zoological secretary to the Linnæan society, hon. LL.D. Aberdeen, late professor of physiology in the royal institution of Great Britain, author of "The philosophy of natural history before and after Darwin," founded the Romanes lecture at Oxford 92. See *Men and Women of the Time*.

Romer, Harry, born at Brixton, Surrey, 18 Nov., 1862; 4s. Charles, gen. CHRIST CHURCH, matric. 15 Oct., 80, aged 17 (from Haileybury), B.A. 84; HONOURS :—3 history 84.

Romestin, rev. Eugene de, born at Dresden 12 May, 1862; o.s. Augustus Henry Eugene, vicar of Froeland, Oxon. NEW COLL., matric. 15 Oct., 81, aged 19 (from Warrington gr. school), B.A. and M.A. 85 (HONOURS :—2 theology 85); curate of Ardleigh, Essex, 88.

Romney, Francis William, born at Tewkesbury, co. Glouc., 25 Nov., 1873; o.s. Churchill, solicitor, deceased. ST. MARY HALL, matric. 18 Oct., 92, aged 18.

Rook, Clarence Henry, born at Faversham, Kent, 1 Dec., 1862; o.s. Henry John, gen. ORIEL, matric. 18 Oct., 81, aged 18 (from Faversham school), scholar 81-6, B.A. 86; HONOURS :—1 classical mods. 82, 2 classics 85.

Rooke, rev. Frederick John, born at Rampisham, Dorset, 23 June, 1862; 4s. Frederick John, rector. ORIEL, matric. 21 May, 80, aged 17 (from Marlborough), B.A. 84; curate of Strathfield Mortimer, Essex, 91.

Rooke, Frederick Darell, born at Rampisham, Dorset, 17 May, 1863; 3s. Frederick John, rector. NON-COLLEGIATE, matric. 30 Oct., 82, aged 19, from Bath coll.

Rooke, Gerald Bradley, born at South Norwood, Surrey, Jan., 1872; 1s. Frederick Henry, solicitor. KEBLE, matric. 20 Oct., 91, aged 19, from Hurstpierpoint coll.

Rooks, rev. Henry Montgomery, born at Monkstown, co. Dublin, 1868; o.s. William Duffield, arm. NON-COLLEGIATE, matric. 13 Oct., 88, aged 20, B.A. 92.

Rooper, Charles Frederick, born at Abbots Ripton, Hunts, July, 1861; 2s. Frederick James, arm. ST. ALBAN HALL, matric. 20 Oct., 81, aged 20, from Malvern coll.

Roos, Gustaf Oscar, born in London 27 Aug., 1868; 2s. Gustaf Ehrewinch, gen. BALLIOL, matric. 19 Oct., 87, aged 18 (from Westminster school), B.A. 91; HONOURS :—3 mathematical mods. 89, 1 law 91.

Rooth, James Augustus, born in London 1869; 3s. John Wilcoxon, arm. UNIVERSITY COLL., matric. 15 Oct., 87, aged 18, B.A. 91; HONOURS :—3 history 90.

Rooth, John, born in London 2 March, 1864; 1s. John Wilcoxon, arm. TRINITY, matric. 15 Oct., 83, aged 19 (from Highgate school), B.A. 88 (HONOURS :—4 law 87); bar.-at-law, Middle Temple, 89.

Roper, Frederic, born at Halifax 17 Nov., 1871; 2s. Frederick, arm. QUEEN'S, matric. 24 Oct., 90, aged 18 (from Bradford school), exhibitioner 90; HONOURS :—2 classical mods. 92.

Roper, Freeman, born in London 8 Sept., 1862; 1s. Freeman C. S., gen. NEW COLL., matric. 15 Oct., 81, aged 19 (from Radley coll.), B.A. 84, M.A. 90; HONOURS :—3 history 84.

Roper, John, born at Kirkby Lonsdale, Westmorland, 20 March, 1869; 1s. Richard, gen. QUEEN'S, matric. 21 Oct., 87, aged 18 (from Macclesfield gr. school), B.A. 90; HONOURS:—3 law 90.

Roper, rev. William, born at Bridport, Dorset, 1862; 2s. John, gen. WORCESTER, matric. 21 Oct., 80, aged 18, B.A. 84, M.A. 87 (HONOURS:—4 theology 84); a missionary (C.M.S.) East Africa 87, now at Waiuku, New Zealand.

Roscoe, Edmund, born at Manchester 6 June, 1864; 1s. sir Henry Enfield, M.P. MAGDALEN, matric. 19 Oct., 83, aged 19 (from Manchester gr. school and Owens coll.); died 2 Jan., 85.

Roscoe, sir Henry Enfield, M.P., created D.C.L. 22 June, 1887; formerly prof. of chemistry at Owens coll.; father of the last-named. See *Men and Women of the Time,* and *Al. Ox.* 2nd series 1224.

Rose, Alexander Wood Hugh, born at Paysandu, So. America, 21 Nov., 1869; 1s. William Baillie. ST. MARY HALL, matric. 18 Oct., 92, aged 22.

Rose, Hamilton, born in London 28 Sept., 1870; 1s. John Henry, cler. EXETER, matric. 13 Oct., 90, aged 19 (from Merchant Taylors' school), exhibitioner 89.

Rose, John William, born at Edinburgh 23 Aug., 1862; 2s. Henry, gen. BALLIOL, matric. 21 Oct., 80, aged 18 (from Clifton coll.), B.A. 84, M.A. 87; HONOURS:—2 classical mods. 82, 3 history 84.

Rosedale, Honyel Gough, born at Willenhall, co. Stafford, May, 1863; 2. William Lewis, cler. CHRIST CHURCH, matric. 4 June, 81, aged 18 (from Merchant Taylors' school), B.A. 85, M.A. 88.

Rosenthal, Eugene Adolphus, born in London 19 June, 1866; 1s. Adolphus Lewis, gen. EXETER, matric. 23 Oct., 85, aged 19, from Uppingham school.

Ross, rev. Alexander George Gordon, born in London 13 April, 1866; 2s. Alexander Henry, major and M.P. Maidstone, deceased. NEW COLL., matric. 16 Oct., 85, aged 19 (from Eton), B.A. 89 (HONOURS:—3 mathematical mods. 87, 2 theology 89); curate of St. Mark, New Swindon, 91.

Ross, Alexander Gordon, born at Esher, Surrey, 9 Sept., 1862; 1s. Henry James, gen. NON-COLLEGIATE, matric. 3 Nov., 83, aged 21; migrated to BALLIOL; HONOURS:—3 history 87.

Ross, Allan, born at Assurghur, East Indies, 1870; 2s. William Henry, arm. CHRIST CHURCH, matric. 11 Oct., 89, aged 19 (from Beaumont coll.); assist. commissioner Burma 91.

Ross, Andrew, born at Lower Wincraig, co. Ross, 4 Aug., 1865; 1s. Philip, gen. WORCESTER, matric. 22 April, 85, aged 19 (from Cheltenham coll.), B.A. 88.

Ross, Benjamin Atkinson, born at Dundalk, co. Armagh, 1861; 6s. Thomas Andrew, gent. NON-COLLEGIATE, matric. 18 Oct., 80, aged 19 (from Brisbane gr. school); migrated to BALLIOL, B.A. 83, M.A. and B.C.L. 87 (HONOURS:—2 history 83, 2 law 84, 1 civil law 85); bar.-at-law, Inner Temple, 86.

Ross, Henry Nickson, born at Lowton, co. Lanc., June, 1867; 3s. John, gen. CHRIST CHURCH, matric. 12 June, 86, aged 19 (from Liverpool coll.), B.A. 89; HONOURS:—Chinese scholarship 88, 2 theology 89.

Ross, Hugo Munro, born at Bexley Heath, Kent, 20 Aug., 1870; o.s. John Callendar, gen. LINCOLN, matric. 17 Oct., 89, aged 19 (from Merchant Taylors' school), exhibitioner 89; HONOURS:—2 classical mods. 91.

Ross, William David, born at Tralee, co. Kerry, 13 July, 1868; 1s. David, banker. HERTFORD, matric. 29 Jan., 89, aged 20 (from Rathmines school and Trinity coll., Dublin, 3rd classical scholar 88); scholar 88, B.A. 92; HONOURS:—1 classical mods. 90, 2 classics 92.

Rossignol, Walter Aubin Le, born at St. Heliers, Jersey, 3 April, 1873; 1s. John Manger, governor H.M. prison, Jersey. EXETER, matric. 22 Oct., 91, aged 18 (from Victoria coll., Jersey), scholar 91; 1st selected candidate Indian C.S. 91.

Rossiter, Francis Seurus, born in London 18 Aug., 1866; 1s. Charles, a master at Uppingham. WADHAM, matric. 19 Oct., 85, aged 19 (from Uppingham school), scholar 84, B.A. 90; HONOURS:—1 classical mods. 87, 2 classics 89, 2 history 90.

Rost, Reinhold, Ph.D., created M.A. 22 June, 1886; librarian at the India office.

Rosthorn, Arthur Von, born at Vienna 1862; 2s. Joseph, arm. NON-COLLEGIATE, matric. 14 Oct., 82, aged 20.

Rostron, Lawrence William Simpson, born at Mitcham 20 June, 1872; 1s. Simpson, bar.-at-law. NEW COLL., matric. 16 Oct., 91, aged 19, from Winchester.

Roth, Walter Edmund, born in London 2 April, 1861; 3s. Matthew, D.Med. MAGDALEN, matric. 9 Dec., 80, aged 19 (from University coll., London), demy 80-5, B.A. 85; HONOURS:—2 natural science 84.

Rotherham, Alan, born at Coventry 1862; 2s. John, gen. BALLIOL, matric. 18 Oct., 81, aged 19 (from Uppingham school), B.A. 86 (HONOURS:—3 classical mods. 83, 2 law 85); bar.-at-law, Lincoln's Inn, 88.

Rothwell, Hugh, born at Darwin, co. Lanc., 27 Nov., 1870; 2a. John, of Adlington, co. Lanc., gen. NON-COLLEGIATE, matric. 17 Oct., 91, aged 20, from Rivington and Blackrod gr. school, and Owens coll., Manchester.

Roundell, Charles Savile, M.A., fellow MERTON 51-74, where see page 97.

Rouse, rev. John, born at "Bay de Verde," Newfoundland, Aug., 1863; 4s. Oliver, cler. KEBLE, matric. 16 Oct., 83, aged 20 (from Stortford school), B.A. 86, M.A. 90 (HONOURS:—1 theology 86); rector of Chicago Holy Trinity (U.S.A.) 91, principal of diocesan theological coll., St. John's, Newfoundland, 90-1.

Routh, Robert Gordon, born at Lee, Kent, 18 Jan., 1869; 3s. Charles Richard, arm. TRINITY, matric. 13 Oct., 88, aged 19 (from Dulwich coll.), B.A. 92; HONOURS:—2 classical mods. 90, 3 classics 92.

Routledge, Frederick, born at Hornsey, Middx., 1867; 4s. Robert Warne, of London, arm. BRASENOSE, matric. 22 Jan., 85, aged 18 (from Harrow); migrated to MARCON'S HALL, B.A. 90.

Rowcliffe, William Charles, born in London Sept., 1867; 1s. William, gen. ORIEL, matric. 19 Oct., 86, aged 19 (from Harrow), B.A. 90.

Rowden, Frederick, M.A., fellow NEW COLL. 57, where see page 205.

Rowden, George Vere, born at Northaw, Middx., 1864; 2s. Charles Wetherall, gen. PEMBROKE, matric. 27 Oct., 83, aged 19, B.A. 87, M.A. 90.

Rowe, Philip Carlos, born at Ballarat, Victoria, 1 July, 1873; 1s. Henry, cler., deceased. NEW COLL., matric. 14 Oct., 92, aged 19, from Wellington coll.

Rowe, Reginald Percy Pfeiffer, born at Liverpool 11 April, 1868; 3s. Charles, deceased. MAGDALEN, matric. 22 Oct., 87, aged 19 (from Clifton coll.), B.A. 91 (HONOURS:—2 history 91), in University eight 89, 90, 91, 92.

Rowland, Alfred Norman, born at Frome, Somerset, 28 May, 1869; 1s. Alfred, congregational minister, Crouch End, London. BALLIOL, matric. 1 May, 90, aged 20, from Mill Hill school.

Rowland, Charles Spencer, born at Martley, co. Wore., 1864; 1s. Charles Browne, cler. ST. JOHN'S, matric. 14 Oct., 82, aged 18, B.A. 86, M.A. 92; HONOURS :—4 theology 86.

Rowland, Percy Fritz, born at Islington 14 April, 1870; 1s. Frederick Arthur Alexander, solicitor. HERTFORD, matric. 14 Oct., 89, aged 19 (from St. Paul's school), scholar 88; HONOURS :—2 classical mods. 91.

Rowlands, Harry Fenn, born in Ceylon 18 Jan., 1870; 2s. William Edward, cler. TRINITY, matric. 13 Oct., 88, aged 18 (from Monkton Combe school), B.A. 92; HONOURS :—4 history 92.

Rowlands, Horace John, born at Birmingham 3 June, 1869; 2s. Joseph, solicitor. EXETER, matric. 16 Oct., 89, aged 20, from Malvern coll.

Rowlands, John Griffith, born at Llanidloes, co. Montgomery, 24 Dec., 1862; 1s. Daniel, arm. JESUS COLL., matric. 18 Oct., 82, aged 19 (from Bangor school), B.A. 86; HONOURS :—2 classical mods. 84, 4 classics 86.

Rowlands, rev. John Hugh, born at Dysart, Flints, 24 Dec., 1863; 3s. David, principal of Bangor training coll. NON-COLLEGIATE, matric. 22 Oct., 87, aged 23, from Friars school, Bangor.

Rowlands, rev. Robert Evan, born at Bangor 20 Aug., 1863; 1s. Owen Robert, gen. NON-COLLEGIATE, matric. 13 Jan., 83, aged 19 (from Bangor coll.); migrated to QUEEN'S, B.A. 86, M.A. 89 (HONOURS :—3 history 86); curate of Pontypridd 86.

Rowlands, William, born at Bangor 1869; 1s. William, gen. JESUS COLL., matric. 16 Oct., 88, aged 19.

Rowley, Charles Edward, born at Oxford 27 July, 1873; 2s. Alfred, gen. NON-COLLEGIATE, matric. 15 Oct., 92, aged 19, from New coll. school, Oxford.

Rowley, Ernest, born at Higher Broughton, co. Lanc., 1870; 1s. Edmund Buller, gen. ORIEL, matric. 25 Oct., 89, aged 19 (from Clifton coll.), B.A. 92; HONOURS :—3 law 92.

Rowley, rev. Herbert Seddon, born at Riccarton, New Zealand, 16 March, 1861; 3s. Thomas, gen. QUEEN'S, matric. 25 Oct., 80, aged 19 (from Elizabeth coll. Guernsey), chorister 78-80, B.A. 83, M.A. 87; curate of Mildenhall, Suffolk, 89.

Rowley, Hugh Edward, born at Willey, Salop, 20 March, 1873; 9s. Thomas, of Guernsey, gent. PEMBROKE, matric. 28 Oct., 92, aged 19 (from Elizabeth coll., Guernsey), exhibitioner 92.

Roxburgh, rev. William John, born at Annan, co. Dumfries, 5 May, 1865; 2s. Alexander, arm. TRINITY, matric. 13 Oct., 88, aged 23 (from Derby school and St. David's coll. Lampeter), B.A. 90 (HONOURS :—3 classical mods. 88, 3 history 90); Trinity college missioner Stratford, Middx., 91.

Royden, Thomas, born at Mossley Hill, co. Lanc., 22 May, 1871; 1s. Thomas Bland, of Liverpool, arm. MAGDALEN, matric. 14 Oct., 90, aged 19 (from Winchester); HONOURS :—2 classical mods. 92.

Royle, Thomas Richard Popplewell, born at Leeds 16 May, 1864; 1s. Thomas Richard Popplewell, of Chester, arm. MAGDALEN, matric. 23 Oct., 85, aged 21 (from Uppingham school) B.A. 80, M.A. and D.Mus. 92.

Ruble, rev. Alfred Edward, born at Portsmouth, Hants, 1864; 4s. John Parsons, gen. BALLIOL, matric. 16 Jan., 83, aged 19 (from Bradfield coll.), exhibitioner BRASENOSE 83, B.A. 86, M.A. 89 (HONOURS :—1 classical mods. 84, 1 classics 86); headmaster of Richmond school, Yorkshire, 90, incumbent of Holy Trinity, Richmond, 91.

Ruck, George, born at Maidstone, Kent, 24 Sept., 1871; 2s. Edwin, cler. NON-COLLEGIATE, matric. 12 Oct., 89, aged 18, from Maidstone gr. school.

Rücker, Arthur William, M.A., hon fellow BRASENOSE 91, where see page 351.

Rudd, D'Arcy Strangways, born at Chesterfield, co. Derby, 8 May, 1869; 2s. George, cler. QUEEN'S, matric. 22 Oct., 89, aged 20 (from Manchester gr. school), B.A. 92; HONOURS :—3 history 92.

Rudd, George Edward, born in York 1866; 1s. George, cler. BRASENOSE, matric. 14 Oct., 84, aged 18 (from Manchester gr. school), scholar 84, B.A. 88, M.A. 91; HONOURS :—2 classical mods. 86, 3 classics 88.

Rudd, Henry Aytone Lindsay, born at St. Heliers, Jersey, 9 July, 1867; 2s. Eric, bar.-at-law. JESUS COLL., matric. 20 Oct., 86, aged 19 (from Tunbridge gr. school), scholar 86, B.A. 90; HONOURS :—3 mathematical mods. 88, 3 mathematics 90.

Ruddach, James Stewart Maynard, born at Leamington 1864; 1s. James Stewart, cler. ORIEL, matric. 27 Oct., 83, aged 19, from Leamington coll.

Rugg, rev. William Robert, born at Debriting, Kent, 1856; 5s. George, gen. EXETER, matric. 12 May, 83, aged 27; migrated to WORCESTER, B.A. 89, M.A. 90 (HONOURS :—3 theology 86) ; vicar of Beoley, co. Worc., 90.

Rumney, Edward, born at Manchester 1852; 1s. William, gen. HERTFORD, matric. 6 June, 82, aged 30.

Rumsey, Henry Langston, M.A., fellow NEW COLL. 57-74, where see page 216.

Rundle, Wilfred Charles, born at Plymouth 17 Jan., 1869; 1s. Charles, gen. LINCOLN, matric. 21 Oct., 87, aged 18 (from the Charterhouse and Bruce Castle school), B.A. 92; HONOURS :—1 history 91.

Rushforth, rev. Collingwood McNeil, born in London 1869; 2s. Daniel, gen. ST. JOHN'S, matric. 16 Oct., 86, aged 17 (from Merchant Taylors' school), scholar 86, B.A. 90, M.A. 92; HONOURS :—2 classical mods. 88, 2 classics 90.

Rushforth, Gordon McNeil, born in London 6 Sept., 1862; 1s. Daniel, gen. ST. JOHN'S, matric. 15 Oct., 81, aged 19 (from Merchant Taylors' school), scholar 81-5, B.A. 85, M.A. 88 (HONOURS :—1 classical mods. 83, 2 classics 85); bar.-at-law, Inner Temple, 89.

Rushton, James Lever, born at Bolton, co. Lanc., 24 May, 1872; 1s. Thomas Henry, gent. BRASENOSE, matric. 21 Oct., 92, aged 20, from Rugby.

Ruskin, John, M.A., hon student CHRIST CHURCH 67, where see page 411.

Russell, Arthur Eustace, born at Leytonstone, Essex, 1866; 2s. Alfred Oliver, cler. BRASENOSE, matric. 23 Oct., 85, aged 19 (from Lancing coll.), exhibitioner 85, B.A. 90, M.A. 92; HONOURS :— 2 classical mods. 87, 1 history 89.

Russell, Arthur Joseph, born in London 1861; 1s. sir Charles, kt., M.P., attorney-gen. NON-COLLEGIATE, matric. 29 April, 81, aged 20 (from Beaumont coll., Windsor); migrated to ORIEL, B.A. 86, M.A. 89 (HONOURS :—4 law 84); bar.-at-law, Inner Temple 86.

Russell, Arthur Oliver Villiers, 2nd baron Ampthill, born at Rome 19 Feb., 1869; 1s. Odo William, 1st baron. NEW COLL., matric. 12 Oct., 88, aged 19 (from Eton), B.A. 92 (HONOURS:—3 history 91), in University eight 89, 90, 91, president of Oxford union society 91.

Russell, Cecil Henry St. Leger, born at Trinidad, West Indies, 18 April, 1862; 1s. Richard, arm. TRINITY, matric. 15 Oct., 81, aged 19 (from Lancing coll.), scholar 81-5, B.A. 86, M.A. 88 (HONOURS:—2 classical mods. 82, Latin verse 82, Greek verse 83, Greek prose 84, 2 classics 85); a master at Clifton coll.

Russell, Charles, born at North Ockendon, Essex, 31 July, 1872; 3s. Champion, esq. HERTFORD, matric. 22 Oct., 92, aged 20 (from Loretto school), scholar 92.

Russell, Charles Martin, born at Cork 2 Oct., 1839; 1s. Garrett John, cler. ST. ALBAN HALL, matric. 16 Oct., 80, aged 41; migrated to MERTON 82; of Stonehouse, co. Glouc.; vicar of Frampton-on-Severn, co. Glouc., 81-8.

Russell, Claud Frederick William, born in London 9 Dec., 1871; 2s. lord Arthur John Edward. BALLIOL, matric. 17 Jan., 91, aged 19; brother of Harold J. H. See Foster's *Peerage*, D. BEDFORD.

Russell, Cyril, born in London 1866; 3s. Charles, knt., attorney-general. UNIVERSITY COLL., matric. 24 Oct., 83, aged 17, B.A. 86; HONOURS:—3 history 86.

Russell, Francis Xavier Joseph, born in London July, 1867; 4s. Charles, knt., attorney-general. ORIEL, matric. 19 Oct., 86, aged 19 (from Haileybury and Beaumont coll., Old Windsor), B.A. 91 (HONOURS:—1 law 90); brother of Arthur J. and of Cyril.

Russell, hon. Frederick Gustavus Hamilton, born 12 June, 1867; 2s. William, viscount Boyne. CHRIST CHURCH, matric. 18 Oct., 86, aged 19, from Eton.

Russell, Harold John Hastings, born in Paris 23 Jan., 1868; 1s. lord Arthur John Edward. BALLIOL, matric. 20 Jan., 87, aged 18, B.A. 90 (HONOURS:—2 history 90); brother of Claud F. W. See Foster's *Peerage*, D. BEDFORD.

Russell, John Francis Stanley, 2nd earl, born 12 Aug., 1865; 1s. John, viscount Amberley. BALLIOL, matric. 16 Oct., 83, aged 18.

Russell, rev. John Francis Vickers, born at Neath, co. Glam., 27 June, 1867; 1s. John, surgeon. NON-COLL., matric. 20 Oct., 86, aged 19 (from Winchester), scholar 86, B.A. 90, HONOURS:—3 classical mods. 88, 3 classics 90; died 25 June, 91.

Russell, John Wellesley, M.A., fellow MERTON 73-90, where see page 98.

Russell, Robert, born at Durban, Natal, 13 May, 1867; o.s. Robert, arm. MERTON, matric. 28 Jan., 86, aged 18 (from Pietermaritzburg school), B.A. 90; HONOURS:—4 law 89, 3 civil law 90.

Russell, Thomas Brownlee, born at Kendal, Westmorland, 5 Aug., 1872; 2s. John, unitarian minister, deceased. PEMBROKE, matric. 28 Oct., 92, aged 19, from Macclesfield gr. school.

Russell, Walter, born at Liverpool 13 Dec., 1868; 2s. Thomas Robert, gent. TRINITY, matric. 15 Oct., 87, aged 18, from Coventry school.

Russell, Western Francis, born at Willesborough, Kent, 1862; 2s. Sydenham Francis, cler. CHRIST CHURCH, matric. 15 Oct., 80, aged 18 (from Cranbrook school), a junior student 80-5, B.A. 84; HONOURS:—2 mathematical mods. 82, 1 mathematics 84.

Russell, William, born in London 1862; y.s. William, gen. EXETER, matric. 20 Oct., 81, aged 19 (from King's coll. school, London.), exhibitioner 81-5, B.A. 85, M.A. 88; HONOURS:—2 classical mods. 83, 2 classics 85.

Russell, William, born at Cambuslang, co. Lanark, 1868; 5s. Archibald, arm. CORPUS CHRISTI, matric. 20 Oct., 86, aged 18 (from Craigmont, Edinburgh), B.A. 90; HONOURS:—3 classical mods. 88, 2 law 90, 3 civil law 91.

Russell, William Arthur Baker, born in London 1865; 1s. William Hugh, gen. NEW COLL., matric. 14 Jan., 90, aged 25, B.Mus. 91.

Rutherford, Alexander Charles, born at Pulborough, Sussex, 13 Sept., 1871; 2s. Samuel, late D.Med., deceased. NON-COLLEGIATE, matric. 26 April, 90, aged 18, from Epsom coll.

Rutherford, Arthur, born at Crosby, co. Lanc., 4 Jan., 1856; 5s. William, gen. WORCESTER, matric. 19 Oct., 82, aged 16 (from Great Crosby school); scholar BRASENOSE 83-5, B.A. 86 (HONOURS:—1 mathematical mods. 84, 1 mathematics 86); bar.-at-law, Middle Temple, 90.

Rutherford, Charles Randall, born at Hackney, Middx., 12 Sept., 1868; o.s. John, solicitor. WADHAM, matric. 15 Oct., 87, aged 19 (from St. John-at-Hackney gr. school), B.A. 91; HONOURS:—2 law 91.

Rutherford, Thomas Dixon, born at Bishop Wearmouth, co. Durham, 3 Dec., 1863; 1s. Thomas, gen. NON-COLLEGIATE, matric. 11 Oct., 90, aged 26, from a Sunderland school and Edinburgh university.

Rutherford, rev. William Gunion, M.A., fellow UNIVERSITY COLL. 83, where see page 34.

Rutter, William Chambers Stuart, born at Ripon, Yorks, 1873; 1s. William Rutter, esq. HERTFORD, matric. 20 Oct., 92, aged 19, from Ripon gr. school.

Rutty, Arthur William Forder, born at Reading 22 Aug., 1872; 1s. Arthur Forster, cler., and headmaster St. John's, Leatherhead. NEW COLL., matric. 16 Oct., 91, aged 19, from Sherborne school.

Ruxton, Arthur Frederick, born at Calcutta 12 June, 1870; 1s. George Rawdon, arm. NEW COLL., matric. 11 Oct., 89, aged 19 (from Wellington coll.); HONOURS:—2 classical mods. 91.

Ryan, William Gladstone, born in London 25 March, 1865; o.s. Charles Lister, arm. TRINITY, matric. 15 Oct., 83, aged 18, from Winchester.

Ryde, Lewis Forbes, born at Melrose, Scotland, 10 March, 1859; 3s. John Gabriel, cler. NON-COLLEGIATE, matric. 18 Oct., 80, aged 21 (from Wellington); migrated to ST. JOHN'S, B.A. 83, M.A. 87; HONOURS:—2 theology 83.

Ryder, Richard Calthorpe Whitmore, M.A., fellow WADHAM 49, where see page 529.

Ryder, William Charles, born at Manchester Oct., 1864; 1s. William Bromwich, arm. CHRIST CHURCH, matric. 18 Jan., 84, aged 19 (from Radley coll.), B.A. and M.A. 91.

Rye, James Bacon, born at Wandsworth, Surrey, 22 July, 1871; 1s. Walter, solicitor. BALLIOL, matric. 17 Oct., 89, aged 18 (from St. Paul's school), scholar 88, B.A. 92; HONOURS:—1 history 92.

Ryley, Arthur Beresford, born at Woolwich, Kent, 4 July, 1868; o.s. James Beresford, D.Med. TRINITY, matric. 15 Oct., 87, aged 18 (from Epsom, and King's coll. school, London). B.A. 90; HONOURS:—3 chemistry 91.

Ryley, Cyril List, born at Camberwell, Surrey, 14 Jan., 1874; 2s. George Buchanan, congregational minister. JESUS COLL., matric. 18 Oct., 92, aged 18, from Southwark school.

Ryley, rev. Geoffrey Charles Edward, born at Sarratt, Herts, 7 Nov., 1866; 1s. Edward, cler. TRINITY, matric. 16 Oct., 86, aged 19 (from Canterbury school), B.A. 89, B.Mus. 91; HONOURS:—3 theology 89.

Ryley, Harold Buchanan, born at Bocking, Essex, 18 July, 1868; 1s. George Buchanan, gen. EXETER, matric. 19 Oct., 87, aged 19 (from Southwark gr. school), scholar 87, B.A. 91; HONOURS:—a classical mods. 89, 4 classics 91.

Ryves, Arthur Edward, born at Allahabad, East Indies, 14 Feb., 1865; o.s. Thomas James, arm. TRINITY, matric. 11 Oct., 84, aged 19 (from Clifton coll.), B.A. 88 (HONOURS:—3 law 87); bar.-at-law, Middle Temple, 88.

Ryves, Robert Hugh, born at Malvern, co. Worcester, 7 Jan., 1870; o.s. Joseph Gore, major R.E. TRINITY, matric. 12 Oct., 89, aged 19 (from Clifton coll.); assist. commissioner central provinces India 91.

Ryves, William Lewis, born at Thornton Heath, Surrey, 1 Dec., 1872; 3s. Edmund Warren Lewis, c.E. JESUS COLL., matric. 20 Oct., 91, aged 18 (from Dulwich coll.), exhibitioner 91; HONOURS:— 2 classical mods. 93.

ORNAMENT FROM NEW COLL.

WOODEN STRING COURSE, ELY CATHEDRAL.—*Pugin.*

S

Sabonadière, Alfred, born at Guernsey 1867; o.s. William Augustus, gen. ST. JOHN'S, matric. 17 Oct., 85, aged 18 (from the Charterhouse); assist. magistrate N.W. provinces, India.

Sadler, Arthur Lindsay, born at Brancaster, Norfolk, 1861; 2s. Ottiwell, cler. PEMBROKE, matric. 30 Oct., 80, aged 19, B.A. 84.

Sadler, Charles, born at Bedford 9 Oct., 1864; 6s. Michael Ferrelxe, cler. EXETER, matric. 18 Oct., 83, aged 19 (from Honiton gr. school), scholar 82, B.A. 87, M.A. 90; HONOURS:—2 classical mods. 85, 3 classics 87.

Sadler, Francis Joseph, born at Barnsley, Yorks, 16 June, 1867; 2s. Michael Thomas, D.Med. WADHAM, matric. 16 Oct., 86, aged 19 (from Rugby); scholar 85 (HONOURS:—3 physiology 90); brother of Michael Ernest.

Sadler, Gilbert Thomas, born at Amoy in China 27 Sept., 1871; 1s. James, missionary, China, L.M.S. NON-COLLEGIATE, matric. 17 Jan., 91, aged 19, from University coll., London.

Sadler, Michael Ernest, born at Barnsley, Yorks. 3 Jan., 1861; 1s. Michael Thomas, D.Med. TRINITY, matric. 16 Oct., 80, aged 19 (from Rugby), scholar 80-5, B.A. 84, M.A. 87, student of CHRIST CHURCH 90, and steward (HONOURS:—1 classical mods. 82, 1 classics 84), president of Oxford union society 82, secretary to delegates of local examinations, and of university extension.

Saer, Benjamin John, born at St. Clear, co. Carmarthen, 1853; 1s. John, gen. NON-COLLEGIATE, matric. 27 Oct., 91, aged 38, from Yale coll., U.S.A.

Sainsbury, Thomas Hugh Langford, born at Beckington, Somerset, 13 Sept., 1869; 1s. Sainsbury Langford, cler. TRINITY, matric. 15 Oct., 87, aged 18 (from Honiton school), B.A. 92.

Saint, Henry John Robert, born at Groombridge, Kent, Nov. 1871; 1s. John James Heath, bar.-at-law. CHRIST CHURCH, matric. 29 May, 91, aged 19, from Westminster school.

St. Aubyn, Bevil le Molesworth, born at Collingham, Yorks, 4 Feb., 1871; 2s. St. Aubyn Hender, vicar. CHRIST CHURCH, matric. 8 June, 89, aged 18 (from Eton), B.A. 92.

St. Aubyn, Guy Stewart, born at Stoke Damarell, Devon, 21 Nov., 1870; 1s. Edward, arm. MERTON, matric. 17 Oct., 88, aged 17, from Eton.

St. Aubyn, Hugh Molesworth, born at Swindon, co. Stafford, 3 Jan., 1865; 1s. St. Aubyn Hender, cler. CHRIST CHURCH, matric. 25 May, 83, aged 18 (from the Charterhouse), B.A. 90.

St. Croix, Sidney de, born at Crockerton, Wilts, 18 Aug., 1866; 3s. Henry Charles, cler. MERTON, matric. 24 Oct., 85, aged 19 (from Haileybury), B.A. 90, M.A. 92; HONOURS:—a history 89.

St. Hill, Edward Ashton, born at Wellington, New Zealand, 4 Feb., 1867; 1s. Henry Woodford, cler. TRINITY, matric. 16 Oct., 86, aged 19 (from Bath coll.), scholar 85, B.A. 90; fellow NEW COLL. 91, tutor 92; HONOURS:—Accessit Hertford scholarship 87, 1 classical mods. 88, 2 classics 90.

St. Hill, Ralph Woodford, born at Wellington, N.Z., 23 Feb., 1874; 4s. Henry Woodford, cler. TRINITY, matric. 15 Oct., 92, aged 18 (from Bath coll.), scholar 91.

St. John, Edward Francis St. John, born at Slinfold, Sussex, July, 1869; o.s. Edward John, lieut.-col. CHRIST CHURCH, matric. 13 Jan., 88, aged 18, B.A. 92.

St. John, Richard Fleming St. Andrew, born at Hilton, Dorset, 12 Sept., 1839; 1s. Henry St. Andrew, vicar. WADHAM, matric. 3 Nov., 58, aged 19; created M.A., 5 June, 88, University teacher of Burmese, late 60th Rifles, and deputy commissioner in British Burmah. See *Al. Ox.* 2nd series 1244.

St. John, Robert, created M.A. 21 June, 1861, of BALLIOL, teacher of Hindustani 80, late capt. 93rd regt.

St. Leger, Edward, born at Scotton, co. Leic., 6 Oct., 1866; 1s. Edward Frederic, rector. NEW COLL., matric. 16 Oct., 85, aged 19, (from Winchester), B.A. 89, M.A. 92 (HONOURS:—2 classical mods. 87, 3 classics 89); 6th viscount Doneraile 91; bar.-at-law, Inner Temple, 91.

St. Quintin, Geoffrey Apsley, born in London 1869; 3s. Matthew Chitty, arm. CHRIST CHURCH, matric. 4 June, 81, aged 19, from Eton.

St. Quinton, William Brandon, born at Blackrock, near Dublin, 1847; 2s. Thomas, arm. ST. EDMUND HALL, matric. 19 April, 80, aged 33, scholar Trinity Hall, Cambridge, 78.

Sale, rev. Thomas Rawlinson, born at Attercliffe, Yorks, 1 April, 1865; 1s. Thomas Walker, vicar of Skendleby. NEW COLL., matric. 15 Oct., 84, aged 19 (from Marlborough), B.A. 88, M.A. 91 (HONOURS:—3 classical mods. 86, 3 classics 88); domestic chaplain and secretary to the bishop of Man 91.

Salisbury, Robert, Marquis of, D.C.L., CHANCELLOR of the University 1869, see part 1, page 1.

Salkeld, Henry Lyde, born at Hyde, Cheshire, 21 Jan., 1873; 3s. Richard, vicar of St. Mark's Dukinfield, Cheshire. NON-COLLEGIATE, matric. 15 Oct., 92, aged 19, from Manchester gr. school.

Salmon, Charles Edward, born at Cheltenham 3 Nov., 1864; 2s. William Percival, of Ashton Keynes, Wilts, late capt. 6oth regt. MAGDALEN, matric. 24 Jan., 84, aged 19, from the Charterhouse.

Salmon, Henry Geoffrey Curwen, born at Manchester 27 June, 1869; 3s. Henry Curwen, gent. JESUS COLL., matric. 16 Oct., 88, aged 19 (from Merchant Taylors' school), scholar 88, B.A. 92; HONOURS :— 2 classical mods. 90, 3 classics 92.

Salmon, Nigel Gordon, born at Harton, co. Durham, 10 May, 1873; 3s. John, of Ryton-on-Tyne, solicitor. UNIVERSITY COLL., matric. 15 Oct., 92, aged 19, from Wellington coll.

Salmon, rev. Robert Cecil, born in London 6 Jan., 1864; 2s. George, gen. TRINITY, matric 15 Oct., 83, aged 19 (from Haileybury), B.A. 86 (HONOURS :—4 history 86); curate of Gt. Ilford, Essex, 87-90.

Salmon, Thomas, born at Brighton 2 Dec., 1873; 1s. Robert Ingham, M.A., rector of Barcombe, Sussex, deceased. MAGDALEN, matric. 18 Oct., 92, aged 18, from Winchester.

Salmond, James Laing, born at Barry, co. Forfar, 1867; 1s. Stewart Dingwall Fordyce, D.D. BALLIOL, matric. 18 Oct., 88, aged 21, from Aberdeen university (HONOURS :—3 classical mods. 90); 1 classics at Aberdeen 88.

Salt, Alexander Edward Wrottesley, born at Stoke-on-Trent, co. Staff., 1874; 1s. Edward, D.A., cler. BALLIOL, matric. 18 Oct., 92, aged 18, from Rugby.

Salt, Frederick John, born at Paddington, Middx., 25 June, 1872; 1s. John Charles, gen. CHRIST CHURCH, matric. 29 May, 91, aged 18, from Rugby.

Salt, George Edmund Stevenson, born at Ilaswick, co. Stafford, 19 Feb., 1873; 3s. Thomas, M.P. and banker. NEW COLL., matric. 16 Oct., 91, aged 18, from the Charterhouse.

Salt, Reginald John, born at Weeping Cross, co. Stafford, 2 March, 1874; 4s. Thomas, gent. NEW COLL., matric. 14 Oct., 92, aged 18, from the Charterhouse.

Salt, Thomas Anderdon, born in London 8 Jan., 1863; 1s. Thomas, arm. ORIEL, matric. 27 Oct., 83, aged 20; student Lincoln's Inn 84.

Salt, Thomas Fosbrooke, born at Baslow, co. Derby, 11 July, 1870; 1s. Thomas Fosbrooke, cler. NEW COLL., matric. 11 Oct., 89, aged 19 (from Repton school); HONOURS :—3 classical mods. 91.

Salter, Henry Stuart, born at Oxford 4 Dec., 1863; 2s. William Charles, cler., principal of St. Alban Hall. ST. ALBAN HALL, matric. 13 June, 81, aged 17 (from Malvern coll.); migrated to EXETER, B.A. 86, M.A. 88.

Salter, rev. Herbert Edward, born in London 6 Feb., 1863; 2s. Henry Hyde, D. Med., deceased. NEW COLL., matric. 14 Oct., 82, aged 19 (from Winchester), scholar 82, B.A. 86, M.A. 89 (HONOURS :—2 classical mods. 83, 1 classics 86, 1 theology 87); vice-principal Leeds clergy school 91.

Salter, William, born at Oxford 31 Dec., 1862; 1s. William Charles, cler., principal of St. Alban Hall. ST. ALBAN HALL, matric. 31 Jan., 82, aged 19 (from Malvern coll.); migrated to MERTON, B.A. 85, M.A. 88; HONOURS :—2 classical mods. 83, 3 classics 85.

Salusbury, rev. Francis Russell, born at Netley, Hants, ———, 1866; 3s. Augustus Pemberton, vicar, EXETER, matric. 18 Oct., 83, aged 17 (from Rossall school), B.A. 86, M.A. 90; curate of St. Bartholomew, Hyde, Manchester, 88.

Salwey, Geoffrey, born at Kildwick, Yorks, 30 Sept., 1872; 1s. Henry, vicar. CHRIST CHURCH, matric. 29 May, 91, aged 18 (from Bradfield coll.); HONOURS :—3 classical mods. 93.

Salwey, Henry, M.A., student CHRIST CHURCH 55-68, where see page 421.

Salwey, Herbert, M.A., senior student CHRIST CHURCH 65-83, where see page 423.

Salwey, rev. John, born at Ewell, Surrey, 6 Aug., 1867; 1s. John, cler. HERTFORD, matric. 22 Oct., 86, aged 19 (from Westminster school), B.A. 89 (HONOURS :—3 classical mods. 88); curate of All Saints, Lambeth, 90.

Salwey, Roger, born at Ludlow, Salop, Oct., 1869; o.s. Alfred, arm. HERTFORD, matric. 28 Jan., 90, aged 20, from Wellington.

Salzmann, Frederick Henry, born at Brighton, Sussex, 23 Feb., 1873; 1s. Frederick William, D. Med. NEW COLL., matric. 14 Oct., 92, aged 19, from Haileybury.

Sammons, Howard, born at Oxford 1861; o.s. Thomas 'Lender, gen. NON-COLLEGIATE, matric. 23 Oct., 80, aged 19.

Sampson, Charles Henry, M.A., fellow BRASENOSE 82, where see page 349.

Sampson, rev. Edward Frank, M.A., senior student CHRIST CHURCH 69, where see page 408.

Sampson, rev. Gerald Victor, born at Ninfield, Sussex, 23 May, 1864; 2s. Thomas, of Moor Hall, Battle, arm. EXETER, matric. 18 Oct., 83, aged 19 (from Westminster school), B.A. 87 (HONOURS :—3 classical mods. 85); curate of St. Barnabas, Pimlico, 87.

Sams, William Henry, born in London 19 Nov., 1871; 1s. William George, gent. WORCESTER, matric. 18 Oct., 92, aged 20, from an Ealing school.

Samson, Edward Mariay, born in London 27 March, 1869; 2s. Ludovic, arm. TRINITY, matric. 15 Oct., 87, aged 18 (from Harrow), B.A. 91; HONOURS :—2 history 91.

Samson, rev. Gavin Hamilton, born at Altrincham, Cheshire, Nov., 1866; 1s. Andrew Gibb, gent. KEBLE, matric. 22 Oct., 85, aged 18 (from Haileybury), B.A. 89, M.A. 92 (HONOURS :—2 theology 89); curate of New Romney, St. Mary-in-the-Marsh, 91.

Samson, Herbert, born at Manchester 5 Dec., 1862; 1s. Henry, gen. NON-COLLEGIATE, matric. 6 March, 82, aged 19 (from Rugby), migrated to ORIEL, B.A. 85 (HONOURS :—3 law 84); student Middle Temple 84.

Samson, Walter, born at Fallowfield, co. Lanc., 9 July, 1864; 2s. Henry, arm. BRASENOSE, matric. 25 May, 83, aged 18 (from Rugby), B.A. 86.

Samuel, Frank Victor, born at Norwich 28 March, 1874; 2s. Benjamin Samuel, merchant, deceased. MAGDALEN, matric. 18 Oct., 92, aged 18 (from Norwich school), exhibitioner 92.

Samuel, Herbert Louis, born at Liverpool 6 Nov., 1870; 4s. Edwin Louis, arm. BALLIOL, matric. 17 Oct., 89, aged 18, from University coll. school, London.

Samuel, rev. Richard Wood, born in London 1860; 4s. Joseph, gen. ST. ALBAN HALL, matric. 19 Oct., 81, aged 21; curate of St. Anne, Soho, 87-91.

Samuelson, Francis (Arthur Edward), born at Torquay, Devon, 26 Feb., 1861; 2s. sir Bernhard, bart., M.P. BALLIOL, matric. 21 Oct., 80, aged 19 (from Cheltenham coll. and Rugby), B.A. 86 (HONOURS :—2 classical mods. 82); student Inner Temple 82.

Samuelson, Godfrey Blundell, born at Banbury, Oxon, 3 June, 1863; 3s. sir Bernhard, bart., M.P. BALLIOL, matric. 17 Oct., 82, aged 19, from Cheltenham coll. and Rugby (HONOURS :—2 classical mods. 83); M.P. co. Gloucester 87-92.

Sandars, Thomas Collett, M.A., fellow ORIEL 49-52, where see page 153.

Sanday, William, M.A., fellow EXETER 83 and 88, where see page 123.

Sandbach, Edward Lister, born at Sale, Cheshire, 27 April, 1874; 1s. Edward, merchant. JESUS COLL., matric. 18 Oct., 92, aged 18, from Queen's coll., Taunton.
Sandbach, Henry, born at Aigburth, co. Lanc., 1863; 3s. Gilbert, cler. NEW COLL., matric. 21 Jan., 82, aged 19 (from Eton), B.A. 85, M.A. 90 (HONOURS:—3 history 85); bar.-at-law, Inner Temple, 87.
Sandberg, Carl, born in London 1872; 1s. John Herman, gen. HERTFORD, matric. 20 Oct., 91, aged 19 (from St. Paul's school), scholar 90; HONOURS:—1 mathematical mods. 92.
Sanders, Alexander Sargent, born at Gloucester 17 Oct., 1868; 3s. Joseph Robert, gen. WORCESTER, matric. 14 Oct., 90, aged 21, from Cheltenham coll. (HONOURS:—2 classical mods. 92); died 21 May, 92.
Sanders, rev. Arthur Andrew, born at Brighton 26 May, 1863; 3s. Lloyd, cler. EXETER, matric. 18 Oct., 82, aged 19 (from the Charterhouse), B.A. 85 (HONOURS:—4 history 85); curate of Whimple, Devon, 91.
Sanders, rev. Henry Lionel Walpole Howard, born at Newport, I.W., 1864; 2s. Gilbert Howard, arm. NON-COLLEGIATE, matric. 18 Oct., 83, aged 19 (from Honiton gr. school); migrated to ST. MARY HALL, B.A. 85; died 8 April, 88.
Sanders, Robert Arthur, born in London 20 June, 1867; 1s. Arthur, arm. BALLIOL, matric. 19 Oct., 86, aged 19 (from Harrow), B.A. 90 (HONOURS:—2 classical mods. 88, 1 law 90); bar.-at-law, Inner Temple, 92.
Sanderson, Anthony Ambrose, born at Ealing, Middx., 21 Aug., 1871; 4s. John, solicitor. UNIVERSITY COLL., matric. 11 Oct., 90, aged 19, from Haileybury.
Sanderson, Archibald, born at Brie Brie in Australia 1870; 4s. John, arm. UNIVERSITY COLL., matric. 13 Oct., 88, aged 18; HONOURS:—3 history 92.
Sanderson, Edward Ainslie Gordon, born in Barbados 1869. NON-COLLEGIATE, matric. 30 Oct. 88, aged 19 (from Harrison coll., Barbados); migrated to ST. JOHN'S, exhibitioner 90; HONOURS:—2 mathematical mods. 90, 3 mathematics 92.
Sanderson, John, born at Cheltenham 1864; 1s. John, gen. ST. JOHN'S, matric. 14 Oct., 82, aged 18 (from Eastbourne coll.), B.A. 85 (HONOURS:—2 theology 85); bar.-at-law, Lincoln's Inn, 89.
Sanderson, John Scott Burdon-, M.A., 27 Feb., 1883 by decree of convocation, and fellow of MAGDALEN 82, where see page 312.
Sandes, John, born at Cork 26 Feb., 1863; 2s. Samuel Dickson, rector of Monewden, Suffolk. MAGDALEN, matric. 21 Jan., 82, aged 18, B.A. 85; HONOURS:—2 classical mods. 83, 4 law 85.
Sandford, Charles Waldegrave, D.D., bishop of Gibraltar, student CHRIST CHURCH 48-72, where see page 418.
Sandford, Francis Follett, born at Bicton, Salop, 1867; 1s. William, cler. CHRIST CHURCH, matric. 16 Oct., 85, aged 18 (from Shrewsbury school), exhibitioner 85, B.A. 89, M.A. 92; HONOURS:—2 classical mods. 87, 3 classics 89.
Sands, William Henry Bethune, born at Edinburgh Dec., 1865; 4s. William John, arm. ORIEL, matric. 23 Oct., 84, aged 18 (from the Charterhouse), B.A. 89; HONOURS:—2 classical mods. 86, 3 history 88.
Sandwith, rev. Edward Pitcairn, born at Sholapore, East Indies, 13 Sept., 1864; 3s. William, arm. CHRIST CHURCH, matric. 14 Oct., 87, aged 23 (from Westminster school), B.A. 90.

Sandwith, rev. William Fitzgerald Gambier, born at Baroch, East Indies, 18 July, 1861; 1s. William, arm. CHRIST CHURCH, matric. 24 Jan., 81, aged 19 (from Westminster school), B.A. 84; vicar of Holkham 87, and rector of Egmere, Norfolk, 88.
Sanford, Edward Charles Percival, born at Combe Flory, Somerset, 20 Feb., 1865; 2s. Edward Aylesford, rector. MAGDALEN, matric. 19 Oct., 83, aged 18 (from Clifton coll.), B.A. 88; bar.-at-law, Inner Temple, 89.
Sanger, William, born in London 1873; 2s. William Albert, gen. CORPUS CHRISTI, matric. 19 Oct., 91, aged 18 (from Wellington), exhibitioner 91; HONOURS:—2 classical mods. 93.
Sanguinetti, Harold Herbert, born in London 27 March, 1872; 2s. Herbert Samuel, g.m. WADHAM, matric. 13 Oct., 90, aged 18, from University coll. school, London.
Sankey, John, born at Moreton-in-Marsh, co. Glouc., 26 Oct., 1866; 2s. Thomas, arm. JESUS COLL., matric. 23 Oct., 85, aged 18 (from Lancing coll.), scholar 85, B.A. 89 (HONOURS:—2 classical mods. 87, 2 history 89, 3 civil law 91); bar.-at-law, Middle Temple, 92.
Sant, Edward, born at Swansea, co. Glamorgan, Feb., 1867; 2s. George, arm. KEBLE, matric. 20 Oct., 85, aged 18 (from Swansea school), B.A. 90; HONOURS:—4 history 89.
Sant, Ivor, born at Oystermouth, co. Glam., 12 April, 1870; 3s. George, artist. JESUS COLL., matric. 15 Oct., 90, aged 20 (from Malvern coll.); HONOURS:—2 classical mods. 92.
Sarel, Sydney Lancaster, born in London June, 1872; 2. Thomas, gen. KEBLE, matric. 20 Oct., 91, aged 19 (from Tonbridge school).
Sargeant, Francis William, born in London 10 Jan., 1870; 4s. Henry, bar.-at-law, deceased. NEW COLL., matric. 11 Oct. 89, aged 19, from Rugby.
Sargent, Arthur John, born at Bromborough, Cheshire, 8 March, 1871; 1s. Arthur James, gen. BRASENOSE, matric. 22 Oct., 91, aged 20 (from King's coll. school, and King's coll., London), exhibitioner 91; HONOURS:—1 classical mods. 93.
Sargent, John Young, M.A., fellow HERTFORD 77, where see page 597.
Sargent, Julian Hilton, born at St. Petersburg 8 April, 1864; 1s. William, assist. master Rugby. EXETER, matric. 18 Oct., 83, aged 19 (from Rugby), scholar 83, B.A. 87; HONOURS:—1 classical mods. 85, 2 classics 87, Latin essay 88.
Sargent, rev. Walter Dmitri, born at Isell, Cumberland, 29 May, 1865; y.s. William, arm. MERTON, matric. 16 Oct., 84, aged 19 (from Rugby), postmaster 83-6, B.A. 88, M.A. 91 (HONOURS:—2 classical mods. 86, 2 classics 88); curate of Aylesbury 89; brother of Julian H.
Sarsfield, James Delacour, born at Dough Cloyne, co. Cork, 20 Sept., 1864; 2s. Dominick Ronayne Patrick, arm. EXETER, matric. 21 Jan., 85, aged 20 (from Cheltenham coll.), B.A. 88; brother of the next.
Sarsfield, Thomas Ronayne, born at Cork 13 April, 1862; 1s. Dominick Ronayne Patrick, of Dough Cloyne, co. Cork, arm. EXETER, matric. 31 Jan., 82, aged 19, from Cheltenham coll.
Sasse, Alfred Edmund, born in London 18 March, 1859; 2s. John, arm. ST. MARY HALL, matric. 18 Jan., 90, aged 30.
Sassoon, David, born in London 1868; 1s. Reuben David, arm. CHRIST CHURCH, matric. 16 April, 86, aged 18, from Eton.
Saul, Ernest Wingate, born at Lancaster March, 1873; 1s. William, D.Med. CHRIST CHURCH, matric. 29 May, 91, aged 18, from Rugby.

Saunders, Arnold Frederick, born at Reigate, Surrey, 4 Dec., 1864; 3s. William Frederick, gen. WADHAM, matric. 23 Oct., 82, aged 17 (from Merchant Taylors' school), scholar 82, B.A. 87; HONOURS:— Hebrew scholarship 84.

Saunders, Arthur Leslie, born in London 1862; 1s. Arthur William, arm. BALLIOL, matric. 1 Nov., 80, aged 18 (from Birmingham oratory); senior judge small cause court, Nagpur, central province India.

Saunders, Arthur Newdigate, born at Magor, co. Mon., 25 July, 1863; 1s. Arthur Cardinal, vicar. ORIEL, matric. 18 Oct., 81, aged 18 (from Marlborough); drowned 83.

Saunders, Arthur Ramsay, born at Woolwich, Kent, Aug., 1872; 1s. Arthur Augustus, lieut.-col. R.A. KEBLE, matric. 9 Feb., 92, aged 19, from Radley coll.

Saunders, Charles James, born at Reigate, Surrey, 1866; 5s. William Frederick, gen. ST. JOHN'S, matric. 16 Oct., 96, aged 18 (from Merchant Taylors' school), scholar 86, B.A. 90 (HONOURS:—2 classical mods. 88, 2 classics 90, Eastern cadetship 91.

Saunders, Edward Arthur, born at Reigate, Surrey, 1866; 4s. William Frederick, gen. ST. JOHN'S, matric. 11 Oct., 84, aged 18 (from Merchant Taylors' school), scholar 84, B.A. 88; HONOURS: —2 physiology 88.

Saunders, George, born at Kathray (? Crathay), Scotland, 1859; 1s. David Mogg, gen. BALLIOL, matric. 18 Oct., 81, aged 22 (from Glasgow university), exhibitioner 81-6, B.A. 66 (HONOURS: —3 classical mods. 83, 3 history 85); student Inner Temple 84.

Saunders, George Eveleigh, M.A., fellow WADHAM 47-58, where see page 531.

Saunders, Godfrey Wadham St. George, born at Chislehurst, Kent, May, 1874; o.s. William Sedgwick, D.Med. CHRIST CHURCH, matric. 14 Oct., 92, aged 18.

Saunders, Herbert Stewart, born in London 18 May, 1872; 1s. Herbert Clifford, Q.C. MAGDALEN, matric. 14 Oct., 90, aged 18, from the Charterhouse.

Saunders, James Vallance, born at Handsworth, co. Stafford, 8 Nov., 1865; o.s. Vallance, gen., deceased. QUEEN'S, matric. 22 Oct., 84, aged 18 (from Birmingham school), scholar 84, B.A. 89, M.A. 91; HONOURS:—2 classical mods. 86, 3 classics 88.

Saunders, Leslie Harry, born at Lahore, East Indies, 11 Nov., 1868; 2s. Leslie Seymour, of Indian C.S. WADHAM, matric. 15 Oct., 87, aged 18 (from Dulwich coll.), exhibitioner 87, assist. commissioner Burmah.

Saunders, Nathaniel Argent, born at Magor, co. Monmouth, 13 Oct., 1873; 2s. Arthur Cardinal, M.A., rector of Lydiard Millicent, Wilts. PEMBROKE, matric. 28 Oct., 92, aged 19 (from Abingdon school), scholar 92.

Saunders, Percival George, born at Chipping Norton, Oxon, 6 April, 1866; 2s. George Henry, solicitor. WADHAM, matric. 16 Oct., 83, aged 17, from Clifton coll.

Saunders, rev. Sidney Charles, born at Chilworth, Surrey, 1851; 3s. James, gen. CHARSLEY'S HALL, matric. 17 Oct., 82, aged 31; migrated to EXETER 82, B.A. 85, M.A. 89; vicar of Cadmore End, Bucks, 90.

Saunders, Thomas Bailey, born at Grahams Town, Cape of Good Hope, 2 Dec., 1862; 2s. George, arm. UNIVERSITY COLL., matric. 15 May, 80, aged 19 (from King's coll., Lond.), B.A. 85, M.A. 88 (HONOURS:—2 classical mods. 82, 2 classics 84); bar.-at-law, Inner Temple, 86.

Saunders, Thomas Dekenn Avening, born at Handsworth, co. Warwick, 29 Dec., 1870; 2s. Cornelius Thomas, of Moseley Wake Green, near Birmingham, solicitor. UNIVERSITY COLL., matric. 12 Oct., 89, aged 18 (from K. Edward's school, Birmingham); HONOURS:—3 classical mods. 91.

Savage, Edwin Louis Livingston, born at New York 1865; o.s. John, arm. NON-COLLEGIATE, matric. 22 Oct., 81, aged 28, from Geneva, Switzerland.

Savage, rev. Edwin Sidney, born at Penge, Surrey, 28 Feb., 1862; 2s. William, of Woodford, Essex, arm. ST. MARY HALL, matric. 21 Jan., 81, aged 18 (from Eastbourne coll.); migrated to MAGDALEN, B.A. 85, M.A. 87; vicar of St. Mark, Barrow-in-Furness, 80.

Savage, Ernest Smallwood, born in Birmingham, Dec., 1869; 2s. Thomas, D.Med. CHRIST CHURCH, matric. 14 Oct., 87, aged 17 (from Birmingham school); B.A. 90.

Savery, rev. John Manly, born at Sherborne, Dorset, 1850; 4s. George, gent. NON-COLLEGIATE, matric. 17 Oct., 81, aged 22; matric. NON-COLL., Cambridge, 21 Oct., 82, B.A. from St. Katherine coll. 84.

Savigny, William Henry, born at St. Paul's coll., Sydney, 1864; 1s. William Henry, cler. NON-COLLEGIATE, matric. 18 Oct., 83, aged 19 (from Launceston church gr. school, Tasmania); migrated to CORPUS CHRISTI, B.A. 87 (HONOURS: —4 Jan. 87); bar.-at-law, Inner Temple, 88.

Savile, rev. Edward Stevenson Gordon, born in London Feb., 1866; 1s. Edward Bourchier, arm. CHRIST CHURCH, matric. 16 Oct., 85, aged 19, B.A. 89 (HONOURS:—4 theology 89); curate of St. Dunstan, Stepney, Middx., 91.

Savile, John Herbert Brad, born at Belfast 29 March, 1866; 1s. William, late capt. 9th Lancers. MAGDALEN, matric. 23 Oct., 85, aged 19, from Eton.

Savory, Albert, born at Weybridge, Surrey, 7 July, 1870; 1s. Albert, arm., deceased. MAGDALEN, matric. 14 Oct., 89, aged 19 (from Winchester (HONOURS:—2 classical mods. 91); 2nd lieut. 4th (Queen's Own) Hussars 92.

Sawyer, rev. Ernest William, born at Fridge, Kent, Oct., 1862; 2s. William Collinson, bishop of Grafton and Armidale. QUEEN'S, matric. 18 Oct., 81, aged 19 (from St. Paul's Coll., Stony Stratford), B.A. 86; curate of St. Stephen Upton Park, E., 91.

Sawyer, rev. Harold Athelstane Parry, born 13 Jan., 1865; 4s. William Collinson, bishop of Grafton and Armidale. QUEEN'S, matric. 22 Oct., 83, aged 18 (from Magdalen coll. school, chorister 74-8), scholar 83, B.A. 87, M.A. 92 (HONOURS:—2 classical mods. 85, 2 classics 87); curate of Lewisham, Kent, 90.

Say, Henry John, born at Puxton, Somerset, 1872; 2s. John, gent. NON-COLLEGIATE, matric. 17 Oct., 91, aged 19, from University coll., Bristol.

Sayce, rev. Archibald Henry, M.A., fellow QUEEN'S 69, where see page 174.

Sayer, rev. James Burchier, born at Finchley; Middlesex, April, 1866; 6s. Edward, gen. QUEEN'S, matric. 30 Oct., 85, aged 19 (from Finchley coll.), B.A. 89, M.A. 92 (HONOURS:—2 history 89); curate of Birkenhead St. Anne 89.

Sayers, rev. Andrew Edward Leslie, born at North Repps, Norfolk, 1868; 3s. Robert, cler. NON-COLLEGIATE, matric. 16 Oct., 86, aged 18 (from Swansea coll.), B.A. 89 (HONOURS:—3 classical mods. 88, 3 history 89); curate of Leicester St. Mark 91.

Sayers, rev. Henry, M.A., chaplain CHRIST CHURCH 79-80 and 84, where see page 425.

Sayle, Charles Edward, born at Cambridge 6 Dec., 1864; s. Robert, gen. NEW COLL., matric. 9 Nov., 83 aged 18 (from Rugby), B.A. 87, M.A. 90 (HONOURS:—2 classical mods. 85, 4 classics 87); incorporated M.A. at CAMBRIDGE 90, from ST. JOHN'S COLL.

Scadding, Samuel William, born at Pearinhall, co. Stafford, 20 Jan., 1866; 1s. Frederick, gen. TRINITY, matric. 16 Oct., 86, aged 20 (from Kingswood school), B.A. 90; HONOURS:—2 chemistry 90.

Scanlen, Arthur Dennison, born at Cradock, Cape of Good Hope, 1870; 2s. Thomas Charles, arm. ORIEL, matric. 25 Oct., 89, aged 19, from Bishop's coll., Capetown.

Scargill, Lionel Walter Kennedy, born at Luton, Beds., 4 Oct., 1871; 1s. Frank Chapman, solicitor. BALLIOL, matric. 11 Feb., 92, aged 20, from Clifton coll.

Scattergood, Bernard Page, born at Leeds 18 May, 1862; 4s. Thomas, gen. QUEEN'S, matric. 4 June, 81, aged 19 (from Leeds gr. school), exhibitioner 81-6, B.A. 85; HONOURS:—2 classical mods. 83, 4 mathematics 84, 2 physics 86.

Schilizzi, Emanuel Stephen, born at Manchester 15 Jan., 1865; 3s. Stephen Peter, gen. NEW COLL., matric. 13 Dec., 86, aged 21 (from Marlborough); HONOURS:—2 classical mods. 88.

Schiller, Ferdinand Canning Scott, born at Othmarschen in Holstein 16 Aug., 1864; 1s. John Christian Ferdinand, gen. BALLIOL, matric. 17 Oct., 82, aged 18 (from Rugby), exhibitioner 81, B.A. 86, M.A. 91 (HONOURS:—1 classical mods. 83, 1 classics 86, Taylorian (German) scholarship 87); brother of the next.

Schiller, Ferdinand Philip Maximilian, born at Ealing, Middx., 28 July, 1866; 3s. John Christian Ferdinand, gen. MAGDALEN, matric. 21 Oct., 85, aged 18 (from Clifton coll.), exhibitioner 86, B.A. 90 (HONOURS:—2 classical mods. 88, 2 classics 90); brother of the last.

Schlesinger, Richard Tolson, born at Lightcliffe, Yorks, Feb., 1869; 1s. Frederick Emil, arm. KEBLE, matric. 11 Oct., 90, aged 21, from Gotha, Germany.

Schleswig-Holstein, prince Christian Victor Albert Lewis Ernest Anton of, born at Windsor Castle 14 April, 1867; 1s. prince Christian of Schleswig-Holstein. MAGDALEN, matric. 26 Jan., 86, aged 18 (from Wellington coll.), G.C.B. hon. lieut. King's Royal Rifles 90.

Schlieman, Henry, created D.C.L. 13 June, 1883, born 6 Jan., 22; died at Naples 27 Dec., 90; buried at Athens. See *Al. Ox.* and series 1261.

Schmid, John William Horace, born at St. Bees, Cumberland, 14 Feb., 1866; 1s. Rudolph, gen. QUEEN'S, matric. 30 Oct., 85, aged 19 (from St. Bees gr. school), exhibitioner 85, B.A. 90; HONOURS:—3 classical mods. 87.

Schneider, Edward Oskar, born at Rusholme, co. Lane., 1865; 1s. Edward Oskar, arm. CORPUS CHRISTI, matric. 23 Oct., 84, aged 19 (from Owens coll., Manchester), B.A. 87; HONOURS:—3 classical mods. 86.

Schœdelin, Emile Thaddée, born at Uffholtz in Alsatia 18 April, 1865; 1s. Francis Xavier, teacher of French. JESUS COLL., matric. 18 Oct., 83, aged 18 (from Bedford school), scholar 83, B.A. 88; HONOURS:—2 classical mods. 85, 2 classics 87, Taylorian (French) exhibition 89.

Schofield, William Shuttlewood, born at Loughborough 1871; 3s. Edward, gen. HERTFORD, matric. 14 Oct., 90, aged 19, from Peterborough school.

Scholefield, Ernest Hall, born at Atherton, co. Lane., 19 Jan., 1873; 2s. James, gen. NEW COLL., matric. 16 Oct., 91, aged 18 (from Rivington and Blackrod school), scholar 91.

Scholefield, Robert Ernest, born at Leeds 1865; y.s. William, gen. CHRIST CHURCH, matric. 11 Oct., 84, aged 19 (from Leeds school), scholar 84, B.A. 88, B. Med. 90, M.A. 91; HONOURS:— 1 physiology 88, Radcliffe fellowship 89.

Schön, rev. James Frederic, created D.D. 24 April, 1884; late missionary on the Niger. See *Al. Ox.* 2nd series 1261.

Schönberg, Edward, born at Wolverhampton 3 Jan., 1863; 2s. Moritz, cler. EXETER, matric. 23 Oct., 85, aged 23 (from Manchester gr. school and Owens coll.), exhibitioner 84; drowned at Oxford 18 Feb., 86.

Schünland, Selmar, Ph.D., created M.A. 4 June, 1889; sub-curator of the Fielding Herbarium.

Schorstein, Gustave Isidore, born at Neuilly, near Paris, 1863; 1s. Lazarus, arm. CHRIST CHURCH, matric. 14 Oct., 81, aged 18 (from city of London school), scholar 81-6, B.A. 85, M.A. and B.Med. 89; HONOURS:—1 classical mods. 83, 2 classics 85.

Schrader, Louis William Conrad, born in London 18 Aug., 1873; 1s. Carl, Ph.D. (Bonn), professor of languages. LINCOLN, matric. 25 Oct., 92, aged 19 (from Highgate school), scholar 92.

Schröder, Bernard Henry, born at Liverpool Feb., 1865; 1s. Bernard Henry, arm. WADHAM, matric. 13 Oct., 88, aged 23, from Eton.

Schulhof, John Maurice, born in London 23 Aug., 1838; o.s. Maurice, D.Med. NON-COLLEGIATE, matric. 13 Oct., 84, aged 26 (from St. Paul's school), exhibitioner EXETER 86, B.A. 87 [HONOURS:—1 classical mods. 86, Ireland scholarship 86 (accessit, twice, 85), Craven scholarship 86, 1 classics 87]; scholar TRINITY COLL., CAMBRIDGE, 77, 12th classic and B.A. 81; assist. master St. Paul's 82.

Schuster, Claud, born at Pendleton, co. Lane., 22 Aug., 1869; o.s. Frederick Leo, arm. NEW COLL., matric. 12 Oct., 88, aged 19 (from Winchester), B.A. 92; HONOURS:—2 history 92.

Schwabe, Cecil Langshaw, born at Lymm, Cheshire, 11 Oct., 1869; 3s. Henry Albert, arm. ORIEL, matric. 20 Oct., 88, aged 19, from Rugby; died 5 May, 91.

Schwabe, Walter George Salis, born in London, 3 March, 1873; 2s. George Salis, colonel and late M.P. TRINITY, matric. 6 Feb., 92, aged 18 (from Marlborough and Cheltenham colls.); HONOURS:— 2 classical mods 93.

Schwann, Henry Sigismund, born at Houghton, Hants, 1869; 1s. Frederick Sigismund, arm. CORPUS CHRISTI, matric. 22 Oct., 87, aged 18 (from Clifton coll.); HONOURS:—2 classical mods. 89; in University eleven 90.

Schwartze, Frederick Walter Helmuth, born in London 1 June, 1870; 3s. Helmutii, gen. WADHAM, matric. 14 Oct., 89, aged 19, from Dulwich coll.

Schweder, Albert Julius, born at Highbury, Middx., 21 Aug., 1863; 4s. Julius Edward, arm. MERTON, matric. 17 Oct., 82, aged 19 (from Eastbourne coll. and Harrow), B.A. 85; HONOURS:—2 history 85.

Sclater, Philip Lutley, M.A., fellow CORPUS CHRISTI 53-62, where see page 382.

Sclater, William Lutley, born in London 23 Sept., 1863; 1s. Philip Lutley, F.R.S. KEBLE, matric. 2 Dec., 81, aged 18 (from Winchester), B.A. 85, M.A. 90; HONOURS:—1 natural science 85.

Scofield, Herbert Harold, born at Stoke Holy Cross, Norfolk, May, 1861; 5s. Edward, arm. CHRIST CHURCH, matric. 10 Oct., 90, aged 29.

Scoones, Offley, born at Langley Marish, Bucks, 2 Jan., 1865; 1s. William Dalton, cler. CHRIST CHURCH, matric. 12 Oct., 83, aged 18 (from Westminster school), scholar 83, B.A. 87; HONOURS:— 2 classical mods. 85, 3 classics 87.

Sootcher, rev. David Fortington, born at Ely, co. Cambr., 25 Feb., 1867; o.s. Edward James, gen. NON-COLLEGIATE, matric. 23 Jan., 86, aged 18 (from Ely school); migrated to WORCESTER, B.A. 89, M.A. 92 (HONOURS:—3 theology 89); curate of Helmsley, Yorks, 90.

Scott, Arthur Edmund Augustine Stewart-, born at Salisbury, Adelaide, South Australia, 16 Nov., 1870; 2s. William, B.A., cler. NON-COLLEGIATE, matric. 2 April, 92, aged 21, from St. John's school, Leatherhead.

Scott, rev. Arthur Shaw Hill, born at Caputh, Perthshire, 21 April, 1863; 1s. Robert Horne, gent. WORCESTER, matric. 17 Oct., 84, aged 21 (from Bedford gr. school), B.A. 87 (HONOURS:—3 theology 88); curate of Gedling, Notts, 89.

Scott, Aylmer Vivian Arthur, born at Horsham, Sussex, April, 1870; 1s. John Henry, cler. KEBLE, matric. 12 Oct., 89, aged 19, from Bedford gr. school.

Scott, Baliol Kenward, born at Paramatta, N.S.W., 17 June, 1873; 1s. Lawrence Hartshorn, captain 11th regt., deceased. UNIVERSITY COLL., matric. 15 Oct., 92, aged 19, from Bath coll.

Scott, Charles Brodrick, D.D., hon student CHRIST CHURCH 75, where see page 412.

Scott, Charles Edward, born at Aughnacloy, co. Tyrone, 20 Nov., 1862; 1s. William, gent. QUEEN'S, matric. 28 Oct., 81, aged 18 (from Bath coll.), scholar 81-5; HONOURS:—2 classical mods. 83.

Scott, Charles Harold, born at Wrexham, co. Denbigh, 1 Dec., 1871; 1s. Thomas, gen. JESUS COLL., matric. 15 Oct., 90, aged 18 (from Wrexham school); HONOURS:—3 classical mods. 92.

Scott, Charles Hepburn, born at Brighton Dec., 1870; 3s. Robert Henry (or Herris) Dudley, arm. HERTFORD, matric. 14 Oct., 90, aged 19.

Scott, Clement Victor Rough, born at East Moulsey, Surrey, May, 1872; 91. Charles, cler. KEBLE, matric. 20 Oct., 91, aged 19.

Scott, David Russell, born at Airdrie, co. Lanark, 1870; 1s. Adam, congregational minister. NON-COLLEGIATE, matric. 22 Oct., 91, aged 21, from Edinburgh university.

Scott, Edwin, born at Polmont, Stirling, 1866; 4s. James Stenhouse, gen. BALLIOL, matric. 15 Oct., 84, aged 18 (from St. Paul's school and University coll., London); assist. to collector and magistrate and agent to the governor of Madras at Godavari.

Scott, Ernest Findlay, born at Thornley, co. Durham, 1868; 1s. Ernest Faithful, cler. BALLIOL, matric. 18 Oct., 88, aged 20 (from Glasgow university, 1 classics and 1 philosophy at Glasgow 88, Ferguson classical scholar 88), exhibitioner 88; HONOURS:—1 classical mods. 90, 2 classics 92.

Scott, Francis McLean, born at Horsham, Sussex, Jan., 1872; 2s. John Arthur Henry, cler. KEBLE, matric. 11 Oct., 90, aged 18, from Bedford gr. school.

Scott, Frederick Ernest, born in London 1855; 6s. Matthew Richard, gen. NON-COLLEGIATE, matric. 19 Jan., 84, aged 29 (from Merchant Taylors' school); migrated to CHRIST CHURCH, B.A. 86, M.A. 92; HONOURS:—2 theology 86.

Scott, George, born at Brisbane 16 Jan., 1866; 1s. Henry, arm. MERTON, matric. 16 Oct., 84, aged 18 (from Brisbane gr. school), B.A. 87, M.A. 91; HONOURS:—2 law 87.

Scott, George Arthur Jervoise, M.A., fellow ALL SOULS, 58-76, where see page 281.

Scott, George Forrester, born at Oulton, Yorks, 1863; 1s. Benjamin Forrester, gen. ST. MARY HALL, matric. 23 Oct., 82, aged 19, B.A. 85; brother of Harold J.

Scott, George Rodney, M.A., fellow MERTON 74, where see page 93.

Scott, Godfrey William Montagu Douglas, born 31 Aug., 1866; 3s. William Henry, duke of Buccleuch. CHRIST CHURCH, matric. 16 April, 86, aged 19 (from Eton); in University eleven 87, 88, 89.

Scott, rev. Gilbert Maxwell, born at Birkenhead 12 Jan., 1863; 2s. Walter, gen. JESUS COLL., matric. 18 Oct., 82, aged 19 (from Blundell's school, Tiverton), B.A. 85, M.A. 89; curate of St. John Evangelist, Reading, 86.

Scott, Godfrey Frederic Charles Baliol, born at Norwich 25 April, 1870; 11. Charles Edmund, col. R.A. MAGDALEN, matric. 28 Jan., 89, aged 18 (from Wellington coll.); and lieut. the King's own Scottish borderers 92.

Scott, rev. Harold John, born at Wilmington, Kent, 31 Dec., 1865; 3s. Benjamin Forrester, gen. MERTON, matric. 24 Oct., 85, aged 19, B.A. 89, M.A. 92; curate of Burghclere, Berks, 90; brother of George F.

Scott, Harold Spencer, born at Wigan, co. Lanc., 9 Sept., 1865; 1s. Edward, solicitor. NEW COLL., matric. 12 Oct., 83, aged 18 (from Ascham school, Bournemouth); HONOURS:—3 history 87; bar.-at-law, Lincoln's Inn, 92.

Scott, lord Henry Francis Montagu Douglas, born 15 Jan., 1868; 4s. William Henry, duke of Buccleuch. CHRIST CHURCH, matric. 15 Oct., 86, aged 18 (from Eton), B.A. 90 (HONOURS:—3 history 90); brother of lords George and John.

Scott, rev. Herbert Reginald, born at Byfleet, Surrey, 30 June, 1861; 2s. Syms, of London, gen. MAGDALEN, matric. 16 Oct., 80, aged 22 (from Brentwood gr. school), B.A., M.A. 87 (HONOURS:—3 theology 84); vicar of Klimeston, Hants, 91.

Scott, Hugh James Elibank, born at Galashiels, Scotland, 1 Oct., 1861; 2s. Hugh, arm. ORIEL, matric. 21 May, 80, aged 18 (from Radley coll.), B.A. 84, M.A. 87.

Scott, John, viscount Encombe, born 8 May, 1870; 1s. John, earl of Eldon. MAGDALEN, matric. 14 Oct., 1889, aged 19 (from Winchester); HONOURS: —3 classical mods. 91.

Scott, John Allen, born at Penge, Surrey, 2 Jan., 1863; 2s. Thomas Scard, cler. NON-COLLEGIATE, matric. 17 Jan., 80, aged 17 (from Felsted gr. school); migrated to WADHAM 19 April, 84.

Scott, John Charles Montagu Douglas, earl of Dalkeith, born 30 March, 1864; 1s. William Henry, duke of Buccleuch. CHRIST CHURCH, matric. 18 Oct., 86, aged 22.

Scott, John Henry Mortimer, born at Saugor, in the East Indies, 19 Aug., 1867; o.s. John Mortimer, arm. ST. MARY HALL, matric. 25 April, 87, aged 19.

Scott, Leslie Frederic, born at Hornsey, Middx., 29 Oct., 69; 1s. John, a judge in Bombay. NEW COLL., matric. 12 Oct., 88, aged 18 (from Rugby); HONOURS:—2 classical mods. 90, 2 classics 92.

Scott, Russell, born at Hampstead, London, 30 March, 1873; 1s. Russell, gen. BALLIOL, matric. 20 Oct., 91, aged 18, from Clifton coll.

Scott, Thomas, born at Plumstead, Kent, 1869; 1s. John, gen. NON-COLLEGIATE, matric. 15 Oct., 87, aged 18 (from Roan school, Greenwich); migrated to BALLIOL, B.A. 90; HONOURS:— 2 chemistry 90.

Scott, Thomas Gilbert, born in London 13 March, 1874; 2s. John Oldrid, of Oxted, Surrey, architect. HERTFORD, matric. 22 Oct., 92, aged 18, from Bradfield coll.

Scott, Walter, M.A., fellow MERTON 79-86, where see page 99.

Scott, rev. William, M.A., KEBLE, where see page 628.

Scott, William, born at Eccles, co. Lanc., 1862; 2s. William Eccles, arm. BRASENOSE, matric. 18 Oct., 81, aged 19 (from Harrow); died 87.

Scrutton, William, M.A., student CHRIST CHURCH 47-72, where see page 416.

Scrimgeour, Alexander Carron, born at Highgate, London, 1868; 1s. Alexander, gen. CHRIST CHURCH, matric. 15 Oct., 86, aged 18 (from Malvern coll.), B.A. 91.

Scrimgeour, John Alexander, born at Highgate March, 1872; 2s. Alexander, gen. CHRIST CHURCH, matric. 16 Oct., 91, aged 19, from the Charterhouse.

Scriven, Francis Thomas, born at Shirley, Hants, June, 1866; 1s. Samuel Charles Augustus, gen. NON-COLLEGIATE, matric. 15 Jan., 87, aged 20, from Bedford gr. school.

Scrivener, Harry Stanley, born in London 1865; o.s. Thomas Partington, chartered accountant. MAGDALEN, matric. 16 Oct., 84, aged 19 (from St. Paul's school), demy 83; B.A. 88 (HONOURS:—2 classical mods. 86, 3 classics 88); bar.-at-law, Middle Temple, 91.

Scroggs, Evelyn Sydney, born in London Oct., 1863; 2s. Sydney Malet, cler. KEBLE, matric. 17 Oct., 82, aged 18 (from Lancing coll.); migrated to CHARSLEY'S HALL, B.A. and M.A. 89.

Scull, Walter (Delaphine), born at Bath 9 Feb., 1863; 1s. Gideon Delaplaine, gen. LINCOLN, matric. 20 Oct., 81, aged 18 (from Rugby), B.A. 84; student of Inner Temple 83.

Seal, Charles Edward, born at Leigh Delamere, Wilts, 1865; 1s. Charles William, gen. NON-COLLEGIATE, matric. 14 Feb., 90, aged 25, from University coll., London.

Sealy, Edward Walker, born in Barbados 21 Jan., 1868; 1s. George Augustus, gen. LINCOLN, matric. 18 Oct., 88, aged 20 (from the Lodge school, Barbados); HONOURS:—3 history 92.

Sealy, George Elliot, born in Barbados 1872; 2s. George Augustus, gen. LINCOLN, matric. 20 Oct., 90, aged 18.

Sears, Frederick William, born at Taunton, Somerset, June, 1870; 2s. Robert Humphrey, gen. KEBLE, matric. 12 Oct., 89, aged 19 (from St. Mark's school, Windsor); HONOURS:—4 history 92.

Seaton, rev. James Buchanan, born at Leeds 1868; 3s. James, arm. CHRIST CHURCH, matric. 15 Oct., 86, aged 18 (from Leeds school), scholar 86, B.A. 90; HONOURS:—1 classical mods. 88, 2 classics 90.

Seaton, James Stuart, born at Manchester 1862; 2.s. William, gent. PEMBROKE, matric. 30 Oct., 80, aged 18 (from Manchester gr. school), scholar 80-5, B.A. 84, M.A. and H.C.L. 87 (HONOURS:—1 classical mods. 81, 1 classics 84, 1 law 85, 1 civil law 86, Vinerian law scholarship 86); examiner in civil law 89, 92; bar.-at-law, Middle Temple, 87; professor of law at Owens coll., Manchester, 91.

Seawell, Arthur Edward, born at Bentley, Hants, 1863; 1s. Arthur Samuel, arm. EXETER, matric. 20 Oct., 81, aged 18 (from Winchester), B.A. 84, M.A. 88.

Seawell, rev. Frederick Yorke, born at Senle, Surrey, July, 1865; 2s. Samuel Arthur, gent. KEBLE, matric. 13 Oct., 83, aged 18 (from Winchester), B.A. 87 (HONOURS:—1 theology 86); died 4 March, 90.

Seccombe, Thomas, born at King's Lynn, Norfolk, 1866; 1s. John Thomas, D.Med. BALLIOL, matric. 24 Oct., 85, aged 19 (from Felsted school), B.A. 89; HONOURS:—Stanhope essay 87, 1 history 89.

Seoker, William Henry, born at Birmingham 3 Nov., 1865; 1s. Thomas Jackson, cler. ST. JOHN'S, matric. 11 Oct., 84, aged 18 (from Rossall school), scholar 84, B.A. 88. M.A. 91; HONOURS:—1 classical mods. 86, 2 classics 88.

Secretan, Bernard, born in London 1863; 3s. Charles Frederick, cler. NON-COLLEGIATE, matric. 14 Oct., 82, aged 19, from St. Paul's school.

Secretan, Douglas Liston, born at Selhurst, Surrey, 1871; 2s. Philip, gen. PEMBROKE, matric. 28 Jan., 90, aged 19 (from Eastbourne coll.).

Seddon, Charles Norman, born at Tranmere, Cheshire, 18 Dec., 1870; 1s. Charles John, gen. BALLIOL, matric. 17 Oct., 89, aged 18 (from Liverpool coll.); assist. collector and magistrate Poona 92.

Sedgwick, Harold James, born at Borobridge, Yorks, 1866; 1s. James, D.Med. EXETER, matric. 16 Oct., 84, aged 18 (from Malvern coll.), B.A. 87, M.A. 91.

Sedgwick, rev. James Henry, born at Stockton-on-Tees, Yorks, 1850; 2s. James, gen. NON-COLLEGIATE, matric. 13 Oct., 84, aged 34 (from church missionary coll., Islington); migrated to PEMBROKE, B.A. 87, M.A. 91 (HONOURS:—Chinese scholarship 85); sometime missionary in China.

Sedgwick, John, D.D., fellow MAGDALEN 54-62, where see page 323.

Sedgwick, rev. Thomas Arnold, born at Watford, Hants, 29 Jan., 1860; y.s. William Fellows, arm. MERTON, matric. 15 May, 80, aged 20 (from Shrewsbury gr. school), B.A. 84, M.A. 87; curate of Christ Church, St. Leonard-on-Sea, 85-6.

Selbie, William Boothby, born at Chesterfield, co. Derby, 1863; 1s. Robert William, cler. BRASENOSE, matric. 19 Oct., 82, aged 19 (from Manchester gr. school), scholar 82, B.A. 86, M.A. 89; HONOURS:—2 classical mods. 84, 2 classics 86, septuagint prize 88.

Selby, Arthur Laidlaw, M.A., fellow MERTON 86, where see page 94.

Selby, Edward, born at Tyldesley, co. Lanc., 13 May, 1869; 5s. Atherton Thomas, gen. QUEEN'S, matric. 25 May, 88, aged 19 (from Bedbergh gr. school), exhibitioner 88, B.A. 92; HONOURS:—2 mathematical mods. 90, 3 mathematics 92.

Selby, Henry Forster Donaldson, born at Louth, co. Lincoln, 18 Sept., 1871; 1s. Henry Donaldson, arm. WORCESTER, matric. 14 Oct., 90, aged 19, from Louth gr. school.

Selby, Prideaux Robert, born in London 9 April, 1873; 1s. William Henry Collingwood, commander R.N., deceased. NEW COLL., matric. 14 Oct., 92, aged 19, from Winchester.

Sélincourt, Ernest de, born at Streatham, Surrey, 24 Sept., 1870; 3s. Charles Alexander, of Rustington Hall, Sussex, arm. UNIVERSITY COLL., matric. 11 Oct., 90, aged 20 (from Dulwich coll.); HONOURS:—2 classical mods. 92.

Sellar, Alexander Kenneth, born at Elgin 1860; 2s. Patrick Plenderleath, arm. ORIEL, matric. 19 Oct., 80, aged 20 (from Fettes coll.), B.A. 84; HONOURS:—2 classical mods. 82, 3 classics 84.

Sellar, Gerard Henry Craig, born in London 20 March, 1871; o.s. Alexander Craig, M.P., deceased. BALLIOL, matric. 17 Oct., 89, aged 18, from Eton.

Sellicks, Francis Joseph, born at Walden, Essex, 1868; 1s. Joseph, gen. NON-COLLEGIATE, matric. 22 Oct., 87, aged 19, from Taunton independent coll.

Sells, Arthur Clement, born at Ewell, Surrey, 2 May, 1873; 1s. William, cler. QUEEN'S, matric. 9 Feb., 92, aged 18, from Malvern coll.

Sells, Vincent Perronet, M.A., NEW COLL., where see page 220.

Selwyn, Sydney George, M.A., fellow NEW COLL. 39-54, where see page 211.

Semsey de, Semse László, born at Budapesth 24 Dec., 1869; o.s. Albert, of Semse, Hungary, arm. TRINITY, matric. 11 Oct., 90, aged 20, from Budapesth university.

Sendyk, Oscar, born at Brixton, Surrey, 5 June, 1863; o.s. Lewis, arm. MERTON, matric. 24 Nov., 81, aged 18.

Sercombe, Rupert Theodore Walton, born at Fairpark near Exeter, 3 Jan., 1861; o.s. Rupert Clampitt, gen. EXETER, matric. 22 Jan., 80, aged 19 (from Westminster school), B.A. 83 (HONOURS: —3 law 83); bar.-at-law, Middle Temple, 85.

Sergeant, Philip Walsingham, born in London 27 Jan., 1872; 1s. Lewis, author. TRINITY, matric. 17 Oct., 91, aged 19 (from St. Paul's school), scholar 89; HONOURS: —1 classical mods. 93.

Serjeantson, rev. Robert Meyrick, born at Titley, co. Hereford, Oct., 1861; 1s. William, cler. KEBLE, matric. 19 Oct., 80, aged 19 (from Rossall school), B.A. 83, M.A. 92 (HONOURS: —2 history 83); curate of St. Sepulchre, Northampton, 87.

Serjeantson, rev. William Frank, born at Acton Burnell, Salop, April, 1864; 3s. William, cler. KEBLE, matric. 16 Oct., 83, aged 19 (from Rossall school), B.A. 87 (HONOURS: —3 classical mods. 85); curate of Rushden, Northants, 88-9.

Serocold, Charles Seymour Pearse, born at Taplow Hill, Bucks, 12 June, 1872; 3s. Charles Pearse, gen. NEW COLL., matric. 16 Oct., 91, aged 19, from Eton.

Servaes, Francis Charles, born at Anfield, near Liverpool, 8 Feb., 1861; 1s. Julius, gen. NEW COLL., matric. 16 Oct., 80, aged 19 (from Uppingham school); matric. 9 Nov., 81, from KING'S COLL., CAMBRIDGE, B.A. 84, M.A. B.Med. and B.Surg. 88; HONOURS: —3 natural science (Cambridge) 84.

Seton, Malcolm Cotter Cariston, born at Buttevant, co. Cork, 1873; 1s. Bertram William, of G.P.O. ORIEL, matric. 27 Oct., 91, aged 18 (from Repton school), scholar 91; HONOURS: —2 classical mods. 93.

Seton, Walter John, born at Calcutta 29 Dec., 1864; 1s. Walter Scott Seton-Karr, B.C.S. NEW COLL., matric. 12 Oct., 83, aged 18 (from Eton), B.A. 87, M.A. 90 (HONOURS: —3 classical mods. 85, 3 classics 87); librarian of Oxford union society 85; bar.-at-law, Inner Temple, 89.

Seward, Harold, born at Wigan, co. Lanc., 10 Oct., 1862; 1s. James, gent. BALLIOL, matric. 21 Oct., 80, aged 18 (from Liverpool institute), scholar 79, B.A. 83; HONOURS: —1 mathematical mods. 81, 2 natural science 83, 1 mathematics 84; and at London university, 1 chemistry 82.

Sewell, Archibald Percy, born at Swaffham, Norfolk, 15 Oct., 1868; 2s. Robert, solicitor. JESUS COLL., matric. 19 Oct., 87, aged 19 (from Grantham gr. school), B.A.

Sewell, Augustine, born at Oxford 1861; 2s. Thomas, pleb. NON-COLLEGIATE, matric. 19 Jan., 89, aged 18, from Oxford central school.

Sewell, Charles William, born at Battle, Sussex, 1859; o.s. William, gen. NON-COLLEGIATE, matric. 2 June, 84, aged 25, from a Folkestone school; died 8 July, 87.

Sewell, rev. Henry, born at Winton, near Kirkby Stephen, Westmorland, 7 March, 1865; 5s. John, gent. QUEEN'S, matric. 22 Oct., 84, aged 19 (from Appleby gr. school), exhibitioner 84, B.A. 88, M.A. 91 (HONOURS: —2 mathematical mods. 86, 3 mathematics 88); curate of Rhosddu, co. Denbigh, 89; brother of James W.

Sewell, James Edwards, D.D., warden of NEW COLL. 60, where see page 204.

Sewell, rev. James Watson, born at Winton, Westmorland, 13 Nov., 1862; 4s. John, gen. QUEEN'S, matric. 23 Oct., 82, aged 19 (from Appleby gr. school), exhibitioner 82-6, B.A. 88 (HONOURS: —3 mathematical mods. 84); curate of Arlecdon, Cumberland, 88-9.

Sewell, rev. John Rowland, born at Patricroft, near Manchester, 31 July, 1860; 1s. John Christmas, gen. ST. ALBAN HALL, matric. 20 April, 82, aged 21 (from Manchester gr. school); migrated to MERTON, B.A. 85 (HONOURS: —1 history 85); missionary in Mashonaland 91.

Sewell, William, M.A., fellow NEW COLL. 56-78, where see page 216.

Seymour, Frederick Beauchamp Paget, admiral lord Alcester, created D.C.L. 17 June, 1885. See *Al. Ox.* and series 1276.

Seymour, Henry Fortescue, M.A., fellow ALL SOULS' 50-5, where see page 279.

Shackleford, Frank, born at Lancaster 24 Aug., 1871; 2s. William Copley, gen. EXETER, matric. 13 Oct., 90, aged 19, from Lancaster gr. school.

Shackleton, Alfred, born at Bradford, Yorks, 1860; 2s. Henry, gen. NEW COLL., matric. 16 Oct., 80, aged 20 (from Bradford gr. school); HONOURS: —3 mathematical mods. 82, 4 mathematics 84.

Shackleton, George Ricketts, born at New Wortley, Yorks, 1865; 1s. Joseph, arm. BRASENOSE, matric. 19 Oct., 82, aged 17 (from Clifton coll.), B.A. 85.

Shacklock, William Lambert, born at Dudley, co. Worc., 1864; 1s. Joshua Ramsbottom, excise officer. NON-COLLEGIATE, matric. 17 Oct., 91, aged 27, from Stourbridge gr. school.

Shadwell, Charles Lancelot, M.A., B.C.L., fellow ORIEL 64, where see page 149.

Shadwell, John Emilius Lancelot, M.A., student CHRIST CHURCH 66-87, where see page 423.

Shallard, rev. George Maddock, born at Marseilles 1864; 1s. Sidney Dillon, arm. NON-COLLEGIATE, matric. 17 Oct., 85, aged 21 (from R.N. school, New Cross, and Warminster gr. school), B.A. 89, M.A. 92 (HONOURS: —4 theology 89); curate of Walkley St. Mary, Yorks, 91.

Shand, Thomas Henry Rodie, M.A., fellow BRASENOSE 52-71, where see page 355.

Sharland, Stanley Cruwys, born at Tiverton, Devon, 2 May, 1865; 4s. Arthur Cruwys, gen. BALLIOL, matric. 16 Oct., 83, aged 18 (from Tiverton school), scholar 83, B.A. 88, M.A. 90 (HONOURS: —2 classical mods. 84, 2 classics 87).

Sharp, rev. Arthur Frederick, born in London 30 Oct., 1869; 4s. William, cler. QUEEN'S, matric. 25 Jan., 88, aged 21 (from St. Mary Magdalen choir school, Paddington), B.A. 91; curate of Chard, Somerset, 91.

Sharp, rev. Charles James, born in London 23 Dec., 1858; 1s. James Wilson, gen. NON-COLLEGIATE, matric. 13 Oct., 84, aged 25 (from a Ramsgate school); migrated to TRINITY, B.A. 87, M.A. 91 (HONOURS: —2 history 87); curate of Acton, Middx., 89.

Sharp, Ernest Hamilton, born at Manchester 26 Sept., 1859; o.s. Edmund Hamilton, gen. LINCOLN, matric. 14 June, 86, aged 26, B.A. 90, M.A. and B.C.L. 93 (HONOURS :—2 law 90, 2 civil law 91); bar.-at-law, Inner Temple, 91.

Sharp, Granville, born at Birmingham 1862; 1s. Alfred John, gen. NON-COLLEGIATE, matric. 23 Oct., 86, aged 24 (from Birmingham gr. school and Spring Hill coll.), B.A. 90; HONOURS :—2 theology 90.

Sharp, Henry, born at Deane, co. Lanc., 1 June, 1869; 2s. Henry, gen. NEW COLL., matric. 12 Oct., 88, aged 19 (from Rugby), B.A. 92; HONOURS :—2 classical mods. 90, 1 classics 92.

Sharp, John Lawrell, born in London 5 Jan., 1867; 6s. Martin Richard, gen. HERTFORD, matric. 12 June, 86, aged 19, B.A. 89; HONOURS :—3 mathematical mods. 87.

Sharp, Lawrence Morton, born at St. Neots, Hunts, 1864; 2s. Henry Morton, gen. ALL SOULS', matric. 16 Oct., 83, aged 19 (from Leamington coll.), bible clerk 83, B.A. 87; HONOURS :—2 history 87.

Sharp, Robert Farquharson, born in London 31 Dec., 1864; 2s. Thomas, gen., deceased. NEW COLL., matric. 12 Oct., 83, aged 18 (from Haileybury), B.A. 87; HONOURS :—3 classical mods. 85, 3 classics 87.

Sharp, William Hastings, born at Masulapatam, East Indies, 17 June, 1865; 1s. John, cler. TRINITY, matric. 11 Oct., 84, aged 19 (from Marlborough), scholar 84, B.A. 88, M.A. 91; HONOURS :—1 classical mods. 86, 1 classics 88.

Sharpe, rev. Charles Henry Dixon, born at Dudley, co. Worc., Nov., 1864; o.s. Robert Dixon, arm. KEBLE, matric. 11 Dec., 83, aged 19 (from Newcastle-under-Lyme school), B.A. 87; curate of Wolverhampton St. George 90.

Sharpe, rev. George Harry, born at East Retford, Notts, 30 Dec., 1859; 2s. Samuel, gen. NON-COLLEGIATE, matric. 28 Jan., 82, aged 22 (from K. Edward's school, E. Retford), exhibitioner LINCOLN 84-5, B.A. 85, M.A. 88 (HONOURS :— 1 classical mods. 83, 2 history 85); vicar of Pory Bar, co. Staff., 91.

Sharpe, Lancelot Lambert, B.D., fellow ST. JOHN'S 61-84, where see page 487.

Sharpe, Wilfred Stanley, born at Richmond, Surrey, 1861; 2s. John Charles, gen. ST. ALBAN HALL, matric. 22 Jan., 80, aged 19.

Sharpley, Hugo, born at Louth, co. Lincoln, 3 March, 1870; 4s. Thomas, gen. CORPUS CHRISTI, matric. 25 Oct., 89, aged 19 (from Shrewsbury school); scholar 88; HONOURS :—1 classical mods. 91.

Shaw, rev. Alfred Ernest, born at Leeds 31 Jan., 1861; 5s. George, gen. QUEEN'S, matric. 15 May, 80, aged 19 (from Leeds gr. school), exhibitioner 80-5, B.A. 84, M.A. 88 (HONOURS :—2 classical mods. 82, 3 classics 84); curate of St. Mary's Lambeth 88.

Shaw, Arthur Barnsley, born at Waterloo, near Liverpool, 5 May, 1861; o.s. Richard, arm. CHRIST CHURCH, matric. 15 Oct., 80, aged 19 (from Christ's hospital), junior student 80, B.A. 84, M.A. 89 (HONOURS :—2 classical mods. 82, 2 classics 84); bar.-at-law, Inner Temple, 86.

Shaw, Arthur Newton, born at Elland, Yorks, 1868; o.s. Henry, gen. NON-COLLEGIATE, matric. 12 Oct., 89, aged 21.

Shaw, Arthur Trevor Ambrose, born at Maes-Gange, East Indies, 13 Aug., 1861; 2s. Clement Robert, of Lucknow, arm. BALLIOL, matric. 28 Oct., 81, aged 19 (from Cheltenham coll.); deputy-commissioner Burmah 86.

Shaw, Bennett Eyre, born at Passage, co. Cork, 1 Feb., 1862; 3s. Edward Francis, cler. NON-COLLEGIATE, matric. 18 Oct., 80, aged 18 (from King's coll. school, London), B.A. 85; brother of Edward D.

Shaw, rev. Charles John Monson, born at Otham, Kent, 24 Nov., 1860; 1s. Charles John, cler. HERTFORD, matric. 7 Feb., 80, aged 19, B.A. 83, M.A. 88; curate of Swanley, Kent, 90.

Shaw, rev. Courtney Albert, born at Swansea 16 Jan., 1866; 5s. John, gen. JESUS COLL., matric. 20 Oct., 86, aged 20 (from Swansea gr. school), scholar 86, B.A. 90 (HONOURS :—2 classical mods. 88, 4 classics 90); curate of Caundle Bishop, Dorset, 90.

Shaw, rev. Edward Domett, born at Cork, 5 Oct., 1860; 2s. Edward Francis, cler. ORIEL, matric. 19 Oct., 80, aged 20 (from Forest school), scholar 79-84, B.A. and M.A. 87 (HONOURS :—3 classical mods. 82, 4 classics 84), in University eleven 82; headmaster Bishops Stortford school 87; brother of Bennett E.

Shaw, George Radcliffe, born at Saddleworth, Yorks, 28 Feb., 1869; o.s. Thomas, gen. QUEEN'S, matric. 25 Oct., 89, aged 20 (from Malvern coll.), B.A. 84; HONOURS :—4 history 84.

Shaw, Harold Lancaster, born at Fairfield, near Manchester, 1874; 1s. William Henry, gent. PEMBROKE, matric. 28 Oct., 92, aged 18 (from Victoria coll., Jersey), scholar 92.

Shaw, rev. Herbert Hyde, born at Stalybridge, co. Lanc., March, 1862; 1s. Abel Hyde, gen. KEBLE, matric. 18 Oct., 81, aged 19 (from Owens coll.), B.A. 85; curate of Dewsbury St. Mark 89-91.

Shaw, rev. Herbert James, born at Bromwich, co. Stafford, 1864; o.s. James, gen. NON-COLLEGIATE, matric. 13 Oct., 83, aged 19; migrated to ST. JOHN's, B.A. 87, M.A. and B.C.L. 90 (HONOURS :—3 law 87, 3 civil law 89); student of Middle Temple 87; curate of St. Andrew Montpelier, Bristol, 91.

Shaw, Herbert Lancaster, born at Lockwood, Yorks, 1864; 6s. Bentley, gen. CHARSLEY'S HALL., matric. 22 April, 84, aged 20.

Shaw, Neville Frederick, born at Cheddleton, co. Staffs, 5 Dec., 1870; 2s. William Frederick, rector of West Stoke, Sussex. MAGDALEN, matric. 14 Oct., 89, aged 18 (from the Charterhouse), B.A. 92; brother of William A.

Shaw, Oliphant, born at Wooriryrite, Victoria, 27 Jan., 1861; 1s. Thomas, arm. MAGDALEN, matric. 29 Oct., 81, aged 20 (from 'Scotch coll.,' Melbourn), B.A. 86; bar.-at-law, Inner Temple, 88.

Shaw, rev. Patrick John, born at Ayr 1869; 2s. Charles George, solicitor. NEW COLL., matric. 14 Oct., 87, aged 18 (from Fettes coll.), B.A. 92 (HONOURS :—3 classical mods. 89); curate of the Abbey Church, Selby, 93.

Shaw, Theodore Frederick Charles Edward, born at Wolverhampton 1859; 1s. Edward Dethick, gen. BALLIOL, matric. 19 Oct., 86, aged 27 (from Tettenhall coll., co. Staffs); M.P. Stafford 92.

Shaw, rev. William Arnold, born at Caverswall, co. Staffs, 2 April, 1868; 1s. William Frederick, rector of West Stoke, Sussex. MAGDALEN, matric. 22 Oct., 87, aged 19 (from the Charterhouse), B.A. 91; curate of Netley, Hants, 91; brother of Neville F.

Shaw, William Hudson, M.A., fellow BALLIOL 50, where see page 64.

Shawcross, John, born at Rochdale, co. Lanc., 17 Sept., 1871; 5s. William Tuer, gen. UNIVERSITY COLL., matric. 11 Oct., 90, aged 19 (from Clifton coll.), scholar 90; HONOURS :—1 classical mods. 92.

Shawcross, rev. John Peter, born at Northwood, co. Stafford, 1863; 2s. William, cler. NON-COLLEGIATE, matric. 13 Oct., 83, aged 20, B.A. 86, M.A. 89 (HONOURS:—1 theology 86); curate of Holt, co. Worcester, 87.

Shawe, Henry Nigel Pole, born in London Jan., 1874; 1s. Henry Cunliffe, esq. CHRIST CHURCH, matric. 14 Oct., 92, aged 18, from Eton.

Shea, Robert Percival, born in London 1861; 2s. John, D.Med. ST. JOHN'S, matric. 15 Oct., 87, aged 16 (from Reading school), scholar 87, B.A. 91; HONOURS:—3 mathematical mods. 89, 4 mathematics 91.

Sheard, Arthur Edward William, born at Oxford 10 Feb., 1868; 2s. Thomas John Walker, gen. NON-COLLEGIATE, matric. 17 March, 88, aged 20 (from Magdalen coll. school), B.A. 91; HONOURS:—2 mathematical mods. 89, 3 mathematics 91.

Sheard, Thomas Frederick Mason, born at Oxford Dec., 1866; 1s. Thomas John Walker, gen. KEBLE, matric. 19 Oct., 86, aged 19 (from Magdalen coll. school), B.A. 90; HONOURS:—2 history 89.

Shearer, Donald Francis, born at Bradford, Yorks, 13 Aug., 1864; 2s. William Campbell, cler. and professor in Independent coll., Bradford. NEW COLL., matric. 14 Oct., 82, aged 18 (from Bradford school), scholar 82, B.A. and B.Med. 90 (HONOURS:—1 mathematical mods. 84, 2 mathematics 86); brother of the next.

Shearer, William Alexander, born at Soham, co. Cambridge, 1863; 1s. William Campbell, cler. EXETER, matric. 20 Oct., 81, aged 18 (from Bradford school), scholar 81-5, B.A. 85 (HONOURS:—1 classical mods. 83, 2 classics 85); brother of the last-named.

Shebbeare, rev. Charles John, born at Wykeham, Yorks, 15 April, 1865; 1s. Charles Hooper, cler. ST. MARY HALL, matric. 20 Oct., 84, aged 19 (from Westminster school); migrated to CHRIST CHURCH 85, B.A. 88 (HONOURS:—2 classical mods. 86, 4 classics 88); curate of Milford, Surrey, 91.

Shebbeare, Ernest Reginald, born at Plaistow, Kent, Dec., 1869; 1s. Reginald John, gen. KEBLE, matric. 12 Oct., 89, aged 19, from Blackheath school.

Shekell, rev. Edleston Donner, born in Edinburgh 30 Oct., 1864; 1s. Thomas Stevens, arm. QUEEN'S, matric. 22 Oct., 84, aged 19 (from Uppingham); migrated to NEW INN HALL (BALLIOL), B.A. 90; curate of Longhope, co. Gloucester, 91.

Sheldon, Henry Gabriel, born at Fonthill, Wilts, 1869; 2s. Robert William, cler. ST. JOHN'S, matric. 15 Oct., 87, aged 18 (from Sherborne school), B.A. 91; HONOURS:—3 law 91.

Sheldon, Thomas Archibald, born at Oxford 1870; 1s. Thomas, gen. NON-COLLEGIATE, matric. 8 June, 89, aged 19.

Sheldon, William Stewart, born at Millbrook, Hants, 1865; 2s. Robert William, cler. UNIVERSITY COLL., matric. 13 Oct., 83, aged 18, B.A. 87.

Shelley, Arrowsmith Hyde, born at Newbury, Berks, 29 March, 1862; o.s. Richard, gen. ST. MARY HALL, matric. 22 Oct., 83, aged 21.

Shelly, John, born at Plymouth, Devon, 1867; 1s. John, gen. ORIEL, matric. 19 Oct., 86, aged 19 (from St. Edmund's coll., Salisbury), B.A. 92.

Shelmerdine, Walter, born at Troutbeck, Westmorland, 6 June, 1870; o.s. Ben, arm., deceased. EXETER, matric. 16 Oct., 89, aged 19, from the Charterhouse.

Shenstone, Frederick Smith, M.A., Fereday fellow, ST. JOHN'S 54-73, where see page 489.

Shepheard, Harold Beaumont, born at Kensington 18 Feb., 1871; o.s. Alfred James, arm. TRINITY, matric. 11 Oct., 90, aged 19 (from Highgate school); HONOURS:—2 classical mods. 92.

Shepherd, Alfred John Parkman, M.A., fellow QUEEN'S 77-82, where see page 182.

Shepherd, Arthur Cunliffe, born in London 20 Feb., 1867; o.s. Henry, cler. QUEEN'S, matric. 25 Oct., 86, aged 19, from Harrow.

Shepherd, Edward Fairbrother, born at Abingdon, Berks, 1865; 1s. Edward Leader, gent. NON-COLLEGIATE, matric. 13 Oct., 84, aged 19 (from Abingdon school), B.A. 88, M.A. 92; HONOURS:—3 classical mods. 86, 3 classics 88.

Shepherd, Edwin Francis, born in Paris 1869; o.s. Edwin Ralph, arm. PEMBROKE, matric. 17 Oct., 88, aged 19, from Eton.

Shepherd, Ernest Bennett Sinclair, born in London 1872; 1s. Frederick, cler. CORPUS CHRISTI, matric. 16 Oct., 90, aged 18 (from Clifton coll.), exhibitioner 90; HONOURS:—1 classical mods. 92.

Shepherd, rev. Frederick Thomas Herbert, born at Bristol 27 May, 1867; 1s. Frederick George, gen. WORCESTER, matric. 22 April, 85, aged 17 (from Ilminster and Chard schools), B.A. 89, M.A. 91; curate of Exeter St. David 90.

Shepherd, Herbert Hutchings, born at Ilminster, Som., 7 April, 1868; o.s. James William, gen. MAGDALEN, matric. 21 Oct., 86, aged 18 (from Harrow), B.A. 90 (HONOURS:—2 law 90, 3 civil law 91); bar.-at-law, Inner Temple, 91.

Shepherd, James Francis, born at Great Grimsby, co. LINCOLN, matric. 31 Aug., 1871; o.s. Robert, cler. LINCOLN, matric. 17 Oct., 89, aged 18, from Hull, and East Riding coll.

Shepherd, Richard Atkinson, born at Bradford, Yorks, 28 Aug., 1863; 2s. Bowman, gen. TRINITY, matric. 14 Oct., 82, aged 19 (from Sedbergh school), scholar 82-6, B.A. 85; fellow ALL SOULS' 87, M.A. 89, B.C.L. 89; HONOURS:—1 classical mods. 83, 1 law 85, 1 civil law 87, Vinerian law scholarship 87, examiner in civil law 91; bar.-at-law, Inner Temple, 89; brother of William 81.

Shepherd, Waldegrave Mutrie, born at Newton Arlosh, Cumberland, 11 Oct., 1870; 1s. William Mutrie, vicar of St. John, Carlisle. NON-COLLEGIATE, matric. 17 Oct., 91, aged 21; from Rossall and Carlisle gr. schools.

Shepherd, Walter Curzon, born at Yealand, co. Lanc., 27 Dec., 1870; o.s. Francis, Edward, arm. QUEEN'S, matric. 22 Oct., 89, aged 18 (from Sedbergh gr. school), scholar 89; HONOURS:—2 classical mods. 91.

Shepherd, William, born at Pudsey, Yorks, 12 Jan., 1861; 1s. Bowman, gent. QUEEN'S, matric. 1 Feb., 81, aged 20 (from Kirkby Lonsdale gr. school); brother of Richard A.

Shepherd, William Lewis, born at Nottingham 7 Jan., 1871; o.s. George Henry, gen. TRINITY, matric. 12 Oct., 89, aged 18 (from Dulwich coll.), B.A. 93; HONOURS:—4 history 92.

Sheppard, Harry Edward, born at Ross, co. Hereford, 20 May, 1867; o.s. Henry Wilson, arm., deceased. NEW COLL., matric. 15 Oct., 86, aged 19 (from Rugby), B.A. 90; HONOURS:—3 classical mods. 88, 1 history 90.

Sheppard, Philip Nevile Fream, born at Chetnoll, Dorset, May, 1871; s. Philip, arm. CHRIST CHURCH, matric. 11 Oct., 89, aged 18, from Radley coll.

Sheppard, William Didsbury, born at Grassendale, co. Lanc., 8 Feb., 1865; 2s. John Edward, gen. NEW COLL., matric. 10 Oct., 84, aged 19 (from Hereford cathedral school); assist. collector and magistrate Kanara, Bombay.

Sheppard, rev. William John Linmer, born at Highworth, Wilts, 21 July, 1861; 1s. William Benjamin, cler. QUEEN'S, matric. 30 Oct., 85, aged 21 (from Salisbury school), B.A. 88, M.A. 92 (HONOURS :—2 theology 88); curate of St. John the Evangelist, Altrincham, Cheshire, 90.

Sherbrooke, Penn Curzon, born at Penn, Bucks, 28 Nov., 1871; 1s. Henry Nevile, cler. CHRIST CHURCH, matric. 27 Oct., 91, aged 19.

Sherwell, Frederick Henry, born at Bristol 1862; 1s. Frederick, gen. NEW COLL., matric. 16 Jan., 85, aged 23.

Sherwen, William Basil, born at Cockermouth 1 Nov., 1869; 2s. William, cler. QUEEN'S, matric. 20 Oct., 88, aged 18 (from K. William coll., isle of Man), exhibitioner 88, B.A. 92; HONOURS :—2 classical mods. 90, 3 theology 92.

Sherwin, Charles, born at Hanley, co. Stafford, 6 April, 1865; 3s. Charles, gen. ST. MARY HALL, matric. 26 Jan., 91, aged 25.

Sherwood, Edward Charles, born at Gateshead, co. Durham, 5 Feb., 1873; 1s. Edward Purvis, gent. MAGDALEN, matric. 18 Oct., 92, aged 19 (from Rotherham gr. school, and Magdalen coll. school), demy 91.

Sherwood, Frederic William, born at Whitley, Berks, 1864; 1s. William, gen. BALLIOL, matric. 16 Oct., 83, aged 19 (from Reading gr. school), exhibitioner 83, B.A. 87 (HONOURS :—1 classical mods. 85, 2 classics 87); bar.-at-law, Middle Temple, 90.

Sherwood, William Harford, M.A., headmaster Magdalen coll. school 1888, where see page 328.

Shew, William Harford, born at Putney, Surrey, 13 Sept., 1867; o.s. William Harford, gen. WORCESTER, matric. 19 Oct., 86, aged 19 (from a Ramsgate school), B.A. 89.

Shields, Cuthbert, M.A., fellow CORPUS CHRISTI 68, where see page 379.

Shillito, Edward, born at Hull, Yorks, 1872; 2s. Francis Thomas, congregational minister. NONCOLLEGIATE, matric. 15 Oct., 92, aged 20, from Owens coll., Manchester.

Shillito, rev. William Francis, born at Putney, Surrey, 1864; 2s. James Francis, arm. ORIEL, matric. 25 Jan., 83, aged 19, B.A. 86, M.A. 89; curate of Putney 89.

Shinner, Oswald Augustus, born at Cheltenham 24 June, 1864; 2s. Arthur John, gent. TRINITY, matric. 15 Oct., 83, aged 19 (from Cheltenham coll.), B.A. 87, M.A. 90.

Shipley, rev. Arthur Glanville, born at Nottingham 15 July, 1867; 3s. Hammond, gen. NON-COLLEGIATE, matric. 5 Nov., 85, aged 18 (from Trent coll., Notts); migrated to WADHAM 19 Oct., 86, B.A. 88; curate of Walsall St. Michael 91.

Shipley, Reginald Heber, born at Murree, East Indies, 1 Aug., 1861; 3s. Reginald Yonge, arm. BALLIOL, matric. 21 Oct., 80, aged 19 (from Winchester), special assist. to collector, and magistrate and agent to the governor of Madras at Godavari.

Shipman, Robert, born at Grantham, co. Linc., 1 July, 1873; 1s. George William, surgeon. TRINITY, matric. 15 Oct., 92, aged 19, from Haileybury.

Shipman, Walter Thomas, born at Northampton 1861; 1s. Walter, gen. ST. JOHN'S, matric. 15 Oct., 81, aged 20.

Shippard, Courtenay Chaworth, born in London May, 1865; 1s. sir Sidney Godolphin Alexander, K.C.M.G. CHRIST CHURCH, matric. 10 Oct., 84, aged 19, B.A. 00; bar.-at-law, Inner Temple, 92.

Shipton, rev. Charles Percy, born at Hull Jan., 1862; 1s. Percival Maurice, cler. ST. EDMUND HALL, matric. 29 Jan., 81, aged 19 (from Stratford-on-Avon school), B.A. 84; curate of St. Neot, Cornwall, 91.

Shirley, Ralph, born at Oxford 30 Dec., 1865; 2s. Walter Waddington, D.D., canon of Christ Church. NEW COLL., matric. 16 Jan., 85, aged 19 (from Winchester), B.A. 90; HONOURS :—2 classical mods. 86.

Shirley, Walter Knight, born at Oxford 5 June, 1864; 1s. Walter Waddington, D.D., late regius prof. of ecclesiastical history. NEW COLL., matric. 12 Oct., 83, aged 19 (from Winchester), scholar 83, B.A. 87; HONOURS :—1 classical mods. 85, 2 classics 87.

Shoppee, Alfred George, born at Penge, Surrey, 1 or 15 July, 1869; 1s. Alfred Collett, gen., deceased. KEBLE, matric. 12 Oct., 89, aged 20 (from Albemarle coll., Penge), academical clerk, MAGDALEN, 90.

Shore, rev. Thomas Edmund Teignmouth, born in London 16 Jan., 1868; 2s. Thomas Teignmouth, cler. MAGDALEN, matric. 21 Oct., 86, aged 18 (from Westminster school), B.A. 90 (HONOURS :—2 classical mods. 88, 2 theology 90); curate of Lewisham, Kent, 91; brother of William F. T.

Shore, William Edward Keith, born at Torquay 1865; 1s. William Woodward, arm. HERTFORD, matric. 18 May, 83, aged 18 (from Sherborne school), scholar 83, B.A. 87; HONOURS :—2 mathematical mods. 85, 2 mathematics 87.

Shore, William Francis Teignmouth, born in London 27 April, 1865; 1s. Thomas, cler. ST. MARY HALL, matric. 22 Oct., 83, aged 17 (from Westminster school); brother of Thomas E. T.

Shorland, Maitland Arthur, born at Silton, Dorset, 18 Jan., 1864; o.s. William Henry, vicar of Oakhill, Bath. WADHAM, matric. 17 Oct., 82, aged 18 (from Sherborne school), B.A. 85; HONOURS :— 4 law 85.

Short, Ambrose, M.A., fellow NEW COLL. 51-64, where see page 215.

Short, Percy, born at Sheffield 15 Nov., 1863; 4s. William, gen. LINCOLN, matric. 11 Feb., 81, aged 17 (from Forest school, Walthamstow), B.A. 84, M.A. and B.C.L. 87; HONOURS :—2 law 84, 2 civil law 86.

Short, Walter Francis, M.A., fellow NEW COLL. 51-83, where see page 214.

Shorthose, William Hartshorne, born at Maison-Lafitte, in France, 1862; o.s. William Townsend, gen. BALLIOL, matric. 18 Oct., 81, aged 19 (from Harrow); HONOURS :—2 classical mods. 82; bar.-at-law, Inner Temple, 87.

Shorto, Denys Edward, born at Exeter 21 May, 1868; o.s. Edward Henry, gen. EXETER, matric. 21 Oct., 86, aged 18 (from Exeter gr. school), scholar 85, B.A. 90; HONOURS :—1 mathematical mods. 87, 1 mathematics 90, 3 physics 91.

Shortt, Alexander Graham, born at Mandair, East Indies, 1865; 2s. Alexander Young, arm. CHRIST CHURCH, matric. 22 Oct., 80, aged 15, B.A. 84 (HONOURS :—3 mathematical mods. 82, 3 mathematics 84), in the University eight 84; lieut. R.A. 86.

Shortt, rev. Joseph Rushton, born at Newcastle-on-Tyne, 17 Dec., 1860; 1s. Edward, cler. EXETER, matric. 22 Oct., 80, aged 19 (from Christ's hospital), scholar 80-5, B.A. 84, M.A. 87 (HONOURS :— 2 classical mods. 81, 1 classics 84), and of Durham M.A. ad eundem 87, classical lecturer 87, and junior censor 87-9; censor 89-91, and bursar Hatfield Hall, Durham, 89.

Shotton, James George, born at Lincoln 1856; 2s. James George, gen. NON-COLLEGIATE, matric. 17 Oct., 85, aged 29, B.A. 89.

Shrubb, John Puyto Charles, born at Ringwood, Hants, 1862; 1s. John Lane, arm. BRASENOSE, matric. 22 Oct., 80, aged 18, from Winchester.

Shuckburgh, Charles James, born in Middx. 1867; 1s. Richard Henry, arm. BRASENOSE, matric. 23 April, 86, aged 21 (from Leamington coll.), B.A. 91; HONOURS:—1 law 91.

Shuckburgh, Henry Frederick Blencowe, born in London 20 May, 1870; 2s. Richard Henry, esquire. WADHAM, matric. 20 Oct., 91, aged 21, from Overslade school, Rugby.

Shuker, Herbert Henry, born at Shrewsbury 30 Oct., 1869; 1s. Herbert, gen. WORCESTER, matric. 29 April, 89, aged 19, from Shrewsbury gr. school.

Shuttlewood, Carlton Aubrey Hamilton Cecil, born at Torquay 1869; 7s. Jesse, gen. NON-COLLEGIATE, matric. 12 Oct., 89, aged 20, from Loughborough gr. school.

Shyngle, Joseph Egerton, born at Bathurst-on-Gambia, in Africa, 1862; 1s. George Newman, gen. CHRIST CHURCH, matric. 31 May, 84, aged 22; bar.-at-law, Inner Temple, 88.

Siam, prince Kkiyakara Varalaksna of, born at Bangkok 8 June, 1873; 1s. Chulalonkon, king of Siam. BALLIOL, matric. 1 May, 90, aged 16.

Siam, prince Rabi Bahhanasakti of, born at Bangkok 1874; 2s. Chulalonkon, king of Siam. CHRIST CHURCH, matric. 27 Oct., 91, aged 17.

Sibree, Ernest, born at Painswick, co. Glouc., 1 Jan., 1859; 2s. John, M.A., Lond. NON-COLLEGIATE, matric. 13 Oct., 83, aged 24 (from Busage House school, Stroud), B.A. 87, M.A. 90; assist. keeper of Indian institute.

Sibree, Francis Joseph, born at Painswick, co. Glouc., 26 June, 1860; 3s. John, gen. NON-COLLEGIATE, matric. 13 Oct., 84, aged 24 (from a Stroud school); migrated to EXETER, B.A. 88, M.A. 93.

Sich, Alexander Ernest, born at Chiswick, Wilts, 1871; 1s. Alexander, gen. LINCOLN, matric. 20 Oct., 90, aged 19 (from St. Paul's school), scholar 90; HONOURS:—2 classical mods. 92.

Sichel, Joshua Sylvester, born at Melbourne, Australia, 22 May, 1873; 1s. Edward Ferdinand, gent. CHRIST CHURCH, matric. 14 Oct., 92, aged 19, from the Charterhouse.

Sidebotham, Henry Samuel, born at St. Peter Port, Guernsey, 5 April, 1871; o.s. Thomas William, cler. ST. JOHN'S, matric. 17 Oct., 91, aged 20.

Sidebotham, Herbert, born at Salford, Cheshire, 1873; 1s. Edward, gen. BALLIOL, matric. 20 Oct., 91, aged 18 (from Manchester gr. school), scholar 90; HONOURS;—Craven scholarship 92.

Sidebottom, rev. Radcliffe Alexander, born at Yatton Keynell, Wilts, March, 1866; 2s. Frederick Radclyffe, cler. KEBLE, matric. 22 Oct., 85, aged 19 (from Bath coll.), B.A. 88 (HONOURS:—3 theology 88); curate of Amport, Hants, 89.

Sidgwick, Alexander Dury, born in London 1873; 2s. Edward, solicitor. UNIVERSITY COLL., matric. 19 Oct., 91, aged 18.

Sidgwick, Arthur, M.A., fellow CORPUS CHRISTI 82, where see page 380.

Sidgwick, Edward Dury, born in London 27 Feb., 1871; 1s. Edward, solicitor. BRASENOSE, matric. 22 Oct., 91, aged 20, from Winchester.

Sidgwick, Henry, D.Litt., created D.C.L. 25 June, 1890; born at Skipton, Yorks, 31 May, 38; 3s. William, cler.; scholar TRINITY COLL., CAMBRIDGE, 57 (from Rugby), B.A. 59, fellow 59-69 and 85, M.A. 62, hon. fellow 81-5, D.Litt. 84, lecturer 59-75, and professor of moral philosophy 83 (HONOURS:—Bell scholarship 56, Craven scholarship 57, Greek epigram 58, 33rd wrangler, senior classic 61, 1st chancellor's medal 61), president Cambridge union society 61; one of the founders of Newnham college, LL.D., Edinburgh, Glasgow, and St. Andrews; brother of Arthur and William Carr. See *Med and Women of the Time*.

Sidgwick, Nevil Vincent, born at Oxford 8 May, 1873; 1s. William Carr, M.A., CHRIST CHURCH, matric. 14 Oct., 92, aged 19 (from Rugby), scholar 91.

Sidgwick, William Carr, M.A., fellow MERTON 57-73, where see page 97.

Sidley, rev. Clarence, born at Godley, co. Lincoln, 8 Oct., 1865; 1s. Samuel, artist. WADHAM, matric. 19 Jan., 84, aged 18 (from Kensington gr. school), B.A. 87, M.A. 91; curate of Manchester St. John 90.

Siebel, John Augustus, born at Kandy, isle of Ceylon, 1861; 1s. John Boyle, arm. ST. JOHN'S, matric. 13 April, 80, aged 18.

Silber, Martin Albert, born at Leyton, Essex, Nov., 1863; 1s. Albert Mark, arm. ST. JOHN'S, matric. 15 Oct., 81, aged 18, from Eton.

Sillar, Alexander Christian Cameron, born at Blackheath, Kent, Feb., 1871; 2s. William Cameron, arm. CHRIST CHURCH, matric. 11 Oct., 89, aged 18 (from Blackheath school); HONOURS:—3 classical mods. 91.

Sillar, Robert Lawrence, born at Upper Norwood, Surrey, 1863; 2s. Thomas Frederick, gen. NON-COLLEGIATE, matric. 14 Oct., 82, aged 19; migrated to WORCESTER 82, B.A. 85, M.A. 89.

Silver, Alexander Claude, born in London 1865; 5s. Hugh Adams, lieut.-col. EXETER, matric. 18 Oct., 83, aged 18 (from Marlborough); migrated to NEW INN HALL, after BALLIOL.

Silver, rev. Ernest Wollaston, born at West Cowes 16 Nov., 1862; 2s. Edgar, cler. CORPUS CHRISTI, matric. 26 Oct., 81, aged 18 (from Marlborough), B.A. 85, M.A. 88 (HONOURS:—2 classics 85); curate of Haggerston St. Paul, London, 87.

Simcox, Arthur Henry Addenbrooke, born at Bampton, Oxon, 26 April, 1870; 1s. Henry Kingdon, rector of Patney, Devizes. NEW COLL., matric. 11 Oct., 89, aged 19 (from Winchester), scholar 89, academical clerk of MAGDALEN 89; HONOURS:—2 classical mods. 91.

Simcox, George Augustus, M.A., fellow QUEEN'S 63, where see page 173.

Simey, George Iliff, born at Bishopwearmouth, co. Durham, 25 Feb., 1866; 2s. Ralph, solicitor. BALLIOL, matric. 24 Oct., 85, aged 19 (from Rugby), exhibitioner 83, B.A. 89; HONOURS:—1 classical mods. 87, 2 classics 89.

Simey, Ralph Iliff, born at Bishopwearmouth, co. Durham, 28 March, 1861; 1s. Ralph, solicitor. CORPUS CHRISTI, matric. 27 Oct., 81, aged 19 (from Rugby), scholar 81-5, B.A. 85 (HONOURS:—1 classical mods. 82, accessit Ireland scholarship 83, 2 classics 85); bar.-at-law, Inner Temple, 87.

Simmonds, Alfred George, born in London 1865; 2s. Benjamin, gen. QUEEN'S, matric. 14 Jan., 90, aged 25.

Simmonds, rev. Mark John, born at Lambeth 17 April, 1862; 1s. John Whateley, gen. BALLIOL, matric. 21 Oct., 80, aged 18 (from Merchant Taylors' school), exhibitioner 79-84, B.A. 84, M.A. 87 (HONOURS:—3 mathematical mods. 82, 3 theology 84, Hebrew scholarship 85); fellow of St. Augustine coll., Canterbury, 86.

Simmons, Graham, born at Bath 18 Aug., 1863; 2s. Henry Argent, arm. MERTON, matric. 17 Oct., 82, aged 19 (from Bath coll.), B.A. 85; HONOURS: —3 law 85.

Simms, Edward Henry, born at Wrexham, co. Denbigh, 1862; 1s. Edward, gen. NON-COLLEGIATE, matric. 17 Oct., 81, aged 19, from Wrexham school.

Simms, Leslie Winfield, born in London 1861; 1s. George, gen. PEMBROKE, matric. 28 Jan., 89, aged 18.

Simms, rev. Spencer Edward, born at Lindfield, Sussex, 1863; o.s. Edward, cler. EXETER, matric. 21 Jan., 82, aged 19 (from Exeter gr. school), B.A. 85, M.A. 90 (HONOURS :—3 classical mods. 83, 3 theology 85); curate of Newington St. Mary, Surrey, 88.

Simon, Arthur Powell, born in London 23 Oct., 1866; 3s. George, arm. NEW COLL., matric. 12 Oct., 88, aged 18 (from Marlborough), B.A. 91; HONOURS: —3 law 91.

Simon, Francis Rupert Powell, born in London 23 Jan., 1866; 6s. George, arm. MERTON, matric. 16 Oct., 84, aged 18, from Rurby.

Simon, John Allsebrook, born at Hulme, co. Lanc., 28 Feb., 1873; 1s. Edwin, congregational minister. WADHAM, matric. 18 Oct., 92, aged 19 (from Fettes coll.), scholar 92.

Simon, Maurice, born at Manchester 16 March, 1874; 1s. Isidore, Jewish clergyman. WADHAM, matric. 18 Oct., 92, aged 18 (from Manchester gr. school), scholar 92.

Simon, Sidney Arthur, born at Eccles, Manchester, 8 July, 1873; 2s. Salis, merchant. CORPUS CHRISTI, matric. 19 Oct., 91, aged 18 (from Manchester gr. school), scholar 91.

Simonds, William Barrow, born at Abbots Barton, Hants, 25 Dec., 1864; 1s. William Barrow, formerly M.P. CHRIST CHURCH, matric. 25 May, 83, aged 18 (from Winchester), B.A. 87, M.A. 91; bar.-at-law, Inner Temple, 90.

Simons, John James Cornelis Diosman, born at Malmesbury, Cape of Good Hope, 4 Dec., 1863; 1s. Arnaud Jacques, D.Med. MERTON, matric. 16 Oct., 82, aged 21, from South African coll., Cape-town.

Simonson, George Adhemar, born in London 1866; 2s. Nathaniel, arm. BALLIOL, matric. 18 May, 83, aged 17, B.A. 88; HONOURS :—2 classical mods. 84, 3 classics 87.

Simonson, Paul Frederick, born in London 1864; 1s. Nathaniel, gen. BALLIOL, matric. 17 Oct., 82, aged 18 (from Stuttgart gymnasium), B.A. 86 (HONOURS :—3 classical mods. 84, 3 classics 86); student of Lincoln's Inn 84; migrated to the Inner Temple, bar.-at-law 89.

Simpson, Alexander Bontein, born in Madras 1868; o.s. Alexander, arm. CHRIST CHURCH, matric. 14 Oct., 87, aged 19, B.A. 91; HONOURS: —2 history 91.

Simpson, Alexander William, born at Adel, near Leeds, 1864; 4s. Henry Trail, cler. NON-COLLEGIATE, matric. 13 Oct., 84, aged 20, from St. Edward's coll., Salisbury.

Simpson, Cyril Edward, born in London 4 Jan., 1867; 3s. Benjamin William, gen. BRASENOSE, matric. 23 Oct., 85, aged 18 (from Hnileybury), B.A. 88, M.A. 92.

Simpson, Edgar Hope, born at Walton, near Liverpool, 11 July, 1873; 6s. John Hope, of Alghurth, gen. BALLIOL, matric. 20 Oct., 91, aged 18, from Liverpool coll.

Simpson, Edmund Kidley, born at Lewisham, Kent, 6 July, 1873; o.s. Abraham Calorius, stockbroker. TRINITY, matric. 15 Oct., 92, aged 19 (from Ipswich school), Ford student 92.

Simpson, Edmund Thornhill Beckett, born at Crofton, Yorks, 5 March, 1867; 1s. Edward, gen. PEMBROKE, matric. 28 Oct., 86, aged 19 (from Harrow), in University eleven 88.

Simpson, Edward Percy, born in London 24 Feb., 1865; 4s. James, C.E. MAGDALEN, matric. 16 Oct., 84, aged 19 (from Wellington coll.), B.A. 89; bar.-at-law, Inner Temple, 92.

Simpson, Elliott, born at Kensington 1872; o.s. William Frederick, gen. ST. JOHN'S, matric. 17 Oct., 91, aged 19, from Winchester.

Simpson, Francis Henry, born at Broughton, co. Lanc., 1866; 1s. Frederick, gen. ST. JOHN'S, matric. 11 Oct., 84, aged 18 (from Preston school), B.A. 88; HONOURS :— 3 mathematical mods. 86, 3 history 88.

Simpson, Frank Douglas, born at Aberdeen 18 Oct., 1870; 3s. Alexander, advocate. EXETER, matric. 13 Oct., 90, aged 19 (from Aberdeen university), exhibitioner 90.

Simpson, Frederick Charles, born in Hackney, London, 28 July, 1874; 1s. Frederick Henry, of Beckenham, stockbroker. QUEEN'S, matric. 27 Oct., 92, aged 18 (from Elstree and Littlehampton schools).

Simpson, Frederick James, born at Portobello, Midlothian, 1857; 4s. Henry, gen. NEW COLL., matric. 27 Jan., 86, aged 29, B.Mus. 17 Dec., 86.

Simpson, rev. George Edward, born at Leeds 1863; o.s. George gen. NON-COLLEGIATE, matric. 13 Oct., 83, aged 20, B.A. 87, M.A. 90; curate of Kellington, Yorks, 91.

Simpson, rev. George Williams, born at Leeds 1863; s. James, gen. ST. JOHN'S, matric. 16 Oct., 88, aged 25, B.A. 92.

Simpson, rev. Henry Edgington, born at Clapham 1858; 1s. Henry, arm. NON-COLLEGIATE, matric. 17 Jan., 80, aged 22; migrated to PEMBROKE 81, B.A. 84, M.A. 86; curate of St. Matthew, Westminster, 84.

Simpson, Herbert Clayton, born at St. Giles, Northampton, 26 Nov., 1892; 2s. Thomas Harrison, H.M. inspector of schools, NON-COLLEGIATE, matric. 17 Oct., 91, aged 18, from Magdalen coll. school.

Simpson, rev. James Gilliland, born in London 16 Oct., 1865; 1s. David Crighton, gen. TRINITY, matric. 11 Oct., 84, aged 18 (from city of London school), scholar 84-8, B.A. 88, M.A. 91 (HONOURS : —2 classical mods. 86, 1 classics 88, 1 theology 89) ; curate of Leeds 89-92, vice-principal of theological college of Scotch episcopal church, Edinburgh, 93.

Simpson, John Hope, born in Liverpool 1868; 3s. John, arm. BALLIOL, matric. 19 Oct., 87, aged 19 (from Liverpool coll.); assist. magistrate N.W. provinces India; brother of Edgar Hope.

Simpson, John Percy, born at Shields, co. Durham, 1862; 2s. Robert James, cler. WORCESTER, matric. 24 Jan., 80, aged 18, B.A. 83; HONOURS: —3 law 83.

Simpson, Percy John, born in London June, 1864; 2s. Benjamin William, gen. CHRIST CHURCH, matric. 25 May, 83, aged 18.

Simpson, Ronald Hugh, born at Ackworth, Yorks, 29 Feb., 1872; 3s. Charles Henry, gen. BRASENOSE, matric. 22 Oct., 91, aged 19, from Eton.

Simpson, Stephen, born at Preston, co. Lanc., 1864; 2s. Stephen, gen. ST. JOHN'S, matric. 21 Jan., 82, aged 18, B.A. 85, M.A. 88; HONOURS :—4 law 85.

Simpson, Thomas Dale, born at Wateringbury, Kent, 19 Dec., 1869; 1s. Thomas Gregson, gent. KEBLE, matric. 12 Oct., 89, aged 19 (from Berkhamstead school), B.A. 92; HONOURS :—3 classical mods. 91.

Simson, David James, born at Edinburgh 2 Jan., 1861; o.s. James, arm., deceased. NEW COLL., matric. 16 Oct., 80, aged 19 (from Fettes coll.), B.A. 83, advocate 85; HONOURS :—2 classical mods. 81, 3 law 83.

Simson, Henry Frew-, born in London 1866; 1s. Henry Knight, arm. CHRIST CHURCH, matric. 15 Oct., 86, aged 20; migrated to CAMBRIDGE, matric. NON-COLL. 22 Oct., 88, B.A. 92; HONOURS : —3 history 92.

Sinclair, rev. the hon. Charles Augustus, born at Aberdeen 11 May, 1865; 3s. James Augustus, arm., after 16th earl of Caithness. TRINITY, matric. 17 Oct., 85, aged 20 (from Aberdeen university), B.A. 89, M.A. 92 (HONOURS:—3 classical mods. 87, 3 classics 89); curate of St. Barnabas, Kensington, 90.

Sinclair, William Hugh Montgomery, born in Dublin 31 Dec., 1868; 1s. Montgomery, arm. BRASENOSE, matric. 2d Oct., 86, aged 17 (from Marlborough), B.A. 89.

Sing, Mark, born at Liverpool April, 1871; 8s. Joshua, gen. CHRIST CHURCH, matric. 11 Oct., 89, aged 18, from Shrewsbury gr. school.

Sinnett, John Parry, born at Llandyssil, co. Carmarthen, 1861; y.s. John, cler. JESUS COLL., matric. 23 Oct., 80, aged 19, B.A. 86.

Sitwell, Edward Sacheverell, born at Stanton Woodhouse, co. Derby, Oct., 1862; 1s. Robert Sacheverell Wilmot, arm. BRASENOSE, matric. 21 May, 80, aged 17, from Eton.

Sitzler, George Christian, born at Surbiton, Surrey, 12 Aug., 1873; 1s. Francis Christian, merchant. NEW COLL., matric. 14 Oct., 92, aged 19, from Haileybury.

Skeffington, hon. Oriel John, born in London 10 Oct., 1871; 1s. Clotworthy John, viscount Massereene. MERTON, matric. 23 Jan., 90, aged 18 (from Eton), B.A. 93.

Skeffington, rev. Sydney William, M.A., fellow UNIVERSITY COLL. See page 99.

Skelton, Arthur Woolfield, born at Twickenham, Middx., 26 March, 1874; o.s. Arthur, of Ireland, revenue officer. NEW COLL., matric. 14 Oct., 92, aged 18 (from Bromsgrove school), scholar 91.

Skene, William Baillie, M.A., student CHRIST CHURCH 90, where see page 409.

Skillicorne, William Nash, born at Cheltenham 10 Jan., 1861; 1s. William Nash, gen. WORCESTER, matric. 21 Oct., 80, aged 19, from Cheltenham coll.

Skilton, Edward Wigram, born at Romford, Essex, 20 April, 1863; 2s. William James, rector of Romford St. Andrew's. LINCOLN, matric. 17 Oct., 84, aged 21 (from Felsted gr. school), B.A. 88; HONOURS :—3 classical mods. 86, 4 classics 88.

Skinner, Henry Bayly, born at Croydon, Surrey, 13 April, 1866; 1s. Henry John Hunt. WORCESTER, matric. 22 Oct., 85, aged 19 (from Highgate school); HONOURS :—4 law 89.

Skinner, John Allan Cleveland, born at Cleveland, America, Sept., 1865; 1s. John Edwin Hilary, arm. KEBLE, matric. 16 Oct., 83, aged 18 (from Wellington); assist. commissioner central provinces India.

Skinner, Stephen Stuart, born at Clevedon, Somerset, 5 Aug., 1872; 1s. Stephen, D.Med. HERTFORD, matric. 20 Oct., 91, aged 19 (from Eton), scholar 90; HONOURS :—2 classical mods. 93.

Skipwith, Grey Hubert, born in London 2 July, 1860; 2s. sir Thomas, bart. TRINITY, matric. 29 Jan., 81, aged 20, B.A. 85; HONOURS :—3 classical mods. 82, 3 history 84.

Skirrow, Benjamin Beck, born at Bingley, Yorks, 1863; 2s. Benjamin Beck, gen. UNIVERSITY COLL., matric. 14 Oct., 82, aged 19 (from Bingley school, and Yorkshire coll., Leeds), scholar 82, B.A. 85, M.A. 91; HONOURS :—1 mathematical mods. 83, junior mathematical scholarship 84, 1 mathematics 85, 2 physics 87.

Skrine, rev. Herbert Henry, born at Charlton, Wilts, 1852; 2s. Wadham Huntley, cler. WORCESTER, matric. 18 Oct., 83, aged 31 (from Marlborough), B.A. 86, M.A. 90 (HONOURS :—2 theology 86); held various curacies 77-90, vicar of Greenham, Berks, 90.

Skrine, rev. John Huntley, M.A., fellow MERTON 71-9, where see page 98.

Skyrme, Frank Elcho, born at Curmannan, co. Glam., 1869; 2s. Edward, gen. BRASENOSE, matric. 19 Oct., 82, aged 19 (from Shrewsbury gr. school), B.A. 86, M.A. 89; HONOURS :—2 classical mods. 84, 3 history 86.

Slack, Humphrey Archer, born at Woolfardisworthy, Devon, 6 April, 1870; 1s. Humphrey Archer, rector. QUEEN'S, matric. 22 Oct., 89, aged 19, from Marlborough.

Slade, George, born at Sydney, Australia, 24 Sept., 1866; 1s. George Pentrevil, solicitor. MAGDALEN, matric. 23 Oct., 85, aged 19 (from the Charterhouse), B.A. 88; HONOURS :—4 law 88.

Slade, George Fitzclarence, M.A., fellow ALL SOULS' 54-8, where see page 260.

Slade, Henry Adolphus Warre, born at Lewknor, Oxon, 17 Sept., 1862; 1s. George Fitzclarence, rector of Buckland, Surrey. NEW COLL., matric. 14 Oct., 87, aged 18 (from Winchester); HONOURS :—3 classical mods. 89.

Slade, Marcus Warre, born at Langford Budville, Somerset, 10 Sept., 1865; 2s. George Fitzclarence, rector of Buckland, Surrey. NEW COLL., matric. 10 Oct., 84, aged 19 (from Clifton coll.), B.A. 89 (HONOURS :—2 history 88); bar.-at-law, Inner Temple, 91.

Slade, Wyndham Neave, born in London 17 Sept., 1867; 1s. Wyndham, arm. BALLIOL, matric. 19 Oct., 86, aged 19 (from Eton), B.A. 90 (HONOURS : —3 classical mods. 88, 3 law 90); bar.-at-law, Inner Temple, 91.

Sladen, David Ramsay, born at Weymouth 1869; 2s. John Ramsay, arm. ST. JOHN'S, matric. 11 Dec., 86, aged 17, from the Charterhouse.

Sladen, Francis Danvers, born in London 1870; 2s. Henry Mainwaring, arm. HERTFORD, matric. 29 Oct., 89, aged 19 (from Canterbury school), matric 88, B.A. 93; HONOURS :—1 classical mods. 90, 3 classics 92.

Sladen, Joseph, born at Allahabad, East Indies, 1866; 1s. Joseph, arm. BALLIOL, matric. 24 Oct., 85, aged 19 (from the Charterhouse), scholar 85, B.A. 88 (HONOURS :—3 Indian languages 88), assist. collector and magistrate Sind 87.

Sladen, Lawrence Banks, born at Woolwich, Kent, 1867; 2s. Joseph, arm. PEMBROKE, matric. 27 Oct., 85, aged 18 (from Elizabeth coll. Guernsey), B.A. 89, M.A. 92; HONOURS :—3 classical mods. 87, 2 classics 89, Ellerton theological essay 91.

Slater, Archibald, born at Darlaston, co. Stafford, 22 July, 1866; 3s. James, solicitor. EXETER, matric. 23 Oct., 85, aged 19 (from Wolverhampton gr. school), B.A. 88.

Slater, David Ansell, born at Worcester 7 Oct., 1866; o.s. David, gen., deceased. MAGDALEN, matric. 23 Oct., 85, aged 19 (from Bromsgrove gr. school), demy 84, B.A. 89; HONOURS :—1 classical mods. 87, 2 classics 89.

Slater, Edward Tilley, born at Darlaston, co. Stafford, 1865; 2s. James, gen. UNIVERSITY COLL., matric. 11 Oct., 84, aged 19 (from Wolverhampton school), B.A. 88 (HONOURS :—2 classics 88); bar.-at-law, Inner Temple, 91.

Slater, Samuel Mills, born at Darlaston, co. Stafford, 1863; 1s. James, solicitor. EXETER, matric. 20 Oct., 81, aged 18 (from Wolverhampton school), B.A. 84, M.A. and B.C.L. 88; HONOURS: —3 law 84, 3 civil law 86.

Slater, rev. Walter, born in London 1861; 1s. Walter, gen. NON-COLLEGIATE, matric. 17 Jan., 80, aged 19 (from Highbury Park school); migrated to WORCESTER, B.A. 83, M.A. 86, B.D. 89 (HONOURS :—4 theology 83); curate of Buckingham 85-91, and of Holywell, Oxford, 91, chaplain Christ Church 90.

Slater, William, born at Heversham, Westmorland, 1860; 2s. Henry, gen. TURRELL'S HALL, matric. 27 April, 89, aged 29.

Slator, Thomas, born at Boston, co. Leicester, 24 April, 1872; 1s. Thomas, gen. PEMBROKE, matric. 25 Oct., 90, aged 18 (from Boston gr. school), scholar 89; HONOURS :—1 mathematical mods. 91, proxime accessit junior mathematical exhibition 92.

Slaughter, Edward Mihill, born at Clifton, co. Glouc., 16 July, 1867; 1s. Edward, arm. TRINITY, matric. 16 Oct., 86, aged 19 (from Rugby, and Trinity coll., Melbourne), B.A. 89; HONOURS :—4 law 89.

Sleasor, Arthur Kerr, born at Headbourne Worthy, Hants, 13 Dec., 1863; 2s. John Henry, rector. CHRIST CHURCH, matric. 12 Jan., 83, aged 19 (from St. Edward's school, Summertown), scholar 84-6, B.A. 87; HONOURS :—2 classical mods. 84, 3 classics 86.

Sleasor, John Henry, M.A., fellow UNIVERSITY COLL. 47-62, where see page 31.

Slight, Andrew Muir, born at Edinburgh 1868; 3s. Alexander, gen. BALLIOL, matric. 19 Oct., 87, aged 19 (from royal coll., Mauritius); assist. to collector and magistrate South Canara, Madras C.S.

Slight, Henry Spencer, B.D., fellow CORPUS CHRISTI 38-50, where see page 382.

Slocock, Arthur Edmund Oliver, born at Chelsea, Middx., 30 Nov., 1863; 2s. Oliver Edmund, cler. MERTON, matric. 17 Oct., 82, aged 18 (from Lancing coll.), postmaster 82, B.A. 86, M.A. 90; HONOURS: —2 classical mods. 84, 3 classics 86.

Slocock, Charles Edward, born at Donnington, Berks, 13 Nov., 1868; 1s. Charles Samuel, arm. MERTON, matric. 22 Oct., 87, aged 18, from Winchester.

Slocock, Edmund, born at Newbury, Berks, 30 April, 1874; 5s. Oliver Edmund, cler., Pembroke, Oxford. MERTON, matric. 18 Oct., 92, aged 18, from Lancing coll.

Slocock, Francis Samuel Alfred, born at Donnington, Berks, 18 July, 1870; 2s. Charles Samuel, arm. TRINITY, matric. 12 Oct., 89, aged 19 (from Marlborough); assist. to collector and magistrate South Arcot, Madras C.S.

Slocock, Richard, born at Winterbourne, Berks, 2 Sept., 1866; 3s. Oliver Edmund, cler. CHRIST CHURCH, matric. 16 Oct., 85, aged 19 (from Lancing coll.), B.A. 89.

Sly, Frederic Charles, born at Salisbury 1866; 3s. Thomas, gen. BALLIOL, matric. 24 Oct., 85, aged 19; assist. commissioner central provinces India.

Smale, rev. Henry John, born in London 1866; 1s. John Jackson, bar.-at-law. EXETER, matric. 8 Dec., 84, aged 18 (from Exeter school), B.A. 88, M.A. 91 (HONOURS :—2 chemistry 88); curate of Worsley, co. Lanc., 91.

Small, Edward Henry Thomas Fewson, born at Downend, near Bristol, Sept., 1869; o.s. Edward Fewson, gent. BRASENOSE, matric. 19 Oct., 89, aged 20 (from King's coll. school), B.A. 86, M.A. 90.

Smalley, Phillips, born at Brooklyn, America, 1866; 1s. Westburn, gen. BALLIOL, matric. 10 Feb., 86, aged 20.

Smallwood, Arthur Irving, born at Bromwich, co. Warwick, 9 Feb., 1870; 2s. John, solicitor. EXETER, matric. 17 Oct., 88, aged 18 (from Marlborough), B.A. 91.

Smallwood, Arthur William, born at Barrow, co. Derby, 24 March, 1873; 1s. George Arthur, cler. CORPUS CHRISTI, matric. 18 Oct., 92, aged 19 (from Repton school), scholar 91.

Smallwood, John Edward, born at Castle Bromwich, co. Warwick, 1869; 1s. John, gen. PEMBROKE, matric. 25 Oct., 87, aged 18 (from Marlborough), B.A. 90.

Smart, John Raesier, born at Cowley, co. Worc., 11 Aug., 1868; 2s. Benjamin, vicar of St. Kea, Cornwall, 83-91. JESUS COLL., matric. 19 Oct., 87, aged 19 (from Truro gr. school), B.A. 92; HONOURS: —2 classical mods. 89, classics 91.

Smart, Newton Reginald, M.A., student CHRIST CHURCH 49-67, where see page 419.

Smart, Roger, born at Cambridge 31 Oct., 1869; 3s. Charles. gen. LINCOLN, matric. 18 Oct., 88, aged 18 (from Perse school, Cambridge), scholar 88, B.A. 92; HONOURS :—2 classical mods. 90, 4 classics 92.

Smart, Sydney Dallow, born at Scarborough 1870; 1s. John, gen. KEBLE, matric. 12 Oct., 89, aged 19 (from Dulwich coll.), scholar 88.

Smeaton, Reginald Gordon Willis, born at Hannington, Wilts, 1864; 2s. James Burn, cler. NON-COLLEGIATE, matric. 14 Oct., 82, aged 18 (from Magdalen coll. school); migrated to HERTFORD, B.A. 88.

Smothurst, rev. James, born at Gartmore, Perthshire, 1856; 2s. Elias, gen. NON-COLLEGIATE, matric. 17 Oct., 81, aged 25 (from Crossby orphanage, Halifax); migrated to WORCESTER 88, B.A. 84; curate of Wells St. Cuthbert 85.

Smith, rev. Alan Gordon, born at Handsworth, co. Staff., 23 Aug., 1863; 3s. George, gen. NEW COLL., matric. 14 Oct., 82, aged 19 (from Birmingham school), B.A. 86 (HONOURS :—3 classical mods. 84, 3 classics 86); curate of St. Saviour, Champion Hill, Surrey, 87.

Smith, Arthur Lionel, M.A., fellow BALLIOL 82, where see page 63.

Smith, Arthur Watson, born at Brooklands, Cheshire, 1871; 6s. Alexander Watson, gen. CORPUS CHRISTI, matric. 16 Oct., 90, aged 19; HONOURS :— 3 classical mods. 92.

Smith, Basil Murray, born at Tedstone Delamere, 11 Jan., 1870; 2s. Isaac Gregory, vicar of Great Malvern. NEW COLL., matric. 12 Oct., 88, aged 18 (from Marlborough), exhibitioner 88, B.A. 92; HONOURS :—1 classical mods. 90, 1 classics 92.

Smith, Beilby Eric, born in London 26 Nov., 1863; 3s. Eric Carrington, arm. CHRIST CHURCH, matric. 13 Oct., 82, aged 18 (from Eton), B.A. 86.

Smith, Bernard, M.A., fellow MAGDALEN 36-9, where see page 321.

Smith, Bertrand Nigel Bosworth-, born at Harrow 20 June, 1873; 4s. Reginald B-S, M.A., assistant master at Harrow. MAGDALEN, matric. 18 Oct., 92, aged 19 (from Harrow), demy 91.

Smith, Boteler Chernocke, born at Hulcote rectory, Beds, Nov., 1873; 7s. Boteler Chernocke, cler. KEBLE, matric. 15 Oct., 92, aged 18, from Bedford gr. school.

Smith, Charles Morden, born at Chevening, Kent, 8 April, 1866; 1s. Richard Goodall, arm., deceased. MAGDALEN, matric. 16 Oct., 84, aged 18, from Eton.

Smith, Charles Purley, born at Dumbleton, co. Glouc., 21 Jan., 1868; 4s. John, arm. EXETER, matric. 19 Oct., 87, aged 19 (from Cheltenham coll.), B.A. 91; HONOURS :—3 history 91.

Smith, Clayton Cozens-, born at Enfield, Middx., 28 April, 1873; 4s. Edward, of Bengeo, Herts, arm. EXETER, matric. 18 Oct., 92, aged 19, from Haileybury.

Smith, Clement Leigh Watson-, born at Islington 28 May, 1862; o.s. Richard, of Faversham, Kent, arm. MAGDALEN, matric. 15 Oct., 81, aged 19 (from Haileybury), exhibitioner 81-5, B.A. 86, M.A. 88 ; HONOURS :—2 classical mods. 83.

Smith, Cyril, born at Lancaster 28 Feb., 1863; 3s. Henry Fielding, cler. QUEEN'S, matric. 23 Oct., 82, aged 19 (from Rugby), exhibitioner 82.

Smith, Ernest, born at Morley, co. Derby, 1870; 2s. William, arm. UNIVERSITY COLL., matric. 15 Oct., 87, aged 17 (from Clifton coll.), scholar 87, B.A. 91 (HONOURS :—2 mathematical mods. 89, 3 mathematics 91), in University eleven 90-91.

Smith, rev. Ernest Albert, born at Sutton Coldfield, co. Warwick, 7 Oct., 1863. MAGDALEN, matric. 11 Dec., 82, aged 19 (from Sutton Coldfield gr. school), B.A. 85, M.A. 90 ; curate of Christ Church, Albany Street, London, 86-91.

Smith, rev. Ernest Dalby Finch, born at Witham, Essex, 22 Oct., 1867; 1s. John Finch, cler. WORCESTER, matric. 17 Oct., 87, aged 19 (from Denstone coll.), B.A. 92 (HONOURS :—4 history 91); curate of Farnham 92.

Smith, Ernest Frederick, born at Cheshunt, Herts, 6 Sept., 1870; o.s. Frederick Warren, gen. LINCOLN, matric. 18 Oct., 86, aged 18 (from Ludlow gr. school), B.A. 92 ; HONOURS :—2 theology 92.

Smith, Francis Edward James, born at Monckton Farleigh, Wilts, 23 Feb., 1865; 3s. John, of Britwell, Berks, arm. NEW COLL., matric. 14 Oct., 82, aged 19 (from Winchester), B.A. 86, M.A. 91; HONOURS :—2 classical mods. 84, 2 classics 86.

Smith, Francis Jagoe, born at Barnet, Herts, 9 Sept., 1873; 1s. Henry Francis, gent. ST. JOHN'S, matric. 15 Oct., 92, aged 19 (from Merchant Taylors' school), scholar 92.

Smith, Francis Robert, born at West Stafford, Dorset, July, 1866 ; 3s. Robert, gen. KEBLE, matric. 17 Oct., 87, aged 21 (from Dorset county school, Charminster), B.A. 90.

Smith, Frederick Edwin, born at Birkenhead, Cheshire, 12 July, 1872; 1s. Frederick, bar.-at-law, deceased. WADHAM, matric. 20 Oct., 91, aged 19 (from Birkenhead school, and University coll., Liverpool), scholar 90 ; HONOURS :—2 classical mods. 93.

Smith, Frederick Herbert Bowden, born at Rugby 17 June, 1861 ; 3s. Philip Bowden, cler. TRINITY, matric. 16 Oct., 80, aged 19 (from Rugby), B.A. 85, M.A. 88 (HONOURS :—3 classical mods. 82) , a master at Shrewsbury school ; brother of Godfrey B.

Smith, rev. Frederick John, M.A., TRINITY, where see page 456.

Smith, George, born at Ayr, Scotland, 15 July, 1867 ; 3s. George, gen. TRINITY, 1 Nov., 87, aged 20 (from Ayr academy and Edinburgh university, 1 classics 88), scholar 85, B.A. 92; HONOURS : —1 classical mods. 89, 1 classics 91.

Smith, George Albert, born in London 1 Aug., 1858 ; 3s. Henry Tilden, gen. CHRIST CHURCH, matric. 13 Oct., 82, aged 24, from Boston gr. school.

Smith, George Frederick Darwall, born in London 6 Jan., 1874 ; o.s. John George, bar.-at-law, assist. registrar Admiralty Court. NEW COLL., matric. 14 Oct., 92, aged 18, from Winchester.

Smith, George Frederick Herbert, born at Edgbaston, co. Warwick, 26 May, 1872 ; 1s. George, cler. NEW COLL., matric. 16 Oct., 91, aged 19 (from Doncaster and Winchester), scholar 90; HONOURS : —1 mathematical mods. 92.

Smith, George Gregory, born at Edinburgh 1865 ; 1s. Henry Gregory Craigie, arm. BALLIOL, matric. 24 Oct., 85, aged 20 (from Feties coll. and Edinburgh university), B.A. 88, M.A. 91 (as G.B.) ; HONOURS :—2 history 88.

Smith, George Herbert, born at Handsworth, co. Staff., 13 Oct., 1860 ; 1s. George, gen. LINCOLN, matric. 23 Oct., 80, aged 20 (from King Edward's school, Birmingham), scholar WORCESTER, 81-4, B.A. 84 ; HONOURS :—2 classical mods. 82, 3 classics 84.

Smith, George Hubert Henry, born at Easingwold, Yorks, 1869 ; 1s. George Hudson, gen. NON-COLLEGIATE, matric. 25 Jan., 88, aged 19, from Easingwold gr. school.

Smith, Gilbert Oswald, born at Croydon, Surrey, Nov., 1872 ; 3s. Robert, gent. KEBLE, matric. 15 Oct., 92, aged 19, from the Charterhouse.

Smith, Godfrey Bowden, born at Rugby, co. Warwick, 27 Nov., 1865 ; 6s. Philip Bowden, cler. BALLIOL, matric. 15 Oct., 84, aged 18 (from Rugby), B.A. 88 ; HONOURS :—1 classical mods. 86, 1 classics 88.

Smith, Goldwin, created D.C.L. 14 June, 1882, hon. fellow UNIVERSITY COLL. 68, etc., where see page 30.

Smith, Gustafkjold Sundius Leeston, born at Penzance 21 Aug., 1859 ; 4s. Frederick James, arm. TRINITY, matric. 29 Jan., 81, aged 21, from Clifton coll.

Smith, Guy Carleton, born at Brighton 18 Dec., 1867 ; 1s. Carleton, arm. WORCESTER, matric. 3 May, 87, aged 19, from Clifton coll.

Smith, Harold Bowden, born at Rugby 5 July, 1868 ; 8s. Philip Bowden, cler., assist. master at Rugby. KEBLE, matric. 17 Oct., 87, aged 19 (from Rugby), B.A. 92.

Smith, Harold Gilbert Brodrick, born at Liverpool 20 April, 1872 ; 1s. George, arm. CHRIST CHURCH, matric. 10 Oct., 90, aged 18, from Rugby.

Smith, Harry Percival, born at Edgbaston, co. Warwick, 1859 ; 1s. Frederic, gen. UNIVERSITY COLL., matric. 11 Oct., 84, aged 25, B.A. 88 ; HONOURS :—3 classical mods. 86, 4 classics 88.

Smith, Harry Senior, born in London 18 Aug., 1867 ; o.s. Theophilus, gen. WORCESTER, matric. 22 Oct., 85, aged 18 (from Leeds gr. school), B.A. 90, M.A. 92.

Smith, Henry Alban, born at Tattenhall, Cheshire, June, 1871 ; 2s. Henry, cler. and inspector of schools. EXETER, matric. 13 Oct., 90, aged 19 (from Rossall school), exhibitioner 90; HONOURS :— 2 classical mods. 92.

Smith, Henry Bompas, born at Hull 29 April, 1867 ; 1s. John Frederick, unitarian minister. WADHAM, matric. 16 Oct., 86, aged 19 (from Mansfield gr. school), scholar 85, B.A. 90; HONOURS :—1 mathematical mods. 87, 1 classics 90.

Smith, Henry Coker, born at Cheltenham 30 Sept., 1870 ; 2s. Arthur Heavans, gen. CORPUS CHRISTI, matric. 25 Oct., 89, aged 19 (from Cheltenham gr. school), exhibitioner 89 ; HONOURS :—2 classical mods. 91.

Smith, Henry Eden, born at Grange-over-Sands, co. Lanc., 1864; 1s. Henry Robert, hon. canon of Carlisle. EXETER, matric. 18 Oct., 83, aged 19 (from the Charterhouse); scholar 83, B.A. 87, M.A. 90; HONOURS:—2 classical mods. 84, 2 classics 87.

Smith, Henry Scott, born at Londonderry May, 1865; 2s. Francis, cler. KEBLE, matric. 14 Oct., 84, aged 19 (from Stratford-on-Avon school); assist. commissioner Punjab.

Smith, Henry Webb, born at Brighton 1865; 1s. William, gen. NON-COLLEGIATE, matric. 15 April, 82, aged 17, from Arundell House school, Brighton.

Smith, Herbert Cecil, born at Rugby 3 March, 1873; 5s. Charles James Eliseo, cler. MERTON, matric. 12 Feb., 92, aged 18 (from Newcastle-under-Lyme high school), postmaster 91.

Smith, Herbert George, born at Toxteth, co. Lanc., 27 July, 1872; 1s. Elisha, of Liverpool, J.P. UNIVERSITY COLL., matric. 11 Oct., 90, aged 18 (from the Charterhouse); HONOURS:—2 classical mods. 92.

Smith, Herbert Maynard, born in London 3 Dec., 1869; 1s. John William, arm. TRINITY, matric. 15 Oct., 87, aged 17 (from Wellington), B.A. 91; HONOURS:—2 history 91.

Smith, Howard, born at Walsall, co. Stafford, 30 Dec., 1866; 4s. Alfred Sidney, gen. MERTON, matric. 24 Oct., 85, aged 18 (from Wolverhampton school), B.A. 89; HONOURS:—3 law 89, 3 civil law 89.

Smith, Isaac Gregory, M.A., fellow BRASENOSE 50-5, where see page 355.

Smith, Hubert Llewellyn, born at Westbury, co. Glouc., 17 April, 1864; 3s. Samuel Wyatt, arm. CORPUS CHRISTI, matric. 19 Oct., 83, aged 19 (from Bristol school), scholar 83, B.A. 87, M.A. 90 (HONOURS:—1 mathematical mods. 84, 1 mathematics 86, Cobden prize 86); a commissioner for labour 93.

Smith James Arthur, born at New Brighton, Cheshire, 5 Feb., 1872; 1s. James, cotton merchant. TRINITY, matric. 15 Oct., 92, aged 20, from Loretto school.

Smith, James Cruickshanks, born at Dun, co. Forfar, 28 Aug., 1867; 1s. James. TRINITY, matric. 13 Oct., 88, aged 21 (from Monirose academy, and Edinburgh university), exhibitioner 88, B.A. 92; HONOURS:—Craven scholarship 89, 1 classical mods. 90, and 1 classics 92; 1 classics at Edinburgh 89, and Ferguson classical scholar 89.

Smith, James Gordon, born at New Brighton, Cheshire, 17 Dec., 1870; 1s. Samuel, arm., M.P. Flints. WADHAM, matric. 20 Jan., 91, aged 20, from Merchiston castle school, Edinburgh.

Smith, rev. James Newland Newland-, born at Greenwich 7 Dec., 1867; 1s. James, cler. EXETER, matric. 19 Oct., 87, aged 19 (from St. Paul's school), scholar 88, B.A. 91 (HONOURS:—2 classical mods. 89, 2 theology 91); curate of Christ Church, Battersea, 91.

Smith, John Alexander, born at Dingwall, co. Ross, 1864; 2s. Andrew, gent. BALLIOL, matric. 28 Jan., 84, aged 20 (from Edinburgh university), Warner exhibitioner 83, B.A. 91, fellow 92 (HONOURS:—1 classical mods. 85, accessit 84, 85, proxime accessit Hertford scholarship 85, accessit Ireland scholarship 85, 1 classics 87, and Jenkyns exhibitioner 87, Ferguson classical scholar 84 (Edinburgh); college lecturer in philosophy.

Smith, rev. John Andrew, born at Liverpool 30 Nov., 1862; o.s. Ebenezer, cler. NON-COLLEGIATE, matric. 14 Oct., 82, aged 19 (from Liverpool coll.), B.A. 85, M.A. 89 (HONOURS:—1 theology 85); curate of St. John Baptist, Toxteth Park, Liverpool, 88.

Smith, John George, born at Dover 24 Jan., 1869; 1s. John George, arm. MAGDALEN, matric. 16 Oct., 88, aged 19 (from Eton), B.A. 92; HONOURS:—2 classical mods. 90, 3 classics 92.

Smith, John Herbert, born at Clifton, co. Derby, 5 Sept., 1868; 3s. William Richard, arm. NEW COLL., matric. 14 Oct., 87, aged 19 (from Repton school), B.A. 90; HONOURS:—a history 90.

Smith, John Hubert, born in London 2 or 9 April, 1872; 3s. John Nathaniel, cler. EXETER, matric. 22 Oct., 91, aged 19 (from Canterbury school), scholar 91; HONOURS:—2 classical mods. 93.

Smith, John Outram, born in London 1871; 2s. John William, gen. PEMBROKE, matric. 26 Oct., 89, aged 18.

Smith, Joseph Lewis Shaw, born at Kircassock, near Lurgan, Ireland, 11 June, 1871; 1s. John Augustus, arm. NEW COLL., matric. 10 Oct., 90, aged 19 (from Clifton coll.), exhibitioner 90; HONOURS:—1 classical mods. 92.

Smith, Leonard William, born at Clapton, Middx., 7 April, 1871; 2s. John Nathaniel, cler. TRINITY, matric. 12 Oct., 89, aged 18 (from Canterbury school), Ford student 89; HONOURS:—2 classical mods. 91.

Smith, rev. Leslie Knight, born at Broughton, Cheshire, 28 Jan, 1868; o.s. Alfred Marshall, gen., deceased. WADHAM, matric. 15 Oct., 87, aged 19 (from Eastbourne coll.), B.A. 91; HONOURS:—2 history 91.

Smith, Lloyd Logan Pearsall, born at Millville, New Jersey 1866; 1s. Robert Pearsall, arm. BALLIOL, matric. 23 April, 88, aged 22 (from Harvard university); HONOURS:—2 classics 91.

Smith, Louis Hilary Shore-, born in London 2 July, 1866; 2s. William, arm. CORPUS CHRISTI, matric. 26 Oct., 85, aged 19 (from Rugby), B.A. 89 (HONOURS:—3 classical mods. 87, 3 law 89); took the name of Nightingale instead of Smith by deed poll 18 April, 93.

Smith, Martin Linton, born at Boston, co. Lincoln, 1869; 2s. James Allan, cler. HERTFORD, matric. 19 Oct., 88, aged 19 (from Repton school), scholar 87, B.A. 92; HONOURS:—2 classical mods. 90, 2 classics 92.

Smith, Molineux Wade, born at Burbage, Wilts, 12 Dec., 1872; 1s. Thomas Wade, vicar of Easton Royal, Wilts. HERTFORD, matric. 20 Oct., 91, aged 18, from St. Edward's school, Summertown.

Smith, Norman Hardwick, born at Maiden Newton, Dorset, 26 Dec., 1859; o.s. John Hardwick, B.A., late congregational minister, deceased. ST. JOHN'S COLL., CAMBRIDGE, matric. 9 Nov., 80, aged 21 (from Shrewsbury school), B.A. 84 (HONOURS:—3 classics 83); incorporated 17 March, 87, NON-COLLEGIATE, M.A. 28 April, 87.

Smith, Nowell Charles, born at Bromley, Kent, 24 Feb., 1871; 1s. Horace, Metropolitan magistrate. NEW COLL., matric. 10 Oct., 90, aged 19 (from Winchester), scholar 89; HONOURS:—1 classical mods. 92.

Smith, Percy, born at Fallowfield, co. Lanc., 1864; 2s. Alexander Watson, gen. CORPUS CHRISTI, matric. 19 Oct., 83, aged 19 (from Clifton coll.), B.A. 88, M.A. 90; HONOURS:—2 classical mods. 85.

Smith, Philip Colville, born at Truro 1865; 2s. Philip Prothero, gen. ST. JOHN'S, matric. 21 Jan., 82, aged 27, M.A. 89; bar.-at-law, Inner Temple, 89.

Smith, Reginald, born at Bishopsthorpe, Yorks, 1863; 4s. Charles Francis, cler. ALL SOULS', matric. 30 Oct., 80, aged 17 (from Clergy Orphan school, Canterbury); bible clerk 80-4.

Smith, Reginald Allender, born in London 4 Jan., 1873; 2s. Thomas Nunn, cler., deceased. UNIVERSITY COLL., matric. 17 Oct., 91, aged 18 (from Christ's hospital), scholar 91; HONOURS:—1 classical mods. 93.

Smith, Reginald Bosworth, M.A., fellow TRINITY 63-5, where see page 453.

Smith, Robert Barr-, born at Adelaide, South Australia, 27 Nov., 1872 ; 3s. Robert Barr, merchant. MAGDALEN, matric. 22 Oct., 91, aged 18, from Glenalmond coll.

Smith, Robert Murray, scholar of Oriel 49 (from Repton), Agent General for Colony of Victoria, in London, created M.A., 27 May, 84. See *Al. Ox.* and series 1319.

Smith, very rev. Robert Payne, D.D., dean of Canterbury, canon of CHRIST CHURCH 65-71, where see page 406.

Smith, Robert Sherbourne, born at Melbourne 20 Oct., 1865 ; 1s. Robert Murray, arm. ORIEL, matric. 8 Dec., 84, aged 19 ; died 17 Nov., 86, at Oxford.

Smith, Robert Summers, born at Milford, co. Derby, 1 March, 1864 ; 1s. William Joseph, gen. WORCESTER, matric. 18 Jan., 83, aged 18 (from Rugby), B.A. 86 ; HONOURS :—3 law 86.

Smith, Robert Talbot, born at Urmritter, East Indies, 1864 ; 3s. Wemyss, late colonel in army. ST. ALBAN HALL, matric. 4 Nov. 81, aged 17.

Smith, Samuel, born at Croix, France, 14 June, 1867 ; 1s. Leonard, gen., deceased. QUEEN'S, matric. 25 Oct., 86, aged 19 (from Bradford gr. school), scholar 86 ; HONOURS :—3 classical mods. 88.

Smith, rev. Shipley Stancliffe, born at Chapeltown, Yorks, 1866 ; 2s. John Edward, gent. KEBLE, matric. 22 Oct., 85, aged 19 (from Highgate school), B.A. 88, M.A. 92 (from HONOURS :—3 theology 88) ; curate of St. Michael, Bowes Park, Middx., 89.

Smith, Thomas, born at Halifax, 1861 ; 2s. Thomas, gen. QUEEN'S, matric. 14 Jan., 90, aged 29, B.Mus. 91.

Smith, Thomas Clark, born at Marl Close, co. Derby, June, 1865 ; 1s. Thomas, pleb. KEBLE, matric. 16 Oct., 83, aged 18, as Thomas (from Ulverston school), B.A. 86, M.A. 90, as T. Clark-Smith ; HONOURS :—3 theology 86.

Smith, Thomas Clifford, born at St. Michael's, Beccles, Suffolk, 25 Feb., 1872 ; 1s. Clifford, esquire. HERTFORD, matric. 20 Oct., 91, aged 19 (from Cheltenham coll.), scholar 90 ; HONOURS :—2 classical mods. 93.

Smith, Thomas Henry Reginald, born in London 1865 ; 1s. Henry George, arm. BRASENOSE, matric. 15 Jan., 83, aged 18, from Russell school, as Henry Reginald.

Smith, Thomas Oliphant, born at New Brighton, Cheshire, 8 May, 1873 ; 2s. James, cotton broker. TRINITY, matric. Cl., 92, aged 19 (from Loretto school), exhibitioner 92.

Smith, Walter John, born at Nottingham 1868 ; 2s. John Benjamin, gen. ST. EDMUND HALL, matric. 18 Oct., 88, aged 20.

Smith, rev. Wemyss Thompson, born at Allahabad, East Indies, 5 May, 1862 ; 2s. colonel Wemyss. ST. ALBAN HALL, matric. 4 Nov., 81, aged 19 (from Stony Stratford coll.) ; migrated to MERTON, B.A. 88 (HONOURS :—3 history 85) ; rector of Lincoln Holy Trinity, Illinois, U.S.A., 90.

Smith, Wilfrid Noel Edmund, born at Sydenham, Kent, 1865 ; 4s. George, arm. ORIEL, matric. 23 Oct., 84, aged 19, from Uppingham school.

Smith, rev. William, born at Salisbury 1868 ; o.s. Henry Edward, cler. ST. EDMUND HALL, matric. 21 Jan., 87, aged 19.

Smith, William Brooke Brooke-, born at Edgbaston, co. Warwick, 4 May, 1862 ; 1s. Brooke, gen. UNIVERSITY COLL., matric. 15 Oct., 81, aged 19, from Clifton coll.

Smith, William Edward (Clifton), born at Clifton, co. Derby, 1866 ; 1s. William Richard, arm. EXETER, matric. 16 Oct., 84, aged 18 (from Repton school), B.A. 88.

Smith, hon. William Frederick Danvers, born at Filey, Yorks, 12 Aug., 1868 ; 1s. right hon. William Henry, 1st lord of the treasury. NEW COLL., matric. 18 Oct., 87, aged 19 (from Eton), B.A. 91 (HONOURS :—3 history 90) ; M.P. for Strand division (London) 91.

Smith, William Garnett, born at Bingley, Yorks, 1 March, 1862 ; 1s. William, gen. QUEEN'S, matric. 4 June, 81, aged 19 (from Leeds gr. school), exhibitioner 81-5, B.A. 85 ; HONOURS :—2 classical mods. 83, Ægrotat classics 85.

Smith, William George, born at Kingsland, Middx., 1864 ; 1s. George, gent. ST. JOHN'S, matric. 14 Oct., 82, aged 18 (from Merchant Taylors' school), scholar 82, senior scholar 88, fellow 89, B.A. 86, M.A. 89 ; HONOURS :—1 classical mods. 84, 1 classics 86, 1 history 87.

Smith, rev. William Henry Payne, M.A., senior student CHRIST CHURCH 75, where see page 408.

Smith, William Seton, born at Plumstead, Kent, 18 Dec., 1868 ; 3s. William Frederick, arm. NEW COLL., matric. 14 Oct., 87, aged 18 (from the Charterhouse), B.A. 91 ; HONOURS :—3 classical mods. 89, 3 law 91.

Smith, William Stephen Montgomery, born at Sutton, Surrey, 1863 ; o.s. William, gen. BALLIOL, matric. 18 Oct., 81, aged 18 (from Winchester), B.A. 86 ; HONOURS :—2 classical mods. 83, 3 classics 85.

Smithe, William Arthur, born at Cheltenham 1864 ; o.s. William Henry, cler. NON-COLLEGIATE, matric. 14 Oct., 82, aged 18 (from St. Edward's school, Summertown), B.A. 85.

Smithwhite, rev. John, born at South Shields, co. Durham, 1840 ; 1s. John, gent. QUEEN'S, matric. 22 May, 82, aged 19, a missionary in Madras; died 14 Feb., 85. See *Crockford*.

Smyth, Edward Herbert Gott, born at Houghton Regis, Beds, Aug., 1862 ; 2s. Hugh Blagg, cler. KEBLE, matric. 30 Oct., 80, aged 18 (from Salisbury school) ; migrated to CHARSLEY'S HALL, B.A. 88.

Smyth, George Muckleston Travers, born at Tenby, co. Pembroke, 29 Jan., 1873 ; 2s. Henry Travers, esq. QUEEN'S, matric. 27 Oct., 91, aged 18 (from Bradfield coll.) ; HONOURS :—2 classical mods. 93.

Smyth, Henry John Watt, born at Lahore, India, 16 June, 1872 ; 1s. John Watt, B.C.S. KEBLE, matric. 17 Oct., 91, aged 19 (from Winchester), scholar 91 ; HONOURS :—2 classical mods. 93.

Smyth, John, born at Newcells, Herts, 5 Aug., 1868 ; o.s. John, gen. QUEEN'S, matric. 21 Oct., 87, aged 19 (from Christ coll., Finchley), B.A. 91 ; HONOURS :—4 law 91.

Smyth, Ralph George, born at Drogheda, co. Louth, 1 Dec., 1864 ; 1s. Ralph, arm. MERTON, matric. 21 Oct., 86, aged 21, from Rugby.

Smyth, William John, born at Sidmouth, Devon, 1869 ; 3s. Henry, arm. BALLIOL, matric. 18 Oct., 88, aged 19 (from Bath coll.), exhibitioner 87, B.A. 93 (HONOURS :—1 classical mods. 90, 3 classics 92) ; selected candidate Indian C.S. 92.

Smythies, Charles Alan, B.A., TRINITY COLL., CAMBRIDGE, 1867 (from Felsted school), M.A. 71, D.D. 83 ; bishop of Central Africa 83, created D.D. 26 June, 90, hon. D.D. Durham university 90 ; vicar of Roath, co. Glamorgan, 80-3.

Snagge, Harold Edward, born in London 28 Dec., 1872 ; 2s. Thomas William, a judge of county courts. NEW COLL., matric. 16 Oct., 91, aged 18, from Eton.

Snagge, Thomas Mordaunt, born in London 25 July, 1868; 1s. Thomas William, a judge of county courts. NEW COLL., matric. 14 Oct., 87, aged 19 (from Eton), B.A. 91; HONOURS:—2 law 91.

Sneath, Donald Aikin, born at Cambridge 1869; 2s. Thomas Aikin, vicar of Bledlow, Bucks. LINCOLN, matric. 18 Oct., 88, aged 19, from Highgate school.

Snell, rev. Charles Dashwood, born in London 1861; 2s. Frederick, arm. ST. JOHN'S, matric. 16 Oct., 80, aged 19 (from Merchant Taylors' school), scholar 80, B.A. 84, M.A. 87 (HONOURS:—2 mathematical mods. 82, 2 mathematics 84); student Inner Temple 82; deputation sec. Church Missionary soc. 91.

Snell, Frederick John, born at Tiverton, Devon, 1863; 1s. Frederick, gen. BALLIOL, matric. 1 Feb., 82, aged 19 (from Tiverton school), Blundell scholar 81-5, B.A. 85, M.A. 90; HONOURS:—2 classical mods. 83, 2 classics 85.

Snelling, Rowland William, born at Sydenham, Kent, 15 Dec., 1869; 1s. William Barham, gen., deceased. NEW COLL., matric. 11 Oct., 89, aged 19 (from Dulwich coll.), exhibitioner 89, B.A. 92; HONOURS:—3 classics 92.

Snook, rev. William Maulkinson, born in London 16 April, 1868; 1s. William, gen. QUEEN'S, matric. 25 Oct., 86, aged 18 (from University coll. school, and King's coll., Lond.), B.A. 89.

Snow, Arthur Edward, born in London 21 Oct., 1862; 2s. John Henry, arm. TRINITY, matric. 15 Oct., 81, aged 18 (from Croydon school), B.A. 87; HONOURS:—2 classical mods. 83, Ægrotat classics 85.

Snow, Thomas Collins, M.A., fellow ST. JOHN'S 75-82, where see page 488.

Snow, William, born at Halifax, Yorks, 10 Aug., 1867; 2s. Thomas, cler. WORCESTER, matric. 19 Oct., 86, aged 19 (from Sedbergh school), scholar 86, B.A. 90, M.A. 93 (HONOURS:—Abbott scholarship 85, 2 classical mods. 88, 3 classics 90); a master at Liverpool institute.

Snowden, Herbert Guy, born in London 5 Nov., 1865; 2s. John Hampden, vicar of Hammersmith. LINCOLN, matric. 17 Oct., 84, aged 18 (from St. Paul's school), scholar 84, B.A. 88, M.A. and B.C.L. 91 (HONOURS:—2 classical mods. 86, 2 classics 88, 2 civil law 90), president of Oxford union soc. 89; bar.-at-law, Middle Temple, 91.

Soames, Edward Roland, born in Herts Nov., 1868; 2s. Stephen, arm. CHRIST CHURCH, matric. 15 Oct., 86, aged 17, from Winchester.

Soames, Francis Archibald, born at Hatfield, Herts, 18 Nov., 1864; 1s. Stephen, arm. TRINITY, matric. 11 Oct., 1884, aged 19 (from Eton), B.A. 88.

Solloway, John, born at Chorley, co. Lane., 1860; o.s. Henry, gen. NON-COLLEGIATE, matric. 3 Nov., 80, aged 23, B.A. 88, M.A. 90.

Solloway, William Major Hatton, born at Oxford 1890; 1s. Major, gen. TURRELL'S HALL, matric. 13 April, 87, aged 28.

Somerset, Raglan George Henry, M.A., student CHRIST CHURCH 49-67, where see page 419.

Soper, Frederick Robert Hawkes, born at Aberystwith, co. Monmouth, 17 Nov., 1868; (gen. fil.) o.s. Isabell MERTON, matric. 22 Oct., 87, aged 18 (from Plymouth coll.), B.A. 91; HONOURS:—3 history 91.

Sorabje, William Francis, born at Rochester 19 July, 1861; 1s. Robert, cler. ORIEL, matric. 19 Oct., 80, aged 19 (from Sutton Valence school), scholar 80-5, B.A. 85; HONOURS:—3 classical mods. 82, 3 classics 84.

Soulsby, Basil Harrington, born at Bessingby, New Zealand, 3 Nov., 1864; o.s. Christopher Percy, arm. CORPUS CHRISTI, matric. 19 Oct., 83, aged 18 (from Cheltenham coll.), B.A. 87; HONOURS:—3 classical mods. 85, 4 history 87.

Southby, Francis Fritz, born at Clifton, co. Glouc., 1868; 3s. Richard William, cler. CORPUS CHRISTI, matric. 22 Oct., 87, aged 19 (from Clifton coll.), B.A. 90; HONOURS:—1 mathematical mods. 88, 2 mathematics 90.

Southcomb, George Hamilton, born at Rose Ash, Devon, 25 July, 1869; o.s. John Hamilton, vicar. WADHAM, matric. 13 Oct., 88, aged 19, B.A. 92.

Southcomb, William Henry Granger, born at Newton Abbot, Devon, 15 April, 1866; 1s. Henry Granger, cler. EXETER, matric. 18 Oct., 85, aged 19 (from Sherborne school), scholar 84, B.A. 89; HONOURS:—2 classical mods. 87, 4 classics 89.

Southern, William Thomas, born at Kenton, Devon, 22 April, 1869; 1s. William, schoolmaster. EXETER, matric. 17 Oct., 88, aged 19 (from Exeter gr. school), scholar 88, B.A. 92; HONOURS:—2 mathematical mods. 90, 2 mathematics 92.

Southey, Ronald, born in London 14 Dec., 1865; 1s. Reginald, D.Med. CHRIST CHURCH, matric. 1 Feb., 86, aged 20, B.A. 89.

Southey, Thomas Castle, M.A., fellow QUEEN'S 59-69, where see page 179.

Southwell, rev. Lionel Jenner, born at Bridgnorth June, 1869; 9s. Thomas Martin, arm. HERTFORD, matric. 19 Jan., 88, aged 18 (from Eastbourne coll.), B.A. 91.

Souttar, Robinson, born at Aberdeen 23 Oct., 1848; 4s. William, gen. NON-COLLEGIATE, matric. 13 Oct., 84, aged 35 (from Aberdeen gymnasium), B.A. 88, M.A. and B.C.L. 91 (HONOURS:—2 history 88, 3 law 89, 1 civil law 90); contested Oxford city 92.

Sowler, Harry, born at Manchester 1869; 2s. Thomas, arm. UNIVERSITY COLL., matric. 15 Oct., 87, aged 18; HONOURS:—3 history 91.

Sowler, Thomas, born at Rusholme, co. Lanc., 11 Sept., 1867; 1s. Thomas, arm. MAGDALEN, matric. 21 Oct., 86, aged 19 (from Harrow), B.A. 89 (HONOURS:—3 history 89); bar.-at-law, Inner Temple, 90.

Spackman, George, born at Farringdon, Berks, 1864; 5s. Frederick Charles, gen. WORCESTER, matric. 26 Jan., 82, aged 18, B.A. 86, M.A. 88.

Sparkes, rev. Charles Ward, born at Barnet, Herts, Oct., 1867; 1s. Charles, cler. KEBLE, matric. 17 Oct., 82, aged 19 (from Canterbury school), B.A. 85 (HONOURS:—4 theology 85); curate of All Saints', Stoke Newington, London, 91.

Sparks, Edmund Jenner, born at Roath, co. Glamorgan, 23 Aug., 1864; y.s. George Davis, cler. JESUS COLL., matric. 18 Oct., 83, aged 19, B.A. 86, M.A. 90; HONOURS:—3 theology 86.

Sparrow, Alan Bertram Hanbury, born at Penn, Salop, 23 Feb., 1863; 4s. Arthur, arm. ORIEL, matric. 29 April, 82, aged 19 (from Rugby), B.A. 85; solicitor.

Sparrow, Hugh Cuthbert Beridge, born at Great Cornard, Suffolk, 27 Aug., 1867; o.s. John Beridge, vicar. ST. JOHN'S, matric. 15 Oct., 87, aged 20 (from Felsted school), B.A. 91.

Sparrow, Isaac, born at Wolverhampton 1871; 1s. John William, gen. CORPUS CHRISTI, matric. 25 Oct., 89, aged 18, from Lanceing coll.

Spaull, rev. Frank William, born at Oswestry, Salop, Oct., 1867; 1s. William Henry, gen. KEBLE, matric. 19 Oct., 86, aged 19 (from Oswestry gr. school), B.A. 90; HONOURS:—4 theology 89.

Speak, Frederick William, born at Baldfield, near Ripon, 4 June, 1871; 1s. John, gen. QUEEN'S, matric. 24 Oct., 90, aged 19 (from Ripon school), exhibitioner 90; HONOURS:—2 classical mods. 92.

Spearing, Martin, born at Southampton 18 Nov., 1873; 1s. James, gent. CHRIST CHURCH, matric. 14 Oct., 92, aged 18 (from the Charterhouse), scholar 92.

Speck, Jocelyn Henry, born in London 25 Dec., 1857; 2s. Edward John, cler. WORCESTER, matric. 25 Jan., 84, aged 26 (from Marlborough), B.A. 87, M.A. 90.

Speke, Frederick John, born at Wallehill, Somerset, 27 Aug., 1871; 2s. Benjamin, late rector of Dowlish Wake, Somerset. CORPUS CHRISTI, matric. 16 Oct., 90, aged 19, from Wellington.

Spence, James Henderson, born at Liverpool 1859; 1s. John, gen. NON-COLLEGIATE, matric. 14 Nov., 84, aged 25, from Liverpool institution.

Spence, William Alfred, born at Bromley, Yorks, 1868; 1s. Joseph, gen. CHRIST CHURCH, matric. 12 Oct., 88, aged 20; HONOURS:—2 history 91 (from Bradford school), scholar 88.

Spencely, Hugh Despencer, born at Liverpool 8 Dec., 1869; 1s. Castle, solicitor. EXETER, matric. 2 May, 90, aged 20, from St. Michael's coll., Tenby, and Harrow.

Spencer, rev. Bertram Stone, born at Maidstone, Kent, 1868; 1s. Alfred, gen. PEMBROKE, matric. 25 Oct., 87, aged 19 (from Canterbury school), B.A. 90; curate of Esh, co. Durham, 91.

Spencer, Charles Gordon, born at Wheatfield, Oxon, 23 Feb., 1869; 4s. Charles Vere, rector. KEBLE, matric. 13 Oct., 88, aged 19 (from Marlborough), exhibitioner 87; Madras c.s. 90.

Spencer, Charles St. David, born at Llandough 1863; 1s. Richard Evans, solicitor. NEW COLL., matric. 15 Oct., 81, aged 18 (from Clifton coll.), exhibitioner 81; B.A. 84; HONOURS:—1 natural science 84.

Spencer, Edmund Vere, born at Wheatfield, Oxon, 13 Nov., 1866; 3s. Charles Vere, rector. KEBLE, matric. 22 Oct., 85, aged 18 (from Haileybury), B.A. 89; HONOURS:—3 classical mods. 87; 4 chemistry 89.

Spencer, Henry Thomas, born at Colchester 11 June, 1869; 1s. Henry, inspector of inland revenue. NON-COLLEGIATE, matric. 11 Oct., 90, aged 21 (from Owens coll., Manchester), B.A., Lond. university, B.S.C., Victoria university.

Spencer, Hugh, born at Bajli, near Allahabad, India, 25 Nov., 1867; 3s. Charles Innes, arm. MAGDALEN, matric. 21 Oct., 86, aged 18 (from Bristol gr. school), deputy 86; assist. magistrate N.W. province India.

Spencer, Hugh Spencer, born at Abingdon, Berks, 1868; 1s. William Henry, arm. NON-COLLEGIATE, matric. 22 Oct., 87, aged 19 (from High Wycombe gr. school), B.A. 91; HONOURS:—3 history 91.

Spencer, John Gordon, born in Barbados 1863; 1s. John Johnson, arm. WADHAM, matric. 26 Jan., 81, aged 18, B.A. 91; HONOURS:—2 classical mods. 82, 3 law 84.

Spencer, Walter Baldwin, born at Stretford, co. Lanc., 23 June, 1860; 1s. Reuben, arm. EXETER, matric. 20 Oct., 81, aged 21 (from Owens coll., Manchester), scholar 81-5, B.A. 84; fellow LINCOLN 86-7 (HONOURS:—1 natural science 84); professor of biology Melbourne university 87.

Spencer, William Cunnington, born in Barbados 1867; 2s. John Johnson, gent. HERTFORD, matric. 16 Dec., 85 (from Harrison coll., Barbados), scholar 85; HONOURS:—1 mathematical mods. 87, 2 mathematics 89.

Spender, Arthur Edmund, born in London Oct., 1871; 2s. Edward, arm. CHRIST CHURCH, matric. 6 June, 90, aged 18, from Radley coll.

Spender, Edward Harold, born at Walcot, near Bath, 22 June, 1864; 2s. John Kent, D.Med. UNIVERSITY COLL., matric. 13 Oct., 83, aged 19 (from Bath coll.), exhibitioner 83, B.A. 88, M.A. 91; HONOURS:—1 classical mods. 84, 1 classics 87.

Spender, John Alfred, born at Bath 23 Dec., 1862; 1s. John Kent, D.Med. BALLIOL, matric. 25 Nov., 81, aged 18 (from Bath coll.), exhibitioner 81-6, B.A. and M.A. 89 (HONOURS:—1 classical mods. 82, 2 classics '85); student Inner Temple 83, journalist.

Spender, Hugh Frederic, born at Walcot, Bath, 1873; 4s. John Kent, of London, D.Med. ORIEL, matric. 27 Oct., 92, aged 19.

Sperling, Arthur Hervey Inker, born at Papworth St. Agnes, Hunts, 7 June, 1856; 1s. Arthur, arm. ST. MARY HALL, matric. 20 Oct., 84, aged 17.

Sperling, Charles Frederick Denne, born at Canterbury 18 March, 1861; 0.s. Charles Brogden of Castle Hedingham, Essex, arm. MAGDALEN, matric. 16 Oct., 80, aged 19 (from Harrow), B.A. 83, M.A. 90; bar.-at-law, Inner Temple, 89.

Sperling, Rowland Arthur Charles, born in London 4 Jan., 1874; 1s. Rowland, commander R.N., deceased. NEW COLL., matric. 14 Oct., 92, aged 18, from Eton.

Spicer, Edward Samuel, born in London 19 Oct., 1873; 1s. Edward, magistrate. WORCESTER, matric. 22 Oct., 91, aged 18.

Spiers, Victor Julian Taylor, born in Paris 1861; 4s. Alexander, arm. UNIVERSITY COLL., matric. 16 Jan., 80, aged 19, exhibitioner 80-3, B.A. 83, M.A. 86; HONOURS:—3 classical mods. 81, Taylorian (French) exhibition 81, 3 history 83.

Spikes, Walter Frederick, born at Tysoe, co. Warwick, 1860; 1s. Frederick, gen. CHARSLEY'S HALL, matric. 17 June, 86, aged 26, B.A. 89.

Spink, Joseph Cooper, born at Walton-on-the-Naze, Essex, 1870; y.s. Daniel, gen. NON-COLLEGIATE, matric. 14 Jan., 88, aged 18, B.A. 92.

Spink, rev. William Jacob, born at Weston-super-Mare 5 Feb., 1866; 4s. Daniel, gent. ST. MARY HALL, matric. 30 April, 85, aged 19, B.A. (NON-COLLEGIATE) 88, M.A. 92; curate of St. Margaret and St. Swithin, Norwich, 90.

Spinks, Frederick William, born in London 1863; 1s. Thomas, Q.C., J.P.; see JOHN'S, matric. 15 Oct., 81, aged 18; bar.-at-law, Inner Temple, 88.

Spooner, Henry Maxwell, M.A., fellow MAGDALEN 68-76, where see page 325.

Spooner, William Archibald, M.A., fellow NEW COLL. 67, where see page 205.

Spooner, Willie Thomas, born at Inglesham, Wilts, 1872; 3s. George Woodbery, vicar. EXETER, matric. 22 Jan., 89, aged 17 (from Magdalen coll. school and Daventry gr. school), B.A. 92; HONOURS:—2 theology 92.

Spottiswoode, Adrian George, born in London 7 Nov., 1867; 1s. George Andrew, arm. MAGDALEN, matric. 21 Oct., 86, aged 18 (from Winchester), B.A. 89.

Spottiswoode, Cyril Andrew, born in London 29 July, 1867; 2s. William, late president royal society. NON-COLLEGIATE, matric. 23 Oct., 86, aged 19 (from Eton); migrated to BRASENOSE.

Spottiswoode, William Hugh, born in London 12 July, 1864; 1s. William, late president royal society. BALLIOL, matric. 17 Oct., 82, aged 18 (from Eton); of Combe Bank, Kent, and of London, Queen's printer.

Spranger, Francis Jefferies Gunner-, born at Malvern, co. Wore., 17 Nov., 1873; 1s. William Francis G.-S., gent. MAGDALEN, matric. 18 Oct., 92, aged 18, from Winchester.

Sproston, Manning Joseph King, born in Demerara 22 Dec., 1868; 4s. Hugh, gen. WORCESTER, matric. 17 Jan., 88, aged 19, from Heidelberg.

Sproston, William Manning Sproston, born at Wolverhampton 1864; 2s. Samuel Thomas, cler. CORPUS CHRISTI, matric. 28 Jan., 82, aged 18, B.A. 85; HONOURS :—4 law 85.

Sproule, Wilfrid Cotton, born at Messingham, co. Lincoln, 21 Jan., 1863; 3s. Thomas Patterson, cler. EXETER, matric. 22 Oct., 80, aged 17 (from Canterbury school), scholar 80-4, B.A. 84; HONOURS :—2 classical mods. 82, 3 classics 84.

Spurling, Cuthbert, born at Blackheath, Kent, Dec., 1868; 6s. Percival, gen. CHRIST CHURCH, matric. 14 Oct. 87, aged 18 (from Blackheath school), scholar 90, B.A. 90; HONOURS :—1 history 90, a civil law 92.

Spurling, rev. Frederick William, M.A., tutor KEBLE 75, where see page 627.

Spurling, Henry Walter, born at Islington, London, 2 Jan., 1874; 1s. Frederick William, cler, NEW COLL., matric. 14 Oct., 92, aged 18 (from Winchester), scholar 91.

Spurrier, rev. Henry Cecil Marriott, born at Roughton, co. Line., 1866; 1s. Henry, rector. PEMBROKE, matric. 28 Oct., 86, aged 20 (from Repton school), B.A. 89; curate of Mottiston with Shorwell, I.W., 90.

Spurrier, rev. Walter Horatio, born at Roughton, co. Lincoln, 2 Oct., 1868; 3s. Henry, rector. BRASE-NOSE, matric. 17 Jan., 88, aged 19 (from Repton school), B.A. 92.

Spyers, Thomas George, born at Weybridge, Surrey, 10 April, 1866; 1s. Henry Almack, cler. MAG-DALEN, matric. 23 Oct., 85, aged 19 (from Radley coll.), demy 84, B.A. 89; HONOURS :—2 classical mods. 87, 2 classics 89.

Spyers, Thomas Roper, born at Faversham, Kent, Dec., 1869; 1s. Thomas Charles, D.Med. KEBLE, matric. 27 Oct., 87, aged 18 (from Radley coll.), B.A. 91; HONOURS :—2 classical mods. 89.

Squire, Frank Reynolds, born in London 6 July, 1862; 3s. William, D.Med. NON-COLLEGIATE, matric. 18 Oct., 80, aged 18 (from Haileybury); migrated to WADHAM 20 Jan., 82, and also to TURRELL'S HALL, B.A. 92.

Squire, William Harold, born in London 14 Feb., 1861; 1s. William Stevens, arm. ST. JOHN'S, matric. 27 April, 81, aged 20 (from Rugby), scholar 84, B.A. 84, M.A. 87; HONOURS :—3 law 84); bar.-at-law, Middle Temple, 86.

Squires, rev. Henry Charles, M.A., WADHAM, where see page 534.

Stacey, Thomas, born at Sleete, co. Glouc., 5 Aug., 1873; 2s. John Thomas Cyril, cler. MERTON, matric. 22 Oct., 91, aged 18, from Eton.

Stafford, George Frederick, born at Anquipa, Peru, 1863; o.s. George, gen. BALLIOL, matric. 17 Oct., 82, aged 19, from Woburn school.

Stafford, Roland Genet, born at Chelsea 8 Sept., 1870; 1s. Henry Edmund, gen. ST. MARY HALL, matric. 14 Oct., 89, aged 19.

Stainer, Charles Lewis, born at Oxford 7 June, 1871; 4s. sir John, prof. of music. CHRIST CHURCH, matric. 8 June, 89, aged 18, from St. Mark's school, Windsor.

Stainer, Edward, born at Oxford 16 Dec., 1869; 2s. sir John, prof. of music. MAGDALEN, matric. 16 Oct., 88, aged 18 (from St. Paul's school), demy 87, B.A. 92; HONOURS :—2 physiology 92.

Stainer, sir John, D.Mus., university professor of music, hon. fellow MAGDALEN 92, where see page 320.

Stainer, John Frederick Randall, born at Oxford 2 Oct., 1866; 1s. sir John, professor of music. MAGDALEN, matric. 23 Oct., 85, aged 19 (from Winchester), exhibitioner 85, B.A. 89, M.A. and B.C.L. 92; HONOURS :—1 classical mods. 87, 2 classics 89.

Stainer, William Edgar, born at Oxford Oct., 1873; 4s. sir John, professor of music. CHRIST CHURCH, matric. 6 Feb., 92, aged 18, from Magdalen coll. school.

Stainton, Nathaniel Evelyn William, born in London. CHRIST CHURCH, matric. 4 June, 1881, aged 18, from Winchester.

Stallard, Frederick Charles Frampton, born in London 4 June, 1871; 3s. William Henry, gen. NON-COLLEGIATE, matric. 11 Oct., 90, aged 19, from St. Edward's school, Summertown, Oxford.

Stallard, Henry Frampton, born at Norwood, Surrey, 3 Aug., 1863; 1s. William Henry, gen. NON-COL-LEGIATE, matric. 13 Oct., 83, aged 20 (from Merchant Taylors' school); migrated to MERTON, B.A. 87, M.A. 90; HONOURS:—2 history 87.

Stallard, Leonard Bristowe, born at Heath, Beds, 11 April, 1873; 4s. Joseph Orlando, cler. KEBLE, matric. 20 Oct., 91, aged 18, from Berkhamstead school.

Stallard, rev. Oswald William, born at Heath, Beds, 7 July, 1869; 3s. Joseph Orlando, cler. KEBLE, matric. 13 Oct., 86, aged 19 (from Berkhamstead school), B.A. 92; HONOURS :—3 classical mods. 90, 2 theology 92.

Stammers, Maurice, born at Hastings 1863; 1s. Frederick, cler. CHARSLEY'S HALL, matric. 25 Jan., 82, aged 18.

Stampa, Lelio, born at Constantinople 14 June, 1873; 1s. George Dominic, late architect and C.E. MAG-DALEN, matric. 18 Oct., 92, aged 19 (from Bedford gr. school), demy 92.

Stamps, Frederick, born at West Bromwich, co. Stafford, 1851; 2s. John, gen. QUEEN'S, matric. 4 Feb., 84, aged 33, B.Mus. 92.

Stanbridge, John William, B.D., fellow ST. JOHN'S 70-82, where see page 487.

Stancomb, William, born at Cirencester 13 May, 1874; 1s. William, M.A., J.P., Wilts. MAGDALEN, matric. 18 Oct., 92, aged 18, from Eton.

Standen, rev. James Edward, born in London 1865; o.s. James William, gen. ST. JOHN'S, matric. 11 Oct., 84, aged 19 (from Merchant Taylors' school), scholar 84, B.A. 88, M.A. 91; HONOURS ; —1 classical mods. 86, 3 classics 88.

Stanfield, Arthur John Charles, born at Wakefield, Yorks, 7 May, 1864 ; 1s. Alfred, arm. UNIVERSITY COLL., matric. 13 Oct., 83, aged 19 (from Westminster school), B.A. 87, M.A. 90; HONOURS :—4 law 87.

Stanford, Charles Villiers, created D.Mus. 14 June, 1883. See *Al. Ox.* and series 1341.

Stanford, rev. Charles Woodward, born at Monkstown, co. Dublin, Jan., 1863; 2s. John Woodward, gen. WORCESTER, matric. 26 Jan., 82, aged 19 (from Denstone coll. and Uppingham), B.A. 84, M.A. 89; curate of Louth St. Michael, co. Line., 88.

Stanhope, hon. and ven. Berkeley Lionel Scudamore, M.A., archdeacon of Hereford, fellow ALL SOULS' 46-58, where see page 279.

Stanhope, hon. Charles Hay Scudamore, born at Llandudno, co. Carnarvon, 28 Aug., 1864 ; 6s. sir Henry Edwyn Chandos, bart. (earl of Chesterfield). NEW COLL., matric. 18 Oct., 88 ; HONOURS :—4 history 87. (from Rugby), B.A. 88

Stanhope, right hon. Edward, B.A., fellow ALL SOULS' 62-70, where see page 281.

Stanhope, rev. Lyonel Scudamore, born at Bosbury, co. Hereford, 9 Dec., 1861; 1s. Berkeley Lionel Scudamore, rector of Byford, co. Hereford. NEW COLL., matric. 16 Oct., 80, aged 18 (from Harrow), B.A. 84, M.A. 89 (HONOURS :—2 classical mods. 82, 4 classics 84); curate of Weymouth Holy Trinity 86.

Stanhope, Philip Bertie Spencer-, born in London 17 Dec., 1868; 4s. Walter Thomas William. CHRIST CHURCH, matric. 15 Jan., 87, aged 18 (from Eton), B.A. 91.

Stanhope, Walter Thomas William Spencer, M.A., student CHRIST CHURCH 47-52, where see page 416.

Stanier, William Sneyd, born at Betley, co. Staff., 5 May, 1871; 3s. Francis. gen. QUEEN'S, matric. 27 Oct., 91, aged 20, from Kadley coll.

Staniland, Alfred Edward, born at Boston, co. Linc., 30 May, 1861; 5s. Meaburn. gen. MAGDALEN, matric. 19 Jan., 80, aged 18 (from Eton), B.A. 84; bar.-at-law, Inner Temple, 85.

Stanistreet, Arthur Handel, born at Clonmel, Ireland, 1859; 5s. Thomas Dawson, gen., incorporated from Trinity coll., Dublin, (NON-COLLEGIATE) 5 Nov., 91, aged 32.

Stanley, rev. Cyril, born at Felsted, Essex, 25 Sept., 1860; 1s. Robert Rainy Pennington, vicar, deceased. QUEEN'S, matric. 24 Jan., 80, aged 19 (from Brighton coll.); curate of Hackney 89.

Stanley, hon. Edward Lyulph, M.A., fellow BALLIOL 62-9, where see page 67.

Stanley, rev. Gerald, born at Felsted, Essex, Aug., 1865; 3s. Robert Rainy Pennington, cler. NON-COLLEGIATE, matric. 19 Jan., 85, aged 19 (from a Cliftonville school, W. Brighton), B.A. 88, M.A. 91; curate of Burgess Hill, Sussex, 90.

Stanley, Henry Morton (originally John Rowlands), African explorer. Created D.C.L. 25 June, 1890 (s. — Rowlands), born near Denbigh 28 Jan., 41; D.C.L. Durham, LL.D. Cambridge 23 Oct., 90. See *Men and Women of the Time*.

Stanley, Herbert James, born at Manchester 25 July, 1872; 1s. Sigismund, esq., deceased. BALLIOL, matric. 20 Oct., 91, aged 19 (from Eton); HONOURS :—3 classical mods. 93.

Stansfeld, John Stedward, born at Walworth, Surrey, 1856; 2s. Alfred, gen. NON-COLLEGIATE, matric. 4 Nov., 86, aged 30 (from Hammersmith middle class school), B.A. 89, M.A. 93.

Stanton, rev. Wilfred James, born at Thelwall, Cheshire, 1862; 2s. Henry, arm. BRASENOSE, matric. 26 Jan., 81, aged 19 (from Eton), B.A. 84, M.A. 87; curate of Wallasey, Cheshire, 85-92.

Stapleton, rev. Gilbert, born in London 11 May, 1862; 1s. John, arm. ORIEL, matric. 20 Oct., 80, aged 18 (from Haileybury), B.A. 84, M.A. 87; vicar of Herriard, Hants, 91.

Stapylton, Robert Miles, born at Manchester April, 1864; 1s. Robert George, arm. ST. JOHN'S, matric. 13 Oct., 83, aged 19 (from Lancaster gr. school), B.A. 87, M.A. 90.

Stapylton, William Chetwynd, M.A., fellow MERTON 47-51, where see page 97.

Stark, William, born at Elgin, co. Moray, 1869; 1s. James, cler. NON-COLLEGIATE, matric. 12 Oct., 89, aged 20, from Aberdeen university.

Starkey, Cyril Edgar Frodsham, born at Bygrave, Herts, 1853; 0.s. Arthur Brydon Cross, rector, PEMBROKE, matric. 26 Oct., 81, aged 18 (from Brighton), scholar 81-5, B.A. 85, M.A. 88; HONOURS :—1 classical mods. 83, 3 classics 85.

Starkie, Edmund Arthur Le Gendre, born at Huntroyd, co. Lanc., 10 Feb., 1871; 1s. Le Gendre Nicholas, arm. CHRIST CHURCH, matric. 12 Oct., 88, aged 17, from Eton.

Starling, rev. John Little, born at Higham, Essex, May, 1862; 1s. Thomas John, arm. KEBLE, matric. 18 Oct., 81, aged 19, B.A. 84, M.A. 91; curate of St. Mark, Denmark Hill, Surrey, 90.

Starling, rev. James Henshaw, born at Higham Ferrers, Northants, Aug., 1863; 2s. Thomas John, arm. KEBLE, matric. 18 Oct., 81, aged 18, B.A. 85, M.A. 88 (HONOURS :—4 history 84); curate of St. Stephen, Guernsey, 91.

Startin, Eliot George Bromley, born at Powyke, co. Worc., 1866; 1s. George Edward, arm. NEW COLL., matric. 16 Oct., 85, aged 19.

Stebbing, rev. Thomas Roscoe Rede, M.A., fellow WORCESTER 60-8, where see page 576.

Stebbing, William, M.A., fellow WORCESTER 56-71, where see page 576.

Stedall, Bertram Pemberton, born in London 19 March, 1869; 1s. Henry, arm. MERTON, matric. 22 Oct., 87, aged 18, from Marlborough.

Steedman, rev. Charles Mackenzie, born at Cape Town 1859; 4s. Daniel, gen. ST. EDMUND HALL, matric. 20 Jan., 81, aged 22 (from Edinburgh university, M.A. 80), B.A. 84, M.A. 87 (HONOURS ; —2 theology 84); curate of Somerton, Wilts, 90.

Steedman, Henry Percy Gormanston, born at Ootacamund, East Indies, 2 March, 1870; 2s. Andrew Harrington, arm. BRASENOSE, matric. 14 Oct., 89, aged 19, from Clifton coll.

Steedman, James William, born at High Ercall, Salop, 1872; 4s. Edward Blackeway, gen. CHRIST CHURCH, matric. 16 Oct., 91, aged 19 (from Shrewsbury school); HONOURS :—3 classical mods. 93.

Steele, Charles Henry, born at Carlisle April, 1868; o.s. Robert, gen. KEBLE, matric. 17 Oct., 87, aged 19 (from Fettes coll.), B.A. 91; HONOURS :—3 classical mods. 89.

Steele, Frederick Augustus Shafto, born at Swanage, Dorset, 22 Aug., 1861; 1s. Frederick Stephen, captain. BRASENOSE, matric. 21 May, 80, aged 18 (from Cheltenham coll.), B.A. 85; bar.-at-law, Inner Temple, 86.

Steele, William Kenneth, born in London 14 Jan., 1865; 2s. John Charles, of Guy's hospital, D. Med. MERTON, matric. 25 Jan., 84, aged 19, from Merchant Taylors' school.

Steevens, George Warrington, born at Sydenham, Kent, 1870; 1s. James, gen. BALLIOL, matric. 18 Oct., 88, aged 18 (from city of London school), scholar 89; fellow PEMBROKE 92, B.A. 93; OXFORD HONOURS :—accessit 88, proxime accessit Hertford scholarship 89, 1 classical mods. 89, 1 classics 92; LONDON HONOURS :—1st in matric. 89, 1 Latin 89, 1 classics 90.

Steinmitz, rev. Bernard, born at Harrow Weald, Middx., 3 Nov., 1866; 3s. John Henry, arm. NEW COLL., matric. 16 Oct., 85, aged 18 (from Harrow), B.A. 89; HONOURS :—3 classical mods. 87, 3 classics 89.

Stenhouse, Frank, born at Hampstead 9 April, 1862; 3s. Thomas, arm. TRINITY, matric. 17 Oct., 85, aged 23 (from Merchant Taylors' school); died 8 Feb., 88.

Stenhouse, Vivian Denman, born at Brixton, Surrey, 1871; 1s. George, born at Maidstone, Kent, 4 May, 1873; 1s. Frederick Stovold, solicitor. ST. JOHN'S, matric. 17 Oct., 91, aged 18 (from Merchant Taylors' school), exhibitioner 91; HONOURS :—3 classical mods. 93.

Stenning, Frank George, born at Battersea, Surrey, 14 Feb., 1868; 2s. Edward, gen. WADHAM, matric. 16 Oct., 86, aged 18 (from Merchant Taylors' school), exhibitioner 86, B.A. 89; senior demy MAGDALEN 92; HONOURS :—Hebrew scholarship 87 and 89, 2 theology 89, Syriac prize 90, 1 Semitic languages 91, theological scholarship 92, Septuagint prize 88 and 92.

Stenning, John Frederick, born at Battersea, Surrey, 14 Feb., 1868; 2s. Edward, gen. WADHAM, matric. 16 Oct., 86, aged 18 (from Merchant Taylors' school), exhibitioner 86, B.A. 90; senior demy MAGDALEN 92; HONOURS :—Hebrew scholarship 87 and 89, 2 theology 89, Syriac prize 90, 1 Semitic languages 91, theological scholarship 92, Septuagint prize 88 and 92.

Stephan, William, born at Ironbridge, Salop, 1848; 3s. Henry, gent. NON-COLLEGIATE, matric. 15 Oct., 92, aged 44, from St. Aidans coll., Birkenhead.

Stephens, Archibald Collingwood, born at Darlington, co. Durham, 18 Nov., 1868; 1s. William Henry, cler. JESUS COLL., matric. 19 Oct., 87, aged 18 (from Rugby), scholar 87, B.A. 92; HONOURS:—2 classical mods. 89, 2 classics 91.

Stephens, Charles Hook, born at Funtington Lavant, Sussex, 10 March, 1874; o.s. rev. William Richard Wood, M.A. CHRIST CHURCH, matric. 14 Oct., '92, aged 18, from Winchester.

Stephens, David Evan, born at Holcwm, co. Carmarthen, 1 July, 1862; 1s. John, arm. MAGDALEN, matric. 16 Oct., 80, aged 18 (from the Charterhouse), B.A. 83.

Stephens, Francis Edward Morse, born at Twickenham 21 May, 1864; 2s. John Edward, D.Med. Edin, WADHAM, matric. 23 Oct., 82, aged 18, from Haileybury.

Stephens, William John, M.A., fellow QUEEN'S 53-69, where see page 179.

Stephenson, Hugh Lansdown, born in London 1871; 5s. Charles, arm. CHRIST CHURCH, matric. 10 Oct., 90, aged 19 (from Westminster school), scholar 90; HONOURS:—2 classical mods. 92.

Stephenson, John Henry Nöell, born at Calcutta 28 Sept., 1872; 1s. John, cler. TRINITY, matric. 17 Oct., 91, aged 19, from Marlborough.

Stephenson, Stuart, born at Buxton, co. Derby, 19 Dec., 1867; 4s. Robert, gen. CORPUS CHRISTI, matric. 26 Oct., 85, aged 17 (from Kingswood school), scholar 85, B.A. 89; HONOURS:—1 mathematical mods. 87, 2 mathematics 89.

Stern, Henry Alfred, born in London 1862; 1s. Henry Aaron, cler. CORPUS CHRISTI, matric. 21 Oct. 80, aged 18 (from St. Paul's school), scholar 80-1 (HONOURS:—2 mathematical mods. 81), from Downing coll., Cambridge, 1 Feb., 82; scholar 84, B.A. 84, M.A. 90 (HONOURS:—35th senior optime.

Sterry, Wascy, born at Stockland, Devon, 26 July, 1866; 1s. Francis, cler. MERTON, matric. 24 Oct., 85, aged 19 (from Eton), exhibitioner 85, B.A. 89 (HONOURS:—2 classical mods. 87, 2 classics 89); bar.-at-law, Lincoln's Inn, 92.

Stert, Lionel Richard, born at Lamarsh, Essex, 25 Feb., 1865; 2s. Arthur Richard, cler. EXETER, matric. 18 Oct., 83, aged 18 (from Cheltenham coll.), exhibitioner 83-5; HONOURS:—3 classical mods. 85.

Stevens, Francis Joseph, born at Enfield, Middx., 27 April, 1867; 5s. Thomas, bar.-at-law. CHRIST CHURCH, matric. 16 June, 87, aged 25 (from Kensington school, St. Bartholomew's and King's coll., Cambridge, matric. 28 Jan., 85), exhibitioner EXETER 87, B.A. 90 (HONOURS:—3 physiology 90); M.R.C.S.

Stevens, George Thomas Edmund, born in London 1861; 1s. George Thomas, arm. NON-COLLEGIATE, matric. 17 Jan., 80, aged 19.

Stevens, rev. Harold, born at Swansea, co. Glamorgan, 1864; 5s. John Sergent, gen. CHRIST CHURCH, matric. 25 May, 83, aged 19, B.A. 87; curate of St. Paul Cliftonville, Margate, Kent, 96.

Stevens, rev. Harry Edward, born in London 1859; 1s. Edward Thomas, cler. NON-COLLEGIATE, matric. 25 Oct., 80, aged 21 (from Rossall school); migrated to TURRELL'S HALL, B.A. 92.

Stevens, Herbert Percy, born at Brockmoor, co. Staff., 25 July, 1869; o.s. Enoch, vicar. ST. JOHN'S, matric. 12 Oct., 89, aged 20 (from Stourbridge school); HONOURS:—3 classical mods. 91.

Stevens, Thomas Moffitt, born at Liverpool 31 Aug., 1860; 1s. Thomas Warner, gen. NON-COLLEGIATE, matric. 17 Jan., 80, aged 19 (from University school, Hastings); migrated to CHRIST CHURCH, B.A. 83, M.A. and R.C.L. 86 (HONOURS:—2 law 83, 2 civil law 85); bar.-at-law, Gray's Inn, 86.

Stevens, William Alan, born at Norwood, Surrey, 1 June, 1871; 1s. William, gen. MERTON, matric. 22 Oct., 91, aged 20, from Uppingham school.

Stevenson, Francis Seymour, born in the Mauritius 1863; 2s. sir William, K.C.B., governor of Mauritius. BALLIOL, matric. 29 Jan., 81, aged 18 (from Harrow), exhibitioner 79-84, B.A. 84 (HONOURS:—2 classical mods. 82, 1 classics 84); a student of Lincoln's Inn 83, M.P. (Eye division) North East Suffolk Dec., 85.

Stevenson, George James Hardress, born at Brighton 1863; o.s. William George, arm. NON-COLLEGIATE, matric. 14 Oct., 82, aged 19, from Eton.

Stevenson, John Sinclair, born at Rathgar, co. Dublin, 4 Feb., 1868; 1s. William Fleming, D.D. LINCOLN, matric. 22 Oct., 86, aged 18 (from Clifton coll.), scholar 86, B.A. 91; HONOURS:—2 classical mods. 88, 3 classics 90.

Stevinson, John Sandbach, born at Cottenham, co. Camb., 12 June, 1872; 1s. John, cler. PEMBROKE, matric. 25 Oct., 90, aged 18 (from Queen's coll., Taunton), scholar 90; HONOURS:—3 classical mods. 92.

Steward, Henry Allan Holden, born at Stafford 18 May, 1865; 2s. Walter Holden, arm. NEW COLL., matric. 8 Dec., 83, aged 18 (from the Charterhouse), B.A. 86 (HONOURS:—1 law 86); bar.-at-law, Inner Temple, 90.

Stewart, Alexander Arthur Grainger, born at Dalkeith, Edinburgh, 1867; 1s. Thomas Grainger, D.Med. CHRIST CHURCH, matric. 14 Oct., 87, aged 20, from Edinburgh university.

Stewart, rev. Alexander Lamont, born at Trinidad 2 June, 1858; 2s. Alexander, gen., deceased. ST. EDMUND HALL, matric. 25 Oct., 81, aged 23 (from Clifton coll.); migrated to MAGDALEN 83, B.A. 85; rector of Aisholt, Somerset, 88.

Stewart, Arthur Henry, born at Worthing, Sussex, 11 April, 1868; o.s. Henry King, arm., deceased. NEW COLL., matric. 18 Oct., 87, aged 19 (from Eton), exhibitioner 87, B.A. 91; HONOURS:—1 morphology 91.

Stewart, Bertrand, born in London Oct., 1872; 1s. Charles. CHRIST CHURCH, matric. 10 Oct., 90, aged 18, from Eton.

Stewart, Charles, born in the Bermudas 1856; 3s. Francis, gen. TURRELL'S HALL, matric. 23 April, 87, aged 31.

Stewart, Charles Edward, born at Paris 1862; o.s. Charles, arm. BRASENOSE, matric. 10 June, 81; aged 19 (from Eton), B.A. 85, M.A. 88; bar.-at-law, Inner Temple, 86.

Stewart, genl. sir Donald Martin, bart, G.C.B., created D.C.L. 17 June, 1891; born 1 March, 24.

Stewart, Francis Hugh, born at Calcutta 5 Nov., 1869; o.s. Robert, arm. MAGDALEN, matric. 14 Oct., 90, aged 20 (from Harrow); HONOURS:—2 classical mods. 92.

Stewart, Francis William Sutton, born at Christ Church, New Zealand, Jan., 1865; 1s. Francis Edward, arm. CHRIST CHURCH, matric. 25 May, 83, aged 18, scholar 86, B.A. 87 (HONOURS:—2 history 87, 3 civil law 88); bar.-at-law, Inner Temple, 87.

Stewart, Gordon Kinross Cumbrae, born at St. Kilda, near Melbourne, 1873; 4s. Francis Edward, arm. CHRIST CHURCH, matric. 29 May, 91, aged 18.

Stewart, Haldane Campbell, born in London 28 Feb., 1868; 3s. John, bar.-at-law. MAGDALEN, matric. 22 Oct., 87, aged 19 (from Magdalen coll. school), exhibitioner 87, B.A. 93; HONOURS :—3 classical mods. 89, 4 classics 91.

Stewart, Hugh, born at Nuneaton, co. Warwick, 1873; o.s. Charles John, arm. CHARSLEY'S HALL, matric. 19 Feb., 87, aged 14.

Stewart, Houston Michael Shaw, born in London 3 Oct., 1871; 3s. Michael Shaw, baronet. CHRIST CHURCH, matric. 10 Oct., 90, aged 19, from Eton.

Stewart, John Alexander, M.A., senior student CHRIST CHURCH 70-5 and 82, where see page 408.

Stewart, Robert Burton, born at Chertsey, Surrey, 20 Dec., 1864; 2s. Robert, arm. TRINITY, matric. 15 Oct., 83, aged 18 (from Dulwich coll.), B.A. 86, M.A. 91 (HONOURS :—3 law 86); student of the Inner Temple 83, assist. collector and magistrate Ahmednagar, Bombay c.s.

Stewart, Robert Bruce, born in London 23 April, 1863; 2s. John, bar.-at-law. MAGDALEN, matric. 16 Oct., 82, aged 19 (from Queen's school, Basingstoke), B.A. 87.

Stewart, Walter James Lionel, born at Notting Hill, London, 9 April, 1866 ; o.s. Robert Walter Daysh, bar.-at-law, deceased. ST. JOHN'S, matric. 17 Oct., 91, aged 25, from Sutton Valence and Worcester schools.

Stewart, William Burton, born at Glasgow 27 Dec., 1872; 1s. James, merchant. BRASENOSE, matric. 22 Oct., 91, aged 18, from Loretto school.

Stickland, Charles Edward, born at Trieste 28 May, 1860; 1s. John, arm. NON-COLLEGIATE, matric. 17 Oct., 81, aged 20 (from Tavistock school), B.A. 84; HONOURS :—3 classical mods. 83.

Stickland, rev. Robert Pattison, born at Millbrook, Hants, 1860; o.s. Robert, arm. MERTON, matric. 26 Feb., 80, aged 20, B.A. 83, M.A. 86; chaplain and secretary Blind school, Southwark, 87.

Stiffe, Norman Cecil, born in London 2 Nov., 1872; 2s. Arthur William, captain (late) Indian Navy. WORCESTER, matric. 22 Oct., 91, aged 18 (from Radley coll.), exhibitioner 92; HONOURS :—2 classical mods. 93.

Still, Arthur Langford, born at Addington, Surrey, 1872; 2s. Henry, gen. CHRIST CHURCH, matric. 16 Oct., 91, aged 19 (from Tonbridge school), exhibitioner 90.

Stillingfleet, Clement Victor, born at Hampton Bishop, co. Hereford, 1873; 6s. Henry James William, cler. ST. JOHN'S, matric. 17 Oct., 91, aged 18, from Hereford school.

Stilwell, Geoffrey Holt, born at Wimbledon, Surrey, 4 July, 1865; 1s. John Pakenham, of Yateley, Hants, arm. MAGDALEN, matric. 24 Jan., 84, aged 18 (from Eton), B.A. 87, M.A. 91.

Stirling, Charles Goodbarne, born at New Malden, Surrey, 23 Jan., 1866; 1s. Charles, cler. EXETER, matric. 23 Oct., 85, aged 19 (from St. Paul's school), B.A. 89, M.A. 93; HONOURS :—3 classical mods. 87.

Stirling, William Hockin, born at New Malden, Surrey, 31 Aug., 1869; 2s. Thomas, cler. ORIEL, matric. 18 Oct., 87, aged 18 (from Monkton Combe school), B.A. 91.

Stobart, St. Clair Kelburn Mulholland, born at Warkton, Northants, 1862; 1s. Henry, cler. ORIEL, matric. 19 Oct., 82, aged 18 (from Winchester), B.A. 88; HONOURS :—4 history 84.

Stock, Edward Innes, born in London 1866; 1s. Edward Ward, bar.-at-law. EXETER, matric. 16 Oct., 84, aged 18 (from Winchester), B.A. 87; died 20 July, 92, at Davos Platz.

Stock, Leslie, born at Windermere 1862; y.s. Edward Poche, cler. EXETER, matric. 20 Oct., 81, aged 19 (from Felstead school), B.A. 86; in University eight 84.

Stock, rev. Osmund, born at Northfield, co. Glouc., 1865; 6s. Thomas Strutt, gen. CHRIST CHURCH, matric. 31 May, 84, aged 18 (from Radley coll.), B.A. 87, M.A. 91; curate of Burwell, eo. Camb., 88.

Stock, Reginald Ashley, born at Douglas, isle of Man, 1852; 3s. St. George Henry, arm. CHARSLEY'S HALL, matric. 17 Jan., 90, aged 38.

Stock, St. George, M.A., PEMBROKE, where see page 556.

Stockdale, Robert, born at Austwick, Yorks, 1865; 1s. William, gen. QUEEN'S, matric. 22 Oct., 84, aged 19 (from Giggleswick school), exhibitioner 84, B.A. 88, M.A. 92; HONOURS :—2 chemistry 88.

Stocken, Stanley Beynon, born at Clapham, Surrey, Nov., 1868; 2s. John Alfred, gen. CHRIST CHURCH, matric. 3 June, 87, aged 18, from Lancing coll.

Stocker, William Nelson, M.A., fellow BRASENOSE 77, where see page 349.

Stocks, Edward Vazielle, born at Salford, co. Lanc., 22 April, 1870; 3s. William, cler. TURRELL'S WADHAM, matric. 14 Oct., 89, aged 19 (from Manchester gr. school); HONOURS :—2 classical mods. 91.

Stocks, William Cecil, born at Market Harborough 2 Sept., 1872; 1s. John Edward, vicar. NEW COLL., matric. 16 Oct., 91, aged 19 (from Winchester); scholar 90; HONOURS :—1 classical mods. 93.

Stoddart, Doveton Vincent, born at Wellington, co. Derby, 1848; 4s. William, cler. TURRELL'S HALL, matric. 16 May, 89, aged 41.

Stoehr, Emil Moritz, born at Fallowfield, co. Lanc., 27 Jan., 1864; 3s. Emil Moritz, gen. BALLIOL, matric. 19 Oct., 87, aged 23, from Rugby and Owens coll., Manchester.

Stoehr, Friedrich Otto, born at Brighton 19 Nov., 1871; 3s. Emil Moritz, arm. TRINITY, matric. 11 Oct., 90, aged 18, from Clifton coll.

Stokes, Arthur Hill, born in London 1863; 3s. Henry James, D.Med. BALLIOL, matric. 17 Oct., 82, aged 19 (from Highgate school); selected candidate Indian c.s. 82.

Stokes, Hopetoun Gabriel, born at Ootacamund, Madras, 1873; 3s. sir Harry Edward, K.C.S.I., Madras c.s. ORIEL, matric. 27 Oct., 92, aged 19 (from Clifton coll.), scholar 92.

Stokes, Whitley, C.S.I., C.I.E., created D.C.L. 17 June, 1885, hon. fellow JESUS COLL. 82, where see page 470.

Stokoe, Cecil George, born at Richmond, Yorks, 9 April, 1867; 2s. Thomas Henry, D.D. TRINITY, matric. 12 Oct., 89, aged 22 (from St. Paul's school), B.A. 92; HONOURS :—4 history 92.

Stokoe, Ernest William, born at Clifton 18 Feb., 1862; 2s. Thomas Henry, D.D. KEBLE, matric. 18 Oct., 81, aged 19 (from Reading gr. school), B.A. 86, M.A. 89.

Stokoe, Henry Robert, born at Uppingham, Rutland, 27 Jan., 1861; 1s. Thomas Henry, D.D. ORIEL, matric. 20 Oct., 80, aged 19 (from Reading and King's coll., London), exhibitioner 80-5, B.A. 85, M.A. 90; HONOURS :—2 classical mods. 82, 3 classics 84.

Stona, rev. John, born at Southampton 17 June, 1859; 1s. John, gen. ST. MARY HALL, matric. 20 Oct., 80, aged 20; migrated to WORCESTER, B.A. 83, M.A. 87 (HONOURS :—3 theology 84); vicar of Mount Hawke, Cornwall, 90.

Stone, Arundell Arthur, born in London 3 Jan., 1871; 1s. William Alfred, chartered accountant. MERTON, matric. 15 Oct., 90, aged 19, from St. Edward's school, Summertown.

Stone, Edward James, of CHRIST CHURCH, M.A., Radcliffe observer 77, see page 426.

Stone, Frederick, born at Summertown, near Oxford, 1859; 2s. John, gen. NON-COLLEGIATE, matric. 13 Oct., 83, aged 24, B.A. 86, M.A. 90; HONOURS:—3 theology 86.

Stone, Henry Charles, born at Govilon-juxta-Abergavenny 13 Sept., 1870; 7s. Henry, capt. of infantry. WADHAM, matric. 14 Oct., 89, aged 19, from Denstone coll., co. Stafford.

Stone, Henry Jessup, born at Sutton, Surrey, 1864; o.s. Henry Robert, gen. BRASENOSE, matric. 15 Jan., 83, aged 19 (from Malden school); of Havering-atte-Bower, Essex.

Stone, Henry Richard, born at Wideombe, near Bath, 1857; 1s. Henry, gen. UNIVERSITY COLL., matric. 15 Oct., 87, aged 30.

Stone, John Rhys, born at Llanblethian, co. Glamorgan, 1866; 4s. Henry, arm. HERTFORD, matric. 18 Oct., 83, aged 17.

Stone, Neville Roper, born at Tunbridge Wells 21 Jan., 1873; 1s. Frank William, solicitor. ORIEL, matric. 27 Oct., 91, aged 18, from Radley coll.

Stone, Park Nelson, born at Fulham, Surrey, 1868; 2s. William, arm. BALLIOL, matric. 19 Oct., 86, aged 18 (from Eton), B.A. 89; HONOURS: —2 law 89.

Stone, William Grannt, born at Liverpool 1867; 1s. William, gen. BALLIOL, matric. 10 Feb., 86, aged 19 (from Eton), B.A. 89; HONOURS : —2 classical mods. 87, 2 classics 89.

Stonehouse, John Robinson, born at West Barnby, Yorks, 1869; 1s. William, gen. NON-COLLEGIATE, matric. 21 Jan., 82, aged 23, from a Middlesborough school.

Stones, Harry, born at Horwich, co. Lanc., 29 Oct., 1868; 1s. James, gen. MERTON, matric. 22 Jan., 91, aged 22 from Owens coll., Manchester; HONOURS:—3 classical mods. 92.

Stoney, rev. Francis Shirley, born at Wolverhampton 1863; 1s. Robert Baker, cler. NON-COLLEGIATE, matric. 17 Oct., 81, aged 18; migrated to ST. JOHN'S 81, B.A. 86, M.A. 88; curate of Aylesbury, Bucks, 89.

Stoney, Ralph Sadleir, born at Ribby-cum-Wren, co. Lanc., 1 Sept., 1872; 1s. Ralph Sadleir, vicar. CHRIST CHURCH, matric. 16 Oct., 91, aged 19, from Rossall school.

Stoney, William, born at Loughborough, co. Leic., 1856; 2s. Robert Baker, cler. CHRIST CHURCH, matric. 16 Oct., 85, aged 19 (from Wolverhampton school), scholar 85; B.A. 89 (HONOURS :—1 mathematical mods. 87, 1 mathematics 89); bar.-at-law, Lincoln's Inn, 91.

Storr, Frank, born at Brenchley, Kent, 10 Feb., 1872; 1s. Charles, cler. NEW COLL., matric. 10 Oct., 90, aged 18 (from Harrow), scholar 89; HONOURS:—2 classical mods. 92.

Storr, Frederick Arnott, born at Rastrick, Yorks, 17 April, 1865; 2s. Thomas Arnott, gen. QUEEN'S, matric. 22 Oct., 84, aged 19 (from Bradford gr. school), exhibitioner 84, B.A. 88; HONOURS:—3 mathematics mods. 86, 4 mathematics 88.

Storr, George Goldthorpe, born at Rastrick, Yorks, 1860; 1s. Thomas Arnott, gen. BRASENOSE, matric. 22 Jan., 80, aged 20 (from Bradford school), scholar 79-84, B.A. 84, M.A. 87; HONOURS:—3 mathematical mods. 81, 3 mathematics 83.

Storr, Vernon Faithfull, born at Mudnapilly, Madras, 4 Dec., 1869; o.s. Edward, arm. QUEEN'S, matric. 20 Oct., 88, aged 18 (from Clifton coll.), scholar 88, B.A. 92; HONOURS :—2 classical mods. 90, 1 classics 92, Aubrey Moore theological studentship 93.

Storrar, John Ireland, born at Grittleton, Wilts, 16 July, 1867; 1s. Robert, gen. EXETER, matric. 23 Oct., 85, aged 18 (from Bath coll.), B.A. 88, M.A. 93.

Story, Thomas William, born at King Moor, near Carlisle, 1863; 1s. John, gen. NON-COLLEGIATE, matric. 22 Jan., 81, aged 18 (from Carlisle high school), B.A. 84, M.A. 87; HONOURS: —a natural science 84.

Story, William, M.A., LL.B., Harvard university, U.S.A.; created D.C.L. 22 June, 1887; commander of the order of the crown of Italy; poet and sculptor (s. Joseph); born 12 Feb., 19. See Al. Ox. and series 1362.

Stote, rev. Walter George, born at Etton, Yorks, 1862; 1s. Arthur, gen. NON-COLLEGIATE, matric. 13 Oct., 88, aged 26 (from Winchester training coll.), B.A. 92.

Stott, rev. George, M.A., fellow WORCESTER 39, where see page 573.

Stott, Herbert Robert, born at Halifax, Yorks, 15 April, 1865; 2s. John, rector of St. James-the-less, Manchester. WADHAM, matric. 11 Oct., 84, aged 19 (from Manchester gr. school), B.A. 87.

Stovin, Cornelius Frederick, born at Mildenhall, Suffolk, 7 March, 1865; 1s. Cornelius Frederick, of Queens Camel, Somerset, D.Med. MAGDALEN, matric. 27 April, 81, aged 18 (from Bruton gr. school), B.A. 86.

Stowe, Alfred, M.A., fellow WADHAM 62, where see page 529.

Stowell, Ernest Alfred Crewe, born at Breadsall, co. Derby, 9 Nov., 1868; 2s. Hugh Ashworth, rector. QUEEN'S, matric. 21 Oct., 87, aged 18 (from Sedbergh school), scholar 87, B.A. 91; HONOURS:—2 classical mods. 89, 2 classics 91.

Stowell, Herbert, born at Gateshend, co. Durham, 4 June, 1869; 6s. William, congregational minister, deceased. NON-COLLEGIATE, matric. 15 Oct., 92, aged 23, from Lewisham congr. school and Glasgow university.

Stowell, John Hilton, born in London 1864; 4s. William, gen. NON-COLLEGIATE, matric. 15 Oct., 87, aged 23 (from Glasgow university), B.A. 90; HONOURS:—2 theology 90.

Stowell, Vere Arthur, born at Breadsall, co. Derby, 12 Sept., 1873; 3s. Hugh Ashworth, rector. CORPUS CHRISTI, matric. 19 Oct., 91, aged 18 (from Rossall school), scholar 91.

Stracey, Gilbert Foard, born at Norwich 29 July, 1868; 1s. Gilbert Hardinge, arm. MERTON, matric. 21 Oct., 86, aged 18, from Eton.

Strachan-Davidson, James Leigh, M.A., fellow BALLIOL 66, where see page 63.

Strachey, Theodore Edward, born at Ashwick, near Bath, 9 June, 1860; 2s. Richard Charles, arm. TRINITY, matric. 21 May, 80, aged 19 (from Sherborne school), B.A. 84 (HONOURS :—3 mathematical mods. 81, 3 law 83); bar.-at-law, Inner Temple, 85.

Strang, Alexander Rankin, born at Blackheath, Kent, 16 Dec., 1868; 4s. William, gen. NEW COLL., matric. 25 Nov., 87, aged 19 (from Winchester); HONOURS :—3 classical mods. 89; died 27 Oct., 90.

Strange, Herbert Pinckney Cother, born at Dulverton, Somerset, Dec., 1863; 2s. William James Stevenson, arm. KEBLE, matric. 16 Oct., 83, aged 19 (from Lancing coll.), B.A. 86.

Strange, William Pirie Heath, born at Hampstead, Middx., April, 1869; 1s. William Heath, D.Med. LINCOLN, matric. 18 Oct., 89, aged 19 (from St. Paul's school), scholar 89.

Strangman, Edward, born at Waterford, Ireland, 1866; 7s. Edward, gen. PEMBROKE, matric. 28 Oct., 86, aged 20 (from Kingsley coll., Westward Ho!), B.A. 90; HONOURS :—3 history 90.

Strangwayes, James de la Hep Swinaston, born at Skelton, Yorks, 9 Sept., 1872; 3s. John Swinaston, arm. CHARSLEY'S HALL, matric. 19 Feb., 87, aged 14.

Strangways, Francis Copleston Fox, born at Weston-super-Mare 14 May, 1870; 2s. Henry Fox, cler. KEBLE, matric. 12 Oct. 89, aged 19, from Sherborne school.

Strangways, Giles Stephen Holland Fox-, lord Stavordale, born in London 31 May, 1874; 1s. Henry Edward, earl of Ilchester. CHRIST CHURCH, matric. 14 Oct., 92, aged 18, from Eton.

Strangways, Maurice Walter Fox, born at Aldershot, Hants, 23 March, 1862; 2s. Walter Aston, arm. BALLIOL, matric. 21 Oct., 80, aged 18 (from the Charterhouse); commissioner of excise, central provinces, India.

Stratton, William Robert, born at Ditton, Kent, 14 Oct., 1871; 1s. John Young, cler. TRINITY, matric. 11 Oct., 90, aged 18 (from Radley coll.); HONOURS :—3 classical mods. 92.

Stredder, Josiah Clifton, born at Llandinam, co. Montgomery, 1870; 1s. Edward William, gen. JESUS COLL., matric. 20 Oct., 91, aged 21, from Bolton church institute.

Street, Frank, born in London 1870; 2s. John Barnfield, arm. CHRIST CHURCH, matric. 11 Oct., 89, aged 19 (from Westminster school), scholar 89; HONOURS :—2 classical mods. 91.

Street, George, born at Ruabon, co. Denbigh, 31 Oct., 1868; o.s. George, gen. WORCESTER, matric. 14 Oct., 89, aged 20, from University coll., London.

Street, George Slythe, born at Wimbledon 18 July, 1867; 2s. Samuel Philip, gen. EXETER, matric. 21 Oct., 86, aged 19 (from the Charterhouse), scholar 86, B.A. 90; HONOURS :—1 classical mods. 88, 2 classics 90.

Street, Oscar William, born in London 18 March, 1869; 1s. Joseph Edward, of Caterham, Surrey, gen. MAGDALEN, matric. 22 Oct., 87, aged 18 (from Eastbourne coll), B.A. 92.

Strickland, Algernon Henry Peter, born in London 19 Dec., 1863; 1s. Algernon, gen. CHRIST CHURCH, matric. 13 Oct., 82, aged 18 (from Eton), B.A. and M.A. 86.

Strickland, Dudley Herbert Cecil, born at Gibraltar 14 Nov., 1869; 1s. Walter Cecil, arm. CHRIST CHURCH, matric. 10 Oct., 90, aged 20, from Lancing coll.

Strickland, Henry Eustace, born in London 4 Nov., 1864; 4s. Walter, arm. MERTON, matric. 19 Oct., 83, aged 18 (from the Charterhouse and King's coll. London), exhibitioner BRASENOSE 84-6 ; migrated to CHARSLEY'S HALL, B.A. 91; HONOURS :—2 classical mods. 85.

Stride, William John Francis Keatley, born at Southampton 16 July, 1865; o.s. William Archer, gen. EXETER, matric. 13 Oct., 90, aged 25, from the Charterhouse.

Strong, Edmund Linwood, born at Burnham, Somerset, 1862; 2s. Robert, cler. ST. JOHN'S, matric. 21 May, 80, aged 18, B.A. 85, M.A. 87.

Strong, rev. Frederick William, born at Chippenham 10 July, 1862; o.s. Thomas Augustus, cler. MERTON, matric. 3 June, 81; aged 19 (from Haileybury), B.A. 85, M.A. 89 (HONOURS :—3 theology 85); curate of Somers Town St. Mary, London, 88.

Strong, rev. Thomas Banks, M.A., student CHRIST CHURCH 88, where see page 409.

Strong, William Arthur, M.A., student CHRIST CHURCH 48-56, where see page 418.

Stroud, Lewis, born at Cheltenham 1866; 1s. Frederick, arm. PEMBROKE, matric. 27 Oct., 84, aged 18, B.A. 88; HONOURS :—3 law 88.

Stroud, William, born at Bristol 2 Feb., 1860; 1s. John, gen. BALLIOL, matric. 24 Feb., 81, aged 21 (from Owens coll., Manchester, and University coll., Bristol), scholar 80-5, B.A. 85 (HONOURS :—1 mathematical mods. 82, 1 mathematics 84, 1 natural science 85), and at LONDON UNIVERSITY 1 chemistry, 1 exper. physics 82, 1 chemistry 82.

Struthers, John, born at Glasgow 1857; 1s. Robert, gen. WORCESTER, matric. 20 Oct., 81, aged 24 (from Glasgow university), exhibitioner 81-5 (HONOURS :—2 classical mods. 83, 1 classics 85); inspector of schools, Scotland, 86.

Strutt, John William, 3rd lord Rayleigh, born 12 Nov., 1842, created D.C.L. 13 June, 83, see *Al. Ox.* and series 1358; fellow of Trinity coll., Cambridge, 66-71, hon. fellow 81 (HONOURS :—Sheepshanks astronomical exhibition 64, senior wrangler 65, 1st Smith's prize 65, Hopkins' prize 82, royal medal of Royal society 82), president of British association 84.

Stuart, Andrew John, born at Dublin 21 Dec., 1841; 1s. hon. Andrew Godfrey, cler. NON-COLLEGIATE, matric. 4 Nov., 80, aged 39 ; of Madras C.S.

Stuart, Henry Charles Villiers, born at Napton-on-the-Hill, co. Warwick, Aug., 1867 ; 1s. Henry Villiers, cler. CHRIST CHURCH, matric. 14 June, 86, aged 18, from Harrow.

Stuart, Louis, born at Calcutta 1870 ; 2s. Kenneth Bruce, D.Med. BALLIOL, matric. 17 Oct., 89, aged 19 (from the Charterhouse); assist. magistrate N.W. provinces India.

Stuart, Simeon Henry Lechmere-, born at Dublin 15 May, 1864 ; o.s. sir Simeon, bart. MAGDALEN, matric. 16 Oct., 82, aged 18 (from Clifton coll.); student of the Inner Temple 84.

Stubbs, John Hamilton, born at Raphoe, co. Donegal, May, 1861 ; 1s. Elias Thackeray, cler. KEBLE, matric. 19 Oct., 80, aged 19 (from Newton Abbott coll., Devon), B.A. 83.

Stubbs, Launcelot Henlock Ayscough, born at Oxford 28 Oct., 1869 ; 2s. William, bishop of Oxford. LINCOLN, matric. 18 Oct., 88, aged 18 (from Merchant Taylors' school), exhibitioner 88, B.A. 92 ; HONOURS :—2 classical mods. 90, Ægrotat law 92.

Stubbs, right rev. William, D.D., bishop of Oxford, hon. fellow ORIEL 88, where see page 151.

Stubbs, William Walter, born 5 Jan., 1866 ; 1s. William, bishop of Oxford. ST. JOHN'S, matric. 11 Oct., 84, aged 18 (from Haileybury), B.A. 88, M.A. 91 ; HONOURS :—4 history 88.

Studholme, John, born at Selwyn, N.Z., Feb., 1863 ; 1s. John, arm. CHRIST CHURCH, matric. 22 Jan., 83, aged 19, B.A. 87.

Studholme, William Paul, born at Christ Church, N.Z., 23 April, 1864 ; 2s. John, of Orpidale House, Sutherlandshire, N.B., arm. MAGDALEN, matric. 16 Oct., 82, aged 18, B.A. 86 (HONOURS :—3 law 86) ; bar.-at-law, Inner Temple, 87.

Sturdy, Charles James, born at Broadwater Down, Sussex, 18 Oct., 1872 ; 2s. William, gen. MERTON, matric. 22 Jan., 91, aged 18, from Eton.

Sturdy, Edward Vyse, born in London 23 Sept., 1873 ; 3s. William, stockjobber. NEW COLL., matric. 14 Oct., 92, aged 19, from Eton.

Sturdy, William Arthur, born in London 17 Jan., 1871 ; 1s. William, of Lindfield, Sussex, gen. MAGDALEN, matric. 20 Jan., 90, aged 19, from Eton.

Sturges, Francis William Murray, born at Kencott, Oxon, 1 June, 1865 ; 3s. Edward, rector of Wokingham. MAGDALEN, matric. 19 Oct., 83, aged 18 (from Winchester), B.A. 88.

Sturges, Hugh Murray, born at Kencott, Oxon, 28 Aug., 1863 ; 2s. Edward, cler. KEBLE, matric. 18 Oct., 81, aged 18 (from Winchester), B.A. 84 ; bar.-at-law, Lincoln's Inn, 89.

Sturrock, Peter Sturrock, born at Edinburgh 26 Dec., 1869; 4s. Robert Maclean, arm. MERTON, matric. 19 Jan., 88, aged 18 (from Watson's coll., Edinburgh), B.A. 90; incorporated B.A. Caius coll., Cambridge, 91.

Sturt, Henry Cecil, born at Mortlake, Surrey, 14 June, 1863; 1s. Henry, gen. QUEEN'S, matric. 23 Oct., 82, aged 19 (from St. Bees gr. school), exhibitioner 82, B.A. 88; HONOURS :—2 classical mods. 84, 1 classics 86, 2 history 87.

Sturton, Charles James, born at Ramsbury, Wilts, 1866; 1s. Jacob, vicar of Little Bedwyn 66. NON-COLLEGIATE, matric. 17 Oct., 85, aged 19 (from Trinity coll., Stratford-on-Avon), B.A. 88.

Sturton, Douglas Phipps, born at Holbench, co. Lincoln, 6 Aug., 1873; o.s. John Phipps, solicitor. NEW COLL., matric. 14 Oct., 92, aged 19, from Rugby.

Sturton, John Anthony, born at Little Bedwyn, Wilts, 1874; 4s. Jacob, D.D., rector of Woodborough. NON-COLLEGIATE, matric. 17 Dec., 92, aged 18.

Statchbury, Harold Owen, born in London 14 Sept., 1873; 1s. George Frederick, accountant. CORPUS CHRISTI, matric. 18 Oct., 92, aged 19 (from St. Paul's school), scholar 91.

Stutfield, Vincent Corbett, born at Broxbourne, Herts, 18 Sept., 1873; 1s. Harton, gent. JESUS COLL., matric. 18 Oct., 92, aged 19 (from St. Paul's school), scholar 92.

Style, Charles Montague, D.D., fellow ST. JOHN'S 49-67, where see page 480.

Style, George Montague, born at Maidstone, Kent, 7 March, 1869; 1s. Albert Frederick, gen. NEW COLL., matric. 12 Oct., 88, aged 19 (from Eton); HONOURS :—4 law 91.

Suckling, Francis Earle, born at Whitwell, Norfolk, 28 May, 1865; 3s. Henry Edward, cler. ST. MARY HALL, matric. 20 Oct., 83, aged 18, from Lynn Regis school.

Suffrin, Aaron Emmanuel, born at Piatra, Roumania, 27 Sept., 1856; 3s. Colman. EXETER, matric. 4 June, 92, aged 36, from Rabbinical school, Roumania, and University of Basle.

Sugars, John Edward, born at Withington, co. Lanc., 19 March, 1869; 4s. William Cooke, gen. PEMBROKE, matric. 25 Oct., 87, aged 18 (from Manchester gr. school), scholar 87; HONOURS :—2 classical mods. 89, 2 classics 91.

Sugden, Albert Hugh, born at Keighley, Yorks, 5 Nov., 1862; 6s. John, arm. LINCOLN, matric. 20 Oct., 81, aged 18, from St. Paul's coll., Stony Stratford.

Sugden, rev. Henry Richard, born at Thames Ditton, Surrey, 13 July, 1862; 2s. rev. and hon. Frank. EXETER, matric. 20 Oct., 81, aged 19 (from the Charterhouse), B.A. 84 (HONOURS :—4 history 84); curate of Bermondsey, Surrey, 88.

Sullivan, rev. Frederick, born at Kimpton, Herts, 28 April, 1865; 1s. Francis William, arm. (after R.C.B.). EXETER, matric. 16 Oct., 84, aged 19 (from Wellington coll.); migrated to CHARSLEY'S HALL, B.A. 90; M.A. (EXETER) 91; curate of Peniston, Yorks, 91.

Sullivan, Patric Donal, born at Dublin 1863; 2s. William Kirby, arm. BALLIOL, matric. 6 May, 84, aged 21, from Queen's coll., Cork.

Sully, Arthur Blount, born at Bridgewater, Somerset, 27 Jan., 1871; 2s. John George, merchant. LINCOLN, matric. 23 Oct., 91, aged 20 (from University coll., Cardiff); scholar 92.

Summers, Herbert William, born at Birkenhead 28 May, 1867; 1s. Augustus William, gen. LINCOLN, matric. 22 Jan., 87, aged 19, B.A. 91.

Summers, Joseph, born at Frome, Somerset, 1843; 7s. George, gen. NEW COLL., matric. 28 April, 87, aged 44.

Sumner, Charles Henry, born at Bishopsbourne, Kent, 9 June, 1862; 2s. John Henry Robert, cler. NON-COLLEGIATE, matric. 18 Oct., 80, aged 18, from Marlborough.

Sumner, rev. George Julian Campbell, born at Burton, Hants, Aug., 1867; y.s. John Maunoir, rector. ORIEL, matric. 5 Feb., 86, aged 19 (from the Charterhouse), B.A. 89; curate of Cranleigh, Surrey, 91.

Surrage, Thomas Lyddon James, born at Wincanton, Somerset, 1866; elder son James, D.Med. HERTFORD, matric. 27 Oct., 85, aged 19, B.A. 88, M.A. and B.C.L. 92; HONOURS :—2 law 88, 2 civil law 89.

Surridge, Charles William West, born in London 1871; 2s. Henry Arthur Dillon, cler. HERTFORD, matric. 20 Oct., 91, aged 27, exhibitioner 91.

Surtees, Charles Henry, born at Holtby, Yorks, 7 Dec., 1870; 5s. Richard, rector. ORIEL, matric. 25 Oct., 89, aged 18 (from Haileybury); HONOURS :— 3 classical mods. 91.

Surtees, Edward Alexander, born at Holtby, Yorks, 12 March, 1863; 2s. Richard, cler. ORIEL, matric. 31 Oct., 82, aged 19 (from Haileybury), B.A. 86, M.A. 89; HONOURS :—2 classical mods. 84, 2 classics 86.

Sutcliffe, Tom, born at Stallingborough, co. Lincoln, 1865; 4s. John, gen. PEMBROKE, matric. 27 Oct., 83, aged 18.

Sutherland, George Humphreys Vivian, born at Derby 21 Feb., 1873; 1s. George, schoolmaster. NEW COLL., matric. 14 Oct., 92, aged 19, from Derby gr. school.

Sutherland, James Garden Blackie, born at Pietermaritzburg 1864; 2s. Peter Cormack, D.Med., surgeon-general colony of Natal. EXETER, matric. 18 Oct., 83, aged 19 (from Fettes coll.), scholar 83-5.

Suttie, sir George Grant, bart., born at Berwick 2 Sept., 1870; o.s. James Grant, baronet. NEW COLL., matric. 11 Oct., 89, aged 19, from Eton.

Sutton, rev. Charles Robert, born at York 1864; 1s. Robert, gen. ST. JOHN'S, matric. 13 Oct., 83, aged 19, B.A. 89, M.A. 90; curate of Idle, Yorks, 89.

Sutton, Edward William, born in London 6 June, 1871; 1s. Edward Gower Vane, gen. TRINITY, matric. 11 Oct., 90, aged 19 (from Brighton coll.); HONOURS :—1 classical mods. 92.

Sutton, Field Flowers, born at Douglas, isle of Man, 11 Nov., 1870; 2s. Henry, vicar of Bordesley Holy Trinity. LINCOLN, matric. 20 Oct., 90, aged 19, from Birmingham school.

Sutton, Frederick Ludlow, born in London Dec., 1863; 2s. Wadham Locke, gen. ST. JOHN'S, matric. 13 Oct., 83, aged 19 (from Highgate school), B.A. 92.

Sutton, John Anthony Leathes, born at Rosliston, co. Derby, 14 March, 1862; 2s. James, cler. MERTON, matric. 3 June, 81, aged 19 (from St. Edward's school, Summertown), B.A. 84.

Sutton, Robert Shuttleworth, M.A., fellow EXETER 40-54, where see page 125.

Sutton, Walter, born at West Hampnett, Sussex, Dec., 1863; 4s. Robert, vicar. NON-COLLEGIATE, matric. 20 April, 84, aged 20 (from Marlborough); migrated to BRASENOSE 84, B.A. 87.

Swabey, Arthur Louis Merttins, born at Charlottetown, P. Edward's island, Canada, 19 Dec., 1863; 2s. Stephen, gen. WADHAM, matric. 11 Oct., 84, aged 20, from St. Edward's school, Summertown.

Swabey, rev. Mark Richard, born in London 14 June, 1861; 2s. Maurice Charles Merttins, D.C.L., late chancellor diocese of Oxford. NEW COLL., matric. 17 Jan., 80, aged 18 (from Winchester), B.A. 83, M.A. 86 (HONOURS :—3 history 82); canon of St. Saviour, Maritzburg.

Swabey, rev. Stephen, born at Charlotte Town, America, 1864; 2s. Henry Birchfield, cler. PEMBROKE, matric. 27 Oct., 83, aged 19 (from Abingdon school), scholar 83-5, B.A. 89 (HONOURS :—3 classical mods. 85); curate of Scotby, Cumberland, 90.

Swainson, rev. Charles Swainson Smith-, born at Grange-over-Sands, co. Lanc., Sept., 1865; 2s. Henry Robert Smith, cler. KEBLE, matric. 14 Oct., 84, aged 19 (from the Charterhouse), B.A. 87; assumed the additional name of Swainson.

Swallow, Ernest, born at Copley, Yorks, March, 1862; 4s. George, arm. KEBLE, matric. 18 Oct., 81, aged 19 (from St. Edward's school, Summertown), B.A. 84; HONOURS:—3 classical mods. 83.

Swan, Charles Robert John Atkin, born at Staplefield, Sussex, 1863; o.s. John Thomas Atkin, cler. KEBLE, matric. 2 Dec., 81, aged 18, B.A. 85, B.Med. 90; HONOURS :—3 natural science 85.

Swann, Frederick Samuel Philip, born at Redhill, Surrey, 8 May, 1871; 2s. Frederick Egerton Brydges, cler., deceased. MAGDALEN, matric. 14 Oct., 90, aged 19 (from Dulwich coll. and Berkhamsted school), exhibitioner 90; HONOURS:— 3 classical mods. 92.

Swann, Nathaniel Emilius Egerton Egerton, born at Dorking, Surrey, 8 May, 1874; 2s. Frederick Brydges, M.A., Camb., cler. WADHAM, matric. 18 Oct., 92, aged 18 (from Berkhamstead school), scholar 91.

Swanston, rev. Frederick John, born in London 1861; 2s. George, gen. WORCESTER, matric. 21 Oct., 80, aged 19, B.A. 84, M.A. 87; curate of Hastings St. Clement 90.

Swanton, Calvert Hutchinson, born at Birkenhead 12 Sept., 1867; 3s. James Hutchinson, arm. QUEEN'S, matric. 25 Oct., 86, aged 19 (from Wesley coll., Sheffield), B.A. 90; HONOURS :— 3 law 90.

Swanwick, Bruce, born at Cirencester 1870 ; 1s. Russell, arm. UNIVERSITY COLL., matric. 12 Oct., 89, aged 19 (from Sherborne school); HONOURS :—3 classical mods. 91.

Swanwick, Eric Drayton, born at Cirencester 11 Aug., 1871; 2s. Russell, gen. UNIVERSITY COLL., matric. 11 Oct., 90, aged 19 from Sherborne school.

Swanzy, Thomas Erskine, born at Newry, co. Down, 25 Nov., 1869; 1s. Thomas Biddall, rector of Newry St. Mary, co. Down, deceased. ST. JOHN'S, matric. 11 Oct., 90, aged 20 (from South Eastern coll., Ramsgate, and Trinity coll., Dublin), senior moderator in mod. lit. 91 at Dublin university.

Swayne, rev. Arthur Wickham, born at Mathon, co. Worcester, April, 1863; 2s. Robert Arthur, gen. KEBLE, matric. 17 Oct., 82, aged 19 (from Birmingham gr. school), B.A. 86, M.A. 90; curate of Scarborough St. Martin's 89.

Swayne, Charles Noel, born at White Parish, Wilts, 10 Jan., 1868; 4s. William John, cler. KEBLE, matric. 14 Dec., 85, aged 18 (from St. Mark's school, Windsor); migrated to WORCESTER, B.A. 90.

Swayne, John Montague, born at Wilton, Wilts, 30 May, 1863; 1s. William James, arm. NEW COLL., matric. 10 Oct., 84, aged 19, from Winchester.

Swayne, rev. William Shuckburgh, born at Whiteparish, Wilts, 19 May, 1862; 1s. William John, vicar of Chitterne, Wilts. NEW COLL., matric. 16 Oct., 80, aged 18 (from St. Paul's coll., Stony Stratford), scholar 81-5, B.A. 84, M.A. 87 (HONOURS :—3 classical mods. 81, 2 classics 84, 1 theology 85) ; a student of the Inner Temple 82 ; vicar of St. Matthew, Walsall, 91.

Sweatman, Frederick John, born at Cowley St. John, Oxon, 20 March, 1873; 3s. William Albert, printer. NON-COLLEGIATE, matric. 17 Oct., 91, aged 18, from New Coll. school, Oxford.

Sweatman, George Albert, born at Oxford 11 Sept., 1868; 1s. William Albert, gen. QUEEN'S, matric. 25 Oct., 86, aged 18 (from Oxford high school), chorister 77-83, B.A. 89.

Sweet, Edward Hoare, born at Colkirk, Norfolk, Aug., 1861; 3s. James Bradley, cler. KEBLE, matric. 19 Oct., 80, aged 19, from Honiton school.

Sweetapple, rev. Henry Darrell Sudell, born at Dulverry, Somerset, 1862; o.s. Thomas, cler. QUEEN'S, matric. 25 Oct., 80, aged 18, B.A. 84, M.A. 87 (HONOURS :— Septuagint prize 83, 1 theology 84); vicar of Gloucester St. James 89.

Sweeting, Edward Thomas, born at Alsager, Cheshire, 1864 ; 1s. Edward, gen. NEW COLL., matric. 25 Jan., 88, aged 24, B.Mus. 89.

Sweeting, Richard Deane Roker, born at Nassau, East Indies, 1856 ; 1s. Richard, D.Med. NON-COLLEGIATE, matric. 21 April, 88, aged 32 (from Malvern coll. and London university); migrated to ST. MARY HALL, B.A. 92.

Swetenham, Roger, born at Holmes Chapel, Cheshire, Jan., 1868 ; 1s. William, cler. CHRIST CHURCH, matric. 15 Oct., 86, aged 18, from Uppingham school.

Swift, Augustus Dickerson, born at Spalding, co. Linc., 1863 ; 3s. Francis, gen. QUEEN'S, matric. 26 Jan., 82, aged 19.

Swift, Benjamin Ryle, born at Bickerink, co. Lanc., 21 Oct., 1866 ; 3s. Benjamin, cler. CORPUS CHRISTI, matric. 23 Oct., 84, aged 18 (from Clifton coll.), scholar 84, B.A. 88, M.A. 92 (HONOURS :—1 classical mods. 86, 1 classics 88); brother of Francis D.

Swift, Francis Darwin, born at Southport, co. Lanc., 28 May, 1864 ; 2s. Benjamin, cler. QUEEN'S, matric. 23 Oct., 83, aged 19 (from Clifton coll.), scholar 83, B.A. 87 (HONOURS :—1 classical mods. 85, 3 classics 87, 2 history 88); brother of Benjamin R.

Swift, Richard Meade (Pratt), born at Dublin July, 1864 ; 1s. Benjamin, D.Med. KEBLE, matric. 16 Oct., 83, aged 19 (from Ockbrook school, Derby), B.A. 86 ; lieut. the royal Dublin fusiliers 91.

Swifte, Ernest Godwin Meade, born at Dublin 1870 ; 1s. Ernest Godwin, arm. UNIVERSITY COLL., matric. 11 Oct., 90, aged 20 (from Shrewsbury school, and Trinity coll., Dublin), exhibitioner 90 ; brother of Latham C.

Swifte, Latham Coddington, born at Dublin 20 Sept., 1871 ; 2s. Ernest Godwin, bar-at-law. NEW COLL., matric. 13 Oct., 90, aged 19 (from Eton) ; selected candidate Indian c.s. 90.

Swinburne, rev. Henry, born at Wemyss Bay, co. Renfrew, 9 Oct., 1865; 6s. Thomas Anthony, of Eilan Shona, Ardgour, N.B., capt. R.N. MAGDALEN, matric. 16 Oct., 84, aged 19 (from Clifton and Fettes colls.), B.A. 89, M.A. 91 ; curate of St. Peter Port, Guernsey, 91.

Swindell, Albert Percy, born at Windsor, Berks, 1872 ; 2s. Thomas Greenall, cler. NON-COLLEGIATE, matric. 11 Oct., 90, aged 18, from Ellesmere coll., Salop.

Swindell, Frederick Smith, born at Upwell, co. Cambridge, 3 Feb., 1855 ; 3s. Thomas, gen. TURRELL'S HALL, matric. 22 April, 85, aged 30 (from Highbury coll.); migrated to EXETER 17 Jan., 87, B.A. 90, M.A. 91.

Swinhoe, Charles, col. Indian staff corps, F.L.S., F.Z.S., hon. M.A. 22 Nov., 1892, born 29 Aug., 38.

Swire, John, born at Aigburth, near Liverpool, 1861; 1s. John Samuel, gen. UNIVERSITY COLL., matric. 15 Oct., 81, aged 20, from Eton.

Swire, Samuel, born at Sale, Cheshire, 22 Jan., 1861; 1s. Samuel Henry, of Ashton-under-Lyne, arm. CHRIST CHURCH, matric. 21 May, 80, aged 19, B.A. 85.

Swire, rev. Samuel, born at Elston, Notts, 2 May, 1866; 2s. Frederick, cler. EXETER, matric. 23 Oct., 85, aged 19 (from St. Paul's school), scholar 84, B.A. 89, M.A. 92 (HONOURS:— 2 classical mods. 87, 2 classics 89); curate of St. Stephen Westminster 90.

Swithinbank, rev. John Edwin, born at Armley, Yorks, 16 June, 1851; 3s. William Chaffers, arm. NON-COLLEGIATE, matric. 10 April, 80, aged 29 (from Leeds gr. school); migrated to QUEEN'S, B.A. 85, M.A. 87; rector of Saltfleetby St. Clement 89.

Sworn, Sidney Augustus, born at Southampton 1866; 1s. William Augustus, gen. BALLIOL, matric. 24 Oct., 85, aged 19 (from Dublin coll. of science), scholar 84, B.A. 88, M.A. 92; HONOURS:— 1 chemistry 88.

Sydenham, Edward Allen, born at Reading, Berks, 19 April, 1873; o.s. Joseph Edward, gent. MERTON, matric. 18 Oct., 92, aged 19, from S. E. coll., Ramsgate.

Sykes, Alan John, born at Cheadle, Cheshire, 11 April, 1868; 2s. Thomas Hardcastle, gen. ORIEL, matric. 19 Oct. 86, aged 18 (from Rugby), B.A. 90; brother of Harold P.

Sykes, Brian Del, born at Basildon, Berks, 25 March, 1870; 1s. Edward John, cler. WORCESTER, matric. 14 Oct., 90, aged 20, from Lancing coll. and Bloxham school.

Sykes, Edward Francis, born at Woodford, Essex, 13 Oct., 1872; 3s. George Frederick Holley, assist. editor of "The New English Dictionary." BALLIOL, matric. 20 Oct., 92, aged 19 (from Magdalen coll. school), exhibitioner 90.

Sykes, Ernest William, born at Wantage, Berks, 13 Sept., 1870; 1s. George Cawthorne, gen. NON-COLLEGIATE, matric. 11 Oct., 90, aged 20, from Owens gr. school, Islington.

Sykes, George William, born at Castleford, Yorks, 1868; 2s. Richard, gen. UNIVERSITY COLL., matric. 15 Oct., 87, aged 19 (from Wakefield school), exhibitioner 87, B.A. 91; HONOURS:— 3 classical mods. 89, 4 history 91.

Sykes, Harold Platt, born at Cheadle, Cheshire, 19 Feb., 1865; 1s. Thomas Hardcastle, gen. ST. JOHN'S, matric. 19 Oct., 83, aged 18 (from Rugby); brother of Alan J.

Sykes, Herbert Rushton, born at Cheadle, Cheshire, 12 Oct., 1870; 1s. Arthur Henry, gen. CHRIST CHURCH, matric. 6 June, 90, aged 19, from Rugby.

Sykes, John Charles Gabriel, born in London 3 Aug., 1869; 1s. John, arm. NEW COLL., matric. 12 Oct., 88, aged 19 (from Winchester), scholar 87, B.A. 92; HONOURS:— 2 classical mods. 90, 1 classics 92.

Sykes, Robert, born at Austwick, Yorks, 3 Nov., 1866; 2s. John Powlett, cler. QUEEN'S, matric. 30 Oct., 85, aged 18 (from Giggleswick gr. school), exhibitioner 85, B.A. 88 (HONOURS:— 2 Indian languages 88); assist. commissioner Punjab.

Sykes, Stephen Frederick, born at Dunsforth, Yorks, 30 Oct., 1871; 2s. Frederick Galland, cler. TRINITY, matric. 11 Oct., 90, aged 18, from Fettes coll.

Sylvester, James Joseph, created D.C.L. 9 June, 1880, and M.A. by decree of convocation 5 Feb., 84, fellow NEW COLL. 83, where see page 206.

Symes, Henry Archibald, born at Clifton, co. Glouc., 9 April, 1868; 2s. Robert Henry, arm. WORCESTER, matric. 3 May, 87, aged 19, from Bath coll.

Symns, Robert Corser Montford, born in London 30 Sept., 1867; 1s. John Edward, cler. BALLIOL, matric. 16 Oct., 85, aged 19 (from Westminster and King's coll., London); assist. commissioner Burmah.

Symon, James David, born at Aberdeen 1867; 1s. David Cruden, merchant. ORIEL, matric. 27 Oct., 92, aged 25 (from Aberdeen university), bible clerk 92.

Symonds, rev. Edward, born at Winterbourne St. Martin, Dorset, 25 Aug., 1859; 2s. Daniel, arm. MERTON, matric. 17 Oct., 82, aged 23 (from Dorset County school), B.A. 86, M.A. 89; curate of Heigham Holy Trinity, Norfolk, 86-91, afterwards in Marlsburgh.

Symonds, Francis Henry, born at Brigg, co. Lincoln, 16 June, 1870; 2s. Christopher Rowland, gen. UNIVERSITY COLL., matric. 12 Oct., 89, aged 19 (from Rossall school), scholar 89; HONOURS:— 1 classical mods. 91.

Symonds, George Davey, born at Nynee Tal, East Indies, 1864; 1s. George Davey, cler. UNIVERSITY COLL., matric. 13 Oct., 83, aged 19 (HONOURS:— 2 classical mods. 85); lieut. R.A. 86.

Symonds, John Addington, M.A., fellow MAGDALEN 62-4; died 19 April, 93, see page 324.

Symonds, Stephen Charles, born at Greystoke, Cumberland, 21 Aug., 1873; 2s. William, cler. NEW COLL., matric. 14 Oct., 92, aged 19, from Winchester.

Symons, Edward William, M.A., Fereday fellow St. John's 80-7, where see page 490.

Symons, Henry, born at Brussels 26 May, 1871; 2s. Bernard, arm. WADHAM, matric. 13 Oct., 90, aged 19 (from city of London school), scholar 89 (HONOURS:— 1 classical mods. 92), 1 Latin et London 91.

Szyrma, Philip Isidore Lach-, born at Truro, Cornwall, March, 1870; 3s. Wladislaw Somerville, cler. KEBLE, matric. 12 Oct., 89, aged 19 (from Sutton Valence school), B.A. 92; HONOURS:— 2 theology 92.

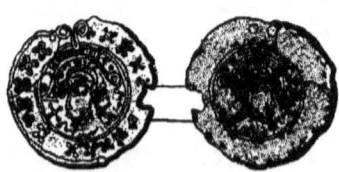

COINS—BODLEIAN.

WOODEN STRING COURSE, ALDENHAM ABBEY.—*Pugin.*

T

Tabberer, Hugh Benjamin, born at Blackheath, Kent, 1866; o.s. Benjamin, gen. BRASENOSE, matric. 23 Oct., 85, aged 19, B.A. 88, M.A. 92; HONOURS: —2 history 88.

Taberer, Henry Melville, born at King William's Town, Africa, Oct., 1870; 1s. Charles, cler. KEBLE, matric. 12 Oct., 89, aged 19, from St. Andrew's Grahamstown.

Tackley, Frederick James, born in London 9 Sept., 1865; 5s. Edward John, gen. QUEEN'S, matric. 27 Jan., 90, aged 24, from King's coll., London.

Tadman, Ernest James, rector of Combe Raleigh, Devon, 1872; 1s. James, rector of Combe Raleigh, Devon. HERTFORD, matric. 14 Oct., 90, aged 18 (from St. John's, Leatherhead), exhibitioner 90; HONOURS :—2 classical mods. 92.

Tait, James, born at Manchester 1863; 1s. Robert, gen. BALLIOL, matric. 15 Oct., 84, aged 21 (from Owens coll., Manchester), exhibitioner 83, B.A. 88; fellow PEMBROKE 91, M.A. 92 (HONOURS :—1 history 87), 1 history at Victoria university 83.

Tait, Walter James, M.A., fellow WORCESTER 64-71, where see page 576.

Talbot, Edward Stuart, D.D., senior student CHRIST CHURCH 66-70, where see page 423.

Talbot, George John, born at Westminster 19 June, 1861; 1s. John Gilbert, M.P. University. CHRIST CHURCH, matric. 15 Oct., 80, aged 19 (from Winchester), scholar 80-5, B.A. 85; fellow ALL SOULS' 86, M.A. 87 (HONOURS :—1 classical mods. 82, 1 classics 84); bar.-at-law, Inner Temple, 87.

Talbot, right rev. Monsignor, the hon. Gilbert Chetwynd, M.A., fellow ALL SOULS' 38-51, where see page 278.

Talbot, John Edward, born in London 14 March, 1870; 3s. John Gilbert, M.P. University. MAGDALEN, matric. 14 Oct., 89, aged 19 (from Eton), demy 88; HONOURS :—1 classical mods. 91.

Talbot, John Gilbert, D.C.L., M.P. for the UNIVERSITY 1878, where see page 2.

Talbot, rev. Reginald Thomas, born at Leamington 1862; 3s. John Thomas, arm. EXETER, matric. 20 Oct., 81, aged 19 (from Clifton coll.), exhibitioner 83-5, B.A. 85, M.A. 88 (HONOURS :—1 theology 85); hon. canon of Durham 89; vicar of Millfield, Sunderland, 93.

Talbot, Walter Stanley, born in London 4 Nov., 1869; 3s. hon. Wellington Patrick. CHRIST CHURCH, matric. 16 Oct., 88, aged 18 (from Wellington); assist. commissioner Punjab 90.

Talcott, James Frederick, born at New York 1866; 1s. James, gen. NON-COLLEGIATE, matric. 11 Nov., 90, aged 24, from Princeton university and union theological college.

Tamplin, rev. John Mainwaring, born at Kingston-on-Thames 1864; 4s. Edward Cowper, gen. UNIVERSITY COLL., matric. 14 Oct., 82, aged 18 (from King's coll. school, London), B.A. 86, M.A. 89 (HONOURS :—3 history 86); curate of Bromley, Kent, 90.

Tamplin, Robert Morgan, born at Purleigh, Essex, 1864; 4s. George Frederick, cler. KEBLE, matric. 17 Oct., 82, aged 18 (from St. Edward's school, Summertown), organ scholar 82-5, B.A. 85; perished in the burning of the new theatre Exeter 5 Sept., 87.

Tandy, Thomas Henry, born at Reddish, co. Worcester, 1860; 2s. Thomas Henry, gen. ST. EDMUND HALL, matric. 18 Oct., 89, aged 29.

Tanner, Archibald Emilius Gosset, born at Bellary, East Indies, 1867; 2s. James, cler. CHRIST CHURCH, matric. 30 May, 85, aged 18 (from Malvern coll.), B.A. 90.

Tanner, Arthur Spencer Gosset, born at Melksham, Wilts, 20 March, 1872; 2s. James, cler. NEW COLL., matric. 16 Oct., 91, aged 19 (from St. Paul's school), scholar 91.

Tanner, Charles Newman, born at Plymouth 25 May, 1869; 1s. Charles Frederick, arm. QUEEN'S, matric. 25 Oct., 86, aged 17, from Plymouth high school, etc.

Taphouse, Charles Milner, born at Oxford 1868; 1s. Thomas William, gen. NEW COLL., matric. 27 Jan., 86, aged 18.

Tapsfield, Charles James, born at Nether Stowey, Somerset, Oct., 1873; 2s. Edward, vicar. ORIEL, matric. 27 Oct., 91, aged 18, from Bradfield coll.

Tapsfield, Hugh Alexander, born at Windsor 31 Jan., 1870; 2s. Edward, vicar of Nether Stowey, Somerset. MAGDALEN, matric. 16 Oct., 88, aged 18 (from Bradfield coll.), academical clerk 88, B.A. 92.

Tarratt, Joseph Fox, born at Edinburgh Feb., 1869; 1s. Fox, arm. CHRIST CHURCH, matric. 11 Oct., 89, aged 20 (from Uppingham school), B.A. 92.

Tarver, Matthew Arthur Joseph, born at Filgrove, Bucks, 18 May, 1869; 3s. Joseph, rector. ORIEL, matric. 20 Oct., 88, aged 19 (from Haileybury), scholar 88; HONOURS :—2 classical mods. 90, 3 classics 92.

Tassell, Alick James, born at Faversham 28 Aug., 1865; 4s. James, solicitor. NEW COLL., matric. 15 Oct., 84, aged 19 (from the Charterhouse), B.A. 88, M.A. 92 (HONOURS :—2 classical mods. 86, 3 classics 88); bar.-at-law, Middle Temple, 90.

Tassell, Douglas Spencer Montague, born at Patrixbourne, Kent, 17 Dec., 1871; o.s. Bradbury William, arm. CHRIST CHURCH, matric. 10 Oct., 90, aged 18 (from Canterbury school), scholar 90; HONOURS: —2 classical mods. 92.

Tate, Charles Richmond, B.D., fellow CORPUS CHRISTI 39-52, where see page 381.

Tate, Ralph Hutchinson, born at Plaxtol, Kent, 10 July, 1873; 3s. James, M.A., cler. LINCOLN, matric. 25 Oct., 92, aged 19 (from Marlborough coll.), exhibitioner 92.

Tate, Robert Franklin, born 24 July, 1859; y.s. George James, gen. NEW COLL., matric. 14 Oct., 87, aged 28, from Oakham school, where he was a master 5 years.

Tatham, Edward Ernst, born at Ryburgh, Norfolk, 2 April, 1866; 4s. George Edmund, cler. ORIEL, matric. 23 Oct., 84, aged 18 (from Haileybury), B.A. 87.

Tatham, Leonard, born at Manchester 26 Jan., 1873; 1s. John Francis Walkinghawse, M.A., D.Med. NEW COLL., matric. 14 Oct., 92, aged 19, from Shrewsbury school.

Tatham, rev. William Mealburn, born at Ryborough, Norfolk, 30 July, 1862; 2s. George Edmund, cler. BRASENOSE, matric. 22 Oct., 80, aged 18 (from Marlborough), B.A. 84, M.A. 87; curate of Kennington St. Agnes, Surrey, 90.

Tattersall, Robert William, born at Howe, Norfolk, 1864; 4s. William, cler. EXETER, matric. 19 April, 82, aged 18 (from Harrow), B.A. 85, M.A. 88; HONOURS:—3 theology 85.

Tattersall, William, born at Bishopsbourne, Kent, 25 May, 1867; 3s. William, cler. MAGDALEN, matric. 23 Oct., 85, aged 18, from Harrow.

Tatton, Robert Grey, M.A., fellow BALLIOL 71-85, where see page 68.

Taverner, Frederick John Winder, born at Skeyby, Notts, 5 Oct., 1868; o.s. Frederick John, cler. EXETER, matric. 19 Oct., 87, aged 19 (from Winchester), B.A. 91; HONOURS:—3 classical mods. 89, 4 history 91.

Tawney, John Archer, born at Wroxton, Oxon, 1869; y.s. Archer Robert, arm. BRASENOSE, matric. 18 Jan., 87, aged 18 (from Winchester), B.A. 90.

Tayler, Alexander Norwich, born at Rothiemay House, Banffshire, N.B., 11 July, 1870; o.s. William James, bar.-at-law, deceased. UNIVERSITY COLL., matric. 15 Oct., 92, aged 22, from Winchester.

Tayler, rev. Ernest Hooper, born at Headingley, Leeds, 1861; 3s. Archdale, cler. QUEEN'S, matric. 15 May, 80, aged 19 (from Leeds school), exhibitioner 80-5, B.A. 84, M.A. 87 (HONOURS:—3 classical mods. 82, 4 classics 84, 3 theology 85); died 21 May, 89, at Auckland, New Zealand.

Tayler, William Fothergill Cooke, born at Bangalore, East Indies, 1869; 1s. John Charles, arm. NON-COLLEGIATE, matric. 28 Jan., 84, aged 15, from St. Kenelm's school, Oxford.

Taylor, Alban Aldersey, born at Isleworth, Middx., 22 Jan., 1865; 1s. Alban, gen. MAGDALEN, matric. 19 Oct., 83, aged 18 (from Harrow), B.A. 86, M.A. 91.

Taylor, Alfred Edward, B.A., fellow MERTON 91, where see page 95.

Taylor, Arnold Charles, born at Kingswood, Surrey, 28 Aug., 1867; 2s. Samuel Barnard, cler. UNIVERSITY COLL., matric. 18 Oct., 86, aged 19 (from Winchester), exhibitioner 86, B.A. 90; HONOURS: 1 classical mods. 88, 1 classics 90.

Taylor, rev. Arthur, born at Manchester 19 March, 1868; 4s. Samuel, gen. CORPUS CHRISTI, matric. 22 Jan., 87, aged 18 (from Manchester gr. school), scholar 86, B.A. 90 (HONOURS:—1 mathematical mods. 88, 1 maths. 90); assist. master Manchester gr. school, and curate of St. Margaret Burnage 91.

Taylor, Arthur Briggs, born at Chatburn, co. Lanc., 20 Dec., 1872; 2s. John, gent. BRASENOSE, matric. 21 Oct., 92, aged 19 (from Clitheroe school), scholar 91.

Taylor, Arthur Ernest, born at Nottingham 1871; 1s. Henry, esq. ST. JOHN'S, matric. 15 Oct., 92, aged 21.

Taylor, Arthur Mould Chapman, born at Headington, Oxon, Jan., 1864; 3s. John William Augustus, cler. BRASENOSE, matric. 19 Oct., 82, aged 18, B.A. 86; died 23 Dec., 89, at Marseilles.

Taylor, Arthur Salem, born in London 1867; 2s. Henry, gen. EXETER, matric. 16 Oct., 84, aged 17 (from the Charterhouse), B.A. 87.

Taylor, rev. Arthur Whitcombe, born at Bradford, Yorks, 21 April, 1867; 1s. William, gen. WORCESTER, matric. 22 Oct., 85, aged 20 (from Abingdon and Westminster schools), B.A. 89; curate of Grantham 90.

Taylor, Coniart de Butts, born at Portland, Dorset, Jan. or Feb., 1869; 3s. Haydon Aldersey, cler. CHRIST CHURCH, matric. 14 Oct., 87, aged 18, from St. Mark's school, London.

Taylor, Douglas Fletcher, born in Bombay Nov., 1867; 1s. James, cler. KEBLE, matric. 13 Oct., 88, aged 20, from Loretto school.

Taylor, Ernest Wesley, born at North Walsham, Norfolk, SS. Simon and Jude's day, 1871; 2s. Alfred, of Kilkhampton, Cornwall, Wesleyan minister. NON-COLLEGIATE, matric. 15 Oct., 92, aged 20, from Kingswood school, Bath.

Taylor, Frank, born in London 8 Nov., 1873; 5s. Horatio, gen. LINCOLN, matric. 25 Oct., 92, aged 19 (from University coll., London), scholar 92.

Taylor, Frank Henning William, born at Kensington 1870; 1s. William, gen. ST. JOHN'S, matric. 17 Oct., 89, aged 19, from University coll., Bristol.

Taylor, Frederick Henry, born in London 1863; 1s. Henry, gen. WORCESTER, matric. 18 Oct., 83, aged 20.

Taylor, Frederick Norman, born in London 31 Oct., 1871; 2s. Joseph, gen. JESUS COLL., matric. 15 Oct., 90, aged 18 (from Southwark gr. school), exhibitioner 90; HONOURS:—2 classical mods. 92.

Taylor, Herbert, born at Unsworth, co. Lanc., 1870; 5s. Ratcliffe, arm. BRASENOSE, matric. 16 Oct., 88, aged 18 (from Bury gr. school, co. Lanc.), exhibitioner 88, B.A. 92; HONOURS:—2 classical mods. 90, 3 classics 92.

Taylor, Horace William, born in London 20 Sept., 1870; o.s. William, arm. WADHAM, matric. 13 Oct., 90, aged 20, from Dulwich coll.

Taylor, James, B.Mus., organist NEW COLL. 65, where see page 220.

Taylor, James Thomas, born at Hastings 1850; 3s. Edward, gen. NON-COLLEGIATE, matric. 15 April, 82, aged 32; migrated to ST. EDMUND HALL, B.A. 87, M.A. 89.

Taylor, James Worsley, born in London 10 July, 1872; 1s. Henry Wilson W.-T., bar.-at-law. BRASENOSE, matric. 21 Oct., 92, aged 20, from Eton.

Taylor, John, M.A., fellow PEMBROKE 56-65, where see page 554.

From Ingram's Memorials.

TAYLOR. —— MATRICULATIONS, 1880 TO 1892. —— TEW.

Taylor, John Charles Marshall, born at Sawtry, Hunts, 23 Sept., 1865; 1s. John, bar.-at-law. NEW COLL., matric. 16 Oct., 85, aged 20 (from Wellington), B.A. 90, M.A. 92; HONOURS :—3 history 89.

Taylor, John Ford, born at Tilberton, Salop, 1874; 2s. Albert, gent. KEBLE, matric. 15 Oct., 92, aged 18, from Newport gr. school.

Taylor, John Francis White, born at Blackheath, Kent, 27 March, 1872; 3s. Richard Stephens, arm. TRINITY, matric. 17 Jan., 91, aged 18 (from Rugby); migrated to DOWNING COLL., CAMB., 21 Oct., 92.

Taylor, John Harryman, born at Brompton, Yorks, 1867; o.s. John, cler. NON-COLLEGIATE, matric. 21 Oct., 89, aged 22.

Taylor, Lionel Alexander Goodenough, born in London 16 July, 1871; o.s. John Howell Goodenough, gen. EXETER, matric. 13 Oct., 90, aged 19, from Tiverton school.

Taylor, rev. Percy Wolryche, born at Little Shelford, co. Camb., 4 June, 1862; 1s. John William, cler. LINCOLN, matric. 20 Oct., 81, aged 19 (from Derby school), scholar 81-5, B.A. 85 (HONOURS :— 1 classical mods. 82, 3 classics 85), in University eight 84 and 85; assist. master Leamington coll. 88-90, and Trinity coll., Glenalmond, 90.

Taylor, Philip Spencer O'Bryen, born at Brighton 3 Dec., 1866; 1s. William, of the Queen's body guard. EXETER, matric. 23 Oct., 85, aged 18 (from the Charterhouse), B.A. 89 (HONOURS :— 4 law 89); bar.-at-law, Lincoln's Inn, 91.

Taylor, Pierre Huyen, born at Framlingham, Suffolk, 1865; 3s. Robert Wager, arm. UNIVERSITY COLL., matric. 13 Oct., 83, aged 18; HONOURS :—4 history 87.

Taylor, Stafford, born at Barton-upon-Irwell, co. Lanc., 15 Nov., 1872; 2s. Henry, solicitor. TRINITY, matric. 17 Oct., 91, aged 18, from Sedbergh school.

Taylor, Thomas Bertrand, born at Bolton-le-Moors, co. Lanc., 21 Dec., 1863; 1s. John Leigh, arm. TRINITY, matric. 21 Jan., 84, aged 20 (from Harrow); died 18 Aug., 92.

Taylor, rev. Walter Buckland, born at Chertsey, Surrey, 17 Aug., 1861; 2s. Samuel, cler. NON-COLLEGIATE, matric. 18 Oct., 80, aged 19 (from Marlborough); migrated to UNIVERSITY COLL. 81, B.A. 84, M.A. 87 (HONOURS :—3 classical mods. 82, 2 history 84); curate of St. John Baptist, Croydon, 86.

Taylor, William Eagle, born in London 1870; y.s. Silas, arm. BRASENOSE, matric. 16 Oct., 88, aged 18, from Bury, co. Lanc., gr. school, and Dulwich coll.

Taylor, William Wilberforce, M.A., QUEEN'S, where see page 184.

Teale, Lionel Henry, born at Leeds 1866; 1s. Thomas Pridgin, B.Med. HERTFORD, matric. 27 Oct., 85, aged 19, from Winchester.

Teale, Michael Aubrey, born at Headingley, near Leeds, Sept., 1867; 2s. Thomas Pridgin, B.Med. CHRIST CHURCH, matric. 6 May, 86, aged 18, from Winchester.

Teale, Reginald Carden, born at Scarborough 1872; 1s. John William, arm. UNIVERSITY COLL., matric. 12 Oct., 89, aged 17.

Tebbs, Stephen Nottidge, B.D., fellow ST. JOHN'S 59, where see page 477.

Teesdale, rev. Edward James, born at Bruges, in Belgium, 13 May, 1866; 4s. Charles Baker, cler. NON-COLLEGIATE, matric. 17 Oct., 85, aged 19 (from Marlborough), B.A. 88; curate of Stretham, Ely, 89.

Teesdale, Kenneth John Marmaduke, born at Edinburgh 25 Jan., 1871; o.s. Frederick Dobree, cler., and of t.w. coll., Ryde. MAGDALEN, matric. 14 Oct., 90, aged 19 (from Winchester), exhibitioner 90; HONOURS :—2 classical mods. 92.

Tempest, Francis Adolphus Vane-, born in London 4 Jan., 1863; 1s. lord Adolphus Vane. BALLIOL, matric. 18 Oct., 81, aged 18 (from Harrow); HONOURS :—3 classical mods. 82.

Tempest, Tristram Tempest, born at Wynberg, South Africa, 10 Jan., 1865; 1s. Robert, arm. (after baronet). CHRIST CHURCH, matric. 10 Oct., 84, aged 19, from Harrow.

Temple, right rev. Frederick, D.D., bishop of London, hon. fellow EXETER 85, where see page 124.

Temple, Michael Henry, born at Douglas, isle of Man, March, 1862; 1s. Charles, arm. KEBLE, matric. 18 Oct., 81, aged 19 (from Leeds gr. school), B.A. 84 (HONOURS :—3 law 84); bar-at-law, Inner Temple, 86.

Temple, Reginald Willock, born at Strensham, co. Worc., 17 Nov., 1868; 1s. William, cler. NEW COLL., matric. 14 Oct., 87, aged 18 (from Sedbergh gr. school), B.A. 91; HONOURS :—3 history 90.

Temple, sir Richard, bart., G.C.S.I., created D.C.L. 9 June, 80. See *Al. Ox.* and series 1399.

Templeman, rev. Burnard Wordsworth, born at Peterborough 1868; 2s. Edward, cler. ST. EDMUND HALL, matric. 21 Oct., 86, aged 18, B.A. 89; curate of Penkridge, co. Staff., 91.

Tepper, Charles William Richard, born at Westminster 10 Aug., 1861; 1s. John, arm. CHRIST CHURCH, matric. 15 Oct., 80, aged 19 (from Westminster school), scholar 80-5, B.A. 84; HONOURS :—2 classical mods. 82, 2 classics 84; died 21 July, 88.

Terry, rev. Douglas, born at Tostock, Suffolk, 15 Oct., 1863; 1s. Charles, cler. HERTFORD, matric. 18 Oct., 82, aged 19 (from Rugby), scholar 81-3; curate of Bridport, Dorset, 91.

Terry, rev. Francis William, born at Wells, Somerset, 26 Oct., 1860; 2s. George, arm. MERTON, matric. 19 Nov., 80, aged 20 (from St. Edward's school, Summertown), B.A. 86; curate of Horsham, Sussex, 86-91, and in Toronto, 91.

Terry, Percival, born at Bradford, Yorks, 15 Sept., 1863; 1s. John Nettleton, surgeon. MAGDALEN, matric. 16 Oct., 82, aged 19 (from Magdalen coll. school), B.A. 86, M.A. 89 (HONOURS :—4 law 86); student Inner Temple 83.

Terry, Richard Runciman, born at Ellington, Northumberland, 1864; 1s. Thomas, gen. NON-COLLEGIATE, matric. 22 Oct., 87, aged 23; migrated 9 May, 89, to King's coll., Cambridge.

Terry, Thomas Robert, M.A., fellow MAGDALEN 77-84, where see page 325.

Teschemaker, William Ernest, born at Thurleston, Devon, Sept., 1866; o.s. Thomas Richard, arm. MERTON, matric. 24 Oct., 85, aged 19 (from Dulwich coll.), B.A. 89; HONOURS :—2 classical mods. 87, 3 classics 89.

Tetley, James George Wynn, born at Badminton, co. Glouc., 2 June, 1873; o.s. James George, M.A., canon of Bristol. PEMBROKE, matric. 28 Oct., 92, aged 19, from Eton.

Tetlow, Henry Parkes, born at St. Heliers, Jersey, 1863; 3s. John Richard, gen. NON-COLLEGIATE, matric. 24 Oct., 87, aged 24.

Tew, Edward Grosvenor, born at Carleton, Yorks, 8 June, 1873; 1s. Thomas William, banker. MAGDALEN, matric. 21 Oct., 91, aged 18, from Shrewsbury gr. school.

Tew, Ernest William, born at Perth 7 Nov., 1873; 5s. Edward, esq. WORCESTER, matric. 18 Oct., 92, aged 19, from Westward Ho! coll.

38

Thackeray, Francis St. John, M.A., fellow LINCOLN 57-61, where see page 242.
Thackeray, rev. Walter Algernon, born at Port George, Nairn, Scotland, 15 Sept., 1868; 4s. Frederick Russell, arm. TRINITY, matric. 15 Oct., 87, aged 19 (from Elizabeth coll. Guernsey), B.A. 90 (HONOURS:—4 theology 90); curate of Scarborough St. Martin's 91.
Thackrah, James Robert, born at Halifax 8 Oct., 1862; 1s. Abraham, gen. QUEEN'S, matric. 23 Oct., 82, aged 20 (from Bradford gr. school), exhibitioner 82-6, B.A. 86, M.A. 92; HONOURS:—4 chemistry 86.
Thatcher, Griffithes Wheeler, born at Melbourne 6 Aug., 1863; o.s. Richard Henry, gen. NON-COLLEGIATE, matric. 12 Oct., 89, aged 26 (from Leipsic university), B.A. 92 (HONOURS:—2 Semitic languages 92), B.A. Melbourne university 83, M.A. 85, B.D. Edinburgh 86.
Thelwall, Francis Walter, born at Challes, Devon, 30 June, 1872; o.s. Sydney, B.A., rector of Radford Semele, co. Warwick. ST. JOHN'S, matric. 17 Oct., 91, aged 19 (from Dean Close memorial school, Cheltenham), scholar 90; HONOURS:—1 classical mods. 93.
Theobald, George Ridley, born at Chale, I.W., 19 Oct., 1869; 2s. Charles, cler. EXETER, matric. 19 Oct., 87, aged 18 (from Radley coll.), exhibitioner 87, B.A. 91; HONOURS:—3 classical mods. 89, 3 classics 91.
Theobald, Henry Studdy, M.A., fellow WADHAM 71-88, where see page 532.
Theobald, James Anwyl, born in London 11 Nov., 1868; 1s. James, gen. WORCESTER, matric. 17 Oct., 87, aged 18 (from St. Leonard's school), B.A. 91; HONOURS:—3 history 91.
Theodosius, Alfred Fletcher, born at Stafford 1867; 4s. James Henry, cler. UNIVERSITY COLL., matric. 16 Oct., 86, aged 19 (from Bath coll.), exhibitioner 86, B.A. 90; HONOURS:—2 mathematical mods. 88, 3 chemistry 90.
Theodosius, Charles Edward, born at Stafford 25 Sept., 1864; 3s. James Henry, cler. WORCESTER, matric. 18 Oct., 83, aged 19 (from Bath coll.), scholar 83, B.A. 87; HONOURS:—1 mathematical mods. 85, 3 history 87.
Thesiger, Arthur Lionel Bruce, born in London 19 Oct., 1872; 1s. hon. Edward Pierson, clerk assist. of the parliament, NEW COLL., matric. 16 Oct., 91, aged 18, from Winchester.
Thesiger, hon. Frederic John Napier, born 12 Aug., 1868; 1s. Frederick Augustus, baron Chelmsford. MAGDALEN, matric. 22 Oct., 87, aged 19 (from Winchester), B.A. 91; fellow ALL SOULS' 92 (HONOURS:—2 classical mods. 89, 1 law 91), in University eleven 88 and 90; bar.-at-law, Inner Temple, 93.
Thicke, Septimus Cox, born at Dulwich, Surrey, 1857; 7s. Charles James, gen. ST. EDMUND HALL, matric. 23 Oct., 85, aged 28.
Thirlwall, Frederic John, born at Nantmel, co. Radnor, 17 May, 1868; 4s. Thomas James, cler. MERTON, matric. 22 Oct., 87, aged 19, from St. Edward's school, Summertown.
Thistlethwaite, Clifton William, born at Whitby, Yorks, 29 June, 1866; 1s. William, gen. EXETER, matric. 16 Oct., 87, aged 21 (from Denstone coll.), B.A. 91.
Thistlethwaite, Richard Thomas, born at Blackpool, co. Lanc., July, 1866; 3s. Richard, cler. KEBLE, matric. 22 Oct., 85, aged 19 (from Preston gr. school), B.A. 88; HONOURS:—4 history 88.
Thomas, Albert Edward, born at Llangyfelach, co. Glam., 19 March, 1868; 1s. John, arm. MERTON, matric. 21 Oct., 86, aged 18 (from Llandovery coll.),

postmaster 85, B.A. 90; HONOURS:—1 mathematical mods. 87, mathematical exhibition 88, 1 mathematics 90, 2 physiology 91.
Thomas, Albert Edward, born at Hammersmith 1871; 1s. Edward James, gen. BALLIOL, matric. 14 Oct., 90, aged 19 (from St. Paul's school), selected candidate Indian C.S. 90.
Thomas, Alfred, born at Loughor, co. Glamorgan, 1859; 4s. William, gen. NON-COLLEGIATE, matric. 20 Oct., 84, aged 25, from Loughor school.
Thomas, Alfred Charles, born at Merthyr Tydvil, co. Glam., 6 March, 1863; 4s. Thomas, gen. ST. MARY HALL, matric. 29 Jan., 86, aged 22 (from Aberystwith coll.); migrated to EXETER 8 June, 87, B.A. 89.
Thomas, Alfred Easton, born at Llangyfelach, co. Glam., 10 Oct., 1869; 2s. John, pleb. JESUS COLL., matric. 16 Oct., 88, aged 19 (from Swansea gr. school), exhibitioner 88; HONOURS:—3 classical mods. 90.
Thomas, Arthur Easton, born at Neath, co. Glamorgan, 20 May, 1868; 1s. Robert Wentmore, arm. TRINITY, matric. 15 Oct., 87, aged 19 (from Bath coll.), exhibitioner 87, B.A. 92; HONOURS:—1 classical mods. 89, 3 classics 92.
Thomas, Arthur Fitzroy Courtenay Vosper, born at Winterbourne, Dorset, 1869; 2s. Samuel, cler. NON-COLLEGIATE, matric. 11 Oct., 90, aged 21, from Wimborne gr. school.
Thomas, rev. Arthur Heber, born at Warmsworth, Yorks, 14 Aug., 1862; 3s. Charles Edward, cler. EXETER, matric. 18 Oct., 82, aged 20 (from Haileybury), B.A. 87; missionary in Madras; died there 2 Nov., 90.
Thomas, Charles Edward, born at Dalston 1870; 1s. Charles, pleb. NON-COLLEGIATE, matric. 12 Oct., 89, aged 19 (from King's coll. school, London), B.A. 92; HONOURS:—2 theology 92.
Thomas, Cyril Meurig, born at St. Asaph, co. Denbigh, 2 Dec., 1871; 2s. David Richard, M.A., F.S.A., archdeacon of Montgomery. JESUS COLL., matric. 15 Oct., 90, aged 18 (from Shrewsbury school), scholar 90; HONOURS:—2 classical mods. 92.
Thomas, rev. Daniel, born at Tycross, co. Carmarthen, 21 Dec., 1854; 2s. Charles, gen. ST. MARY HALL, matric. 18 May, 89, aged 34; curate of Pudsey 85-8, and of Sowerby Bridge, (both) Yorks, 88.
Thomas, Daniel Lleufer, born at Llidth-Enoch, co. Carmarthen, 1863; 2s. William, gen. NON-COLLEGIATE, matric. 27 Oct., 83, aged 20 (from Llandovery coll.), B.A. 87 (HONOURS:—3 law 87); bar.-at-law, Lincoln's Inn, 89.
Thomas, David, M.A., fellow TRINITY 60-72, where see page 452.
Thomas, David, born at Ystalyfera, co. Glam., 15 March, 1873; 3s. Jenkin, gen. EXETER, matric. 22 Oct., 91, aged 18 (from Llandovery coll.), scholar 91.
Thomas, Edward Aubrey, born at Titley, co. Hereford, 1 May, 1872; 1s. Edward David, of Fishponds, Netley Abbey, Hants, J.P. MAGDALEN, matric. 11 Oct., 90, aged 18, from the Charterhouse.
Thomas, Edward Swayne, born at Fishponds, Bristol, 15 Sept., 1872; 2s. Edward, gen. QUEEN'S, matric. 27 Oct., 91, aged 19 (from Clifton coll.), scholar 91; HONOURS:—2 classical mods. 93.
Thomas, Evan Lorimer, born at Llandegni, co. Carnarvon, 21 Feb., 1872; 1s. David Walter, canon of Bangor. JESUS COLL., matric. 20 Oct., 91, aged 19 (from Westminster, and Friars school, Bangor), scholar 91; HONOURS:—2 classical mods. 93.
Thomas, Francis Inigo, born at Warmsworth, Yorks, 1866; 5s. Charles Edward, cler. PEMBROKE, matric. 30 Jan., 84, aged 18; brother of George P.

Thomas, George Holt, born at Clapham, Surrey, 31 March, 1870; 7s. William Luson, founder and director of "The Graphic" newspaper. QUEEN'S, matric. 20 Oct., 88, aged 18, from King's coll. school, London.

Thomas, George Pelham, born at Warnsworth, Yorks, 18 April, 1864; 5s. Charles Edward, cler. MERTON, matric. 17 Jan., 83, aged 18 (from Haileybury), B.A. 87; brother of Francis I.

Thomas, rev. John Arthur, born at Wrexham, co. Denbigh, 3 Sept., 1867; 3s. William, gen. JESUS COLL., matric. 20 Oct., 86, aged 19 (from Wrexham school), B.A. 90; HONOURS:—2 classical mods. 88, 3 classics 90.

Thomas, John Lewis, born at Llandilo, co. Carmarthen, 1862; 1s. John Lewis, arm. PEMBROKE, matric. 9 May, 81, aged 19, B.A. 85, M.A. 90; of Caerglas, co. Carm.

Thomas, rev. John Llewellyn Pugh, born at Oswestry, Salop, Feb., 1863; 1s. John, arm. CHRIST CHURCH, matric. 14 Jan., 87, aged 24, B.A. 91.

Thomas, John Owen, born at Bangor 8 or 18 Sept., 1862; 1s. Josiah, presbyterian minister. NON-COLLEGIATE, matric. 13 Oct., 83, aged 21 (from Liverpool coll., and Glasgow university); migrated to NEW COLL., B.A. 87, M.A. 91; HONOURS:—2 classical mods. 85, 2 classics 87.

Thomas, John Richard William, born in London 1865; o.s. Richard, gen. ST. EDMUND HALL, matric. 19 Jan. 88, aged 23; HONOURS:—2 classical mods. 89, 3 classics 91.

Thomas, Lionel George, born at Clifton, co. Glouc., June, 1868; 5s. William John, gen. KEBLE, matric. 17 Oct., 87, aged 19 (from Clifton coll.), B.A. 91; HONOURS:—3 classical mods. 89.

Thomas, Llewellyn, M.A., fellow JESUS COLL. 72, where see page 509.

Thomas, rev. Penson Charles, born at Stockingford, co. Warwick, 5 Jan., 1862; 1s. John, cler. NON-COLLEGIATE, matric. 14 Oct., 82, aged 20 (from Marlborough); migrated to WORCESTER, B.A. 87; curate of Lower Mitton 89-90, and of Barford, (both) co. Worcester, 90.

Thomas, rev. Philip Cadwallader, born in London 1864; 1s. Cadwallader, gen. NON-COLLEGIATE, matric. 4 June, 81, aged 17 (from city of London school); migrated to BALLIOL 81, B.A. 84; HONOURS:—3 natural science 84.

Thomas, Pryse Lewis, born at Amlwch, isle of Anglesey, 1871; 1s. Meshach, gen. NON-COLLEGIATE, matric. 12 Oct., 89, aged 18, from Bonumaris school; died 16 April, 90.

Thomas, Rhys Goring, born at Ferryhill, co. Carmarthen, Aug., 1864; 1s. Rees Goring, arm. KEBLE, matric. 17 Oct., 84, aged 18, from Eton.

Thomas, Richard James Francis, born in London 20 Aug., 1873; 1s. George, coroner for London and Middx. BRASENOSE, matric. 21 Oct., 92, aged 19, from Harrow.

Thomas, Richard Rice, born at Fishguard, co. Pembroke, 30 July, 1872; 2s. John Richard, surgeon-major. KEBLE, matric. 20 Oct., 91, aged 19, from Haverfordwest gr. school.

Thomas, Ritchie, born at Brynbella, Llandinorwic, co. Carnarvon, 8 June, 1873; 2s. Richard Owen. JESUS COLL., matric. 18 Oct., 92, aged 19, from S. Oswald's coll., Ellesmere.

Thomas, Robert, M.A., MERTON, where see page 100.

Thomas, Robert Curre, B.A., HERTFORD, where see page 604.

Thomas, Robert D'Oyley Freeman, born in London Feb., 1866; 1s. Henry John, arm. CHRIST CHURCH, matric. 2 Feb., 86, aged 19, from Eton.

Thomas, Robert Edwin, born at Oxford 1857; 1s. Richard, gen. NON-COLLEGIATE, matric. 4 June, 81, aged 24, B.A. 84, M.A. 89.

Thomas, rev. Walter Webb, born at Southease, Sussex, 12 July, 1865; 1s. Samuel Webb, rector. WORCESTER, matric. 17 Dec., 84, aged 19, B.A. 88; curate of Wavertree St. Mary 89-90, and of St. Matthew, Toxteth Park, Liverpool, 90.

Thomas, Walter William, born at West Derby, Liverpool, 1864; 2s. Augustus William, merchant. ST. JOHN'S, matric. 17 Oct., 91, aged 27 (from Paris university); HONOURS:—Taylorian scholarship (French) 92, 2 classical mods. 93.

Thomas, William Beach, born at Godmanchester 1868; 2s. Daniel George, cler. CHRIST CHURCH, matric. 14 Oct., 87, aged 19 (from Shrewsbury school; scholar 91, B.A. 91; HONOURS:—3 classical mods. 89, 3 classics 91.

Thomas, William Edwin, born at Oxford 1867; 1s. Edwin James, gen. ST. EDMUND HALL, matric. 23 Oct., 85, aged 18 (chorister CHRIST CHURCH 78-83), B.Mus. 88.

Thomas, William Henry Griffith, born at Oswestry, Salop, 1861; 1s. William, gen. NON-COLLEGIATE, matric. 17 Oct., 91, aged 30.

Thomas, William Llewellyn, born at Brecon April, 1872; 4s. David William Jones, solicitor. KEBLE, matric. 20 Oct., 91, aged 19 (from Brecon coll.); HONOURS:—3 classical mods. 93.

Thomas, William Rowland, born at Haverfordwest, co. Pembroke, 8 June, 1867; o.s. Samuel, gen. QUEEN'S, matric. 30 Oct., 85, aged 18 (from Haverfordwest gr. school), scholar 85, B.A. 89; HONOURS:—2 classical mods. 87, 1 mathematical mods. 87, 2 mathematics 88, 3 classics 90.

Thomas, William Vincent Howell, born at Carmarthen, 10 May, 1865; 1s. John, gen. WORCESTER, matric. 17 Oct., 84, aged 19, from Shrewsbury gr. school.

Thompson, rev. Arnold Thewlis, born at Kirkburton, Yorks, 1 March, 1869; 1s. Robert Boyle, cler. CORPUS CHRISTI, matric. 20 Oct., 88, aged 19 (from Leeds gr. school), B.A. 92; HONOURS:—4 history 92.

Thompson, Arthur, born at Kirkby Stephen, Westmorland, 28 Jan., 1871; 4s. Joseph, gen. QUEEN'S, matric. 22 Oct., 89, aged 18 (from Appleby gr. school), exhibitioner 89; HONOURS:—2 classical mods. 91.

Thompson, Arthur Huxley, born at Worcester 8 July, 1872; 1s. John David, solicitor. JESUS COLL., matric. 18 Oct., 92, aged 20 (from Malvern coll.), scholar 91.

Thompson, Austin Henry, born at Malta 29 April, 1870; 2s. John Baylis, lieut.-col. late R.A. ST. EDMUND HALL, matric. 18 Oct., 89, aged 19 (from King's school, Canterbury); HONOURS:—2 classical mods. 91.

Thompson, Charles Henry, born at Sheffield 18 Jan., 1865; 1s. Henry Lynn, gent. QUEEN'S, matric. 22 Oct., 83, aged 18 (from Ripon and Hoddesdon schools), scholar 83, B.A. 86; student of CHRIST CHURCH 90, M.A. 90 [HONOURS:—accessit junior math. scholarship 84 and 85, 1 math. mods. 84, 1 maths. 86, senior math. scholarship 89 (accessit 87)]; lecturer in maths. St. David's coll., Lampeter 89, 90, and Durham college of science, Newcastle-upon-Tyne, 91.

Thompson, rev. Charles Howard, born at Westerham, 1866; 1s. Charles Robert, gen. CHRIST CHURCH, matric. 31 May, 84, aged 18 (from Radley coll.), B.A. 88, M.A. 90 (HONOURS:—3 theology 88); curate of Lee St. Margaret, Kent, 89.

Thompson, Edward Maunde; created D.C.L. 25 June, 1890, hon. fellow UNIVERSITY COLL. 1892, where see page 31.

Thompson, Ernest Alfred, born at Wootton-under-Edge, co. Gloucester, 7 Oct., 1862; 3s. William, cler. NON-COLLEGIATE, matric. 18 Oct., 80, aged 18 (from Haileybury); migrated to NEW COLL. 81, B.A. 83; HONOURS:—3 classical mods. 82, 3 theology 83.

Thompson, Francis Robert, born at Port Elizabeth, South Africa, 1857; 2s. Francis, M. L. C. KEBLE, matric. 21 Oct., 92, aged 35.

Thompson, Frank Edward Rogers, born at Bedale, Yorks, 7 Aug., 1868; 3s. John, cler., deceased. NON-COLLEGIATE, matric. 11 Oct., 90, aged 22.

Thompson, George Ernest, born at Bristol 2 Sept., 1871; 2s. Frederic, arm., deceased. BALLIOL, matric. 14 Oct., 90, aged 18 (from Edinburgh high school); HONOURS:—3 classical mods 92.

Thompson, Gerard Elyetson, arm.; (2s.) born at Kirkby Stephen, Westmorland, 3 March, 1864. EXETER, matric. 27 May, 82, aged 18 (from Marlborough), B.A. 87, M.A. 89.

Thompson, Harry Thompson Arnall-, born at Belgrave, co. Leic., 7 April, 1865; 1s. Joseph, of Stoneygate, Leicester, solicitor. BRASENOSE, matric. 15 Jan., 83, aged 18 (from Rugby); of Belgrave Grange, co. Leic., in University eleven 86; assumed additional final surname of Thompson 85.

Thompson, Henry Lewis, M.A., student CHRIST CHURCH 56-72, where see page 422.

Thompson, James Neville, born at Wootton-under-Edge, co. Glouc., 1865; 4s. William, cler. ORIEL, matric. 27 Oct., 83, aged 18 (from Bromsgrove gr. school), B.A. (NON-COLLEGIATE) 87.

Thompson, John Barclay, M.A., senior student CHRIST CHURCH 69, where see page 407.

Thompson, John Vickers, born at Salisbury 22 May, 1866; 1s. Thomas, Wesleyan minister. WADHAM, matric. 11 Oct., 84, aged 18 (from Kingswood school), scholar 83, B.A. 88, M.A. 92; HONOURS: —1 classical mods. 86, 2 classics 88.

Thompson, Percy, born at Whalley, co. Lanc., 18 Dec., 1872; 6s. Richard, gen. BRASENOSE, matric. 27 Jan., 91, aged 18 (from Rugby); HONOURS:— 2 mathematical mods. 92.

Thompson, rev. Reginald Beviss, born in London 22 Aug., 1852; 1s. Reginald Ward, cler. WORCESTER, matric. 19 Oct., 82, aged 30 (from Marlborough coll.), B.A. 86, M.A. 90 (HONOURS:—3 classical mods. 84, 3 history 86); assist. master 89, and chaplain Oxford military coll. 89.

Thompson, Richard Boville, born at Kirkby Stephen, Westmorland, 1862; 1s. Matthew, arm. ST. JOHN's, matric. 16 Oct., 80, aged 18; of Stobars, Westmorland, J.P., D.L.

Thompson, William, born at Burton-on-Trent, co. Stafford, 1860; 3s. Francis, gen. NON-COLLEGIATE, matric. 13 Oct., 83, aged 23 (from Malvern coll.), B.A. 86; HONOURS:—3 law 86.

Thompson, William Driggs, born at Brampton, Cumberland, 13 July, 1867; 1s. James Hutherington, arm. ORIEL, matric. 19 Oct., 86, aged 19 (from Rugby), B.A. 89 (HONOURS:—3 law 89, 3 civil law 90); bar.-at-law, Inner Temple, 92.

Thompson, William James, born at Epsom, Surrey, 14 June, 1868; o.s. William James, gen. EXETER, matric. 17 Oct., 88, aged 20, from Eton.

Thompson, William Robert, born at Horsley, co. Derby, 28 Sept., 1869; 1s. Grammer, cler. TRINITY, matric. 13 Oct., 88, aged 19 (from Repton school), B.A. 92; HONOURS:—3 law 91.

Thompson, William Scott, born at Standish, co. Lanc., 26 Aug., 1861; 1s. Robert, gen. QUEEN's, matric. 15 May, 80, aged 18 (from Sedbergh school), exhibitioner 80-5, B.A. 84 (HONOURS:—2 mathematical mods. 81, 1 mathematics 84, 3 civil law 85); bar.-at-law, Lincoln's Inn, 88.

Thomson, Adam Smith, born at Aberdeen 23 June, 1860; 3s. David, gen. LINCOLN, matric. 23 Oct., 82, aged 22 (from King's coll., Aberdeen), scholar 82-6, B.A. 86; HONOURS:—1 classical mods. 84, 2 classics 86.

Thomson, Allen, D.Med., F.R.S., created D.C.L. 14 June, 1882. See *All. Ox.* 2nd series 1412.

Thomson, Andrew, born at Edinburgh 1861; 1s. John Comrie, arm. BALLIOL, matric. 16 Oct., 83, aged 19 (from Aberdeen university, and Leibnitz Real schule, Hanover); selected candidate Indian C.S. 83; died 3 July, 90.

Thomson, Archibald Steele, born at Plymouth 20 June, 1868; 1s. Arthur, gen. EXETER, matric. 21 Oct., 86, aged 18 (from the Charterhouse and Mannamead schools), scholar 86, B.A. 90; HONOURS:—2 classical mods. 88, 3 classics 90, 2 theology 91.

Thomson, Arthur, of EXETER COLL.; M.A. by decree of convocation 9 June, 85, lecturer in human anatomy university museum 86; M.R.C.S.; see page 130.

Thomson, Arthur Ramsay, born at Sale, Cheshire, 10 Oct., 1870; 1s. John, arm. TRINITY, matric. 12 Oct., 90, aged 20 (from Rugby); HONOURS:—3 classical mods. 92.

Thomson, Basil Home, born at Queen's coll., Oxford, 21 April, 1861; 3s. William, archbishop of York. NEW COLL., matric. 17 Jan., 80, aged 18, from Eton.

Thomson, Charles Fox, born at Dulwich, Kent, 25 July, 1870; 2s. Thomas, arm. MERTON, matric. 17 Oct., 88, aged 18, from Uppingham school.

Thomson, Clement Reynolds, born at Tunbridge Wells, Kent, 30 July, 1870; 1s. John Radford arm. TRINITY, matric. 12 Oct., 89, aged 19 (from Mill Hill school); HONOURS:—3 classical mods. 92.

Thomson, Courtauld Greenwood, born at Edinburgh 1866; 2s. Robert William, arm., deceased. MAGDALEN, matric. 23 April, 84, aged 18, from Eton.

Thomson, Guy, born at Baldon, Oxon, 15 Aug., 1873; 1s. John, banker. NEW COLL., matric. 14 Oct., 92, aged 19, from Winchester.

Thomson, William, born at Corbridge, Northumberland, 1863; 2s. William Cunningham, gen. BALLIOL, matric. 17 Oct., 82, aged 19 (from St. Andrews university); scholar HERTFORD 82-6, B.A. 86, M.A. 89; HONOURS:—2 classical mods. 83, 3 classics 86; Guthrie scholarship at St. Andrews 82.

Thomson, William Edwin, born at Weston-super-Mare 1866; 1s. William, gen. BALLIOL, matric. 24 Oct., 85, aged 19 (from St. Andrews university), Bible clerk ORIEL 86, B.A. 89 (HONOURS:—2 classical mods. 87, 2 classics 89), Guthrie scholarship St. Andrews 85, and Fergusson classical scholar 87; died 5 June, 91.

Thorley, George Earlam, M.A., warden of WADHAM 81, where see page 528.

Thorley, Robert, born at Manchester 10 April, 1868; o.s. Joshua Hartford, gen. CHRIST CHURCH, matric. 12 Oct., 88, aged 20 (from St. Paul's school), scholar 88.

Thorne, Charlton, born in London 1868; 2s. Joseph, arm. CHRIST CHURCH, matric. 14 Oct., 87, aged 19, from Brighton coll.

Thorne, rev. Ernest Anderson, born at Hendon, Middx., 12 Dec., 1868; 2s. Frederick, cler. NON-COLLEGIATE, matric. 15 Oct., 87, aged 18 (from St. Paul's school, Oxford); migrated to EXETER, B.A. 90 (HONOURS:—2 theology 90); curate of Langley Marish, Bucks, 91.

Thorne, Frederick Gruetber, born at Ramsgate 1868; 1s. John Finch, gen. CORPUS CHRISTI, matric. 22 Oct., 87, aged 19 (from Hobart Town, Tasmania), B.A. 91; HONOURS:—2 classical mods. 89, 2 classics 91.

Thorne, Herbert Sandford, born in Barbados 1865; o.s. Elliot Sandford, cler. ST. JOHN's, matric. 11 Oct., 84, aged 19, B.A. 89 (HONOURS:—3 classical mods. 86, 4 law 88); bar.-at-law, Middle Temple, 91.

Thorneycroft, William, born at Brierley Hill, co. Stafford, 1862; 3s. John, gen. QUEEN'S, matric. 16 March, 92, aged 30.

Thornhill, Charles Edward, M.A., CHRIST CHURCH, where see page 426.

Thornton, Cyril Minshull, born in London 1870; o.s. Richard Napoleon, bar.-at-law. PEMBROKE, matric. 25 Oct., 89, aged 19, from Eton.

Thornton, Henry Samuel Robinson, born at Leamington 13 July, 1867; o.s. Samuel, D.D., bishop of Ballarat. TRINITY, matric. 15 Oct., 87, aged 20 (from Harrow), scholar 87, B.A. 91; HONOURS:—a classical mods. 89, 3 classics 91.

Thornton, Henry Welch-, born at East Cowes, I.W., 3 July, 1870; o.s. Henry Samuel, arm. MERTON, matric. 15 Oct., 90, aged 20.

Thornton, Hugh Aylmer, born at Wereham, Norfolk, 10 May, 1872; 3s. Thomas, gen. CHRIST CHURCH, matric. 16 Oct., 91, aged 19 (from Cheltenham coll.), scholar 91; HONOURS:—1 classical mods. 93.

Thornton, John, born at Dewsbury, Yorks, 1870; 1s. Joseph, gen. UNIVERSITY COLL., matric. 13 Oct., 88, aged 18 (from Wakefield school), exhibitioner 88.

Thornton, John Gidley, born at Epsom, Surrey, 26 Jan., 1867; 1s. Robinson, D.D. KEBLE, matric. 26 Jan., 86, aged 19 (from Winchester), B.A. 89, M.A. 92; HONOURS:—2 classical mods. 87, 3 classics 89.

Thornton, Richard, born at Sydenham, Surrey, 22 Aug., 1873; 1s. Richard. MERTON, matric. 18 Oct., 92, aged 19, from Eton.

Thornton, Robert Gidley, born at Epsom Surrey, 20 July, 1868; 2s. Robinson, D.D. KEBLE, matric. 17 Oct., 87, aged 19 (from Westminster school), B.A. 92.

Thornton, Robinson, D.D., prebendary St. Paul's; fellow ST. JOHN'S 43-55, where see page 480.

Thornton, Samuel, D.D., fellow QUEEN'S 58-61, where see page 180.

Thornton, Thomas Henry, D.C.L., fellow ST. JOHN'S 51-62, where see page 483.

Thorold, Algar Labouchere, born 9 Aug., 1866; o.s. Anthony Wilson, bishop of Winchester. CHRIST CHURCH, matric. 31 May, 84, aged 17.

Thorold, Algernon Herbert, born at Shanklin, I.w., Jan., 1872; 1s. Algernon Charles Edward, cler. KEBLE, matric. 11 Oct., 90, aged 18, from Lancing coll.

Thorold, right rev. Anthony Wilson, D.D., hon. fellow QUEEN'S 90, where see page 176.

Thorold, Arthur Charles Campbell, born at Trant, Kent, 13 Sept., 1873; 2s. Algernon Charles Edward, M.A., cler. WORCESTER, matric. 18 Oct., 92, aged 19 (from Marlborough coll.), exhibitioner 92.

Thorold, rev. Edmund, M.A., fellow MAGDALEN 57-9, where see page 324.

Thorold, Harry Grant-, born at Cleo, co. Lincoln, 1870; 2s. Alexander William Thorold, arm. CORPUS CHRISTI, matric. 25 Oct., 83, aged 19 (from Eton), B.A. 92; HONOURS:—3 history 92.

Thorold, rev. John Leofric de Buckenhold, born at Warkleigh, Devon, 13 July, 1864; 3s. William, rector. NEW COLL., matric. 12 Oct., 83, aged 19 (from Rugby), B.A. 87, M.A. 90; HONOURS:—a classical mods. 84, 2 classics 87); rector of Warkleigh 91.

Thoroton, rev. Levett Edward Wanley, born at Hersham, Surrey, 1869; 2s. Richard. CHRIST CHURCH, matric. 15 Oct., 86, aged 17, B.A. (NON-COLLEGIATE) 91.

Thorp, rev. Sidney Benson, born at Hedington, Essex, 1865; 1s. Sidney, gen. ST. EDMUND HALL, matric. 16 Jan., 83, aged 18, B.A. 86.

Thorpe, Frederick Follett Younghusband, born at Nottingham 11 April, 1865; 1s. Frederick Scadding, gen. MAGDALEN, matric. 13 Jan., 83, aged 17, B.A. 86; bar.-at-law, Inner Temple, 89.

Thralfall, William, born at Wood Plumpton, co. Lanc., 27 Jan., 1863; 2s. Richard, arm. ORIEL, matric. 17 Feb., 82, aged 19 (from Clifton coll.), B.A. 85.

Thring, Laurence Theodore, born at Liverpool 16 April, 1863; 5s. Theodore, arm. NEW COLL., matric. 14 Oct., 82, aged 19 (from Winchester), scholar 82-6, B.A. 86, M.A. 90; HONOURS:—2 classical mods 84, 2 classics 86.

Throckmorton, Oliver, born at Centreville, America, 1860; 3s. Oliver Perry, arm. CHARSLEY'S HALL, matric. 16 Dec., 81, aged 21.

Thrupp, rev. Herbert Inglis, born at Seaton, Devon, 24 June, 1866; 5s. Hornee William, cler. ST. MARY HALL, matric. 19 Oct., 85, aged 19, B.A. 89; curate of Seaton 90.

Thurburn, Martin Lloyd, born at Norwood, Surrey, 1872; 3s. Felix Augustus Victor, colonel in the army. ORIEL, matric. 27 Oct., 92, aged 20, from Dulwich coll.

Thurn, Johannes Douglas, count, born at Gratz, in Austria, 1864; 1. John Douglas, count T. CHRIST CHURCH, matric. 14 Oct., 81, aged 17.

Thurnall, Arthur, born at Bedford 17 July, 1865; 2s. William, gent. WADHAM, matric. 11 Oct., 84, aged 19 (from Bedford gr. school), scholar 83, B.A. 88; HONOURS:—1 classical mods. 86, 2 classics 88.

Thursby, Harvey William Gustavus, born at Wormleighton, co. Warwick, June, 1867; 2s. Arthur Harvey, gen. PEMBROKE, matric. 25 Oct., 87, aged 20, from Wellington.

Thursfield, James Hugh, born at Leamington 29 July, 1869; 1s. Thomas William, D.Med. TRINITY, matric. 13 Oct., 88, aged 19 (from Leamington coll.), exhibitioner 87, B.A. 92; HONOURS:—1 classical mods. 90, 2 classics 92.

Thursfield, James Richard, M.A., fellow JESUS COLL. 64-81, where see page 513.

Thursfield, William Heath, born at Leamington 1871; 2s. Thomas William, D.Med. UNIVERSITY COLL., matric. 12 Oct., 89, aged 18 (from Leamington coll.), scholar 89; HONOURS:—2 classical mods. 91.

Thurstans, John Aubrey, born at Tettenhall, co. Stafford, 1864; 1s. John, gen. NON-COLLEGIATE, matric. 12 May, 83, aged 19.

Thurston, Edward de Basset, born at Blandford, Dorset, 12 June, 1867; 2s. Hugh Kingsmill, arm. TRINITY, matric. 16 Oct., 86, aged 19 (from Sherborne school), B.A. 89; HONOURS:—4 history 89.

Thynne, lord Alexander George, born in London 17 Feb., 1873; 3s. John Alexander, marquis of Bath. BALLIOL, matric. 20 Oct., 91, aged 18, from Eton.

Thynne, John Alexander Roger, born in London 2 Sept., 1863; 3s. (lord) Henry Frederick. NEW COLL., matric. 12 Oct., 83, aged 20 (from Eton); HONOURS:—2 classical mods. 85.

Thynne, Thomas Henry, viscount Weymouth, born 15 July, 1862; 1s. John Alexander, marquis of Bath. BALLIOL, matric. 20 Jan., 81, aged 18 (from Eton), B.A. 86, M.A. 88 (HONOURS:—4 history 84); M.P. Somersetshire (Frome division) July 86—Aug. 92.

Tibbits, Charles John, born at Chester 1861; 3s. George, gen. NON-COLLEGIATE, matric. 18 Oct., 80, aged 19 (from Albion house school, Chester), B.A. 86.

Tibbits, John Knox, born at Troy, New York State, 13 Jan., 1870; o.s. Charles Edward Dudley, gent. NON-COLLEGIATE, matric. 15 Oct., 92, aged 22, from Yale university, U.S.A.

Tibbs, John Harding, born at Roseren, Ireland, 16 March, 1863; 1s. Philip Graydon, S.T.P. WORCESTER, matric. 22 Jan., 85, aged 21, scholar 84, B.A. 89 (HONOURS:—1 classical mods. 86, 2 classics 88), scholar Trinity coll., Dublin, B.A. 82, and 2nd classical scholar 84, 1 classics and Greek medal Dublin university 85.

Ticehurst, Rowland Francis, born at Cheltenham 1872; 1s. Rowland, arm. UNIVERSITY COLL., matric. 11 Oct., 90, aged 18.

Tickell, George, B.A., Stowell fellow UNIVERSITY COLL. 37-40, where see page 34.

Tidd, Edgar Mason, born at Herne Hill, Kent, 4 April, 1868; 1s. Walter Robert, gen. NEW COLL., matric. 14 Oct., 87, aged 19 (from the Charterhouse), B.A. 92; HONOURS:—3 classical mods. 89.

Tidman, Arthur, born in London July, 1865; 1s. Paul Frederic, gen. CHRIST CHURCH, matric. 10 Oct., 84, aged 19, B.A. 87, M.A. 91.

Tidmarsh, rev. Thomas William, born at Steeple Claydon, Bucks, 25 Dec., 1857; 1s. Thomas, pleb. NON-COLLEGIATE, matric. 13 Oct., 83, aged 24 (from St. John's school, Oxford, and St. Mark's coll., Chelsea); exhibitioner EXETER 86, B.A. 87, M.A. 90 (HONOURS:—2 theology 87); curate of Plympton St. Mary, Devon, 90.

Tidswell, Walter Ingham, born at Thornbury, parish of Calverley, Yorks, 23 March, 1873; 1s. Alfred Ingham, of Frisinghall, Bradford, merchant. QUEEN'S, matric. 27 Oct., 92, aged 19 (from Bradford school), exhibitioner 92.

Tiffen, Herbert Joseph, born at Sledmere, Yorks, 11 July, 1869; 3s. Joseph, gen. WORCESTER, matric. 16 Oct., 88, aged 19 (from Malvern coll.), B.A. 92; HONOURS:—2 classical mods. 90, 3 classics 92.

Tillyard, Francis, born at Sprowston, Norfolk, 1865; 4s. Isaac, gen. BALLIOL, matric. 16 Oct., 83, aged 18 (from city of London school), exhibitioner 82, B.A. 87 (HONOURS:—1 mathematical mods. 84, 1 mathematics 86, 1 law 88, Vinerian law scholarship 88); bar.-at-law, Middle Temple, 90.

Tilney, Robert Henry, born at Liverpool 1866; 1s. Robert John, gen. BRASENOSE, matric. 23 Oct., 85, aged 19, from Eton.

Timbrell, rev. William Frederick John, born at Islington 1869; o.s. William, gen. NON-COLLEGIATE, matric. 13 Oct., 88, aged 19, B.A. 92 (HONOURS:—4 theology 92); curate of Buckingham.

Timmis, George Dunstan, born at Waterloo, co. Lanc., 1866; 2s. Thomas Sutton, gen. CHRIST CHURCH, matric. 10 Oct., 84, aged 18, B.A. 88.

Timmis, Thomas Sutton, born at Aigburth, co. Lanc., 1867; 3s. Thomas Sutton, arm. CHRIST CHURCH, matric. 30 May, 85, aged 17 (from the Charterhouse), B.A. 89 (HONOURS:—3 law 89); bar.-at-law, Lincoln's Inn, 91.

Tindall, Gilbert John, born at Scarborough, Yorks, 1872; 1s. John, banker. CORPUS CHRISTI, matric. 19 Oct., 91, aged 19 (from Clifton coll.), exhibitioner 91; HONOURS:—2 classical mods. 93.

Tingey, John Cottingham, born at Ellingham, Norfolk, 1861; 1s. John, gen. EXETER, matric. 28 Jan., 81, aged 19 (from Norwich gr. school), B.A. and M.A. 87.

Tinkler, Robert Nicolas, born at Whiston, co. Lanc., 24 March, 1866; 2s. John, M.A. (Camb.), vicar of Caunton, Notts. NON-COLLEGIATE, matric. 15 Oct., 92, aged 26.

Tinniswood, Joseph, born at Glassonby, Cumberland, 8 May, 1868; 2s. Joseph, gen. QUEEN'S, matric. 21 Oct., 87, aged 19 (from St. Bees gr. school), B.A. 91; HONOURS:—2 classical mods. 89, 2 classics 91.

Tissot, Lucien Ernest Robert, born at Chaux-de-Fonds, Switzerland, 1854; 2s. Charles Olivier, arm. NON-COLLEGIATE, matric. 29 April, 81, aged 27, B.A. and M.A. 88.

Titchener, Edward Bradford, born at Chichester 11 Jan., 1867; 1s. John, gent. BRASENOSE, matric. 23 Oct., 85, aged 18 (from Malvern coll.), scholar 85, B.A. 90; HONOURS:—1 classical mods. 87, 1 classics 89.

Titherington, rev. Arthur Fluitt, born at Chester 14 Nov., 1865; 3s. William, arm. QUEEN'S, matric. 22 Oct., 84, aged 18 (from Magdalen coll. school), scholar 84, B.A. 88, M.A. 91 (HONOURS:—2 classical mods. 86, 2 classics 88, 2 history 89) stroke of University eight 87; assist. master Radley coll. 89.

Titherington, Richard Handfield, born at Chester 2 Oct., 1861; 2s. William, arm. MAGDALEN, matric. 16 Oct., 80, aged 19 (from Winchester), demy 80-3; HONOURS:—accessit Hertford scholarship 82, 1 classical mods. 82, 3 classics 84.

Tod, Walter MacLeod, born at Woolton, near Liverpool, 28 June, 1865; 5s. Archibald, gen. PEMBROKE, matric. 2 May, 88, aged 22, B.A. 92.

Todd, David Bansall, born at Sydney, N.S.W., 31 Jan., 1867; 4s. John, gen. LINCOLN, matric. 3 Feb., 86, aged 19 (from Uppingham school), B.A. 89; HONOURS:—3 history 89.

Todhunter, Arthur Louis, born at Cambridge 28 Sept., 1868; 2s. Isaac, M.A., late fellow St. John's, Cambridge (senior wrangler 48). CORPUS CHRISTI, matric. 22 Oct., 87, aged 19 (from the Charterhouse), B.A. 92; HONOURS:—3 classical mods. 89.

Todhunter, Francis Gerald, born at Cambridge 18 June, 1872; 3s. Isaac, M.A., late fellow St. John's, Cambridge (senior wrangler 48). NEW COLL., matric. 16 Oct., 91, aged 19, from Marlborough.

Toke, Leslie Alexander St. Lawrence, born at Camberley, Surrey, 10 Aug., 1871; 2s. col. John Leslie, of Godinton, Kent. BALLIOL, matric. 20 Oct., 91, aged 20, from Clifton coll.

Tolcher, Henry Edward Archer, born at Newton Abbot, Devon, 1862; 1s. Henry John, arm. CHARSLEY'S HALL, matric. 25 Jan., 82, aged 20.

Toler, Thomas Clayton, born in London 1863; 1s. John Merton, arm. CHRIST CHURCH, matric. 22 Jan., 83, aged 20, from Eton.

Toler, William Brabazon Lindesay Graham, 4th earl of Norbury, born 2 July, 1862; 1s. Hector, earl of Norbury. CHRIST CHURCH, matric. 13 Oct., 82, aged 20, from Harrow.

Tollinton, Henry Phillips, born at York 1870; 2s. Richard Bartram, gen. BALLIOL, matric. 17 Oct., 89, aged 19 (from Leamington coll.), exhibitioner 89; HONOURS:—1 classical mods. 91.

Tollinton, rev. Richard Bartram, born at Heworth, Yorks, 1866; 1s. Richard Bartram, gen. BALLIOL, matric. 24 Oct., 85, aged 19 (from Leamington coll.), exhibitioner 85, B.A. 89, M.A. 93; HONOURS:—1 classical mods. 87, 2 classics 89.

Tollit, Arthur Henry, born at Oxford 4 Feb., 1869; 2s. Henry James, architect. LINCOLN, matric. 21 Oct., 87, aged 18 (from Magdalen coll. school), scholar 87, B.A. 91 (HONOURS:—ægrotat classics 91); brother of Percy K.

Tollit, Charles Rowland, born at Holywell, Oxford, 1873; 4s. Henry James, architect. LINCOLN, matric. 23 Oct., 91, aged 18 (from Magdalen coll. school), scholar 91.

Tollit, Percy Kitto, born at Oxford 1 Aug., 1863; 1s. Henry James, architect. MAGDALEN, matric. 15 Oct., 81, aged 18 (from Magdalen coll. school), demy 81-6, B.A. 86, M.A. 88; HONOURS:—1 mathematical mods. 82, accessit junior mathematical scholarship 83, 1 mathematics 85, 1 physics 86.

Tomaszewski, Alfred Hugo, born at Edinburgh 9 Feb., 1871; 1s. Hugh Frederick, gen. JESUS COLL., matric. 14 Oct., 89, aged 18 (from Southwark gr. school); HONOURS:—3 classical mods. 91, Taylorian (German) exhibition 91.

Tombleson, James Bennett, born at Barton-on-Humber, co. Lincoln, 7 Nov., 1872; 2s. James Bennett, arm. CORPUS CHRISTI, matric. 17 Oct., 90, aged 17 (from St. Paul's school), scholar 90.

Tomkins, James George, born at Lutterworth, co. Leic., 10 July, 1861; 4s. James Peebles Oman, cler. BALLIOL, matric. 21 Oct.; 80, aged 19, B.A. 84 (HONOURS:—3 classical mods. 82, 3 classics 84); died 1 April, 87.

Tomkins, Percy Smith, born in London 25 June, 1871; 2s. Samuel Leith, gent. KEBLE, matric. 15 Oct., 92, aged 21, from St. Paul's school.

Tomlin, Harry Marmaduke, born in London 1866; 2s. John Leonard, gen. BALLIOL, matric. 16 Oct., 83, aged 17 (from Leamington coll.); died 15 Nov., 91.

Tomlin, James William Sackett, born at Canterbury 18 July, 1871; 1s. George Taddy, bar.-at-law. NEW COLL., matric. 10 Oct., 90, aged 19, from Harrow (HONOURS:—2 classical mods. 92); brother of Thomas J. C.

Tomlin, Morton James Baring, born in London 9 March, 1862; 1s. John Leonard, solicitor. NEW COLL., matric. 15 Oct., 81, aged 20 (from Eton), B.A. 84, M.A. 88.

Tomlin, Thomas James Chesshyre, born at Canterbury 6 May, 1867; 1s. George Taddy, bar.-at-law. NEW COLL., matric. 16 Oct., 85, aged 18 (from Harrow), B.A. 89, M.A. and B.C.L. 92 (HONOURS:—3 classical mods. 87, 1 law 89, 2 civil law 91); bar.-at-law, Middle Temple, 91; brother of James W. S.

Tomlinson, Bernard Dixon, born at Manchester 1862; 3s. Thomas, gen. BRASENOSE, matric. 18 Oct., 81, aged 19 (from Manchester gr. school), scholar 81, B.A. 86; HONOURS:—1 classical mods. 83, 2 classics 85.

Tomlinson, Charles Henry, M.A., fellow WORCESTER 64-70, where see page 576.

Tomlinson, rev. James Frederic, born at Bradly, co. Derby, March, 1863; 5s. William, gen. CHRIST CHURCH, matric. 22 Oct., 83, aged 20 (from Derby school), B.A. 86, M.A. 90 (HONOURS:—3 history 86); curate of Berners Roding, Essex, 86-9, Cavendish, Suffolk, 89-90.

Tomlinson, Robert George, born at Winshill, co. Derby, 30 March, 1869; 1s. Henry George, arm. MAGDALEN, matric. 16 Oct., 88, aged 19 (from Repton school); HONOURS:—2 classical mods. 90.

Tonge, Arthur William, born at Aston near Birmingham 9 Oct., 1869; 1s. George, cler. BRASENOSE, matric. 16 Oct., 88, aged 19 (from Repton school), scholar 88; HONOURS:—1 classical mods. 90, 2 classics 92.

Toogood, Charles Frederick Strangways Gwynne, born at Calcutta 1867; o.s. Octavius, arm. NON-COLLEGIATE, matric. 20 Nov., 80, aged 19 (from Eton); migrated to EXETER 28 Jan., 81.

Topham, Arthur George, born at Elson, Salop, Feb., 1869; y.s. Robert, cler. KEBLE, matric. 17 Oct., 87, aged 18 (from Oswestry gr. school), B.A. 91; brother of Robert.

Topham, rev. George Saint John, born at Biggin, co. Derby, 1864; 3s. Robert, cler. WORCESTER, matric. 22 April, 82, aged 18, B.A. 85, M.A. 88 (HONOURS:—4 history 85); curate of St. Anne, Birkenhead, 87-91.

Topham, Robert, born at Ellesmere, Salop, 1867; 1s. Robert, cler. KEBLE, matric. 19 Oct., 86, aged 18 (from Oswestry gr. school); brother of Arthur G.

Torr, William George, born at Tavistock, Devon, 1853; 4s. John, gen. NON-COLLEGIATE, matric. 4 Nov., 86, aged 33 (from Adelaide university); migrated to ST. JOHN'S, B.A. 89 (HONOURS: —4 theology 89, 3 civil law 91); migrated to DOWNING COLL., CAMB., 21 Oct., 89, incorporated (B.A.) 12 Dec., 89; bar.-at-law, Inner Temple, 91.

Tottenham, Francis Robert Loftus, born at Torquay 31 July, 1873; 7s. John Francis, capt. R.N. QUEEN'S, matric. 9 Feb., 92, aged 18 (from Clifton coll.), scholar 92; HONOURS:—1 classical mods. 93.

Tottenham, Edward Hyacinth, born at St. Leonards, Sussex, 1861; 2s. John W., cler. EXETER, matric. 15 May, 80, aged 19 (from Harrow), B.A. 90, M.A. 91.

Tourtel, rev. William Ernest, born at Alderney 1865; 2s. John, gen. PEMBROKE, matric. 28 Oct., 86, aged 21, B.A. 90 (HONOURS:—4 theology 90); curate of Guernsey St. Martin 90.

Tout, Thomas Frederick, M.A. fellow PEMBROKE 83-90, where see page 555.

Tower, David Eric, born at Leicester 1870; 5s. Ferdinand Ernest, cler. HERTFORD, matric. 14 Oct., 90, aged 20, from Dover coll.

Tower, rev. Frederick, born at East Chilton, co. Leicester, 10 Dec., 1863; 2s. Ferdinand Ernest, cler. HERTFORD, matric. 14 Oct., 84, aged 20 (from Lancing coll.), scholar 83, B.A. 87, M.A. 91; curate of St. Mary with St. Nicholas, Beverley, 89.

Tower, rev. Henry, born at Hurstpierpoint, Sussex, 1866; 1s. Ferdinand Ernest, cler. HERTFORD, matric. 18 Oct., 82, aged 18 (from Lancing coll.), scholar 81-6, B.A. 86, M.A. 89; curate of Leicester St. Andrew 86.

Tower, Noel Percival, born at Chilmark, Wilts, Oct., 1863; 5s. Charles, cler. KEBLE, matric. 16 Oct., 83, aged 19 (from Lancing coll.), B.A. 87, M.A. 90.

Towers, Robert Montagu, born in London 11 Dec., 1867; 1s. Robert, cler. CHRIST CHURCH, matric. 15 Oct., 86, aged 18 (from Westminster school), scholar 86, B.A. 90; HONOURS:—2 classical mods. 88, 2 classics 90, 2 history 92.

Townend, Douglas Abner, born at Clapham, Surrey, 1866; 3s. Arthur Powell, gen. ST. JOHN'S, matric. 12 Oct., 89, aged 23 (from King's coll. school, Lond.), scholar 93; HONOURS:—2 classical mods. 91.

Townend, Henry, born at Cullingworth, Yorks, 17 Aug., 1864; 3s. Joseph, gen. HERTFORD, matric. 18 Oct., 83, aged 19 (from Rugby), scholar 82; HONOURS:—2 classical mods. 85, 3 classics 87.

Townend, Henry Charles Wise, born at Loddiswell, Devon, 1868; 1s. Henry, cler. NON-COLLEGIATE, matric. 25 Jan., 88, aged 20, from Appleby gr. school.

Townley, rev. Stuart Augustus, born in London 1859; 2s. Charles Augustus, gen. NON-COLLEGIATE, matric. 13 Oct., 84, aged 25 (from Wick school, Brighton); migrated to ST. MARY HALL, B.A. and M.A. 92.

Townsend, James, born at Abingdon, Berks, 10 Dec., 72; 4s. Thomas, gen. PEMBROKE, matric. 26 Oct., 91, aged 18 (from Abingdon school), scholar 91; HONOURS:—2 classical mods 93.

Townshend, Arthur Edward, born at Myross, co. Cork, 1863; 4s. John Handcock, arm. CORPUS CHRISTI, matric. 23 Oct., 84, aged 21.

Townshend, Brian Chambré, born in London 9 April, 1874; 1s. Chambrey Corker, architect. NEW COLL., matric. 19 Oct., 92, aged 18, from Sedbergh school.

Townson, George Benjamin, born at Barrow-in-Furness, co. Lanc., 1 Aug., 1871; 2s. Benjamin, gen. ST. MARY HALL, matric. 20 Oct., 90, aged 19.

Townson, rev. Robert Walter, born at Grayrigg, Westmorland, 1864; 2s. Robert, cler. ST. JOHN'S, matric. 16 Oct., 86, aged 22 (from Rossall school), B.A. 89 (HONOURS:—3 theology 89); curate of Warkworth, Northumberland, 91.

Tozer, Ernest Evan Morgan, born at Birkenhead, Cheshire, 1864; 1s. Morgan, arm. JESUS COLL., matric. 18 Oct., 83, aged 19 (from Llandovery coll.), scholar 83.

Tozer, Ferris, born at Exeter 1858; o.s. John Ferris, gen. QUEEN'S, matric. 15 Jan., 91; aged 33. B.Mus. 91.

Tozer, rev. Henry Fanshawe, M.A., fellow EXETER 50-68, 82-93, where see page 123.

Tracey, rev. Frederick, born at Dartmouth, Devon, 10 March, 1858; 4s. John, cler. LINCOLN, matric. 30 Jan., 82, aged 23 (from Honiton and Uppingham schools), exhibitioner EXETER 82-3, B.A. 84 (HONOURS:—3 mathematical mods. 83); M.A. university of Sydney 85, vice-warden of St. Paul coll., Sydney university, 85-6, second master Colston's gr. school, Bristol, 86-8, principal of All Souls' coll., etc., Bath, 88, chaplain to bishop of Bath 91.

Tracey, John, born at Dartmouth, Devon, 29 April, 1862; 6a. John, cler. BRASENOSE, matric. 18 Oct., 81, aged 19 (from Winchester), scholar 81, B.A. 85, M.A. 88, tutor KEBLE 87; HONOURS:—1 classical mods. 85.

Trafford, Guy Rawson, born at Tenby, co. Pembroke, 1863; 4s. Charles Guy, arm. EXETER, matric. 18 Oct., 83, aged 20, B.A. 87.

Traill, Henry Duff, D.C.L., fellow ST. JOHN'S 61-79, where see page 484.

Traill, William Frederick, D.C.L., fellow ST. JOHN'S 56, where see page 477.

Treadgold, Arthur Newton Christian, born at Gonerby, co. Lincoln, 1863; 1s. Thomas George, gen. HERTFORD, matric. 18 Oct., 82, aged 19 (from Grantham school), scholar 81-6, B.A. 87, M.A. 89; HONOURS:—2 classical mods. 83, 2 classics 86.

Trefusis, hon. Charles John Robert, born 18 Jan., 1863; 1s. Charles Henry Rolle, baron Clinton. CHRIST CHURCH, matric. 4 June, 81, aged 18, from Eton.

Tregarthen, Greville Philipps, born in London 19 April, 1864; 2s. William Francis, cler., late inspector of schools. UNIVERSITY COLL., matric. 14 Oct., 82, aged 18 (from Sherborne school), exhibitioner 83-4.

Tregarthen, Hugh Philipps, born at Osmington, Dorset, 22 Dec., 1860; 1s. William Francis, cler., inspector of schools. UNIVERSITY COLL., matric. 16 Oct., 80, aged 19 (from Sherborne school), scholar 80-5, B.A. and M.A. 87 (HONOURS:—2 classical mods. 82, 2 classics 84); in government statistical department; died 9 Sept., 90.

Treharne, Everson James, born at Aberdare, co. Glamorgan, 1871; 2s. Treharne, gen. ST. EDMUND HALL, matric. 11 Feb., 90, aged 21.

Treharne, Lionel Belville, born in London 30 Nov., 1863; 5s. Henry, of Somerset House. QUEEN'S, matric. 31 Jan., 82, aged 18, from Godolphin gr. school, Hammersmith.

Tremenheere, Hugh Seymour, C.B., M.A., fellow NEW COLL. 24-56, where see page 209.

Trench, Frederic Herbert, born at Midleton, co. Cork, 12 Nov., 1865; 1s. William Wallace, arm. KEBLE, matric. 14 Oct., 84, aged 18 (from Haileybury), exhibitioner 84, B.A. 88; fellow ALL SOULS', 89, M.A. 92 (HONOURS:—1 history 88); in the education department, home office.

Trench, Frederic Oliver, 3rd baron Ashtown, born 2 Feb., 1868; 1s. Frederic Sydney Charles, baron Ashtown. MAGDALEN, matric. 22 Oct., 87, aged 19, from Eton.

Trendall, Edwin Percival, born at Abingdon, Berks, 17 Aug., 1873; 1s. William Henry, gent. WORCESTER, matric. 18 Oct., 92, aged 19, from St. Edward's school, Summertown.

Trepté, George Herbert, born at Chelsea 25 April, 1869; 1s. George Frederick, schoolmaster. EXETER, matric. 17 Oct., 88, aged 19 (from Bedford gr. school), scholar 88, B.A. 92; HONOURS:—2 classical mods. 90, 3 classics 92.

Trethewy, Antony William, born at Silsoe, Beds, 1 March, 1864; 2s. Henry, gen. TRINITY, matric. 14 Oct., 82, aged 18 (from Winchester), B.A. 85 (HONOURS:—2 law 85); joint magistrate N.W. provinces India.

Trethewy, Thomas Langdon, born at Silsoe, Beds, 30 May, 1867; 4s. Henry, gen. TRINITY, matric. 17 Oct., 85, aged 18 (from Marlborough); lieut. the Duke of Cornwall's light infantry 91.

Trevelyan, Francis, born at Wolverhampton, Bucks, 21 Oct., 1862; 4s. William Pitt, cler. KEBLE, matric. 30 Oct., 80, aged 18, from Winchester.

Trevelyan, right hon sir George Otto, bart., created D.C.L. 17 June, 1885. See *Al. Ox.* and series 1437.

Trevelyan, sir Walter John, bart., born at Goldsithney, Cornwall, 28 Jan., 1866; o.s. Willoughby John, arm. EXETER, matric. 21 Oct., 86, aged 20, from Newton Abbot coll.

Trewby, Cecil, born at New Wandsworth, Surrey, 22 Nov., 1873; 5s. William George, draper. WADHAM, matric. 18 Oct., 92, aged 18 (from Merchant Taylors' school), exhibitioner 92.

Trewby, Norman, born in London 1868; 4s. William George, gen. HERTFORD, matric 22 Oct., 86, aged 18 (from St. Paul's school), scholar 85, B.A. 90; HONOURS:—2 classical mods. 88, 2 classics 90.

Trier, Emil Antony, born at Camberwell, Surrey, 22 June, 1863; y.s. Theodore, gent. TRINITY, matric. 14 Oct., 82, aged 19 (from University coll., London), B.A. 86, M.A. 90 (HONOURS:—3 history 86); bar.-at-law, Inner Temple, 90.

Trimmer, rev. Charles, M.A., fellow CORPUS CHRISTI 51, where see page 379.

Trimmer, Robert, M.A., fellow WADHAM 46-7, where see page 531.

Trinder, rev. Arthur Robert Burn, born at Teddington, Middx., 21 Jan., 1865; 2s. Daniel, vicar of Highgate. HERTFORD, matric. 18 Oct., 83, aged 18, B.A. 87, M.A. 90; curate of Gainsborough 88-91, and of New Somerby, (both) co. Lanc., 91.

Tringham, Stuart William George, born at Busbridge, Surrey, 1867; 1s. William, cler. ST. JOHN'S, matric. 16 Jan., 85, aged 18.

Tripp, Henry, M.A., fellow WORCESTER 45-58, where see page 575.

Tripp, Owen Howard, born at Winford, near Bristol, 6 Jan., 1862; 1s. Henry, cler. NON-COLLEGIATE, matric. 18 Oct., 80, aged 18, from Bradfield coll.

Tristram, Charles Edward, born in London 1869; 2s. Thomas Hutchinson, D.C.L., Q.C. BRASENOSE, matric. 20 Oct., 87, aged 18 (from Hereford school), scholar 87 (HONOURS:—3 classical mods. 89); and lieut. the Dorsetshire regt. 91.

Tristram, Henry Barrington, born at Greetham, co. Durham, 5 Sept., 1861; 1s. Henry Baker, canon of Durham, D.C.L. HERTFORD, matric. 19 Oct., 81, aged 20 (from Loretto school), scholar 80-5, B.A. 85, M.A. 89; HONOURS:—2 classical mods. 83, 2 classics 85.

Tristram, James Floyd, born at Hulme, co. Lanc., 19 Oct., 1864; 1s. George, arm. MERTON, matric. 19 Oct., 83, aged 19 (from Manchester gr. school), postmaster 83, B.A. 87; HONOURS:—2 mathematical mods. 85, 2 chemistry 87; 1 chemistry at London 86.

Tristram, John Christopher, born at Penton, Hants, 1864; 3s. Henry Baker, canon of Durham. EXETER, matric. 18 Oct., 83, aged 19, from the Charterhouse.

Tristram, Percy Preston, born at Bolton, co. Lanc., 1862; 3s. William, arm. BRASENOSE, matric. 10 June, 81, aged 19 (from Clifton coll.), B.A. 84, M.A. 88.

Trollope, Andrew Harvey, born at Streatham, Surrey, 1861; 6s. George Francis, gen. UNIVERSITY COLL., matric. 16 Jan., 80, aged 19 (from the Charterhouse), B.A. 83, M.A. 86; HONOURS:—3 classical mods. 81, 4 history 83.

Trollope, rev. Mark Napier, born in London 28 March, 1862; 2s. Charles Brown, arm. NEW COLL., matric. 15 Oct., 81, aged 19 (from Lancing coll.), B.A. 86, M.A. 88 (HONOURS:—2 classical mods. 83, 3 classics 85); missionary (S.P.G.) at Seoul, Corea, 90, and bishop's chaplain.

Trotman, Clement Newsham, born at Calcutta 7 Aug., 1871; 2s. William Charles, arm. NEW COLL., matric. 10 Oct., 90, aged 19 (from Bruton gr. school); HONOURS:—2 classical mods. 92.

Trotman, Edward Fiennes, B.C.L., fellow NEW COLL. 47-59, where see page 213.

Trotter, rev. Archibald Owen, born at Newnham, co. Glouc., 1861; 5s. John, gen. ST. EDMUND HALL, matric. 25 Oct., 80, aged 19, B.A. 84; curate of Stroud (H.T.) 90.

Troughton, rev. Leslie Wycliffe, born at Bebington, Cheshire, Oct., 1866; 5s. George, cler. KEBLE, matric. 22 Oct., 85, aged 19 (from Liverpool coll.), B.A. 88 (HONOURS:—2 theology 88); curate of Chester (Christ Church) 89.

Trounoer, Harold Moltke, born at Kingston, Surrey, 20 Feb., 1871; 3s. John Henry, of Surbiton, D. Med. UNIVERSITY COLL., matric. 11 Oct., 90, aged 19 (from Eastbourne coll.), scholar 90; HONOURS: —2 mathematical mods. 91, twice.

Troup, Charles Edward, born at Huntley, Aberdeenshire, 1858; 1s. Robert, cler. BALLIOL, matric. 21 Jan., 80, aged 22 (from Aberdeen university), exhibitioner 77-83, B.A. 63 (HONOURS:—Cobden prize 83); 1 philosophy at Aberdeen 76; bar.-at-law, Middle Temple 88.

Trow, Edwyn Buckley, born at Kerry, co. Montgomery, 15 Oct., 1868; 1s. Alfred, gen. NON-COLLEGIATE, matric. 17 Oct., 91, aged 22, from Saltley coll., Birmingham.

Trower, Cuthbert Fetherston, born in London 1861; 6s. George, arm. ST. JOHN'S, matric. 27 April, 81, aged 20, B.A. 86, M.A. 88.

Trower, Gerard, born at Hook, Yorks, Dec., 1860; 5s. Arthur, gen. KEBLE, matric. 18 Oct., 81, aged 20 (from Merchant Taylors' school), B.A. 85, M.A. 88; HONOURS:—3 theology 85.

Trueman, Henry Joseph, born in London 1862; 1s. Joseph, gent. CHRIST CHURCH, matric. 27 Jan., 86, aged 24.

Trustram, Edward Jones, born at Tunbridge Wells 1865; 1s. William Prince, gen. WORCESTER, matric. 18 Oct., 83, aged 18, B.A. 86, M.A. 90; HONOURS:—4 law 86.

Trye, Richard Norwood, born at Hartshill, co. Warwick, 6 June, 1873; 2s. Henry Norwood, J.P. ST. EDMUND HALL, matric. 19 Oct., 92, aged 19, from Nuneaton gr. school.

Tubbs, Henry Arnold, born at Crumpsall, co. Lanc., 1865; 1s. Henry Harmer, gent. PEMBROKE, matric. 17 Oct., 83, aged 18 (from Manchester gr. school), scholar 83-7, B.A. 87, B.A. 87, M.A. 91; HONOURS:— 1 classical mods. 84, 1 classics 87, Craven travelling fellowship 88, Arnold essay 89.

Tucker, Alexander Lungun Pendock, born in London 2 Nov., 1861; 1s. Henry Pendock St. George, arm. BALLIOL, matric. 21 Oct., 80, aged 18 (from Winchester); 1st assist.-agent at Indore to governor-general India.

Tucker, Alfred Robert, born at Woolwich 1849; 2s. Edward, gent. NON-COLLEGIATE, matric. 11 Oct., 79, aged 30, B.A. from CHRIST CHURCH 82, M.A. 86, created D.D. 16 June, 91; curate of St. Andrew-the-less, Clifton, 82-5, and of St. Nicholas, Durham, 85-90, hon. D.D. Durham 91, bishop of Eastern equatorial Africa 90.

Tucker, rev. Charles Cartwright, born at Ashburton, Devon, 1865; 2s. Robert Coard, gen. ST. EDMUND HALL, matric. 22 Oct., 84, aged 19, B.A. 88, M.A. 91; curate of Prickwillow, Ely, 89.

Tucker, Charles Comyns, M.A., fellow UNIVERSITY COLL. 69-80, where see page 33.

Tucker, Charles Marwood, born in London 7 Oct., 1864; o.s. Marwood, bar.-at-law. MAGDALEN, matric. 19 Oct., 83, aged 19, from Eton.

Tucker, Frederick Howell, born at Northam, Devon, 1862; 4s. William, gen. EXETER, matric. 15 May, 80, aged 18, from Shrewsbury gr. school.

Tucker, John Savile, born at Westbury, co. Glouc., 1867; 1s. John Henry, gent. BALLIOL, matric. 19 Oct., 86, aged 19 (from Bristol gr. school), scholar 85, B.A. 89 (HONOURS:—1 mathematical mods. 87, junior 88, and senior mathematical exhibition 87, junior 88, and senior mathematical scholarship 90); 1 mathematics at London 88.

Tucker, Robert Frank Wrentmore, born at Bristol 1854; o.s. Robert, gen. MERTON, matric. 18 Oct., 81, aged 27, from a Clifton school.

Tucker, rev. Sydney Herbert Thomas, born at South Molton, Devon, Dec., 1865; 3s. William, gent. KEBLE, matric. 22 Oct., 85, aged 19 (from Heavitree coll.), B.A. 88, M.A. 92.

Tucker, William Lyddon, born at Bristol 16 Feb., 1867; 1s. William, gen. NON-COLLEGIATE, matric. 13 Oct., 88, aged 21 (from Bristol gr. school and University coll., London); migrated to EXETER, B.A. 92; HONOURS:—3 theology 91.

Tuckett, Philip Debell, born in London 22 Dec., 1868; 1s. Philip Debell, arm. TRINITY, matric. 15 Oct., 87, aged 18 (from Marlborough), B.A. 90 (HONOURS:—Ægrotat history 90), in University eight 90.

Tuckey, Charles Sprot, born at Tenby, co. Pembroke, 7 July, 1867; o.s. Charles Rickards, R.N. WADHAM, matric. 19 Oct., 85, aged 18 (from Warrington gr. school), B.A. 92.

Tuckey, James Grove White, born at Canterbury 5 June, 1864; 2s. Charles Caulfield, B.Med. TRINITY, matric. 15 Oct., 83, aged 19 (from Canterbury school), Ford student 83, B.A. 88, M.A. 90 (HONOURS:—1 classical mods. 85, 3 classics 87); lecturer in modern languages at Durham university.

Tuckwell, Henry Matthews, M.A., D.Med. LINCOLN, where see page 246.

Tuckwell, William, M.A., fellow NEW COLL. 48-59, where see page 213.

611   TUDBALL. —— MATRICULATIONS, 1880 TO 1892. —— TURNOR.   612

Tudball, William, born at Callian, East Indies, 1866; 2s. Charles, arm. CHRIST CHURCH, matric. 16 Oct., 85, aged 19 (from Bedford modern school), scholar 85; assist. magistrate N.W. provinces India 87.

Tufnell, Charles Edward, born at Stourpaine, Dorset, Sept., 1865; 1s. Charles, vicar. KEBLE, matric. 14 Oct., 84, aged 19 (from Uppingham school), B.A. 88.

Tufnell, right rev. Edward Wyndham, D.D., bishop of Brisbane 59-75, fellow WADHAM 39-67, where see page 531.

Tufnell, rev. Frederick, born at Chelsea, Middx., 21 Oct., 1860; 3s. Edward Carleton, arm. MAGDALEN, matric. 16 Oct., 80, M.A. 87 (HONOURS:—4 classical coll.), B.A. 84, M.A. 87 (HONOURS:—4 history 84); curate of North Mundham, Sussex, 85-8.

Tullook, Hector St. John, born at Bangalore, East Indies, 1863; 2s. Hector, arm. BALLIOL, matric. 17 Oct., 82, aged 19, from Harrow.

Tupholme, Hugh Seymour, born at Ealing 6 Dec., 1869; 2s. Benjamin Seymour, vicar of Ealing St. Stephen's. HERTFORD, matric. 20 Oct., 91, aged 22, from an Ealing school.

Tupholme, Wilfrid Seymour, born at Ealing, Middx., 1867; 1s. Benjamin Seymour, cler. CORPUS CHRISTI, matric. 20 Oct., 86, aged 19 (from St. Paul's school), B.A. 91; HONOURS:—3 classical mods. 88, 4 classics 90.

Tupper, Henry Bingham de Vic, born at St. Peter's Port, Guernsey, 9 Feb., 1867; o.s. de Vic, colonel. LINCOLN, matric. 27 Oct., 85, aged 18 (from Q. Elizabeth coll., Guernsey), B.A. 89; HONOURS: —3 history 89.

Tupper, John Lucas, born at Rugby 9 Oct., 1872; 2s. John Lucas, gent. QUEEN'S, matric. 27 Oct., 91, aged 19 (from Rugby), scholar 91; HONOURS:—2 classical mods. 93.

Turing, James Walter, born at Rotterdam 3 Jan., 1862; o.s. sir Robert F. (*sol disant*), bart. CHRIST CHURCH, matric. 20 Jan., 82, aged 20, from Eton.

Turing, Julius Mathison, born at Edwinstowe, Notts, 9 Nov. 1874; 2s. John Robert, cler., M.A., Camb. CORPUS CHRISTI, matric. 18 Oct., 92, aged 18 (from Bedford school), scholar 92.

Turnbull, Charles Cuthbert Ingram, born at Carlton, Notts, 26 July, 1867; 3s. William Stephenson, cler. WORCESTER, matric. 19 Oct., 86, aged 19, from Stratford-on-Avon school.

Turnbull, William Whiteford, born in island of Rum, in the Hebrides, 3 March, 1869; 1s. George, D.Med. NON-COLLEGIATE, matric. 11 Oct., 90, aged 21 (from Kelso high school); drowned at Godslow 23 Sept., 91.

Turner, Arthur Beresford, born at Farley, Hants, 24 Aug., 1862; o.s. Charles Beresford, cler. KEBLE, matric. 2 Dec., 81, aged 19 (from Marlborough), B.A. 85.

Turner, Arthur Frederick, born at Sydney 3 Oct., 1870; 5s. John Andrew, arm. TRINITY, matric. 12 Oct., 89, aged 19, from Sherborne school.

Turner, Augustus, born at Torquay, Devon, 4 Aug., 1864; 3s. Augustus, cler. TRINITY, matric. 15 Oct., 83, aged 19 (from Bath coll.), B.A. 86, M.A. 90; HONOURS:—2 classical mods. 85.

Turner, sir Charles Arthur, K.C.I.E., M.A., fellow EXETER 55-66, where see page 127.

Turner, Charles Henry, born at Islington 1867; 1s. William, gen. CORPUS CHRISTI, matric. 20 Oct., 86, aged 19 (from University coll. school, London), B.A. 90; HONOURS:—2 classical mods. 88, 2 classics 90.

Turner, Charles McLellan, born at Bristol 5 Dec., 1869; 4s. John Robert, arm. TRINITY, matric. 13 Oct., 88, aged 18 (from Clifton coll.), B.A. 92; HONOURS:—3 classical mods. 90, Ægrotat history 92.

Turner, Charles Westall, born in London 1863; 1s. Henry James, gent. EXETER, matric. 19 April, 82, aged 19 (from Harrow), B.A. 85, M.A.

Turner, Cuthbert Hamilton, M.A., fellow MAGDALEN 89, where see page 315.

Turner, Edward Reginald, born in London 3 March, 1862; 2s. Edward Goldwin, solicitor. ST. JOHN'S, matric. 22 April, 82, aged 20 (from Cheltenham coll.); died 20 Feb., 86.

Turner, rev. Edward Tindal, M.A., fellow BRASENOSE 45, where see page 349.

Turner, Ernest Edward, born at Ulverstone, co. Lanc., 22 Nov., 1871; 1s. William Barrow, arm. EXETER, matric. 13 Oct., 90, aged 18, from Harrow.

Turner, rev. Francis William Tudsbery-, born at Storeton, Cheshire, 1857; 1s. William, arm. NON-COLLEGIATE, matric. 4 Nov., 80, aged 23 (from a Birkenhead school); migrated to ORIEL 84, B.A. 88; solicitor 79-89; curate of St. Thomas, Toxteth Park, Liverpool, 90; brother of William T.

Turner, Frank Herbert, born at Sydney, Australia, 1861; 3s. John Andrew, arm. PEMBROKE, matric. 4 Feb., 80, aged 19.

Turner, Frederick Charles, born in London 22 Aug., 1872; 2s. James, gen. UNIVERSITY COLL., matric. 17 Oct., 91, aged 19 (from Christ's hospital), exhibitioner 91; HONOURS:—2 classical mods. 93.

Turner, John Ernest Priestley, born at Harrogate, Yorks, 6 May, 1865; 1s. John Francis, arm. MERTON, matric. 21 Oct., 86, aged 21 (from Trinity coll., Harrogate), B.A. 90 (HONOURS:—3 law 90); bar.-at-law, Lincoln's Inn, 92.

Turner, Montagu Cecil Scott, born at Liverpool 1 Dec., 1870; 3s. Henry Scott, arm. BRASENOSE, matric. 14 Oct., 89, aged 18 (from Rugby), B.A. 92.

Turner, Percy Shearman-, born in London 5 March, 1874; 4s. William, banker. EXETER, matric. 22 Oct., 91, aged 17, from Forest school, Walthamstow.

Turner, Raymond Cecil, born at Nottingham 2 July, 1870; 3s. Benjamin Thorne, arm. WORCESTER, matric. 14 Oct., 90, aged 20, from Tiverton school.

Turner, Reginald, born in London 2 June, 1869; o.s. Reginald, arm. MERTON, matric. 17 Oct., 88, aged 19 (from Hurstpierpoint coll.), B.A. 92; HONOURS: —3 history 92.

Turner, sir William, created D.C.L. 25 June, 1890, M.R.C.S.Eng. 53, gold medallist, and B.Med. London 57, demonstrator 54, and professor of anatomy in the university of Edinburgh 67, university examiner in anatomy in Oxford and Edinburgh, knighted 8 March, 86, hon. LL.D. Glasgow and Durham, F.R.S. London and Edinburgh; born at Lancaster 32. See *Men and Women of the Time*.

Turner, William Derington, born at Norbury, co. Stafford, 1865; 1s. William Derington, gen. EXETER, matric. 18 Oct., 84, aged 19 (from Newport gr. school, Salop), B.A. 88.

Turner, William Tudsbery, born at Storeton, Cheshire, 3 Oct., 1871; 3s. William Tudsbery, esq. MERTON, matric. 22 Oct., 91, aged 20, from Birkenhead school; brother of Francis W. T.

Turney, Horace George, born at Camberwell, Surrey, 26 Oct., 1860; 2s. George Leonard, gen. TRINITY, matric. 17 Jan., 80, aged 19 (from Dulwich coll.), B.A. 84, M.A. and B.Med. 88.

Turnor, Christopher Hatton, born at Toronto, Canada, 23 Nov., 1873; 1s. Christopher Hatton, gent. CHRIST CHURCH, matric. 18 Oct., 92, aged 18.

Turpin, Julian James, born at Grahamstown, Cape Colony, Jan., 1872; 5s. William Homun, cler. KEBLE, matric. 15 Oct., 92, aged 20, from Hurstpierpoint coll.

Turral, Joseph, born in London 1870; 1s. Joseph, gen. QUEEN'S, matric. 16 March, 92, aged 22.

Turrell, Arthur George, born at Oxford 1866; 3s. Henry Joseph, cler. TURRELL'S HALL, matric. 6 May, 83, aged 17, B.A. 92.

Turrell, Harry Joseph, born at Oxford 1864; 1s. Henry Joseph, cler. TURRELL'S HALL, matric. 4 June, 81, aged 17, B.A. 84; migrated to EXETER, M.A. and D.C.L. 88 (HONOURS:—3 law 85, a civil law 87); bar.-at-law, Inner Temple, 87.

Turrell, rev. Henry Joseph, M.A. (LINCOLN), master of TURRELL'S HALL. See *Al. Ox.* and series, 1452.

Turrell, Walter John, born at Oxford 9 April, 1865. 2s. Henry Joseph, cler. TURRELL'S HALL, matric. 4 June, 81, aged 16, B.A. 86, M.A. and B.Med. 90, D.Med. 92.

Tuson, George Baily, born at Bath July, 1867; 4s. Henry, cler. KEBLE, matric. 19 Oct., 86, aged 19, from Felsted school.

Tuting, rev. William Chomell, born at Peshawur, East Indies, 25 Dec., 1861; o.s. Thomas, chaplain C.M.S. NON-COLLEGIATE, matric. 21 Jan., 82, aged 20 (from Merchant Taylors' school, London, and Monckton Combe, near Bath); migrated to LINCOLN 5 April, 83, B.A. 85, M.A. 88 (HONOURS:—2 theology 85); London diocesan home missioner at Isleworth 89.

Tweddell, Ralph Brown, born at Newcastle-on-Tyne 12 May, 1870; 1s. George, gent. ST. EDMUND HALL, matric. 16 Oct., 90, aged 20, from Newcastle royal gr. school.

Tweed, Henry Earle, M.A., fellow ORIEL 1852-64, where see page 153.

Tweedy, Charles Winstanley, born at Redruth, Cornwall, 7 March, 1867; 1s. Charles, gent. QUEEN'S, matric. 30 Oct., 85, aged 18 (from Truro gr. school), exhibitioner 85, B.A. 89; HONOURS:—2 classical mods. 87, 2 classics 89.

Twemlow, Jesse Alfred, born at Liverpool 8 Aug., 1867; 2s. Jesse, gen. CHRIST CHURCH, matric. 6 Feb., 90, aged 22 (from Liverpool Institute and University coll., Liverpool), scholar 91.

Twentyman, Arthur Edward, born at Hammersmith 1867; 1s. John, cler. BRASENOSE, matric. 20 Oct., 87, aged 20 (from Shrewsbury and King's coll. school, London), exhibitioner 87, B.A. 91; HONOURS:—3 classical mods. 89, 2 history 91.

Twidell, John Cook, born at Worthing, Sussex, 13 Oct., 1870; 1s. William Thomas, gen. TRINITY, matric. 12 Oct., 89, aged 19 (from Oxford high school), scholar 89; HONOURS:—1 classical mods. 91.

Twigg, Edward Bernard, born at Wednesbury, co. Stafford, Aug., 1866; 2s. Richard, cler. KEBLE, matric. 22 Oct., 85, aged 19 (from Bruton and Stony Stratford schools), B.A. 90; HONOURS:—3 theology 89.

Twiss, Frederick Alexander, born at Forest Hill, Kent, July, 1866; 1s. Alexander, cler. KEBLE, matric. 22 Oct., 85, aged 19 (from Bath coll.), B.A. 88.

Twiss, Quintin William Francis, M.A., student CHRIST CHURCH 1853-61, where see page 420.

Twiss, sir Travers, Q.C., D.C.L., hon. fellow UNIVERSITY COLL. 1864, where see page 30.

Twist, rev. George Cecil, born at Rusholme, co. Lanc., 6 Sept., 1869; 2s. John James, cler. TRINITY, matric. 15 Oct., 87, aged 18 (from Radley coll.), B.A. 91; HONOURS:—4 history 91.

Twist, James Frederick, born at Birch in Rusholme, co. Lanc., 1864; 1s. John James, cler. EXETER, matric. 18 Oct., 82, aged 18 (from Winchester), B.A. 87, M.A. 89.

Twycross, rev. George Francis, born at Wokingham, Berks, 1866; 1s. George, gent. NON-COLLEGIATE, matric. 19 Jan., 85, aged 19 (from Tonbridge school); migrated to HERTFORD, B.A. 88 (HONOURS:—2 history 88); curate of Kentish Town, London, 91.

Tyacke, Richard Trevise, born at St. Breage, Cornwall, 1848; y.s. Nicholas, gent. NON-COLLEGIATE, matric. 14 Oct., 82, aged 34, from Exeter high school.

Tylecote, Charles Brandon Lea, M.A., Fereday fellow ST. JOHN'S 1873, where see page 478.

Tylecote, Edward Ferdinande Sutton, M.A., Fereday fellow ST. JOHN'S 1868, where see page 478.

Tyler, Charles William, born at Welsh Newton, co. Hereford, 1864; 1s. George Griffin, of Newton Court, co. Mon., banker. ORIEL, matric. 8 Dec., 83, aged 19 (from Bury St. Edmunds' school), B.A. 87, M.A. 90; brother of the next.

Tyler, George Endell, born at Welsh Newton, co. Hereford, 24 Jan., 1866; 2s. George Griffin, of Newton Court, co. Mon., banker. MAGDALEN, matric. 23 Oct., 85, aged 19 (from Bury St. Edmunds' school), B.A. 88; brother of the last.

Tylor, Edward Burnett, of BALLIOL, D.C.L., keeper of the museum 1883, see page 70.

Tyringham, Roger William Giffard, born at Tyringham, Bucks, 5 Aug., 1870; 1s. William Backwell, arm. CHRIST CHURCH, matric. 1 June, 88, aged 17, from Eton.

Tyrrell, William George, born at Naini, East Indies, 1866; o.s. William Henry, arm. BALLIOL, matric. 24 Oct., 85, aged 19 (from Bonn university); HONOURS:—3 classical mods. 87.

Tyrwhitt, rev. Cecil Robert, born at Oxford 25 Dec., 1862; 2s. Richard St. John, cler. CHRIST CHURCH, matric. 21 May, 80, aged 17, B.A. 84, M.A. 88, chaplain Christ Church 90; curate of Cowley St. John, Oxon, 90.

Tyrwhitt, Richard St. John, M.A., student CHRIST CHURCH 1845-59, where see page 415.

Tyrwhitt, Walter Spencer Stanhope, M.A., CHRIST CHURCH, where see page 426.

Tyson, Dudley Thomas, born in London 1861; o.s. Thomas, arm. NEW INN HALL, matric. 31 Jan., 84, aged 23.

Tyson, rev. Henry, born at New Brighton, Cheshire, 28 Sept., 1864; 3s. John Dawson, gen. MAGDALEN, matric. 23 April, 84, aged 19 (from a Wallasey school, Cheshire), B.A. 87, M.A. 91; curate of Crewe (Christ Church), 91.

WOODEN ORNAMENT, NEW COLLEGE.

WOODEN STRING COURSE, TRINITY CHURCH, STRATFORD-ON-AVON.—*Pugin.*

U

Underdown, William Goodwin, born at Faversham, Kent, 6 April, 1873; o.s. Frederick William, architect. WADHAM, matric. 20 Oct., 91, aged 18 (from Faversham gr. school); HONOURS :—3 classical mods. 93.

Underhill, Charles Bernard, born at Oxford 23 July, 1873; 2s. Charles Maitland, gent. BALLIOL, matric. 20 Oct., 92, aged 18 (from Oxford high school, and Kelly coll., Tavistock), scholar 90; HONOURS :—1 mathematical mods. 92, junior mathematical scholarship 93.

Underhill, George Edward, M.A., fellow MAGDALEN 1862, where see page 312.

Underhill, Percy Arthur, born at Oxford 1862; 3s. William, gent. NON-COLLEGIATE, matric. 22 Oct., 81, aged 19, B.A. 87, M.A. 88.

Underhill, Reginald Stanley, born at Oxford 22 Feb., 1870; 1s. Ernest Augustus, gen. JESUS COLL., matric. 14 Oct., 89, aged 18 (from Magdalen coll. school); HONOURS :—2 mathematical mods. 91.

Underwood, Joseph William, born at Sevenoaks, Kent, April, 1865; 1s. Frederick James, arm. CHRIST CHURCH, matric. 31 May, 84, aged 18; lieut. 4th (the Queen's Own) Hussars 89.

Underwood, Ormsby Charles Henry, born at Lahore in East Indies 8 April, 1869; o.s. Thomas Ormsby, arm. TRINITY, matric. 13 Oct., 88, aged 19 (from Blair lodge, Edinburgh); assist. commissioner Burma 90.

Underwood, William Thomas, born at Rugby 10 April, 1869; 1s. Enoch, gent. NON-COLLEGIATE, matric. 15 Oct., 92, aged 23, from Milton coll., Ullesthorpe, co. Warwick.

Unlacke, Richard Gordon Fitzgerald, born at Frogmore, Herts. 19 Aug., 1867; 1s. Robert Fitzgerald, cler. TRINITY, matric. 17 Oct., 85, aged 18 (from Repton school), B.A. 89; HONOURS :—3 history 88.

Unsworth, Recce, born at Litherland, co. Lanc., 31 Jan., 1871; 3s. John Taylor, late of Southport, merchant, deceased. UNIVERSITY COLL., matric. 11 Oct., 90, aged 19, from Rossall school.

Unwin, Frederick Herbert, born at Brookfield, Sheffield, 21 Feb., 1873; 1s. Herbert, gen. TRINITY, matric. 17 Oct., 91, aged 18, from Marlborough.

Unwin, rev. William Sully, born at Rotherham, Yorks, 27 July, 1869; 1s. William, arm. NON-COLLEGIATE, matric. 21 Jan., 89, aged 19 (from Magdalen coll. school); migrated to MAGDALEN 82, B.A. 86, M.A. 93; in Oxford eight 83-86, Wingfield sculls 84-85; curate of Caversham 88.

Upcott, William Edward Crosse, born at Knowle, Devon, 1871; 1s. William, gen. ST. MARY HALL, matric. 20 Oct., 90, aged 19.

Upstone, rev. Philip, born at Shipton-under-Wychwood, Oxon, 1861; o.s. Philip, gent. NON-COLLEGIATE, matric. 16 Oct., 86, aged 25 (from Burford school), B.A. 90, M.A. 93 (HONOURS :—3 history 90); curate of Wotton-under-Edge, co. Glouc., 90.

Upton, Archer Mowbray, born in London 1869; 1s. James Richard, gen. PEMBROKE, matric. 25 Oct., 87, aged 18 (from Winchester), B.A. 90.

Upton, Ralph Daubeny, born in London Feb., 1871; 2s. James Richard, solicitor. BRASENOSE, matric. 14 Oct., 89, aged 18 (from Winchester), B.A. 90.

Upton, William Judd, M.A., fellow NEW COLL. 1833-48, where see page 211.

Uran, rev. John Arthur, born at Boston Spa, Yorks, 1865; o.s. James Pascoe, gent. NON-COLLEGIATE, matric. 19 Jan., 85, aged 20, B.A. 88 (HONOURS :—4 theology 88); curate of Devonport St. Michael 91.

Uroh, Frank, born at Birmingham 23 June, 1873; 1s. Frank, of Equitable Assurance Society, U.S.A. CHRIST CHURCH, matric. 14 Oct., 92, aged 19 (from Westminster school), scholar 92.

Ure, John Francis Frederick Whall, born at York Feb., 1867; 1s. John, D.Med. CHRIST CHURCH, matric. 12 June, 86, aged 19 (from Blackheath school), B.A. 90; HONOURS :—2 history 90, 3 civil law 92.

Urquhart, Francis, born at Geneva 1 Sept., 1868; 2s. David, late M.P. Stafford, deceased. BALLIOL, matric. 14 Oct., 90, aged 22 (from Beaumont and Stonyhurst colls.), exhibitioner 90.

Urwick, Edward Johns, born at Hatherlow, Cheshire, 20 June, 1867; 3s. William, congregational minister. WADHAM, matric. 16 Oct., 86, aged 18 (from Uppingham school), B.A. 90; HONOURS :—2 classical mods. 88, 1 classics 90.

Urwick, William Eddowes, born at Hatherlow, Cheshire, 3 June, 1864; 1s. William, gent. TRINITY, matric. 15 Oct., 83, aged 19 (from Uppingham school), B.A. 87, M.A. 90; HONOURS :—2 classical mods. 85, 2 classics 87.

Usborne, Charles Frederick, born in London 18 Feb., 1874; 1s. Thomas, of Bradfield, Berks, gent. BALLIOL, matric. 18 Oct., 92, aged 18, from the Charterhouse.

Ussher, Beverley Grant, born at Dublin 19 Feb., 1867; 1s. Richard John, arm. NEW COLL., matric. 23 Oct., 85, aged 18 (from Marlborough), scholar 84, B.A. 90, M.A. 92; HONOURS :—1 classical mods. 87, 1 classics 89, 1 history 90.

[615] [616]

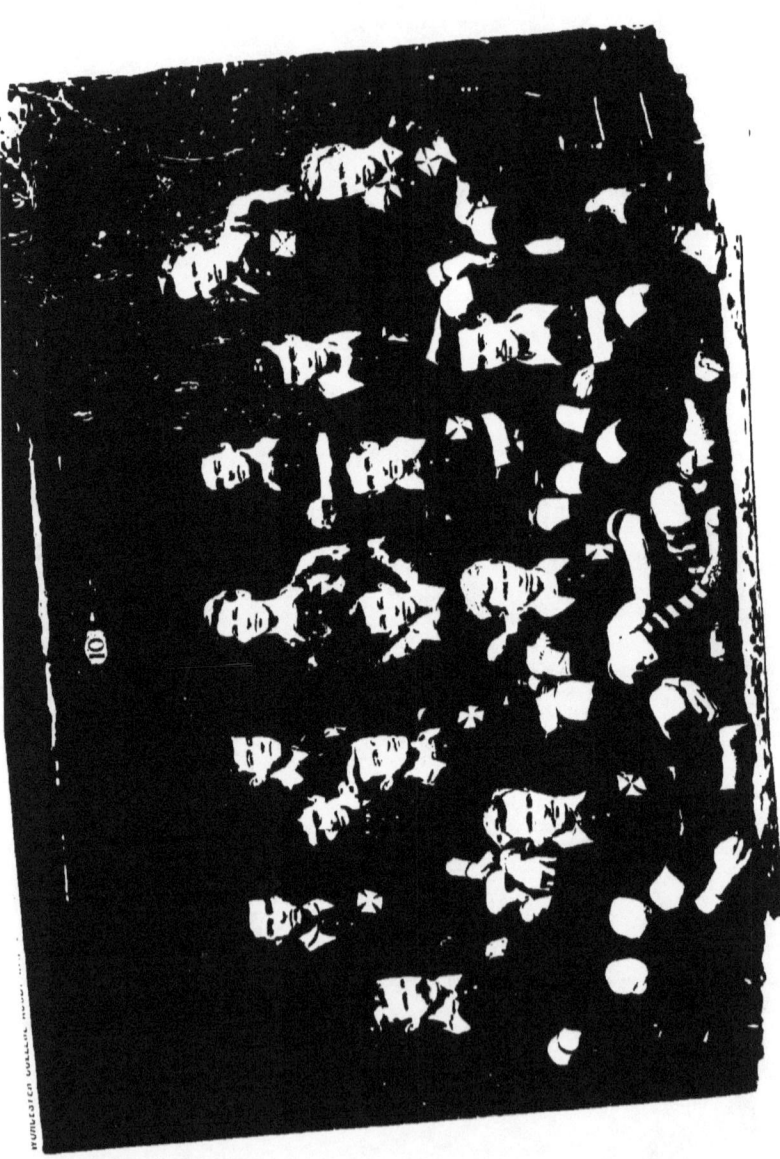

V

Vaillant, Wilfred Bernard, born at Weybridge, Surrey, 1864; 3s. Albert, arm. CHRIST CHURCH, matric. 25 May, 83, aged 18 (from Radley coll.), B.A. 90, M.A. 91.

Vale, Alfred Conduit, born at Boulogne-sur-Mer 1868; 5s. William Croxton, cler. ST. JOHN'S, matric. 17 Jan., 91, aged 23.

Vallance, Henry Wellington, born in London 1867; o.s. Henry Fletcher, gent. PEMBROKE, matric. 1 Feb., 86, aged 19 (from Dulwich coll.), B.A. 89 (HONOURS :—3 law 89); bar.-at-law, Lincoln's Inn, 91.

Vallance, rev. William Howard Aymer, born in London March, 1862; 1s. Thomas William, arm. ORIEL, matric. 4 June, 81, aged 19 (from Harrow), B.A. 85, M.A. 88.

Vallings, rev. George Ross, born at Calcutta 4 March, 1867; 1s. Frederick Ross, cler. WORCESTER, matric. 19 Oct., 85, aged 19 (from St. Edmund's, Salisbury), B.A. 90; HONOURS :—2 history 90.

Vanes, Sidney Albert, born at Carmarthen 7 Jan., 1864; 8s. John, cler. JESUS COLL., matric. 18 Oct., 82, aged 18 (from Kingswood school), scholar 82-6, B.A. 86; HONOURS :—1 mathematical mods. 84, 2 mathematics 86.

Van Langenburgh, James Arthur, see Langenburgh page 358.

Vann, Alfred George Collins, born at Northampton 1859; 1s. Thomas Collins, gent. ST. MARY HALL, matric. 20 Oct., 90, aged 31.

Vanneck, Arthur Percy, born in London 1870; o.s. John Grant, gen. BALLIOL, matric. 18 Oct., 88, aged 18 (from University coll. school, Lond.); HONOURS :—3 classical mods. 90, 1 law 92.

Van Norden, Theodore Langdon, born at New Orleans, La., U.S.A., 26 Feb., 1869; 1s. Warner, of New York, banker. NON-COLLEGIATE, matric. 22 Oct., 90, aged 23, from Columbia coll. and union theological seminary, New York.

Vargas, Albert Charles, born in London 20 Nov., 1872; 2s. Clunaco, merchant. WORCESTER, matric. 22 Oct., 91, aged 18, from Harrow.

Varley, Frederick John, born in London 4 May, 1872; 1s. John, solicitor. ORIEL, matric. 27 Oct., 91, aged 19 (from Westminster school), scholar 91; HONOURS :—2 classical mods. 93.

Vasey, Walter, born in London 11 Oct., 1867; 6s. Charles, M.R.C.S. QUEEN'S, matric. 3 Nov., 86, aged 19 (from Haughton gr. school, etc.), B.A. 90.

Vassall, Archer, born at Hardington Mandeville, Somerset, 1874; 5s. William, M.A., cler. KEBLE, matric. 15 Oct., 92, aged 18 (from the Charterhouse), scholar 92.

Vassall, Harry Greame, born at Frenchay, near Bristol, 21 Jan., 1865; 4s. Robert Lowe Grant, arm. TRINITY, matric. 15 Jan., 83, aged 17 (from Marlborough), B.A. 90.

Vaughan, Edward William, B.A., fellow ST. JOHN'S 1890-94, where see page 479.

Vaughan, Francis Philip, born at St. Leonard's-on-Sea 4 June, 1870; 6s. Charles Lyndhurst, cler. NEW COLL., matric. 11 Oct., 89, aged 19 (from Winchester), B.A. 92; HONOURS :—3 law 92.

Vaughan, George Frederick, born at Darlaston, co. Stafford, 1856; 1s. Joshua, gent. NON-COLLEGIATE, matric. 17 Jan., 80, aged 24, scholar ST. JOHN'S 81-4, B.A. 83, M.A. 88; HONOURS :—1 classics 83.

Vaughan, Herbert Millingchamp, born at Penmorfa, co. Cardigan, July, 1870; 1s. John, arm. KEBLE, matric. 12 Oct., 89, aged 19 (from Clifton coll.), B.A. 92; HONOURS :—2 history 92.

Vaughan, Hugh John Stanley, born at Thurlstone, Devon, July, 1871; 1s. Hugh Coffin, arm. KEBLE, matric. 11 Oct., 90, aged 19, from Bradfield coll.

Vaughan, William Wyamar, born in London 25 Feb., 1865; o.s. Henry Halford, regius professor of modern history 48-58. NEW COLL., matric. 10 Oct., 84, aged 19 (from Rugby), B.A. 88; HONOURS :—2 classical mods. 85, 2 classics 88.

Vaughton, Rowland Griffith, born at Alverstoke, Hants, 27 Aug., 1869; o.s. Theophilus, arm. PEMBROKE, matric. 25 Oct., 87, aged 18 (from Eastbourne coll.), B.A. 91; HONOURS :—2 mathematical mods. 89, 1 mathematics 91.

Vaux, Richard Augustus, born in London 19 Sept., 1869; 2s. William Sandys Wright, arm. LINCOLN, matric. 18 Oct., 88, aged 19 (from Lancing coll.), B.A. 92; HONOURS :—3 classical mods. 90, 3 classics 92.

Vavasour, Richard St. John, born at Ashby-de-la-Zouch, co. Leicester, 5 Feb., 1869; 1s. John Francis, cler. WORCESTER, matric. 16 Oct., 88, aged 19 (from Rossall school), exhibitioner 88, B.A. 93; HONOURS :—2 classical mods. 90, 3 classics 92.

Vavasseur, Robert, born at Knockholt, Kent, 4 July, 1865; 2s. James, arm. CHRIST CHURCH, matric. 10 Oct., 84, aged 19 (from Westminster school), scholar 84, B.A. 88; HONOURS :—1 classical mods. 86, 2 classics 88.

Vawdrey, Alexander Allen Clement Neale, born at Mabe, Cornwall, 23 Nov., 1870; 1s. Alexander Allen, cler. EXETER, matric. 20 Jan., 90, aged 19, from Bristol gr. school.

Vawdrey, Daniel, M.A., fellow BRASENOSE 1830-43, where see page 36.

Veale, Rawdon Augustus, born at Hampsthwaite, Yorks, 13 March, 1873; 2s. Richard Selby, D.Med. Edinburgh, deceased. MAGDALEN, matric. 27 Oct., 92, aged 19 (from Rossall school), scholar 92.

Veale, William George, born at Bristol 1872; 3s. Edward John, gent. PEMBROKE, matric. 26 Oct., 81, aged 19 (from Bristol gr. school), scholar 81-3, B.A. 85, M.A. 88; HONOURS :—2 mathematical mods. 83, 3 law 85.

Veley, Victor Herbert, M.A., UNIVERSITY COLL., where see page 36.

Venables, William Alfred, born in New York, U.S.A., 21 Oct., 1872; 2s. Charles Edward Cumberland, major-general, C.B., late R.E. MAGDALEN, matric. 22 Oct., 91, aged 18, from St. Mark's school, Windsor, and the Charterhouse.

Venn, Clement Francis, born at Uffculme, Devon, 25 Aug., 1864; 1s. Robert Warren, gent. LINCOLN, matric. 19 Oct., 83, aged 19 (from Sherborne school), B.A. 88, M.A. 90.

Venning, Alfred John Mybohm, born at Devonport, Devon, 1865; 1s. John James Edgcombe, arm. BRASENOSE, matric. 20 Oct., 86, aged 21, B.A. 89.

Vernède, Arthur Henry, born in London 30 Sept., 1872; 1s. Oscar, solicitor. UNIVERSITY COLL., matric. 19 Oct., 91, aged 19 (from St. Paul's school), scholar 91; HONOURS :—2 classical mods. 93.

Verney, hon. Richard Greville, born in London 29 March, 1869; 1s. Henry, baron Willoughby de Broke. NEW COLL., matric. 12 Oct., 88, aged 19 (from Eton), B.A. 92; HONOURS:—3 law 92.

Vernon, Alfred Samuel Edward Russell Stone, born at Islington 1865; o.s. Edward, D.Med. ST. MARY HALL, matric. 14 Oct., 89, aged 24.

Vernon, Bowater George Hamilton, born at Hanbury, co. Worcester, 12 Sept., 1865; 1s. Henry, arm. BRASENOSE, matric. 7 June, 84, aged 18, from Eton.

Vernon, Charles Venables, born at Old Trafford, co. Lanc., 1872; 2s. George Venables, F.R.C.S. and F.R.S. CHRIST CHURCH, matric. 16 Oct., 91, aged 19 (from Manchester gr. school), scholar 91; HONOURS:—1 classical mods. 93.

Vernon, Cyril John, born at Cheriton, Kent, 1866; 1s. John Richard, cler. ST. JOHN'S, matric. 16 Oct., 86, aged 20 (from Merchant Taylors' school), B.A. 90.

Vernon, Herbert Evelyn Harcourt, born at Colgrave, Notts., 12 Jan., 1863; 4s. Evelyn Hardolph, cler. KEBLE, matric. 18 Oct., 81, aged 18, from Uppingham school.

Vernon, Horace Middleton, born in London 3 Oct., 1870; 2s. Thomas Hygate, arm. MERTON, matric. 17 Oct., 88, aged 18 (from Dulwich coll.), scholar 88, B.A. 91; HONOURS:—1 chemistry 91.

Vernon, Thomas Henry, born in Middlesex 8 Nov., 1862; 2s. John, arm. CHRIST CHURCH, matric. 17 Oct., 81, aged 18 (from Merchant Taylors' school), exhibitioner 82-4, B.A. 84, M.A. 90; HONOURS:—2 law 84.

Vernon, William Edward, born at Forest Hill, Surrey, 1864; 3s. John, gent. ST. JOHN'S, matric. 13 Oct., 83, aged 19 (from Merchant Taylors' school), scholar 85, senior scholar 90, B.A. 89, M.A. and B.C.L. 92 (HONOURS:—2 law 87; 1 civil law 89, Vinerian law scholarship 89); bar.-at-law, Middle Temple, 89.

Versohoyle, Charles John, born at Tanrass, co. Sligo, 13 April, 1867; 3s. Richard John. MERTON, matric. 24 March, 87, aged 19 (from Ramsgate coll.), B.A. 90.

Vesey, Sidney Philip Charles, born at Ballyellen Goresbridge, co. Kilkenny, 9 March, 1873; 1s. William Muschamp, J.P. CHRIST CHURCH, matric. 14 Oct., 92, aged 19, from Rugby.

Vessey, rev. George Bass, born at Wilton, co. Lanc., 1866; 1s. John Henry, arm. UNIVERSITY COLL., matric. 11 Oct., 84, aged 18 (from Eton), B.A. 87, M.A. 91 (HONOURS:—3 history 87); curate of Croydon 90.

Veysey, John Waldegrave, born at Salisbury 24 Feb., 1870; 1s. John, vicar of Purton, Wilts. PEMBROKE, matric. 26 Oct., 89, aged 19 (from Abingdon school), scholar 89; HONOURS:—3 classical mods. 91.

Vian, Alsager Richard, born at Lewisham, Kent, 1865; 2s. William John, gen. BALLIOL, matric. 18 Oct., 81; aged 18 (from the Charterhouse), B.A. 85; HONOURS:—2 classical mods. 83, 3 classics 85.

Vickers, Charles William, born at St. Louis, Missouri, 21 Feb., 1871; 2s. Charles Kirsop, of Redgate Hall, co. Durham, arm. ST. JOHN'S, matric. 11 Oct., 90, aged 19, from Dulwich coll.

Vickers, Edgar George, born in London 1863; 2s. George Naylor, gent. UNIVERSITY COLL., matric. 15 Oct., 81, aged 18 (from Clifton coll.), B.A. and M.A. 88; bar.-at-law, Inner Temple, 87.

Vickers, Muschamp, born at Brixton (Surrey), 1868; 2s. Cuthbert Bainbridge, arm. NON-COLLEGIATE, matric. 15 Oct., 87, aged 19; migrated to BALLIOL, B.A. 91; HONOURS:—4 history 90.

Vickers, Randall Hugh Wentworth, born at Coatham, Yorks, 14 July, 1871; 1s. Randal William, vicar of Nafturn, Yorks. BALLIOL, matric. 14 Oct., 90, aged 19, from Winchester.

Vickers, Ronald, born at Barlborough, co. Derby, 3 May, 1869; 2s. Thomas Edward, arm. BRASENOSE, matric. 16 Oct., 88, aged 19 (from Marlborough), scholar 88, B.A. 92; HONOURS:—2 classical mods. 90, 2 classics 92.

Vickers, Shirley Frank, born in London 28 March, 1866; 4s. Henry Joseph, gent. WORCESTER, matric. 17 Oct., 84, aged 18 (from King's coll., Lond.), B.A. 89.

Vidal, rev. George Studley Sealy, born at Cornborough, Devon, 12 Feb., 1862; 8s. Edward, arm. NEW COLL., matric. 15 Oct., 81, aged 19 (from Winchester coll.), scholar 81-5, B.A. 85, M.A. 88 (HONOURS:—2 classical mods. 83, 3 classics 85); treasurer 84, and president of Oxford union society 85; curate of St. Giles 88, and chaplain of St. John's coll. 88, and of New coll. 89.

Viener, Harry Dan Leigh, born at Blackpool, co. Lanc., 1869; o.s. Adolph Moritz, gent. ST. JOHN'S, matric. 10 Jan., 89, aged 20 (from Malvern coll.); HONOURS:—3 classical mods. 90, 4 classics 92.

Villiers, Charles Hyde, born at Thole St. Knights, near Colchester, 1862; 1s. Charles, cler. NON-COLLEGIATE, matric. 18 Oct., 80, aged 18 (from Marlborough); HONOURS:—4 history 83.

Villiers, Charles Walter, born at Closeburne, co. Dumfries, 23 Sept., 1873; 2s. Frederick Ernest, arm. CHRIST CHURCH, matric. 29 May, 91, aged 17, from Eton.

Villiers, Henry Montagu, born at Adisham, Kent, 30 March, 1863; 1s. Henry Montagu, cler. KEBLE, matric. 17 Oct., 82, aged 19, from Canterbury school.

Vincent, rev. Edward Cecil, born at Longdon, co. Stafford, 2 April, 1864; 4s. John Charles Frederick, D.D. KEBLE, matric. 17 Oct., 82, aged 18 (from Marlborough), B.A. 85, M.A. 89 (HONOURS:—3 history 85); curate of Longdon 91.

Vincent, very rev. John Ranulph, born at Crockham, Kent, 22 Oct., 1859; 3s. Richard, cler. NON-COLLEGIATE, matric. 14 Oct., 80, aged 22 (from Haileybury); migrated to ST. JOHN'S, B.A. 85, M.A. 89 (HONOURS:—4 theology 85); dean of Blomfontein 92.

Vincent, Ralph Harry, born at Leyton, Essex, 20 Dec., 1870; 1s. Ralph, solicitor. ST. MARY HALL, matric. 27 Oct., 91, aged 20.

Vincent, Thomas Augustine, born at Wantage, Berks, 1863; 1s. Thomas, cler. WORCESTER, matric. 20 Oct., 81, aged 18 (from Lancing coll.), B.A. 84.

Vines, Sydney Howard, M.A., D.Sc. Camb., fellow MAGDALEN, where see page 315.

Vines, Thomas Humfrey, born at Echington, co. Worc., 9 Oct., 1864; 1s. Thomas Hotchkin, cler. JESUS COLL., matric. 18 Oct., 83, aged 19 (from Rossall school), scholar 83, B.A. 87; HONOURS:—3 classical mods. 85, 3 classics 87.

Vines, Walter Stuart Menteith, born at Birmingham 1867; 2s. Thomas, cler. ST. JOHN'S, matric. 16 Oct., 86, aged 19 (from Rossall school), B.A. 92; HONOURS:—3 history 90.

Vingoe, Alexander Luke, born at Penzance 1852; 1s. Alexander Mills, gent. QUEEN'S, matric. 16 March, 92, aged 40.

Virchow, Dr. Rudolf von, hon. D.C.L. 23 March, 1890; rector magnificus of the university of Berlin and prof. of pathological anatomy 56, hon. D.Sc. Camb. 21 March, 93, Copley medallist 92, and Croonian lecturer royal society 93; born at Schivelbein, in Pomerania, 13 Oct., 21, prof. of pathological anatomy at Wurzburg 49. For list of his writings, see *Men and Women of the Time*.

Viret, Henry Marriott, born in London June, 1868; 2s. Benjamin Pope, gen. ST. EDMUND HALL, matric. 18 Oct., 88, aged 20 (from a London school), B.A. 92.

Vitré, George Theodosius Denis Denis de, born in London 28 Jan., 1862; 1s. Henry, of Charlton House, Wantage, Berks, gent. MAGDALEN, matric. 16 Oct., 80, aged 18 (from Winchester), B.A. 83.

Vitré, John Durham Denis de, born at Wantage, Berks, Aug., 1870; 3s. Henry, arm. CHRIST CHURCH, matric. 8 June, 89, aged 18 (from Radley coll.), B.A. 92.

Vivian, Herbert Leigh, born at Hampstead 31 Aug., 1861; 5s. William, gent. TRINITY, matric. 29 Jan., 81, aged 19 (from Rugby), B.A. 84; died March, 86.

Vlasto, Augustus Alexander, born at Clapham Park, Surrey, 11 Nov., 1872; 4s. Alexander Anthony, gen. TRINITY, matric. 17 Oct., 91, aged 18, from the Charterhouse.

Voeux, sir Henry Dalrymple des, bart., M.A., fellow ALL SOULS' 1847-64, where see page 279.

Voysey, rev. Annesley Montagu, born at Alderley Edge, Cheshire, 17 Sept., 1859; 3s. Richard, cler. NON-COLLEGIATE, matric. 17 Oct., 81, aged 22 (from Christ's hospital); migrated to MERTON, B.A. 85 (HONOURS:—3 theology 85); curate of Lower Brixham, Devon, 89.

Voysey, Ellison Annesley, born at Helaugh, Yorks, 20 Aug., 1867; 4s. Charles, vicar. LINCOLN, matric. 22 Oct., 86, aged 19 (from Dulwich coll.), B.A. 91.

ARCH IN THE VESTRY OF ST. EBBE'S CHURCH.—*From Ingram.*

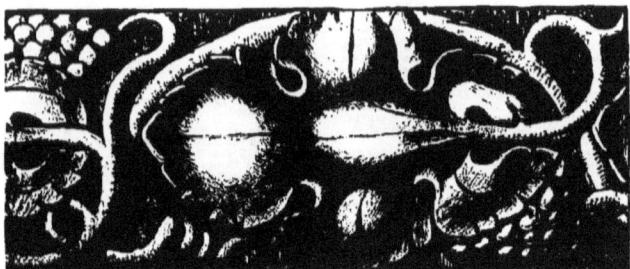

STONE STRING COURSE, YORK MINSTER.—*Pugin.*

W

Wace, rev. Henry Charles, born in London 10 Sept., 1867; 1s. Henry, principal of King's coll., London, D.D. NEW COLL., matric. 15 Oct., 86, aged 19 (from the Charterhouse), B.A. 90 (HONOURS :— 2 classical mods. 88, 2 classics 90, 1 theology 91); curate of Ramsgate 91.

Waddell, George Ralston Peddie, born at Edinburgh 9 Feb., 1874; 1s. Alexander Peddie, w.s. NEW COLL., matric. 14 Oct., 92, aged 18, from Glenalmond coll.

Waddilove, Edward Granville, born in London 19 Sept., 1862; 1s. Edward, arm. ORIEL, matric. 18 Oct., 81, aged 19 (from Marlborough), B.A. and M.A. 92 (HONOURS :—4 law 85); bar.-at-law, Lincoln's Inn, 87.

Waddilove George Hope, born at Wall, Northumberland, Jan., 1864; o.s. George Marmaduke, arm. PEMBROKE, matric. 27 Oct., 83, aged 18 (from Eton), B.A. 89.

Waddington, Charles Willoughby, born at Poonah, East Indies, 29 Dec., 1865; 1s. Thomas, arm. ORIEL, matric. 23 Oct., 84, aged 18 (from the Charterhouse), scholar 84, B.A. 89; HONOURS :—1 classical mods. 86, 2 classics 88.

Waddington, Evelyn de Burgh, born at Clifton, co. Glouc., 26 Dec., 1869; 2s. Horace, inspector of schools. TRINITY, matric. 27 April, 89, aged 19 (from the Charterhouse); HONOURS :—a classical mods. 90; passed for the army.

Waddington, Horace Penderell, born at Clifton, co. Glouc., 1865; 1s. Horace, inspector of schools. ORIEL, matric. 8 Dec., 84, aged 19.

Waddington, Pomfrett, born at Southampton 14 May, 1865; 1s. William Wilks, arm. ST. MARY HALL, matric. 20 Oct., 84, aged 19.

Waddington, William Henry, created D.C.L. 22 June, 1892, ambassador extraordinary and minister plenipotentiary from the French republic at the court of St. James's 83-93; born in Paris 11 Dec., 26, of Trinity coll., Cambridge, 45 (from Rugby), scholar 47, B.A. 49, hon. fellow 81, and hon. LL.D. 84 (HONOURS :—3rd senior optime, 2 classics and Chancellor's medal 49), in University eight 49.

Wade, Armigel, born at Eastoft, Yorks, 1865; 4s. George Frederick, cler. ALL SOULS', matric. 22 Oct., 85, aged 20 (from York school), bible clerk 85, B.A. 90; HONOURS :—2 classical mods. 87, 3 history 89.

Wade, Charles Edward, born at Haworth, Yorks, 1864; 1s. John, cler. ST. JOHN'S, matric. 11 Oct., 84, aged 20 (from Bradford school), B.A. 88, M.A. 91; HONOURS :—2 classical mods. 86, 3 classics 88, 3 history 89.

Wade, Charles Gregory, born at Singleton, N.S.W., 26 Jan., 1863; 1s. William Burton, gen. MERTON, matric. 18 Oct., 80, aged 17 (from King's school, Parramatta, N.S.W.), B.A. 85 (HONOURS :— 3 classical mods. 82, 3 classics 84); bar.-at-law, Inner Temple, 85.

Wade, George Herbert, born at Eastoft, Yorks, 1s. George Frederick, cler. BALLIOL, matric. 21 Oct., 80, aged (from York school), exhibitioner 79-84, B.A. 84, M.A. 90; HONOURS :—2 mathematical mods. 81, 3 classical mods. 82, 3 theology 83, 3 classics 85.

Wade, George Herbert, born at Haworth, Yorks, 14 Aug., 1868; 2s. John, cler. ST. JOHN'S, matric. 13 Oct., 88, aged 20 (from Bradford school), B.A. 92; HONOURS :—3 classical mods. 90, 4 history 92.

Wade, Harry Kipton, born at Shrewsbury 1865; o.s. Henry, gent. BRASENOSE, matric. 22 Oct., 83, aged 18, from Shrewsbury gr. school.

Wade, Richard Ramsden, born at Caterham, Surrey, 2 Oct., 1871; 3s. Thomas, cler. EXETER, matric. 13 Oct., 90, aged 19, from the Charterhouse.

Wadmore, Beauchamp, born at Clapton, Middx., Aug., 1861; 3s. James Foster, arm. CHRIST CHURCH, matric. 31 Jan., 81, aged 19, from Tonbridge school.

Wadsworth, John Hartley, born at Newport, co. Monmouth, 9 July, 1864; 2s. John, cler. JESUS COLL., matric. 18 Oct., 83, aged 19 (from Clifton coll.), B.A. 87, M.A. 90.

Waggett, rev. Philip Napier, born in London 27 Feb., 1862; 2s. John, D.Med. CHRIST CHURCH, matric. 22 Oct., 80, aged 18 (from the Charterhouse), exhibitioner 80-5, B.A. 84, M.A. 87 (HONOURS :— 1 natural science 84, 2 theology 85); curate of Southwark (H. T.) 89.

Wagner, Charles Ernest, born at Blue Bell, Montgomery co., Pa., U.S.A., 10 Oct., 1864; 1s. Samuel Grose, of Allentown, Penn., D.D. NON-COLLEGIATE, matric. 22 Oct., 91, aged 27, from Mecklenberg coll., Pa.

Wagner, Orlando Henry, born at Hertford 7 Dec., 1867; 1s. Orlando Henry, gent. WORCESTER, matric. 19 Oct., 66, aged 18 (from Christ's hospital), B.A. 90.

Wahl, Adelbert Emil August, born at Mannheim, in Germany, 1872; 2s. Rudolf Frederick, gen. CORPUS CHRISTI, matric. 16 Oct., 90, aged 18 (from Bonn university); HONOURS:—2 classical mods. 92.

Wain, Harris, born at Brynmawr, co. Brecon, 7 June, 1866; 3s. Richard, gent. QUEEN'S, matric. 22 Oct., 84, aged 18 (from Magdalen coll. school), B.A. 88.

Wainewright, John Bannerman, born at Wycfield, Kent, 3 July, 1871; 1s. John Hertslet, bar.-at-law. NEW COLL., matric. 10 Oct., 90, aged 19 (from Winchester), scholar 89; HONOURS:—1 classical mods. 92.

Wainwright, George Edward, born at Redcar, Yorks, 1862; 1s. David, gent. UNIVERSITY COLL., matric. 16 Oct., 80, aged 18 (from Bradford gr. school), exhibitioner 80-1, scholar 81-5; HONOURS:—2 classical mods. 82, 3 classics 84.

Wainwright, James Charles, born at Aughton, co. Lanc., 1865; o.s. Josiah. QUEEN'S, matric. 15 Jan., 91, aged 26.

Wainwright, Leonard Dart, born at Altrincham, Cheshire, 8 April, 1868; 2s. Frederick, cler. WORCESTER, matric. 17 Oct., 87, aged 19 (from Manchester gr. school), scholar 87, B.A. 91; HONOURS:—1 classical mods. 89, 1 classics 91.

Wait, Hamilton Wilfrid Killigrew, born at Clifton, co. Gloucester, 11 Jan., 1865; 1s. William Killigrew, formerly M.P. TRINITY, matric. 15 Oct., 83, aged 18 (from Winchester), B.A. 86, M.A. 90; HONOURS:—3 history 86.

Waite, Anthony Temple, born at Cheltenham 25 June, 1860; o.s. William, arm. ST. MARY HALL, matric. 13 April, 80, aged 19.

Waite, William, born at Leatherhead, Surrey, 1860; 4s. Edward, gent. NON-COLLEGIATE, matric. 18 Oct., 80, aged 20 (from Blackheath gr. school), exhibitioner BALLIOL 80-4, B.A. 84, M.A. 87; HONOURS:—3 history 84.

Waithman, Charles Anthony, born at Halifax, Yorks, 1855; 1s. Charles William, arm. HERTFORD, matric. 26 Feb., 86, aged 31.

Waitt, rev. Thomas Brace, born at Bamborough, Northumberland, 28 Feb., 1862; 1s. Thomas, gent. LINCOLN, matric. 19 Oct., 83, aged 21 (from Whitgift school, Croydon), B.A. 86, M.A. 90 (HONOURS: —1 history 86); senior assist. master Weymouth coll. 87-91, missioner St. Andrew, Sarum, 91.

Wake, Edwin St. Aubyn, born at Brampton, Northants, 20 July, 1862; 2s. Charles, vice-admiral R.N. CHRIST CHURCH, matric. 14 Oct., 81, aged 19 (from the Charterhouse); lieut. the Liverpool regt. 84, squadron officer 10th Bengal Lancers 91.

Wake, Herewand Eyre, born at Sutton-in-the-Forest, Yorks, 8 June, 1869; 1s. Baldwyn Eyre, cler. WORCESTER, matric. 16 Oct., 88, aged 19 (from Rossall school), B.A. 92.

Wakefield, Richard Dunster, born at Dalston, Middx., 1860; 3s. Richard, gent. PEMBROKE, matric. 30 Oct., 80, aged 20, B.A. 84, M.A. 87; HONOURS:— 4 theology 84.

Wakefield, William Henry, born at Sedgwick, Westmorland, 28 May, 1870; 3s. William Henry, banker, deceased. NEW COLL., matric. 11 Oct., 89, aged 19 (from the Charterhouse); HONOURS:—3 classical mods. 91.

Wakeling, George Henry, born in London 18 July, 1859; 1s. George, arm. TRINITY, matric. 15 Oct., 87, aged 28, B.A. 90; HONOURS:—1 history 90.

Wakeman, Henry Offley, M.A., fellow ALL SOULS' 73, where see page 272.

Wakemnn, Maurice Reginald, born at Warminster, Wilts, 8 Aug., 1872; 2s. Herbert John, solicitor. ST. JOHN'S, matric. 17 Oct., 91, aged 19 (from Clifton coll.), exhibitioner 93; HONOURS:—2 classical mods. 93.

Waloot, John Owen Halliwell, born at Ryde, I.W., 31 March, 1873; 1s. Owen Charles, of Mytton House, Salop, J.P. HERTFORD, matric. 19 Feb., 92, aged 18, from Shrewsbury school.

Walde, Cornelius Paul, born at Sowerby near Halifax, Yorks, 9 Oct., 1872; 1s. Menachem Niphdeh, rector of Linkenholt, Hants. NEW COLL., matric. 16 Oct., 91, aged 19 (from Winchester), scholar 90; HONOURS:—1 classical mods. 93.

Walden, Allan Frederick, born at Ware, Herts, 16 Sept., 1871; 1s. Keith, congregational minister. MAGDALEN, matric. 22 Oct., 91, aged 20 (from Bradford gr. school), exhibitioner 90.

Waldock, Frederick William, born at Candy, Ceylon, 18 March, 1866; 1s. Frederick David, baptist missionary. LINCOLN, matric. 27 Oct., 85, aged 19 (from Blackheath school), scholar HERTFORD 85, B.A. 90; HONOURS:—2 classical mods. 87, 3 classics 89.

Waldron, James Ballard, born at Launceston in Tasmania 4 July, 1871; 1s. James Ballard, solicitor. CORPUS CHRISTI, matric. 16 Oct., 90, aged 19 from Launceston church gr. school.

Waldy, John Bradshaw de Garmundesway, born 10 April, 1864; 2s. John Edward, rector of Claverton, Somerset. MAGDALEN, matric. 19 Oct., 83, aged 19 (from Bath coll.), B.A. 88.

Waldy, Lionel St. Clair, born at Affpuddle, Dorset, 20 April, 1863; 1s. William Thomas Jervis, of 43rd L.I. EXETER, matric. 16 Oct., 89, aged 26, from Clifton coll. and Tiverton school.

Wales, Frank Howard, born at Belfast April, 1867; 7s. George Frederick, D.Med. KEBLE, matric. 22 Oct., 85, aged 18 (from Queen's coll., Belfast), B.A. 88, M.A. 92; HONOURS:—3 history 88.

Wales, John Adolphus Gaigens, born at Hull 15 June, 1871; 1s. Alfred, gen. LINCOLN, matric. 17 Oct., 89, aged 18 (from Hull and East Riding coll.), scholar 90; HONOURS:—1 classical mods. 91.

Waley, John Felix, born in London 30 Dec., 1862; 3s. Jacob, late bar.-at-law, professor. BALLIOL, matric. 18 Oct., 81, aged 18 (from Harrow), B.A. 85, M.A. 89 (HONOURS:—2 classical mods. 83, 3 classics 85); bar.-at-law, Lincoln's Inn, 92.

Walker, Arthur Henry, born at Bristol 14 Feb., 1871; 1s. Henry John, schoolmaster. HERTFORD, matric. 14 Oct., 89, aged 18 (from Bristol gr. school), scholar 88; HONOURS:—1 classical mods. 91.

Walker, Arthur John, born at Hartsey, Yorks, 23 Dec., 1869; 1s. Edmund, arm., deceased. NEW COLL., matric. 12 Oct., 88, aged 18 (from Harrow); HONOURS:—3 classical mods. 90.

Walker, Arthur Thomas John, born in Dundee 22 April, 1867; 3s. Thomas, gent. TRINITY, matric. 16 Oct., 86, aged 19 (from Dundee and Glenalmond coll.), B.A. 90; HONOURS:—4 history 89.

Walker, Bernard Stevens, born at Walkhampton, Devon, 25 March, 1873; 2s. Charles Henry, vicar. ORIEL, matric. 16 Oct., 91, aged 18, from Marlborough.

Walker, Charles Henry Hirst, born at Bootle, co. Lanc., 1870; 1s. Charles James, gen. UNIVERSITY COLL., matric. 12 Oct., 89, aged 19 (from Wakefield school), exhibitioner 89.

Walker, Charles William, born at Durham 1867; 1s. William, gen. NON-COLLEGIATE, matric. 15 Oct., 87, aged 20, from Durham gr. school.

Walker, rev. Dawson, born at Bradford, Yorks, 20 Dec., 1868; 1s. Richard Fehris, gent. CORPUS CHRISTI, matric. 22 Oct., 87, aged 18 (from Bradford gr. school), scholar 87, B.A. 91; HONOURS:— 1 classical mods. 89, 2 classics 91.

Walker, rev. Edward Mewburn, M.A., fellow QUEEN'S 81, where see page 175.

Walker, Edward Russell, born at Ringley Bury, co. Lanc., 16 Feb., 1874; 1s. John Russell, M.A., cler., deceased. MAGDALEN, matric. 18 Oct., 92, aged 18, from Winchester.

Walker, Ernest, born at Malabar Hill, Bombay, 15 July, 1870; 1s. Edward, gen. BALLIOL, matric. 19 Oct., 87, aged 17 (from South Norwood coll.), B.A. 91 (HONOURS:—2 classical mods. 89, 2 classics 91); associate royal college of music.

Walker, Ernest William, born at Barnsley, Yorks, 27 Jan., 1871; 1s. William Henry, cler. CHRIST CHURCH, matric. 10 Oct., 90, aged 19 (from Kingswood and Colwyn Bay schools), scholar 89; HONOURS:— a mathematical mods. 92.

Walker, Francis Philip, born at Chidham, Essex, 1861; 3s. George Alfred, cler. NON-COLLEGIATE, matric. 18 Oct., 80, aged 19, from Cranleigh school by Guildford.

Walker, Frederick Edmund, born at Harlsey, Yorks, 29 March, 1871; 2s. Edmund, arm. MERTON, matric. 23 Jan., 90, aged 18 (from Harrow), B.A. 93.

Walker, Fredrick William, M.A., fellow CORPUS CHRISTI 59-67, where see page 383.

Walker, Frederick William, born at Walmesley, co. Lanc., 1864; 4s. John Scholes, arm. TRINITY, matric. 15 Oct., 83, aged 19 (from Marlborough), B.A. 88.

Walker, Frederick William George, born at Beverley, Yorks, 5 Oct., 1862; 1s. Frederick James, arm. CHRIST CHURCH, matric. 27 May, 82, aged 19 (from Eton), B.A. 87.

Walker, Harry Banes, born at Alford, co. Lincoln, 3 June, 1865; o.s. Banes, solicitor. LINCOLN, matric. 19 Oct., 83, aged 18 (from Louth gr. school), B.A. 87.

Walker, Herbert Turpin, born at Oxford 1868; 6s. William Henry, gent. NON-COLLEGIATE, matric. 19 Jan., 84, aged 16 (from an Oxford school), B.A. 87, M.A. 91.

Walker, Hugh, born at Kilbirnie, Ayrshire, 1855; 1s. James, gent. BALLIOL, matric. 22 Jan., 80, aged 25 (from Glasgow university), exhibitioner 80-5, B.A. 83, M.A. 86 (HONOURS:— 2 classical mods. 81, 1 classics 83); an advocate.

Walker, Hugh Carmichael, born at Crawfordton, co. Dumfries, 13 Jan., 1871; 4s. George Guthrie, colonel of militia. EXETER, matric. 17 Oct., 88, aged 17 (from Marlborough), B.A. 91.

Walker, James, M.A., CHRIST CHURCH 83, where see page 426.

Walker, James, born at Aberdeen 1864; 1s. Alexander, gent. BALLIOL, matric. 16 Oct., 83, aged 19 (from Aberdeen university), assist. commissioner central provinces India.

Walker, rev. James Manders, born at Kirk Andrews, Isle of Man, Jan., 1860; 1s. Samuel Sharpe, cler. WADHAM, matric. 16 Oct., 80, aged 20 (from K. William's coll., isle of Man), scholar 79-84, B.A. 84, M.A. 87 (HONOURS:— 2 classical mods. 82, 3 classics 84), F.R.G.S. 85, F.R.H.S. 89; assist. master Bedford school, and curate of Bodford St. Paul 91.

Walker, James Ronald, born in London 5 Feb., 1873; 1s. James Douglas, Q.C. ORIEL, matric. 27 Oct., 91, aged 18, from Rugby.

Walker, John Alison, born at Plumtree, Notts, 30 Nov., 1871; o.s. Matthew Williamson, merchant. MAGDALEN, matric. 22 Oct., 91, aged 19, from Shrewsbury school.

Walker, John Michael Stanhope, born at Averham, Notts, 6 Aug., 1871; 4s. Joseph, cler. BRASENOSE, matric. 15 Oct., 90, aged 19, from Repton school.

Walker, rev. John William Faulkner, born at Degbrooke, Oxon, 1861; 3s. James, gent. NON-COLLEGIATE, matric. 18 Oct., 80, aged 19 (from Woodstock gr. school, and Christ Church cathedral school, Oxford), B.A. 84, M.A. 87; vicar of Tovil, Kent, 91.

Walker, Joseph, M.A., fellow BRASENOSE 32-44, where see page 351.

Walker, rev. Joseph Cyril, born at Averham, Notts, 25 April, 1866; 1s. Joseph, rector. MAGDALEN, matric. 26 Jan., 86, aged 19 (from Eton), B.A. 89; curate of Fulham St. Clement 91.

Walker, Reginald Edmund, born at Foston Hall, Yorks, 27 June, 1866; 2s. sir James Robert, bart. CHRIST CHURCH, matric. 16 Oct., 85, aged 19 (from Harrow), B.A. 89.

Walker, Richard Johnson, born at Cheetham Hill, co. Lanc., 11 May, 1868; o.s. Frederick William, headmaster of St. Paul's school. BALLIOL, matric. 19 Oct., 87, aged 19 (from St. Paul's), scholar 86, B.A. 91; HONOURS:— 1 classical mods. 89, Hertford scholarship 87, Craven scholarship 88 (necessit 87), Ireland scholarship 90 (necessit 89), 2 law 91.

Walker, Richard Zouche, M.A., fellow MAGDALEN 56-62, where see page 323.

Walker, rev. Robert Peard, born at Wolverhampton 1864; o.s. Robert Percy, gent. EXETER, matric. 28 Jan., 81, aged 19 (from Wolverhampton gr. school), B.A. 84; died 5 Feb., 88, at Dunedin, New Zealand.

Walker, Thomas, born at Londonderry 13 Sept., 1859; 1s. Robert, gent. WADHAM, matric. 11 Oct., 84, aged 19 (from Trinity coll. Dublin), Hebrew exhibitioner 84, B.A. 85, M.A. 89; HONOURS:— Syriac prize 85, Hebrew scholarship 86 and 87; 2nd Wall Biblical scholarship at Dublin university 83.

Walker, Thomas Alexander Draycott, born at Abbots Morton, co. Worcester, 7 May, 1867; 1s. Thomas, cler. LINCOLN, matric. 17 Oct., 89 aged 22 (from Bromsgrove and Hampstead schools); HONOURS: — 2 classical mods. 91.

Walker, Thomas Hollis, born at Spilsby, co. Lincoln, 1861; 3s. John West, B.Med. CHRIST CHURCH, matric. 21 May, 80, aged 19 (from Epsom coll.), scholar 80-5, B.A. 83 (HONOURS:— 2 mathematical mods. 81, 2 mathematics 83); assist. master Epsom college, bar.-at-law, Inner Temple, 86.

Walker, Thomas Jesse, born at Northampton 1863; 2s. Aston, gen. NON-COLLEGIATE, matric. 17 Oct., 91, aged 28, from Durham university.

Walker, William George, born at Naini Tal, East Indies, 29 May, 1863; 1s. William, B.Med. ST. JOHN'S, matric. 15 Oct., 81, aged 18 (from Haileybury), B.A. 84, M.A. 88; lieut. the Suffolk regt. 85, wing officer 1st. battalion 4th Goorkhas 90.

Walker, William Greaves, born at Sheffield, Yorks, 26 Jan., 1865; 4s. Horace, gent. WORCESTER, matric. 25 Jan., 84, aged 18 (from Malvern coll.), B.A. 87, M.A. 91.

Walker, William Holmes, born at Alverthorpe, near Wakefield, 17 May, 1872; 1s. John Young, schoolmaster. UNIVERSITY COLL., matric. 15 Oct., 92, aged 19 (from Wakefield gr. school), exhibitioner 92.

Wall, Charles Calvert, born at Brighton 1865; 1s. Charles Heron, gent. NON-COLLEGIATE, matric. 18 Oct., 83, aged 18.

Wall, Reginald Cecil Bligh, born 16 Oct., 1869; 2s. Reginald Bligh, gen. QUEEN'S, matric. 22 Oct., 89, aged 20 (from Bradfield coll.), exhibitioner 89; HONOURS:— 2 classical mods. 91.

Wallace, Alfred Russell, F.R.S., created D.C.L. 26 Nov., 1889; born at Usk, co. Monmouth, 8 Jan., 22, educated at Hertford grammar school, royal medallist royal society 68, gold medallist société de géographie of Paris 70, president Land Nationalisation Society, hon. LL.D. Dublin 82, Darwin medallist (royal society) 90, royal medallist (royal Geogr. society) 92.

Wallace, George Williamson, born at Greenock, near Renfrew, 1862; 2s. James, D.Med. CORPUS CHRISTI, matric. 26 Oct., 81, aged 19 (from Fettes coll.), exhibitioner 82-5, B.A. 86, M.A. 90; HONOURS :—2 classical mods. 82, 2 classics 85.

Wallace, Houston Stewart, born at Glasgow 1870; 2s. Houston Stewart, gen. ST. JOHN'S, matric. 12 Oct., 89, aged 19, from Fettes coll.

Wallace, Lewis Alexander Richard, born in London Sept., 1866; 1s. Richard, gent. UNIVERSITY COLL., matric. 17 Oct., 85, aged 19 (from Eton), B.A. 89; HONOURS :—2 physiology 89.

Wallace, Percy Maxwell, born at Loughborough, co. Leic., 20 Jan., 1863; 1s. James, cler., late headmaster Loughborough gr. school. LINCOLN, matric. 20 Oct., 81, aged 18 (from Malvern coll.), scholar 81-5, B.A. 85, M.A. 90; HONOURS :—2 classical mods. 83, 3 classics 85.

Wallace, Robert Hugh, born at Downpatrick, co. Down, 1860; 2s. William Nevin, gent. NON-COLLEGIATE, matric. 17 Jan., 80, aged 19 (from Harrow); migrated to BRASENOSE 80, B.A. 84, M.A. 87; bar.-at-law, Inner Temple, 86.

Wallace, William, M.A., fellow MERTON 67, where see page 93.

Waller, David Grierson, born at Sawaut Warrie, East Indies, 4 July, 1872; 4s. William Francis Frederick, arm. TRINITY, matric. 17 Jan., 91, aged 18 (from Bath coll.), scholar 90; HONOURS :—2 classical mods. 92.

Waller, Edmund, born at Pakington, co. Warwick, 24 Oct., 1871; 2s. Ernest Alfred, M.A., hon. canon of Worcester. UNIVERSITY COLL., matric. 11 Oct., 90, aged 18, from Marlborough.

Waller, John Theodore, born at Amsterdam 1863; 1s. Hendrick, arm. ST. JOHN'S, matric. 17 Jan., 80, aged 17, B.A. 84, M.A. 86; HONOURS :— 4 history 83.

Wallernried, Maximilian Rudolf Carl Velth von, born at Dresden in Saxony July, 1872; 3s. Wilhelm, colonel. KEBLE, matric. 20 Oct., 91, aged 19, from Lancing coll.

Wallis, Arthur Bertram Ridley, born at Reading 13 May, 1864; 2s. William Marshall, cler. WORCESTER, matric. 14 June, 84, aged 20 (from King's school, Canterbury), B.A. 88, M.A. and B.C.L. 91 (HONOURS :—2 law 88); brother of the next.

Wallis, Henry Thomas Masterman, born at Bucklebury, Berks, 1860; 1s. William Marshall, cler. UNIVERSITY COLL., matric. 16 Oct., 80, aged 20 (from Canterbury school), B.A. 84 (HONOURS :— 3 mathematical mods. 82, 4 mathematics 84); brother of the last-named.

Wallis, Henry Weston, born in Calcutta 1851; 2s. Charles Balfour, arm. NON-COLLEGIATE, matric. 4 Nov., 80, aged 29 (from St. Paul's, London, and Caius coll., Cambridge); HONOURS :—a natural science 84.

Wallis, Henry White, born at Stockwell, Surrey, 1861; 3s. Joseph, cler. NON-COLLEGIATE, matric. 14 Oct., 82, aged 21.

Wallis, James Appleton, born near Ware, Herts, 12 Dec., 1873; 2s. William, actuary. TRINITY, matric. 15 Oct., 92, aged 18 (from the Charterhouse), scholar 91.

Wallop, hon. Arthur George Edward, born 12 Oct., 1867; 5s. Isaac Newton, earl of Portsmouth. CHRIST CHURCH, matric. 11 Oct., 89, aged 21 (from Uppingham school), B.A. 92; HONOURS :—3 theology 92.

Wallop, (hon) Frederick Henry Arthur, born 22 Feb., 1870; 6s. Isaac Newton, earl of Portsmouth. CHRIST CHURCH, matric. 18 Jan., 89, aged 18.

Wallop, hon. Robert Gerald Valoynes, born 6 July, 1864; 4s. Isaac Newton, earl of Portsmouth. NON-COLLEGIATE, matric. 14 Oct., 82, aged 18.

Walmsley, Hugh, born at Kingston-on-Thames 13 Aug., 1871; 3s. Samuel, gen. NON-COLLEGIATE, matric. 11 Oct., 90, aged 19 (from a Hereford school); exhibitioner MERTON 91; HONOURS :—2 classical mods. 92.

Walmsley, rev. John, born at Hereford 1867; 1s. George, gent. BRASENOSE, matric. 14 Oct., 84, aged 17 (from Hereford school), scholar 84, B.A. 88, M.A. 91 (HONOURS :—2 classical mods. 86, 3 classics 88, 2 theology 89, Greek Testament prize 90); curate of Stokenham with Chivelstone and Shenfard, Devon, 90.

Walmsley, John Bankes, born at Wavertree, co. Lanc., 1872; 3s. John Bankes, gen. UNIVERSITY COLL., matric. 11 Oct., 90, aged 18, from Liverpool royal institution school.

Walrond, Henry Humphrey, born at St. Leonards, Sussex, 1862; 1s. Henry, arm. EXETER, matric. 20 Oct., 81, aged 19 (from a Southampton school), B.A. 86; of Dulford, Devon.

Walrond, Main Swete Osmond, born in London 1870; 4s. Main Swete Alexander, vicar of St. Lawrence, Jewry, with St. Mary Magdalen, Milk-street, 73. BALLIOL, matric. 17 Oct., 89, aged 19, from Harrow.

Walrond, Seymour Henry, born at Cookham, Berks, 13 Oct., 1861; 2s. Theodore, C.B. BALLIOL, matric. 20 Oct., 80, aged 19 (from Rugby); HONOURS :—2 classical mods. 82.

Walrond, Theodore Hunter Hastings, born at Glasgow 5 Dec., 1871; 1s. Francis Charles, of Rugby, gen. BALLIOL, matric. 20 Oct., 91, aged 18, from Rugby.

Walsh, Cecil Henry, born at South Leigh, Oxon, 1869; 3s. Perceval, solicitor. ST. JOHN'S, matric. 15 Oct., 87, aged 18 (from Honiton school), B.A. 90; HONOURS :—3 history 90.

Walsh, Correa Moylan, born at Newburgh, In America, 1862; 3s. Joseph Correa, arm. BALLIOL, matric. 18 Oct., 88, aged 26, from Harvard university.

Walsh, Ernest, born in London 1860; 3s. Robert, gent. NON-COLLEGIATE, matric. 14 Oct., 82, aged 22 (from Hurstpierpoint coll.), B.A. 86; HONOURS :—4 theology 86.

Walsh, rev. Henry William, born at Oxford 14 Aug., 1861; 1s. William Henry, solicitor. LINCOLN, matric. 23 Oct., 80, aged 19 (from Haileybury), B.A. 84, M.A. 87 (HONOURS :—3 classical mods. 82, 4 classics 84); curate of Battersea St. Philip 87.

Walsh, rev. John Ernest, born at Oxford 9 Sept., 1862; 2s. William Henry, of Oxford, solicitor. NON-COLLEGIATE, matric. 17 Dec., 84, aged 22 (from Haileybury); migrated to EXETER 21 Oct., 85, B.A. 87, M.A. 91 (HONOURS :—1 law 87); died 25 July, 92.

Walsh, hon. Nigel Christopher, born 2 April, 1867; 5s. Arthur, lord Ormathwaite. CHRIST CHURCH, matric. 20 May, 85, aged 18, B.A. 89; HONOURS :—4 law 89.

Walsh, Thomas Preston, born in the Indian Ocean 1857; o.s. Thomas Prendergast, arm. NON-COLLEGIATE, matric. 19 Jan., 89, aged 32 (from Wellington coll.); HONOURS :—2 Indian languages 92.

Walsh, rt. rev. William, gent. ST. ALBAN HALL, matric. 10 April, 56, aged 19, B.A. 59, M.A. 62; migrated to MERTON 82, created D.D. 4 Dec., 90; perpetual curate St. Andrew's, Watford, 73-8, chaplain at Rome 78-9, vicar of St. Matthew's, Newington, Surrey, 79-86, prebendary of St. Paul's 89, bishop of Mauritius 91.

Walsh, William Trevor Hayne, born in London 1866; 1s. William, cler. ST. JOHN'S, matric. 17 Oct., 85, aged 19 (from Merchant Taylors' school), scholar 85, B.A. 89; HONOURS :—2 classical mods. 87, 3 classics 89.

Waltenberg, rev. Theophilus Ralph, born at Sereje, Poland, 17 Sept., 1855; 1s. Charles, D. Med. NON-COLLEGIATE, matric. 9 June, 82, aged 26 (from Durham university, B.A., and Queen's coll. Birmingham); migrated to EXETER 16 Oct., 83, B.A. 86, M.A. 89 (HONOURS :—2 theology 86); held various curacies 78-89, Lichfield missioner (Ch. Miss. Soc.), and headmaster Harris school, Tripheane, Madras, 89.

Walter, Hubert, born in London 12 March, 1870; 8s. John, of Dearwood, Berks, M.P. NON-COLLEGIATE, matric. 12 Oct., 88, aged 18 (from Winchester), B.A. 92; HONOURS :—3 classical mods. 90, 4 classics 92.

Walter, John Russell, born at Taunton, Somerset, 1864; 2s. Octavius Gardner, solicitor. NON-COLLEGIATE, matric. 24 Feb., 81, aged 17 (from Taunton collegiate school); brother of William A. G.

Walter, Robert, born at Woolwich, Kent, 22 Oct., 1873; 2s. Frederic Edward, major R.A. (retired). WORCESTER, matric. 18 Oct., 92, aged 18 (from Marlborough coll.), scholar 92.

Walter, Stackhouse William, born at Sutcombe, Devon, 1863; 1s. Edward, gent. NON-COLLEGIATE, matric. 3 Nov., 83, aged 20; migrated to CHARSLEY HALL, B.A. 87; HONOURS :—4 theology 87.

Walter, William Ardagh Gardner, born at Taunton, Somerset, 1860; 1s. Octavius Gardner, solicitor. NON-COLLEGIATE, matric. 23 Oct., 80, aged 20 (from Taunton collegiate school); migrated to EXETER, Lent term, 81; brother of John R.

Walters, David, born at Llanwonno, co. Glam., 10 Feb., 1871; 1s. Morgan Jones, gen. MERTON, matric. 15 Oct., 90, aged 19, from Brecon coll.

Walters, rev. Ernest William Richard, born at Cheltenham 1862; 1s. Richard Ernest, gent. KEBLE, matric. 17 Oct., 82, aged 20 (from Ardingly school), B.A. 85; curate of Warden with Newbrough, Northumberland, 89.

Walters, Frederick Wilfrid, born at Winchester 11 Oct., 1863; 5s. Alfred Vaughan, cler. NON-COLLEGIATE, matric. 13 Jan., 83, aged 19; scholar EXETER 84-6, B.A. 86 (HONOURS :—2 theology 86); curate of Sydenham St. Philip 91.

Walters, Hubert Alexander, born at Redhill, Surrey, 1867; 2s. Charles, cler. HERTFORD, matric. 27 Oct., 87, aged 20.

Walters, Hugh Melmoth, born at Ewell, Surrey, 7 April, 1868; 3s. William Melmoth, arm. ORIEL, matric. 19 Oct., 86, aged 18 (from Haileybury), B.A. 90; died 27 Nov., 90, of a football accident.

Walters, John Edgar, born at Oldham, co. Lanc., 20 April, 1874; o.s. Charles, national schoolmaster. WORCESTER, matric. 18 Oct., 92, aged 18 (from Manchester gr. school), scholar 92.

Walters, John Stewart, born at Reigate, Surrey, July, 1866; 1s. John, arm. ORIEL, matric. 23 Oct., 84, aged 18 (from Winchester), B.A. 87.

Walters, Percy Melmoth, born at Ewell, Surrey, 1863; 1s. William Melmoth, gent. ORIEL, matric. 18 Oct., 81, aged 18 (from the Charterhouse), B.A. 87, M.A. 89 (HONOURS :—3 law 85); bar.-at-law, Lincoln's Inn, 88.

Walters, rev. Reginald Edward, born at Bosworth, co. Lincoln, 21 May, 1861; 1s. Thomas, cler. LINCOLN, matric. 23 Oct., 80, aged 19 (from Tavistock gr. school), B.A. 84, M.A. 87 (HONOURS: —3 theology 84); assist. master Clergy Orphan school, Canterbury, 84.

Walton, Arthur David William, born at Marlborough Feb., 1865; 2s. Alexander, gent. WORCESTER, matric. 18 Oct., 83, aged 18, from Stratford-on-Avon school.

Walton, Cyril Medd Baskerville, born at Oxford 3 Oct., 1870; 3s. Henry Baskerville, late vicar of Holywell, Oxford, deceased. NON-COLLEGIATE, matric. 21 Oct., 89, aged 19, from Brighton coll.

Walton, Francis William, born at Handsworth, co. Staff.; o.s. Daniel Nathaniel, cler. KEBLE, matric. 16 Oct., 83, aged (from Tonbridge school), B.A. 87; HONOURS :—3 physiology 87.

Walton, Harry Boughey, born at Boulogne-sur-Mer 2 April, 1871; o.s. Henry Valentine, E.I.C.S., deceased. NEW COLL., matric. 16 Oct., 91, aged 20 (from Haileybury); HONOURS :—3 classical mods. 93.

Walton, Herbert Fitzgerald Reed Haynes, born in London 28 March, 1861; 3s. Henry Haynes, gent. LINCOLN, matric. 23 Oct., 80, aged 19 (from the Charterhouse); died 12 Dec., 80.

Walton, Herbert Henry Bishop, born at Oxford 3 May, 1863; 1s. Henry Baskerville, vicar of Holywell. NEW COLL., matric. 15 Oct., 81, aged 18 (from Malvern coll.), B.A. 85; HONOURS :—2 classical mods. 83, 1 classics 85, 1 history 86.

Walton, James William, born at Mellor, co. Lanc., 1866; 1s. James, gen. NON-COLLEGIATE, matric. 13 Oct., 88, aged 22 (from Blackburn gr. school); migrated to BALLIOL 89, B.A. 92.

Walton, Walter Edward Baskerville, born at Oxford 12 Jan., 1865; 2s. Henry Baskerville, cler. TRINITY, matric. 16 Oct., 83, aged 18 (from Magdalen coll. school), B.A. 87, M.A. and B.C.L. 90; HONOURS :—2 classical mods. 85, 2 law 87, 2 civil law 88.

Walwyn, Hugh Wallwyn Shepheard-, born at Ashover vicarage, 22 Oct., 1874; 7t. son Clement Carus Wilson S.-W., late rector of Sacombe, Herts, deceased. HERTFORD, matric. 22 Oct., 92, aged 17, from Matfield school, Staplehurst.

Wansbrough, rev. Alfred Ernest, born at Watchet, Somerset, May, 1863; 1s. Alfred Colmer, gent. NON-COLLEGIATE, matric. 14 Oct., 82, aged 19 (from Clifton coll.); migrated to CHRIST CHURCH, B.A. 87, M.A. 92; curate of Taunton St. Mary Magdalen 91.

Wansey, Henry Raymond, born at Stoke Bishop, Bristol, 16 Oct., 1873; 2s. Arthur Henry, solicitor. UNIVERSITY COLL., matric. 15 Oct., 92, aged 19, from Clifton school.

Warburton, rev. Acton, born at Iffley, Oxon, 13 March, 1867; 1s. Thomas Acton, cler. KEBLE, matric. 22 Oct., 85, aged 18 (from St. Mark's school, Windsor); migrated to WORCESTER, B.A. 90; curate of Leavesden, Herts, 91.

Warburton, Arthur Rolle, born at Winchester 14 Oct., 1868; 4s. William Parsons, canon of Winchester. EXETER, matric. 19 Oct., 87, aged 19 (from Honiton school), scholar 87, B.A. 91; HONOURS :—2 classical mods. 89, 3 classics 91.

Warburton, Barclay Harding, born at Philadelphia 1866; 1s. Charles Edward, gen. CHRIST CHURCH, matric. 13 Jan., 88, aged 22.

Warburton, Frederick, born at Elton, co. Lanc., Sept., 1870; 2s. Mark, gen. KEBLE, matric. 11 Oct., 90, aged 20, from Bury Lane. school.

Warburton, George, born at Iffley, Oxon 24 Aug., 1868; 2s. Thomas Acton, cler. WORCESTER, matric. 17 Oct., 87, aged 19, from St. Mark's school, Windsor.

Warburton, Harris Grant, born at Ryde, I.W., 1867; 2s. Augustus Frederick, arm. BALLIOL, matric. 24 Oct., 85, aged 17 (from Dover coll.); assist. magistrate N.W.P., and of the finance department government of India 87.

Warburton, Philip Egerton Bass, born at Kilmington, Somerset, 9 July, 1873; o.s. Mark, B.D., rector. QUEEN'S, matric. 9 Feb., 92, aged 18, from Clifton coll.

Warburton, William Parsons, M.A., fellow ALL SOULS, 49-53, where see page 279.

Ward, Alfred Haden Melville, born at Rowley Regis, co. Stafford, 1860; 4s. Thomas, cler. NON-COLLEGIATE, matric. 14 Oct., 82, aged 22, B.A. 86.

Ward, Arthur, born at Aymestrey, co. Hereford, 3 Aug., 1870; 3s. John George Rodney, of Yatton Court, co. Hereford, arm. MAGDALEN, matric. 14 Dec., 88, aged 18 (from Rudley coll.), demy 88.

Ward, Bernard Rowland, born at Winchester 16 Jan., 1863; 1s. Bernard Edward, arm. BALLIOL, matric. 20 Jan., 87, aged 24 (from Winchester); capt. R.E. 91, of the military works department India.

Ward, Charles Crosbie, born at Monkstown, co. Dublin, 26 March, 1868; y.s. hon. Somerset Richard Hamilton, KEBLE, matric. 17 Oct., 87, aged 19, from Glenalmond coll.

Ward, rev. Charles Fenwick, born at Manchester 1862; 2s. John Charles, gent. NON-COLLEGIATE, matric. 14 Oct., 82, aged 20, B.A. 85, M.A. 89; curate of Chadderton (Christ Church), co. Lanc., 91.

Ward, Charles Osman, born at Bramber, Sussex, 1870; 2s. Thomas William, cler. NON-COLLEGIATE, matric. 12 Oct., 89, aged 19 (from Reading school), B.A. 92.

Ward, Francis, born at Meerut, East Indies, 12 Jan., 1872; 4s. George Ernest, late Indian C.S. NON-COLLEGIATE, matric. 30 Jan., 90, aged 18 (from Clifton coll.); migrated to WADHAM 16 Jan., 91; brother of George next-named.

Ward, George, born at Meerut, East Indies, 1871; 3s. George Ernest, arm. NON-COLLEGIATE, matric. 30 Jan., 90, aged 19 (from Clifton coll.); brother of Francis last-named.

Ward, George Ernest, M.A., WADHAM, where see page 534.

Ward, George Herbert, born at Oxford 1862; 1s. George Sturton, cler., fellow of Hertford coll. HERTFORD, matric. 18 May, 80, aged 18 (from Malvern coll.), scholar 79-84, B.A. 86, M.A. 88; HONOURS:—1 mathematical mods. 81, 1 mathematics 84.

Ward, rev. George Sturton, M.A., fellow HERTFORD 74, where see page 597.

Ward, Herbert, born at Bradford, Yorks, 2 May, 1866; 1s. Samson, gent. CORPUS CHRISTI, matric. 26 Oct., 85, aged 19 (from Bradford gr. school), scholar 85, B.A. 89, M.A. 92; HONOURS:—1 classical mods. 87, 1 classics 89, English essay 90.

Ward, rev. Hugh Herbert Edward Nelson-, born at Radstock, near Bath, 1863; 3s. Horatio Nelson, cler. BRASENOSE, matric. 19 Oct., 82, aged 19 (from Bruton gr. school) B.A. 86 (HONOURS:—4 theology 86); curate of Ashbourne with Mapleton 90.

Ward, rev. Lionel, born at Winchester 29 Feb., 1864; 2s. Bernard Edward, lieut.-col. LINCOLN, matric. 23 Oct., 82, aged 18 (from Winchester), B.A. 86, M.A. 89 (HONOURS:—2 history 86); curate of Southampton All Saints 91.

Ward, Maurice Suckling, born at Pinner, Middx., 26 Jan., 1873; 2s. Nelson, registrar in Chancery. NEW COLL., matric. 16 Oct., 91, aged 18 (from Harrow); brother of the next-named.

Ward, Nelson, born at Pinner, Middx., 19 Feb., 1865; 1s. Nelson, registrar in Chancery. NEW COLL., matric. 18 Jan., 84, aged 18 (from Harrow), B.A. 87 (HONOURS:—2 classical mods. 85, 4 law 87); brother of the last-named.

Ward, Robert Bruce, born at Middleton, co. Lanc., June, 1868; 3s. Charles Bruce, cler. KEBLE, matric. 13 Oct., 88, aged 20 (from Denstone coll.), B.A. 91; HONOURS:—2 history 91.

Ward, Stanhope Edgar, born at Wrecclesham, Surrey, 1863; 5s. Owen Lewis, arm. PEMBROKE, matric. 23 Oct., 82, aged 19, B.A. 86. (NON-COLLEGIATE) 87, M.A. 90.

Ward, Thomas Clare, born at Market Overton, Rutland, 1870; 1s. Thomas William, cler. CHARSLEY'S HALL, matric. 20 May, 86, aged 16, B.A. 90.

Ward, Thomas Humphrey, M.A., fellow BRASENOSE 69-72, where see page 356.

Ward, rev. Thomas Wilfred, born at Street, Somerset, 23 March, 1868; 1s. John, cler. NON-COLLEGIATE, matric. 13 Oct., 88, aged 20 (from Leatherhead school); migrated to WORCESTER, B.A. 91.

Ward, William Carey, born at Cardiff 1867; o.s. James Lewis Carey, gent. NON-COLLEGIATE, matric. 13 Oct., 84, aged 17, B.A. 88, M.A. 92; HONOURS:—theology 88.

Ward, William Erroll, born at Brighton 1872; 3s. Thomas William, cler. NON-COLLEGIATE, matric. 20 Oct., 90, aged 18, from Cranleigh-by-Guildford school.

Ward, William Henry, born at Coventry 27 July, 1871; o.s. Joseph, gen., deceased. ST. JOHN'S, matric. 11 Oct., 90, aged 19 (from Coventry school), scholar 90; HONOURS:—2 classical mods 92.

Ward, rev. William John, born at Ashburton, Devon, 23 March, 1861; 2s. William Baker, gent. EXETER, matric. 20 Oct., 81, aged 20 (from Wesleyan coll., Taunton), scholar 80-5, B.A. 85 (HONOURS:—2 mathematical mods. 83, 2 mathematics 85); chaplain to the forces 90.

Ward, William Shaw, born at Madras 1844; 1s. Ferdinand de Wilton, D.D. NON-COLLEGIATE, matric. 20 Oct., 90, aged 46.

Wardell, Harold Piper, born at Tunbridge Wells, Kent, 1861; 1s. John Richard, D.Med. CHRIST CHURCH, matric. 21 May, 80, aged 19, from Eton.

Wardell, Warren Henry, born at St. Heliers, Jersey, 1866; 1s. William Henry, arm. PEMBROKE, matric. 27 Oct., 85, aged 19 (from Canterbury school), scholar 85.

Wardrop, John Oliver, born at Lambeth, Surrey, 10 Oct., 1864; 1s. Thomas Caldwell, gen. BALLIOL, matric. 18 Oct., 88, aged 24 (from Cowper Street gr. school, London), B.A. 91; HONOURS:—Taylorian exhibition, Spanish 88, French 89, and Italian 90, 1 history 91.

Ware, Hugh Robert Webb, born at Heidelberg, Australia, 1865; 4s. Thomas, arm. ST. JOHN'S, matric. 21 Oct., 84, aged 19, B.A. 89.

Ware, John Hubert, born at Utlingworth, co. Hereford, 1865; 1s. John Middleton, cler. BRASENOSE, matric. 19 Oct., 82, aged 19 (from Hereford school), scholar 82-6, B.A. 86, M.A. 90; HONOURS:—3 classical mods. 84, 4 history 86.

Ware, Sedley Lynch, born at Jackson, Mississippi, U.S.A., 15 Nov., 1868; o.s. William, southern planter. NON-COLLEGIATE, matric. 15 Oct., 92, aged 23, from coll. St. Barbe, Paris, LL.B. university of France.

Ware, Walter Patrick Webb-, born at Melbourne 1871; 6s. Thomas, gent. ST. JOHN'S, matric. 12 Oct., 89, aged 18 (from St. Edward's school, Summertown), B.A. 92.

Wareing, Thomas, born at Southport, co. Lanc., 1862; o.s. Thomas, gent. CHRIST CHURCH, matric. 14 Oct., 81, aged 19 (from Rossall school), exhibitioner 81-5, B.A. 85; HONOURS:—2 classical mods. 83, 3 theology 85.

Warman, Arthur Seager, born at Richmond, Yorks, 29 June, 1870; 1s. John Seager, cler. CORPUS CHRISTI, matric. 25 Oct., 89, aged 19 (from Marlborough school), scholar 89; HONOURS :—2 classical mods. 91.

Warman, Frederick Sumpter Guy, born in London 5 Nov., 1872; 2s. Frederick, architect. PEMBROKE, matric. 25 Oct., 90, aged 17 (from Merchant Taylors' school), scholar 90; HONOURS :—2 classical mods. 92.

Warneford, rev. Harry Launcelot, born at Halifax 26 June, 1860; 2s. John Henry, cler. HERTFORD, matric. 23 Jan., 80, aged 20 (from Cheltenham coll.), B.A. 85 (HONOURS :—3 law 84) ; curate of Pokesdown, Hants, 91.

Warner, Basil Hale, born at Snitterby, co. Lincoln, 1861; 2s. Richard Edward, rector. NONCOLLEGIATE, matric. 12 Oct., 89, aged 18, from St. Edward's school, Summertown.

Warner, Ernest Thomas, born at Croydon, Surrey, 1874; 1s. Thomas Lenty, gent. CHRIST CHURCH, matric. 14 Oct., 92, aged 18 (from Croydon school), scholar 92.

Warner, Harrie Leonard, born at Wandsworth, Surrey, 13 May, 1863; 2s. Algernon, arm. ORIEL, matric. 18 Oct., 81, aged 18 (from Winchester), B.A. 85; HONOURS :—3 law 84.

Warner, James, born at Ramsgate 1868 ; 1s. James, gen. ST. EDMUND HALL, matric. 18 Oct., 88, aged 20.

Warner, Pelham Francis, born at Port of Spain, Trinidad, 2 Oct., 1873; 3s. Charles William, attorney-general Trinidad. ORIEL, matric. 10 Dec., 92, aged 19, from Rugby.

Warner, Raymond John Richmond, born in London 1861; 3s. Charles William, arm. PEMBROKE, matric. 30 Oct., 80, aged 19.

Warner, Robert Townsend, born at Torquay, Devon, 10 Oct., 1868; 2s. George Townsend, cler., and headmaster of Newton Abbot coll. NEW COLL., matric. 14 Oct., 87, aged 19 (from Winchester), scholar 87; HONOURS :—2 classical mods. 89, 2 classics 91.

Warner, rev. William, M.A., senior student CHRIST CHURCH 74, where see page 408.

Warner, William Charles, born at Hampstead 1872; 1s. William Henry, gen. UNIVERSITY COLL., matric. 11 Oct., 90, aged 18.

Warrack, Charles, born at Aberdeen 1861 ; 1s. Charles, arm. BALLIOL, matric. 17 Oct., 82, aged 21 (from Aberdeen university); exhibitioner 82-5, B.A. 88, M.A. 90; HONOURS :—3 classical mods. 83, 1 classics 86, Green moral philosophy prize 90; died 13 Sept., 91.

Warre, Edmond, D.D., fellow ALL SOULS' 59-62, where see page 281.

Warre, Ernald Roger, born at Eton, Berks, 31 Oct., 1872; 3s. Edmond, D.D., head master of Eton. BALLIOL, matric. 18 Oct., 92, aged 19, from Eton coll.

Warren, Alfred Thomas, born at Lambeth 1863; 1s. Thomas, cler. CORPUS CHRISTI, matric. 27 Oct., 81, aged 19 (from Christ's hospital), scholar 81-6, B.A. 86; HONOURS :—1 mathematical mods. 82, 1 mathematics 85.

Warren, Edward Perry, born at Waltham, Massachusetts, 8 June, 1860; 3s. Samuel Dennis, gent. NEW COLL., matric. 12 Oct., 83, aged 22 (from Harvard university), B.A. 88; HONOURS :—1 classical mods. 85.

Warren, Frederick Edward, B.D., fellow ST. JOHN'S 61-82, where see page 487.

Warren, Richard Bertram Scott-, born at Birdbrook, Essex, 1866; 1s. Richard, cler. KEBLE, matric. 5 Nov., 84, aged 18, B.A. 88, M.A. 91; HONOURS :—3 classical mods. 86, 2 theology 88.

Warren, Samuel Lickendey, M.A., fellow WADHAM 61-70, where see page 532.

Warren, Thomas Herbert, M.A., president MAGDALEN 85, where see page 308.

Warren, William Meade King, born at Exton rectory, Somerset, 2 Aug., 1874; 2s. Frederic King, M.A., clkt. ORIEL, matric. 27 Oct., 92, aged 18, from Malvern coll.

Warrington, Thomas Cotterill, born at Stoke-on-Trent 16 Sept., 1869; 1s. James. NON-COLLEGIATE, matric. 6 Feb., 92, aged 22 (from University coll., Aberystwith) ; exhibitioner of JESUS COLL. 92, scholar 93.

Warry, Ernest Arthur Bragg, born at Combe Rawleigh, Devon, Feb., 1867; 2s. William, arm. ST. JOHN'S, matric. 23 Jan., 86, aged 18 (from the Charterhouse), B.A. 89; HONOURS :—3 history 89.

Warry, George Taylor, born in London 3 Dec., 1861; 1s. George Deedes, Q.C. ORIEL, matric. 27 April, 81, aged 19 (from Winchester), B.A. 90 (HONOURS :—3 classical mods. 82, 3 law 84) ; bar.-at-law, Inner Temple, 88.

Warschauer, Joseph, born at Posen, Germany, 4 Nov., 1869; o.s. Hermann, Dr. Phil. EXETER, matric. 22 Oct., 91, aged 21, from Breslau gymnasium.

Wart, Reginald Bramley Van, born at Liverpool 13 Nov., 1871; o.s. Harry, arm., deceased. ST. JOHN'S, matric. 11 Oct., 90, aged 18 (from Reading gr. school), scholar 90; HONOURS :—3 mathematical mods. 92.

Warter, Henry Gordon, born at Terez de la Frontera, Spain, 1868 ; o.s. Joseph, gen. PEMBROKE, matric. 26 Oct., 89, aged 21, from Uppingham school.

Warwick, Harry Sidney, born at Driffield, Yorks, Feb., 1871; y.s. Francis, gen. KEBLE, matric. 12 Oct., 89, aged 18 (from York school), B.A. 92.

Wason, Leighton Sandys, born in London 31 Dec., 1867; 1s. Rigby Melvill, arm. CHRIST CHURCH, matric. 29 April, 89, aged 21 (from Westminster school); some time in the artillery.

Waterfield, Arthur Swainson, born at Allahabad, East Indies, 16 July, 1866; 2s. Edward, arm. NON-COLLEGIATE, matric. 16 Oct., 86, aged 20 (from Westminster school); migrated to MERTON, B.A. 89; HONOURS :—2 chemistry 89.

Waterfield, Nevill, born at Peshawur, India, 2 Dec., 1864; 1s. William Yarrow, colonel. NEW COLL., matric. 12 Oct., 83, aged 18 (from Eton), B.A. 87.

Waterfield, Reginald, born at Dorking, Surrey, 20 Dec., 1867 ; 3s. Edward, of the Indian c.s. NEW COLL., matric. 15 Oct., 86, aged 18 (from Winchester), scholar 85, B.A. 91 ; HONOURS :—1 classical mods. 88, 1 classics 90.

Waterhouse, Alfred Maurice, born in London 19 April, 1868; 2s. Alfred, R.A. BALLIOL, matric. 19 Oct., 86, aged 18 (HONOURS :—3 mathematical mods. 88, 3 classics 90); died 24 Dec., 90; brother of Amyas, Paul and Samuel H.

Waterhouse, Amyas Theodore, born in London 19 Nov., 1872; 2s. Alfred, R.A., of Yattendon Court, Berks. BALLIOL, matric. 20 Oct., 91, aged 18, from Eton.

Waterhouse, Paul, born at Rusholme, co. Lanc., 20 Oct., 1861; 1s. Alfred, R.A. BALLIOL, matric. 21 Oct., 80, aged 18 (from Eton); HONOURS :—2 classical mods. 82, 2 classics 84.

Waterhouse, Samuel Hugh, born in London 1863; 3s. Alfred, R.A. ORIEL, matric. 18 Oct., 81, aged 18, B.A. 84 ; bar.-at-law, Middle Temple, 86.

Waterhouse, William John, born at Southport, co. Lanc., 1871 ; 2s. John Harrison, gent. CHRIST CHURCH, matric. 14 Oct., 90, aged 21 (from University coll., Liverpool), exhibitioner 91.

Waterlow, Mark, born in London 13 March, 1873; 1s. Herbert Jameson, gent. MAGDALEN, matric. 18 Oct., 92, aged 19, from Harrow.

Waterman, Arthur Nunneley, born at Clifton, co. Glouc., 15 July, 1868; o.s. Edward, gen. MAGDALEN, matric. 22 Oct., 87, aged 19 (from Clifton coll.), B.A. 91; HONOURS :—3 classical mods. 89, 4 classics 91.

Waters, Cyril Aubrey, born at Tredegar, co. Monmouth, 1861; 3s. Richard, arm. NON-COLLEGIATE, matric. 17 Jan., 80, aged 19, B.A. 83, M.A. 88.

Waters, George Thorold, born at Thornbury, co. Glouc., 22 Aug., 1873; 1s. Thomas Waters, rector of Staverton, Northants. NEW COLL., matric. 14 Oct., 92, aged 19 (from Winchester), scholar 91.

Waters, John William, born at Freethorpe, Norfolk, 1871; 1s. William, arm. ST. JOHN'S, matric. 14 Oct., 90, aged 19.

Waters, Sampson, born at Truro, Cornwall, June, 1864; 1s. John, arm. CHRIST CHURCH, matric. 13 Oct., 82, aged 18 (from Harrow), B.A. 86; bar.-at-law, Inner Temple, 89.

Waters, Thomas, M.A., student CHRIST CHURCH 58-73, where see page 422.

Waters, William Arthur Pernow, born at Hindringham, Norfolk, Oct., 1868; 1s. William George, arm. BRASENOSE, matric. 17 Jan., 86, aged 19 (from Clifton coll.), B.A. 91; HONOURS :—3 classical mods. 89, 2 physiology 91.

Wathen, rev. Percy Montague, born at Great Malvern, co. Worcester, 1 Jan., 1863; 3s. John Bateman, cler. UNIVERSITY COLL., matric. 21 Jan., 82, aged 19 (from Malvern coll.), B.A. 85, M.A. 89 (HONOURS:—4 theology 85); curate of Almondbury, Yorks, 90.

Watkins, Christopher D'Oyly, born at Bangor 10 Dec., 1861; 3s. John, gent. JESUS COLL., matric. 19 Oct., 81, aged 19 (from Brecon coll.), scholar 81-5; HONOURS :—3 classical mods. 83.

Watkins, Frederick Edmund, born at Treeton, Yorks, 21 March, 1862; 10s. Richard Edward, of Lawkland Hall, Clapham, Yorks, cler. WADHAM, matric. 19 Oct., 85, aged 23 (from Giggleswick gr. school), B.A. 89.

Watkins, George Nueces, born at Walworth, Surrey, 1856; 3s. Thomas William, gen. NON-COLLEGIATE, matric. 10 April, 80, aged 24, from Birkbeck school, Peckham.

Watkins, Harry, born at Beckenham, Kent, 12 Sept., 1869; 4s. William, gent. EXETER, matric. 17 Oct., 88, aged 19 (from a Blackheath school); died 30 July, 89.

Watkins, Philip Morgan, born at Ottery St. Mary, Devon, 26 Aug., 1867; 1s. Morgan George, cler. BRASENOSE, matric. 20 Oct., 86, aged 19 (from Winchester), scholar 86, B.A. 91; HONOURS :—2 classical mods. 88, 2 classics 90.

Watkins, Sidney Cornish, born at Ottery St. Mary, Devon, 16 Feb., 1871; 2s. Morgan George, cler. KEBLE, matric. 11 Oct., 90, aged 19, from Hereford school.

Watkinson, Frank, born at Egerton, Yorks, Dec., 1867; 3s. James, gen. BRASENOSE, matric. 20 Oct., 87, aged 19 (from Shrewsbury school), B.A. 92.

Watling, Henry John Wyatt, born at Cheltenham 3 Sept., 1872; 2s. Henry Fairchild, cler. LINCOLN, matric. 20 Oct., 90, aged 18.

Watney, Claude, born in London 4 Nov., 1866; 2s. James, M.P. NEW COLL., matric. 16 Oct., 85, aged 18, from Eton.

Watney, John Sanders, born at Redhill, Surrey, 1866; 1s. John, gent. CORPUS CHRISTI, matric. 26 Oct., 85, aged 19 (from Winchester), B.A. 88, M.A. 92; HONOURS:—3 law 88.

Watson, rev. Albert, M.A., principal BRASENOSE 86-9, where see page 348.

Watson, Archibald Ralph, born at Charlecombe, Somerset, 7 Jan., 1870; 5s. Edward Dyot, lieut.-general Bengal army. TRINITY, matric. 12 Oct., 89, aged 19 (from Bath coll.) ; HONOURS :—2 classical mods. 91.

Watson, Archibald Watson, born at Akola, East Indies, 13 Nov., 1864; 1s. Archibald, gent. BALLIOL, matric. 16 Oct., 83, aged 18 (from Rugby), B.A. 87 (HONOURS :—2 classical mods. 85, 3 history 87) ; bar.-at-law, Inner Temple, 90.

Watson, Arthur George, D.C.L., fellow ALL SOULS' 53-65, where see page 280.

Watson, rev. Arthur Hawtree, born at Saltfleetby St. Peter, co. Lincoln, June, 1865 ; 1s. William Richards, cler. KEBLE. matric. 14 Oct., 84, aged 19 (from Derby school), B.A. 87.

Watson, rev. Arthur Herbert, born at Plumbland, Cumberland, 15 May, 1864; 1s. Shepley Watson, cler. TRINITY, matric. 15 Oct., 83, aged 19 (from Marlborough), exhibitioner QUEEN'S 84, B.A. 87, M.A. 91 (HONOURS:—3 classical mods. 85) ; curate of St. Luke, Beeston Hill, Leeds, 90.

Watson, Arthur Kenelm, born at Harrow, Middx., 23 March, 1867; 1s. Arthur George, D.C.L. BALLIOL, matric. 24 Oct., 85, aged 18 (from Harrow), exhibitioner 85, B.A. 89 (HONOURS :—1 classical mods. 87, 2 classics 89), in University eleven 89.

Watson, Christopher, born at Woodford, Northants, 6 June, 1862; 3s. George Augustus Frederick, vicar of Abbotsley, Hunts. NON-COLLEGIATE, matric. 13 Oct., 83, aged 19 from Brampton school, Hunts); migrated to WADHAM 25 Jan., 86, B.A. 87; HONOURS :—4 theology 87.

Watson, rev. Edwin Walton, born at Bradford, Yorks, 1856; 3s. Matthew, arm. NON-COLLEGIATE, matric. 22 Jan., 81, aged 25 (from Yorkshire coll., Leeds); migrated to QUEEN'S 81, B.A. 83, M.A. 87; vicar of Mumby St. Leonard, co. Linc., 88.

Watson, Ernest Henry Poole, born at Hounslow, Middx., Jan., 1869; o.s. George Henry, gen. KEBLE, matric. 6 March, 88, aged 19 (from Merchant Taylors' school), B.A. 91; HONOURS :— 3 theology 91 ; died 1 Nov., 92.

Watson, Francis Edward, born at Cottesnck, Northants, 1870; 4s. William, cler. ST. EDMUND HALL, matric. 16 Oct., 90, aged 20.

Watson, Frederick Harvey, born at Tring, Herts, 1867; 3s. Henry George, cler. PEMBROKE, matric. 27 Oct., 85, aged 18 (from St. Mark's, Windsor), scholar 85 ; HONOURS :—3 mathematical mods. 87.

Watson, Harry de Vitré, born at Bareilli 18 Nov., 1872; 6s. Edward Dyot, lieut.-genl. Bengal army. TRINITY, matric. 17 Oct., 91, aged 18, from Bath coll.

Watson, Henry Gordon, born at Ryde, I.W., Nov., 1862; o.s. Francis Gordon Deggs, arm. BRASENOSE, matric. 29 April, 82, aged 19 (from Eton), B.A. 87, M.A. 90.

Watson, Henry James John, born at Tring, Herts, 1864; 1s. Henry George, cler. ST. JOHN'S, matric. 13 Oct., 83, aged 19 (from Merchant Taylors' school), scholar 83, B.A. 87, M.A. 91 ; HONOURS :—1 classical mods. 85, 2 classics 87.

Watson, Herbert Sarsfield, born at Llandaff, co. Glamorgan, 1864; 1s. Jonah, gent. ORIEL, matric. 30 Jan., 83, aged 18, B.A. 87; HONOURS:— 3 natural science 85.

Watson, Hubert Digby, born at Harrow, Middx., 31 Dec., 1869; 2s. Arthur George, D.C.L. BALLIOL, matric. 18 Oct., 88, aged 18 (from Harrow), exhibitioner 88, B.A. 93 (HONOURS:— 1 classical mods. 90, 2 classics 92), in University eleven 91; lieut. and batt. and (Prince of Wales' own), Gorkha (rifle) regt., 90, selected candidate Indian C.S. 92.

Watson, rev. John Collinson, born at Lincoln 20 Dec., 1858; 2s. Henry, gen. NON-COLLEGIATE, matric. 21 April, 88, aged 19 (from Lincoln gr. school); migrated to WORCESTER, B.A. 91.

Watson, Walter Crum, born at Northfield, Largs, Ayrsh., 1871; 3s. Charles, D.D., minister F.C. Scot. NEW COLL., matric. 11 Oct., 89, aged 18 (from Harrow); HONOURS:—2 classical mods. 91.

Watson, William Donald Paul, born in London 19 April, 1872; 1s. William Clarence, arm. BRASENOSE, matric. 15 Oct., 90, aged 18, from the Charterhouse.

Watson, William Farnell, born at Mowbray, Cape of Good Hope, 7 July, 1869; y.s. Thomas, gen. WADHAM, matric. 14 Oct., 89, aged 20, from Lancing coll.

Watson, William Floyd, born at Elsham, co Lincoln, 11 June, 1869; 2s. Hickman Barratt, gen. EXETER, matric. 17 Oct., 88, aged 19 (from Clifton coll.), scholar 88, B.A. 92; HONOURS:— 2 classical mods. 90, 3 classics 92.

Watson, William John Ross, born at Milnton, Ross-sh., 17 Feb., 1865; 1s. Hugh, pleb. MERTON, matric. 26 April, 88, aged 23 (from Aberdeen university, 1 classics 86), exhibitioner 88; HONOURS:— 1 classical mods. 89, 1 classics 91.

Watt, Arthur Fowler, born in London 4 Feb., 1874; 1s. Arthur Chorley, late district judge Bo. C.S., deceased. UNIVERSITY COLL., matric. 15 Oct., 92, aged 18 (from Clifton coll.), scholar 92.

Watt, James, born at Edinburgh 1871; 2s. James, gen. BALLIOL, matric. 14 Oct., 90, aged 19 (from Dumfries academy and Edinburgh university, 1 classics 90), scholar 89; HONOURS:—2 classical mods. 92.

Watt, James Gordon, born at Aberdeen 19 Sept., 1868; 1s. James, gen. NON-COLLEGIATE, matric. 21 Oct., 89, aged 21 (from Aberdeen university, 1 mathematics 89), B.A. 92; HONOURS:—Hebrew scholarship 91, 1 theology 92, Denyer and Johnson theological scholarship 93.

Wattie, James Macpherson, born at Aberdeen 1863; o.s. Archibald, gen. PEMBROKE, matric. 30 Jan., 84, aged 21 (from Aberdeen university, 1 classics and 1 mathematics 89), scholar 83, B.A. 87; HONOURS:—1 classical mods. 85, 1 mathematical mods. 85, 1 classics 87.

Watts, George Frederick, R.A., created D.C.L. 14 June, 1882. See Al. Ox. and series page 1512.

Watts, Harold Sellon, born at Freefolk, Hants, 1867; 6s. Robert Edward Reginald, cler. CHRIST CHURCH, matric. 14 Oct., 87, aged 20 (from Bedford gr. school), exhibitioner 87, B.A. 92; HONOURS:—3 classical mods. 89.

Watts, Henry Langford, born at Stainland, Yorks, 6 Sept., 1861; o.s. Langford Lovell, vicar. QUEEN'S, matric. 27 May, 82, aged 20, from Thorp Arch grange school, Yorks.

Watts, Hugh Alban, born at Dyserth, Flints, 1863; o.s. Edmund Thomas, D.Med. ST. JOHN'S, matric. 14 Oct., 82, aged 19, B.A. 85.

Watts, James Henry, born at Oxford 24 June, 1864; 1s. Arthur, gent. NEW COLL., matric. 9 Dec., 81, aged 17 (from New Coll. school), chorister QUEEN'S 74-9, B.A. 85, M.A. 89; HONOURS:—3 classical mods. 83, 3 history 85.

Watts, John, M.A., BALLIOL, where see page 70.

Watts, Thomas Henry John, born at Steynton, co. Pembroke, 1865; 1s. Thomas Martin, gent. BALLIOL, matric. 22 Jan., 85, aged 20 (from Llandovery coll.), exhibitioner 83.

Watts, Thomas Owen, born at Chorley, co. Lanc., 1865; 1s. Thomas Burgoyne, arm. NEW INN HALL, matric. 24 Jan., 84, aged 19.

Wauchope, David Maitland, born at Church Lawford, co. Warwick, 4 March, 1864; o.s. David, cler. KEBLE, matric. 17 Oct., 82, aged 18 (from Marlborough), B.A. 85, M.A. 91; HONOURS:—4 history 85.

Waugh, Arthur, born at Midsomer Norton, Somerset, 24 Aug., 1866; 1s. Alexander, D.Med. NEW COLL., matric. 23 Jan., 86, aged 19 (from Sherborne school), B.A. 89; HONOURS:—3 classical mods. 87, English verse 88, 3 classics 89.

Waugh, William Laurence, born at Wroughton, Wilts, Feb., 1871; 3s. James Charles, cler. KEBLE, matric. 11 Oct., 90, aged 19, from Shrewsbury gr. school.

Way, Bromley George Vere, born at Stapleton rectory, co. Glouc., 20 Nov., 1873; 1s. William Henry Bromley, rector of Duntsbourne Abbots, co. Glouc. NEW COLL., matric. 14 Oct., 92, aged 18, from Wellington coll.

Way, Henry Edward Hugh, born at Henbury, Somerset, April, 1862; 1s. John Hugh, cler. NON-COLLEGIATE, matric. 21 Jan., 82, aged 19, from Malvern coll.

Way, hon. Samuel James, created D.C.L. 17 June, 1891 (s. rev. James), born at Portsmouth 11 April, 36; South Australian bar.-at-law 61, Q.C. 71, attorneygeneral 75, chief justice 76, and lieutenant-governor of South Australia, administered the government 77, 8, 9, 83-9, vice-chancellor 76, and chancellor university of Adelaide 83. See *Men and Women of the Time*.

Way, William Archer, born at Blackheath, Kent, 9 May, 1869; 2s. Edward, gen. TRINITY, matric. 15 Oct., 87, aged 18 (from Christ's Hospital), scholar 85; HONOURS:—2 classical mods. 89, 3 classics 91.

Waylen, Robert Francis, born at Devizes 1839; 1s. Robert, gent. NON-COLLEGIATE, matric. 15 Oct., 81, aged 42; migrated to BALLIOL 81, B.A. 85, M.A. 88; HONOURS:—4 classics 85.

Wayte, John, born at Meriden, co. Warwick, 24 Jan., 1862; 2s. Allin, arm. TRINITY, matric. 16 Oct., 80, aged 18 (from Rochester school), B.A. 83, B.Med. and M.A. 88; HONOURS:—3 classical mods. 82.

Wayte, Samuel William, B.D., president TRINITY 66-78, where see page 447.

Weall, Stanley, born at Brixton, Surrey, 1862; 2s. William, arm. ST. JOHN'S, matric. 17 Jan., 80, aged 18, scholar 83-5, B.A. 83, M.A. 89 (HONOURS:—3 history 83); bar.-at-law, Inner Temple, 84.

Weallens, rev. Robert Stephenson, born at Newcastle-on-Tyne May, 1860; 3s. William, gent. CHARSLEY'S HALL, matric. 27 Oct., 80, aged 20 (from Uppingham school), B.A. 84; curate of St. John Evangelist, Leeds, 89.

Wearing, James Williamson, born at Lancaster 1864; 1s. Stephen Wright, arm. BRASENOSE, matric. 20 Oct., 86, aged 22 (from a Lancaster school), B.A. 89, M.A. 93 (HONOURS:—2 law 89); bar.-at-law, Middle Temple, 88.

Weatherall, John Henry, born at Liverpool 23 Sept., 1868; 2s. William, cler. NON-COLLEGIATE, matric. 11 Oct., 90, aged 22 (from Waverree national school, and Owens coll.); migrated to EXETER 21 Jan., 91.

Weatherly, Alec John Frederic Hugh, born at Oxford 9 Dec., 1873; o.s. Frederic Edward, bar.-at-law. BRASENOSE, matric. 12 Feb., 92, aged 18, from Rugby.

Weatherly, Cecil Octavius, born at Portishead, Somerset, 7 May, 1869; 8s. Frederick, gen. QUEEN'S, matric. 20 Oct., 88, aged 19 (from Rossall school), scholar 88, B.A. 92; HONOURS:— 2 classical mods. 90, 2 classics 92.

Weatherly, Lewis Gatty, born at Portishead, Somerset, 12 Jan., 1863; 7s. Frederick, gent. NON-COLLEGIATE, matric. 10 April, 80, aged 17.

Weaver, rev. William, born at Hampton Wick, Middx., 31 Aug., 1867; 2s. William, gent. QUEEN'S, matric. 25 Oct., 86, aged 19 (from Kingston-upon-Thames gr. school), B.A. 90 (HONOURS:—4 theology 90); curate of East Dulwich St. Clement 91.

Webb, rev. Alfred Ernest, born at Chorlton-on-Medlock, co. Lanc., 1863; 1s. John Stubbins, arm. BRASENOSE, matric. 19 Oct., 82, aged 19 (from Manchester gr. school), exhibitioner 82-6, B.A. 86, M.A. 89 (HONOURS:—2 classical mods. 84, 2 classics 86); curate of St. Mary the Virgin, Stockport, 89.

Webb, Allan Becher, D.D., fellow UNIVERSITY COLL. 63-8, where see page 32.

Webb, Allan Cyprian Bourne, born at Avon Dassett, co. Warwick, Sept., 1870; 1s. Allan Becher, D.D., bishop of Grahamstown. ORIEL, matric. 10 Dec., 88, aged 18 (from St. Edmund's coll., Salisbury); HONOURS:—2 history 92.

Webb, Arthur Sapte, born in London 1867; 2s. Henry, arm. CHRIST CHURCH, matric. 30 May, 85, aged 18, B.A. 89.

Webb, Clement Charles Julian, born in London 25 June, 1865; 3s. Benjamin, cler. CHRIST CHURCH, matric. 10 Oct., 84, aged 19 (from Westminster school), scholar 84, B.A. 88; fellow MAGDALEN 89, tutor 90, M.A. 91; HONOURS:—2 classical mods. 86, 1 classics 88.

Webb, Ernest Walter, born at Oxford May, 1866; 1s. George Walter, gen. NON-COLLEGIATE, matric. 13 Oct., 84, aged 18 (from Oxford high school); scholar KEBLE 85, B.A. 88; HONOURS:— 3 history 88.

Webb, Frederick Edward, born at Oxford 4 July, 1868; o.s. William Edward, gen. QUEEN'S, matric. 21 Oct., 87, aged 19 (from Oxford high school), scholar 87; HONOURS:—2 classical mods. 89, 2 classics 91.

Webb, Godfrey, born 8 July, 1872; 5s. Edward, gen. EXETER, matric. 21 Jan., 91, aged 18, from Winchester.

Webb, James Howard, born at Wellington, Salop, 27 Jan., 1865; 2s. James, gent. NON-COLLEGIATE, matric. 13 Oct., 84, aged 19 (from Denstone coll.); migrated to EXETER, B.A. 87, M.A. 92; HONOURS:—3 classical mods. 86.

Webb, Maurice Lancelot, born at Bagshot, Surrey, 7 Dec., 1870; 4s. Edward, gen. NEW COLL., matric. 11 Oct., 89, aged 18 (from Winchester), B.A. 92; HONOURS:—2 law 92.

Webb, William Harold, born at Worcester 14 June, 1870; 3s. Walter, of Baltenhall, co. Worc., gen. HERTFORD, matric. 25 Oct., 89, aged 19 (from Worcester cathedral gr. school), scholar 87; HONOURS:—2 classical mods. 91.

Webber, Amhurst, born at Cannes, France, 25 Oct., 1867; o.s. Felix Wherry, R.N. NEW COLL., matric. 18 Oct., 87, aged 19 (from Marlborough), B.Mus. 89.

Webber, William Henre Incledon, born at Bromley, Kent, 17 Jan., 1872; 2s. Edward Chichester, gent. PEMBROKE, matric. 25 Oct., 90, aged 18 (from Merchant Taylors' school), scholar 89; HONOURS: —2 classical mods. 92.

Webber, William Thomas Thornhill, bishop of Brisbane, created D.D. 13 May, 1885. See *Al. Ox.* 2nd series 1518.

Weber, Arthur Frederick Clarence, born at Georgetown, Demerara, British Guiana, 12 March, 1873; 2s. Arthur, merchant, and consul general, Demerara. MERTON, matric. 18 Oct., 92, aged 19, from Queen's coll., Demerara.

Webster, Herbert William, born at Bruera, Cheshire, 23 Feb., 1864; 2s. John, vicar of King's Heath, Birmingham. MAGDALEN, matric. 19 Oct., 83, aged 19 (from Birmingham gr. school), clerk 83.

Webster, rev. John, born at Bruern, Cheshire, 1860; 1s. John, cler. HERTFORD, matric. 18 Oct., 80, aged 20 (from Birmingham school), B.A. 83, M.A. 87 (HONOURS:—4 history 83); curate of King's Heath 83-5, of Parkwood 85-90, and of Vacor and Mansel Heath, (all) co. Hereford, 90.

Wedd, Henry George, born in London 1 Dec., 1870; 1s. Henry Arthur, arm. BRASENOSE, matric. 15 Oct., 90, aged 19, from Harrow.

Wedel, count Georg Erhard, born at Evenburg, in Hanover, 1851; 1s. count Charles. BALLIOL, matric. 16 May 84, aged 23, from Vitzthum gymnasium, Dresden.

Weeden, Edward St. Clair, born at Eccles, co. Lanc., 12 July, 1867; o.s. Edward Charles, arm. NEW COLL., matric. 15 Oct., 86, aged 19 (from Rugby), B.A. 90; HONOURS:—3 classical mods. 88, 4 classics 90.

Weekes, Charles Hampton, born at Haywards Heath, Sussex, 1866; 1s. Charles Hampton, cler. CORPUS CHRISTI, matric. 26 Oct., 85, aged 19 (from Harrow); migrated to CHARSLEY'S HALL, B.A. 90, M.A. (MARCON'S HALL) 92.

Weekes, Lawrence Carey Hampton, born at Lindfield, Sussex, 5 Sept., 1872; 2s. Charles Hampton, cler. TRINITY, matric. 17 Oct., 91, aged 19 (from the Charterhouse), exhibitioner 90; HONOURS:—2 classical mods. 93.

Weigall, Cecil Edward, born at Sydney, in Australia, 25 March, 1870; 1s. Albert Bythesea, headmaster of Sydney gr. school. CORPUS CHRISTI, matric. 25 Oct., 89, aged 19 (from Sydney gr. school); HONOURS:—2 classical mods. 91.

Weigall, Edward Mitford, M.A., fellow PEMBROKE 56-9, where see page 554.

Weigall, FitzRoy Henry Francis, born at Wandsworth, Surrey, 5 Aug., 1867; 1s. Henry, arm. CHRIST CHURCH, matric. 30 May, 85, aged 17 (from Winchester), B.A. 89; HONOURS:—2 history 89.

Weigall, rev. Harold Wilkie, born in London July, 1865; 5s. Alfred, gent. NON-COLLEGIATE, matric. 26 Oct., 85, aged 20 (from Salisbury school), B.A. 88, M.A. 93; domestic chaplain to bishop of Nassau, Bahamas, 90.

Weigall, James William Wellesley, born in London 30 Dec., 1868; 2s. Henry, arm. UNIVERSITY COLL., matric. 15 Oct., 87, aged 18 (from Wellington), B.A. 91; HONOURS:—2 classical mods. 89, 3 classics 91.

Weir, Clement Burnett, born at Enfield, Middx., 21 Jan., 1871; 5s. Archibald, cler. TRINITY, matric. 12 Oct., 89, aged 18 (from Harrow), B.A. 93.

Weir, John Campbell, born at Malvern Link, co. Worc., 1864; 1s. Archibald, D.Med. UNIVERSITY COLL., matric. 13 Jan., 83, aged 19, from the Charterhouse.

Weiss, Henry Gillott, born at Edgbaston, co. Warwick, 25 Aug., 1866; o.s. Henry, arm. MERTON, matric. 24 Oct., 85, aged 19 (from Harrow), B.A. 90, M.A. 92.

Welburn, William Gustavus, born at Netherbury, Dorset, July, 1871; 1s. Frederick William, cler. KEBLE, matric. 11 Oct., 90, aged 19, from St. Edward's school, Summertown.

Welby, Charles Glynne Earle, born at Denton Manor, Notts, 11 Aug., 1865; 1s. sir William Earle, bart. CHRIST CHURCH, matric. 25 May, 83, aged 17 (from Eton); HONOURS :—3 history 86.

Welby, Edward Everard Earle, born at Norton Lees, co. Derby, 22 Dec., 1870; 1s. Edward Montagu Earle, county court judge, Sheffield. CORPUS CHRISTI, matric. 25 Oct., 89, aged 18 (from Eton); HONOURS:—2 classical mods. 91.

Welby, John Earle, M.A., fellow MAGDALEN 40-72, where see page 321.

Welby, Montague Earle, M.A., fellow MAGDALEN 53-7, where see page 323.

Welch, William Whitmore, born at Camberwell, Surrey, 1862; 3s. Frederick Isaac, gen. NON-COLLEGIATE, matric. 24 May, 88, aged 26, from Shrewsbury gr. school and King's coll., London.

Welchman, rev. Harold de Vere, born at Lichfield 1861; 5s. Charles Edward Eliot, D.Med. HERTFORD, matric. 19 Oct., 81, aged 20 (from Christ's hospital), scholar 80-6, B.A. 86, M.A. 88 (HONOURS:—1 classical mods. 83, 3 classics 85); assist. master Chigwell gr. school 86.

Wellby, Stanley, born at Balham, Surrey, 19 Feb., 1870; 3s. Daniel, gen. TRINITY, matric. 19 Jan., 89, aged 18 (from Clifton coll.), scholar 88, B.A. 92; HONOURS :—3 classical mods. 90, 4 chemistry 92.

Welldon, rev. Charles Edward, born at Tunbridge, Kent, 1861; 2s. Edward Ind, cler. KEBLE, matric. 22 Jan., 80, aged 18, B.A. 83, M.A. 87 (HONOURS :—4 theology 83); vicar of Faringdon, Berks, 91.

Weller, Samuel Gardner, born at Red Wing, in America, 1868; 2s. Edward Randolph, bishop of . NON-COLLEGIATE, matric. 13 Oct., 88, aged 20.

Wells, Blyth, born at Broomhall Place, Sheffield, 1864; 4s. Henry Jollie, gent. ST. JOHN'S, matric. 15 Oct., 92, aged 28.

Wells, Frederick Burd, born at Cheltenham 20 March, 1860; 5s. Walter Warwick, surgeon. NON-COLLEGIATE, matric. 17 Jan., 80, aged 19 (from Cheltenham coll.); migrated to BALLIOL Easter term 80; died in college 3 June, 81.

Wells, rev. Herbert Methuen, born at Wallingford, Berks, 1862; 2s. Thomas Frederick, gent. UNIVERSITY COLL., matric. 14 Oct., 82, aged 20 (from Magdalen coll. school), B.A. 85 (HONOURS:—3 classical mods. 84, 3 theology 85); rector of Gunthorpe with Bale, Norfolk, 90.

Wells, John George Percy, born at Booth Ferry, Yorks, 17 May, 1868; o.s. John, gen., deceased. WADHAM, matric. 13 Oct., 88, aged 20, from Repton.

Wells, Joseph, M.A., fellow WADHAM 82, where see page 529.

Wells, Richard Busk Paterson, born at Codicote, Herts, Dec., 1873; 1s. Harry Morland, of Scarletts, Twyford, cler. MAGDALEN, matric. 18 Oct., 92, aged 18, from Eton.

Welsh, Hugh Russell, born at Calcutta 5 June, 1864; 2s. David, arm. TRINITY, matric. 15 Oct., 83, aged 19 (from Bruton school), B.A. 86 (HONOURS : —3 classical mods. 85); a medical student; died 92.

Weltoh, Henry Herbert, born at Bromyard, co. Hereford, July, 1865; 1s. Henry William, cler. KEBLE, matric. 14 Oct., 84, aged 19, from Bath coll.

Wenborn, George Frederick, born at Lea, Kent, 10 June, 1868; 1s. George Frederick, accountant. EXETER, matric. 21 Oct., 86, aged 18 (from St. Leonards school), B.A. 91.

Wendt, Ernest Henry, born in London 1865; 1s. Ernest Emil, D.C.L. CHRIST CHURCH, matric. 31 May, 84, aged 19.

Wentworth, William Charles, born at Wimborne, Dorset, 1 Sept., 1871; 1s. Fitzwilliam, arm. NEW COLL., matric. 18 Oct., 90, aged 19, from Wellington.

Were, Edward Ash, born at Clifton, co. Glouc., 14 Nov., 1846; 2s. Thomas Bonville, arm. NEW COLL., matric. 20 Oct., 65, aged 18 (from Rugby), B.A 70, M.A. 72; created D.D. 22 Oct., 89 (HONOURS:—1 classical mods. 67, 2 classics 69); assist. master 72-80, and chaplain Winchester coll. 77-80, vicar of North Bradley, Wilts, 80-5, preb. of Southwell 85, vicar of St. Werburgh, Derby, 89, and suffragan bishop of Derby 89.

West, rev. Arthur George Bainbridge, born at Dunholme, co. Lincoln, 21 Jan., 1854; 2s. John, pleb. NEW COLL., matric. 12 Oct., 83, aged 19 (from Tonbridge school), B.A. 88, M.A. 92 (HONOURS :— 3 classical mods. 85, 3 history 87); curate of St. Mary, South Shields, 91.

West, Bertrand George Sackville-, born in London 20 Nov., 1872; 3s. hon. William Edward. CHRIST CHURCH, matric. 29 May, 91, aged 18 (from Winchester); brother of Lionel E. S.

West, Charles Ernest, born at Great Crosby, co. Lanc., 23 March, 1873; 2s. Charles Percy, gen. BALLIOL, matric. 20 Oct., 91, aged 18 (from Great Crosby school), scholar 90; HONOURS :—1 classical mods. 93.

West, Charles Frederick Cumber, D.D., fellow ST. JOHN'S 53-75, where see page 483.

West, Charles Hamilton, born at Wherwell, Hants, 1863; 2s. Joseph, cler. NON-COLLEGIATE, matric. 12 March, 81, aged 18, from St. Edward's school, Summertown.

West, Francis George, born at Alnwick, Northumberland, 3 Aug., 1864; 1s. George, cler. HERTFORD, matric. 21 Jan., 85, aged 20.

West, Frederick Malcolm, born at Hawarden, Flints, 26 Feb., 1862; 3s. William, cler. NON-COLLEGIATE, matric. 18 Oct., 83, aged 21 (from Glenalmond and school for the Blind, Worcester); migrated to TRINITY, B.A. 87, M.A. 91; HONOURS :—3 classical mods. 85, 2 history 87.

West, Frederick William, born in Dublin 1871; o.s. Raymond, equitis. CHRIST CHURCH, matric. 21 Jan., 90, aged 19 (from Dulwich coll.), scholar 89; HONOURS :—1 classical mods. 93.

West, rev. John Oliver, born at Llandona, isle of Anglescy, 1852; 1s. Henry, gent. NON-COLLEGIATE, matric. 13 Oct., 84, aged 32, B.A. 88 (HONOURS :—2 theology 88); held various curacies 83-91, vicar of Duddeston, co. Warwick, 91.

West, Leslie Wilberforce, born at Lewisham, Kent, May, 1872; 4s. Thomas John, cler. KEBLE, matric. 20 Oct., 91, aged 19, from a Blackheath school.

West, Lionel Charles Cranfield Sackville-, viscount Cantelupe, born 1 Jan., 1868; 1s. Reginald Windsor, earl Delawarr. CHRIST CHURCH, matric. 22 April, 85, aged 17; drowned 7 Nov., 90.

West, Lionel Edward Sackville-, born in London 15 May, 1867; 1s. hon. William Edward, lieut.-col. CHRIST CHURCH, matric. 30 May, 85, aged 18, B.A. 88 (HONOURS :—3 history 88); brother of Bertrand G. S.

West, Percival Carey, born at East Sheen, Surrey, 1873; 3s. Lewis Borrett, gent. ORIEL, matric. 27 Oct., 92, aged 19, from Marlborough.

West, Richard Bowerman, born at Streatham, Surrey, 1866; 1s. Richard Thornton, arm. CHRIST CHURCH, matric. 31 May, 84, aged 18, B.A. 89.

West, Thomas Brookes Charles, born in London 1864; o.s. Thomas, gent. ST. JOHN'S, matric. 14 Oct., 82, aged 18.

West, Thomas Temple, born at Norwood, Surrey, 1873; 1s. Thomas Edward, bar.-at-law. ALL SOULS', matric. 20 Oct., 92, aged 19 (from Shrewsbury school), bible clerk 92.

West, Tom, born at Langton Grange, near Northallerton, Yorks, 7 Feb., 1874; 2s. Jack, of Bridlington Quay, gent. QUEEN'S, matric. 27 Oct., 92, aged 18, from Giggleswick gr. school.

West, Washbourne, B.D, fellow LINCOLN 45, where see page 241.

West, William Willoughby, born at Cheddington, Dorset, Sept., 1866; 1s. William Henry, cler. CHRIST CHURCH, matric. 15 Oct., 86, aged 20 (from Winchester), B.A. 90.

Westacott, Charles Frederick, born in London 25 June, 1872; 6s. George, gent. QUEEN'S, matric. 1 Feb., 81, aged 21 (from a Littlehampton school), B.A. 84, M.A. 89; HONOURS:—1 mathematical mods. 90, junior mathematical exhibition 91.

Westall, rev. William Hawkesley, born at Grenstead Green, near Colchester, 1860; 1s. William, cler. ST. EDMUND HALL, matric. 22 Oct., 84, aged 24; migrated to MAGDALEN COLL., CAMBRIDGE, 22 Oct., 88; curate of Castle-thorpe, Stony Stratford, 90.

Westcott, Brooke Foss, created D.C.L. 22 June, 1881; bishop of Durham 90, see *Al. Ox.* 2nd series 1508.

Westcott, George John Biles, born at Ringwood, Hants, 20 Aug., 1870; 1s. John George Jennings, arm. QUEEN'S, matric. 22 Oct., 89, aged 19 (from Portsmouth gr. school), scholar 88; HONOURS:—1 mathematical mods. 90, junior mathematical exhibition 91.

Westington, William, born at Tavistock, Devon, 1858; 5s. John, pleb. NON-COLLEGIATE, matric. 17 May, 80, aged 28, from Tavistock gr. school.

Westlake, Sidney St. John, born at Colaba, East Indies, 8 June, 1865; 1s. John, gent. BALLIOL, matric. 16 Oct., 83, aged 18 (from Cheltenham coll.); student Inner Temple 84; assist. commissioner Burmah; died 17 May, 92, at Mandalay, Burmah.

Westmacott, Charles Rendel, born at Benwell, Northumberland, 1870; 4s. Percy Graham Buchanan, C.E. BRASENOSE, matric. 16 Oct., 88, aged 18 (from Winchester), B.A. 92; HONOURS:— 3 law 92.

Westmacott, Henry Armstrong, born at Gateshead-on-Tyne, co. Durham, 1864; 5s. Percy Graham Buchanan, C.E. EXETER, matric. 31 May, 82, aged 18.

Weston, Frank, born at Norwood, Surrey, 13 Sept., 1871; 4s. Robert William Gibbs, arm. TRINITY, matric. 11 Oct., 90, aged 19, from Dulwich coll.

Westropp, Lionel Erskine, born at Bombay Sept., 1866; 2s. sir Michael, knt. PEMBROKE, matric. 28 Oct., 86, aged 20, from Sherborne school.

Westwood, Henry Samuel, born at Handsworth, co. Stafford, 18 Feb., 1868; 3s. Henry, gent. WORCESTER, matric. 19 Oct., 86, aged 18 (from Bromsgrove gr. school), B.A. 91.

Wethered, Arthur James, born at St. James, Westminster, 11 May, 1869; 2s. Florence Thomas, cler. CHRIST CHURCH, matric. 21 March, 91, aged 21, from Winchester.

Wethered, rev. Edmund Peel, born at Exeter 7 Jan., 1863; 1s. Florence Thomas, cler. CHRIST CHURCH, matric. 4 June, 81, aged 18 (from the Charterhouse), B.A. 84, M.A. 88; curate of St. John Bapt., Tue Brook, Liverpool, 88.

Wethered, Francis Owen, born at Marlow, Bucks, 13 Dec., 1864; 1s. Owen Peel, arm. CHRIST CHURCH, matric. 13 Oct., 82, aged 17 (from Eton), B.A. 86, M.A. 89; in University eight 85, 6, 7.

Wethered, Herbert Newton, born at Bristol 1870; 3s. Henry, arm. CORPUS CHRISTI, matric. 20 Oct., 88, aged 18 (from Clifton coll.), B.A. 92; HONOURS:—2 history 91.

Wethered, Owen Henry, born at Great Marlow, Bucks, 19 Dec., 1867; 2s. Owen Peel, arm. CHRIST CHURCH, matric. 16 Oct., 85, aged 18 (from Eton), B.A. 88, M.A. 92; HONOURS:—3 law 88.

Wethered, Vernon, born at Bristol 1865; 2s. Henry, arm. ORIEL, matric. 23 Oct., 84, aged 19 (from Clifton coll.), scholar 84, B.A. 88; HONOURS: —2 classical mods. 86, 2 classics 88.

Weymouth, George Augustus, born at Plymouth 29 Oct., 1869; 1s. Richard Francis, doctor and head-master Mill Hill school. LINCOLN, matric. 17 Oct., 84, aged 18 (from Mill Hill school), exhibitioner 84, B.A. 88; HONOURS:—3 classical mods. 86, 2 classics 88.

Whalley, Arthur Henry, born at Sydney, Australia, 1 Nov., 1863; o.s. Arthur John. MERTON, matric. 18 Oct., 81, aged 18.

Whalley, rev. Oswald Philip, born at Terrington St. Clement, Norfolk, Jan., 1861; 2s. Richard Ambrose, cler. ST. EDMUND HALL, matric. 26 Jan., 84, aged 23, B.A. 87, M.A. 90 (HONOURS:—1 theology 87); died 19 Sept., 91.

Whapham, Richard Henry William, born at Crickdade, Wilts, 10 Jan., 1869; 2s. Thomas, M.R.C.V.S. JESUS COLL., matric. 14 Oct., 89, aged 20 (from Cowbridge gr. school, and University coll., Cardiff), scholar 89; HONOURS:—1 mathematical mods. 91.

Wharton, Edward Ross, M.A., fellow JESUS COLL. 68-71 and 82, where see page 510.

Wharton, rev. George Henry Lawrence, born at Gilling, Yorks, Sept., 1865; 2s. James Charles, cler. CHRIST CHURCH, matric. 16 Oct., 85, aged 20 (from the Charterhouse), B.A. 89, M.A. 92; curate of Leeds 90.

Whately, Arthur Pepys, M.A., student CHRIST CHURCH 47-63, where see page 417.

Whatley, rev. Charles Lawson, born at Peopleton, co. Worc., 1868; 2s. Henry Lawson, cler. PEMBROKE, matric. 25 Oct., 87, aged 19 (from Hereford school), B.A. 90; curate of Blockley, co. Worc., 91.

Whatley, Frederick Lawson, born at Aston Ingham, co. Hereford, 13 Dec., 1873; 4s. Henry Lawson, cler. ST. EDMUND HALL, matric. 16 Oct., 92, aged 18, from St. Edward's school, Summertown.

Wheat, rev. Charles Templer, born at Mildmay, Middx., 1866; 4s. Godfrey Charles, gent. NON-COLLEGIATE, matric. 26 Oct., 85, aged 19 (from Brighton coll.), B.A. 89 (HONOURS:—2 history 88); curate of Grimsby, co. Line., 89.

Wheat, Henry, born at Wensbeton, Somerset, 22 Feb., 1870; 1s. Samuel, arm. TRINITY, matric. 12 Oct., 89, aged 19 (from Coventry school), B.A. 93.

Wheatley, Robert Albert, born at Salford, Manchester, 27 March, 1873; 1s. Joseph Larke, solicitor. EXETER, matric. 22 Oct., 91, aged 18, from Rugby.

Wheeler, Charles Bickersteth, born at Coppenhall, Cheshire, 27 March, 1862; 2s. John Bluchor, cler. NON-COLLEGIATE, matric. 22 Jan., 81, aged 18 (from Merchant Taylors' school); migrated to NEW COLL. 81, B.A. 84, M.A. 88; HONOURS:— 2 classical mods. 82, 2 law 84.

Wheeler, Daniel William, born at Berrow, Somerset, 7 Sept., 1867; 1s. William Handcock, cler. EXETER, matric. 21 Oct., 86, aged 19 (from New Plymouth, N.Z., high school), B.A. 90; HONOURS: —1 history 90.

Wheeler, Emmanuel, born at Birmingham 23 Nov., 1869; 2s. George, gen. NON-COLLEGIATE, matric. 17 Jan., 91, aged 21, from Birmingham high school and Mason coll.

Wheeler, George William, born at Oxford 1863; 3s. William, pleb. BALLIOL, matric. 18 May, 83, aged 20 (from Oxford central school), B.A. 89, M.A. 90 (HONOURS: —2 classical mods. 84, 2 classics 87), assistant Bodleian library.

Wheeler, Thomas William Ogle, born at St. Mary Cray, Kent, 30 June, 1868; 2s. Thomas, arm. UNIVERSITY COLL., matric. 15 Oct., 87, aged 19, (from Westminster school), B.A. 90; HONOURS:— 3 law 90.

Wheeler, rev. Walter Compton, born at Wolford, co. Warwick, 1860; 3s. George Domvile, vicar. WORCESTER, matric. 24 Jan., 80, aged 19 B.A. 83; vicar of Wolford 90.

Wheeler, William Albert, born at Pollington, Yorks, 25 Feb., 1863; 3s. William Cheslin, cler. KEBLE, matric. 16 Oct., 83, aged 20 (from Haileybury), B.A. 86.

Wheelwright, Edwin Whitfield, born at Idle, Yorks, 1868; 2s. Thomas Whitfield, gen. BALLIOL, matric. 18 Oct., 88, aged 20 (from Yorkshire coll., Leeds), scholar 88; HONOURS :— 1 chemistry 91.

Wheen, Richard, born in London 22 Jan., 1871; 1s. Richard, gen. MAGDALEN, matric. 14 Oct., 90, aged 19 (from Winchester); HONOURS :— 2 classical mods. 92.

Whelor, Granville Charles Hastings, born at Otterden, Kent, Oct., 1872; 1s. Charles Wheler, esq. CHRIST CHURCH, matric. 16 Oct., 91, aged 19, from Eton.

Whicker, Robert Bricknell, born at St. Peter Port, Guernsey, PEMBROKE, matric. 17 Oct., 88, aged 18 (from Elizabeth coll., Guernsey), scholar 89, B.A. 92 ; HONOURS ;—3 classical mods. 90, 3 classics 92.

Whicker, rev. Walter George Samuel, born at St. Peter Port, Guernsey, 12 July, 1865; 1s. Samuel George, gent. CORPUS CHRISTI, matric. 23 Oct., 83, aged 19 (from Elizabeth coll., Guernsey), scholar 84, B.A. 88, M.A. 91 (HONOURS :—1 classical mods. 86, 2 mathematical mods. 86, 2 classics 88); curate of Basing, Hants, 88.

Whigham, Harry James, born at Drumley, Ayrshire, 24 Dec., 1869; 2s. David Dundas, advocate. QUEEN'S, matric. 20 Oct., 88, aged 18 (from Sedbergh gr. school), exhibitioner 88 ; HONOURS :—2 classical mods. 90, 3 classics 92.

Whinfield, Charles Richard, born at Jarrow, co. Durham, 7 Dec., 1870; 1s. Charles Edgar, gen. ST. MARY HALL, matric. 2 Feb., 91, aged 20.

Whinfield, rev. Herbert Edward, born in London 1862; 1s. Edward Wrey, arm. HERTFORD, matric. 19 Oct., 81, aged 19, B.A. 84; curate of Findbury, co. Worcester, 91.

Whinfield, rev. Walter Grenville, born at South Elkington, co. Linc., 2 Nov., 1865; 3s. Edward Wrey, of Severn Grange, Worcester, arm. MAGDALEN, matric. 23 Oct., 85, aged 19 (from Magdalen coll. and Uppingham schools), B.A. 88, B.Mus. 90 (HONOURS :—3 history 88); curate of Eastbourne 91.

Whipham, Thomas Rowland Charles, born in London 4 Jan., 1871; 1s. Thomas Tillyer, D.Med. NEW COLL., matric. 11 Oct., 89, aged 18, from Rugby.

Whishaw, Bernhard, born at Chipping Norton, Oxon, 8 Feb., 1867; 1s. Alexander, cler. QUEEN'S, matric. 15 May, 80, aged 23 (from Leamington and Clifton colls.), B.A. 83; HONOURS :—2 history 83.

Whitaker, Bernard, born at Hampton Hall, Salop, 23 March, 1873; 2s. James, esq. EXETER, matric. 18 Oct., 92, aged 19, from Cheltenham coll.

Whitaker, rev. Charles Probart, born at Walcot, Bath, 28 Jan., 1858; 2s. John, artist. EXETER, matric. 20 Oct., 81, aged 23 (from Hermitage school, Bath), exhibitioner 81-5, B.A. 84, M.A. 88 (HONOURS :—2 classical mods. 83, 1 theology 85) ; rector of High Bray, Devon, 90.

Whitaker, Dugald Robert, born at Westbury, Salop, 24 Dec., 1869; 3s. John, arm. EXETER, matric. 16 Oct. 89, aged 19 (from Shrewsbury gr. school), B.A. 92.

Whitaker, Harold Thomas, born in London 1870; 2s. John, gen. CHRIST CHURCH, matric. 11 Oct., 89, aged 19 (from Westminster school), exhibitioner 89; HONOURS :—2 classical mods. 91.

Whitaker, Henry Ernest, born at Worthen, Salop, 19 Jan., 70. James, arm. EXETER, matric. 16 Oct., 89, aged 19 (from Wellington coll. and Shrewsbury gr. school), B.A. 92.

Whitaker, Hugh Edward, born at Stanton, co. Derby, April, 1870; o.s. Edward Wright, arm. CHRIST CHURCH, matric. 18 Jan., 89, aged 18.

Whitaker, Milo, born at Salford, co. Lanc., 1870; 3s. Charles, cler. NON-COLLEGIATE, matric. 17 Jan., 91, aged 21.

Whitaker, William, born at Holbeck, Leeds, 28 Sept., 1869; 2s. Joseph, gen. EXETER, matric. 22 Oct., 91, aged 22.

Whitby, Hugh Owen, born at Ottery St. Mary, Devon, 12 April, 1864; 3s. Charles William, D.Med., Aberdeen. LINCOLN, matric. 19 Oct., 83, aged 19 (from Leamington coll.), B.A. 90, M.A. 92; in University eleven 84, 5, 6, 7.

Whitcombe, Robert Henry, born at Milton-juxta-Gravesend 18 July, 1802; 2s. Philip, surgeon. NEW COLL., matric. 15 Oct., 81, aged 19 (from Winchester), scholar 81-5, B.A. 85, M.A. 88 (HONOURS :—1 mathematical mods. 82, 1 natural science 85); student Inner Temple 83.

White, Ambrose, born at Grayingham, co. Linc., Jan., 1864 ; 5s. John, cler. KEBLE, matric. 17 Oct., 82, aged 18 (from Stony Stratford coll.), B.A. 86 (HONOURS :—3 classical mods. 84, 3 classics 86); brother of Leonard H.

White, Arthur Meadows, born at Stonehouse, co. Glouc., 9 Jan., 1866; 1s. William Darren, vicar. QUEEN'S, matric. 20 Oct., 84, aged 18, from Wellington coll.

White, Cecil Alban, born at St. Albans, Muswellbrook, N.S.W., 29 Sept., 1869; 2s. William Edward, M.A., Oxford, canon Christ Church, Newcastle, N.S.W. NEW COLL., matric. 12 Oct., 88, aged 19 (from Paramatta school), B.A. 93; HONOURS :—2 classical mods. 90, 2 classics 92.

White, rev. Charles, born at Ampthill, Beds, 1863; 4s. William, gen. NON-COLLEGIATE, matric. 19 Jan., 85, aged 22, B.A. 89; curate of Long Whatton, co. Leic., 91.

White, Edward Alfred, born at Eckington, co. Wore., 1870; 1s. Alfred, gen. HERTFORD, matric. 19 Oct., 88, aged 18 (from Worcester cathedral school), scholar 87, B.A. 92; HONOURS :—proxime accessit junior mathematical exhibition 90, 1 mathematical mods. 90, 1 mathematics 92.

White, rev. Frederick Ernest, born in London 1853 ; 1s. John, cler. NON-COLLEGIATE, matric. 14 Oct., 82, aged 29, B.A. 85, M.A. 89 (HONOURS ; —3 theology 85) ; curate of St. Stephen, South Dulwich, Kent, 91.

White, Frederick Lumley, born at Mortimer, Hants, 13 Dec., 1862; 3s. Adolphus Leighton, cler. ST. JOHN'S, matric. 14 Oct., 82, aged 19, B.A. 86.

White, Frederick Meadows, Q.C., M.A., recorder of Canterbury, fellow MAGDALEN 65-7, where see page 324.

White, rev. Henry Alcock, born in London 15 Oct., 1864; 1s. Henry Master, archdeacon of Grahamstown, South Africa. NEW COLL., matric. 12 Oct., 83, aged 19 (from King's coll. school, London), II.A. 87, fellow 89, M.A. 90; HONOURS :—1 classical mods. 84, Greek testament prize 86, 1 classics 87, 1 theology 88, Hebrew scholarship 91.

White, Herbert Meadows Frith, born in London 9 Dec., 1867; 2s. Robert Holmes, solicitor. NEW COLL., matric. 15 Oct., 86, aged 18 (from Eton), B.A. 89; HONOURS :—3 history 89.

White, John, M.A., fellow QUEEN'S 63, where see page 173.

White, rev. John, born in London 21 Oct., 1863; 3s. Lewis Borrett, D.D. QUEEN'S, matric. 25 Jan., 83, aged 19 (from Merchant Taylors' school), B.A. 86, M.A. 89 (HONOURS :—3 classical mods. 84, 4 history 86); curate of Spratton 86-91, and of Towcester, (both) Northants, 91.

White, John, born at Deddington, Oxon, 13 Feb., 1870; 1s. John, gen. QUEEN'S, matric. 20 Oct., 88, aged 18 (from Oxford high school), scholar 88, B.A. 92; HONOURS :—1 mathematical mods. 89, 2 mathematics 92.

White, John Edward, D.C.L., fellow NEW COLL. 50-88, where see page 214.

White, John Joseph, born at Nantenan, co. Limerick, 21 Oct., 1863; 1s. John Patrick, arm. TRINITY, matric. 21 Jan., 82, aged 18 (from Stonyhurst), B.A. 85; of Nantenan, lieut. in Shropshire Light Infantry 90.

White, Joseph John Fisher, born at Clifton, co. Glouc., May, 1865; 1s. John, cler. ORIEL, matric. 27 Oct., 83, aged 18 (from Monkton Combe school, Bath), B.A. 87.

White, Leonard Hamilton, born at Grayingham, co. Lincoln, April, 1867; 7s. John, cler. CORPUS CHRISTI, matric. 26 Oct., 85, aged 18 (from Tonbridge school), B.A. 89, M.A. 92 (HONOURS :—2 classical mods. 87, 3 classics 89); brother of Ambrose.

White, Lewis Borrett, D.D., fellow QUEEN'S 51-9, where see page 179.

White, Ralph Lavard, born in London 16 Feb., 1872; 3s. Robert Holmes, solicitor. NEW COLL., matric. 10 Oct., 90, aged 18 (from Eton); HONOURS : —3 classical mods. 92.

White, Robert Eaton, born in London 6 Nov., 1861; 1s. Robert Holmes, solicitor. NEW COLL., matric. 12 Oct., 83, aged 18 (from Eton), B.A. 87 (HONOURS : —2 history 87) ; bar.-at-law, Inner Temple, 90.

White, Robert Thomas, born at Marden 1871; 1s. Robert, gen. QUEEN'S, matric. 16 March, 92, aged 21.

White, Stuart Arthur Frank, born at Portsmouth 27 Aug., 1870; 1s. Francis Symons, gen. LINCOLN, matric. 15 Oct., 87, aged 17 (from Portsmouth gr. school), scholar 86, B.A. 92 (HONOURS :—1 mathematical mods. 88, junior mathematical exhibition 89, 1 mathematics 90, and 1 physics 92, proxime accessit senior mathematical scholarship 93, and Herschel astronomical prize 93.

White, Theodore Henry, born at Reading 1842; 2s. John, gent. NON-COLLEGIATE, matric. 18 Oct., 80, aged 38, B.A. 84.

White, Thomas Armstrong, born at Caehar, East Indies, 1865; 1s. Thomas Augustus, gent. HERTFORD, matric. 27 Oct., 85, aged 19, B.A. 90; HONOURS :—2 history 89.

White, Wallis Harry Brinsley, born at Warminster, Wilts, 21 Oct., 1871; 1s. Charles Henry, gen. LINCOLN, matric. 20 Oct., 90, aged 18 (from Bruton gr. school); HONOURS :—3 classical mods. 92.

White, rev. William Edward, born at Winchester 10 March, 1867; 3s. John, cler. WADHAM, matric. 19 Oct., 85, aged 18 (from Monkton Combe school), B.A. 89, M.A. 92 ; curate of Christ Church, Folkestone, 90.

Whitehead, Charles Balston, born at East Farleigh, Kent, 5 Feb., 1867; 1s. Charles, gent. WORCESTER, matric. 19 Oct., 86, aged 19 (from Tonbridge school), B.A. 89.

Whitehead, George Hugh, born in London 30 Oct., 1861; 1s. James (after lord mayor, bart., and M.P.). TRINITY, matric. 16 Oct., 80, aged 18 (from Clifton coll.); B.A. 84, M.A. 87 (HONOURS :—3 history 84); stockbroker; brother of Rowland E. and Wilfred.

Whitehead, Henry, M.A., fellow TRINITY 77, where see page 449.

Whitehead, Joseph Louis, born at Quebec 17 July, 1854; 1s. Joseph Whiston, gent. NON-COLLEGIATE, matric. 17 Oct., 85, aged 18 (from Queen's coll., Belfast); migrated to NEW COLL. 87, exhibitioner EXETER 87, B.A. 89; HONOURS :— Stanhope essay 88, 2 history 89.

Whitehead, Rowland Edward, born in London 1863; 2s. James (after lord mayor, bart., and M.P.). UNIVERSITY COLL., matric. 14 Oct., 82, aged 19 (from Clifton coll.), B.A. 86, M.A. 89 (HONOURS :—2 classical mods. 83, 1 history 86); bar.-at-law, Inner Temple, 88; brother of George H. and Wilfred James.

Whitehead, Stanley, born at Maidstone, Kent, 7 July, 1863; 3s. Arthur, cler. TRINITY, matric. 15 Oct., 81, aged 18 (from Sherborne school); died.

Whitehead, Wilfred James, born at Catford Bridge, Kent or Surrey, 6 Jan., 1873; 4s. sir James, bart. TRINITY, matric. 6 Feb., 92, aged 19 (from Rugby); brother of George H. and Rowland E.

Whitehead, William Hingeston, born at Barming, Kent, May, 1873; 3s. Charles, gent. ORIEL, matric. 27 Oct., 92, aged 19, from Tonbridge school.

Whitehouse, Arthur Statham Wildman, born at Brighton 25 Sept., 1865; 1s. Edward Orange Wildman, arm. ORIEL, matric. 23 Oct., 84, aged 19 (from Winchester), scholar 84-6; HONOURS :—3 classical mods. 86.

Whitehouse, Howard Sidney Chavasse, born at Sedgley, co. Stafford, 1864; 1s. Henry Nieberton, gent. HERTFORD, matric. 18 Oct., 83, aged 19, B.A. 87, M.A. 92.

Whitelaw, Walter Hugh, born at Rugby, co. Warwick, 1873; 3s. Robert, M.A., assist. master at Rugby. NEW COLL., matric. 14 Oct., 92, aged 19, from Rugby.

Whitelocke, Richard Henry Anglin, born at Westmorland, Jamaica, W.I., 13 Aug., 1861; 3s. Hugh Anthony, district judge, Jamaica. LINCOLN, matric. 28 April, 92, aged 30, from Owens coll. and Edinburgh university.

Whiteside, rev. Joseph, born at Thrimby, Westmorland, 14 May, 1861; 2s. Stephen, cler. TRINITY, matric. 16 Oct., 80, aged 19 (from Durham gr. school), B.A. 84 (HONOURS :—3 classical mods. 82); curate of Stranton, co. Durham, 90.

Whitfeld, rev. Arthur Lewis, born at Lewes, Sussex, 31 July, 1861; 5s. George, arm. MAGDALEN, matric. 15 Oct., 81, aged 19 (from Malvern coll.), B.A. 85, M.A. 88; rector of Little Easton, Essex, 91.

Whitfield, George, born at Modreeny, co. Tipperary, 19 Oct., 1870; 2s. George, arm. MAGDALEN, matric. 20 Jan., 90, aged 19, from Wellington.

Whitham, rev. Arthur Richard, born at Rawdon, Yorks, 13 April, 1863; 1s. William, arm. MAGDALEN, matric. 15 Oct., 81, aged 18 (from Bradford gr. school), demy 81-6, B.A. 86, M.A. 88 (HONOURS: —2 classical mods. 83, 1 classics 85, 1 history 86); rector of Little Easton, Essex, 91.

Whiting, Algernon Oswald, born in London 1861; y.s. George, arm. MERTON, matric. 18 Oct., 80, aged 19 (from Sherborne school), in University eleven 81-2.

Whitley, Edward William, born at Wokingham, Berks, 1868; 1s. Henry Edward, arm. KEBLE, matric. 17 Oct., 87, aged 19 (from Crewkerne school), B.A. 92; HONOURS:—3 history 90.

Whitman, George Ashley, born at Chicago Sept., 1869; o.s. George Ralph, arm. CHRIST CHURCH, matric. 8 June, 89, aged 19.

Whitmore, Charles Algernon, M.A., fellow ALL SOULS' 74, where see page 272.

Whittaker, Thomas, born at Walton le Dale, co. Lanc., 1865; 1s. Robert, gent. ORIEL, matric. 27 Oct., 83, aged 18, from Winchester.

Whittingham, rev. George Napier, born in London 18 Nov., 1865; 2s. Ferdinand, arm. WORCESTER, matric. 17 Oct., 84, aged 18 (from Haileybury), B.A. 89, M.A. 92; curate of Powyke, co. Worc., 91.

Whittington, Benjamin George Collett, born in London 1865; 1s. Benjamin Thomas, gent. ST. EDMUND HALL, matric. 5 Nov., 85, aged 20.

Whittington, Charles Sellon Ashmore, born in London 5 March, 1870; 3s. Richard, preb. of St. Paul's. ST. JOHN'S, matric. 13 Oct., 88, aged 18 (from Merchant Taylors' school), scholar 88, B.A. 92; HONOURS:—Hebrew scholarship 88, 2 classical mods. 90, Septuagint prize 91, 1 theology 92.

Whittington, rev. Frederick Benjamin Brandon, born in London 19 Nov., 1864; 1s. Thomas, solicitor. WADHAM, matric. 16 Oct., 83, aged 19 (from Merchant Taylors' school and King's coll., London), B.A. 89, M.A. 92; curate of Dodworth, Yorks, 90.

Whittington, Richard, born in London 6 Jan., 1869; 2s. Benjamin Thomas, gen. MERTON, matric. 19 Oct., 89, aged 20, from King's coll., London.

Whittington, Richard Piers, born at Thornhill Lees, Yorks, July, 1869; 1s. Richard Thomas, cler. KEBLE, matric. 15 Oct., 88, aged 19 (from Winchester), B.A. 92; HONOURS:—3 classical mods. 90, 3 history 92.

Whittington, rev. Robert Wheeler, born in London 1866; 2s. Richard, canon of St. Paul's. WADHAM, matric. 11 Oct., 84, aged 18 (from Merchant Taylors' school), B.A. 88 (HONOURS:—3 theology 88); curate of Long Eaton, Notts, 91.

Whittuck, Charles Augustus, M.A., fellow BRASENOSE 73-89, where see page 357.

Whittuck, Edward Arthur, M.A., ORIEL, where see page 154.

Whitworth, rev. Joe Pentycross, born at Huddersfield 1862; 2s. Gordon Pentycross, arm. NON-COLLEGIATE, matric. 17 Oct., 81, aged 19 (from King's school, Chester), migrated to BRASENOSE 82, B.A. 84, M.A. 88; curate of Barwell 85.

Whitworth, Robert Henry, born at Up Lyme, Devon, 19 Sept., 1863; o.s. James, arm. ST. MARY HALL, matric. 21 Jan., 89, aged 25 (from Melcombe Regis gr. school); migrated to EXETER, B.A. 92.

Whyatt, Herbert, born at Cheetham Hill, co. Lanc., 6 Feb., 1866; 1s. Robert, gent. EXETER, matric. 16 Oct., 84, aged 18 (from Cheltenham coll); bar.-at-law, Inner Temple, 92.

Wickes, rev. William, D.D., created M.A., 14 Feb., 1888. See *Al. Ox.* 2nd series 1547.

Wickham, rev. Charles Townshend, born at Twyford, Hants, 11 June, 1862; 2s. Latham, cler. CHRIST CHURCH, matric. 21 May, 80, aged 17 (from Harrow), B.A. 84, M.A. 87; headmaster Twyford school 88.

Wickham, Edward Charles, M.A., fellow NEW COLL. 52-74, where see page 215.

Wickham, Frederick, born in London 30 March, 1862; y.s. John, gent. WORCESTER, matric. 21 Oct., 80, aged 18 (from Southwark gr. school); HONOURS:—3 classical mods. 82.

Wickham, Frederick Peers, M.A., fellow NEW COLL. 52-75, where see page 215.

Wickham, Henry John, M.A., fellow NEW COLL. 56-88, where see page 216.

Wickham, Henry John, M.A., fellow NEW COLL. 48-61, where see page 213.

Wickham, Herbert Wykeham, born at Maidstone, Kent, Oct., 1865; y.s. George, arm. CHRIST CHURCH, matric. 31 May, 84, aged 18; bar.-at-law, Middle Temple, 90; lieut. 3rd batt. the Oxfordshire L.I. 92.

Wickham, rev. Lawrence Hawtrey, born at Winchester 1868; 6s. Charles, cler. NON-COLLEGIATE, matric. 15 Oct., 87, aged 19 (from St. Mark's, Windsor), B.A. 90.

Wickham, Reginald William, born at Wetherby, Yorks, 4 March, 1871; 2s. William, of Boston Spa, Yorks, arm. MAGDALEN, matric. 14 Oct., 89, aged 18, from Harrow.

Wicks, Frederick, born at Norwich 1863; 1s. James, merchant. KEBLE, matric. 17 Oct., 82, aged 19 (from Norwich school); scholar 82, until his death, 20 Aug., 85.

Wicksteed, Joseph Hartley, born at Dukinfield, Cheshire, 8 June, 1870; 1s. Philip Henry, cler. LINCOLN, matric. 17 Oct., 89, aged 19 (from Lancaster school), B.A. 92; HONOURS:—4 history 92.

Widdrington, Gerard, born at Shillootel, Northumberland, 20 May, 1871; 1s. Shalcross Fitzherbert, arm. ORIEL, matric. 22 Oct., 90, aged 19, from Winchester.

Widnell, Edward Herbert, born at Lasswade, near Edinburgh, 16 March, 1859; o.s. Henry, gent., deceased. MAGDALEN, matric. 16 Oct., 80, aged 21, B.A. 84, M.A. 89; bar.-at-law, Lincoln's Inn, 87.

Wigan, Arthur Lawford, born at East Sheen, Surrey, 22 Oct., 1868; 2s. Frederic, gent. BALLIOL, matric. 19 Oct., 86, aged 18 (from Eton), B.A. 90; HONOURS:—3 classical mods. 88, 3 classics 90.

Wigan, Ernest Edward, born at Mortlake, Surrey, 22 Oct., 1864; 3s. James, gent. UNIVERSITY COLL., matric. 13 Oct., 83, aged 18 (from Rugby), B.A. 86, M.A. 90 (HONOURS:—4 law 86); a solicitor 91.

Wigan, Herbert, born at St. Leonard's, Sussex, Sept., 1862; 3s. Alfred, cler. ORIEL, matric. 1 June, 82, aged 19 (from Radley coll.), B.A. 87, M.A. 89.

Wigan, Hugh John George, born at Malling, Kent, 3 Aug., 1865; 5s. William Lewis, vicar. MERTON, matric. 21 Oct., 86, aged 21.

Wigan, rev. Percy Frederick, born at Maidstone, Kent, 6 Nov., 1867; 3s. Lewis Davis, arm. MERTON, matric. 21 Oct., 86, aged 18 (from Harrow), B.A. 90; HONOURS:—3 history 90.

Wigfall, William Elliott, born at West Mallon, Yorks, 26 Nov., 1861; 2s. John, gent. QUEEN'S, matric. 23 Oct., 82, aged 20 (from Doncaster gr. school), B.A. 87, M.A. 89.

Wigg, rev. Montagu John Stone, born at Rusthall, near Tunbridge Wells, 1861; 3s. John Stone, arm. UNIVERSITY COLL., matric. 16 Oct., 80, aged 19 (from Winchester), B.A. 83, M.A. 87 (HONOURS :—3 classical mods. 82, 4 history 83); curate 89-91, and vicar of St. John's pro-cathedral, Brisbane, 91, and chaplain to the bishop 91.

Wiggett, Henry Edward Allan, born at Binfield, Berks, 31 July, 1868; 1s. James Allan, arm. BRASENOSE, matric. 18 Jan., 87, aged 18 (from Winchester), B.A. 89.

Wightman, Owen William, born at York 29 Dec., 1869; o.s. William Arnett, cler. EXETER, matric. 17 Oct., 88, aged 18, from Radley coll.

Wigram, Ernest Money, born in London 20 Nov., 1862; 2s. Money, arm. ORIEL, matric. 18 Oct., 81, aged 18, from Winchester.

Wigram, Robert, born in London 25 June, 1874; 1s. Robert, director National provincial bank. MERTON, matric. 18 Oct., 92, aged 18, from the Charterhouse.

Wigram, Spencer Robert, M.A., BALLIOL, see page 70.

Wilbraham, Cecil Grenville, born at Hartford, Cheshire, 29 Dec., 1866; 2s. Henry, bar.-at-law. MERTON, matric. 10 April 86, aged 19 (from Clifton coll.), B.A. 90 (HONOURS :—3 law 89) ; bar.-at-law, Middle Temple, 91.

Wilbraham, Donald Fortescue, born at Bowdon, Cheshire, 14 Nov., 1865; 1s. Henry, bar.-at-law. TRINITY, matric. 17 Oct., 85, aged 19 (from Clifton coll.), B.A. 88 (HONOURS :—3 classical mods. 87, 4 law 88); bar.-at-law, Lincoln's Inn, 91.

Wilbraham, William Robartes, born in London 14 May, 1871; 5s. Roger William, arm. BRASENOSE, matric. 23 Jan., 90, aged 18, from Eastbrook school, Wokingham.

Wild, Charles Edmund, born at Bromley, Middx., 1869; 1s. Robert, gen. BALLIOL, matric. 19 Oct., 87, aged 18 (from city of London school); assist. magistrate N.W. provinces India 89.

Wild, Herbert Louis, born at Uffington, Salop, 2 July, 1865; 1s. Robert Lewis, cler. EXETER, matric. 16 Oct., 84, aged 19 (from the Charterhouse), scholar 84, B.A. 88, M.A. 91 (HONOURS :—1 classical mods. 86, 2 classics 88.

Wild, rev. Herbert Robert, born at Salford, co. Lanc., 7 Nov., 1865; 1s. William Rigby, arm. MERTON, matric. 16 Oct., 84, aged 18 (from Owens coll., Manchester), B.A. 87, M.A. 91 ; curate of Tynemouth 89.

Wilder, rev. Percival Hampson Elwin, born at Brandeston, Norfolk, 1868; 3s. John McMahon, rector. PEMBROKE, matric. 25 Oct., 87, aged 19, B.A. 90 ; curate of Blyth, Northumberland, 91.

Wilder, rev. William Burnard Chichester, born at Brandeston, Norfolk, 1866; 2s. John McMahon, rector. EXETER, matric. 21 Oct., 86, aged 20, B.A. 89 ; curate of Tynemouth St. Augustine's 90.

Wilford, John Womersley, born at Birchencliffe, Yorks, 8 July, 1870; 1s. Robert Crone, cler. EXETER, matric. 17 Oct., 88, aged 18 (from Huddersfield and Lancing colls.), B.A. 91 ; HONOURS :—3 law 91.

Wilford, Thomas Ernest Robert, born at Huddersfield 1874; 2s. Robert Crosse, cler. ST. EDMUND HALL, matric. 19 Oct., 92, aged 18, from Huddersfield coll.

Wilgress, Edward Heberden, born at Cuddesdon, Oxon, 1871; 2s. George Frederick, cler. KEBLE, matric. 11 Oct., 90, aged 19, from St. Edward's school, Summertown.

Wilgress, rev. George Frederick, born at Cuddesdon, Oxon, Aug., 1868; 1s. George Frederick, cler. KEBLE, matric. 17 Oct., 87, aged 19 (from Lancing coll.), B.A. 90; curate of Grimsby St. James 91.

Wilkes, Alpheus Nelson Paget, born at Titchwell, Norfolk, 19 Jan., 1871; 2s. Alpheus, B.A., cler. LINCOLN, matric. 25 Oct., 92, aged 21 (from Bedford school), exhibitioner 92.

Wilkes, Lewis Chitty Vaughan, born at Stowmarket, Suffolk, 15 Sept., 1869 ; 1s. Alpheus, rector of Whitton, Suffolk. HERTFORD, matric. 19 Oct., 88, aged 19 (from Perase school, Cambridge), scholar 87 ; HONOURS :—2 classical mods. 90, 2 classics 92.

Wilkins, Harold, born at Doncaster, Yorks, 1869 ; 3s. John, cler. NEW COLL., matric. 25 Jan., 88, aged 19.

Wilkins, Henry John, born at Appleton, Berks, 1866 ; 2s. Alfred William, gent. NON-COLLEGIATE, matric. 16 Feb., 84, aged 18, B.A. 87, M.A. 91 ; HONOURS :—4 classics 87.

Wilkins, rev. Laurence, born at Richmond, Yorks, 21 Dec., 1861 ; 4s. Thomas, actuary. NEW COLL., matric. 14 Oct., 80, aged 20 (from Richmond gr. school), B.A. 85, M.A. 90 (HONOURS :—3 classical mods. 84) ; curate of Derby St. Andrew 91.

Wilkins, Roland Field, born at Manchester 3 Jan., 1872 ; 1s. Augustus Samuel, professor of Latin at Owens coll., Manchester. BALLIOL, matric. 14 Oct., 90, aged 18 (from Sedbergh gr. school and Owens coll.), exhibitioner 89 ; HONOURS :—1 classical mods. 92, accessit Craven scholarship 92.

Wilkins, William Herbert Francis, born at St. Petersburg 27 Oct., 1871 ; 2s. George Francis, a Russian noble. HERTFORD, matric. 14 Oct., 90, aged 18 (from St. Edward's school, Summertown), exhibitioner 90 ; HONOURS :—3 classical mods. 92.

Wilkinson, Bernard Kedington Rodwell, born at Highgate, Middx., 14 Nov., 1872; 3s. Josiah, bar.-at-law. NEW COLL., matric. 16 Oct., 91, aged 18 (from the Charterhouse) ; HONOURS :—2 classical mods. 93.

Wilkinson, Charles John Royal, born at Edgbaston, co. Warwick, 1868 ; 1s. Charles Thomas, D.D. ORIEL, matric. 18 Oct., 87, aged 19, from Plymouth school.

Wilkinson, Charles Robert, born at Andreas, isle of Man, 7 March, 1873 ; 5s. James Siely, M.A., vicar of Kirk Loman, I.M. HERTFORD, matric. 22 Oct., 92, aged 19 (from Christ's hospital), scholar 91.

Wilkinson, Ernest Goden, born at Ripley, co. Derby, 20 Nov., 1868 ; 3s. Thomas, Wesleyan minister. JESUS COLL., matric. 19 Oct., 87, aged 18 (from Kingswood college), B.A. 91 ; B.A. 91 ; HONOURS : —1 classical mods. 89, 2 classics 91.

Wilkinson, Francis Henry Green, born in London 28 April, 1856 ; o.s. Henry, lieut.-colonel. CHRIST CHURCH, matric. 10 Oct., 84, aged 18, from Wellington.

Wilkinson, Frederick, born at Melbourne 1866 ; 4s. Frederick, bar.-at-law, Middle Temple, and master in equity, supreme court Victoria. BRASENOSE, matric. 28 Jan., 88, aged 22 (from Trinity coll., Melbourne), in University eight 91.

Wilkinson, Henry Arthur, born at Kirkleatham, Yorks, 18 June, 1863 ; 2s. Thomas Henry, cler. WORCESTER, matric. 22 April, 85, aged 21 (from Felsted school), B.A. 88 ; HONOURS :—4 theology 88.

Wilkinson, Hiram Parkes, born at Yokohama, Japan, 1866; 1s. Hiram Shaw, D.Med. EXETER, matric. 16 Oct., 84, aged 18 (from Methodist coll., Belfast) ; B.A. 87 (HONOURS :—3 law 87, 3 civil law 90) ; bar.-at-law, Middle Temple, 89.

Wilkinson, rev. John Herbert, born at Burley, Leeds, 30 April, 1862; 3s. James Henshall, gent. QUEEN'S, matric. 4 June, 81, aged 19 (from Leeds school), exhibitioner 80, B.A. 85, M.A. 88 (HONOURS:—1 classical mods. 83, 1 classics 85); curate of Richmond, Surrey, 89.

Wilkinson, rev. John Richard, born at Liskeard, Cornwall, 24 Feb., 1865; 1s. John, cler. WORCESTER, matric. 14 June, 84, aged 19 (from Newcastle-on-Tyne gr. school), scholar 83, B.A. 87, M.A. 93 (HONOURS:—1 mathematical mods. 85, proxime accessit junior mathematical exhibition 86, 1 mathematics 87, 3 classics 89); curate of South Hackney, London; 91.

Wilkinson, Lancelot Campbell, born at Ruyton-Eleven-Towns, Salop, 14 Aug., 1863; 3s. Frederick, cler. MERTON, matric. 17 Oct., 82, aged 19 (from St. Edward's school, Summertown), B.A. 86, M.A. 90; HONOURS:—3 history 86.

Wilkinson, Leonard Rodwell, born at Highgate, near London, 1869; 2s. Josiah. CHRIST CHURCH, matric. 14 Oct., 87, aged 18 (from the Charterhouse), exhibitioner 87, B.A. 92; HONOURS: —2 classical mods. 89, 3 classics 91.

Wilkinson, Robert Wigley, born at Shrewsbury, Salop, 1867; 1s. Robert Josiah, gent. CHRIST CHURCH, matric. 15 Oct., 86, aged 19 (from Shrewsbury school), exhibitioner 85.

Wilkinson, Walter George, M.A., fellow WORCESTER 53-66, where see page 576.

Wilkinson, Wilfred Edward, born at Goldsborough, Yorks, June, 1869; 4s. Percival Spearman, arm. KEBLE, matric. 13 Oct., 88, aged 19 (from Durham gr. school), B.A. 92.

Wilkinson, William, born at Everton, co. Lanc., 29 Sept., 1859; 1s. William, gent. NON-COLLEGIATE, matric. 19 Jan., 85, aged 25, from Westminster training coll.

Wilkinson, William Edward, born at Ashton-in-Makerfield 3 March, 1858; 4s. John, master of Ashton national school. QUEEN'S, matric. 25 Oct., 80, aged 22, from a Margate school.

Willan, Ferdinand Howard Douglas, born at Dover Jan., 1866; 2s. Stanhope Leonard, arm. ST. JOHN'S, matric. 1 May, 86, aged 20, B.A. 89.

Willert, Paul Ferdinand, M.A., fellow EXETER 67-87, where see page 124.

Willes, Edmund Henry Lacon, M.A., fellow QUEEN'S 56-65, where see page 180.

Willett, Arthur Augustus Saltren, born at Monkleigh, Devon, March, 1862; 2s. Charles, cler. ORIEL, matric. 21 May, 80, aged 18 (from Eton), B.A. and M.A. 87; bar.-at-law, Lincoln's Inn, 87.

Willett, Basil Wickham, born at Lakenham, Norfolk, 2 April, 1869; 1s. Louis Edward, arm. MAGDALEN, matric. 16 Oct., 88, aged 19 (from Repton school), B.A. 93; HONOURS:—3 history 92.

Willett, Cecil George Wilmer, born at Surbiton, Surrey, 30 Jan., 1870; 1s. Lewis Wilmer, arm. BRASENOSE, matric. 14 Oct., 89, aged 19, from Malvern coll.

Willett, Herbert Burrows, born in London 1870; 1s. Alfred, arm. UNIVERSITY COLL., matric. 13 Oct., 88, aged 18, B.A. 92; HONOURS:— 3 law 91.

Willett, John Abernethy, born in London 14 June, 1872; 2s. Alfred, F.R.C.S. UNIVERSITY COLL., matric. 11 Oct., 90, aged 18, from Westminster school.

Willey, Frederick, born at Rawdon, Yorks, 1870; 2s. Thomas, gen. LINCOLN, matric. 20 Oct., 90, aged 20, from Leeds gr. school.

Williams, Albert, born at Lisbon 1865; 2s. Daniel, gen. NEW COLL., matric. 14 Jan., 90, aged 25, B.Mus. 91.

Williams, rev. Alfred William Addams, born at Pantag, co. Monmouth, 6 Jan., 1865; 1s. Alfred, arm. ORIEL, matric. 27 Oct., 83, aged 18 (from Marlborough), B.A. 86, M.A. 90, student Inner Temple 84; curate of Llangattock-Caerleon, co. Mon., 90.

Williams, Archibald, born at Kingston Lisle, Berks, 14 July, 1871; 4s. Daniel Rowland, cler. KEBLE, matric. 11 Oct., 90, aged 19 (from Christ's coll., Finchley); HONOURS:—2 classical mods. 92.

Williams, Arthur Dyson, born at Neath, co. Glamorgan, 1860; 2s. Leonard Dyson, arm. CORPUS CHRISTI, matric. 21 Oct., 80, aged 20, B.A. 86, M.A. 87 (HONOURS:—3 classical mods. 82, treasurer 83, and president of Oxford union society 84; bar.-at-law, Inner Temple, 84.

Williams, Arthur Frederick Basil, born in London 4 April, 1867; o.s. Frederick George Adolphus, bar.-at-law. NEW COLL., matric. 15 Oct., 86, aged 19 (from Marlborough), scholar 86, B.A. 91; HONOURS:—1 classical mods. 88, 2 classics 90.

Williams, Arthur Scott, born at Woodland, Dorset, 5 Sept., 1864; 4s. Montagu, arm. NEW COLL., matric. 4 Dec., 82, aged 18 (from Harrow), B.A. 86, M.A. 89 (HONOURS:—3 history 86); brother of Herbert S.

Williams, Arthur Theodore, born at Reigate, Surrey, 1866; 3s. Walter Davis, D.Med. WADHAM, matric. 19 Oct., 85, aged 19 (from Eastbourne coll.), B.A. 89, M.A. 92; HONOURS:—4 classics 89.

Williams, Bernard Francis, born at Chislehurst, Kent, Feb., 1868; 3s. Edward Pote, cler. KEBLE, matric. 17 Oct., 87, aged 19, from Beccles gr. school.

Williams, Charles Francis Abdy, born at Dawlish, Devon, 1856; o.s. Charles Abdy, arm. CHRIST CHURCH, matric. 18 Jan., 89, aged 33, B.Mus. 89.

Williams, Claude, born at Bengeo, Herts, 11 Feb., 1870; o.s. William Morgan, gen. NON-COLLEGIATE, matric. 13 Oct., 88, aged 18 (from Lancing coll.); migrated to LINCOLN 25 Jan., 89, B.A. 92; HONOURS:—3 theology 92.

Williams, rev. David, born at Tymwydd, near Lampeter, 1860; 3s. John. NON-COLLEGIATE, matric. 28 Jan., 84, aged 24 (from Lampeter coll.), B.A. 90 (HONOURS:—3 classical mods. 83, 3 theology 86); prof. of classics and mathematics in Huron theol. coll., London, Ontario, 87; curate of St. Paul's cathedral, Huron, 89.

Williams, David James, born at Caerphilly, near Cardiff, 18 Feb., 1870; 7s. Thomas James, gen. WORCESTER, matric. 14 Oct., 89, aged 19 (from Llandovery coll.), scholar 88; HONOURS:—1 mathematical mods. 91.

Williams, David Thomas Clarke, born at Bridgend, co. Glam., 2 Nov., 1871; 1s. Rees, cler. JESUS COLL., matric. 15 Oct., 90, aged 17, from Brecon coll. and Cowbridge gr. school.

Williams, Douglas Watkin Wynn, born at Christchurch, N.Z., 1863; 1s. William Henry, bar.-at-law. EXETER, matric. 28 Jan., 81, aged 18 (from Christchurch gr. school, N.Z.); bar.-at-law, Inner Temple, 86.

Williams, Edmund, born at Henllan, co. Denbigh, 1862; 2s. Edmund, gent. ST. MARY HALL, matric. 22 Jan., 83, aged 21, B.A. 87.

Williams, Edward Geoffry, born at Oswestry, Salop, 23 March, 1871; 1s. Edward, gen. MERTON, matric. 19 Oct., 89, aged 18, from Oswestry gr. school.

Williams, Ernest Wynne, born at Llandrillo, co. Monmouth, 1871; o.s. Thomas, cler. CORPUS CHRISTI, matric. 16 Oct., 90, aged 18, from Oswestry school.

From Ingram's Memorials.

Williams, Frederick Billingsley Ambrose, born at Harwich 3 Dec., 1870; y.s. Oliver John, late foreign consul at Harwich. WADHAM, matric. 14 Oct., 89, aged 18; migrated to CHARSLEY'S HALL, Christmas, 90; re-admitted to WADHAM 10 July, 91.

Williams, Frederick Ernest Albert, born in London 20 Jan., 1870; 4s. Frederick, superintendent Oxford industrial schools. NON-COLLEGIATE, matric. 15 Oct., 92, aged 22, from New coll. school, Oxford.

Williams, Frederick Horne Tait, born at Battiscombe, Dorset, March, 1871; 1s. Frederick, cler. NON-COLLEGIATE, matric. 12 Oct., 89, aged 18, from All Hallows' school, Honiton.

Williams, rev. Frederick Hubert Augustus, born at Drayton, Oxon, 5 Aug., 1869; 4s. Arthur James, cler. WORCESTER, matric. 16 Oct., 88, aged 19 (from Bromsgrove gr. school), exhibitioner 87, B.A. 92; HONOURS:—2 theology 92.

Williams, George Cooke, born at Mold, Flints, 1861; 1s. Peter, gent. ST. JOHN'S, matric. 13 Oct., 83, aged 22, from University coll., Bangor.

Williams, George Frederick Charles, born at Ashtonunder-Lyne, 1864; o.s. Frederick, cler. ST. EDMUND HALL, matric. 22 Oct., 84, aged 20.

Williams, rev. Griffith, born at Wrenfaur, co. Carnarvon, 1859; 1s. Thomas, gent. JESUS COLL., matric. 23 Oct., 80, aged 21; curate of Bishops Knoyle, Wilts, 89.

Williams, Henry Harcourt, born at Trendrea, Cornwall, 18 March, 1869; 1s. Michael Henry, arm. MERTON, matric. 22 Oct., 87, aged 18 (from Eton), B.A. 90.

Williams, Henry Herbert, born at Poppleton, Yorks, 19 Dec., 1872; 1s. John, cler. QUEEN'S, matric. 27 Oct., 91, aged 18 (from York school), exhibitioner 91; HONOURS:—2 classical mods. 93.

Williams, Henry Richard, born in London 23 Dec., 1862; o.s. Henry Richard, gent. QUEEN'S, matric. 28 Oct., 81, aged 18 (from University coll. school and University coll., London), exhibitioner 81; HONOURS:—2 classical mods. 83; died same year.

Williams, Henry Wedgwood Vaughan-, born at Ockley, Surrey, 14 April, 1869; 1s. Arthur Charles, vicar of Down Ampney, deceased. NEW COLL., matric. 12 Oct., 88, aged 19 (from the Charterhouse); HONOURS:—2 classical mods. 90, 3 classics 92.

Williams, rev. Herbert Allan, born at St. Albans, Herts, 1854; 1s. Herbert, cler.; B.A. from ST. JOHN'S, CAMBRIDGE, 78, M.A. 81; incorporated 6 Nov., 90, aged 36; chaplain CHRIST CHURCH 90; curate of St. Giles, Oxford, 90.

Williams, Herbert Scott, born at Woolland, Dorset, 4 Sept., 1869; 2s. Montagu, arm. MERTON, matric. 19 Nov., 80, aged 20, B.A. 84, M.A. 87; brother of Arthur 8.

Williams, Hugh Clement, born at Uppingham 21 March, 1872; 3s. Bennett Hesketh, M.A., cler. WORCESTER, matric. 18 Oct , 92, aged 20, from Leatherhead school.

Williams, rev. Hugh Howard, born in Kensington, Middx., April, 1866 ; 3s. Watkin Wynn, of Brixton, Surrey, arm. CHRIST CHURCH, matric. 31 May, 84, aged 18 (from Radley coll.), B.A. 88 (HONOURS: —2 theology 88); curate of St. John's, Bethnal Green, 90.

Williams, Hugh Noel, born at Newport, co. Mon., 1870; 2s. William, arm. ST. JOHN'S, matric. 13 Oct., 88, aged 18 (from Clifton coll.), B.A. 92; HONOURS :—3 history 92.

Williams, James, M.A., fellow LINCOLN 90, where see page 241.

Williams, John Basil Llewellyn, born at Guernsey 16 May, 1870 ; 3s. Charles Henry, arm. LINCOLN, matric. 17 Oct., 89, aged 19, from Bristol gr. school.

Williams, John Evan, born at Bedwas, co. Monmouth, 30 Dec., 1862; 2s. William, cler. TRINITY, matric. 13 Oct., 81, aged 18 (from Marlborough), B.A. 84, M.A. 88 (HONOURS :—3 law 84); solicitor.

Williams, John Fischer, born at Kensington 26 Feb., 1870; o.s. John, arm. NEW COLL., matric. 12 Oct., 88, aged 18 (from Harrow), scholar 87, fellow 92, B.A. 92 ; HONOURS :—1 classical mods. 90, 1 classics 92, Arnold essay prize 93.

Williams, John Larden, born at Wavertree, near Liverpool, 1872 ; 2s. Owen Hugh, merchant. UNIVERSITY COLL., matric. 19 Oct., 91, aged 19, from Radley coll.

Williams, John Tudor, born at Llandudno, co. Carnarvon, 25 Dec., 1868; 1s. William, gen. NON-COLLEGIATE, matric. 11 Oct., 90, aged 21, from Llandudno collegiate school, and University coll., Bangor.

Williams, John Wodehouse, born at Matala, Ceylon, 30 Jan., 1869; 1s. George Sanders, of Ceylon c.s., arm. MAGDALEN, matric. 18 Jan., 86, aged 18 (from Wellington coll.); HONOURS :—3 classical mods. 89, 2 history 93.

Williams, Leonard, born at Swansea, co. Glamorgan, 1871 ; 3s. Leonard Dyson, arm. BALLIOL, matric. 14 Oct., aged 19, from Clifton coll.

Williams, Llewellyn Stanley, born at Fulshaw, Cheshire, Nov., 1869; 1s. William, gen. BRASENOSE, matric. 20 Oct., 87, aged 17 (from Manchester gr. school), scholar 87; HONOURS :—3 classical mods. 89.

Williams, Mark Penry Fenton Garnons, born at Abercannaid, co. Brecon, 25 April, 1867 ; 6s. Garnons, cler. CHARSLEY'S HALL, matric. 2 Nov., 86, aged 19.

Williams, Morris Price, M.A., fellow JESUS COLL. 86-90, where see page 514.

Williams, rev. Owen Kyffin, born at Bodfian, co. Carnarvon, 1864 ; 2s. Owen Kyffin, cler. JESUS COLL., matric. 24 Jan., 82, aged 18, B.A. 85 ; curate of Church Stretton, co. Hereford, 91.

Williams, Percy Wyndham, born at Poole, Dorset, 14 March, 1863 ; 3s. John Lewis, cler. NON-COLLEGIATE, matric. 14 Oct., 82, aged 19 (from Bromsgrove gr. school and Hurstpierpoint coll.); migrated to WORCESTER, B.A. 86, M.A. 89.

Williams, Philip, M.A., B.C.L., fellow NEW COLL. 44-51, where see page 129.

Williams, Philip Henry Oakley, born at Dadington, Somerset, 28 April, 1869 ; 1s. Llewellyn, cler. NON-COLLEGIATE, matric. 15 Oct., 88, aged 19 (from Wiesbaden and Heidelberg coll.), exhibitioner QUEEN'S 90; HONOURS :—3 history 92.

Williams, rev. Reginald Henry, born at Winferton, co. Hereford, 28 May, 1864 ; 2s. Daniel Roland, of Cawnpore, cler. CHRIST CHURCH, matric. 22 Oct., 83, aged 19 (from Westminster school), scholar 83, B.A. 87 (HONOURS :—2 classical mods. 85, 1 morphology 87); curate of Odd-Rode, Cheshire, 89.

Williams, rev. Reuben, born at Ystradmeurig, co. Monmouth, 1859 ; 1s. David, pleb. NON-COLLEGIATE, matric. 27 Oct., 81, aged 22 (from University coll., Aberystwyth), B.A. 85, M.A. 90 (HONOURS :—2 theology 85); curate of St. Mark, Woodhouse, Leeds, 88.

Williams, Rhys, born at Llantrissant, co. Glam., 20 Oct., 1865 ; 1s. Gwilym, arm. ORIEL, matric. 23 Oct., 84, aged 19, B.A. 87 ; bar.-at-law, Inner Temple, 90.

Williams, rev. Robert, born at Llanystymdwy, co. Carnarvon, 1860; 4s. John, gent. NON-COLLEGIATE, matric. 18 Oct., 80, aged 20 (from Bangor school); migrated to KEBLE, B.A. 84 (HONOURS:—1 theology 84); vicar of Dolwyddelan, co. Carnarvon, 87.

Williams, rev. Robert, born at Caron-is-y-Clawdd, co. Cardigan, 1862; 1s. William, gent. MERTON, matric. 21 Oct., 86, aged 24 (from St. Davids coll., Lampeter), exhibitioner 86, B.A. 89, M.A. 92 (HONOURS:—1 history 88); professor of Welsh and mod. history St. Davids coll.

Williams, Robert Edward, M.A., fellow JESUS COLL. 67-72, where see page 513.

Williams, Roland Edmund Lomax Vaughan, born in London 21 Oct., 1866; o.s. sir Roland Vaughan. MERTON, matric. 21 Oct., 86, aged 19, B.A. 92; HONOURS:—2 history 90.

Williams, sir Roland Lomax Vaughan, M.A., judge of the high court, student CHRIST CHURCH 56-65, where see page 421.

Williams, Samuel Cornelius, born in London 1867; 3s. Frederick, gen. CHARSLEY'S HALL, matric. 10 Oct., 87, aged 20, B.A. 90.

Williams, Stephen Glynn, born at Rewe, Devon, 13 July, 1864; 3s. Philip, cler. CORPUS CHRISTI, matric. 19 Oct., 83, aged 19 (from Marlborough), B.A. 88 (HONOURS:—2 classical mods. 85, 3 law 87), in University eight 87.

Williams, Thomas, M.A., fellow JESUS COLL. 46-53, where see page 512.

Williams, Thomas Benjamin, born at Wolverhampton 29 Aug., 1852; 2s. George, gent. WADHAM, matric. 16 Oct., 83, aged 31, B.A. 87, M.A. 90 (HONOURS:—3 classical mods. 85, 2 classics 87); assist. master Oxford high school.

Williams, Thomas Beynon, born at Llangibby, co. Carm., 10 Sept., 1861; y.s. Thomas, gent. JESUS COLL., matric. 18 Oct., 83, aged 21 (from University coll., Aberystwith), B.A. 87, M.A. 90; HONOURS:—2 classical mods. 85, 3 classics 87.

Williams, Thomas Erskine, born at Bettiscombe, Dorset, 3 Dec., 1872; 2s. Francis, cler. EXETER, matric. 13 Oct., 90, aged 17, from Honiton school.

Williams, Thomas Gwynne Horsley, born at the Hutt, Wellington, N.Z., 11 May, 1874; 4s. Thomas Coldham, gent. BRASENOSE, matric. 21 Oct., 92, aged 18, from Wangamis collegiate school.

Williams, Thomas James, born at Kensington 1868; o.s. Thomas, gen. PEMBROKE, matric. 25 Oct., 87, from Victoria coll., Jersey; scholar 87, B.A. 91; HONOURS:—2 classical mods. 89, 3 classics 91.

Williams, Thomas Reece, born at Chelsea, Middx., 13 July, 1863; 1s. Thomas, rector of Aston Clinton, Bucks. JESUS COLL., matric. 18 Oct., 82, aged 19 (from Sherborne school), B.A. 88.

Williams, Trevor Tudor, born at Bridgend, co. Gloue., 1870; 1s. Charles Carne, cler. NON-COLLEGIATE, matric. 12 Oct., 89, aged 19, from Monmouth gr. school.

Williams, Walter David, born at Osgathorpe, co. Leic., 7 Dec., 1869; 1s. Walter Augustus, rector. LINCOLN, matric. 17 Oct., 89, aged 19.

Williams, Walter George, born at Bristol 15 Dec., 1870; 5s. James, arm. BRASENOSE, matric. 14 Oct., 89, aged 18 (from Bristol gr. school), scholar 88; HONOURS:—1 mathematical mods. 91.

Williams, Watkin Salusbury, born at Llangar, co. Merioneth, 1856; o.s. Watkin, cler. EXETER, matric. 16 Oct., 84, aged 18, from Marlborough.

Williams, rev. William, born at Tregarfon, co. Cardigan, 1867; o.s. Rees, cler. NON-COLLEGIATE, matric. 16 Oct., 85, aged 19 (from Brecon coll.); migrated to JESUS COLL., B.A. 89 (HONOURS:—3 history 89); curate of Neath with Llantwit, co. Glam., 90.

Williams, rev. William, born at Penpontbrew, co. Cardigan, 29 Nov., 1863; 1s. Rhys, gen. JESUS COLL., matric. 8 May, 90, aged 30 (from St. David's coll., Lampeter), exhibitioner 90, B.A. 92; HONOURS:—2 classical mods. 90, 2 classics 92.

Williams, William Griffith, born at Bangor, co. Carnarvon, 6 Dec., 1867; 1s. Richard, gent. WORCESTER, matric. 22 Oct., 85, aged 17 (from Friars school, Bangor), B.A. 88; HONOURS:—3 law 88.

Williams, rev. William Henry, born at Amersham, Bucks, 1863; 1s. William Henry, cler. NON-COLLEGIATE, matric. 13 Oct., 83, aged 20 (from Hereford cathedral school), B.A. 87; curate of Portishead, Somerset.

Williams, William John, born at Reigate, Surrey, 22 Dec., 1863; 2s. Walter Davis, gen. QUEEN'S, matric. 21 Oct., 87, aged 24 (from Chichester theological coll.), B.A. 90 (HONOURS:—3 history 89); matric. 2 Oct., 85, from Corpus Christi coll., Cambridge.

Williams, William Llewellyn, born at Llansadwrn, co. Carm., 1867; 2s. Morgan, gent. BRASENOSE, matric. 23 Oct., 85, aged 18 (from Llandovery coll.), exhibitioner 85; HONOURS:—2 history 89.

Williams, rev. William Samuel, born in London 1865; 3s. Edward Valentine, cler. WORCESTER, matric. 23 April, 83, aged 18, B.A. 87, M.A. 89; curate of Hersham, Surrey, 89.

Williams, William Smith Gittings, born at Baltimore, 20 Oct., 1863; 2s. George Hawkins, senator for Baltimore, Maryland. TRINITY, matric. 15 Oct., 81, aged 17 (from the Charterhouse), B.A. 84, M.A. 92; attorney at New York.

Williams, rev. William Thomas, born at Llanthety, co. Brecon, 1867; 1s. David, cler. CHARSLEY'S HALL, matric. 14 Dec., 89, aged 22; migrated to ST. MARY HALL; HONOURS:—2 theology 92.

Williamson, Andrew Cochrane, born in Edinburgh 1866; 1s. Robert Cochrane, arm. ST. JOHN'S, matric. 16 Oct., 86, aged 20 (from Edinburgh academy), B.A. 90 (HONOURS:—3 law 90); brother of William C.

Williamson, Benjamin, M.A., Sc.D., fellow Trinity coll., Dublin, 1852, F.R.S. 79; created D.C.L. 22 June, 92 (HONOURS:—1 mathematics 48, and Law mathematical prize 49, at Dublin university); professor of natural philosophy, Dublin, B.A. See *Men and Women of the Time.*

Williamson, Harold, born at Weaste, Salford, co. Lanc., 17 Nov., 1872; 3s. Samuel, arm. BALLIOL, matric. 20 Oct., 91, aged 18 (from Manchester gr. school), exhibitioner 90; HONOURS:—accessit Craven scholarship 92, 1 classical mods. 93.

Williamson, Hedworth, born in London 23 May, 1867; 1s. sir Hedworth, bart. CHRIST CHURCH, matric. 16 April, 86, aged 18.

Williamson, John Bruce, born at Glasgow 1859; 2s. John, gent. BALLIOL, matric. 29 Jan., 81, aged 22 (from Glasgow university), scholar 81-5, B.A. 85 (HONOURS:—Stanhope essay 83, 2 history 84); bar.-at-law, Middle Temple, 87.

Williamson, rev. John Ernest, born at Catterick, Yorks, 13 March, 1867; 1s. William Edward, of Ashbourne, arm. MAGDALEN, matric. 20 Oct., 85, aged 18 (from Haileybury), B.A. 89; curate of Kippax, Yorks, 90.

Williamson, Percy, born in London 12 June, 1871; 2s. John, arm. CHRIST CHURCH, matric. 10 Oct., 90, aged 19 (from Westminster school), scholar 91; HONOURS:—2 classical mods. 92.

Williamson, Victor Alexander, C.M.G., M.A., student CHRIST CHURCH 57-71, where see page 422.

Williamson, William Christian, born at Shandon, near Dumbarton, 1867; 2s. Robert, arm. BALLIOL, matric. 19 Oct., 86, aged 19 (from Edinburgh academy); brother of Andrew.

Willimott, Andrew Beauchamp, born at Caerhays, Cornwall, 11 May, 1872; 3s. William, rector of Laverton. WADHAM, matric. 20 Oct., 91, aged 19 (from Lancing coll.), scholar 90; HONOURS:—2 classical mods. 93.

Willing, John Rhea Barton, born at Philadelphia, America, 1864; o.s. Edward Shippen, arm. CHRIST CHURCH, matric. 15 Oct., 86, aged 22.

Willis, Charles Francis, M.A., fellow CORPUS CHRISTI 63-62, where see page 382.

Willis, Cyril Hamer, born at Rockferry, Cheshire, 1866; 2s. Matthew Marwood, gent. ST. JOHN'S, matric. 11 Oct., 84, aged 18; brother of Rawdon.

Willis, Evelyn d'Anyers, born at Wellingborough, Northants, 18 Nov., 1873; 2s. Frederic William, rector of Warrington. CORPUS CHRISTI, matric. 18 Oct., 92, aged 18, from Bradfield coll.

Willis, Frederic Earle d'Anyers, born at Wendover, Bucks, 13 July, 1869; 1s. Frederic William, M.A., rector of Warrington. CORPUS CHRISTI, matric. 25 Oct., 89, aged 20 (from Marlborough), B.A. 93; HONOURS :—3 history 92.

Willis, John, born at St. Germain, isle of Man, 7 Sept., 1864; 1s. John, gen. QUEEN'S, matric. 27 Oct., 91, aged 26, from Douglas gr. school.

Willis, Joseph George, born at Redcliffe, Bristol, 5 Sept., 1861; 1s. Joseph, gent. CHRIST CHURCH, matric. 15 Oct., 80, aged 19 (from Bristol school), scholar 80-5, B.A. 84; HONOURS :—1 classical mods. 82, 1 classics 84; and at London 1 Latin 80, and 1 classics 83.

Willis, Rawdon Marwood, born at Birkenhead 1864; 1s. Matthew Marwood, gent. ST. JOHN'S, matric. 14 Oct., 82, aged 18, B.A. 85, M.A. 89; brother of Cyril.

Willis, Richard Atherton de Anyers, born at Halewood, co. Lanc., March, 1871; o.s. Henry Ralph de Anyers, arm. CHRIST CHURCH, matric. 10 Oct., 90, aged 19, from Eton.

Willoughby, rev. James Mason, born at Plymouth, 2 Nov., 1867; 3s. Joseph, gen. JESUS COLL., matric. 20 Oct., 86, aged 18 (from Selwyn coll., Pembroke, matric. 21 Oct., 84), B.A. 90 (HONOURS :—2 classical mods. 88, 2 classics 90); curate of Holy Trinity, Bristol, 92.

Willoughby, William, born at Plymouth 1866; 3s. William, gen. NON-COLLEGIATE, matric. 25 Jan., 88, aged 22 (from Plymouth gr. school), B.Mus. 92.

Wills, Arthur James Hamilton, born in London 1 May, 1868; 1s. Frederick, gen. MAGDALEN, matric. 21 Oct., 86, aged 18 (from Clifton coll.), B.A. 89; HONOURS:—1 history 89.

Wills, Edgar John, born in London 14 Oct., 1869; 2s. Cuthbert, of Putney Common, arm. HERTFORD, matric. 14 Oct., 90, aged 20 (from Harrow), scholar 89.

Wills, Francis John, born at Nailsworth, co. Glouc., 13 Dec., 1872; 4s. Samuel, merchant. MAGDALEN, matric. 22 Oct., 91, aged 18, from Clifton coll.

Willshaw, rev. John William, born at Rushton, Cheshire, 1815; o.s. George, gent. NON-COLLEGIATE, matric. 9 June, 82, aged 67 (from Didsbury coll. Manchester, and Lichfield theological coll.); curate of Brierley Hill 80-8, Wednesbury 88-91, and of Chasetown, (all) co. Stafford, 88.

Willson, Dallas Alexander Wynne, born at Lambeth 18 July, 1865; 1s. William Wynne, rector of Codford St. Mary, Wilts. TRINITY, matric. 11 Oct., 84, aged 19 (from Cheltenham coll.), B.A. 87 (HONOURS :—3 classical mods. 86, 4 classics 88); a master at St. Edward's school, Summertown.

Willson, William Richard, born in London 1861; o.s. William Thomas, gent. PEMBROKE, matric. 4 Feb., 81, aged 20, B.A. 85; bar.-at-law, Middle Temple, 88.

Willson, William Wynne, M.A., fellow ST. JOHN'S 54-64, where see page 483.

Willy, Alexander Cavendish, born at Petersham, Surrey, 1864; 1s. Parkes, clcr. NON-COLLEGIATE, matric. 13 Oct., 88, aged 24, B.A. 92.

Wilmot, rev. Richard Hurt, born at Milford, co. Derby, 1 March, 1864; 3s. Edmund, arm. MERTON, matric. 19 Oct., 83, aged 19 (from Malvern coll.), B.A. 87, M.A. 90; curate of Fairford, co. Glouc., 88.

Wilshire, Alured Nathaniel Myddelton, born at Corhampton, Hants, 27 Feb., 1872; 1s. Ebenezer Stibbs, cler. HERTFORD, matric. 14 Oct., 90, aged 18 (from Bristol gr. school), scholar 89; HONOURS :—classical mods. 92.

Wilson, Alfred Alexander Ball, born at Moxley, co. Stafford, 31 May, 1864; 4s. John Patrick, D.D. NON-COLLEGIATE, matric. 6 Feb., 92, aged 27, from Bromsgrove and Almondbury gr. schools.

Wilson, Alfred FitzRoy, born at Stowlangtoft, Suffolk, Jan., 1872; 1s. Cyril FitzRoy, cler. CHRIST CHURCH, matric. 16 Oct., 91, aged 19, from Uppingham school.

Wilson, Ambrose John, D.D., fellow QUEEN'S 76-81, where see page 182.

Wilson, Andrew Brockett, born at Dublin 1861; 4s. James Moncrieff, gent. BALLIOL, matric. 29 Jan., 81, aged 20 (from a Birkenhead school), B.A. 86 (HONOURS :— 1 law 84) ; bar.-at-law, Inner Temple, 87.

Wilson, Archibald Herdmore Buchanan, born at Chinchilla, Queensland, 15 Oct., 1868; 1s. John George Hannay, arm. TRINITY, matric. 15 Oct., 87, aged 19 (from Bath coll.), B.A. 91 (HONOURS : —3 law 91); brother of Theophilus.

Wilson, Archibald Wayet, born at Pinchbeck, co. Lincoln, 1870; 5s. Plumpton Stravenson, cler. KEBLE, matric. 30 Jan., 90, aged 20 (from Rossall school, and Royal coll. of music); organ scholar 89, B.Mus. 91; organist at East Moulsey.

Wilson, Arthur Cecil Henry Carus-, born at Hutton, Essex, 1874; 2s. William (C.-W.), cler. NON-COLLEGIATE, matric. 17 Oct., 91, aged 17, from Oakham gr. school.

Wilson, Charles Edward, born at Plymouth 1867; 1s. Charles, cler. NON-COLLEGIATE, incorporated 1 Feb., 89, aged 22, matric. from Christ's coll., Cambridge, 21 Oct., 85 (from Plymouth coll. and Leys school, Cambridge), B.A. Cambridge 89, M.A. 93.

Wilson, Charles Robert, born at Old Charlton, Kent, 27 March, 1863; o.s. Charles, gent. WADHAM, matric. 17 Oct., 82, aged 19 (from city of London school), scholar 81, B.A. 87, M.A. 89; HONOURS :—1 mathematical mods. 83, 1 classics 86.

Wilson, col. sir Charles William, K.C.B., K.C.M.G., born 16 March, 1836, created D.C.L. 13 June, 83, hon. M.E. (engineering) Dublin 92. See Al. Ox. and series 1581.

Wilson, rev. Charles William Goodall, born at Moxley, co. Stafford, 1860; 3s. John Patrick, cler. PEMBROKE, matric. 30 Oct., 80, aged 20 (from Bromsgrove gr. school), B.A. 83, M.A. 87 (HONOURS :—2 history 83); curate of Upper St. Leonards-on-sea 88.

Wilson, Clarence Chesney, born at Melbourne March, 1873; 3s. sir Samuel, kt., M.P. CHRIST CHURCH, matric. 4 June, 92, aged 19, from Eton.

Wilson, rev. Clifford Plumpton, born at Diss, Norfolk, Dec., 1862; 3s. Plumpton Stravenson, cler. KEBLE, matric. 18 Oct., 81, aged 18 (from Rossall school), scholar 81-5, B.A. 85, M.A. 88 (HONOURS :—1 classical mods. 83, 3 classics 85); chaplain Clifton coll., Bristol, 89.

Wilson, Cyril Raynold, born at Balderston, Yorks, 6 March, 1867; 2s. William Reginald, cler. EXETER, matric. 23 Oct., 85, aged 18 (from Haileybury), B.A. 90.

Wilson, Daniel Berners, born at Birkenhead, Cheshire, 10 Nov., 1874; 1s. Daniel, merchant. TRINITY, matric. 15 Oct., 92, aged 18, from Wellington coll.

Wilson, Daniel Ferguson, born at Kilmarnock, co. Ayr, 1859; 2s. John, pleb. NEW COLL., matric. 12 Feb., 83, aged 24, B.Mus. 86.

Wilson, David Landale, born at Hurlet, near Glasgow, 1864; 2s. George, arm. ORIEL, matric. 23 Oct., 84, aged 20, B.A. 88.

Wilson, David Lorraine, born at Clifton 27 July, 1862; o.s. James, arm. BRASENOSE, matric. 17 March, 81, aged 18 (from Haileybury), capt. the Black Watch (Royal Highlanders) 91, served in the Nile expedition 84-5, medal with two clasps, etc.

Wilson, Donald, born at Kingston-upon-Hull 20 Dec., 1861; o.s. William, gent. NON-COLLEGIATE, matric. 14 April, 83, aged 20; migrated to LINCOLN 84, B.A. 86; HONOURS :—4 classics 86.

Wilson, rev. Edmund Algernon, born at Smethcote, Salop, 21 Aug., 1863; 6s. Theodore Percival, cler. NEW COLL., matric. 4 Dec., 82, aged 19, B.A. 85, M.A. 89 (HONOURS :—2 classical mods. 83, 3 classics 85); curate of Upton, Devon, 86.

Wilson, Ernest William, born at Whitechurch, co. Mon., 1870; 6s. Ernest William, gen. NON-COLLEGIATE, matric. 27 April, 89, aged 19, from Merchant Taylors' school.

Wilson, Frederick Augustus (Basford de), born at Lytham, co. Lanc. 1867; 1s. Frederick Augustus, cler. CHARSLEY'S HALL, matric. 20 Oct., 80, aged 23 (from Magdalen coll. school); migrated to EXETER 18 Oct., 83, B.A. 85, M.A. 87.

Wilson, Frederick Robert Leyland, born at Oxford 1870; 3s. John Charles, arm. KEBLE, matric. 13 Oct., 88, aged 18 (from Radley), scholar 88, B.A. 92 (HONOURS :—2 chemistry 92); brother of William Hawkins.

Wilson, rev. George, born at Newcastle-on-Tyne 1860; 1s. Wilson, pleb. KEBLE, matric. 22 Oct., 85, aged 25 (from St. Andrews university), M.A. 85, B.A. 89 (HONOURS :—3 theology 88); curate of Battle, Sussex, 92.

Wilson, George Herbert, born at Alfreton, co. Derby, 13 May, 1870; 2s. Joseph George, solicitor. ST. JOHN'S, matric. 12 Oct., 89, aged 19 (from Cheltenham coll.), B.A. 92; HONOURS :—3 history 92.

Wilson, George Herbert, born in London 16 May, 1871; 3s. Arthur, judge in high court Calcutta. EXETER, matric. 13 Oct., 90, aged 19, from Rugby.

Wilson, George John, born at Cork 1857; 6s. Edward Henry, arm. CHRIST CHURCH, matric. 1 Feb., 86, aged 29, B.A. 88, M.A. 92.

Wilson, George Lindsay, born at Melbourne 1868; 2s. William, gen. UNIVERSITY COLL., matric. 15 Oct., 87, aged 19 (from Brighton coll.), B.A. 92; in University eleven 90, 1.

Wilson, George Rowland Holt, born at Redgrave, Norfolk, 26 Feb., 1867; 1s. George Holt, arm. ORIEL, matric. 19 Oct., 86, aged 19 (from Rugby), B.A. 91.

Wilson, Gordon Chesney, born at Melbourne, Australia, Aug., 1865; 1s. sir Samuel, knt. CHRIST CHURCH, matric. 30 May, 85, aged 19, from Eton.

Wilson, Graham Lionel John, born at Bembridge, I.W., 5 April, 1864; 1s. John Wilson, arm. EXETER, matric. 24 Jan., 84, aged 19, B.A. 88, M.A. 91; bar.-at-law, Inner Temple, 92.

Wilson, Henry Austin, M.A., fellow MAGDALEN 76, where see page 312.

Wilson, Herbert, born at Sevenoaks, Kent, 1868; 2s. Alfred, arm. MAGDALEN, matric. 22 Oct., 87, aged 19, from Winchester coll.

Wilson, Herbert Edward, born at Eccleshall, Yorks, 1865; 5s. George, gent. CHRIST CHURCH, matric. 12 Oct., 83, aged 18; migrated to BALLIOL, B.A. 87.

Wilson, Herbert Wrigley, born at Linthwaite, Yorks, 25 Oct., 1866; 1s. George Edward, cler. TRINITY, matric. 17 Oct., 85, aged 18 (from Durham gr. school), scholar 85, B.A. 92; HONOURS :—1 classical mods. 87, 2 classics 89.

Wilson, Horace Ernest, born at Durham 10 April, 1871; o.s. Horace, cler. WORCESTER, matric. 14 Oct., 90, aged 19 (from Clifton coll.), scholar 90; HONOURS :—2 classical mods. 92.

Wilson, James Christopher Hill, born at Ambleside, Westmorland, 19 Nov., 1865; 1s. James Christopher, arm. MERTON, matric. 24 Oct., 85, aged 19; capt. 3rd batt. (militia) border regiment 89.

Wilson, James Edward Bowles, born at Wimbledon, Surrey, 6 May, 1865; 1s. James Leonard, gent. TRINITY, matric. 15 Oct., 83, aged 18 (from Marlborough), B.A. 87, M.A. 92; HONOURS :—4 chemistry 87.

Wilson, James Henry Gilchrist, born at York 13 March, 1868; 3s. James Gilchrist, cler. QUEEN'S, matric. 21 Oct., 87, aged 19 (from York school), exhibitioner 87; HONOURS :—3 classical mods. 89.

Wilson, John Charles, M.A., B.C.L., EXETER, where see page 130.

Wilson, John Cook, M.A., fellow ORIEL 74, where see page 150.

Wilson, John Plumpton, born at Horbling, co. Lincoln, 1 June, 1868; 4s. Plumpton Stravenson, cler. QUEEN's, matric. 21 Oct., 87, aged 19 (from Rossall school), exhibitioner 88, B.A. 90; HONOURS :— 3 classical mods. 89, 3 theology 91.

Wilson, Joseph Maitland, born at Bury St. Edmund's 22 Dec., 1868; 3s. Fuller Maitland, arm. CHRIST CHURCH, matric. 3 June, 87, aged 18, from Eton.

Wilson, Percy William Alfred, born at Boston, co. Lincoln, 14 Nov., 1870; 1s. Charles Jonathan, gen. WADHAM, matric. 13 Oct., 90, aged 19 (from Boston gr. school), exhibitioner 89; HONOURS :— 1 mathematical mods. 92.

Wilson, Reginald Francis, born at Stowlangtoft rectory, Suffolk, 22 Oct., 1873; 2s. Cyril FitzRoy, M.A., cler. CORPUS CHRISTI, matric. 18 Oct., 92, aged 18, from Uppingham.

Wilson, Robert Henry, born at Wandsworth, Surrey, 2 May, 1870; 1s. Henry Weymouth Mitchell, gen. ST. JOHN'S, matric. 12 Oct., 89, aged 19 (from Cheltenham coll.); HONOURS :—2 classical mods. 91.

Wilson, rev. Robert James, M.A., warden of KEBLE 88, where see page 627-8.

Wilson, Robert Spedding, M.A., fellow BRASENOSE 55-76, where see page 356.

Wilson, Robert Walton Williams, born at Londonderry, 1 Feb., 1861 ; 1s. Robert, gent. CORPUS CHRISTI, matric. 21 Oct., 80, aged 19 (from Rugby school); died 21 Sept., 87.

Wilson, Sidney Edward, born at Liverpool 14 April, 1869 ; 2s. Charles Bowman, D.Med. TRINITY, matric. 15 Oct., 87, aged 18, from Liverpool coll.

Wilson, Stephen Miller, born at Wanstead, Essex, 28 June, 1873 ; 2s. Lewis Miller Wilmot, stockbroker. NEW COLL., matric. 14 Oct., 92, aged 19, from Haileybury coll.

Wilson, Theophilus Stuart Beatty, born at Brisbane, in Australia, 13 Aug., 1870 ; 2s. John George Hannay, of Torquay, arm. TRINITY, matric. 12 Oct., 89, aged 19 (from Bath coll.); in University eleven 92; brother of Archibald H. H.

Wilson, Thomas Corby, born at Liverpool 9 Nov., 1862; 1s. Thomas, of Leeds, gent. TRINITY, matric. 15 Oct., 81, aged 18 (from Clifton coll.), exhibitioner 81; deputy commissioner Burmah 83.

Wilson, Thomas Dobinson, born at Victoria, British Columbia, 4 Aug., 1872; 2s. Thomas, gen. TRINITY, matric. 17 Oct., 91, aged (19 from Faversham school); HONOURS:—2 classical mods. 93.

Wilson, Thomas Horrocks, born at Preston, co. Lanc., 1861; 1s. Thomas, solicitor. EXETER, matric. 22 Oct., 80, aged 19, from the Charterhouse.

Wilson, Thomas Needham, born at Southampton 3 Aug., 1863; 1s. Robert, arm. TRINITY, matric. 21 Jan., 82, aged 18 (from Harrow), B.A. 85, M.A. 88; bar.-at-law, Inner Temple, 87.

Wilson, Walter Frederick, born at St. Kilda, Melbourne, 31 Jan., 1863; o.s. Walter Horace, arm. TRINITY, matric. 13 Oct., 81, aged 18 (from Brisbane gr. school), B.A. 84, M.A. 88 (HONOURS: —3 history 84); bar.-at-law, Middle Temple, 85; practising at Brisbane.

Wilson, William Elliot, born Waterbeach, co. Cambridge, 10 June, 1868; 2s. William, cler. KEBLE, matric. 19 Oct., 86, aged 18 (from Winchester), B.A. 90.

Wilson, William Gilchrist, born at West Heslerton, Yorks, 21 July, 1865; 2s. James Gilchrist, cler. WORCESTER, matric. 22 Oct., 85, aged 20 (from York school), exhibitioner 85, B.A. 89, M.A. 92; HONOURS :—3 classical mods. 87, 3 history 89.

Wilson, William Hawkins, born at Crookham, Hants, Feb., 1866; 3s. John Charles, arm. KEBLE, matric. 14 Oct., 84, aged 18 (from Radley coll.), scholar 84, B.A. 88, M.A. 91 (HONOURS :—1 physiology 88, Radcliffe fellowship 91); brother of Frederick R. L.

Wilson, William Mortimer, born at Alfreton, co. Derby, 30 Sept., 1865; 1s. Joseph George, gent. ST. JOHN'S, matric. 11 Oct., 84, aged 19 (from Cheltenham coll.), B.A. 87, M.A. 91; HONOURS : —3 history 87.

Wilton, Charles Henry Jones, born at Foye, co. Hereford, Oct., 1864; 1s. Charles Turner, vicar. KEBLE, matric. 16 Oct., 83, aged 18 (from Winchester), B.A. 86, M.A. 90.

Wimberley, Herbert Irvine Arabin, born at Hartlip, Kent, Jan., 1868; 2s. Charles Irvine, vicar. KEBLE, matric. 17 Oct., 87, aged 19 (from Canterbury school), B.A. 90.

Wimbush, rev. James Sedgwick, born at Terrington, Yorks, 20 Feb., 1866; 3s. Samuel, cler. ORIEL, matric. 23 Oct., 85, aged 19 (from Haileybury), B.A. 89, M.A. 92 (HONOURS :—3 classical mods. 87, 3 history 89); curate of St. Columba, Southwick, Sunderland, 91.

Winbolt, Samuel Edward, born in London 24 Feb., 1868; 1s. Edward Grove, arm. CORPUS CHRISTI, matric. 22 Oct., 87, aged 19 (from Christ's hospital), scholar 87, B.A. 91; HONOURS :—1 classical mods. 89, 2 classics 91.

Winch, Richard Bluett, born at Chatham, Kent, 1869; 2s. George, gen. PEMBROKE, matric. 25 Oct., 87, aged 18 (from the Charterhouse), B.A. 90.

Winch, Tom Moningu, born at Chatham, Kent, 17 Feb., 1873; 1s. Thomas, gen. MERTON, matric. 22 Oct., 91, aged 18, from Sherborne school.

Winckworth, Harry Gordon, born at Woodford, Essex, 1859; 2s. Laurence Henry, arm. ST. JOHN'S, matric. 17 Jan., 80, aged 21; migrated to NEW INN HALL, B.A. and M.A. 86.

Winder, Edward Humphreys, born at Chirk, co. Denbigh, 1869; 5s. John Green, gen. NEW COLL., matric. 12 Oct., 89, aged 19 (from Manchester gr. school), exhibitioner 88, B.A. 92; HONOURS :—Ægrotat chemistry 92.

Windle, Percival Webbe, born at Kirtling, co. Cambridge, 2 Sept., 1860; 3s. William, cler. QUEEN'S, matric. 22 Oct., 83, aged 23, from St. Paul's school.

Windley, Francis, born at Nottingham 5 Jan., 1865; 5s. William, gent. TRINITY, matric. 11 Oct., 84, aged 19 (from Repton school), B.A. 88; living at Vryberg, Bechuanaland.

Windsor, Francis Duncan, born at Kingston, Canada, 1867; y.s. Samuel Dampfylde, cler. NON-COLLEGIATE, matric. 16 Oct., 86, aged 19 (from Forest school), B.A. 90, M.A. 93.

Winfield, Alfred, clinical lecturer in surgery, Radcliffe infirmary, 83, see page 8.

Wingate, John Bruce, born at Manse, in the island of Shetland, 1869; 1s. Thomas Daniel, cler. BALLIOL, matric. 18 Oct., 88, aged 19 (from Aberdeen university); assist. commissioner Burma 90.

Wingate, Philip Bernard, born at Ludford, co. Linc., 24 Nov., 1867; 2s. William, gen. WORCESTER, matric. 9 Feb., 92, aged 24, from Dorset county school, Charminster.

Wingfield, Charles Lee, M.A., fellow ALL SOULS' 55-71, where see page 480.

Wingfield, Edward, M.A., B.C.L., fellow NEW COLL. 50-72, where see page 214.

Winkfield, John, born at Penge, Surrey, 1863 o.s. John Thomas Cox, gent. WORCESTER, matric. 20 Oct., 81, aged 18, B.A. 86, M.A. 88 (HONOURS: —3 classical mods. 83); bar.-at-law, Lincoln's Inn, 89.

Winkworth, Stephen Dickenson, born at Manchester 3 June, 1864; 1s. Stephen, gent. BALLIOL, matric. 17 Oct., 82, aged 18 (from Clifton coll.), B.A. and M.A. 89; HONOURS :—3 law 86.

Winn, Charles James, born at Liverpool 1870; 1s. James, gen. ST. JOHN'S, matric. 12 Oct., 89, aged 19 (from Liverpool coll.), B.A. 92; HONOURS: —3 theology 92.

Winnifrith, Bertram Thomas, born at Hythe, Kent, 1868; 2s. Alfred, cler. CHARLSEY'S HALL, matric. 2 Nov., 89, aged 21.

Winter, rev. Alexander Bassell, born at New Amsterdam, British Guiana, 23 Sept., 1859; 2s. Alexander, arm. NON-COLLEGIATE, matric. 18 Oct., 80, aged 21 (from Blackheath school); migrated to NEW COLL., B.A. 84, M.A. 88 (HONOURS :—2 classics 84); curate of St. John, Bethnal Green, 85-9, chaplain at Jersey 89-90, curate of West Hackney, London, 90.

Winter, Edward Stuart, born at Brighton Nov., 1866; 1s. Robert Reynolds, cler. KEBLE, matric. 19 Oct., 86, aged 19, from Uppingham school.

Winterbotham, Henry Noel, born at South Cleeve, co. Glouc., 13 Dec., 1873; 2s. John Brand, of Cheltenham, solicitor. CORPUS CHRISTI, matric. 18 Oct., 92, aged 18, from Clifton coll.

Winterbotham, Reginald John, born at South Clewe, co. Glouc., 12 July, 1872; 1s. John Brand, solicitor. TRINITY, matric. 17 Oct., 91, aged 19, from Clifton coll.

Wintle, Frederic Thomas, born at Brown Condover, Hants, 11 May, 1864; 1s. Frederic Thomas William, rector of Bere Ferrers, Devon. ST. EDMUND HALL, matric. 16 Jan., 84, aged 18 (from Godolphin school, Hammersmith), B.A. 86.

Winton, Frederick Henry de, M.A., fellow JESUS COLL. 76, where see page 309.

Winton, Robert Francis Chiappini de, born at Boughrood, co. Radnor, 6 Sept., 1868; 6s. Henry, archdeacon of Brecon. EXETER, matric. 19 Oct., 87, aged 19 (from Marlborough), exhibitioner 89; HONOURS :—2 classical mods. 89, 2 classics 91.

Wintour, Evelyn, born at Hawerby, co. Lincoln, Dec., 1864; 3s. Fitzgerald, cler. CHRIST CHURCH, matric. 12 Oct., 83, aged 18, from Canterbury school.

Wise, Henry Edward Disbrowe, born at Woodcote, co. Warwick, 20 Oct., 1868; o.s. Henry Christopher, arm., deceased. NEW COLL., matric. 14 Oct., 87, aged 18 (from Harrow), B.A. 91; HONOURS:—3 history 90.

Wise, William John, M.A., fellow ST. JOHN'S 35-42, where see page 479.

Wither, William Henry Walter Bigg, M.A., R.C.L., fellow NEW COLL. 28-71, where see page 209.

Witherby, Walter Henry, born in London 1864; o.s. Walter, gent. ST. JOHN'S, matric. 14 Oct., 82, aged 18 (from Merchant Taylors' school), scholar 82, B.A. 86, M.A. 91; HONOURS:—2 classical mods. 84, 2 classics 86, 2 history 87.

Witherington, Charles Townsend, born at Bradfield, Berks, 1864; 1s. Charles, gent. ST. JOHN'S, matric. 13 Oct., 83, aged 19. B.A. 88.

Withers, Harry Livingston, born at Aigburth, co. Lanc., 1865; 3s. Harry Hartley, gent. BALLIOL, matric. 16 Oct., 83, aged 18 (from King's coll. school, London), scholar 82, B.A. 87 (HONOURS :— 1 classical mods. 84, 1 classics 87); brother of the next.

Withers, Hartley, born at Aigburth, co. Lanc., 15 July, 1867; 4s. Harry Hartley, gent. CHRIST CHURCH, matric. 15 Oct., 86, aged 19 (from Westminster school), scholar 86, B.A. 90; HONOURS:— 1 classical mods. 88, 3 classics 90.

Withers, John Herbert, born at Bury, co. Lanc., 3 Jan., 1872; 3s. Bigland, cler. EXETER, matric. 13 Oct., 90, aged 18 (from Bury, co. Lanc., gr. school), scholar 90; HONOURS :—2 classical mods. 92.

Withington, Archibald Edward, born in London 28 Oct., 1870; 2s. Edward, cler. ST. JOHN'S, matric. 27 April, 89, aged 18, from Eton.

Withington, Thomas Ellames, M.A., MERTON, where see page 102.

Witt, Alfred Robert, born at Leyton, Essex, 1863; 4s. Alexander King, gent. NON-COLLEGIATE, matric. 28 Jan., 82, aged 19 (from Wimborne gr. school), B.A. 86, M.A. 90.

Witt, Robert Clermont, born at Camberwell, Surrey, 16 Jan., 1872; 1s. Gustavus Andrew, gen. NEW COLL., matric. 10 Oct., 90, aged 18, from Clifton coll.

Wodehouse, Edmond Henry, M.A., student CHRIST CHURCH 55-64, where see page 421.

Wodehouse, Walker, M.A., fellow MERTON 41-7, where see page 96.

Wolfe, Franke, born at Brooklyn, U.S.A., 19 May, 1873; 1s. merchant, deceased. ST. JOHN'S, matric. 15 Oct., 92, aged 19, from Liverpool institute.

Wolfe, Benjamin Spencer, born at Swansea, co. Glam., 7 Dec., 1871; 4s. Edwin John, cler. MAGDALEN, matric. 14 Oct., 90, aged 18 (from Clifton coll.), demy 90; HONOURS:—1 mathematical mods. 92.

Wolfendale, Thomas Arthur, born at Tutbury, co. Stafford, 1864; 1s. James, gen. NON-COLLEGIATE, matric. 23 Oct., 86, aged 22 (from Bruton gr. school), matric. 22 Oct., 83, from St. John's coll., Cambridge, and HONOURS:—2 theology 86; B.A. 86, M.A. 90.

Wollaston, William Monro, M.A., fellow EXETER 55-64, where see page 127.

Wolstenholme, William, born at Blackburn, co. Lanc., 24 Feb., 1865; 1s. James, arm. WORCESTER, matric. 13 Dec., 89, aged 21 (from Blind coll., Worcester), B.Mus. 27 Oct., 87.

Womack, Arthur Shaw, born at Wakefield, Yorks, 1861; 3s. James, arm. BALLIOL, matric. 21 Oct., 80, aged 19 (from Marylebone school); junior judge small cause court, central provinces, India.

Wonnacott, rev. Bryant, born at Morley, Yorks, 17 Feb., 1859; 2s. James, gent. ST. MARY HALL, matric. 29 Oct., 85, aged 26.

Wonnacott, rev. William John Blight, born at Devonport 28 Sept., 1860; 1s. John, gent. NON-COLLEGIATE, matric. 17 Oct., 81, aged 21 (from a Devonport school), B.A. and M.A. 91; acting chaplain to the forces at Singapore 86-8, and Hong Kong 88, curate of St. Michael, Hackney, London, 89.

Wood, rev. Alan Philip, born at Saddington, co. Leicester, July, 1865; y.s. William Paul, cler. KEBLE, matric. 16 Oct., 83, aged 18 (from Harlow coll.), B.A. 86, M.A. 90 (HONOURS :—4 history 86); curate of Ellesmere, Salop, 89.

Wood, rev. Alfred, born at Canterbury 1862; 1s. George Frederick, gent. NON-COLLEGIATE, matric. 14 Oct., 82, aged 20, B.A. 86, M.A. 89 (HONOURS;—2 theology 86); curate of Sheffield, Yorks, 88.

Wood, Alfred Herbert, born at Frizinhall, Yorks, 10 Nov., 1865; o.s. Benjamin, of Shipley Fields, Leeds, arm. MAGDALEN, matric. 16 Oct., 84, aged 18, from Wellington coll.

Wood, Alfred Herbert, born at Portsmouth 1866; 3s. Robert, gent. BRASENOSE, matric. 23 Oct., 85, aged 19 (from Portsmouth gr. school), scholar 85, B.A. 89, M.A. 92; HONOURS :—2 mathematical mods. 87, 3 mathematics 89.

Wood, Arthur Henry, born at Reading 8 Nov., 1870; 3s. Robert, cler. NEW COLL., matric. 11 Oct., 89, aged 18 (from Cranbrook school); HONOURS :—2 classical mods. 91.

Wood, Arthur Syms, born at Lancaster 29 Dec., 1861; 2s. James, gent. BALLIOL, matric. 17 Oct., 82, aged 20 (from Lindon Grove school, and Owens coll., Manchester), B.A. 87 (HONOURS:—3 classical mods. 84, 3 classics 86); student Inner Temple 84.

Wood, Charles Henry Thursfield, born at Cheltenham 1869; 1s. Joseph, D.D., headmaster of Tonbridge school. CHRIST CHURCH, matric. 12 Oct., 88, aged 19 (from Clifton and Lemmington colls.), scholar 88, B.A. 92 (HONOURS :—1 classical mods. 90, 2 classics 92); brother of John Barry.

Wood, Charles John, born at St. Michaels, Lichfield, 1861; 3s. Walter, gen. QUEEN'S, matric. 16 March, 92, aged 31.

Wood, hon. Charles Reginald Lindley, born 17 July, 1870; elder son of Charles Lindley, viscount Halifax. CHRIST CHURCH, matric. 11 Oct., 89, aged 19 (from Eton); died 6 Sept., 90.

Wood, rev. Edward James, born at Chatburn, co. Lanc., 1861; 2s. John, cler. NON-COLLEGIATE, matric. 4 June, 81, aged 20, B.A. 85 (HONOURS :—2 history 85); assist. tutor and chaplain Exeter diocesan training college 85-8, curate of Blackburn St. Peter 89-91, and of Prescot 91.

Wood, Ernest Montagu, born in London 5 Aug., 1861; 8s. (Peter) Almeric Leheup, cler. MERTON, matric. 18 Oct., 81, aged 20 (from Eton), postmaster 81-5, B.A. 86; HONOURS :—2 classical mods. 83, 2 classics 85.

Wood, Fergus Henry, born at Bolton, co. Lanc., 16 March, 1861; 1s. Joseph Reynolds, gent. LINCOLN, matric. 19 Oct., 83, aged 22, B.A. 86, M.A. 90; HONOURS;—3 history 86.

Wood, Frederick, born at Bradford, Yorks, 1865; 3s. William, gent. ST. JOHN'S, matric. 11 Oct., 84, aged 19 (from Bradford school), scholar 84, B.A. 88 (HONOURS :—2 classical mods. 86, 3 classics 88); bar.-at-law, Inner Temple, 89.

Wood, George, M.A., fellow PEMBROKE 75, where see page 553.

Wood, George Arnold, born at Salford, co. Lanc., 1865; 1s. George Stanley, gent. BALLIOL, matric. 24 Oct., 85, aged 20 (from Owens coll., Manchester), scholar 86, B.A. 90, M.A. 92 (HONOURS: —1 history 88, Stanhope essay 89), professor of modern history at Sydney university 90.

Wood, George Robert, born at Reading, Berks, Dec., 1865; 1s. Robert, cler. KEBLE, matric. 14 Oct., 84, aged 18 (from Haileybury), B.A. 88, M.A. 91.

Wood, George Ronald, born at Evesham, co. Worc., 11 March, 1869; 3s. Matthew, cler. MERTON, matric. 17 Oct., 88, aged 19 (from Shrewsbury gr. school), postmaster 88, B.A. 92 (HONOURS :—2 mathematical mods. 89, 3 mathematics 92); brother of Walter Birkbeck.

Wood, Gordon Edward Boileau, born at Ealing, Middx., July, 1866; 1s. Edward, arm. CHRIST CHURCH, matric. 14 Jan., 87, aged 20.

Wood, John Barry, born at Cheltenham 27 April, 1870; 2s. Joseph, D.D., headmaster of Tonbridge school. BALLIOL, matric. 17 Oct., 89, aged 19 (from Marlborough), exhibitioner 88 (HONOURS :—1 classical mods. 91), in University eleven 92; brother of Charles H. T.

Wood, John Bertram, born at Withycombe, Devon, 4 March, 1872; o.s. John, gent. TRINITY, matric. 15 Oct., 92, aged 20, from Lancing coll.

Wood, John Thomas, born at Clitheroe, co. Lanc., 1863; 3s. John, cler. NON-COLLEGIATE, matric. 22 Oct., 87, aged 24 (from Wigan gr. school); migrated to HERTFORD; HONOURS :—3 mathematical mods. 89, 4 mathematics 91.

Wood, rev. Joseph, D.D., Fereday fellow ST. JOHN'S 65-8, where see page 490.

Wood, Kenneth Forbes, born at Brighton 29 April, 1863 ; 1s. William, B.D. CHRIST CHURCH, matric. 13 Oct., 82, aged 19 (from Eton), scholar 82-6, B.A. 86 (HONOURS :—2 classical mods. 84, 3 classics 86) ; bar.-at-law, Lincoln's Inn, 91 ; brother of Michael H. M.

Wood, Lancelot John Swettenham, born at Oxford 4 Sept., 1866; 3s. Charles James, arm. NEW COLL., matric. 16 Oct., 85, aged 19, from Radley coll.

Wood, rev. Michael Henry Mansel, born at Prestwood, Bucks, 16 Nov., 1864 ; 2s. William, D.D. TRINITY, matric. 15 Oct., 83, aged 18 (from Eton), scholar 83, B.A. 87, M.A. 90 (HONOURS :—2 classical mods. 84, Greek prose 86, 2 classics 87, 2 theology 88); curate of Wantage 89-91 ; brother of Kenneth F.

Wood, Richard Boardman, born at Bromsgrove 8 July, 1871; 1s. Richard, D.Med. HERTFORD, matric. 14 Oct., 90, aged 19 (from Bromsgrove gr. school); scholar 89; HONOURS :—1 classical mods. 92.

Wood, rev. Robert Gifford, born at Swansea, co. Glamorgan, 30 May, 1853 ; o.s. Gifford, captain and commander India and China naval service. WADHAM, matric. 25 Feb., 85, aged 31 (from St. Davids coll., Lampeter, B.A. 72, D.D. 82), B.A. 89, M.A. 92 (HONOURS :—3 classical mods. 84) ; headmaster Swansea collegiate school 77-85, and of Kirby Ravensworth gr. school 85.

Wood, Walter Birkbeck, born at Hampton, co. Worc., 15 April, 1866 ; 1s. Matthew, cler. WORCESTER, matric. 22 Oct., 85, aged 19 (from Rugby), scholar 84, B.A. 89 (HONOURS :—1 classical mods. 87, 1 classics 89) ; brother of George Ronald.

Wood, Walter John, born at Portsmouth 31 May, 1869 ; 5s. Robert, gen. MAGDALEN, matric. 22 Oct., 87, aged 18 (from Portsmouth gr. school), demy 87, B.A. 91 ; HONOURS :—2 mathematical mods. 89, 2 mathematics 91.

Wood, William, D.D., fellow TRINITY 51-67, where see page 451.

Wood, William Henry, born in London 1854 ; 1s. Charles Henry, gent. ST. ALBAN HALL, matric. 4 June, 80, aged 26.

Wood, William Key, born at San Francisco 1865 ; 2s. John Key, arm. ST. JOHN'S, matric. 22 Jan., 84, aged 19.

Woodard, Arthur Mortimer Wilmot, born 1867; 1s. Mortimer Neville, bar.-at-law, deceased. HERTFORD, matric. 22 Oct., 86, aged 19, from Lancing coll.

Woodard, Ernest Henry James, born at Hulme, co. Lanc., 13 Dec., 1873; 4s. Mortimer Neville, bar.-at-law, deceased. NON-COLLEGIATE, matric. 15 Oct., 92, aged 18, from Malvern coll.

Woodbridge, Cecil Mercer, born at Hillingdon, Middx., Feb., 1866 ; 1s. Henry William, arm. ORIEL, matric. 8 Dec., 84, aged 19, B.A. 88 (from the Charterhouse), B.A. 88.

Woodcock, Charles, M.A., student CHRIST CHURCH 28-35, where see page 413.

Woodcock, John Neville, born at Wigan, co. Lanc., 26 April, 1873 ; 3s. Henry, of Holnore, Sussex, arm. MAGDALEN, matric. 18 Oct., 92, aged 19, from Winchester.

Woodhouse, Edward John, born at Otterhampton, Somerset, 1869 ; 1s. Thomas, rector. ORIEL, matric. 20 Oct., 88, aged 19, B.A. 93 ; HONOURS:—2 classical mods. 90, 2 classics 92.

Woodhouse, George, born at Cheetham Hill, co. Lanc., 14 Feb., 1874 ; 1s. William, of Macclesfield, gent. ST. JOHN'S, matric. 15 Oct., 92, aged 18 (from Macclesfield gr. school), exhibitioner 92.

Woodhouse, Sidney Chawner, born at Fulham, Middx., 1871 ; 2s. Thomas James, D.Med. CHRIST CHURCH, matric. 11 Oct., 89, aged 18 (from Westminster school), scholar 89 ; HONOURS: —1 classical mods. 91.

Woodhouse, William John, born at Clifton, Westmorland, 7 Nov., 1866; 1s. Richard, gent. QUEEN'S, matric. 20 Oct., 84, aged 18 (from Sedburgh school), exhibitioner 85, B.A. 89 ; HONOURS :— 1 classical mods. 87, 1 classics 89, archæological studentship at Athens 89, Craven travelling fellowship 91.

Woodin, Stanley Hassall, born at Kingston-on-Thames 1871 ; o.s. Alfred, cler. EXETER, matric. 16 Oct., 89, aged 18.

Woodman, Edward Polly, born at East Lavant, Sussex, 1855 ; 3s. John Sibley, cler. WORCESTER, matric. 24 Jan., 80, aged 25.

Woodman, Henry Charles, born at Old East Hartlepool, co. Durham, 27 March, 1874 ; 1s. Henry, vicar of St. Peter's, Stockton-on-Tees, BRASENOSE, matric. 22 Oct., 92, aged 18 (from Durham school), exhibitioner 92.

Woodroffe, John George, born at Calcutta 1866 ; 1s. James Tisdall, arm. UNIVERSITY COLL., matric. 11 Oct., 84, aged 18; migrated to CHARSLEY'S HALL, B.A. 88, M.A. 91 (HONOURS: —2 law 88, 2 civil law 89); bar.-at-law, Inner Temple, 89.

Woods, Francis Cunningham, born in London 29 Aug., 1862; 2s. Alfred, gent. ST. MARY HALL, matric. 22 Oct., 83, aged 21; migrated to EXETER, 18 Jan., 87; B.A. 89, M.A. 90, B.Mus. 92; organist BRASENOSE 84-6, and EXETER Jan., 87; brother of William M.

Woods, Francis Henry, B.D., fellow ST. JOHN'S 76-83, where see page 488.

Woods, Henry George, D.D., president of TRINITY 87, where see page 448.

Woods, James Haughton, born at Boston, Mass., 1865; 2s. Joseph Wheeler, gen. NON-COLLEGIATE, matric. 23 April, 91, aged 26; graduated in America.

Woods, Richard Edward Cotterell, born at Malins-Lee, in Dawley, Salop, 1874; 1s. Richard, cler. CHRIST CHURCH, matric. 14 Oct., 92, aged 18, from Shrewsbury.

Woods, rev. William Maldnad, born in London 4 Jan., 1864; 3s. Alfred, gent. ST. MARY HALL, matric. 16 April, 83, aged 19; migrated to EXETER, B.A. 89, M.A. (ST. MARY HALL) 90; rector of Thursday island, Queensland; brother of Francis C.

Woodward, Agathos Arthur, born at Oxford 10 July, 1861; 2s. William, gent. NON-COLLEGIATE, matric. 18 Oct., 80, aged 19, B.A. 86.

Woodward, rev. Frederick William Morris, born at Geelong, Australia, 1861; 1s. William, gent. NON-COLLEGIATE, matric. 13 Oct., 81, aged 23 (from Trinity coll., Melbourne, B.A. 82); scholar HERTFORD 84, B.A. 89 (HONOURS :— 1 classical mods. 86, 2 classics 88); curate of Whitechapel 91.

Woodward, George Deward, born in London 11 Oct., 1865; o.s. Francis Edgar, gen., deceased. NON-COLLEGIATE, matric. 17 Oct., 91, aged 26 (from Brighton gr. school, and University coll. school, London); migrated to BALLIOL 92; LL.D. university of London.

Woodward, Michael Edward Parnell, born at Folke-stone Sept., 1872; 3s. Matthew, vicar. KEBLE, matric. 15 Oct., 92, aged 20, from St. Edward's school, Summertown.

Woodward, rev. William Edward, born at Saham Toney, Norfolk, 1867; 2s. William, cler. BALLIOL, matric. 19 Oct., 87, aged 20 (from Trent coll.), B.A. 91 (HONOURS :— 2 classical mods. 89, 2 theology 91); curate of Sandy, Beds, 92.

Woodyatt, Roger Gresley, born in London 25 July, 1866; 2s. George, cler. UNIVERSITY COLL., matric. 11 Oct., 84, aged 18 (from Rugby), B.A. 88 (HONOURS :— 1 classical mods. 86, 3 law 88); bar.-at-law, Inner Temple, 93.

Wooldridge, George Frederic, born at Haseley, co. Worcester, Aug., 1861; 2s. Benjamin, gent. KEBLE, matric. 18 Oct., 80, aged 19 (from Malvern coll.), B.A. 84, M.A. 87; HONOURS :— 3 mathematical mods. 82.

Woollacott, Francis James, born at New Maiden, Surrey, 7 Jan., 1866; 2s. James Oliver, gent. QUEEN'S, matric. 22 Oct., 84, aged 18 (from city of London school); scholar 84, B.A. 88, B.Med. 92; HONOURS :— 2 mathematical mods. 86, 3 physiology 88.

Woollcombe, rev. Arthur Augustus, born at Petrockstow, Devon, 1861; 3s. Louis, rector. NON-COLLEGIATE, matric. 17 Jan., 80, aged 19; migrated to ST. MARY HALL, B.A. 84; curate of East and West Stower, Dorset, 87.

Woollcombe, Charles Kenneth, born at Plympton St. Maurice, Devon, 8 Nov., 1871; 5s. William John, gen. WORCESTER, matric. 23 April, 91, aged 19, from Forest school, Walthamstow.

Woollcombe, George Penrose, born at Loudwater, Bucks, 1867; 1s. William Penrose, cler. CHRIST CHURCH, matric. 30 May, 85, aged 18, B.A. 88; HONOURS :— 3 history 88.

Woollcombe, Henry St. John Stirling, born at Highampton, Devon, 27 Dec., 1869; 1s. George, rector. KEBLE, matric. 12 Oct., 89, aged 19 (from Clifton coll.), B.A. 92; HONOURS :— 3 history 92.

Woollcombe, Herbert Louis, born at Exeter 1 Aug., 1862; 4s. Henry, archdeacon of Barnstaple. KEBLE, matric. 18 Oct., 81, aged 19 (from Winchester), B.A. 85; HONOURS :— 4 theology 85.

Woollcombe, rev. Thomas Clement, born at Heavitree, Devon, 2 July, 1864; 5s. Henry, archdeacon of Barnstaple. KEBLE, matric. 16 Oct., 83, aged 19 (from Clifton coll.); migrated to CHARSLEY'S HALL, B.A. 88; M.A. from KEBLE 90; curate of Roath, co. Glam., 89.

Woolley, Charles, born at Cardington, Cheshire, 1868; 2s. John, gen. KEBLE, matric. 18 Jan., 90, aged 21.

Woolley, Francis Alfred, born at Lewes, Sussex, 1862; 3s. Frederick, cler. NON-COLLEGIATE, matric. 17 Oct., 81, aged 19, B.A. 87.

Woolley, Joseph Edmund, born at Barrow-on-Soar, co. Leicester, 1861; 5s. William John, gent. PEMBROKE, matric. 20 May, 80, aged 19, B.A. 86.

Woolner, rev. Ernest Henry George, born at Stockwell, Surrey, 31 March, 1861; o.s. George Augustus, gent. QUEEN'S, matric. 4 May, 81, aged 20 (from Radley coll.), B.A. 84, M.A. 89; curate of Brighton St. Paul 85.

Woolrych, rev. Bertram Best, born at Enfield, Middx., 26 May, 1859; 2s. William Henry, cler. NON-COLLEGIATE, matric. 15 Oct., 87, aged 28 (from King's coll. school, London); migrated to EXETER, B.A. 90 (HONOURS :— 3 history 90); curate of Bishops Lavington, Wilts, 90.

Woolsey, rev. William George, born at Cork, Ireland, 1869; 1s. William Myers, cler. ALL SOULS', matric. 11 Feb., 81, aged 19 (from Magdalen coll. school, chorister 71-5), bible clerk 81-4, B.A. 84, M.A. 89; curate of St. Mary, Tothill Fields, London, 87.

Wootten, Aubrey Francis Wootten, born at Headington, Oxon, 19 Sept., 1866; 5s. William, gent. ORIEL, matric. 5 Feb., 86, aged 19 (from Rugby), B.A. 89 (HONOURS :— 2 law 89); bar.-at-law, Inner Temple, 92; brother of the next.

Wootten, Herbert Edward Wootten, born at Headington, Oxon, 3 April, 1864; 4s. William, arm. BRASENOSE, matric. 18 April, 83, aged 19 (from Rugby); migrated to NEW INN HALL and BALLIOL; brother of the last.

Wootton, Thomas John, born at Ealing, Middx., 19 Nov., 1865; 1s. John Cardy, gent. ORIEL, matric. 27 Oct., 83, aged 18 (from Winchester), B.A. 86, M.A. 90.

Wordsworth, right rev. John, D.D., bishop of Sarum, hon. fellow BRASENOSE 93, where see page 351.

Wordsworth, John Roundell, born at Perth 14 Feb., 1866; 4s. Charles, bishop of St. Andrews. NON-COLLEGIATE, matric. 15 Oct., 84, aged 18 (from Glenalmond coll.); lieut. 2nd batt. N. Staffs. regt.; died 15 April, 90.

Worfield, Ethelbert Dudley, born at Lexington, America, 1861; 2s. William, gent. WADHAM, matric. 17 Oct., 82, aged 21.

Workman, Arthur Skeete, born at Reading 26 Feb., 1864; o.s. Francis, gent. HERTFORD, matric. 22 Nov., 82, aged 18 (from Cheltenham coll.), B.A. 85, M.A. 89; HONOURS :— 3 classical mods. 84.

Worrall, Arthur Hartley, born at Nottingham 1868; 1s. Robert, gent. ST. JOHN'S, matric. 16 Oct., 86, aged 18 (from Grantham school); scholar 86, B.A. 90; HONOURS :— 1 classical mods. 88, 2 classics 90.

Worrall, rev. Thomas Pryse, born at Llanwrda, co. Carmarthen, 30 Oct., 1860; 2s. John, gent. LINCOLN, matric. 22 Jan., 80, aged 19 (from Llandovery coll.), B.A. 82; curate of Crakehall, Yorks, 90.

Worrall, Walter, born at Liverpool 11 March, 1862; 1s. Joseph, gent. WORCESTER, matric. 21 Oct., 80, aged 18 (from Liverpool institute), scholar 80-5, B.A. 84; HONOURS :—2 classical mods. 82, 2 classics 84.

Worsey, Frederick William, born at Burton-on-Trent, co. Staff., 22 March, 1873; 1s. Frederick, of Cheltenham, gent. CORPUS CHRISTI, matric. 18 Oct., 92, aged 19, from Cheltenham coll.

Worsfold, William Basil, born at Wolvey, co. Warwick, 5 Dec., 1858; 2s. John Napper, cler. UNIVERSITY COLL., matric. 22 Jan., 80, aged 21 (from Wakefield school), exhibitioner 80-3, B.A. 83, M.A. 86 (HONOURS :—1 classical mods. 81, 2 classics 83); bar.-at-law, Middle Temple, 87.

Worsley, Edward, M.A., fellow MAGDALEN 67-72, where see page 335.

Worsley, Frederick Stanhope, born at Patna, East Indies, 15 Dec., 1865; 1s. Charles Fortescue, of Indian c.s. MAGDALEN, matric. 16 Oct., 82, aged 18, from Wellington coll.

Worsley, William Henry Arthington, born 12 Jan., 1861; elder son of Arthington, arm., deceased. NEW COLL., matric. 16 Oct., 80, aged 19 (from Eton), B.A. 84 (HONOURS :—3 classical mods. 82, 2 classics 84), treasurer 83, and president of Oxford union society 84.

Worthington, Frank, born at Stretford, co. Lanc., 1865; 1s. John, arm. UNIVERSITY COLL., matric. 11 Oct., 84, aged 19 (from Shrewsbury gr. school), B.A. 88 (HONOURS :—3 law 87); bar.-at-law, Lincoln's Inn, 89.

Worthington, Harry, born at Stretford, co. Lanc., 1867; 2s. John, gent. CHRIST CHURCH, matric. 12 June, 86, aged 19 (from Shrewsbury gr. school), B.A. 89.

Worthington, rev. Henry Brooke, born at Oxton, Cheshire, 21 Jan., 1863; 3s. Joseph Hall, arm. MERTON, matric. 17 Oct., 82, aged 19 (from Birkenhead school), B.A. 87, M.A. 92 (HONOURS :—2 classical mods. 84, 2 classics 86); curate of St. John Evangelist, Sheffield, 88.

Worthington, rev. Herbert Edward, born at Frittenden, Kent, 15 April, 1863; 2s. John, cler. MERTON, matric. 18 Oct., 81, aged 18 (from Oundle gr. school), B.A. 85 (HONOURS :—2 theology 85); rector of Cadeby, co. Leic., 91.

Worthington, Percy Scott, born at Cheetham Hill, co. Lanc., 1864; 1s. Thomas, gent. CORPUS CHRISTI, matric. 19 Oct., 83, aged 19 (from Clifton coll.), B.A. 87, M.A. 90; HONOURS :—2 classical mods. 85.

Worthington, William Clark, born at Addlestone, Surrey, 31 July, 1870; 2s. Charles John, arm. WADHAM, matric. 13 Oct., 88, aged 18, from Eastbourne coll.

Worthington, William Worthington, born at Wellington, co. Derby, Dec., 1871; 1s. Albert Octavius, arm. NEW COLL., matric. 10 Oct., 90, aged 18, from the Charterhouse.

Wotherspoon, Charles Grey, born at Kensington 25 Aug., 1869; 2s. Charles Grey, bar.-at-law. EXETER, matric. 17 Oct., 88, aged 19 (from Malvern coll.), B.A. 92.

Wragge, rev. Walter, born at Chester 2 Oct., 1865; 5s. Alfred, gent. JESUS COLL., matric. 16 Oct., 84, aged 19 (from Oxford high school and Dulwich coll.), scholar 84, B.A. 88, M.A. 91 (HONOURS :—3 classical mods. 86, 3 classics 88); curate of Stockwell St. Andrew, Surrey, 91.

Wreford, rev. Charles Herbert, born at Clannaborough, Devon, 9 Oct., 1866; 3s. John, gent. WORCESTER, matric. 20 Oct., 85, aged 19 (from Winchester), B.A. 90, M.A. 92; curate of East Ham 91.

Wren, John Albert Edward, born at Leith, near Edinburgh, 29 Jan., 1863; 4s. George, gent. EXETER, matric. 21 Oct., 86, aged 23, B.A. 89.

Wren, Joseph, born at Leith, in Midlothian, 1857; 2s. George, gen. EXETER, matric. 26 April, 88, aged 31, B.A. 91.

Wrey, Albany Bourchier Sherard, born at Ashburton, Devon, 4 Jan., 1861; 3s. Herny Bourchier Toke, arm. HERTFORD, matric. 18 Oct., 80, aged 19, B.A. 87, M.A. 89.

Wright, rev. Albert Leslie, born at Osmaston, co. Derby, 23 Feb., 1862; 1s. Henry, cler. CHRIST CHURCH, matric. 14 Oct., 81, aged 19 (from Marlborough), B.A. 90.

Wright, Arthur Columbine, born at Bradford, Yorks, 26 July, 1871; 1s. Jonathan, gen. MAGDALEN, matric. 14 Oct., 89, aged 18 (from Bradford gr. school), demy 88 ; HONOURS :—3 mathematical mods. 90.

Wright, Arthur Cory, born at Highgate, Middx., 18 Nov., 1869; 1s. Francis Cory, arm. MERTON, matric. 17 Oct., 88, aged 18 (from Harrow), B.A. 91.

Wright, Arthur Samuel, born at Drattleby Hall, co. Linc., 1868; 2s. Samuel, arm. NEW COLL., matric. 15 Oct., 86, aged 18 (from the Charterhouse) ; HONOURS :—2 classical mods. 88, 4 classics 90 ; brother of Philip C.

Wright, rev. Benjamin, born at Wilsden, Yorks, Aug., 1865; 9s. Joseph, gent. KEBLE, matric. 22 Oct., 85, aged 20 (from Bingley school, and Yorkshire coll., Leeds), exhibitioner 85, B.A. 88 (HONOURS :—1 history 88); curate of St. Luke Pallion, co. Durham, 89-90.

Wright, Charles Beaufoy, born at Clapham, Surrey, 12 July, 1863; 3s. Edward John, D.Med. PEMBROKE, matric. 23 Oct., 82, aged 19, from Westminster school.

Wright, Charles Edward Leigh, born at Wigan, co. Lanc., 19 Sept., 1865; 1s. Egerton Leigh, arm. WORCESTER, matric. 17 Oct., 84, aged 19 (from Eton), B.A. 87; HONOURS :—3 history 87.

Wright, Charles Ernest, born at Sunderland 29 July, 1872; 1s. Charles, solicitor. ORIEL, matric. 27 Oct., 91, aged 19, from Harrow.

Wright, Charles Henry Conrad, born at Chicago, U.S.A., 15 Nov., 1869; o.s. Charles Henry, gen. TRINITY, matric. 17 Oct., 91, aged 21, from Harvard coll., U.S.A.

Wright, Dudley Cory-, born at Hornsey, Middx., 2 Dec., 1872; 2s. Francis Cory, shipowner. MERTON, matric. 22 Oct., 91, aged 18, from Highgate school.

Wright, rev. Harry Walter Banks, born at Shelton, Notts, 22 June, 1865; 1s. Henry Banks, arm. MAGDALEN, matric. 23 Oct., 85, aged 20 (from Bradfield and Cheltenham colls.), B.A. 89.

Wright, Henry Francis, born at Swanwick, co. Derby, 15 Feb., 1864; 3s. Henry, cler. CHRIST CHURCH, matric. 25 May, 83, aged 19 (from Marlborough and Eton), B.A. 86, M.A. 90 ; HONOURS :—3 history 86.

Wright, Henry Nelson, born in Manipuri, East Indies, 1870; 1s. Francis Nelson, of Indian c.s. CORPUS CHRISTI, matric. 20 Oct., 88, aged 18 (from Eton) ; assist. magistrate N.W. provinces, India, 90.

Wright, Henry Woodley (Boscawen), born at Caledon 22 June, 1865; 1s. Henry Boscawen, capt. 15th King's hussars. MERTON, matric. 17 Jan., 83, aged 18 (from Cheltenham coll.), B.A. 86, M.A. 90 (HONOURS :—3 law 86) ; bar.-at-law, Middle Temple, 87.

43

Wright, rev. James Paget, born at Worksop, Notts, 14 June, 1865; y.s. Henry Henton, cler. NON-COLLEGIATE, matric. 20 Oct., 84, aged 19 [from Sheffield collegiate school]; migrated to WADHAM 20 Jan., 85, B.A. 87, M.A. 91; curate of Woodford Wells, Essex, 90; brother of Walter N.

Wright, rev. John Charles, born at Bolton, co. Lanc., 1861; 1s. Joseph Farrell, cler. MERTON, matric. 18 Oct., 80, aged 19 [from Manchester gr. school], postmaster 80-4, B.A. 84, M.A. 87 (HONOURS :—2 classical mods. 81, 2 classics 84); curate of Bradford, Yorks, 88.

Wright, Joseph, Ph.D., created M.A. 9 June, 1891, deputy professor of comparative philology 91.

Wright, Philip Chetwood, born at Brattleby Hall, co. Lincoln, 10 May, 1866; 1s. Samuel Wright, arm. MAGDALEN, matric. 27 April, 85, aged 18 [from Haileybury], B.A. 89; brother of Arthur S.

Wright, Reginald Guy, born at Maidstone, Kent, 1873; 1s. Charles Edward, arm. UNIVERSITY COLL., matric. 23 Jan., 90, aged 17 [from Maidstone gr. school], exhibitioner 90.

Wright, Robert James, born at Damascus, Syria, 16 May, 1873; 3s. William, D.D., editorial supt. British and Foreign Bible Society. BRASENOSE, matric. 21 Oct., 92, aged 19 [from Dulwich coll.], scholar 92.

Wright, hon. sir Robert Samuel, M.A., B.C.L., hon. fellow ORIEL 82, where see page 151.

Wright, Thomas Howard, M.A., fellow MERTON 75-90, where see page 99.

Wright, Walter Norton, born at Sheffield 1864; 3s. Henry Henton, cler. NON-COLLEGIATE, matric. 18 Oct., 83, aged 19 [from Sheffield collegiate school]; migrated to UNIVERSITY COLL., B.A. 86, M.A. 91 (HONOURS :—4 mathematics 86); brother of James P.

Wright, Walter Reginald, born at Trichinopoli, India, 3 Nov., 1869; 3s. William Edward, arm. WADHAM, matric. 13 Oct., 88, aged 18 [from Merchant Taylors' school], exhibitioner 88, B.A. 92; HONOURS :—Hebrew scholarship 90, 1 theology 92.

Wright, Walter Southey, born in London 1860; 3s. John Freeman, gent. BALLIOL, matric. 17 Oct., 82, aged 20 [from Epsom coll.], B.A. 87.

Wright, William, LL.D., professor of Arabic in Cambridge and Dublin, created D.C.L. 22 June, 1887; died 22 May, 89. See Al. Ox. and series, 1616.

Wright, William Aldis, vice-master Trinity coll., Camb., fellow 78, created D.C.L. 30 June, 1886. See Al. Ox. and series, 1616.

Wright, William Edward Fellowes, born at Tullamore, Ireland, 1848; 1s. John, gen. NON-COLLEGIATE, matric. 29 Jan., 81, aged 32; HONOURS :—2 mathematical mods. 82.

Wright, William Maurice, born at Wold Newton, co. Lincoln, 10 July, 1873; 1s. William, esq., deceased. ST. JOHN'S, matric. 15 Oct., 92, aged 19, from Malvern coll.

Wright, rev. William Peter, born at Sheffield 16 Aug., 1864; o.s. Charles Sisum, cler. TRINITY, matric. 11 Oct., 84, aged 20 [from Repton school], B.A. 87, M.A. 91; curate of Stokesley, Yorks, 89.

Wrigley, George Frederick, born at Audenshaw, co. Lanc., 26 Dec., 1865; 2s. Charles Harrop, arm. MERTON, matric. 19 Oct., 83, aged 17 [from Manchester gr. school], postmaster 83, B.A. 87, M.A. 91; HONOURS :—2 classical mods. 85, 3 classics 87.

Wrottesley, hon. Charles, M.A., fellow ALL SOULS 47, where see page 271.

Wrottesley, hon. Victor Alexander, born at Wrottesley, co. Stafford, 18 Sept., 1873; 2s. Arthur, lord W. CHRIST CHURCH, matric. 4 June, 92, aged 18.

Wurm, John Lewis, born at Southampton 1866; 2s. John Evangelist, gent. HERTFORD, matric. 22 Oct., 86, aged 20, from Dulwich coll.

Wyatt, Edward, born at Haywards Heath, Sussex, 16 March, 1872; 3s. Robert Edward, cler. EXETER, matric. 22 Oct., 91, aged 19, from Lancing coll.

Wyatt, Edward Gerald Penfold, born at Hawley, Hants, Feb., 1869; 3s. John Ingram Penfold, cler. CHRIST CHURCH, matric. 3 June, 87, aged 18 [from Winchester]; HONOURS :—3 classical mods. 89, 3 history 91.

Wyatt, Harold Digby, born at Barton under Needwood, co. Stafford, 25 March, 1866; 5s. Arthur Harvey, cler. NON-COLLEGIATE, matric. 23 Jan., 86, aged 19 [from Rossall school]; migrated to EXETER, B.A. 90.

Wyatt, John, born at Norwood, Surrey, 2 Jan., 1870; o.s. John Frederick, of Newfoundland, merchant, deceased. BALLIOL, matric. 17 Oct., 89, aged 19 [from Blundell's school, Tiverton]; HONOURS :—3 classical mods. 91.

Wyatt, John Holland, born at Acton, co. Stafford, 1867; 3s. Robert, arm. NON-COLLEGIATE, matric. 22 Oct., 87, aged 20, B.A. 90.

Wyatt, Johnson Charles, born at Bengal 1852; 3s. Alexander, arm. CHRIST CHURCH, matric. 27 April, 81, aged 29.

Wyatt, Robert Harvey Lyle, born at Acton, co. Stafford, 1867; 1s. Robert, gent. NON-COLLEGIATE, matric. 23 Jan., 86, aged 19 [from Rossall school], B.A. 89.

Wybergh, Cecil Hilton, born at Weeton, Yorks, 1 Aug., 1871; 2s. Christopher, late rector of Serayingham, Yorks. HERTFORD, matric. 14 Oct., 90, aged 19, from Sherborne school.

Wykes, John Theodore, born at Derby 20 Jan., 1864; 1s. John Louth, assist. registrar Derby county court. JESUS COLL., matric. 18 Oct., 82, aged 18 [from Derby school], B.A. 86; HONOURS :—2 chemistry 86.

Wyld, Charles Edward, born in London 27 Jan., 1870; 1s. Edward, arm. MERTON, matric. 17 Oct., 88, aged 18, from Harrow.

Wylie, Daniel, born at Edinburgh 1857; 2s. John, gen. QUEEN'S, matric. 16 March, 92, aged 35.

Wylie, Francis James, born at Bromley, Kent, 1866; 2s. Richard Northcote, gent. BALLIOL, matric. 15 Oct., 84, aged 18 [from St. Edward's school, Summertown, and Glasgow university], exhibitioner 84, B.A. 88; fellow of BRASENOSE 92, M.A. 92; HONOURS :—1 classical mods. 86, 1 classics 88.

Wynoh, Lionel Maling, born at Horringer, Suffolk, 21 July, 1864; 2s. William Maling, arm. BALLIOL, matric. 17 Oct., 82, aged 18 [from Bedford gr. school], B.A. 85 (HONOURS :—2 law 85); deputy director department of land records and agriculture.

Wyndham, hon. George O'Brien, born in London 17 Nov., 1868; 1s. Henry, baron Leconfield. NEW COLL., matric. 15 Oct., 86, aged 17 [from Eton], B.A. 91; HONOURS :—2 history 90.

Wyndham, Howard James, born at Finchley, Middx., 4 April, 1865; o.s. Charles, gen. ST. MARY HALL, matric. 24 Oct., 85, aged 20.

Wyndham, Percy, born at Cockermouth, Cumberland, 22 Dec., 1867; 3s. Horace Robert, gen., deceased. QUEEN'S, matric. 25 Oct., 86, aged 18 [from Giggleswick school], scholar 86, B.A. 89 (HONOURS :—2 mathematical mods. 87, 2 law 89); assist. commissioner Oudh 88.

Wyndham, Percy Charles Hugh, born at Berlin 23 Sept., 1864; 1s. George Hugh, C.B., minister at Belgrade. NEW COLL., matric. 4 Dec., 85, aged 21 (from Eton), B.A. 88; HONOURS:—3 history 88.

Wynksop, Wooddrop Crispin, born at Philadelphia 1860; o.s. Alfred, arm. NON-COLLEGIATE, matric. 1 Feb., 81, aged 21.

Wynn, Charles Watkin Williams, M.A., student CHRIST CHURCH 39-53, where see page 414.

Wynn, Frederick Rowland Williams, born in London 19 Feb., 1865; 3s. Charles Watkin, arm. UNIVERSITY COLL., matric. 13 Oct., 83, aged 18, B.A. 85; HONOURS:—4 history 86.

Wynn, Robert William Herbert Watkin Williams, born at Cefn Hall, co. Denbigh, 3 June, 1862; s. Herbert Watkin Williams-. CHRIST CHURCH, matric. 4 June, 81, aged 19, B.A. 91.

Wynne, rev. George, born at Guernsey 1861; 1s. George Henry, cler. BRASENOSE, matric. 10 June, 80, aged 19 (from Lancing coll.), B.A. 84, M.A. 88; curate of St. Andrew, Wolverhampton, 85.

Wynne, George Robert Llewellyn, born at Holywood co. Down, 23 Oct., 1873; 1s. George Robert, archdeacon, D.D. ST. JOHN'S, matric. 29 Oct., 91, aged 18, from St. Columba's coll., near Dublin.

Wynne, John Henry, B.C.L., fellow ALL SOULS' 41-51, where see page 278.

Wynne, rev. Owen, born at Belchalwell, Dorset, 5 May, 1864; 2s. George Henry, cler. KEBLE, matric. 16 Oct., 83, aged 19 (from Marlborough), B.A. 86, M.A. 90; curate of St. Saviour's, Leicester, 89.

Wynne, Richard, born at Wavertree, co. Lanc., 1864; 4s. Walter William, gent. WORCESTER, matric. 19 Oct., 82, aged 18 (from Wellington), B.A. 86; HONOURS:— 2 classical mods. 84, 3 classics 86.

Wynne, William Lifton, born at Ruthin, co. Denbigh, 1 June, 1865; 1s. Walter, gent. JESUS COLL., matric. 16 Oct., 84, aged 19 (from Ruthin gr. school), scholar 84, B.A. 88, M.A. 92; HONOURS: —3 classical mods. 86, 3 classics 88.

Wynyard, William Bingham Ashton, born at Mussoori, East Indies, Oct., 1863; 2s. William, arm. EXETER, matric. 27 May, 82, aged 18 (from Marlborough), B.A. 87, M.A. 90.

Wythes, Ernest James, born at Bickley, Kent, 1 Sept., 1868; 2s. George Edward, arm. CHRIST CHURCH, matric. 14 Oct., 87, aged 19, from Eton.

STONE BRACKET YORK MINSTER.—*Pugin*

WOODEN ORNAMENT, ROUEN CATHEDRAL.—*Pugin.*

Y

Yardley, Frank, born at Birmingham 1864; 2s. Edwin, gent., deceased. EXETER, matric. 16 Oct., 84, aged 19 (from Malvern coll.), B.A. 90, M.A. 91.

Yates, rev. Arthur George, born at Rastrick, Yorks, 1861; 3s. David, gent. KEBLE, matric. 22 Jan., 80, aged 19 (from Owens coll., Manchester); scholar 79-83, B.A. 83, M.A. 86 (HONOURS:—2 mathematical mods. 81, 2 mathematics 83); chaplain to royal navy and naval infirmary 83.

Yates, Frederic Peel, born at Valetta, Malta, Oct., 1868; 5s. Henry Peel, arm. HERTFORD, matric. 19 Oct., 88, aged 19 (from Newton Abbot coll.), B.A. 91.

Yates, George James, born at Birmingham 27 July, 1861; 1s. George, gent. QUEEN'S, matric. 28 Oct., 81, aged 20 (from Birmingham gr. school), scholar 81-5, B.A. 85, M.A. 89; HONOURS:—2 mathematical mods. 83, 3 mathematics 85.

Yates, John William, born at Birmingham 19 Dec., 1864; y.s. George, arm. MERTON, matric. 16 Oct., 84, aged 19 (from Birmingham gr. school), exhibitioner 84-5, B.A. 88, M.A. 91; HONOURS:—2 classical mods. 86, 3 classics 88.

Yates, Joseph Hollis, born at Gloucester 1861; 2s. Thomas, arm. NON-COLLEGIATE, matric. 13 Jan., 1883, aged 22, from Gloucester gr. school.

Yates, Stanley, born at Cleckheaton, Yorks, 14 Sept., 1873; 1s. Henry, manufacturer. MERTON, matric. 18 Oct., 92, aged 19, from Bradford gr. school.

Yates, William, M.A., fellow BRASENOSE 53-67, where see page 356.

Yatman, William, born at Winscombe, Somerset, March, 1864; 1s. John Augustus, cler. EXETER, matric. 27 May, 82, aged 18, from Radley coll.

Yearsley, John Herbert, born at Welshpool, co. Montgomery, 28 Jan., 1869; 3s. William Pryce, gen. QUEEN'S, matric. 21 Oct., 87, aged 18 (from Christ's coll., Finchley), B.A. 92; HONOURS:—3 classical mods. 89, 3 classics 91.

Yeo, Gerald, born at Streatham, Surrey, 1866; 2s. Robert, arm. UNIVERSITY COLL., matric. 11 Oct., 84, aged 18, B.A. 88 (HONOURS:—1 law 88); bar.-at-law, Inner Temple, 91.

Yeomans, Robert, born at Burton-on-Trent, co. Stafford, 1871; 2s. John, gen. BALLIOL, matric. 20 Oct., 91, aged 20 (from King's coll. school, London); HONOURS:—2 classical mods. 93.

Yonge, rev. Charles Burell, born at Newton Ferrers, Devon, April, 1866; 2s. Duke, rector. KEBLE, matric. 14 Oct., 84, aged 18 (from Forest school, Walthamstow), B.A. 87, M.A. 91; rector of Newton Ferrers 91.

Yonge, rev. Geoffrey, born at Newton Ferrers, Devon, 20 Sept., 1867; 3s. Duke, rector. KEBLE, matric. 24 April, 88, aged 20, B.A. 91 (HONOURS:—4 theology 91); curate of Old Swindon, Wilts, 91.

Yonge, John, born at Newton Ferrers, Devon, 18 Dec., 1864; 1s. Duke, cler. WORCESTER, matric. 25 Jan., 84, aged 19 (from Winchester), B.A. 88.

Yonge, Edward, arm. CHRIST CHURCH, matric. 30 May, 85, aged 17, from Harrow.

Yorke, John Cecil, born at Preston, Yorks, 10 March, 1867; 1s. Edward, arm. CHRIST CHURCH, matric. 30 May, 85, aged 17, from Harrow.

Yorke, Philip Chesney, born at Eaton Bishop, co. Hereford, 28 Aug., 1865; 3s. Reginald, rear-admiral R.N., deceased. MAGDALEN, matric. 1 March, 86, aged 20 (from Marlborough), B.A. 89, M.A. 92; HONOURS:—2 history 89.

Youard, Wilfred Wadham, born at Dewsbury, Yorks, 6 Dec., 1869; 1s. Henry George, cler. EXETER, matric. 17 Oct., 88, aged 18 (from Rossall school), B.A. 92.

Young, rev. Alexander, born at Brixton, Surrey, 29 Nov., 1863; y.s. William, gent. KEBLE, matric. 18 Oct., 81, aged 17 (from Southwark gr. school), B.A. 85, M.A. 89 (HONOURS:—2 classical mods. 83, 2 classics 85, 2 theology 86); curate of Long Whatton, co. Leic., 86-8, and St. Mark, Peterborough, 88-9; died 23 Feb., 92.

Young, Alfred Joseph Karney, born in British Columbia 1 Aug., 1864; 2s. William Alexander George, C.M.G., lieut.-governor British Guiana. MAGDALEN, matric. 24 Jan., 84, aged 18 (from St. Mark's school, Windsor), B.A. 87; bar.-at-law, Inner Temple, 89.

Young, Charles Philip Radford, born at Brighton 1865; 2s. Charles, cler. PEMBROKE, matric. 27 Oct., 84, aged 19 (from Eton), scholar 84, B.A. 88; HONOURS:—2 classical mods. 86, 2 classics 88.

Young, Dalhousie James, born at Gurdaspur, East Indies, 1867; 3s. Ralph, general officer. BALLIOL, matric. 24 Oct., 85, aged 18 (from Clifton coll.), B.A. 89; M.A. 92; HONOURS :—4 classics 89.

Young, Francis Gordon, born at Dulwich, Surrey, 11 Jan., 1868; 3s. William, gen. CORPUS CHRISTI, matric. 22 Oct., 87, aged 19 (from Wellington coll.), B.A. 92; HONOURS :—3 classical mods. 89.

Young, Francis Samuel, born at Harlow, Essex, 14 Oct., 1871; 1s. Samuel, gen. QUEEN'S, matric. 24 Oct., 90, aged 19, from Nonconformist coll., Bishop Stortford.

Young, Frederic Coxwell, born at North Witham, co. Lincoln, 31 Oct., 1862; 5s. l'ctor, rector. KEBLE, matric. 17 Oct., 82, aged 19 (from Haileybury), B.A. 86; HONOURS :—3 classical mods. 84, 3 history 86.

Young, George James, born at Wallaroo, Australia, 13 Feb., 1866; o.s. Gavin David, of Adelaide, arm. TRINITY, matric. 11 Oct., 84, aged 18 (from Marlborough], B.A. 87.

Young, George Walter, born 17 Dec., 1852; 2s. William, gent. QUEEN'S, matric. 22 Oct., 83, aged 30, B.A. 86, M.A. 90, a schoolmaster.

Young, Henry Thenkstone, born at Great Crosby, co. Lanc., March, 1868; 5s. James Stephen Gordon, cler. KEBLE, matric. 19 Oct., 86, aged 18 (from Rishworth gr. school), B.A. 91; HONOURS :—2 classical mods. 88, 3 classics 90.

Young, James Allen, born in London 1867; 2s. Charles Florence, gent. BRASENOSE, matric. 23 Oct., 85, aged 18, from Winchester.

Young, James Frederick, born at Wolverhampton 23 March, 1867; 1s. John, cler. CORPUS CHRISTI, matric. 22 Oct., 86, aged 19 (from Swansea school and matric. 21 Oct., 84, St. John's coll., Cambridge), scholar 86, B.A. 90; HONOURS :—1 mathematical mods. 87, 2 mathematics 90.

Young, John Herbert, born at Holywell, Oxford, 2 April, 1869; s. (———), master of Swansea gr. school. JESUS COLL., matric. 8 May, 90, aged 21 (from Brecon coll., and matric. 21 Oct., 89, Christ's coll., Cambridge), B.A. 92.

Young, John Joseph Baldwin, born at Mansfield, Notts, 7 Aug., 1868; 1s. Bernard Joseph, arm. TRINITY, matric. 13 Oct., 88, aged 20 (from Beaumont and Stonyhurst colls.), B.A. 91 (HONOURS: —3 law 91); law-at-law, Inner Temple, 91.

Young, John William Alexander, born at Galgarm Castle, co. Antrim, 2 June, 1873; 4s. right hon. John, P.C. NON-COLLEGIATE, matric. 3 Nov., 92, aged 19 (from Shrewsbury gr. school); migrated to NEW COLL. Jan., 93.

Young, Newton Barton, M.A., fellow NEW COLL. 25-52, where see page 209.

Young, Percy Frederick, born at Isleworth, Middx., 5 March, 1869; 2s. Charles, gen. WADHAM, matric. 13 Oct., 88, aged 19 (from Lancing coll.), B.A. 92.

Young, Samuel, born at Cardigan 28 April, 1868; 1s. John, gen. JESUS COLL., matric. 22 Jan., 89, aged 21, from Cardigan collegiate school.

Young, Telford Mackenzie, born at Adelaide, Australia, 17 March, 1867; 1s. Edmund, gent. EXETER, matric. 23 Oct., 85, aged 18 (from Harrow), B.A. 90.

Young, Thomas, born at Keele, co. Stafford, 19 April, 1868; 2s. James, gen. JESUS COLL., matric. 15 Oct., 90, aged 22 (from Newcastle-under-Lyne school, and University coll., Aberystwith), scholar 90 (HONOURS :—1 classical mods. 92), 1 classics at London 89.

Young, Walter George, born at Louth, co. Lincoln, 10 Dec., 1866; 3s. Anthony William, arm. MAGDALEN, matric. 16 Oct., 84, aged 18 (from Eton), exhibitioner, 84, B.A. 88; HONOURS :—1 mathematical mods. 85, 2 mathematics 88.

Younger, Robert, born at Alloa, co. Clackmannan, 1862; 4s. James, gent. BALLIOL, matric. 17 April, 80, aged 18 (from Edinburgh academy), B.A. 83 (HONOURS :—3 classical mods. 81, 2 law 83); bar.-at-law, Inner Temple, 84.

Younger, Robert Edward Nelson, born at Newmarket 1871; 1s. Robert Edward, arm. BALLIOL, matric. 14 Oct., 90, aged 19 (from Ipswich gr. school), scholar 89; HONOURS :—1 classical mods. 92, accessit 91, and Craven scholarship 92.

Younger, William, born at Edinburgh 1863; 1s. William, gent. WORCESTER, matric. 22 April, 82, aged 19.

Younghusband, Ernest Robert, born at Rugby 18 July, 1870; 5s. Robert Romer, C.B., general in the army. NEW COLL., matric. 11 Oct., 89, aged 19, from Clifton coll.

Younghusband, Oswald, born at Clifton, co. Glouc., 30 Nov., 1872; 6s. Robert Romer, C.B., general in the army. TRINITY, matric. 15 Oct., 92, aged 19, from Clifton coll.

Youngman, rev. George Mallows, born at Saffron Walden, Essex, 1857; 1s. John Mallows, gent. WORCESTER, matric. 21 Oct., 80, aged 23, B.A. 83, M.A. 87 (HONOURS :—1 theology 83); curate of Greenwich, Kent, 83.

Yule, Charles John Francis, M.A., fellow MAGDALEN 73, where see page 312.

Z

Zachary, Arthur, born at Cirencester, co. Glouc., 31 May, 1872; 5s. Henry, gent. NON-COLLEGIATE, matric. 15 Oct., 92, aged 18, from Lancing coll.

Zachary, Francis Edward, born at Cirencester Sept., 1870; 4s. Henry, gen. LINCOLN, matric. 24 Jan., 89, aged 18, from Lancing coll.

Zedlitz, George William Ernest Edward von, born at Herrmannswaldarn, In Silesia, 10 March, 1871; o.s. George William Frederic Sigismund, Reichsfreiherr von Zedlitz. TRINITY, matric. 12 Oct., 89, aged 18 (from Wellington), scholar 88; HONOURS : —2 classical mods. 91.

Ziohy, count Antal, born at Buda Pesth, Hungary, 1859; 1s. count Frans de Paula. CHRIST CHURCH, matric. 20 Oct., 82, aged 23.

Zwezdakoff, Victor (3s.), born at Geneva Oct., 1871; his father, a Polish exile. LINCOLN, matric. 23 Oct., 91, aged 19, from Harwarden gr. school and Lancing coll.

COINS—BODLEIAN.

INDIANS, ETC.

IN CHRONOLOGICAL ORDER.

Syed Hassan, born at Teheran, Persia, 1859; 2s. Syed Mohommed. BALLIOL, matric. 21 Oct., 80, aged 21.

Ibrahim, Ahmed, born at Calcutta 1863; 1s. Ahmed Wali. BALLIOL, matric. 18 Oct., 81, aged 18 (from Calcutta), bar.-at-law, Inner Temple, 86.

Syed Mohammed Habib Ullah, born at Harrah, East Indies, 1863; 3s. Syed Riaz Uddin. NON-COLLEGIATE, matric. 14 Oct., 82, aged 19 (from M. A. O. coll, Aligarh, Indin); bar.-at-law, Middle Temple, 84.

Mancherji (Pestonji) Khareghat, born at Bombay 1865; 2s. Pestonji. BALLIOL, matric. 17 Oct., 82, aged 17 (from St. Francis Xavier's coll., Bombay); a selected candidate Indian C.S. 82.

Suresh Chundra Biswas, born at Calcutta 1862; 3s. Cally Prosoni. BALLIOL, matric. 11 Dec., 82, aged 20 (from Presidency coll., Calcutta), B.A. 87, M.A. 90 (HONOURS :—4 law 86); bar.-at-law, Middle Temple, 86.

Bunyiu Nanjio, a Japanese student; created M.A. 18 March, 1884.

Ganpat vas Shravenras Gaikward, born at Baroda 1866; 2s. prince Shraven. BALLIOL, matric. 29 Oct., 84, aged 18 (from Baroda high school); bar.-at-law, Middle Temple, 90.

Moung Kyaw, born in Mandalay 1866; 1s. prince Strain Zan. BALLIOL, matric. 29 Oct., 84, aged 18; bar.-at-law, Middle Temple, 89.

Lakshman Gangadhan Bhadbhade, born at Belgaum, East Indies, 1861; 2s. Gangadhar Suram. BALLIOL, matric. 22 Jan., 85, aged 24 (from Deccan coll., and Government law school, Bombay), B.A. 87 (HONOURS :—Boden Sanskrit scholarship 85, 2 Indian languages 87); bar.-at-law, Middle Temple, 88.

Sampatras Kashiras Gaikward, born at Kavalana, East Indies, 1865; 3s. prince Kashiras. NON-COLLEGIATE, matric. 26 Jan., 85, aged 20.

Mohsin Badroodeen Tyabjee, born at Cambury, East Indies, 1866; 1s. Badroodeen. BALLIOL, matric. 24 Oct., 85, aged 19 (from St. Francis Xavier's coll., Bombay); a selected candidate Indian C.S. 85.

Kekhosru Punthaki, born at Bombay 9 Nov., 1864; 1s. Kekobad Kanasjée. CHRIST CHURCH, matric. 15 Oct., 86, aged 21.

Pestonji Sorabji Kotval, born in Bombay 1868; 2s. Sorabji Dosaubhoy. NON-COLLEGIATE, matric. 23 Oct., 86, aged 18 (from St. Francis Xavier's coll., Bombay); migrated to BALLIOL, B.A. 89 (HONOURS :—3 law 89); bar.-at-law, Inner Temple, 89.

Jagundra Nath Das Gupta, born at Calcutta 9 Nov., 1870; 1s. Hari Hav. BALLIOL, matric. 20 Jan., 87, aged 19 (from Calcutta metropolitan institution), B.A. 90 (HONOURS :—2 history 89, 2 law 90); bar.-at-law, Middle Temple, 90.

On Wah Wei, born at Hong Kong, China, 13 Sept., 1866; y.s. Kong Wah. CHRIST CHURCH, matric. 3 June, 87, aged 18 (from Cheltenham coll.), B.A. 92.

Manmohan Ghose, born at Bhagulpore, East Indies, 1869; 2s. Krishna Dan, D.Med.

Christ Church, matric. 14 Oct., 87, aged 18 (from St. Paul's school), scholar 87; HONOURS :—2 classical mods. 89.

Satis Chandra Mookerjee, born at Calcutta 12 Feb., 1868; 1s. Soshibhoosan. QUEEN'S, matric. 21 Oct., 87, aged 19 (from Calcutta university); bar.-at-law, Lincoln's Inn, 91, of Indian C.S. 90.

Abdul Majid Khan, born at Dhagalpur, in Bengal, 1870; 1s. Molir Abdul. NON-COLLEGIATE, matric. 14 Jan., 88, aged 18; bar.-at-law, Inner Temple, 92.

Syad Zainulabidin Bilgrami, born at Belgaum in Oude, East Indies, 1865; 1s. Syad Hosain. CHRIST CHURCH, matric. 24 April, 88, aged 21.

Kamalkrishna Shelley Bonnerjee, born at Entally, near Calcutta, 5 March, 1870; 1s. Woomes Chunder, advocate, high court. NEW COLL., matric. 12 Oct., 88, aged 18 (from Rugby), B.A. 91; HONOURS :—4 classics 91.

Mohamed Nujmul Huda, born at Patna, East Indies, 1870; 3s. Mohamed Shumshul. NON-COLLEGIATE, matric. 12 Oct., 89, aged 19 (from Patna collegiate school); bar.-at-law, Middle Temple, 92.

Khalil Khayyat, born at Tannurin 1872; 2s. Abdullah, D.Med. NON-COLLEGIATE, matric. 18 Jan., 90, aged 18, from American coll., Beyrout.

Syed Hashim Bilgrami, born at Belgaum, in East Indies, 1870; 2s. Syed. BALLIOL, matric. 1 May, 90, aged 20 (from Madrasi Alla, Hyderabad); migrated to Cambridge, NON-COLLEGIATE, 22 Oct., 89.

Jyun Takakusu, born at Kobe, in Japan, 25 May, 1868; 1s. Magosaburo, merchant. NON-COLLEGIATE, matric. 11 Oct., 90, aged 23 (from Kioto gr. school, Japan); HONOURS :—Chinese scholarship 92.

Richard Kaikhusroo Sorabji, born at Belgaum, East Indies, 11 July, 1872; o.s. Sorabji Kharsedji, of Poona, India, cler. BALLIOL, matric. 14 Oct., 90, aged 18, from Poona, and s.E. coll., Ramsgate.

Mir Aun Ali, born at Bombay 1871; 2s. Khan, Bahadur. NON-COLLEGIATE, matric. 29 Oct., 90, aged 19, from Bombay.

Mahimohan Ghose, born at Calcutta 1872; 1s. Manomohan, arm. BALLIOL, matric. 1 Nov., 90, aged 18; of Indian C.S. 90.

Gorind Dinanuth Madgavkar, born at Bombay 1872; 1s. Dinanuth Vishnu. BALLIOL, matric. 17 Jan., 91, aged 19 (from St. Francis Xavier's coll., Calcutta); of Indian C.S. 90.

Murari Lal Taitri, born at Baghra, E. Indies, 1873; 2s. Duarka Prasada. NON-COLLEGIATE, matric. 17 Jan., 91, aged 18 (from Canning coll., Lucknow); a student of Gray's Inn.

Jnanandranath Gupta, born at Patna, East Indies, 1872; 1s. Babu Ghanashyam. NON-COLLEGIATE, matric. 27 Jan., 91, aged 19 (from Calcutta university); of Indian C.S. 90.

Hari Das Bose, born at Calcutta Oct., 1870; 1s. Umbica Charan. NON-COLLEGIATE, matric. 29 Jan., 91, aged 20 (from Government Presidency coll., Calcutta); migrated to WADHAM 26 April, 92.

Manockji Pestonjee Asavaid, born at Bombay 1871; 3s. Pestonjee Dadabhai. NON-COLLEGIATE, matric. 16 May, 91, aged 20, from Neech coll., Bombay.

MATRICULATIONS, INDIANS, 1880 TO 1892.

Hafiz Muniruddai, Ahmed, born at Sangharhi, central provinces, India, 1869; 1s. Hafiz Naizeruddin, pleader in high court. NON-COLLEGIATE, matric. 17 Oct., 91, aged 22, from Saugor high school and Jubbulpore coll.

Mufti Fida Mahomed Khan, born at Peshawur, India, 1871; 5s. Mufti Mohamed Khan, land-holder. NON-COLLEGIATE, matric. 17 Oct., 91, aged 20, from Punjab university, Lahore.

Tomotake Minami-iwakura, born at Kyoto, Japan, 1870; 3s. baron Somoyoski Minamiiwakura. NON-COLLEGIATE, matric. 6 Feb., 92, aged 22, from Noble's coll., Tokyo.

Abdur Rasul, born at Guniauk, Tipperah, India, 10 April, 1874; 1s. Golam Rasul, zemindar, deceased. ST. JOHN'S, matric. 9 Feb., 92, aged 17, from Dacca coll., India, from Liverpool institute and King's coll., London.

Joseph Augustus Maung Gyi, born at Moulmein, Lower Burmah, 1872; 1s. Edward Moung Kheem. NON-COLLEGIATE, matric. 18 Feb., 92, aged 20, from St. Paul's coll., Rangoon, and St. Mary's coll., Peckham, Surrey, etc.

Shumboo Nath, born at Gujrat, Punjab, 1866; 1s. Bhola Nath, landed proprietor, etc. NON-COLLEGIATE, matric. 26 Feb., 92, aged 26.

Syed Sirajul Hassan, born at Etawah, N.W.P., India, 31 Aug., 1872; 1s. late Syed Riazul Hassan, the first Talugdar to H. H. the Nizam of Hyderabad c.s. MERTON, matric. 18 Oct., 92, aged 20, from Government high school and Nizam's coll., Hyderabad.

Jogerchundra Chandhuri, born at Bag Pubna, Bengal, 1864; 2s. Durjadas ChandurnZamindar op Pubna, late sub-divisional magistrate Chooadanga. NON-COLLEGIATE, matric. 1 Dec., 92, aged 28.

STONE BRACKET, YORK MINSTER.—*Pugin.*

PATERAS, BEAUCHAMP CHAPEL, WARWICK.—*Pugin*.

www.ingramcontent.com/pod-product-compliance
Lightning Source LLC
Chambersburg PA
CBHW051900300426
44117CB00006B/475